UNIVERSITY CASEBOOK SERIES

EDITORIAL BOARD

DAVID L. SHAPIRO
DIRECTING EDITOR
Professor of Law, Harvard University

ROBERT C. CLARK
Dean of the School of Law, Harvard University

DANIEL A. FARBER
Professor of Law, University of Minnesota

OWEN M. FISS
Professor of Law, Yale Law School

GERALD GUNTHER
Professor of Law, Stanford University

THOMAS H. JACKSON
President, University of Rochester

HERMA HILL KAY
Dean of the School of Law, University of California, Berkeley

HAROLD HONGJU KOH
Professor of Law, Yale Law School

ROBERT L. RABIN
Professor of Law, Stanford University

CAROL M. ROSE
Professor of Law, Yale Law School

For Eve

PREFACE

"Business crime," as the term is used in these materials, is a crime committed during the normal course of business operations, for economic reasons, by or on behalf of a legitimate business organization. Business crimes are not crimes of intentional violence, although some do result in physical harm. I have used the term "business crime" rather than "white collar crime" because the latter tends to emphasize the socio-economic class of the offender and ignore the broader context of the offense. My focus of study, however, is more on the nature of the offense and its institutional character. Nevertheless, the materials do explore some crimes which may not be business crimes in the narrow sense (such as RICO, mail fraud, and insider trading), but which have come to have a significant legal and strategic impact in the business crime area.

The study of business crime fits at the intersection of the business, criminal law, and criminal procedure curricula. Few law school courses dealing with the regulation of business conduct even acknowledge the potential for criminal liability under the statutes being considered, let alone explore the proper place for such liability. Few criminal law courses have time to explore the issues of organizational crime occurring within a regulatory framework. Few criminal procedure courses are able to explore the issues raised in complex criminal litigation, with numerous potential defendants, difficult factual problems, and lurking civil liability.

My main goal in writing this casebook, therefore, has been to organize a course of study which focuses systematically on these otherwise unaddressed areas. In addition, I hope that the casebook accomplishes two, more specific objectives. The first is to raise questions about business crime issues, some of which go to very basic problems (such as why should there be corporate criminal liability). The second is to provide business crime "literacy." This means conveying to the student some of the rich legal and factual history involved in the business crime area. The case selection, therefore, tends to include older foundational cases along with current cases, and the text Notes attempt to provide context for the case analysis. I also believe that literacy requires some familiarity with the great controversies of the day, whether it is railroad rebating of the 1900s or foreign improper payments of the 1970s. I have therefore edited the cases with as much an eye to providing this kind of information as to providing an understanding of the law. I should note that to facilitate easier reading, I have omitted supporting citations and footnotes from cases and articles, unless otherwise indicated.

PREFACE

I was originally drawn to the study of business crime out of an interest in exploring different legal methods for controlling improper corporate behavior. If there is a bias in these materials, then, it is a bias in favor of using the criminal law as a sanction to punish and deter such behavior. Hopefully, though, these materials have gone far beyond being a brief for corporate criminal liability. My intention is to provide a window into the complexities of using the criminal law and the criminal process in this area. Only if we understand the impact that the law can have on people and institutions in the business world today can we make progress in solving the legal and policy problems involved in applying the criminal law to business behavior.

HARRY FIRST

New York, New York
October, 1989

ACKNOWLEDGMENTS

I would like to thank the students in my seminar in Business Crime at New York University Law School for their comments and assistance with earlier drafts of these materials. My research assistants, who have been tremendously helpful, have included Donna Avergun, Lisa Barkan, Neil Corwin, Tom Davis, John Genovese, Ken Goldberg, Lisa Lefkovic Jacobs, and Richard Nevins. I would also like to thank Miriam Sparrow for her assistance with regard to organization theory. Martha Derby and Carole Sparkes assisted greatly in the preparation of the manuscript. This project was funded, in part, by research grants from the Filomen D'Agostino and Max E. Greenberg Research Fund at New York University School of Law and from the New York University Law Center Foundation.

HF

*

SUMMARY OF CONTENTS

	Page
PREFACE	v
ACKNOWLEDGMENTS	vii
TABLE OF STATUTES	xxi
TABLE OF CASES	xxv

PART ONE. PROBLEMS OF SUBSTANTIVE CRIMINAL LAW

CHAPTER 1. BUSINESS CRIMES — 1
A. Statutory Overview — 1
B. The Decision to Criminalize — 13
C. Federal Statutes of General Application — 80

CHAPTER 2. PRINCIPLES OF LIABILITY — 167
A. Entity Liability — 167
B. Individual Liability — 227

CHAPTER 3. SANCTIONS — 297
A. Sentencing Guidelines — 297
B. Individual Sanctions — 323
C. Entity Sanctions — 354

PART TWO. PROBLEMS OF CRIMINAL PROCEDURE

CHAPTER 4. CORPORATE PRIVILEGES — 382
A. Constitutional — 382
B. Common Law: Attorney–Client Privilege — 401

CHAPTER 5. THE GRAND JURY — 435
A. Fundamentals of Grand Jury Power — 435
B. Conducting The Grand Jury Inquest — 450
C. Multiple Representation and Conflicts of Interest — 477

CHAPTER 6. GOVERNMENT EVIDENCE GATHERING — 496
A. Immunity — 496
B. Search Warrants — 528
C. Subpoenas and Summonses — 580

CHAPTER 7. INTERPLAY BETWEEN CIVIL AND CRIMINAL PROCEEDINGS — 623
A. Order of Litigation — 624
B. Fifth Amendment Issues — 645
C. Grand Jury Materials — 668

SUMMARY OF CONTENTS

	Page
Appendix	680
Index	697

TABLE OF CONTENTS

	Page
PREFACE	v
ACKNOWLEDGMENTS	vii
TABLE OF STATUTES	xxi
TABLE OF CASES	xxv

PART ONE. PROBLEMS OF SUBSTANTIVE CRIMINAL LAW

CHAPTER 1. BUSINESS CRIMES 1

A. Statutory Overview 1
   Scope Note 1
   Essay: Three Regulatory Periods 1

Notes

     (1) International Trade 7
     (2) Financial Institutions 9
     (3) Federal Criminal Code 12
     (4) Bibliography 12

B. The Decision to Criminalize 13
   Scope Note 13
   United States v. Patterson 15

Notes and Queries

     (1) Constitutionality of the Sherman Act 24
     (2) Subsequent Vagueness Cases 25
     (3) Brandeis' View 27
     (4) Criminal Monopolization 27
     (5) Political Motivations 32
   United States v. Dowling 33

Notes and Queries

     (1) Queries 42
     (2) Protecting Soft Property 43
     (3) The IBM–Hitachi Affair 45
     (4) Criminalizing Infringement of Patents or Trademarks? 46
     (5) Privatization of Criminal Law Enforcement 47
   Readings 52
      Clarence Darrow, Address to the Prisoners in the Cook County Jail 62
      J. Hall, Theft, Law and Society 66
      L. Friedman, A History of American Law 71
      E. Sutherland, White Collar Crime 73

TABLE OF CONTENTS

	Page
B. The Decision to Criminalize—Continued	
Kadish, Some Observations on the Use of Criminal Sanctions in Enforcing Economic Regulations	76
C. Federal Statutes of General Application	80
Scope Note	80
1. Racketeer Influenced and Corrupt Organizations Act ("RICO")	81
United States v. Turkette	81

Notes and Queries

(1) Discovering RICO	87
(2) RICO Paradigm	87
(3) Corporations as RICO Defendants	93
(4) Prosecutorial Discretion	98
(5) Forfeiture Penalty	100
(6) Civil RICO	103
2. Fraud	107
McNally v. United States	107

Notes and Queries

(1) History and Elements of Mail Fraud	116
(2) Queries	117
(3) Political Corruption	118
(4) Unfaithful Employees	122
(5) Unfaithful Lawyers	125
(6) Corporate Mail Fraud	132
(7) Interpreting McNally	133
(8) Congress Decides	137
Chiarella v. United States	138

Notes and Queries

(1) Queries	145
(2) Tippee Liability	146
(3) Duty to Employers	148
(4) Enforcement Policy	152
(5) Profiling the Criminals	154
(6) Corporate Criminal Liability for Insider Trading	159
(7) Congressional Response	163
(8) What's Wrong With Insider Trading?	164
(9) Doonesbury on Insider Trading	166
CHAPTER 2. PRINCIPLES OF LIABILITY	167
A. Entity Liability	167
Scope Note	167
Three Analytical Models	167
New York Central And Hudson River Railroad Co. v. United States	174

TABLE OF CONTENTS

Page

A. Entity Liability—Continued
   Notes and Queries
   (1) Black Letter Law 178
   (2) History—The Concept of Corporate Criminal Liability 179
   (3) Criminal Liability for Non-Corporate Entities 182
   (4) State Prosecutions of Corporations for Homicide 184
   (5) People v. Film Recovery Systems 187
   (6) Safety in the Workplace 190

   Standard Oil Company of Texas v. United States 192

   Notes and Queries
   (1) Queries 197
   (2) On Winking 197

   United States v. Hilton Hotels Corporation 202

   Notes and Queries
   (1) Compliance Programs 206
   (2) Employee Level 207
   (3) State Common Law Crimes 208
   (4) Proposed Federal Criminal Code 209
   (5) Is Compliance Possible? 211

   United States v. FMC Corporation 213

   Notes and Queries
   (1) Who Killed the Birds? 219
   (2) Collective Knowledge/Collective Action 219
   (3) Is Systems Failure Criminal? 224

   Endnote: Toward a Theory of Organizational Crime 225

B. Individual Liability 227
   Scope Note 227
   1. Intent 228
      United States v. United States Gypsum Company 228

   Notes and Queries
   (1) Legislative History 239
   (2) Constitutional Implications of Gypsum 239
   (3) Mistake of Law 241
   (4) Reading Statutes—When Does "Knowingly" Require Knowledge of the Law? 242

   United States v. Garber 247

   Notes and Queries
   (1) Queries 256
   (2) Subsequent Cases 256
   (3) Reliance on Advice of Counsel 258
   (4) Reliance on Official Interpretation 259

   2. Managerial Liability 261
      Scope Note 261

TABLE OF CONTENTS

B. Individual Liability—Continued
      United States v. Dotterweich 262
      United States v. Park 267

Notes and Queries
      (1) The "Responsible Share" Test 276
      (2) A Model II View of Park 277
      (3) Applying the Responsible Share Test Outside the Food and Drug Area 279
      (4) Taking Responsibility 282
      (5) Proposed Federal Criminal Code 287
   3. Subordinate Liability 288
      United States v. Natelli 288

Notes and Queries
      (1) Queries 295
      (2) Following Orders 295

CHAPTER 3. SANCTIONS 297
A. Sentencing Guidelines 297
  Scope Note 297
   1. Sentencing Reform Act of 1984 297

Notes and Queries
      (1) Legislative Background 306
      (2) Queries 308
      (3) Constitutional Issues 308
   2. Sentencing Guidelines 316
      United States Sentencing Commission, Sentencing Guidelines And Policy Statements 316

Notes and Queries
      (1) How to Do It 319
      (2) Controversy Over Drafting the Guidelines 319
      (3) The Guidelines Process and the Role of Defense Counsel 320
      (4) How Do Judges Judge? 321
B. Individual Sanctions 323
  Scope Note 323
   1. Specific Guidelines 324
      United States v. Reich 324

Notes and Queries
      (1) Applying the Guidelines 331
      (2) A Conversation With Judge Sweet 331
      (3) How Do We Judge Equality? 333
      (4) Examining Disparity in White Collar Crime Cases 335
      Guidelines for Antitrust Offenses 337
      Queries 339

TABLE OF CONTENTS

Page

B. Individual Sanctions—Continued
    2. Sentencing Alternatives 340
        Renfrew, The Paper Label Sentences: An Evaluation 341

Notes and Queries

        (1) Queries 348
        (2) Community Service 348
        (3) House Arrest 349
        (4) Alternative Sanctions Under the Guidelines 351
        (5) Occupational Restrictions 352
        (6) Where Do They Go to Jail? 353

C. Entity Sanctions 354
    Scope Note 354
    1. Fines 355
        United States Sentencing Commission, Discussion Draft of Sentencing Guidelines and Policy Statements for Organizations 355

Notes and Queries

        (1) Understanding the Theory 357
        (2) Three Details 360
        (3) Queries 361
        (4) Collateral Consequences 362
        (5) Equity Fine 362
    2. Probation 364
        United States v. Missouri Valley Construction Company 364

Notes and Queries

        (1) Charitable Contributions Under the Sentencing Reform Act 369
        (2) The Purposes of Corporate Probation 370
        (3) Just Desserts 370
        (4) Limits on the Cost of Probationary Conditions 373
        United States Sentencing Commission, Discussion Draft of Sentencing Guidelines and Policy Statements for Organizations 373

Notes and Queries

        (1) The Commission's Proposal and the Sentencing Reform Act 374
        (2) Alternative Proposal 375
        (3) Debarment 376
        (4) Imprisonment 377
        (5) Endnote 381

TABLE OF CONTENTS

PART TWO. PROBLEMS OF CRIMINAL PROCEDURE

	Page
CHAPTER 4. CORPORATE PRIVILEGES	382
A. Constitutional	382
Scope Note	382
Hale v. Henkel	382
Notes and Queries	
(1) Understanding the Context of Hale v. Henkel	390
(2) Queries	392
(3) Developing Hale's Fifth Amendment Theory	393
(4) The Partnership Entity	397
(5) The Constitutional Rights of Corporations	399
(6) Double Jeopardy	400
B. Common Law: Attorney–Client Privilege	401
Scope Note	401
1. Qualifying for the Privilege	402
Upjohn Co. v. United States	402
Notes and Queries	
(1) The Court's Choices	411
(2) Internal Investigations	412
(3) E.F. Hutton Internal Investigation	416
(4) Lying During an Investigation	418
2. Losing the Privilege	419
In Re Grand Jury Proceedings (FMC Corp.)	419
Queries	422
Commodity Futures Trading Commission v. Weintraub	423
Notes and Queries	
(1) Who Can Waive the Privilege?	429
(2) Remember—Who Is the Client?	432
(3) Endnote	434
CHAPTER 5. THE GRAND JURY	435
A. Fundamentals of Grand Jury Power	435
Scope Note	435
Hale v. Henkel	435
Blair v. United States	439
Notes and Queries	
(1) Role and Function of the Grand Jury—Some History	442
(2) Constitutional Protection?	445
(3) Coverage of the Grand Jury Clause: States and Corporations	446
(4) Executive Control Over the Grand Jury	449
B. Conducting the Grand Jury Inquest	450
Scope Note	450

TABLE OF CONTENTS

Page

B. Conducting the Grand Jury Inquest—Continued
  1. Grand Jury Secrecy 451
    Federal Rules of Criminal Procedure, Rule 6(e) 451

Notes and Queries

    (1) Reasons for Secrecy 453
    (2) Debriefing Witnesses 454
    (3) How Secret Are Grand Jury Proceedings? 455
  2. Presenting Evidence to the Grand Jury 456
    In Re Grand Jury 79–01 456
    United States v. Deerfield Specialty Papers, Inc 459

Notes and Queries

    (1) Should There Be Any Duty? 461
    (2) Tactical Choices 462
  3. Challenging the Decision to Indict 465
    Bank Of Nova Scotia v. United States 465

Notes and Queries

    (1) Queries 472
    (2) Post–Conviction Attacks on Grand Jury Errors 472
    (3) Constitutional Error 476
    (4) Endnote—Indict a Ham Sandwich? 477
C. Multiple Representation and Conflicts of Interest 477
  Pirillo v. Takiff 477

Notes and Queries

    (1) Tactics—Who Wants Multiple Representation? 483
    (2) Constitutional Right to Counsel 485
    (3) Separate Representation and the Joint Defense Privilege 490

CHAPTER 6. GOVERNMENT EVIDENCE GATHERING 496
A. Immunity 496
  Scope Note 496
  Counselman v. Hitchcock 496
  Brown v. Walker 499

Notes and Queries

    (1) Resist Beginnings? 504
    (2) Transactional v. Use Immunity 506
    (3) Prosecutions for Perjury 510
    (4) Fear of Foreign Prosecution 511
  Murphy v. Waterfront Commission 514

Notes and Queries

    (1) Queries 517
    (2) Defense Witness Immunity 518
    (3) Enforcing "Non–Statutory" Grants of Immunity 522
    (4) Talking to the Government 524

TABLE OF CONTENTS

	Page
B. Search Warrants	528
Scope Note	528
1. Protection of Business Premises	530
Marshall v. Barlow's, Inc	530

Notes and Queries

(1) Constitutional Background—Administrative Searches ... 535
(2) Pervasively Regulated Industries ... 537
(3) Reasonable Expectations of Privacy? ... 542
(4) Queries ... 545

  2. Scope of a Lawful Search ... 546
    Warden v. Hayden ... 546

Notes and Queries

(1) Expanding the Scope of the Search ... 550
(2) Privacy Protection Act ... 553
(3) Law Office Searches ... 554

  3. Specificity ... 558
    Andresen v. Maryland ... 558

Notes and Queries

(1) Queries ... 563
(2) Is Specificity Possible? ... 563

  4. Remedy ... 568
    Massachusetts v. Sheppard ... 568

Notes and Queries

(1) The Rationale for the "Good Faith Exception" ... 572
(2) Queries ... 575
(3) Motions for Return of Unlawfully Seized Evidence ... 577

  5. Endnote ... 579

C. Subpoenas and Summonses ... 580
Scope Note ... 580
Oklahoma Press Publishing Co. v. Walling ... 581

Notes and Queries

(1) The Correct Analogy? ... 587
(2) Grand Jury Subpoenas ... 589
(3) Searches Followed by Subpoenas—The Fruits Problem ... 589
(4) Subpoenas to Third Parties—Notice to Targets ... 592
(5) Subpoenas to Third Parties—Paying the Costs ... 596

Fisher v. United States ... 598

Notes and Queries

(1) Developing Fifth Amendment Doctrine ... 607
(2) What Does Fisher Mean—Round 1 ... 607
(3) What Does Fisher Mean—Round 2 ... 612
(4) What Is Testimonial? ... 617

TABLE OF CONTENTS

Page

CHAPTER 7. INTERPLAY BETWEEN CIVIL AND CRIMINAL PROCEEDINGS 623

    Scope Note 623

A. Order of Litigation 624

    United States v. LaSalle National Bank 624

        Notes and Queries

        (1) Aftermath of LaSalle 629

        (2) Institutional Good Faith 629

        (3) Agency Investigation and the Criminal Referral 630

        (4) Why Permit Simultaneous Government Civil and Criminal Proceedings? 635

        (5) Bargaining Over the Criminal Referral 637

    Note: Staying Parallel Proceedings 643

B. Fifth Amendment Issues 645

    Pillsbury Co. v. Conboy 645

        Notes and Queries

        (1) Blocking Civil Litigation 651

        (2) When Are You Entitled to Assert the Fifth? 653

        (3) Taking the Fifth After Conviction 654

        (4) The Costs of Taking the Fifth 655

        (5) Answering the Complaint 656

        (6) Taking the Fifth Amendment at Trial 658

    In Re Grand Jury Subpoena 659

        Notes and Queries

        (1) Queries 666

        (2) Granting a Stay 667

C. Grand Jury Materials 668

    Douglas Oil Co. v. Petrol Stops Northwest 668

        Notes and Queries

        (1) Queries 675

        (2) Particularized Need—Taking the Fifth 675

        (3) Government as Civil Plaintiff 676

Appendix 680

Index 697

TABLE OF STATUTES

References are to pages where the text of important statutes has been reproduced or where the substance thereof is stated.

UNITED STATES

UNITED STATES CONSTITUTION

Amend.	Page
4	560
	607
5	512
	514
	560
	607
	617
	651
	653
	654
	655
	666

UNITED STATES CODE ANNOTATED

7 U.S.C.A.—Agriculture

Sec.	Page
13	4

15 U.S.C.A.—Commerce and Trade

Sec.	Page
13a	3
24	261
78m(b)(2)	7
78u(d)(2)(A)	163
78dd–1	7
78dd–2	7
78ff	7
78ff(a)	242
2068	5
2070	5
2615(b)	6

18 U.S.C.A.—Crimes and Criminal Procedure

Sec.	Page
215	9
656	9
657	9
981	11
1116(d)	47
1343	116
1344	9
1356(b)	12
1357(b)	11

UNITED STATES CODE ANNOTATED

18 U.S.C.A.—Crimes and Criminal Procedure

Sec.	Page
1357(d)	11
1510	418
1512	418
1863	369
1956(a)(1)	11
1957	11
1961(1)	98
1963(a)(1)	103
1964(c)	103
2113	9
2314	44
2320	46
3551 et seq.	297
3551(c)	369
3553	298
3553(a)(2)	370
3555	299
3556	299
3559	300
3561	300
3561(a)(3)	352
3563	300
3571	302
	362
3572	302
	361
3572(a)(4)	207
3582	303
3742	297
6002	509
	511
	512
	517
	522
	651
	654
6003	512
	517
	518
	522

26 U.S.C.A.—Internal Revenue Code

Sec.	Page
7602	629

TABLE OF STATUTES

UNITED STATES CODE ANNOTATED

28 U.S.C.A.—Judiciary and Judicial Procedure

Sec.	Page
991 et seq.	303
994	304
994(d)	319

29 U.S.C.A.—Labor

Sec.	Page
666	5

31 U.S.C.A.—Money and Finance

Sec.	Page
5313	11
5322(b)	219

33 U.S.C.A.—Navigation and Navigable Waters

Sec.	Page
1319(c)(1)	5

42 U.S.C.A.—The Public Health and Welfare

Sec.	Page
2000aa et seq.	553
2000aa–11	553
2000aa–12	554
6928(d)	6
7413(c)	5

49 U.S.C.A.—Transportation

Sec.	Page
10741	2
10751	2
11903	2
11904(b)	2

50 U.S.C.A.App.—War and National Defense

Sec.	Page
2402(5)	7
2407	7
2410	7

STATUTES AT LARGE

Year	Page
1906, June 29, P.L., 59–337, 34 Stat. 584	2
1906, June 29, P.L., 59–337, 34 Stat. 587	2
1906, June 29, P.L., 59–337, 34 Stat. 588	2
1909, Mar. 4, P.L., 60–343, 35 Stat. 1075	3
1909, Mar. 4, P.L., 60–343, 35 Stat. 1082	3
1982, Sept. 3, P.L., 97–248, 96 Stat. 324	629

STATUTES AT LARGE

Year	Page
1984, Oct. 10, P.L., 98–376, 98 Stat. 1264	163
1986, Oct. 27, P.L., 99–570, 100 Stat. 3207–18	11, 12
1986, Oct. 27, P.L., 99–570, 100 Stat. 3207–25	11
1986, Oct. 27, P.L., 99–570, §§ 1351–1367, 100 Stat. 3027–28	11
1986, Oct. 27, P.L., 99–570, § 1356(b), 100 Stat. 3207–23	12
1986, Oct. 27, P.L., 99–570, § 1357(b), 100 Stat. 3207–26	11
1986, Oct. 27, P.L., 99–570, § 1357(d), 100 Stat. 3207–26	11
1987, Dec. 11, P.L., 100–185, 101 Stat. 1279	302
1988, Aug. 23, P.L., 100–418, 102 Stat. 1107	8
1988, Aug. 23, P.L., 100–418, § 5001ff, 102 Stat. 1415	8
1988, Nov. 18, P.L., 100–690, § 7603, 102 Stat. 4508	137
1988, Nov. 19, P.L., 100–704, 102 Stat. 4677	163

POPULAR NAME ACTS

BANK SECRECY ACT

Tit.	Page
II	11

CLAYTON ACT

Sec.	Page
14	261

INTERSTATE COMMERCE ACT

Sec.	Page
10	2

PRIVACY PROTECTION ACT OF 1980

Tit.	Page
I	553
II	553

RIVERS & HARBORS ACT OF 1899

Sec.	Page
13	259
16	259

ROBINSON–PATMAN ACT

Sec.	Page
3	3

TABLE OF STATUTES

SECURITIES EXCHANGE ACT OF 1934

Sec.	Page
10(b)	148
10b	4
32(a)	242

SENTENCING REFORM ACT OF 1984

Sec.	Page
235(b)(1)	297

SHERMAN ACT

Sec.	Page
1	2
	8
2	2

STATE STATUTES

WEST'S FLORIDA STATUTES ANNOTATED

Sec.	Page
921.001	308

MINNESOTA STATUTES ANNOTATED

Sec.	Page
244.08	308

FEDERAL RULES OF CIVIL PROCEDURE

Rule	Page
8(d)	656

FEDERAL RULES OF CRIMINAL PROCEDURE

Rule	Page
6	450
	679
6(a)	450
6(d)	451
	473
6(e)	451
	453
	455
	456
	679
6(e)(3)(C)(i)	676
6(f)	450
16	675
41	578
41(e)	577

CODE OF FEDERAL REGULATIONS

Tit.	Page
28, § 50.18	7
28, §§ 59.1–59.6	554

FEDERAL REGISTER

Vol.	Page
49, p. 13099	7

TABLE OF CASES

Principal cases are in italic type. Non-principal cases are in roman type. References are to Pages.

Abrams, United States v., 418
Adamo, United States v., 461
Aitken, United States v., 258
Albany, Corporation of, People v., 180
Allegheny Bottling Co., United States v., 695 F.Supp. 856, p. 379
Allegheny Bottling Co., United States v. 1988–2 Trade Cas. ¶68,350, p. 380
American Radiator & Standard Sanitary Corp., United States v., 227
American Tobacco Co., United States v., 31 S.Ct. 632, p. 391
American Tobacco Co., United States v., 191 F. 371, p. 392
Amrep Corp., United States v., 560 F.2d 539, p. 227
Amrep Corp., United States v., 405 F.Supp. 1053, p. 645
Andresen v. Maryland, 558
Angelilli, United States v., 87
Antitrust Grand Jury, In re, 423
Apfelbaum, United States v., 510
Appeal of (see name of party)
Application of (see name of party)
A & P Trucking Company, United States v., 182, 195
Armored Transport, Inc., United States v., 446
Armour & Co., United States v., 206

Badders v. United States, 116
Bain, Ex parte, 442
Ballard v. United States, 451
Baltimore and Ohio Railroad, United States v., 182
Bank of New England, N.A., United States v., 12, 219
Bank of Nova Scotia v. United States, 465, 472, 476, 477
Basic Const. Co., United States v., 206
Baxter v. Palmigiano, 655, 657
Bellis v. United States, 397
Bennett v. Berg, 97
Bennett v. United States Trust Co. of New York, 97
Bernstein, United States v., 296
Beusch, United States v., 197, 206, 207
B.F. Hirsch v. Enright Refining Co., Inc., 97
Blair, In re, 446
Blair v. United States, 435, 439, 442, 445, 661

Bottone, United States v., 43
Boyce Motor Lines v. United States, 27
Boyd v. United States, 392
Bracy v. United States, 462
Branzburg v. Hayes, 589
Braswell v. United States, 612
Brennan, United States v., 87
Briggs & Stratton Corp. v. Baldrige, 9
Bronston, United States v., 125
Brown v. Walker, 496, 499, 504, 507
Burton, United States v., 257

Cadillac Overall Supply Co., United States v., 197, 206
Calandra, United States v., 442, 451, 589, 591
California, State of v. United States, 182
Camara v. Municipal Court of City and County of San Francisco, 535, 545
Canadian Fur Trappers' Corporation, People v., 208
Cardassi, In re, 512
Carpenter v. United States, 133, 137
Carpenter, United States v., 148, 149
Carter, United States v., 197
Chiarella v. United States, 80, 138, 148, 152
Christy Pontiac–GMC, Inc., State v., 208
Ciambrone, United States v., 461
C.I.T. Corporation v. United States, 206
City of (see name of city)
Clark v. United States, 422
Commonwealth v. ____(see opposing party)
Commodity Futures Trading Com'n v. Weintraub, 423
Commonwealth of (see name of Commonwealth)
Computer Sciences Corp., United States v., 97
Core Laboratories, Inc., United States v., 9
Corporation of (see name of corporation)
Corrugated Container Antitrust Litigation, In re, 675
Costello v. United States, 451
Counselman v. Hitchcock, 496
Cox, United States v., 449
Curcio v. United States, 612
Curtis, United States v., 257

Dahlstrom, United States v., 257

TABLE OF CASES

Danilow Pastry Co., Inc., United States v., 370
Davis, United States v., 87
Deerfield Speciality Papers, Inc., United States v., 459, 522
DePalma, United States v., 88
Diaz, United States v., 575
Dirks v. S.E.C., 146, 148
Doe v. United States, 617
Doe, Inc. I, John, United States v., 679
Doe, United States v., 607
Donovan v. Dewey, 537, 538, 542, 545
Dotterweich, United States v., 228, 262, 276, 281, 287
Douglas Oil Co. of California v. Petrol Stops Northwest, 623, *668,* 675, 676
Dow Chemical Co. v. United States, 542
Dowling v. United States, 33, 42, 43, 118, 132
Dowling, United States v., 42
Dunn v. United States, 228
Dye Const. Co., United States v., 207

Eisenstein, United States v., 258
Ex parte (see name of party)

Fagan, United States v., 133
Farmers and Merchants Bank, United States v., 596, 598
Fields, United States v., 637
Film Recovery Systems, People v., 187
First Nat. Bank of Boston v. Bellotti, 400
First Nat. Bank of Clark, State v., 180
Fisher v. United States, 393, 580, *598,* 612, 617
Florida v. Riley, 545
FMC Corp., United States v., 167, *213,* 219
Folding Carton Antitrust Litigation, In re, 654
Ford Motor Co., State v., 184
Forsythe, United States v., 87
Fountain, United States v., 475
Frank v. State of Maryland, 536
Frezzo Bros., Inc., United States v., 6, 279

GAF Corp., United States v., 666
Garber, United States v., 247, 256
Gibson Products Co., Inc., United States v., 206
Gilboe, In re, 512
Ginsburg, United States v., 103
Gold, United States v., 197, 295, 296
Golden Quality Ice Cream Co., Inc. v. Deerfield Specialty Papers, Inc., 645
Government of Virgin Islands v. Smith, 518
Grand Jury Empanelled October 18, 1979 (Malfitano), In re, 589
Grand Jury Investigation of Ocean Transp., In re, 429
Grand Jury Proceedings, In re, 454, *419*
Grand Jury Proceedings, Detroit, Mich., Aug. 1977, In re, 432

Grand Jury 79–01, In re, 456
Grand Jury Proceedings, In re, 604 F.2d 798, p. *419*
Grand Jury Proceedings, In re, 558 F.Supp. 532, p. 454
Grand Jury Subpoena Duces Tecum Dated November 16, 1974, Matter of, 490
Grand Jury Subpoena Duces Tecum Dated Sept. 15, 1983, In re, 423
Grayson, United States v., 307
Groder v. United States, 629
Grzywacz, United States v., 87
Gulf Oil Corp., United States v., 279

Hague v. CIO, 399
Hale, In re, 444
Hale v. Henkel, 382, 390, 391, 392, 397, 401, 435, 442, 443, 444, 445, 504, 580, 587, 589
Hamel, United States v., 7
Hancock Free Bridge Corp., Commonwealth v., 180
Harford, United States v., 380
Haroco, Inc. v. American Nat. Bank and Trust Co. of Chicago, 97, 98
Harper & Row Publishers, Inc. v. Decker, 412
Hartley, United States v., 93
Hayes Intern. Corp., United States v., 6
Herzog, United States v., 256
Hilton Hotels Corp., United States v., 3, 167, *202,* 206, 208
H.J. Inc. v. Northwestern Bell Telephone Co., 106
Hoffman v. United States, 653
Holloway v. Arkansas, 485
Holzer, United States v., 133
Hooks, United States v., 522
Huber, United States v., 100
Hurtado v. People of State of California, 444, 446

Illinois Cent. R. Co., Com. v., 180
Indelicato, United States v., 106
Ingredient Technology Corp., United States v., 257
In re (see name of party)
International Harvester Co. of America v. Commonwealth of Kentucky, 25, 27
International Minerals & Chemical Corp., United States v., 242
Interstate Cigar Co., Inc., United States v., 373

Johnson & Towers, Inc., United States v., 6
Joudis, United States v., 512

Kastigar v. United States, 507, 517, 647
Katz v. United States, 529
Kenney International Corp., United States v., 8
Key Line Freight, Inc. v. United States, 2
Klimavicius, United States v., 512
Kordel, United States v., 636

TABLE OF CASES

Lafayette Academy, Inc., Application of, 563, 575
LaSalle Nat. Bank, United States v., 623, *624,* 625, 630
L. Cohen Grocery Co., United States v., 25, 27
Ledesma, United States v., 117
Leon, United States v., 569, 572, 575, 577, 592
L'Hoste, United States v., 100
Liparota v. United States, 243
Lizza Industries, Inc., United States v., 98, 103
Lord, United States v., 522
Louisville & N. R. Co., United States v., 411

MacAndrews & Forbes Co., United States v., 391
Magnolia Motor & Logging Company v. United States, 228
Mallas, United States v., 257
Mandel, United States v., 862 F.2d 1067, p. 133
Mandel, United States v., 591 F.2d 1347, p. 118
Mangan, United States v., 117
Margiotta, United States v., 116
Marine Midland Bank v. John E. Russo Produce Co., Inc., 658
Marshall v. Barlow's Inc., 529, *530,* 535, 536, 537, 545, 587
Martindell v. International Tel. and Tel. Corp., 667
Martin Linen Supply Co., United States v., 400
Massachusetts v. Sheppard, 568, 575, 592
Matter of (see name of party)
Maze, United States v., 116
McAlister v. Henkel, 391
McKenzie, State v., 240
McNally v. United States, 80, 107, 116, 118, 131, 133, 137
Mechanik, United States v., 472, 475, 476
Meyer, United States v., 9
Minneapolis & St. L. R. Co. v. Beckwith, 400
Mishima v. United States, 512
Missouri Valley Const. Co., United States v., 364, 369, 370, 380
Mistretta v. United States, 297, 309
Morris Canal & Banking Co., State v., 180
Morrison v. Olson, 446
Morse, United States v., 464
Murphy, United States v., 349
Murphy v. Waterfront Commission of New York Harbor, 496, *514,* 517

Nash v. United States, 24, 25, 27
Natelli, United States v., 228, *288,* 295
National Acceptance Co. of America v. Bathalter, 656

National Dairy Products Corp., United States v., 3, 279
Navarro–Ordas, United States v., 103
Newberry v. United States, 446
New York v. Burger, 538, 542, 545
New York Cent. & H. R. R. Co. v. United States, 2, 167, *174,* 178, 179, 184, 195, 208, 227, 354
Nye & Nissen v. United States, 261

O'Connor v. Johnson, 554
O'Connor v. Ortega, 545
Oklahoma Press Pub. Co. v. Walling, 580, *581,* 587, 588, 589
Olmstead, United States v., 464

Pacific Powder Co., State v., 180
Page, United States v., 461
Palmieri v. State of N.Y., 666
Park, United States v., 228, 262, *267,* 276, 277, 287
Patten, United States v., 239
Patterson v. United States, 24
Patterson, United States v., 15, 24, 25, 27, 42, 117
Pennsylvania, Commonwealth of v. Derry Const. Co., Inc., 98
Pennsylvania Indus. Chemical Corp., United States v., 259
People v. _____(see opposing party)
Pereira v. United States, 116
Petrol Stops Northwest v. Continental Oil Co., 675
Phelps Dodge Corp., United States v., 7
Philadelphia, City of v. Westinghouse Elec. Corp., 411
Pickel v. United States, 625
Pillsbury Co. v. Conboy, 517, 623, *645,* 651, 653, 675
Pirillo v. Takiff, 477, 483, 485, 495
Powell, United States v., 105 S.Ct. 471, p. 228
Powell, United States v., 85 S.Ct. 248, pp. 588, 627
Precision Medical Laboratories, Inc., United States v., 261
President of Susquehannah & Bath Turnpike Rd. Co. v. People, 180
Procter & Gamble Co., United States v., 78 S.Ct. 983, pp. 453, 456
Procter & Gamble Co., United States v., 47 F.Supp. 676, pp. 132, 133

Rachal, United States v., 279
Radiant Burners, Inc. v. American Gas Ass'n, 411
Rae v. Union Bank, 97
Reich, United States v., 324
Roberts v. United States, 577, 579
Rodriguez, United States v., 333
Rogers, United States v., 103
Rose, United States v., 453
Rubin, United States v., 512

TABLE OF CASES

Runnels, United States v., 133
Russello v. United States, 101, 102, 103

Sandstrom v. Montana, 239
San Mateo County v. Southern Pac. R. Co., 399
Santa Clara County v. Southern Pac. R. Co., 399
Schmuck v. United States, 116
Schreiber Distributing Co. v. Serv-Well Furniture Co., Inc., 98
Screws Antitrust Litigation, In re, 675
Sealed Case, In re, 446
Search Warrant B–21778, In re, 554
S.E.C. v. Dresser Industries, Inc., 630
S.E.C. v. Jerry T. O'Brien, Inc., 592, 598
Security Nat. Bank, United States v., 400
Sedima, S.P.R.L. v. Imrex Co., Inc., 104, 105
See v. City of Seattle, 535, 545
Sells Engineering, Inc., United States v., 676
Shelbyville, Corporation of, State v., 180
Silverthorne Lumber Co. v. United States, 589
Smyth v. Ames, 400
Spiezio, United States v., 296
Standard Drywall Corp., United States v., 117
Standard Oil Co. of Tex. v. United States, 167, *192,* 197, 200
Standard Sanitary Mfg. Co. v. United States, 643
Standard Sanitary Mfg. Co., United States v., 522
State v. ____(see opposing party)
State of (see name of state)
States, United States v., 116
Steere Tank Lines, Inc. v. United States, 198

Thompson, United States v., 87
Torkington, United States v., 47
Trammel v. United States, 589
Turkette, United States v., 80, 81, 87
Turkish, United States v., 519

Ullmann v. United States, 504, 507
(Under Seal), United States v., 512
Union Pac. R. Co. v. United States, 182
United States v. ____(see opposing party)
Upjohn Co. v. United States, 402, 411, 412, 429, 434, 630
U. S. Gypsum Co., United States v., 146, 206, *228,* 239, 241

Valencia, United States v., 522
Vasquez v. Hillery, 451, 473, 476, 477
Velsicol Chemical Corp. v. Parsons, 429
Von Barta, United States v., 122, 124

Walsh, In re, 589
Warden, Md. Penitentiary v. Hayden, 546, 550, 563
Washington, United States v., 451
Wehling v. Columbia Broadcasting System, 667
Weiss v. United States, 116
Western Laundry & Linen Rental Co. v. United States, 184
Western Turf Ass'n v. Greenburg, 400
Wheat v. United States, 485
White v. Mapco Gas Products, Inc., 645
White, United States v., 393, 397, 607
Williams v. United States, 9
Wilson v. United States, 612
Winans, United States v., 149
Wise, United States v., 279
Wolfson, United States v., 589
Wood v. Georgia, 442

Yamashita, Application of, 282
Yellow Freight System, Inc., United States v., 449
Yermian, United States v., 247
Young v. United States ex rel. Vuitton et Fils S.A., 48

Zicarelli v. New Jersey State Commission of Investigation, 511
Zurcher v. Stanford Daily, 550, 553, 554, 588

BUSINESS CRIME

CASES AND MATERIALS

*

Part One

PROBLEMS OF SUBSTANTIVE CRIMINAL LAW

Chapter 1

BUSINESS CRIMES

A. STATUTORY OVERVIEW

SCOPE NOTE

The materials in this Section are intended to provide broad familiarity with the history and basic content of many of the substantive federal business crimes which the student will encounter in this casebook. The Section begins with an Essay describing the three major regulatory periods during which Congress enacted important business crime legislation. Following this Essay are four Notes. The first two describe substantive areas which do not fit neatly within this historical treatment, but which are, nevertheless, significant—international trade and financial institutions. The third Note describes the failed effort to enact a Federal Criminal Code. The Section concludes with a bibliographical Note, containing references to books which deal generally with business crime.

ESSAY: THREE REGULATORY PERIODS

Federal regulatory legislation is essentially the product of three historical periods: 1) the initial era of federal regulation of the economy, 1887 to 1914; 2) the New Deal era, 1932 to 1940; and 3) the "environmental-consumerist" era, 1968 to 1977.[1] Even though federal regulatory legislation imposes both criminal and civil liability, these statutes have generally not been thought of as "criminal laws" in the same way that a legislature would think of murder as a "crime." Rather, the criminal sanction has been included as an additional tool which could be used by the government to achieve the regulatory goals sought in the legislation. In many of these statutes, criminal provisions were included with virtually no Congressional debate as to why the criminal sanction was desirable, or when criminal remedies should be used rather than civil, or against whom the criminal sanction should be invoked. Legislative attention was generally directed at the broader question whether it was appropriate or constitutional to enact any

---

[1]. For a good review of these regulatory periods, albeit without reference to criminal enforcement, see Rabin, Federal Regulation in Historical Perspective, 38 Stan.L. Rev. 1189 (1986).

regulatory legislation at all. Once the propriety of legislation was accepted, the inclusion of a criminal sanction was often accepted as a matter of course.

The initial era of federal regulation began with the Interstate Commerce Act of 1887. This statute established the first major federal regulatory agency, the Interstate Commerce Commission, and gave the Commission jurisdiction over a number of railroad practices, many of which involved discrimination in price or service between shippers or regions.[2] Section 10 of the Act created the first important "business crime," making it a misdemeanor, punishable by fine, willfully to violate the Act. This meant, for example, that it would be a crime to charge a customer a different rate than the one established in the railroad's "tariff" (a public listing of all the railroad's charges), or to give a customer a "rebate" (i.e., a refund of part of the money previously paid to the railroad).

These price discrimination provisions were enforced with some vigor and became the substantive setting for a number of important business crime cases.[3] Congress subsequently attempted to strengthen this prohibition, through passage of the Elkins Act of 1903 and the Hepburn Act of 1906, eventually extending criminal liability to the "knowing" grant or acceptance of a discriminatory price or rebate.[4] This provision still remains in force for railroad pricing.[5]

The second major federal business crime of this era was the Sherman Act of 1890.[6] This statute, directed at the "trusts" (i.e., large corporations) of the day, prohibited agreements "in restraint of trade" (Section 1) and prohibited "monopolization" (Section 2). The Act gave the Attorney General the power to seek an injunction against violations of the statute, and gave private parties the right to sue for three times their damages caused by a violation of the Act. In addition Sections 1 and 2 provided that "every person" who violated the Act could be imprisoned for up to one year and/or fined a maximum of $5,000. These penalties were increased in 1974. Maximum imprisonment was raised to three years (making the crime a felony rather than a misdemeanor). The fine was increased to a maximum of $100,000 for individuals, or $1 million for corporations.[7] Despite the breadth of the

---

2. The power to establish just and reasonable railroad rates was not given to the Commission until 1906, when Congress passed the Hepburn Act. See 34 Stat. 584 (1906).

3. See, e.g., New York Central & H.R.R. Co. v. United States, infra p. 174.

4. See Hepburn Act, 34 Stat. 587, 588 (1906).

5. See 49 U.S.C.A. §§ 10741, 11903. The Motor Carrier Act of 1935, regulating entry and pricing in the trucking industry, contained a similar provision, see 49 U.S.C.A. § 11904(b). For an interesting application, see Key Line Freight, Inc. v. United States, 570 F.2d 97 (6th Cir.1978) (giving shippers expense-paid trip to Kentucky Derby violates statute). But see 49 U.S.C.A. § 10751 (such business entertainment expenses no longer illegal).

6. The provisions are set out in the Statutory Appendix, infra.

7. The penalties described in this Essay for this and all other federal crimes are those authorized by the statute describing the offense. The Sentencing Reform Act of 1984, which was part of the Comprehensive Crime Control Act of 1984, classified all federal offenses by a letter grade (e.g., "Class A"), and then provided a new range

statutory language, criminal enforcement of the antitrust laws has been limited almost exclusively to cases where competitors have agreed to fix the prices of the goods or services they sell.[8] Nevertheless, the criminal provisions of this statute have been a major component of federal business crime prosecutions, although the intensity of enforcement has varied over time.[9]

The third important statute enacted in this initial period was the Pure Food and Drug Act of 1906, the product of contemporary outrage over unsanitary conditions in the food industry. This Act gave the government the power to seize foods and drugs which were adulterated or misbranded, and made it a crime, punishable by up to one year imprisonment, to manufacture, distribute, or sell such adulterated or misbranded foods or drugs. This Act is particularly important because it is considered the source of what has been termed "no fault public welfare offenses." [10]

Although Congress enacted other regulatory statutes during this period,[11] this era ended with the enactment of major economic regulatory legislation which did *not* include criminal provisions. The Clayton Act of 1914 strengthened the Sherman Act by more clearly prohibiting certain business practices, such as anticompetitive mergers and the use of certain exclusive dealing agreements. The legislation also included a prohibition on price discrimination. Despite the precedent of the Interstate Commerce Act, a proposal to criminalize price discrimination in general was abandoned as the legislation went through Congress, and the Act provided only civil remedies.[12]

The next major period of federal economic regulatory legislation was the New Deal. Although Congress brought many industries under federal control during that period—e.g., trucking, airlines, electric power, natural gas, radio—most of these regulatory schemes relied more on the grant of regulatory pre-approval to control business conduct than on after-the-fact sanctions for business misconduct. An important exception to this pattern, however, was the securities industry. Rather than providing for an administrative agency which would

---

of penalties. Although the term of imprisonment remains the same as provided in the statute describing the offense, the maximum fine, in some cases, may be higher. Thus, for example, the maximum criminal fine which can be imposed on individuals convicted of violating the Sherman Act was increased from $100,000 to $250,000 or twice the gain or loss from the offense (whichever is greater). These provisions are discussed at greater length, infra Chapter 3A.

8. For a rare example of a criminal antitrust boycott case, see United States v. Hilton Hotels, infra p. 202.

9. For further discussion of criminal antitrust enforcement, see L. Schwartz, J. Flynn & H. First, Free Enterprise and Economic Organization: Antitrust 18–19 (6th ed. 1983).

10. Discussed infra, p. 262.

11. The Copyright Act of 1909, for example, made it a crime to infringe a copyright "willfully and for profit." 35 Stat. 1075, 1082 (1909).

12. Congress subsequently criminalized certain types of price discrimination in Section 3 of the Robinson Patman Act of 1935. See 15 U.S.C.A. § 13a. This provision has rarely been invoked. For an example, see United States v. National Dairy Prods. Corp., 372 U.S. 29, 83 S.Ct. 594, 9 L.Ed.2d 561 (1963) (upholding the constitutionality of the statute, as applied in the particular case, against a claim of vagueness).

review stock offerings before they were sold, and then permit only financially sound corporations to issue stock, Congress decided to regulate the issuance and sale of securities through a system of required disclosures made directly to investors.

The two major securities statutes were the Securities Act of 1933 and the Securities Exchange Act of 1934. The 1933 Act required the filing of a registration statement and prospectus, prior to issuance of stock, which would disclose to investors all "material" facts about the corporation, so that the investors themselves could accurately determine whether to invest in the particular stock offering. The 1934 Act required periodic reporting of all material facts relating to a publicly traded corporation's financial posture, required disclosures in connection with the solicitation of proxies for the election of corporate directors, and, in Section 10b, added the general provision forbidding the use of any "manipulative or deceptive device" "in connection with the purchase or sale" of any security.

Although Congress established a regulatory commission to oversee the securities industry and the disclosure requirements (the Securities and Exchange Commission), a critical part of the remedial scheme necessarily involved sanctions imposed in the event a person failed to comply with the disclosure requirements. Further, the fraud-like nature of selling stock without disclosing important facts about the company in which the buyer would be investing made it natural to provide for criminal penalties where such conduct was done "willfully." [13] Given the critical importance of the stock markets to a properly functioning economy, the broad coverage of the securities acts with regard to corporate financial practices, and the opportunities the stock markets provide for outright swindles, the securities laws have been an important component of business crime enforcement.[14]

The third major period for the enactment of business crime legislation is the "environmental-consumerist" period, from 1968 to 1977. Congressional attention during this period was focused on some of the social costs of a successful industrial economy—unsafe products and workplaces, and polluted air and water. As with the Pure Food and Drug Act of 1906, this business behavior was a reflection of profit-seeking in the marketplace, and was also close to a major concern of the criminal law—personal safety. Criminal penalties would thus seem appropriate to punish and deter this behavior; but, as in the case of legislation enacted earlier, Congress included criminal sanctions, along

---

13. The criminal provisions of the 1933 and 1934 Acts are reprinted in the Statutory Appendix, infra. The criminal provisions of the 1933 and 1934 Acts are explored in Herlands, Criminal Law Aspects of the Securities Act of 1933, 67 U.S.L.Rev. 562 (1933), and Herlands, Criminal Law Aspects of the Securities Exchange Act of 1934, 21 Va.L.Rev. 139 (1934). For a review of the problems in criminal securities law prosecutions, see H. Friedman, Securities and Commodities Enforcement: Criminal Prosecutions and Civil Injunctions (1981).

14. Trading in other types of markets has also been protected through the criminal law. See, e.g., Commodity Futures Trading Commission Act of 1974, 7 U.S.C.A. § 13.

with a wide variety of civil remedies, without paying much attention to the question whether such criminal penalties were appropriate or, even, effective.

The first important statutes of this period were passed in 1970. In the Occupational Safety and Health Act, Congress established the Occupational Safety and Health Administration ("OSHA") and gave it broad powers to promulgate national workplace safety standards, and to inspect businesses for violations. Although the Act relied heavily on "civil penalties" (i.e., money fines, but no imprisonment), criminal penalties were provided for "willful" violations of any OSHA regulation causing death to an employee.[15] In the same year Congress passed the Clean Air Amendments to the Air Quality Act of 1967. The 1970 Amendments, inter alia, introduced criminal penalties for certain air pollution offenses, giving the Administrator of the Environmental Protection Agency ("EPA") authority to seek either injunctive relief, civil penalties, or, for willful violations of the Act, fine and/or imprisonment.[16]

In 1972 Congress amended the Federal Water Pollution Control Act, establishing a comprehensive scheme of licenses and permits to make it unlawful to discharge pollutants into navigable waters without either securing a permit issued by the EPA or acting under an approved state program. As in the case of air pollution, criminal sanctions previously had not been part of the general regulatory scheme. And, as in the case of air pollution, the EPA was given a choice of injunctive, civil, and criminal penalty provisions, although criminal liability under the Water Pollution Act could be imposed either for "willful" or "negligent" violations.[17]

In 1972 Congress also enacted the Consumer Product Safety Act, which responded to the concern that many consumer products posed an unreasonable risk of injury, or even death. The Act established the Consumer Product Safety Commission ("CPSC"), giving it the power to promulgate federal safety standards for consumer products (dealing with, e.g., performance, design, or labelling) and to ban the sale of those products it found hazardous. As with the environmental legislation, there were a number of predecessor statutes dealing with the safety of specific types of products. Although some of these statutes had criminal provisions, their criminal provisions had rarely been invoked. A criminal provision was included in this new statute as well, providing that "knowing and willful" violations, occurring after receipt of notice of noncompliance from the Commission, could be punished by a fine of up to $50,000 and/or imprisonment of up to one year.[18]

---

15. For the criminal provision of the Act, see 29 U.S.C.A. § 666.

16. The Act's criminal penalties were strengthened in the Clean Air Act Amendments of 1977. See 42 U.S.C.A. § 7413(c).

17. See 33 U.S.C.A. § 1319(c)(1). For a discussion of these provisions, see Glenn, The Crime of "Pollution": The Role of Federal Water Pollution Criminal Sanctions, 11 Am.Crim.L.Rev. 835 (1973).

18. See 15 U.S.C.A. §§ 2068, 2070.

Two other important environmental laws were enacted in 1976 to deal with the problems caused by hazardous substances in the environment. One was the Toxic Substances Control Act. This Act addressed the concern that new chemicals were being brought to market each year which could have severe harmful effects in the future, including cancer and genetic mutation. Congress believed then-current legislation was inadequate, because the legislation focused either on too narrow a group of products (e.g., food and drugs) or focused on the medium being polluted (e.g., air and water) rather than on the substance causing the pollution.

The Toxic Substances Control Act gave the EPA the power to evaluate the potential hazards of new chemical substances prior to manufacture. Those thought to pose an "unreasonable risk" to health or environment had to be tested prior to marketing; depending on the results, the chemical substance could then be banned from manufacture, or subject to mandatory labelling. "Knowing or willful" violations of the Act were subject to fines of $25,000 per day and/or up to one year imprisonment. Interestingly, although the chemical industry was strongly opposed to the passage of the bill, their witnesses did not question the inclusion of criminal penalties, perhaps reflecting an assumption that these penalties were not likely to be invoked (an assumption borne out to date).[19]

The other important environmental statute enacted in 1976 was the Resource Conservation and Recovery Act ("RCRA"). The bill was designed to deal with the end of the distribution chain—the disposal of "hazardous wastes." Recognizing that chemicals and other substances were being discarded with little concern for their longevity, or the security of the place or container in which they were being "stored," the Act required the EPA to establish criteria for identifying and listing hazardous wastes, and empowered the EPA to issue permits to operators of hazardous waste disposal sites. The EPA was given a broad array of powers—inspections, compliance orders, and civil penalties. Criminal penalties were provided for the "knowing" transportation of hazardous wastes without a permit, and for misrepresentations knowingly made with regard to any permit or on any shipping manifest.[20] Despite the importance of this statute to public health, this—and other statutes of this period—have received only sporadic criminal enforcement.[21]

19. For the criminal provision of the Act, see 15 U.S.C.A. § 2615(b).

20. For the criminal provisions of the Act, see 42 U.S.C.A. § 6928(d).

21. For criminal cases under RCRA, see United States v. Hayes International Corp., 786 F.2d 1499 (11th Cir.1986) (knowledge of illegal disposal of waste inferred from extremely low price paid by the defendants for the "disposal"); United States v. Johnson & Towers, Inc., 741 F.2d 662 (3d Cir. 1984) (criminal provisions cover employees as well as employers; knowledge of lack of permit may be inferred for individuals who hold responsible positions within the corporation), certiorari denied 469 U.S. 1208, 105 S.Ct. 1171, 84 L.Ed.2d 321 (1985). For criminal cases under the Federal Water Pollution Control Act, see, e.g., United States v. Frezzo Bros., Inc., 602 F.2d 1123 (3d Cir.1979) (held: government can maintain a criminal proceeding under the Act without first instituting a civil action or giving notice of the alleged violation), certi-

NOTES

(1) *International Trade.* Two significant statutes were enacted in the late 1970s to deal with perceived improper behavior by United States corporations doing business in foreign countries. The first was the Foreign Corrupt Practices Act of 1977 ("FCPA"), which generally prohibited domestic companies from giving anything of value to any "foreign official" or any "foreign political party" or candidate for "foreign political office" for the purpose of influencing their official actions so as to obtain or retain business.[22] The second was the Export Administration Act of 1979, and, specifically, the antiboycott program mandated by the Act.[23] This statute generally barred United States firms from taking certain actions with intent to support a boycott against a country "friendly to the United States," including refusing to do business in the boycotted country or furnishing information about the firm's business relationships with or in the boycotted country or with firms already subject to the boycott. Both statutes provided potentially severe criminal penalties, including imprisonment of up to five years.

Although the two statutes punish different kinds of business behavior, they bear certain similarities. Both can be viewed as an attempt to carry over into the international business sphere American attitudes of business morality, notions which many United States business firms believe are inappropriate and harmful to U.S. business interests abroad. Both statutes were also preceded by enforcement activities under other statutes. The Foreign Corrupt Practices Act was preceded by a series of investigations undertaken by the Securities and Exchange Commission in the mid-1970s involving "questionable payments" by United States firms abroad; failure to disclose such widespread payments, it was argued, violated the Securities Acts, and a number of corporations "voluntarily" audited their foreign practices and agreed to stop making such undisclosed payments. Similarly, the antiboycott provisions of the Export Administration Act were enacted in the wake of a 1977 civil suit brought by the Justice Department against the

orari denied 444 U.S. 1074, 100 S.Ct. 1020, 62 L.Ed.2d 756 (1980); United States v. Hamel, 551 F.2d 107 (6th Cir.1977) (circumstantial evidence held sufficient to connect defendant to illegal discharge); United States v. Phelps Dodge Corp., 391 F.Supp. 1181 (D.Ariz.1975) (defining "navigable waters" broadly; motion to dismiss indictment denied). For a discussion of some of the difficulties in prosecuting environmental crimes, see Note, Putting Polluters in Jail: The Imposition of Criminal Sanctions on Corporate Defendants Under Environmental Statutes, 20 Land & Water L.Rev. 93 (1985); "Against Heavy Odds, EPA Tries to Convict Polluters and Dumpers," Wall St.J., Jan. 7, 1985, p. 1 (noting lack of investigators and scientific resources; focus has been on "small-time" cases; "I don't think we should become a national criminal law-enforcement agency," says EPA enforcement official).

22. See 15 U.S.C.A. §§ 78m(b)(2), 78dd–1, 78dd–2, 78ff. For Justice Department regulations providing for pre-transaction review, see 28 C.F.R. § 50.18.

23. This provision expired by its terms on September 30, 1983. President Reagan subsequently signed an Executive Order purporting to continue the provisions of the Act until Congress enacted a new bill. See 49 Fed.Reg. 13099 (April 3, 1984). The antiboycott provisions were reenacted in 1985. See 50 U.S.C.A.App. §§ 2402(5), 2407, 2410 (Supp.).

Bechtel Company, an international construction firm, for violating Section 1 of the Sherman Act by allegedly agreeing to boycott subcontractors who were on the Arab League's boycott list.[24] The antiboycott legislation is, perhaps, the more overtly political of the two statutes, because its most obvious target is the Arab League's boycott of Israel; but United States' uncovering of foreign "payments" has also had its political repercussions.[25]

Both statutes are also similar for having drawn much criticism from the business community, and little heavy criminal enforcement from the Justice Department. The Reagan Administration supported efforts to amend the Foreign Corrupt Practices Act beginning in the early 1980s.[26] In 1985 the Administration linked the FCPA to the trade deficit, arguing that changes in the Act would "'reduce disincentives' to exports" by allowing U.S. business firms aggressively to pursue overseas business.[27] There have been a few well-publicized criminal convictions under the Act,[28] but the Justice Department has investigated far more cases than it has prosecuted.[29] Congress finally responded to the criticism of the Foreign Corrupt Practices Act, substantially amending it in 1988.[30] The antiboycott provision has likewise not been

24. The litigation was settled by consent decree. See 796 ATRR A–17, E–1 (1977).

25. See, e.g., "Two Japanese Guilty of Bribery in Lockheed Case," Wall St.J., June 9, 1982, p. 33 (reporting conviction of two former Japanese government officials for bribery in connection with Lockheed payments in Japan; payments surfaced in 1976 Senate report of $2 million in payments to Japanese government officials in connection with sale of TriStar in Japan, touching off Japan's "worst political scandal since World War II").

26. See, e.g., "White House Seeks Eased Bribery Act," N.Y.Times, May 21, 1981, p. 1. For a discussion of various proposals, see Bader & Shaw, Amendment of the Foreign Corrupt Practices Act, 15 J.Int'l L & P 627 (1983).

27. See "Reagan Attacks Unfair Trade Practices By Foreign Nations With Modest Plan," Wall St.J., Sept. 24, 1985, p. 3; "Recent Charges of Payoffs by Companies Coincide With Bid to Relax Law Barring Overseas Bribes," Wall St.J., July 10, 1986, p. 54.

28. The first criminal conviction was United States v. Kenney International Corp., 516 Sec.Reg. & L.Rep. (BNA) at A–2 (D.D.C.1979) (guilty plea for payment related to postage stamp distribution in the Cook Islands). The most widely publicized criminal cases have involved payments to Pemex, Mexico's national oil company. See "Pemex Case Convictions," N.Y.Times, April 6, 1985, p. 29 (no contest pleas by four defendants); "Federal Jury Clears Harvester Ex–Official of Bribery Charges," Wall St.J., May 14, 1985, p. 15 (defendant argued at trial that he was "turned into a 'scapegoat'" by his employer, from whom he is seeking "millions of dollars in damages" for allegedly "singl[ing] him out for punishment after the payments to Mexican officials during the late 1970s were uncovered").

29. See Witherspoon, Multinational Corporations—Governmental Regulations of Business Ethics under the Foreign Corrupt Practices Act of 1977: An Analysis, 87 Dickinson L.Rev. 531, 551 (1983) (eighty-five investigations pending). For an interesting account of one series of payments, see "Ashland Oil Criticizes Its Payments to Libyan to Get Oman's Crude," Wall St.J., May 24, 1983, p. 1 (included payments of $2.3 million invested in sausage casings venture and $26 million in a worthless Rhodesian chromium mine). The internal investigation of Ashland is discussed infra, p. 412.

30. See Omnibus Trade and Competitiveness Act of 1988, Pub.L. 100–418, § 5001 et seq., 102 Stat. 1107, 1415 (1988) (adding intent standard to accounting provisions; permitting: payments for "routine governmental action," payments which are lawful in the recipient's country, and payments which are for bona fide expenses incurred by the recipient).

a favorite of enforcement officials. Although some civil penalties have been assessed against major corporations, the amounts have generally been small and no criminal cases have yet been brought.[31]

(2) *Financial Institutions.* Financial institutions have historically been a special concern of federal criminal law. Criminal statutes have long protected banks from having their funds taken improperly, whether by outsiders (robbery) or by insiders ("misapplication" and embezzlement).[32] In recent years federal prosecutorial attention to criminal problems in the banking industry has increased, particularly with the partial deregulation of the banking industry. In 1984, for example, there were 1900 federal convictions for bank fraud, and 8000 cases were pending. In the same year Congress strengthened federal bank fraud and bank bribery legislation, broadening the language of the bank fraud statute [33] and enacting a bank bribery statute which appeared to criminalize the receipt of even small "gratuities" by bank employees.[34] Nevertheless, bank fraud has continued to grow, with estimates of losses from fraud in 1986 amounting to $1.1 billion.[35] With the failure of numerous savings and loans in 1988, criminal enforcement was expected to increase once again.[36]

One of the most spectacular prosecutions involving financial institutions was the case brought in 1985 against E.F. Hutton and Co. for a widespread system of overdrafting its bank accounts. Hutton entered a

---

31. See "'Pariah' Boycott Office Lacks Muscle," Legal Times, Dec. 15, 1986, p. 1 (Kaiser Corp. pays $5,500 for twenty-two violations; 41 cases settled in 1985; "'There are a few people here who are not eager for me to do my job. I'm a trade disincentive,'" says director of enforcement office). For civil cases, see United States v. Meyer, 808 F.2d 912 (1st Cir.1987) (in proceeding to enforce penalty, statute of limitations begins when administrative decision is final, rather than on date of violation). Contra, United States v. Core Laboratories, Inc., 759 F.2d 480 (5th Cir.1985). See also Briggs & Stratton Corp. v. Baldridge, 728 F.2d 915 (7th Cir.) (declaratory judgment action; statute held constitutional), certiorari denied 469 U.S. 826, 105 S.Ct. 106, 83 L.Ed.2d 50 (1984). Compare "Boycott Law Enforcement is Toughened," Wall St.J., Dec. 9, 1982, p. 31 (reporting 48 U.S. companies charged by Commerce Department with boycott-related offenses in fiscal 1982, up from 22 in 1981; amount of fines collected nearly doubled); "Antiboycott Office Steps Up Enforcement Actions," Legal Times of Washington, Oct. 11, 1982, p. 4 (noting increased enforcement; but also notes that no case has ever been brought to federal court, and all but five of 1982 cases were resolved by negotiated settlements).

32. See 18 U.S.C.A. §§ 656, 657, 2113.

33. See 18 U.S.C.A. § 1344. The statute was part of the Comprehensive Crime Control Act of 1984; it was modeled on the mail fraud statute, discussed infra Section C. Among other things, the statute was intended to cover "check kiting," a practice which the Supreme Court had held was not covered by the bank false statement statute. See Williams v. United States, 458 U.S. 279, 102 S.Ct. 3088, 73 L.Ed.2d 767 (1982).

34. See 18 U.S.C.A. § 215. Although there was some concern that the statute was written broadly enough to allow prosecution of customers who took their bankers to lunch, Justice Department guidelines subsequently made clear that the Department would confine prosecution to "acts of corruption in the banking industry," and would not prosecute "inconsequential conduct," such as the "occasional receipt of meals, entertainment, or other gifts of modest or nominal value." See 10 Department of Justice Manual, tit. 9–40.539.B (1988).

35. See "Financial Fraud: Theories Behind Nationwide Surge in Bank Swindles," Wall St.J., Oct. 2, 1987, p. 23 (FBI data).

36. See Corp.Crime Rep., Feb. 13, 1989, at 5 (budget proposal for $50 million for prosecutorial task force; fraud and insider abuse believed to have accounted for 25% of bank failures).

plea of guilty to 2,000 counts of mail and wire fraud, and paid a fine of $2.75 million.

The Hutton case illustrates a number of issues which frequently arise in today's complex business crime prosecutions. First, under what circumstances should the government accept a plea of guilty from a corporation in return for its agreement not to prosecute any individuals? Despite the large fine and guilty plea in the Hutton case, the Department of Justice was criticized for agreeing not to prosecute any of the individuals involved in the scheme. Second, how vigorously should prosecutors push for a negotiated plea in cases which they recognize are legally and factually complex, but which the corporate defendant, for business reasons, might prefer not to contest? In Hutton, the government was never forced to test the validity of the underlying legal theories, which were admittedly "rather unconventional." [37] Third, how should defense counsel weigh the risks and benefits of accepting such an agreement? Despite the hope of Hutton's management, the guilty pleas and fine did not put an end to the matter, but set in motion a complex chain of events, including Congressional investigations, investigations by state securities regulators, and a resulting loss of business.[38] Fourth, when is it appropriate for the corporation to conduct an internal investigation of its own behavior, how should such an investigation be handled, and what should happen as a result? Fifteen days after entering the plea, Hutton hired Griffin Bell, a former federal judge and Attorney General in the Carter Administration, to perform such an investigation. Bell's lengthy report led to the resignation of three senior company executives, the reprimand of eleven lower-level officials, and a $20 million defamation suit brought against him and Hutton by one of the reprimanded Hutton employees.[39]

The other significant area involving financial institutions relates to the efforts of the federal government to combat illegal drug trafficking. The drug business generates large amounts of cash, and drug dealers must get the cash into legitimate banking channels to make full use of it. Accordingly, Congress decided to use the banks (and other financial institutions, such as stock brokerage firms) to help trace the flow of cash. The initial statutory effort was the Bank Secrecy Act of 1970, generally requiring financial institutions to file a cash transaction report ("CTR") within fifteen days of any "payment, receipt, or trans-

---

37. See "Hutton Overdrafting Case Was Settled Only After Some Miscues on Both Sides," Wall St.J., April 9, 1986, p. 26 (prosecution's primary goal was to negotiate guilty plea without any indictment, avoiding risks of trial; lead government attorney acknowledged that threats of prosecuting Hutton and executives were "'all part of trying to force the company to sit down and bargain with me. It was like playing hardball.'")

38. For Hutton's situation approximately one year after the plea, see "Hutton Group Suffers A Series of Reverses in Wake of Overdrafts," Wall St.J., April 9, 1986, p. 1.

39. See "Hutton's Vice Chairman, 2 Others Agree to Step Down Following Check Probe," Wall St.J., Sept. 6, 1985, p. 3. The problems associated with the Hutton internal investigation are explored infra p. 416.

fer" of U.S. currency in excess of $10,000.[40] Criminal penalties were provided for failure to file the forms.

Enforcement of the Act directly against financial institutions (as opposed to employees or customers) did not begin until the mid-1980s.[41] The most significant case occurred in February of 1985, when the Bank of Boston pleaded guilty to "knowingly and willfully" failing to report $1.22 billion in cash transactions. The bank was fined $500,000.[42] This plea and fine prodded other banks to review their own compliance with the law (which had been in effect for fifteen years!) and led a number of banks voluntarily to disclose past violations of the Act to the Treasury Department and pay substantial civil penalties.[43] Compliance with this statute continues to be a significant problem for financial institutions.

Despite the increased enforcement of the Bank Secrecy Act, Congress felt that stronger legislation was required. The result was the "Money Laundering Control Act of 1986."[44] This statute went beyond the reporting approach of the Bank Secrecy Act and, for the first time, made it a federal crime knowingly to engage in financial transactions designed to "conceal or disguise" the source of illegally derived funds.[45] The statute also made it a crime "knowingly" to engage in a monetary transaction (defined as a deposit, withdrawal, transfer, or exchange of funds) of more than $10,000, where the funds are derived from specified unlawful activity.[46] This complex statute provided for heavy criminal penalties (up to twenty years in jail), increased the civil fines under the Bank Secrecy Act,[47] provided for forfeiture of property representing the "gross receipts" traceable to a violation of the statute,[48] and permitted private recovery of treble damages for those injured by violations of the statute.[49] Note that this combination of civil and criminal remedies is

---

40. See 31 U.S.C.A. § 5313. These provisions are part of Title II of the Bank Secrecy Act, known as the Currency and Foreign Transactions Reporting Act.

41. See "Bank in Florida Pleads Guilty in Drug–Money Case," Wall St.J., April 17, 1984, p. 2 (first corporation to be charged with multiple felony violations of the Act).

42. See "Bank of Boston Unit Violated Law on Reporting," Wall St.J., Feb. 8, 1985, p. 3. A subsequent report by the bank's outside directors criticized the bank for its "'extensive'" noncompliance with the law. See Wall St.J., July 25, 1985, p. 6.

43. See "Treasury Fines Crocker Unit $2,250,000 For Failing to Report Cash Transactions," Wall St.J., Aug. 28, 1985, p. 3 (failure to report 7,877 transactions; follows fines of $1.2 million against four New York banks; sixty other banks under investigation). See also "U.S. Fines 2 Banks To Settle Charges on Cash Reporting," Wall St.J., May 23, 1986, p. 4 (sixty banks had disclosed violations over past year, with largest fine being $4.7 million; no bank which voluntarily disclosed received a civil fine in excess of 25% of the maximum $1000 per transaction for transactions prior to 1984).

44. Pub.L. 99–570, §§ 1351–1367, 100 Stat. 3207–18 (1986).

45. See 18 U.S.C.A. § 1956(a)(1) (Supp.) ("laundering of monetary instruments").

46. See 18 U.S.C.A. § 1957 (Supp.) ("engaging in monetary transactions in property derived from unlawful activity"). Note that this statute is not limited to financial institutions.

47. The civil fine was increased to a $100,000 maximum against a financial institution. The statute also authorized a $500 fine for negligent violations. See §§ 1357(b), (d), 100 Stat. 3207–18, 3207–25, 3207–26 (1986).

48. See 18 U.S.C.A. §§ 981 (civil forfeiture), 982 (criminal forfeiture) (Supp.).

49. The Act made the money laundering provisions one of the predicate offenses under RICO, which is then subject to pri-

consistent with the approach that Congress has taken to business crimes since the enactment of the first business crime statute in 1887. Note, also, that from the point of view of the ordinary operations of legitimate financial institutions, a critical issue in enforcement and interpretation of this statute will be the extent to which criminal liability can be imposed on financial institutions which are lax in instituting procedures to ensure compliance with the legislation.[50]

(3) *Federal Criminal Code.* The United States has never had a single criminal "code" with consistent definitions, nonduplicative provisions, or consistent penalties. In 1966 Congress began an effort to produce such a code. It established the "National Commission on Reform of Federal Criminal Laws" to study the diverse criminal provisions of federal law and draft a comprehensive federal criminal code which would consolidate and clarify federal criminal law. The Commission submitted a proposed draft code to Congress in 1971. In 1978 a version of the Code passed the Senate, but not the House; in 1980 another proposed draft was reported by the Judiciary Committees of both houses, but again failed to pass. The final effort was the Criminal Code Reform Act of 1981, but it, too, failed to win Congressional support.[51]

All these bills would have had substantial impact in the business crime area. Fines would have been increased; mail and wire fraud and "racketeering" statutes strengthened; the principles governing organizational liability clarified; states of culpability defined; and new penalties would have been provided for certain acts of "endangerment." Given the breadth of areas covered, however, the bills were criticized from many sides. Business groups thought the legislation too harsh on business conduct; civil liberties groups complained of restrictive bail and conspiracy provisions; some conservative groups thought the legislation too soft on obscenity and sexual offenses. With such political opposition, comprehensive consolidation and codification of federal criminal law does not appear likely,[52] although in 1984 Congress did enact a statute which attempted to rationalize federal sentencing practices and provisions.[53]

(4) *Bibliography.* There has been an increase in attention to the area of business crime in recent years. This has resulted in the publication of a number of treatises, as well as the introduction of

vate treble-damage suits. See § 1356(b), 100 Stat. 3207–18, 3207–23 (1986). For discussion of RICO, and its private remedy, see pp. 81–106, infra.

50. For a case raising this issue in the context of the Bank Secrecy Act, see United States v. Bank of New England, N.A., infra p. 219.

51. See S. 1630, 97th Cong., 1st Sess. (1981); Criminal Code Reform Act of 1981, Sen.Jud.Comm., S.Rep. No. 97–307, 97th Cong., 1st Sess. (1982). For a report on the reform effort to 1977, see L.B. Schwartz, Reform of the Federal Criminal Laws: Issues, Tactics and Prospects, 41 Law & Contemp.Probs. 1 (1977).

52. See "Crime Code Bill Seems Dead in Congress With Right and Left Uniting in Opposition," Wall St.J., April 28, 1982. The work of the original National Commission is collected in Working Papers, Nat'l Comm'n on Reform of Federal Criminal Law (1970) (2 vols.).

53. The Sentencing Reform Act of 1984 is discussed infra, Chapter 3.

several specialized reporter services. For a good treatise covering substantive criminal law provisions, see K. Brickey, Corporate Criminal Liability: A Treatise on the Criminal Liability of Corporations, Their Officers and Agents (1984) (3 vols.). For a treatise which also covers procedural problems, see S. Arkin et al., Business Crime: Criminal Liability of the Business Community (1981) (6 vols. with update). Guides primarily directed at the practicing bar include Glekel et al., Business Crimes: A Guide for Corporate and Defense Counsel (1982), and Pickholz et al., Guide to White Collar Crime: A Practical Approach (1986, with forms). For keeping up with current developments, BNA's Criminal Law Reporter includes business crime cases within its overall coverage of criminal law matters. A more specialized reporter is the Corporate Crime Reporter, which tracks caselaw developments and reports on the initiation and settlement of business crime prosecutions. Early issues of this Reporter also contain excellent bibliographies of relevant Congressional Hearings (in vol. 1, no. 3, April 27, 1987) along with listings of current books and law review articles. Also useful is the White–Collar Crime Reporter, which publishes short articles dealing with issues important in the business crime area and reports briefly on caselaw developments.

The social science literature relating to business crime is extensive. The "original" is E. Sutherland, White Collar Crime (originally published in 1949 and republished in "uncut" form in 1983). More recent studies include M. Clinard and P. Yeager, Corporate Crime (1980); G. Geis and E. Stotland, eds., White Collar Crime: Theory and Research (1980). For an excellent description of what business crime lawyers do (at least in New York City), see K. Mann, Defending White Collar Crime: A Portrait of Attorneys At Work (1985).

B. THE DECISION TO CRIMINALIZE

SCOPE NOTE

"Crime in the executive suites has come to command media attention of a sort formerly reserved for ax murderers." So began an article in the December, 1980, issue of Fortune Magazine, titled "How Lawless Are Big Companies?". In 1985 the New York Times wrote that "a corporate crime wave appears to be exploding across the nation." The Times reported a public opinion survey showing that only 32% of those polled thought most American corporate executives were honest, while 55% thought they were not.[54]

Certainly the 1980s has brought a number of highly visible criminal prosecutions against major companies. Nevertheless, despite the notion, as Fortune Magazine put it, that "big companies have recently been surprisingly lawless," the extent to which business crime occurs is actually unclear. Further, it is uncertain whether it is increasing, or

---

54. "White Collar Crime: Booming Again," N.Y. Times, June 9, 1985, p. F1; "Low Marks for Executive Honesty," N.Y. Times, June 9, 1985, p. F.1.

even whether the government is more vigorously prosecuting it.[55] All that is clear is that we perceive a rise in business crime—and that Americans have periodically perceived such rises.[56]

Our perception that business crime constitutes an increasing problem might lead one to assume that we have a fairly good idea why we call certain behavior by business organizations "crimes." Traditionally we have assigned four reasons for using the criminal sanction: retribution, deterrence (both "specific" and "general"), rehabilitation, and the protection of society by removing the criminal.[57] All these reasons, however, presuppose that the condemned behavior is "bad." They are reasons for punishing behavior. They do not explain why certain behavior should be criminalized in the first place.

The materials in this Section are designed to open the inquiry into the decision to criminalize. Students should examine this issue from the point of view of the legislator and the prosecutor: 1) Should the conduct in question have been made criminal? 2) Could the statute have been written more clearly so as to indicate what behavior would be criminal? 3) Should the prosecutor have chosen a civil remedy (e.g., injunction), rather than the criminal law, to enforce the legislation? 4) Does the lack of clarity in purpose and remedy give the prosecutor excessive discretion?

55. Data on business crime prosecutions are not collected for every crime, nor are they centrally collected. Overall Justice Department data on "white collar" crimes indicate that approximately 6,000 defendants were convicted of such crimes in 1985 (not counting counterfeiting, forgery, and embezzlement); this was about an 18% increase over 1980. The major increase was in miscellaneous fraud (which includes government program fraud). With regard to antitrust cases, government criminal antitrust cases rose from 20 cases filed in 1976 to 100 filed in 1984, but then dropped back to 47 in 1985. Prosecutions subsequently increased, to 53 in 1986 and 92 in 1987. Nearly 70% of the criminal cases filed by the Antitrust Division from 1980 through 1985 involved conspiracies to rig bids on public highway and airport construction projects. For earlier data on criminal antitrust enforcement, see J. Clabault & M. Block, Sherman Act Indictments: 1955–1980 (1981). The number of criminal tax prosecutions increased considerably between 1973 and 1976, as did the number of criminal securities cases referred by the SEC to the Department of Justice. But see "IRS Statistics Show Decline In Prosecuting of Tax Frauds," N.Y. L.J., April 19, 1982, p. 1 (reporting decline between 1979 and 1982 in investigations, recommendations for prosecution, and filings of indictments or information). For earlier data, see Rubin, A Statistical Study of Federal Criminal Prosecutions, 1 Law & Contemp.Prob. 494 (1934) (data for 1922 through 1933); Fisher, The Proposed Food and Drugs Act: A Legal Critique, 1 Law & Contemp.Prob. 74, 109–110 (1933) (data for Food & Drug Act prosecutions, 1906 through 1932).

56. See Warner & Cabot, Changes in the Administration of Criminal Justice During the Past Fifty Years, 50 Harv.L. Rev. 583, 586 (1937): "At the same time that crime has been getting more complicated and criminals better organized, the public has become more cynical in its attitude toward crime. The feeling that the robber is merely using crude methods to get his share of the 'cut', which those in high places obtain with greater finesse, has certainly not been lessened by recent revelations of the practices of leaders of finance and industry."

57. See, e.g., G. Fletcher, Rethinking Criminal Law 414 (1978).

UNITED STATES v. PATTERSON

United States District Court, Southern District of Ohio, 1912.
201 Fed. 697.

HOLLISTER, DISTRICT JUDGE. The indictment contains three counts, which may briefly and very generally be described as (1) a charge of conspiracy in restraint of interstate trade in cash registers during the three years preceding the date of the indictment, in the manner and by the means set forth; (2) a charge of creating a monopoly, during the same three years, of the cash register business by the means and in the manner set forth in the first count; (3) a charge of monopolizing such business, built up and augmented prior to the three years prior to the date of the indictment, through the conspiracy and by the means in the first count described, by continuing the business during those years.

The validity of the indictment is challenged on a number of grounds:

1. Because the matters and things set forth and charged do not constitute an offense against the laws of the United States.

2. Because the provisions of the act of Congress of July 2, 1890, entitled "An act to protect trade and commerce against unlawful restraints and monopolies" are too vague, uncertain, and indefinite to create a criminal offense.[58]

3. Because said act, in so far as it attempts to create offenses and impose penalties, is repugnant to the Constitution of the United States, and especially to section 1 of article 1, and to the provision of the fifth amendment, that no person shall be deprived of life, liberty, or property without due process of law, and to the provision of the sixth amendment, that in all criminal prosecutions the accused shall enjoy the right to be informed of the nature and cause of the accusation, and to the tenth amendment.

4. Because the averments are too general, vague, indefinite, and uncertain to inform the defendants of the nature and cause of the accusation against them, or to apprise them with such reasonable certainty of the offense with which they are charged or what they may expect to meet on the trial as to enable them to make their defense.

* * *

The first count describes cash registers, with the statement that for the past 20 years many concerns have been engaged in the business of manufacturing and selling them, and sets forth the names of some 33 different cash register companies, and avers that of the total business of making cash registers the National Cash Register Company has done from approximately 80 per cent., early in the period of the 20 years, to approximately 95 per cent. at the latter end thereof. It then avers that all the cash register companies during that time have sold the greater

---

58. [The text of Sections 1 and 2 of the Sherman Act are set out in the Statutory Appendix, infra.—Ed.]

portion of their product to users and dealers in all other parts of the United States than those wherein the registers were manufactured, and have consigned registers for sale to dealers, and to their own agents, in other states, and shipping the same to these various persons, the number of which would be impracticable, if not impossible, to set forth. It then sets forth a list of names of some 137 individuals, who were officers and agents of the National Cash Register Company, and the dates at which each had been actively engaged in the management of the business and the nature of his official relation to the company. Included in the list are the names of 30 persons who are the defendants in the case, and the count charges that by virtue of their official relation to the company they controlled and directed its business from the dates when they became officers or agents, and that they knowingly and consciously participated in a corrupt conspiracy in undue, unreasonable, direct, and oppressive restraint of the interstate trade described and carried on by the several concerns other than the National Cash Register Company; that is to say, a conspiracy to restrain, and which did restrain, such commerce, and by divers unfair, oppressive, tortious, illegal, and unlawful means, and means which, "consideration being given to the advantage over said other concerns held by the said National Cash Register Company in consequence of its resources being, as they were, so great as compared with those of such other concerns, respectively," the defendants "have unlawfully, wrongfully, and irresistibly excluded others from engaging in that trade and commerce, none of which has been justified or warranted by any letters patent."

[The following is from a subsequent opinion by the court of appeals describing the evidence presented by the Government at trial:

We think it clear that there was substantial evidence to the effect that there was a conspiracy on the part of those officers and agents of the National Company who then had to do with competition against most, if not all, of the competitors named who were in existence before the American of Columbus came into existence, which was not later than the early part of 1907, except the Peninsular, Burdick–Corbin, and Dial, as long as they were in existence within the 20-year period, and that this conspiracy included the use of some, if not all, of the means specified, and other means not specified aimed to be covered by the eleventh item, and that when that company came into existence there was a generic conspiracy against all competitors, at least all who might endanger the National's supremacy, which generic conspiracy had been in existence at least from the beginning of the 20 years. In an issue of a publication of the company seemingly for distribution amongst its officers and agents, of date May 1, 1892, occur these statements:

"If the opposition knew what is in store for them, they would not waste any more time and money staying in the business. They are all beginning to realize that there is no hope for them."

"It is only a question of whether we propose to spend the money to keep down opposition. If we continue, it is absolutely certain no opposition company can stand against this company and its agents. If necessary, we will spend five times as much money as we have already done, in order to down opposition. If they really believe this, they will throw up the sponge and quit."

"We are receiving overtures to buy out opposition. We will not buy them out. We do not buy out; we knock out."

In an issue August 1, 1895, occurs this statement:

"We are determined to absolutely control the cash register business."

And in an issue of date March 25, 1897, after setting forth the policy of the company of frankly informing a competitor of the purpose to drive him out of business, occurs this statement:

"This, it is true, is what is called 'securing a monopoly'; but we think there can be no possible economic or other objection to it. Cash registers are not a necessity of life. Any one who chooses can do business without them, thus contributing nothing to the 'monopoly.'"

It is then stated that "this monopoly" "is managed upon a liberal and broad-minded plan." And at a convention of the district managers held at Dayton July 22, 1907, the defendant John H. Patterson, president, thus expressed himself to them:

"We want Mr. Anderson of the competition department to give you a little idea of how we are going to control competition. We want Mr. Hayward also to give you a little talk. We want Mr. Muzzy to tell you how we are going to absolutely control the competition of the world, because we want you to feel this way. The first thing we aim to do is to keep down competition."

And again:

"I asked the Standard Oil Company what was the secret of their success, and they said this question could be answered in a very few words. Men, nothing but men; men well organized; they will keep down competition and make things succeed."

In the publications of the company and in the communications between the officers and agents having to do with competition, terms of warfare were not infrequently used, such as battle, fight, enemy, ammunition, shot, whipped, victory, and flags flying. During that time all the competitors named then in existence retired from the field. The American of Philadelphia, Boston, Hallwood, International, Hubinger & Carroll, and Latimer quit. The National does not seem to have been the cause of the Latimer quitting. The Century, Chicago, Cuckoo, Globe, Ideal, Kruse, Lamson, Metropolitan, Navy, Osborn, Standard, Simplex, Sun, Toledo, Union, and Weller sold out to the National, and it discontinued their business. The American of Philadelphia and Boston quit because of infringement suits brought against them by the National, in which it was successful. The result of this litigation may possibly have had something to do with other competitors quitting or selling out. Infringement suits were brought against most, if not all, the others, and these suits had more or less to do with their quitting or selling out. There was evidence tending to show in some of these instances at least that the claim of infringement was unfounded and known to be so, and that the suits for infringement were not brought in good faith, but for the sole purpose of aiding in driving the competitors from the field. The government claims that such was the case in all instances. In most, if not all, of these instances, some, if not all, of the other means were resorted to, and it is not unlikely that in some instances at least they were more effective than the suits. And such means were resorted to in some, if not all, the cases where the suits were successful. The Hallwood, International, Century, Chicago, Cuckoo, Globe, Ideal, Metropolitan, Navy, Osborn, Simplex, Sun, Toledo, Union, and Western retired from the field during the 7 years prior to 1907. Most, if not all, of the others retired before then, and mainly in the early part of the 20–year period.

In justice to the National Company and the defendants it should be noted that it was the pioneer in the cash register business and developed it. It owned the basic patents and must have acquired in a proper manner a very great number of improvement patents. In addition to this, it had the advantage of very great capacity in the management of its affairs. These two considerations together, without reference to any unfair treatment of its competitors, are sufficient in themselves to account in a large measure for the success it has attained. And it is not unlikely that its trade was pirated by other competitors besides the American of Philadelphia and the Boston, against whom it obtained decrees of infringement, and that these, as well as others, in their competition with it, resorted to some of the tactics complained of here.

We think it clear, also, that there was substantial evidence to the effect that this generic conspiracy was directed against the American of Columbus when it came into existence, and became specific as to it, and that it continued up until just shortly before the beginning of the 3–year period. The only other competitors then in existence were the Peninsular, Burdick–Corbin, and Dial, neither of which, as stated, was of much consequence. That company was the successor of the International, and it in turn of the Hallwood. The Hallwood during its existence, which covered a number of years, was one of the National's most stubborn competitors. It went into the hands of a receiver in 1903 or 1904. There was evidence tending to show that an effort was made, whilst its assets were in such hands, by the National, to acquire them without its being known in the transaction. The International acquired them, and then the American. Its connection with the Hallwood not unlikely aided it in getting established in business soon after entering the field. So identified with the Hallwood was it that its machines were frequently called Hallwood, and it, sometimes, the Hallwood Company. In view of its connection with the Hallwood Company, one would expect the generic conspiracy to be directed against it as soon as it came into existence, and so the government's evidence tended to show. May 4, 1907, the district manager at Detroit, Henry F. James, wrote to the assistant head of the competition department, Joseph E. Warren, that the Hallwood (i.e., American) situation in Detroit looked rather serious, and suggested the employment of the plaintiff in error Alexander W. Sinclair, then off the roll, to hire the Hallwood agent at that point. Warren answered that the competition did not warrant placing Sinclair on the roll again, and suggested that he (James) was in a better position to hire the agent than Sinclair. There was no evidence of anything else of a specific character during this year. But there were general statements as to competition which could not have had reference to any one but the American. Such was the statement of plaintiff in error John H. Patterson, at the convention of district managers July 22, 1907. June 20, 1907, the general manager, Hugh Chalmers, wrote to all the sales agents and salesmen, suggesting that they call on the users of competing machines and point out to them the weaknesses and deficiencies thereof, so that, even if they could not make a trade, they would cease to be a "plugger" for the opposition. And September 6, 1907, the head of the competition department, C.D. Anderson, wrote James at Detroit that the company was never in better shape to take care of competition than at that time, and for that reason they did not intend to let it increase again.

March 1, 1908, the plaintiff in error Sinclair entered the employ of the American and located at Detroit. It is possible that he was then still off the National's roll. He continued in its employ there until September 24, 1908. During this time a vigorous effort was made to drive him from the field, and it finally succeeded, when he re-entered the National's employ as a company salesman, and so continued until the trial. The plaintiffs in error Pflum, then general manager, Harned, then executive secretary, and Watson, then sales manager, participated in this effort. The method of attack was to prevent him from making sales of American machines and to displace such as he made. The way in which the former was attempted was by offering Hallwoods owned by the National Company at low prices—i.e., 30 cents on the dollar—in competition. The intention was to construct a machine specially for that purpose. In letter from James to Harned of date March 16, 1908, he stated that he needed a proper tool with which to fight Sinclair's competition, and requested that 10 or 12 Hallwoods be sent him, "as our machine parallel to Hallwood will not be ready for some time," and Harned in his answer said that work on drawer-operated machine—which was the character of the American—was being pushed and they would be able to give it to him sooner than he had stated. But whether this machine was used in this connection does not appear. The way in which the displacements were brought about was by offering the regular National machines on unusual terms. Both methods were unfair. Their purpose was to drive Sinclair and the American which he represented off the field, so that the National might have it to itself. May 16, 1908, Harned wrote James, congratulating him on displacing six Hallwoods taken in part pay for six Nationals, and stated that all at the factory, including plaintiff in error Deeds, were pleased and gratified at the outcome, and that he had put a crimp in Sinclair from which he would have difficulty in recovery. June 9, 1908, James wrote Pflum that since Sinclair had taken hold he had blocked 25 of his sales and displaced 9. September 4, 1908, plaintiff in error Watson issued a circular to the selling force empowering them to sell Hallwoods at 30 cents on the dollar. There was evidence of unfair means being used during this same time at Los Angeles to prevent the sale of the American machine, the details of which need not be given. And September 10, 1908, James, in whose territory Grand Rapids, Mich., was located, wrote plaintiff in error Watson, wanting to know the conclusion of himself and plaintiff in error Pflum as to the situation at that place, and whether they had succeeded in hiring Cleaves, the agent of the American, and saying that, if they could not hire him, they should have some special men—i.e., company salesmen—there until they ran him out of business.

After Sinclair returned to the service of the National, he was sent to Toledo, Ohio, where he remained at least until in November, 1908. Whilst there he adopted the same tactics that had been used against him in Detroit to drive out the agents of the American at that point. Finally, in the middle of January, 1909, James, the district manager at Detroit left the service of the National, and in breach of a contract that he had with it at once entered the employ of the American and was placed in charge of several states, with headquarters at Detroit. In the early part of February, 1909, certainly not as late as the 22d of that month, the new district manager appointed to take the place of James at Detroit was installed. At a meeting of the sales agents and salesmen who were to be under him, held on that occasion, the plaintiff in error Watson was present and undertook to outline the policy of the National in meeting competition, and in the course of his remarks, according to one witness, he said that it would be necessary to use every means possible to put James out of business, and according to another that they did not want him to get a foothold in Detroit, and that they would move their executive offices to Detroit, but that they would put him out of business.

* * * Here, according to defendants, was all that was done. In 22 instances sales agents and salesmen of the National attempted to induce purchasers of American machines, who had not paid for them, to repudiate their contracts by seller's talk and offering to allow them what they had paid on the purchase price of Nationals, in two, and possibly three, of which instances the attempt was successful. They occurred in 14 different states and 17 different localities. Ten of them occurred in 1909, 7 in 1910, and 5 in 1911. Defendants would have it that these were all such instances, but the tendency of the testimony of Steubenrauch is to establish 8 others, 6 of which were in 1910 and 2 in 1912, in Connecticut. In addition to these acts in restraint covered by the government's evidence were the display in March, 1909, by the National's sales agents at Los Angeles, in California, in his show window, smashed-up Hallwood cash registers with a card bearing this inscription:

> "Hundreds of merchants have exchanged unsatisfactory Hallwood cash registers for Nationals. We sell them at 30 cents on the dollar. But as they have no commercial value and do not sell, we are compelled to break them up to make room and will sell as Old Junk"

—an unsuccessful attempt by the sales agent of the National at Dallas, Tex., in the winter of 1909–10 to bribe a drayman in the employ of the American agent to tell him where he delivered every American machine, and an unsuccessful attempt by the sales agent of the National at Los Angeles, Cal., May 1, 1910, to induce the American agent at that point to leave its employ and enter that of the National.

The district court's opinion continues:]

Among others, the broad question is here presented whether or not there can be any criminal prosecution under the Sherman Anti–Trust Act. The question is of the utmost importance. There is apparently much diversity of opinion upon it, and the Supreme Court have not yet directly passed upon the subject.

Counsel for defendants admit—as they must, in view of the many decisions of the Supreme Court sustaining civil actions under the act, brought either by the government or by individuals by virtue of express provisions of the act—that civil actions may be prosecuted, but contend that . . . [as] the statute itself fixes no standard of lawfulness or unlawfulness to which the conduct of individuals or corporations may be referred, no criminal prosecution can be based upon it.

[They argue that no] man is advised by the statute whether any act contemplated by him is unreasonable or not; and that, as he cannot know, neither can any 12 men who are called upon to determine the quality of his acts, and that one jury might take one view and another jury a different view of the same conduct. Predicating their case on these assumptions, the defendants cite important authorities in support of their conclusion.

[After a discussion of various cases, the district court continued:]

I hold . . . that the Sherman Anti–Trust Act is a valid criminal statute, sufficiently clear in itself to inform the accused of the nature and cause of the accusation against them, and that criminal prosecutions under it in no way deprive the defendants of liberty or property without due process of law.

If this conclusion is right, the defendants are presumed to know the law applicable to their acts or contemplated acts, and are presumed to intend the consequences of them as heretofore shown. The discussion might end here; but other considerations suggest themselves, which, while perhaps not necessary for decision, are so pertinent as to warrant some reference.

Having in view the purposes of the common law and of the exception which has grown up in its evolution, and appreciating that these purposes are the same, there seem to be compelling reasons for the conclusion that moral considerations are involved in the question of the intent with which an act in restraint of trade is done. Judge Hook puts it this way:

> "There is more of the decalogue in the common law respecting the trading of merchants than is sometimes supposed." United States v. Standard Oil Co. (C.C.) 173 Fed. 177, 196.

Eminent authority, beginning with Lord Chief Justice Hale, have declared that the Christian religion is a part of the law of England. There are in a number of states decisions to the effect that the same is true of the law of the United States, and it is said by Justice Brewer in Church of Holy Trinity v. United States, 143 U.S. 457, 12 Sup.Ct. 511, 36 L.Ed. 226, that the United States is a Christian nation. No finding on this question is here made, for it is not necessary; but it may safely be said that civilization, as we understand it, so far as the recognition of the individual in the community and his rights are concerned, is the outgrowth of the appreciation that, among many other things, dealings between man and man must be on terms of justice, and justice requires that no man shall build up his business by acts whose purpose is to put the purchasing public at his mercy or to exploit others for his advantage, and destroy thereby the opportunities of others to exercise their talents and desires in the same field of mercantile activity. The common law in many of its phases developed through the appreciation of these rights and is based upon justice in the abstract. It may therefore be said to have a moral basis.

The ancient law against some voluntary restraint put by contract on an individual's right to carry on his particular trade or calling was established because it was deemed that such restraints were injurious to the public as well as to the individuals who made them; and the evils of monopoly are:

> "(1) The power which the monopoly gave to the one who enjoyed it to fix the price and thereby injure the public; (2) the power which it engendered of enabling a limitation on production; and (3) the danger of deterioration in quality of the monopolized article which it was deemed was the inevitable resultant of the monopolistic control over its production and sale." Standard Oil Case, 221 U.S. 52, 31 Sup.Ct. 512, 55 L.Ed. 619, 34 L.R.A. (N.S.) 834.

It was unjust to the community that a man should contract away his right to do business, and thereby possibly become, with his family, a charge on the community. It was unjust to the community to monopolize a product, and thereby enhance, or have the power to enhance, the prices the public were to pay for it. It was unjust to deprive an individual of his right and power of freely contracting, and of carrying on any lawful business he desired, and selling his product at prices fixed by free competition; and it was recognized that when the evils were brought about by the purpose to inflict them then that purpose was wrongful, and wrongful because unjust. If in a remote and comparatively barbarous civilization every contract in restraint of trade was deemed wrong, hence unlawful, because it was thought to work an injury to the public and to individuals, and if in our own time of advanced civilization the contract in restraint of trade is held to be wrong, hence unlawful, because its purpose is to bring about the same injuries, then the motive underlying the contract is the criterion by which the contract is to be judged.

If in the doing of a thing a man entertains a wrongful purpose, he knows it better than anybody else can know it. And if, under the law, a man is presumed to intend the consequences of his acts, how much the more must he be held blameworthy when his deliberate purpose is to bring about the evils condemned by the common law from the beginning—condemned because restraints of trade were wrongful to the community and to the individual and wrongful because they were unjust?

It is hard to sympathize with the often-repeated expression that a merchant is not advised by the anti-trust act of the character of a contemplated act. If the act is wrong under commonly accepted moral or ethical standards, it was wrong at common law, and wrong under the exception to the common law, and always was and always must be wrong, so long as there is community life, with common and relative rights belonging to each individual in the community and to the public as a whole. How can any fair-minded man engaged in trade, whose deliberate purpose in his acts and contracts in trade is to work injustice to his competitors and to the public, honestly claim want of knowledge of the quality of his acts? The Golden Rule may not as yet be the standard by which the law requires contracts in restraint of trade to be measured, but the ancient adage, "Live and let live," has its application to trade and is a safe rule to go by.

But it is said that contracts and acts in restraint of trade were not criminal at common law. It is unnecessary to decide whether they were or not, for they are made criminal by the anti-trust act, and by it the defendants were advised either that it meant every contract in restraint of trade, a construction which would hamper rather than encourage trade, or that it meant such contract, the purpose of which was wrongful in the sense so often hereinbefore stated.

[The district court upheld the validity of the indictment.] [59]

59. The court of appeals later held that there was sufficient evidence to submit to the jury the question whether the defendants conspired to restrain trade, but reversed the convictions on other grounds. See United States v. Patterson, 222 Fed. 599 (6th Cir.), certiorari denied 238 U.S. 635, 35 S.Ct. 939, 59 L.Ed. 1499 (1915).

NOTES AND QUERIES

(1) *Constitutionality of the Sherman Act.* The year after the district court's decision in *Patterson* the Supreme Court authoritatively settled the argument over whether the Sherman Act was unconstitutionally vague. In *Nash v. United States*,[60] the defendants were indicted for conspiring to restrain and monopolize trade in spirits of turpentine by, inter alia, setting the price of turpentine below the cost of production, circulating false statements as to turpentine stocks, and attempting to bribe employees of competitors to obtain information. Defendants demurred, on the ground that the statute was too vague. The Court, per Justice Holmes, upheld the overruling of the demurrer:[61]

> The objection to the criminal operation of the statute is thought to be warranted by The Standard Oil Co. v. United States, 221 U.S. 1, and United States v. American Tobacco Co., 221 U.S. 106. Those cases may be taken to have established that only such contracts and combinations are within the act as, by reason of intent or the inherent nature of the contemplated acts, prejudice the public interests by unduly restricting competition or unduly obstructing the course of trade. And thereupon it is said that the crime thus defined by the statute contains in its definition an element of degree as to which estimates may differ, with the result that a man might find himself in prison because his honest judgment did not anticipate that of a jury of less competent men. The kindred proposition that "the criminality of an act cannot depend upon whether a jury may think it reasonable or unreasonable. There must be some definiteness and certainty," is cited from the late Mr. Justice Brewer sitting in the Circuit Court.
>
> But apart from the common law as to restraint of trade thus taken up by the statute the law is full of instances where a man's fate depends on his estimating rightly, that is, as the jury subsequently estimates it, some matter of degree. If his judgment is wrong, not only may he incur a fine or a short imprisonment, as here; he may incur the penalty of death. "An act causing death may be murder, manslaughter, or misadventure according to the degree of danger attending it" by common experience in the circumstances known to the actor. "The very meaning of the fiction of implied malice in such cases at common law was, that a man might have to answer with his life for consequences which he neither intended nor foresaw." Commonwealth v. Pierce, 138 Massachusetts, 165, 178. Commonwealth v. Chance, 174 Massachusetts, 245, 252. "The criterion in such cases is to examine whether common social duty would, under the circumstances, have suggested a more circumspect conduct." 1 East P.C. 262. If a man

---

60. 229 U.S. 373, 33 S.Ct. 780, 57 L.Ed. 1232 (1913).

61. 229 U.S. at 376–78, 33 S.Ct. at 781, 57 L.Ed. at 1235–36.

should kill another by driving an automobile furiously into a crowd he might be convicted of murder however little he expected the result. If he did no more than drive negligently through a street he might get off with manslaughter or less. And in the last case he might be held although he himself thought that he was acting as a prudent man should.

Queries. Are cases distinguishing murder from manslaughter relevant in this area? Does the problem in *Patterson* involve the defendant's intent with respect to the result achieved? Or does the vagueness claim ultimately rest on the argument that the defendant lacked "consciousness of wrongdoing" and the statute failed to define what aspects of business conduct would henceforth be deemed illegal? Do you think Patterson's behavior "wrong"? As a legislator, do you think there should be a connection between "wrong behavior" and the decision to criminalize?

(2) *Subsequent Vagueness Cases.* The year after *Nash* the Supreme Court struck down Kentucky's antitrust statute. That statute permitted combination for the purpose of controlling prices unless the purpose or effect was to fix a price greater or less than "the real value of the article." In *International Harvester Co. v. Commonwealth of Kentucky,*[62] Holmes, writing for the Court, found it unreasonable that "a combination invited by law is required to guess at its peril what its product would have sold for if the combination had not existed. . . ." He continued:[63]

> [*Nash*] held that a criminal law is not unconstitutional merely because it throws upon men the risk of rightly estimating a matter of degree,—what is an undue restraint of trade. . . . It goes no further than to recognize that . . . between the two extremes of the obviously illegal and the plainly lawful there is a gradual approach, and that the complexity of life makes it impossible to draw a line in advance without an artificial simplification that would be unjust. The conditions are as permanent as anything human, and a great body of precedents on the civil side, coupled with familiar practice, make it comparatively easy for common sense to keep to what is safe.

The statute in *International Harvester*, on the other hand, dealt with "an imaginary condition other than facts." Requiring defendants to "divine prophetically what the reaction of only partially determinate facts would be upon the imaginations and desires of purchasers, is to exact gifts that mankind does not possess."

See also *United States v. L. Cohen Grocery Co.,*[64] involving the constitutionality of the Lever Act, originally enacted in 1917 and reenacted in 1919:

62. 234 U.S. 216, 34 S.Ct. 853, 58 L.Ed. 1284 (1914).

63. 234 U.S. at 223, 34 S.Ct. at 855, 58 L.Ed. at 1288.

64. 255 U.S. 81, 41 S.Ct. 298, 65 L.Ed. 516 (1921).

> That it is hereby made unlawful for any person willfully . . . to make any unjust or unreasonable rate or charge in handling or dealing in or with any necessaries; to conspire, combine, agree, or arrange with any other person . . . (e) to exact excessive prices for any necessaries . . . Any person violating any of the provisions of this section upon conviction thereof shall be fined not exceeding $5,000 or be imprisoned for not more than two years, or both: . . .

The defendant was charged with selling approximately 50 pounds of sugar for $10.07, and with selling a 100-pound bag of sugar for $17.50. The Court held that the statute did not provide "an ascertainable standard of guilt . . . adequate to inform persons accused of violation thereof of the nature and cause of the accusation against them."

Observe that the section forbids no specific or definite act. It confines the subject-matter of the investigation which it authorizes to no element essentially inhering in the transaction as to which it provides. It leaves open, therefore, the widest conceivable inquiry, the scope of which no one can foresee and the result of which no one can foreshadow or adequately guard against. In fact, we see no reason to doubt the soundness of the observation of the court below, in its opinion, to the effect that, to attempt to enforce the section would be the exact equivalent of an effort to carry out a statute which in terms merely penalized and punished all acts detrimental to the public interest when unjust and unreasonable in the estimation of the court and jury.

The Court cited in support of its view the "conflicting results" produced by the "attempts of enlightened judges" to carry out the statute.[65]

---

65. [From Footnote 1 of the Court's opinion.] Judge McCall, of the Western District of Tennessee, in his charge to the grand jury, stated that, if a shoe dealer bought two orders of exactly the same kind of shoes at different times and at different prices, the first lot at $8 per pair and the second lot after the price had gone up to $12 per pair "and then he sells both lots of those shoes at eighteen dollars, he is profiteering clearly upon the first lot of [shoes] that only cost him $8. Now he does that upon the theory that if he sells these shoes out and goes into the market and buys again he will have to pay the higher price, but that doesn't excuse him. He is entitled to make a reasonable profit, but he certainly hasn't the right to take advantage of the former low purchase and take the same profit on them that he gets on the twelve dollar shoes."

* * *

District Judge Hand, of the Northern District of New York, in his charge to the grand jury, said:

"Furthermore, it is not the particular profits that the individual himself makes which is the basis of the unreasonable charge, but it is whether the charge is such as gives unreasonable profit—not to him, but if established generally in the trade. The law does not mean to say that all people shall charge the same profit. If I am a particularly skillful merchant or manufacturer and I can make profits which are greater than the run of people in my business, I am allowed to make those profits. So much am I allowed. But if I am charging more than a reasonable price, taking the industry as a whole, I am not allowed to keep that profit because on other items I am sustaining a loss."

* * *

In *United States v. Culbertson, etc., Co.*, District Judge Rudkin, of the Eastern District of Washington, on the trial of defendant on July 8, 1920, charged the jury, among other things, that as a matter of law, defendant was entitled to sell its goods on the basis of the actual *market value* at

Nash was distinguished as a case in which "a standard of some sort was afforded."

Query. Do you find the Kentucky antitrust statute and the Lever Act more vague than the Sherman Act's prohibition on "contracts, combinations, or conspiracies" in "unreasonable" restraint of trade? (Note that the word "unreasonable" is a judicial gloss on the Sherman Act and does not appear in the Act.) Did the defendants in *Patterson* have adequate notice? Would it be so difficult for a legislature to write a statute clearly specifying those "restraints of trade" it considers criminal?

(3) *Brandeis' View.* Consider the following argument advanced by Louis Brandeis while still in private law practice: [66]

> I have been asked many times as regard to particular practices or agreements as to whether they were legal or illegal under the Sherman law. One gentlemen said to me, "We do not know where we can go." To which I replied, "I think your lawyers or anyone else can tell you where a fairly safe course lies. If you are walking along a precipice no human being can tell you how near you can go to that precipice without falling over, because you may stumble on a loose stone, you may slip and go over; but anybody can tell you where you can walk perfectly safe within convenient distance of that precipice." The difficulty which men have felt generally in regard to the Sherman law has been rather that they have wanted to go the limit rather than that they have wanted to go safely.

Recall the conduct and statutes involved in *Patterson, Nash, International Harvester,* and *L. Cohen.* Using Brandeis' approach, would there be any concern about lack of notice in any of those cases?

(4) *Criminal Monopolization.* Consider the following criminal information.[67] Is it clear that the conduct described in Paragraph 26 should be viewed (or was viewed by the defendants) as criminal? Would you have charged them with the separate crimes of conspiracy to restrain trade (Section 1 of the Sherman Act), monopolization (Section 2), and conspiracy to monopolize (Section 2)? The Government did.

INFORMATION FOR SHERMAN ACT VIOLATION

In the District Court of the United States for the Eastern District of Kentucky

---

the time and place of sale over and above the expense of handling the goods, and a reasonable profit, and that the original cost price became immaterial, except as it threw some light upon the market value.

66. Hearings before Sen. Comm. on Interstate Commerce, S.Res. No. 98, 62nd Cong., 1st Sess. 1161 (1911). See also Boyce Motor Lines, Inc. v. United States, 342 U.S. 337, 340, 72 S.Ct. 329, 331, 96 L.Ed. 367, 371 (1952) ("Nor is it unfair to require that one who deliberately goes perilously close to an area of proscribed conduct shall take the risk that he may cross the line.")

67. At the time, violation of the Sherman Act was only a misdemeanor, and therefore an indictment was not required.

No. 6670 (CRIMINAL)

UNITED STATES OF AMERICA

v.

THE AMERICAN TOBACCO COMPANY, ET AL.

UNITED STATES OF AMERICA,
Eastern District of Kentucky, ss:

INFORMATION

At the June 1940 Term of the District Court of the United States of America for the Eastern District of Kentucky, held at Lexington, Kentucky, in said District, comes the United States of America, acting through John T. Metcalf, United States Attorney in and for said District, and, leave of the Court having first been obtained, informs the Court as follows:

FIRST COUNT

The defendants

1. The following named corporations, principally engaged in that substantial part of the trade and commerce among the several States of the United States and with foreign nations which consists in the purchase, handling, transportation, manufacture and sale of tobacco, are hereby made defendants herein. Tobacco, as referred to in this information, means the leaf of the tobacco plant, in any one or more phases of its transition from the growing leaf to and including one or more of the manufactured forms in which it is sold for use, as indicated by the context. Each of said corporations is duly authorized to do business under the laws of the state of its incorporation as indicated:

Corporate Defendants	Abbreviated Names	State of Incorporation	Principal Place of Business in the United States
The American Tobacco Company	American	New Jersey	New York, N.Y.
Liggett & Myers Tobacco Company	Liggett & Myers	New Jersey	St. Louis, Mo.
R.J. Reynolds Tobacco Company	Reynolds	New Jersey	Winston–Salem, N.C.
P. Lorillard Company	Lorillard	New Jersey	New York, N.Y.
The Imperial Tobacco Co. (of Great Britain and Ireland), Ltd.	Imperial	Great Britain	Richmond, Va.
British–American Tobacco Company Limited	British–American	Great Britain	Richmond, Va.
Philip Morris & Co., Ltd., Incorporated	Philip Morris	Virginia	New York, N.Y.
Universal Leaf Tobacco Company, Inc.	Universal	Virginia	Richmond, Va.

* * *

26. (a) The defendant major tobacco companies, as the principal purchasers of leaf tobacco, have attempted to support, build up, and maintain marketing systems and marketing conditions for leaf tobacco intentionally designed to deprive the growers thereof of any substantial bargaining power in connection with its sale, and to permit said defendants to control the instrumentalities through which leaf tobacco is marketed in order that defendants might purchase it under conditions unnaturally, unreasonably and artificially favorable to themselves, and unnaturally, unreasonably and arbitrarily restrictive, oppressive and unfair to the growers, sellers, other purchasers and other handlers of such tobacco. Defendants have in fact accomplished these objectives through domination of the boards of trade, and members thereof, in the several marketing localities, and of the Tobacco Association of the United States, through which, as well as through other channels, they jointly foster and enforce regulations and practices with respect to the terms, methods, conditions, places and times of sales of leaf tobacco.

(b) Within the framework of the marketing systems and conditions so brought about and maintained, defendants have further attempted arbitrarily to fix, establish, maintain, manipulate and tamper with the prices of leaf tobacco, including that purchased by themselves, with the purpose and effect of enabling them to purchase leaf tobacco at such prices and unreasonably to restrain and dominate the trade of the growers thereof, and with the further purpose and effect of unreasonably eliminating and tending to eliminate and restrain competition among themselves, competition from other purchasers and handlers of leaf tobacco, and competition from other manufacturers and potential manufacturers of tobacco products, particularly the manufacturers of ten cent cigarettes. Defendants have in fact accomplished these objectives by understandings in advance of the openings of the marketing seasons, and from time to time throughout such seasons, with respect to the prices to be paid for leaf tobacco; and by intentionally formulating their grades, buying instructions, and products so as to avoid competition among themselves for the same or similar kinds of tobacco, at the same times, in the same markets.

(c) Defendants the Big Four and Philip Morris have further pursued a common policy of fixing, controlling, manipulating and tampering with the factory prices of their products, for the purpose and with the effect of unreasonably and unduly restraining and eliminating price competition among themselves and enabling said defendants to exact unreasonably high and monopolistic prices, and with the further purpose and effect of developing and maintaining a system of artificial controls over price manipulable, and in fact manipulated, by said defendants as a weapon for suppressing, eliminating, and unreasonably restraining, competition from other manufacturers of tobacco products. Pursuant to this policy said defendants have for many years maintained identical factory prices for certain of their major products, with substantially identical discounts and terms, including inventory adjustment terms.

(d) Defendants the Big Four and Philip Morris have further pursued a common policy of domination over the practices and policies of distributors of their products, for the purpose and with the effect of developing and maintaining a distributive mechanism favorable to their products and unfavorable to those of existing and potential competitors. Such domination has been achieved by selling direct to less than one per cent of the distributors of their products and refusing to sell to the other distributors thereof, by maintaining a substantial identity in their direct customer lists, by granting to and withholding favors from distributors, and by other means, including those set out in the paragraph hereof numbered 26(e).

(e) Defendants the Big Four and Philip Morris have further pursued a common policy of fixing, regulating, controlling and tampering with the wholesale and retail prices of their own and other tobacco manufacturers' products, for the purpose and with the effect of unreasonably and unduly restraining and eliminating price competition among themselves, of suppressing, eliminating, and unreasonably restraining, competition from other manufacturers, and of unreasonably and unduly restraining and controlling the trade of retailers and jobbers in defendants' and other manufacturers' products. Pursuant to this policy said defendants have by extensive and continuous nation-wide advertising and various sales promotion schemes created and maintained such a public acceptance and demand for their major brands that, the offering of such products for sale being a necessary adjunct to the conduct of numerous wholesale, retail, and service establishments, such establishments are forced to handle the products of defendants and others even on unreasonable and arbitrary terms, and at such prices. Said defendants have further effectuated such control over resale prices by selling direct to selected retail outlets at wholesale terms denied to the great majority of retailers, by limited offers of advertising allowances, special "deals" or "free goods," and of other favors, to selected distributors from time to time, by advertising retail prices for their own brands—and in some instances for brands of other manufacturers—over the heads of retailers and such other manufacturers, and by other means, including those set out in the paragraph hereof numbered 26(d).

* * *

Second Count

30. Each and every allegation contained in the paragraphs of this information numbered 1 through 23 is here realleged with the same force and effect as though said paragraphs were here set forth in full.

The Monopoly

31. Before and during the period of three years next preceding the filing of this information, and continuing to the date of the filing thereof, defendants, and others to the United States Attorney unknown, well knowing the foregoing facts, have, in the United States, and particularly in the Eastern District of Kentucky, wrongfully and unlawfully monopolized the aforesaid interstate and foreign trade and commerce in tobacco, in violation of Section Two of the Act of Congress of July 2, 1890, entitled "An Act to protect trade and commerce against unlawful restraints and monopolies" (U.S.C.A. Title 15, Sec. 2), commonly known as the Sherman Act, that is to say:

32. Defendants by concerted action have unlawfully attempted to fix, establish, maintain, control, manipulate and tamper with the prices, conditions and instrumentalities of the marketing of tobacco in interstate and foreign commerce as aforesaid; have in fact unlawfully fixed, established, maintained, controlled, manipulated and tampered with said prices, conditions and instrumentalities; and have bought and sold tobacco in interstate and foreign commerce, as aforesaid, at prices, under conditions, and through instrumentalities thus unlawfully fixed, established, maintained, controlled, manipulated and tampered with. In so doing defendants have unlawfully attempted to restrict, eliminate, suppress, and unreasonably and unduly restrain, and have in fact unlawfully restricted, eliminated, suppressed, and unreasonably and unduly restrained, competition among themselves in interstate and foreign commerce in tobacco, the interstate and foreign trade and commerce of others in tobacco, and the ability of others to compete with defendants in the aforesaid interstate and foreign trade and commerce.

* * *

Effects

34. Said unlawful monopolization has had the effects, among others, of permitting a few companies to attain control of a bottleneck in a great industry, through which a major farm commodity, on which several million are dependent, must pass, on its way through the hands of jobbers and retailers, to the many millions of people who use tobacco products; of enabling these few companies to abuse their resulting strategic and dominant position, by making the income of growers of leaf tobacco lower than it otherwise would have been; by making the income of distributors and other manufacturers of tobacco products lower than it otherwise would have been; and by keeping from all other groups in the industry, and from consumers, the benefits which otherwise would flow from free, vigorous and normal competition.[68]

[68]. The defendants were convicted at trial on all counts. Their convictions were affirmed on appeal, 147 F.2d 93 (6th Cir. 1944), and (on a limited issue) by the Supreme Court, 328 U.S. 781, 66 S.Ct. 1125, 90 L.Ed. 1575 (1946). The Court found, inter alia, no double jeopardy violation in the three counts.

(5) *Political Motivations.* Vaguely worded statutes, criminalizing conduct not clearly immoral, can open up the possibility for politically selective enforcement. Consider "U.S. Charges: Japan's View," N.Y. Times, August 5, 1982, p. D1: [69]

Not long ago, a cartoon in Asahi Shimbun, a leading Japanese newspaper, showed Ronald Reagan, his sleeves rolled up, pummeling small, mole-like creatures with a huge mallet.

The small creatures, of course, were supposed to be Japanese companies, and the idea was to depict what trade specialists call "Japan bashing," or punishing Japan for the success of its export drive.

Although as political caricatures go, this one was singularly unsubtle, it did capture the sense of aggrieved innocence that many Japanese are feeling these days over recent moves by the United States Government against Japanese companies.

Accused of Thefts

On June 22, employees of Hitachi Ltd. and the Mitsubishi Electric Corporation were charged with conspiring to steal computer secrets from the International Business Machines Corporation.

On July 20, the American subsidiary of Mitsui & Company was indicted for conspiring to sell steel in the United States at artificially low prices. The following day, Mitsui, a giant trading company, pleaded guilty.

Then, last week, it was disclosed that the Justice Department was investigating possible price-fixing by six Japanese companies selling sophisticated semiconductor chips in the American market.

The indictments and the investigation come at a time when America's huge trade deficit with Japan is widening. Last Wednesday, the Commerce Department reported that in the first half of 1982, the deficit was more than $10 billion, a record for a six-month period.

Despite repeated proclamations by American officials that the cases are unrelated to trade disputes, most Japanese simply do not believe it.

In Japan, lawsuits are comparatively rare. Taking legal action against an individual or company is viewed as a last resort. Grievances are typically resolved by negotiation, not by litigation, as in the United States. Thus the recent indictments and investigation are widely taken to be symbols of American hostility toward Japan.

Furthermore, big business and government in Japan work together, much more so than in the United States, where the public and private sectors often are adversaries. So the Japanese, not surprisingly, think it is only logical that the recent Justice Department steps represent a collective effort by American business and government to blunt competition from Japanese companies.

"Japanese tend to have an ethnocentric view of this—that the American actions are a plot," said Noritake Kobayashi, director of the Keio Business School.

Mr. Kobayashi, who attended Harvard University, added that the widespread view that there was an American conspiracy against Japan was "a big

69. Copyright © 1982 by The New York Times Company. Reprinted with permission.

mistake"—and one that could further sour trade relations between the two nations.

Though Japanese Government officials are upset by the recent Justice Department actions, none go so far as to characterize them as a "conspiracy," either publicly or privately.

'A Perception Gap'

Most Government officials say these are law enforcement matters that should be kept at arm's length from trade issues. And most officials express confidence that this can be done.

"There is a perception gap between the two nations concerning these three incidents, and that is important to deal with," said Osamu Watanabe, a senior official at the Ministry of International Trade and Industry. "But I do not think that these incidents will have a lasting effect on our trade relations with the United States."

The investigation of Japanese semiconductor producers is perhaps most irksome to Japanese officials. Just a few months earlier, Reagan Administration officials expressed concern that Japanese companies were selling 64k RAM chips (random access memory chips that can store 64,000 units of information) at prices that were too low, hurting American producers. In recent months, the Japanese Government has warned its companies not to price chips so low that they could be accused of "dumping"—selling products at artificially low prices.

But now the Justice Department is apparently investigating possible cartel-like price-fixing by Japanese companies, which would increase the price of chips.

"We have taken a cooperative approach on this issue," one official said, "and we would like to see some consistency from the American Government."

"Frankly," he added, "the Reagan Administration has lacked consistency, and that has made them difficult to deal with."

UNITED STATES v. DOWLING

Supreme Court of the United States, 1985.
473 U.S. 207, 105 S.Ct. 3127, 87 L.Ed.2d 152.

JUSTICE BLACKMUN delivered the opinion of the Court.

The National Stolen Property Act provides for the imposition of criminal penalties upon any person who "transports in interstate or foreign commerce any goods, wares, merchandise, securities or money, of the value of $5,000 or more, knowing the same to have been stolen, converted or taken by fraud." 18 U.S.C. § 2314. In this case, we must determine whether the statute reaches the interstate transportation of "bootleg" phonorecords, "stolen, converted or taken by fraud" only in the sense that they were manufactured and distributed without the consent of the copyright owners of the musical compositions performed on the records.

I

After a bench trial in the United States District Court for the Central District of California conducted largely on the basis of a stipulated record, petitioner Paul Edmond Dowling was convicted of one count of conspiracy to transport stolen property in interstate commerce, in violation of 18 U.S.C. § 371; eight counts of interstate transportation of stolen property, in violation of 18 U.S.C. § 2314; nine counts of copyright infringement, in violation of 17 U.S.C. § 506(a); and three counts of mail fraud, in violation of 18 U.S.C. § 1341.[70] The offenses stemmed from an extensive bootleg record operation involving the manufacture and distribution by mail of recordings of vocal performances by Elvis Presley.[71] The evidence demonstrated that sometime around 1976, Dowling, to that time an avid collector of Presley recordings, began in conjunction with codefendant William Samuel Theaker to manufacture phonorecords of unreleased Presley recordings. They used material from a variety of sources, including studio outtakes, acetates, soundtracks from Presley motion pictures, and tapes of Presley concerts and television appearances.[72] Until early 1980, Dowling

---

70. [Court's footnote 1.] Only the § 2314 counts concern us here. Counts Two through Seven of the indictment, referring to the statute, charged:

"On or about the dates listed below and to and from the locations hereinafter specified, defendants THEAKER and DOWLING knowingly and willfully caused to be transported in interstate commerce phonorecords, as the defendants then and there well knew, were stolen, converted and taken by fraud, in that they were manufactured without the consent of the copyright proprietors.

* * *

71. [Court's footnote 2.] A "bootleg" phonorecord is one which contains an unauthorized copy of a commercially unreleased performance. As in this case, the bootleg material may come from various sources. For example, fans may record concert performances, motion picture soundtracks, or television appearances. Outsiders may obtain copies of "outtakes," those portions of the tapes recorded in the studio but not included in the "master," that is, the final edited version slated for release after transcription to phonorecords or commercial tapes. Or bootleggers may gain possession of an "acetate," which is a phonorecord cut with a stylus rather than stamped, capable of being played only a few times before wearing out, and utilized to assess how a performance will likely sound on a phonorecord.

Though the terms frequently are used interchangeably, a "bootleg" record is not the same as a "pirated" one, the latter being an unauthorized copy of a performance already commercially released.

72. [Court's footnote 3.] For example, according to the stipulated testimony of the Presley archivist at RCA Records, which held the exclusive rights to manufacture and distribute sound recordings of Presley performances from early in his career through the time of trial in this case, the "Elvis Presley Dorsey Shows" contained performances from Presley's appearances on a series of six television shows in January, February, and March 1956; "Elvis Presley From the Waist Up" contained performances from three appearances on "The Ed Sullivan Show" in September and October 1956 and January 1957; "Plantation Rock" included a version of the title song recorded from an acetate, which other testimony indicated Dowling had purchased from the author of the song; "The Legend Lives On" included material from unreleased master tapes from the RCA Records inventory; "Rockin' with Elvis New Year's Eve" derived from a recording by an audience member at a 1976 concert in Pittsburgh; and "Elvis on Tour" came from the master tape or the film source of the film of the same name. With the exceptions of "Plantation Rock" and "Elvis on Tour," quantities of each of these albums were included in the shipments giving rise to the § 2314 counts.

and Theaker had the records manufactured at a record-pressing company in Burbank, Cal. When that company later refused to take their orders, they sought out other record-pressing companies in Los Angeles and, through codefendant Richard Minor, in Miami, Fla. The bootleg entrepreneurs never obtained authorization from or paid royalties to the owners of the copyrights in the musical compositions.[73]

In the beginning, Dowling, who resided near Baltimore, handled the "artistic" end of the operation, contributing his knowledge of the Presley subculture, seeking out and selecting the musical material, designing the covers and labels, and writing the liner notes, while Theaker, who lived in Los Angeles and had some familiarity with the music industry, took care of the business end, arranging for the record pressings, distributing catalogs, and filling orders. In early 1979, however, having come to suspect that the FBI was investigating the West Coast operation, Theaker began making shipments by commercial trucking companies of large quantities of the albums to Dowling in Maryland. Throughout 1979 and 1980, the venturers did their marketing through Send Service, a labeling and addressing entity, which distributed at least 50,000 copies of their catalog and advertising flyers to addresses on mailing lists provided by Theaker and Dowling. Theaker would collect customers' orders from post office boxes in Glendale, Cal., and mail them to Dowling in Maryland, who would fill the orders. The two did a substantial business: the stipulated testimony establishes that throughout this period Dowling mailed several hundred packages per week and regularly spent $1,000 per week in postage. The men also had occasion to make large shipments from Los Angeles to Minor in Miami, who purchased quantities of their albums for resale through his own channels.

The eight § 2314 counts on which Dowling was convicted arose out of six shipments of bootleg phonorecords from Los Angeles to Baltimore and two shipments from Los Angeles to Miami. The evidence established that each shipment included thousands of albums, that each album contained performances of copyrighted musical compositions for the use of which no licenses had been obtained nor royalties paid, and that the value of each shipment attributable to copyrighted material exceeded the statutory minimum.

Dowling appealed from all the convictions save those for copyright infringement, and the United States Court of Appeals for the Ninth Circuit affirmed in all respects.

73. [Court's footnote 4.] The Copyright Act requires record manufacturers to obtain licenses and pay royalties to copyright holders upon pressing records that contain performances of copyrighted musical compositions. 17 U.S.C. § 115.

While motion-picture copyrights protect the soundtracks of Presley's movies, Congress did not extend federal copyright protection to sound recordings until the Sound Recording Act of 1971, and then only to sound recordings fixed after February 15, 1972. Therefore, most of the sound recordings involved in this case, as opposed to the musical compositions performed, are apparently not protected by copyright. In any event, the § 2314 counts rely solely on infringement of copyrights to musical compositions. See n. 1, supra.

* * *

We granted certiorari to resolve an apparent conflict among the Circuits concerning the application of the [National Stolen Property Act] to interstate shipments of bootleg and pirated sound recordings and motion pictures whose unauthorized distribution infringed valid copyrights.

II

* * *

A

[W]e examine at the outset the statutory language. Section 2314 requires, first, that the defendant have transported "goods, wares, [or] merchandise" in interstate or foreign commerce; second, that those goods have a value of "$5,000 or more"; and, third, that the defendant "kno[w] the same to have been stolen, converted or taken by fraud." Dowling does not contest that he caused the shipment of goods in interstate commerce, or that the shipments had sufficient value to meet the monetary requirement. He argues, instead, that the goods shipped were not "stolen, converted or taken by fraud." In response, the Government does not suggest that Dowling wrongfully came by the phonorecords actually shipped or the physical materials from which they were made; nor does it contend that the objects that Dowling caused to be shipped, the bootleg phonorecords, were "the same" as the copyrights in the musical compositions that he infringed by unauthorized distribution of Presley performances of those compositions. The Government argues, however, that the shipments come within the reach of § 2314 because the phonorecords physically embodied performances of musical compositions that Dowling had no legal right to distribute. According to the Government, the unauthorized use of the musical compositions rendered the phonorecords "stolen, converted or taken by fraud" within the meaning of the statute.[74] We must deter-

74. [Court's footnote 7.] The Government argues in the alternative that even if the unauthorized use of copyrighted musical compositions does not alone render the phonorecords contained in these shipments "stolen, converted or taken by fraud," the record contains evidence amply establishing that the bootleggers obtained the source material through illicit means. The Government points to testimony, for example, that the custodians of the tapes containing the outtakes which found their way onto Dowling's records neither authorized their release nor permitted access to them by unauthorized persons. According to the Government, the wrongfully obtained tapes which contained the musical material should be considered "the same" as the phonorecords onto which the sounds were transferred, which were therefore "stolen, converted or taken by fraud" within the meaning of § 2314.

For several reasons, we decline to consider this alternative basis for upholding Dowling's convictions. The § 2314 counts in the indictment were founded exclusively on the allegations that the shipped phonorecords, which contained "Elvis Presley performances of copyrighted musical compositions," were "stolen, converted and taken by fraud, in that they were manufactured without the consent of the copyright proprietors." See n. 1, supra. * * * Moreover, even assuming that the stipulated testimony contained sufficient evidence to establish the unlawful procurement of the source material, the Government made no attempt in the District Court to address the difficult problems of valuation under its alternative theory. For example, it in-mine, therefore, whether phonorecords that include the performance of copyrighted musical compositions for the use of which no authorization has been sought nor royalties paid are consequently "stolen, converted or taken by fraud" for purposes of § 2314. We conclude that they are not.

The courts interpreting § 2314 have never required, of course, that the items stolen and transported remain in entirely unaltered form. See, e.g., United States v. Moore, 571 F.2d 154, 158 (CA3) (counterfeit printed Ticketron tickets "the same" as stolen blanks from which they were printed), cert. denied, 435 U.S. 956, 98 S.Ct. 1589, 55 L.Ed.2d 808 (1978). Nor does it matter that the item owes a major portion of its value to an intangible component. See, e.g., United States v. Seagraves, 265 F.2d 876 (CA3 1959) (geophysical maps identifying possible oil deposits); United States v. Greenwald, 479 F.2d 320 (CA6) (documents bearing secret chemical formulae), cert. denied, 414 U.S. 854, 94 S.Ct. 154, 38 L.Ed.2d 104 (1973). But these cases and others prosecuted under § 2314 have always involved physical "goods, wares, [or] merchandise" that have themselves been "stolen, converted or taken by fraud." This basic element comports with the common-sense meaning of the statutory language: by requiring that the "goods, wares, [or] merchandise" be "the same" as those "stolen, converted or taken by fraud," the provision seems clearly to contemplate a physical identity between the items unlawfully obtained and those eventually transported, and hence some prior physical taking of the subject goods.

In contrast, the Government's theory here would make theft, conversion, or fraud equivalent to wrongful appropriation of statutorily protected rights in copyright. The copyright owner, however, holds no ordinary chattel. A copyright, like other intellectual property, comprises a series of carefully defined and carefully delimited interests to which the law affords correspondingly exact protections.

* * *

For example, § 107 of the Copyright Act "codifies the traditional privilege of other authors to make 'fair use' of an earlier writer's work." Likewise, § 115 grants compulsory licenses in nondramatic musical works. Thus, the property rights of a copyright holder have a character distinct from the possessory interest of the owner of simple "goods, wares, [or] merchandise," for the copyright holder's dominion is subjected to precisely defined limits.

It follows that interference with copyright does not easily equate with theft, conversion, or fraud. The Copyright Act even employs a separate term of art to define one who misappropriates a copyright: "'Anyone who violates any of the exclusive rights of the copyright

troduced no evidence that might have established the value of the tapes allegedly stolen from the RCA archives, nor how that value might relate to the value of the goods ultimately shipped. Instead, its evidence concerning the value of the interstate shipments of records attempted to isolate the value attributable to the copyrighted musical compositions. Under these circumstances, we assess the validity of Dowling's convictions only under the allegations made in the indictment.

owner,' that is, anyone who trespasses into his exclusive domain by using or authorizing the use of the copyrighted work in one of the five ways set forth in the statute, 'is an infringer of the copyright.' " There is no dispute in this case that Dowling's unauthorized inclusion on his bootleg albums of performances of copyrighted compositions constituted infringement of those copyrights. It is less clear, however, that the taking that occurs when an infringer arrogates the use of another's protected work comfortably fits the terms associated with physical removal employed by § 2314. The infringer invades a statutorily defined province guaranteed to the copyright holder alone. But he does not assume physical control over the copyright; nor does he wholly deprive its owner of its use. While one may colloquially link infringement with some general notion of wrongful appropriation, infringement plainly implicates a more complex set of property interests than does run-of-the-mill theft, conversion, or fraud. As a result, it fits but awkwardly with the language Congress chose—"stolen, converted or taken by fraud"—to describe the sorts of goods whose interstate shipment § 2314 makes criminal.

* * *

B

In light of the ill-fitting language, we turn to consider whether the history and purpose of § 2314 evince a plain congressional intention to reach interstate shipments of goods infringing copyrights. Our examination of the background of the provision makes more acute our reluctance to read § 2314 to encompass merchandise whose contraband character derives from copyright infringement.

Congress enacted § 2314 as an extension of the National Motor Vehicle Theft Act, currently codified at 18 U.S.C. § 2312. Passed in 1919, the earlier Act was an attempt to supplement the efforts of the States to combat automobile thefts. Particularly in areas close to state lines, state law enforcement authorities were seriously hampered by car thieves' ability to transport stolen vehicles beyond the jurisdiction in which the theft occurred. Legislating pursuant to its commerce power, Congress made unlawful the interstate transportation of stolen vehicles, thereby filling in the enforcement gap by "strik[ing] down State lines which serve as barriers to protect [these interstate criminals] from justice." 58 Cong.Rec. 5476 (1919) (statement of Rep. Newton).

Congress acted to fill an identical enforcement gap when in 1934 it "extend[ed] the provisions of the National Motor Vehicle Theft Act to other stolen property" by means of the National Stolen Property Act. . . . Again, Congress acted under its commerce power to assist the States' efforts to foil the "roving criminal," whose movement across state lines stymied local law enforcement officials. As with its progenitor, Congress responded in the National Stolen Property Act to "the need for federal action" in an area that normally would have been left to state law.

No such need for supplemental federal action has ever existed, however, with respect to copyright infringement, for the obvious reason that Congress always has had the bestowed authority to legislate directly in this area. Article I, § 8, cl. 8, of the Constitution provides that Congress shall have the power

> "To promote the Progress of Science and useful Arts, by securing for limited Times to Authors and Inventors the exclusive Right to their respective Writings and Discoveries."

By virtue of the explicit constitutional grant, Congress has the unquestioned authority to penalize directly the distribution of goods that infringe copyright, whether or not those goods affect interstate commerce. Given that power, it is implausible to suppose that Congress intended to combat the problem of copyright infringement by the circuitous route hypothesized by the Government. Of course, the enactment of criminal penalties for copyright infringement would not prevent Congress from choosing as well to criminalize the interstate shipment of infringing goods. But in dealing with the distribution of such goods, Congress has never thought it necessary to distinguish between intrastate and interstate activity. Nor does any good reason to do so occur to us. In sum, the premise of § 2314—the need to fill with federal action an enforcement chasm created by limited state jurisdiction—simply does not apply to the conduct the Government seeks to reach here.

C

The history of copyright infringement provisions affords additional reason to hesitate before extending § 2314 to cover the interstate shipments in this case. Not only has Congress chiefly relied on an array of civil remedies to provide copyright holders protection against infringement, see 17 U.S.C. §§ 502–505, but in exercising its power to render criminal certain forms of copyright infringement, it has acted with exceeding caution.

The first full-fledged criminal provisions appeared in the Copyright Act of 1909, and specified that misdemeanor penalties of up to one year in jail or a fine between $100 and $1,000, or both, be imposed upon "[a]ny person who willfully and for profit" infringed a protected copyright.[75] This provision was little used. In 1974, however, Congress amended the section, substantially to increase penalties for record piracy. The new version retained the existing language, but supplemented it with a new subsection (b), which provided that one who "willfully and for profit" infringed a copyright in sound recordings

---

75. [Court's footnote 14.] * * * Congress first provided criminal penalties for copyright infringement in the Act of January 6, 1897, 29 Stat. 481, which made a misdemeanor punishable by imprisonment for one year of the unlawful performance or presentation, done willfully and for profit, of a copyrighted dramatic or musical composition. See also Act of May 31, 1790, § 2, 1 Stat. 124 (fixed civil penalties, one-half payable to the United States, for unauthorized copying of copyrighted book, chart, or map).

* * *

would be subject to a fine of up to $25,000 or imprisonment for up to one year, or both. The legislative history demonstrates that in increasing the penalties available for this category of infringement, Congress carefully calibrated the penalty to the problem: it had come to recognize that "record piracy is so profitable that ordinary penalties fail to deter prospective offenders." Even so, because it considered record piracy primarily an economic offense, Congress, after serious consideration, rejected a proposal to increase the available term of imprisonment to three years for a first offense and seven years for a subsequent offense.

When in 1976, after more than 20 years of study, Congress adopted a comprehensive revision of the Copyright Act, it again altered the scope of the criminal infringement actions, albeit cautiously. . . . [D]espite the urging of representatives of the film industry, . . . Congress declined once again to provide felony penalties for copyright infringement involving sound recordings and motion pictures.

Finally, by the Piracy and Counterfeiting Amendments Act of 1982, Congress chose to address the problem of bootlegging and piracy of records, tapes, and films by imposing felony penalties on such activities. Section 5 of the 1982 Act revised 17 U.S.C. § 506(a) to provide that "[a]ny person who infringes a copyright willfully and for purposes of commercial advantage or private financial gain shall be punished as provided in section 2319 of title 18." Section 2319(b)(1), in turn, was then enacted to provide for a fine of up to $250,000, or imprisonment of up to five years, or both, if the offense "involves the reproduction or distribution, during any one-hundred-and-eighty-day period, of at least one thousand phonorecords or copies infringing the copyright in one or more sound recordings [or] at least sixty-five copies infringing the copyright in one or more motion pictures or other audiovisual works." Subsection (b)(2) provides for a similar fine and up to two years' imprisonment if the offense involves "more than one hundred but less than one thousand phonorecords or copies infringing the copyright in one or more sound recordings [or] more than seven but less than sixty-five copies infringing the copyright in one or more motion pictures or other audiovisual works." And subsection (b)(3) provides for a fine of not more than $25,000 and up to one year's imprisonment in any other case of willful infringement.

* * *

Thus, the history of the criminal infringement provisions of the Copyright Act reveals a good deal of care on Congress' part before subjecting copyright infringement to serious criminal penalties. First, Congress hesitated long before imposing felony sanctions on copyright infringers. Second, when it did so, it carefully chose those areas of infringement that required severe response—specifically, sound recordings and motion pictures—and studiously graded penalties even in those areas of heightened concern. This step-by-step, carefully considered approach is consistent with Congress' traditional sensitivity to the special concerns implicated by the copyright laws.

In stark contrast, the Government's theory of this case presupposes a congressional decision to bring the felony provisions of § 2314, which make available the comparatively light fine of not more than $10,000 but the relatively harsh term of imprisonment of up to 10 years, to bear on the distribution of a sufficient quantity of any infringing goods simply because of the presence here of a factor—interstate transportation—not otherwise thought relevant to copyright law. The Government thereby presumes congressional adoption of an indirect but blunderbuss solution to a problem treated with precision when considered directly. To the contrary, the discrepancy between the two approaches convinces us that Congress had no intention to reach copyright infringement when it enacted § 2314.

D

The broad consequences of the Government's theory, both in the field of copyright and in kindred fields of intellectual property law, provide a final and dispositive factor against reading § 2314 in the manner suggested.

* * *

[T]he Government's theory . . . would as easily encompass the law of patents and other forms of intellectual property. . . . [T]he intangible idea protected by a patent [would] be made tangible by its embodiment in an article manufactured in accord with patented specifications. Thus, [the Government's] view of the statute would readily permit its application to interstate shipments of patent-infringing goods. Despite its undoubted power to do so, however, Congress has not provided criminal penalties for distribution of goods infringing valid patents.[76] Thus, the rationale supporting application of the statute under the circumstances of this case would equally justify its use in wide expanses of the law which Congress has evidenced no intention to enter by way of criminal sanction.[77] This factor militates strongly against the reading proffered by the Government.

III

No more than other legislation do criminal statutes take on straightjackets upon enactment. In sanctioning the use of § 2314 in the manner urged by the Government here, the Courts of Appeals

---

76. [Court's footnote 19.] Congress instead has relied on provisions affording patent owners a civil cause of action. 35 U.S.C. §§ 281–294. Among the available remedies are treble damages for willful infringement. The only criminal provision relating to patents is 18 U.S.C. § 497, which proscribes the forgery, counterfeiting, or false alteration of letters patent, or the uttering thereof. See also 35 U.S.C. § 292 ($500 penalty, one-half to go to person suing and one-half to the United States, for false marking of patent status).

77. [Court's footnote 20.] The Government's rationale would also apply to goods infringing trademark rights. Yet, despite having long and extensively legislated in this area, see federal Trademark Act of 1946 (Lanham Act), 15 U.S.C. § 1051 et seq., in the modern era Congress only recently has resorted to criminal sanctions to control trademark infringement. See Trademark Counterfeiting Act of 1984, Pub.L. 98–473, ch. XV, 98 Stat. 2178.

understandably have sought to utilize an existing and readily available tool to combat the increasingly serious problem of bootlegging, piracy, and copyright infringement. Nevertheless, the deliberation with which Congress over the last decade has addressed the problem of copyright infringement for profit, as well as the precision with which it has chosen to apply criminal penalties in this area, demonstrates anew the wisdom of leaving it to the legislature to define crime and prescribe penalties. Here, the language of § 2314 does not "plainly and unmistakably" cover petitioner Dowling's conduct; the purpose of the provision to fill gaps in state law enforcement does not couch the problem under attack; and the rationale employed to apply the statute to petitioner's conduct would support its extension to significant bodies of law that Congress gave no indication it intended to touch. In sum, Congress has not spoken with the requisite clarity. Invoking the "time-honored interpretive guideline" that " 'ambiguity concerning the ambit of criminal statutes should be resolved in favor of lenity,' " we reverse the judgment of the Court of Appeals.

It is so ordered.

[Justice Powell, joined by Chief Justice Burger and Justice White, dissented. Justice Powell wrote, inter alia, that "Dowling's unauthorized duplication and commercial exploitation of the copyrighted performances were intended to gain for himself the rights and benefits lawfully reserved to the copyright owner" and that "Dowling and his partners 'could not have doubted the criminal nature of their conduct . . . .' "]

NOTES AND QUERIES

(1) *Queries.* Compare the behavior in *Dowling* with the behavior in *Patterson*. Which defendants do you think had clearer notice of the illegality of their acts? From a legislator's point of view, whose behavior do you think it more appropriate to criminalize?

Note that the defendants in *Dowling* were convicted of a number of criminal charges, including mail fraud and criminal copyright infringement. All the charges rested on the same conduct. The defendants appealed the mail fraud and National Stolen Property Act convictions to the Court of Appeals (but not their copyright convictions); the Supreme Court limited its grant of certiorari to the National Stolen Property Act issue.[78]

Should the Court's narrow interpretation of the National Stolen Property Act have placed so much emphasis on the existence of the carefully tailored criminal provisions of the Copyright Act? Why bother to construe one federal criminal statute narrowly when there are a host of others in the prosecutor's arsenal? As a prosecutor, after *Dowling* would you feel it appropriate to bring a similar case only under the Copyright Act, or would you look for the broadest statute

78. For the Court of Appeals decision, see 739 F.2d 1445 (9th Cir.1984), certiorari granted 469 U.S. 1157, 105 S.Ct. 901, 83 L.Ed.2d 917 (1985).

available to "get" the defendant? Note that the mail fraud statute is one of the vaguest and most pliable statutes available to prosecutors seeking convictions for "improper" behavior.[79]

(2) *Protecting Soft Property.* The property involved in *Dowling* can be thought of as "soft property"—that is, the right to exclude others from using information in various forms—as opposed to the "hard property" of tangible goods. Prior to *Dowling,* the leading case in the area was *United States v. Bottone,* 365 F.2d 389 (2d Cir.1966). In reading the Court of Appeals' opinion, consider whether the result would be the same after *Dowling:*

> Friendly, Circuit Judge:
>
> The convictions here under appeal stem from a scheme for the massive extraction from Lederle Laboratories, a division of American Cyanamid Company located in Pearl River, N.Y., of microorganisms used in the production of three antibiotics and a steroid,[80] and instructions for the drugs' manufacture. Although the drugs were covered by patents and specimen cultures were required to be deposited in collections available for purchase by the public at minimal cost, improved strains of the microorganisms and detailed manufacturing processes developed by Lederle which were not in the public domain offered vastly greater output from the same physical plant. The combination of this with the lack of patent protection in certain foreign countries created a market for stolen cultures and secret processes and furnished a substantial incentive for theft to disloyal employees and persons willing to do business with them. The enterprise that was the subject of this indictment involved stealing and preserving cultures Lederle had developed, temporarily removing and copying documents that outlined manufacturing procedures, and then selling the cultures and the copies primarily for ultimate exportation to Europe. As in so many criminal trials, the Government's case was presented mainly through the chief culprits, two former Lederle employees, Sidney Fox and John Cancelarich, and their lieutenant, Leonard Fine, all of whom pleaded guilty to the charges against them and were rewarded for their cooperation with light sentences of six-months' imprisonment. The serious crimes charged against the appellants, Salb, Sharff and Bottone, were on the receiving end.
>
> * * *
>
> The only serious point of law raised by appellants is whether the transportation of papers describing the Lederle processes constituted the transportation in interstate or foreign commerce of "any goods, wares, merchandise, securities or money, of the value of $5,000 or more, knowing the same to have been stolen, converted or taken by fraud." 18 U.S.C. § 2314. The problem is not any

---

79. Mail fraud is explored further, infra pp. 107–138.

80. [Court's footnote 1.] The antibiotics were tetracycline (TC), sold as Achromycin; chlortetracycline (CTC), sold as Aureomycin; and demethyl-chlortetracycline (DMCTC), sold as Declomycin. The steroid was triamcinolone, sold as Aristocort.

doubt on our part that papers describing manufacturing procedures are goods, wares, or merchandise. . . . Neither do we have any concern over the value of these papers, since we dismiss out of hand the contentions that secret processes for which European drug manufacturers were willing to pay five and six figures and in whose illicit exploitation appellants eagerly invested a large portion of their time and an appreciable amount of their fortunes were not worth the $5,000 required to subject them to federal prosecution. . . . The serious question is whether, on the facts of this case, the papers showing Lederle processes that were transported in interstate or foreign commerce were "goods" which had been "stolen, converted or taken by fraud" in view of the lack of proof that any of the physical materials so transported came from Lederle's possession. The standard procedure was for Fox and Cancelarich to remove documents from Lederle's files at Pearl River, N.Y., take these to Fox' home within New York state, make photocopies, microfilms or notes, and then restore the purloined papers to the files; only the copies and notes moved or were intended to move in interstate or foreign commerce. The case differs in this respect from [other cases in which the copies were] made in the company's office, on its paper and with its equipment.

We are not persuaded, however, that a different result should obtain simply because the intangible information that was the purpose of the theft was transformed and embodied in a different physical object. To be sure, where no tangible objects were ever taken or transported, a court would be hard pressed to conclude that "goods" had been stolen and transported within the meaning of § 2314; the statute would presumably not extend to the case where a carefully guarded secret formula was memorized, carried away in the recesses of a thievish mind and placed in writing only after a boundary had been crossed. The situation, however, is quite different where tangible goods are stolen and transported and the only obstacle to condemnation is a clever intermediate transcription or use of a photocopy machine. In such a case, when the physical form of the stolen goods is secondary in every respect to the matter recorded in them, the transformation of the information in the stolen papers into a tangible object never possessed by the original owner should be deemed immaterial. It would offend common sense to hold that these defendants fall outside the statute simply because, in efforts to avoid detection, their confederates were at pains to restore the original papers to Lederle's files and transport only copies or notes, although an oversight would have brought them within it. We have been instructed to "free our minds from the notion that criminal statutes must be construed by some artificial and conventional rule." Such considerations have particular force when, as here, the defendants could not have doubted the criminal nature of their conduct, and the sole issue is whether they subjected themselves to punishment by the United States as well as by a state.

* * *

Affirmed.

(3) *The IBM–Hitachi Affair.* One of the more celebrated cases involving the allegedly improper acquisition of confidential information (in the form of trade secrets) is described as follows: [81]

> On November 20, 1980, a computer scientist left his employment at IBM to work for another computer firm, [signing] a pledge that he was taking no confidential information with him. This pledge was not fulfilled. Instead, he took with him ten volumes of IBM workbooks involving IBM plans for a new generation of computers. These workbooks eventually made their way to Japan, to the offices of Hitachi, Ltd.
>
> Hitachi, as a manufacturer of IBM-compatible computers, had a strong incentive to keep as well-informed about IBM plans as possible. IBM, of course, preferred to keep its plans secret and its "lead-time" as long as possible, so that it could reap the maximum rewards from its innovations prior to being forced to compete with imitating products. When Hitachi engineers began to study the workbooks, they became interested in obtaining more information about the computer project the workbooks described. Unfortunately for Hitachi, the consultant to whom they turned in the United States—a consultant who had previously worked for Hitachi in securing information about IBM products—decided to inform IBM that Hitachi was in possession of copies of these confidential workbooks.

* * *

> IBM [subsequently] linked up with an ongoing FBI undercover operation known as Pengem ("Penetration of the Gray Electronics Market"), which was designed, in part, to deal with the problem of the diversion of sophisticated somiconductor chips to the Soviet Union. In fact, IBM had shortly before agreed to help train the FBI agents involved with Pengem. Operation Pengem had established an undercover consulting firm in Silicon Valley, named Glenmar Associates. Hitachi's consultant introduced a Hitachi representative to an IBM security man, posing as a retired lawyer, who then introduced the Hitachi representative to an employee of Glenmar, who was, in reality, an FBI agent. Over a period of nearly eight months, the FBI agent and the IBM security man then worked together to feed Hitachi sensitive IBM information; in fact, the information was so sensitive that IBM executives began to wonder whether they were giving away too much. The operation finally ended on June 22, 1982, when FBI agents arrested two Hitachi employees who were about to exchange $525,000 for a large group of documents relating to IBM's new computer system.

* * *

81. First, Protecting Soft Property Through the Criminal Law: The Emerging View from the United States, 2 Nihon University Comp.L. 1 (1985).

Hitachi and its employees were not prosecuted for theft of trade secrets. There is no such federal crime. Rather, they were indicted for conspiracy to violate the National Stolen Property Act. . . .

What were the "goods" which were stolen? Were they the actual books and documents which belonged to IBM? Or could the "goods" simply be the "trade secrets" contained in these documents? On one occasion, a Hitachi employee took photographs of a new IBM memory device in which Hitachi was interested. The device was installed at a Pratt & Whitney plant, rather than at an IBM plant. Were these photographs stolen "goods"? We have no answers to these questions because the case did not go to trial.[82]

. . .

On February 8, 1983, Hitachi, and two of its employees, pleaded guilty; the corporation was fined $10,000, and the employees fined $10,000 and $4000 respectively. IBM was not content to rest with criminal prosecution. In subsequent civil litigation Hitachi eventually agreed to pay IBM its legal costs stemming from the incident (reportedly, an amount in excess of $40 million), admitted that software being used on certain of its computers infringed IBM software copyrights, agreed to pay royalties for an eight year period (reportedly, approximately $300 million), and agreed to allow IBM to inspect all new Hitachi data-processing products before release over the next five years.[83]

(4) *Criminalizing Infringement of Patents or Trademarks?* In *Dowling* the Court expressed concern that the government's theory could easily be expanded to criminalize patent infringement, a step that Congress has not yet taken. The Court also acknowledged that other forms of intellectual property might similarly be covered.

Even if the Court is properly reluctant to expand a vague statute into an area where Congress has not spoken, why should Congress be so reluctant? In fact, in 1984 Congress passed the first law providing criminal protection for trademarks since 1879 (when the Trademark Act of 1870 was declared unconstitutional).[84] The statute does not

---

82. [Footnote from original.] The indictment charged the defendants with conspiring to transport "documents and other personal property of IBM Corporation." Although there was some indignation in Japan over this indictment, criminal prosecutions for this type of behavior are hardly unknown in Japan. See, e.g., "Guilty Ruling Upheld on 4 Men For Buying Stolen Textile Files," Japan Times, Nov. 30, 1983, p. 2 (defendants found guilty of purchasing stolen property, consisting of classified documents of competitor; prison terms ranged from six to eight months, with one-year stay of execution). See also Affidavit of Kenneth C. Thompson, accompanying complaint in United States v. Nakazawa, June 21, 1982 (quoting conversation between FBI agent and Hitachi employee to effect that "secrecy was important since the laws in the United States made it 'dangerous to sell this product,' " to which Hitachi employee responded "the laws were 'same in Japan' ").

83. The Antitrust Division of the Department of Justice subsequently began an investigation to determine whether the *settlement* violated the antitrust laws. The investigation was subsequently terminated without taking any enforcement action.

84. See Trademark Counterfeiting Act of 1984, 18 U.S.C.A. § 2320 (Supp.). For a thorough discussion of the need for such

make every trademark infringement a "crime." It only forbids the intentional "trafficking" in goods and services on which a "counterfeit" mark is knowingly used. For a mark to be considered counterfeit it must be identical to, or substantially indistinguishable from, a registered mark, and it must be used in a way "likely to cause confusion, to cause mistake, or to deceive." Substantial penalties were provided—for first offenders, a maximum sentence of five years in jail and a fine of $250,000 ($1 million for a corporation).

The statute grew out of the efforts of the "International Anti-Counterfeiting Coalition," an association formed in 1978 by more than seventy major manufacturers. This group stressed the danger to health and safety from counterfeits; examples given were counterfeit aircraft parts and pharmaceutical drugs. In addition, though, the Coalition argued that counterfeit goods had become highly competitive with "legitimate" goods, because they were made with "cheap materials, unskilled labor, and little or no quality controls." The Coalition pointed out that "commercial counterfeiting has become an important part of the economies of a number of foreign countries, particularly in Southeast Asia." This concern was reiterated in Congressional debate on the legislation.

Would you have voted for a broad criminal counterfeiting bill? Where is the harm if you buy a cheap copy of an expensive watch (say, for $10 from a sidewalk vendor)? Who is being "confused"? [85] Does it matter if the copyist has included the "expensive" trademark on the face of the watch? Should it be a crime to sell such a watch even if there is no counterfeit mark on it? Might you have voted for a narrower (broader?) statute than the one Congress passed?

(5) *Privatization of Criminal Law Enforcement.* Are public enforcement resources adequate to deal with misuses of soft property? To the extent that significant economic interests are involved, there will often be sufficient incentive for injured parties to pursue the "perpetrator." If we believe that civil actions for monetary damages are inadequate to deter this kind of behavior, should we provide private parties with some kind of criminal enforcement power? Note, for example, the role IBM played in helping the FBI in the IBM–Hitachi affair, supra, where, in a sense, the FBI became an extension of IBM, protecting IBM's commercial interests. Note, also, that the Trademark Counterfeiting Act of 1984 gave the trademark owner the right to obtain a court issued seizure order which is analogous to a government issued search and seizure warrant.[86] Won't private parties, who know the cost of the infringing behavior better than public authorities, be more likely

legislation, see Rakoff & Wolff, Commercial Counterfeiting and the Proposed Trademark Counterfeiting Act, 20 Am. Crim.L.Rev. 145 (1982).

85. See United States v. Torkington, 812 F.2d 1347 (11th Cir.1987) ("causing confusion" under 1984 Act can include confusion to other potential purchasers of trademark holder's goods; denying motion to dismiss indictment).

86. See 15 U.S.C.A. § 1116(d) (Supp.).

to enforce these provisions "efficiently" (i.e., because they will act only if the benefits of enforcement outweigh they costs of enforcement)?

Consider in this connection *Young v. U.S. ex rel. Vuitton et Fils, S.A.*, 481 U.S. 787, 107 S.Ct. 2124, 95 L.Ed.2d 740 (1987):

> Justice Brennan delivered the opinion of the Court with respect to Parts I, II, III–A, and IV, and an opinion with respect to Part III–B, in which Justice Marshall, Justice Blackmun, and Justice Stevens join.
>
> Petitioners in these cases were found guilty of criminal contempt by a jury, pursuant to 18 U.S.C. § 401(3), for their violation of the District Court's injunction prohibiting infringement of respondent's trademark. They received sentences ranging from six months to five years.[87] On appeal to the Court of Appeals for the Second Circuit, petitioners urged that the District Court erred in appointing respondent's attorneys, rather than a disinterested attorney, to prosecute the contempt. The Court of Appeals affirmed, and we granted certiorari. We now reverse, exercising our supervisory power, and hold that counsel for a party that is the beneficiary of a court order may not be appointed to undertake contempt prosecutions for alleged violations of that order.

I

> The injunction that petitioners violated in these cases is a result of the settlement of a lawsuit brought in December 1978, in the District Court for the Southern District of New York, by Louis Vuitton, S.A., a French leather goods manufacturer, against Sol Klayminc, his wife Sylvia, his son Barry (the Klaymincs), and their family-owned businesses, Karen Bags, Inc., Jade Handbag Co., Inc., and Jak Handbag, Inc. Vuitton alleged in its suit that the Klaymincs were manufacturing imitation Vuitton goods for sale and distribution. . . . Vuitton and the Klaymincs then entered into a settlement agreement in July 1982. Under this agreement, the Klaymincs agreed to pay Vuitton $100,000 in damages, and consented to the entry of a permanent injunction prohibiting them from, inter alia, "manufacturing, producing, distributing, circulating, selling, offering for sale, advertising, promoting or displaying any product bearing any simulation, reproduction, counterfeit, copy, or colorable imitation" of Vuitton's registered trademark.
>
> In early 1983, Vuitton and other companies concerned with possible trademark infringement were contacted by a Florida investigation firm with a proposal to conduct an undercover "sting" operation. The firm was retained, and Melvin Weinberg and Gunner Askeland, two former Federal Bureau of Investigation agents, set out to pose as persons who were interested in purchas-

---

87. [Court's footnote 1.] The petitioners' sentences were as follows: Sol Klayminc, five years; Gerald Young, two and one-half years; Barry Klayminc, nine months; George Cariste, nine months; Nathan Helfand, six months.

ing counterfeit goods. Weinberg expressed this interest to petitioner Nathan Helfand, who then discussed with Klayminc and his wife the possibility that Weinberg and Askeland might invest in a Haitian factory devoted to the manufacture of counterfeit Vuitton and Gucci goods. Klayminc signed documents that described the nature of the factory operation and that provided an estimate of the cost of the counterfeited goods. In addition, Klayminc delivered some sample counterfeit Vuitton bags to Helfand for Weinberg and Askeland's inspection.

Four days after Helfand met with Klayminc, on March 31, 1983, Vuitton attorney J. Joseph Bainton requested that the District Court appoint him and his colleague Robert P. Devlin as special counsel to prosecute a criminal contempt action for violation of the injunction against infringing Vuitton's trademark. Bainton's affidavit in support of this request recounted the developments with Helfand and Klayminc, and pointed out that he and Devlin previously had been appointed by the court to prosecute Sol Klayminc for contempt of an earlier preliminary injunction in the Vuitton lawsuit. Bainton also indicated that the next step of the "sting" was to be a meeting among Sol and Barry Klayminc, Weinberg, and Askeland, at which Sol was to deliver twenty-five counterfeit Vuitton handbags. Bainton sought permission to conduct and videotape this meeting, and to continue to engage in undercover investigative activity.

The court responded to Bainton on the day of this request. It found probable cause to believe that petitioners were engaged in conduct contumacious of the court's injunctive order, and appointed Bainton and Devlin to represent the United States in the investigation and prosecution of such activity, as proposed in Bainton's affidavit. A week after Bainton's appointment, on April 6, the court suggested that Bainton inform the United States Attorney's Office of his appointment and the impending investigation. Bainton did so, offering to make available any tape recordings or other evidence, but the Chief of the Criminal Division of that Office expressed no interest beyond wishing Bainton good luck.

Over the course of the next month, more than 100 audio and video tapes were made of meetings and telephone conversations between petitioners and investigators. On the basis of this evidence, Bainton requested and the District Court signed an order on April 26, directing the petitioners to show cause why they and other parties should not be cited for contempt for either violating or aiding and abetting the violation of the court's July 1982 permanent injunction. [T]wo of the defendants subsequently entered guilty pleas. Sol Klayminc ultimately was convicted, following a jury trial, of criminal contempt under 18 U.S.C. § 401(3), and the other petitioners were convicted of aiding and abetting that contempt. . . .

II

[The Court held that the federal courts have authority to prosecute contempt actions, and to appoint private attorneys to initiate such prosecutions.]

While a court has the authority to initiate a prosecution for criminal contempt, its exercise of that authority must be restrained by the principle that "only '[t]he least possible power adequate to the end proposed' should be used in contempt cases." . . .

This principle of restraint in contempt counsels caution in the exercise of the power to appoint a private prosecutor. We repeat that the rationale for the appointment authority is necessity. If the Judiciary were completely dependent on the Executive Branch to redress direct affronts to its authority, it would be powerless to protect itself if that branch declined prosecution. The logic of this rationale is that a court ordinarily should first request the appropriate prosecuting authority to prosecute contempt actions, and should appoint a private prosecutor only if that request is denied. Such a procedure ensures that the court will exercise its inherent power of self-protection only as a last resort.

In practice, courts can reasonably expect that the public prosecutor will accept the responsibility for prosecution. Indeed, the United States Attorney's Manual § 9–39.318 (1984) expressly provides: "In the great majority of cases the dedication of the executive branch to the preservation of respect for judicial authority makes the acceptance by the U.S. Attorney of the court's request to prosecute a mere formality. . . ." Referral will thus enhance the prospect that investigative activity will be conducted by trained prosecutors pursuant to Justice Department guidelines.

In this case, the District Court did not first refer the case to the U.S. Attorney's Office before the appointment of Bainton and Devlin as special prosecutors. We need not address the ramifications of that failure, however. Even if a referral had been made, we hold, in the exercise of our supervisory power, that the court erred in appointing as prosecutors counsel for an interested party in the underlying civil litigation.

III

A

In Berger v. United States, 295 U.S. 78, 88, 55 S.Ct. 629, 633, 79 L.Ed. 1314 (1935), this Court declared:

> "The United States Attorney is the representative not of an ordinary party to a controversy, but of a sovereignty whose obligation to govern impartially is as compelling as its obligation to govern at all; and whose interest, therefore, in a criminal prosecution is not that it shall win a case, but that justice shall be done. As such, he is in a peculiar and very

definite sense the servant of the law, the two fold aim of which is that guilt shall not escape nor innocence suffer."

* * *

... The concern that representation of other clients may compromise the prosecutor's pursuit of the Government's interest rests on recognition that a prosecutor would owe an ethical duty to those other clients. "Indeed, it is the highest claim on the most noble advocate which causes the problem—fidelity, unquestioned, continuing fidelity to the client." Brotherhood of Locomotive Firemen & Enginemen v. United States, 411 F.2d 312, 319 (CA5 1969).

Private attorneys appointed to prosecute a criminal contempt action represent the United States, not the party that is the beneficiary of the court order allegedly violated. . . .

. . . The government's interest is in dispassionate assessment of the propriety of criminal charges for affronts to the judiciary. The private party's interest is in obtaining the benefits of the court's order. While these concerns sometimes may be congruent, sometimes they may not. . . .

Regardless of whether the appointment of private counsel in this case resulted in any prosecutorial impropriety (an issue on which we express no opinion), that appointment illustrates the *potential* for private interest to influence the discharge of public duty. Vuitton's California litigation had culminated in a permanent injunction and consent decree in favor of Vuitton against petitioner Young relating to various trademark infringement activities. This decree contained a liquidated damages provision of $750,000 for violation of the injunction. The prospect of such a damage award had the potential to influence whether Young was selected as a target of investigation, whether he might be offered a plea bargain, or whether he might be offered immunity in return for his testimony. In addition, Bainton was the defendant in a defamation action filed by Klayminc arising out of Bainton's involvement in the litigation resulting in the injunction whose violation was at issue in this case. This created the possibility that the investigation of Klayminc might be shaped in part by a desire to obtain information useful in the defense of the defamation suit. Furthermore, Vuitton had various civil claims pending against some of the petitioners. These claims theoretically could have created temptation to use the criminal investigation to gather information of use in those suits, and could have served as bargaining leverage in obtaining pleas in the criminal prosecution. In short, as will generally be the case, the appointment of counsel for an interested party to bring the contempt prosecution in this case at a minimum created *opportunities* for conflicts to arise, and created at least the *appearance* of impropriety.[88]

---

88. [Court's footnote 17.] The potential for misconduct that is created by the appointment of an interested prosecutor is not outweighed by the fact that counsel for the beneficiary of the court order may often be most familiar with the allegedly con-

* * *

. . . The exercise of supervisory authority is especially appropriate in the determination of the procedures to be employed by courts to enforce their orders, a subject that directly concerns the functioning of the judiciary. We rely today on that authority to hold that counsel for a party that is the beneficiary of a court order may not be appointed as prosecutor in a contempt action alleging a violation of that order.

B

[This part of Justice Brennan's opinion, to the effect that the error could not be "harmless," is omitted.]

IV

Between the private life of the citizen and the public glare of criminal accusation stands the prosecutor. That state official has the power to employ the full machinery of the state in scrutinizing any given individual. Even if a defendant is ultimately acquitted, forced immersion in criminal investigation and adjudication is a wrenching disruption of everyday life. For this reason, we must have assurance that those who would wield this power will be guided solely by their sense of public responsibility for the attainment of justice. A prosecutor of a contempt action who represents the private beneficiary of the court order allegedly violated cannot provide such assurance, for such an attorney is required by the very standards of the profession to serve two masters. The appointment of counsel for Vuitton to conduct the contempt prosecution in these cases therefore was improper. Accordingly, the judgment of the Court of Appeals is *Reversed.*

[The concurring opinions of Justices Blackmun and Scalia are omitted. Justice Powell, joined by Chief Justice Rehnquist, would have remanded to determine whether the error was harmless. Justice White would have affirmed the Court of Appeals decision.]

READINGS

"A Roster of Wrongdoing," Fortune Magazine, December 1, 1980, pp. 58–61.[89]

The following is a list of the major successful federal cases against big companies between 1970 and 1980. Fortune canvassed the 1,043 companies that appeared at some point during that period in its lists of the 800 largest industrial and non-industrial corporations; 117—11%—turned out to be offenders.

tumacious conduct. That familiarity may be put to use in *assisting* a disinterested prosecutor in pursuing the contempt action, but cannot justify permitting counsel for the private party to be in control of the prosecution.

89. By Irwin Ross, © 1980 Time Inc. All rights reserved.

COMPANY	OFFENSE
Allied Chemical	1974—Fixing prices of dyes. Pleaded nolo contendere. 1979—Tax fraud related to paying kickbacks. Nolo plea on some charges.
Amerada Hess	1976—Fixing prices of gasoline. Convicted after trial. Executive acquitted. Conviction being appealed.
American Airlines	1973—Illegal campaign contributions of $55,000. Guilty plea. 1975—CAB charges related to slush fund used for contributions. Settlement. 1977—SEC charges related to same. Consent decree.
American Bakeries	1972—Fixing prices of bread. Nolo plea.
Amer. Beef Packers	1975—Company and president charged with defrauding a creditor. Both found guilty on some counts. 1976—SEC charges related to same matter. Injunction against president.
American Brands	1978—James B. Beam subsidiary and two executives charged with bribery of state liquor official. All pleaded guilty.
American Can	1976—Company and executive charged with fixing prices of folding cartons. Nolo pleas by both.
American Cyanamid	1974—Fixing prices of dyes. Nolo plea.
American Export Ind.	1979—American Export Lines subsidiary charged with fixing prices of ocean shipping. Nolo plea.
Anheuser-Busch	1977—SEC charges concerning $2.7 million in payments to customers. Consent decree. 1978—Treasury Dept. charges about same matter. Settlement and $750,000 fine.
Archer-Daniels-Midland	1976—Defrauding grain buyers by shortweighting. Nolo plea.
Arden-Mayfair	1971—Company and executive charged with fixing prices of dairy products. Nolo pleas. 1977—SEC charges related to $4.4 million in rebates and off-book accounts. Consent decree. 1978—Price fixing of dairy products. Nolo plea.
Armco	1973–77—Three cases of fixing prices of steel reinforcing bars. Nolo pleas by company and three executives.
Ashland Oil	1973—Illegal political contribution of $100,000. Guilty plea. 1975—SEC charges about allegedly illegal payments. Consent de-

COMPANY	OFFENSE
	cree. **1977**—Fixing prices of resins used to make paint. Nolo plea. **1980**—Ashland-Warren subsidiary pleaded guilty in three cases involving bid rigging in highway construction. Fined a total of $1.5 million.
Associated Milk Prod.	**1974**—Illegal political contributions. Guilty plea.
Beatrice Foods	**1974**—Fixing prices of toilet seats. Company and president of Beneke division pleaded nolo. **1978**—SEC charges about improper accounting for $11.7 million in rebates. Consent decree.
Bethlehem Steel	**1973-74**—Two cases of fixing prices of steel reinforcing bars. Company and one employee pleaded nolo; another convicted after trial. **1980**—Mail fraud related to bribes paid for ship-repair business. Guilty plea.
Boise Cascade	**1978**—Fixing prices of corrugated containers. Nolo pleas by company and two plant managers.
Borden	**1974 & 1977**—Two cases of fixing prices of dairy products. Company and three executives pleaded nolo.
Borg-Warner	**1971**—Fixing prices of plastic pipe fittings. Nolo plea.
Braniff International	**1973**—Illegal political contribution of $40,000. Guilty pleas by company and chairman. **1975**—CAB allegations about contribution. Settlement. **1976**—SEC charges related to $900,000 slush fund and contributions. Consent decree. **1977**—Criminal restraint of trade. Nolo plea.
CPC International	**1977**—Fixing prices of industrial sugar. Nolo plea.
Carnation	**1971**—Fixing prices of dairy products. Company and executive pleaded nolo. **1973**—Illegal political contributions of $9,000. Company and chairman pleaded guilty. **1974**—Fixing prices of dairy products. Nolo pleas by company and general manager.
Carter Hawley Hale	**1974**—Bergdorf Goodman subsidiary charged with fixing prices of women's clothing. Company and executive pleaded nolo.
Ceco	**1973-77**—Three cases involving fixing prices of steel reinforcing bars. Company and one

COMPANY	OFFENSE
	executive pleaded nolo; another executive convicted after trial.
Celanese	1971—Fixing prices of plastic pipe fittings. Company pleaded nolo; executive acquitted.
Cenco	1976—SEC charges related to falsifying inventory. Seven of eight former executives signed consent decrees. 1979—Seven executives indicted on criminal charges of mail fraud related to the same scheme. Three pleaded guilty, three convicted after trial, and one acquitted of fraud charges. Convictions are being appealed.
Champion Intl.	1974—Bid rigging in purchase of timber from public lands. Company found guilty after trial. Executive acquitted. 1976—Fixing prices of folding cartons. Nolo plea.
Chemical New York	1977—Chemical Bank charged with violations of Bank Secrecy Act in scheme by two branch officials to launder money for alleged narcotics dealer. Officials pleaded guilty to tax charges and company to reduced charges.
Chicago Milwaukee	1976—SEC allegations of improper use of assets and political contributions. Consent decree.
Combustion Engin.	1973—Fixing prices of chromite sand. Company and executive pleaded nolo.
Consolidated Foods	1974—Fixing prices of refined sugar. Nolo plea.
Continental Group	1976—Fixing prices of paper bags. Company and one executive convicted after trial; two others acquitted. Company fined $750,000.
Cook Industries	1976—Defrauding grain customers by short-weighting. Company pleaded nolo and five executives pleaded guilty.
Dean Foods	1977—Price fixing of dairy products. Nolo pleas by company and executive.
Diamond International	1974—Illegal campaign contributions of $6,000. Company and executive pleaded guilty. 1974—Fixing prices of paper labels. Nolo pleas by company and two executives. 1976—Fixing prices of folding cartons. Company and seven executives pleaded nolo.

COMPANY	OFFENSE
Diversified Industries	1976—SEC charges related to alleged short-weighting of customers in metal-recovery processes. Consent decree.
Du Pont	1974—Fixing prices of dyes. Nolo plea.
Equity Funding	1973—SEC charges relating to $2 billion in fictitious insurance policies. Consent decree. 1973—Former chairman and 21 other former executives charged with fraud. All pleaded guilty to some counts.
FMC	1976—Fixing prices of persulfates. Company and executive pleaded nolo.
Federal Paper Board	1976—Fixing prices of folding cartons. Company and two executives pleaded nolo.
Federated Dept. Stores	1976—I. Magnin subsidiary charged with fixing prices of women's clothing. Nolo plea.
Fibreboard	1976—Fixing prices of folding cartons. Company and executive pleaded nolo.
Firestone	1976—SEC charges about slush fund and allegedly illegal political contributions of $330,000. Consent decree. **1979**—False tax-return charges related to $13 million in set-aside income. Guilty plea on some counts.
Flavorland Industries	1979—Fixing prices of meat. Nolo plea.
Flintkote	1973—Fixing prices of gypsum board. Company, chairman, and president pleaded nolo.
Franklin New York	1974—SEC charges against nine executives relating to the bankruptcy of Franklin National Bank. Company and eight executives signed consent decree. **1975**—Eight former executives and employees of bank charged with fraud. All pleaded guilty. **1978**—Three other former executives charged with fraud. All convicted after trial.
Fruehauf	1975—Company, chairman, and vice president charged with criminal tax evasion. All convicted after trial.
GAF	1974—Fixing prices of dyes. Nolo plea.
GTE	1977—SEC charges relating to political contributions and payments to local officials. Consent decree.
General Dynamics	1977—SEC allegations of improper accounting to disguise political contributions. Consent decree.

COMPANY	OFFENSE
General Host	1972—Fixing prices of bread. Nolo plea.
General Tire & Rubber	1976—SEC charges concerning slush fund and allegedly illegal political contributions. Consent decree.
Genesco	1974—Fixing prices of women's clothing. Nolo plea.
Gimbel Bros.	1974 & 1976—Saks & Co. subsidiary charged with two cases of fixing prices of women's clothing. Company and executive pleaded nolo.
B.F. Goodrich	1978—Tax evasion related to slush fund used for illegal political contributions. Nolo plea by company; charges against an executive dropped.
Goodyear	1973—Illegal political contribution of $40,000. Company and chairman pleaded guilty. 1977—SEC charges concerning slush fund of $500,000 for contributions. Consent decree.
Great Western United	1974—Great Western Sugar subsidiary charged with fixing prices of refined sugar. Nolo plea.
Greyhound	1974—Illegal campaign contributions of $16,000. Guilty plea.
Gulf Oil	1973—Illegal political contributions of $100,000. Company and executive pleaded guilty. 1975—SEC charges about $10-million slush fund used for political contributions. Consent decree. 1977—Company and two employees charged with giving illegal gifts to an IRS agent. Company pleaded guilty, one employee pleaded nolo, the other convicted after trial. 1978—Fixing prices of uranium. Pleaded guilty.
Gulf & Western	1976—Brown Co. subsidiary charged with fixing prices of folding cartons. Company and two executives pleaded nolo.
Hammermill Paper	1978—Palmer Paper Co. unit charged with fixing prices of paper products. Company and executive pleaded nolo.
Heublein	1978—Bribery of state liquor official. Guilty plea.
Hoerner Waldorf	1976—Fixing prices of folding cartons. Company and four executives pleaded nolo.

COMPANY	OFFENSE
	1978—Fixing prices of corrugated containers. Nolo plea.
ITT	1972—ITT Continental Baking subsidiary charged with fixing prices of bread. Nolo plea.
Inland Container	1978—Fixing prices of corrugated containers. Nolo plea by company and executive.
International Paper	1974—Fixing prices of paper labels. Company and two executives pleaded nolo. 1976—Fixing prices of folding cartons. Company and four executives pleaded nolo. 1978—Fixing prices of corrugated containers. Nolo plea. Fined $617,000.
Walter Kidde	1977—SEC charges against U.S. Lines subsidiary related to $2.5 million in allegedly illegal rebates. Consent decree. 1978—Federal Maritime Commission charges related to same. Settlement. 1979—U.S. Lines charged with fixing prices of ocean shipping. Nolo plea. Fined $1 million.
Koppers	1979—Bid rigging in connection with sale of road tar to State of Connecticut. Nolo plea.
LTV	1978—Agriculture Dept. charges against Wilson Foods subsidiary related to alleged illegal payoffs to customers. Settlement.
Liggett Group	1978—Paddington Corp. subsidiary charged with bribery of state liquor official. Guilty plea.
Litton Industries	1974—Fixing prices of paper labels. Convicted after trial.
3M	1973—Illegal campaign contribution of $30,000. Company and chairman pleaded guilty. 1975—SEC charges related to $634,000 slush fund for contributions. Consent decree.
Marcor	1976—Container Corp. subsidiary charged with fixing prices of folding cartons. Company and eight executives pleaded nolo. 1978—Subsidiary charged with fixing prices of corrugated boxes. Company and two executives pleaded nolo.
Martin Marietta	1978—Martin Marietta Aluminum subsidiary charged with fixing prices of titanium products. Company and executive pleaded nolo.

COMPANY	OFFENSE
Mattel	1974—SEC charges related to false disclosures to influence stock prices. Consent decree. 1978—Former president indicted on criminal charges related to same matter. Nolo plea.
J. Ray McDermott	1976—SEC charges related to slush fund of more than $800,000 used for commercial bribes and illegal political contributions. Consent decree. 1978—Wire fraud and racketeering charges relating to the bribes and contributions. Guilty plea. 1978—Bid rigging and allocation of contracts relating to pipeline and offshore-oil-rig construction. Company president, and three other executives pleaded nolo. Company fined $1 million.
Mead	1976—Fixing prices of folding cartons. Company and executive pleaded nolo.
National Distillers	1978—Bribery of state liquor official. Pleaded guilty. 1980—Treasury Dept. allegations of illegal payments to customers. Settlement and $750,000 fine.
Northern Natural Gas	1972—Mail fraud related to bribery of local officials to obtain right-of-way permits for pipeline construction. Company and one executive pleaded nolo to some counts; charges against another executive dropped.
Northrop	1974—Illegal campaign contributions of $150,000. Company and two executives pleaded guilty. 1975—SEC charges related to slush fund for $500,000 in domestic contributions. Consent decree.
Occidental Petroleum	1974—Illegal campaign contribution of $54,000. Executive and later the chairman pleaded guilty. 1977—SEC charges related to $200,000 slush fund for contributions in the U.S. and abroad. Consent decree.
Olinkraft	1978—Fixing prices of corrugated containers. Company and one executive pleaded nolo; another executive acquitted.
Owens–Illinois	1978—Fixing prices of corrugated containers. Company and one executive pleaded nolo; two others acquitted.
Pan American	1975—Illegal fare cutting. Nolo plea. 1977—Fixing prices of military fares. Nolo plea.

COMPANY	OFFENSE
Peavey	1977—Defrauding grain customers by short-weighting. Nolo plea.
Penn Central	1974—SEC charges of fraud relating to the bankruptcy of the railroad. Consent decree.
PepsiCo	1970—Frito–Lay subsidiary charged with fixing prices of snack food. Nolo plea. 1977—Parent company charged with fixing prices of industrial sugar. Nolo plea. 1979—Parent company and two executives of Monsieur Henri subsidiary charged with bribing a union official. All pleaded guilty.
Pet	1970—Fixing prices of snack foods. Nolo plea.
Phillips Petroleum	1973—Illegal campaign contribution of $100,000. Company and chairman pleaded guilty. 1975—SEC charges related to $2.8-million slush fund, a portion of which was allegedly used for domestic illegal political contributions. Consent decree. 1975—Fixing prices of gasoline. Nolo plea. 1976—Tax evasion related to the slush fund. Guilty plea.
Pittston	1977—Brink's Inc. subsidiary charged with bid rigging and fixing prices of security services. Company and five executives pleaded nolo. Company fined $625,000.
H.K. Porter	1974—Fixing prices of steel reinforcing bars. Nolo plea.
Potlatch	1976—Fixing prices of folding cartons. Company and one executive pleaded nolo; another executive acquitted.
Purolator	1978—Bid rigging and allocation of markets for security services. Nolo plea.
Rapid-American	1978—Schenley subsidiary and three executives charged with bribery of a state liquor official. All pleaded guilty. 1979—SEC charges against Schenley related to $6 million in allegedly illegal payments to customers. Consent decree.
Reichhold Chemicals	1977—Fixing prices of resins used to make paints. Company and executive pleaded nolo.
R.J. Reynolds Ind.	1977—Federal Maritime Commission charges against Sea–Land Services subsidiary relating to illegal payments to customers. Settlement and $4 million fine. 1978—SEC suit against

COMPANY	OFFENSE
	Sea-Land related to $25 million in allegedly illegal rebates and political contributions. Consent decree. **1979**—Fixing prices of ocean shipping. Nolo plea. Fined $1 million.
Rockwell International	**1978**—Fixing prices of gas meters. Pleaded guilty.
St. Regis Paper	**1976**—Fixing prices of folding cartons. Company and executive pleaded nolo.
F. & M. Schaefer	**1978**—Treasury Dept. allegations of $600,000 in illegal rebates to customers. Settlement.
Jos. Schlitz Brewing	**1977**—SEC charges related to $3 million in illegal rebates to customers. Consent decree. **1977**—Fixing prices of beer. Company and executive pleaded nolo. **1978**—Treasury Dept. allegations of illegal marketing practices and rebates. Consent decree and $750,000 fine.
Joseph E. Seagram	**1977**—SEC charges related to over $1 million in allegedly illegal rebates to customers and political contributions. Consent decree. **1978**—Seagram Distillers, three other subsidiaries, and four executives charged with bribery of a state liquor official. All pleaded guilty. **1979**—Illegal payments to members of a state liquor-control board. Guilty plea. Fined $1.5 million.
Seatrain Lines	**1978**—Payment of illegal rebates and violation of currency regulations. Guilty plea in criminal case and $2.5 million fine paid in Federal Maritime Commission case. **1979**—Fixing prices of ocean shipping. Nolo plea. **1980**—SEC suit related to $14 million in rebates to customers. Consent decree.
Singer	**1975**—Illegal campaign contribution of $10,000. Guilty plea.
SuCrest	**1977**—Fixing prices of industrial sugar. Nolo plea.
Tenneco	**1976**—Packaging Corp. subsidiary charged with fixing prices of folding cartons. Company and four executives pleaded nolo. **1978**—Mail fraud in connection with bribery of a local official. Guilty plea.
Textron	**1978**—Fixing prices of gas meters. Pleaded guilty.

COMPANY	OFFENSE
Time Inc.	1976—Eastex Packaging subsidiary charged with fixing prices of folding cartons. Nolo plea.
Trans World Corp.	1975—TWA charged with illegal fare cutting. Nolo plea. 1977—Fixing prices of military fares. Nolo plea.
Uniroyal	1977—SEC charges related to allegedly illegal political contributions. Consent decree.
United Brands	1975—SEC charges related to improper use of funds to pay a $1.2 million bribe to a Honduran official. Consent decree. 1978—Wire fraud charges related to the same matter. Guilty plea.
U.S. Steel	1973—Fixing prices of steel reinforcing bars. Company and an executive pleaded nolo.
Jim Walter	1978—Knight Paper subsidiary charged with fixing prices of paper products. Company and executive pleaded nolo.
Ward Foods	1972—Fixing prices of bread. Nolo plea. 1978—Fixing prices of meat. Nolo plea.
Weyerhaeuser	1976—Fixing prices of folding cartons. Company and three executives pleaded nolo. 1978—Fixing prices of corrugated boxes. Company pleaded nolo, fined $632,000. Two executives acquitted.
Wheelabrator-Frye	1976—A.L. Garber subsidiary charged with fixing prices of folding cartons. Nolo plea.
Zale	1977—SEC charges related to slush fund to reimburse executives for political contributions. Consent decree.

CLARENCE DARROW, ADDRESS TO THE PRISONERS IN THE COOK COUNTY JAIL
(1902).[90]

If I looked at jails and crimes and prisoners in the way the ordinary person does, I should not speak on this subject to you. The reason I talk to you on the question of crime, its cause and cure, is that I really do not in the least believe in crime. There is no such thing as a crime as the word is generally understood. I do not believe there is any sort of distinction between the real moral conditions of the people in and out of jail. One is just as good as the other. The people here can no more help being here than the people outside can avoid being outside. I do

---

90. From Attorney For The Damned, A. Weinberg, Editor. © 1957, reprinted with the permission of Lila Weinberg.

not believe that people are in jail because they deserve to be. They are in jail simply because they cannot avoid it on account of circumstances which are entirely beyond their control and for which they are in no way responsible.

* * *

Most of you probably have nothing against me, and most of you would treat me the same as any other person would, probably better than some of the people on the outside would treat me, because you think I believe in you and they know I do not believe in them. While you would not have the least thing against me in the world, you might pick my pockets. I do not think all of you would, but I think some of you would. You would not have anything against me, but that's your profession, a few of you. Some of the rest of you, if my doors were unlocked, might come in if you saw anything you wanted—not out of any malice to me, but because that is your trade. There is no doubt there are quite a number of people in this jail who would pick my pockets. And still I know this—that when I get outside pretty nearly everybody picks my pocket. There may be some of you who would hold up a man on the street, if you did not happen to have something else to do, and needed the money; but when I want to light my house or my office the gas company holds me up. They charge me one dollar for something that is worth twenty-five cents. Still all these people are good people; they are pillars of society and support the churches, and they are respectable.

When I ride on the streetcars I am held up—I pay five cents for a ride that is worth two and a half cents, simply because a body of men have bribed the city council and the legislature, so that all the rest of us have to pay tribute to them.

If I do not want to fall into the clutches of the gas trust and choose to burn oil instead of gas, then good Mr. Rockefeller holds me up, and he uses a certain portion of his money to build universities and support churches which are engaged in telling us how to be good.

Some of you are here for obtaining property under false pretenses—yet I pick up a great Sunday paper and read the advertisements of a merchant prince—"Shirtwaists for 39 cents, marked down from $3.00."

When I read the advertisements in the paper I see they are all lies. When I want to get out and find a place to stand anywhere on the face of the earth, I find that it has all been taken up long ago before I came here, and before you came here, and somebody says, "Get off, swim into the lake, fly into the air; go anywhere, but get off." That is because these people have the police and they have the jails and the judges and the lawyers and the soldiers and all the rest of them to take care of the earth and drive everybody off that comes in their way.

A great many people will tell you that all this is true, but that it does not excuse you. These facts do not excuse some fellow who reaches into my pocket and takes out a five-dollar bill. The fact that the gas company bribes the members of the legislature from year to year, and fixes the law, so that all you people are compelled to be "fleeced" whenever you deal with them; the fact that the streetcar companies and the gas companies have control of the streets; and the fact that the landlords own all the earth—this, they say, has nothing to do with you.

Let us see whether there is any connection between the crimes of the respectable classes and your presence in the jail. Many of you people are in jail because you have really committed burglary; many of you, because you have stolen something. In the meaning of the law, you have taken some other person's property. Some of you have entered a store and carried off a pair of shoes because you did not have the price. Possibly some of you have committed murder. I cannot tell what all of you did. There are a great many people here who have done some of these things who really do not know themselves why they did them. I think I know why you did them—every one of you; you did these things because you were bound to do them. It looked to you at the time as if you had a chance to do them or not, as you saw fit; but still, after all, you had no choice. There may be people here who had some money in their pockets and who still went out and got some more money in a way society forbids. Now, you may not yourselves see exactly why it was you did this thing, but if you look at the question deeply enough and carefully enough you will see that there were circumstances that drove you to do exactly the thing which you did. You could not help it any more than we outside can help taking the positions that we take. The reformers who tell you to be good and you will be happy, and the people on the outside who have property to protect—they think that the only way to do it is by building jails and locking you up in cells on weekdays and praying for you Sundays.

I think that all of this has nothing whatever to do with right conduct. I think it is very easily seen what has to do with right conduct. Some so-called criminals—and I will use this word because it is handy, it means nothing to me—I speak of the criminals who get caught as distinguished from the criminals who catch them—some of these so-called criminals are in jail for their first offenses, but nine tenths of you are in jail because you did not have a good lawyer and, of course, you did not have a good lawyer because you did not have enough money to pay a good lawyer. There is no very great danger of a rich man going to jail.

* * *

Long ago, Mr. Buckle, who was a great philosopher and historian, collected facts, and he showed that the number of people who are arrested increased just as the price of food increased. When they put up the price of gas ten cents a thousand, I do not know who will go to jail, but I do know that a certain number of people will go. When the meat combine raises the price of beef, I do not know who is going to jail, but I know that a large number of people are bound to go. Whenever the Standard Oil Company raises the price of oil, I know that a certain number of girls who are seamstresses, and who work night after night long hours for somebody else, will be compelled to go out on the streets and ply another trade, and I know that Mr. Rockefeller and his associates are responsible and not the poor girls in the jails.

First and last, people are sent to jail because they are poor. Sometimes, as I say, you may not need money at the particular time, but you wish to have thrifty forehanded habits, and do not always wait until you are in absolute want. Some of you people are perhaps plying the trade, the profession, which is called burglary. No man in his right senses will go into a strange house in the dead of night and prowl around with a dark lantern through unfamiliar rooms and take chances of his life, if he has plenty of the good things of the world in his own home. You would not take any such chances as that. If a man had clothes in his clothes-press and beefsteak in his pantry and money in the bank, he would not navigate around nights in houses where he knows nothing about the premises whatever. It always requires experience and education for this profession, and people who fit themselves for it are no more to blame than I am for being a lawyer. A man would not hold up another man on the street if he had plenty of money in his own pocket. He might do it if he had one dollar or two dollars, but he wouldn't if he had as much money as Mr. Rockefeller has. Mr. Rockefeller has a great deal better hold-up game than that.

* * *

. . . If every man and woman and child in the world had a chance to make a decent, fair, honest living, there would be no jails and no lawyers and no courts. There might be some persons here or there with some peculiar formation of their brain, like Rockefeller, who would do these things simply to be doing them; but they would be very, very few, and those should be sent to a hospital and treated, and not sent to jail; and they would entirely disappear in the second generation, or at least in the third generation.

* * *

. . . These people who have property fix it so they can protect what they have. When somebody commits a crime it does not follow that he has done something that is morally wrong. The man on the outside who has committed no crime may have done something. For instance: to take all the coal in the United States and raise the price two dollars or three dollars when there is no need of it, and thus kill thousands of babies and send thousands of people to the poorhouse and tens of thousands to jail, as is done every year in the United States—this is a greater crime than all the people in our jails ever committed; but the law does not punish it. Why? Because the fellows who control the earth make the laws. If you and I had the making of the laws, the first thing we would do would be to punish the fellow who gets control of the earth. Nature put this coal in the ground for me as well as for them and nature made the prairies up here to raise wheat for me as well as for them, and then the great railroad companies came along and fenced it up.

* * *

And this has been the history of the world. It's easy to see how to do away with what we call crime. It is not so easy to do it. I will tell you how to do it. It can be done by giving the people a chance to live—by destroying special privileges. So long as big criminals can get the coal fields, so long as the big criminals have control of the city council and get the public streets for streetcars and gas rights—this is bound to send thousands of poor people to jail. So long as men are allowed to monopolize all the earth, and compel others to live on such terms as these men see fit to make, then you are bound to get into jail.

The only way in the world to abolish crime and criminals is to abolish the big ones and the little ones together. Make fair conditions of life. Give men a chance to live. Abolish the right of private ownership of land, abolish monopoly, make the world partners in production, partners in the good things of life. Nobody would steal if he could get something of his own some easier way. Nobody will commit burglary when he has a house full. No girl will go out on the streets when she has a comfortable place at home. The man who owns a sweatshop or a department store may not be to blame himself for the condition of his girls, but when he pays them five dollars, three dollars, and two dollars a week, I wonder where he thinks they will get the rest of their money to live. The only way to cure these conditions is by equality. There should be no jails. They do not accomplish what they pretend to accomplish. If you would wipe them out there would be no more criminals than now. They terrorize nobody. They are a blot upon any civilization, and a jail is an evidence of the lack of charity of the people on the outside who make the jails and fill them with the victims of their greed.

J. HALL, THEFT, LAW AND SOCIETY
pp. 62–70, 77–79 (1952).[91]

The era of discoveries and the Commercial Revolution whose advent substantially coincided with them poured into Europe specie in quantities sufficient to turn existing values topsy-turvy. This influx of specie, vastly increasing the supply of liquid capital, must be regarded as one potent factor in stimulating economic enterprise.

Moreover, by shifting trade routes from land to sea the discoveries made possible the carriage of merchandise in bulk theretofore unknown. A trade which had been limited largely to spices and other luxuries now became available to sugar, tobacco, tea—and in quantities sufficient to broaden the market enormously and to multiply transactions geometrically. At the same time, England, in particular, moved into the focus of trade, indeed, in time, into a position almost analogous to that the Italian cities had occupied in the days of the caravan.

---

91. © 1952. Reprinted with the permission of Jerome Hall.

Late-comer in the exploration, England's road ran over conquest. Her sailors, led by Drake, preyed on the Spanish fleets—while Elizabeth hanged petty thieves at home. Beginning in 1607, advancing rapidly with the emigration consequent on the civil disturbances, the colonial expansion followed, 1640–1664 presenting a peak.

Immediately the colonies served a double purpose. They supplied raw materials. They also furnished a market for the sale of goods manufactured at home; and the home manufacturers were prompt to protect that market. The tremendous change in the organization of industry is the first development of major importance which closely touches the law of the eighteenth century. Trade became increasingly impersonal and free from supervision. In this transformation of the economic organization of England, it will be recalled, four stages are usually distinguished. In the Middle Ages goods were produced by individuals, their families and neighbors, for local consumption. Next came regulation and close supervision by crafts and gilds in villages and small towns. This was still rather largely a primary group organization until the modern period set in. There followed a period of individual and group production, but with an increasing trend toward large-scale marketing. And, finally, with the Industrial Revolution, came large-scale production.

All this was accompanied by changes in the economic organization of society. The growing wool industry aided by the recurrent enclosure movements had swept and continued to sweep away a vast number of tenant farmers. This movement was a symptom of the transition from an agricultural economy toward a dominantly manufacturing system. It permitted the introduction of more modern methods of raising sheep; it supplied labor for expanding industries; it led to the rise of cities.

There was another eighteenth century development of the greatest importance, namely, the rise of credit and banking facilities and the use of modern instruments to facilitate trade. Banking had been of slow growth in England. Up to the end of the sixteenth century, financial affairs had remained largely in the control of foreigners. But the new possibilities of accumulation of large amounts of precious metals had effect. In 1545 it became legal to lend money at interest rates not exceeding ten per cent. Overseas trade and expansion of business made financing essential. The goldsmiths, who had long functioned as depositories for precious metals, began to make loans. Their rates were very high; the risk of defalcation was great. Thus, when Charles II in 1672 repudiated a debt of almost one and a half million pounds to the goldsmiths, they in turn were unable to meet their obligations to the merchants who had deposited these funds.

In 1691 William Paterson made his famous proposal to establish a Bank of England which would loan money at reasonable rates, do a general banking business, and assure security. For political reasons, in reality, but avowedly because the government objected to the legalizing of paper money, Paterson's scheme was rejected. However, it was taken up later and arrangements for loans to the government being made, the Bank was organized in 1694. The growth of provincial banks, however, was a very slow process. Burke stated in 1750, and his opinion is generally accepted, that there were not more than "twelve banker's shops out of London"; and the Clearing House was not established until 1775. From the middle of the century on, however, the careers of many prominent merchants gravitated from business to banking; and by 1793 there were over four hundred county banks in England. In 1759, the Bank of England, which had not issued notes for less than £20, began to issue £10 notes. Paper had, indeed, been used for several centuries by merchants, but ordinary traders were compelled in the eighteenth century to carry considerable amounts of coin with them. Payment by check apparently did not begin until the end of the eighteenth century.

This growth in banking and the use of paper currency and instruments of credit affected the law of theft in several important respects. The effect upon the law of embezzlement was direct and sharply marked. We have met the Act of 1742, the first true embezzlement statute passed by a Whig parliament, anxious to protect the greatest Whig mercantile institution in the country; but this, it will be recalled, applied only to officers and servants of the Bank of England. Just prior to the passage of this Act, one John Waite, a cashier of the Bank, had taken six East India bonds of the value of 13,300 pounds. He could not be convicted under the common law rule incorporated into 2 Geo. II, and was discharged. The second embezzlement statute, enacted in 1751, applied to officers and employees of the South Sea Company; and the third (1763) extended only to employees of the Post Office. This last followed a large number of cases involving the theft of paper money and valuable instruments sent through the mail. These three statutes were enacted between the years 1742 and 1763. In 1799 Bazeley's Case . . . brought on the first general embezzlement statute.

Whig mercantile interests and the importance of the three corporations concerned account for the special acts. In all three statutes the offense was made a felony without benefit of clergy. The appearance of the general act of 1799 followed shortly after the organization of some four hundred banks in the last decade of the century.

The pattern of conditions which gave rise to embezzlement may therefore be delineated as follows: (1) the expansion of mercantile and banking credit and the use of credit mechanisms, paper money, and securities; (2) the employment of clerks in important positions with reference to dealing with and, in particular, receiving valuables from third persons; (3) the interests of the commercial classes and their representation in Parliament; (4) a change in attitude regarding the public importance of what could formerly be dismissed as merely a private breach of trust; and (5) a series of sensational cases of very serious defalcation which set the pattern into motion and produced immediate action.[92]

---

92. [Footnote from original.] "Peculiarly interesting results are obtained by the intensive study of criminal statistics in particular countries. It appears that in

Fast upon the heels of the sixteenth and seventeenth century colonization and as a phase of the changing financial organization, came the joint-stock companies, promoted for the conduct of the new colonial commerce. These companies required enormous investment of capital and led to the formation of a type of limited partnership and to popular investment which grew very rapidly and soon took on huge proportions.

The first true joint-stock company was the Russia Company, formed in 1553 with 240 shareholders who had paid £25 each. The Hudson Bay Company was chartered in 1670. Between these dates the Levant, the East India, the Virginia, and other stock companies were formed. These companies paid enormous dividends. The stock of the East India Company, to pick an extreme case, paid 245 per cent in profits in 1676. But extreme cases fire popular fancy. The South Sea venture is familiar to all; but there had been previous investment "phrensies" in 1694, 1695 and 1698. "London, at this time [1698] abounded with many new projects and schemes promising mountains of gold, the Royal Exchange was crowded with projects, wagers, airy companies of new manufactures and inventions, and stock-jobbers, and the like."

The South Sea Company itself was formed in 1711 with the encouragement of the government. Its stock rose like a meteor from £100 to over £1000. Brokerage offices were opened everywhere. In coffee houses, bars, at milliners and dressmakers, men and women in all walks of life placed their orders for stock—and not only in the South Sea Company, but in dozens of others promoted upon most fantastic projects.[93]

In 1721 came the crash. The panic which ensued recalls the United States in 1930. Public indignation demanded strong repressive measures against the directors of the South Sea Company.[94] Walpole, although he had himself made a neat fortune in this stock, was recalled into office as the one man who could exercise some control in the crisis. Even he could not prevent the passage of drastic legislation to satisfy the public clamor. The Chancellor of the Exchequer was impeached. A bill was carried to compensate the victims out of the private assets of the promoters. The grandfather of Gibbon, the historian, forfeited almost his entire fortune of £60,000; others suffered like treatment.

nations whose modern economic development is recent or as yet incomplete the more involved forms of dishonesty increase rapidly from year to year. We therefore expect to find, and do find, that in Germany and Austria, frauds, embezzlements and forgeries are for the time being on the increase. On the other hand, a nation that is advancing very slowly in economic standing, such as Italy, or scarcely at all, such as Spain, displays no increase in these more refined offenses of modern life, while retaining a conspicuously high average in the unpremeditated and savage crimes, such as homicide, rape, assault and battery." Raymond B. Fosdick, European Police Systems (1915) 12.

93. [Footnote from original.] Companies were organized for the purpose of making salt water fresh, planting mulberry trees and breeding silk-worms in Chelsea Park, importing jackasses from Spain, "as if, remarks a later writer with some severity, there were not already jackasses enough in London alone."

94. [Footnote from original.] Cf. the prosecution of bankers in the United States in the 1930's.

"There is," writes Thorold Rogers, "I believe, no other instance in our history in which a fraud has been punished by an ex post facto law." Prior to this financial panic the Bubble Act of 1719 had been passed, ironically enough at the instigation of directors of the South Sea Company in order to check competition. It prohibited the formation of companies with transferable shares unless chartered by the Crown or Parliament. In 1734 an act was passed "to prevent the infamous Practice of Stock Jobbing." But although speculation stopped for a time, it began again and by 1769 had become common. Still, the more flagrant practices of promoters were checked, and most people turned to safer investments.

So striking and far-reaching was this experience in the promotion of stock that it must necessarily have formed an important factor in the change of social attitudes regarding false representations, which expressed itself later in the criminal law. Yet the connection was not avowed. Repression of fraudulent stock promotion did take specific form, but the thought did not transfer itself to ordinary commercial transactions for some time. Nevertheless, it is impossible to read the vivid accounts of wholesale ruin produced by reliance upon fraudulent representations without placing stock speculation high among the factors that changed attitudes regarding misrepresentations in general. And it will be recalled that the major emphasis in Young's Case was that protection must be afforded "the weaker part of mankind."

There were a number of other less dramatic developments which influenced the law of criminal fraud. They were the disappearance of gild regulation, the concomitant rise of intercommunity transactions; and the development of vast, new types of business enterprise, particularly at the end of the eighteenth century.

* * *

With the growth of large scale production and the marketing of goods on a wide national basis the personal, immediate relationship that existed between manufacturer, merchant and buyer in the manorial system and under the gilds gave way to an impersonal, distant relationship. As a result, buyers of merchandise were without the firsthand protection they had previously enjoyed.

Instead, the rule caveat emptor was invoked, and buyers were required to safeguard their own interests, lest trade be smothered by claims raised after sale. Yet the combination of large-scale marketing and the purchase of goods at a distance in reliance on representations of the seller, produced conditions which in due course could be seen to make safeguards against fraud necessary. Again, the transition from a system of cash on delivery transactions to a credit economy made the sale of goods on time a vital factor. Accordingly it became necessary to safeguard merchants against an extension of credit upon misrepresentations. Finally, the breakdown of primary groups by a succession of enclosure movements concomitant with greatly increased mobility in population and the rise of cities produced new alignments of persons unknown to one another—a condition of affairs which lent itself to fraud quite apart from commercial transactions.

* * *

We may summarize and conclude this discussion by noting that the last twenty years of the eighteenth century produced the most rapid and extensive growth of the entire law of theft. What conditions influenced this accelerated development? To the continuing and cumulative effects of the social and economic conditions described thus far, it is necessary to add that trade was increasing at enormous strides as the Commercial Revolution advanced to its peak. But most important were the effects of the Industrial Revolution. Both of these factors were aspects of the same movement.

* * *

Set against this the principal changes in the law: Pear's Case in 1779 marks the inception of a vastly accelerated growth of the entire law of theft. In 1782 the thief's testimony is admitted against the receiver. 30 Geo. II expands in 1789, with Young's Case, to include false pretenses in a modern sense. That same year comes Pasley v. Freeman, and ten years later the first general embezzlement statute.

Whether regarded as the peak of the Commercial Revolution or regarded partly as the era which also ran well into the Industrial Revolution or as a transition, there is unanimity that with reference to the volume of business done, the nature of commerce, and the prevailing types of social and economic organization, the century, as a whole, stands out clearly against all preceding periods in English history. It would be extraordinary if this had left no mark on the growth of the law on crimes against property without violence.

L. FRIEDMAN, A HISTORY OF AMERICAN LAW
pp. 295–98 (1973).[95]

Between 1847 and 1900, the population swelled; the cities grew enormously; the Far West was settled; the country became a major industrial power; transportation and communication vastly improved; overseas expansion began. New inventions and new techniques made life easier and healthier; at the same time, the social order became immeasurably more complex, and perhaps more difficult for the average man to grasp. New social cleavages developed. The North–South cleavage was bandaged over in the 1860's and 1870's. The black man was put back in his subordinate place. When the blood of the Civil War dried, the Gilded Age began. This was the factory age, the age of money, the age of the robber barons, of capital and labor at war. And the frontier died. The pioneer, the frontier individualist, had been the American culture hero, free, self-reliant, unencumbered by weakness that inhered in the cities. The frontier had been a symbol of an open society; opportunity was as unlimited as the sky. In 1893, Frederick Jackson Turner wrote his famous essay, "The Significance of the

---

95. A History of American Law, copyright © 1973 by Lawrence M. Friedman. Reprinted by permission of Simon & Schuster, Inc.

Frontier in American History." He traced the influence of the frontier on American character and institutions; but when he wrote the essay, Turner also announced that the frontier was irrevocably dead.

What really passed was not the frontier, but the idea of the frontier. This inner sense of change was one of the most important influences on American law. Between 1776 and the Civil War, dominant public opinion exuberantly believed in growth, believed that resources were virtually unlimited; that there would be room and wealth for all. The theme of American law before 1850 was the release of energy, in Willard Hurst's phrase. Develop the land; grow rich; all segments will gain. By 1900, if one can speak about so slippery a thing as dominant public opinion, that opinion saw a narrowing sky, a dead frontier, life as a struggle for position, competition as a zero-sum game, the economy as a pie to be divided, not a ladder stretching out beyond the horizon. By 1900 the theme was: hold the line. Many trends and movements give indirect evidence of the basic cultural change already discussed. One such piece of evidence was the propensity of Americans to form groups. The United States became a "nation of joiners." De Tocqueville had already noted in his travels a magnificent flowering of clubs and societies in America. "Americans," he wrote, "of all ages, all stations in life, and all types of disposition are forever forming associations . . . religious, moral, serious, futile, very general and very limited, immensely large and very minute." But organization in the last half of the 19th century was more than a matter of clubs and societies. Noticeably, many strong interest groups developed—labor unions, industrial combines, farmers' organizations, occupational associations—to jockey for position and power in society. These groups molded, dominated, shaped American law.

A group or association has two aspects: it defines some persons in, and some persons out. People joined together in groups not simply for mutual help, but to exclude, to define an enemy, to make common cause against outsiders. Organization was a law of life, not merely because life was so complicated, but also because life seemed so much a zero-sum game.

The consequences were fundamental. Open-arms immigration laws were replaced by Chinese exclusion laws, demands for literacy tests, and (ultimately, in 1924) the quota system. Resources, in 1800, looked inexhaustible; by 1900, it seemed clear that natural resources could be chopped, burned, and eroded past recovery; a conservation movement was already under way. Government, in 1840, was boosting railroads; in 1880, it was trying to control them, or pretending to try. In general, before the Civil War, leaders of opinion looked at government, and law, as ways to unleash the capacity of the nation. After the war, government's role began slowly to change to that of regulator and trustee. There was bitter opposition, of course, to this new-minted role. Much of the opposition was couched in ideological terms. But the fundamental issues were issues of economic and political strength. The Revolutionary generation had been suspicious of *any* governmental power. The generation of the Gilded Age was still suspicious of imbalance of power. But significant segments of the public saw danger, not merely from one but from various sides: not only from government, but from populists, or trusts, or farmers, or the urban proletariat. American optimism was balanced by a growing pessimism; that the charmed life of America might come to an end, unless people mounted a major battle against creeping decay.

In an important sense, the increasing formation of groups, in American life, merely carried on a major trend of prior generations. Classic English law was a law of and for an elite. In America, more and more people had a stake in the system. This meant that law was necessary, and accessible, to a broad and diverse middle class; that law could serve as a social instrument of great power. Hence the struggle to control the operations of law. Each session of an American legislature was a cockpit of contention between interests. In the Midwest, in the early 1870's, the organized farmers had their day. Their legislation (the Granger laws) merely paid railroads and grain elevators back for what *they* had done to farmers when *they* were at the helm. Or so the farmers thought. Less dramatically, in the 1890's, there was a great rush to pass occupational licensing laws: for plumbers, barbers, horseshoers, lawyers, pharmacists, midwives, and nurses. These laws cemented the power of the group that lobbied for their passage: the organized profession. It is naive to think of them as hostile regulation.

The struggle against industrial combines—the dreaded trusts—was part of the general struggle for a "fair share" of the economy, as the various interest groups viewed it. It was not a struggle to keep free enterprise pure. It would be a mistake to read much economic theory into the passage of the Sherman Anti-Trust Act (1890). Small business, farmers, independent professionals, all feared the *power* of the trusts; antitrust laws were an attempt to use law to cut that power down to size. Regulation, trust-busting, licensing, labor legislation: all these were part of the same general battle of all against all, a battle for security, wealth, prestige, authority, for all the social goods. The power of the state—the law, in short—was both a means and an end in the battle; a way to achieve social goods, and a charter of the dominance of one set of norms and values. Of course, the typical outcome of contention in the legislative chamber was some sort of compromise. No one group was ever absolute. Law was made by hammering out bargains, some explicit, some not.

E. SUTHERLAND, WHITE COLLAR CRIME
pp. 12–13, 229–32 (1949).[96]

The financial cost of white collar crime is probably several times as great as the financial cost of all the crimes which are customarily regarded as "the crime problem." An officer of a chain grocery store in

---

96. Reprinted by permission of the copyright holder, Yale University Press © 1949.

one year embezzled $600,000, which was six times as much as the annual losses from five hundred burglaries and robberies of the stores in that chain. Public enemies number one to six secured $130,000 by burglary and robbery in 1938, while the sum stolen by Ivar Krueger is estimated at $250,000,000, or nearly two thousand times as much. The New York Times in 1931 reported four cases of embezzlement in the United States with a loss of more than a million dollars each and a combined loss of nine million dollars. Although a million-dollar burglar or robber is practically unheard of, the million-dollar embezzler is a small-fry among white collar criminals. The estimated loss to investors in one investment trust from 1929 to 1935 was $580,000,000, due primarily to the fact that 75 percent of the values in the portfolio were in securities of affiliated companies, although this investment house advertised the importance of diversification in investments and its expert services in selecting safe investments. The claim was made in Chicago around 1930 that householders lost $54,000,000 in two years during the tenure of a city sealer who granted immunity from inspection to stores which provided Christmas baskets for his constituents. This financial loss from white collar crime, great as it is, is less important than the damage to social relations. White collar crimes violate trust and therefore create distrust; this lowers social morale and produces social disorganization. Many of the white collar crimes attack the fundamental principles of the American institutions. Ordinary crimes, on the other hand, produce little effect on social institutions or social organization.

* * *

The corporate form of business organization . . . has the advantage of increased rationality. The corporation probably comes closer to the "economic man" and to "pure reason" than any other person or any other organization. The executives and directors not only have explicit and consistent objectives of maximum pecuniary gain but also have research and accounting departments by which precise determination of results is facilitated, and have discussions of policies by directors with diverse abilities and diverse interests, so that the sentiments of one person are canceled by those of another. This general advantage does not deny the disadvantages of corporate organization. Two principal disadvantages have been pointed out in the literature. First, the directors do not necessarily have their attention fixed on the balance sheet of the corporation, but often engage in log-rolling for personal advantages, just as is true in politics. Second, the corporation, like a government, tends to become bureaucratic with all of the limitations of bureaucratic organization.

In the earlier days the corporation aimed at technological efficiency; in the later days it has aimed more than previously at the manipulation of people by advertising, salesmanship, propaganda, and lobbying. With this recent development the corporation has developed a truly Machiavellian ideology and policy. It has reached the conclusion that practically anything is possible if resources, ingenuity, and strenuous efforts are used. It has appropriated the physical and biological sciences and applied them to its objectives of technological efficiency, and in the process has made significant contributions to those sciences. Similarly, it has appropriated the social and psychological sciences and applied them to the objective of manipulating people.

Three aspects of the rationality of the corporation in relation to illegal behavior may be mentioned. First, the corporation selects crimes which involve the smallest danger of detection and identification, and against which victims are least likely to fight. The crimes of corporations are similar in this respect to professional thefts: both are carefully selected and both are similar to taking candy from a baby, in that the victim is a weak antagonist. The advantage of selecting weak victims was stated explicitly by Daniel Drew in the decade of the eighties:

> I began to see that it is poor policy for big men in Wall Street to fight each other. When I am fighting a money-king, even my victories are dangerous. Take the present situation. I had scooped a fine profit out of the Erie deal and it was for the most part in solid cash. But—and here was the trouble—it had all come out of one man—Vanderbilt. Naturally it had left him very sore. And being so powerful, he was able to fight back. As has been seen, he did fight back. He had put me and my party to a lot of inconvenience. That always happens when you take money from a man on your own level. On the other hand, if I had taken these profits from outsiders, it would in the aggregate have amounted to the same sum, but the losers would have been scattered all over the country and so wouldn't have been able to get together and hit back. By making my money from people on the outside, an insider like myself could make just as much in the long run, and not raise up any one enemy powerful enough to cause him discomfort.

The victims of corporate crimes are seldom in a position to fight against the management of the corporation. Consumers are scattered, unorganized, lacking in objective information as to qualities of commodities, and no one consumer suffers a loss in a particular transaction which would justify him in taking individual action. Stockholders seldom know the complex procedures of the corporation which they own, cannot attend annual meetings, and receive little information regarding the policies or the financial status of the corporation. Even if stockholders suspect illegal behavior by the management, they are scattered, unorganized, and frequently cannot even secure access to the names of other stockholders. In their conflicts with labor, the corporations have the advantage of a friendly press and of news commentators whose salaries are paid by business corporations, so that their unfair labor practices can be learned generally only by consulting official reports.

The ordinary case of embezzlement is a crime by a single individual in a subordinate position against a strong corporation. It is, therefore, one of the most foolish of white collar crimes. The weakness of the embezzler, in comparison with the corporation, is illustrated in the case of J.W. Harriman. He was indicted for embezzlement in 1933 and later convicted. No criminal complaint was made against the banks which were accessory to this crime, and which were discovered in the course of the investigation. Their crimes included loans to one corporation in excess of the limit set by law, a pool formed by the officers of the bank to trade in the stock of the bank in violation of law, concealment of the embezzlement by officers of the bank and of the clearing house, and refusal by many of the banks to meet the losses of the Harriman bank which they had agreed to do on condition that the embezzlement be concealed.

A second aspect of corporate rationality in relation to crime is the selection of crimes in which proof is difficult. In this respect, also, white collar crime is similar to professional theft. The selection of crimes on this basis is illustrated by advertising: since a little puffing is regarded as justifiable, the proof of unreasonable puffing is difficult. . . .

KADISH, SOME OBSERVATIONS ON THE USE OF CRIMINAL SANCTIONS IN ENFORCING ECONOMIC REGULATIONS
30 U.Chi.L.Rev. 423 (1963).[97]

The kind of economic regulations whose enforcement through the criminal sanction is the subject of this inquiry may be briefly stated: those which impose restrictions upon the conduct of business as part of a considered economic policy. This includes such laws as price control and rationing laws, antitrust laws and other legislation designed to protect or promote competition or prevent unfair competition, export controls, small loan laws, securities regulations, and, perhaps, some tax laws. Put to one side, therefore, are regulations directly affecting business conduct which are founded on interests other than economic ones; for example, laws regulating the conduct of business in the interest of public safety and general physical welfare. Also to one side are laws indirectly affecting business conduct by their general applicability; for example, embezzlement, varieties of fraud and related white-collar offenses.

The class of regulations so defined possesses several characteristics that have a direct bearing upon the uses and limits of the criminal sanction as a means of achieving compliance. The first is the very feature suggested as the identifying characteristic of such legislation; that is, the nature of the interest protected. Certainly the use of criminal sanctions to protect interests of an economic character is not a contemporary departure. The extension of the classic larceny offense by courts and legislatures to embrace fraud, embezzlement and similar varieties of misappropriation that threatened newly developing ways of

---

[97]. Reprinted by permission of the copyright holder.

transacting business is a well documented chapter in the history of the criminal law. Indeed the process continues today. But there is an important difference between the traditional and expanded property offenses and the newer economic regulatory offenses—a difference reflecting the shift from an economic order that rested on maximum freedom for the private entrepreneur to one committed to restraints upon that freedom. The traditional property offenses protect private property interests against the acquisitive behavior of others in the furtherance of free private decision. The newer offenses, on the other hand, seek to protect the economic order of the community against harmful use by the individual of his property interest. The central purpose, therefore, is to control private choice, rather than to free it. But the control imposed (and this too has significance) is not total, as it would be in a socialistic system. Private economic self-determination has not been abandoned in favor of a wholly state regulated economy. Indeed, the ideal of free enterprise is maintained, the imposed regulations being regarded as necessary to prevent that ideal from consuming itself. Whether the criminal sanction may safely and effectively be used in the service of implementing the large-scale economic policies underlying regulatory legislation of this kind raises fundamental questions.

A second relevant feature of these laws concerns the nature of the conduct restrained. Since it is not criminal under traditional categories of crime and, apart from the regulatory proscription, closely resembles acceptable aggressive business behavior, the stigma of moral reprehensibility does not naturally associate itself with the regulated conduct. Moreover, the conduct is engaged in by persons of relatively high social and economic status; since it is motivated by economic considerations, it is calculated and deliberate rather than reactive; it is usually part of a pattern of business conduct rather than episodic in character; and it often involves group action through the corporate form.

The third noteworthy attribute of this legislation is the role provided for the criminal sanction in the total scheme of enforcement. Typically the criminal penalty is only one of a variety of authorized sanctions which may include monetary settlements, private actions (compensatory or penal), injunctions, inspections, licensing, required reporting or others. Its role, therefore, is largely ancillary and takes either or both of two forms. On the one hand, the criminal penalty may serve as a means to insure the functioning of other sanctions, as, for example, penalties for operating without a license, or without prior registration or reporting. On the other hand, the criminal sanction may serve as a separate and supplementary mode of enforcement by directly prohibiting the conduct sought to be prevented, as in the Sherman Act. Furthermore, implicit in the legislative scheme is the conception of the criminal sanction as a last resort to be used selectively and discriminatingly when other sanctions fail. The array of alternative non-penal sanctions appears unmistakably to carry this message.

That this is assumed by enforcement authorities is apparent from the relative infrequency of the use of the criminal as compared to other sanctions, and in the occasional appearance of published criteria of enforcement policy. And in some legislation, of course, the message of selective enforcement is explicit in the law. Finally, the responsibility for investigation, detection and initiating prosecution is often vested in a specialized agency or other body rather than left with the usual institutions for policing and prosecuting criminal violations. Moreover, these bodies, such as the Office of Price Administration during the war, or the Securities and Exchange Commission, commonly are not specialized organs of criminal enforcement, but are the agencies broadly charged with administering the legislative scheme.

* * *

A common explanation of the failure of the criminal sanction is simply that the powerful business interests affected do not want these laws enforced and employ their power and position in American life to block vigorous enforcement. Influence is exercised over the legislatures to keep enforcement staffs impoverished and sanctions safely inefficacious. Enforcement officials, as prospective counsel for business interests, and judges as former counsel, identify with these interests and resist criminal enforcement. Moreover, news media, under the control of these same groups, work to create hostility to these laws and their vigorous enforcement and sympathy for the violators. In short, "those who are responsible for the system of criminal justice are afraid to antagonize businessmen. . . . The most powerful group in medieval society secured relative immunity from punishment by 'benefit of clergy,' and now our most powerful group secures relative immunity by 'benefit of business.'"

It would be dogmatic to assert that influences of this kind do not exist, but it may be doubted that they play a dispositive role. Business surely constitutes a powerful interest group in American life; but the profusion of regulatory legislation over the ardent protests of important economic interests in the past thirty years is some evidence that it is not all-powerful. Opposing forces have been able to marshal considerable public sentiment against a variety of business practices. Moreover, it is perhaps an oversimplification to identify all business as united in monolithic opposition. There is less a single business interest than a substantial variety of business interests. What then, in addition to business propaganda and influence, has accounted for the failure of the criminal sanction? Or, if we must have a villain, how has it been that business, which has not always gotten its way, has been this successful in devitalizing the use of that sanction?

It is a plausible surmise that the explanation is implicated in another feature of the behavior regulated by these laws; namely, that it is not generally regarded as morally reprehensible in the common view, that, indeed, in some measure it is the laws themselves that appear bad, or at least painful necessities, and that the violators by and large turn out to be respectable people in the respectable pursuit of profit. It is not likely that these popular attitudes are wholly products of a public-relations campaign by the affected business community. The springs of the public sentiment reach into the national ethos, producing the values that the man of business himself holds, as well as the attitude of the public toward him and his activities. Typically the conduct prohibited by economic regulatory laws is not immediately distinguishable from modes of business behavior that are not only socially acceptable, but affirmatively desirable in an economy founded upon an ideology (not denied by the regulatory regime itself) of free enterprise and the profit motive. Distinctions there are, of course, between salutary entrepreneurial practices and those which threaten the values of the very regime of economic freedom. And it is possible to reason convincingly that the harms done to the economic order by violations of many of these regulatory laws are of a magnitude that dwarf in significance the lower-class property offenses. But the point is that these perceptions require distinguishing and reasoning processes that are not the normal governors of the passion of moral disapproval, and are not dramatically obvious to a public long conditioned to responding approvingly to the production of profit through business shrewdness, especially in the absence of live and visible victims. Moreover, in some areas, notably the antitrust laws, it is far from clear that there is consensus even by the authors and enforcers of the regulation—the legislators, courts and administrators—on precisely what should be prohibited and what permitted, and the reasons therefor. And as Professor Freund observed, "if a law declares a practice to be criminal, and cannot apply its policy with consistency, its moral effect is necessarily weakened."

The consequences of the absence of sustained public moral resentment for the effective use of the criminal sanction may be briefly stated. The central distinguishing aspect of the criminal sanction appears to be the stigmatization of the morally culpable. At least it tends so to be regarded in the community. Without moral culpability there is in a democratic community an explicable and justifiable reluctance to affix the stigma of blame. This perhaps is the basic explanation, rather than the selfish machinations of business interests, for the reluctance of administrators and prosecutors to invoke the criminal sanction, the reluctance of jurors to find guilt and the reluctance of judges to impose strong penalties. And beyond its effect on enforcement, the absence of moral opprobrium interferes in another more subtle way with achieving compliance. Fear of being caught and punished does not exhaust the deterrent mechanism of the criminal law. It is supplemented by the personal disinclination to act in violation of the law's commands, apart from immediate fear of being punished. One would suppose that especially in the case of those who normally regard themselves as respectable, proper and law-abiding the appeal to act in accordance with conscience is relatively great. But where the violation is not generally regarded as ethically reprehensible, either by the community at large or by the class of businessmen itself, the private appeal to conscience is at its minimum and being convicted and fined may have little more impact than a bad selling season.

C. FEDERAL STATUTES OF GENERAL APPLICATION

SCOPE NOTE

Business crimes are not always prosecuted under specific economic regulatory legislation, as has already been seen from some of the cases in Section B. The materials in this Section are designed to acquaint the student with some of the most important federal criminal statutes of general application, which federal prosecutors have often used in business crime settings.

The materials begin with an exploration of the Racketeer Influenced and Corrupt Organizations Act, commonly known as "RICO." The lead case is the Supreme Court's decision in *United States v. Turkette*, included in the materials to indicate the overall principles of construction of the Act which the Supreme Court has adopted. The Notes are not intended to provide a complete survey of all the problems encountered under RICO, but have been chosen for their specific importance to business crime prosecutions.

Part 2 of this Section focuses on two groups of statutes relating to fraud, the mail and wire fraud statutes and the antifraud provisions of the Securities Acts. The materials on mail and wire fraud focus on the development of the "intangible rights" doctrine, beginning with the Supreme Court's decision in *United States v. McNally*. The Notes following *McNally* explore the wisdom of the intangible rights doctrine in a number of settings. The materials then move to a discussion of securities fraud, and, particularly, the question of insider trading. The lead case here is *Chiarella v. United States;* also included are materials describing the surge in insider trading prosecutions which began with the prosecution of Chiarella in 1978.

Certain problems run through this Section. 1) Do broad interpretations of these statutes reach too far into "normal" business operations (or, indeed, interfere with permissible economic behavior)? 2) To what extent should prosecutors use these statutes as "add-ons" to other, more specific, charges? 3) Do these statutes apply to corporations as well as individuals? (The general principle of corporate criminal liability will be explored more fully in Chapter 2.) 4) How should we account for the existence of private remedies under these statutes?

1. RACKETEER INFLUENCED AND CORRUPT ORGANIZATIONS ACT ("RICO")

UNITED STATES v. TURKETTE

Supreme Court of the United States, 1981.
452 U.S. 576, 101 S.Ct. 2524, 69 L.Ed.2d 246.

JUSTICE WHITE delivered the opinion of the Court.

Chapter 96 of Title 18 of the United States Code, 18 U.S.C. §§ 1961–1968, entitled Racketeer Influenced and Corrupt Organizations (RICO), was added to Title 18 by Title IX of the Organized Crime Control Act of 1970, Pub.L. 91–452, 84 Stat. 941. The question in this case is whether the term "enterprise" as used in RICO encompasses both legitimate and illegitimate enterprises or is limited in application to the former. The Court of Appeals for the First Circuit held that Congress did not intend to include within the definition of "enterprise" those organizations which are exclusively criminal. This position is contrary to that adopted by every other circuit that has addressed the issue. We granted certiorari to resolve this conflict.

I

Count Nine of a nine-count indictment charged respondent and 12 others with conspiracy to conduct and participate in the affairs of an enterprise [98] engaged in interstate commerce through a pattern of racketeering activities, in violation of 18 U.S.C. § 1962(d).[99] The indictment described the enterprise as "a group of individuals associated in fact for the purpose of illegally trafficking in narcotics and other dangerous drugs, committing arsons, utilizing the United States mails to defraud insurance companies, bribing and attempting to bribe local police officers, and corruptly influencing and attempting to corruptly influence the outcome of state court proceedings. . . ." The other eight counts of the indictment charged the commission of various substantive criminal acts by those engaged in and associated with the criminal enterprise, including possession with intent to distribute and distribution of controlled substances, and several counts of insurance fraud by arson and other means. The common thread to all counts was respondent's alleged leadership of this criminal organization through which he orchestrated and participated in the commission of the

---

98. [Court's footnote 2.] Title 18 U.S.C. § 1961(4) provides:

"'enterprise' includes any individual, partnership, corporation, association, or other legal entity, and any union or group of individuals associated in fact although not a legal entity."

99. [Court's footnote 3.] Title 18 U.S.C. § 1962(d) provides that "[i]t shall be unlawful for any person to conspire to violate any of the provisions of subsections (a), (b), or (c) of this section." Pertinent to these charges, subsection (c) provides:

"It shall be unlawful for any person employed by or associated with any enterprise engaged in, or the activities of which affect, interstate or foreign commerce, to conduct or participate, directly or indirectly, in the conduct of such enterprise's affairs through a pattern of racketeering activity or collection of unlawful debt."

various crimes delineated in the RICO count or charged in the eight preceding counts.

After a 6-week jury trial, in which the evidence focused upon both the professional nature of this organization and the execution of a number of distinct criminal acts, respondent was convicted on all nine counts. He was sentenced to a term of 20 years on the substantive counts, as well as a 2-year special parole term on the drug count. On the RICO conspiracy count he was sentenced to a 20-year concurrent term and fined $20,000.

On appeal, respondent argued that RICO was intended solely to protect legitimate business enterprises from infiltration by racketeers and that RICO does not make criminal the participation in an association which performs only illegal acts and which has not infiltrated or attempted to infiltrate a legitimate enterprise. The Court of Appeals agreed. We reverse.

II

In determining the scope of a statute, we look first to its language. If the statutory language is unambiguous, in the absence of "a clearly expressed legislative intent to the contrary, that language must ordinarily be regarded as conclusive." * * *

Section 1962(c) makes it unlawful "for any person employed by or associated with any enterprise engaged in, or the activities of which affect, interstate or foreign commerce, to conduct or participate, directly or indirectly, in the conduct of such enterprise's affairs through a pattern of racketeering activity or collection of unlawful debt." The term "enterprise" is defined as including "any individual, partnership, corporation, association, or other legal entity, and any union or group of individuals associated in fact although not a legal entity." Id., § 1961(4). There is no restriction upon the associations embraced by the definition: an enterprise includes any union or group of individuals associated in fact. On its face, the definition appears to include both legitimate and illegitimate enterprises within its scope; it no more excludes criminal enterprises than it does legitimate ones. Had Congress not intended to reach criminal associations, it could easily have narrowed the sweep of the definition by inserting a single word, "legitimate." But it did nothing to indicate that an enterprise consisting of a group of individuals was not covered by RICO if the purpose of the enterprise was exclusively criminal.

The Court of Appeals, however, clearly departed from and limited the statutory language. It gave several reasons for doing so, none of which is adequate. First, it relied in part on the rule of ejusdem generis, an aid to statutory construction problems suggesting that where general words follow a specific enumeration of persons or things, the general words should be limited to persons or things similar to those specifically enumerated. * * *

Section 1961(4) describes two categories of associations that come within the purview of the "enterprise" definition. The first encompasses organizations such as corporations and partnerships, and other "legal entities." The second covers "any union or group of individuals associated in fact although not a legal entity." The Court of Appeals assumed that the second category was merely a more general description of the first. * * * But that assumption is untenable. Each category describes a separate type of enterprise to be covered by the statute—those that are recognized as legal entities and those that are not. The latter is not a more general description of the former. The second category itself not containing any specific enumeration that is followed by a general description, ejusdem generis has no bearing on the meaning to be attributed to that part of § 1961(4).

A second reason offered by the Court of Appeals in support of its judgment was that giving the definition of "enterprise" its ordinary meaning would create several internal inconsistencies in the Act. With respect to § 1962(c), it was said that:

> "If 'a pattern of racketeering' can itself be an 'enterprise' for purposes of section 1962(c), then the two phrases 'employed by or associated with any enterprise' and 'the conduct of such enterprise's affairs through [a pattern of racketeering activity]' add nothing to the meaning of the section. The words are coherent and logical only if they are read as applying to legitimate enterprises."

This conclusion is based on a faulty premise. That a wholly criminal enterprise comes within the ambit of the statute does not mean that a "pattern of racketeering activity" is an "enterprise." In order to secure a conviction under RICO, the Government must prove both the existence of an "enterprise" and the connected "pattern of racketeering activity." The enterprise is an entity, for present purposes a group of persons associated together for a common purpose of engaging in a course of conduct. The pattern of racketeering activity is, on the other hand, a series of criminal acts as defined by the statute. 18 U.S.C. § 1961(1). The former is proved by evidence of an ongoing organization, formal or informal, and by evidence that the various associates function as a continuing unit. The latter is proved by evidence of the requisite number of acts of racketeering committed by the participants in the enterprise. While the proof used to establish these separate elements may in particular cases coalesce, proof of one does not necessarily establish the other. The "enterprise" is not the "pattern of racketeering activity"; it is an entity separate and apart from the pattern of activity in which it engages. The existence of an enterprise at all times remains a separate element which must be proved by the Government.[1]

---

1. [Court's footnote 5.] The Government takes the position that proof of a pattern of racketeering activity in itself would not be sufficient to establish the existence of an enterprise: "We do not suggest that any two sporadic and isolated offenses by the same actor or actors ipso facto constitute an "illegitimate" enterprise; rather, the existence of the enterprise as an independent entity must also be shown." Petitioner's Reply Brief, at 4. * * *

Apart from § 1962(c)'s proscription against participating in an enterprise through a pattern of racketeering activities, RICO also proscribes the investment of income derived from racketeering activity in an enterprise engaged in or which affects interstate commerce as well as the acquisition of an interest in or control or any such enterprise through a pattern of racketeering activity. 18 U.S.C. § 1962(a) and (b). The Court of Appeals concluded that these provisions of RICO should be interpreted so as to apply only to legitimate enterprises. If these two sections are so limited, the Court of Appeals held that the proscription in § 1962(c), at issue here, must be similarly limited. Again, we do not accept the premise from which the Court of Appeals derived its conclusion. It is obvious that § 1962(a) and (b) address the infiltration by organized crime of legitimate businesses, but we cannot agree that these sections were not also aimed at preventing racketeers from investing or reinvesting in wholly illegal enterprises and from acquiring through a pattern of racketeering activity wholly illegitimate enterprises such as an illegal gambling business or a loan-sharking operation. There is no inconsistency or anomoly in recognizing that § 1962 applies to both legitimate and illegitimate enterprise. Certainly the language of the statute does not warrant the Court of Appeals' conclusion to the contrary.

Similarly, the Court of Appeals noted that various civil remedies were provided by § 1964, including divestiture, dissolution, reorganization, restrictions on future activities by violators of RICO and treble damages. These remedies it thought would have utility only with respect to legitimate enterprises. As a general proposition, however, the civil remedies could be useful in eradicating organized crime from the social fabric, whether the enterprise be ostensibly legitimate or admittedly criminal. The aim is to divest the association of the fruits of its ill-gotten gains. Even if one or more of the civil remedies might be inapplicable to a particular illegitimate enterprise, this fact would not serve to limit the enterprise concept. Congress has provided civil remedies for use when the circumstances so warrant. It is untenable to argue that their existence limits the scope of the criminal provisions.

Finally, it is urged that the interpretation of RICO to include both legitimate and illegitimate enterprises will substantially alter the balance between federal and state enforcement of criminal law. This is particularly true, so the argument goes, since included within the definition of racketeering activity are a significant number of acts made criminal under state law. 18 U.S.C. § 1961(1). But even assuming that the more inclusive definition of enterprise will have the effect suggested, the language of the statute and its legislative history indicate that Congress was well aware that it was entering a new domain of federal involvement through the enactment of this measure. Indeed, the very purpose of the Organized Crime Control Act of 1970 was to enable the Federal Government to address a large and seemingly neglected problem. * * *

Contrary to the judgment below, neither the language nor structure of RICO limits its application to legitimate "enterprises." Applying it also to criminal organizations does not render any portion of the statute superfluous nor does it create any structural incongruities within the framework of the Act. The result is neither absurd nor surprising. On the contrary, insulating the wholly criminal enterprise from prosecution under RICO is the more incongruous position.

Section 904(a) of RICO, 84 Stat. 947, directs that "the provisions of this Title shall be liberally construed to effectuate its remedial purposes." With or without this admonition, we could not agree with the Court of Appeals that illegitimate enterprises should be excluded from coverage. We are also quite sure that nothing in the legislative history of RICO requires a contrary conclusion.[2]

III

The statement of findings that prefaces the Organized Crime Control Act of 1970 reveals the pervasiveness of the problem that Congress was addressing by this enactment:

> "The Congress finds that (1) organized crime in the United States is a highly sophisticated, diversified, and widespread activity that annually drains billions of dollars from America's economy by unlawful conduct and the illegal use of force, fraud, and corruption; (2) organized crime derives a major portion of its power through money obtained from such illegal endeavors as syndicated gambling, loan sharking, the theft and fencing of property, the importation and distribution of narcotics and other dangerous drugs, and other forms of social exploitation; (3) this money and power are increasingly used to infiltrate and corrupt legitimate business and labor unions and to subvert and corrupt our democratic processes; (4) organized crime activities in the United States weaken the stability of the Nation's economic system, harm innocent investors and competing organizations, interfere with free competition, seriously burden interstate and foreign commerce, threaten the domestic security, and undermine the general welfare of the Nation and its citizens; and (5) organized crime continues to grow because of defects in the evidence-gathering process of the law inhibiting the development of the legally admissible evidence necessary to bring criminal and other sanctions or remedies to bear on the unlawful activities of those engaged in organized crime and because the sanctions and remedies available to the Government are unnecessarily limited in scope and impact." 84 Stat., at 922–923.

In light of the above findings, it was the declared purpose of Congress, "to seek the eradication of organized crime in the United States by strengthening the legal tools in the evidence-gathering process, by establishing new penal prohibitions, and by providing enhanced

---

2. [Court's footnote 10.] We find no occasion to apply the rule of lenity to this statute. "[T]hat 'rule,' as is true of any guide to statutory construction, only serves as an aid for resolving an ambiguity; * * *"

sanctions and new remedies to deal with the unlawful activities of those engaged in organized crime." Id., at 923. The various titles of the Act provide the tools through which this goal is to be accomplished. Only three of those titles create substantive offenses, Title VIII, which is directed at illegal gambling operations, Title IX, at issue here, and Title XI, which addresses the importation, distribution and storage of explosive materials. The other titles provide various procedural and remedial devices to aid in the prosecution and incarceration of persons involved in organized crime.

Considering this statement of the Act's broad purposes, the construction of RICO suggested by respondent and the court below is unacceptable. Whole areas of organized criminal activity would be placed beyond the substantive reach of the enactment. For example, associations of persons engaged solely in "loan sharking, the theft and fencing of property, the importation and distribution of narcotics and other dangerous drugs," would be immune from prosecution under RICO so long as the association did not deviate from the criminal path. Yet these are among the very crimes that Congress specifically found to be typical of the crimes committed by persons involved in organized crime, see 18 U.S.C. § 1961(1), and as a major source of revenue and power for such organizations. Along these same lines, Senator McClellan, the principal sponsor of the bill, gave two examples of types of problems RICO was designed to address. Neither is consistent with the view that substantive offenses under RICO would be limited to legitimate enterprises: "Organized criminals, too have flooded the market with cheap reproductions of hit records and affixed counterfeit popular labels. They are heavily engaged in the illicit prescription drug industry." 116 Cong.Rec. 592 (1970). In view of the purposes and goals of the Act, as well as the language of the statute, we are unpersuaded that Congress nevertheless confined the reach of the law to only narrow aspects of organized crime, and, in particular, under RICO, *only* the infiltration of legitimate business.

This is not to gainsay that the legislative history forcefully supports the view that the major purpose of Title IX is to address the infiltration of legitimate business by organized crime. The point is made time and again during the debates and in the hearings before the House and Senate. But none of these statements requires the negative inference that Title IX did not reach the activities of enterprises organized and existing for criminal purposes.

On the contrary, these statements are in full accord with the proposition that RICO is equally applicable to a criminal enterprise that has no legitimate dimension or has yet to acquire one. Accepting that the primary purpose of RICO is to cope with the infiltration of legitimate businesses, applying the statute in accordance with its terms, so as to reach criminal enterprises, would seek to deal with the problem at its very source. Supporters of the bill recognized that organized crime uses its primary sources of revenue and power—illegal gambling, loan-sharking and illicit drug distribution—as a springboard into the sphere of legitimate enterprise. * * *

As a measure to deal with the infiltration of legitimate businesses by organized crime, RICO was both preventive and remedial. Respondent's view would ignore the preventive function of the statute. If Congress had intended the more circumscribed approach espoused by the Court of Appeals, there would have been some positive sign that the law was not to reach organized criminal activities that give rise to the concerns about infiltration. The language of the statute, however,—the most reliable evidence of its intent—reveals that Congress opted for a far broader definition of the word "enterprise," and we are unconvinced by anything in the legislative history that this definition should be given less than its full effect.

The judgment of the Court of Appeals is accordingly *Reversed*.

[JUSTICE STEWART dissented.]

NOTES AND QUERIES

(1) *Discovering RICO.* RICO was virtually forgotten immediately after its passage in 1970.[3] It was not until the mid-1970s that federal prosecutors began invoking the statute. Since that time, however, the statute has grown enormously in popularity. In addition to using RICO to prosecute "gangs of crooks," as in *Turkette*, the government has made active use of RICO to prosecute governmental corruption.[4] These cases are often far from "organized crime." Is there anything wrong, however, with applying the statute outside of the area of original concern? Is it stretching the statute, for example, to find that the "Office of the Governor" is a RICO "enterprise"?[5]

(2) *RICO Paradigm.* However broad the language of RICO may sweep, it is clear that Congress was most concerned with the infiltration of legitimate businesses by "organized crime," and RICO has in fact been used to prosecute such behavior. The paradigmatic case

---

3. The legislative history and early development is described in Bradley, Racketeers, Congress and the Courts: An Analysis of RICO, 65 Iowa Law Review 837 (1980). For a comprehensive overview of later developments, see Lynch, RICO: The Crime of Being A Criminal, 87 Colum.L. Rev. 661, 920 (1987).

4. See, e.g., United States v. Davis, 707 F.2d 880 (6th Cir.1983) (two members of an Ohio County Sheriff's Office charged with soliciting and accepting bribes in exchange for certain favors such as overlooking violations of state motor vehicle regulations); United States v. Brennan, 798 F.2d 581 (2d Cir.1986) (judge convicted of soliciting and accepting bribes to fix cases; Queens County Court held to be a RICO "enterprise"); United States v. Grzywaiz, 603 F.2d 682 (7th Cir.1979) (three members of the Madison, Illinois, police department prosecuted for accepting bribes in exchange for protection of illegal activity such as prostitution and operating after closing hours); United States v. Forsythe, 560 F.2d 1127 (3d Cir.1977) (magistrates, constables, and minor court officials in Allegheny County prosecuted for receiving bribes from a bail bond agency in return for referral of defendants to the agency).

5. Held: within the statute—United States v. Thompson, 685 F.2d 993 (6th Cir.) (en banc), reversing 669 F.2d 1143 (6th Cir.), certiorari denied 459 U.S. 1072, 103 S.Ct. 494, 74 L.Ed.2d 635 (1982). See also United States v. Angelilli, 660 F.2d 23 (2d Cir.1981) (holding that city's civil court is an "enterprise" for purposes of RICO), certiorari denied 455 U.S. 945, 102 S.Ct. 1442, 71 L.Ed.2d 657 (1982).

involved activities surrounding the operation and bankruptcy of The Westchester Premiere Theatre, located in the suburbs of New York City. Although this case gave rise to a number of prosecutions, the opinion in *United States v. DePalma*, 461 F.Supp. 778 (S.D.N.Y.1978), indicates how a number of the major issues were decided:

> Sweet, District Judge.
>
> The Indictment in this action was filed on June 2, 1978 and alleges a pattern of racketeering activity by the defendants centering on the corporate enterprise known as the Westchester Premier Theatre ("the Theatre") (Count One), a securities fraud (Counts Two through Twelve), a bankruptcy fraud (Counts Thirteen through Twenty-three) and an obstruction of justice (Count Twenty-four). The events giving rise to the charges occurred over a period from 1971 through 1978. The Indictment resulted from extensive electronic interceptions, data obtained from informants, and the admissions of certain of the defendants. There are ten defendants named. Not surprisingly defendants have filed extensive pretrial motions challenging the adequacy of the various counts of the Indictment, the propriety of joinder of the counts in the Indictment, seeking severance, dismissal of certain counts as a consequence of prosecutorial misconduct, striking certain material from the Indictment, requesting a bill of particulars, production of documents for inspection, and seeking a continuance. * * *
>
> * * *
>
> I. COUNT ONE CHARGES AN OFFENSE.
>
> Count One charges defendants Weisman, DePalma and Fusco with violating 18 U.S.C. § 1962(c) ("RICO"), in that they are alleged to have participated in a pattern of racketeering activity in the conduct of the affairs of the Theatre through the commission of acts of securities fraud and bankruptcy fraud. . . .
>
> Title IX, entitled Racketeer Influenced and Corrupt Organizations, proscribes, inter alia, "the operation of any enterprise engaged in interstate commerce through a 'pattern' of 'racketeering activity.'" H.R.Rep. No. 1549, 91st Cong., 2nd Sess. reprinted in 2 U.S.Code Cong. & Ad.News, pp. 4007, 4010 (1970). Section 1961(1) of Title IX defines racketeering activity to include bankruptcy and securities fraud. A review of the legislative history relating to this statute evinces the concern of Congress in eliminating the influence of organized crime activities in our society. The Senate Report on the Organized Crime Control Act states as follows:
>
>> Obviously, the time has come for a frontal attack on the subversion of our economic system by organized criminal activities. That attack must begin, however, with the frank recognition that our present laws are inadequate to remove criminal influences from legitimate endeavor organizations.
>
> * * * * * * * *

Title IX recognizes that present efforts to dislodge the forces of organized crime from legitimate fields of endeavor have proven unsuccessful. To remedy this failure, the proposed statute adopts the most direct route open to accomplish the desired objective. Where an organization is acquired or run by defined racketeering methods, then the persons involved can be legally separated from the organization, either by the criminal law approach of fine, imprisonment and forfeiture, or through a civil law approach of equitable relief broad enough to do all that is necessary to free the channels of commerce from all illicit activity.

S.Rep. No. 617, 91st Cong., 1st Sess. 78–79 (1969). This attitude was consistently endorsed in both the House and the Senate during hearings on this bill. It is in this context that the defendants' motions must be viewed.

A. *The Indictment Properly Alleges a Pattern of Racketeering.*

Defendant Weisman asserts that in order to establish a violation of 18 U.S.C. § 1962(c) the two acts of racketeering activity necessary to establish a "pattern" must be related. Claiming that the activities with respect to the alleged securities fraud are not related to the activities of the alleged bankruptcy fraud, Weisman seeks dismissal of Count One. The motion is denied.

The statutory definition of pattern of racketeering activity is unambiguous and contains no reference to any requirement of "relatedness." A review of the legislative history establishes that Congress was concerned with proscribing illegal activities of legitimate business, and that the only relation it deemed necessary for the two predicate acts is that they both be in the conduct of the affairs of the same enterprise. 18 U.S.C. § 1962(c) (1970).[6]

Two significant amendments to the definition of pattern of racketeering, prior to the enactment of the statute, lend further support to this view. Prior to these amendments the definition was as follows: "The term pattern of racketeering activity includes at least one act occurring after the effective date of this chapter." S.Rep. No. 617, supra at 122. Since "the term 'pattern' indicates that what is intended to be proscribed is not a single isolated act of 'racketeering activity,' but at least two such acts" (id) the statute was amended to read as follows: "The term 'pattern of racketeering activity' means at least two acts, one of which occurred after the effective date of this chapter." Id. There was no requirement that the two acts be related to each other. In fact, at that point there was no requirement that the two acts even be related in time. This was the cause of some concern to those who commented on the

---

6. [Court's footnote 4.] "A 'pattern of racketeering activity' means simply two or more acts of racketeering activity, one of which . . . must have occurred subsequent to the enactment of the title." 116 Cong.Rec. H35, 295 (daily ed. Oct. 7, 1970) (remarks of Rep.Poff).

proposed bill. Such concerns led to the enactment of the ten year limitation in the statute. It was this ten year limitation that provided any requirement of nexus between the two predicate acts. In its final form the statute simply required that the person commit at least two acts of racketeering activity within a ten year period.

Considering the time and effort spent by Congress on this definition, had it wanted to provide for any "relatedness", it had ample opportunity to do so. Instead Congress must have realized that the definition of "pattern of racketeering activity" would necessarily be interpreted in the context of the statute to which it applies (18 U.S.C. § 1962). Thus, the term "pattern", when used in this context, applies to the relationship of the acts to the enterprise, and no more. The definition of "racketeering activity" in the section and the additional definition of "pattern of racketeering activity", taken together, results in the conclusion that the "pattern" definition states a minimum but not necessarily an exclusive definition. A main focus of Title IX was the enterprise,[7] not only the persons committing the acts, and Congress felt that the "pattern" would be supplied by this common factor.

* * *

The Indictment here satisfies the definition of "pattern of racketeering activity"; both frauds are alleged to have been committed in the conduct of the Theatre's affairs and related to the essential functions that the Theatre served in the regular conduct of its affairs.

In fact, the alleged frauds are of exactly the type with which Congress was concerned when it enacted the Organized Crime Control Act. As noted by Senator Thurmond during hearings on the bill,

> One of the favorite devices of organized crime is to infiltrate a company, build it up, and then let it go broke so that it can take advantage of certain tax provisions and other devices thus disposing of or protecting a large treasury of illegally obtained dollars. This provision will help in curbing this activity.

---

7. [Court's footnote 5.] It was noted during the Congressional hearings that

"While prosecutions and convictions of leaders of organized crime and their confederates are increasing each year as the Federal Government's organized crime program gains momentum, it is becoming increasingly apparent that such convictions alone, which simply remove the leaders from control of syndicate-owned enterprises but do not attack the vested property interests whose control passes on to other Cosa Nostra leaders, are not adequate to demolish the structure of the surviving organizations which they run. The legislative proposals contained in title IX of this act, entitled 'Racketeer influenced and corrupt organizations,' constitute a carefully structured program which can drastically curtail—and eventually eradicate—the vast expansion of organized crime's economic power which operates outside the rules of fair competition of the American marketplace."

116 Cong.Rec. S607 (daily ed. Jan. 21, 1970) remarks of Sen. Byrd.

116 Cong.Rec. S607 (daily ed. Jan. 23, 1970). Congress recognized that "[i]n business, the mob bleeds a firm of assets, then takes bankruptcy" (176 Cong.Rec. S591 (daily ed. Jan. 21, 1970) (remarks of Sen. McClellan)) and sought to protect the public from such occurrences. It is this type of situation which is alleged in this case.

Furthermore, even if the term "pattern" requires that the predicate acts themselves be interrelated, such exists between the alleged frauds:

(i) Defendants Weisman, Fusco and DePalma allegedly were each involved in both frauds.

(ii) The frauds allegedly were with respect to the same entity.

(iii) The stock fraud allegedly defrauded investors in the sale of the securities. The bankruptcy fraud allegedly defrauded these same investors, who would have been entitled to any remaining assets in the event the Chapter XI reorganization was successful.

(iv) The frauds allegedly had the same common goal of enriching those in control of and related to the Theatre through the use of illegal acts.

(v) Both frauds allegedly were committed well within the statutory requirement of ten years.

(vi) The alleged skimming activities bridge the gap between the securities fraud and the bankruptcy fraud, implying that both were anticipated by those in control of and related to this enterprise. Although the alleged skimming activities here cannot be considered, in themselves, as predicate acts necessary to prove a RICO violation, they still may be considered to prove a nexus between the two frauds. The Indictment sufficiently alleges a pattern of racketeering activity.

B. *The Alleged Predicate Offenses are Sufficient.*

Defendant Weisman next asserts that the alleged securities fraud and bankruptcy fraud are insufficient predicate offenses under RICO. With respect to the securities fraud Weisman claims that, although 18 U.S.C. § 1961(1) specifically includes fraud in the sale of securities as a predicate offense, the sale of the securities in this instance, the alleged securities fraud, was not in the conduct of the affairs of the enterprise (18 U.S.C. § 1962(c)), having been committed prior to the formation of the Theatre and therefore not in the conduct of its affairs.

The Indictment alleges that Weisman was involved in the formation of the corporate entity known as the Westchester Premier Theatre and was employed by and associated with such from or about January 1, 1971. The sale of the securities, in 1973, was "in order to create the Theatre as a going concern", but not to establish the enterprise; such already existed and pursuant to the securities laws of the United States had to be in existence prior to the offering for sale of any securities of the enterprise. The Indictment relates to the corporate entity, and not merely to the building which housed the Theatre. To conclude otherwise would be to deny reality.

Weisman's claim that the alleged bankruptcy fraud was not part of the day to day activities of the enterprise, and therefore not in the conduct of the enterprise's affairs, is also unrealistically technical. The statute in question specifically provides that an offense involving bankruptcy fraud is a predicate offense (18 U.S.C. § 1961(1)(D) (1970)) and the legislative history of the statute evidences Congress' concern with fraudulent bankruptcies. There is nothing in the statute requiring that the racketeering activity be part of the day to day business operation of an enterprise. The statute merely refers to the enterprise's affairs—bankruptcy is such. The affairs of an entity in Chapter XI, as was the enterprise in question here, are in fact controlled by the bankruptcy proceedings. An assertion that these proceedings are not in the conduct of the affairs of the enterprise is frivolous.

C. *The RICO Count and the Other Counts are Not Multiplicious.*

Defendants Fusco and DePalma assert that the alleged securities fraud and bankruptcy fraud counts are included in the RICO count and that therefore the Indictment is multiplicious.[8]

Offenses "are the 'same' only when 'the evidence required to support a conviction upon one of them would have been sufficient to warrant a conviction upon the other.'" Defendant DePalma asserts that proof of the conspiracy charges in Counts Two and Thirteen would establish the RICO count without further proof. As discussed, supra, the RICO count requires proof of additional facts—that a pattern of (two or more) racketeering activity existed and that the defendants' alleged racketeering activity was in the conduct of an enterprise's affairs.

Furthermore, there is nothing in the RICO statute or legislative history to indicate that Congress intended to substitute the RICO charge and penalties for those of the criminal acts constituting the pattern of racketeering activity. A single criminal conspiracy or a single criminal act can constitute two or more separate offenses, and Congress may choose to punish each offense without offending the double jeopardy clause. It appears that Congress intended a similar result when it enacted the Organized Crime Control Act. The Statement of Findings and Purpose to the law states as follows:

---

8. [Court's footnote 10.] Count I alleges the RICO violation, which includes the alleged securities fraud and the bankruptcy fraud as predicate offenses. Count II alleges a securities fraud conspiracy. Counts III to XII allege substantive securities

It is the purpose of this Act to seek the eradication of organized crime in the United States by *strengthening* the legal tools in the evidence-gathering process, by establishing *new* penal prohibitions, and by providing *enhanced* sanctions and *new* remedies to deal with the unlawful activities of those engaged in organized crime. (Emphasis added.)

Pub.Law 91–452, 84 Stat. 922 (1970).

Further proof of this intent is evident from the language of the statute itself. Section 1961(5) requires that the two predicate acts must occur within ten years, *excluding any period the perpetrator was in confinement.* See H.R.Rep. No. 1549, 91st Cong., 2nd Sess. 56 (1970). This indicates that even though the perpetrator had been convicted of, and served time for, the first predicate act, he could be prosecuted for that act under Title IX. The Indictment is not multiplicious.

* * *

(3) *Corporations as RICO Defendants.* Using RICO against individual (but "organized") criminals might have been at the core of Congressional concern, but can RICO also be used against corporate defendants? Consider *United States v. Hartley,* 678 F.2d 961 (11th Cir.1982), certiorari denied 459 U.S. 1170, 103 S.Ct. 815, 74 L.Ed.2d 1014 (1983):

* * *

Treasure Isle, Inc., is a Florida corporation specializing in the production of breaded seafood products. Its production of frozen breaded shrimp for consumption by the military provided the basis of the thirty-three count indictment. G. Cecil Hartley serves as one of Treasure Isle's vice presidents; Travis Dell occupies the position of plant manager. Count one charged the defendants with conspiring to defraud the United States Government by supplying breaded shrimp that did not conform to designated military specifications. The shrimp contained too much breading, were of inadequate size, and had not been properly cleaned. Counts two through fifteen concerned mail fraud violations regarding invoices sent to the government seeking payment for the nonconforming shrimp. Counts sixteen through eighteen charged mail fraud violations for invoices directly related to sample production lots under investigation. Counts nineteen through thirty-two charged defendants with the interstate transportation of money obtained by fraud which consisted of United States Treasury checks corresponding to the invoices involved in counts two through eighteen. The RICO count charged that the activities outlined in the previous thirty-two counts established a pattern of racketeering.

After approximately ten weeks of trial, a jury convicted the three defendants of all thirty-three counts. Treasure Isle was fined

fraud charges. Count XIII alleges a bankruptcy fraud conspiracy. Counts XIV to XXIII are substantive bankruptcy fraud charges. Count XXIV alleges obstruction of justice. The securities and bankruptcy fraud conspiracies and the substantive counts with respect thereto are not multiplicious vis-a-vis each other.

$167,000 for its participation in the first thirty-two counts and was sentenced to perform community service for its conviction under the RICO statute.[9] The District Court sentenced Hartley and Dell to one year with three year's probation and a special condition of community service. Hartley additionally received a $25,000 fine.

The District Court denied the defendants' post-trial motions for an arrest of judgment, a judgment of acquittal, and a new trial.

At the center of this case are the imaginatively deceptive schemes designed to circumvent the inspection procedures implemented by the government to assure the quality of the shrimp purchased. * * *

* * *

In count thirty-three, the government charged the defendants with a violation of 18 U.S.C. § 1962(c), a subpart of the Racketeering Influenced and Corrupt Organization Act [RICO].[10] * * * Treasure Isle contends that it cannot simultaneously be the defendant and the enterprise under RICO. * * *

We have exhausted the plethora of case law on RICO and the numerous interpretations of its statutory language, but find no express prohibition of Treasure Isle's dual role in the present case. Thus, for the reasons articulated below we hold that a corporation can simultaneously be named as a defendant *and* satisfy the "enterprise" requirement under RICO. * * *

* * *

Under 18 U.S.C. § 1962(c) the government must prove: "(1) the existence of an enterprise which affects interstate or foreign commerce; (2) that the defendant 'associated with' the enterprise; (3) that the defendant participated in the conduct of the enterprise's affairs; and (4) that the participation was through a pattern of racketeering activity. . . ."

Recently, in United States v. Turkette, 452 U.S. 576, 101 S.Ct. 2524, 69 L.Ed.2d 246 (1981), the United States Supreme Court reemphasized the separate and distinct identity of two RICO elements, the "enterprise" and the "pattern of racketeering activity." The Court read the statute broadly to include wholly illegitimate "enterprises" within its purview. If it were to do otherwise, "[w]hole areas of organized criminal activity would be placed beyond the substantive reach of the enactment." Id. at 589, 101 S.Ct. at 2532. Congress, itself, directed a liberal construction of the act "to effectuate its remedial purposes."

* * *

---

9. [Where is this penalty mentioned in RICO? Do you think it appropriate "punishment"?—Ed.]

10. [Court's footnote 40.] 18 U.S.C. § 1962(c) (1976) provides:

It shall be unlawful for any person employed by or associated with any enterprise engaged in, or the activities of which affect, interstate or foreign commerce, to conduct or participate, directly or indirectly, in the conduct of such enterprise's affairs through a pattern of racketeering activity or collection of unlawful debt.

* * * We are presented with a situation in which the entity clearly satisfies the "enterprise" requirement, and may clearly be a defendant. The question is whether the same entity can be both simultaneously.

Section 1961(4) of Title 18 defines an "enterprise" as including "any individual, partnership, corporation, association, or other legal entity, and any union or group of individuals associated in fact although not a legal entity." Not even the appellants contest the inclusion of Treasure Isle within the literal reading of the statute. This relieves us of the arduous task of statutory interpretation, but does not resolve the issue.

Section 1962(c) prohibits "any *person* employed by or associated with any enterprise" from committing the proscribed conduct. 18 U.S.C. § 1962(c) (1976). " '[P]erson' includes any individual or entity capable of holding a legal or beneficial interest in property." 18 U.S.C. § 1961(3) (1976). Clearly Treasure Isle fits this definition.

Considering the broad reading given the term "enterprise" in *Turkette*, the Court's willingness to expand the scope of RICO's application, and absent any prohibition of Treasure Isle assuming a dual role, we answer our inquiry in the affirmative. A corporation may be simultaneously both a defendant and the enterprise under RICO.

Appellants suggest that if we allow the conviction to stand, we have "effectively eliminated" the enterprise element from section 1962(c). This simply is not true. "The enterprise is an entity, for present purposes a group of persons associated together for a common purpose of engaging in a course of conduct. . . . [It] is proved by evidence of an ongoing organization, formal or informal, and by evidence that the various associates function as a continuing unit." 452 U.S. at 583, 101 S.Ct. at 2528. The Fourth Circuit Court of Appeals suggested a form of proof for satisfaction of the enterprise element if a corporation was named as the enterprise. "Presumably . . . it would involve proof simply of the 'legal' existence of the corporation. . . . Neither the actual nor ostensible purpose of such an enterprise would seem directly relevant to proof of a RICO violation. . . ." Thus, it would appear that evidence of Treasure Isle's corporate existence would supply the requisite proof of the enterprise element, a separate and distinct burden in satisfaction of the Supreme Court's mandate in *Turkette*.[11]

---

11. [Court's footnote 43.] Appellants complain that Treasure Isle's corporate status, allowing for the government's alleged "emasculation of the enterprise element," is "particularly grievous" in view of the doctrine of corporate liability. Since a corporation is liable for the acts of its agents and employees, it permits an employee's activities to serve as proof of the two predicate acts required by section 1962(c). This is simply a reality to be faced by corporate entities. With the advantages of incorporation, must come the appendant responsibilities.

We are further persuaded of the soundness of our decision by the logic propounded by the government and the dictates of common sense. The government hypothesizes that if an individual were named as the enterprise,[12] and a group of persons engaged in a pattern of racketeering with that individual, it would defy reason to suggest that the central figure (the enterprise) could not also be prosecuted under RICO. We agree.

The government also suggests, and the defendants concede, this problem would never have surfaced had it charged the defendants collectively as an "association in fact" and charged Treasure Isle singly as the enterprise. This is reminiscent of the old adage, "a rose by any other name." *"There is no distinction, for 'enterprise' purposes, between a duly formed corporation that elects officers and holds annual meetings and an amoebalike infra-structure that controls a secret criminal network." In fact, the former Fifth Circuit in discussing the distinction between a "legal entity" or a "group of individuals associated in fact although not a legal entity," has stated "there is no logical or statutory reason to force the government to choose between alternative enterprise theories . . . as long as the indictment is otherwise sufficient." Had the government elected to charge the defendants in this manner, it would certainly have alleviated this lengthy discussion. Regardless, as long as the "enterprise" is established as an independent element under RICO, we perceive no problem with the form of the indictment in this case.

A third plausible rationale can be derived from basic corporations law. Although a corporation is a distinct legal entity, "[i]n rare, special circumstances, . . . courts will 'pierce the corporate veil'. . . ." We do not intend to analyze this issue under corporate doctrines, but by analogy Treasure Isle, Inc., can be dissected and viewed in a different light for each of the roles it assumes in this case. As a defendant, it can maintain its separate legal status as an ongoing business venture. By piercing through this sterile exterior, however, it can be revealed as an association of employees, officers, and agents working as a unit to effectuate a common purpose—to defraud the government. Viewed in this manner, it takes the form of a "group of individuals associated in fact," or in the words of the Court, "a group of persons associated together for a common purpose of engaging in a course of conduct." 452 U.S. at 583, 101 S.Ct. at 2528. Evidence of its ongoing nature, and "that the various associates function as a continuing unit" satisfies the enterprise element of RICO. Treasure Isle's problem lies in the fact that its corporate structure admits the characteristics essential to the formation of an association in fact—a fate which renders its

---

12. [Court's footnote 44.] 18 U.S.C. § 1961(4) includes an individual in its definition of an enterprise.

argument concerning the elimination of the enterprise element nugatory.

It would be anomalous indeed if the mere format chosen by the government could circumvent the proper application of RICO to the case presented. We refuse to allow this to happen. We hold that a corporate defendant may simultaneously be named in the indictment as the enterprise through which defendants conduct a pattern of racketeering.

Query. Are you convinced by the court's reading of 1962(c)? Most courts have not been.[13] In *Haroco Inc. v. American Nat'l Bank & Trust Co.*,[14] a civil suit, the Seventh Circuit reasoned as follows:

> We do not doubt that a corporation may satisfy the section 1961 definitions of both "person" and "enterprise," as the court observed in *Hartley*. But we focus our attention on the language in section 1962(c) requiring that the liable person be "employed by or associated with any enterprise" which affects interstate or foreign commerce. The use of the terms "employed by" and "associated with" appears to contemplate a person distinct from the enterprise. If Congress had meant to permit the same entity to be the liable person and the enterprise under section 1962(c), it would have required only a simple change in language to make that intention crystal clear. Also, we do not think the general principle of liberal interpretation of RICO can be used to stretch section 1962(c) to reach this situation in the face of the subsection's own limits.
>
> * * *
>
>   * * *
>
> Discussion of this person/enterprise problem under RICO can easily slip into a metaphysical or ontological style of discourse—after all, when is the person truly an entity "distinct" or "separate" from the enterprise? We are therefore reluctant to base our conclusion on the statutory language without also examining the relevant policies and potential consequences of our conclusion.
>
>   * * *
>
> * * * In our view, the plaintiffs here and the court in *Hartley* are correct when they argue that the corporate enterprise should be liable where it is the perpetrator, or the central figure in the criminal scheme. In that situation, the corporate deep pocket should certainly be subject to RICO liability. At the same time, the defendants here * * * are surely correct in saying that the corporation-enterprise should not be liable when the corporation is

---

13. See, e.g., United States v. Computer Sciences Corp., 689 F.2d 1181 (4th Cir. 1982), certiorari denied 459 U.S. 1105, 103 S.Ct. 729, 74 L.Ed.2d 953 (1983); Bennett v. Berg, 685 F.2d 1053 (8th Cir.1982), affirmed in pertinent part en banc, 710 F.2d 1361 (8th Cir.1983); B.F. Hirsch v. Enright Refining Co., Inc., 751 F.2d 628 (3d Cir. 1984); Rae v. Union Bank, 725 F.2d 478 (9th Cir.1984); Bennett v. United States Trust Co. of New York, 770 F.2d 308 (2d Cir.1985). Note that, except for *Computer Sciences*, these are all civil RICO cases.

14. 747 F.2d 384 (7th Cir.1984), affirmed on other grounds 473 U.S. 606, 105 S.Ct. 3291, 87 L.Ed.2d 437 (1985).

itself the victim or target, or merely the passive instrument for the wrongdoing of others.

In our view, the tensions between these policies may be resolved sensibly and in accord with the language of section 1962 by reading subsection (c) together with subsection (a). As we read subsection (c), the "enterprise" and the "person" must be distinct. However, a corporation-enterprise may be held liable under subsection (a) when the corporation is also a perpetrator. As we parse subsection (a), a "person" (such as a corporation-enterprise) acts unlawfully if it receives income derived directly or indirectly from a pattern of racketeering activity in which the person has participated as a principal within the meaning of 18 U.S.C. § 2, and if the person uses the income in the establishment or *operation* of an enterprise affecting commerce. Subsection (a) does not contain any of the language in subsection (c) which suggests that the liable person and the enterprise must be separate. Under subsection (a), therefore, the liable person may be a corporation using the proceeds of a pattern of racketeering activity in its operations. This approach to subsection (a) thus makes the corporation-enterprise liable under RICO when the corporation is actually the direct or indirect beneficiary of the pattern of racketeering activity, but not when it is merely the victim, prize, or passive instrument of racketeering. This result is in accord with the primary purpose of RICO, which, after all, is to reach those who ultimately profit from racketeering, not those who are victimized by it.[15]

* * *

(4) *Prosecutorial Discretion*. Review the list of "predicate offenses" under RICO (sec. 1961(1), reproduced in the Statutory Appendix, infra p. 682). Most of these offenses are already federal crimes. On what basis should a federal prosecutor decide to "add" a RICO count? Is it permissible to do so as an additional bargaining tool which might convince the defendant(s) to accept a negotiated plea to the predicate offenses in return for dropping the RICO charge? Note that even if a federal crime is not a predicate offense, it is often easy to add a mail or wire fraud count thereby bringing the conduct within RICO's sweep.[16] If, for example, the government includes a mail fraud count in an indictment for price-fixing under Section 1 of the Sherman Act, should it add RICO as well?[17]

The Department of Justice has issued Guidelines governing the institution of RICO prosecutions. The Guidelines, however, are not

---

15. *Haroco*'s preference for finding corporate liability under 1962(a) has been followed by other courts. See, e.g., Schreiber Distributing Co. v. Serv-Well Furniture Co., 806 F.2d 1393 (9th Cir.1986); Commonwealth of Pa. v. Derry Construction Co., 617 F.Supp. 940 (W.D.Pa.1985).

16. Mail and wire fraud are discussed infra, pp. 107–138.

17. The government has done so, apparently in cases where bids to governmental agencies are rigged (a violation of the Sherman Act) and there are accompanying bribes or payments to governmental officers. See United States v. Lizza Industries, Inc., 775 F.2d 492 (2d Cir.1985), certiorari denied 475 U.S. 1082, 106 S.Ct. 1459, 89 L.Ed.2d 716 (1986).

intended to create any legal rights, and specifically disclaim any intent to bind the government legally in the event that the Guidelines are violated.[18] These Guidelines provide, in part:

9–110.200 *RICO Guidelines Preface*

* * *

Despite the broad statutory language of RICO and the legislative intent that the statute ". . . shall be liberally construed to effectuate its remedial purpose," it is the policy of the criminal Division [of the Department of Justice] that RICO be selectively and uniformly used. It is the purpose of these guidelines to make it clear that not every case in which technically the elements of a RICO violation exist will result in the approval of a RICO charge. Further, it is not the policy of the criminal Division to approve "imaginative" prosecutions under RICO which are far afield from the Congressional purpose of the RICO statute. Stated another way, a RICO count which merely duplicates the elements of proof of a traditional Hobbs Act, Travel Act, mail fraud, wire fraud, gambling or controlled substances cases, will not be added to an indictment unless it serves some special RICO purpose as enumerated herein.

Further, it should be noted that only in exceptional circumstances will approval be granted when RICO is sought merely to serve some evidentiary purpose, rather than to attack the activity which Congress most directly addressed—the infiltration of organized crime into the nation's economy.

* * *

9–110.311 Commentary [Considerations Prior to Seeking Indictment]

All-encompassing examples are difficult, if not impossible, to formulate when discussing RICO; however, by way of illustration only:

A. When a diversified course of criminal conduct involving division of labor and functional responsibilities exists, for which other conspiracy statutes are inadequate, charging a RICO conspiracy may be appropriate;

B. When the course of criminal conduct has aspects which aggravate the seriousness of the crime (including prior criminal activity by a RICO defendant) which realistically can be foreseen as grounds for the sentencing judge imposing a heavier sentence under RICO than for the underlying acts, a RICO count may be appropriate;

C. When, subject to all of the guidelines, an essential portion of the evidence of the criminal conduct in a pattern of racketeering

---

18. See United States Attorneys' Manual, tit. 9–110.200 (1984). The Guidelines are also reproduced in 10 Department of Justice Manual, tit. 9–110.200 (1988) (published by Prentice Hall).

activity can be shown to be admissible only under RICO, and not under other evidentiary theories (such as: prior similar acts, continuing crime or conspiracy), a RICO count may be appropriate;

D. When a substantial prosecutive interest will be served by forfeiting an individual's interest in or source of influence over the enterprise which he has acquired, maintained, operated or conducted in violation of 18 U.S.C. § 1962, RICO may be appropriate.

* * *

. . Inclusion of a RICO count in an indictment solely or even primarily to create a bargaining tool for later plea negotiations on lesser counts would not be appropriate. . . .

* * *

9–110.340 *Charging a Violation of 18 U.S.C. § 1962(c)*

No indictment shall be brought charging a violation of 18 U.S.C. § 1962(c) based upon a pattern of racketeering activity growing out of a single criminal episode or transaction.

9–110.341 *Commentary*

The purpose of this guideline is to prevent a pattern of racketeering activity being charged which lacks the attributes which Congress had in mind but which is literally within the language of the statute.

(5) *Forfeiture Penalty.* Note that in addition to a jail term and fine, RICO provides for the forfeiture of any interest "acquired or maintained" in violation of § 1962, or any "interest in" an enterprise conducted in violation of § 1962 (see § 1963(a)(1), reproduced in the Statutory Appendix).[19] Is the forfeiture penalty excessive in light of the other penalties available? Does the court have any discretion not to impose forfeiture once a violation is found? Consider *United States v. Huber*, 603 F.2d 387 (2d Cir.1979):[20]

> We do not say that no forfeiture sanction may ever be so harsh as to violate the Eighth Amendment. But at least where the provision for forfeiture is keyed to the magnitude of a defendant's criminal enterprise, as it is in RICO, the punishment is at least in some rough way proportional to the crime. We further note that where the forfeiture threatens disproportionately to reach untainted property of a defendant, for example, if the criminal and legitimate aspects of the "enterprise" have been commingled over time, section 1963 permits the district court a certain amount of discretion in avoiding draconian (and perhaps potentially unconstitutional) applications of the forfeiture provision. Section 1963(c) provides:

---

19. For a general discussion, see W. Taylor, Forfeiture Under 18 U.S.C.A. § 1963—RICO's Most Powerful Weapon, 17 Am.Crim.L.Rev. 379 (1980).

20. But see United States v. L'Hoste, 609 F.2d 796 (5th Cir.) (holding forfeiture mandatory), certiorari denied 449 U.S. 833, 101 S.Ct. 104, 66 L.Ed.2d 39 (1980).

> Upon conviction of a person under this section, the court shall authorize the Attorney General to seize all property or other interest declared forfeited under this section upon such terms and conditions as the court shall deem proper.

In this case, Judge Tenney provided in his sentence that the seizure

> shall be on the following terms and conditions: (1) that defendant may redeem and repossess himself of said entities at any time within six months of the date of this judgment upon payment or delivery to the Attorney General of cash or other property satisfactory to the Attorney General having a value of $100,000. . . .

We certainly cannot say that the forfeiture provision is unconstitutional as applied to these circumstances, even if there were some doubt about its application to others.

The Supreme Court construed the forfeiture provision in *Russello v. United States*.[21] Russello was convicted under RICO for his part in an arson ring. One of the fires burned his office building. He received insurance payments of $340,043.09, out of which he paid $30,000 to the insurance adjuster who was part of the ring. The government sought forfeiture of the $340,043.09; the district court and court of appeals held the forfeiture proper. In the Supreme Court Russello argued that the money constituted "profits or proceeds" of racketeering, but was not an "interest" acquired or maintained in violation of the Act. The Supreme Court disagreed. Justice Blackmun, for a unanimous Court, wrote:

> The term "interest" is not specifically defined in the RICO statute. This silence compels us to "start with the assumption that the legislative purpose is expressed by the ordinary meaning of the words used." The ordinary meaning of "interest" surely encompasses a right to profits or proceeds. See Webster's Third New International Dictionary 1178 (1976), broadly defining "interest," among other things, as a "good," "benefit," or "profit." Random House Dictionary of the English Language (1979) defines interest to include "profit," "welfare," or "benefit." Black's Law Dictionary 729 (5th ed., 1979) provides a significant definition of "interest": "The most general term that can be employed to denote a right, claim, title or legal share in something." It is thus apparent that the term "interest" comprehends all forms of real and personal property, including profits and proceeds.
>
> * * *
>
> Petitioner himself has not attempted to define the term "interest" as used in § 1963(a)(1). He insists, however, that the term does not reach money or profits because, he says: " 'Interest,' by definition, includes of necessity an interest in something." Petitioner then asserts that the "something" emerges from the wording

---

21. 464 U.S. 16, 104 S.Ct. 296, 78 L.Ed. 2d 17 (1983).

of § 1963(a)(1) itself, that is, an interest "acquired . . . in violation of section 1962," and thus derives its meaning from the very activities barred by the statute. In other words, a direct relationship exists between that which is subject to forfeiture as a result of racketeering activity and that which constitutes racketeering. This relationship, it is said, means that forfeiture is confined to an interest in an "enterprise" itself. . . .

We do not agree. Every property interest, including a right to profits or proceeds, may be described as an interest in something. Before profits of an illegal enterprise are divided, each participant may be said to own an "interest" in the ill-gotten gains. After distribution, each will have a possessory interest in currency or other items so distributed. We therefore conclude that the language of the statute plainly covers the insurance proceeds petitioner received as a result of his arson activities.

* * *

If it is necessary to turn to the legislative history of the RICO statute, one finds that that history does not reveal, as petitioner would have us hold, a limited congressional intent.

* * *

The legislative history leaves no doubt that, in the view of Congress, the economic power of organized crime derived from its huge illegal profits. See Blakey, The RICO Civil Fraud Action in Context: Reflections on Bennett v. Berg, 58 Notre Dame L.Rev. 237, 249–256 (1982). Congress could not have hoped successfully to attack organized crime's economic roots without reaching racketeering profits. During the congressional debates, the sources and magnitude of organized crime's income were emphasized repeatedly. See, e.g., 115 Cong.Rec. 5873, 5884–5885 (1969); 116 Cong.Rec. 590, 592 (1970) (remarks of Sen. McClellan). From all this, the intent to authorize forfeiture of racketeering profits seems obvious.

It is true that Congress viewed the RICO statute in large part as a response to organized crime's infiltration of legitimate enterprises. United States v. Turkette, 452 U.S., at 591, 101 S.Ct., at 2532. But Congress' concerns were not limited to infiltration. The broader goal was to remove the profit from organized crime by separating the racketeer from his dishonest gains. Forfeiture of interest in an enterprise often would do little to deter; indeed, it might only encourage the speedy looting of an infiltrated company. It is unlikely that Congress intended to enact a forfeiture provision that provided an incentive for activity of this kind while authorizing forfeiture of an interest of little worth in a bankrupt shell.

* * *

Congress subsequently enacted the Comprehensive Forfeiture Act of 1984 (as part of the Comprehensive Crime Control Act of 1984). In addition to the required forfeiture of "any interest" acquired or maintained in violation of RICO (the provision construed in *Russello*), the 1984 amendment added forfeiture of "any property constituting, or derived from, any proceeds which the person obtained, directly or indirectly" from a violation of RICO. Note that this new provision makes no mention of "profits." The accompanying Senate Report, however, indicates that the term "proceeds" was used in lieu of the term "profits," so that the government would not have the "unreasonable burden" of having to prove "what the defendant's overhead expenses were." [22]

Query. How clear is the meaning of "profits" (mentioned in *Russello*) or "proceeds" (as used in the 1984 Act)? Consider *United States v. Lizza Industries, Inc.,* 775 F.2d 492 (2d Cir.1985), certiorari denied 475 U.S. 1082, 106 S.Ct. 1459, 89 L.Ed.2d 716 (1986), decided after *Russello* but under the original language of 1963(a)(1). In *Lizza* the defendants were found guilty of mail fraud and RICO charges arising out of a conspiracy to fix bids for building and paving roads. The court held that "gross" profits, rather than "net" profits, were a forfeitable "interest" under the statute. Gross profits were defined as the amount received for the jobs minus direct expenses; net profits would have allowed a deduction for general overhead and business expenses. Could you have thought of any other way to compute "profits"? [23] Would the result have been different under the 1984 amendment?

(6) *Civil RICO.* RICO is similar to other business crime statutes in that it provides a private civil remedy in addition to its criminal penalties. In Section 1964(c), Congress provided that anyone injured in their "business or property" could sue for three-times their damages, plus reasonable attorneys fees. This provision was modeled directly on Section 4 of the Clayton Act, which provides for treble-damages in antitrust cases.[24]

Just as prosecutors paid little attention to RICO immediately after its passage, civil litigators likewise ignored the statute.[25] In the early 1980s, however, private plaintiffs began to realize that the broad substantive coverage of RICO held out tremendous possibilities for private recoveries, including recoveries for securities law violations

---

22. See S.Rep. No. 225, 98th Cong., 1st Sess., at p. 199, reprinted in U.S.Code Cong. & Admin.News, p. 3382 (1984). The legislative history of this part of the Comprehensive Forfeiture Act is discussed in United States v. Rogers, 602 F.Supp. 1332, 1339–1341 (D.Colo.1985) (noting that the provision was drafted before *Russello* and was intended to clarify the split in the Circuits then existing).

23. For other cases construing the forfeiture provision, see, e.g., United States v. Ginsburg, 773 F.2d 798 (7th Cir.1985) (lawyer, one of two partners in firm, must forfeit half of firm's legal fees received for representing clients in tax cases in which lawyer bribed board of tax appeals); United States v. Navarro–Ordas, 770 F.2d 959 (11th Cir.1985) (forfeiting the amount of loans fraudulently obtained).

24. See Note, The Conflict Over RICO's Private Treble Damages Action, 70 Cornell L.Rev. 902, 905 (1985). For discussion of civil RICO, see generally, e.g., Note, Civil RICO: A Primer, 31 Loy.L.Rev. 989 (1986); Wexler, Civil RICO Comes of Age: Some Maturational Problems and Proposals for Reform, 35 Rut.L.Rev. 285 (1983); Blakey, The RICO Civil Fraud Action in Context: Reflections on Bennett v. Berg, 58 Notre Dame L.Rev. 237 (1983).

25. Of 270 civil district court decisions construing RICO prior to 1985, only nine were decided in the 1970s; one-third of all the cases were decided in 1983 and forty-three percent were decided in 1984. See ABA Section on Corporation, Banking and Business Law, Report of the Ad Hoc Civil RICO Task Force, at 55 (1985).

(this despite the provision for private causes of action under the antifraud provisions of the securities acts). As civil cases were filed, district courts reacted by construing RICO's provisions narrowly (a curious reversal of the usual presumption in statutory construction that *criminal* statutes be narrowly construed).

In *Sedima S.P.R.L. v. Imrex Co., Inc.*,[26] the Supreme Court made clear that it would not construe RICO more narrowly in civil than in criminal litigation. Sedima, a Belgian corporation, had entered into a joint business venture with Imrex, a New York exporter of aviation parts. Believing it had been cheated through overbilling, Sedima filed a RICO suit against Imrex and two of its officers, alleging mail and wire fraud as predicate acts. The Second Circuit held that a plaintiff cannot bring a RICO suit unless the defendant had already been convicted of the predicate acts alleged (or of the RICO violation). The Court of Appeals also held that the plaintiff must show "racketeering injury," not simply injury in fact; this concept was imported from the antitrust laws, which require proof of "antitrust injury." The Supreme Court, however, disagreed on both points:[27]

Underlying the Court of Appeals' holding was its distress at the "extraordinary, if not outrageous," uses to which civil RICO has been put. Instead of being used against mobsters and organized criminals, it has become a tool for everyday fraud cases brought against "respected and legitimate 'enterprises.'" Yet Congress wanted to reach both "legitimate" and "illegitimate" enterprises. United States v. Turkette, supra. The former enjoy neither an inherent incapacity for criminal activity nor immunity from its consequences. The fact that § 1964(c) is used against respected businesses allegedly engaged in a pattern of specifically identified criminal conduct is hardly a sufficient reason for assuming that the provision is being misconstrued. . . .

It is true that private civil actions under the statute are being brought almost solely against such defendants, rather than against the archetypal, intimidating mobster.[28] Yet this defect—if defect it is—is inherent in the statute as written, and its correction must lie with Congress. It is not for the judiciary to eliminate the private action in situations where Congress has provided it simply because plaintiffs are not taking advantage of it in its more difficult applications.

---

26. 473 U.S. 479, 105 S.Ct. 3275, 87 L.Ed.2d 346 (1985).

27. 473 U.S. at 499–500, 105 S.Ct. at 3287, 87 L.Ed.2d at 360–361.

28. [Court's footnote 16.] The ABA Task Force found that of the 270 known civil RICO cases at the trial court level, 40% involved securities fraud, 37% common-law fraud in a commercial or business setting, and only 9% "allegations of criminal activity of a type generally associated with professional criminals." ABA Report, at 55–56. Another survey of 132 published decisions found that 57 involved securities transactions and 38 commercial and contract disputes, while no other category made it into double figures. American Institute of Certified Public Accountants, The Authority to Bring Private Treble-Damage Suits Under "RICO" Should be Removed 13 (Oct. 10, 1984).

We nonetheless recognize that, in its private civil version, RICO is evolving into something quite different from the original conception of its enactors. Though sharing the doubts of the Court of Appeals about this increasing divergence, we cannot agree with either its diagnosis or its remedy. The "extraordinary" uses to which civil RICO has been put appear to be primarily the result of the breadth of the predicate offenses, in particular the inclusion of wire, mail, and securities fraud, and the failure of Congress and the courts to develop a meaningful concept of "pattern." We do not believe that the amorphous standing requirement imposed by the Second Circuit effectively responds to these problems, or that it is a form of statutory amendment appropriately undertaken by the courts.[29]

In the wake of *Sedima*, critics of the RICO private treble-damage remedy have sought legislative change. Frequently advanced proposals would, inter alia, eliminate mail, wire, and securities fraud as predicate offenses for the private remedy, impose a prior criminal conviction requirement, tighten the "pattern" requirement, reduce the treble-damage remedy, and eliminate the "racketeering" label. Congress has not enacted any of these proposals; but it seems highly likely that legislative change will continue to be sought in the future.[30]

As for activity in the courts, *Sedima* itself offered a suggestion on how to narrow the sweep of RICO. As indicated above, the Court complained about the failure to develop a "meaningful concept of 'pattern.'" In footnote 14 of its opinion the Court wrote:

> As many commentators have pointed out, the definition of a "pattern of racketeering activity" differs from the other provisions in § 1961 in that it states that a pattern "*requires* at least two acts of racketeering activity," § 1961(5) (emphasis added), not that it "means" two such acts. The implication is that while two acts are necessary, they may not be sufficient. Indeed, in common parlance two of anything do not generally form a "pattern." The legislative history supports the view that two isolated acts of racketeering

---

29. Justice Marshall, joined in dissent by Justices Brennan, Blackmun, and Powell, strongly objected to the use of civil RICO against respected businesses in ordinary commercial settings, arguing that in creating the civil RICO remedy, Congress did not intend to "bring about dramatic changes in the nature of commercial litigation." See 473 U.S. at 500, 105 S.Ct. at 3292, 87 L.Ed.2d at 361.

30. The proposal which received the most serious consideration in the 99th Congress was H.R. 5445, which passed the House in an amended version but was tabled in the Senate. See 132 Cong.Rec. H9365–66 (Oct. 7, 1986). Amendments to RICO failed in the 100th Congress as well; a major problem was whether to make the changes retroactive so that they would cover conduct which occurred prior to the enactment of the legislation. See Corp. Crim.Rep., Oct. 24, 1988, p. 4. For a thorough review of the arguments for and against the civil RICO remedy, by one who strongly favors retaining a private right of action (although with some limitations), see Goldsmith, Civil RICO Reform: The Basis for Compromise, 71 Minn.L.Rev. 827 (1987). For the text of reform bills considered in the 99th Congress, see id. at 884–911. For the 100th Congress, see, e.g., S. 1523, 100th Cong., 1st Sess. (1987), reported favorably by the Senate Judiciary Committee, see S.Rep. No. 100–459, 100th Cong., 2d Sess. (1988).

activity do not constitute a pattern. As the Senate Report explained: "The target of [RICO] is thus not sporadic activity. The infiltration of legitimate business normally requires more than one 'racketeering activity' and the threat of continuing activity to be effective. It is this factor of *continuity plus relationship* which combines to produce a pattern." S.Rep. No. 91–617, p. 158 (1969) (emphasis added). Similarly, the sponsor of the Senate bill, after quoting this portion of the Report, pointed out to his colleagues that "[t]he term 'pattern' itself requires the showing of a relationship. . . . So, therefore, proof of two acts of racketeering activity, without more, does not establish a pattern. . . ." 116 Cong. Rec. 18940 (1970) (statement of Sen. McClellan). See also id., at 35193 (statement of Rep. Poff) (RICO "not aimed at the isolated offender"); House Hearings, at 665. Significantly, in defining "pattern" in a later provision of the same bill, Congress was more enlightening: "[c]riminal conduct forms a pattern if it embraces criminal acts that have the same or similar purposes, results, participants, victims, or methods of commission, or otherwise are interrelated by distinguishing characteristics and are not isolated events." 18 U.S.C. § 3575(e). This language may be useful in interpreting other sections of the Act.

Four years after *Sedima*, in *HJ. Inc. v. Northwestern Bell Telephone Co.*[31] the Court adopted its "suggestions" from footnote 14, holding that "pattern" means "continuity plus relationship," not simply two predicate acts.[32] Justice Brennan wrote: "[T]o prove a pattern of racketeering activity a plaintiff or prosecutor must show that the racketeering predicates are related, *and* that they amount to or pose a threat of continued criminal activity." For "relatedness," the Court relied on the factors in § 3575(e) (quoted in footnote 14). The Court found "continuity" a more difficult concept. Continuity can be "a closed period of repeated conduct" or "past conduct that by its nature projects into the future with a threat of repetition." Applying these factors, the Court reversed the Eighth Circuit's holding that multiple illegal schemes were required. Justice Scalia, in his concurring opinion (joined in by the Chief Justice and Justices O'Connor and Kennedy), was highly critical of the majority's test, but admitted to being unable to do much better. He hinted at a constitutional challenge: Because RICO must "possess the degree of certainty required for criminal laws," the failure of the Court to provide "more than today's meager guidance bodes ill for the day when that [constitutional] challenge is presented."

31. __ U.S. __, 109 S.Ct. 2893, 106 L.Ed.2d 195 (1989).

32. For a thorough review of the cases construing "pattern" between *Sedima* and *H.J. Inc.* see United States v. Indelicato, 865 F.2d 1370 (2d Cir.1989) (en banc) (multiple mob murders, proximate in time; held: could constitute a pattern).

2. FRAUD

McNALLY v. UNITED STATES
Supreme Court of the United States, 1987.
483 U.S. 350, 107 S.Ct. 2875, 97 L.Ed.2d 292.

JUSTICE WHITE delivered the opinion of the Court.

This action involves the prosecution of petitioner Gray, a former public official of the Commonwealth of Kentucky, and petitioner McNally, a private individual, for alleged violation of the federal mail fraud statute, 18 U.S.C. § 1341. The prosecution's principal theory of the case, which was accepted by the courts below, was that petitioners' participation in a self-dealing patronage scheme defrauded the citizens and government of Kentucky of certain "intangible rights," such as the right to have the Commonwealth's affairs conducted honestly. We must consider whether the jury charge permitted a conviction for conduct not within the scope of the mail fraud statute.

We accept for the sake of argument the Government's view of the evidence, as follows. The petitioners and a third individual, Howard P. "Sonny" Hunt, were politically active in the Democratic Party in the Commonwealth of Kentucky during the 1970's. After Democrat Julian Carroll was elected Governor of Kentucky in 1974, Hunt was made chairman of the state Democratic Party and given de facto control over selecting the insurance agencies from which the State would purchase its policies. In 1975, the Wombwell Insurance Company of Lexington, Kentucky (Wombwell), which since 1971 had acted as the Commonwealth's agent for securing a workmen's compensation policy, agreed with Hunt that in exchange for a continued agency relationship it would share any resulting commissions in excess of $50,000 a year with other insurance agencies specified by him. The commissions in question were paid to Wombwell by the large insurance companies from which it secured coverage for the State.

From 1975 to 1979, Wombwell funneled $851,000 in commissions to 21 separate insurance agencies designated by Hunt. Among the recipients of these payments was Seton Investments, Inc. (Seton), a company controlled by Hunt and petitioner Gray and nominally owned and operated by petitioner McNally.

Gray served as Secretary of Public Protection and Regulation from 1976 to 1978 and also as Secretary of the Governor's Cabinet from 1977 to 1979. Prior to his 1976 appointment, he and Hunt established Seton for the sole purpose of sharing in the commissions distributed by Wombwell. Wombwell paid some $200,000 to Seton between 1975 and 1979, and the money was used to benefit Gray and Hunt. Pursuant to Hunt's direction, Wombwell also made excess commission payments to the Snodgrass Insurance Agency, which in turn gave the money to McNally.

On account of the foregoing activities, Hunt was charged with and pleaded guilty to mail and tax fraud and was sentenced to three years' imprisonment. The petitioners were charged with one count of conspiracy and seven counts of mail fraud, six of which were dismissed before trial. The remaining mail fraud count was based on the mailing of a commission check to Wombwell by the insurance company from which it had secured coverage for the State. This count alleged that petitioners had devised a scheme (1) to defraud the citizens and government of Kentucky of their right to have the Commonwealth's affairs conducted honestly, and (2) to obtain, directly and indirectly, money and other things of value by means of false pretenses and the concealment of material facts. The conspiracy count alleged that petitioners had (1) conspired to violate the mail fraud statute through the scheme just described and (2) conspired to defraud the United States by obstructing the collection of federal taxes.

After informing the jury of the charges in the indictment,[33] the District Court instructed that the scheme to defraud the citizens of Kentucky and to obtain money by false pretenses and concealment could be made out by either of two sets of findings: (1) that Hunt had de facto control over the award of the workmen's compensation insurance contract to Wombwell from 1975 to 1979; that he directed payments of commissions from this contract to Seton, an entity in which he had an ownership interest, without disclosing that interest to persons in state government whose actions or deliberations could have been affected by the disclosure; and that petitioners, or either of them, aided and abetted Hunt in that scheme; or (2) that Gray, in either of his appointed positions, had supervisory authority regarding the Commonwealth's workmen's compensation insurance at a time when Seton received commissions; that Gray had an ownership interest in Seton and did not disclose that interest to persons in state government whose actions or deliberations could have been affected by that disclosure; and that McNally aided and abetted Gray (the latter finding going only to McNally's guilt).

The jury convicted petitioners on both the mail fraud and conspiracy counts, and the Court of Appeals affirmed the convictions. In affirming the substantive mail fraud conviction, the court relied on a line of decisions from the Courts of Appeals holding that the mail fraud statute proscribes schemes to defraud citizens of their intangible rights to honest and impartial government. See, e.g., United States v. Mandel, 591 F.2d 1347 (CA4 1979), aff'd in relevant part, 602 F.2d 653

---

33. [Court's footnote 4.] The instruction summarized the charge as follows:

"Count 4 of the Indictment charges in part that the defendants devised a scheme or artifice to:

"(a)(1) defraud the citizens of the Commonwealth of Kentucky and its governmental departments, agencies, officials and employees of their right to have the Commonwealth's business and its affairs conducted honestly, impartially, free from corruption, bias, dishonesty, deceit, official misconduct, and fraud; and,

"(2) obtain (directly and indirectly) money and other things of value, by means of false and fraudulent pretenses, representations, and promises, and the concealment of facts. * * *"

(en banc), cert. denied, 445 U.S. 961, 100 S.Ct. 1647, 64 L.Ed.2d 236 (1980). Under these cases, a public official owes a fiduciary duty to the public, and misuse of his office for private gain is a fraud. Also, an individual without formal office may be held to be a public fiduciary if others rely on him " 'because of a special relationship in the government' " and he in fact makes governmental decisions. 790 F.2d, at 1296 (quoting United States v. Margiotta, 688 F.2d 108, 122 (CA2 1982), cert. denied, 461 U.S. 913, 103 S.Ct. 1891, 77 L.Ed.2d 282 (1983)). The Court of Appeals held that Hunt was such a fiduciary because he "substantially participated in governmental affairs and exercised significant, if not exclusive, control over awarding the workmen's compensation insurance contract to Wombwell and the payment of monetary kickbacks to Seton." 790 F.2d, at 1296.

We granted certiorari, and now reverse.

The mail fraud statute clearly protects property rights, but does not refer to the intangible right of the citizenry to good government. As first enacted in 1872, as part of a recodification of the postal laws, the statute contained a general proscription against using the mails to initiate correspondence in furtherance of "any scheme or artifice to defraud." The sponsor of the recodification stated, in apparent reference to the anti-fraud provision, that measures were needed "to prevent the frauds which are mostly gotten up in the large cities . . . by thieves, forgers, and rapscallions generally, for the purpose of deceiving and fleecing the innocent people in the country." Insofar as the sparse legislative history reveals anything, it indicates that the original impetus behind the mail fraud statute was to protect the people from schemes to deprive them of their money or property.

Durland v. United States, 161 U.S. 306, 16 S.Ct. 508, 40 L.Ed. 709 (1896), the first case in which this Court construed the meaning of the phrase "any scheme or artifice to defraud," held that the phrase is to be interpreted broadly insofar as property rights are concerned, but did not indicate that the statute had a more extensive reach. The Court rejected the argument that "the statute reaches only such cases as, at common law, would come within the definition of 'false pretenses,' in order to make out which there must be a misrepresentation as to some existing fact and not a mere promise as to the future." Id., at 312. Instead, it construed the statute to "includ[e] everything designed to defraud by representations as to the past or present, or suggestions and promises as to the future." Id., at 313. Accordingly, the defendant's use of the mails to sell bonds which he did not intend to honor was within the statute. The Court explained that "[i]t was with the purpose of protecting the public against all such intentional efforts to despoil, and to prevent the post office from being used to carry them into effect, that this statute was passed. . . ." Id., at 314.

Congress codified the holding of *Durland* in 1909, and in doing so gave further indication that the statute's purpose is protecting property rights. The amendment added the words "or for obtaining money or property by means of false or fraudulent pretenses, representations, or promises" after the original phrase "any scheme or artifice to defraud." Act of Mar. 4, 1909, ch. 321, § 215, 35 Stat. 1130.[34] The new language is based on the statement in Durland that the statute reaches "everything designed to defraud by representations as to the past or present, or suggestions and promises as to the future." 161 U.S., at 313. However, instead of the phrase "everything designed to defraud" Congress used the words "[any scheme or artifice] for obtaining money or property."

After 1909, therefore, the mail fraud statute criminalized schemes or artifices "to defraud" or "for obtaining money or property by means of false or fraudulent pretenses, representation, or promises. . . ." Because the two phrases identifying the proscribed schemes appear in the disjunctive, it is arguable that they are to be construed independently and that the money-or-property requirement of the latter phrase does not limit schemes to defraud to those aimed at causing deprivation of money or property. This is the approach that has been taken by each of the Courts of Appeals that has addressed the issue: schemes to defraud include those designed to deprive individuals, the people or the government of intangible rights, such as the right to have public officials perform their duties honestly.

As the Court long ago stated, however, the words "to defraud" commonly refer "to wronging one in his property rights by dishonest methods or schemes," and "usually signify the deprivation of something of value by trick, deceit, chicane or overreaching." Hammerschmidt v. United States, 265 U.S. 182, 188 (1924). The codification of the holding in *Durland* in 1909 does not indicate that Congress was departing from this common understanding. As we see it, adding the second phrase simply made it unmistakable that the statute reached false promises and misrepresentations as to the future as well as other frauds involving money or property.

We believe that Congress' intent in passing the mail fraud statute was to prevent the use of the mails in furtherance of such schemes. The Court has often stated that when there are two rational readings of a criminal statute, one harsher than the other, we are to choose the harsher only when Congress has spoken in clear and definite language. As the Court said in a mail fraud case years ago, "There are no constructive offenses; and before one can be punished, it must be shown that his case is plainly within the statute." Fasulo v. United States, 272 U.S. 620, 629, 47 S.Ct. 200, 202, 71 L.Ed. 443 (1926). Rather than construe the statute in a manner that leaves its outer boundaries ambiguous and involves the Federal Government in setting standards

---

34. [Court's footnote 7.] The new language was suggested in the Report of the Commission to Revise and Codify the Criminal and Penal Laws of the United States, which cited Durland in the margin of its Report. See S.Doc. No. 68, pt. 2, 57th Cong., 1st Sess. 63, 64 (1901). The sponsor of the 1909 legislation did not address the significance of the new language, stating that it was self-explanatory. 42 Cong.Rec. 1026 (1908) (remarks of Sen. Heyburn).

of disclosure and good government for local and state officials, we read § 1341 as limited in scope to the protection of property rights. If Congress desires to go further, it must speak more clearly than it has.

For purposes of this action, we assume that Hunt, as well as Gray, was a state officer. The issue is thus whether a state officer violates the mail fraud statute if he chooses an insurance agent to provide insurance for the State but specifies that the agent must share its commissions with other named insurance agencies, in one of which the officer has an ownership interest and hence profits when his agency receives part of the commissions. We note that as the action comes to us, there was no charge and the jury was not required to find that the Commonwealth itself was defrauded of any money or property. It was not charged that in the absence of the alleged scheme the Commonwealth would have paid a lower premium or secured better insurance. Hunt and Gray received part of the commissions but those commissions were not the Commonwealth's money. Nor was the jury charged that to convict it must find that the Commonwealth was deprived of control over how its money was spent. Indeed, the premium for insurance would have been paid to some agency, and what Hunt and Gray did was to assert control that the Commonwealth might not otherwise have made over the commissions paid by the insurance company to its agent. Although the Government now relies in part on the assertion that the petitioners obtained property by means of false representations to Wombwell, there was nothing in the jury charge that required such a finding. We hold, therefore, that the jury instruction on the substantive mail fraud count permitted a conviction for conduct not within the reach of § 1341.

It may well be that Congress could criminalize using the mails to further a state officer's efforts to profit from governmental decisions he is empowered to make or over which he has some supervisory authority, even if there is no state law proscribing his profiteering or even if state law expressly authorized it. But if state law expressly permitted or did not forbid a state officer such as Gray to have an ownership interest in an insurance agency handling the State's insurance, it would take a much clearer indication than the mail fraud statute evidences to convince us that having and concealing such an interest defrauds the State and is forbidden under federal law.

* * *

The judgment of the Court of Appeals is reversed and the case remanded for proceedings consistent with this opinion.

It is so ordered.

JUSTICE STEVENS, with whom JUSTICE O'CONNOR joins as to Parts I, II and III, dissenting.

Congress has broadly prohibited the use of the United States mails to carry out "any scheme or artifice to defraud." 18 U.S.C. § 1341. The question presented is whether that prohibition is restricted to fraudulent schemes to deprive others of money or property, or whether it also includes fraudulent schemes to deprive individuals of other rights to which they are entitled. Specifically, we must decide whether the statute's prohibition embraces a secret agreement by state officials to place the State's workmen's compensation insurance with a particular agency in exchange for that company's agreement to share a major portion of its commissions with a list of agents provided by officials, including sham agencies under the control of the officials themselves.

The same question of statutory construction has arisen in a variety of contexts over the past few decades. In the public sector, judges, state Governors, chairmen of state political parties, state cabinet officers, city aldermen, congressmen and many other state and federal officials have been convicted of defrauding citizens of their right to the honest services of their governmental officials.[35] In most of these cases, the officials have secretly made governmental decisions with the objective of benefiting themselves or promoting their own interests, instead of fulfilling their legal commitment to provide the citizens of the State or local government with their loyal service and honest government. Similarly, many elected officials and their campaign workers have been convicted of mail fraud when they have used the mails to falsify votes, thus defrauding the citizenry of its right to an honest election.[36] In the private sector, purchasing agents, brokers, union leaders, and others with clear fiduciary duties to their employers or unions have been found guilty of defrauding their employers or unions by accepting kickbacks or selling confidential information.[37] In other cases, defen-

---

35. [Footnote 1 in original.] See, e.g., United States v. Holzer, 816 F.2d 304 (CA7 1987) (county judge); United States v. Silvano, 812 F.2d 754 (CA1 1987) (city budget director); United States v. Barber, 668 F.2d 778 (CA3) (state Alcoholic Beverage Control Commissioner), cert. denied, 459 U.S. 829 (1982); United States v. Margiotta, 688 F.2d 108 (CA2 1982) (party leader), cert. denied, 461 U.S. 913 (1983); United States v. Diggs, 198 U.S.App.D.C. 255, 613 F.2d 988 (1979) (Congressman), cert. denied, 446 U.S. 982 (1980); United States v. Mandel, 591 F.2d 1347 (CA4 1979) (Governor of Maryland), cert. denied, 445 U.S. 961 (1980); United States v. Brown, 540 F.2d 364 (CA8 1976) (city building commissioner); United States v. Bush, 522 F.2d 641 (CA7 1975) (city Director of Public Relations), cert. denied, 424 U.S. 977 (1976); United States v. Keane, 522 F.2d 534 (CA7 1975) (city Alderman), cert. denied, 424 U.S. 976 (1976); United States v. Staszcuk, 502 F.2d 875 (CA7 1974) (city alderman), cert. denied, 423 U.S. 837 (1975); United States v. Isaacs, 493 F.2d 1124 (CA7) (ex-Governor of Illinois & ex-Director of Illinois Department of Revenue), cert. denied, 417 U.S. 976 (1974); United States v. Classic, 35 F.Supp. 457 (ED La.1940) (election commissioner).

36. [Footnote 2 in original.] See, e.g., United States v. Girdner, 754 F.2d 877 (CA10 1985) (candidate for state legislature); United States v. Odom, 736 F.2d 104, 116, n. 13 (CA4 1984) (sheriff); United States v. Clapps, 732 F.2d 1148, 1153 (CA3 1984) (party chairman), cert. denied, 469 U.S. 1085 (1984); United States v. States, 488 F.2d 761 (CA8 1973) (candidates for city office), cert. denied, 417 U.S. 909 (1974).

37. [Footnote 3 in original.] See, e.g., United States v. Price, 788 F.2d 234 (CA4 1986), cert. pending sub nom. McMahan v. United States, No. 86–632; United States v. Boffa, 688 F.2d 919, 930–931 (CA3 1982); United States v. Curry, 681 F.2d 406 (CA5 1982) (chairman of political action committee); United States v. Bronston, 658 F.2d 920 (CA2 1981) (attorney), cert. denied, 456 U.S. 915 (1982); United States v. Von Barta, 635 F.2d 999 (CA2 1980) (securities trader), cert. denied, 450 U.S. 998 (1981); United States v. Bohonus, 628 F.2d 1167 (CA9) (insurance manager), cert. denied, 447 U.S. 928 (1980); United States v. Bryza, 522 F.2d 414 (CA7 1975) (purchasing agent), cert. denied, 426 U.S. 912 (1976); United States v. George, 477 F.2d 508 (CA7) (purchasing agent), cert. denied, 414 U.S. 827 (1973); United States v. Proctor &

dants have been found guilty of using the mails to defraud individuals of their rights to privacy, and other nonmonetary rights.[38] All of these cases have something in common—they involved what the Court now refers to as "intangible rights." They also share something else in common. The many federal courts that have confronted the question whether these sorts of schemes constitute a "scheme or artifice to defraud" have uniformly and consistently read the statute in the same, sensible way. They have realized that nothing in the words "any scheme or artifice to defraud," or in the purpose of the statute, justifies limiting its application to schemes intended to deprive victims of money or property.

* * *

I

The mail fraud statute sets forth three separate prohibitions. It prohibits the use of the United States mails for the purpose of executing "[1] *any* scheme or artifice to defraud, [2] *or* for obtaining money or property by means of false or fraudulent pretenses, representations, or promises, [3] *or* to sell, dispose of, loan, exchange, alter, give away, distribute, supply, or furnish or procure for unlawful use any counterfeit or spurious coin, obligation, security, or other article, or anything represented to be or intimated or held out to be such counterfeit or spurious article . . ." 18 U.S.C. § 1341 (emphasis and brackets added).

As the language makes clear, each of these restrictions is independent. One can violate the second clause—obtaining money or property by false pretenses—even though one does not violate the third clause—counterfeiting. Similarly, one can violate the first clause—devising a scheme or artifice to defraud—without violating the counterfeiting provision. Until today it was also obvious that one could violate the first clause by devising a scheme or artifice to defraud, even though one did not violate the second clause by seeking to obtain money or property from his victim through false pretenses. Every court to consider the matter had so held. Yet, today, the Court, for all practical purposes, rejects this longstanding construction of the statute by imposing a requirement that a scheme or artifice to defraud does not violate the statute unless its purpose is to defraud someone of money or property. I am at a loss to understand the source or justification for this holding. Certainly no canon of statutory construction requires us to ignore the plain language of the provision.

In considering the scope of the mail fraud statute it is essential to remember Congress' purpose in enacting it. Congress sought to protect

Gamble Co., 47 F.Supp. 676 (Mass.1942) (attempt to bribe competitor's employee).

38. [Footnote 4 in original.] See, e.g., United States v. Condolon, 600 F.2d 7 (CA4 1979) (wire fraud conviction related to bogus talent agency designed to seduce women); United States v. Louderman, 576 F.2d 1383 (CA9) (scheme to fraudulently obtain confidential personal information), cert. denied, 439 U.S. 896 (1978); see also United States v. Castor, 558 F.2d 379, 383 (CA7 1977) (fraudulent information on application for liquor license), cert. denied, 434 U.S. 1010 (1978).

the integrity of the United States mails by not allowing them to be used as "instruments of crime." "The focus of the statute is upon the misuse of the Postal Service, not the regulation of state affairs, and Congress clearly has the authority to regulate such misuse of the mails. See Badders v. United States, 240 U.S. . . . 391 (1916)." Once this purpose is considered, it becomes clear that the construction the Court adopts today is senseless. Can it be that Congress sought to purge the mails of schemes to defraud citizens of money but was willing to tolerate schemes to defraud citizens of their right to an honest government, or to unbiased public officials? Is it at all rational to assume that Congress wanted to ensure that the mails not be used for petty crimes, but did not prohibit election fraud accomplished through mailing fictitious ballots? . . .

* * *

III

To support its crabbed construction of the Act, the Court makes a straight-forward but unpersuasive argument. Since there is no explicit, unambiguous evidence that Congress actually contemplated "intangible rights" when it enacted the mail fraud statute in 1872, the Court explains, any ambiguity in the meaning of the criminal statute should be resolved in favor of lenity. The doctrine of lenity is, of course, sound, for the citizen is entitled to fair notice of what sort of conduct may give rise to punishment. But the Court's reliance on that doctrine in this case is misplaced for several reasons.

To begin with, "although criminal statutes are to be construed strictly . . . this does not mean that every 'criminal statute must be given the narrowest possible meaning in complete disregard of the purpose of the legislature.'" McElroy v. United States, 455 U.S., at 658, quoting United States v. Bramblett, 348 U.S. 503, 509–510 (1955). Especially in light of the statutory purpose, I believe that § 1341 unambiguously prohibits all schemes to defraud that use the United States mails—whether or not they involve money or property.

In any event, this asserted ambiguity in the meaning of the word "defraud," if it ever existed, was removed by judicial construction long ago. [T]he series of Court of Appeals' opinions applying this very statute to schemes to defraud a State and its citizens of their intangible right to honest and faithful government, notwithstanding the absence of evidence of tangible loss, [have] removed any relevant ambiguity in this statute. Surely these petitioners knew that it would be unlawful to place Kentucky's insurance coverage with an agent who would secretly make hundreds of thousands of dollars available for the private use of petitioners, their relatives, and their paramours. This is, indeed, a strange application of the doctrine of lenity.[39]

---

39. [Footnote 9 in original.] When considering how much weight to accord to the doctrine of lenity, it is appropriate to identify the class of litigants that will benefit from the Court's ruling today. They are not uneducated, or even average, citizens. They are the most sophisticated practitioners of the art of government among us.

I recognize that there may have been some overly expansive applications of § 1341 in the past. With no guidance from this Court, the Courts of Appeals have struggled to define just when conduct which is clearly unethical is also criminal. In some instances, however, such as voting fraud cases, the criminality of the scheme and the fraudulent use of the mails could not be clearer. It is sometimes difficult to define when there has been a scheme to defraud someone of intangible rights. But it is also sometimes difficult to decide when a tangible loss was caused by fraud. The fact that the exercise of judgment is sometimes difficult is no excuse for rejecting an entire doctrine that is both sound and faithful to the intent of Congress.

IV

Perhaps the most distressing aspect of the Court's action today is its casual—almost summary—rejection of the accumulated wisdom of the many distinguished federal judges who have thoughtfully considered and correctly answered the question this case presents. The quality of this Court's work is most suspect when it stands alone, or virtually so, against a tide of well-considered opinions issued by state or federal courts. In this case I am convinced that those judges correctly understood the intent of the Congress that enacted this statute. Even if I were not so persuaded, I could not join a rejection of such a longstanding, consistent interpretation of a federal statute.

In the long run, it is not clear how grave the ramifications of today's decision will be. Congress can, of course, negate it by amending the statute. Even without Congressional action, prosecutions of corrupt officials who use the mails to further their schemes may continue since it will frequently be possible to prove some loss of money or property.[40] But many other types of fraudulent use of the mail will now be immune from prosecution. The possibilities that the decision's impact will be mitigated do not moderate my conviction that the Court has made a serious mistake. Nor do they erase my lingering questions about why a Court that has not been particularly receptive to the rights of criminal defendants in recent years has acted so dramatically to protect the elite class of powerful individuals who will benefit from this decision.

There is an element of fiction in the presumption that every citizen is charged with a responsibility to know what the law is. But the array of government executives, judges, and legislators who have been accused, and convicted, of mail fraud under the well-settled construction of the statute that the Court renounces today are people who unquestionably knew that their conduct was unlawful. Cf. Nash v. United States, 229 U.S. 373, 377 (1913).

40. [Footnote 10 in original.] When a person is being paid a salary for his loyal services, any breach of that loyalty would appear to carry with it some loss of money to the employer—who is not getting what he paid for. Additionally, "[i]f an agent receives anything as a result of his violation of a duty of loyalty to the principal, he is subject to a liability to deliver it, its value, or its proceeds, to the principal." Restatement (Second) of Agency § 403 (1958). This duty may fulfill the Court's "money or property" requirement in most kickback schemes.

* * *

I respectfully dissent.

NOTES AND QUERIES

(1) *History and Elements of Mail Fraud.* As the Court indicates in *McNally,* Congress enacted the first mail fraud statute in 1872. A product of the Reconstruction Era, the statute was apparently aimed at large scale swindles and "get rich quick" schemes which were then only imperfectly regulated by state law.[41] The statute's language is broad, however, and, prior to *McNally,* the courts had been quite willing to interpret it expansively.

The elements of the offense are 1) a scheme to defraud; and 2) the mailing of a letter for the purpose of executing the scheme. The ostensible purpose of the mail fraud statute being to prevent misuse of the mails,[42] a defendant can be charged separately for each use of the mails even if there is only one scheme to defraud.[43] Nevertheless, use of the mails need not be an essential part of the scheme to defraud; it need only be "incidental" to an essential part.[44] As for the meaning of "fraud" in the statute, one court has written, "[t]he law does not define fraud; it needs no definition; it is as old as falsehood and as versatile as human ingenuity."[45]

The mail fraud statute has often been used to attack "new" frauds until particularized legislation can be passed to deal more directly with the perceived problem. Examples include securities fraud, loan sharking, real estate fraud, and credit card fraud.[46] More recently, the Justice Department used it against companies which paid bribes to foreign officials prior to the passage of the Foreign Corrupt Practices

---

41. For the background history, see Rakoff, The Federal Mail Fraud Statute (I), 18 Duquesne L.Rev. 771, 779–86, 809–10, 816–20 (1980).

42. See United States v. States, 488 F.2d 761 (8th Cir.1973), certiorari denied 417 U.S. 909, 94 S.Ct. 2605, 41 L.Ed.2d 212 (1974). Schemes to defraud which use wire, radio, or television are prohibited by the Wire Fraud statute, 18 U.S.C.A. § 1343.

43. See Badders v. United States, 240 U.S. 391, 394, 36 S.Ct. 367, 368, 60 L.Ed. 706, 708 (1916). Compare United States v. Margiotta, 646 F.2d 729 (2d Cir.1981) (allowing indictment charging fifty separate mailings in one count; no unfairness and defendant does not have to be separately charged).

44. Pereira v. United States, 347 U.S. 1, 8, 74 S.Ct. 358, 362, 98 L.Ed. 435, 444 (1954). Compare Schmuck v. United States, ___ U.S. ___, 109 S.Ct. 1443, 103 L.Ed.2d 734 (1989) (continuing scheme to sell used cars to dealers after rolling back odometers; only use of mails was by unsuspecting used car dealers who mailed title application forms to the State Department of Transportation; held (5–4): within statute; mailings, although innocent, were "part of the execution of the scheme" because continuation of Schmuck's business relationships with customers depended on smooth passage of title) with United States v. Maze, 414 U.S. 395, 94 S.Ct. 645, 38 L.Ed.2d 603 (1974) (defendant's misuse of credit card not within statute; mailing of invoices by merchants to banks and billing of card holder not "sufficiently closely related" to scheme to be "in furtherance").

45. Weiss v. United States, 122 F.2d 675, 681 (5th Cir.), certiorari denied 314 U.S. 687, 62 S.Ct. 300, 86 L.Ed. 550 (1941).

46. See United States v. Maze, 414 U.S. 395, 405–07, 94 S.Ct. 645, 651, 38 L.Ed.2d 603, 611–12 (1974) (Burger, C.J., dissenting).

Act.⁴⁷ Even after remedial legislation has been passed, prosecutors may continue to charge defendants under the mail fraud statute, or under the mail fraud statute and the new statute. Although some courts have expressed reservations about "the Government's use of the mail fraud statute as a basis for additional counts in an indictment the gravamen of which was the violation of other federal criminal statutes," ⁴⁸ the courts have nevertheless held that simultaneous prosecution under the mail fraud and other statutes based on the same substantive conduct does not place the defendant in double jeopardy.⁴⁹

(2) *Queries.* As Justice Stevens indicates in his dissent in *McNally*, the argument that the mail fraud statute protects "intangible rights" had been accepted by all the courts of appeals which had passed on it. This construction of the statute consequently gave the Justice Department a significant prosecutorial tool which it employed in a wide variety of settings, from governmental corruption to "private" breaches of loyalty. Although this statutory construction was well accepted by the courts, commentators generally disapproved, arguing that the term "scheme to defraud" was being interpreted to cover so many diverse patterns of "misbehavior" that defendants were no longer being given adequate notice of what conduct might be deemed "criminal." ⁵⁰

1) To what extent should the Supreme Court have given more weight to the views of the courts of appeals? After all, these courts had reviewed many cases over a significant period of time; apparently, they had not yet reached the point where they felt that the Justice Department had overstepped prosecutorial bounds.

2) Justice White reminds us that there are "no constructive crimes" and that harsh constructions of penal statutes are to be avoided "unless Congress has spoken in clear and definite language." Has the Court consistently applied these principles of clarity and strict construction? Reconsider *Patterson* and the Notes following, supra p. 15.

3) Can we tolerate "loose texture" criminal statutes, such as mail fraud (and, indeed, many business crime statutes), which the courts are then left to interpret in the usual common law way? Consider Justice Stevens' argument regarding the "notice" which these defendants had as to the potential criminality of their conduct. Do you think this "notice" was adequate? Do you think they were surprised at having

---

47. See Comment, Mail and Wire Fraud Prosecutions for Bribery, 9 Ga.J.Int'l. & Comp.L. 49 (1979).

48. United States v. Mangan, 575 F.2d 32, 49 (2d Cir.1978). Compare United States v. Standard Drywall Corporation, 617 F.Supp. 1283 (E.D.N.Y.1985) (indictment did not pyramid charges of mail fraud on top of charges of tax fraud, where indictment alleged that corporate defendant and its principals made fraudulent mailings that related to tax liabilities of persons other than themselves).

49. See, e.g., United States v. Ledesma, 632 F.2d 670 (7th Cir.), certiorari denied 449 U.S. 998, 101 S.Ct. 539, 66 L.Ed.2d 296 (1980).

50. See Coffee, The Metastasis of Mail Fraud: The Continuing Story of the Evolution of White Collar Crime, 21 Am.Crim.L. Rev. 1, 27–28 (1983). See also Hurson, Limiting the Federal Mail Fraud Statute: A Legislative Approach, 20 Am.Crim.L. Rev. 423 (1983).

their conduct labelled "criminal"? Should that decide the issue of statutory construction? Reconsider *Dowling,* supra p. 33.

4) Based on the facts given in the Court's opinion, could McNally have been convicted even under the Court's construction of the statute? As prosecutor, how would you have argued the matter to the jury?

Notes (3), (4), and (5), infra, present pre–*McNally* cases, decided by the Courts of Appeals under the "intangible rights" doctrine. Each of these cases was referred to by either the majority or dissent in *McNally.* When reading these cases, keep in mind the above four questions and reconsider your initial answers when you finish.

(3) *Political Corruption.* In *United States v. Mandel,*[51] Maryland's Governor, Marvin Mandel, was charged with mail fraud in connection with legislation increasing the number of racing days at a Maryland racetrack. Mandel first vetoed the legislation, for a reason unconnected with the increase in racing days. Seven months after this veto, the owners of the racetrack sold it to a group of investors who were at the same time involved with Mandel in a waterfront land investment. The new racetrack owners concealed their identity from the public, but caused a letter to be sent to the legislature urging an override of the Governor's veto. A legislative ally of Mandel's told several legislators that Mandel would not mind his veto being overridden. The legislature did override the veto, thereby doubling the track's racing days. Two months later a bill was introduced further increasing the track's racing days. Although Mandel lobbied strenuously for this bill, the legislation was not enacted. There was evidence that Mandel had long supported such legislation.

Evidence was introduced that Mandel received three gifts of clothing and one gift of jewelry from some of the racetrack investors; two of the gifts predated and two post-dated the events in question. There was also a question as to the adequacy of the consideration Mandel gave these investors for his participation in the waterfront land investment and in a subsequent office building investment. Finally, several senators testified that had they known the true identities of the investors in the racetrack and their business relationships and gifts to Governor Mandel, they would have considered such information relevant to their vote on the veto override and to their decision on the bill increasing racing days.

The Government charged in Count 1 of the indictment, paragraph 13, that Mandel and the other investors had devised a scheme:

> "(a) To defraud the citizens of the State of Maryland, and its governmental departments, agencies, officials and employees, both executive and legislative, of their right to the conscientious, loyal, faithful, disinterested and unbiased services, actions and performance of official duties of MARVIN MANDEL, in his official capacities as Governor of the State of Maryland,

---

51. 591 F.2d 1347 (4th Cir.), convictions aff'd en banc, 602 F.2d 653 (4th Cir.1979), certiorari denied 445 U.S. 961, 100 S.Ct. 1647, 64 L.Ed.2d 236 (1980).

free from bribery, corruption, partiality, willful omission, bias, dishonesty, deceit, official misconduct and fraud;

"(b) To defraud the citizens of the State of Maryland, and its governmental departments, agencies, officials and employees, both executive and legislative, of their right to have the state's business and its affairs conducted honestly, impartially, free from bribery, corruption, bias, dishonesty, deceit, official misconduct and fraud, and in accordance with the laws and Code of Ethics of the State of Maryland;

"(c) To defraud the citizens of the State of Maryland, and its governmental departments, agencies, officials and employees, both executive and legislative, of their right to have available and to be made aware of all relevant and pertinent facts and circumstances when:

(1) drafting, considering and deliberating upon proposed legislation for the State of Maryland with respect to the Maryland horse racing industry and to other matters;

(2) administering the laws of the State of Maryland with respect to the Maryland horse racing industry and to other matters; and

(3) transacting business for and on behalf of the State of Maryland;

"(d) To obtain, directly and indirectly, money, property and other things of value, by means of false and fraudulent pretenses, representations, and promises, and the concealment of material facts, relating to the Marlboro Race Track, the Bowie Race Track, the Security Investment Company, Ray's Point, Inc., and to other matters."

Writing the initial panel decision for the Court of Appeals, Judge Widener stated:

> For the most part, courts have broadly construed the words, "scheme or artifice to defraud." The result has been to include within that term many schemes involving deception which employ the mails in their execution if they are contrary to public policy and fail to measure up to accepted moral standards and notions of honesty and fair play. In Badders v. United States, 240 U.S. 391, 393, 36 S.Ct. 367, 368, 60 L.Ed. 706 (1916), the Court stated, "Whatever the limits to [Congress'] power, it may forbid any such acts done in furtherance of a scheme that it regards as contrary to public policy. . . ." This public policy reference has been followed by some courts as setting the outer limits to the term "scheme or artifice to defraud" as that term is used in the mail fraud statute, i.e., any scheme contrary to public policy that involves deception can be prosecuted under the mail fraud statute if the mails are used in the execution of the scheme. Other cases have used accepted moral standards and notions of honesty and

fair play as setting the outer limits to the term "scheme to defraud." * * *

* * * As a result of the failure to limit the term "scheme or artifice to defraud" to common law definitions of fraud and false pretenses and schemes prohibited by State law, the mail fraud statute generally has been available to prosecute a scheme involving deception that employs the mails in its execution that is contrary to public policy and conflicts with accepted standards of moral uprightness, fundamental honesty, fair play and right dealing.

* * *

As to whether a scheme involving the bribery of a public official satisfies the fraud element of the mail fraud statute, the question has long since been answered in the affirmative. Although most mail fraud prosecutions of public officials that allege bribery also allege that a state bribery law or law prohibiting the taking of additional fees has been violated, such an allegation is not necessary to bring the alleged scheme within the purview of the mail fraud statute * * *.

[When a] public official is not exercising his independent judgment in passing on official matters * * * [a] fraud is perpetrated upon the public to whom the official owes fiduciary duties, e.g., honest, faithful and disinterested service. When a public official has been bribed, he breaches his duty of honest, faithful and disinterested service. While outwardly purporting to be exercising independent judgment in passing on official matters, the official has been paid for his decisions, perhaps without even considering the merits of the matter. Thus, the public is not receiving what it expects and is entitled to, the public official's honest and faithful service.

From the foregoing discussion, it is clear that the allegations contained in paragraphs 13(a) and (b) and 27 of count 1 of the indictment in this case constitute a scheme to defraud that is cognizable under § 1341. Those paragraphs essentially allege that Governor Mandel, in return for certain financial and other benefits, took certain positions on racetrack legislation that was before the Maryland legislature. This is a plain and simple bribery allegation; that Governor Mandel did not exercise his independent judgment on these legislative matters; rather, he was paid by some or all of the Appellants for the positions he took.

The question of whether non-disclosure or concealment, or both, of material information satisfies the fraud element of the mail fraud statute and, thus, is cognizable as a "scheme or artifice to defraud" under § 1341 is not as clear-cut as the bribery issue.

It should first be noted that a duty to disclose material information need not necessarily be based upon the existence of some statute or regulation prescribing such a duty. Rather, the duty to disclose may exist because of the relationship between the one possessing the material information and another * * *.

Although failure by a public official to disclose material information would constitute a breach of fiduciary duty, that breach, standing alone, could never be cognizable under the mail fraud statute, for the mail fraud statute only reaches schemes or artifices to defraud. Thus, the breach of fiduciary duty must be linked with some actionable fraud in order for the proscriptions of the mail fraud statute to apply.

There are two situations relevant to this case in which nondisclosure or concealment, or both, of material information may constitute actionable fraud under the mail fraud statute as well as a breach of fiduciary duties.[52] The first situation is where a public official fails to disclose the existence of a direct interest in a matter that he is passing on. Provided the requisite intent is shown, the official's failure to disclose the existence of a direct interest in a matter that he is passing on defrauds the public and pertinent public bodies of their intangible right to honest, loyal, faithful and disinterested government.

* * *

The other situation applicable here in which we think fraudulent non-disclosure or concealment of facts may be evidence to support a conviction under the mail fraud statute is when there has been a fraudulent statement of facts, or a deliberate concealment thereof, to a public body, in order to receive a benefit by action of the public body. The scheme to defraud can in such a case be said to encompass not only the receipt of the illicit benefit, but also the deprivation of the public of the right to have its officials act on other than false information.[53]

* * *

As these principles apply to the case at hand, it is apparent that the mail fraud case could have been submitted on either or both of two theories on the indictment and record now before us. First, that Governor Mandel had either been bribed as a part of a scheme to defraud or that attempts had been made to bribe Governor Mandel as a part of such scheme. Second, that false information was presented to, or true information concealed from, the Maryland General Assembly or Maryland Racing Commission, or both, in order to induce those bodies to take favorable action toward those interested in [the race tracks]. . . .[54]

---

52. [Court's footnote 11.] Of course, since fraud is a crime requiring specific intent, before non-disclosure or concealment of material information could be deemed actionable fraud cognizable under the mail fraud statute, a specific intent to defraud would have to be proven.

53. [Court's footnote 12.] At this point, we note that * * * we would not adopt the construction of the mail fraud statute . . . to the effect that pecuniary or property injury is necessary.

54. The remainder of the panel's opinion, reversing the conviction on a different ground, is omitted. On rehearing en banc, the Fourth Circuit reversed the panel and affirmed Mandel's conviction.

(4) *Unfaithful Employees.* Note the definition of a "scheme to defraud" enunciated in *Mandel:* one that is "contrary to public policy and conflicts with accepted standards of moral uprightness, fundamental honesty, fair play and right dealing." Consider this standard in connection with the employee behavior revealed in *United States v. Von Barta:* [55]

> In the instant case, we are asked to construe two seemingly limitless provisions, the mail and wire fraud statutes, in the context of the employer-employee relationship. The Government urges us to hold that these statutes are violated whenever an employee, acting to further a scheme for pecuniary gain, intentionally breaches a fiduciary duty of honesty or loyalty he owes his employer. The defendant decries this "overcriminalization" of the employment relationship, and asks us to declare his alleged conduct exempt from criminal sanction. While we reject the sweeping theory advanced by the Government, we find that the mail and wire fraud statutes do reach the conduct with which the defendant is charged. Accordingly, we reverse the district court's dismissal of the indictment.

* * *

> From 1976, until the indictment against him was filed in 1979, Von Barta was employed as a salesman and trader of government bonds at Malon S. Andrus, Inc. ("Andrus"), a small securities firm in New York City. When Von Barta was hired, he was admonished "never to jeopardize the firm's banking relationships and always to advise Mr. Andrus if the firm's repurchase agreements 'were in trouble.'" As this warning indicates, Von Barta enjoyed an especially powerful and trusted position at Andrus. He had considerable discretion to open new customer accounts, knowing his decisions in that regard would not be re-examined by another member of the firm.
>
> Von Barta conducted many of his trades with William Harty,[56] a salesman in the government securities department at Blyth Eastman Dillon & Co. ("Blyth"), a large New York brokerage firm. In or about July 1978, Harty formed the Piwacket Corp. ("Piwacket"), to which he and Von Barta each contributed $5,000 as their capital investment. They decided to use Piwacket as their vehicle for trading in government bonds, and agreed to share equally in any profits made by their corporation. Von Barta then opened an account for Piwacket with Andrus, without telling Mr. Andrus of Piwacket's meagre capitalization or of his involvement with the firm. Piwacket became one of Andrus's most active accounts, generating substantial commissions for both Andrus and Von

---

55. 635 F.2d 999 (2d Cir.1980), certiorari denied 450 U.S. 998, 101 S.Ct. 1703, 68 L.Ed.2d 199 (1981).

56. [Court's footnote 5.] Harty was named in the indictment returned against Von Barta as an unindicted "co-schemer." He was also charged in an information similar to the indictment filed against Von Barta, and pled guilty to those charges.

Barta. Piwacket ultimately speculated in government bonds worth more than $50 million, and incurred liabilities vastly in excess of the combined ability of Andrus and Piwacket to secure Piwacket's creditors against loss. The volume of Piwacket's trading attracted the attention of Andrus and Blyth, but Von Barta continued to conceal his involvement, falsely telling Mr. Andrus that Piwacket was an established Long Island arbitrageur and misrepresenting to Blyth that Harty was Piwacket's sole principal.

At first, Piwacket's trades were very successful, generating profits of nearly $200,000. Later, however, the bond market weakened. When Von Barta indicated that Piwacket could not cover its losses, Andrus terminated the Piwacket account. Piwacket's resultant insolvency forced Andrus and Blyth to bear a $2 million loss.

The Government alleges that by trading through Piwacket, Von Barta speculated in the government bond market using the fraudulently obtained credit of Blyth and Andrus. It charges further that by limiting Piwacket's liability to $10,000 (the amount of the capital investment), Von Barta attempted to shield himself from the risk accompanying his speculative transactions. In effect, the Government claims, Von Barta shifted the risk from himself to Andrus. If his trades were successful, he reaped the profit; if they failed, Andrus bore the loss. Finally, the Government charges that Von Barta concealed material information from Andrus. According to the Government, Andrus never would have allowed Von Barta to open or to continue trading in the Piwacket account had it known Piwacket was undercapitalized, that Von Barta was involved with the firm, or that neither Andrus nor Piwacket had sufficient assets to cover Piwacket's losses.

In setting out its theory of the indictment, the Government has repeatedly refused to rely on allegations that Von Barta intended to defraud Andrus of any tangible interest. Rather, the Government charges that "Von Barta, by abusing his fiduciary position as an employee of Andrus, and concealing material information, defrauded Andrus of its right to his honest and faithful services, as well as of its right to decide what business risks to bear with all the facts before it." Thus, we are asked to decide whether Von Barta's alleged scheme to defraud his employer of only these intangible interests violates the mail and wire fraud statutes.

* * *

* * * [I]t is now generally accepted that the object of the fraudulent scheme need not be the deprivation of a tangible interest. Artifices designed to cause losses of an intangible nature also violate the statute. * * *

Despite the broad language contained in some opinions, several courts have held that the breach of an employee's fiduciary duty, without more, does not violate the mail fraud statute. The additional element which frequently transforms a mere fiduciary breach into a criminal offense is a violation of the employee's duty to disclose material information to his employer. * * *

Our discussion is not to be construed as holding that an employee's duty to disclose material information to his employer must be imposed by state or federal statute. Indeed, the employment relationship, by itself, may oblige an employee not to conceal, and in fact to reveal, information he has reason to believe is material to the conduct of his employer's business.

In light of these precedents, and taking the facts as alleged by the Government, we have no difficulty holding that Von Barta was under a duty to apprise Andrus of material information concerning Piwacket's trading in government bonds. Von Barta was admonished to warn Mr. Andrus if the firm's repurchase agreements "were in trouble." But he said nothing upon opening an account for an allegedly undercapitalized firm, knowing, as an experienced trader for Andrus, that if Piwacket became insolvent, Andrus would be liable for any losses. Nor can we overlook the fact that by trading in millions of dollars, Von Barta exposed Andrus to liabilities greatly in excess of Andrus's limited ability to meet them. When Mr. Andrus became concerned, however, and inquired about Piwacket, Von Barta dissimulated, telling his employer that Piwacket was backed by credit worthy arbitrageurs from Long Island. Von Barta's alleged scheme to speculate in the bond market using Andrus's credit was eminently successful. At first, Von Barta pocketed nearly $100,000 from Piwacket's trades, but when the market collapsed, Andrus was left with nothing but a responsibility for heavy debts.

The Government's charges reveal that Von Barta's relationship with Andrus was special in several respects. Von Barta was advised to keep his employer informed of adverse market developments, and he occupied a position of great trust and considerable power, apparently possessing the authority to extend his employer's credit beyond Andrus's capacity to cover losses. These special circumstances are the source of Von Barta's duty of disclosure. Thus, we need not decide whether all employees risk prosecution for mail fraud if they fail to reveal material information to their employers. Nor must we express any opinion as to what constitutes material information. We simply hold that on the facts alleged by the Government, Von Barta's breach of his duty of disclosure subjects him to prosecution for mail fraud.

Accordingly, we reverse the district court's order dismissing the indictment, and remand for further proceedings not inconsistent with this opinion.

Query. Does the Court of Appeals decision in *Von Barta* suggest any limitations on what misrepresentations will constitute mail fraud? Why should there be any limitations? [57]

---

57. See generally Note, Intra–Corporate Mail and Wire Fraud: Criminal Liability for Fiduciary Breach, 94 Yale L.J. 1427 (1985); Coffee, From Tort to Crime: Some

(5) *Unfaithful Lawyers.* Consider *United States v. Bronston:* [58]

Mansfield, Circuit Judge:

Jack E. Bronston appeals from a judgment of the Southern District of New York entered after a jury trial before Judge Milton Pollack, convicting him of two counts of mail fraud, based on the government's allegations that he fraudulently violated his fiduciary duty as an attorney by helping to further the efforts of Convenience and Safety Corporation ("C & S") and Saul Steinberg, chairman of C & S, to obtain a bus stop shelter franchise from the City of New York at the same time when the law firm in which he was a partner, Rosenman, Colin, Freund, Lewis & Cohen ("Rosenman Colin"), was representing a group of investors in BusTop Shelters, Inc. ("BusTop"), the then current holder of the franchise and a participant in the competition for its renewal. We affirm. The evidence was sufficient to allow the jury to convict Bronston of mail fraud based on his breach of his duty of loyalty to his firm's clients, his concealment from the clients of his promotion to their harm of the interests of Steinberg and C & S in obtaining the franchise, his specific intent thereby to defraud his firm's client of the very economic value his firm had been retained to protect, and his mailing of two letters in furtherance of the fraudulent scheme.

On May 8, 1975, BusTop obtained an interim franchise from the City of New York to build and maintain shelters at bus stops over a three-year period. In the spring of 1977, as the end of the interim franchise was drawing near, BusTop began seeking outside capital with which it could expand its business and improve its chances of persuading the City that a 20-year renewal of its franchise was in order. After extensive negotiations, two venture capital companies, Citicorp Venture Capital Limited (a subsidiary of Citicorp) and Fifty-Third Street Ventures, Inc. (collectively "the investors" or "the minority investors"), tentatively agreed to make a substantial investment in BusTop. On June 1, 1977, the investors contacted Samuel ("Sandy") Lindenbaum, a partner in the Rosenman Colin firm, and retained the firm to advise them in making the investment.

At approximately the same time Jack Bronston, who was then a partner in the Rosenman Colin firm and a state senator from Queens, learned that his friend and client, Saul Steinberg, was also interested in retaining Rosenman Colin to assist him in his efforts to obtain the bus stop shelter franchise. Acting on Steinberg's behalf, Bronston met with Lindenbaum on May 17, 1977, to tell him that Steinberg wanted to retain Rosenman Colin to represent him in his bus stop shelter endeavors, and that he wanted Lindenbaum to appear on his behalf before the Board of Estimate. Lindenbaum immediately declined to undertake the representation,

---

Reflections on the Criminalization of Fiduciary Breaches and the Problematic Line Between Law and Ethics, 19 Am.Crim.L. Rev. 117 (1981).

[58]. 658 F.2d 920 (2d Cir.1981), certiorari denied 456 U.S. 915, 102 S.Ct. 1769, 72 L.Ed.2d 174 (1982). Judge Van Graafeiland's dissenting opinion is omitted.

however, because, although BusTop was not itself a client of Rosenman Colin (and the representation of the minority investors had not yet begun), Lindenbaum did not feel he could work against BusTop, in view of his personal friendships with BusTop's public relations consultant and attorney. Despite this reaction from Lindenbaum, Bronston went ahead on Steinberg's behalf and had a Rosenman Colin associate set up a Delaware corporate shell under the name of "Convenience and Safety Corporation," which would serve as Steinberg's vehicle in the bus stop shelter competition. C & S was incorporated on June 2, 1977.

On June 9, 1977, Bronston, by this time aware that Rosenman Colin had been retained as counsel by the BusTop investors, wrote a memorandum to his firm's new business committee, suggesting that the firm take on the representation of C & S

> "which will serve as an investment vehicle for the erection of public bus shelters in New York City, Philadelphia, Chicago and Seattle. This may involve conflict with other clients of the office and should be discussed."

Murray Cohen, a member of the committee, was the first to receive Bronston's memo, and immediately returned it to him with the notation: "We should not do anything further on this until Sandy [Lindenbaum], you and I talk about it. There is a definite conflict." At trial, Cohen testified that at a subsequent meeting with Bronston and Lindenbaum he told Bronston that the firm could not represent C & S because its interests were "inimical" to those of the investors in BusTop. The situation was described by Cohen:

> "The investors were proposing to invest, over a period of time, $1,300,000 in BusTop and obviously were counting on BusTop obtaining a renewal of its franchise, and Convenience and Safety was going to be a competitor of BusTop for that franchise and, therefore, if we were successful on behalf of Convenience and Safety, we would have jeopardized the financial investment of the investors in BusTop."

Despite this clear response from Cohen rejecting his proposal that the firm accept the C & S representation, Bronston went back to Cohen on July 5, and proposed that he authorize the establishment of a client billing number for C & S "just in case at some time in the future something developed in which there was not a conflict." Cohen acceded to Bronston's request, but expressly instructed him that no work was to be performed on behalf of C & S without his prior approval. The memorandum written by Bronston to the firm's bookkeeper makes it clear that Bronston understood the very limited nature of Cohen's acquiescence:

> "This new matter memorandum has been approved by Murray Cohen subject to the understanding that no further work will be performed on this matter without his explicit consent."

In August, 1977, representation of C & S's effort to acquire the New York City franchise was transferred to the law firm of Stein Rosen & Ohrenstein.

Thus, no later than June 9, 1977, the Rosenman Colin firm had made the decision to represent the BusTop investors rather than C & S in the competition for New York City's bus stop shelter franchise, and this decision had been authoritatively communicated to Jack Bronston. For the next two months Rosenman Colin attorneys labored on behalf of the minority investors in negotiating the exact terms of their participation in BusTop. * * *

At the same time when these efforts were being made by Rosenman Colin lawyers on behalf of the BusTop investors, Bronston was secretly continuing his relationship with C & S. At the first meeting of C & S's board of directors, on June 17, 1977, Bronston was elected to a one-year term as the corporation's assistant secretary. On 15 separate occasions between August 25, 1977, and February 6, 1978, Bronston met with Steinberg and later filled out time tickets at his law firm indicating that the time spent was billable to C & S.[59] Bronston's time tickets reflected an additional half dozen meetings with other C & S officials during this same period, with the time recorded as billable to C & S.

Despite the fact that the legal representation of C & S's efforts to obtain the New York City franchise was formally transferred to Stein Rosen & Ohrenstein in August, 1977, Bronston continued thereafter to attend meetings at which C & S business in New York was discussed, and was kept informed about the progress of the C & S bid. Important internal documents dealing with the New York bid prepared by C & S or by lawyers for Stein Rosen were routinely sent to Bronston, occasionally by messenger. Finally, the billing records of David Simpson, the Stein Rosen partner principally responsible for the C & S account, indicated that on at least six occasions between December, 1977, and June, 1978, Bronston participated in conference calls or meetings which Simpson billed to C & S.

There was also evidence that, during the period when Bronston was secretly working in the interests of C & S against those of BusTop and his firm's clients, Lindenbaum was meeting with the clients (Venture Capital and Fifty-Third Street Ventures), was actively engaged in negotiating their agreement to invest in Bus-Top, was unaware of Bronston's activities on behalf of C & S, and was conferring with Bronston with respect to the clients' investment in BusTop. These conferences were billed by Lindenbaum to the clients. At the same time Bronston made out tickets to bill C & S for time spent in discussing with Steinberg Bronston's conver-

---

59. [Court's footnote 3.] At no time was any bill based on these time tickets sent to C & S. This may have been due to the fact that under firm billing procedures Bronston could not bill C & S directly, since all bills were screened by the firm's billing committee prior to transmittal.

sations with Lindenbaum. Billing records reveal that some of these Lindenbaum–Bronston meetings which were followed by Bronston–Steinberg conferences occurred at points of critical importance to the clients and to C & S in pursuing their competing and conflicting interests. For instance, on October 21, 1977, the day after the New York City Board of Estimate was to consider BusTop's application for the bus stop franchise, Lindenbaum and Bronston had a one-hour breakfast discussion which Lindenbaum billed to the BusTop investors as clients. Three hours later Bronston had a 2½-hour meeting with Steinberg and others which he noted for billing to C & S. His firm's clients, the BusTop investors, were not informed of his activities on behalf of C & S in conflict with their interests.

The indictment against Bronston charged him with two counts of mail fraud, growing out of the sending of two letters allegedly intended to increase C & S's chances of wresting the New York bus stop shelter franchise from BusTop. The first count involved a letter sent by Stein Rosen on C & S's behalf to the members of the New York City Board of Estimate. The letter was prepared after Bronston had met with Steinberg and Samuel Stein of Stein Rosen on August 25, 1977. It was decided at that meeting that a letter should be sent to the Board publicly announcing C & S's interest in presenting to the City a plan for building and operating bus stop shelters, and introducing Stein Rosen as counsel for C & S. The letter was drafted by Stein Rosen lawyers, but before it was sent a copy of the draft was hand-delivered to Steinberg for review. Steinberg went over the letter with Bronston, and Bronston then telephoned Stein at Stein Rosen to let him know that he thought it was a good letter. Bronston then noted to bill C & S for five hours of services on August 25, specifically including his "review of letter with Saul Steinberg." He also noted an additional half hour spent on C & S business on August 26 for his telephone conference with "Sam Stein re letter." When the City subsequently responded to the August 26 letter, Bronston participated in a meeting with Steinberg and Stein to evaluate the response, and filled out a time ticket in the name of C & S for the time spent.

The second count grew out of a letter which Bronston himself drafted and sent on his official New York State Senate stationery to Richard Wells, Executive Assistant to New York City Comptroller Goldin, on October 28, 1977. In relevant part, the letter read as follows:

> "I enclose some figures in connection with the existing franchise which I am sure you have, but which I would like to reiterate. Obviously, a renewal of the existing franchise would not appear to be in the public interest since it might be taken for a reward for non-performance."

The enclosure consisted of a one-page summary of the status of the BusTop's performance under the interim franchise, emphasizing BusTop's failure to comply with the terms of the agreement. * * * The letter was typed on Bronston's official Senate stationery by his Rosenman Colin secretary and was mailed by her with the enclosure. Bronston then noted to bill C & S for a "letter to Richard Wells."

For its services to the BusTop investors Rosenman Colin billed approximately $52,000, which the investors paid without being aware that Bronston had been working for Steinberg and C & S and against their interests. In addition, there was evidence at trial from which the jury could have inferred that Bronston was paid $12,500 by Steinberg for his efforts on behalf of C & S. On December 9, 1977, Bronston wrote to Steinberg, detailing his time charges to date and indicating that he would not ask for payment "until you and your partners decide on a format through which this can be done." On June 28, 1978, Bronston received a personal check from Steinberg (which was never recorded on C & S's books) for $12,500, the precise amount which Bronston had previously estimated to Rosenman Colin as the retainer that would be forthcoming in 1978 if the C & S representation were accepted.[60]

* * *

DISCUSSION

Bronston's principal contention is that in order to show a violation of the mail fraud statute based on a fraudulent breach of fiduciary duty, the government must prove that the defendant used his breach in some way that would benefit himself or harm the victim of the fraud and that the trial judge erred in failing to instruct the jury accordingly. Under this test, Bronston argues, the conviction must be reversed since the evidence was insufficient to permit the jury to find that he used his fiduciary status as a partner of Rosenman Colin to benefit himself or C & S at the expense of the BusTop investors. We disagree.

Although a mere breach of fiduciary duty, standing alone, may not necessarily constitute a mail fraud, the concealment by a fiduciary of material information which he is under a duty to disclose to another under circumstances where the non-disclosure could or does result in harm to the other is a violation of the statute. United States v. Von Barta, 635 F.2d 999 (2d Cir.1980); * * * As we noted in *Von Barta*, supra, proof that the fiduciary relationship was used or manipulated in some way is not necessary.

* * *

In the present case the indictment charged that Bronston, in disregard of the fiduciary duty he owed as a member of the

---

60. [Court's footnote 4.] * * * At trial, defense counsel introduced in evidence a check from Bronston to Steinberg for $12,500 dated July 19, 1978, and marked "repayment of exchange."

Rosenman Colin firm to the BusTop investors and for the purpose of benefiting Steinberg and C & S to their detriment, promoted the interests of Steinberg and C & S in their efforts to obtain a bus shelter franchise from the City of New York and "did conceal from, and fail to disclose to, the BusTop minority investors and BusTop the fact that he was advising and promoting the interests of Steinberg and C & S." These allegations, coupled with the charge that Rosenman Colin received $50,000 from BusTop for services to it, that Bronston received a check for $12,500 from Steinberg for promoting the interests of Steinberg and C & S with the intent of harming BusTop, and that Bronston caused two letters to be mailed in furtherance of the scheme, were sufficient to state a violation of the mail fraud statute.

Applying these standards, the evidence before the jury was sufficient to support a conviction for the alleged mail fraud. It is clear beyond doubt that as a member of the Rosenman Colin firm Bronston owed a fiduciary duty to its clients, the BusTop investors, and that in promoting the interests of Steinberg and C & S in competition and conflict with those of his firm's clients, Bronston violated that duty. DR5–105, Code of Professional Responsibility. Having retained the Rosenman Colin firm as their counsel, the BusTop investors were entitled to the undivided loyalty of its partners.

* * *

The element of concealment of a material fact, necessary to prove the alleged scheme to defraud, was also established. At no time did Bronston reveal to the BusTop investors that he was working hand in glove with Steinberg and C & S to obtain the franchise for C & S to their detriment. The materiality of this fact is self-evident. This was no mere technical failure on a law firm's part to disclose all potential conflicts of interest to its clients. One can imagine few nondisclosures more crucial to an attorney-client relationship than the fact that the law firm which the client has retained is actively engaged in efforts designed to frustrate the precise endeavor which the client had engaged the firm to pursue.

The record is equally clear that the scheme to defraud BusTop and its investors of the bus stop shelter franchise was designed to inflict actual economic harm on the BusTop investors and was capable of doing so. * * *

* * * In any event, as alleged in the indictment, Bronston, by means of his fraudulent conduct, benefited to the extent of receiving a check for $12,500 from Steinberg which was returned only after his fraudulent activities were discovered by his firm's clients, and, in addition to the prospective harm the clients faced from BusTop's potential loss of the franchise, they suffered actual loss to the extent of paying the Rosenman Colin firm as their counsel $52,000 for undivided loyalty which they did not receive. Moreover, although use or manipulation of Bronston's breach of fiduciary relationship was not a prerequisite to conviction, the proof that Bronston, immediately following a conference with Lindenbaum regarding their clients' investment in BusTop, discussed the conversation with Steinberg provided the basis for an inference that such activity occurred. * * *

Finally, the evidence at trial was sufficient to support the jurisdictional predicate contained in the mail fraud statute that the defendant be found to have "place[d] in any post office or authorized depository for mail matter, any matter or thing whatever to be sent or delivered by the Postal Service," in furtherance of his fraudulent scheme. The letter which Bronston drafted and had sent to Richard Wells falls within the statutory language, as Bronston seems to concede. While it is true that Bronston's participation in the preparation and mailing of the letter to the members of the Board of Estimate was less active, it was sufficient under the cases to support conviction. * * *

Bronston argues that a decision upholding his conviction "would render every disloyal or ethically questionable act which is accompanied by the mailing of a letter a crime." We disagree. Although a hypothetical can be posed in which one could be prosecuted for mail fraud on the basis of a breach of fiduciary duty accompanied by little more than a failure to disclose the breach to the person to whom the duty was owed, without any prospect of substantial economic harm to the victim, this is not such a case. Here we are faced with a straight-forward economic fraud in which the object of the scheme was not merely to deprive the victims of a law firm's undivided loyalty, for which they paid $52,000, but to deprive BusTop and its minority investors of the BusTop franchise. A partner in a law firm used the mails with the specific intent of defrauding one of his firm's own clients of the precise interest which it had been retained to defend. This falls within the ambit of the mail fraud statute.

* * *

Queries. Under the Court of Appeals' decision, how could Bronston have avoided criminal liability? Would there have been a crime had Bronston disclosed to his partners his representation of C & S and then set up a "Chinese Wall" to screen himself from any information about BusTop (a common practice when a lawyer in a firm has a personal conflict, e.g., prior involvement as a government official with a particular case or client)? Would there have been a crime if Bronston's law firm routinely obtained the written permission of its clients to represent conflicting interests? Under *McNally,* could Bronston have been convicted on the same evidence? Does your answer depend on whether BusTop or C & S received the franchise?

(6) *Corporate Mail Fraud.* Consider *United States v. Procter & Gamble Co.:* [61]

> Six of the defendants have filed demurrers to the indictment * * *. These defendants are Procter & Gamble Company, The Procter & Gamble Distributing Company, The Procter & Gamble Manufacturing Company, Raymond J. Lamping, D. Paul Smelser, and Cleo W. Knappenberger. * * *
>
> The six demurrers * * * attack the indictment on the principal ground that the offenses charged therein are not schemes to defraud within the meaning of 18 U.S.C.A. § 338. * * *
>
> Broadly, "fraud" has been defined as "any artifice whereby he who practises it gains, or attempts to gain, some undue advantage to himself, or to work some wrong or do some injury to another, by means of a representation which he knows to be false, or of an act which he knows to be against right or in violation of some positive duty." * * * "To try to delimit 'fraud' by definition would tend to reward subtle and ingenious circumvention and is not done."
>
> The alleged scheme to defraud covered by the counts of this indictment consists of the payment of gratuities or bribes by the defendant Procter & Gamble Company, its subsidiaries and agents, to certain employees of Lever Brothers Company in exchange for which the employees obtained from their employer possession of certain experimental cakes of soap, secret processes, formulas, facts and figures, etc., belonging to Lever Brothers Company, which they turned over to the Procter & Gamble Company, its agents and subsidiaries.
>
> The normal relationship of employer and employee implies that the employee will be loyal and honest in all his actions with or on behalf of his employer, and that he will not wrongfully divulge to others the confidential information, trade secrets, etc., belonging to his employer. See Restatement of the Law of Agency, Section 395, Comment: a. and b.; * * *. When one tampers with that relationship for the purpose of causing the employee to breach his duty he in effect is defrauding the employer of a lawful right. The actual deception that is practised is in the continued representation of the employee to the employer that he is honest and loyal to the employer's interests. The employee, in using the employment relationship for the express purpose of carrying out a scheme to obtain his employer's confidential information and other property, as alleged in the indictment, would be guilty of deliberately producing a false impression on his employer in order to cheat him. Such conduct would constitute a positive fraud * * *.

Query. Reconsider the discussion in *Dowling,* supra p. 33, detailing the caution shown by Congress with regard to imposing criminal liability on the unauthorized use of information "owned" by someone

---

61. 47 F.Supp. 676 (D.Mass.1942).

else. In light of this general policy, is it proper to use the mail fraud statute in a case like *Procter & Gamble*, particularly where the underlying "theft" of trade secrets is not criminally punishable under federal law (although it may give rise to civil or criminal liability under state law [62])?

(7) *Interpreting McNally.* The Supreme Court's first opportunity to interpret *McNally* [63] came in *Carpenter v. United States*, 484 U.S. 19, 108 S.Ct. 316, 98 L.Ed.2d 275 (1987):

Justice White delivered the opinion of the Court.

Petitioners Kenneth Felis and R. Foster Winans were convicted of violating . . . the federal mail and wire fraud statutes, and were convicted for conspiracy under 18 U.S.C. § 371. Petitioner David Carpenter, Winans' roommate, was convicted for aiding and abetting. . . .

I

In 1981, Winans became a reporter for the Wall Street Journal (the Journal) and in the summer of 1982 became one of the two writers of a daily column, "Heard on the Street." That column discussed selected stocks or groups of stocks, giving positive and negative information about those stocks and taking "a point of view with respect to investment in the stocks that it reviews." Winans regularly interviewed corporate executives to put together interesting perspectives on the stocks that would be highlighted in upcoming columns, but, at least for the columns at issue here, none contained corporate inside information or any "hold for release" information. Because of the "Heard" column's perceived quality and integrity, it had the potential of affecting the price of the stocks which it examined. The District Court concluded on the basis of testimony presented at trial that the "Heard" column "does have an impact on the market, difficult though it may be to quantify in any particular case."

The official policy and practice at the Journal was that prior to publication, the contents of the column were the Journal's confidential information. Despite the rule, with which Winans was familiar, he entered into a scheme in October 1983 with Peter Brant and

---

62. For a review of state legislation, see Epstein, Criminal Liability for the Misappropriation of Trade Secrets, in 12 B Business Organizations, Milgrim on Trade Secrets App. B–5 (1979).

63. For lower court interpretations, compare, e.g., United States v. Holzer, 840 F.2d 1343 (7th Cir.1988) (reversing conviction of judge convicted under intangible rights doctrine for accepting bribes; rejects argument that judge is "constructive trustee" for bribe and therefore deprived state of property right) with United States v. Runnels, 833 F.2d 1183 (6th Cir.1987) (accepting constructive trust argument) and United States v. Fagan, 821 F.2d 1002 (5th Cir.1987) (employee acceptance of kickbacks; employer had property right in control over money paid to supplier who might have taken lower price), certiorari denied ___ U.S. ___, 108 S.Ct. 697, 98 L.Ed.2d 649 (1988). Governor Mandel sought to have his conviction vacated and his fine returned on the basis of *McNally*, although he had already served his sentence. He was successful. See United States v. Mandel, 862 F.2d 1067 (4th Cir.1988).

petitioner Felis, both connected with the Kidder Peabody brokerage firm in New York City, to give them advance information as to the timing and contents of the "Heard" column. This permitted Brant and Felis and another conspirator, David Clark, a client of Brant, to buy or sell based on the probable impact of the column on the market. Profits were to be shared. The conspirators agreed that the scheme would not affect the journalistic purity of the "Heard" column, and the District Court did not find that the contents of any of the articles were altered to further the profit potential of petitioners' stocktrading scheme. Over a four-month period, the brokers made prepublication trades on the basis of information given them by Winans about the contents of some 27 Heard columns. The net profits from these trades were about $690,000.

In November 1983, correlations between the "Heard" articles and trading in the Clark and Felis accounts were noted at Kidder Peabody and inquiries began. Brant and Felis denied knowing anyone at the Journal and took steps to conceal the trades. Later, the Securities and Exchange Commission began an investigation. Questions were met by denials both by the brokers at Kidder Peabody and by Winans at the Journal. As the investigation progressed, the conspirators quarreled, and on March 29, 1984, Winans and Carpenter went to the SEC and revealed the entire scheme. This indictment and a bench trial followed. Brant, who had pled guilty under a plea agreement, was a witness for the Government.

The District Court found, and the Court of Appeals agreed, that Winans had knowingly breached a duty of confidentiality by misappropriating prepublication information regarding the timing and contents of the "Heard" columns, information that had been gained in the course of his employment under the understanding that it would not be revealed in advance of publication and that if it were, he would report it to his employer. It was this appropriation of confidential information that underlay . . . [the] mail and wire fraud counts. . . .

In affirming the mail and wire fraud convictions, the Court of Appeals ruled that Winans had fraudulently misappropriated "property" within the meaning of the mail and wire fraud statutes and that its revelation had harmed the Journal. It was held as well that the use of the mail and wire services had a sufficient nexus with the scheme to satisfy §§ 1341 and 1343. The petition for certiorari challenged these conclusions.

* * *

II

Petitioners assert that their activities were not a scheme to defraud the Journal within the meaning of the mail and wire fraud statutes; and that in any event, they did not obtain any "money or property" from the Journal, which is a necessary element of the crime under our decision last Term in McNally v. United States, 483 U.S. 350, 107 S.Ct. 2875, 97 L.Ed.2d 292 (1987). We are unpersuaded by either submission and address the latter first.

We held in *McNally* that the mail fraud statute does not reach "schemes to defraud citizens of their intangible rights to honest and impartial government," and that the statute is "limited in scope to the protection of property rights." Petitioners argue that the Journal's interest in prepublication confidentiality for the "Heard" columns is no more than an intangible consideration outside the reach of § 1341; nor does that law, it is urged, protect against mere injury to reputation. This is not a case like *McNally*, however. The Journal, as Winans' employer, was defrauded of much more than its contractual right to his honest and faithful service, an interest too ethereal in itself to fall within the protection of the mail fraud statute, which "had its origin in the desire to protect individual property rights." *McNally*, supra, at ——, n. 8, 107 S.Ct., at 2881, n. 8. Here, the object of the scheme was to take the Journal's confidential business information—the publication schedule and contents of the "Heard" column—and its intangible nature does not make it any less "property" protected by the mail and wire fraud statutes. *McNally* did not limit the scope of § 1341 to tangible as distinguished from intangible property rights.

Both courts below expressly referred to the Journal's interest in the confidentiality of the contents and timing of the "Heard" column as a property right, and we agree with that conclusion. Confidential business information has long been recognized as property. "Confidential information acquired or compiled by a corporation in the course and conduct of its business is a species of property to which the corporation has the exclusive right and benefit, and which a court of equity will protect through the injunctive process or other appropriate remedy." 3 W. Fletcher, Cyclopedia of Law of Private Corporations § 857.1, p. 260 (rev. ed. 1986) (footnote omitted). The Journal had a property right in keeping confidential and making exclusive use, prior to publication, of the schedule and contents of the "Heard" columns. As the Court has observed before:

> "[N]ews matter, however little susceptible of ownership or dominion in the absolute sense, is stock in trade, to be gathered at the cost of enterprise, organization, skill, labor, and money, and to be distributed and sold to those who will pay money for it, as for any other merchandise." International News Service v. Associated Press, 248 U.S. 215, 236, 39 S.Ct. 68, 71, 63 L.Ed. 211 (1918).

Petitioners' arguments that they did not interfere with the Journal's use of the information or did not publicize it and deprive the Journal of the first public use of it miss the point. The confidential information was generated from the business and the business had a right to decide how to use it prior to disclosing it to the public. Petitioners cannot successfully contend based on *Associated Press* that a scheme to defraud requires a monetary loss, such as giving the information to a competitor; it is sufficient that the Journal has been deprived of its right to exclusive use of the information, for exclusivity is an important aspect of confidential business information and most private property for that matter.

We cannot accept petitioners' further argument that Winans' conduct in revealing prepublication information was no more than a violation of workplace rules and did not amount to fraudulent activity that is proscribed by the mail fraud statute. Sections 1341 and 1343 reach any scheme to deprive another of money or property by means of false or fraudulent pretenses, representations, or promises. As we observed last Term in *McNally*, the words "to defraud" in the mail fraud statute have the "common understanding" of " 'wronging one in his property rights by dishonest methods or schemes,' and 'usually signify the deprivation of something of value by trick, deceit, chicane or overreaching.' " The concept of "fraud" includes the act of embezzlement, which is " 'the fraudulent appropriation to one's own use of the money or goods entrusted to one's care by another.' " Grin v. Shine, 187 U.S. 181, 189, 23 S.Ct. 98, 101, 47 L.Ed. 130 (1902).

The District Court found that Winans' undertaking at the Journal was not to reveal prepublication information about his column, a promise that became a sham when in violation of his duty he passed along to his co-conspirators confidential information belonging to the Journal, pursuant to an ongoing scheme to share profits from trading in anticipation of the "Heard" column's impact on the stock market. In Snepp v. United States, 444 U.S. 507, 515, n. 11, 100 S.Ct. 763, 768, n. 11, 62 L.Ed.2d 704 (1980) (per curiam), although a decision grounded in the provisions of a written trust agreement prohibiting the unapproved use of confidential government information, we noted the similar prohibitions of the common law, that "even in the absence of a written contract, an employee has a fiduciary obligation to protect confidential information obtained during the course of his employment." As the New York courts have recognized, "It is well established, as a general proposition, that a person who acquires special knowledge or information by virtue of a confidential or fiduciary relationship with another is not free to exploit that knowledge or information for his own personal benefit but must account to his principal for any profits derived therefrom." Diamond v. Oreamuno, 24 N.Y.2d 494, 497, 301 N.Y.S.2d 78, 80, 248 N.E.2d 910, 912 (1969); see also Restatement (Second) of Agency §§ 388, Comment *c*, 396(c) (1958).

We have little trouble in holding that the conspiracy here to trade on the Journal's confidential information is not outside the reach of the mail and wire fraud statutes, provided the other elements of the offenses are satisfied. The Journal's business information that it intended to be kept confidential was its property; the declaration to that effect in the employee manual merely removed any doubts on that score and made the finding of specific intent to defraud that much easier. Winans continued in the employ of the Journal, appropriating its confidential business information for his own use, all the while pretending to perform his duty of safeguarding it. In fact, he told his editors twice about leaks of confidential information not related to the stock-trading scheme, demonstrating both his knowledge that the Journal viewed information concerning the "Heard" column as confidential and his deceit as he played the role of a loyal employee. Furthermore, the District Court's conclusion that each of the petitioners acted with the required specific intent to defraud is strongly supported by the evidence.

Lastly, we reject the submission that using the wires and the mail to print and send the Journal to its customers did not satisfy the requirement that those mediums be used to execute the scheme at issue. The courts below were quite right in observing that circulation of the "Heard" column was not only anticipated but an essential part of the scheme. Had the column not been made available to Journal customers, there would have been no effect on stock prices and no likelihood of profiting from the information leaked by Winans.

The judgment below is *Affirmed.*

Query. Does *Carpenter* indicate that *McNally* will be liberally read? Could Bronston have been convicted under *Carpenter*? Could Von Barta?

(8) *Congress Decides.* On November 18, 1988, the Anti–Drug Abuse Act of 1988 was enacted into law. It includes the following provision: [64]

> For the purposes of this chapter [which includes mail fraud, wire fraud, and bank fraud], the term "scheme or artifice to defraud" includes a scheme or artifice to deprive another of the intangible right of honest services.

Senator Biden, explaining this provision on the floor of the Senate, stated: [65]

> This section overturns the decision in McNally v. United States in which the Supreme Court held that the mail and wire fraud statutes protect property but not intangible rights. Under the amendment, those statutes will protect any person's intangible

---

64. Pub.L. 100–690, § 7603, 102 Stat. 4508 (1988).

65. 134 Cong.Rec. S17360, 17376 (Nov. 10, 1988). Rep. Conyers drafted this provision as a substitute for one previously introduced by Senator Biden. Both proposals came at the end of the 100th Congress, and did not receive extensive legislative attention. For a description, see Franklin, "McNally: A Dead Letter?", N.Y.L.J., Oct. 27, 1988, p. 5. For criticism, see Rakoff, "Congressional Macho," N.Y.L.J., Nov. 17, 1988, p. 3.

right to the honest services of another, including the right of the public to the honest services of public officials. The intent is to reinstate all of the pre-*McNally* caselaw pertaining to the mail and wire fraud statutes without change.

Queries. Do you agree that the language will do what its drafters say it is intended to do? What does "honest services" mean (the legislation doesn't define the term)? How would the language apply to the defendants in *McNally* itself? To the defendants in the other intangible rights cases in this section? Would you have voted for this bill? Do you think we are now through with the intangible rights controversy?

CHIARELLA v. UNITED STATES
Supreme Court of the United States, 1980.
445 U.S. 222, 100 S.Ct. 1108, 63 L.Ed.2d 348.

MR. JUSTICE POWELL delivered the opinion of the Court.

The question in this case is whether a person who learns from the confidential documents of one corporation that it is planning an attempt to secure control of a second corporation violates § 10(b) of the Securities Exchange Act of 1934 if he fails to disclose the impending takeover before trading in the target company's securities.

I

Petitioner is a printer by trade. In 1975 and 1976, he worked as a "markup man" in the New York composing room of Pandick Press, a financial printer. Among documents that petitioner handled were five announcements of corporate takeover bids. When these documents were delivered to the printer, the identities of the acquiring and target corporations were concealed by blank spaces or false names. The true names were sent to the printer on the night of the final printing.

The petitioner, however, was able to deduce the names of the target companies before the final printing from other information contained in the documents. Without disclosing his knowledge, petitioner purchased stock in the target companies and sold the shares immediately after the takeover attempts were made public. By this method, petitioner realized a gain of slightly more than $30,000 in the course of 14 months. Subsequently, the Securities and Exchange Commission (Commission or SEC) began an investigation of his trading activities. In May 1977, petitioner entered into a consent decree with the Commission in which he agreed to return his profits to the sellers of the shares. On the same day, he was discharged by Pandick Press.

In January 1978, petitioner was indicted on 17 counts of violating § 10(b) of the Securities Exchange Act of 1934 (1934 Act) and SEC Rule

10b–5.[66] After petitioner unsuccessfully moved to dismiss the indictment, he was brought to trial and convicted on all counts.

The Court of Appeals for the Second Circuit affirmed petitioner's conviction. We granted certiorari, and we now reverse.

II

Section 10(b) of the 1934 Act, 15 U.S.C. § 78j, prohibits the use "in connection with the purchase or sale of any security .. [of] any manipulative or deceptive device or contrivance in contravention of such rules and regulations as the Commission may prescribe." Pursuant to this section, the SEC promulgated Rule 10b–5 which provides in pertinent part [67] that

> "It shall be unlawful for any person, directly or indirectly, by the use of any means or instrumentality of interstate commerce, or of the mails or of any facility of any national securities exchange,
>
> "(a) To employ any device, scheme, or artifice to defraud, [or]
>
> . . .
>
> "(c) To engage in any act, practice, or course of business which operates or would operate as a fraud or a deceit upon any person, in connection with the purchase or sale of any security." 17 CFR § 240.10b–5 (1979).

This case concerns the legal effect of the petitioner's silence. The District Court's charge permitted the jury to convict the petitioner if it found that he willfully failed to inform sellers of target company securities that he knew of a forthcoming takeover bid that would make their shares more valuable. In order to decide whether silence in such circumstances violates § 10(b), it is necessary to review the language and legislative history of that statute as well as its interpretation by the Commission and the federal courts.

Although the starting point of our inquiry is the language of the statute, § 10(b) does not state whether silence may constitute a manipulative or deceptive device. Section 10(b) was designed as a catchall clause to prevent fraudulent practices. But neither the legislative history nor the statute itself affords specific guidance for the resolution of this case. When Rule 10b–5 was promulgated in 1942, the SEC did not discuss the possibility that failure to provide information might run afoul of § 10(b).

66. [Court's footnote 3.] Section 32(a) of the 1934 Act sanctions criminal penalties against any person who willfully violates the Act. 15 U.S.C.A. § 78ff(a) (1972–1978 Supp.). Petitioner was charged with 17 counts of violating the Act because he had received 17 letters confirming purchase of shares.

67. [Court's footnote 5.] Only Rules 10b–5(a) and (c) are at issue here. Rule 10b–5(b) provides that it shall be unlawful "[t]o make any untrue statement of a material fact or to omit to state a material fact necessary in order to make the statements made, in the light of the circumstances under which they were made, not misleading." 17 CFR § 240.10b–5(b) (1979). The portion of the indictment based on this provision was dismissed because the petitioner made no statements at all in connection with the purchase of stock.

The SEC took an important step in the development of § 10(b) when it held that a broker-dealer and his firm violated that section by selling securities on the basis of undisclosed information obtained from a director of the issuer corporation who was also a registered representative of the brokerage firm. In Cady, Roberts & Co., 40 S.E.C. 907 (1961), the Commission decided that a corporate insider must abstain from trading in the shares of his corporation unless he has first disclosed all material inside information known to him. * * *

That the relationship between a corporate insider and the stockholders of his corporation gives rise to a disclosure obligation is not a novel twist of the law. At common law, misrepresentation made for the purpose of inducing reliance upon the false statement is fraudulent. But one who fails to disclose material information prior to the consummation of a transaction commits fraud only when he is under a duty to do so. And the duty to disclose arises when one party has information "that the other [party] is entitled to know because of a fiduciary or similar relation of trust and confidence between them." In its *Cady, Roberts* decision, the Commission recognized a relationship of trust and confidence between the shareholders of a corporation and those insiders who have obtained confidential information by reason of their position with that corporation. This relationship gives rise to a duty to disclose because of the "necessity of preventing a corporate insider from [taking] . . . unfair advantage of the uninformed minority stockholders."

The Federal courts have found violations of § 10(b) where corporate insiders used undisclosed information for their own benefit. E.g., SEC v. Texas Gulf Sulphur Co., 401 F.2d 833 (CA2 1968), cert. denied, 404 U.S. 1005, 92 S.Ct. 561, 30 L.Ed.2d 558 (1972). The cases also have emphasized, in accordance with the common-law rule, that "[t]he party charged with failing to disclose market information must be under a duty to disclose it." * * *

* * *

Thus, administrative and judicial interpretations have established that silence in connection with the purchase or sale of securities may operate as a fraud actionable under § 10(b) despite the absence of statutory language or legislative history specifically addressing the legality of nondisclosure. But such liability is premised upon a duty to disclose arising from a relationship of trust and confidence between parties to a transaction. Application of a duty to disclose prior to trading guarantees that corporate insiders, who have an obligation to place the shareholder's welfare before their own, will not benefit personally through fraudulent use of material nonpublic information.

III

In this case, the petitioner was convicted of violating § 10(b) although he was not a corporate insider and he received no confidential information from the target company. Moreover, the "market information" upon which he relied did not concern the earning power or operations of the target company, but only the plans of the acquiring company. Petitioner's use of that information was not a fraud under § 10(b) unless he was subject to an affirmative duty to disclose it before trading. In this case, the jury instructions failed to specify any such duty. In effect, the trial court instructed the jury that petitioner owed a duty to everyone; to all sellers, indeed, to the market as a whole. The jury simply was told to decide whether petitioner used material, nonpublic information at a time when "he knew other people trading in the securities market did not have access to the same information."

The Court of Appeals affirmed the conviction by holding that "[a]nyone—corporate insider or not—who regularly receives material nonpublic information may not use that information to trade in securities without incurring an affirmative duty to disclose." Although the court said that its test would include only persons who regularly receive material nonpublic information, its rationale for that limitation is unrelated to the existence of a duty to disclose. The Court of Appeals, like the trial court, failed to identify a relationship between petitioner and the sellers that could give rise to a duty. Its decision thus rested solely upon its belief that the federal securities laws have "created a system providing equal access to information necessary for reasoned and intelligent investment decisions." The use by anyone of material information not generally available is fraudulent, this theory suggests, because such information gives certain buyers or sellers an unfair advantage over less informed buyers and sellers.

This reasoning suffers from two defects. First not every instance of financial unfairness constitutes fraudulent activity under § 10(b). Second, the element required to make silence fraudulent—a duty to disclose—is absent in this case. No duty could arise from petitioner's relationship with the sellers of the target company's securities, for petitioner had no prior dealings with them. He was not their agent, he was not a fiduciary, he was not a person in whom the sellers had placed their trust and confidence. He was, in fact, a complete stranger who dealt with the sellers only through impersonal market transactions.

We cannot affirm petitioner's conviction without recognizing a general duty between all participants in market transactions to forgo actions based on material, nonpublic information. Formulation of such a broad duty, which departs radically from the established doctrine that duty arises from a specific relationship between two parties, should not be undertaken absent some explicit evidence of congressional intent.

[N]o such evidence emerges from the language or legislative history of § 10(b). Moreover, neither the Congress nor the Commission ever has adopted a parity-of-information rule. Instead the problems caused by misuse of market information have been addressed by detailed and sophisticated regulation that recognizes when use of market information may not harm operation of the securities markets. For example, the Williams Act [68] limits but does not completely prohibit a tender offeror's purchases of target corporation stock before public announcement of the offer. Congress' careful action in this and other areas contrasts, and is in some tension, with the broad rule of liability we are asked to adopt in this case.

* * *

* * * Section 10(b) is aptly described as a catch-all provision, but what it catches must be fraud. When an allegation of fraud is based upon nondisclosure, there can be no fraud absent a duty to speak. We hold that a duty to disclose under § 10(b) does not arise from the mere possession of nonpublic market information. The contrary result is without support in the legislative history of § 10(b) and would be inconsistent with the careful plan that Congress has enacted for regulation of the securities markets.

IV

In its brief to this Court, the United States offers an alternative theory to support petitioner's conviction. It argues that petitioner breached a duty to the acquiring corporation when he acted upon information that he obtained by virtue of his position as an employee of a printer employed by the corporation. The breach of this duty is said to support a conviction under § 10(b) for fraud perpetrated upon both the acquiring corporation and the sellers.

We need not decide whether this theory has merit for it was not submitted to the jury. * * *

* * *

The jury instructions demonstrate that petitioner was convicted merely because of his failure to disclose material, nonpublic information to sellers from whom he bought the stock of target corporations. The jury was not instructed on the nature or elements of a duty owed by petitioner to anyone other than the sellers. Because we cannot affirm a criminal conviction on the basis of a theory not presented to the jury, we will not speculate upon whether such a duty exists, whether it has been breached, or whether such a breach constitutes a violation of § 10(b).

The judgment of the Court of Appeals is *Reversed.*

[Justice Stevens, in a concurring opinion, approved the majority's refusal to address the question whether petitioner's breach of the duty "unquestionably" owed to his employer and the acquiring corporations who had entrusted information to his employer could give rise to criminal liability under Rule 10b–5; "[r]espectable arguments could be made in support of either position." 445 U.S. at 238, 100 S.Ct. at 1119, 63 L.Ed.2d at 362. Justice Brennan, in a separate concurring opinion, agreed with Chief Justice Burger's dissenting view, infra, that a person

---

68. [Court's footnote 15.] 15 U.S.C. § 78m(d)(1) permits a tender offeror to purchase 5% of the target company's stock prior to disclosure of its plans for acquisition.

violates § 10b "whenever he improperly obtains or converts to his own benefit nonpublic information which he then uses in connection with the purchase or sale of securities," id. at 239, 100 S.Ct. at 1120, 63 L.Ed. 2d at 363; but did not believe the jury was properly charged on the theory.]

MR. CHIEF JUSTICE BURGER, dissenting.

I believe that the jury instructions in this case properly charged a violation of § 10(b) and Rule 10b–5, and I would affirm the conviction.

I

As a general rule, neither party to an arm's length business transaction has an obligation to disclose information to the other unless the parties stand in some confidential or fiduciary relation. See Prosser, The Law of Torts § 106. This rule permits a businessman to capitalize on his experience and skill in securing and evaluating relevant information; it provides incentive for hard work, careful analysis, and astute forecasting. But the policies that underlie the rule also should limit its scope. In particular, the rule should give way when an informational advantage is obtained, not by superior experience, foresight, or industry, but by some unlawful means. One commentator has written:

> "[T]he way in which the buyer acquires the information which he conceals from the vendor should be a material circumstance. The information might have been acquired as the result of his bringing to bear a superior knowledge, intelligence, skill or technical judgment; it might have been acquired by chance; or it might be acquired by means of some tortious action on his part. . . . *Any time information is acquired by an illegal act it would seem that there should be a duty to disclose that information.*" Keeton, Fraud—Concealment and Non–Disclosure, 15 Tex.L.Rev. 1, 25–26 (1936) (emphasis added).

I would read § 10(b) and Rule 10b–5 to encompass and build on this principle: to mean that a person who has misappropriated nonpublic information has an absolute duty to disclose that information or to refrain from trading.

The language of § 10(b) and of Rule 10b–5 plainly support such a reading. By their terms, these provisions reach *any* person engaged in *any* fraudulent scheme. This broad language negates the suggestion that congressional concern was limited to trading by "corporate insiders" or to deceptive practices related to "corporate information." Just as surely Congress cannot have intended one standard of fair dealing for "white collar" insiders and another for the "blue collar" level. The very language of § 10(b) and Rule 10b–5 "by repeated use of the word 'any' [was] obviously meant to be inclusive."

The history of the statute and of the rule also support this reading. The antifraud provisions were designed in large measure "to assure that dealing in securities is fair and without undue preferences or advantages among investors." H.R.Conf.Rep. No. 94–229, 94th Cong., 1st Sess., 91–92 (1975), U.S. Code Cong. & Admin. News 1975, p. 323. These provisions prohibit "those manipulative and deceptive practices which have been demonstrated to fulfill no useful function." S.Rep. No. 792, 73d Cong., 2d Sess., 6 (1934). An investor who purchases securities on the basis of misappropriated nonpublic information possesses just such an "undue" trading advantage; his conduct quite clearly serves no useful function except his own enrichment at the expense of others.

* * *

[I]t bears emphasis that this reading of § 10(b) and Rule 10b–5 would not threaten legitimate business practices. So read, the antifraud provisions would not impose a duty on a tender offeror to disclose its acquisition plans during the period in which it "tests the water" prior to purchasing a full 5% of the target company's stock. [In such a case,] trading is accomplished on the basis of material nonpublic information, but the information has not been unlawfully converted for personal gain.

II

[In Part II of his opinion, Chief Justice Burger discussed the adequacy of the jury instructions under the theory of securities fraud discussed in Part I. The Chief Justice concluded:]

In sum, the evidence shows beyond all doubt that Chiarella, working literally in the shadows of the warning signs in the printshop, misappropriated—stole to put it bluntly—valuable nonpublic information entrusted to him in the utmost confidence. He then exploited his ill-gotten informational advantage by purchasing securities in the market. In my view, such conduct plainly violates § 10(b) and Rule 10b–5. Accordingly, I would affirm the judgment of the Court of Appeals.

MR. JUSTICE BLACKMUN, with whom MR. JUSTICE MARSHALL joins, dissenting.

Although I agree with much of what is said in Part I of the dissenting opinion of The Chief Justice, I write separately because, in my view, it is unnecessary to rest petitioner's conviction on a "misappropriation" theory. The fact that petitioner Chiarella purloined, or, to use The Chief Justice's word, "stole," information concerning pending tender offers certainly is the most dramatic evidence that petitioner was guilty of fraud. He has conceded that he knew it was wrong, and he and his co-workers in the print shop were specifically warned by their employer that actions of this kind were improper and forbidden. But I also would find petitioner's conduct fraudulent within the meaning of § 10(b) of the Securities Exchange Act of 1934, 15 U.S.C. § 78j(b), and the Securities and Exchange Commission's Rule 10b–5, 17 CFR § 240.10b–5 (1979), even if he had obtained the blessing of his employer's principals before embarking on his profiteering scheme. Indeed, I think petitioner's brand of manipulative trading, with or without such approval, lies close to the heart of what the securities laws are intended to prohibit.

* * *

I, of course, agree with the Court that a relationship of trust can establish a duty to disclose under § 10(b) and Rule 10b–5. But I do not agree that a failure to disclose violates the Rule only when the responsibilities of a relationship of that kind have been breached. As applied to this case, the Court's approach unduly minimizes the importance of petitioner's *access* to confidential information that the honest investor no matter how diligently he tried, could not legally obtain. * * *

The common law of actionable misrepresentation long has treated the possession of "special facts" as a key ingredient in the duty to disclose. Traditionally, this factor has been prominent in cases involving confidential or fiduciary relations, where one party's inferiority of knowledge and dependence upon fair treatment is a matter of legal definition, as well as in cases where one party is on notice that the other is "acting under a mistaken belief with respect to a material fact." Even at common law, however, there has been a trend away from strict adherence to the harsh maxim *caveat emptor* and toward a more flexible, less formalistic understanding of the duty to disclose.

* * *

* * *

* * * I would hold that persons having access to confidential material information that is not legally available to others generally are prohibited by Rule 10b–5 from engaging in schemes to exploit their structural informational advantage through trading in affected securities. To hold otherwise, it seems to me, is to tolerate a wide range of manipulative and deceitful behavior.

Whatever the outer limits of the Rule, petitioner Chiarella's case fits neatly near the center of its analytical framework. He occupied a relationship to the takeover companies giving him intimate access to concededly material information that was sedulously guarded from public access. The information, in the words of Cady, Roberts & Co., 40 S.E.C., at 912, was "intended to be available only for a corporate purpose and not for the personal benefit of anyone." Petitioner, moreover, knew that the information was unavailable to those with whom he dealt. And he took full, virtually riskless advantage of this artificial information gap by selling the stocks shortly after each takeover bid was announced. By any reasonable definition, his trading was "inherent[ly] unfair[ ]." Ibid. This misuse of confidential information was clearly placed before the jury. Petitioner's conviction, therefore, should be upheld and I dissent from the Court's upsetting that conviction.

NOTES AND QUERIES

(1) *Queries.* How does the fact that this is a criminal, rather than a civil, case affect the views of the majority and the dissents? Could

(should) the Court have explicitly recognized that Section 10b is to be interpreted differently when the penalties sought are criminal?[69] Does the majority's emphasis on the lack of a clear duty to the victim(s) make more sense in light of the common law's general reluctance to impose criminal liability for failures to act where the defendant owes no duty to the victim?[70] Does the emphasis in the dissenting opinions on the method used to acquire the inside information merely revisit the central issue in the law of theft since the thirteenth century—the need to punish defendants who acquire property by trickery?[71]

What is the harm Section 10b is intended to prevent?[72] Is there some public, economic harm involved, which calls for the application of the criminal law? Does such harm depend on the way the information was obtained? On the way it was used? On the identity of the user? It is clearly legal for the tender offeror to buy up to five percent before announcing a takeover (see n. 68, supra). How, then, can it be a crime for others to do the same thing? Would there be any liability if 1) Pandick Press had encouraged its printers to trade on the information, as a way to increase their compensation; 2) Pandick had traded on the information in lieu of its printing fee; 3) officials of the tender offeror traded on the information?

(2) *Tippee Liability.* Dirks v. SEC[73] was a *civil* case in which the SEC charged an officer of an investment analysis firm with insider trading under the following circumstances: Secrist, an officer of Equity Funding of America, reported to Dirks that the assets of Equity Funding were vastly overstated because of systematic fraudulent practices. Secrist made these disclosures for the purpose of having Dirks investigate and disclose the fraud publicly. During the two weeks that Dirks investigated (by personally interviewing Equity Funding employees), he also informed his firm's clients about what he had discovered. These clients sold more than $15 million of Equity Funding stock, and the stock price fell by more than forty percent. Dirks also made several contacts with reporters from the Wall Street Journal, but did not directly contact the SEC. The SEC finally asked to interview Dirks nearly three weeks after Secrist told him about the fraud; a front-page article published by the Journal six days later pushed Equity Funding into receivership.

The SEC, in an administrative proceeding, found that Dirks committed securities fraud, even though he was only a "tippee." The

69. For an example of such a decision, see United States v. United States Gypsum Co., infra p. 228.

70. See Hughes, Criminal Omissions, 67 Yale L.J. 590 (1958).

71. See, e.g., J. Hall, Theft, Law & Society (1952).

72. The literature on insider trading is voluminous, particularly with respect to the problems of "inside" and "outside" (or, "market") information. See, e.g., Barry, The Economics of Outside Information and Rule 10b–5, 129 U.Pa.L.Rev. 1307 (1981); Brudney, Insiders, Outsiders and Informational Advantages Under the Federal Securities Laws, 93 Harv.L.Rev. 322 (1979); Fleischer, Mundheim and Murphy, An Initial Inquiry Into the Responsibility to Disclose Market Information, 121 U.Pa.L.Rev. 798 (1973).

73. 463 U.S. 646, 103 S.Ct. 3255, 77 L.Ed.2d 911 (1983).

Supreme Court reversed. Reaffirming the principle "set forth in *Chiarella*" that equal information among all traders was not required by the securities laws, the Supreme Court (per Justice Powell) stated: [74]

> [T]he tippee's duty to disclose or abstain is derivative from that of the insider's duty. . . . [T]ippees must assume an insider's duty to the shareholders not because they receive inside information, but rather because it has been made available to them *improperly*. . . . Thus, a tippee assumes a fiduciary duty to the shareholders only when the insider has breached his fiduciary duty to the shareholders by disclosing the information to the tippee and the tippee knows or should know that there has been a breach. . . .
>
> In determining whether a tippee is under an obligation to disclose or abstain, it thus is necessary to determine whether the insider's "tip" constituted a breach of the insider's fiduciary duty. All disclosures of confidential corporate information are not inconsistent with the duty insiders owe to shareholders. In contrast to the extraordinary facts of this case, the more typical situation in which there will be a question whether disclosure violates the insider's . . . duty is when insiders disclose information to analysts. . . .
>
> In some situations, the insider will act consistently with his fiduciary duty to shareholders, and yet release of the information may affect the market. For example, it may not be clear—either to the corporate insider or to the recipient analyst—whether the information will be viewed as material nonpublic information. Corporate officials may mistakenly think the information already has been disclosed or that it is not material enough to affect the market. Whether disclosure is a breach of duty therefore depends in large part on the purpose of the disclosure. . . .
>
> Thus, the test is whether the insider personally will benefit, directly or indirectly, from his disclosure. Absent some personal gain, there has been no breach of duty to stockholders. And absent a breach by the insider, there is no derivative breach.

Applying this test, the Court concluded:

> Under the inside-trading and tipping rules set forth above, we find that there was no actionable violation by Dirks.[75] It is

---

74. Id. at 647, 665–667, 103 S.Ct. at 3257–58, 3267–68, 77 L.Ed.2d at 917, 928–30.

75. [Court's footnote 25.] Dirks contends that he was not a "tippee" because the information he received constituted unverified allegations of fraud that were denied by management and were not "material facts" under the securities laws that required disclosure before trading. He also argues that the information he received was not truly "inside" information, i.e., intended for a confidential corporate purpose, but was merely evidence of a crime. The Solicitor General agrees. We need not decide, however, whether the information constituted "material facts," or whether information concerning corporate crime is properly characterized as "inside information." For purposes of deciding this case, we assume the correctness of the SEC's findings, accepted by the Court of Appeals, that petitioner was a tippee of material inside information.

undisputed that Dirks himself was a stranger to Equity Funding, with no pre-existing fiduciary duty to its shareholders.[76] He took no action, directly or indirectly, that induced the shareholders or officers of Equity Funding to repose trust or confidence in him. There was no expectation by Dirk's sources that he would keep their information in confidence. Nor did Dirks misappropriate or illegally obtain the information about Equity Funding. Unless the insiders breached their . . . duty to shareholders in disclosing the nonpublic information to Dirks, he breached no duty when he passed it on to investors as well as to the Wall Street Journal.

It is clear that neither Secrist nor the other Equity Funding employees violated their . . . duty to the corporation's shareholders by providing information to Dirks.[77] The tippers received no monetary or personal benefit for revealing Equity Funding's secrets, nor was their purpose to make a gift of valuable information to Dirks. As the facts of this case clearly indicate, the tippers were motivated by a desire to expose the fraud. In the absence of a breach of duty to shareholders by the insiders, there was no derivative breach by Dirks. Dirks therefore could not have been "a participant after the fact in [an] insider's breach of a fiduciary duty." *Chiarella*, 445 U.S., at 230, n. 12.

Queries. In its opinion, the Court does not mention the fact that *Chiarella* was a criminal case, nor does it attempt to draw any different standard for a civil case. Should the fact that *Dirks* was a civil case have led the Court to place more emphasis on the harm done to shareholders or securities markets, and less emphasis on the means of acquiring the information? In assessing breach of fiduciary duties, did the Court or the SEC overlook any fiduciary duties owed by Dirks directly—to his employer? customers? the SEC? "the market"? Review the mail fraud cases, supra. Could (should?) Dirks have been prosecuted for mail or wire fraud?

(3) *Duty to Employers.* In *Carpenter v. United States,* discussed supra p. 133, in addition to mail fraud, the defendants were also prosecuted for securities fraud under Section 10(b). The Court of

---

76. [Court's footnote 26.] Judge Wright found that Dirks acquired a fiduciary duty by virtue of his position as an employee of a broker-dealer. See 220 U.S.App.D.C., at 325–327, 681 F.2d at 840–842. The SEC, however, did not consider Judge Wright's novel theory in its decision, nor did it present that theory to the Court of Appeals. The SEC also has not argued Judge Wright's theory in this Court. The merits of such a duty are therefore not before the Court.

77. [Court's footnote 27.] In this Court, the SEC appears to contend that an insider invariably violates a fiduciary duty to the corporation's shareholders by transmitting nonpublic corporate information to an outsider when he has reason to believe that the outsider may use it to the disadvantage of the shareholders. "Thus, regardless of any ultimate motive to bring to public attention the derelictions at Equity Funding, Secrist breached his duty to Equity Funding shareholders." . . . In fact, the SEC did not charge Secrist with any wrongdoing, and we do not understand the SEC to have relied on any theory of a breach of duty by Secrist in finding that Dirks breached his duty to Equity Funding's shareholders. . . . Moreover, to constitute a violation of Rule 10b–5, there must be fraud.

Appeals for the Second Circuit affirmed their convictions.[78] The Court, per Judge Pierce, wrote with regard to the securities fraud charge:

> We hold that section 10(b) of the Securities Exchange Act of 1934 and Rule 10b–5 proscribe an employee's unlawful misappropriation from his employer, a financial newspaper, of material nonpublic information in the form of the newspaper's forthcoming publication schedule, in connection with a scheme to purchase and sell securities to be analyzed or otherwise discussed in future columns in that newspaper. . . .
>
> * * *
>
> Although the facts render the securities fraud issue herein one of first impression, we do not write on a clean slate in assessing whether this case falls within the purview of the "misappropriation" theory of section 10(b) and Rule 10b–5 thereunder. In 1980, the Supreme Court left open the question of the viability of that theory, Chiarella v. United States, 445 U.S. 222, 100 S.Ct. 1108, 63 L.Ed.2d 348 (1980), with the concurring and dissenting opinions suggesting that had the theory been presented to the jury, Chiarella's conviction might have been affirmed. Since then, the theory has been applied twice by this court. See SEC v. Materia, 745 F.2d 197 (2d Cir.1984), cert. denied 471 U.S. 1053, 105 S.Ct. 2112, 85 L.Ed.2d 477 (1985); United States v. Newman, 664 F.2d 12 (2d Cir. 1981), affirmed after remand 722 F.2d 729 (2d Cir.), cert. denied, 464 U.S. 863, 104 S.Ct. 193, 78 L.Ed.2d 170 (1983). It is clear that defendant Winans, as an employee of the Wall Street Journal, breached a duty of confidentiality to his employer by misappropriating from the Journal confidential prepublication information, regarding the timing and content of certain newspaper columns, about which he learned in the course of his employment. We are presented with the question of whether that unlawful conduct may serve as the predicate for the securities fraud charges herein.
>
> * * *
>
> The core of appellants' argument is that *Newman* and *Materia* are inapposite because in those cases the information was misappropriated by employees who owed a duty of confidentiality not only to their employers, but also to their employers' clients, the corporation whose securities were traded. In other words, appellants argue, the misappropriation theory may be applied only where the information is misappropriated by corporate insiders or so-called quasi-insiders, Dirks v. SEC, 463 U.S. 646, 655 n. 14, 103 S.Ct. 3255, 3262 n. 14, 77 L.Ed.2d 911 (1983), who owe to the corporation and its shareholders a fiduciary duty of abstention or disclosure. . . .
>
> Appellants read *Newman* and *Materia* and interpret the misappropriation theory too narrowly. Notwithstanding the existence of

---

78. 791 F.2d 1024 (2d Cir.1986). The district court opinion is United States v. Winans, 612 F.Supp. 827 (S.D.N.Y.1985).

corporate clients of the employers in *Newman* and *Materia*, the misappropriation theory more broadly proscribes the conversion by "insiders" or others of material non-public information in connection with the purchase or sale of securities. See Materia, 745 F.2d at 203 (liability may arise merely because one "misappropriates non-public information in breach of a fiduciary duty and trades on that information to his advantage"); . . . cf. SEC v. Musella, 578 F.Supp. 425, 438 (S.D.N.Y.1984) (*Newman* "gave legal effect to the commonsensical view that trading on the basis of improperly obtained information is fundamentally unfair, and that distinctions premised on the source of the information undermine the prophylactic intent of the securities law"). It is precisely such conversion that serves as the predicate for the convictions herein.

* * *

Further, we think that the application of the misappropriation theory herein promotes the purposes and policies underlying section 10(b) and Rule 10b–5. . . .

The legislative intent of the 1934 Act is . . . broad-reaching. As this Court has noted in applying the misappropriation theory, "the antifraud provision was intended to be broad in scope, encompassing all 'manipulative and deceptive practices which have been demonstrated to fulfill no useful function.'" We perceive nothing "useful" about defendants' scheme. Nor, in our view, could any purported function of the scheme be considered protected given Congress' stated concern for the perception of fairness and integrity in the securities markets and the potential costs of foresaking such legislated concerns, including fewer market participants and greater reliance on fraud as a means of competing in the market.

* * *

. . . There are disparities in knowledge and the availability thereof at many levels of market functioning that the law does not presume to address. However, the critical issue is found in the district judge's careful distinction between "information" and "conduct." Whatever may be the legal significance of merely using one's privileged or unique position to obtain material, nonpublic information, here we address specifically whether an employee's use of such information in breach of a duty of confidentiality to an employer serves as adequate predicate for a securities violation. Obviously, one may gain a competitive advantage in the marketplace through conduct constituting skill, foresight, industry and the like. Certainly this is as true in securities law as in antitrust, patent, trademark, copyright and other fields. But one may not gain such advantage by conduct constituting secreting, stealing, purloining or otherwise misappropriating material nonpublic information in breach of an employer-imposed fiduciary duty of confidentiality. Such conduct constitutes chicanery, not competition; foul play, not fair play. Indeed, underlying section 10(b) and the major securities laws generally is the fundamental promotion of

" 'the highest ethical standards . . .' in every facet of the securities industry." SEC v. Capital Gains Research Bureau, 375 U.S. 180, 186–187, 84 S.Ct. 275, 279–281, 11 L.Ed.2d 237 (1963). . . .

* * *

As to the "in connection with" standard [in Rule 10b(5)], the use of the misappropriated information for the financial benefit of the defendants and to the financial detriment of those investors with whom appellants traded supports the conclusion that appellants' fraud was "in connection with" the purchase or sale of securities under section 10(b) and Rule 10b–5. We can deduce reasonably that those who purchased or sold securities without the misappropriated information would not have purchased or sold, at least at the transaction prices, had they had the benefit of that information. Certainly the protection of investors is the major purpose of section 10(b) and Rule 10b–5. Further, investors are endangered equally by fraud by non-inside misappropriators as by fraud by insiders.

* * *

Appellants argue that it is anomalous to hold an employee liable for acts that his employer could lawfully commit. Admittedly, the employers in *Newman* were investment banks that would be barred by federal securities laws from trading in securities of their clients, while in the present case the Wall Street Journal or its parent, Dow Jones Company, might perhaps lawfully disregard its own confidentiality policy by trading in the stock of companies to be discussed in forthcoming articles. But a reputable newspaper, even if it could lawfully do so, would be unlikely to undermine its own valued asset, its reputation, which it surely would do by trading on the basis of its knowledge of forthcoming publications. Although the employer may perhaps lawfully destroy its own reputation, its employees should be and are barred from destroying their employer's reputation by misappropriating their employer's informational property. Appellants' argument that this distinction would be unfair to employees illogically casts the thief and the victim in the same shoes. . . .

Thus, because of his duty of confidentiality to the Journal, defendant Winans—and Felis and Carpenter, who knowingly participated with him—had a corollary duty, which they breached, under section 10(b) and Rule 10b–5, to abstain from trading in securities on the basis of the misappropriated information or to do so only upon making adequate disclosure to those with whom they traded.

* * *

Finally, we do not agree with the position taken in the brief of amici curiae that the district court's decision portends First Amendment infringements. The confidentiality restrictions stem from the Wall Street Journal and Dow Jones company rules, not from any action by the government. Moreover, we cannot see how the convictions will chill free speech. If Winans had respected his employer's reasonable confidentiality policy, he would have had nothing to fear by publishing his "Heard" columns. Indeed, where a columnist uses his position to profit in transactions, at least one court has held that he may be compelled to disclose to his readers his potential financial stake in the impact of his columns. The First Amendment generally empowers a journalist with no "special privilege" merely for the exercise of his craft, and the securities laws require of him, no less than of others, compliance therewith in the pursuit of his financial interests. . . .

* * *

Query. On review of the securities fraud charge, the Supreme Court affirmed the conviction by an equally divided Court. What arguments might have convinced four Justices that Winans' conduct was not fraud under the Securities Acts, even though they all agreed that it was fraud under the Mail Fraud Act? Does it make any sense to believe that Congress could intend to cover this behavior under one fraud provision but not another? Does it make any difference?

(4) *Enforcement Policy.* Chiarella's was the first federal criminal case brought for insider trading since the Securities Exchange Act was passed in 1934. After *Chiarella,* however, enforcement attention focused on the area and, with the election of President Reagan in 1980, policing insider trading violations became a high priority. This was in some contrast to SEC enforcement policy in the Carter Administration, which had been concerned with issues of "management integrity," such as the making of "improper payments" to foreign government officials to win business in foreign countries.[79]

As enforcement attention to the area increased, more violations were uncovered. In a little over six years (from the end of 1980 through the early part of 1987), sixty-three separate criminal insider trading cases were filed by the United States Attorney's Office in the Southern District of New York (the office primarily responsible for criminal insider trading prosecutions).[80] Defendants have included attorneys, stock brokers, law firm employees, including office managers, word processor operators, and proof readers, investment bankers, securities analysts, financial printers(!), a director of a corporation, and a New York City police officer. These investigations have spawned at least two books, one a thinly-disguised novel about one of the early insider trading cases, the other an autobiographical account by one of the most "legally famous" insider-traders.[81]

---

79. See, e.g., "The Dispute over the S.E.C.," N.Y. Times, April 21, 1982, p. D1 (reporting shift to insider trading and fraud, and away from accounting practices and corporate governance; change criticized as demonstrating "too narrow" a view of the SEC's role in protecting the integrity of the capital markets).

80. The cases are listed in Corporate Crime Reporter, v. 1, no. 1, April 13, 1987, at 12–16.

81. See Winans, Trading Secrets: Seduction and Scandal at The Wall Street Journal (1986); Stanfill, Shadows and Light (1984) (reviewed in Herman, "Taking the Novel Route," Wall St.J., Nov. 14, 1984, p. 30).

Two of these cases stand out for the sheer amount of money they involve. The first is the prosecution against Dennis Levine, who was charged with engaging in illegal insider trading over a 5½ year period, during which time he worked for four major Wall Street investment banking firms. In 1986 he pleaded guilty to earning profits of $12.6 million on his trades.[82] He also agreed to cooperate with the government in its continuing investigations, and to lead the government to at least four other "less major" traders.

Levine also led the government to the other, even more spectacular case—Ivan Boesky. Ivan Boesky was perhaps the most prominent "risk arbitrager" (professional traders who invest for themselves and others in the stock of takeover targets) on Wall Street, earning large amounts of money in the wave of mergers which began in the late 1970s. In November 1986 the government announced that Boesky had agreed to plead guilty to one count of insider trading, to cooperate with the government, to accept a permanent bar from working in the United States' securities industry (after an 18–month phase-out period), and to pay $100 million in penalties ($50 million of which was turned over immediately in cash or cash-equivalents). The amount of this civil penalty was unprecedented, although this did not prevent some from criticizing the SEC as "too lenient" toward Boesky.[83]

The full benefit from Boesky's agreement to plead guilty may turn out to come from Boesky's agreement to cooperate with the government. In September 1988, apparently on the strength of information supplied by Boesky, the investment banking firm of Drexel Burnham Lambert was charged in a civil complaint by the SEC with a wide array of securities violations in sixteen transactions (mostly takeovers). In December 1988, facing a potential RICO charge and having already reportedly spent $175 million in legal fees and expenses, Drexel agreed to plead guilty to six felony counts of securities fraud and pay $650 million in fines and restitution.[84]

82. For information on the Levine case, see, e.g., "Drexel Official Accused by SEC of Insider Trades," Wall St.J., May 13, 1986, p. 3 (SEC terms case "the largest insider trading case ever"); Wall St.J., May 23, 1986, p. 8 (listing deals involved); "Letter Unravelled Levine Case, N.Y. Times, June 10, 1986, p. D1 (describing how case uncovered through anonymous letter sent from Caracas to Merrill Lynch in 1985); "Insider Pleads Guilty in $12.6 Million Stock Case," N.Y. Times, June 6, 1986, p. 1 (four felony counts; in civil SEC settlement, will turn over "almost all his estimated wealth of $11.5 million").

83. For information on Boesky, see, e.g., "Big Trader To Pay U.S. $100 Million For Insider Abuses," N.Y. Times, Nov. 15, 1986, p. 1; "Boesky's Rise and Fall Illustrate a Compulsion to Profit by Getting Inside Track on Market," Wall St.J., Nov. 17, 1986, p. 28 ("No one on Wall Street ever flew as high or crashed as hard as Ivan F. Boesky."); "U.S. Said to Issue Subpoenas Linked to Boesky Trading," N.Y. Times, Nov. 17, 1986, p. 1 (describing SEC settlement); "Boesky Terms: Too Lenient?", N.Y. Times, Nov. 20, 1986, p. D2; "Boesky Pact May Give SEC $13 Million Less Than Believed, Court Files Indicate," Wall St.J., July 2, 1987, p. 3.

84. See "Drexel Agrees to Plead Guilty and Pay Out A Record $650 Million," Wall St.J., Dec. 22, 1988, p. 1; "SEC Accuses Drexel of a Sweeping Array of Securities Violations," Wall St.J., Sept. 8, 1988, p. 1. Still to be determined is the fate of Michael Milken, head of Drexel's junk bond operation and a major target of the Drexel investigation. See "Milken's Defense Likely to be Hurt By Drexel's Accord," Wall St.J., Dec. 22, 1988, p. A7

As in other areas of business crime enforcement, note that many of the most significant cases have been settled without any litigation. Cooperation with the government, in return for some reduction in possible charges, has been frequent. Consider the implications of this pattern. As a prosecutor, is it "just" to agree to reduce charges against one spectacular trader because he can finger someone even more spectacular? And what charges would you threaten a suspect with? How about RICO, threatened in the Drexel case? [85] Recall, in particular, the forfeiture provisions of RICO, which reach the "proceeds" of a RICO violation and property "derived from" the proceeds, and note that the government can seek a bond to insure that sufficient assets will be on hand to cover the forfeiture if the defendant is convicted. In these major insider trading cases, the government might be able to put a brokerage company out of business simply by the size of the bond.[86] Consider, also, whether you would treat these as "ordinary" criminal cases. Would you be certain that these defendants were arrested at their place of business, in full view of their co-workers, and taken away in handcuffs? [87] Would you seek high bail? [88] Is it possible (or even desirable) to treat these cases just like "normal" criminal prosecutions?

(5) *Profiling the Criminals.* What might lead people who are already wealthy by anyone's standards to engage in criminal insider trading? Consider the following (not atypical) account. Stewart and Hertzberg, "Unhappy Ending: The Wall Street Career of Martin Siegel Was A Dream Gone Wrong," Wall St.J., Feb. 17, 1987, p. 1.[89]

Last Nov. 14, 38-year-old Martin A. Siegel, one of Wall Street's leading investment bankers, was spending the afternoon in the Park Avenue offices of Martin Lipton, an eminent takeover lawyer and a man Mr. Siegel had come to regard almost as a father.

Suddenly a federal marshal burst in upon the two men, thrusting a subpoena into Mr. Siegel's hand. When Mr. Siegel read the subject matter of

(Drexel agrees to cooperate with government; Drexel employees may testify against Milken).

85. Justice Department Guidelines for RICO prosecutions are set out supra, N(4), p. 98. The first RICO charge in an insider trading case was brought in August 1988. See "Racketeering Charges May Be Common in Future Insider-Trading Prosecutions," Wall St.J., Sept. 2, 1988, p. 4 (RICO charged in case where defendant allegedly made $687,187; Justice Department defends use of RICO, saying case is "just as serious as arson or insurance fraud or mail fraud").

86. See "Dread of RICO Law Is Likely to Grow, But May Inspire Push for Mob-Only Use," Wall St.J., Dec. 22, 1988, p. A6 (describing bond required in case involving partners in Princeton/Newport L.P., charged with RICO for tax fraud, and its effect on Drexel; "'The horrors of RICO are so fearsome and threatening that a company will abandon what otherwise might be a valid defense,'" says white-collar crime lawyer).

87. Yes: "Insider-Trading Scandal Implicates High Aides at Goldman, Kidder," Wall St.J., Feb. 13, 1987 ("brigade" of federal marshalls, in "full view of the firm's stunned traders," placed vice president of Kidder, Peabody "against the wall, frisked and handcuffed [him], and led [him] away in tears").

88. Yes: "$5 Million Bail in S.E.C. Case," N.Y. Times, May 14, 1986, p. D24 (personal recognizance bond for Levine, secured by cash, Manhattan cooperative apartment and furnishings, and shares in investment banking firm; also required to surrender passport).

89. Reprinted by permission of The Wall Street Journal, © Dow Jones & Company, Inc., 1987. All Rights Reserved.

the investigation—Ivan F. Boesky—and the accompanying list of his own takeover deals at Kidder, Peabody & Co. in the 1980s, he knew his career was over. He began sobbing, as a horrified Mr. Lipton rushed to comfort him.

The public end to Mr. Siegel's career, once one of the most spectacular success stories on Wall Street, came last Friday. He resigned his year-old position as co-head of mergers and acquisitions at Drexel Burnham Lambert Inc. and pleaded guilty in federal court to two felony counts for his role in the Boesky scandal. Coming just a day after the stunning arrests of three top Wall Street professionals, Mr. Siegel's pleas still managed to shock Wall Street. More than anyone else so far implicated in the scandal, Mr. Siegel personified the American dream.

* * *

This is the story of Mr. Siegel's rise and abrupt fall. * * *

In the eyes of many Wall Street observers, the takeover boom came of age on Aug. 26, 1982, when Bendix Corp. launched a $1.5 billion hostile bid for Martin Marietta Corp., the opening salvo in what became the now-legendary four-way battle involving Bendix, Martin Marietta, United Technologies Corp. and Allied Corp. And thrust into the center of the action, in his role as Martin Marietta's chief strategist, was a young, hitherto little-known merger specialist at Kidder Peabody named Martin Siegel.

By the time of the Bendix bid, Mr. Siegel had known Ivan F. Boesky for years. Kidder Peabody, where Mr. Siegel was the key mergers and acquisitions strategist, didn't have an arbitrage department so Mr. Siegel couldn't use his own firm for the information about stock positions and company valuations that is crucial to takeover strategy and is the arbitragers' stock-in-trade. He had come to rely on Mr. Boesky, whose persistent phone calls had led to a close relationship. Indeed, they spoke on the phone for five years before they met in person in 1980.

Mr. Siegel had become awed by the vast wealth he saw Mr. Boesky amassing. Two years before the Bendix bid, Mr. Siegel had been invited to dinner at Mr. Boesky's sprawling estate in suburban Westchester County; the Boesky house dwarfed the house that Mr. Siegel was planning to build on Long Island Sound. On two other occasions, Mr. Boesky had come out to the Siegel home to play tennis, a game Mr. Siegel loved and played well. Mr. Boesky arrived in his pink Rolls-Royce.

Mr. Siegel's awe at Mr. Boesky's possessions was all the more pronounced because he came from a modest family background that had been marked by financial struggle. When he was 20 years old, his father, then in his 40s, had filed for bankruptcy, an event that left an indelible impression on the son. Indeed, friends say that Mr. Siegel was haunted by the fear that someday, like his father, he would fail just as he reached the prime of life.

For the same reason, he saved money compulsively. For years, he had lived as a bachelor on his relatively modest $50,000 annual salary at Kidder Peabody, saving all of his much larger bonuses. But in 1981 he married his second wife, another investment banker at Kidder Peabody, and they had their first child the next year. They built a large home in Greens Farms, one of the most exclusive enclaves on the Connecticut coast. They had a New York apartment as well and hired a nurse for the child. Mr. Siegel's salary wasn't enough to cover these burgeoning expenses; he was depleting his carefully saved capital.

Several days before the Bendix bid, Mr. Siegel, then 33, trim, dark-haired and strikingly handsome, pushed through the double doors of the grill room at New York's Harvard Club. Mr. Siegel spotted Mr. Boesky, and the two settled down for what would become a fateful conversation.

Mr. Siegel aired some of his personal financial concerns to Mr. Boesky. He must have known that to do so in front of an arbitrager was like placing red meat before a lion. "I'll make some investments for you," Mr. Boesky volunteered, and one thing led to another. By the end of that conversation, the two had forged an agreement: In return for information furnished by Mr. Siegel, Mr. Boesky would pay him an unspecified percentage of Mr. Boesky's own profits from trading on the information.

At the beginning, Mr. Siegel didn't expect to be leaking inside information; he thought he would simply be using his expertise as an investment banker to identify companies he deemed likely takeover targets. Indeed, Mr. Boesky had agreed that to trade on inside information just before a deal was publicly announced, or during the course of a deal, was too risky. The goal was to get Mr. Boesky into a takeover stock so early that the purchases couldn't possibly attract the interest of the Securities and Exchange Commission or other market watchers.

The 'PacMan' Defense

Bendix/Martin Marietta, however, provided an opportunity too good to resist. Martin Marietta, Mr. Siegel's client, had responded to the Bendix bid with the most audacious of tactics: the "PacMan" defense, named after the video game, in which the target tries to devour its suitor with a counterbid. Martin Marietta offered to pay $1.5 billion for Bendix.

In some ways, the tactic showed Mr. Siegel at his best. Although it wasn't the first time it had been employed, "it was wildly creative to do it on this scale," recalls one participant. Says another colleague, "You see the creative impulse in the literary and artistic worlds, only rarely in law or business. Marty had it."

But the PacMan defense, to be effective, needed some market momentum to get Bendix into play, pushing up its stock price so it would realize the market was taking the Martin Marietta attack seriously. So just before Martin Marietta's bid was unveiled, Mr. Siegel called Mr. Boesky and leaked the top secret plan, fully aware that he had just crossed the line of illegality. It was the last time he ever used the telephone to convey inside information to Mr. Boesky; shortly after, his feelings of guilt manifested themselves in a paranoid belief that his phone was tapped.

Using Mr. Siegel's information, Mr. Boesky bought Bendix stock, eventually realizing a profit of about $120,000. The PacMan defense succeeded. Bendix lost its independence and was acquired by Allied, and Martin Marietta survived, though at a cost so high that the PacMan defense has never again been attempted on such a scale. The battle was a coup for Mr. Siegel, thrusting him into the limelight just as the nation's takeover boom erupted. And it put Kidder Peabody, considered an established but sleepy firm in decline, at the forefront of merger-defense work.

Thriving Practice

Mr. Siegel parlayed that fame into a thriving defense-oriented merger practice, modeled in part on the successful takeover law firms. Mr. Siegel tirelessly traveled around the country, persuading chief executives of major corporations to pay Kidder Peabody a retainer to defend them should they become the target of a hostile corporate raid. Over time, he succeeded in scores of instances. "Marty was the most persuasive, most charming investment banker I'd ever met," recalls one chief executive who joined the Kidder Peabody fold. "He had a terrific bedside manner with [chief executive officers] and boards."

But his success wasn't immediately reflected in a significantly higher salary. Over the years he complained about Kidder Peabody's stinginess, its refusal to recognize his contributions to the firm and its penchant for doling out money to unproductive senior partners. In December 1982, a few months after the Bendix/Martin Marietta battle began, he turned to Mr. Boesky and asked the arbitrager for a cash payment of $125,000.

Mr. Boesky readily agreed even though the sum exceeded his profits from Mr. Siegel's information about Bendix. To avoid detection, Mr. Boesky placed the cash in a suitcase and gave it to a courier who met Mr. Siegel in a public place. Mr. Siegel gave the courier an agreed-upon password, and he handed over the suitcase. Mr. Siegel kept the cash hoard, dipping into it throughout the year to pay employees, such as his child's nurse, and for spending money. He thought of the money as a "consulting fee."

With the exchange of money, Mr. Siegel's relationship with Mr. Boesky settled into a pattern. When Mr. Boesky wanted information, or when Mr. Siegel had information he wanted to leak, the two got in touch by telephone. The signal was "Let's have coffee," and they then met in person to exchange the information, first in an alley behind 55 Water St., the financial-district building where Mr. Boesky worked, and later, after Mr. Boesky moved into the former Fifth Avenue offices of fugitive commodities trader Marc Rich, at a nearby midtown coffee shop.

In early 1983, Mr. Siegel leaked inside information about a bid by Diamond Shamrock Corp. for Natomas Inc. and a bid for Pargas Inc., later acquired by Freeport–McMoRan Inc. In September he told Mr. Boesky that Gordon Getty, one of Mr. Siegel's clients, was dissatisfied with the management of Getty Oil Co. and that a sale of the company was likely; it was eventually acquired by Texaco Inc. In 1984, he told Mr. Boesky about a bid for Midlands Energy Co. and used inside information about Carnation Co. to predict it would be sold. Nestle S.A. eventually acquired Carnation, and Mr. Boesky earned a profit of more than $28.3 million on that deal alone.

The insider trading in these instances was extremely clever. In at least three cases, Natomas, Getty and Carnation, Mr. Siegel used inside information to make an educated prediction that a major corporate transaction would ensue. Mr. Boesky was thus able to take enormous stock positions ahead of any final decision to make a bid. Even if detected by the authorities, such trading didn't look like it could possibly be insider trading. And in every instance, it could be argued that Mr. Siegel's leaks actually worked to his client's benefit by driving up the stock price at which they were eventually acquired, and to Kidder Peabody's benefit by boosting its fees that were based on the sale price.

Increasing Anxiety

At the end of both 1983 and 1984, Mr. Boesky and Mr. Siegel met to tally up Mr. Siegel's fee. Mr. Boesky began by saying, "What did you do for me this year?" and Mr. Siegel responded with an analysis of his leaks. The two end-of-year cash payments totaled $575,000.

Mr. Siegel, however, was becoming increasingly anxious about the scheme. . . . He vowed to stop passing inside information, even though he couldn't bring himself to tell Mr. Boesky, and he accepted the 1984 payment.

* * *

At Kidder Peabody, Mr. Siegel had developed into the model investment banker, idolized by many he worked with. The firm began having its annual summer party for interns at Mr. Siegel's home in Connecticut, the message being, as one participant recalls, "that if you come to Kidder and work hard, you're going to be like Marty—a beautiful home, beautiful wife, beautiful kids. It was like a stage set for 'The Great Gatsby.'"

Mr. Siegel commuted from the house to lower Manhattan by helicopter. At home, he pursued his two hobbies, tennis and sailing on adjacent Long Island Sound. Colleagues say Mr. Siegel was never swept up into the fast-paced whirl of Manhattan society. "He disdained the charity-ball set," says one friend. "He was not a social climber. He didn't globe-trot. His main interest was his children." (In addition to a daughter, the Siegels had twins, a boy and a girl, who were born in 1985.)

Despite his growing success, Mr. Siegel was coming under mounting pressure from within Kidder Peabody. Many of its areas were not doing well, and many partners feared for the firm's future. In March 1984, Ralph DeNunzio, the firm's chief executive, told Mr. Siegel that in addition to his merger and acquisitions work, Mr. Siegel had to help create an arbitrage department. The firm allotted $30 million to that effort.

The directive seemed to undermine the "Chinese Wall" that is supposed to limit the exchange of information between arbitrage departments and mergers and acquisition departments at investment-banking firms. Evidently in recognition of the inherent conflicts in having the firm's top mergers and acquisitions specialist directly involved in trading on takeover rumors, Mr. DeNunzio also indicated that Mr. Siegel's involvement in arbitrage not be disclosed publicly; it never was.

* * *

Despite pressures from the firm's officials to generate large profits, Kidder Peabody didn't have the resources to succeed at arbitrage. . . . Mr. Siegel despaired that the unit could generate legitimate profits and complained at the time that his own role in arbitrage was untenable.

Extraordinary Performance

Apparently, the result was the alleged arrangement with Robert Freeman, the head of arbitrage at Goldman Sachs, who, when he was arrested by the government last week, was charged with entering into an agreement with Mr. Siegel to swap inside information. It was information that gave Mr. Siegel a tremendous edge in his own merger and acquisitions work. Mr. Freeman, too, became a highly valued strategist on Goldman Sachs merger deals.

The arrangement turned Kidder Peabody's arbitrage unit, virtually overnight, into one of the firm's principal profit centers. In an extraordinary first-year performance that aroused amazement within the firm, the arbitrage unit accounted for more than 25% of Kidder Peabody's pretax profits the first year it existed.

* * *

Then, in January 1986, Mr. Siegel decided to move to Drexel as co-head of its merger and acquisitions department, in part because the pressures of sustaining the Kidder Peabody arbitrage operation while building the firm's mergers and acquisitions practice had become nearly unbearable. * * *

But at Drexel, Mr. Siegel put inside trading behind him. He severed his ties with Mr. Freeman. He had come to Drexel to wed his defense expertise to Drexel's legendary financing capabilities, and the result was hugely successful. . . .

Last summer, Mr. Boesky tried several times to get in touch with Mr. Siegel. In August, almost exactly four years after their fateful Harvard Club meeting, Mr. Boesky called to say, "I must meet with you" to discuss their "arrangement." Mr. Siegel resisted, then suggested a public place—the Harvard Club. Mr. Boesky said it had to be private; Mr. Siegel declined. Mr. Boesky was presumably wired at the time, but the government never obtained convincing recorded evidence of Mr. Siegel's guilt.

On Nov. 14, the question of the government's evidence became moot. After news of Mr. Boesky's settlement with the government and after he sobbed in Mr. Lipton's office, Mr. Siegel determined almost immediately to plead guilty. . . .

Though he kept coming into the office, he ceased active participation in pending transactions. The Connecticut home he loved was hastily sold. He moved his family away from New York. He quickly agreed to the government's offer of a guilty plea to two felony counts; negotiations with the SEC over the financial terms of his settlement took longer. Under his agreement, he is paying $9 million to settle the charges. When he resigned from Drexel, he also forfeited approximately $11 million—$7 million in compensation due him and about $4 million in Drexel stock.

* * *

Mr. Siegel faces a maximum of 10 years in jail and a $260,000 fine on the two charges. He also settled, without admitting or denying guilt, SEC charges that he tipped Mr. Boesky about six takeover stocks.

Mr. Siegel was permanently barred from working in the securities industry. In a statement . . . Mr. Siegel said, "I hope that, by accepting responsibility for my mistakes, I have begun to make up for the anguish I have caused my family, friends and colleagues."

In the end, it was Mr. Siegel, seemingly blessed with nearly every attribute for success, who was his own worst enemy. By embracing the use of inside information for personal gain, to advance his career, and to benefit his firm, Mr. Siegel sealed his fate. Mr. Siegel's fears that his career, like that of his father's, would end in financial ruin, proved self-fulfilling.

(6) *Corporate Criminal Liability for Insider Trading.* Should financial institutions be indicted for insider trading committed by their employees? Prior to 1988, insider trading violations had been brought only against individuals. In 1988, however, several investment banking firms were charged with insider trading violations (including Drexel Burnham, discussed supra); and a non-financial corporation (GAF) was indicted over the alleged manipulation, by one of its officers, of stock it owned in another company. For an idea of the stakes and strategies involved in such a charge, consider the following account. Stewart and

Guyon, "Damage Control: How GE and Kidder Managed to Ward Off An Impending Disaster," Wall St. J., June 8, 1987, p. 1.[90]

A group of top managers of General Electric Co. were having lunch at the company's Fairfield, Conn., headquarters last Feb. 12 when a secretary burst into their private dining room with terrible news.

Federal marshals had that morning entered the New York offices of Kidder, Peabody & Co., a securities firm acquired by GE only eight months earlier, and led away one of its top executives in handcuffs.

Events quickly took a turn for the worse.

Two days later, on Saturday, Feb. 14, Manhattan U.S. Attorney Rudolph W. Giuliani and Gary Lynch, head of the Securities and Exchange Commission's enforcement unit, met with Kidder representatives and told them the firm was to be indicted on criminal insider-trading charges. Mr. Giuliani bluntly suggested that Kidder plead guilty.

Bleak Prospect

For Kidder and GE, the prospect was devastating. Criminal prosecution and conviction, thought lawyers for the two companies, would shatter Kidder's already damaged reputation. Kidder would be barred from money management, barred from the mutual-fund business, banned from broker-dealer offerings. Its municipal-bond business could collapse. Every local and state regulator in the country would be investigating the firm, threatening even more restrictions. Foreign governments would also shun Kidder.

Then there were the likely civil suits. If convicted of a crime, the firm would be bound by findings of wrongdoing that could fuel racketeering lawsuits and treble-damage claims of untold millions. GE suddenly faced the prospect of writing off its entire $600 million investment in Kidder as worthless.

But last Thursday, 16 weeks after the trauma began, Kidder was given a new lease on life: Mr. Giuliani announced that he wouldn't prosecute the firm. Although public attention was focused primarily on the $25.3 million Kidder is paying to settle SEC charges—the second-largest settlement in the SEC's history—Mr. Giuliani's decision was considered a victory by Kidder and GE and climaxed one of the most stunning turnarounds in the annals of corporate scandal. How it happened is a story with important implications for other firms swept into Wall Street's biggest insider-trading scandal and for any company that finds itself suddenly confronted with crime in its midst.

Implications Spelled Out

At their first meeting that Saturday in February, Mr. Giuliani laid out the implications of the week's events for Kidder, which is 80% owned by GE. Martin A. Siegel, once Kidder's foremost takeover specialist, had just pleaded guilty to two felonies and described a scheme in which, he said, he swapped inside information about impending takeover attempts with Robert M. Freeman, the head of arbitrage at Goldman, Sachs & Co.

Mr. Siegel said that he passed on the information to Richard Wigton, the Kidder official arrested on Feb. 12, and Timothy Tabor, a former Kidder

---

90. Reprinted by permission of The Wall Street Journal, © Dow Jones & Company, Inc., 1987. All Rights Reserved.

arbitrager who had been arrested the day before. Kidder had earned millions of dollars by trading on the information allegedly received from Goldman.

* * *

By the end of the Saturday meeting, any peaceful settlement, let alone one that wouldn't involve criminal charges, looked highly unlikely. Given the suddenness of events, there wasn't much the Kidder people could say. They didn't know the facts, and they were still reeling from the public arrests.

Kidder's lawyers from Sullivan & Cromwell, the securities firm's longstanding outside counsel, took a combative approach close to that of Goldman, which vowed to fight the charges against its employee with all the resources it could muster. At the Saturday meeting, Sullivan & Cromwell lawyers seemed to irritate Mr. Giuliani, belittling Mr. Siegel's reliability and questioning the strength of the government's case.

But GE wasn't so sure that Sullivan & Cromwell's approach was the right one. On Feb. 12, the day the case broke, GE had put its deputy general counsel, Joseph Handros, in charge of the case. Mr. Handros, a career GE lawyer, in 1985 had negotiated an end to a suspension of GE's government contracts, a suspension imposed after GE was charged with defrauding the Defense Department. The company later pleaded guilty.

* * *

GE launched an investigation the afternoon of the 14th, using its own highly regarded audit staff. The auditors, coincidentally, had descended on Kidder the previous Monday for a thorough review of the firm's operations. Using government subpoenas in the case as a guide to suspect transactions, they pored over reams of Kidder trading records and Goldman records obtained from Goldman.

They conducted intensive interviews of Kidder employees. Exhaustive research was done to uncover every bit of public information about the takeover deals under investigation, in the hope of coming up with alternative, innocent explanations for the investments made by Kidder's arbitrage department. . . .

Discouraging Results

The results of the investigation were discouraging. The trading records provided strong corroboration of what was expected to be Mr. Siegel's testimony. Although Kidder's trading in some of the stocks under investigation . . . looked like it might be plausibly defended based on publicly available information, other situations were devastating.

* * *

During the investigation of possible criminal liability, the GE auditors picked up the pace of their broader investigation of the firm. GE officials were appalled by their discoveries. "The situation was abysmal," says one person involved in the audit. "There were no systems and controls. It was basically run like a family business." . . .

GE swiftly decided to take control of Kidder, a decision it immediately incorporated into its strategy for dealing with Mr. Giuliani. Sullivan & Cromwell, which had continued to argue that Kidder should fight the government's charges, was dismissed from the negotiations with the government and was replaced by Mr. Naftalis [a white-collar crime lawyer] and his firm, Kramer Levin. GE decided that no Kidder executives . . . would be directly involved in further negotiations with the government. The company ordered

Kidder employees to make no comments to the press like that of a Goldman employee who had vowed to "bring Giuliani down."

GE's Goal in Talks

GE's goal was to show Mr. Giuliani that GE was taking control and cleaning house. "We were trying to convince the man that the Kidder that existed then and had been involved in the Siegel situation wouldn't be the future Kidder," says a GE executive.

On March 7, Lawrence A. Bossidy, one of two GE vice chairmen and chief executive of General Electric Financial Services Inc., the holding company for GE's financial-services businesses met with Mr. Giuliani at the U.S. attorney's offices in lower Manhattan. The GE/Kidder team viewed it as a make-or-break meeting that would probably seal Kidder's fate.

Mr. Bossidy, a man of impressive stature who gave up a potential career in professional baseball to work at GE, pulled out the stops. He emphasized that GE knew nothing about the situation when it bought the firm. He described GE's investigation and acknowledged the discovery of serious problems, though he stopped short of acknowledging criminal wrongdoing. He promised sweeping management changes. And he announced that Kidder would get out of risk arbitrage. Mr. Bossidy argued that it wouldn't be fair to punish Kidder's 7,000 innocent employees and 300,000 customers with criminal sanctions that might destroy the firm.

GE's bold proposals and its candor seemed to make a strong impression on Mr. Giuliani. "He indicated we were a breath of fresh air compared to what he was hearing from other firms involved in the scandal," says one participant. Mr. Giuliani asked if Kidder would cooperate in the government's investigation, and the GE/Kidder negotiators agreed that it would. The government made no promises. Nonetheless, for the first time, the GE and Kidder negotiators saw a glimmer of hope that Mr. Giuliani might be swayed.

* * *

Late in March the GE and Kidder negotiators again met with Mr. Giuliani. This time, Mr. Giuliani set forth the conditions Kidder would have to meet, principally that it would have to reach a settlement with the SEC. It was implicit that if the conditions were met, Kidder wouldn't be indicted. "We were ecstatic," says one of the participants.

* * *

Kidder's negotiations with the SEC began the following week in Washington.

* * *

In the midst of the SEC negotiations, GE/Kidder made good on many of its representations to the government about GE's taking control and cleaning house. On May 14, GE assumed direct control of Kidder, ousting three top executives . . . and named a GE director to head the firm. . . .

Ultimately . . . Kidder agreed to pay $25.3 million—including $13.7 million in alleged illegal profits—to settle the SEC's . . . cases. It also agreed to SEC supervision of controls planned by the firm to prevent insider trading and breaches of confidentiality. By Sunday, May 31, all but a few minor details of the Kidder settlement had been hammered out.

With the settlement in hand, GE and Kidder officials waited anxiously over the weekend for the final word from Mr. Giuliani. They heard nothing. Then, last Tuesday, Messrs. Bossidy and Handros got the word they had been waiting for: Mr. Giuliani said he wouldn't prosecute.

As part of the final agreement between GE/Kidder and the government, Mr. Giuliani agreed to issue a statement announcing that Kidder wouldn't be indicted. GE and Kidder weren't allowed to see it in advance, but it was an unusually warm endorsement of an institution that, four months before, Mr. Giuliani thought should be criminally sanctioned. At a later press conference he praised GE as a "responsible corporate citizen."

Kidder's troubles aren't entirely over. The government's investigation of individuals at Kidder involved in the alleged parking scheme continues. Civil lawsuits by individuals and companies claiming damages from insider trading, breaches of confidentiality and other securities-law violations are a near-certainty.

But to those at GE and Kidder who knew just how close Kidder had come to criminal indictment, the transformation of Kidder from potential defendant to corporate good citizen in the eyes of the government seemed only slightly less than miraculous.

* * *

(7) *Congressional Response.* Despite the increase in criminal prosecutions for insider trading described above, Congress has believed that the sanctions provided in the Securities Exchange Act were inadequate to deter the practice. This led to the enactment, first, of the Insider Trading Sanctions Act of 1984.[91] This statute gives the SEC authority to bring an action in federal district court for a "civil penalty" for insider trading, the amount to be determined by the court "in light of the facts and circumstances" of the case but which could be as much as "three times the profit gained or loss avoided" as a result of the unlawful purchase or sale.[92]

This statute was then amended by the Insider Trading and Securities Fraud Enforcement Act of 1988.[93] This statute adds liability for those who control "directly or indirectly" anyone who engages in insider trading. Such "controlling persons" can be liable if they "knew or recklessly disregarded" the fact that the controlled person was likely to engage in insider trading and failed to take appropriate steps to prevent such activity. In addition, if the "controlling person" is a securities broker or dealer, or an investment adviser, they can be liable if they failed to "establish, maintain, and enforce" written "policies and procedures" to prevent the misuse of material, nonpublic information. The Act provides an alternate penalty for controlling persons of twice the gain or loss, or $1 million, whichever is higher. The Act also leaves the SEC and the Justice Department free to pursue any other remedies provided by law for insider trading. In fact, the Act substantially increases criminal penalties for violations of the 1934 Act, raising fines

---

91. See Pub.L. 98–376, 98 Stat. 1264 (1984). For discussion of the Act, see, e.g., Langevoort, The Insider Trading Sanctions Act of 1984 and Its Effect on Existing Law, 37 Vand.L.Rev. 1273 (1985); Note, A Critique of the Insider Trading Sanctions Act of 1984, 71 Va.L.Rev. 455 (1985).

92. See 15 U.S.C.A. § 78u(d)(2)(A) (Supp.).

93. See Pub.L. 100–704, 102 Stat. 4677 (1988). For legislative history, see U.S. Code Cong. & Admin.News p. 6043 (1988).

for individuals from $100,000 to $1 million; for corporations, from $500,000 to $2.5 million; and doubling the maximum jail sentence, from five to ten years.[94] What the Act does not do, however, is define insider trading with any greater precision than current caselaw provides (the Act applies to those who violate the 1934 Act "by purchasing or selling a security while in possession of material, nonpublic information"), despite the urging of many critics that Congress ought to give greater guidance.

(8) *What's Wrong With Insider Trading?* Is it clear to you that insider trading should be a crime? Some people argue that insider trading should not be criminal. In fact, some argue that it is beneficial. Consider the following version of this argument, "Insider Trading as Victimless Crime," Regulation Magazine, May/June 1985, p. 8.[95] What value would you place on "public confidence" in the integrity of the securities markets?

> Few corporate-governance issues arouse as much indignation in the general press as insider trading. Allowing executives to reap trading profits based on their knowledge of internal corporate developments is widely viewed as grossly unfair—though it is not always clear who is victimized by this unfairness. Sometimes the companies that the insiders work for suffer harm, but other times they welcome the trading. Outside shareholders may envy the profits of inside traders, but proving that they are harmed by the practice is much more difficult. On the whole, the most common grievance against insider trading is simply that it reduces public confidence, and therefore public participation, in the stock market.
>
> From the applause that greets each new prosecution of a suspected inside trader . . . one would hardly guess that the merits of this sort of regulation are being increasingly questioned in academic circles. Insider trading seems to be one of those cases where regulators are moving in the opposite direction from academic opinion.
>
> The standard defense of the practice is still Henry G. Manne's 1966 volume *Insider Trading and the Stock Market,* which has been followed by more recent work by a number of other scholars. These critics argue that insider trading enhances the efficiency of the capital market by enabling stock prices to adjust more quickly to reflect underlying economic realities. If insiders are allowed to trade they will tend to push prices in the "right" direction, and faster than if the market had to wait for formal public disclosure.

---

94. The increase in maximum imprisonment will not likely have an effect on actual sentences, however, given the Sentencing Guidelines currently in effect in federal court. The Guidelines for insider trading are explored infra, Chapter 3B.

95. Reprinted with the permission of the American Enterprise Institute for Public Policy Research. See also Carlton & Fischel, The Regulation of Insider Trading, 35 Stan.L.Rev. 857 (1983) (arguing that firms should be permitted to decide whether their employees can trade on inside information because it may be an efficient way to compensate corporate managers).

Moreover, the ultimate price adjustment attributable to a piece of news may be smoother than the sharp price "cliff" that would result if insider trading were perfectly suppressed until the news became public.

* * *

There is no general common law rule prohibiting insider trading, nor do firms seem to make much of an effort to prohibit it through internal regulation. . . .

It should not be very costly for firms to develop internal rules against insider trading. The cost to a firm of writing restrictions into executives' contracts should be minimal, and the informal sanction of dismissal is probably the most powerful sanction in very many cases anyway. The general absence of such restraints, both now and before the legal assault on insider trading got into gear in the 1960s, suggests that they are not of great value to investors.

There is an exception: law firms and financial printers often go to significant lengths to prevent insider trading by their employees. This exception makes sense in several ways. First, such trading is unlikely to serve as compensation for unusual creative services. Second, the stock bought is most often not that of the client firm, but that of a merger partner, and such purchases may drive up the price the client must pay. Moreover, the confidential information is generated by, and belongs to, the customer, not the trader's own firm. Since the clients are unlikely to look favorably on such trading, these firms, which depend on their reputations in the corporate community, have strong incentives to adopt internal controls.

* * *

Like other victimless crimes, insider trading is hard to stamp out. In a 1980 article, Michael Dooley of the University of Virginia analyzed both SEC enforcement and private damage actions under the insider trading laws and concluded that "the present enforcement system has not deterred insider trading appreciably." Stocks still rise before good news is made public and fall before bad news is made public; a 1981 study by Arthur Keown and John Pinkerton of takeovers between 1975 and 1978 found that close to half the price run-up typically occurred before the takeover was announced. This is not surprising, given the substantial sums involved. What would be surprising is if corporate America and the financial community could not between them find a way to cash in on nonpublic information without leaving a trail for the SEC and the plaintiff's securities bar.

* * *

(9) *Doonesbury On Insider Trading.*

DOONESBURY/By Garry Trudeau [96]

96. Doonesbury, © 12/1/86, 4/14/87, 4/17/87, G.B. Trudeau, reprinted with permission of Universal Press Syndicate. All rights reserved.

Chapter 2

PRINCIPLES OF LIABILITY

A. ENTITY LIABILITY

SCOPE NOTE

A critical issue in any criminal case is "who did it." In business crime cases, however, this issue takes on added difficulty. Business crime is organizational crime. How can we tell when "the organization" did it? More critically, why should we even bother prosecuting the organization criminally? Why is it not sufficient to prosecute the individuals responsible for criminal behavior? Are (large) organizations something more than, or different from, their human constituents? If so, does this make application of the criminal sanction appropriate?

The materials in this Section focus on the above issues, and are organized as follows. The Section begins with an exploration of three models of organizational behavior, models which are useful for analyzing the legal rules subsequently explored. Following this is *New York Central & Hudson River R.R. Co. v. United States,* the case which settled the principle that it is appropriate to apply the criminal law to corporations. The Notes after *New York Central* focus on whether corporate criminal liability really is a sensible idea. Subsequent materials in this Section explore the problems of applying the rule established in *New York Central.* The main cases are: *Standard Oil Co. v. United States,* involving the issue of acting "for the benefit" of the corporation; *United States v. Hilton Hotels Corp.,* involving corporate compliance programs; and *United States v. FMC Corp.,* involving questions of collective action. The Section concludes with an Endnote reviewing possible legal theories for organizational crime.

HOW DO ORGANIZATIONS BEHAVE?

THREE ANALYTICAL MODELS

If business crime is primarily organizational crime, then it presumably would be helpful to have some idea how organizations work (or should work) so that we can correctly determine under what circumstances an organization should be found liable and what we should do to the organization by way of sanction. There is no single way to describe organizational behavior, however. What follows are three models which can be used to describe organizations. The models presented were developed in the context of government organizations,

G. ALLISON, ESSENCE OF DECISION: EXPLAINING THE CUBAN MISSILE CRISIS
(1971).[1]

Model I: The Rational Actor

When confronted by a puzzling international event, how does one proceed? Let the reader consider, for example, how he would respond to the assignment "Explain the Soviet installation of missiles in Cuba." The typical analyst or layman begins by considering various aims that the Soviets might have had in mind—for example, to probe American intentions, to defend Cuba, or to improve their bargaining position. By examining the problems the Soviets faced and the character of the action they chose, the analyst eliminates some of these aims as implausible. When he is able to construct a calculation that shows how, in a particular situation, with certain objectives, he could have chosen to place missiles in Cuba, the analyst has explained the action. . . . The attempt to explain international events by recounting the aims and calculations of nations or governments is the trademark of the Rational Actor Model.

. . . To see how deeply this framework is engrained in our thinking, it is useful to consider the language used in writing or speaking about international events. We speak of occurrences not as unstructured happenings but rather as "the Soviet *decision* to abstain from attack," "the Chinese *policy* concerning defense of the mainland," and "Japanese *action* in surrendering." To summarize the relevant aspects of a state of the world as a nation's "decision" or "policy" is—at least implicitly—to slip into the rational actor framework. These terms derive their meaning from a conceptual web, the major strands of which constitute the classical model. *Decision* presupposes a decider and a choice among alternatives with reference to some goal. *Policy* means the realization in a number of particular instances of some agent's objectives. These concepts identify phenomena as actions performed by purposeful agents. This identification involves a simple extension of the pervasive everyday assumption that what human beings do is at least "intendedly rational," an assumption fundamental to most understanding of human behavior.

This everyday assumption of human purposiveness has a counterpart that plays a central role in the social sciences. One strand of social science concentrates on the reactive aspects of human behavior, specifying regularities of behavior in certain typical situations. But the central tradition in the social sciences examines the purposive, calculated, and planned aspects of human behavior. Thus economics,

---

1. © Scott Foresman, Inc., 1971. Reprinted by permission.

political science, and to a large extent sociology and psychology study human behavior as purposive, goal-directed activity.

Classical "economic man" and the rational man of modern statistical decision theory and game theory make optimal choices in narrowly constrained, neatly defined situations. In these situations rationality refers to an essentially Hobbesian notion of consistent, value-maximizing *reckoning* or adaptation within specified constraints. In economics, to choose rationally is to select the most efficient alternative, that is, the alternative that maximizes output for a given input or minimizes input for a given output. Rational consumers purchase the amount of goods, A, B, and C, etc., that maximizes their utility (by choosing a basket of goods on the highest possible indifference curve.) Rational firms produce at a point that maximizes profits (by setting marginal costs equal to marginal revenue). In modern statistical decision theory and game theory, the rational decision problem is reduced to a simple matter of selecting among a set of given alternatives, each of which has a given set of consequences: the agent selects the alternative whose consequences are preferred in terms of the agent's utility function which ranks each set of consequences in order of preference.

* * *

Dominant Inference Pattern. If a nation performed a particular action, that nation must have had ends toward which the action constituted a maximizing means. The Rational Actor Model's explanatory power stems from this inference pattern. The puzzle is solved by finding the purposive pattern within which the occurrence can be located as a value-maximizing means.

Model II: Organizational Process

For some purposes, governmental behavior can be usefully summarized as action chosen by a unitary, rational decisionmaker: centrally controlled, completely informed, and value maximizing. But this simplification must not be allowed to conceal the fact that a government consists of a conglomerate of semi-feudal, loosely allied organizations, each with a substantial life of its own. Government leaders do sit formally and, to some extent, in fact, on top of this conglomerate. But governments perceive problems through organizational sensors. Governments define alternatives and estimate consequences as their component organizations process information; governments act as these organizations enact routines. Governmental behavior can therefore be understood, according to a second conceptual model, less as deliberate choices and more as *outputs* of large organizations functioning according to standard patterns of behavior.

* * *

The preeminent feature of organizational activity is its programmed character: the extent to which behavior in any particular case is an enactment of preestablished routines. In producing outputs, the activity of each organization is characterized by:

1. *Goals: Constraints Defining Acceptable Performance.* The operational goals of an organization are seldom revealed by formal mandates. Rather, each organization's operational goals emerge as a set of constraints defining acceptable performance. Central among these constraints is organizational health, defined usually in terms of bodies assigned and dollars appropriated. The set of constraints emerges from a mix of the expectations and demands of other organizations in the government, statutory authority, demands from citizens and special interest groups, and bargaining within the organization. . . .

2. *Sequential Attention to Goals.* The existence of conflict among operational constraints is resolved by the device of sequential attention. As a problem arises, the subunits of the organization most concerned with that problem deal with it in terms of the constraints they take to be most important. When the next problem arises, another cluster of subunits deals with it, focusing on a different set of constraints.

3. *Standard Operating Procedures.* Organizations perform their "higher" functions, such as attending to problem areas, monitoring information, and preparing relevant responses for likely contingencies, by doing "lower" tasks—for example, preparing budgets, producing reports, and developing hardware. Reliable performance of these tasks requires standard operating procedures (SOPs). Rules of thumb permit concerted action by large numbers of individuals, each responding to basic cues. The rules are usually simple enough to facilitate easy learning and unambiguous application. Since procedures are "standard" they do not change quickly or easily. Without such standard procedures, it would not be possible to perform certain concerted tasks. But because of them, organizational behavior in particular instances appears unduly formalized, sluggish, and often inappropriate. Some SOPs are simply conventions that make possible regular or coordinated activity. But most SOPs are grounded in the incentive structure of the organization or even in the norms of the organization or the basic attitudes and operating style of its members. The stronger the grounding, the more resistant SOPs are to change.

4. *Programs and Repertoires.* Organizations must be capable of performing actions in which the behavior of hundreds of individuals is precisely coordinated. Assured performance requires sets of rehearsed SOPs for producing specific actions, e.g., fighting enemy units or answering an embassy's cable. Each cluster comprises a "program" (in the language of drama and computers) that the organization has available for dealing with a situation. The list of programs relevant to a type of activity, e.g., fighting, constitutes an organizational repertoire. The number of programs in a repertoire is always quite limit-

ed. When properly triggered, organizations execute programs; programs cannot be substantially changed in a particular situation. The more complex the action and the greater the number of individuals involved, the more important are programs and repertoires as determinants of organizational behavior.

* * *

7. *Organizational Learning and Change.* The parameters of organizational behavior mostly persist. In response to nonstandard problems, organizations search and routines evolve, assimilating new situations. Such learning and change follow in large part from existing procedures, but marked changes in organizations do sometimes occur. Conditions in which dramatic changes are more probable include:

   a. *Budgetary Feast.* Typically, organizations devour budgetary feasts by proceeding down the existing shopping list. Nevertheless, government leaders who control the budget and are committed to change can use extra funds to effect changes.

   b. *Prolonged Budgetary Famine.* Though a single year's famine typically results in few fundamental changes in organizational structure and procedures, it often causes a loss of effectiveness in performing certain programs. Prolonged famine, however, forces major retrenchment.

   c. *Dramatic Performance Failures.* Dramatic change occurs usually in response to major disasters. Confronted with an undeniable failure of procedures and repertoires, authorities outside the organization demand change, existing personnel are less resistant to change, and key members of the organization are replaced by individuals committed to change.

* * *

. . . Each organization's propensities and routines can be affected by the intervention of government leaders. Central direction and persistent control of organizational activity, however, is not possible. The relations among organizations and between organizations and government leaders depend critically on a number of structural variables, including the (1) nature of the job, (2) performance measures and information available to government leaders, (3) system of rewards and punishments for organizational members, and (4) procedures by which human and material resources get committed. For example, to the extent that rewards and punishments for the members of an organization are distributed by higher authorities, these authorities can exercise some control by specifying criteria for evaluating organizational output. These criteria become constraints within which organizational activity proceeds. Constraints, however, are crude instruments of control. . . .

Intervention by government leaders does sometimes change the activity of an organization in an intended direction, but instances are fewer than might be expected. . . .

Dominant Inference Pattern. If a nation performs an action of a certain type today, its organizational components must yesterday have been performing (or have had established routines for performing) an action only marginally different from today's action. At any specific point in time, t, a government consists of an established conglomerate of organizations, each with existing goals, programs, and repertoires. The characteristics of a government's action in any instance follows from those established routines, and from the choice made by government leaders—on the basis of information and estimates provided by existing routines—among established programs. The best explanation of an organization's behavior at t is $t-1$; the best prediction of what will happen at $t+1$ is t. Model II's explanatory power is achieved by uncovering the organizational routines and repertoires that produced the outputs that comprise the puzzling occurrence.

Model III: Governmental Politics

Model II's grasp of government action as organizational output, partially coordinated by a unified group of leaders, balances the classical model's efforts to understand government behavior as choices of a unitary decisionmaker. But the fascination of Model II analysis should not be allowed to blur a further level of investigation. The "leaders" who sit on top of organizations are not a monolithic group. Rather, each individual in this group is, in his own right, a player in a central, competitive game. The name of the game is politics: bargaining along regularized circuits among players positioned hierarchically within the government. Government behavior can thus be understood according to a third conceptual model, not as organizational outputs but as results of these bargaining games. In contrast with Model I, the Governmental (or Bureaucratic) Politics Model sees no unitary actor but rather many actors as players—players who focus not on a single strategic issue but on many diverse intra-national problems as well; players who act in terms of no consistent set of strategic objectives but rather according to various conceptions of national, organizational, and personal goals; players who make government decisions not by a single, rational choice but by the pulling and hauling that is politics.

The apparatus of each national government constitutes a complex arena for the intra-national game. Political leaders at the top of the apparatus are joined by the men who occupy positions on top of major organizations to form a circle of central players. Those who join the circle come with some independent standing. Because the spectrum of foreign policy problems faced by a government is so broad, decisions have to be decentralized—giving each player considerable baronial discretion.

The nature of foreign policy problems permits fundamental disagreement among reasonable men about how to solve them. Analyses yield conflicting recommendations. Separate responsibilities laid on the shoulders of distinct individuals encourage differences in what each sees and judges to be important. But the nation's actions really matter. A wrong choice could mean irreparable damage. Thus responsible men are obliged to fight for what they are convinced is right.

Men share power. Men differ about what must be done. The differences matter. This milieu necessitates that government decisions and actions result from a political process. In this process, sometimes one group committed to a course of action triumphs over other groups fighting for other alternatives. Equally often, however, different groups pulling in different directions produce a result, or better a resultant—a mixture of conflicting preferences and unequal power of various individuals—distinct from what any person or group intended. In both cases, what moves the chess pieces is not simply the reasons that support a course of action, or the routines of organizations that enact an alternative, but the power and skill of proponents and opponents of the action in question.

This characterization captures the thrust of the bureaucratic politics orientation. If problems of foreign policy arose as discrete issues, and decisions were determined one game at a time, this account would suffice. But most "issues"—e.g., Viet Nam, or the proliferation of nuclear weapons—emerge piecemeal over time, one lump in one context, a second in another. Hundreds of issues compete for players' attention every day. Each player is forced to fix upon his issues for that day, deal with them on their own terms, and rush on to the next. Thus the character of emerging issues and the pace at which the game is played converge to yield government "decisions" and "actions" as collages. Choices by one player (e.g., to authorize action by his department, to make a speech, or to refrain from acquiring certain information), resultants of minor games (e.g., the wording of a cable or the decision on departmental action worked out among lower-level players), resultants of central games (e.g., decisions, actions, and speeches bargained out among central players), and "foul-ups" (e.g., choices that are not made because they are not recognized or are raised too late, misunderstandings, etc.)—these pieces, when stuck to the same canvas, constitute government behavior relevant to an issue. To explain why a particular formal governmental decision was made, or why one pattern of governmental behavior emerged, it is necessary to identify the games and players, to display the coalitions, bargains, and compromises, and to convey some feel for the confusion.

* * *

Dominant Inference Pattern. If a nation performed an action, that action was the *resultant* of bargaining among individuals and groups within the government. Model III's explanatory power is achieved by displaying the game—the action-channel, the positions, the players, their preferences, and the pulling and hauling—that yielded, as a resultant, the action in question. Where an outcome was for the most part the triumph of an individual (e.g., the President) or group (e.g., the President's men or a cabal) this model attempts to specify the details of the game that made the victory possible. But with these as with "orphan" actions, Model III tries not to neglect the sharp differences, misunderstandings, and foul-ups that contributed to what was actually done.

NEW YORK CENTRAL AND HUDSON RIVER RAILROAD CO. v. UNITED STATES

Supreme Court of the United States, 1909.
212 U.S. 481, 29 S.Ct. 304, 53 L.Ed. 613.

MR. JUSTICE DAY delivered the opinion of the court.

This is a writ of error to the Circuit Court of the United States for the Southern District of New York, sued out by the New York Central and Hudson River Railroad Company, plaintiff in error. In the Circuit Court the railroad company and Fred L. Pomeroy, its assistant traffic manager, were convicted for the payment of rebates to the American Sugar Refining Company and others, upon shipments of sugar from the city of New York to the city of Detroit, Michigan. The indictment was upon seven counts and was returned against the company, its general traffic manager and its assistant traffic manager.[2] The first count, covering the offering of a rebate, was withdrawn from the jury by the district attorney, and it is unnecessary to consider it. The second count charges the making and publishing of a through tariff rate upon sugar by certain railroad companies, including the plaintiff in error, fixing the rate at twenty-three cents per 100 pounds from New York city to Detroit, and charges the railroad company's general traffic manager and assistant traffic manager with entering into an unlawful agreement and arrangement with the shippers, the American Sugar Refining Company of New York and the American Sugar Refining Company of New Jersey, and the consignees of the sugar, W.H. Edgar & Son, of

---

2. [The indictment was brought under the Elkins Act of 1903, which provided in part:

[I]t shall be unlawful for any person, persons, or corporation to offer, grant, or give or to solicit, accept, or receive any rebate, concession, or discrimination in respect of the transportation of any property in interstate or foreign commerce by any common carrier subject to said Act to regulate commerce and the Acts amendatory thereto whereby any such property shall by any device whatever be transported at a less rate than that named in the tariffs published and filed by such carrier, as is required by said Act to regulate commerce and the Acts amendatory thereto, or whereby any other advantage is given or discrimination is practiced. Every person or corporation who shall offer, grant, or give or solicit, accept or receive any such rebates, concession, or discrimination shall be deemed guilty of a misdemeanor, and on conviction thereof shall be punished by a fine of not less than one thousand dollars nor more than twenty thousand dollars. In all convictions occurring after the passage of this Act for offenses under said Acts to regulate commerce, whether committed before or after the passage of this Act, or for offenses under this section, no penalty shall be imposed on the convicted party other than the fine prescribed by law, imprisonment wherever now prescribed as part of the penalty being hereby abolished.—Ed.]

Detroit, whereby it was agreed that for sugar shipped over the line, the full tariff rate being paid thereon, the railroad company should give a rebate of five cents for each 100 pounds. This count charges that during the months of April and May, 1904, shipments were made under this agreement and the regular tariff rates paid thereon. On July 14 of that year a claim for a rebate in the sum of $1,524.99 was presented by the agents of the shipper and consignees and paid on the thirty-first day of August to Lowell M. Palmer, agent of the sugar company, for the benefit of the shippers and consignees. In each of the counts, except the sixth, the lawful rate is charged to have been 23 cents per 100 pounds. During the month of June, 1904, the same was reduced to 21 cents per 100 pounds, and the rebate agreed to and paid being 3 cents per 100 pounds. The second count covers the shipments of April and May, 1904; the third count, the shipments for July and August, 1904; the fourth for September, 1904; the fifth for October, 1904; the sixth for June, 1904, and the seventh for April and May, 1904. In each of these counts there is an allegation of the payment of the published rate, the presentation of the claim for the rebate, and the statement of a specific sum allowed and paid on account thereof.

Upon the trial there was a conviction upon all of the six counts, two to seven inclusive. The assistant traffic manager was sentenced to pay a fine of $1,000 upon each of the counts; the present plaintiff in error to pay a fine of $18,000 on each count, making a fine of $108,000 in all.

* * *

Numerous objections and exceptions were taken at every stage of the trial to the validity of the indictment and the proceedings thereunder. The principal attack in this court is upon the constitutional validity of certain features of the Elkins act. 32 Stat. 847. That act, among other things, provides:

"(1) That anything done or omitted to be done by a corporation common carrier subject to the act to regulate commerce, and the acts amendatory thereof, which, if done or omitted to be done by any director or officer thereof, or any receiver, trustee, lessee, agent or person acting for or employed by such corporation, would constitute a misdemeanor under said acts, or under this act, shall also be held to be a misdemeanor committed by such corporation, and upon conviction thereof it shall be subject to like penalties as are prescribed in said acts, or by this act, with reference to such persons, except as such penalties are herein changed.

* * * * * * * * * *

"In construing and enforcing the provisions of this section, the act, omission or failure of any officer, agent or other person acting for or employed by any common carrier, acting within the scope of his employment, shall in every case be also deemed to be the act, omission or failure of such carrier, as well as of that person."

It is contended that these provisions of the law are unconstitutional because Congress has no authority to impute to a corporation the commission of criminal offenses, or to subject a corporation to a criminal prosecution by reason of the things charged. The argument is that to thus punish the corporation is in reality to punish the innocent stockholders, and to deprive them of their property without opportunity to be heard, consequently without due process of law. And it is further contended that these provisions of the statute deprive the corporation of the presumption of innocence, a presumption which is part of due process in criminal prosecutions. It is urged that as there is no authority shown by the board of directors or the stockholders for the criminal acts of the agents of the company, in contracting for and giving rebates, they could not be lawfully charged against the corporation. As no action of the board of directors could legally authorize a crime, and as indeed the stockholders could not do so, the arguments come to this: that owing to the nature and character of its organization and the extent of its power and authority, a corporation cannot commit a crime of the nature charged in this case.

Some of the earlier writers on common law held the law to be that a corporation could not commit a crime. It is said to have been held by Lord Chief Justice Holt that "a corporation is not indictable, although the particular members of it are." In Blackstone's Commentaries, chapter 18, § 12, we find it stated: "A corporation cannot commit treason, or felony, or other crime in its corporate capacity, though its members may in their distinct individual capacities." The modern authority, universally, so far as we know, is the other way. In considering the subject, Bishop's New Criminal Law, § 417, devotes a chapter to the capacity of corporations to commit crime, and states the law to be: "Since a corporation acts by its officers and agents their purposes, motives, and intent are just as much those of the corporation as are the things done. If, for example, the invisible, intangible essence of air, which we term a corporation, can level mountains, fill up valleys, lay down iron tracks, and run railroad cars on them, it can intend to do it, and can act therein as well viciously as virtuously." Without citing the state cases holding the same view, we may note Telegram Newspaper Company v. Commonwealth, 172 Massachusetts, 294, in which it was held that a corporation was subject to punishment for criminal contempt, and the court, speaking by Mr. Chief Justice Field, said: "We think that a corporation may be liable criminally for certain offenses of which a specific intent may be a necessary element. There is no more difficulty in imputing to a corporation a specific intent in criminal proceedings than in civil. A corporation cannot be arrested and imprisoned in either civil or criminal proceedings, but its property may be taken either as compensation for a private wrong or as punishment for a public wrong." It is held in England that corporations may be criminally prosecuted for acts of misfeasance as well as nonfeasance. Queen v. Great North of England Railway Company, 9 Queen's Bench, 315.

It is now well established that in actions for tort the corporation may be held responsible for damages for the acts of its agent within the scope of his employment.

And this is the rule when the act is done by the agent in the course of his employment, although done wantonly or recklessly or against the express orders of the principal. In such cases the liability is not imputed because the principal actually participates in the malice or fraud, but because the act is done for the benefit of the principal, while the agent is acting within the scope of his employment in the business of the principal, and justice requires that the latter shall be held responsible for damages to the individual who has suffered by such conduct.

A corporation is held responsible for acts not within the agent's corporate powers strictly construed, but which the agent has assumed to perform for the corporation when employing the corporate powers actually authorized, and in such cases there need be no written authority under seal or vote of the corporation in order to constitute the agency or to authorize the act.

In this case we are to consider the criminal responsibility of a corporation for an act done while an authorized agent of the company is exercising the authority conferred upon him. It was admitted by the defendant at the trial that at the time mentioned in the indictment the general freight traffic manager and the assistant freight traffic manager were authorized to establish rates at which freight should be carried over the line of the New York Central and Hudson River Company, and were authorized to unite with other companies in the establishing, filing and publishing of through rates, including the through rate or rates between New York and Detroit referred to in the indictment. Thus the subject-matter of making and fixing rates was within the scope of the authority and employment of the agents of the company, whose acts in this connection are sought to be charged upon the company. Thus clothed with authority, the agents were bound to respect the regulation of interstate commerce enacted by Congress, requiring the filing and publication of rates and punishing departures therefrom. Applying the principle governing civil liability, we go only a step farther in holding that the act of the agent, while exercising the authority delegated to him to make rates for transportation, may be controlled, in the interest of public policy, by imputing his act to his employer and imposing penalties upon the corporation for which he is acting in the premises.

It is true that there are some crimes, which in their nature cannot be committed by corporations. But there is a large class of offenses, of which rebating under the Federal statutes is one, wherein the crime consists in purposely doing the things prohibited by statute. In that class of crimes we see no good reason why corporations may not be held responsible for and charged with the knowledge and purposes of their agents, acting within the authority conferred upon them. 2 Morawetz on Corporations, § 733; Green's Brice on Ultra Vires, 366. If it were not so, many offenses might go unpunished and acts be committed in violation of law, where, as in the present case, the statute requires all persons, corporate or private, to refrain from certain practices forbidden in the interest of public policy.

It is a part of the public history of the times that statutes against rebates could not be effectually enforced so long as individuals only were subject to punishment for violation of the law, when the giving of rebates or concessions enured to the benefit of the corporations of which the individuals were but the instruments. This situation, developed in more than one report of the Interstate Commerce Commission, was no doubt influential in bringing about the enactment of the Elkins Law, making corporations criminally liable.

This statute does not embrace things impossible to be done by a corporation; its objects are to prevent favoritism, and to secure equal rights to all in interstate transportation, and one legal rate, to be published and posted and accessible to all alike.

We see no valid objection in law, and every reason in public policy, why the corporation which profits by the transaction, and can only act through its agents and officers, shall be held punishable by fine because of the knowledge and intent of its agents to whom it has intrusted authority to act in the subject-matter of making and fixing rates of transportation, and whose knowledge and purposes may well be attributed to the corporation for which the agents act. While the law should have regard to the rights of all, and to those of corporations no less than to those of individuals, it cannot shut its eyes to the fact that the great majority of business transactions in modern times are conducted through these bodies, and particularly that interstate commerce is almost entirely in their hands, and to give them immunity from all punishment because of the old and exploded doctrine that a corporation cannot commit a crime would virtually take away the only means of effectually controlling the subject-matter and correcting the abuses aimed at.

There can be no question of the power of Congress to regulate interstate commerce, to prevent favoritism and to secure equal rights to all engaged in interstate trade. It would be a distinct step backward to hold that Congress cannot control those who are conducting this interstate commerce by holding them responsible for the intent and purposes of the agents to whom they have delegated the power to act in the premises.

* * *

We find no error in the proceedings of the Circuit Court, and its judgment is *Affirmed.*

NOTES AND QUERIES

(1) *Black Letter Law.* *New York Central* articulates what can be considered "Black Letter Law" for when to impose corporate criminal

liability: "[L]iability is . . . imputed . . . [when] the act is done for the benefit of the principal, while the agent is acting within the scope of his employment in the business of the principal. . . ." The rule is based on a "strict imputation" theory; that is, the act of the agent is imputed to, and "becomes," the act of the principal.

As the case indicates, the rule was taken over from the law of torts. Consider the application of such a rule in the tort context. Are the policies for the rule any different there than they are in the criminal law context? Should the Court have been so willing to borrow the concept? What Model of organizational behavior do you think the Court had in mind?

Consider the argument advanced by counsel for the defense in *New York Central* to the effect that a criminal prosecution of the corporation will punish only the stockholders, who are, after all, innocent. How did the Court deal with that argument? If the railroad had been owned by one individual (and not in corporate form), would criminal liability still have been appropriate?

In considering the above questions, it might be helpful to have in mind some of the history behind the Elkins Act, the statute involved in *New York Central*. The original Interstate Commerce Act of 1887 made willful violations a misdemeanor, subject only to a maximum fine of $5,000. That statute was amended in 1889 to allow also for a maximum of two years imprisonment for rate discrimination. The statute did not, however, provide for corporate criminal liability.

Congress passed the Elkins Act in 1903 to remedy this deficiency. Although the Elkins Act added corporate criminal liability, it also eliminated imprisonment as a possible penalty for individuals. Two reasons were advanced for these statutory changes. First, the Chairman of the Interstate Commerce Commission stated that liability ought to be imposed upon "the real offender, the corporation, which is the beneficiary of the illegal arrangement. . . ." Second, he stated that railroad officials are "a sort of fraternity" and are "personally intimate with each other." As a result they had refused to give evidence "when the result of that disclosure might be to inflict punishment and suffering upon some friend or send some associate to jail."

Interestingly, the railroads themselves were ardent supporters of the Elkins Act. The major features of the Act (including repeal of imprisonment) were at least suggested, if not actually drafted, by the Pennsylvania Railroad.[3] These railroads felt that the only way to stop selective rate-cutting—which was often demanded by large shippers— was to enlist the federal government to prosecute railroads that gave rebates or discriminatory low prices to certain shippers.

(2) *History—The Concept of Corporate Criminal Liability.* Although *New York Central* firmly established the principle that corporations could be subject to criminal prosecution, this case was not the first

---

3. See G. Kolko, Railroads and Regulation: 1876–1916, 94–101 (1965).

case which so held. Criminal liability for corporate entities was developed slowly through the course of the nineteenth century. The courts, both in England and later in the United States, were inheritors of the view, expressed by Blackstone, that a corporation could not commit "treason, or felony, or other crime in its corporate capacity." [4] However accurate this statement was with regard to treason or to felonies, English courts even before Blackstone had imposed liability on governmental entities for nuisance arising out of a failure to keep up bridges and roads.[5] This willingness to impose criminal responsibility on an entity for nonfeasance was taken over by United States courts and applied to entities which performed these governmental services, but were privately owned.[6] By the mid–1850s the courts had also allowed entity criminal liability for misfeasance, thereby moving another step closer to full criminal responsibility.[7]

Prosecutions for misfeasance or nonfeasance did not require proof of criminal intent. Where a corporation violated a duty imposed by statute, which made no mention of an intent requirement, the courts could avoid the question whether a corporation with "no soul" could have "actual wicked intent."[8] It was thus relatively easy to find criminal liability.

Where a criminal statute required proof of intent, however, the courts had more difficulty, and generally were unreceptive to corporate criminal liability. The issue was often posed as one of statutory interpretation; that is, given the intent requirement, could the corporation be a "proper subject" of criminal liability under the statute in question?[9] Note that the courts were not troubled by the question of how to determine whether to attribute particular criminal conduct to the entity, an issue of central concern for the law today. Without much analysis, courts were willing to accept the concept of a corporate

---

4. 1 W. Blackstone, Commentaries 476 (1765).

5. See L. Leigh, The Criminal Liability of Corporations in English Law 16 (1969).

6. See, e.g., Commonwealth v. Hancock Free Bridge Corp., 68 Mass. 58 (1854) (deteriorated road); State v. Morris Canal & Banking Co., 22 N.J.L. 537 (1850) (decaying bridges); President of Susquehannah & Bath Turnpike Rd. Co. v. People, 15 Wend. 267 (N.Y.Sup.Ct.1836) (deteriorated road); cf. State v. Corporation of Shelbyville, 36 Tenn. 176 (1856) (malodorous slaughterhouses) (governmental entity); People v. Corporation of Albany, 11 Wend. 539 (N.Y. Sup.Ct.1834) (polluted river basin) (governmental entity).

7. These developments are detailed in Elkins, Corporations and the Criminal Law: An Uneasy Alliance, 65 Ky.L.J. 73, 93–96 (1976). See also Collier, Impolicy of Modern Decision and Statute Making Corporations Indictable and the Confusion of Morals Thus Created, 71 Cent.L.J. 421, 422–24 (1910).

8. See State v. First Nat'l Bank of Clark, 2 S.D. 568, 571, 51 N.W. 587 (1892) (corporations cannot commit intent crimes, but could be indicted for the "public offense" charged).

9. This issue was often presented in the context of arguments that corporations, with "no body," could not be imprisoned, and therefore were not the proper subject for criminal liability under statutes where imprisonment was the only punishment provided. See Commonwealth v. Illinois Cent. RR Co., 152 Ky. 320, 328, 153 S.W. 459, 463 (1913); H. Henn & J. Alexander, Law of Corporations sec. 184 (3d ed. 1983). This statutory argument can sway even modern courts. See State v. Pacific Powder Co., 226 Or. 502, 507, 360 P.2d 530, 532 (1961) (no corporate liability for manslaughter).

"entity" as distinct from its human members and attribute the resulting harm to the "corporation," at least where there was no need to find proof of intent.[10]

Whatever problems courts and commentators were having with the notion of corporate criminal liability, however, legislators did not share them when they turned their attention to the economic issues of the late nineteenth century. Reacting to the pressures of substantial economic change—industrialization, the growth of a national economy, the rise of the railroads—legislators were attempting to regulate corporate behavior so as to prevent abuse. Criminal law was an essential component of this economic regulation:

> In every state, every extension of governmental power, every new form of regulation brought in a new batch of criminal law. Every important statute, governing railroads, banks, and corporations, or the marketing of milk, cheese, fruit, or coal . . . trailed with it at the end a sentence or two imposing criminal sanctions on violators.[11]

These statutes made clear that corporations would be proper subjects for criminal prosecution. In this way, legislators effectively overcame the formalistic judicial objections to corporate criminal liability.[12]

Legislative clarification that particular criminal statutes were to apply to corporations, and subsequent judicial acceptance of this result, have placed the notion of corporate criminal liability beyond doubt. The familiarity of the principle, however, should not obscure the fact that, as a general matter, neither legislatures nor courts have devoted much analysis to the question whether such liability actually serves the goals of the criminal law. Indeed, commentators' views on the subject, in general, have been mixed.[13] Do you think the question whether corporations should be subject to criminal penalties depends (only?) on whether such penalties can be effective in deterring improper behavior? Or can the case for criminal liability also be supported by an argument that corporations can be "blameworthy," and hence deserve punishment? Can a corporation have "wicked intent"?

10. See, e.g., V. Morawetz, A Treatise on the Law of Private Corporations, sec. 732 (2d ed. 1886).

11. L. Friedman, A History of American Law 510 (1973).

12. For further discussion of the development of corporate criminal liability, see, e.g., Elkins, Corporations and the Criminal Law: An Uneasy Alliance, 65 Ky.L.J. 73, 89–96 (1976). The late-nineteenth century view of the problem is well presented in Hamilton, Indictment of Corporations, 6 Crim.Law Mag. 317 (1885).

13. For a thorough review of arguments for and against corporate criminal liability, see Fisse, Reconstructing Corporate Criminal Law: Deterrence, Retribution, Fault, and Sanctions, 56 S.Cal.L.Rev. 1141 (1983) (arguing that corporate criminal liability is necessary for deterrence; that retribution justifies liability; that corporations can be "at fault"; and that a range of punishments beyond fines can be utilized). See also, e.g., Friedman, Some Reflections on the Corporation as Criminal Defendant, 55 Notre Dame Law. 173 (1979) (discussing problems of finding corporate criminal liability where intent is required); Note, Developments in the Law—Corporate Crime: Regulating Corporate Behavior Through Criminal Sanctions, 92 Harv.L.Rev. 1227, 1365–75 (1979) (arguing against corporate criminal liability).

(3) *Criminal Liability for Non–Corporate Entities.* Do the arguments favoring corporate criminal liability extend to entities other than the familiar privately-owned limited liability corporation? How about a corporation established by special act of Congress, and financed and partly owned by the federal government?[14] How about a City or a State?[15] Can we sensibly think of such entities as "criminals"?

With regard to criminal prosecutions of non-corporate entities, the most common (although still relatively rare) prosecutions are those involving partnerships. The leading case is *United States v. A & P Trucking Company*.[16] Justice Harlan wrote for the majority:

> Appellees, two partnerships, were charged, as entities, in separate informations with violations of 18 U.S.C. § 835, which makes it criminal knowingly to violate Interstate Commerce Commission regulations for the safe transportation in interstate commerce of "explosives and other dangerous articles." Appellee A & P Trucking Company was also charged with numerous violations of 49 U.S.C. § 322(a). The District Court dismissed, on motion, the informations on the ground that a partnership entity cannot be guilty of violating the statutes involved. The Government appealed directly to this Court under the Criminal Appeals Act, and we noted probable jurisdiction. For reasons set forth below we hold that the informations were erroneously dismissed.
>
> 49 U.S.C. § 322(a), the comprehensive misdemeanor provision of the Motor Carrier Act, provides that "any person knowingly and willfully violating any provision of this chapter [Part II of the Interstate Commerce Act], or any rule, regulation, requirement, or order [of the Interstate Commerce Commission] thereunder, or any term or condition of any certificate, permit, or license, for which a penalty is not otherwise herein provided, shall, upon conviction thereof, be fined. . . ." The Motor Carrier Act also contains its own definition of the word "person": "The term 'person' means any individual, firm, *copartnership,* corporation, company, association, or joint-stock association; . . . ." (Italics supplied.) 49 U.S.C. § 303(a).
>
> 18 U.S.C. § 835 provides that "whoever knowingly violates any such regulation [ICC regulations pertaining to the safe transport of

---

14. The Consolidated Rail Corporation ("Conrail") was such a corporation, formed in 1976 mainly to take over and run the bankrupt Penn Central Company. In United States v. Baltimore & Ohio RR Co., Crim. No. 81–00396 (D.D.C., filed Oct. 13, 1981), Conrail, along with four other railroads, was indicted for antitrust violations. Conrail pleaded nolo contendere and was fined $1 million, $900,000 of which was suspended. See 1035 ATRR A–11, 1037 ATRR A–16 (1981).

15. Cf. California v. United States, 320 U.S. 577, 64 S.Ct. 352, 88 L.Ed. 322 (1944) (State of California and City of Oakland violated Shipping Act by giving certain shippers undue preferences in wharf cargo storage fees; governmental agencies that own wharves are "persons" under the Shipping Act) (civil case); Union Pac. RR Co. v. United States, 313 U.S. 450, 61 S.Ct. 1064, 85 L.Ed. 1453 (1941) (Kansas City, Kansas, held to have violated Elkins Act for assisting railroad company in giving discriminatory advantages to certain shippers) (civil case).

16. 358 U.S. 121, 79 S.Ct. 203, 3 L.Ed.2d 165 (1958).

dangerous articles] shall be fined not more than $1,000 or imprisoned not more than one year, or both; . . . ." The section makes such regulations binding on "all common carriers" engaged in interstate commerce. And 1 U.S.C. § 1, part of a chapter entitled "Rules of Construction" and in light of which § 835 must be read, provides that "in determining the meaning of any Act of Congress, unless the context indicates otherwise— . . . the words 'person' and 'whoever' include corporations, companies, associations, firms, *partnerships,* societies, and joint stock companies, as well as individuals; . . . ." (Italics supplied.) The word "whoever" in 18 U.S.C. § 835 must, therefore, be construed to include partnerships "unless the context indicates otherwise."

We think that partnerships as entities may be proceeded against under both § 322(a) and § 835. The purpose of both statutes is clear: to ensure compliance by motor carriers, among others, with safety and other requirements laid down by the Interstate Commerce Commission in the exercise of its statutory duty to regulate the operations of interstate carriers for hire. In the effectuation of this policy it certainly makes no difference whether the carrier which commits the infraction is organized as a corporation, a joint stock company, a partnership, or an individual proprietorship. The mischief is the same, and we think that Congress intended to make the consequences of infraction the same.

True, the common law made a distinction between a corporation and a partnership, deeming the latter not a separate entity for purposes of suit. But the power of Congress to change the common-law rule is not to be doubted. We think it beyond dispute that it has done so in § 322(a) for, as we have seen, "person" in that section is expressly defined in the Motor Carrier Act to include partnerships. We think it likewise has done so in § 835, since we find nothing in that section which would justify our not applying to the word "whoever" the definition given it in 1 U.S.C. § 1, which includes partnerships. Section 835 makes regulations promulgated by the ICC for the transportation of dangerous articles binding on *all* common carriers. In view of the fact that many motor carriers are organized as partnerships rather than as corporations, the conclusion is not lightly to be reached that Congress intended that some carriers should not be subject to the full gamut of sanctions provided for infractions of ICC regulations merely because of the form under which they were organized to do business. More particularly, we perceive no reason why Congress should have intended to make partnership motor carriers criminally liable for infractions of § 322(a), but not for violations of § 835.[17]

17. [Court's footnote 4.] The fact that § 835 provides for imprisonment, as well as fine, for its violation, whereas § 322(a) provides only for fines, does not lead to a different conclusion.

It is argued that the words "knowingly" (§ 835) and "knowingly and willfully" (§ 322(a)) by implication eliminate partnerships from the coverage of the statutes, because a partnership, as opposed to its individual partners, cannot so act. But the same inability so to act *in fact* is true, of course, with regard to corporations and other associations; yet it is elementary that such impersonal entities can be guilty of "knowing" or "willful" violations of regulatory statutes through the doctrine of respondeat superior.

* * *

The policy to be served in this case is the same. The business entity cannot be left free to break the law merely because its owners . . . do not personally participate in the infraction. The treasury of the business may not with impunity obtain the fruits of violations which are committed knowingly by agents of the entity in the scope of their employment. Thus pressure is brought on those who own the entity to see to it that their agents abide by the law.

We hold, therefore, that a partnership can violate each of the statutes here in question quite apart from the participation and knowledge of the partners as individuals. The corollary is, of course, that the conviction of a partnership cannot be used to punish the individual partners, who might be completely free of personal guilt. As in the case of corporations, the conviction of the entity can lead only to a fine levied on the firm's assets.[18]

Query. Suppose one of the partners *and* the partnership had been found criminally liable. Would it be proper to fine both the partner and the partnership? Or would this subject the partner to double jeopardy? [19] In a civil suit, a judgment against a partnership would not be limited to partnership assets. Why, as Justice Harlan writes, should a fine be so limited?

(4) *State Prosecutions of Corporations for Homicide.* Are there any crimes that corporations "cannot" commit? Suppose that death results from the activities of corporate employees. Would it be inappropriate to apply the imputation rule of *New York Central?* Note that in recent years there have been an increasing number of state prosecutions of corporations under homicide statutes for deaths arising out of industrial accidents, improper product design, or improper operation of facilities open to the public.[20] Should local prosecutors bring more homicide

---

18. Justice Douglas, joined by Justices Black, Frankfurter, and Whittaker, dissented in part, arguing that Congress had spoken clearly only in the case of the Motor Carrier Act, and that since the "entity" theory of partnership had been adopted only in a minority of states, the Court should require a clear statement of Congressional intent before treating a partnership as an entity subject to criminal liability for acts of employees.

19. No: Western Laundry & Linen Rental Co. v. United States, 424 F.2d 441 (9th Cir.), certiorari denied 400 U.S. 849, 91 S.Ct. 41, 27 L.Ed.2d 87 (1970).

20. One of the most highly publicized cases was the prosecution of the Ford Motor Company for reckless homicide arising out of the design of the Pinto. See State v. Ford Motor Co., No. 5324 (Ind.Super.Ct. 1980), acquittal reported, N.Y. Times, March 14, 1980, p. A–1. The Pinto prose-

cases against corporations in these circumstances? Or is this another case where a more "targeted" statute would be preferable? Compare the approaches advocated in the following two excerpts:

June 27, 1985

TO: ALL POLICE CHIEFS

In re: REQUEST FOR HOMICIDE INVESTIGATIONS OF INDUSTRIAL DEATHS

Every year there are over 100 industrial deaths in Los Angeles County. Many of these are caused by unsafe working conditions. When employers and management personnel are grossly negligent, and that negligence results in an employee death, the employer should be prosecuted for involuntary manslaughter, and in some cases, second degree murder. I am writing to request your assistance in conducting the type of investigation of these cases which is necessary for criminal prosecution.

Due to my concern about the lack of a prosecutorial presence in this area, I created a new Occupational Safety and Health Section in the District Attorney's Office. . . . Unfortunately, Cal/OSHA safety engineers are not trained in criminal investigation techniques, nor are they always promptly called to the scene of a death. Further, the Cal/OSHA Bureau of Investigations, which has responsibility for criminal investigations, has only five field personnel statewide. These investigators are not equipped with radio communication equipment, and are not called to the scene of a death. With only one investigator assigned for the greater Los Angeles area, many cases are not investigated or are underinvestigated.

For an effective prosecution program we must obtain physical evidence before it is destroyed and witness statements before they decide not to be candid because of fear of losing their jobs. Meaningful prosecution can be accomplished if you direct your homicide investigators to conduct a preliminary investigation at the scene of an occupational death, secure all physical evidence, assure that photographs are taken, and obtain witness statements.

* * *

Very truly yours,
Ira Reiner, District Attorney [21]

cution was criticized in, e.g., Epstein, "Is Pinto A Criminal," Regulation, March/April 1980, p. 15; Wheeler, "The Public's Costly Mistrust of Cost–Benefit Safety Analysis," Nat'l L.J., Oct. 13, 1980, p. 24. Other cases include People v. Sabine Consolidated Inc., reported in Corp.Crim.Rep., April 20, 1987, p. 4 (nolo contendere plea to negligent homicide in connection with deaths of two employees); State v. Six Flags Corp., No. 650–9–84 (N.J.Super.Ct. Ocean Co. 1984) (amusement park ride), acquittal reported, N.Y. Times, July 21, 1985, p. A–1.

21. Quoted in Corporate Crime Reporter, April 13, 1987, at p. 4. Reprinted by permission.

METZGER, CORPORATE CRIMINAL LIABILITY FOR DEFECTIVE PRODUCTS: POLICIES, PROBLEMS, AND PROSPECTS
73 Geo.L.J. 1, 74–77 (1984).[22]

Courts could employ existing criminal statutes, assuming these were properly worded or sympathetically interpreted, to assess criminal penalties in the manufacturing context. Reckless conduct that causes the death of a human being supports an involuntary-manslaughter or reckless-homicide prosecution in most states. And while most states require more than ordinary tort negligence for manslaughter, a few states have defined manslaughter as negligently causing the death of another. Products that produce nonfatal injuries could also give rise to criminal liability, because reckless or negligent conduct that causes bodily harm supports a battery indictment in most jurisdictions. Indeed, actual harm is not always a necessary predicate to corporate criminal liability, since some jurisdictions have passed "endangerment" statutes which make criminal the reckless creation of a risk of harm to others and which could arguably be used against manufacturers of products that embody such a risk.

Using traditional criminal statutes appears less than desirable, however. The most obvious problem is the ex post facto application of traditional criminal statutes in a new context. Certainly it is questionable whether legislatures ever intended criminal statutes to apply in the manufacturing context. Doing so arguably contravenes basic criminal-law principles of nullem crimen sine lege and nulla poena sine lege. Novel application of broadly worded, traditional statutes would afford prosecutors undue discretion in deciding which cases to prosecute. A traditional statute provides no express guidance about how to resolve the many difficult issues of, inter alia, manufacturing costs, technological feasibility, and safety choices inherent in product-related cases, and would create the risk of "lawless" verdicts based on jury antipathy [to cost-benefit analysis]. The jury might also find it difficult to apply traditional criminal-law terms like "reckless" or "negligent" to new situations. Defendants would have little or no guidance concerning courses of conduct that would minimize their chances of future liability. A further difficulty is that general criminal statutes furnish no guidance on whether compliance with federal regulatory standards should provide a defense against liability. There are significant due process concerns about the ability of the state to punish a manufacturer for conduct that has conformed to such standards.

Product-related prosecutions under existing criminal statutes also raise disturbing problems of multiple punishment similar to those encountered in civil cases. Although multiple prosecutions for the "same offense" violate the fifth amendment's double jeopardy clause,

---

22. Reprinted with permission.

multiple prosecutions for similar product-related offenses appear to be possible.

Individuals within the corporate hierarchy could thus conceivably face multiple indictments for one allegedly wrong product decision. Manufacturers exposed to multiple prosecutions would face the prospect of multiple cash . . . fines, or the daunting prospect of several courts ordering disparate internal structural reforms under judicially imposed restructuring.

It seems obvious that criminal statutes drafted expressly for regulating the products area are required.

(5) *People v. Film Recovery Systems.* In this case the defendant corporation and three of its officers (O'Neil, Kirschbaum, and Rodriguez) were charged with involuntary manslaughter and "reckless conduct" arising out of the death of an employee, Stefan Golab. From the transcript of proceedings in Cook County Circuit Court, June 14, 1985 (No. 83–11091):[23]

THE COURT:

I hereby make the following findings:

No. 1: Stefan Golab died of acute cyanide toxicity. I arrived at that conclusion in the following way: Many witnesses testified as to the conditions of the air in the plant; not only workers, but independent witnesses as well, such as insurance inspectors, OSHA inspectors, Environmental Protection Agency inspectors, police officers and other service representatives.

The testimony of the police investigators is the most important because although we do not know the actual amount of hydrogen cyanide gas in the air on February 10, 1983, the date of the death of Stefan Golab, the police officers testified as to the air quality on the date in question. They were the investigating officers after the incident had occurred, and their symptoms were classical symptoms, which, according to the Material Safety Data Sheet, would occur if exposed to hydrogen cyanide gas at high levels.

These symptoms were nausea, burning throat, burning eyes, difficult breathing, plus others.

No. 2. I believe also the Medical Examiner, because in the Medical Examiner and toxicologist reports, the victim had a blood cyanide level of 3.45 micrograms per millilitre, which is a lethal dose and can be fatal.

---

23. See also Brickey, Death in the Workplace: Corporate Liability for Criminal Homicide, 4 Notre Dame J. of Law, Ethics & Pub.Pol. 753 (1987) (discussion of *Film Recovery* using unpublished trial record; argues that OSHA cannot adequately deal with problem). For a discussion of the question whether the OSH Act preempts state law criminal prosecution, see Note, Getting Away With Murder: Federal OSHA Preemption of State Criminal Prosecutions for Industrial Accidents, 101 Harv.L.Rev. 535 (1987) (arguing against preemption). See also People v. Chicago Magnet Wire Corp., 126 Ill.2d 356, 128 Ill. Dec. 517, 534 N.E.2d 962 (1989) (holding that state aggravated battery prosecutions for workplace injuries were not preempted by OSH Act) (reported in Corp.Crim.Rep., Feb. 6, 1989).

The manufacturer states that sodium cyanide, which has a brand name or trade name of Cyanogran, which is manufactured by the DuPont Company, when mixed with a weak alkali, with water in this case, which is a weak alkali, has a pH of approximately seven, will create hydrogen cyanide gas.

I find that the conditions under which the workers in the plant performed their duties was totally unsafe. There was an insufficient amount of safety equipment present on the premises. There were no safety instructions given to the workers. The workers were not properly warned of the hazards and dangers of working with cyanide.

The warning signs were totally inadequate. The warning signs were written in Spanish and English. The warning signs stated the words "poison" and "veneno," meaning poison in Spanish.

The problem with that is that there were more than Spanish and American workers working in this plant. Aside from the Spanish and American workers, there was Stefan Golab, plus other Polish workers.

The evidence has shown that Stefan Golab did not speak English, could not read or write English, so a sign in Spanish had no benefit to that man at all.

The Cyanogran label, which is on all the drums that were delivered to Film Recovery, which is Exhibit 13, if I recall correctly, which is the brand name for sodium cyanide, states that there are three ways in which cyanide gas can be fatal; one being inhalation of the gas hydrogen cyanide; one being ingestion of the sodium cyanide, and third, the absorption into the skin of the sodium cyanide or the liquid that was produced by the sodium cyanide in water.

This was not told to the workers, and most of the workers, including Stefan Golab, could not read the label because they could not read English; therefore, he had no knowledge of the potential danger from inhalation or absorption into their bodies.

I also find that the defendants were totally knowledgeable in the dangers which are associated with the use of cyanide.

This I ascertained through the testimony of the witnesses, including the defendants. The defendants knew that the workers were becoming nauseated and vomiting. The workers complained to all three of the defendants.

Steven O'Neil testified on May 28, 1985 as stated in the transcript on page 5–4, and I quote, "I was aware of all of the hazardous nature of cyanide." He knew hydrogen cyanide gas was present. He knew hydrogen cyanide gas, if inhaled, could be fatal.

Charles Kirschbaum saw workers vomiting. He was given a Material Safety Data Sheet. He read the label, and he knew what it said. He said that he did not wear the same equipment the workers did because he did not do the same work as the workers did, even though he testified to the contrary.

Daniel Rodriguez knew the workers got sick at the plant. He testified to that. He could read the label, and he read it many times.

I also find that Steven O'Neil, who was the President of Film Recovery Systems, President of Metallic Marketing Systems, Metallic Marketing Systems owning fifty percent of Film Recovery Systems, was in control and exercised control over both Film Recovery Systems and Metallic Marketing Systems before and after the death of Stefan Golab, which was on February 10, 1983.

Using all the facts stated above and all other evidence pertinent to this case, I find that the conditions present in the work place which caused sickness and injury to workers was reckless conduct.

I also find that the death of Stefan Golab was not accidental but in fact murder.

I also find that the defendants created the conditions present in the plant by their acts of omission and commission.

I also find that the defendants were either officers or high managerial personnel of both Film Recovery Systems and Metallic Marketing Systems, Inc.

I also find that to state that a corporation cannot be convicted of a crime because it has no mind and it cannot therefore have a mental state in order to infer knowledge on a corporation is totally erroneous.

It is my belief that the mind and mental state of a corporation is the mind and mental state of the directors, officers and high managerial personnel because they act on behalf of the corporation for both the benefit of the corporation and for themselves; and if the corporation's officers, directors and high managerial personnel act within the scope of their corporate responsibilities and employment for their benefit and for the benefit of the profits of the corporations, the corporations must be liable for what occurred in the work place.

Therefore, it is the decision of this Court that . . . because of the negligence and reckless behavior of both Film Recovery Systems, Inc. and Metallic Marketing Systems as corporate entities in allowing their officers and high managerial personnel to operate the corporations in such a manner as to cause death to one worker and injuries to other workers, that the defendant corporations Film Recovery Systems and Metallic Marketing Systems, the corporations, are guilty of involuntary manslaughter and fourteen counts of reckless conduct.

I hereby find that Film Recovery Systems and Metallic Marketing Systems are guilty as charged and enter judgment on all the findings, as to the fourteen counts of reckless conduct and involuntary manslaughter.

(6) *Safety in the Workplace.* How serious is the problem of workplace safety? What are the underlying causes of workplace injuries? Consider again the question of federal administrative regulation vs. state criminal law enforcement, in light of Simison, "Safety Last: Job Deaths and Injuries Seem to be Increasing After Years of Decline," Wall St. J., March 18, 1986, p. 1.[24]

Safety and health conditions in the nation's workplaces have stopped improving and appear to be deteriorating.

After declining for four straight years, the rates of work-related injuries, illnesses and deaths began rising across a broad front in 1984, the latest year for which statistics are available. Occupational safety and health professionals expect the 1985 rates to show a continued increase. They say that workplace safety simply has become less urgent to employers than it once was.

On a drilling rig near Gillette, Wyo., the top priority last Sept. 17 was saving time and money. Despite state safety regulations against the practice, Exeter Drilling Co. began a test for oil and natural gas long before daylight. To do that is dangerous because the lights needed to operate in the dark increase the risk that a stray electrical spark will ignite the hydrocarbons. Just such an explosion occurred about 7:30 a.m., killing John E. Nelson, a 30-year-old rig hand, and injuring four other people.

Wyoming safety authorities cited Exeter for the violation, and Exeter is appealing. To have waited for daylight, an Exeter official says, would have raised costs by as much as $6,000 because of the time the rig and its crew would have been idle. Just a month after Exeter's fatal accident, a huge piece of drilling pipe came loose and crushed another Exeter worker to death. "In hurrying to do a job fast, somebody must have done something in the wrong sequence," says Douglas Basey, Exeter's administrative manager. "You've got to cut corners out there."

Less Stress on Safety

Corner-cutting accounts for some of the rise in accidents. During the recession of the early 1980s companies reduced sharply their spending on health and safety. Then, with the recovery, many employers hired a significant number of inexperienced workers, which further contributed to the increase in mishaps. The Reagan administration has de-emphasized the writing and enforcement of safety rules. And employers have put greater stress on competitiveness, often at the expense of safety, specialists say.

The number of workplace fatalities in 1984 rose 21% from 1983, to 3,740, and injuries, 13% to 5.3 million. Workplace accidents in 1984 cost the economy $33 billion in lost wages, medical expenses, property damage and indirect costs, the National Safety Council estimates. The total excludes the effects of exposures to toxic substances, which can cause occupational illnesses that don't become evident for years.

* * *

24. Reprinted by permission of The Wall Street Journal, © Dow Jones & Company, Inc., 1986. All Rights Reserved.

Safety conditions appear to have deteriorated most in construction, manufacturing, and oil and gas extraction. Much of the decline seems to reflect the shrinkage of certain depressed industries and greater emphasis on competition in others.

* * *

For oil and gas extraction, the injury rate shot up 22% in 1984, more than for any other industrial category. Some in the industry, however, believe that the rate declined in 1985. But declining oil prices and drilling activity have idled thousands of rigs, making remaining rig operators intensely cost-conscious.

"How do you cut costs? First, you let the safety engineers go," observes a Wyoming safety official. . . .

A number of recent industrial accidents indicate a pattern of neglect of safety-related maintenance and training. Nuclear Regulatory Commission investigators found that inadequate safety training contributed to the Jan. 4 chemical leak at Kerr–McGee Corp.'s Gore, Okla., uranium-processing plant that killed one worker and injured 32 other people.

On July 23, 1984, a Unocal Corp. refinery in Lemont, Ill., erupted in an immense fireball, rocking the ground for 50 miles. The accident killed 17 and injured 17. In proposing fines totaling $31,000, OSHA cited the company for improper inspection and maintenance of pressure vessels and lack of training for fire-brigade members, among other things. Unocal, which is contesting the charges, argues that it didn't break any safety rules.

* * *

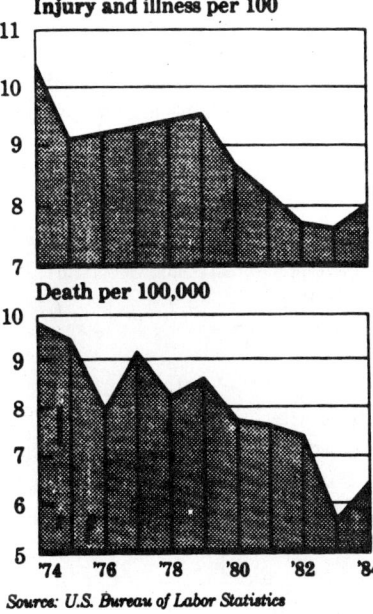

Illness, Injury And Death on the Job
Occupational incidence rates for nonfarm employers of 11 or more

Source: U.S. Bureau of Labor Statistics

The federal safety agency, established in 1970, has always faced a Herculean task in attempting to regulate the nation's 4.6 million workplaces. But budget cutbacks and Reagan administration policy changes have shrunk what Congress's Office of Technology Assessment last year called "an already weak regulatory effort." At the end of 1985, OSHA had 1,089 inspectors, down 15% from 1979.

Perhaps most controversial has been OSHA's practice of conducting a full-scale inspection only if a facility's accident rate exceeds the national average. After examining the safety records of Film Recovery Systems Inc. near Chicago, an OSHA inspector left without inspecting the plant. Several months later, in 1983, a worker there died after inhaling cyanide fumes. Three Film Recovery officials were convicted of murder last year because of the unsafe conditions.

* * *

Critics . . . fault the Reagan administration for issuing few new workplace-safety rules or exposure standards. OSHA has been working since 1980 on grain-dust rules intended to prevent explosions in grain elevators. In 1983, the agency sent a proposed standard to the Office of Management and Budget, which took nearly a year to approve less stringent wording. A weakened rule is to be published later this year. Meanwhile, since 1983, the number of grain-elevator explosions has risen steadily, to 22 last year; there were four deaths in 1985.

Because a rash of trench cave-ins killed 42 workers last year, OSHA is stepping up efforts to inspect trenches. "Trenches are easy to dig, but people don't know how to do it safely," one OSHA official observes. OSHA has issued a civil citation against Kelran Constructors Inc. of Sedalia, Colo., in the cave-in deaths of four workers last July. In proposing civil fines totaling $50,000, OSHA cited the company for, among other things, failing to shore the walls of the 34-foot-deep trench.

* * *

And, more and more, local prosecutors are stepping in. . . .

But the jury is still out on whether the wave of prosecutions will help. "It's a good idea, but it only gets the clear, outrageous violations," observes Nicholas Ashford, a Massachusetts Institute of Technology professor and a former chairman of the National Advisory Committee on Occupational Safety and Health. "What characterizes most workplace hazards is their insidious nature."

STANDARD OIL COMPANY OF TEXAS v. UNITED STATES
United States Court of Appeals, Fifth Circuit, 1962.
307 F.2d 120.

JOHN R. BROWN, CIRCUIT JUDGE.

This appeal by two corporate defendants, from fines imposed on judgments of conviction under the Connally Hot Oil Act, raises this basic question. May a corporate employer be held liable for a crime committed by employees who, although ostensibly acting in the performance of their duties, were really cooperating with a third person in the accomplishment of a criminal purpose for the benefit of that third person, and whose acts not only did not benefit the employer, but in some instances, at least, result in a theft of its property? . . .

* * *

Standard and Pasotex are corporate affiliates. Pasotex, a wholly owned subsidiary of Standard, is a common carrier by pipe line within Texas. It maintained and operated an extensive gathering system in the Kelly–Snyder Field of Scurry County, Texas. Additionally, and primarily for account of Standard, it transported a very large quantity of oil from the Field to Standard's Refinery at El Paso from which substantial quantities of refined products subsequently moved in interstate commerce. All oil gathered and transported by Pasotex was handled under intrastate tariffs filed with the Railroad Commission of Texas, the regulatory agency for oil and gas matters in the State.

Standard's activities were even more comprehensive. The Kelly–Snyder Field, discovered in 1948, is a large field both in geographical area and in petroleum reserves. Covering an area of approximately five miles by seventeen miles, it included over 1300 wells. For conservation and operational efficiency, the Field was unitized into Segments 1, 2, and 3 of SACROC. Standard as an owner of approximately 19% of the total production in the Unit was the operator of Segment 1, located in the northerly part of the Unit.

Because it is of importance later on, it is helpful to point out here that Segment 1 included the wells on the Jesse Brown Leases. Oil from Segment 1 moved through Pasotex Pumping Station No. 1. Pumping Station No. 1 is important because of the movement through it of oil from the Jesse Brown Leases into the main El Paso trunk line, and also because most of the oil gathered at Pumping Station No. 2 moved through Station No. 1 and thence into the El Paso trunk line. Pumping Station No. 2 was the collecting point for oil run from the Thompson Leases through the gathering lines of Pasotex. Ultimately there were nine Thompson wells. None of these leases was in the SACROC Unit. The wells were, therefore, operated wholly by Thompson's employees. The interest of Pasotex was limited to gathering and transportation of the Thompson oil. Standard's interest was limited to that of a purchaser having a statutory duty of buying oil tendered to it by Thompson and other producers in the field. § 8, Art. 6049a, Texas Rev. Civ.Stat.

It is in this setting that the plot was hatched, the minimum effect of which was to give Thompson credit for production in excess of that which some of his wells were making and, as to other phases, involved the actual misappropriation of large quantities of oil purchased by Standard from the Jesse Brown Segment 1 leases and for which Standard paid Thompson. Here individuals start to play the indispensable part to any corporate crime. The cast of characters includes Morgan, Ware and Purcell.

The scheme was really very simple in origin and execution. Nothing was subtle. Thompson has nine wells. Some were capable of producing their daily allowable under rules of the Texas Railroad Commission. Some of them could not. But under the Texas Conservation Laws and Regulations, the underage from one lease may not be made up from other commonly owned leases which have a capacity in excess of their assigned allowables. Oil swapped in this fashion is most certainly hot oil under the Connally Act which, forbidding "the transportation in interstate commerce * * * of contraband oil * * *," 15 U.S.C.A. § 715b, defines this as "petroleum which, * * * was produced * * * or withdrawn * * * in excess of the amounts permitted to be produced * * * or withdrawn * * * under the laws of a State * * *," 15 U.S.C.A. § 715a(1).

Over a period of approximately twelve months, Morgan (or Hart as his relief) issued false run tickets covering oil supposedly received at Pumping Station No. 2 from or produced by specified Thompson wells. Some of these purported to show that the oil actually received (and receipted for) was produced by a given well rather than the one from which it was known by Morgan (or Hart) to have come. But in numerous other instances, a false run ticket was used showing receipt of Thompson oil which had never been produced or received at all. For rendering this vital and knowing participation in these two schemes which benefited Thompson, these two Pasotex employees were paid or received substantial sums in cash or merchandise from Thompson.[25]

In those instances where, though receipted for, no oil was actually received at Pumping Station No. 2, a new problem came up. Oil received at Station No. 2 moved to Station No. 1 where Purcell was in charge. But since Station No. 2 had less oil than it had receipted for, the shortage continued at Station No. 1 when No. 2 "moved" all of its oil to No. 1. This was an actual shortage of oil in contrast to mere swapping of oil among leases. This shortage had to be made up or the whole scheme would collapse.

This is where Standard becomes involved.[26] As operator of Segment 1 of SACROC, it operated all of the wells including those on the Jesse Brown leases. It therefore had control over the movement of the oil from the leases. More than that, by reason of the unitizing agreement Standard was an owner of a substantial undivided interest (approximately 19%) in all such oil. Purcell, aware of the continuing shortages from Station No. 2, gave instructions to pumpers to increase production from Segment 1 sufficient to make up the shortage. This amounted to 6,000 or so barrels every month for a considerable period. Records, of course, had to be falsified so that this "excess" oil moving through Station No. 1 to make up Station No. 2 "shortages" would be concealed. Standard had still another role. It was the purchaser of the oil. Since this make-up of Station No. 2 shortage was the only way Standard was getting oil ostensibly purchased earlier by it from Thomp-

25. [Court's footnote 8.] These transactions were covered by counts 1 through 8. Pasotex was named together with these individuals. Standard was not named in these counts. Standard and Pasotex, Purcell and other individuals. Only as to two of them, counts 11 and 12, did the Court find evidence sufficient to hold the corporate defendants guilty.

26. [Court's footnote 9.] This was the subject of counts 9 through 15 charging

son at Station No. 2, Standard was, in effect, paying Thompson for oil which belonged to Standard (and the other Unit co-owners).

How Standard or Pasotex may be held criminally liable for "knowingly violating" [27] the statute by transportation of oil " * * * produced * * * in excess of the amounts permitted to be produced * * * under the laws of [the] state" of Texas when all of such oil came into the custody of each corporation solely as a result of a deliberate purpose by unfaithful employees to cheat or steal is the legal question for our determination. Adding irony to what some might regard as amazement is the fact that the very first moment knowledge of this activity came to light, Pasotex, after preliminary verification of its suspicions, reported the matter immediately to the Texas Railroad Commission. Thereafter followed this prosecution.

We start with the proposition that what is involved is statutory construction. We may assume that Congress can subject corporations to criminal accountability for acts of this kind committed by unfaithful servants. But the question is whether any such purpose was intended with regard to the Connally Hot Oil Act.

Since the record is absolutely barren of even the most remote whisper of suspicion that this was the case of corporations winking at dereliction by energetic, zealous employees, the Government stresses, for both a legal and psychological purpose, the contention that the two corporations received some benefit. But as we point out later, no benefit was either intended or obtained.

We have some difficulty in understanding the contentions which the Government makes in its effort to support the District Court's finding of guilt which, in turn, was based almost wholly on the idea that what these unfaithful agents were doing was their usual function for the corporation.

* * *

The corporations can be found guilty . . . only if the evidence shows that each, acting through its human agents, deliberately did these acts, that is, with the corporation "knowing" that they were being done for it. Inquiry along this line brings us face-to-face with the everyday problem of imputing knowledge to a corporation.

* * *

[After reviewing the Supreme Court's holdings in *New York Central* and *A & P Trucking* supra, the Court continued:]

Of course the defendants do not contend, nor could they, that criminal accountability and actual benefit are equated. There have been many cases, and there may well be others in the future, in which

---

27. [Court's footnote 10.] The penal provisions of the Connally Act are found in § 715e:

"Any person knowingly violating any provision of this chapter or any regulation prescribed thereunder shall upon conviction be punished by a fine of not to exceed $2,000 or by imprisonment for not to exceed six months, or by both such fine and imprisonment." 15 U.S.C.A. § 715e.

the corporation is criminally liable even though no benefit has been received in fact. But while benefit is not essential in terms of result, the purpose to benefit the corporation is decisive in terms of equating the agent's action with that of the corporation. For it is an elementary principle of agency that "an act of a servant is not within the scope of employment if it is done with no intention to perform it as a part of or incident to a service on account of which he is employed." Restatement of the Law of Agency (2d) § 235.

It is for this reason that the simple "function" test applied by the District Court—while obviously a factor of relevance—is alone insufficient upon which to rest convictions here.[28] Thus the taking in or paying out of money by a bank teller, while certainly one of his regular functions, would hardly cast the corporation for criminal liability if in such "handling" the faithless employee was pocketing the funds as an embezzler or handing them over to a confederate under some ruse.

* * *

On the facts of this record, only the most hypercritical, artificial view would find any benefit intended by the actions of Morgan, Hart or Purcell. As to oil from SACROC's Segment No. 1, this was taking Standard's oil and giving it to Thompson. Standard's oil was either stolen from it or it was, through these faithless agents, compelled to pay twice for oil supposedly purchased by it from Thompson. While the matter is not a spectacular theft as to Pasotex, it is equally positive that no benefit was conferred, nor, as the critical thing, was one intended by the actions taken at Pumping Station No. 2 by Hart and Morgan. They were not interested in doing Pasotex's work. As ostensible employees of Pasotex, they were each in the secret pay of Thompson for the purpose of assisting him in violating Texas (and hence federal) law through the movement and sale of oil produced in violation of applicable Texas statutes and regulations. Their purpose was to aid Thompson in his criminal enterprise. Of course it could not succeed for Thompson unless, through these false run tickets, the oil could be channeled into legitimate commercial transportation facilities. Without Pasotex and its pipeline transportation, and without Standard's purchase of such "hot" or non-existent oil, Thompson could not succeed. But Hart and Morgan were doing their usual tasks in handling run tickets not to advance or further the interest of Pasotex. This was done to further the criminal enterprise of which they were an indispensable part.

Hart and Morgan and Purcell each knew what he did and what he was doing. But to say that acts done by servants actuated by such evil and specifically unlawful motives were the acts of the very corporations thus sought to be cheated or implicated in practices known to be in

28. [Court's footnote 15.] The District Court applied the "function" test as the sole determinant. In its memorandum decision the Court stated, "The test, in deciding whether the conduct and knowledge of these employees should be imputed to the employer, does not turn on action consistent with or contrary to company policy, but instead *the touchstone is the function of the employee.*" (emphasis added).

serious violation of law and, moreover, to impute not only accountability but "knowledge" of such acts to the corporations, would be to disregard every accepted notion of respondeat superior. For these corporations to be found guilty of violating the Connally Hot Oil Act we may assume that it is not necessary to prove that through imputation each corporation consciously knew that the acts being done were in violation of the law. But to subject these corporations to criminal accountability it was necessary on accepted principles of imputation for each to know that these acts of Morgan, Hart and Purcell were being done. Under a statute requiring that there be "a specific wrongful intent," and the "presence of culpable intent as a necessary element of the offense * * *," the corporation does not acquire that knowledge or possess the requisite "state of mind essential for responsibility," through the activities of unfaithful servants whose conduct was undertaken to advance the interests of parties other than their corporate employer.

Consequently, the Court ought to have entered a judgment of acquittal on these counts, and the judgments must be reversed and here rendered.

* * *

NOTES AND QUERIES

(1) *Queries.* The "for the benefit" requirement is well-accepted as a component of the "Black Letter Law" rule for corporate criminal liability. As *Standard Oil* indicates, the courts have not required, however, that the corporation actually receive a benefit.[29] Nor have the courts required that the agent be acting exclusively for the benefit of the principal.[30]

What is the policy reason for the "for the benefit" requirement? Review the statement of this requirement in *New York Central,* supra, on which the Fifth Circuit relied in *Standard Oil.* Did either court explain the reason for such a requirement? In terms of the policy of corporate criminal liability, why should it matter what the agent's purpose was in committing the illegal act?

(2) *On Winking.* Can you think of any other way to test whether "the corporation" in *Standard Oil* had committed an illegal act? The Court suggests that the result might have been different if this had been a case of a corporation "winking" at employee derelictions. How does a corporation "wink"? Why should "winking" be sufficient to make the corporation criminally liable?

29. See, e.g., United States v. Cadillac Overall Supply Co., 568 F.2d 1078, 1090 (5th Cir.1978); United States v. Carter, 311 F.2d 934, 942 (6th Cir.), certiorari denied 373 U.S. 915, 83 S.Ct. 1301, 10 L.Ed.2d 415 (1963).

30. See, e.g., United States v. Gold, 743 F.2d 800, 823 (11th Cir.1984); United States v. Beusch, 596 F.2d 871, 877–78 & n. 7 (9th Cir.1979).

Consider, in this connection, *Steere Tank Lines, Inc. v. United States,* 330 F.2d 719 (5th Cir.1963). What Model of the corporation does the Court have in mind?

Griffin B. Bell, Circuit Judge.

Appellant, a motor common carrier operating under the authority of the Interstate Commerce Commission, was convicted on each of fourteen counts [31] of a criminal information after jury trial of violating the following regulation, 49 CFR, § 195.8(a) promulgated by the Commission in that drivers' logs were falsified:

"(a) Every motor carrier shall require that a driver's daily log shall be made in duplicate by every driver employed or used by it and every driver who operates a motor vehicle shall make such a log. Form BMC–59 and the instructions for its use, which form and instructions are set forth below, shall be used for this purpose.

* * *

"1. Drivers and motor carriers will be held responsible for the proper maintenance of the daily logs. Drivers shall keep the log current to the time of the last change of duty status. Failure to make logs, failure to make required entries therein, falsification of entries, or failure to file logs with the motor carrier will make both the driver and the carrier liable to prosecution."

The punishment provided for violation of this regulation is set out in Title 49 U.S.C.A. § 322(a) as follows:

"Any person knowingly and wilfully violating any provision of this chapter, or any rule, regulation, requirement, or order thereunder, or any term or condition of any certificate, permit, or license, for which a penalty is not otherwise herein provided, shall, upon conviction thereof, be fined not less than $100 nor more than $500 for the first offense and not less than $200 nor more than $500 for any subsequent offense."

There is no contention that the regulation is invalid, or that violation of it is not otherwise subject to the punishment. And, as appellant notes in its brief, having had a former conviction under

---

31. [Court's footnote 1.] Count 1 of the information will suffice as an example of the nature of each of the counts:

"On or about the 3rd day of May, 1961, at Dumas, State and Northern District of Texas, Amarillo Division, Steere Tank Lines, Inc., defendant, a corporation, a common carrier by motor vehicle, did knowingly and wilfully fail to require D.R. Kiser, a driver in its employ, to make and keep a driver's daily log in the form and manner prescribed by the Motor Carrier Safety Regulations (49 CFR 190 to 196), in that the driver's daily log, received and accepted by said defendant from said driver as a record of the work performed by said driver for said defendant on said day, contained entries showing that said driver was off duty from 7:00 p.m. to 11:59 p.m. at Mancos, Colorado, whereas, in truth and in fact, as defendant well knew, said driver was driving a motor vehicle and performing other work for said defendant at 9:26 p.m. at Fort Garland, Colorado, on said day. (49 CFR 195.8; 49 U.S. Code 322(a)."

this regulation, the punishment was assessed by the trial judge at the minimum of two hundred dollars on each count. This appeal is from the judgment of conviction, and the errors assigned go to a claimed fault in the charge, and to the admission in evidence, over objection, of testimony concerning discrepancies in logs other than those charged in the information.

Appellant had its main office in Dallas, Texas and its Safety Department in Albuquerque, New Mexico. In December 1960, it leased certain trucks, to be driven by drivers who were to be in its employ but who were theretofore assigned to the trucks and employed by the lessors, from a terminal in Dumas, Texas for the purpose of hauling asphalt from Dumas to points in the State of Colorado. The log violations charged involved drivers operating out of this terminal, and occurred in May 1961. The lease agreement was cancelled in August 1961.

The evidence showed that an Interstate Commerce Commission inspector had conferred with appellant with regard to log violations in 1956, 1957, 1958 and 1960. The government presented the testimony of six drivers who were involved in the violations charged in twelve of the fourteen counts. They testified in substance that they had made a practice of preparing and filing logs with appellant containing false entries as to the times they were off duty and that the practice was followed in operations from Dumas to the points in Colorado, including the trips involved in the respective counts of the information. Their purpose was to earn extra money by driving over and above the lawful number of hours allowed by the regulations.[32] There was also evidence, aside from the fact that the drivers wanted to make the extra money, that the extra hours were necessary in order for appellant to handle the business on hand with the available equipment and manpower.

One of the two lessors served as dispatcher for appellant at the Dumas terminal and had knowledge of the falsification of the logs. The logs were sent by him to the Safety Department in Albuquerque. A simple comparison of these records with port of entry records obtained by each driver from the State of Colorado and turned in to the dispatcher would have disclosed the falsification. These port of entry records were sent from Dumas to the main office of appellant in Dallas instead of to the Albuquerque office and, of course, one of the contentions of appellant on the trial was that they had no knowledge that such a comparison would have shown the discrepancies, and that the Safety Department in Albuquerque did not have access to the Dallas office records.

The evidence disclosed that during or near the period of the violations charged, one hundred twenty five false logs were filed by thirty five drivers operating from four different terminals of appel-

---

32. [Court's footnote 2.] The regulations require that a driver must have eight hours off duty after having driven ten consecutive hours before he can drive again.

lant relating to trips to Colorado. This disclosure resulted from a comparison by a safety inspector for the Interstate Commerce Commission of approximately three hundred of the Colorado port of entry receipts with the driver's daily logs. . . .

* * *

It is clear from the case of United States v. Illinois Central R. Co., supra, that "knowingly" and "wilfully" are separate elements of the violation, but that neither term connotes an act done with evil purpose or criminal intent. The Supreme Court there pointed out:

> "Mere omission with knowledge of the facts is not enough. The penalty may not be recovered unless the carrier is also shown 'willfully' to have failed. In statutes denouncing offenses involving turpitude, 'willfully' is generally used to mean with evil purpose, criminal intent or the like. But in those denouncing acts not in themselves wrong, the word is often used without any such implication. Our opinion in United States v. Murdock, 290 U.S. 389, 394 [54 S.Ct. 223, 78 L.Ed. 381, 384], shows that it often denotes that which is 'intentional, or knowing, or voluntary, as distinguished from accidental,' and that it is employed to characterize 'conduct marked by careless disregard whether or not one has the right so to act.' The significance of the word 'willfully' as used in § 3 now before us, was carefully considered by the circuit court of appeals for the eighth circuit in St. Louis & S.F. R. Co. v. United States (C.C.A. 8th) 169 Fed. 69. Speaking through Circuit Judge Van Devanter, now Mr. Justice Van Devanter, the court said (p. 71): ' "Willfully" means something not expressed by "knowingly," else both would not be used conjunctively * * *. But it does not mean with intent to injure the cattle or to inflict loss upon their owner because such intent on the part of a carrier is hardly within the pale of actual experience or reasonable supposition. * * * So, giving effect to these considerations, we are persuaded that it means purposely or obstinately and is designed to describe the attitude of a carrier, who, having a free will or choice, either intentionally disregards the statute or is plainly indifferent to its requirements.'"

There is no doubt that the evidence here was sufficient to support a finding by the jury of violations, knowingly and wilfully done, by appellant but that is not the end of the matter. We held in Standard Oil Company of Texas v. United States, 5 Cir., 1962, 307 F.2d 120, a case involving the prosecution of corporations under the Connally Hot Oil Act, Title 15 U.S.C.A. § 715, et seq., where the violation was through the act of employees, ostensibly in the performance of their duties, but actually in cooperation with a third person in the accomplishment of a criminal purpose for the benefit of the third person, and whose acts did not benefit the employer, but in some instances resulted in the theft of its properties, that this did not amount to acts knowingly done by the corporation. The employees were not acting for the benefit of the corporation. The question of wilfulness was not there involved as it was not an element of the statute, and the statute was analogized with those where "knowingly" was held to mean that the corporation must have acted with specific wrongful intent. . . .

The statute under consideration here is of the malum prohibitum class but, as stated, proof of both knowledge and wilfulness is required, and this brings up the issue of whether, under the charge, and in spite of the abundance of evidence to support the verdict, the court erred with respect to the instruction that appellant was bound by the knowledge that its truck drivers, alone, had of falsifications. This brings into focus, not only proof of knowledge in such manner, but the additional element of attributing wilfulness to the corporation through acts of the truck drivers alone. After giving a proper charge on the meaning of "knowingly" and "wilfully", and stating that it was not necessary to show that an evil or criminal intent existed, the court went into the subject of a corporation acting through agents and employees, and how knowledge was attributed to the corporation. So much of the charge as includes, or bears on this instruction in question is set out in the margin.[33]

Appellant states that the crux of this appeal is the answer to one question, contending that this is the meaning of the instruction: Is the appellant corporation guilty of the offenses charged simply because its drivers falsified logs, or must the government prove acts or failure to act on the part of agents of the corporation other than its drivers? This is a clear statement of the issue based on the sense of the instruction. This issue is present only because of the addition of the words "such as truck drivers", or more explicitly, if these words were to be used, because of the failure to go further and charge that knowledge sufficient to serve as a basis for a finding of a violation knowingly and wilfully done would depend on knowledge on the part of agents and employees of the corporation other than the truck drivers doing the falsifying. This necessarily follows from our holding in Standard Oil of Texas, supra, for if the falsifications were for the benefit of the truck

---

33. [Court's footnote 3.] The defendant company, as a corporation, is a legal entity, that is an intangible being, and, in the nature of things, can act, know, reason, choose or have discernment only through the medium of persons working as its managers, or agents, or any of the lesser rank of employees, and in practical necessity it is liable for the acts of such persons done within the bounds of their authority and duty as one doing some part of the work of the corporation. Knowledge affecting the corporation, which has been gained by any officer, agent or employees thereof in the course of his work for the company is attributed to the corporation, and this includes subordinate employees, such as truck drivers. The corporation cannot be shielded from such imputed knowledge on the ground that an employee in doing his regular work for the company committed a violation of some instruction by the company.

drivers only, and unknown to any other agent or employee of the corporation, they could not rise to the level of proscribed violations.

. . . While the charge as given here is technically a correct statement of law, it nevertheless may have engendered confusion and ambiguity and over emphasis in the background of the evidence that each of the truck drivers acted for his own benefit. The charge as given was erroneous in light of the evidence, and we must determine whether it constituted harmful error.

* * *

Viewing the error in the light of the whole record, the following facts become paramount. The violations occurred out of the Dumas terminal. The manager of the terminal was the agent of appellant. He knew of the falsifications. It is true that the drivers falsified the records to make extra money, but it is also true that the situation of insufficient equipment and a shortage of drivers for the rush of business made a rife situation for falsification. The "word" to at least one of the drivers at this terminal was to follow the practice which resulted in a falsified log if he was to keep his job. Moreover, appellant had been repeatedly warned of falsified logs, and had records in its possession, although in separate offices, which would have easily disclosed the falsifications. We hold that it affirmatively appears from the whole record that the error in the charge had but slight effect, if any, on the jury and was therefore harmless.

It follows that the judgment appealed from should be, and it is affirmed.

UNITED STATES v. HILTON HOTELS CORPORATION

United States Court of Appeals, Ninth Circuit, 1972.
467 F.2d 1000, certiorari denied 409 U.S. 1125, 93 S.Ct. 938,
35 L.Ed.2d 256 (1973).

BROWNING, CIRCUIT JUDGE:

This is an appeal from a conviction under an indictment charging a violation of section 1 of the Sherman Act, 15 U.S.C. § 1.

Operators of hotels, restaurants, hotel and restaurant supply companies, and other businesses in Portland, Oregon, organized an association to attract conventions to their city. To finance the association, members were asked to make contributions in predetermined amounts. Companies selling supplies to hotels were asked to contribute an amount equal to one per cent of their sales to hotel members. To aid collections, hotel members, including appellant, agreed to give preferential treatment to suppliers who paid their assessments, and to curtail purchases from those who did not.

I

The jury was instructed that such an agreement by the hotel members, if proven, would be a per se violation of the Sherman Act. Appellant argues that this was error.

[The Court rejected the argument.]

II

Appellant's president testified that it would be contrary to the policy of the corporation for the manager of one of its hotels to condition purchases upon payment of a contribution to a local association by the supplier. The manager of appellant's Portland hotel and his assistant testified that it was the hotel's policy to purchase supplies solely on the basis of price, quality, and service. They also testified that on two occasions they told the hotel's purchasing agent that he was to take no part in the boycott. The purchasing agent confirmed the receipt of these instructions, but admitted that, despite them, he had threatened a supplier with loss of the hotel's business unless the supplier paid the association assessment. He testified that he violated his instructions because of anger and personal pique toward the individual representing the supplier.

Based upon this testimony, appellant requested certain instructions bearing upon the criminal liability of a corporation for the unauthorized acts of its agents. These requests were rejected by the trial court. The court instructed the jury that a corporation is liable for the acts and statements of its agents "within the scope of their employment," defined to mean "in the corporation's behalf in performance of the agent's general line of work," including "not only that which has been authorized by the corporation, but also that which outsiders could reasonably assume the agent would have authority to do." The court added:

> "A corporation is responsible for acts and statements of its agents, done or made within the scope of their employment, even though their conduct may be contrary to their actual instructions or contrary to the corporation's stated policies."

Appellant objects only to the court's concluding statement.

* * *

[W]e think the construction of the Act that best achieves its purpose is that a corporation is liable for acts of its agents within the scope of their authority even when done against company orders.

It is obvious from the Sherman Act's language and subject matter that the Act is primarily concerned with the activities of business entities. The statute is directed against "restraint upon commercial competition in the marketing of goods or services." Apex Hosiery Co. v. Leader, 310 U.S. 469, 495, 60 S.Ct. 982, 993, 84 L.Ed. 1311 (1940). In

1890, as now, the most significant commercial activity was conducted by corporate enterprises.

Despite the fact that "the doctrine of corporate criminal responsibility for the acts of the officers was not well established in 1890", the Act expressly applies to corporate entities. 15 U.S.C. § 7. The preoccupation of Congress with corporate liability was only emphasized by the adoption in 1914 of section 14 of the Clayton Act to reaffirm and emphasize that such liability was not exclusive, and that corporate agents also were subject to punishment if they authorized, ordered, or participated in the acts constituting the violation.

Criminal liability for the acts of agents is more readily imposed under a statute directed at the prohibited act itself, one that does not make specific intent an element of the offense. . . . The Sherman Act is aimed at consequences. Specific intent is not an element of any offense under the Act except attempt to monopolize under section 2, and conscious wrongdoing is not an element of that offense. The Sherman Act is violated if "a restraint of trade or monopoly results as the consequence of a defendant's conduct or business arrangements."

The breadth and critical character of the public interests protected by the Sherman Act, and the gravity of the threat to those interests that led to the enactment of the statute, support a construction holding business organizations accountable, as a general rule, for violations of the Act by their employees in the course of their businesses. In enacting the Sherman Act, "Congress was passing drastic legislation to remedy a threatening danger to the public welfare. . . ." United Mine Workers v. Coronado Coal Co., 259 U.S. 344, 392, 42 S.Ct. 570, 576, 66 L.Ed. 975 (1922). The statute "was designed to be a comprehensive charter of economic liberty aimed at preserving free and unfettered competition as the rule of trade. It rests on the premise that the unrestrained interaction of competitive forces will yield the best allocation of our economic resources, the lowest prices, the highest quality and the greatest material progress, while at the same time providing an environment conducive to the preservation of our democratic political and social institutions." Northern Pacific Ry. v. United States, 356 U.S. at 4, 78 S.Ct. at 517.

With such important public interests at stake, it is reasonable to assume that Congress intended to impose liability upon business entities for the acts of those to whom they choose to delegate the conduct of their affairs, thus stimulating a maximum effort by owners and managers to assure adherence by such agents to the requirements of the Act.

Legal commentators have argued forcefully that it is inappropriate and ineffective to impose criminal liability upon a corporation, as distinguished from the human agents who actually perform the unlawful acts (see Francis, Criminal Responsibility of the Corporation, 18 Ill. L.Rev. 305 (1924); Canfield, Corporate Responsibility for Crime, 14 Colum.L.Rev. 469 (1914)), particularly if the acts of the agents are unauthorized. See Mueller, Mens Rea and the Corporation, 19 U.Pitt.

L.Rev. 21, 45 (1957). But it is the legislative judgment that controls, and "the great mass of legislation calling for corporate criminal liability suggests a widespread belief on the part of legislators that such liability is necessary to effectuate regulatory policy." ALI Model Penal Code, Comment on § 2.07, Tentative Draft No. 4, p. 149 (1956). Moreover, the strenuous efforts of corporate defendants to avoid conviction, particularly under the Sherman Act, strongly suggests that Congress is justified in its judgment that exposure of the corporate entity to potential conviction may provide a substantial spur to corporate action to prevent violations by employees.

Because of the nature of Sherman Act offenses and the context in which they normally occur, the factors that militate against allowing a corporation to disown the criminal acts of its agents [34] apply with special force to Sherman Act violations.

Sherman Act violations are commercial offenses. They are usually motivated by a desire to enhance profits.[35] They commonly involve large, complex, and highly decentralized corporate business enterprises, and intricate business processes, practices, and arrangements. More often than not they also involve basic policy decisions, and must be implemented over an extended period of time.

Complex business structures, characterized by decentralization and delegation of authority, commonly adopted by corporations for business purposes, make it difficult to identify the particular corporate agents responsible for Sherman Act violations. At the same time, it is generally true that high management officials, for whose conduct the corporate directors and stockholders are the most clearly responsible, are likely to have participated in the policy decisions underlying Sherman Act violations, or at least to have become aware of them.

Violations of the Sherman Act are a likely consequence of the pressure to maximize profits that is commonly imposed by corporate owners upon managing agents and, in turn, upon lesser employees. In the face of that pressure, generalized directions to obey the Sherman Act, with the probable effect of foregoing profits, are the least likely to be taken seriously. And if a violation of the Sherman Act occurs, the corporation, and not the individual agents, will have realized the profits from the illegal activity.

In sum, identification of the particular agents responsible for a Sherman Act violation is especially difficult, and their conviction and

---

34. [Court's footnote 3.] See generally Sutherland, White Collar Crime 53–54, 217–220, 229–233 (1949); ALI Model Penal Code Comment on § 207, Tentative Draft No. 4, 148–149 (1955); Watkins, Electrical Equipment Antitrust Cases—Their Implications for Government and for Business, 29 U.Chi.L.Rev. 97, 105–106 (1961); Comment, Criminal Prosecutions for Violations of the Sherman Act: In Search of a Policy, 48 Geo.L.J. 530, 538–541 (1965); Note, Corporate Criminal Liability for Acts in Violation of Company Policy, 50 Geo.L.J. 547, 552–554 (1962).

35. [Court's footnote 4.] A purpose to benefit the corporation is necessary to bring the agent's acts within the scope of his employment. Standard Oil Co. v. United States, 307 F.2d 120, 128–129 (5th Cir. 1962).

punishment is peculiarly ineffective as a deterrent. At the same time, conviction and punishment of the business entity itself is likely to be both appropriate and effective.

For these reasons we conclude that as a general rule a corporation is liable under the Sherman Act for the acts of its agents in the scope of their employment, even though contrary to general corporate policy and express instructions to the agent.

Thus the general policy statements of appellant's president were no defense. Nor was it enough that appellant's manager told the purchasing agent that he was not to participate in the boycott. The purchasing agent was authorized to buy all of appellant's supplies. Purchases were made on the basis of specifications, but the purchasing agent exercised complete authority as to source. He was in a unique position to add the corporation's buying power to the force of the boycott. Appellant could not gain exculpation by issuing general instructions without undertaking to enforce those instructions by means commensurate with the obvious risks.

* * *

NOTES AND QUERIES

(1) *Compliance Programs.* Subsequent cases have followed *Hilton Hotels'* holding that a corporation can be liable for employee action even when done contrary to express instructions.[36] Although *Hilton Hotels* was decided at a time when courts thought that there was no intent requirement for Sherman Act violations,[37] subsequent cases have not drawn this distinction. The courts have applied *Hilton Hotels'* holding even to corporate offenses that require proof of intent.[38]

Despite the acceptance of *Hilton Hotels,* courts have been willing to allow juries to consider the existence of compliance programs under other theories. In *United States v. Beusch* the Ninth Circuit approved a jury instruction allowing consideration of "corporate policies" as it might bear on the question whether the agent was acting within the scope of authority or for the benefit of the corporation.[39] In *United States v. Basic Construction Co.* the Fourth Circuit similarly approved

---

36. See, e.g., United States v. Basic Construction Co., 711 F.2d 570, 573 (4th Cir. 1983); United States v. Beusch, 596 F.2d 871, 877–78 (9th Cir.1979); United States v. Cadillac Overall Supply Co., 568 F.2d 1078, 1090 (5th Cir.1978); United States v. Gibson Products Co., Inc., 426 F.Supp. 768, 770 (S.D.Tex.1976). For earlier cases, see United States v. Armour & Co., 168 F.2d 342 (3d Cir.1948); C.I.T. Corp. v. United States, 150 F.2d 85, 90 (9th Cir.1945).

37. The intent requirement was not imposed until 1978. See United States v. United States Gypsum Co., discussed infra, p. 228.

38. See United States v. Basic Construction Co., supra, 711 F.2d at 573 (decision in *Gypsum* does not require separate consideration of corporate and employee intent); United States v. Beusch, supra, 596 F.2d at 877–78 (violation of Bank Secrecy Act, requiring finding of willfulness; rejects argument that instruction allows strict liability).

39. 596 F.2d at 878.

consideration of compliance programs in connection with the question whether the agent was acting for the benefit of the corporation.[40]

Should compliance programs be relevant to the question of corporate criminal liability? Consider this question in connection with three issues: 1) Is consideration of such programs consistent with the imputation rule for corporate criminal liability established in *New York Central?* 2) Would the policies behind corporate criminal liability be advanced by considering compliance programs? 3) Which Model of corporate organizational behavior would argue for the consideration of compliance programs?

If compliance programs were to be considered as a defense to corporate criminal liability, would it then be necessary to set some standards as to what constitutes a meaningful compliance program? Note that courts which have considered such programs have cautioned that the programs must be thoroughly done.[41] As counsel to a corporation, how would you set up such a program? Would you require employees to listen to lectures on the requirements of the law? Presently on the market are several movies designed to convince employees that horrible results will follow from violating the law. Would it be adequate to make certain that these movies are viewed by employees?

Without regard to the extent to which the law currently recognizes compliance programs as a defense to corporate criminal liability, would you as a prosecutor take them into account? Do you think it would be unfair to indict a corporation for acts done contrary to a vigorously enforced compliance program, on the theory that the corporation had done the best it could?[42] Note that in the Sentencing Reform Act of 1984 Congress explicitly accepted the relevance of compliance programs as a mitigating factor in sentencing corporations.[43]

(2) *Employee Level.* The imputation rule does not distinguish among employees at different levels in the corporate hierarchy. The standard view is that the acts of any employee can render the corporation criminally liable. *United States v. Dye Construction Co.,* a prosecution for willful violation of OSHA regulations for failing properly to shore up a trench, resulting in the death of a worker, states the standard view:[44]

> We find no merit in the further contention that the corporation cannot be guilty of willfulness based on the acts, conduct and inferentially the states of mind of the employees. Contrary to

---

40. 711 F.2d at 573.

41. See, e.g., United States v. Beusch, 596 F.2d 871, 878 (9th Cir.1979) ("Merely stating or publishing such instructions and policies without diligently enforcing them is not enough to place the acts of an employee who violates them outside the scope of his employment.").

42. Cf. Note, Developments in the Law—Corporate Crime: Regulating Corporate Behavior Through Criminal Sanctions, 92 Harv.L.Rev. 1227, 1242 (1979).

43. See 18 U.S.C.A. § 3572(a)(4) (in imposing fine, consider "if the defendant is an organization, any measure taken by the organization to discipline its employees or agents responsible for the offense or to insure against a recurrence of such an offense").

44. 510 F.2d 78, 82 (10th Cir.1975).

Dye's argument, the president [of the corporation] is not the only individual whose state of mind would be relevant. The cases recognize that corporations are responsible for the acts and omissions of their authorized agents acting in the scope of their employment. There is no doubt as to the authority of the superintendent, the foreman and the back hoe operator [who had observed the trench prior to the cave-in].

Query. Should there be any requirement that "higher-ups" be involved if there is to be corporate criminal liability? Does the treatment of compliance programs shed any light on this question?

(3) *State Common Law Crimes.* In contrast to the approach of *Hilton Hotels,* some state courts have required proof of higher authority when common law crimes are involved. Consider *People v. Canadian Fur Trappers Corp.,* 248 N.Y. 159, 161 N.E. 455 (1928).[45] The defendant corporation was owned by four brothers, the Dornfeldts, who were its only officers. The State claimed that the corporation resold (many times over) fur coats on which customers had placed a deposit, substituting a different coat should any of the customers return to pay the balance due. In the course of reversing the conviction for grand larceny, Judge Crane first discussed *New York Central,* and then wrote:

> This [the rule in *New York Central*] is the law for corporations whose servants violate positive prohibitions or commands of statutes regarding corporate acts. Such offenses do not necessarily embody the element of intent to commit a crime. The corporation would be guilty of the violation in many instances irrespective of intent or knowledge.
>
> When it comes, however, to such crimes as larceny, there enters as a necessary element the intent accompanying the act. There must be the intent to steal, to misappropriate, to apply the property of another to the use of the corporation to constitute the crime. The mere knowledge and intent of the agent of the servant to steal would not be sufficient in and of itself to make the corporation guilty. While a corporation may be guilty of larceny, may be guilty of the intent to steal, the evidence must go further than in the cases involving solely the violation of prohibitive statutes. The intent must be the intent of the corporation and not merely that of the agent. How this intent may be proved or in what cases it becomes evident depends entirely upon the circumstances of each case. Probably no general rule applicable to all situations could be stated. It has been said that the same evidence which in a civil case would be sufficient to prove a specific or malicious intention upon the part of a corporation defendant would be sufficient to show a like intention upon the part of a corporation charged criminally with the doing of an act prohibited by law (U.S.

---

45. See also Minnesota v. Christy Pontiac–GMC, 354 N.W.2d 17 (Minn.1984) (upholding theft and forgery charges; for liability, criminal acts must be "authorized, tolerated, or ratified" by corporate management).

v. Kelso Co., 86 Fed.Rep. 304), and Judge Hough in U.S. v. New York Herald Co. (159 Fed.Rep. 296) said: "To fasten this species of knowledge upon a corporation requires no other or different kind of legal inference than has long been used to justify punitive damages in cases of tort against an incorporated defendant." . . . Sufficient to say that in this case the law was correctly laid down to the jury by the trial judge when he said: "The defendant is liable in a prosecution for larceny only for acts which it authorizes through action of its officers or which is done with the acquiescence of its officers, and unless the jury find beyond a reasonable doubt such authority or acquiescence, there must be an acquittal." This in my judgment was a correct statement of the law . . . .

There may be cases where the single act of an officer will constitute larceny by a corporation, but we are not dealing with such a case here, and as I have stated, it would probably be unwise to attempt to place limits upon corporate criminal liability. The rule is, however, that the acts must be corporate acts authorized by it.

* * *

Under the law as correctly charged in this case by the trial judge, the defendant corporation was criminally liable only for such felonious acts as it had authorized through the Dornfeldts, the officers of the corporation, or for such acts as through a course of business must have been known to the corporation and its officers, and thus authorized by them. The People failed to prove that the officers or any one acting as manager of the Buffalo store, in the place and stead of the officers had authorized a resale of the complainant's coat; and further, that if the complainant's coat was resold, the resale of purchased coats was a continuous and established practice in the defendant's establishment.

(4) *Proposed Federal Criminal Code.* In 1971, the Final Report of the National Commission on Reform of Federal Criminal Laws proposed:

§ 402. Corporate Criminal Liability.

(1) Liability Defined. A corporation may be convicted of:

(a) any offense committed by an agent of the corporation within the scope of his employment on the basis of conduct authorized, requested or commanded, by any of the following or a combination of them:

[(a) any offense committed in furtherance of its affairs on the basis of conduct done, authorized, requested, commanded, ratified or recklessly tolerated in violation of a duty to maintain effective supervision of corporate affairs, by any of the following or a combination of them:]

(i) the board of directors;

(ii) an executive officer or any other agent in a position of comparable authority with respect to the formulation of corporate policy or the supervision in a managerial capacity of subordinate employees;

(iii) any person, whether or not an officer of the corporation, who controls the corporation or is responsibly involved in forming its policy;

(iv) any other person for whose act or omission the statute defining the offense provides corporate responsibility for offenses;

(b) any offense consisting of an omission to discharge a specific duty of affirmative conduct imposed on corporations by law;

(c) any misdemeanor committed by an agent of the corporation within the scope of his employment; or

(d) any offense for which an individual may be convicted without proof of culpability, committed by an agent of the corporation within the scope of his employment.

(2) Defense Precluded. It is no defense that an individual upon whose conduct liability of the corporation for an offense is based has been acquitted, has not been prosecuted or convicted or has been convicted of a different offense, or is immune from prosecution, or is otherwise not subject to justice.

The Commission recognized that this provision differed from the "black letter rule" that a corporation may be held responsible for the acts of its agents which violate the law "if such acts are done in behalf of the corporation and within the scope of the agent's employment . . . ."[46] The Commission further noted that "[i]nvolvement of the corporation's managerial or supervisory personnel is not regarded by the Federal courts as a necessary condition of corporate liability. Thus it has been held that the status of the employee violating the law in the corporate hierarchy is immaterial, and that all that is necessary is that he be acting in the area of responsibility assigned to him."[47]

The last version of the Federal Criminal Code introduced into Congress, however, had the following provision:[48]

---

[46] Working Papers of the National Commission on Reform of Federal Criminal Laws, p. 168 (1970). Note that the National Commission's provision closely resembles the Model Penal Code section on corporate liability. See Model Penal Code § 2.07 (1962).

[47] Working Papers, at p. 170.

[48] S. 1630, 97th Cong., 2d Sess., § 402 (1982).

§ 402. Liability of an Organization for Conduct of an Agent

Except as otherwise expressly provided, an organization is criminally liable for an offense if the conduct constituting the offense—

(a) is conduct of its agent, and such conduct—

(1) occurs in the performance of matters within the scope of the agent's employment or authority and is intended by the agent to benefit the organization; or

(2) is thereafter ratified or adopted by the organization; or

(b) involves a failure by the organization or its agent to discharge a specific duty of conduct imposed on the organization by law.

According to the Senate Report, "[t]his section is designed to codify current Federal law with respect to the circumstances in which the conduct of an organization may be imputed for purposes of criminal liability to the organization itself. Unlike the proposal of the National Commission, this section . . . continues existing laws rendering organizations criminally liable for the act of any agent within the area of duties or functions entrusted to him." [49]

For which proposal would you vote?

(5) *Is Compliance Possible?* Consider Landro, "Analysis of ITT's Report Shows Problems in Halting Questionable Foreign Payments," Wall St.J., June 3, 1982, p. 27.[50]

Can "questionable foreign payments" by U.S. corporations abroad ever be halted?

An analysis of the experience of International Telephone & Telegraph Corp. suggests that it will be difficult. The big multinational's latest report on its own problems, issued last month, describes a stern effort to curb the practice—and discloses millions of dollars of previously unrevealed payments, some made after passage of the Foreign Corrupt Practices Act of 1977.

"There's no way in a situation like this that you can come away with any kind of guarantee—it's just not doable," says Harry Wellington, dean of the Yale University law school. "You can promulgate strict rules, get contractual commitments that it won't happen, but there's no sure way of knowing if there is a questionable payment. It may just be built into the normal process of doing business in a foreign country."

Sitting in Review

Mr. Wellington acted as an independent "review person" for the report prepared by a special committee of the ITT board of directors. In an interview, he identifies the key problem for U.S. firms abroad as the necessity of dealing with independent agents abroad whose records aren't always available for scrutiny.

---

49. Report on the Criminal Code Reform Act of 1981, Sen. Comm. on the Judiciary, 97th Cong., 1st Sess. 83–84 (1981).

50. Reprinted by permission of The Wall Street Journal, © Dow Jones & Company, Inc., 1981. All Rights Reserved.

"There's no way American business abroad doesn't have to deal with local enterprises who act as agents," says the dean. "You can't force them to comply with the Foreign Corrupt Practices Act. And even if they did open their books to you, it probably wouldn't tell you much. That was one of our frustrations in trying to conduct this review."

ITT, with its far-flung foreign subsidiaries, was a prominently mentioned U.S. firm in the foreign payments furor of the mid 1970s. As previously reported, the new report, supplementing one made in 1978 under a consent decree with the Securities and Exchange Commission, sets a total of $13.9 million in payments for the years 1971 to 1975—up from the previously known total of $8.7 million for those years.

Company Policies

In addition, the report (a copy of which is filed with the district court in Washington, D.C.) tells of $5.7 million in newly discovered payments made after 1975, some of them as recent as last year. ITT issued policies forbidding such payments in 1976.

Without naming names, the report sets the blame on former ITT management, which, it says, made insufficient efforts to stop the practice of questionable payments. Harold S. Geneen, ITT chairman during the years in question, stepped down in 1980.

According to the special committee's report, "The highest levels of the company were aware of the reluctance of foreign managers to accept what many of them viewed as exported American morality." However, it adds, "Management's efforts were insufficient to impress upon foreign managers the importance of complying," and says ITT's lawyers and comptrollers "failed carefully and thoroughly to follow up leads to possibly questionable payments."

The investigators give much higher marks to the new ITT management under Chief Executive Rand V. Araskog. Shortly after taking over from Mr. Geneen, Mr. Araskog, appointed an ITT attorney, Herbert Steinke, to the job of compliance officer, giving him a special auditing staff and promising direct access to outside counsel, the board of directors and Mr. Araskog himself.

Drawing a Bead

"I don't think it's fair to say former ITT management was indifferent to the problem," says Mr. Steinke. "It just wasn't focused on the effort to solve it. Under the present management, the effort is very focused." He says ITT hasn't hesitated to fire managers at high levels who haven't complied with company policy.

* * *

In some cases, ITT managers overseas appeared to ignore company policies, or made "misrepresentations" to ITT headquarters, as the report puts it, about questionable payments. In February 1980, for instance, ITT learned that a European subsidiary acquired in 1973 had made questionable payments before the acquisition and after it.

There were "grease payments" too—amounts of less than $2,000 paid to various government officials for assistance in influencing the award of business. But ITT wasn't able to uncover many of those payments at the time, the report says, because foreign executives didn't reveal them. Similarly, ITT headquarters managers and Arthur Andersen & Co., the company's auditors, failed to communicate that they knew of some payments, the report asserts. (A spokesman for Andersen says: "We are aware of the report. It speaks for itself.")

The report doesn't go into much detail about where questionable payments were made, asserting that it would violate certain foreign laws to disclose the information, particularly in countries that are making their own investigations. ITT says also that lives could be endangered if names were revealed.

Shareholder suits against ITT executives and directors, pending in the Supreme Court for the state of New York, charge officials with concealing and condoning the questionable payments. One suit charges ITT with making payments to get business in Nigeria, Mexico and Austria. Austrian payments, to contractors building the Vienna General Hospital, have been widely publicized. ITT has denied the allegations.

ITT's compliance officer, Mr. Steinke, acknowledges that problems persist, such as lawyers and executives who accept thin explanations for payments that may be questionable. "But we're getting better on that," he says. "It takes time to get the message across in a company as far-flung as ITT." He spends one week a month traveling to ITT's foreign outposts, and his auditors conduct frequent spot checks, "like the Army's Inspector General," he says.

"Inevitably, in some remote country, some ITT employe will decide it's in his interest to make a questionable payment," he says. "It will be our job to identify it and correct the situation."

UNITED STATES v. FMC CORPORATION
United States Court of Appeals, Second Circuit, 1978.
572 F.2d 902.

MOORE, CIRCUIT JUDGE:

This is an appeal from a judgment of conviction entered after a jury trial against FMC Corporation ("FMC"), for violation of the Migratory Bird Treaty Act, by killing 92 migratory birds in violation of 16 U.S.C. § 703. The jury convicted defendant FMC of 18 counts of the 36 counts in the indictment.

The indictment charged that FMC between April 23, 1975 and June 25, 1975 (exact dates unknown) "did unlawfully by means of toxic and noxious waters kill migratory birds included in the terms of the conventions between [specifically naming treaties between the United States of America and Great Britain (1916), the United Mexican States (1936), and the Government of Japan (1972)], all in violation of Title 16, United States Code, section 703".

Each count of the indictment specifies the date of discovery of the alleged killing, the number of birds killed, ranging from 1 bird in each of 24 counts to 2 to 26 birds in the remaining 12 counts. The varieties of birds were described in the indictment by their ornithological and more common titles and included the Eremophila alpestris (Horned Lark), the Butorides virescens (Green Heron) and Brata canadensis (Canada Goose). They will be referred to herein as "birds".

Defendant was fined $100 on each of the 18 counts, but the fine was remitted on all but 5 counts.

The 18 counts selected by the jury for conviction covering alleged killings between April 25, 1975 and June 9, 1975 and the 18 counts for acquittal between April 23, 1975 and June 25, 1975, present no clue useful on appellate review unless there were jurors disposed favorably to the Ringbilled Gull and Shortbilled Dowicher (Counts 10 and 13) and less favorably to the Least Sandpiper and the Migratory Fringillid (Counts 8 and 36). Equally baffling is the trial court's remission of the fines except for 5 birds found dead between April 25 and May 7 (Counts 3, 4, 5, 7 and 9), because fines were imposed on 18 counts between April 25 and May 29.

So far as pertinent, the Migratory Bird Treaty Act ("MBTA") provides:

> ". . . it shall be unlawful at any time, by any means or in any manner, to . . . kill . . . any migratory bird . . . included in the terms of the conventions between the United States and Great Britain . . . [Mexico] . . . [and Japan]. . . ." 16 U.S.C. § 703.

A separate section provides for the penalties under the MBTA:

> "(a) . . . any person . . . or corporation who shall violate . . . section 703 . . . shall be deemed guilty of a misdemeanor and upon conviction thereof shall be fined not more than $500 or be imprisoned not more than six months, or both." 16 U.S.C. § 707.

The issue before us, as it was before the trial court and as charged to the jury, is clearly framed: does the statute require that the violation be intentional or in other words, where a crime is involved and a criminal penalty imposed for the violation thereof, must the violator have a mens rea.

I. THE CHARGE OF THE COURT

With the undisputed fact that the birds died as a result of the noxious waters in the pond, the Court's charge was virtually a directed verdict. The Court charged:

> "Such legislation [the statute here in issue] dispenses with the conventional requirement for criminal conduct; namely, awareness of wrongdoing and the specific intent to violate the law.
>
> * * * * * * * *
>
> In order to protect this public interest has lead [sic] to the creation of this particular statute which prohibits the killing of birds regardless of the means or manner. Therefore, under the law good will and good intention and measures taken to prevent the killing of the birds are not a defense. Therefore, if you find that the birds were killed by the products emitted from the FMC plant then you must return a verdict of guilty. . . ."

To make doubly sure that intent was not a factor to be considered, the charge continued:

> "The Government in this case does not have to prove that the defendant intended to kill the birds. You may convict the corpora-

tion even if you find that the killing of the birds was accidental or unintentional provided that you find that the FMC Corporation did kill the birds as charged in the indictment. . . ."

Lack of necessity for establishing intent is further emphasized by the court's feeling of an obligation to tell the jury that the remedial steps taken by FMC to avoid the casualties are "under the Law . . . not a defense".

The Government argues that the statute makes it "unlawful at any time, by any means or in any manner, to . . . kill, [or] attempt to . . . kill . . . any migratory bird . . ." and that there is no requirement of intent. FMC on the other hand, claims that the very use of the word "kill" imports an intentional act and that this interpretation is buttressed by the word "attempt" which, of necessity, would require an affirmative voluntary act.

II. FACTS

FMC operates a plant in Middleport, New York which manufactures various pesticides including carbofuran [51] and dithiocarbamates. Production of the dithio carbamates requires large amounts of wastewater. This wastewater was stored in a ten acre pond which held approximately 12 million gallons of water. This pond also held small amounts of wash water from the production of carbofuran. Before any wash water from the carbofuran operation went into the pond, it was chemically treated in a sump to breakdown the carbofuran into environmentally safe constituents. Thus, carbofuran itself, as opposed to the dithiocarbamates, should not have been present in the pond.

The size of the open water area attracted waterfowl during migration. In April of 1975, dead birds were discovered at the pond. Five dead birds were originally discovered on or about April 11, 1975. In the process of removing them on April 23, 1975 additional dead birds (26 Canadian Geese and 8 or 9 ducks) were discovered. On April 25 representatives of New York State Fish and Wildlife visited the site after hearing reports on dead birds. At that time the cause of the deaths was unknown, but a chemist from the Department of Environmental Conservation visited FMC on May 7 in an effort to determine the cause of death.

Dead birds continued to be found throughout April and May, and FMC attempted various measures to keep birds away from the pond. They tried using styrofoam floats to frighten the birds. There was some evidence that rather than frighten the birds, the floats acted like hunting decoys and attracted more birds. On May 16 a federal Fish and Wildlife Agent visited the FMC plant. He suggested various methods of repelling the birds, including zon guns (loud cannons), cracker shells (loud shotgun shells) and netting over the pond. FMC

---

51. [Court's footnote 3.] Carbofuran is primarily used on corn for the control of rootworms and various insects.

tried the zon guns, but they disturbed nearby citizens at night. On May 29 FMC was informed that carbofuran was the suspected cause of death. Analysis of the water in the pond indicated an extremely high concentration of carbofuran of approximately 75 parts per million which is roughly 200 times greater than the level which could cause a significant probability of death to birds. On June 13 FMC employed guards to keep the birds away, but the guards were derelict in their duties, sometimes sleeping on the job, and bird deaths continued. By the end of June, FMC had analyzed the sump used to breakdown the carbofuran and discovered it was ineffective and that carbofuran was being pumped directly into the pond.

On July 30 the indictment was handed down covering the period from April 11 to June 25, 1975. Measures taken after the time period covered by the indictment proved more effective in stopping the bird kills. During July the guard system became effective, avalarms were installed (loud pitched alarms which stimulate the distress cry of a bird), chemicals were added to the pond to break down the carbofuran, and nets were installed over the pond. By the time of trial the pond was completely graded over, having been replaced by a wastewater treatment facility.

III. DISCUSSION

Where there is no help to be had from legislative history or decisional authority, as in this specific situation, resort must be had to a rule of reason or even better, common sense. That the penalty is only a $500 fine or imprisonment for not more than six months, or both, does not affect the propriety of a criminal conviction. Were a corporate officer to have been added as a defendant he would not regard as de minimis a sentence of only six-months which, if consecutive on 36 counts, would be 18 years. Of course, this is a reductio ad absurdum argument but so is the Government's claim that the statute as to killing is "without limitation". Certainly construction that would bring every killing within the statute, such as deaths caused by automobiles, airplanes, plate glass modern office buildings or picture windows in residential dwellings into which birds fly, would offend reason and common sense. As stated in one of the early decisions under the Act, "[a]n innocent technical violation on the part of any defendant can be taken care of by the imposition of a small or nominal fine." United States v. Schultze, 28 F.Supp. 234, 236 (W.D.Ky.1939). Such situations properly can be left to the sound discretion of prosecutors and the courts.

* * *

FMC was manufacturing a powerful pesticide. For the protection of its employees it had to wash down the areas where carbofuran was manufactured. The washwater was pumped into a sump where it was to decompose into safe constituents before entering the pond. As a result of more frequent washdown procedures, instituted in the prior few months to protect workers, the carbofuran did not remain in the sump long enough to decompose. The washwater was pumped into the pond and in such quantities that migratory birds were killed. It can be assumed that FMC did not know for some weeks that carbofuran was the cause of the deaths; that it took remedial measures in an effort to keep the birds from the pond; that it conferred with State and Federal Conservation agencies and gave them full cooperation as to ways and means of avoiding the danger. Yet the fact remains that it was FMC's product which killed the birds.

FMC contends that . . . there must be "an intent to harm birds culminating in their death for there to be a conviction." FMC argues that it had no intention to kill birds, that it took no affirmative act to do so, possessed no scienter, and thus should not be held liable under the Act. It argues that, even in public welfare offenses, some "act" must be intended.

* * *

Here FMC did perform an affirmative act—it engaged in the manufacture of a pesticide known to be highly toxic. Then it failed to act to prevent this dangerous chemical from reaching the pond where it was dangerous to birds and other living organisms that ingested, or came into close contact with, the chemical. Such a situation is analogous to the situations in the various tort notions of strict liability which have insinuated themselves into American law since the English case of Rylands v. Fletcher, 3 Hurl. & C. 774 (1865), L.R. 1 Ex. 265 (1866), L.R. 3 H.L. 330 (1868). In that case a reservoir was built on the site of an abandoned coal mine. When the reservoir was filled, water leaked through the unused shaft and into an adjoining mine. The plaintiff was granted damages for the injury to his mine caused by the flooding. In so finding, the Exchequer Chamber stated:

> "We think that the true rule of law is that the person who for his own purposes brings on his lands and collects and keeps there anything likely to do mischief if it escapes, must keep it at his peril and if he does not do so, is prima facie answerable for all the damage which is the natural consequence of its escape." L.R. 1 Ex. 265, 279 (1866).

Subsequently, strict liability has been deemed to apply in various Rylands v. Fletcher situations and also when a person engages in extrahazardous activities. It has been applied to such areas as filth in a cesspool, blasting, and crop dusting. Strict liability has also been adopted by the Restatement (Second) of Torts, Tentative Draft No. 10 (April 24, 1964):

> "(1) One who carries on an abnormally dangerous activity is subject to liability for harm to the person, land or chattels of another resulting from the activity, although he has exercised the utmost care to prevent such harm.
>
> (2) Such strict liability is limited to the kind of harm, the risk of which makes the activity abnormally dangerous." Id. § 519.

The principle here is the same as in the tort situation even though in this case the carbofuran remained on the property of FMC, and the birds found their way to the attracting FMC pond. When one enters into a business or activity for his own benefit, and that benefit results in harm to others, the party should bear the responsibility for that harm.

> " 'The principle of law behind all these cases is, it is submitted, if a man takes a risk, which he ought not to take without also taking upon his shoulders the consequence of that risk, he shall pay for any damage that ensues.' . . . It means that the enterprise, involving as it does unusual hazards, considering the time and the locality, must pay its way." (footnote omitted). Harper & James, The Law of Torts 801 (1956).

Some 60 years ago a Congressman in proposing protective legislation said, in the rather florid language of the day:

> "Let the songbird live to herald to the world its happy and joyous anthem proclaiming the goodness of God to all its creatures . . .
>
> Civilization, ever advancing along the world's pathway, pleads for humanity, for the birds, so helpless and yet so useful."

As civilization advances so have other protections for individuals against convictions without scienter or even knowledge that a crime is being committed. But as science, with its technological achievements, produces an ever widening array of poisonous pesticides for the destruction of food-and-grain destroying insects, so the manufacturers of such products will have to be ever on guard lest the waste created in the manufacturing process causes damage. The vast areas of our national industry, including pesticide manufacturing, which have come under the scrutiny of the Environmental Protection Agency, attest to the difficulty of avoiding conflict between crop destruction by insects and the dangers to wildlife resulting from noxious pesticides, designed to avoid such destruction.

Although FMC was not aware of the lethal-to-birds quality of the water in its pond (and in fairness to FMC this may be assumed) nevertheless it was aware of the danger of carbofuran to humans—a fact which caused FMC to wash down the carbofuran areas more frequently, which activity in turn pumped contaminated water into the pond. Imposing strict liability on FMC in this case does not dictate that every death of a bird will result in imposing strict criminal liability on some party. However, here the statute does not include as an element of the offense "wilfully, knowingly, recklessly, or negligently"; implementation of the statute will involve only relatively minor fines; Congress recognized the important public policy behind protecting migratory birds; FMC engaged in an activity involving the manufacture of a highly toxic chemical; and FMC failed to prevent this chemical from escaping into the pond and killing birds. This is sufficient to impose strict liability on FMC.

Accordingly, we affirm.

NOTES AND QUERIES

(1) *Who Killed the Birds?* Is the decision in *FMC* to find the corporation criminally liable consistent with the imputation rule set out in the cases above? What principle did the court use for corporate criminal liability? Did the court inquire into which employee killed the birds, so that the employee's acts could be imputed to the corporation? In fact, who did kill the birds?

(2) *Collective Knowledge/Collective Action.* Can a corporation be found criminally liable based on the sum of its employees' knowledge or action, even if no individual employee either did an illegal act which caused harm or had the requisite level of knowledge? Consider *United States v. Bank of New England, N.A.*, 821 F.2d 844 (1st Cir.), certiorari denied, ___ U.S. ___, 108 S.Ct. 328, 98 L.Ed.2d 356 (1987):

Bownes, Circuit Judge.

The Bank of New England appeals a jury verdict convicting it of thirty-one violations of the Currency Transaction Reporting Act (the Act). Department of Treasury regulations promulgated under the Act require banks to file Currency Transaction Reports (CTRs) within fifteen days of customer currency transactions exceeding $10,000. The Act imposes felony liability when a bank willfully fails to file such reports "as part of a pattern of illegal activity involving transactions of more than $100,000 in a twelve-month period. . . ." 31 U.S.C. § 5322(b).

I. THE ISSUES

The Bank was found guilty of having failed to file CTRs on cash withdrawals made by James McDonough. It is undisputed that on thirty-one separate occasions between May 1983 and July 1984, McDonough withdrew from the Prudential Branch of the Bank more than $10,000 in cash by using multiple checks—each one individually under $10,000—presented simultaneously to a single bank teller. The Bank contends that such conduct did not trigger the Act's reporting requirements. . . . The Bank also argues that the trial judge's instructions on willfulness were fatally flawed, and that, in any event, the evidence did not suffice to show that it willfully failed to file CTRs on McDonough's transactions. Finally, the Bank submits that during her charge to the jury, the trial judge erroneously alluded to evidence of the Bank's conduct after the dates specified in the indictment.

The Bank had been named in a federal grand jury indictment which was returned on October 15, 1985. Count One of the indictment alleged that between May 1983 and May 1985, James McDonough, the Bank, and Carol Orlandella and Patricia Murphy—both of whom were former head tellers with the Bank's Prudential Branch—unlawfully conspired to conceal from the IRS thirty-six of McDonough's currency transactions. The trial court directed a verdict of acquittal on this count. Defendants Murphy and Orlandella were found not guilty of charges that they individually aided and abetted the failure to file CTRs on McDonough's transactions.

The bulk of the indictment alleged that the Bank, as principal, and McDonough, as an aider and abettor, willfully failed to file CTRs on thirty-six occasions between May 1983 and July 1984. Five counts were dismissed because, on those occasions, McDonough received cashier's checks from the Bank, rather than currency. McDonough was acquitted of all charges against him. The Bank was found guilty on the thirty-one remaining counts. We affirm.

II. THE REPORTABILITY OF McDONOUGH'S TRANSACTIONS

[The Court held the Act was violated by multiple simultaneous transactions, even though each transaction was less than $10,000.]

IV. WILLFULNESS OF THE BANK'S CONDUCT

A. *The Trial Court's Instruction on Willfulness*

Criminal liability under 31 U.S.C. § 5322 only attaches when a financial institution "willfully" violates the CTR filing requirement. A finding of willfulness under the Reporting Act must be supported by "proof of the defendant's knowledge of the reporting requirements and his specific intent to commit the crime." . . . Willfulness can rarely be proven by direct evidence, since it is a state of mind; it is usually established by drawing reasonable inferences from the available facts.

The Bank contends that the trial court's instructions on knowledge and specific intent effectively relieved the government of its responsibility to prove that the Bank acted willfully. The trial judge began her instructions on this element by outlining generally the concepts of knowledge and willfulness:

> Knowingly simply means voluntarily and intentionally. It's designed to exclude a failure that is done by mistake or accident, or for some other innocent reason. Willfully means voluntarily, intentionally, and with a specific intent to disregard, to disobey the law, with a bad purpose to violate the law.

The trial judge properly instructed the jury that it could infer knowledge if a defendant consciously avoided learning about the reporting requirements. The court then focused on the kind of proof that would establish the Bank's knowledge of its filing obligations. The judge instructed that the knowledge of individual employees acting within the scope of their employment is imputed to the Bank. She told the jury that "if any employee knew that multiple checks would require the filing of reports, the bank knew it, provided the employee knew it within the scope of his employment,. . . ."

The trial judge then focused on the issue of "collective knowledge":

> In addition, however, you have to look at the bank as an institution. As such, its knowledge is the sum of the knowledge of all of the employees. That is, the bank's knowledge is the totality of what all of the employees know within the scope of their employment. So, if Employee A knows one facet of the currency reporting requirement, B knows another facet of it, and C a third facet of it, the bank knows them all. So if you find that an employee within the scope of his employment knew that CTRs had to be filed, even if multiple checks are used, the bank is deemed to know it. The bank is also deemed to know it if each of several employees knew a part of that requirement and the sum of what the separate employees knew amounted to knowledge that such a requirement existed.

After discussing the two modes of establishing knowledge—via either knowledge of one of its individual employees or the aggregate knowledge of all its employees—the trial judge turned to the issue of specific intent:

> There is a similar double business with respect to the concept of willfulness with respect to the bank. In deciding whether the bank acted willfully, again you have to look first at the conduct of all employees and officers, and, second, at what the bank did or did not do as an institution. The bank is deemed to have acted willfully if one of its employees in the scope of his employment acted willfully. So, if you find that an employee willfully failed to do what was necessary to file these reports, then that is deemed to be the act of the bank, and the bank is deemed to have willfully failed to file.
>
> . . .
>
> Alternatively, the bank as an institution has certain responsibilities: as an organization, it has certain responsibilities. And you will have to determine whether the bank as an organization consciously avoided learning about and observing CTR requirements. The Government to prove the bank guilty on this theory, has to show that its failure to file was the result of some flagrant organizational indifference. In this connection, you should look at the evidence as to the bank's effort, if any, to inform its employees of the law; its effort to check on their compliance; its response to various bits of information that it got in August and September of '84 and February of '85; its policies, and how it carried out its stated policies.
>
> . . .
>
> If you find that the Government has proven with respect to any transaction either that an employee within the scope of his employment willfully failed to file a required report or that the

bank was flagrantly indifferent to its obligations, then you may find that the bank has willfully failed to file the required reports.

The Bank contends that the trial court's instructions regarding knowledge were defective because they eliminated the requirement that it be proven that the Bank violated a known legal duty. It avers that the knowledge instruction invited the jury to convict the Bank for negligently maintaining a poor communications network that prevented the consolidation of the information held by its various employees. The Bank argues that it is error to find that a corporation possesses a particular item of knowledge if one part of the corporation has half the information making up the item, and another part of the entity has the other half.

A collective knowledge instruction is entirely appropriate in the context of corporate criminal liability. . . . The acts of a corporation are, after all, simply the acts of all of its employees operating within the scope of their employment. The law on corporate criminal liability reflects this. Similarly, the knowledge obtained by corporate employees acting within the scope of their employment is imputed to the corporation. Steere Tank Lines, Inc. v. United States, 330 F.2d 719, 722 (5th Cir.1963). Corporations compartmentalize knowledge, subdividing the elements of specific duties and operations into smaller components. The aggregate of those components constitutes the corporation's knowledge of a particular operation. It is irrelevant whether employees administering one component of an operation know the specific activities of employees administering another aspect of the operation . . . . Since the Bank had the compartmentalized structure common to all large corporations, the court's collective knowledge instruction was not only proper but necessary.

Nor do we find any defects in the trial court's instructions on specific intent. The court told the jury that the concept of willfulness entails a voluntary, intentional, and bad purpose to disobey the law. Her instructions on this element, when viewed as a whole, directed the jury not to convict for accidental, mistaken or inadvertent acts or omissions. It is urged that the court erroneously charged that willfulness could be found via flagrant indifference by the Bank toward its reporting obligations. With respect to federal regulatory statutes, the Supreme Court has endorsed defining willfulness, in both civil and criminal contexts, as "a disregard for the governing statute and an indifference to its requirements." Trans World Airlines, Inc. v. Thurston, 469 U.S. 111, 127 & n. 20 (1985); United States v. Illinois Central R. Co., 303 U.S. 239 (1938). . . . Accordingly, we find no error in the court's instruction on willfulness.

B. *Evidence of Willfulness*

The Bank asserts that the evidence did not suffice to show that it had willfully failed to comply with the Act's reporting requirements. We review the evidence in the light most favorable to the government.

As already discussed, the language of the Treasury regulations itself gave notice that cash withdrawals over $10,000 were reportable, regardless of the number of checks used. Primary responsibility for CTR compliance in the Bank's branch offices was assigned to head tellers and branch managers. Head tellers Orlandella and Murphy, who knew of the nature of McDonough's transactions, also knew of the CTR filing obligations imposed by the Bank. The jury heard testimony from former bank teller Simona Wong, who stated that she knew McDonough's transactions were reportable, and that the source of her knowledge was head teller Murphy.

Even if some Bank personnel mistakenly regarded McDonough as engaging in multiple transactions, there was convincing evidence that the Bank knew that his withdrawals were reportable. An internal memo sent in May 1983 by project coordinator Jayne Brady to all branch managers and head tellers stated that " '[r]eportable transactions are expanded to include multiple transactions which aggregate more than $10,000 in any *one day.*' This includes deposits or withdrawals by a customer to or from more than one account." (Emphasis in original.) The Prudential Branch Manual instructed that if Bank personnel know that a customer has engaged in multiple transactions totalling $10,000 or more, then such transactions should be regarded as a single transaction. In addition, since 1980, the instructions on the back of CTR forms have directed that reports be filed on multiple transactions which aggregate to over $10,000. Finally, a Bank auditor discussed with Orlandella and Murphy, the Bank's obligation to report a customer's multiple transactions in a single day which amount to more than $10,000. We do not suggest that these evidentiary items in themselves legally bound the Bank to report McDonough's transactions; it is the language of the regulations that impose such a duty. This evidence, however, proved that the Bank had ample knowledge that transactions like McDonough's came within the purview of the Act.

Regarding the Bank's specific intent to violate the reporting obligation, Simona Wong testified that head teller Patricia Murphy knew that McDonough's transactions were reportable but, on one occasion, deliberately chose not to file a CTR on him because he was "a good customer." In addition, the jury heard testimony that bank employees regarded McDonough's transactions as unusual, speculated that he was a bookie, and suspected that he was structuring his transactions to avoid the Act's reporting requirements. An internal Bank memo, written after an investigation of the McDonough transactions, concluded that a "person managing the branch would have to have known that something strange was going on." Given the suspicions aroused by McDonough's banking practices and the abundance of information indicating that his transactions were reportable, the jury could have concluded that the failure by Bank personnel to, at least, inquire about the reportability of McDonough's transactions constituted flagrant indifference to the obligations imposed by the Act.

We hold that the evidence was sufficient for a finding of willfulness.

* * *

Affirmed.

Queries. (1) Was the bank's conviction affirmed because the banks "consciously avoided learning about" the CTR requirements and showed "flagrant organizational indifference" to compliance? What acts qualified under this standard? What more should the bank have done to avoid liability? (2) Was the bank's conviction affirmed on the basis that there was sufficient evidence that an employee acted willfully, with the conduct imputed to the bank under the normal imputation rule? Note, in this connection, that all the charged employees were acquitted. If they did not act willfully, who did? (3) Suppose the tellers involved had been bribed by McDonough. Could the bank still have been convicted? Under what theory? Review, in this connection, the *Standard Oil* case, supra p. 192.

(3) *Is Systems Failure Criminal?* How can we tell when "systems failure" rises to the level of criminality? Consider "Boston Bank Cites 'Systems Failure,'" N.Y. Times, Feb. 12, 1985, p. D6: [52]

The Bank of Boston said today that its failure to report $1.22 billion in cash transfers with foreign banks stemmed from mistakes by at least 10 to 12 of the bank's departments as well as its auditors.

William L. Brown, the chairman of the bank, depicted the problem as merely a "systems failure," caused by a misinterpretation of the Federal Register, which informs banks about new Government regulations.

Mr. Brown also insisted that there was "absolutely" no connection between the bank's failure to file the Federal currency reports and any illegal activity.

'Knowingly and Willfully'

The bank last week pleaded guilty to a felony charge of "knowingly and willfully" failing to report the $1.22 billion in cash transfers with nine foreign banks and was fined $500,000, a record. The currency law, which requires banks to report all cash transactions of more than $10,000, including international interbank transfers, was designed to help Federal authorities trace cash illicitly generated through narcotics, gambling and loan sharking, among other activities.

"There is nothing illegal or unsavory" about the business of transferring large sums of cash to and from foreign banks, Mr. Brown contended. "The only legal issue was our failure to file the required reports with the Internal Revenue Service," he asserted. He spoke at a highly unusual news conference at the bank's brown marble headquarters.

* * *

As for how the bank failed to make the reports, Richard A. Wiley, the bank's executive vice president, described it as merely an "internal administrative glitch." He said that "easily 10 to a dozen different departments or

---

[52]. Copyright © 1988 by The New York Times Company. Reprinted by permission.

divisions" were at fault for not catching the new regulation in the Federal Register in 1980, when it went into effect.

Mr. Brown said the bank's auditors, Coopers & Lybrand, had also not caught the error. Clark Chandler, the partner at the auditing firm who handles the bank's account, said he had no comment on Mr. Brown's statement.

And, "U.S. Says Bank of Boston Unit Was Told It Broke Law 2 Years Before Compliance," Wall St. J., Feb. 28, 1985: [53]

Federal bank examiners said they notified First National Bank of Boston that it failed to report foreign cash transactions about two years before the bank began to comply with the law requiring such reports.

For the past two weeks, the bank has maintained that it began to comply with the law shortly after it was notified of the violations. It said that it learned of the violations in June 1984 during a probe by the New England organized-crime strike force into the bank and began reporting the cash transactions in October 1984.

H. Joe Selby, acting comptroller of the currency, said in a letter to a House Banking subcommittee on oversight and investigations that the Comptroller determined First National was in violation of the currency reporting law during an examination of the bank in September 1982. Mr. Selby attributed the violations partly to the bank's "unfamiliarity with regulations concerning international transactions."

Mr. Selby wrote that the violations were noted in a report to the bank and that the bank promised "corrective action."

* * *

In addition, Mr. Selby's letter disclosed that at about the time of its examination of the bank, the Treasury Department had been in contact with First National's "officer in charge of currency operations." Mr. Selby said that official was "not completely familiar with the provisions of the Bank Secrecy Act regulations."

A source familiar with one of the current investigations of the bank said that Daniel Dormer, First National vice president for coin and currency, is the bank official who contacted the Treasury Department. According to the source, Mr. Dormer was told that the law required that the bank file cash-transaction reports on foreign interbank transfers. Mr. Dormer wouldn't comment yesterday.

Since 1974, banks have been required to report cash transactions of more than $10,000 with individuals or companies. That law was amended in July 1980 to include cash transfers between domestic and foreign banks. The currency-transaction law was designed to give federal authorities a tool to investigate cases involving drug deals, corruption and organized crime, where large amounts of cash change hands.

ENDNOTE: TOWARD A THEORY OF ORGANIZATIONAL CRIME

The imputation rule of *New York Central* was adopted in the context of a crime which could be committed by a single employee (or

---

[53]. Reprinted by permission of The Wall Street Journal, © Dow Jones & Company, Inc., 1985. All Rights Reserved.

an identifiable group of employees) and which required no proof of intent. In such a setting, the imputation rule has worked quite well (assuming, of course, that there should be corporate criminal liability). Not every crime, however, fits this neat mold. Particularly troubling are those crimes where it is difficult to pinpoint responsibility in particular employees, and those crimes where the intent requirement carries some sense of moral opprobrium. As the above materials indicate, many crimes for which corporations are being prosecuted today fall into these categories. Current corporate behavior is marked by organizational complexity; and the harms caused are more frequently of the sort that trigger statutes requiring proof of "willful" behavior.

Note, also, that the imputation rule was developed in the tort context. Respondeat superior was accepted in the tort area to shift to the enterprise civil liability for activity which benefits the enterprise. This not only serves the tort law policy of compensating for loss. It also serves economic policy, insuring that enterprises internalize in their cost structures all the costs of doing business, and that a proper trade-off is made between the cost of accidents and the cost of prevention. Tort law seeks to deter inefficient behavior. Criminal law shares an element of deterrence, but its goal is to deter and punish blameworthy behavior. "Improper" behavior may be "inefficient," but the two do not necessarily overlap.

The question, then, is whether the analytical approach to corporate criminal responsibility taken by the courts today is adequate to deal with crimes of organizational complexity, requiring some proof of intent. Rather than focusing on imputing the conduct of a particular employee to the corporate entity, is it possible to develop a "second track" which looks at the behavior of the entity totally apart from what the particular erring employee did?

A review of the above materials suggests the outlines of such an approach, even though the courts have not clearly articulated it. The analytical structure would require inquiry into three traditional criminal law problems: 1) the nature of the act which gives rise to liability; 2) the level of intent required for culpability; and 3) the causal connection between the act and the resulting harm.

> (1) The nature of the act: In reviewing the above cases, for what acts is the corporation being held accountable? Is it really the act of the employee who, e.g., agrees with an employee of a competitor to fix a price? Or is the corporation really being held accountable for failing to keep its employees within the law, or for putting its employees "in position" to commit violations of the law? In analyzing "organizational crime" should not the focus be on what the organization has done which led to the improper behavior? Consider, again, the relevance of the Model II approach to organizational behavior, particularly the importance of standard operating procedures used by the corporation to bring information up to management and down to employees.

(2) The level of intent: To what extent should statutory standards of "knowing" and "willful" require, for corporate liability, greater culpability than simply the acts of one employee (even if *those* acts are done "willfully")? Do courts instinctively look for such involvement, even if they do not articulate this as a requirement for liability? If more involvement is required, however, can culpability be shown only through high management involvement or ratification? Or is such a requirement overly stringent in the context of today's multidivisional corporations? Would not a sharper focus on organizational responses and structures permit the development of rules on what kinds of organizational behavior should be characterized as "willful" (much as we have developed rules for what constitutes individual willful behavior)?

(3) Causation: The cases discussed above do not explicitly focus on the question of causation. If one were to look more closely at organizational behavior, however, it would then become necessary to determine whether there was any causal link between the conduct and the harm. Criminal liability for having improper operating procedures would seem unwarranted, for example, if the actual harm were done by a faithless employee whose behavior could not have been controlled even by the best set of operating procedures.

This "second track" for analyzing corporate criminal liability is premised on the concept that the corporation, as an entity, is distinct from any of its individual employees or managers. It is a separate subject for the criminal sanction. Whether such an approach is either necessary or useful, of course, is an open question. What do you think?

B. INDIVIDUAL LIABILITY

SCOPE NOTE

The materials in this Section explore issues which relate to the problem of establishing the criminal liability of individuals. Corporate agents, of course, are responsible for the crimes they personally commit. It is no defense that the employee committed the crime in a "representative" capacity.[54] A corporate agent acting on behalf of the corporation, and within his or her scope of authority, can be convicted of the same crime for which the corporation can be convicted under *New York Central*'s imputation rule.[55] In fact, courts do not require

---

54. See, e.g., United States v. Amrep Corp., 560 F.2d 539 (2d Cir.1977), certiorari denied 434 U.S. 1015, 98 S.Ct. 731, 54 L.Ed. 2d 759 (1978); United States v. American Radiator & Standard Sanitary Corp., 433 F.2d 174 (3d Cir.1970), certiorari denied 401 U.S. 948, 91 S.Ct. 928, 28 L.Ed.2d 231 (1971).

55. New York Central & H.R.R. Co. v. United States, 212 U.S. 481, 495–497, 29 S.Ct. 304, 308, 53 L.Ed. 613, 622–23 (1909).

consistent verdicts, so that it is possible for a jury to convict the employee but acquit the corporation.[56]

The Section is divided into three parts. The first explores problems of intent which can arise in business crime cases. The lead case, *United States v. United States Gypsum Co.*, stresses the importance of an intent requirement. The Notes and cases following explore the intent requirement in the context of vaguely worded business crime legislation, particularly questioning the interaction between the law's vagueness and the relevant intent standards. Among the questions raised: Is it fair to punish individuals who may be engaging in what they reasonably believe to be aggressive competition? Is it fair to punish them if they did not (or could not) "know" the law? Can they rely on counsel's advice that their course of conduct is legal?

The second and third parts of this Section focus, respectively, on managerial and subordinate liability. The question whether "higher-ups" in the corporate hierarchy can be liable for the conduct of lower level employees is an issue of great importance in business crime prosecutions. The main cases here are *United States v. Dotterweich* and *United States v. Park;* the Notes following explore the implications of the "test" set out in these cases for determining who in the corporation might be criminally liable. The issue of subordinate liability for performing one's job "under orders" is explored in the concluding case, *United States v. Natelli* and the Notes following.

1. INTENT

UNITED STATES v. UNITED STATES GYPSUM COMPANY

Supreme Court of the United States, 1978.
438 U.S. 422, 98 S.Ct. 2864, 57 L.Ed.2d 854.

MR. CHIEF JUSTICE BURGER delivered the opinion of the Court.

This case presents the following [question]: whether intent is an element of a criminal antitrust offense. . . .

I

Gypsum board, a laminated type of wall board composed of paper, vinyl or other specially treated coverings over a gypsum core, has in the last 30 years substantially replaced wet plaster as the primary component of interior walls and ceilings in residential and commercial construction. The product is essentially fungible; differences in price, credit terms and delivery services largely dictate the purchasers' choice between competing suppliers. Overall demand, however, is governed by the level of construction activity and is only marginally affected by price fluctuations.

---

56. See, e.g., United States v. Dotterweich, 320 U.S. 277, 279, 64 S.Ct. 134, 88 L.Ed. 48 (1943); Magnolia Motor & Logging Co. v. United States, 264 F.2d 950, 953 (9th Cir.1959); cf. United States v. Powell, 469 U.S. 57, 105 S.Ct. 471, 83 L.Ed.2d 461 (1984); Dunn v. United States, 284 U.S. 390, 52 S.Ct. 189, 76 L.Ed. 356 (1932).

The gypsum board industry is highly concentrated with the number of producers ranging from nine to 15 in the period 1960–1973. The eight largest companies accounted for some 94% of the national sales with the seven "single plant producers" accounting for the remaining 6%. Most of the major producers and a large number of the single plant producers are members of the Gypsum Association which since 1930 has served as a trade association of gypsum board manufacturers.

Beginning in 1966, the Justice Department, as well as the Federal Trade Commission, became involved in investigations into possible antitrust violations in the gypsum board industry. In 1971, a grand jury was empaneled and the investigation continued for an additional 28 months. In late 1973, an indictment was filed in the United States District Court for the Western District of Pennsylvania charging six major manufacturers and various of their corporate officials with violations of § 1 of the Sherman Act.[57]

The indictment charged that the defendants had engaged in a combination and conspiracy "[b]eginning sometime prior to 1960 and continuing thereafter at least until sometime in 1973," in restraint of interstate trade and commerce in the manufacture and sale of gypsum board. The alleged combination and conspiracy consisted of:

> "A continuing agreement understanding and concert of action among the defendants and co-conspirators to (a) raise, fix, maintain and stabilize the prices of gypsum board; (b) fix, maintain and stabilize the terms and conditions of sale thereof; and (c) adopt and maintain uniform methods of packaging and handling such gypsum board."

The indictment proceeded to specify some 13 types of actions taken by conspirators "in formulating and effectuating" the combination and conspiracy, the most relevant of which, for our purposes, is specification (h) which alleged that the conspirators:

> "telephoned or otherwise contacted one another to exchange and discuss current and future published or market prices and published or standard terms and conditions of sale and to ascertain alleged deviations therefrom.

The bill of particulars provided additional details about the continuing nature of the alleged exchanges of competitive information and the role played by such exchanges in policing adherence to the various other illegal agreements charged.

---

57. [Court's footnote 2.] The corporate defendants named in the indictment were: United States Gypsum Company, National Gypsum Company, Georgia Pacific Corporation, Kaiser–Gypsum Company, Inc., the Celotex Corporation, and the Flintkote Company. The individual defendants included: the Chairman of the Board and the Executive Vice–President of United States Gypsum, the Chairman of the Board and Vice–President for Sales of National Gypsum, the President of Georgia Pacific, the President and the Vice–President and General Manager of Kaiser–Gypsum, the President of Celotex, and the Chairman of the Board and the President of Flintkote. The Gypsum Association was named as an unindicted co-conspirator as were two other gypsum board producers—Johns–Manville Corporation and Fibreboard Corporation.

... [N]ine of the defendants entered pleas of *nolo contendere* and were sentenced. The trial of the remaining seven defendants commenced on March 3, 1975, and lasted some 19 weeks.

The focus of the Government's price fixing case at trial was interseller price verification—that is, the practice allegedly followed by the gypsum board manufacturers of telephoning a competing producer to determine the price currently being offered on gypsum board to a specific customer. The Government contended that these price exchanges were part of an agreement among the defendants, had the effect of stabilizing prices and policing agreed upon price increases, and were undertaken on a frequent basis until sometime in 1973. Defendants disputed both the scope and duration of the verification activities, and further maintained that those exchanges of price information which did occur were for the purposes of complying with the Robinson–Patman Act[58] and preventing customer fraud. These purposes, in defendants' view, brought the disputed communications among competitors within a "controlling circumstance" exception to Sherman Act liability—at the extreme, precluding, as a matter of law, consideration of verification by the jury in determining defendants' guilt on the price fixing charge, and at the minimum, making the defendants' purposes in engaging in such communications a threshold factual question.

The instructions on the verification issue given by the trial judge provided that if the exchanges of price information were deemed by the jury to have been undertaken "in a good faith effort to comply with the Robinson–Patman Act," verification standing alone would not be sufficient to establish an illegal price fixing agreement. The paragraphs immediately following, however, provided that the purpose was essentially irrelevant if the jury found that the effect of verification was to raise, fix, maintain or stabilize prices. The instructions on verification closed with the observation that

> "[t]he law presumes that a person intends the necessary and natural consequences of his acts. Therefore, if the effect of the exchanges of pricing information was to raise, fix, maintain and stabilize prices, then the parties to them are presumed, as a matter of law, to have intended that result."

* * *

[The jury returned guilty verdicts against each defendant. The Court of Appeals for the Third Circuit reversed, holding that the trial judge erred in instructing the jury that an effect on prices resulting

---

58. [The Robinson–Patman Act makes it unlawful to sell goods of "like grade and quality" at different prices to different purchasers, where the effect may be substantially to lessen competition. One defense to a Robinson–Patman Act charge is that the discriminatory low price was made "in good faith to meet an equally low price of a competitor." Defendants contended that to be certain they were acting "in good faith" and were meeting "an equally low price of a competitor," they needed to verify the price that the buyer claimed to have been offered. Without verification, the defendants claimed, they could not be certain the discriminatory price being given to meet competition was "equally low." After all, the buyer making the claim might be lying.—Ed.]

from an agreement to exchange price information made out a Sherman Act violation even if respondents' sole purpose was to establish a defense to price discrimination charges.]

II

We turn first to consider the jury instructions regarding the elements of the price-fixing offense charged in the indictment. Although the trial judge's instructions on the price fixing issue are not without ambiguity, it seems reasonably clear that he regarded an effect on prices as the crucial element of the charged offense. The jury was instructed that if it found interseller verification had the effect of raising, fixing, maintaining or stabilizing the price of gypsum board, then such verification could be considered as evidence of an agreement to so affect prices. They were further charged, and it is this point which gives rise to our present concern, that "if the effect of the exchanges of pricing information was to raise, fix, maintain, and stabilize prices, then the parties to them are presumed, *as a matter of law,* to have intended that result."

The Government characterizes this charge as entirely consistent with "this Court's long-standing rule that an agreement among sellers to exchange information on current offering prices violates Section 1 of the Sherman Act if it has either the purpose or the effect of stabilizing prices". . . .

[W]e hold that a defendant's state of mind or intent is an element of a criminal antitrust offense which must be established by evidence and inferences drawn therefrom and cannot be taken from the trier of fact through reliance on a legal presumption of wrongful intent from proof of an effect on prices. Cf. Morissette v. United States, 342 U.S. 246, 274–275, 72 S.Ct. 240, 255, 96 L.Ed. 288. Since the challenged instruction, as we read it, had this prohibited effect, it is disapproved. We are unwilling to construe the Sherman Act as mandating a regime of strict liability criminal offenses.[59]

A

We start with the familiar proposition that "[t]he existence of a mens rea is the rule of, rather than the exception to, the principles of Anglo–American criminal jurisprudence." In a much cited passage in Morissette v. United States, 342 U.S. 246, 250–251, 72 S.Ct. 240, 243, 96 L.Ed. 288, Mr. Justice Jackson speaking for the Court observed:

> "[T]he contention that an injury can amount to a crime only when inflicted by intention is no provincial or transient notion. It is as universal and persistent in mature systems of law as belief in

---

59. [Court's footnote 13.] Our analysis focuses solely on the elements of a criminal offense under the antitrust laws, and leaves unchanged the general rule that a civil violation can be established by proof of either an unlawful purpose or an anticompetitive effect. Of course, consideration of intent may play an important role in divining the actual nature and effect of the alleged anticompetitive conduct.

freedom of the human will and a consequent ability and duty of the normal individual to choose between good and evil. A relation between some mental element and punishment for a harmful act is almost as instinctive as the child's familiar exculpatory 'But I didn't mean to,' and has afforded the rational basis for a tardy and unfinished substitution of deterrence and reformation in place of retaliation and vengeance as the motivation for public prosecution. Unqualified acceptance of this doctrine by English common law in the Eighteenth Century was indicated by Blackstone's sweeping statement that to constitute any crime there must first be a 'vicious will.'"

Although Blackstone's requisite "vicious will" has been replaced by more sophisticated and less colorful characterizations of the mental state required to support criminality, see ALI Model Penal Code § 2.02 (Prop Official Draft 1962), intent generally remains an indispensable element of a criminal offense. This is as true in a sophisticated criminal antitrust case as in one involving any other criminal offense.

This Court, in keeping with the common-law tradition and with the general injunction that "ambiguity concerning the ambit of criminal statutes should be resolved in favor of lenity," has on a number of occasions read a state of mind component into an offense even when the statutory definition did not in terms so provide. Indeed, the holding in *Morissette* can be fairly read as establishing, at least with regard to crimes having their origin in the common law, an interpretative presumption that mens rea is required. "[M]ere omission . . . of intent [in the statute] will not be construed as eliminating that element from the crimes denounced"; instead Congress will be presumed to have legislated against the background of our traditional legal concepts which render intent a critical factor, and "absence of contrary direction [will be] taken as satisfaction with widely accepted definitions, not as a departure from them." 342 U.S., at 263, 72 S.Ct., at 250.

While strict liability offenses are not unknown to the criminal law and do not invariably offend constitutional requirements, see Shevlin–Carpenter Co. v. Minnesota, 218 U.S. 57, 30 S.Ct. 663, 54 L.Ed. 930 (1910), the limited circumstances in which Congress has created and this Court has recognized such offenses attest to their generally disfavored status. See generally ALI Model Penal Code § 2.05 comments, at 140 (Tent. 4th Draft 1955); LaFave & Scott, Criminal Law 222–223 (1972). Certainly far more than the simple omission of the appropriate phrase from the statutory definition is necessary to justify dispensing with an intent requirement. In the context of the Sherman Act, this generally inhospitable attitude to non-mens rea offenses is reinforced by an array of considerations arguing against treating antitrust violations as strict liability crimes.

B

The Sherman Act, unlike most traditional criminal statutes, does not, in clear and categorical terms, precisely identify the conduct which it proscribes. Both civil remedies and criminal sanctions are authorized with regard to the same generalized definitions of the conduct proscribed—restraints of trade or commerce and illegal monopolization—without reference to or mention of intent or state of mind. Nor has judicial elaboration of the Act always yielded the clear and definitive rules of conduct which the statute omits; instead open-ended and fact-specific standards like the "rule of reason" have been applied to broad classes of conduct falling within the purview of the Act's general provisions.

Although in United States v. Nash, 229 U.S. 373, 376–378, 33 S.Ct. 780, 781–782, 57 L.Ed. 1232, the Court held that the indeterminancy of the Sherman Act's standards did not constitute a fatal constitutional objection to their criminal enforcement; nevertheless, this factor has been deemed particularly relevant by those charged with enforcing the Act in accommodating its criminal and remedial sanctions. The 1955 Report of the Attorney General's National Committee to Study the Antitrust Laws concluded that the criminal provisions of the Act should be reserved for those circumstances where the law was relatively clear and the conduct egregious:

> "The Sherman Act, inevitably perhaps, is couched in language broad and general. Modern business patterns moreover are so complex that market effects of proposed conduct are only imprecisely predictable. Thus, it may be difficult for today's businessman to tell in advance whether projected actions will run afoul of the Sherman Act's criminal structures. With this hazard in mind, we believe that criminal process should be used only where the law is clear and the facts reveal a flagrant offense and plain intent unreasonably to restrain trade." Report of the Attorney General's National Committee to Study the Antitrust Laws 349 (1955).

The Antitrust Division of the Justice Department took a similar though slightly more moderate position in its enforcement guidelines issued contemporaneously with the 1955 Report of the Attorney General's Committee:

> "In general, the following types of offenses are prosecuted criminally: (1) price fixing; (2) other violations of the Sherman Act where there is proof of a specific intent to restrain trade or to monopolize; (3) a less easily definable category of cases which might generally be described as involving proof of use of predatory practices (boycotts for example) to accomplish the objective of the combination or conspiracy; (4) the fact that a defendant has previously been convicted of or adjudged to have been, violating the antitrust laws may warrant indictment for a second offense. . . . The Division feels free to seek an indictment in any case where a

prospective defendant has knowledge that practices similar to those in which he is engaging have been held to be in violation of the Sherman Act in a prior suit against other persons." [60]

While not dispositive of the question now before us, the recommendations of the Attorney General's Committee and the guidelines promulgated by the Justice Department highlight the same basic concerns which are manifested in our general requirement of mens rea in criminal statutes and suggest that these concerns are at least equally salient in the antitrust context.

Close attention to the type of conduct regulated by the Sherman Act buttresses this conclusion. With certain exceptions for conduct regarded as per se illegal because of its unquestionably anticompetitive effects, see e.g., United States v. Socony–Vacuum Oil Co., 310 U.S. 150, 60 S.Ct. 811, 84 L.Ed. 1129, the behavior proscribed by the Act is often difficult to distinguish from the gray zone of socially acceptable and economically justifiable business conduct. Indeed, the type of conduct charged in the indictment in this case—the exchange of price information among competitors—is illustrative in this regard.[61] The imposition of criminal liability on a corporate official, or for that matter on a corporation directly, for engaging in such conduct which only after the fact is determined to violate the statute because of anti-competitive effects, without inquiring into the intent with which it was undertaken, holds out the distinct possibility of overdeterrence; salutary and procompetitive conduct lying close to the borderline of impermissible conduct might be shunned by businessmen who chose to be excessively cautious in the face of uncertainty regarding possible exposure to criminal punishment for even a good-faith error of judgment.[62] Fur-

---

60. [Court's footnote 15.] In 1967, the Antitrust Division refined its guidelines to emphasize that criminal prosecutions should only be brought against willful violations of the law. See The President's Commission on Law Enforcement and Administration of Justice, Task Force Report: Crime and Its Impact—An Assessment 110 (1967).

61. [Court's footnote 16.] The exchange of price data and other information among competitors does not invariably have anticompetitive effects; indeed such practices can in certain circumstances increase economic efficiency and render markets more rather than less competitive. For this reason, we have held that such exchanges of information do not constitute a per se violation of the Sherman Act.

A number of factors including most prominently the structure of the industry involved and the nature of the information exchanged are generally considered in divining the pro or anticompetitive effects of this type of interseller communication. Exchanges of current price information, of course, have the greatest potential for generating anticompetitive effects and although not per se unlawful have consistently been held to violate the Sherman Act.

62. [Court's footnote 17.] The possibility that those subjected to strict liability will take extraordinary care in their dealings is frequently regarded as one advantage of a rule of strict liability. See Hall, General Principles of Criminal Law 344 (1960); LaFave & Scott, Criminal Law 222–223 (1972). However, where the conduct prescribed is difficult to distinguish from conduct permitted and indeed encouraged, as in the antitrust context, the excessive caution spawned by a regime of strict liability will not necessarily redound to the public's benefit. The antitrust laws differ in this regard from, for example, laws designed to insure that adulterated food will not be sold to consumers. In the latter situation, excessive caution on the part of producers is entirely consistent with the legislative purpose.

ther, the use of criminal sanctions in such circumstances would be difficult to square with the generally accepted functions of the criminal law. The criminal sanctions would be used not to punish conscious and calculated wrongdoing at odds with statutory proscriptions, but instead simply to *regulate* business practices regardless of the intent with which they were undertaken. While in certain cases we have imputed a regulatory purpose to Congress in choosing to employ criminal sanctions, the availability of a range of nonpenal alternatives to the criminal sanctions of the Sherman Act negates the imputation of any such purpose to Congress in the instant context.[63]

For these reasons, we conclude that the criminal offenses defined by the Sherman Act should be construed as including intent as an element.

C

Having concluded that intent is a necessary element of a criminal antitrust violation, the task remaining is to treat the practical aspects of this requirement.[64] As we have noted, the language of the Act provides minimal assistance in determining what standard of intent is appropriate and the sparse legislative history of the criminal provisions is similarly unhelpful. We must therefore turn to more general sources and traditional understandings of the nature of the element of intent in the criminal law. In so doing, we must try to avoid "the variety, disparity and confusion" of judicial definitions of the "requisite but elusive mental element" of criminal offenses.

The ALI Model Penal Code is one source of guidance upon which the Court has relied to illuminate questions of this type.

. . . Recognizing that "mens rea is not a unitary concept," the Code enumerates four possible levels of intent—purpose, knowledge, recklessness and negligence. In dealing with the kinds of business decisions upon which the antitrust laws focus, the concepts of recklessness and negligence have no place. Our question instead is whether a criminal violation of the antitrust laws requires, in addition to proof of anticompetitive effects, a demonstration that the disputed conduct was undertaken with the "conscious object" of producing such effects or whether it is sufficient that the conduct is shown to have been under-

63. [Court's footnote 10.] Congress has recently increased the criminal penalties for violation of the Sherman Act. Individual violations are now treated as felonies punishable by a fine not to exceed $100,000, or by imprisonment for up to three years, or both. Corporate violators are subject to a $1 million fine. 15 U.S.C. § 1. The severity of these sanctions provides further support for our conclusion that the Sherman Act should not be construed as creating strict liability crimes. Respondents here were not prosecuted under the new penalty provisions since they were indicted prior to the December 21, 1974, effective date for the increased sanctions.

64. [Court's footnote 20.] In a conspiracy, two different types of intent are generally required—the basic intent to agree, which is necessary to establish the existence of the conspiracy, and the more traditional intent to effectuate the object of the conspiracy. See LaFave and Scott, Criminal Law 464–465 (1972). Our discussion here focuses only on the second type of intent.

taken with knowledge that the proscribed effects would most likely follow. While the difference between these formulations is a narrow one, see ALI Model Penal Code § 2.02, comment, at 125 (Tent. Draft 4 1955), we conclude that action undertaken with knowledge of its probable consequences and having the requisite anticompetitive effects can be a sufficient predicate for a finding of criminal liability under the antitrust laws.[65]

Several considerations fortify this conclusion. The element of intent in the criminal law has traditionally been viewed as a bifurcated concept embracing either the specific requirement of purpose or the more general one of knowledge or awareness.

> "[I]t is now generally accepted that a person who acts (or omits to act) intends a result of his act (or omission) under two quite different circumstances: (1) when he consciously desires that result, whatever the likelihood of that result happening from his conduct; and (2) when he knew that the result is practically certain to follow from his conduct, whatever his desire may be as to that result."

LaFave & Scott, Criminal Law 196 (1972).

Generally this limited distinction between knowledge and purpose has not been considered important since "there is good reason for imposing liability whether the defendant desired or merely knew of the practical certainty of the result." LaFave & Scott, supra, at 197. See also ALI Model Penal Code, § 2.02 comments, at 125 (Tent. Draft 4, 1955). In either circumstance, the defendants are consciously behaving in a way the law prohibits, and such conduct is a fitting object of criminal punishment. See Working Papers of the National Commission on Reform of Federal Criminal Laws, Vol. I, 124 (1970).

Nothing in our analysis of the Sherman Act persuades us that this general understanding of intent should not be applied to criminal antitrust violations such as charged here. The business behavior which is likely to give rise to criminal antitrust charges is conscious behavior normally undertaken only after a full consideration of the desired results and a weighing of the costs, benefits and risks. A requirement of proof not only of this knowledge of likely effects, but also of a conscious desire to bring them to fruition or to violate the law would seem, particularly in such a context, both unnecessarily cumulative and unduly burdensome. Where carefully planned and calculated conduct is being scrutinized in the context of a criminal prosecution, the perpetrator's knowledge of the anticipated consequences is a sufficient predicate for a finding of criminal intent.

---

65. [Court's footnote 21.] In so holding, we do not mean to suggest that conduct undertaken with the purpose of producing anticompetitive effects would not also support criminal liability, even if such effects did not come to pass. We hold only that this elevated standard of intent need not be established in cases where anticompetitive effects have been demonstrated; instead, proof that the defendant's conduct was undertaken with knowledge of its probable consequences will satisfy the Government's burden.

D

When viewed in terms of this standard, the jury instructions on the price-fixing charge cannot be sustained. "A conclusive presumption [of intent], which testimony could not overthrow would effectively eliminate intent as an ingredient of the offense." The challenged jury instruction, as we read it, had precisely this effect; the jury was told that the requisite intent followed, *as a matter of law,* from a finding that the exchange of price information had an impact on prices. Although an effect on prices may well support an inference that the defendant had knowledge of the probability of such a consequence at the time he acted, the jury must remain free to consider additional evidence before accepting or rejecting the inference. Therefore, although it would be correct to instruct the jury that it may infer intent from an effect on prices, ultimately the decision on the issue of intent must be left to the trier of fact alone. The instruction given invaded this factfinding function.

* * *

Accordingly, the judgment of the Court of Appeals is *Affirmed.*

MR. JUSTICE REHNQUIST concurring in part and dissenting in part.

I concur in Part I . . . I dissent from the remaining portions of the opinion, and set forth as briefly as possible my reasons for doing so.

Part II of the Court's opinion uses as its point of departure jury instructions on pricefixing which the Court correctly characterizes as "not without ambiguity." But these jury instructions are but a starting point for the discourse in Part II of the Court's opinion, dealing with the element of intent in a criminal case, a discourse which I believe goes beyond any reasoning necessary to dispose of the contentions with respect to that point in this case.

I do not find it necessary to decide the intent which Congress required as a prerequisite for criminal liability under the Sherman Act, because I believe that the instructions given by the District Court, when considered as a whole and in connection with the objections made to them, are sufficiently close to respondent's tendered instructions so as to afford respondents no basis upon which to challenge the verdict. The jury instructions in this case take up some 40 pages of the record and are both detailed and complex.

* * *

The portions of Part II which I find most troubling are not those which expressly address the congressionally prescribed requirement of intent for criminal liability under the Sherman Act, but those which discourse at length upon the role of intent in the imposition of criminal liability in general, particularly those which might be taken to import any special constitutional difficulty if criminal liability is imposed without fault. While the Court emphasizes that its result is not constitutionally required, the Court's broad policy statements may be misread by the lower courts. I also feel bound to say that while I am willing to respectfully defer to the views of the distinguished authors of the American Law Institute's Model Penal Code, and to the authors of law review articles such as those sprinkled throughout the text of Part II of the Court's opinion, I have serious reservations about the undiscriminating emphasis and weight which the Court appears to give them in this case.

* * *

MR. JUSTICE STEVENS, concurring in part and dissenting in part.

* * *

In 1955 I subscribed to the view that criminal enforcement of the Sherman Act is inappropriate unless the defendants have deliberately violated the law.[66] I adhere to that view today. But since 1890 when the Sherman Act was enacted, the statute has had the same substantive reach in criminal and civil cases. No matter how wise the new rule that the Court adopts today may be, I believe it is an amendment only Congress may enact.

If I were fashioning a new test of criminal liability, I would require proof of a specific purpose to violate the law rather than mere knowledge that the defendants' agreement has had an adverse effect on the market.

* * *

. . . I am afraid that the new civil-criminal dichotomy may work mischief in the civil enforcement of the prohibition against tampering with prices in a free market. Conclusive presumptions play a central role in the enforcement, both civil and criminal, of the Sherman Act. Thus, an agreement to charge the same price, or to adopt a common purchasing policy that determines the market price is unreasonable, and therefore unlawful, without any proof of the purpose or the actual effect of the agreement. The law presumes that those who entered the price-fixing agreement knew that forbidden effects would follow, and it also presumes, conclusively, that those effects will follow. In a criminal prosecution for price-fixing in violation of the Sherman Act it is, therefore, irrelevant whether the prices fixed were reasonable or whether the defendant's intentions were good.[67]

* * *

66. [Footnote 1 in original.] Report of the Attorney General's National Committee to Study the Antitrust Laws 349–351 (1955). [Justice Stevens was a member of the Committee—Ed.]

67. [Before retrial, the government dropped the criminal charges against the defendant corporations in return for their agreement to pay income taxes on approximately $12.3 million, part of the $35 million in business-expense deductions taken for payments made to settle earlier civil suits. Had the corporations lost the criminal retrial, the entire $35 million deduction would have been disallowed. The government stated that the settlement was the best result it could hope to obtain because the complexity and age of the case would have made successful prosecution " 'unusually difficult here.' " See Wall St. J., March 4, 1980, p. 14.—Ed.]

NOTES AND QUERIES

(1) *Legislative History.* There is nothing in the debates over the Sherman Act to indicate that Congress ever considered the question presented in *Gypsum,* although a predecessor bill did contain some "specific intent" language (condemning agreements "made with a view or which tend to prevent full and free competition"). The Supreme Court had previously discussed the intent requirement in *United States v. Patten,* 226 U.S. 525, 33 S.Ct. 141, 57 L.Ed. 333 (1913). In *Patten* the defendants were charged with trying to corner the market ("running a corner") in cotton. The Court wrote:

> It well may be that running a corner tends for a time to stimulate competition; but * * * [u]pon the corner becoming effective, there could be no trading in the commodity save at the will of the conspirators and at such price as their interests might prompt them to exact. And so, the conspiracy was to reach and to bring within its dominating influence the entire cotton trade of the country.
>
> Bearing in mind that such was the nature, object and scope of the conspiracy, we regard it as altogether plain that by its necessary operation it would directly and materially impede and burden the due course of trade and commerce among the States and therefore inflict upon the public the injuries which the Anti-trust Act is designed to prevent. And that there is no allegation of a specific intent to restrain such trade or commerce does not make against this conclusion, for, as is shown by prior decisions of this court, the conspirators must be held to have intended the necessary and direct consequences of their acts and cannot be heard to say the contrary. In other words by purposely engaging in a conspiracy which necessarily and directly produces the result which the statute is designed to prevent, they are, in legal contemplation, chargeable with intending that result.

Query. Are *Patten* and *Gypsum* consistent?

(2) *Constitutional Implications of Gypsum.* Is the decision in *Gypsum,* regarding the jury charge, of Constitutional dimension? Consider *Sandstrom v. Montana,* 442 U.S. 510, 99 S.Ct. 2450, 61 L.Ed.2d 39 (1979), where the trial court instructed the jury that "[t]he law presumes that a person intends the ordinary consequences of his voluntary acts." After holding that the jury could have believed this to be an irrebuttable presumption, Justice Brennan continued for the Court:

> The petitioner here was charged with and convicted of deliberate homicide, committed purposely or knowingly, under 1947 Mont. Rev.Codes § 94–5–102(a) (Crim.Code of 1973). It is clear that under Montana law, whether the crime was committed purposely or knowingly is a fact necessary to constitute the crime of deliberate

homicide.[68] Indeed, it was the lone element of the offense at issue in Sandstrom's trial, as he confessed to causing the death of the victim, told the jury that knowledge and purpose were the only questions he was controverting, and introduced evidence solely on those points. Moreover, it is conceded that proof of defendant's "intent" would be sufficient to establish this element. Thus, the question before this Court is whether the challenged jury instruction had the effect of relieving the State of the burden of proof [beyond a reasonable doubt] on the critical question of petitioner's state of mind. We conclude that under either of the two possible interpretations of the instruction set out above, precisely that effect would result, and that the instruction therefore represents constitutional error.

We consider first the validity of a conclusive presumption. This Court has considered such a presumption on at least two prior occasions. In Morissette v. United States, 342 U.S. 246, 72 S.Ct. 240, 96 L.Ed. 288 (1952), the defendant was charged with willful and knowing theft of government property. Although his attorney argued that for his client to be found guilty, "'the taking must have been with felonious intent'," the trial judge ruled that "'[t]hat is presumed by his own act.'" Id., at 249, 72 S.Ct. at 243. After first concluding that intent was in fact an element of the crime charged, and after declaring that "[w]here intent of the accused is an ingredient of the crime charged, its existence is a . . . jury issue," *Morissette* held:

> "*It follows that the trial court may not withdraw or prejudge the issue by instruction that the law raises a presumption of intent from an act.* It often is tempting to cast in terms of a 'presumption' a conclusion which a court thinks probable from given facts. . . . [But] [w]e think presumptive intent has no place in this case. *A conclusive presumption which testimony could not overthrow would effectively eliminate intent as an ingredient of the offense.* A presumption which would permit but not require the jury to assume intent from an isolated fact would prejudge a conclusion which the jury should reach of its own volition. A presumption which would permit the jury to make an assumption which all the evidence considered together does not logically establish would give to a proven fact an artificial and fictional effect. In either case, this *presumption would conflict with the overriding presumption of innocence*

---

68. [Court's footnote 10.] . . . In State v. McKenzie, 177 Mont. 280, 581 P.2d 1205, 1232 (1978), the Montana Supreme Court stated:

"In Montana, a person commits the offense of deliberate homicide if he purposely or knowingly causes the death of another human being. Sections 94–5–102(1)(a), 94–5–101(1), R.C.M. 1947. *The statutorily defined elements of the offense, each of which the State must prove beyond a reasonable doubt, are therefore causing the death of another human being with the knowledge that you are causing or with the purpose to cause death of that human being.*" (Emphasis added)

with which the law endows the accused and which extends to every element of the crime." 342 U.S., at 274–275, 72 S.Ct. at 255–256. (Emphasis added.)

Just last Term, in United States v. United States Gypsum, 438 U.S. 422, 98 S.Ct. 2864, 57 L.Ed.2d 854 (1978), we reaffirmed the holding of *Morissette*. In that case defendants, who were charged with criminal violations of the Sherman Act, challenged the following jury instruction:

> "The law presumes that a person intends the necessary and natural consequences of his acts. Therefore, if the effect of the exchanges of pricing information was to raise, fix, maintain and stabilize prices, then the parties to them are presumed, as a matter of law, to have intended that result." Id., at 430, 98 S.Ct. at 2869.

After again determining that the offense included the element of intent, we held

> "[A] defendant's state of mind or *intent is an element of a criminal antitrust offense which . . . cannot be taken from the trier of fact through reliance on a legal presumption* of wrongful intent from proof of effect on prices. Cf. Morissette v. United States. . . .
>
> "Although an effect on prices may well support an inference that the defendant had knowledge of the probability of such a consequence at the time he acted, the jury must remain free to consider additional evidence before accepting or rejecting the inference. . . . [U]ltimately the decision on the issue of intent must be left to the trier of fact alone. The instruction given invaded this factfinding function." 438 U.S., at 435, 446, 98 S.Ct. at 2872, 2878 (emphasis added).

As in *Morissette* and *United States Gypsum*, a conclusive presumption in this case would "conflict with the overriding presumption of innocence with which the law endows the accused and which extends to every element of the crime," and would "invade [the] factfinding function" which in a criminal case the law assigns solely to the jury. The instruction announced to David Sandstrom's jury may well have had exactly these consequences. Upon finding proof of one element of the crime (causing death), and of facts insufficient to establish the second (the voluntariness and "ordinary consequences" of defendant's action), Sandstrom's jurors could reasonably have concluded that they were directed to find against defendant on the element of intent. The State was thus not forced to prove "beyond a reasonable doubt . . . every fact necessary to constitute the crime . . . charged," 397 U.S., at 364, 90 S.Ct. at 1073, and defendant was deprived of his constitutional rights [to have his guilt proved beyond a reasonable doubt].

(3) *Mistake of Law.* Was the real problem in *Gypsum* a mistake of law? The defendants' argument was that the system of interseller

verification was necessary to insure that they could assert the Robinson–Patman Act's "good faith meeting of competition" defense (see n. 58, supra p. 230). It turns out that the defendants were wrong. The Robinson–Patman Act does not require interseller price verification before a seller can, in good faith, meet an equally low price of a competitor. This legal point was not settled, however, until the *Gypsum* case itself (it was addressed in the remainder of the Court's opinion, not reproduced in these materials).

Should the defendants' mistaken (but allegedly good faith) purpose to comply with the Robinson–Patman Act have been a defense to the Sherman Act prosecution? Should business people be held to anticipate decisions of the Supreme Court at their peril? The only point at which the Court addressed this issue is in the following footnote (n. 23, prior to the remainder of the Court's opinion). Do you think it satisfactory? Does it throw any light on the wisdom of the intent standard adopted by the Court (and reconsider the one Justice Stevens would have adopted)?

> This question [whether price verification done to comply with the Robinson–Patman Act is a defense to Sherman Act liability] was not resolved by the prior discussion [regarding the need to prove intent] because a purpose of complying with the Robinson–Patman Act by exchanging price information is not inconsistent with knowledge that such exchanges of information will have the probable effect of fixing or stabilizing prices. Since we hold knowledge of the probable consequences of conduct to be the requisite mental state in a criminal prosecution like the instant one where an effect on prices is also alleged, a defendant's purpose in engaging in the proscribed conduct will not insulate him from liability unless it is deemed of sufficient merit to justify a general exception to the Sherman Act's proscriptions.

(4) *Reading Statutes—When Does "Knowingly" Require Knowledge of the Law?* Many business crime statutes require proof that the defendant acted "knowingly." Can lack of knowledge of the law then be a defense? The standard view, of course, is that ignorance of the law is no defense, unless knowledge of the law is an element of the offense.[69] Usually, the statute does not make clear, however, whether it is the law the defendant must know, or just the facts.[70]

A leading case is *United States v. International Minerals & Chemical Corporation.*[71] There the Supreme Court was called upon to construe a statute which made it a crime "knowingly" to violate any regulation promulgated by the Interstate Commerce Commission. The district court had dismissed the case because it was not alleged that the defendant knew of the regulation in question. The Supreme Court

---

69. See W. LaFave & A. Scott, Criminal Law sec. 5.1(a) (2d Ed.1986).

70. Compare Sec. 32(a) of the Securities Exchange Act of 1934, 15 U.S.C.A. § 78ff(a), relieving the defendant from imprisonment (but not criminal liability) on proof that the defendant lacked knowledge of the rule or regulation violated.

71. 402 U.S. 558, 91 S.Ct. 1697, 29 L.Ed. 2d 178 (1971).

reversed. The prosecution need show only that the defendant had knowledge of the relevant facts (shipping acids without placing the words "corrosive liquid" on the shipping papers): "The principle that ignorance of the law is no defense applies whether the law be a statute or a duly promulgated and published regulation. . . . [T]he meager legislative history . . . makes unwarranted the conclusion that Congress abandoned the general rule and required knowledge of . . . the pertinent law. . . ."[72]

A more recent decision is *Liparota v. United States,* 471 U.S. 419, 105 S.Ct. 2084, 85 L.Ed.2d 434 (1985):

> Justice Brennan delivered the opinion of the Court.
>
> The federal statute governing food stamp fraud provides that "whoever knowingly uses, transfers, acquires, alters, or possesses coupons or authorization cards in any manner not authorized by [the statute] or the regulations" is subject to a fine and imprisonment. 7 U.S.C. § 2024(b). The question presented is whether in a prosecution under this provision the Government must prove that the defendant knew that he was acting in a manner not authorized by statute or regulations.
>
> I
>
> Petitioner Frank Liparota was the co-owner with his brother of Moon's Sandwich Shop in Chicago, Illinois. He was indicted for acquiring and possessing food stamps in violation of § 2024(b). The Department of Agriculture had not authorized petitioner's restaurant to accept food stamps. At trial, the Government proved that petitioner on three occasions purchased food stamps from an undercover Department of Agriculture agent for substantially less than their face value. On the first occasion, the agent informed petitioner that she had $195 worth of food stamps to sell. The agent then accepted petitioner's offer of $150 and consummated the transaction in a back room of the restaurant with petitioner's brother. A similar transaction occurred one week later, in which the agent sold $500 worth of coupons for $350. Approximately one month later, petitioner bought $500 worth of food stamps from the agent for $300.
>
> In submitting the case to the jury, the District Court rejected petitioner's proposed "specific intent" instruction, which would have instructed the jury that the Government must prove that "the defendant knowingly did an act which the law forbids, purposely intending to violate the law." Concluding that "[t]his is not a specific intent crime" but rather a "knowledge case," the District Court instead instructed the jury as follows:

72. 402 U.S. at 563, 91 S.Ct. at 1701, 29 L.Ed.2d at 182.

"When the word 'knowingly' is used in these instructions, it means that the Defendant realized what he was doing, and was aware of the nature of his conduct, and did not act through ignorance, mistake, or accident. Knowledge may be proved by defendant's conduct and by all of the facts and circumstances surrounding the case."

The District Court also instructed that the Government had to prove that "the Defendant acquired and possessed food stamp coupons for cash in a manner not authorized by federal statute or regulations" and that "the Defendant knowingly and wilfully acquired the food stamps." Petitioner objected that this instruction required the jury to find merely that he knew that he was acquiring or possessing food stamps; he argued that the statute should be construed instead to reach only "people who knew that they were acting unlawfully." The judge did not alter or supplement his instructions, and the jury returned a verdict of guilty.

Petitioner appealed his conviction to the Court of Appeals for the Seventh Circuit, arguing that the District Court erred in refusing to instruct the jury that "specific intent" is required in a prosecution under 7 U.S.C. § 2024(b). The Court of Appeals rejected petitioner's arguments. Because this decision conflicted with recent decisions of three other Courts of Appeals, we granted certiorari. We reverse.

II

The controversy between the parties concerns the mental state, if any, that the Government must show in proving that petitioner acted "in any manner not authorized by [the statute] or the regulations." The Government argues that petitioner violated the statute if he knew that he acquired or possessed food stamps and if in fact that acquisition or possession was in a manner not authorized by statute or regulations. According to the Government, no mens rea, or "evil-meaning mind," is necessary for conviction. Petitioner claims that the Government's interpretation, by dispensing with mens rea, dispenses with the only morally blameworthy element in the definition of the crime. To avoid this allegedly untoward result, he claims that an individual violates the statute if he knows that he has acquired or possessed food stamps *and* if he also knows that he has done so in an unauthorized manner.[73] Our task is to determine which meaning Congress intended.

---

73. [Court's footnote 5.] The required mental state may of course be different for different elements of a crime. In this case, for instance, both parties agree that petitioner must have known that he acquired and possessed food stamps. They disagree over whether any mental element at all is required with respect to the unauthorized nature of that acquisition or possession.

We have also recognized that the mental element in criminal law encompasses more than the two possibilities of "specific" and "general" intent. The Model Penal Code, for instance, recognizes four mental states—purpose, knowledge, recklessness, and negligence. ALI Model Penal Code § 2.02 (Prop.Off.Draft 1962). In this case, petitioner argues that with respect to the

The definition of the elements of a criminal offense is entrusted to the legislature, particularly in the case of federal crimes, which are solely creatures of statute.[74] With respect to the element at issue in this case, however, Congress has not explicitly spelled out the mental state required. Although Congress certainly intended by use of the word "knowingly" to require *some* mental state with respect to *some* element of the crime defined in § 2024(b), the interpretations proffered by both parties accord with congressional intent to this extent. Beyond this, the words themselves provide little guidance. Either interpretation would accord with ordinary usage. The legislative history of the statute contains nothing that would clarify the congressional purpose on this point.

Absent indication of contrary purpose in the language or legislative history of the statute, we believe that § 2024(b) requires a showing that the defendant knew his conduct to be unauthorized by statute or regulations.[75] . . . Thus, in United States v. United States Gypsum Co., 438 U.S. 422, 438, 98 S.Ct. 2864, 2874, 57 L.Ed. 2d 854 (1978), we noted that "[c]ertainly far more than the simple omission of the appropriate phrase from the statutory definition is necessary to justify dispensing with an intent requirement" and that criminal offenses requiring no mens rea have a "generally disfavored status." Similarly, in this case, the failure of Congress explicitly and unambiguously to indicate whether mens rea is required does not signal a departure from this background assumption of our criminal law.

This construction is particularly appropriate where, as here, to interpret the statute otherwise would be to criminalize a broad range of apparently innocent conduct. For instance, § 2024(b) declares it criminal to use, transfer, acquire, alter, or possess food stamps in any manner not authorized by statute or regulations. The statute provides further that "[c]oupons issued to eligible households shall be used by them only to purchase food in retail

element at issue, knowledge is required. The Government contends that no mental state is required with respect to that element.

74. [Court's footnote 6.] Of course, Congress must act within any applicable constitutional constraints in defining criminal offenses. In this case, there is no allegation that the statute would be unconstitutional under either interpretation.

75. [Court's footnote 9.] The Dissent repeatedly claims that our holding today creates a defense of "mistake of law." Our holding today no more creates a "mistake of law" defense than does a statute making knowing receipt of stolen goods unlawful. In both cases, there is a legal element in the definition of the offense. In the case of a receipt of stolen goods statute, the legal element is that the goods were stolen: in this case, the legal element is that the "use, transfer, acquisition," etc. were in a manner not authorized by statute or regulations. It is not a defense to a charge of receipt of stolen goods that one did not know that such receipt was illegal, and it is not a defense to a charge of a § 2024(b) violation that one did not know that possessing food stamps in a manner unauthorized by statute or regulations was illegal. It *is*, however, a defense to a charge of knowing receipt of stolen goods that one did not know that the goods were stolen, just as it is a defense to a charge of a § 2024(b) violation that one did not know that one's possession was unauthorized. . . .

food stores which have been approved for participation in the food stamp program *at prices prevailing in such stores.*" This seems to be the *only* authorized use. A strict reading of the statute with no knowledge of illegality requirement would thus render criminal a food stamp recipient who, for example, used stamps to purchase food from a store that, unknown to him, charged higher than normal prices to food stamp program participants. Such a reading would also render criminal a nonrecipient of food stamps who "possessed" stamps because he was mistakenly sent them through the mail due to administrative error, "altered" them by tearing them up, and "transferred" them by throwing them away. Of course, Congress *could* have intended that this broad range of conduct be made illegal, perhaps with the understanding that prosecutors would exercise their discretion to avoid such harsh results. However, given the paucity of material suggesting that Congress did so intend, we are reluctant to adopt such a sweeping interpretation.

In addition, requiring mens rea is in keeping with our long-standing recognition of the principle that "ambiguity concerning the ambit of criminal statutes should be resolved in favor of lenity." . . . Application of the rule of lenity ensures that criminal statutes will provide fair warning concerning conduct rendered illegal and strikes the appropriate balance between the legislature, the prosecutor, and the court in defining criminal liability. Although the rule of lenity is not to be applied where to do so would conflict with the implied or expressed intent of Congress, it provides a time-honored interpretive guideline when the congressional purpose is unclear. In the instant case, the rule directly supports petitioner's contention that the Government must prove knowledge of illegality to convict him under § 2024(b).

* * *

[T]he Government contends that the § 2024(b) offense is a "public welfare" offense, which the Court defined in United States v. Morissette, 342 U.S., at 252–253, 72 S.Ct., at 244–245, to "depend on no mental element but consist only of forbidden acts or omissions." Yet the offense at issue here differs substantially from those "public welfare offenses" we have previously recognized. In most previous instances, Congress has rendered criminal a type of conduct that a reasonable person should know is subject to stringent public regulation and may seriously threaten the community's health or safety. Thus, in United States v. Freed, 401 U.S. 601, 91 S.Ct. 1112, 28 L.Ed.2d 356 (1971), we examined the federal statute making it illegal to receive or possess an unregistered firearm. In holding that the Government did not have to prove that the recipient of unregistered hand grenades knew that they were unregistered, we noted that "one would hardly be surprised to learn that possession of hand grenades is not an innocent act." Id., at 609, 91 S.Ct., at 1118. See also United States v. International

Minerals & Chemical Corp., 402 U.S. 558, 564–565, 91 S.Ct. 1697, 1701–1702, 29 L.Ed.2d 178 (1971). Similarly, in United States v. Dotterweich, 320 U.S. 277, 284, 64 S.Ct. 134, 138, 88 L.Ed. 48 (1943), the Court held that a corporate officer could violate the Food and Drug Act when his firm shipped adulterated and misbranded drugs, even "though consciousness of wrongdoing be totally wanting." The distinctions between these cases and the instant case are clear. A food stamp can hardly be compared to a hand grenade, see Freed, nor can the unauthorized acquisition or possession of food stamps be compared to the selling of adulterated drugs, as in Dotterweich.

III

We hold that in a prosecution for violation of § 2024(b), the Government must prove that the defendant knew that his acquisition or possession of food stamps was in a manner unauthorized by statute or regulations. This holding does not put an unduly heavy burden on the Government in prosecuting violators of § 2024(b). To prove that petitioner knew that his acquisition or possession of food stamps was unauthorized, for example, the Government need not show that he had knowledge of specific regulations governing food stamp acquisition or possession. Nor must the Government introduce any extraordinary evidence that would conclusively demonstrate petitioner's state of mind. Rather, as in any other criminal prosecution requiring mens rea, the Government may prove by reference to facts and circumstances surrounding the case that petitioner knew that his conduct was unauthorized or illegal.[76]

Reversed.[77]

UNITED STATES v. GARBER

United States Court of Appeals, Fifth Circuit, En Banc, 1979.
607 F.2d 92.

CHARLES CLARK, CIRCUIT JUDGE:

Dorothy Clark Garber was indicted for willfully and knowingly attempting to evade a portion of her income tax liability for the years 1970, 1971, and 1972 by filing a false and fraudulent income tax return on behalf of herself and her husband. A jury found her innocent of the charges for 1970 and 1971 but convicted her under 26 U.S.C.A. § 7201

---

76. [Court's footnote 17.] In this case, for instance, the Government introduced evidence that petitioner bought food stamps at a substantial discount from face value and that he conducted part of the transaction in a back room of his restaurant to avoid the presence of the other patrons. Moreover, the Government asserts that food stamps themselves are stamped "nontransferable." A jury could have inferred from this evidence that petitioner knew that his acquisition and possession of the stamps was unauthorized.

77. Justice Powell did not participate in the decision. The dissenting opinion of Justice White, which Chief Justice Burger joined, is omitted. Cf. United States v. Yermian, 468 U.S. 63, 104 S.Ct. 2936, 82 L.Ed.2d 53 (1984) (crime of "knowingly and willfully" making false statement in any matter within jurisdiction of federal government does not require proof of knowledge of federal jurisdiction; statute's meaning not ambiguous in light of statutory language and legislative history).

for knowingly misstating her income on her 1972 tax return. She was sentenced to 18 months imprisonment—all but 60 days of which was suspended—placed on probation for 21 months, and fined $5,000 exclusive of any civil tax liability. The taxability of the money received by Garber presents a unique legal question. Because of trial errors which deprived defendant of her defense on the element of willfulness, we reverse the conviction.

Some time in the late 1960's after the birth of her third child, Dorothy Garber was told that her blood contained a rare antibody useful in the production of blood group typing serum. Dade Reagents, Inc. (Dade Reagents), a manufacturer of diagnostic reagents used in clinical laboratories and blood banks, had made the discovery and in 1967 induced her to enter into a contract for the sale of her blood plasma. By a technique called plasmapheresis, a pint of whole blood was extracted from her arm, plasma was centrifugally separated, and the red cells were returned to her body. The process was then repeated. The two bleeds produced one pint of plasma from two pints of blood, and took a total of from one and a half to two and a half hours.

Plasmapheresis is often preceded by a stimulation of the donor whereby the titre or concentration of the desired antibody in the blood is artifically increased by an injection of an incompatible blood type. Both stimulation and plasmapheresis are accompanied by pain and discomfort and carry the risks of hepatitis and blood clotting.

In exchange for Garber's blood plasma, Dade Reagents agreed to pay her for each bleed on a sliding scale dependent on the titre or strength of the plasma obtained. Dade Reagents then marketed the substance for the production of blood group typing serum.

Because Garber's blood is so rare—she is one of only two or three known persons in the world with this antibody—she was approached by other laboratories which lured her away from Dade Reagents by offering an increasingly attractive price for her plasma. By 1970, 1971, and 1972, the three years covered in the indictment, she was receiving substantial sums of money in exchange for her plasma.[78] For two of those years she was selling her blood under separate contract to Associated Biologicals, Inc. (Associated) and to Biomedical Industries, Inc. (Biomedical), in both cases receiving in exchange a sum of money dependent on the strength of the antibody in each unit sold. In addition, Biomedical offered a weekly salary of $200, provided a leased automobile, and in 1972 added a $25,000 bonus. In that last year Garber sold her plasma to Biomedical exclusively, producing the coveted body fluid as often as six times a month.

For all three years involved, Biomedical had treated the regular $200 weekly payments as a salary subject to withholding taxes and provided Garber with a yearly W—2 form noting the taxes withheld.

78. [Court's footnote 1.] Sale of her plasma allegedly brought her $80,200 in 1970, $71,400 in 1971, and $87,200 in 1972.

Every year, Garber attached those W—2 forms to her income tax return (which was filed jointly with her husband whom she has since divorced), declared the $200 per week as income, and paid the taxes due. All other payments, both from Biomedical and from Associated, had been paid directly to defendant by check. No income taxes were withheld by the companies; she received no W—2 forms, and paid no taxes on the money received. Biomedical did, however, file a Form 1099 Information Return with the IRS which showed a portion of Garber's donor fees not subject to withholding. Garber was provided a copy of each 1099, which plainly states that it is for information only and is not to be attached to the income tax return. She had never before received Information Returns, and, while she was receiving checks from both Biomedical and Associated, only Biomedical provided this information.

In this prosecution for the felony of willful evasion of income taxes the government had the burden of proving every element of the crime beyond a reasonable doubt. This required proof of a tax deficiency, an affirmative act constituting evasion or attempted evasion of the tax due, and willfulness. The element we find lacking here was willfulness.

At trial, outside the presence of the jury, the government proffered the testimony of Jacquin Bierman, a professor of law and practicing attorney in the City of New York, who stated his opinion that Garber had made available her bodily functions or products for a consideration which constituted taxable gross income. His conclusion was based on section 61(a) of the Internal Revenue Code (Code) which defines gross income as all income from whatever source derived, including (but not limited to) the following items:

(1) Compensation for services, including fees, commissions, and similar items;

. . .

(3) Gains derived from dealings in property;

26 U.S.C.A. § 61(a). While admitting that this case is the first of its kind, Bierman opined that if the exchanges were considered the sale of a product, there would be no tax basis or original cost for the product sold, and the entire sales price would constitute gain subject to tax under section 61(a)(3). Alternatively, he considered categorizing the transactions as the rendition of a service, in which case he was of the opinion that the entire sales price similarly would be fully taxable under section 61(a)(1).

The defense proffered to the court the testimony of Daniel Nall, a Certified Public Accountant and former revenue agent, who concluded that the money received by Garber was not within the legal definition of income in section 61(a) and that she had therefore participated in tax-free exchanges. He patterned his reasoning on early case law resting on Doyle v. Mitchell Brothers, 247 U.S. 179, 38 S.Ct. 467, 62 L.Ed. 1054 (1918), which held that funds obtained by the conversion of capital assets and which represented only the actual value of such assets was not taxable income. According to Nall, the Attorney General in a 1918 opinion considered the human body a kind of capital asset. Following the reasoning in *Doyle,* the opinion held that the proceeds of an accident insurance policy were not subject to tax because the proceeds of the insurance policy represented a conversion of the capital loss which the injured taxpayer had suffered. Nall mentioned similar opinions finding settlements received for personal injury not taxable income. Eventually the Code was amended to include a specific provision covering the tax consequences of compensation for injuries or sickness. Nevertheless, Nall explained, the theory has reappeared in situations involving the exchange of something so personal that its value is not susceptible to measurement. In these transactions—such as property settlements in divorce actions or damage awards for alienation of affection or for defamation of character—the value received is deemed equal to the value given, resulting in no taxable gain. Nall compared blood plasma, a part of the body which no one can value, and concluded that it too must be worth its market value. He therefore reasoned that its exchange produces no gain.

The district court heard the testimony of these two experts but refused to admit either opinion in the evidence which went to the jury because it considered the question of taxability to be one of law for the court and not the jury to decide. However, the court did permit the government to introduce testimony by an Internal Revenue Service agent who qualified as an expert in the field of accounting and taxation. This agent offered his opinion that additional taxable income was due but not reported in the years in question. His testimony was received over defense objection that it was based on his conclusion that the compensation received was income and taxable. During cross examination, the witness conceded that the taxability of money received for giving up a part of one's body is a unique and undecided question in tax law. He also agreed that money received as a return on a capital product is not subject to tax. Yet, he based his calculations on his opinion that the blood plasma donations here were taxable personal services. His view was, in turn, based solely on a Revenue Ruling which declared donations of whole blood to be a service for purposes of determining the deductibility of a charitable contribution. The court sustained objections to the relevancy of further inquiry regarding the nature or value of blood plasma.

The defense argued to the court that the expert testimony of Daniel Nall should be presented to the jury to rebut the government's expert IRS agent, to show that doubt existed as to whether a tax was due because it was incapable of being computed, and to demonstrate the vagueness of the law, which would preclude a willful intent to violate it. The court recognized that Nall's theory could be relevant to its judicial resolution of the legal conflict. It ruled however that since Nall had never discussed his opinion of the law with the defendant, it had no relevancy to the fact issue of Garber's intent. The jury never heard the testimony. It did, however, hear considerable factual evidence relating to Garber's actual intent.[79]

After hearing all the evidence, the court ruled as a matter of law that the moneys Garber received for her blood plasma, whether considered a personal service or a product, were income subject to federal income taxation. Consistent with that ruling the jury was instructed that the funds Garber received from the sale of her blood plasma were taxable income. . . .

We hold that the combined effect of the trial court's evidentiary rulings excluding defendant's proffered expert testimony and its requested jury charge prejudicially deprived the defendant of a valid theory of her defense. No court has yet determined whether payments received by a donor of blood or blood components are taxable as income. If, as the government contends, by subjecting herself to the plasmapheresis process Garber has performed a service, her compensation would be taxable under section 61(a)(1) of the Code. In some ways, Garber's activity does resemble work: artificial stimulation, which is not a necessary prerequisite to plasma extraction, causes nausea and dizziness; the ordeal of plasmapheresis can be extremely painful if a nerve is struck, can cause nausea, blackouts, dizziness and scarring, and increases the risks of blood clotting and hepatitis. These efforts of production may logically compare to the performance of a service.

On the other hand, blood plasma, like a chicken's eggs, a sheep's wool, or like any salable part of the human body, is tangible property which in this case commanded a selling price dependent on its value. The amount of Garber's compensation for any given pint of plasma was

---

79. [Court's footnote 3.] To prove that Garber had to have been actually aware of her tax liability, the government offered testimony from an employee of Dade Reagents, contradicted by defendant's own statements, that in Garber's early dealings with that company not only had she been advised of the taxable element of her payments but the company had also opened a savings account in her name and regularly deposited a portion of her earnings allegedly for income tax purposes. The IRS agent who first investigated the Garbers took the stand and testified that, in his initial interview with both Mr. and Mrs. Garber concerning their 1971 joint return, defendant denied having received any income other than the reported $200 per week salary from Biomedical. However, that same afternoon following the interview, defendant called the agent, explained that she and her husband were about to be divorced, and arranged a second interview in which she discussed her plasma donations and disclosed all monies received. The agent admitted that Garber was cooperative in the absence of her husband; she produced all relevant records including the 1099 forms received from Biomedical.

The defense offered affirmative evidence to show that Garber did not willfully misstate her income. An accountant had prepared all three joint returns from information supplied by Mr. Garber, who was not indicted, without consulting with defendant. Furthermore, it was undisputed that all payments to defendant were made by check, payable to her, and deposited in her bank account. Payments were never made in cash; there was no duplicative bookkeeping or other clandestine financial dealings indicative of an attempt to secrete earnings. Her returns for the years in question disclosed Biomedical as a source of income. In addition, Garber produced a copy of her 1969 tax return on which she declared no taxable income but noted "I have no W—2 forms as my income was made up entirely from donating blood plasma from various blood banks." The defendant herself testified that she thought, after speaking with other blood donors, that because she was selling a part of her body the money received was not taxable.

directly related to the strength of the desired antibodies. The greater their concentration, the more she was paid; her earnings were in no way related to the amount of work done, pain incurred, or time spent producing one pint of plasma.

Of course, the product/service distinction is relevant only if the sale of the product results in no taxable gain. The experts testifying for both parties here concede that section 61(a)(3) includes in income only the profit gained through the sale or conversion of capital assets. They do not, however, agree on the computation of gain, because they differ in their theories as to how the value of the product before its sale is to be established. . . .

. . . However, we need not and do not undertake the complex task of resolving what the law should be, nor is it necessary to decide whether, as the trial court concluded, the question is purely one of law for the court and not the jury to resolve. Rather, because the district court refused to permit Bierman, the expert for the government, and Nall, the expert for the defense, to testify and because it reserved to itself the job of unriddling the tax law, thus completely obscuring from the jury the most important theory of Garber's defense—that she could not have willfully evaded a tax if there existed a reasonable doubt in the law that a tax was due—her trial was rendered fundamentally unfair.

A tax return is not criminally fraudulent simply because it is erroneous. Willfulness is an essential element of the crime charged. As such, the government must prove beyond a reasonable doubt that the defendant willfully and intentionally attempted to evade and defeat income taxes for each year in question by filing with the IRS tax returns which she knew were false. . . .

When the taxability of unreported income is problematical as a matter of law, the unresolved nature of the law is relevant to show that defendant may not have been aware of a tax liability or may have simply made an error in judgment. Furthermore, the relevance of a dispute in the law does not depend on whether the defendant actually knew of the conflict. . . .

. . . To hold otherwise would advocate convicting an unsophisticated taxpayer who failed to seek expert advice as to whether certain income was taxable while setting free a wise taxpayer who could find advice that taxes were not due on the identical type of debatable taxable income.

* * *

The tax treatment of earnings from the sale of blood plasma or other parts of the human body is an uncharted area in tax law. The parties in this case presented divergent opinions as to the ultimate taxability by analogy to two legitimate theories in tax law. The trial court should not have withheld this fact, and its powerful impact on the issue of Garber's willfulness, from the jury. In a case such as this where the element of willfulness is critical to the defense, the defendant is entitled to wide latitude in the introduction of evidence tending to show lack of intent. The defendant testified that she subjectively thought that proceeds from the sale of part of her body were not taxable. By disallowing Nall's testimony that a recognized theory of tax law supports Garber's feelings, the court deprived the defendant of evidence showing her state of mind to be reasonable.

This error was compounded by the court's instructions to the jury which took from them the question of the validity of the tax. In effect, the court adopted the government's position that a tax was owing as a matter of law. Garber admitted receiving unreported money and disclosed its source; the defense in this case rested entirely on a denial of the necessary criminal intent to evade taxes. The court erred by refusing to instruct the jury that a reasonable misconception of the tax law on her part would negate the necessary intent. . . .

* * *

[T]he government presented persuasive evidence showing that the defendant knowingly and willfully evaded her taxes. She received a significant amount of money over a three year period, but reported none of it. The proof also showed that those with whom she dealt advised her that they thought the proceeds were taxable. Nevertheless, the tax question was completely novel and unsettled by any clearly relevant precedent. A criminal proceeding pursuant to section 7201 is an inappropriate vehicle for pioneering interpretations of tax law. The conviction is reversed and the cause is remanded for retrial.

Reversed and Remanded.

TJOFLAT, CIRCUIT JUDGE, with whom AINSWORTH and ALVIN B. RUBIN, CIRCUIT JUDGES, join, dissenting:

* * *

. . . [T]he critical issue in the case . . . [is] a factual one: whether Garber acted with the requisite willfulness in failing to pay taxes on the sums in question. To be admissible, the proffered testimony must be relevant to this issue, Fed.R.Evid. 402, and its probative value must outweigh the danger of unfair prejudice, confusion of the issues, or misleading the jury. Fed.R.Evid. 403. I conclude that Nall's testimony is not relevant to Garber's intent, and that it certainly fails the weighing test. I would hold, therefore, that Judge Fulton properly excluded the evidence. It is necessary to examine closely this relevance issue to show the dangers created by the majority opinion.

The factual question for the jury, narrowly stated, was whether Garber had an honest belief that the money she had received for her blood plasma was nontaxable. The inquiry is a subjective one. Garber's belief does not have to have been reasonable; in fact, if her asserted belief had been reasonable, presumably the indictment should be dismissed for failure to charge an offense. The majority opinion obscures the subjective nature of the issue: "The court erred by refusing to instruct the jury that a reasonable misconception of the tax law on her part would negate the necessary intent." By drawing the notion of reasonableness into the inquiry, the majority improperly broadens the scope of relevancy, causing certain evidence to appear admissible although it would be excluded if the factual issue were correctly identified.

Fed.R.Evid. 401 defines relevant evidence as evidence "having any tendency to make the existence of any fact that is of consequence to the determination of the action more probable or less probable than it would be without the evidence." Garber sought to introduce expert testimony that the taxability of the plasma sales proceeds was in doubt. Conceivably, there are two ways in which such testimony might be relevant. It might provide evidence of the defendant's state of mind, or it might indirectly buttress her explanation of her actions. Concededly, there was never any communication between Garber and Nall. Since Nall neither influenced Garber's opinion nor learned of her opinion, it follows that he could have nothing to say that would bear directly on Garber's intent. So if Nall's proffered testimony is relevant at all, it can only be relevant through reinforcing the credibility of Garber's explanation.

On direct examination, Garber was asked whether, at the time she entered into the plasma sale contracts, she had come to any conclusion concerning whether the monies she was to receive were taxable. She replied:

> I had arrived in my own mind that it was definitely not taxable, that this was their gain, a part of me, it was my body, it was a very human element . . ., and I felt that it definitely was not taxable, that it was like I said, part of me, something—

Garber testified that she had discussed this idea that sales of portions of the human body are inherently nontaxable with fellow donors and with her husband, but that she had never sought any professional advice about her theory.

On the proffer of his testimony, Nall, like Garber, stated that he considered the proceeds of the plasma sales nontaxable, but that is the extent of the similarity between his testimony and Garber's. Nall bases his opinion solely on his reading of the law. For example, when he was asked, "Sir, when would you say that, if somebody, based upon what you say, sold his plasma, that there is no income because there is no way of determining the basis?", he responded:

> Under this particular concept of the Supreme Court definition of income, the amount received for the part of the body . . . if a person did sell a part of their body, no, there would not be a taxable transaction.
>
> I might add, if I may . . . that the Solicitor's Opinion 132 said, "No, these things are not income by reason of the definition of income. . . ."

In deciding the relevancy of this testimony, the trial judge should have, in essence, asked himself whether a reasonable juror could believe that the proffered testimony makes it more probable that Garber actually believed no tax was due on the money. See, e.g., McCormick, Evidence § 185, at 438 (2d ed. 1972). I am certain that what this professional accountant concluded after studying the law could not make one whit more or less probable the truth of Garber's explanation that she had not paid taxes on what she had received for plasmapheresis because "in my heart I did not feel it was taxable. . . ." Therefore, the proffer does not pass the rule 401 test, and the testimony should be excluded.

The relevance issue could possibly be resolved differently if the expert's testimony bore some relation to the context of the defendant's explanation. For example, an accountant might testify, "I have advised twenty laypeople concerning the taxability of transactions analogous to the ones in the instant case. None of them have communicated with Mrs. Garber, and none of them have had any more legal training than Mrs. Garber. Seventeen of the twenty told me that they had a gut feeling—like the feeling Mrs. Garber testified she had—that the monies they had received were not taxable." Putting aside the hearsay problem, it appears that a juror might reasonably infer from this statement that since other people have the belief that Garber says she had, it is slightly more likely that Garber did indeed have the belief. On the other hand, such an inference would not be reasonable if it could be shown: that the expert was somehow not qualified to present the proffered testimony; that the seventeen people did not state their opinions in good faith; or that the situations were not truly analogous. Consequently, on the proffer of such testimony, the Government would have been entitled to cross-examine the expert in an effort to exclude his opinion altogether. Failing that, the Government would have the option to call each of the seventeen people and to cross-examine them in order to destroy the foundation of the expert's testimony and thus to demonstrate its irrelevancy for lack of probative value. Cross-examination and rehabilitation could go on forever, and the principal issues in the trial would be lost in this sea of collateral nonsense.

* * *

The majority's failure adequately to consider the consequences of the rule of evidence that it has fashioned is particularly grave because what we decide today may prove irretrievable. I suspect that in future criminal trials involving the defendant's state of mind, the introduction of expert testimony concerning the state of the law will be initiated by the defense.[80] . . .

---

80. [Footnote 10 in original.] For example, in a criminal antitrust prosecution arising from a complex series of business transactions, a defendant may admit the alleged transactions but contend that he had not believed his actions unlawfully anticompetitive. The defense is that the defendant has not acted with the mens rea required for a criminal conviction. See United States v. United States Gypsum Co., 438 U.S. 422, 431–433, 98 S.Ct. 2864, 2876–78, 57 L.Ed.2d 854 (1978). The antitrust defendant would surely welcome the opportunity to put a law professor or some other expert on the stand to testify as to vagueness in the law or to the reasonableness of the defendant's belief in the legality of his conduct.

Because I conclude that the district court correctly decided the issues of law before it and properly excluded "expert" testimony concerning the state of the law, I would affirm Garber's conviction.[81]

NOTES AND QUERIES

(1) *Queries.* What is the theory underlying *Garber*? a) Is the theory that given the legal uncertainties of her situation, Mrs. Garber could not possibly have had notice of what the law required in these circumstances, and, accordingly, could not have "willfully" violated it? If so, is this really a "due process as applied" argument? If this is the underlying basis of the decision, does it matter whether the defendant had any actual knowledge as to what the legal disputes were? Could this defense be applied in any case in which the defendant claims that the law was uncertain, or only in unusual cases? b) Is the theory underlying the decision that Mrs. Garber could not have "willfully" violated the law because she had a "good faith" belief that her conduct was lawful, her good faith being shown by proof of the law's uncertainty? If this is the basis of the decision, then could the expert testimony on the state of the law ("uncertain") be admissible as relevant if she did not in fact rely on legal advice, or did not even know what the expert's theory was? How, then, is she to prove her good faith?

What is the harm from admitting the expert testimony offered by Mrs. Garber? Is the concern that juries might be confused by differing views of the state of the law? If this concern is justifiable, doesn't this actually support the defense argument that the legal uncertainty should negate willfulness (or, at least, that the defendant could have had a good faith belief that his or her conduct was lawful)? If jury confusion is a problem, should the question of uncertainty then be decided by the court? On the other hand, is the real concern that defendants could too easily avoid criminal liability by finding some "expert" who would say that the tax laws are confusing? Who has ever claimed that the tax laws *aren't* confusing?

Is *Garber* limited to tax cases? Should it only be in criminal tax cases that we allow defendants to argue that they did not act willfully because the law was unclear or because they thought in good faith that their behavior was lawful? Can we rationally limit this defense to the Internal Revenue Code? How about other business crimes? Traditional "common law" crimes?

(2) *Subsequent Cases.* Subsequent cases have not treated *Garber* well. In a Fifth Circuit case decided one year after *Garber*, *United States v. Herzog*,[82] the Court of Appeals refused to permit a tax law professor to testify about the uncertainty of the legal theory the defendant claimed to be following (that the exchange of his work for wages was not "profit or gain" to him and hence was not taxable). The

---

81. The opinion of Judge Hill, specially concurring, and the dissenting opinion of Judge Ainsworth, in which Judges Godbold, Tjoflat and Alvin Rubin joined, are omitted.

82. 632 F.2d 469 (5th Cir.1980).

Court, distinguishing *Garber*, held that the proffered testimony was not relevant because the defendant was being prosecuted for filing fraudulent withholding statements, rather than for failing to pay income tax. However, in a 1984 prosecution for willful failure to file tax returns, *United States v. Burton*,[83] the Fifth Circuit again rejected, on evidentiary grounds, expert testimony regarding this "exchange theory." Expert testimony regarding the uncertainty of taxing wages under this theory "may be relevant to the credibility of a defendant's claim" that he had a good faith belief in legality, the court wrote. Nevertheless, this testimony was held inadmissible because the "marginal contribution" of that testimony must be weighed "against potential prejudice and confusion, keeping in mind that the judge remains the jury's source of information regarding the law." Under this approach, the Court noted, surveys showing that the defendant's view "was shared by others" might lead to a different result when ruling on admissibility. The Court of Appeals then described *Garber* as follows:

> Given the unique, indeed near bizarre, facts [in *Garber*], we recoiled at the use of criminal prosecution to 'pioneer' the tax law. Critically, the level of uncertainty was so high we did not require a connection between the legal uncertainty and Garber's claim. Awareness of legal debate thus was virtually presumed; however, we did not hold that in the absence of such a level of uncertainty—approaching legal vagueness—that we could not require a defendant to link his own belief to the evidence of legal uncertainty.

> We are persuaded that, apart from those few cases where the legal duty pointed to is so uncertain as to approach the level of vagueness, the abstract question of legal uncertainty of which a defendant was unaware is of marginal relevance. In short, we read *Garber* no more broadly than its facts. . . . Evidence of legal uncertainty, except as it relates to defendant's effort to show the source of his state of mind, need not be received, at least where, as here, the claimed uncertainty does not approach vagueness and is neither widely recognized nor related to a novel or unusual application of the law.[84]

---

83. 737 F.2d 439 (5th Cir.1984).

84. 737 F.2d at 444. See also United States v. Curtis, 782 F.2d 593 (6th Cir.1986) (proffered testimony to the effect that law governing corporate distributions was unsettled and complex; held: inadmissible, absent proof that defendant was confused or relied on expert's advice; rejects *Garber* approach allowing testimony without proof of a connection between external facts and defendant's state of mind); United States v. Mallas, 762 F.2d 361 (4th Cir.1985) (reversing twelve year imprisonment term arising out of selling tax shelters; question of tax liability "novel" and "governing law offers no clear guidance"; because defendants "could not have ascertained the legal standards applicable to their conduct," criminal prosecution violates constitutional duty to warn citizens whether conduct is unlawful; uncertainty of tax law is a question for the judge, rather than jury); United States v. Dahlstrom, 713 F.2d 1423 (9th Cir.1983) (tax fraud prosecution arising out of sale of tax shelters; legality of shelters in question "completely unsettled by any clearly relevant precedent" decided before acts charged in indictment; due process requires "a person be given fair notice as to what constitutes illegal conduct"), certiorari denied 466 U.S. 980, 104 S.Ct. 2363, 80 L.Ed.2d 835 (1984); United States v. Ingredient Technology Corp., 698 F.2d 88, 97 (2d Cir.) (rejecting *Garber* because case

(3) *Reliance on Advice of Counsel.* A critical issue in *Garber* is whether to admit expert testimony with regard to uncertain legal theories when the defendant had no knowledge of these uncertain legal theories at the time the offense allegedly was committed. Such a problem would not occur, of course, if the defendant had sought counsel prior to deciding what his or her tax liability should be. Do you agree with the Court's argument in *Garber* as to why such consultation with counsel should not be required?

Suppose, however, that a defendant does consult counsel, who tells the defendant that the actions the defendant is about to undertake are lawful. Is the defendant then free to go ahead and perform the actions, even though it turns out later that counsel's advice was inaccurate? Should this be a defense in every criminal case where intent is required, or only in cases which require "willfulness"? Suppose counsel's advice is that "there is an eighty percent chance that the proposed conduct will not be found to be illegal"? Sixty percent?

Are there any restrictions on what a defendant must show when asserting the defense? In *United States v. Eisenstein,* a prosecution for failing to file currency transaction reports under the Bank Secrecy Act, the Fifth Circuit Court of Appeals wrote: [85]

> Only *willful* failures to file CTRs are subject to criminal penalties under the Act. The law of this circuit is well established that, as it is used in the currency reporting statute, the term '*willful* require[s] proof of the defendant's knowledge of the reporting requirement and his specific intent to commit the crime.' Congress no doubt made the failure to file CTRs a specific intent crime because, without knowledge of the reporting requirement, a would-be violator cannot be expected to recognize the illegality of his otherwise innocent act.
>
> A defendant charged with violating the reporting statute can attempt to negate proof of specific intent by establishing the defense of good faith reliance on advice of counsel. In order to take advantage of this defense, the defendant must show that he relied in good faith after first making a full disclosure of all facts that are relevant to the advice for which he consulted the attorney. When

---

permits juries to find that uncertainty in the law negates willfulness "whether or not the defendants are actually confused about the extent of their tax liability"; and because submitting opposing opinions on the law to the jury would be confusing), certiorari denied 462 U.S. 1131, 103 S.Ct. 3111, 77 L.Ed.2d 1366 (1983); Note, Criminal Liability for Willful Evasion of an Uncertain Tax, 81 Colum.L.Rev. 1348 (1981) ("willfulness" does not depend on the certainty or uncertainty of the law but on what the defendant honestly believes; for uncertainty to negate willfulness, there must be reliance; *Garber* is better analyzed as a vagueness case); cf. United States v. Aitken, 755 F.2d 188 (1st Cir.1985) ("willfulness" under tax laws is based on subjective intent, rather than the objective reasonableness of defendant's views with regard to the legality of conduct; general doctrine that mistake of law is seldom a defense in criminal prosecutions is "inappropriate" in tax cases; cases have recognized that internal revenue reporting and filing requirements are "an enclave apart").

85. 731 F.2d 1540, 1543–44 (11th Cir. 1984).

the defendant presents evidence that he disclosed all relevant facts to his attorney and relied on the attorney's advice based on the disclosure, the trial court must instruct the jury on the defense of good faith reliance on counsel.[86]

(4) *Reliance on Official Interpretation.* Consider *United States v. Pennsylvania Industrial Chemical Corp.,* 411 U.S. 655, 93 S.Ct. 1804, 36 L.Ed.2d 567 (1973). This was a prosecution for dumping industrial refuse into the Monongehela River in violation of Section 13 of the Rivers and Harbors Act of 1899. One of the questions presented was whether the defendant "was entitled to assert as a defense its alleged reliance on the Army Corps of Engineers' longstanding administrative construction of § 13 as limited to water deposits that impede or obstruct navigation." Under Section 16 of the Act, "[e]very person and every corporation that shall violate, or that shall knowingly aid, abet, authorize or instigate a violation" of the statute is guilty of a misdemeanor. Justice Brennan wrote for the Court:

> [T]he Court of Appeals' alternative ground for reversing PICCO's conviction [was] that in light of the longstanding, official administrative construction of § 13 as limited to those water deposits that tend to impede or obstruct navigation, PICCO may have been "affirmatively misled" into believing that its conduct was not criminal.[87] We agree with the Court of Appeals that PICCO should have been permitted to present relevant evidence to establish this defense.
>
> At the outset, we observe that the issue here is not whether § 13 in fact applies to water deposits that have no tendency to affect navigation. For, although there was much dispute on this question in the past, in United States v. Standard Oil Co. [decided in 1966, four years before the discharges involved in this case], we held that "the 'serious injury' to our watercourses .. sought to be remedied [by the 1899 Act] was caused in part by obstacles that impeded navigation and in part by pollution," and that the term "refuse" as used in § 13 "includes all foreign substances and pollutants. . . ." 384 U.S., at 228–229, 230. Since then, the lower courts have almost universally agreed, as did the courts below, that § 13 is to be read in accordance with its plain language as imposing a flat ban on the unauthorized deposit of foreign substances into navigable waters, regardless of the effect on navigation.
>
> Nevertheless, it is undisputed that prior to December 1970 the Army Corps of Engineers consistently construed § 13 as limited to water deposits that affected navigation. Thus, at the time of our decision in Standard Oil, the published regulation pertaining to § 13 read as follows:

---

86. But see W. La Fave & A. Scott, Criminal Law § 5.1(d)(4), at p. 419 (2d ed. 1986) (cases "uniformly hold" that defense of reliance on counsel is not available).

87. [Court's footnote 22.] It was conceded for purposes of this case that the refuse matter involved was not of a nature that would impede or obstruct navigation.

"§ 209.395. Deposit of refuse. Section 13 of the River and Harbor Act of March 3, 1899 (30 Stat. 1152; 33 U.S.C. 407), prohibits the deposit in navigable waters generally of 'refuse matter of any kind or description whatever other than that flowing from streets and sewers and passing therefrom in a liquid state.' The jurisdiction of the Department of the Army, derived from the Federal laws enacted for the protection and preservation of the navigable waters of the United States, is limited and directed to such control as may be necessary to protect the public right of navigation. Action under section 13 has therefore been directed by the Department principally against the discharge of those materials that are obstructive or injurious to navigation." 33 CFR § 209.395 (1967).

In December 1968, the Corps of Engineers published a complete revision of the regulations pertaining to navigable waters. The new regulations pertaining to §§ 9 and 10 of the Rivers and Harbors Act of 1899, 33 U.S.C. §§ 401 and 403, dealing with construction and excavation in navigable waters, stated for the first time that the Corps would consider pollution and other conservation and environmental factors in passing on applications under those sections for permits to "work in navigable waters." 33 CFR § 209.120(d) (1969). But notwithstanding this reference to environmental factors and in spite of our intervening decision in *Standard Oil*, the new regulation pertaining to § 13 of the 1899 Act continued to construe that provision as limited to water deposits that affected navigation. . . .

At trial, PICCO offered to prove that, in reliance on the consistent, longstanding administrative construction of § 13, the deposits in question were made in good-faith belief that they were permissible under law. PICCO does not contend, therefore, that it was ignorant of the law or that the statute is impermissibly vague, but rather that it was affirmatively misled by the responsible administrative agency into believing that the law did not apply in this situation.

Of course, there can be no question that PICCO had a right to look to the Corps of Engineers' regulations for guidance. The Corps is the responsible administrative agency under the 1899 Act, and "the rulings, interpretations and opinions of the [responsible agency] . . ., while not controlling upon the courts by reason of their authority, do constitute a body of experience and informed judgment to which . . . litigants may properly resort for guidance." Moreover, although the regulations did not of themselves purport to create or define the statutory offense in question, it is certainly true that their designed purpose was to guide persons as to the meaning and requirements of the statute. Thus, to the extent that the regulations deprived PICCO of fair warning as to what conduct the Government intended to make criminal, we think there can be no doubt that traditional notions of fairness inherent in our system of criminal justice prevent the Government from proceeding with the prosecution. See Newman, Should Official Advice Be Reliable?—Proposals as to Estoppel and Related Doctrines in Administrative Law, 53 Col.L.Rev. 374 (1953); Note, Applying Estoppel Principles in Criminal Cases, 78 Yale L.J. 1046 (1969).

The Government argues, however, that our pronouncement in *Standard Oil* precludes PICCO from asserting reliance on the Corps of Engineers' regulations and that, in any event, the revised regulation issued in 1968, when considered in light of other pertinent factors,[88] was not misleading to persons in PICCO's position. But we need not respond to the Government's arguments here, for the substance of those arguments pertains, not to the issue of the availability of reliance as a defense, but rather to the issues whether there was in fact reliance and, if so, whether that reliance was reasonable under the circumstances—issues that must be decided in the first instance by the trial court. At this stage, it is sufficient that we hold that it was error for the District Court to refuse to permit PICCO to present evidence in support of its claim that it had been affirmatively misled into believing that the discharges in question were not a violation of the statute.

Accordingly, the judgment of the Court of Appeals is modified to remand the case to the District Court for further proceedings consistent with this opinion.

It is so ordered.

2. MANAGERIAL LIABILITY

SCOPE NOTE

Criminal liability can be imposed not only on corporate employees who "did" the crime, but also on higher level supervisors, officers, or directors. In some cases such liability has been rested on traditional "aiding and abetting" grounds.[89] In other cases, prosecutors have invoked provisions of some federal regulatory statutes which specifically permit liability for individual "directors, officers, or agents of such corporation who shall have authorized, ordered, or done" any acts which violate the statute in question.[90] Liability under either theory, however, does not present problems unique to the business crime area

---

88. [Court's footnote 26.] The other factors that the Government argues must be taken into consideration are post-1968 regulations issued with respect to other sections of the 1899 Act and with respect to other acts, and certain Corps of Engineers press releases and periodic publications.

89. See, e.g., Nye & Nissen v. United States, 336 U.S. 613, 69 S.Ct. 766, 93 L.Ed. 919 (1949) (president of corporation, although not directly tied to false invoices in question, was "promoter" of the scheme; makers of false invoices were his subordinates); United States v. Precision Medical Laboratories, Inc., 593 F.2d 434, 442 (2d Cir.1978) (despite fact that president did not sign false claim forms, he authorized employees to do so and can therefore be found guilty as an aider and abetter).

90. Clayton Act, Section 14, 15 U.S.C.A. § 24.

because liability rests on active behavior of the kind encountered in other areas of the criminal law.

Managerial criminal liability presents the greatest difficulty when it is premised on inaction, rather than on active approval or command. A failure to supervise, or a failure to correct a known problem, or a failure to discover a problem can all be thought of as "contributing" to the commission of an offense. Sometimes, as when the harm is the result of a malfunction in the manufacturing process, the failures of higher-level management can be seen as more serious than the actual mistake of the lower-level line employee. Despite frequent demands to prosecute the "real offenders," however, legal principles have been slow to develop which are capable of selecting the proper defendants out of the managerial hierarchy of today's large corporations.

The area which has seen the greatest development in this regard is the Food, Drug and Cosmetic Act, and the materials which follow concentrate on this area. The Section begins with the two leading cases, *United States v. Dotterweich* and *United States v. Park*. The Notes following explore the problems of imposing criminal liability for failing to discharge adequately one's managerial responsibilities.

UNITED STATES v. DOTTERWEICH

Supreme Court of the United States, 1943.
320 U.S. 277, 64 S.Ct. 134, 88 L.Ed. 48.

[Digest: Dotterweich and the Buffalo Pharmacal Company were prosecuted for three violations of the Federal Food, Drug and Cosmetic Act. The first count was based on a shipment of a bottle of cascara compound, which was alleged to be misbranded because the label listed strychnine sulphate as an ingredient when this ingredient had been removed several months before from the formula for the pills as stated in the official National Formulary. The other two counts related to a shipment of a bottle of digitalis tablets, alleging that they were adulterated and misbranded because the tablets were analyzed to have less than one-half the represented potency. Both shipments were made in the course of filling an order received by the company from a physician. The company had purchased the drugs from a wholesale manufacturer and repackaged them for shipment. Dotterweich had no personal connection with either shipment. He was in general charge of the company's business and had given general instructions to its employees to fill orders received from physicians. The jury found him guilty on all counts, but acquitted the corporation. He was fined $500 on each count, with payment suspended on the second and third counts, and given 60 days probation concurrently on each count.]

MR. JUSTICE FRANKFURTER delivered the opinion of the Court.

* * *

... The informations were based on § 301 of that Act (21 U.S.C. § 331), paragraph (a) of which prohibits "The introduction or delivery for introduction into interstate commerce of any . . . drug . . . that is adulterated or misbranded." "Any person" violating this provision is, by paragraph (a) of § 303, made "guilty of a misdemeanor."

* * *

... The Circuit Court of Appeals, one judge dissenting, reversed the conviction on the ground that only the corporation was the "person" subject to prosecution unless, perchance, Buffalo Pharmacal was a counterfeit corporation serving as a screen for Dotterweich. On that issue, after rehearing, it remanded the cause for a new trial. We then brought the case here, on the Government's petition for certiorari, because this construction raised questions of importance in the enforcement of the Federal Food, Drug, and Cosmetic Act.

The court below drew its conclusion not from the provisions defining the offenses on which this prosecution was based (§§ 301(a) and 303(a)), but from the terms of § 303(c). That section affords immunity from prosecution if certain conditions are satisfied. The condition relevant to this case is a guaranty from the seller of the innocence of his product. So far as here relevant, the provision for an immunizing guaranty is as follows:

> "No person shall be [penalized] for having violated section 301(a) or (d), if he establishes a guaranty or undertaking signed by, and containing the name and address of, the person residing in the United States from whom he received in good faith the article, to the effect, in case of an alleged violation of section 301(a), that such article is not adulterated or misbranded, within the meaning of this Act, designating this Act . . ."

The Circuit Court of Appeals found it "difficult to believe that Congress expected anyone except the principal to get such a guaranty, or to make the guilt of an agent depend upon whether his employer had gotten one." And so it cut down the scope of the penalizing provisions of the Act to the restrictive view, as a matter of language and policy, it took of the relieving effect of a guaranty.

The guaranty clause cannot be read in isolation. The Food and Drugs Act of 1906 was an exertion by Congress of its power to keep impure and adulterated food and drugs out of the channels of commerce. By the Act of 1938, Congress extended the range of its control over illicit and noxious articles and stiffened the penalties for disobedience. The purposes of this legislation thus touch phases of the lives and health of people which, in the circumstances of modern industrialism, are largely beyond self-protection. Regard for these purposes should infuse construction of the legislation if it is to be treated as a working instrument of government and not merely as a collection of English words. The prosecution to which Dotterweich was subjected is based on a now familiar type of legislation whereby penalties serve as effective means of regulation. Such legislation dispenses with the conventional requirement for criminal conduct—awareness of some wrongdoing. In the interest of the larger good it puts the burden of acting at hazard upon a person otherwise innocent but standing in responsible relation to a public danger. And so it is clear that shipments like those now in issue are "punished by the statute if the article is misbranded [or adulterated], and that the article may be misbranded [or adulterated] without any conscious fraud at all. It was natural enough to throw this risk on shippers with regard to the identity of their wares . . ."

The statute makes "any person" who violates § 301(a) guilty of a "misdemeanor." It specifically defines "person" to include "corporation." § 201(e). But the only way in which a corporation can act is through the individuals who act on its behalf. New York Central & H. R.R. Co. v. United States, 212 U.S. 481. . . . If, then, Dotterweich is not subject to the Act, it must be solely on the ground that individuals are immune when the "person" who violates § 301(a) is a corporation, although from the point of view of action the individuals are the corporation. As a matter of legal development, it has taken time to establish criminal liability also for a corporation and not merely for its agents. See New York Central & H. R.R. Co. v. United States, supra. The history of federal food and drug legislation is a good illustration of the elaborate phrasing that was in earlier days deemed necessary to fasten criminal liability on corporations. Section 12 of the Food and Drugs Act of 1906 provided that, "the act, omission, or failure of any officer, agent, or other person acting for or employed by any corporation, company, society, or association, within the scope of his employment or office, shall in every case be also deemed to be the act, omission, or failure of such corporation, company, society, or association as well as that of the person." By 1938, legal understanding and practice had rendered such statement of the obvious superfluous. Deletion of words—in the interest of brevity and good draftsmanship [91]— superfluous for holding a corporation criminally liable can hardly be found ground for relieving from such liability the individual agents of the corporation. To hold that the Act of 1938 freed all individuals, except when proprietors, from the culpability under which the earlier legislation had placed them is to defeat the very object of the new Act. Nothing is clearer than that the later legislation was designed to enlarge and stiffen the penal net and not to narrow and loosen it. This purpose was unequivocally avowed by the two committees which reported the bills to the Congress. . . . If the 1938 Act were construed as it was below, the penalties of the law could be imposed only in the rare case where the corporation is merely an individual's alter ego. Corporations carrying on an illicit trade would be subject only to what the House Committee described as a "license fee for the conduct of an illegitimate business." A corporate officer, who even with "intent to

---

91. [Court's footnote 1.] "The bill has been made shorter and less verbose than previous bills. That has been done without deleting any effective provisions." S.Rep. No. 152, 75th Cong., 1st Sess., p. 2.

defraud or mislead" (§ 303b), introduced adulterated or misbranded drugs into interstate commerce could not be held culpable for conduct which was indubitably outlawed by the 1906 Act. This argument proves too much. It is not credible that Congress should by implication have exonerated what is probably a preponderant number of persons involved in acts of disobedience—for the number of non-corporate proprietors is relatively small. Congress, of course, could reverse the process and hold only the corporation and allow its agents to escape. In very exceptional circumstances it may have required this result. But the history of the present Act, its purposes, its terms, and extended practical construction lead away from such a result. . . .

The Act is concerned not with the proprietory relation to a misbranded or an adulterated drug but with its distribution. In the case of a corporation such distribution must be accomplished, and may be furthered, by persons standing in various relations to the incorporeal proprietor. If a guaranty immunizes shipments of course it immunizes all involved in the shipment. But simply because if there had been a guaranty it would have been received by the proprietor, whether corporate or individual, as a safeguard for the enterprise, the want of a guaranty does not cut down the scope of responsibility of all who are concerned with transactions forbidden by § 301. To be sure, that casts the risk that there is no guaranty upon all who according to settled doctrines of criminal law are responsible for the commission of a misdemeanor. To read the guaranty section, as did the court below, so as to restrict liability for penalties to the only person who normally would receive a guaranty—the proprietor—disregards the admonition that "the meaning of a sentence is to be felt rather than to be proved." It also reads an exception to an important provision safeguarding the public welfare with a liberality which more appropriately belongs to enforcement of the central purpose of the Act.

The Circuit Court of Appeals was evidently tempted to make such a devitalizing use of the guaranty provision through fear that an enforcement of § 301(a) as written might operate too harshly by sweeping within its condemnation any person however remotely entangled in the proscribed shipment. But that is not the way to read legislation. Literalism and evisceration are equally to be avoided. To speak with technical accuracy, under § 301 a corporation may commit an offense and all persons who aid and abet its commission are equally guilty. Whether an accused shares responsibility in the business process resulting in unlawful distribution depends on the evidence produced at the trial and its submission—assuming the evidence warrants it—to the jury under appropriate guidance. The offense is committed, unless the enterprise which they are serving enjoys the immunity of a guaranty, by all who do have such a responsible share in the furtherance of the transaction which the statute outlaws, namely, to put into the stream of interstate commerce adulterated or misbranded drugs. Hardship there doubtless may be under a statute which thus penalizes the transaction though consciousness of wrongdoing be totally wanting.

Balancing relative hardships, Congress has preferred to place it upon those who have at least the opportunity of informing themselves of the existence of conditions imposed for the protection of consumers before sharing in illicit commerce, rather than to throw the hazard on the innocent public who are wholly helpless.

It would be too treacherous to define or even to indicate by way of illustration the class of employees which stands in such a responsible relation. To attempt a formula embracing the variety of conduct whereby persons may responsibly contribute in furthering a transaction forbidden by an Act of Congress, to wit, to send illicit goods across state lines, would be mischievous futility. In such matters the good sense of prosecutors, the wise guidance of trial judges, and the ultimate judgment of juries must be trusted. Our system of criminal justice necessarily depends on "conscience and circumspection in prosecuting officers," Nash v. United States, 229 U.S. 373, 378, even when the consequences are far more drastic than they are under the provision of law before us. See United States v. Balint, supra (involving a maximum sentence of five years). For present purposes it suffices to say that in what the defense characterized as "a very fair charge" the District Court properly left the question of the responsibility of Dotterweich for the shipment to the jury, and there was sufficient evidence to support its verdict.

Reversed.

Mr. Justice Murphy, dissenting:

Our prime concern in this case is whether the criminal sanctions of the Federal Food, Drug, and Cosmetic Act of 1938 plainly and unmistakably apply to the respondent in his capacity as a corporate officer. He is charged with violating § 301(a) of the Act, which prohibits the introduction or delivery for introduction into interstate commerce of any adulterated or misbranded drug. There is no evidence in this case of any personal guilt on the part of the respondent. There is no proof or claim that he ever knew of the introduction into commerce of the adulterated drugs in question, much less that he actively participated in their introduction. Guilt is imputed to the respondent solely on the basis of his authority and responsibility as president and general manager of the corporation.

It is a fundamental principle of Anglo–Saxon jurisprudence that guilt is personal and that it ought not lightly to be imputed to a citizen who, like the respondent, has no evil intention or consciousness of wrongdoing. It may be proper to charge him with responsibility to the corporation and the stockholders for negligence and mismanagement. But in the absence of clear statutory authorization it is inconsistent with established canons of criminal law to rest liability on an act in which the accused did not participate and of which he had no personal knowledge. Before we place the stigma of a criminal conviction upon any such citizen the legislative mandate must be clear and unambiguous. Accordingly that which Chief Justice Marshall has called "the tenderness of the law for the rights of individuals" entitles each person, regardless of economic or social status, to an unequivocal warning from the legislature as to whether he is within the class of persons subject to vicarious liability. Congress cannot be deemed to have intended to punish anyone who is not "plainly and unmistakably" within the confines of the statute.

Moreover, the fact that individual liability of corporate officers may be consistent with the policy and purpose of a public health and welfare measure does not authorize this Court to impose such liability where Congress has not clearly intended or actually done so. Congress alone has the power to define a crime and to specify the offenders. It is not our function to supply any deficiencies in these respects, no matter how grave the consequences. Statutory policy and purpose are not constitutional substitutes for the requirement that the legislature specify with reasonable certainty those individuals it desires to place under the interdict of the Act.

Looking at the language actually used in this statute, we find a complete absence of any reference to corporate officers. There is merely a provision in § 303(a) to the effect that "any person" inadvertently violating § 301(a) shall be guilty of a misdemeanor. . . .

* * *

The dangers inherent in any attempt to create liability without express Congressional intention or authorization are illustrated by this case. Without any legislative guides, we are confronted with the problem of determining precisely which officers, employees and agents of a corporation are to be subject to this Act by our fiat. To erect standards of responsibility is a difficult legislative task and the opinion of this Court admits that it is "too treacherous" and a "mischievous futility" for us to engage in such pursuits. But the only alternative is a blind resort to "the good sense of prosecutors, the wise guidance of trial judges, and the ultimate judgment of juries." Yet that situation is precisely what our constitutional system sought to avoid. Reliance on the legislature to define crimes and criminals distinguishes our form of jurisprudence from certain less desirable ones. The legislative power to restrain the liberty and to imperil the good reputation of citizens must not rest upon the variable attitudes and opinions of those charged with the duties of interpreting and enforcing the mandates of the law. I therefore cannot approve the decision of the Court in this case.

MR. JUSTICE ROBERTS, MR. JUSTICE REED and MR. JUSTICE RUTLEDGE join in this dissent.

UNITED STATES v. PARK

Supreme Court of the United States, 1975.
421 U.S. 658, 95 S.Ct. 1903, 44 L.Ed.2d 489.

MR. CHIEF JUSTICE BURGER delivered the opinion of the Court.

We granted certiorari to consider whether the jury instructions in the prosecution of a corporate officer under § 301(k) of the Federal

Food, Drug, and Cosmetic Act were appropriate under United States v. Dotterweich, 320 U.S. 277, 64 S.Ct. 134, 88 L.Ed. 48 (1943).

Acme Markets, Inc., is a national retail food chain with approximately 36,000 employees, 874 retail outlets, 12 general warehouses, and four special warehouses. Its headquarters, including the office of the president, respondent Park, who is chief executive officer of the corporation, are located in Philadelphia, Pa. In a five-count information filed in the United States District Court for the District of Maryland, the Government charged Acme and respondent with violations of the Federal Food, Drug and Cosmetic Act. Each count of the information alleged that the defendants had received food that had been shipped in interstate commerce and that, while the food was being held for sale in Acme's Baltimore warehouse following shipment in interstate commerce, they caused it to be held in a building accessible to rodents and to be exposed to contamination by rodents. These acts were alleged to have resulted in the food's being adulterated within the meaning of 21 U.S.C. §§ 342(a)(3) and (4),[92] in violation of 21 U.S.C. § 331(k).[93]

Acme pleaded guilty to each count of the information. Respondent pleaded not guilty. The evidence at trial demonstrated that in April 1970 the Food and Drug Administration (FDA) advised respondent by letter of insanitary conditions in Acme's Philadelphia warehouse. In 1971 the FDA found that similar conditions existed in the firm's Baltimore warehouse. An FDA consumer safety officer testified concerning evidence of rodent infestation and other insanitary conditions discovered during a 12–day inspection of the Baltimore warehouse in November and December 1971.[94] He also related that a second inspec-

---

92. [Court's footnote 1.] Section 402 of the Act, 21 U.S.C. § 342, provides in pertinent part:

"A food shall be deemed to be adulterated—

"(a) . . . (3) if it consists in whole or in part of any filthy, putrid, or decomposed substance, or if it is otherwise unfit for food; or (4) if it has been prepared, packed, or held under insanitary conditions whereby it may have become contaminated with filth, or whereby it may have been rendered injurious to health . . . .."

93. [Court's footnote 2.] Section 301 of the Act, 21 U.S.C. § 331, provides in pertinent part:

"The following acts and the causing thereof are prohibited:

. . .

"(k) The alteration, mutilation, destruction, obliteration, or removal of the whole or any part of the labeling of, or the doing of any other act with respect to, a food, drug, device, or cosmetic, if such act is done while such article is held for sale (whether or not the first sale) after shipment in interstate commerce and results in such article being adulterated or misbranded."

94. [Court's footnote 4.] The witness testified with respect to the inspection of the basement of the "old building" in the warehouse complex:

"We found extensive evidence of rodent infestation in the form of rat and mouse pellets throughout the entire perimeter area and along the wall.

"We also found that the doors leading to the basement area from the rail siding had openings at the bottom or openings beneath part of the door that came down at the bottom large enough to admit rodent entry. There were also roden[t] pellets found on a number of different packages of boxes of various items stored in the basement, and looking at this document, I see there were also broken windows along the rail siding." On the first floor of the "old building," the inspectors found:

"Thirty mouse pellets on the floor along walls and on the ledge in the hanging meat

tion of the warehouse had been conducted in March 1972.[95] On that occasion the inspectors found that there had been improvement in the sanitary conditions, but that "there was still evidence of rodent activity in the building and in the warehouses and we found some rodent-contaminated lots of food items."

The Government also presented testimony by the Chief of Compliance of the FDA's Baltimore office, who informed respondent by letter of the conditions at the Baltimore warehouse after the first inspection.[96] There was testimony by Acme's Baltimore division vice president, who had responded to the letter on behalf of Acme and respondent and who described the steps taken to remedy the insanitary conditions discovered by both inspections. The Government's final witness, Acme's vice president for legal affairs and assistant secretary, identified respondent as the president and chief executive officer of the company and read a bylaw prescribing the duties of the chief executive officer.[97] He testified that respondent functioned by delegating "normal operating duties," including sanitation, but that he retained "certain things, which are the big, broad, principles of the operation of the company," and had "the responsibility of seeing that they all work together."

At the close of the Government's case in chief, respondent moved for a judgment of acquittal on the ground that "the evidence in chief has shown that Mr. Park is not personally concerned in this Food and Drug violation." The trial judge denied the motion, stating that United States v. Dotterweich, 320 U.S. 277, 64 S.Ct. 134, 88 L.Ed. 48 (1943), was controlling.

Respondent was the only defense witness. He testified that, although all of Acme's employees were in a sense under his general direction, the company had an "organizational structure for responsibil-

room. There were at least twenty mouse pellets beside bales of lime Jello and one of the bales had a chewed rodent hole in the product. . . ."

95. [Court's footnote 5.] The first four counts of the information alleged violations corresponding to the observations of the inspectors during the November and December 1971 inspection. The fifth count alleged violations corresponding to observations during the March 1972 inspection.

96. [Court's footnote 6.] The letter, dated January 27, 1972, included the following:

"We note with much concern that the old and new warehouse areas used for food storage were actively and extensively inhabited by live rodents. Of even more concern was the observation that such reprehensible conditions obviously existed for a prolonged period of time without any detection, or were completely ignored. . . .

. . .

"We trust this letter will serve to direct your attention to the seriousness of the problem and formally advise you of the urgent need to initiate whatever measures are necessary to prevent recurrence and ensure compliance with the law."

97. [Court's footnote 7.] The bylaw provided in pertinent part:

"The Chairman of the board of directors or the president shall be the chief executive officer of the company as the board of directors may from time to time determine. He shall, subject to the board of directors, have general and active supervision of the affairs, business, offices and employees of the company. . . .

"He shall, from time to time, in his discretion or at the order of the board, report the operations and affairs of the company. He shall also perform such other duties and have such other powers as may be assigned to him from time to time by the board of directors."

ities for certain functions" according to which different phases of its operation were "assigned to individuals who, in turn, have staff and departments under them." He identified those individuals responsible for sanitation, and related that upon receipt of the January 1972 FDA letter, he had conferred with the vice president for legal affairs, who informed him that the Baltimore division vice president "was investigating the situation immediately and would be taking corrective action and would be preparing a summary of the corrective action to reply to the letter." Respondent stated that he did not "believe there was anything [he] could have done more constructively than what [he] found was being done."

On cross-examination, respondent conceded that providing sanitary conditions for food offered for sale to the public was something that he was "responsible for in the entire operation of the company," and he stated that it was one of many phases of the company that he assigned to "dependable subordinates." Respondent was asked about and, over the objections of his counsel, admitted receiving, the April 1970 letter addressed to him from the FDA regarding insanitary conditions at Acme's Philadelphia warehouse.[98] He acknowledged that, with the exception of the division vice president, the same individuals had responsibility for sanitation in both Baltimore and Philadelphia. Finally, in response to questions concerning the Philadelphia and Baltimore incidents, respondent admitted that the Baltimore problem indicated the system for handling sanitation "wasn't working perfectly" and that as Acme's chief executive officer he was responsible for "any result which occurs in our company."

At the close of the evidence, respondent's renewed motion for a judgment of acquittal was denied. The relevant portion of the trial judge's instructions to the jury challenged by respondent is set out in the margin.[99] Respondent's counsel objected to the instructions on the

---

98. [Court's footnote 8.] The April 1970 letter informed respondent of the following "objectionable conditions" in Acme's Philadelphia warehouse:

"1. Potential rodent entry ways were noted via ill fitting doors and door in irrepair at Southwest corner of warehouse; at dock at old salvage room and at receiving and shipping doors which were observed to be open most of the time.

"2. Rodent nesting, rodent excreta pellets, rodent stained bale bagging and rodent gnawed holes were noted among bales of flour stored in warehouse.

"3. Potential rodent harborage was noted in discarded paper, rope, sawdust and other debris piled in corner of shipping and receiving dock near bakery and warehouse doors. Rodent excreta pellets were observed among bags of sawdust (or wood shavings)."

99. [Court's footnote 9.] "In order to find the Defendant guilty on any count of the Information, you must find beyond a reasonable doubt on each count. . . .

. . .

"Thirdly, that John R. Park held a position of authority in the operation of the business of Acme Markets, Incorporated.

"However, you need not concern yourselves with the first two elements of the case. The main issue for your determination is only with the third element, whether the Defendant held a position of authority and responsibility in the business of Acme Markets.

. . .

"The statute makes individuals, as well as corporations, liable for violations. An individual is liable if it is clear, beyond a reasonable doubt, that the elements of the adulteration of the food as to travel in

ground that they failed fairly to reflect our decision in United States v. Dotterweich, supra, and to define "'responsible relationship.'" The trial judge overruled the objection. The jury found respondent guilty on all counts of the information, and he was subsequently sentenced to pay a fine of $50 on each count.[1]

The Court of Appeals reversed the conviction and remanded for a new trial. That court viewed the Government as arguing "that the conviction may be predicated solely upon a showing that . . . [respondent] was the President of the offending corporation," and it stated that as "a general proposition, some act of commission or omission is an essential element of every crime." It reasoned that, although our decision in United States v. Dotterweich, supra, 320 U.S., at 281, 64 S.Ct., at 136–137, had construed the statutory provisions under which respondent was tried to dispense with the traditional element of "'awareness of some wrongdoing,'" the Court had not construed them as dispensing with the element of "wrongful action." The Court of Appeals concluded that the trial judge's instructions "might well have left the jury with the erroneous impression that Park could be found guilty in the absence of 'wrongful action' on his part," and that proof of this element was required by due process. It held, with one dissent, that the instructions did not "correctly state the law of the case," and directed that on retrial the jury be instructed as to "wrongful action," which might be "gross negligence and inattention in discharging . . . corporate duties and obligations or any of a host of other acts of commission or omission which would 'cause' the contamination of food."

The Court of Appeals also held that the admission in evidence of the April 1970 FDA warning to respondent was error warranting reversal, based on its conclusion that, "as this case was submitted to the jury and in light of the sole issue presented," there was no need for the evidence and thus that its prejudicial effect outweighed its relevancy.

. . .

interstate commerce are present. As I have instructed you in this case, they are, and that the individual had a responsible relation to the situation, even though he may not have participated personally.

"The individual is or could be liable under the statute, even if he did not consciously do wrong. However, the fact that the Defendant is pres[id]ent and is a chief executive officer of the Acme Markets does not require a finding of guilt. Though, he need not have personally participated in the situation, he must have had a responsible relationship to the issue. The issue is, in this case, whether the Defendant, John R. Park, by virtue of his position in the company, had a position of authority and responsibility in the situation out of which these charges arose."

First Business Crime UCB—11

1. [Court's footnote 10.] Sections 303(a) and (b) of the Act, 21 U.S.C. § 333(a) and (b), provide:

"(a) Any person who violates a provision of section 331 of this title shall be imprisoned for not more than one year or fined not more than $1,000, or both.

"(b) Notwithstanding the provisions of subsection (a) of this section, if any person commits such a violation after a conviction of him under this section has become final, or commits such a violation with the intent to defraud or mislead, such person shall be imprisoned for not more than three years or fined not more than $10,000, or both."

We granted certiorari because of an apparent conflict among the Courts of Appeals with respect to the standard of liability of corporate officers under the Federal Food, Drug, and Cosmetic Act as construed in United States v. Dotterweich, supra, and because of the importance of the question to the Government's enforcement program. We reverse.

I

[The Court here reviewed United States v. Dotterweich.]

II

The rule that corporate employees who have "a responsible share in the furtherance of the transaction which the statute outlaws" are subject to the criminal provisions of the Act was not formulated in a vacuum. Cf. Morissette v. United States, 342 U.S. 246, 258, 72 S.Ct. 240, 96 L.Ed. 288 (1952). Cases under the Federal Food and Drugs Act of 1906 reflected the view both that knowledge or intent were not required to be proved in prosecutions under its criminal provisions, and that responsible corporate agents could be subjected to the liability thereby imposed. Moreover, the principle had been recognized that a corporate agent, through whose act, default, or omission the corporation committed a crime, was himself guilty individually of that crime. The principle had been applied whether or not the crime required "consciousness of wrongdoing," and it had been applied not only to those corporate agents who themselves committed the criminal act, but also to those who by virtue of their managerial positions or other similar relation to the actor could be deemed responsible for its commission.

In the latter class of cases, the liability of managerial officers did not depend on their knowledge of, or personal participation in, the act made criminal by the statute. Rather, where the statute under which they were prosecuted dispensed with "consciousness of wrongdoing," an omission or failure to act was deemed a sufficient basis for a responsible corporate agent's liability. It was enough in such cases that, by virtue of the relationship he bore to the corporation, the agent had the power to prevent the act complained of.

The rationale of the interpretation given the Act in *Dotterweich* as holding criminally accountable the persons whose failure to exercise the authority and supervisory responsibility reposed in them by the business organization resulted in the violation complained of, has been confirmed in our subsequent cases. Thus, the Court has reaffirmed the proposition that "the public interest in the purity of its food is so great as to warrant the imposition of the highest standard of care on distributors." In order to make "distributors of food the strictest censors of their merchandise," the Act punishes "neglect where the law requires care, or inaction where it imposes a duty." Morissette v. United States, supra, 342 U.S., at 255, 72 S.Ct., at 246. "The accused, if he does not will the violation, usually is in a position to prevent it with no more care than society might reasonably expect and no more exertion than it might reasonably exact from one who assumed his responsibilities." Id., at 256, 72 S.Ct., at 246. Cf. Hughes, Criminal Omissions, 67 Yale L.J. 590 (1958). Similarly, in cases decided after *Dotterweich,* the Courts of Appeals have recognized that those corporate agents vested with the responsibility, and power commensurate with that responsibility, to devise whatever measures are necessary to ensure compliance with the Act bear a "responsible relationship" to, or have a "responsible share" in, violations.

Thus *Dotterweich* and the cases which have followed reveal that in providing sanctions which reach and touch the individuals who execute the corporate mission—and this is by no means necessarily confined to a single corporate agent or employee—the Act imposes not only a positive duty to seek out and remedy violations when they occur but also, and primarily, a duty to implement measures that will insure that violations will not occur. The requirements of foresight and vigilance imposed on responsible corporate agents are beyond question demanding, and perhaps onerous, but they are no more stringent than the public has a right to expect of those who voluntarily assume positions of authority in business enterprises whose services and products affect the health and well-being of the public that supports them.

The Act does not, as we observed in *Dotterweich,* make criminal liability turn on "awareness of some wrongdoing" or "conscious fraud." The duty imposed by Congress on responsible corporate agents is, we emphasize, one that requires the highest standard of foresight and vigilance, but the Act, in its criminal aspect, does not require that which is objectively impossible. The theory upon which responsible corporate agents are held criminally accountable for "causing" violations of the Act permits a claim that a defendant was "powerless" to prevent or correct the violation to "be raised defensively at a trial on the merits." United States v. Wiesenfeld Warehouse Co., 376 U.S. 86, 91, 84 S.Ct. 559, 563, 11 L.Ed.2d 536 (1964). If such a claim is made, the defendant has the burden of coming forward with evidence, but this does not alter the Government's ultimate burden of proving beyond a reasonable doubt the defendant's guilt, including his power, in light of the duty imposed by the Act, to prevent or correct the prohibited condition. Congress has seen fit to enforce the accountability of responsible corporate agents dealing with products which may affect the health of consumers by penal sanctions cast in rigorous terms, and the obligation of the courts is to give them effect so long as they do not violate the Constitution.

III

We cannot agree with the Court of Appeals that it was incumbent upon the District Court to instruct the jury that the Government had the burden of establishing "wrongful action" in the sense in which the

Court of Appeals used that phrase. The concept of a "responsible relationship" to, or a "responsible share" in, a violation of the Act indeed imports some measure of blameworthiness; but it is equally clear that the Government establishes a prima facie case when it introduces evidence sufficient to warrant a finding by the trier of the facts that the defendant had, by reason of his position in the corporation, responsibility and authority either to prevent in the first instance, or promptly to correct, the violation complained of, and that he failed to do so. The failure thus to fulfill the duty imposed by the interaction of the corporate agent's authority and the statute furnishes a sufficient causal link. The considerations which prompted the imposition of this duty, and the scope of the duty, provide the measure of culpability.

* * *

Reading the entire charge satisfies us that the jury's attention was adequately focused on the issue of respondent's authority with respect to the conditions that formed the basis of the alleged violations. Viewed as a whole, the charge did not permit the jury to find guilt solely on the basis of respondent's position in the corporation; rather, it fairly advised the jury that to find guilt it must find respondent "had a responsible relation to the situation," and "by virtue of his position . . . had . . . authority and responsibility" to deal with the situation. The situation referred to could only be "food . . . held in unsanitary conditions in a warehouse with the result that it consisted, in part, of filth or . . . may have been contaminated with filth."

* * *

IV

Our conclusion that the Court of Appeals erred in its reading of the jury charge suggests as well our disagreement with that court concerning the admissibility of evidence demonstrating that respondent was advised by the FDA in 1970 of insanitary conditions in Acme's Philadelphia warehouse. We are satisfied that the Act imposes the highest standard of care and permits conviction of responsible corporate officials who, in light of this standard of care, have the power to prevent or correct violations of its provisions. Implicit in the Court's admonition that "the ultimate judgment of juries must be trusted," United States v. Dotterweich, 320 U.S., at 285, 64 S.Ct., at 138, however, is the realization that they may demand more than corporate bylaws to find culpability.

Respondent testified in his defense that he had employed a system in which he relied upon his subordinates, and that he was ultimately responsible for this system. He testified further that he had found these subordinates to be "dependable" and had "great confidence" in them. By this and other testimony respondent evidently sought to persuade the jury that, as the president of a large corporation, he had no choice but to delegate duties to those in whom he reposed confidence, that he had no reason to suspect his subordinates were failing to insure compliance with the Act, and that, once violations were unearthed, acting through those subordinates he did everything possible to correct them.[2]

Although we need not decide whether this testimony would have entitled respondent to an instruction as to his lack of power, had he requested it,[3] the testimony clearly created the "need" for rebuttal evidence. That evidence was not offered to show that respondent had a propensity to commit criminal acts, or that the crime charged had been committed; its purpose was to demonstrate that respondent was on notice that he could not rely on his system of delegation to subordinates to prevent or correct insanitary conditions at Acme's warehouses, and that he must have been aware of the deficiencies of this system before the Baltimore violations were discovered. The evidence was therefore relevant since it served to rebut respondent's defense that he had justifiably relied upon subordinates to handle sanitation matters. And, particularly in light of the difficult task of juries in prosecutions under the Act, we conclude that its relevance and persuasiveness outweighed any prejudicial effect.

Reversed.

MR. JUSTICE STEWART, with whom MR. JUSTICE MARSHALL and MR. JUSTICE POWELL join, dissenting.

Although agreeing with much of what is said in the Court's opinion, I dissent from the opinion and judgment, because the jury instructions in this case were not consistent with the law as the Court today expounds it.

As I understand the Court's opinion, it holds that in order to sustain a conviction under § 301(k) of the Federal Food, Drug, and Cosmetic Act the prosecution must at least show that by reason of an individual's corporate position and responsibilities, he had a duty to use care to maintain the physical integrity of the corporation's food products. A jury may then draw the inference that when the food is found to be in such condition as to violate the statute's prohibitions, that condition was "caused" by a breach of the standard of care imposed upon the responsible official. This is the language of negligence, and I agree with it.

To affirm this conviction, however, the Court must approve the instructions given to the members of the jury who were entrusted with determining whether the respondent was innocent or guilty. Those

---

2. [Court's footnote 18.] In his summation to the jury, counsel for respondent argued:

> "Now, you are Mr. Park. You have his responsibility for a thousand stores— I think eight hundred and some stores— lots of stores, many divisions, many warehouses. What are you going to do, except hire people in whom you have confidence to whom you delegate the work? . . .
>
> . . . .
>
> ". . . What I am saying to you is that Mr. Park, through his subordinates, when this was found out, did everything in the world they [sic] could."

3. [Court's footnote 19.] Assuming, arguendo, that it would be objectively impossible for a senior corporate agent to control fully day-to-day conditions in 874 retail outlets, it does not follow that such a corporate agent could not prevent or remedy promptly violations of elementary sanitary conditions in 16 regional warehouses.

instructions did not conform to the standards that the Court itself sets out today.

The trial judge instructed the jury to find Park guilty if it found beyond a reasonable doubt that Park "had a responsible relation to the situation .... The issue is, in this case, whether the Defendant, John R. Park, by virtue of his position in the company, had a position of authority and responsibility in the situation out of which these charges arose." Requiring, as it did, a verdict of guilty upon a finding of "responsibility," this instruction standing alone could have been construed as a direction to convict if the jury found Park "responsible" for the condition in the sense that his position as chief executive officer gave him formal responsibility within the structure of the corporation. But the trial judge went on specifically to caution the jury not to attach such a meaning to his instruction, saying that "the fact that the Defendant is pres[id]ent and is a chief executive officer of the Acme Markets does not require a finding of guilt." "Responsibility" as used by the trial judge therefore had whatever meaning the jury in its unguided discretion chose to give it.

The instructions, therefore, expressed nothing more than a tautology. They told the jury: "You must find the defendant guilty if you find that he is to be held accountable for this adulterated food." In other words: "You must find the defendant guilty if you conclude that he is guilty."

* * *

We deal here with a criminal conviction, not a civil forfeiture. It is true that the crime was but a misdemeanor and the penalty in this case light. But under the statute even a first conviction can result in imprisonment for a year, and a subsequent offense is a felony carrying a punishment of up to three years in prison. So the standardless conviction approved today can serve in another case tomorrow to support a felony conviction and a substantial prison sentence. However highly the Court may regard the social objectives of the Food, Drug, and Cosmetic Act, that regard cannot serve to justify a criminal conviction so wholly alien to fundamental principles of our law.

* * *

But before a person can be convicted of a criminal violation of this Act, a jury must find—and must be clearly instructed that it must find—evidence beyond a reasonable doubt that he engaged in wrongful conduct amounting at least to common-law negligence. There were no such instructions, and clearly, therefore, no such finding in this case.

For these reasons, I cannot join the Court in affirming Park's criminal conviction.

NOTES AND QUERIES

(1) *The "Responsible Share" Test.* Review the Supreme Court's articulation in *Dotterweich* and *Park* of the test for determining when a

managerial employee might be found criminally liable. How helpful is this test?

Is the "responsible share" test applicable only to cases where the statute involved dispenses with "consciousness of wrongdoing"? Consider whether this test is analytically related to the intent requirement at all. Does the "no fault" aspect of the Food, Drug and Cosmetic Act only explain why it was permissible to hold someone liable without proof of negligent (or willful) discharge of his or her duty effectively to manage the company? Can the "no fault" intent requirement explain why it was proper to hold *Park* liable, as opposed to (or in addition to) any other corporate manager, including particularly the vice president in charge of the Baltimore Division to whom the responsibility for sanitation at the Baltimore warehouse had been given?

(2) *A Model II View of Park.* Consider Note, Decisionmaking Models and the Control of Corporate Crime, 85 Yale L.J. 1091, 1115–1120 (1976): [4]

> Prosecutors faced with the decision of whether to seek an indictment or file a criminal information against a corporate decisionmaker often work with statutes manifesting no particular conception of how the proscribed corporate offense takes place. That Model II insights can be valuable to prosecutors even in the absence of Model II statutes is illustrated by the recent case of United States v. Park.
>
> * * *
>
> The prosecutor sought to integrate the evidence into a theory of the case which bore a striking resemblance to the Organizational Process Model approach. In his cross-examination of Park, the prosecutor alluded to the inefficacy of the "system" of sanitation. In his closing argument, the prosecutor referred to the FDA letter to Park following the 1970 Philadelphia warehouse inspection as a warning given to Park that the "system wasn't working." Despite the warning, the prosecutor argued to the jury, Park did not change the system. "[O]ther people were part of the system," he noted, "[but] the man at the top, the man who sets the system, . . . should be responsible."
>
> The *Park* trial can be fruitfully analyzed in Model II terms. The prosecutor's contention was that the violation resulted from the operation of flawed SOPs. The evidence about the Philadelphia warehouse inspection was significant in two respects. First, it revealed that one or more sanitation SOPs were malfunctioning in divisions other than Baltimore. Second, it demonstrated that corporate management was notified of the ineffectiveness of the SOPs well before the malfunction for which Park was being prosecuted.
>
> As Model II would suggest, the prosecution and the defense both focused during the trial on the power of Park to modify the

---

4. Reprinted by permission of The Yale Law Journal Company and Fred B. Rothman & Company from The Yale Law Journal Company, Vol. 85, pp. 1115–1120.

SOPs and on his knowledge of their inadequacy by reason of the 1970 warning. The prosecutor introduced into evidence the corporate by-laws, indicating the overall authority of Park as chief executive officer. During cross-examination he drew from Park the admission that Park had read the 1970 letter from the FDA. Park's counsel, on the other hand, underscored the scope of Acme operations and the many levels of subordinates under Park who were authorized to oversee various corporate activities. Counsel for the defendant also claimed that Park had reasonably relied on his subordinates to handle the sanitation problem once it was brought to their attention. Apparently the jury was persuaded that Park had both the knowledge of the malfunctioning SOPs and the power to change them, for it returned a verdict of guilty.

It is not clear from the *Park* trial transcript how thoroughly the prosecutor probed the Acme decisionmaking process. If the prosecutor had taken full advantage of the insights of Model II, he would have posed certain questions that would have helped identify how the SOP malfunction occurred: Which decisionmaking units in Acme (e.g., local warehouses, regional divisions, corporate headquarters) were involved with sanitation problems? What SOPs did these units have in order to foster the flow of information about sanitation problems? unannounced inspections by the corporation's chief sanitation engineer? periodic reports by warehouse staffs? circulation of FDA observation lists? What SOPs did Acme units have in order to generate policy alternatives about sanitation problems? a research and development program within the engineering division? a conference of sanitation managers from the various regional divisions? a special advisory group reporting to the president? What SOPs did Acme units have in order to implement alternative courses of action to resolve sanitation problems? directives from the president to the division managers? training programs for inventory workers? amendments to the company's employee manual? If some of these SOPs were nonexistent, how did the units involved with sanitation problems negotiate areas of responsibility and allocation of resources among themselves to mitigate uncertainty? These Model II questions attempt to locate criminal responsibility for the unlawful warehouse conditions. Answers to them would have helped the prosecutor to understand the decisionmaking process at Acme and, thereby, to determine whether the recurrent lawbreaking could be halted most effectively by prosecuting the chief executive officer of the corporation.

However, these questions were neither expressly asked nor fully answered at the *Park* trial. It is not surprising, therefore, that the trial judge, despite the Model II tone of the trial presentations, relied in his jury instructions on a vague "responsible relation" standard inherited from another, arguably distinguishable case. Had the judge been aware of Model II, he would have been better prepared for the case presented in his courtroom and could have tailored his explanation of criminal liability to the specific facts of *Park*.

The judges and Justices who reviewed the *Park* trial on appeal might likewise have benefited from familiarity with Model II in resolving an evidentiary dispute in the case. Testimonial and documentary evidence about the 1970 FDA inspection of Acme's Philadelphia warehouse was admitted at trial over Park's objection that the introduction of evidence of alleged prior crimes was prejudicial. The Court of Appeals for the Fourth Circuit reversed Park's conviction, partly on that ground. The Supreme Court held that the evidence was admissible since it "served to rebut [Park's] defense that he had justifiably relied upon subordinates to handle sanitation matters." However, the Supreme Court did not indicate whether such evidence was essential for Park's conviction. Had the Court taken a Model II approach to the case it would have held expressly that if Park were responsible for promulgation of Acme sanitation SOPs, then he would also be responsible for ensuring that information about their inadequacy reached him; prior government notice would therefore be superfluous to criminal liability.

(3) *Applying the Responsible Share Test Outside the Food and Drug Area.* Consider *United States v. Wise*, 370 U.S. 405, 82 S.Ct. 1354, 8 L.Ed.2d 590 (1962):[5]

Mr. Chief Justice Warren delivered the opinion of the Court.

A grand jury returned an indictment charging the National Dairy Products Corporation with engaging "in a combination and conspiracy to eliminate price competition in the sale of milk in the Greater Kansas City market in unreasonable restraint of . . . trade and commerce, in violation of Section 1" of the Sherman Act, 15 U.S.C. § 1. Two counts incorporated by reference the alleged illegal acts of the corporation and named the appellee as codefendant. In a bill of particulars the Government charged that the appellee had "been acting solely in his capacity as an officer, director, or agent who authorized, ordered, or did some of the acts" constituting the violation. The appellee moved for a dismissal on the ground that the indictment, as particularized by the bill, failed to charge a crime. According to appellee, the Sherman Act does not apply to corporate officers acting in a representative capacity; he contends that the statute exclusively applicable to these officers

---

5. For other examples, see United States v. Frezzo Bros., 602 F.2d 1123, 1130 n. 11 (3d Cir.1979) (conviction of principal corporate officers for willful and negligent violations of Federal Water Pollution Control Act), certiorari denied 444 U.S. 1074, 100 S.Ct. 1020, 62 L.Ed.2d 756 (1980); United States v. Gulf Oil Corp., 408 F.Supp. 450, 470–72 (W.D.Pa.1975) (denying motion to dismiss indictment charging defendant, who was executive vice president and director of Gulf Oil, with willful violations of regulations issued under Economic Stabilization Act); cf. United States v. National Dairy Products Corp., 372 U.S. 29, 83 S.Ct. 594, 9 L.Ed.2d 561 (1963) (Robinson–Patman Act) (intentional sales below cost); United States v. Rachal, 473 F.2d 1338, 1341 (5th Cir.) (officers of corporate issuer charged under Securities Act of 1933), certiorari denied 412 U.S. 927, 93 S.Ct. 2750, 37 L.Ed.2d 154 (1973).

is § 14 of the Clayton Act, 15 U.S.C. § 24. Over the Government's opposition the dismissal was ordered by the district judge. An appeal was perfected pursuant to 18 U.S.C. § 3731, and we noted probable jurisdiction.

Although the Sherman Act has been in existence for over 70 years and although corporate officers have been indicted under that Act for almost as long,[6] this question is one of first impression for this Court. The impetus for raising this issue at such a late date comes from the fact that in 1955 the Congress raised the penalty provision in the Sherman Act from $5,000 to $50,000 without making a corresponding increase in the $5,000 penalty found in the Clayton Act.

Section 1 of the Sherman Act imposes criminal sanctions upon "every person" who violates that provision, 15 U.S.C. § 1. The Government contends that a corporate officer is obviously a "person" within the Act. The appellee, however, distinguishes between a corporate officer who represents his corporation and one who acts on his own account. In the latter case the appellee agrees that the Sherman Act applies. But, when the officer is acting solely for his corporation, the appellee contends that he is no longer a "person" within the Act. The rationale for this distinction is that the activities of an officer, however illegal and culpable, are chargeable to the corporation as the principal but not to the individual who perpetrates them.

No substantial support for such an artificial interpretation of a seemingly clear statute is provided by the legislative history. . . .

The appellee points to § 8 of the Sherman Act, 15 U.S.C. § 7, which defines "person" "to include corporations and associations." He argues that, since corporations are included within the term, individual corporate officers are thereby excluded. This is a non sequitur. The mere fact that the term is given a broad construction does not alter its basic meaning, and no such inference can be drawn from the express inclusion of corporations as "persons." The reason for this inclusion is readily understandable. The doctrine of corporate criminal responsibility for the acts of the officers was not well established in 1890. See New York Central & H.R.R. Co. v. United States, 212 U.S. 481. When a criminal statute proscribed conduct by "persons," corporate defendants contended that only natural persons were included. . . .

This Court was faced with the same problem in United States v. Dotterweich, 320 U.S. 277, involving the construction of the Federal Food, Drug, and Cosmetic Act, 21 U.S.C. §§ 301–392. . . . This Court reversed the Court of Appeals, rejecting substantially the same argument that is advanced by the appellee in this

---

6. [Court's footnote 1.] In the Government's brief the Solicitor General cites 40 cases in which corporate officers were indicted under the Sherman Act between 1890 and 1914.

case. The reason for the rejection is equally applicable to the case at bar. No intent to exculpate a corporate officer who violates the law is to be imputed to Congress without clear compulsion; else the fines established by the Sherman Act to deter crime become mere license fees for illegitimate corporate business operations. Following *Dotterweich,* we construe § 1 of the Sherman Act in its common-sense meaning to apply to all officers who have a responsible share in the proscribed transaction.

* * *

In 1914 the Congress passed . . . the Clayton Act. Section 14 of that Act provided:

> "That whenever a corporation shall violate any of the penal provisions of the antitrust laws, such violation shall be deemed to be also that of the individual directors, officers, or agents of such corporation who shall have authorized, ordered, or done any of the acts constituting in whole or in part such violation, and such violation shall be deemed a misdemeanor, and upon conviction therefor of any such director, officer, or agent he shall be punished by a fine of not exceeding $5,000 or by imprisonment for not exceeding one year, or by both, in the discretion of the court."

The appellee contends that § 14 is an entirely new provision added by Congress to provide for the criminal responsibility of corporate officers who act in a representative capacity. The Government contends that § 14 is merely supplemental and that appellee's construction results in an implied repeal of part of § 1 of the Sherman Act.

Appellee asserts that § 14 would not literally apply to the officer who acted on his own account because his misconduct would not be attributed to the corporation. From this premise he argues that since § 14 of the Clayton Act applies only to an officer acting in a representative capacity, § 1 of the Sherman Act only applies to an officer acting on his own account.

We do not agree. The reasons for § 14 are sufficiently revealed by the legislative history. . . . The proponents of the bill agreed that the Sherman Act did cover officers whose conduct constituted the offense (without distinction as to the capacity in which the officer was acting), but were disappointed in the sympathy shown to corporate officers by judges, juries, and prosecutors. Second, the proponents feared that the present Sherman Act did not cover officers who merely authorized or ordered the commission of the offense. These ideas were clearly expressed by Representative Floyd, a House manager:

> "The purpose we had was to make it clear that, when a corporation had been guilty, those officers, agents, and directors of the corporation that either authorized, ordered, or did the thing prohibited should be guilty. Under the existing law,

and without that provision of the statute, the person who did the things would undoubtedly be guilty; but in the enforcement of the criminal provisions of the Sherman law, experience has demonstrated that both juries and courts are slow to convict men who have simply done acts authorized or ordered by some officers of the concern higher up, and the words 'authorized' and 'ordered' were introduced to reach the real offenders, the men who caused the things to be done. . . ." 51 Cong.Rec. 9609.

* * *

Section 14 was intended to be a reaffirmation of the Sherman Act's basic penal provisions and a mandate to prosecutors to bring all responsible persons to justice. In the light of the congressional purpose revealed on the face of the statute and by the legislative history, this Court cannot construe § 14 as a restriction of § 1 of the Sherman Act. Thus, insofar as § 14 relates to the corporate officer who participates in the Sherman Act violation, whether or not in a representative capacity, no change was either intended or effected.

* * *

Based upon the foregoing, we hold that a corporate officer is subject to prosecution under § 1 of the Sherman Act whenever he knowingly participates in effecting the illegal contract, combination, or conspiracy—be he one who authorizes, orders, or helps perpetrate the crime—regardless of whether he is acting in a representative capacity. It follows that the District Court erred when it dismissed the indictment against the appellee. The case is reversed and remanded for proceedings consistent with this opinion.

Reversed and remanded.

Mr. Justice Frankfurter took no part in the consideration or decision of this case.

(4) *Taking Responsibility.* Do you believe that the "Chief Executive" should "take responsibility" for the mistakes of subordinates? Are you willing to include criminal responsibility? Or, do you think that Dotterweich and Park were, in fact, convicted only because of their title, and that this was improper?

Consider your views in connection with the following case, *In re Yamashita,* 327 U.S. 1, 66 S.Ct. 340, 90 L.Ed. 499 (1946):

Mr. Chief Justice Stone delivered the opinion of the Court.

No. 61 Miscellaneous is an application for leave to file a petition for writs of habeas corpus and prohibition in this Court. No. 672 is a petition for certiorari to review an order of the Supreme Court of the Commonwealth of the Philippines (28 U.S.C. § 349), denying petitioner's application to that court for writs of habeas corpus and prohibition. As both applications raise substantially like questions, and because of the importance and novelty of some of those presented, we set the two applications down for oral argument as one case.

From the petitions and supporting papers it appears that prior to September 3, 1945, petitioner was the Commanding General of the Fourteenth Army Group of the Imperial Japanese Army in the Philippine Islands. On that date he surrendered to and became a prisoner of war of the United States Army Forces in Baguio, Philippine Islands. On September 25th, by order of respondent, Lieutenant General Wilhelm D. Styer, Commanding General of the United States Army Forces, Western Pacific, which command embraces the Philippine Islands, petitioner was served with a charge prepared by the Judge Advocate General's Department of the Army, purporting to charge petitioner with a violation of the law of war. On October 8, 1945, petitioner, after pleading not guilty to the charge, was held for trial before a military commission of five Army officers appointed by order of General Styer. The order appointed six Army officers, all lawyers, as defense counsel. Throughout the proceedings which followed, including those before this Court, defense counsel have demonstrated their professional skill and resourcefulness and their proper zeal for the defense with which they were charged.

On the same date a bill of particulars was filed by the prosecution, and the commission heard a motion made in petitioner's behalf to dismiss the charge on the ground that it failed to state a violation of the law of war. On October 29th the commission was reconvened, a supplemental bill of particulars was filed, and the motion to dismiss was denied. The trial then proceeded until its conclusion on December 7, 1945, the commission hearing two hundred and eighty-six witnesses, who gave over three thousand pages of testimony. On that date petitioner was found guilty of the offense as charged and sentenced to death by hanging.

* * *

The charge. Neither congressional action nor the military orders constituting the commission authorized it to place petitioner on trial unless the charge preferred against him is of a violation of the law of war. The charge, so far as now relevant, is that petitioner, between October 9, 1944 and September 2, 1945, in the Philippine Islands, "while commander of armed forces of Japan at war with the United States of America and its allies, unlawfully disregarded and failed to discharge his duty as commander to control the operations of the members of his command, permitting them to commit brutal atrocities and other high crimes against people of the United States and of its allies and dependencies, particularly the Philippines; and he . . . thereby violated the laws of war."

Bills of particulars, filed by the prosecution by order of the commission, allege a series of acts, one hundred and twenty-three in number, committed by members of the forces under petitioner's command during the period mentioned. The first item specifies the execution of "a deliberate plan and purpose to massacre and exterminate a large part of the civilian population of Batangas Province, and to devastate and destroy public, private and religious property therein, as a result of which more than 25,000 men, women and children, all unarmed noncombatant civilians, were brutally mistreated and killed, without cause or trial, and entire settlements were devastated and destroyed wantonly and without military necessity." Other items specify acts of violence, cruelty and homicide inflicted upon the civilian population and prisoners of war, acts of wholesale pillage and the wanton destruction of religious monuments.

It is not denied that such acts directed against the civilian population of an occupied country and against prisoners of war are recognized in international law as violations of the law of war. Articles 4, 28, 46, and 47, Annex to the Fourth Hague Convention, 1907, 36 Stat. 2277, 2296, 2303, 2306–7. But it is urged that the charge does not allege that petitioner has either committed or directed the commission of such acts, and consequently that no violation is charged as against him. But this overlooks the fact that the gist of the charge is an unlawful breach of duty by petitioner as an army commander to control the operations of the members of his command by "permitting them to commit" the extensive and widespread atrocities specified. The question then is whether the law of war imposes on an army commander a duty to take such appropriate measures as are within his power to control the troops under his command for the prevention of the specified acts which are violations of the law of war and which are likely to attend the occupation of hostile territory by an uncontrolled soldiery, and whether he may be charged with personal responsibility for his failure to take such measures when violations result. That this was the precise issue to be tried was made clear by the statement of the prosecution at the opening of the trial.

It is evident that the conduct of military operations by troops whose excesses are unrestrained by the orders or efforts of their commander would almost certainly result in violations which it is the purpose of the law of war to prevent. . . .

* * *

[There was] plainly imposed on petitioner, who at the time specified was military governor of the Philippines, as well as commander of the Japanese forces, an affirmative duty to take such measures as were within his power and appropriate in the circumstances to protect prisoners of war and the civilian population. This duty of a commanding officer has heretofore been recognized, and its breach penalized by our own military tribunals.[7] . . .

We do not make the laws of war but we respect them so far as they do not conflict with the commands of Congress or the Constitution. There is no contention that the present charge, thus read, is without the support of evidence, or that the commission held petitioner responsible for failing to take measures which were beyond his control or inappropriate for a commanding officer to take in the circumstances.[8] We do not here appraise the evidence on which petitioner was convicted. We do not consider what measures, if any, petitioner took to prevent the commission, by the troops under his command, of the plain violations of the law of war detailed in the bill of particulars, or whether such measures as he may have taken were appropriate and sufficient to discharge the duty imposed upon him. These are questions within the peculiar competence of the military officers composing the commission and were for it to decide. It is plain that the charge on which petitioner was tried charged him with a breach of his duty to control the operations of the members of his command, by permitting them to commit the specified atrocities. This was enough to require the commission to hear evidence tending to establish the culpable failure of petitioner to perform the duty imposed on him by the law of war and to pass upon its sufficiency to establish guilt.

* * *

[T]he petition for certiorari, and leave to file in this Court petitions for writs of habeas corpus and prohibition should be, and they are Denied.

Mr. Justice Jackson took no part in the consideration or decision of these cases.

Mr. Justice Murphy, dissenting.

* * *

. . . The Fifth Amendment guarantee of due process of law applies to "any person" who is accused of a crime by the Federal Government or any of its agencies. No exception is made as to

---

7. [Court's footnote 3.] Failure of an officer to take measures to prevent murder of an inhabitant of an occupied country committed in his presence. Gen. Orders No. 221, Hq.Div. of the Philippines, August 17, 1901. And in Gen. Orders No. 264, Hq. Div. of the Philippines, September 9, 1901, it was held that an officer could not be found guilty for failure to prevent a murder unless it appeared that the accused had "the power to prevent" it.

8. [Court's footnote 4.] In its findings the commission took account of the difficulties "faced by the Accused with respect not only to the swift and overpowering advance of American forces, but also to the errors of his predecessors, weaknesses in organization, equipment, supply . . ., training, communication, discipline and morale of his troops," and the "tactical situation, the character, training and capacity of staff officers and subordinate commanders as well as the traits of character . . . of his troops." It nonetheless found that petitioner had not taken such measures to control his troops as were "required by the circumstances." We do not weigh the evidence. We merely hold that the charge sufficiently states a violation against the law of war, and that the commission, upon the facts found, could properly find petitioner guilty of such a violation.

those who are accused of war crimes or as to those who possess the status of an enemy belligerent. Indeed, such an exception would be contrary to the whole philosophy of human rights which makes the Constitution the great living document that it is. The immutable rights of the individual, including those secured by the due process clause of the Fifth Amendment, belong not alone to the members of those nations that excel on the battlefield or that subscribe to the democratic ideology. They belong to every person in the world, victor or vanquished, whatever may be his race, color or beliefs. They rise above any status of belligerency or outlawry. They survive any popular passion or frenzy of the moment. No court or legislature or executive, not even the mightiest army in the world, can ever destroy them. Such is the universal and indestructible nature of the rights which the due process clause of the Fifth Amendment recognizes and protects when life or liberty is threatened by virtue of the authority of the United States.

* * *

The failure of the military commission to obey the dictates of the due process requirements of the Fifth Amendment is apparent in this case. . . .

. . . [Petitioner] was not charged with personally participating in the acts of atrocity or with ordering or condoning their commission. Not even knowledge of these crimes was attributed to him. It was simply alleged that he unlawfully disregarded and failed to discharge his duty as commander to control the operations of the members of his command, permitting them to commit the acts of atrocity. The recorded annuals of warfare and the established principles of international law afford not the slightest precedent for such a charge. . . .

In my opinion, such a procedure is unworthy of the traditions of our people or of the immense sacrifices that they have made to advance the common ideals of mankind. . . . No one in a position of command in an army, from sergeant to general, can escape those implications. Indeed, the fate of some future President of the United States and his chiefs of staff and military advisers may well have been sealed by this decision. . . .

* * *

Mr. Justice Rutledge dissenting.

* * *

[T]here is not a suggestion in the findings that petitioner personally participated in, was present at the occurrence of, or ordered any of these incidents, with the exception of the wholly inferential suggestion noted below. Nor is there any express finding that he knew of any one of the incidents in particular or of all taken together. The only inferential findings that he had knowledge, or that the commission so found, are in the statement that the "crimes *alleged to have been permitted* by the Accused in violation of the laws of war may be grouped into three categories" set out below,[9] in the further statement that "the Prosecution presented evidence to show that the crimes were so extensive and widespread, both as to time and area, that *they must* either have been *wilfully permitted* by the Accused, *or secretly ordered* by" him; and in the conclusion of guilt and the sentence. (Emphasis added.) Indeed the commission's ultimate findings draw no express conclusion of knowledge, but state only two things: (1) the fact of widespread atrocities and crimes; (2) that petitioner "failed to provide effective control . . . as was required by the circumstances."

This vagueness, if not vacuity, in the findings runs throughout the proceedings, from the charge itself through the proof and the findings, to the conclusion. It affects the very gist of the offense, whether that was wilful, informed and intentional omission to restrain and control troops *known* by petitioner to be committing crimes or was only a negligent failure on his part to *discover* this and take whatever measures he then could to stop the conduct.

Although it is impossible to determine from what is before us whether petitioner in fact has been convicted of one or the other or of both these things, the case has been presented on the former basis and . . . it must be taken that the crime charged and sought to be proved was only the failure, with knowledge, to perform the commander's function of control, although the Court's opinion nowhere expressly declares that knowledge was essential to guilt or necessary to be set forth in the charge.

* * *

(5) *Proposed Federal Criminal Code.* Consider the following rule for supervisory liability, proposed in 1971 in the Final Report of the National Commission on Reform of Federal Criminal Law. Does the proposal differ from the state of the law as set out in *Dotterweich* and *Park*? Would you have voted for it?

§ 403. Individual Accountability for Conduct on Behalf of Organizations.

* * *

(4) **Default in Supervision.** A person responsible for supervising relevant activities of an organization is guilty of an offense if he manifests his assent to the commission of an offense for which the organization may be convicted by his willful default in supervi-

---

9. [Footnote 13 in the original.] Namely, "(1) Starvation, execution or massacre without trial and maladministration generally of civilian internees and prisoners of war; (2) Torture, rape, murder and mass execution of very large numbers of residents of the Philippines, including women and children and members of religious orders, by starvation, beheading, bayoneting, clubbing, hanging, burning alive, and destruction by explosives; (3) Burning and demolition without adequate military necessity of large numbers of homes, places of business, places of religious worship, hospitals, public buildings, and educational institutions. In point of time, the offenses extended throughout the period the Accused was in command of Japanese troops in the Philippines. In point of area, the crimes extended throughout the Philippine Archipelago, although by far the most of the incredible acts occurred on Luzon."

sion within the range of that responsibility which contributes to the occurrence of that offense. Conviction under this subsection shall be of an offense of the same class as the offense for which the organization may be convicted, except that if the latter offense is a felony, conviction under this subsection shall be for a Class A misdemeanor.

3. SUBORDINATE LIABILITY

UNITED STATES v. NATELLI

United States Court of Appeals for the Second Circuit, 1975.
527 F.2d 311, certiorari denied 425 U.S. 934, 96 S.Ct. 1663,
48 L.Ed.2d 175 (1976).

GURFEIN, CIRCUIT JUDGE:

Anthony M. Natelli and Joseph Scansaroli appeal from judgments of conviction entered in the United States District Court for the Southern District of New York on December 27, 1974 after a four week trial before the Hon. Harold R. Tyler and a jury. Judge Tyler imposed a one year sentence and a $10,000 fine upon Natelli, suspending all but 60 days of imprisonment, and a one year sentence and a $2,500 fine upon Scansaroli, suspending all but 10 days of the imprisonment.

Both appellants are certified public accountants. Natelli was the partner in charge of the Washington, D.C. office of Peat, Marwick, Mitchell & Co. ("Peat"), a large independent firm of auditors, and the engagement partner with respect to Peat's audit engagement for National Student Marketing Corporation ("Marketing"). Scansaroli was an employee of Peat, assigned as audit supervisor on that engagement.

Appellants were charged and tried only on Count Two of a multi-count indictment against other defendants connected with Marketing.

Count Two of the indictment charged that, in violation of Section 32(a) of the Securities Exchange Act of 1934, 15 U.S.C. § 78ff(a),[10] four of Marketing's officers and the appellants, as independent auditors, "wilfully and knowingly made and caused to be made false and misleading statements with respect to material facts" in a proxy statement for Marketing dated September 27, 1969 and filed with the Securities and Exchange Commission (SEC) in accordance with Section 14 of the 1934 Act, 15 U.S.C. § 78n.

The proxy statement was issued by Marketing in connection with a special meeting of its stockholders to consider inter alia a charter amendment increasing its authorized capital stock and the merger of

---

10. [Court's footnote 1.] Section 32(a) provides in relevant part:

"Any *person* . . . *who willfully and knowingly makes, or causes to be made, any statement in any application, report, or document required to be filed under this chapter or any rule or regulation thereunder* or any undertaking contained in a registration statement as provided in subsection (d) of section 78o of this title, *which statement was false or misleading with respect to any material fact,* shall upon conviction be fined not more than $10,000, or imprisoned not more than two years, . . ." (Emphasis added.)

six companies, including Interstate National Corporation ("Interstate") into Marketing.

Count Two of the indictment further charged that appellants, in attempting to reconcile net sales and earnings as originally reported in the annual report for the fiscal year ending August 31, 1968 with the amounts shown in the statement of earnings in the proxy statement, filed less than a year later, created an explanatory footnote that was materially false and misleading.[11] It was alleged that "as the defendants well knew but failed to disclose . . . (a) approximately one million dollars, or more than 20%, of the 1968 'net sales originally reported' had proven to be nonexistent by the time the proxy statement was filed and had been written off on [Marketing's] own internal books of account; (b) net sales and profits of 'pooled companies reflected retroactively' were substantially understated; and (c) net sales and profits of [Marketing] were substantially overstated."

Count Two charged further that the proxy statement also contained an unaudited statement of earnings for the nine months ended May 31, 1969 which was materially false and misleading in that it stated "net sales" as $11,313,569 and "net earnings" as $702,270, when, in fact, as the defendants well knew, "net sales" for the period were less than $10,500,000 and Marketing had no earnings at all.

In order to understand the theory of the government's case, we must retrace our steps to the beginning of the Peat engagement at Marketing. The jury could permissibly have found the following facts.

Marketing was formed in 1966 by Cortes W. Randell. It provided to major corporate accounts a diversified range of advertising, promotional and marketing services designed to reach the youth market. In April 1968 Marketing had its first and only public offering of stock. Peat was not its auditor at the time.

Peat took on the engagement in August 1968 after checking with the previous auditors that there had been no professional disagreement with management. Natelli, the partner in charge of Peat's Washington office, undertook the engagement to audit the financial statements of Marketing for the fiscal year ended August 31, 1968, and Natelli assigned Scansaroli to serve as supervisor on the engagement.

In late September or early October 1968 (after the close of the fiscal year), Randell and Bernard Kurek, Marketing's Comptroller, met with both appellants and discussed the method of accounting that Marketing

11. [Court's footnote 2.] The footnote read in relevant part:

"Net sales and earnings as originally reported to stockholders in the annual report [for the year 1968] and the amounts as shown in the statement of earnings in this proxy statement are reconciled as follows:

Net sales	1968
Originally reported	$ 4,989,446
Pooled companies reflected retroactively	6,552,449
Per statement of earnings	$11,541,895

Net earnings	
Originally reported	$ 388,031
Pooled companies reflected retroactively	385,121
Per statement of earnings	$ 773,152

had been using with respect to fixed-fee programs. In the fixed-fee program, Marketing would develop overall marketing programs for the client to reach the youth market by utilizing a combination of the mailings, posters and other advertising services offered by Marketing. Randell explained that Marketing and the client agreed upon a fixed fee to be charged for participating in the various programs. Randell stated that the company believed that it was proper to recognize income on these fixed-fee contracts at the time the clients committed themselves to participate in the programs presented to them by the account executives, and that this was the accounting method that had been used in preparing the financial statements for the period ended May 31, 1968, which had been distributed to stockholders.

After considering alternative methods of accounting, Natelli concluded that he would use a percentage-of-completion approach to the recognition of income on these commitments, pursuant to which the company would accrue that percentage of the gross income and related costs on a client's "commitment" that was equal to the proportion of the time spent by the account executive on the project before August 31, 1968 to the total time it was estimated he would have to spend to complete the project.

The difficulty immediately encountered was that the "commitments" had not been booked during the fiscal year, and were not in writing. The Marketing stock which had initially been sold at $6 per share was selling in the market by September 1968 for $80, an increase of $74 in five months. A refusal to book the oral "commitments" would have resulted in Marketing's showing a large loss for the fiscal year—according to Kurek's computations, a loss of $232,000.

Scansaroli, upon Natelli's order, attempted to verify the "commitments," the sales not previously included in the company records, in a rather haphazard manner by telephone to representatives of companies which had purportedly indicated some intent to use Marketing's services. Pursuant to Randell's urging, Scansaroli did not seek any written verifications. He accepted a schedule prepared by Kurek which showed about $1.7 million in purported "commitments." He also received from the account executives forms indicating estimates of the gross amount of the client's commitment, the printing and distribution costs to be incurred on the program, and the account executive's estimate of the percentage of completion of the program.

On the basis of the above, Natelli decided not only to recognize income on a percentage-of-completion basis, but to permit adjustment to be made on the books after the close of the fiscal year in the amount of $1.7 million for such "unbilled accounts receivable." This adjustment turned the loss for the year into a handsome profit of $388,031, showing an apparent doubling of the profit of the prior year.

Appellants were not charged with a criminal violation with respect to this decision. It may be observed, however, that in the footnote to the audited financial statement for 1968 explaining this method of accounting for "Contracts in Progress," no indication is given of the flimsy nature of the evidence that such client "commitments" actually existed.

After the 1968 audit had been given a full certificate by the auditors on November 14, 1968, Natelli in December 1968 told the officers of Marketing that in the future Peat would allow income to be recorded only on written commitments, supported by contemporaneous logs kept by the account executives with respect to each contract. A form letter was drafted to spell out a binding contractual commitment to be signed by each client.

In the meantime, following the issuance of the 1968 audited annual report and before the September 1969 proxy statement, seven companies were acquired largely in exchange for Marketing stock, in reliance on the 1968 annual report.

Things began to happen with respect to the $1.7 million of "sales" that had been recorded as income after fiscal year end. Within five months of publication of the annual report, by May 1969, Marketing had written off over $1 million of the $1.7 million in "sales" which the auditors had permitted to be booked.

Of the total $1 million written off, $748,762 was attributable to "sales" purportedly made by one Ronald Michaels, an account executive who was fired for taking kickbacks and who was said to be dishonest. The other quarter of a million dollars of sales written off had nothing to do with Michaels. When accrued costs were taken into account, the effect of the write-off of the Michaels contracts was to reduce 1968 income by $209,750. It appeared that of the $1 million of sales requiring retroactive write-off, $350,000 had already been written off by the company by subtracting these "sales" from 1969 *current* year figures. An additional $678,000 was to be written off sales for the prior year 1968, and appellants were asked to design the write-off. The write-off suggested by appellants was accepted and entered in the general ledger as a journal voucher entry sometime in late April or early May.

That entry wrote off the $678,000 retroactively as a deduction from 1968 sales. Instead of reducing 1968 earnings commensurately, however, no such reduction was made. Appellants were informed by tax accountants in Peat's employ that a certain deferred tax item should be reversed, resulting in a tax credit that happened to be approximately the same amount as the profit to be written off. Scansaroli "netted" this extraordinary item (the tax credit) with an unrelated ordinary item (the write-off of sales and profits). By this procedure he helped to conceal on the books the actual write-off of profits, further using the device of rounding off the tax item to make it conform exactly to the write-off. The effect of the netting procedure was to bury the retroactive adjustment which should have shown a material decrease in earnings for the fiscal year ended August 31, 1968.

The Proxy Statement

A. *The Footnote*

As part of the proxy statement, appellants set about to draft a footnote purporting to reconcile the Company's prior reported net sales and earnings from the 1968 report with restated amounts resulting from pooled companies reflected retroactively. The earnings summary in the proxy statement included companies acquired after fiscal 1968 and their pooled earnings. The footnote was the only place in the proxy statement which would have permitted an interested investor to see what Marketing's performance had been in its preceding fiscal year 1968, as retroactively adjusted, separate from the earnings and sales of the companies it had acquired in fiscal 1969.

At Natelli's direction, Scansaroli subtracted the written-off Marketing sales from the 1968 sales figures for the seven later acquired pooled companies without showing any retroactive adjustment for Marketing's own fiscal 1968 figures. There was no disclosure in the footnote that over $1 million of previously reported 1968 sales of Marketing had been written off. All narrative disclosure in the footnote was stricken by Natelli. This was a violation of Accounting Principles Board Opinion Number 9, which requires disclosure of prior adjustments which affect the net income of prior periods.

B. *The False Nine–Months Earnings Statement*

The proxy statement also required an unaudited statement of nine months earnings through May 31, 1969. This was prepared by the Company, with the assistance of Peat on the same percentage of completion basis as in the 1968 audited statement. A commitment from Pontiac Division of General Motors amounting to $1,200,000 was produced two months after the end of the fiscal period. It was dated April 28, 1969.

The proxy statement was to be printed at the Pandick Press in New York on August 15, 1969. At about 3 A.M. on that day, Natelli informed Randell that the "sale" to the Pontiac Division for more than $1 million could not be treated as a valid commitment because the letter from Pontiac was not a legally binding obligation. Randell responded at once that he had a "commitment from Eastern Airlines" in a somewhat comparable amount attributable to the nine months fiscal period (which had ended more than two months earlier). Kelly, a salesman for Marketing, arrived at the printing plant several hours later with a commitment letter from Eastern Airlines, dated August 14, 1969, purporting to confirm an $820,000 commitment ostensibly entered into on May 14, just before the end of the nine-month fiscal period of September 1, 1968 through May 31, 1969. When the proxy statement was printed in final form, the Pontiac "sale" had been deleted, but the Eastern "commitment" had been inserted in its place.

Soon after the incident at Pandick Press, Douglas Oberlander, an accountant at Peat assigned by Natelli to review Marketing's accounts, discovered $177,547 worth of "bad" contracts from 1968 which were known to Scansaroli in May as doubtful, but which had not been written off. Oberlander suggested to Kurek that these contracts and others amounting to over $320,000, in addition to the $1 million in bad contracts previously disposed of, be written off. Kurek consulted Scansaroli, who, after consulting with Natelli, decided against the suggested write-off.

The proxy statement was filed with the SEC on September 30, 1969. There was no disclosure that Marketing had written off $1 million of its 1968 sales (over 20%) and over $2 million of the $3.3 million in unbilled sales booked in 1968 and 1969. A true disclosure, which was not made, would have shown that without these unbilled receivables, Marketing had no profit in the first nine months of 1969.

Each appellant contends that the evidence was insufficient to support his conviction. We shall consider each appellant separately.

I

Natelli—Sufficiency of Evidence

[The Court upheld Natelli's conviction.]

II

Scansaroli—Sufficiency of Evidence

The claim of Scansaroli with respect to insufficiency of the evidence is somewhat more difficult. As Judge Tyler noted after both sides had rested, "It is a close question, I think frankly as to Scansaroli, as I see it. Certainly if I were the factfinder, I would be more troubled with his case for a variety of reasons."

Scansaroli contends that there was insufficient evidence to prove beyond a reasonable doubt that (1) he participated in a criminal act with respect to the footnote or (2) that he made an accounting judgment permitting Marketing to include in sales certain contracts-in-progress with the requisite criminal intent. We hold that there was enough evidence to establish the former, but not the latter. For reasons relating to the form of the charge, we will reverse and remand for a new trial.

A. *The Footnote*

The essence of Scansaroli's argument on his conviction with respect to the false footnote is that he was really convicted for his conduct during the 1968 audit, for which he was not indicted. This misses the thrust of the Government's claim. The unjustifiable manner of treating the unbilled commitments in the 1968 audit bore upon the illegal acts connected with the 1969 proxy statement in two ways: (a) it created a motive to conceal the accounting errors made in the 1968 audit; and (b) the 1968 audited statement was part of the 1969 proxy statement and was not disclosed therein to have been wrong in the light of the subsequent known write-offs. In view of the established motive to conceal, the jury could properly find, as we have seen, that both the netting of the tax credit against earnings and the subsequent subtracting of the write-offs from the pooled earnings in the footnote without further explanation were done in order to conceal the true retroactive decrease in the Marketing earnings for fiscal 1968.

There is some merit to Scansaroli's point that he was simply carrying out the judgments of his superior Natelli. The defense of obedience to higher authority has always been troublesome. There is no sure yardstick to measure criminal responsibility except by measurement of the degree of awareness on the part of a defendant that he is participating in a criminal act, in the absence of physical coercion such as a soldier might face. Here the motivation to conceal undermines Scansaroli's argument that he was merely implementing Natelli's instructions, at least with respect to concealment of matters that were within his own ken.

We think the jury could properly have found him guilty on the specification relating to the footnote. Scansaroli himself wrote the journal entry in Marketing's books which improperly netted the tax credit with earnings, the true effect never being pointed out in the financial statement. This, with the background of Scansaroli's implication in preparation of the 1968 statement, could be found to have been motivated by intent to conceal the 1968 overstatement of earnings.

Scansaroli participated in the decision to subtract in the proxy statement footnote $678,000 of written-off Marketing sales from the figures for later-acquired pooled companies instead of from its own figures, without further disclosure. Even if Scansaroli did not write the footnote, he supplied the misleading computations and subtractions though he was conscious of the true facts.

B. *The Eastern Commitment*

Having concluded that there was sufficient evidence to convict both appellants on the footnote specification, we turn to the nine-months earnings statement which, in turn, included two items, the Eastern contract and the doubtful commitments discovered by Oberlander. We put aside the decision to ignore Oberlander's questioning of certain commitments on the ground that, if it stood alone, the evidence would have been too equivocal to support proof beyond a reasonable doubt that this was not a mere error of judgment.

With respect to the major item, the Eastern commitment, we think Scansaroli stands in a position different from that of Natelli. Natelli was his superior. He was the man to make the judgment whether or not to object to the last-minute inclusion of a new "commitment" in the nine-months statement. There is insufficient evidence that Scansaroli engaged in any conversations about the Eastern commitment at the

Pandick Press or that he was a participant with Natelli in any check on its authenticity. Since in the hierarchy of the accounting firm it was not his responsibility to decide whether to book the Eastern contract, his mere adjustment of the figures to reflect it under orders was not a matter for his discretion. As we have seen, Natelli bore a duty in the circumstances to be suspicious of the Eastern commitment and to pursue the matter further. Scansaroli may also have been suspicious, but rejection of the Eastern contract was not within his sphere of responsibility. Absent such duty, he cannot be held to have acted in reckless disregard of the facts.

* * *

NOTES AND QUERIES

(1) *Queries.* Do you agree with the Court's statement that "[t]he defense of obedience to higher authority has always been troublesome?" Didn't Scansaroli do the actual act of adjusting the figures to take account of the Eastern "commitment"? As a certified public accountant, isn't it likely that he did this act "willfully and knowingly"? Why is it relevant that he did this act "under orders"?

(2) *Following Orders.* With *Natelli* compare *United States v. Gold*, 743 F.2d 800 (11th Cir.1984). In *Gold* the defendants were convicted for defrauding the government by willfully filing false Medicare claims. Gold, a "hard-driving businessman" with an "obsessive concern for the bottom line," was the owner of a chain of retail eyeware stores. Highsmith was the manager of one of Gold's stores. He was convicted on proof that he followed certain of the fraudulent billing practices engaged in by other branches, and also initiated some new practices of his own which spread to some other stores. The Court of Appeals wrote:

> The final objection to the court's jury instructions is raised by Highsmith, who challenges the trial judge's refusal to charge the jury as follows:
>
>> With respect to Defendant Gary Highsmith, if you determine that he prepared or submitted the Medicare claims alleged and described in the indictment in the counts pertaining to him and that he did so as instructed by his employers and superiors obeying their orders and instructions and following their standard office procedure, then you must find him not guilty.
>
> . . . What Highsmith has failed to understand, however, is that "following orders" can only be a defense where a defendant has no idea that his conduct is criminal—a critical limitation that Highsmith's proposed instruction does not reflect. If Highsmith was aware of the illegality of his conduct, the fact that it was authorized by a superior clearly cannot insulate him from criminal liability. . . . If, on the other hand, Highsmith was genuinely ignorant of the criminal nature of his actions, then he was not guilty

because he lacked the knowledge and specific intent necessary to be convicted under the applicable statutes. Since the trial court carefully instructed the jury that they must find that the defendants had acted knowingly and willfully in order to convict them, we conclude that there is no merit to appellant Highsmith's objection.

Query. Do you think there will be many cases in which the defendant will be able successfully to assert the defense suggested in *Gold?* Note that there are very few cases in which employees attempt to avoid liability by arguing that they were acting under orders.[12] Might the reason for the lack of cases be that prosecutors have not generally brought criminal cases against low-level employees? If the lack of cases connects to prosecutorial discretion, what factors would you, as a prosecutor, look for to determine whether to charge an employee who "did it," but who has a low position in the corporate hierarchy?

---

12. For other cases mentioning this defense, see United States v. Bernstein, 533 F.2d 775, 788 (2d Cir.) (proper to disqualify employee's defense counsel paid for by employer; employee could assert conflicting defense that employers "were the guilty ones because she was only obeying the orders of her superiors and following standard office procedure") (employee convicted on proof of active involvement), certiorari denied 429 U.S. 998, 97 S.Ct. 523, 50 L.Ed.2d 608 (1976); United States v. Spiezio, 523 F.Supp. 264, 279 (E.D.Pa.1981) (although employee claimed he was only "following the directions of his superior," court found to the contrary; no discussion on question whether this would have been a good legal defense).

Chapter 3

SANCTIONS

A. SENTENCING GUIDELINES

SCOPE NOTE

November 1, 1987, was an historic date for the development of the law relating to sanctions in business crime cases. For it was on that date that the Sentencing Guidelines promulgated by the United States Sentencing Commission became effective. These Guidelines, issued pursuant to the Sentencing Reform Act of 1984, are the first attempt to apply a single approach to sentencing to the entire body of federal criminal law. The hope of the Sentencing Reform Act and the Guidelines is to remove sentencing from the unreviewed discretion of each individual federal district court judge and to bring all federal sentences under a single coherent framework.

Our study of sanctions for business crime begins with the Sentencing Reform Act itself. The first part of this Section provides relevant excerpts from the Act. The Notes which follow provide background on the Act; included is *Mistretta v. United States,* the Supreme Court case which upheld the constitutionality of the basic Guidelines system.

The second part of this Section focuses on the actual Guidelines. This part begins with a description of the Guidelines prepared by the Sentencing Commission. The Notes which follow provide the student with some idea of the mechanics of how the Guidelines are supposed to work, along with a description of the controversy which surrounded the drafting of the Guidelines.

The Sentencing Reform Act, and the Guidelines, now provide the overall architecture for criminal remedies under federal law. Whether the approach taken in the Act and the Guidelines is either wise or feasible, however, is the overall question posed in this Section of the Chapter.

1. SENTENCING REFORM ACT OF 1984[1]

18 U.S.C.A. § 3551 et seq.

§ 3551. Authorized sentences

(a) **In general.**—Except as otherwise specifically provided, a defendant who has been found guilty of an offense described in any Federal statute . . . shall be sentenced in accordance with the provisions of

---

[1]. Among the sections of the Act omitted here are those which abolish the parole system, see Sentencing Reform Act, § 235(b)(1), and which permit the prosecution and defense to appeal the sentence imposed, see 18 U.S.C.A. § 3742.

this chapter so as to achieve the purposes set forth in subparagraphs (A) through (D) of section 3553(a)(2) to the extent that they are applicable in light of all the circumstances of the case.

(b) **Individuals.**—An individual found guilty of an offense shall be sentenced, in accordance with the provisions of section 3553, to—

(1) a term of probation as authorized by subchapter B;

(2) a fine as authorized by subchapter C; or

(3) a term of imprisonment as authorized by subchapter D.

A sentence to pay a fine may be imposed in addition to any other sentence. A sanction authorized by section 3554, 3555, or 3556 may be imposed in addition to the sentence required by this subsection.

(c) **Organizations.**—An organization found guilty of an offense shall be sentenced, in accordance with the provisions of section 3553, to—

(1) a term of probation as authorized by subchapter B; or

(2) a fine as authorized by subchapter C.

A sentence to pay a fine may be imposed in addition to a sentence to probation. A sanction authorized by section 3554, 3555, or 3556 may be imposed in addition to the sentence required by this subsection.

§ 3553. Imposition of a sentence

(a) **Factors to be considered in imposing a sentence.**—The court shall impose a sentence sufficient, but not greater than necessary, to comply with the purposes set forth in paragraph (2) of this subsection. The court, in determining the particular sentence to be imposed, shall consider—

(1) the nature and circumstances of the offense and the history and characteristics of the defendant;

(2) the need for the sentence imposed—

(A) to reflect the seriousness of the offense, to promote respect for the law, and to provide just punishment for the offense;

(B) to afford adequate deterrence to criminal conduct;

(C) to protect the public from further crimes of the defendant; and

(D) to provide the defendant with needed educational or vocational training, medical care, or other correctional treatment in the most effective manner;

(3) the kinds of sentences available;

(4) the kinds of sentence and the sentencing range established for the applicable category of offense committed by the applicable category of defendant as set forth in the guidelines that are issued by the Sentencing Commission pursuant to 28 U.S.C. 994(a)(1) and that are in effect on the date the defendant is sentenced;

(5) any pertinent policy statement issued by the Sentencing Commission pursuant to 28 U.S.C. 994(a)(2) that is in effect on the date the defendant is sentenced;

(6) the need to avoid unwarranted sentence disparities among defendants with similar records who have been found guilty of similar conduct; and

(7) the need to provide restitution to any victims of the offense.

(b) **Application of guidelines in imposing a sentence.**—The court shall impose a sentence of the kind, and within the range, referred to in subsection (a)(4) unless the court finds that there exists an aggravating or mitigating circumstance of a kind, or to a degree, not adequately taken into consideration by the Sentencing Commission in formulating the guidelines that should result in a sentence different from that described. . . .

(c) **Statement of reasons for imposing a sentence.**—The court, at the time of sentencing, shall state in open court the reasons for its imposition of the particular sentence, and, if the sentence—

(1) is of the kind, and within the range, described in subsection (a)(4) and that range exceeds 24 months, the reason for imposing a sentence at a particular point within the range; or

(2) is not of the kind, or is outside the range, described in subsection (a)(4), the specific reason for the imposition of a sentence different from that described.

If the court does not order restitution, or orders only partial restitution, the court shall include in the statement the reason therefor. . . .

* * *

§ 3555. Order of notice to victims

The court, in imposing a sentence on a defendant who has been found guilty of an offense involving fraud or other intentionally deceptive practices, may order, in addition to the sentence that is imposed pursuant to the provisions of section 3551, that the defendant give reasonable notice and explanation of the conviction, in such form as the court may approve, to the victims of the offense. The notice may be ordered to be given by mail, by advertising in designated areas or through designated media, or by other appropriate means. In determining whether to require the defendant to give such notice, the court shall consider . . . the cost involved in giving the notice as it relates to the loss caused by the offense, and shall not require the defendant to bear the costs of notice in excess of $20,000.

§ 3556. Order of restitution

The court, in imposing a sentence on a defendant who has been found guilty of an offense under this title . . . may order, in addition to the sentence that is imposed pursuant to the provisions of section 3551, that the defendant make restitution to any victim of the offense in accordance with the provisions of sections 3663 and 3664.

§ 3559. Sentencing classification of offenses

(a) **Classification.**—An offense that is not specifically classified by a letter grade in the section defining it, is classified if the maximum term of imprisonment authorized is—

    (1) life imprisonment, or if the maximum penalty is death, as a Class A felony;

    (2) twenty-five years or more, as a Class B felony;

    (3) less than twenty-five years but ten or more years, as a Class C felony;

    (4) less than ten years but five or more years, as a Class D felony;

    (5) less than five years but more than one year, as a Class E felony;

    (6) one year or less but more than six months, as a Class A misdemeanor;

    (7) six months or less but more than thirty days, as a Class B misdemeanor;

    (8) thirty days or less but more than five days, as a Class C misdemeanor; or

    (9) five days or less, or if no imprisonment is authorized, as an infraction.

(b) **Effect of classification.**—An offense classified under subsection (a) carries all the incidents assigned to the applicable letter designation, except that the maximum term of imprisonment is the term authorized by the law describing the offense.

§ 3561. Sentence of probation

(a) **In general.**—A defendant who has been found guilty of an offense may be sentenced to a term of probation unless—

    (1) the offense is a Class A or Class B felony and the defendant is an individual;

    (2) the offense is an offense for which probation has been expressly precluded; or

    (3) the defendant is sentenced at the same time to a term of imprisonment for the same or a different offense.

(b) **Authorized terms.**—The authorized terms of probation are—

    (1) for a felony, not less than one nor more than five years;

    (2) for a misdemeanor, not more than five years; and

    (3) for an infraction, not more than one year.

§ 3563. Conditions of probation

(a) **Mandatory conditions.**—The court shall provide, as an explicit condition of a sentence of probation—

(1) for a felony, a misdemeanor, or an infraction, that the defendant not commit another Federal, State, or local crime during the term of probation; and

(2) for a felony, that the defendant also abide by at least one condition set forth in subsection (b)(2), (b)(3), or (b)(13).

If the court has imposed and ordered execution of a fine and placed the defendant on probation, payment of the fine or adherence to the court-established installment schedule shall be a condition of the probation. . . .

(b) Discretionary conditions.—The court may provide, as further conditions of a sentence of probation, to the extent that such conditions are reasonably related to the factors set forth in section 3553(a)(1) and (a)(2) and to the extent that such conditions involve only such deprivations of liberty or property as are reasonably necessary for the purposes indicated in section 3553(a)(2), that the defendant—

(1) support his dependents and meet other family responsibilities;

(2) pay a fine . . .;

(3) make restitution to a victim of the offense pursuant to the provisions of section 3556;

(4) give to the victims of the offense the notice ordered pursuant to the provisions of section 3555;

(5) work conscientiously at suitable employment or pursue conscientiously a course of study or vocational training that will equip him for suitable employment;

(6) refrain, in the case of an individual, from engaging in a specified occupation, business, or profession bearing a reasonably direct relationship to the conduct constituting the offense, or engage in such a specified occupation, business, or profession only to a stated degree or under stated circumstances;

* * *

(11) remain in the custody of the Bureau of Prisons during nights, weekends, or other intervals of time, totaling no more than the lesser of one year or the term of imprisonment authorized for the offense, during the first year of the term of probation;

(12) reside at, or participate in the program of, a community corrections facility (including a facility maintained or under contract to the Bureau of Prisons) for all or part of the term of probation;

* * *

(21) satisfy such other conditions as the court may impose.

* * *

§ 3571. Sentence of fine[2]

(a) **In general.**—A defendant who has been found guilty of an offense may be sentenced to pay a fine.

(b) **Fines for individuals.**—Except as provided in subsection (e) of this section, an individual who has been found guilty of an offense may be fined not more than the greatest of—

(1) the amount specified in the law setting forth the offense;

(2) the applicable amount under subsection (d) of this section;

(3) for a felony, not more than $250,000;

(4) for a misdemeanor resulting in death, not more than $250,000;

(5) for a Class A misdemeanor that does not result in death, not more than $100,000;

(6) for a Class B or C misdemeanor that does not result in death, not more than $5,000; or

(7) for an infraction, not more than $5,000.

(c) **Fines for organizations.**—[A]n organization that has been found guilty of an offense may be fined not more than the greatest of—

(1) the amount specified in the law setting forth the offense;

(2) the applicable amount under subsection (d) of this section;

(3) for a felony, not more than $500,000;

(4) for a misdemeanor resulting in death, not more than $500,000;

(5) for a Class A misdemeanor that does not result in death, not more than $200,000;

(6) for a Class B or C misdemeanor that does not result in death, not more than $10,000; and

(7) for an infraction, not more than $10,000.

(d) **Alternative fine based on gain or loss.**—If any person derives pecuniary gain from the offense, or if the offense results in pecuniary loss to a person other than the defendant, the defendant may be fined not more than the greater of twice the gross gain or twice the gross loss, unless imposition of a fine under this subsection would unduly complicate or prolong the sentencing process.

* * *

§ 3572. Imposition of a sentence of fine and related matters

(a) **Factors to be considered.**—In determining whether to impose a fine, and the amount, time for payment, and method of payment of a fine, the court shall consider, in addition to the factors set forth in section 3553(a)—

---

2. §§ 3571 and 3572 were added by the Criminal Fine Improvements Act of 1987, Pub.L. 100–185, 101 Stat. 1279 (1987). For legislative history, see 3 U.S.Code Cong. & Admin.News, 100th Cong., 1st Sess., p. 2137 (1987).

(1) the defendant's income, earning capacity, and financial resources;

(2) the burden that the fine will impose upon the defendant, any person who is financially dependent on the defendant, or any other person (including a government) that would be responsible for the welfare of any person financially dependent on the defendant, relative to the burden that alternative punishments would impose;

(3) any pecuniary loss inflicted upon others as a result of the offense;

(4) whether restitution is ordered or made and the amount of such restitution;

(5) the need to deprive the defendant of illegally obtained gains from the offense;

(6) whether the defendant can pass on to consumers or other persons the expense of the fine; and

(7) if the defendant is an organization, the size of the organization and any measure taken by the organization to discipline any officer, director, employee, or agent of the organization responsible for the offense and to prevent a recurrence of such an offense.

(b) Fine not to impair ability to make restitution.—If, as a result of a conviction, the defendant has the obligation to make restitution to a victim of the offense, the court shall impose a fine or other monetary penalty only to the extent that such fine or penalty will not impair the ability of the defendant to make restitution.

* * *

§ 3582. Imposition of a sentence of imprisonment

(a) **Factors to be considered in imposing a term of imprisonment.**—The court, in determining whether to impose a term of imprisonment, and, if a term of imprisonment is to be imposed, in determining the length of the term, shall consider the factors set forth in section 3553(a) to the extent that they are applicable, recognizing that imprisonment is not an appropriate means of promoting correction and rehabilitation. In determining whether to make a recommendation concerning the type of prison facility appropriate for the defendant, the court shall consider any pertinent policy statements issued by the Sentencing Commission pursuant to 28 U.S.C. 994(a)(2).

* * *

28 U.S.C.A. § 991 et seq.

§ 991. United States Sentencing Commission: establishment of purposes

(a) There is established as an independent commission in the judicial branch of the United States a United States Sentencing Commission which shall consist of seven voting members and one nonvoting member. The President . . . shall appoint the voting members of the Commission, by and with the advice and consent of the Senate. . . . At least three of the members shall be Federal judges. . . . Not more than four of the members of the Commission shall be members of the same political party. The Attorney General, or his designee, shall be an ex officio, nonvoting member of the Commission. . . .

(b) The purposes of the United States Sentencing Commission are to—

(1) establish sentencing policies and practices for the Federal criminal justice system that—

(A) assure the meeting of the purposes of sentencing as set forth in section 3553(a)(2) of title 18, United States Code;

(B) provide certainty and fairness in meeting the purposes of sentencing, avoiding unwarranted sentencing disparities among defendants with similar records who have been found guilty of similar criminal conduct while maintaining sufficient flexibility to permit individualized sentences when warranted by mitigating or aggravating factors not taken into account in the establishment of general sentencing practices; . . .

§ 994. Duties of the Commission

(a) The Commission . . . shall promulgate and distribute to all courts of the United States . . .—

(1) guidelines, as described in this section, for use of a sentencing court in determining the sentence to be imposed in a criminal case, including—

(A) a determination whether to impose a sentence to probation, a fine, or a term of imprisonment;

(B) a determination as to the appropriate amount of a fine or the appropriate length of a term of probation or a term of imprisonment;

(C) a determination whether a sentence to a term of imprisonment should include a requirement that the defendant be placed on a term of supervised release after imprisonment, and, if so, the appropriate length of such a term; . . .

(2) general policy statements regarding application of the guidelines or any other aspect of sentencing or sentence implementation that in the view of the Commission would further the purposes set forth in section 3553(a)(2) of title 18 . . .

(b) . . .

(2) If a sentence specified by the guidelines includes a term of imprisonment, the maximum of the range established for such a term shall not exceed the minimum of that range by more than the greater of 25 percent or 6 months, except that, if the minimum

term of the range is 30 years or more, the maximum may be life imprisonment.

(c) The Commission, in establishing categories of offenses . . . shall take . . . into account only to the extent that they do have relevance—

(1) the grade of the offense;

(2) the circumstances under which the offense was committed which mitigate or aggravate the seriousness of the offense;

(3) the nature and degree of the harm caused by the offense, including whether it involved property, irreplaceable property, a person, a number of persons, or a breach of public trust;

(4) the community view of the gravity of the offense;

(5) the public concern generated by the offense;

(6) the deterrent effect a particular sentence may have on the commission of the offense by others; and

(7) the current incidence of the offense in the community and in the Nation as a whole.

(d) The Commission in establishing categories of defendants . . . shall take . . . into account only to the extent that they do have relevance—

(1) age;

(2) education;

(3) vocational skills;

(4) mental and emotional condition to the extent that such condition mitigates the defendant's culpability or to the extent that such condition is otherwise plainly relevant;

(5) physical condition, including drug dependence;

(6) previous employment record;

(7) family ties and responsibilities;

(8) community ties;

(9) role in the offense;

(10) criminal history; and

(11) degree of dependence upon criminal activity for a livelihood.

The Commission shall assure that the guidelines and policy statements are entirely neutral as to the race, sex, national origin, creed, and socioeconomic status of offenders.

(e) The Commission shall assure that the guidelines and policy statements, in recommending a term of imprisonment or length of a term of imprisonment, reflect the general inappropriateness of considering the education, vocational skills, employment record, family ties and responsibilities, and community ties of the defendant.

* * *

(j) The Commission shall insure that the guidelines reflect the general appropriateness of imposing a sentence other than imprisonment in cases in which the defendant is a first offender who has not been convicted of a crime of violence or an otherwise serious offense, and the general appropriateness of imposing a term of imprisonment on a person convicted of a crime of violence that results in serious bodily injury.

(k) The Commission shall insure that the guidelines reflect the inappropriateness of imposing a sentence to a term of imprisonment for the purpose of rehabilitating the defendant or providing the defendant with needed educational or vocational training, medical care, or other correctional treatment.

* * *

(m) The Commission shall insure that the guidelines reflect the fact that, in many cases, current sentences do not accurately reflect the seriousness of the offense. . . . The Commission shall not be bound by . . . average sentences, and shall independently develop a sentencing range that is consistent with the purposes of sentencing. . . .

(n) The Commission shall assure that the guidelines reflect the general appropriateness of imposing a lower sentence than would otherwise be imposed, including a sentence that is lower than that established by statute as a minimum sentence, to take into account a defendant's substantial assistance in the investigation or prosecution of another person who has committed an offense.

* * *

(p) The Commission . . . shall report to the Congress any amendments of the guidelines promulgated pursuant to subsection (a)(1), and a report of the reasons therefor, and the amended guidelines shall take effect one hundred and eighty days after the Commission reports them, except to the extent the effective date is enlarged or the guidelines are disapproved or modified by Act of Congress.

* * *

(s) The Commission shall give due consideration to any petition filed by a defendant requesting modification of the guidelines utilized in the sentencing of such defendant, on the basis of changed circumstances unrelated to the defendant, including changes in—

   (1) the community view of the gravity of the offense;

   (2) the public concern generated by the offense; and

   (3) the deterrent effect particular sentences may have on the commission of the offense by others.

* * *

NOTES AND QUERIES

(1) *Legislative Background.* Federal criminal laws have historically permitted a judge to choose from a range of penalties, rather than

requiring a judge to impose any specific fixed sentence.[3] A judge could thus sentence an offender to a term of imprisonment, or a fine, or both; or could suspend all or part of a sentence and place a defendant on probation. Further, once the defendant was sentenced to a term of imprisonment, the length of time that would actually be served was determined by a parole commission which had the power to shorten significantly the sentence imposed by the court.

This approach ("indeterminate sentencing") gave wide discretion for two reasons. First, this approach emphasized the tailoring principle, that is, the principle that the sentence should be tailored to the specific characteristics of the offender (still taking into account, of course, the overall gravity of the crime). Second, the main goal of this approach was rehabilitation, with the offender being released when (but only when) the offender was ready to return to society as a productive citizen. This system of indeterminate sentencing received major scholarly endorsement in 1962 in the Model Penal Code.[4]

By the early 1970s, however, criticisms of this approach to sentencing began to appear. The criticisms had two major prongs. One prong was the argument that a system of indeterminate sentences produced significant disparities in sentences both among offenders and among offenses.[5] The other prong was a direct attack on rehabilitation as a primary goal of criminal punishment. Some critics preferred a sentencing philosophy that emphasized retribution ("just deserts"); others sought surer deterrence.[6] Both groups of critics, however, argued that fixed, determinate sentences would more likely achieve the sentencing goal they felt proper.

One solution that emerged from this criticism was to remove discretion from courts by appointing a sentencing commission which would issue guidelines for sentencing based on offense and offender characteristics. The function of the sentencing judge would then be to place the defendant in the appropriate spot on a sentencing grid which would account for the two variables.[7]

During the same period that indeterminate sentencing was being criticized, efforts were underway to reform the entire body of federal

3. For a concise review of the shifts in philosophy between determinate and indeterminate sentencing, see United States v. Grayson, 438 U.S. 41, 45–47, 98 S.Ct. 2610, 2613–14, 57 L.Ed.2d 582, 586–87 (1978).

4. See Model Penal Code § 6.06 (Official Draft 1962).

5. See the Comptroller General, Report to the Congress of the United States, Reducing Federal Judicial Sentencing and Prosecution Disparities: A Systematic Approach Needed (1979); A. Partridge & W. Eldridge, The Second Circuit Sentencing Study: A Report to the Judges of the Second Circuit (1974); both discussed in Frankel & Orland, Sentencing Commissions and Guidelines, 73 Geo.L.J. 225, 226–27 n. 9 (1984).

6. See, e.g., A. von Hirsch, Doing Justice: The Choice of Punishments (1976); F. Allen, The Decline of the Rehabilitative Ideal (1981); N. Morris, The Future of Imprisonment (1974); Becker, Crime and Punishment: An Economic Approach, 76 J.Pol.Econ. 169 (1968).

7. See, e.g., A. von Hirsch, supra, 132–140. For a highly influential description of the basic proposal, see M. Frankel, Criminal Sentences: Law Without Order 111–124 (1973).

criminal law by adopting a uniform federal criminal code.[8] The idea of moving toward determinate sentencing under guidelines became part of this overall effort, and sentencing reform was included in criminal code reform bills introduced in Congress beginning in the mid–1970s.[9] Further support for determinate sentencing came from various "model act" proposals adopted in the late 1970s,[10] as well as the adoption of sentencing guideline systems in a number of states.[11]

The Sentencing Reform Act was enacted as part of the "Comprehensive Crime Control Act of 1984." This bill was more patch-work than comprehensive, and it did not contain a federal criminal code.[12] Thus, of the entire effort to reform the structure of federal criminal law, sentencing reform is the only part that succeeded.

(2) *Queries.* (a) How does the language of the Sentencing Reform Act reflect the shift in sentencing philosophies discussed in Note (1)? Does the Act choose one particular sentencing philosophy?

(b) Review the offense and offender characteristics set out in Section 994(c) and (d). Are they consistent with the purposes of the Act (or with other sections of the Act)? Would a guidelines system which took account of these factors be readily administrable? Is there a connection between ease of administrability and consistency in sentencing? Section 991(b) seeks certainty and flexibility. Is this possible?

(c) What sections of the Sentencing Reform Act have particular relevance to business crime cases? Does the Act indicate a Congressional desire to have the Sentencing Commission increase or decrease penalties in these cases? What effect does the Act have on the maximum penalties which can be imposed in business crime cases?

(3) *Constitutional Issues.* Following enactment of the Sentencing Reform Act, commentators began questioning the Act's constitutionality on two major grounds, improper delegation by Congress and separation of powers.[13] When the Guidelines finally became effective in November 1987, there was a wave of litigation as defendants through-

---

8. These efforts are described supra, p. 12.

9. See Criminal Code Reform Act of 1977, S.1437, 95th Cong., 1st Sess., Part III (1977); Criminal Code Reform Act of 1979, S.1722, 96th Cong., 1st Sess. (1979); Criminal Code Reform Act of 1981, S.1630, 97th Cong., 1st Sess., Titles I, III (1981).

10. See, e.g., Model Sentencing and Corrections Act (1979) (National Conference of Commissioners on Uniform State Laws); 3 American Bar Ass'n, Standards for Criminal Justice, Sentencing Alternatives and Procedures ch. 18 (2d ed. 1980).

11. See, e.g., Minn.Stat.Ann. 244.08 (adopted 1980); Fla.Stat.Ann. 921.001 (adopted 1982).

12. For sentencing reform proposals introduced in the Senate of the 98th Congress, see S. 688, 98th Cong., 1st Sess. (1983); S. 829, 98th Cong., 1st Sess. (1983). Parts of § 829 became the Comprehensive Crime Control Act of 1983, S.1762, 98th Cong., 1st Sess. (1983). For Judiciary Committee Reports, see S.Rep. No. 98–223, 98–225, 98th Cong., 1st Sess. The House Judiciary Committee had favorably reported a different sentencing proposal, H.R. 6012, 98th Cong., 2d Sess. (1984); see H.Rep. No. 98–1017, 98th Cong., 2d Sess. (1984); but the House finally agreed to the Senate's version in the waning days of the 98th Congress.

13. See, e.g., Note, The Constitutional Infirmities of the United States Sentencing Commission, 96 Yale L.J. 1363 (1987).

out the country challenged their constitutionality. By one count, as of May of 1988 the Guidelines had been challenged in more than 105 cases in 53 judicial districts; the Sentencing Commission had been declared unconstitutional in thirty-two cases and upheld in twenty-three.[14]

The issue was finally settled by the Supreme Court in *Mistretta v. United States*.[15] After reviewing the background of the Act and its basic provisions, Justice Blackmun wrote:

III

Delegation of Power

Petitioner argues that in delegating the power to promulgate sentencing guidelines for every federal criminal offense to an independent Sentencing Commission, Congress has granted the Commission excessive legislative discretion in violation of the constitutionally based nondelegation doctrine. We do not agree.

The nondelegation doctrine is rooted in the principle of separation of powers that underlies our tripartite system of government. The Constitution provides that "[a]ll legislative Powers herein granted shall be vested in a Congress of the United States," U.S. Const., Art. I, § 1, and we long have insisted that "the integrity and maintenance of the system of government ordained by the Constitution," mandate that Congress generally cannot delegate its legislative power to another Branch. Field v. Clark, 143 U.S. 649, 692, 12 S.Ct. 495, 504, 36 L.Ed. 294 (1892). We also have recognized, however, that the separation-of-powers principle, and the non-delegation doctrine in particular, do not prevent Congress from obtaining the assistance of its coordinate Branches. In a passage now enshrined in our jurisprudence, Chief Justice Taft, writing for the Court, explained our approach to such cooperative ventures: "In determining what [Congress] may do in seeking assistance from another branch, the extent and character of that assistance must be fixed according to common sense and the inherent necessities of the government co-ordination." J.W. Hampton, Jr., & Co. v. United States, 276 U.S. 394, 406, 48 S.Ct. 348, 351, 72 L.Ed. 624 (1928). So long as Congress "shall lay down by legislative act an intelligible principle to which the person or body authorized to [exercise the delegated authority] is directed to conform, such legislative action is not a forbidden delegation of legislative power." Id., at 409, 48 S.Ct., at 352.

* * *

[W]e harbor no doubt that Congress' delegation of authority to the Sentencing Commission is sufficiently specific and detailed to meet constitutional requirements. [The Court here reviewed, inter alia, the statutory goals set out in 28 U.S.C. § 991(b)(1) and 18 U.S.C. § 3553(a)(2); the limitations on sentences provided in 28

---

14. See Obermaier, Sentencing Redux VII, N.Y.L.J., May 3, 1988, p. 1.

15. ___ U.S. ___, 109 S.Ct. 647, 102 L.Ed.2d 714 (1989).

U.S.C. § 994(b); and the offender/offense characteristics in 28 U.S.C. § 994(c) and (d).]

In addition to these overarching constraints, Congress provided even more detailed guidance to the Commission about categories of offenses and offender characteristics. Congress directed that guidelines require a term of confinement at or near the statutory maximum for certain crimes of violence and for drug offenses, particularly when committed by recidivists. § 994(h). Congress further directed that the Commission assure a substantial term of imprisonment for an offense constituting a third felony conviction, for a career felon, for one convicted of a managerial role in a racketeering enterprise, for a crime of violence by an offender on release from a prior felony conviction, and for an offense involving a substantial quantity of narcotics. § 994(i). Congress also instructed "that the guidelines reflect . . . the general appropriateness of imposing a term of imprisonment" for a crime of violence that resulted in serious bodily injury. On the other hand, Congress directed that guidelines reflect the general inappropriateness of imposing a sentence of imprisonment "in cases in which the defendant is a first offender who has not been convicted of a crime of violence or an otherwise serious offense." § 994(j). Congress also enumerated various aggravating and mitigating circumstances, such as, respectively, multiple offenses or substantial assistance to the Government, to be reflected in the guidelines. §§ 994(*l*) and (n). In other words, although Congress granted the Commission substantial discretion in formulating guidelines, in actuality it legislated a full hierarchy of punishment—from near maximum imprisonment, to substantial imprisonment, to some imprisonment, to alternatives—and stipulated the most important offense and offender characteristics to place defendants within these categories.

We cannot dispute petitioner's contention that the Commission enjoys significant discretion in formulating guidelines. The Commission does have discretionary authority to determine the relative severity of federal crimes and to assess the relative weight of the offender characteristics that Congress listed for the Commission to consider. See §§ 994(c) and (d) (Commission instructed to consider enumerated factors as it deems them to be relevant). The Commission also has significant discretion to determine which crimes have been punished too leniently, and which too severely. § 994(m). Congress has called upon the Commission to exercise its judgment about which types of crimes and which types of criminals are to be considered similar for the purposes of sentencing.

* * *

Developing proportionate penalties for hundreds of different crimes by a virtually limitless array of offenders is precisely the sort of intricate, labor-intensive task for which delegation to an expert body is especially appropriate. Although Congress has delegated significant discretion to the Commission to draw judgments from its analysis of existing sentencing practice and alternative sentencing models, "Congress is not confined to that method of executing its policy which involves the least possible delegation of discretion to administrative officers." We have no doubt that in the hands of the Commission "the criteria which Congress has supplied are wholly adequate for carrying out the general policy and purpose" of the Act.

IV

Separation of Powers

* * *

Mistretta argues that. . . . Congress, in constituting the Commission as it did, effected an unconstitutional accumulation of power within the Judicial Branch while at the same time undermining the Judiciary's independence and integrity. Specifically, petitioner claims that in delegating to an independent agency within the Judicial Branch the power to promulgate sentencing guidelines, Congress unconstitutionally has required the Branch, and individual Article III judges, to exercise not only their judicial authority, but legislative authority—the making of sentencing policy—as well. Such rulemaking authority, petitioner contends, may be exercised by Congress, or delegated by Congress to the Executive, but may not be delegated to or exercised by the Judiciary.

At the same time, petitioner asserts, Congress unconstitutionally eroded the integrity and independence of the Judiciary by requiring Article III judges to sit on the Commission, by requiring that those judges share their rulemaking authority with nonjudges, and by subjecting the Commission's members to appointment and removal by the President. According to petitioner, Congress, consistent with the separation of powers, may not upset the balance among the Branches by co-opting federal judges into the quintessentially political work of establishing sentencing guidelines, by subjecting those judges to the political whims of the Chief Executive, and by forcing judges to share their power with nonjudges.

. . . Although the unique composition and responsibilities of the Sentencing Commission give rise to serious concerns about a disruption of the appropriate balance of governmental power among the coordinate Branches, we conclude, upon close inspection, that petitioner's fears for the fundamental structural protections of the Constitution prove, at least in this case, to be "more smoke than fire," and do not compel us to invalidate Congress' considered scheme for resolving the seemingly intractable dilemma of excessive disparity in criminal sentencing.

A

Location of the Commission

The Sentencing Commission unquestionably is a peculiar institution within the framework of our Government. Although placed by the Act in the Judicial Branch, it is not a court and does not exercise judicial power. Rather, the Commission is an "independent" body comprised of seven voting members including at least three federal judges, entrusted by Congress with the primary task of promulgating sentencing guidelines. 28 U.S.C. § 991(a). Our constitutional principles of separated powers are not violated, however, by mere anomaly or innovation. . . . Congress' decision to create an independent rulemaking body to promulgate sentencing guidelines and to locate that body within the Judicial Branch is not unconstitutional unless Congress has vested in the Commission powers that are more appropriately performed by the other Branches or that undermine the integrity of the Judiciary.

* * *

[The] sentencing function long has been a peculiarly shared responsibility among the Branches of government and has never been thought of as the exclusive constitutional province of any one Branch. For more than a century, federal judges have enjoyed wide discretion to determine the appropriate sentence in individual cases and have exercised special authority to determine the sentencing factors to be applied in any given case. Indeed, the legislative history of the Act makes clear that Congress' decision to place the Commission within the Judicial Branch reflected Congress' "strong feeling" that sentencing has been and should remain "primarily a judicial function." Report, at 159. That Congress should vest such rulemaking in the Judicial Branch, far from being "incongruous" or vesting within the Judiciary responsibilities that more appropriately belong to another Branch, simply acknowledges the role that the Judiciary always has played, and continues to play, in sentencing.[16]

Given the consistent responsibility of federal judges to pronounce sentence within the statutory range established by Congress, we find that the role of the Commission in promulgating guidelines for the exercise of that judicial function bears considerable similarity to the role of this Court in establishing rules of procedure under the various enabling acts. Just as the rules of

---

16. [Court's footnote 17.] Indeed, had Congress decided to confer responsibility for promulgating sentencing guidelines on the Executive Branch, we might face the constitutional questions whether Congress unconstitutionally had assigned judicial responsibilities to the executive or unconstitutionally had united the power to prosecute and the power to sentence within one Branch. The Justice Department testified before the Senate to this very effect: "If guidelines were to be promulgated by an agency outside the judicial branch, it might be viewed as an encroachment on the sentencing function. . . ." S.Rep. No. 98–225 (1983), p. 159.

procedure bind judges and courts in the proper management of the cases before them, so the Guidelines bind judges and courts in the exercise of their uncontested responsibility to pass sentence in criminal cases. . . .

* * *

[W]e recognize that the task of promulgating rules regulating practice and pleading before federal courts does not involve the degree of political judgment integral to the Commission's formulation of sentencing guidelines.[17] To be sure, all rulemaking is nonjudicial in the sense that rules impose standards of general application divorced from the individual fact situation which ordinarily forms the predicate for judicial action. Also, this Court's rulemaking under the enabling acts has been substantive and political in the sense that the rules of procedure have important effects on the substantive rights of litigants. Nonetheless, the degree of political judgment about crime and criminality exercised by the Commission and the scope of the substantive effects of its work does to some extent set its rulemaking powers apart from prior judicial rulemaking.

We do not believe, however, that the significantly political nature of the Commission's work renders unconstitutional its placement within the Judicial Branch. . . .

First, although the Commission is located in the Judicial Branch, its powers are not united with the powers of the Judiciary in a way that has meaning for separation-of-powers analysis. Whatever constitutional problems might arise if the powers of the Commission were vested in a court, the Commission is not a court, does not exercise judicial power, and is not controlled by or accountable to members of the Judicial Branch. The Commission, on which members of the Judiciary may be a minority, is an independent agency in every relevant sense. In contrast to a court's exercising judicial power, the Commission is fully accountable to Congress, which can revoke or amend any or all of the Guidelines as it sees fit either within the 180-day waiting period, see § 235(a)(1)(B)(ii)(III) of the Act, or at any time. In contrast to a court, the Commission's members are subject to the President's limited powers of removal. In contrast to a court, its rulemaking is subject to the notice and comment requirements of the Administrative Procedure Act, 28 U.S.C. § 994(x). . . .

Second, although the Commission wields rulemaking power and not the adjudicatory power exercised by individual judges when passing sentence, the placement of the Sentencing Commission in the Judicial Branch has not increased the Branch's

---

17. [Court's footnote 18.] Under its mandate, the Commission must make judgments about the relative importance of such considerations as the "circumstances under which the offense was committed," the "community view of the gravity of the offense," and the "deterrent effect a particular sentence may have on the commission of the offense by others." 28 U.S.C. § 994(c)(2), (4), (6).

authority. Prior to the passage of the Act, the Judicial Branch, as an aggregate, decided precisely the questions assigned to the Commission: what sentence is appropriate to what criminal conduct under what circumstances. It was the everyday business of judges, taken collectively, to evaluate and weigh the various aims of sentencing and to apply those aims to the individual cases that came before them. The Sentencing Commission does no more than this, albeit basically through the methodology of sentencing guidelines, rather than entirely individualized sentencing determinations. . . .

Nor do the Guidelines, though substantive, involve a degree of political authority inappropriate for a nonpolitical branch. Although the Guidelines are intended to have substantive effects on public behavior (as do the rules of procedure), they do not bind or regulate the primary conduct of the public or vest in the Judicial Branch the legislative responsibility for establishing minimum and maximum penalties for every crime. They do no more than fetter the discretion of sentencing judges to do what they have done for generations—impose sentences within the broad limits established by Congress. Given their limited reach, the special role of the Judicial Branch in the field of sentencing, and the fact that the Guidelines are promulgated by an independent agency and not a court, it follows that as a matter of "practical consequences" the location of the Sentencing Commission within the Judicial Branch simply leaves with the Judiciary what long has belonged to it.

* * *

B

Composition of the Commission

* * *

We are somewhat more troubled by petitioner's argument that the Judiciary's entanglement in the political work of the Commission undermines public confidence in the disinterestedness of the Judicial Branch. While the problem of individual bias is usually cured through recusal, no such mechanism can overcome the appearance of institutional partiality that may arise from judiciary involvement in the making of policy. The legitimacy of the Judicial Branch ultimately depends on its reputation for impartiality and nonpartisanship. That reputation may not be borrowed by the political Branches to cloak their work in the neutral colors of judicial action.

Although it is a judgment that is not without difficulty, we conclude that the participation of federal judges on the Sentencing Commission does not threaten, either in fact or in appearance, the impartiality of the Judicial Branch. We are drawn to this conclusion by one paramount consideration: that the Sentencing Commission is devoted exclusively to the development of rules to rationalize a process that has been and will continue to be performed exclusively by the Judicial Branch. In our view, this is an essentially neutral endeavor and one in which judicial participation is peculiarly appropriate. Judicial contribution to the enterprise of creating rules to limit the discretion of sentencing judges does not enlist the resources or reputation of the Judicial Branch in either the legislative business of determining what conduct should be criminalized or the executive business of enforcing the law. Rather, judicial participation on the Commission ensures that judicial experience and expertise will inform the promulgation of rules for the exercise of the Judicial Branch's own business—that of passing sentence on every criminal defendant. To this end, Congress has provided, not inappropriately, for a significant judicial voice on the Commission.

* * *

C

Presidential Control

[The Court held that the President's power to appoint and remove judges from the Commission does not compromise judicial independence.]

V

We conclude that in creating the Sentencing Commission—an unusual hybrid in structure and authority—Congress neither delegated excessive legislative power nor upset the constitutionally mandated balance of powers among the coordinate Branches. The Constitution's structural protections do not prohibit Congress from delegating to an expert body located within the Judicial Branch the intricate task of formulating sentencing guidelines consistent with such significant statutory direction as is present here. Nor does our system of checked and balanced authority prohibit Congress from calling upon the accumulated wisdom and experience of the Judicial Branch in creating policy on a matter uniquely within the ken of judges. Accordingly, we hold that the Act is constitutional.[18]

---

18. Justice Scalia dissented, stressing that the Commission's decisions will be "heavily laden" with "value judgments and policy assessments" (noting, as an example, the antitrust guideline discussed infra p. 337). Justice Scalia concluded that the establishment of the Sentencing Commission as "a sort of junior-varsity Congress," exercising the power to make laws but insulated from the political process, was "a pure delegation of legislative power," and therefore unconstitutional.

2. SENTENCING GUIDELINES

UNITED STATES SENTENCING COMMISSION,
SENTENCING GUIDELINES AND POLICY STATEMENTS
(April 13, 1987.)

* * *

3. *The Basic Approach*

* * *

A philosophical problem arose when the Commission attempted to reconcile the differing perceptions of the purposes of criminal punishment. . . . Some argue that appropriate punishment should be defined primarily on the basis of the moral principle of "just deserts." Under this principle, punishment should be scaled to the offender's culpability and the resulting harms. Thus, if a defendant is less culpable, the defendant deserves less punishment. Others argue that punishment should be imposed primarily on the basis of practical "crime control" considerations. Defendants sentenced under this scheme should receive the punishment that most effectively lessens the likelihood of future crime, either by deterring others or incapacitating the defendant.

Adherents of these points of view have urged the Commission to choose between them, to accord one primacy over the other. Such a choice would be profoundly difficult. The relevant literature is vast, the arguments deep, and each point of view has much to be said in its favor. A clear-cut Commission decision in favor of one of these approaches would diminish the chance that the guidelines would find the widespread acceptance they need for effective implementation. As a practical matter, in most sentencing decisions both philosophies may prove consistent with the same result.

For now, the Commission has sought to solve both the practical and philosophical problems of developing a coherent sentencing system by taking an empirical approach that uses data estimating the existing sentencing system as a starting point. It has analyzed data drawn from 10,000 presentence investigations, crimes as distinguished in substantive criminal statutes, the United States Parole Commission's guidelines and resulting statistics, and data from other relevant sources, in order to determine which distinctions are important in present practice. After examination, the Commission has accepted, modified, or rationalized the more important of these distinctions.

* * *

The Commission has not simply copied estimates of existing practice as revealed by the data (even though establishing offense values on this basis would help eliminate disparity, for the data represent averages). Rather, it has departed from the data at different points for various important reasons. Congressional statutes, for example, may suggest or require departure, as in the case of the new drug law that imposes increased and mandatory minimum sentences. In addition, the data may reveal inconsistencies in treatment, such as punishing economic crime less severely than other apparently equivalent behavior.

Despite these policy-oriented departures from present practice, the guidelines represent an approach that begins with, and builds upon, empirical data. The guidelines will not please those who wish the Commission to adopt a single philosophical theory and then work deductively to establish a simple and perfect set of categorizations and distinctions. The guidelines may prove acceptable, however, to those who seek more modest, incremental improvements in the status quo, who believe the best is often the enemy of the good, and who recognize that these initial guidelines are but the first step in an evolutionary process. . . .

* * *

4. *The Guidelines' Resolution of Major Issues*

* * *

(b) *Departures.*

The new sentencing statute permits a court to depart from a guideline-specified sentence only when it finds "an aggravating or mitigating circumstance . . . that was not adequately taken into consideration by the Sentencing Commission. . . ." 18 U.S.C. § 3553(b). Thus, in principle, the Commission, by specifying that it had adequately considered a particular factor, could prevent a court from using it as grounds for departure. In this initial set of guidelines, however, the Commission does not so limit the courts' departure powers. The Commission intends the sentencing courts to treat each guideline as carving out a "heartland," a set of typical cases embodying the conduct that each guideline describes. When a court finds an atypical case, one to which a particular guideline linguistically applies but where conduct significantly differs from the norm, the court may consider whether a departure is warranted. [With a few] specific exceptions, however, the Commission does not intend to limit the kinds of factors (whether or not mentioned anywhere else in the guidelines) that could constitute grounds for departure in an unusual case.

* * *

(c) *Plea Agreements.*

Nearly ninety percent of all federal criminal cases involve guilty pleas, and many of these cases involve some form of plea agreement. . . .

The Commission has decided that these initial guidelines will not, in general, make significant changes in current plea agreement practices. The court will accept or reject any such agreements primarily in accordance with the rules set forth in Fed.R.Crim.P. 11(e). . . .

The Commission nonetheless expects the initial set of guidelines to have a positive, rationalizing impact upon plea agreements for two reasons. First, the guidelines create a clear, definite expectation in respect to the sentence that a court will impose if a trial takes place. Insofar as a prosecutor and defense attorney seek to agree about a likely sentence or range of sentences, they will no longer work in the dark. This fact alone should help to reduce irrationality in respect to actual sentencing outcomes. Second, the guidelines create a norm to which judges will likely refer when they decide whether, under Rule 11(e), to accept or to reject a plea agreement or recommendation. Since they will have before them the norm, the relevant factors (as disclosed in the plea agreement), and the reason for the agreement, they will find it easier than at present to determine whether there is sufficient reason to accept a plea agreement that departs from the norm.

(d) *Probation and Split Sentences.*

The statute provides that the guidelines are to "reflect the general appropriateness of imposing a sentence other than imprisonment in cases in which the defendant is a first offender who has not been convicted of a crime of violence or an otherwise serious offense . . ." 28 U.S.C. § 994(j). Under present sentencing practice, courts sentence to probation an inappropriately high percentage of offenders guilty of certain economic crimes, such as theft, tax evasion, antitrust offenses, insider trading, fraud, and embezzlement, that in the Commission's view are "serious." If the guidelines were to permit courts to impose probation instead of prison in many or all such cases, the present sentences would continue to be ineffective.

The Commission's solution to this problem has been to write guidelines that classify as "serious" (and therefore subject to mandatory prison sentences) many offenses for which probation is now frequently given. At the same time, the guidelines will permit the sentencing court to impose short prison terms in many such cases. The Commission's view is that the definite prospect of prison, though the term is short, will act as a significant deterrent to many of these crimes, particularly when compared with the status quo where probation, not prison, is the norm.

More specifically, the guidelines work as follows in respect to a first offender. For offense levels one through six, the sentencing court may elect to sentence the offender to probation (with or without confinement conditions) or to a prison term. For offense levels seven through ten, the court may substitute probation for a prison term, but the probation must include confinement conditions (community confinement or intermittent confinement). For offense levels eleven and twelve, the court must impose at least one half the minimum confinement sentence in the form of prison confinement, the remainder to be served on supervised release with a condition of community confinement. The Commission, of course, has not dealt with the single acts of aberrant behavior that still may justify probation at higher offense levels through departures.

* * *

NOTES AND QUERIES

(1) *How To Do It.* Section 1B1.1 of the Guidelines explains how to apply the Guidelines. The Guidelines are grouped by types of offenses (e.g., Part N—Offenses Involving Food, Drugs, Agricultural Products, and Odometer Laws) and then further divided by specific Guidelines for types of violations (e.g., § 2N2.1, covering violations of statutes dealing with "any food, drug, biological product, device, cosmetic, or agricultural product"). The first step, therefore, is to determine which Guideline is closest to the crime for which the defendant has been convicted, because a single Guideline could cover a number of statutory offenses. The second step is to read the Guideline itself, which will state a "base offense level" (a Guideline might specify "6") and "specific offense characteristics" which increase or decrease that level (for example, raising the offense level depending on the dollar value involved). The third step is to apply relevant "adjustments" to the offense level previously computed; these include the type of victim ("vulnerable"), the defendant's role in the offense ("organizer" or "manager or supervisor"), and the defendant's acceptance of responsibility. The fourth step is to determine the defendant's criminal history category. The fifth step is to consult the "Sentencing Table" (reproduced in the Statutory Appendix, infra p. 694) to find the appropriate sentencing range based on the offense level and the criminal history category. Based on this sentencing range, the Guidelines then indicate the appropriate mix of penalties (such as imprisonment, probation, supervised release, fines, and restitution). The indicated sentence may then be modified by the application of a final set of "Policy Statements." These involve the specific offender characteristics set out in 28 U.S.C. § 994(d); the amount of assistance "in the investigation or prosecution of another" that the defendant provided to authorities; and a list of further aggravating or mitigating circumstances which might not otherwise have been accounted for in the basic Guideline (for example, "disruption of governmental function" or committing a crime to avoid a greater harm). The Guidelines conclude with provisions relating to the sentencing hearing.

(2) *Controversy Over Drafting the Guidelines.* The guidelines process and the Sentencing Commission were surrounded by controversy from the beginning, first as to appointments to the Commission and then as to the content of the Guidelines.[19] Although the Sentencing Reform Act had provided that the Guidelines were "due" by November 1, 1986, Congress was forced to amend the statute to give the Commission an additional year. The first draft of the Guidelines was completed in September of 1986, but met with substantial opposition from many in the criminal justice community (including judges) in part because the proposed Guidelines were felt to be overly complex,

---

19. See Wermiel, "Commission on Criminal Sentencing Is Tangled in Controversy About Its Makeup and Its Mission," Wall St. J., Jan. 29, 1987, p. 60 (efforts marked by "disarray, personal rivalries and a lack of direction").

mechanical, and harsh.[20] The Guidelines were then substantially rewritten, based on the approach described above. This final version drew a strong dissent from one of the Commissioners, particularly for its reliance on averages of past sentences and for its refusal to choose a consistent sentencing philosophy for all the Guidelines, which could assist judges who feel it appropriate to depart from the Guidelines.[21] A last-minute attempt to convince Congress to postpone the Guidelines failed, and they became effective as of November 1, 1987. With the basic constitutional issues resolved by *Mistretta,* supra, the courts and the Commission are now free to develop the Guidelines in an on-going process.

(3) *The Guidelines Process and the Role of Defense Counsel.* Even before examining the specifics of the current Guidelines, students should consider the wisdom of the basic decision to embark on the guidelines process. Constitutional doctrine to the side, is the Commission really the proper body to control sentences in all federal criminal cases? If the range of penalties that Congress has provided in a particular statute is too broad, shouldn't Congress decide how to narrow it? And do we really want a truly determinate sentencing system? Determinate sentencing might be uniform, but at what cost?

Consider these views of Judge Jack Weinstein, Chief Judge of the United States District Court for the Eastern District of New York: [22]

> Let me emphasize again that these new sentencing guidelines present a difficult challenge to the trial bar. Indeed, they may well have the effect of dehumanizing defendants. The defendant may be seen not as a person, but as an objective sum of points and levels.
>
> The procedure may relieve the tensions of some judges in sentencing. Most judges find it extremely difficult to look into the eye of another human being and punish that person severely, particularly when the defendant's spouse and children are standing by, about to suffer more than the defendant. Real people compel us to face hard choices and to deal with our innate compassion. Recent history has taught us that cruelty and punishment are easier to administer when dehumanization has taken place. Substituting numbers for the person is a first step toward denigration: since the numbers compel the result, there may be a reduced sense of the judge's obligation to consider the whole human being before the court. Why lose sleep struggling with justice and morality and the effect on people awaiting judgment, when we can comfortably delegate these matters to mathematics?

---

20. See Kohn, "U.S. Judges Ask Changes in Plan for Sentencing," N.Y.L.J., Dec. 4, 1986, p. 1 (joint statement by District Court and Second Circuit Judges).

21. See Dissenting View of Commissioner Paul H. Robinson on the Promulgation of Sentencing Guidelines by the United States Sentencing Commission (May 1, 1987).

22. "The Role of Attorneys Under the New Sentencing Guidelines," N.Y.L.J., Dec. 16, 1987, p. 1.

Already software is being developed so that much of the calculation can be done by computer. The Court of Appeals, without even seeing the person being sentenced, can "recompute."

How much the computer, the bottom line, and a narrow view of economic utilitarianism take over from the human element and push out wisdom and mercy in our criminal law depends to a large extent on the defense bar. The commission has invited appropriate departures, and the defense lawyer's work may make such departures precedents for amelioration. It is largely up to attorneys and the judges.

(4) *How Do Judges Judge?* In thinking about the play between direction and discretion, it might be helpful to know how judges themselves think about sentencing. Consider the following description, based on interviews with fifty-one judges in seven federal districts, with the primary emphasis being on districts with heavy white collar crime caseloads. The excerpt is from S. Wheeler, K. Mann, and A. Sarat, Sitting in Judgment: The Sentencing of White–Collar Criminals 19–22 (1988): [23]

> Our basic thesis is that judges apply a common normative lens to the task of sentencing, a normative lens that has a rich tradition in Anglo–American law and cultural experience. The normative lens through which judges view the cases is neither so varied nor idiosyncratic as is commonly believed. There is a broad consensus, across a wide range of judges of otherwise different temperaments and styles, on the core principles that ought to be applied in the sentencing of offenders. . . .
>
> At the heart of this common moral lens lie three core legal norms that are deeply rooted in the history of Anglo–American jurisprudence. The first is the norm that offenses should be treated differently according to the *harm* they produce. . . .
>
> In assessing harm, judges are not limited to harm as it is defined in one or another section of the criminal code, for instance, "deprivation of revenue to the treasury." They work with an *expanded conception* of harm that may include matters (like amount of loss) that are also reflected in legislative grading, but they may also include matters (like duration of offense or whether the victim was an individual or an organization) that are often only implicit, if that, in legislation.
>
> The second principle is the norm of *blameworthiness:* Offenders should be treated differently according to the blameworthiness of their actions. As with harm, judges found it virtually impossible to discuss a case without some assessment of the moral culpability of the offender. Some spoke bluntly ("You have to realize this was really a bad guy—thoroughly corrupt and dishonest") while others were less direct. The consistency with which their concern re-

---

23. Reprinted with permission. ©
Yale University Press

turned to assessment of the elements of the moral character of offenders convinces us that it lies at the heart of judicial thought.

* * *

The conventional elements of criminal intent that are essential to establishing grounds for conviction in a criminal case are often the starting point for a judge's consideration of blameworthiness. But this consideration usually reaches beyond the starting point to include a broader moral sphere. That sphere may reach into the earlier history of the defendant, into the details of the defendant's role in the crime, into a character assessment based on how the defendant reacted to the fact of arrest and conviction, or into whether the defendant was moved by need or by greed, matters rarely relevant for purposes of guilt determination. The broad general principle of blameworthiness encompasses all of them.

* * *

Although the moral forces of judgments of harm and blameworthiness sometimes pull in opposite directions—a petty offense by a habitual criminal, a major economic crime by a first offender—some qualities seem to adhere both to the offense and the offender. One of these qualities is especially significant in white-collar cases: the violation of trust. When persons in positions of significant financial or public trust violate that trust in the commission of crimes, they add both to the harm done—by threatening the fabric of trust on which transactions in the society are often based—and to the blameworthiness of the defendant—by adding to his criminal responsibility the added moral opprobrium that attaches to one who lets others down by violating the trust placed in him. Thus, the most serious of white-collar crimes are often judged to be those in which huge economic gains are made at the expense of trusting victims.

For our judges, if there is primarily a "just deserts" concern behind their examination of harm and blameworthiness, there is also a utilitarian concern. In cases of white-collar crime, as in other crimes, greater harm brings greater punishment in order to provide greater protection to society. But greater blameworthiness, or a more vicious will, as some would say, is also a measure of the degree of injury caused to society. A carefully planned fraud committed with stealth and cover-up must warrant more punishment because it causes greater injury to the citizens' sense of security.

As important as the twin norms of harm and blameworthiness are, they do not exhaust judges' views about sentences. A third principle is that of *consequence*. . . . The primary social consequence in the judge's view is deterrence or general prevention. Judges worry much about the message they are implicitly sending to the community by virtue of the sanction they give. They often find it difficult to elevate the concern for deterrence to the level granted judgments about the harm caused by the offense and the blameworthiness of the offender, and they find it difficult to sanction for general deterrence purposes alone, if they cannot also justify that sanction on grounds of moral culpability or gravity of offense. Nevertheless, especially in white-collar cases, general deterrence is a most relevant consequence.

Concern for deterrence is a generalized element of consequence affecting the whole society. A second element of consequence is more personal. It asks, What will be the effect of the sanction on the person sanctioned, or on his or her immediate family or work associates? Because white-collar offenders are often new to the criminal justice system, because their families often have status in the community, because these offenders are often employers whose own workers will suffer if they are imprisoned, the personal as well as the societal effects of the sanction loom large in white-collar cases.

Consequence is no more easily reduced to a measurable phenomenon than harm or blameworthiness. . . . Indeed, its diverse elements more often pull in opposite directions than the indicators of harm and blameworthiness. But it is a norm (or series of norms) that appears in almost every judge's account of why they sentence as they do, and along with harm and blameworthiness completes the foundation of judicial reflection and judgment about the sentencing of offenders.

B. INDIVIDUAL SANCTIONS

SCOPE NOTE

The major issue with regard to sanctions for individuals in business crime cases can be reduced to one word: jail. Should these defendants be sent to jail at all, or are alternative sanctions preferable? If they should go to jail, for how long should they be incarcerated? Both questions often involve a difficult question of equity. Should business crime defendants be treated differently than other defendants? Before jumping to a conclusion on this question, be aware that if you believe that sentences for these defendants have not been harsh enough, you might prefer inequality.

The materials in this Section are organized as follows. The first part explores the Guidelines provisions for two important business crime offenses, insider trading and antitrust. The purpose of these examples is not only to see the results produced by the Guidelines in these two areas, but also to provide some concrete settings for the exploration of the proper approach to sentencing individuals in business crime cases. The second part of this Section explores some of the alternatives to jail.

1. SPECIFIC GUIDELINES

UNITED STATES v. REICH

United States District Court for the Southern District of New York, 1987.
661 F.Supp. 371.

SWEET, DISTRICT JUDGE.

Defendant Ilan Reich ("Reich") has timely moved pursuant to Fed. R.Crim.P. 35 to reduce his sentence of one year and a day imposed on January 23, 1987 as punishment for the crime of securities fraud. The government submitted a letter in opposition to the motion on April 15, 1987. For the reasons set forth below, the motion is denied.

The primary ground for a reduced sentence asserted by Reich's skilled counsel is disparity between the sentences imposed upon Reich and others in the scheme. In particular counsel refers to the year and a day sentence imposed on Robert Wilkis, an investment banker who entered pleas to securities fraud, mail fraud and tax evasion which arose out of transactions with Dennis Levine, a broker who received inside information from Reich, Wilkis and others.

> Deponent believes that a comparison of the facts and circumstances of all of the recent insider trading cases demonstrates that Mr. Reich's culpability is among the lowest; yet his sentence ranks as one of the harshest. Affidavit of Robert G. Morvillo, sworn to March 11, 1987 [hereinafter cited as "Morvillo Affidavit"].

According to the Morvillo Affidavit, the government said in its submission with respect to the Wilkis sentence that "Cecola and Reich . . . were less culpable than Wilkis." Ira Sokolow, who it is alleged committed a similar insider trading violation and profited to the extent of $140,000, also received a sentence of one year and a day, which recently has been reduced to eight months.[24] According to the Morvillo Affidavit, David Brown, apparently an investment banker who committed a similar offense, received a sentence of thirty days to be served on weekends.

The Morvillo Affidavit also states that a reporter was told by a staff member of the Sentencing Commission (the "Commission") that the difference between the treatment accorded Reich, Sokolow, Wilkis and Levine is a justification for the recently promulgated Sentencing Guidelines. The Commission has not sought from the court a copy of Reich's Presentence Report ("PSI"), or inquired of the court as to its reason for its sentence, or the extent to which it considered sentences

---

24. [Court's footnote 1.] Since the original imposition of sentence, the Honorable John F. Keenan reduced the sentence of one of the members of the scheme, Ira Sokolow, from one year and one day to eight months, United States v. Sokolow, 86 Cr. 762 (Apr. 30, 1987), on the grounds that at the time of sentence the court had misapprehended the amount of time that Sokolow would actually serve. With respect to so-called "real time"—the amount of time that an offender actually spends behind bars—this is a reduction from approximately 8 months to approximately 6 months.

previously imposed in security frauds cases. The Commission completed its Sentencing Guidelines and Policy Statements for the Federal Courts (the "Guidelines") on April 13, 1987, and this final draft has been submitted to Congress for review. Unless Congress acts to the contrary, the Guidelines will automatically become effective November 1, 1987.[25]

Reich's application also states that the national press reported that the sentence imposed on him "surprised lawyers because it came 11 days after investment banker David S. Brown received a much lighter term. . . ." Morvillo Affidavit at 5.

Reich has submitted exhibits showing the sentences imposed on other defendants, some of whom were part of Levine's scheme and some of whom were also convicted of insider trading offenses. Levine himself received a two-year term, three of the other four members who participated with him (including Reich) received one year and one day, and the remaining member received 30 days and 300 hours of community service. In addition, a sentence of two months was imposed on one member of another insider trading scheme and the rest received probation. The government proceeded against each defendant separately, with the result that the members of the two schemes have been sentenced by a total of four different judges. Of course, because of the confidentiality that surrounds Presentence Reports, see Fed.R.Crim.P. 31(c), this court is not privy to the details of the cases of defendants sentenced by other judges. There presently exists no mechanism, formal or informal, for obtaining information about sentences in other cases except through counsel, and counsel is, of course, also barred access to other defendants' Presentence Reports. . . .

As I attempted to make clear at the time of sentence, the essence of this crime was not the acquisition of dollars (or not in Reich's case) but rather the destruction of trust in the integrity of the financial marketplace and in the specialized lawyers and professionals who are essential to the creation and management of the multimillion—and occasionally billion—dollar transactions. From this point of view, the difference between Sokolow's $140,000 profit and Reich's zero does not affect the essence of the willful criminal behavior. To adjust sentences in crimes of this nature by the amount of profits taken (or available to be taken) would reduce the search for a just result to an accounting.

In addition, Reich's counsel points to the $485,000 that the Securities and Exchange Commission ("SEC") obtained from Reich under its consent decree. Clearly the administrative agency charged with overseeing the financial markets concluded that Reich's action merited a substantial financial penalty. The SEC action, however, neither satisfied the government nor relieved this court of its duty to consider incarceration in addition to the payments obtained from Reich.

25. [Judge Sweet's opinion was handed down May 20, 1987—Ed.]

Reich has sought relief, therefore, primarily on the grounds of disparity, a contention which deserves serious consideration because of the currency of the issue. With little meaningful empirical data,[26] the shibolleth of disparity swept the Congress, created the Sentencing Commission, and has resulted in the Guidelines. Because of Reich's claim of disparity, the court has examined that sentence in the light cast by the draft Guidelines submitted by the Commission to Congress. This examination demonstrates that the Guidelines will require time-consuming calculations on issues tangential to the case, that they will create a host of litigable uncertainties for appeal, as well as a number of other undesirable side effects, but that they will fail to eliminate disparity in any meaningful way.[27]

Under the Guidelines a district court could impose a sentence upon Ilan Reich ranging from probation, a condition of which is 6 months at a halfway house, to about two and one-half years in jail—before even considering departing from the standard guideline range. This is a broader range for Reich alone than the Southern District actually employed for all of the members of the Levine ring, and suggests— given that the Guidelines are society's most recent manifestation of offense severity—that the sentence previously imposed upon Reich is on the low side, if anything.

To arrive at Ilan Reich's sentence under the Guidelines, the court would have to proceed through the following steps. The first task is to identify the proper "Offense of Conduct." Here, Reich falls within the terms of § 2F1.2, titled "Insider Trading." The Guidelines direct that the "Base Offense Level" for insider trading is 8. The derivation of this 8 is neither explained nor made the subject of rational analysis, nor are the "base scores" for other offenses.

The next step under the Guidelines is to modify this "Base Offense Level" figure by taking into account any "Specific Offense Characteristics." For insider trading, that means increasing the Base Offense Level "by the number of levels from the table in § 2F1.1 corresponding

---

26. [Court's footnote 6.] A 1983 review of the literature by the National Research Council revealed scant support for so radical a revamping of the sentencing process: "While substantial disparities in sentencing *probably* exist, the relative magnitude of disparity *is not known.* Furthermore, both normative disagreements and measurement problems *make it difficult to determine how much of the disparity is unwarranted.*" Panel on Sentencing Research, Committee on Research on Law Enforcement and the Administration of Justice, Commission on Behavioral and Social Sciences and Education, National Research Council, 2 Research on Sentencing: The Search for Reform 19 (1983) (emphasis added).

27. [Court's footnote 7.] The recent reduction of the sentence imposed upon Ira Sokolow noted above, has been the subject of post-motion correspondence from Reich's counsel, again stressing the claim of disparity. To bottom such a claim on a two-month difference in time served is to exalt the concept beyond the capacity of any system, including the recently promulgated Sentencing Guidelines.

Of course, one advantage of the new Guidelines is that they stand for so-called "truth in sentencing," without an estimate for the effect of parole.

to the gain resulting from the defendant's conduct." Guidelines § 2F1.2(b)(1), at 2.58. The table provides:

	Loss	Increase in Level
(A)	$2,000 or less	no increase
(B)	$2,001–$5,000	add 1
(C)	$5,001–$10,000	add 2
(D)	$10,001–$20,000	add 3
(E)	$20,001–$50,000	add 4
(F)	$50,001–$100,000	add 5
(G)	$100,001–$200,000	add 6
(H)	$200,001–$500,000	add 7
(I)	$500,001–$1,000,000	add 8
(J)	$1,000,001–$2,000,000	add 9
(K)	$2,000,001–$5,000,000	add 10
(L)	Over $5,000,000	add 11

As already discussed, the dollar amount of loss or gain is not—or, at least, should not be—the point here. Nevertheless, here, Reich has admitted that approximately $300,000 was placed in an account for him by Levine. Presumably, Levine himself also profited substantially from Reich's tips. The commentary to the section directs that the figure to be used when consulting the chart is "the total increase in value realized by the defendant or tippees through trading in securities based upon inside information." Id. at 2.60.[28] For the sake of this discussion, it could be assumed that Levine's profits should be added to Reich's $300,000, and, consequently, that the total increase in market gain is between $500,001 and $1,000,000. This means that 8 levels should be added to the Base Level score, which brings Reich's total to 16.

Parenthetically, the notion of using dollar amounts as indices for moving from one box on the sentencing grid may open an entire new class of post-conviction attacks. Although the Guidelines themselves suggest that a court "need only make an estimate of the range of loss that is reasonable given the available information." Id., at 2.59, since the 1940's defendants have enjoyed a constitutional right to be sentenced on the basis of accurate facts. To have a sentence vacated on the grounds that it was predicated on inaccurate information, a defendant has to show that the court did indeed rely on erroneous information, that is, that the bad information affected the sentence. . . . Under the Guidelines, the court must make an explicit finding in order to be able to sum up the numbers, which may move an offender's sentence from one box in a grid to another, and thus impact a due process right. Consequently, post-conviction due process attacks on sentences may enjoy a new vitality.

* * *

28. [Court's footnote 9.] The court would expect the parties to litigate the question of whether Reich "realized" any profits at all for the sake of this calculation. After all, he never did accept a penny of the $300,000.

As to role in the offense, however, there are several potential adjustments, at least one of which would certainly be the subject of heated litigation. First, there is the potential adjustment under § 3B1.3, titled "Abuse of Position of Trust or Use of Special Skill." Obviously, in Reich's case, this is the very heart of the issue. Bad enough, under the Guidelines, the court must struggle through so many tangential calculations before even getting to this line in the work sheet. Worse, the Guidelines are phrased so that the court may be unable to face the issue squarely even here.

The Guidelines direct that if an offender has abused a trust or a special skill, then the court should add 2 to his score. § 3B1.3 However, the section directs that this enhancement is *not* made "if an abuse of trust or skill is included in the base offense level or specific offense characteristic." Id. This question is thus presented: Is a breach of trust or skill built into a notion of insider trading? There is no insider trading violation "where the person who has traded in inside information 'was not [the corporation's] agent, . . . was not a fiduciary, [or] was not a person in whom the sellers [of the securities] had placed their trust and confidence.'" Dirks v. SEC, 463 U.S. 646, 654, 103 S.Ct. 3255, 3261, 77 L.Ed.2d 911 (1983) (quoting Chiarella v. United States, 445 U.S. 222, 232, 100 S.Ct. 1108, 1117, 63 L.Ed.2d 348 (1980)). On other hand, perhaps there is a workable difference between the special skills of a lawyer at a prominent law firm and, say, a financial printer. The issue might turn on the technical elements of insider trading and their interrelation with the Guidelines, rather than on this particular defendant's breach of trust. Depending on how this issue was resolved, Reich's score at this stage would be either 16 or 18.

Also in the Role in the Offense category is the question of the extent of Reich's participation in the scheme, because the Guidelines allow for mitigation for those with lesser roles. § 3B1.2. If the defendant was "a minimal participant in any criminal activity" then his score is decreased by 4 points. However, if he is but a "minor participant", then the court is to subtract only 2 points. Finally, the Guidelines direct: "In cases falling between (a) and (b), decrease by 3 levels." Twice Reich withdrew from the scheme, and he never touched any of the profits Levine cached for him, which suggests that he might be entitled to the discount. On the other hand, a partner in the Mergers and Acquisitions department of a respected law firm is far from the example in the Guidelines of one who offloads a single marijuana shipment in an otherwise large smuggling operation. Guidelines § 3B1.2(a) commentary, at 3.4. Thus after this step, Reich could have a score as low as 12 or as high as 18.

Finally, the court would have to adjust for Acceptance of Responsibility. The Guidelines allow a court to reduce a defendant's score by 2 if he "clearly demonstrates a recognition and affirmative acceptance of personal responsibility for the offense of conviction." § 3E1.1, at 3.13. Awarding this discount is almost entirely in the discretion of the sentencing judge, because the sentencer, as opposed to the Court of

Appeals, is the one who has had the opportunity to look the defendant in the eye. "For this reason, the determination of the sentencing judge is entitled to great deference on review and should not be disturbed unless without foundation." Id. commentary, at 3.13. Reich's guilty plea and his willingness to be "debriefed" by the U.S. Attorney's office evidence acceptance of responsibility, as have his statements to the court, and the court would award him the 2 point remorse discount. Consequently, after this stage, Reich's score could be as low as 10 or as high as 16, depending on the previous decisions. Whichever number it is, it is his final "Offense Level" score.

As an aside, this maze of necessary factual findings may fundamentally affect the nature of plea bargaining. Rather than resolving the charge and the total possible exposure of the defendant, prosecutors and defense counsel presumably will be forced to enter detailed negotiations respecting each category of fact that will affect a sentence. The Guidelines specifically envision "a written stipulation of facts" that "set forth the relevant facts and circumstances of the actual offense conduct and offender characteristics," yet which do "not contain misleading facts." § 6B1.4(a)(1), (2).

However, after parties have gone to the trouble of negotiating this stipulation, the court is not bound by it, "but may with the aid of the presentence report, determine the facts relevant to sentencing," § 6B1.4(d), although it is hard to see how those facts can be determined in the light of any agreement. It appears that the court will either be in a straight jacket fashioned by the parties or on a frolic of its own, unaided by the parties. . . .

Before sentence is imposed, the court must also calculate Reich's "Criminal History Category." Like many white collar criminals, Reich has no record. Because of this, he is in "Criminal History Category I." With the "Offense Level" score and the "Criminal History Category," the sentencer would then turn to the "Sentencing Table". . . .

Referring to the grid, if the court determines that Reich has an Offense Level score of 10, the sentencing range in the grid would be 6 to 12 months. When the Guidelines allow a sentence of 6 months, the court may instead impose a sentence of probation, § 5B1.1(2), a condition of which is alternative confinement in a community center such as a half-way house, § 5C2.1(c)(2). Thus Reich's minimum sentence under the Guidelines is probation, a condition of which is one-half year in a half-way house.

On the other hand, if the court determines that Reich's Offense Level score is 16, the range would instead be 21 months to 27 months. Thus the maximum that Reich could receive under the Guidelines is about two and one-half years in jail.

This is a greater level of disparity than the difference between the sentences actually imposed in the Southern District on Reich and all the other defendants in the scheme. Thus, if it is true that the Sentencing Commission is pointing to Reich, Sokolow, Wilkis, and

Levine as a justification for their grid, their reliance appears misplaced. Finally, the amount and cost of litigation that would be expended in a case like this on tangential issues fail to serve any public purpose.

But perhaps even more importantly, the idea of restraining discretion through grids, columns, and various scores belittles the gravity of the social statement that attends the imposition of a criminal sentence. The formulae and the grid distance the offender from the sentencer—and from the reasons for punishment—by lending the process a false aura of scientific certainty. If it is determined, contrary to the views here expressed, that this sentence demonstrates the need for greater uniformity in sentencing, then the Guidelines should be replaced by a rule of law enunciated by our appellate courts evolving from a case by case analysis.

Aside from the claim of disparity, what lies at the heart of Reich's position is his demonstrated withdrawal from the securities fraud before it was discovered, his plea, constituting his admission of responsibility for the criminal acts, and his personal situation. If punishment for Reich alone were the sole element to be considered in the imposition of this sentence, as was stated at that time, the result would have been other than it was. However, visibility is part of Reich's reality, and, consequently, deterrence is a significant factor in his sentence.

Reich was preeminent in his field. His firm is one of the most highly regarded in the mergers and acquisition practice. His position and the prestige of his firm have raised his sentence to national notice. As long as our system of justice is based upon individual responsibility—as it always has been and should be—then Reich must bear the substantial consequences of his acts, and these consequences extend well beyond dollars gained or lost by him individually.

Another aspect of this sentence is the suffering imposed on Reich, his wife, his young children, his mother and father, and his wife's mother. All have already been damaged, emotionally and financially, and that damage will undoubtedly be intensified as Reich's service of his sentence continues. The pattern is painful and all too familiar.

However, here the family unit is far stronger than that which exists for many defendants whose children face not only separation but a threat of subsistence and whose remaining parent is left without resources of any kind. The issue is not the comparative harm to the innocent family members who are affected in virtually every case, but rather the penalty to be imposed upon the guilty for flouting the laws by which our society seeks to govern itself. Life, death, deprivation and separation are at stake for the innocent in varying degrees in every sentence. Here, painful as these consequences may be, they were anticipated at the time of sentence and do not outweigh the considerations stated at that time.

The imperfection of man and his effort to create a just society is manifest from time to time, and perhaps this opinion is one such manifestation. However, it is the effort and the goal which validates our system of laws and the imposition of punishment for the disobedience of those laws.

IT IS SO ORDERED.

NOTES AND QUERIES

(1) *Applying the Guidelines.* Although the *Reich* case was decided before the effective date of the Guidelines, Judge Sweet's attempt to apply them provides some indication of the potential difficulties they entail. Are you convinced that the range of offense levels and sentences that Judge Sweet says are possible are really likely? Based on the facts given by the court, wouldn't you expect that, in fact, most judges would come out within one or two offense levels of each other if they had to sentence Reich? (What level would you choose?)

In any event, isn't the more interesting question how disparate Reich's sentence would be from the sentence others in the "Levine ring" [29] would have received under the Guidelines? Indeed, this was the heart of the argument made by Reich's counsel. Even if we knew what sentence the other defendants would have received under the Guidelines, however, would that necessarily satisfy our questions about disparity (and equality)? When we seek equal treatment, what factors do we use to judge whether equality has been achieved? If each member of the ring were given the identical sentence, would that be equality?

Review the Sentencing Table in the Appendix, p. 694. Is selecting the exact offense level absolutely critical? Before reaching a conclusion on this question, you should be aware that the court has discretion to avoid prison completely if the minimum sentence is zero months; that "community confinement" can substitute completely for imprisonment if the minimum is six months or less; and that where the minimum is more than ten months, it must be entirely satisfied by imprisonment.[30]

(2) *A Conversation With Judge Sweet.* From Adam Smith, "The Seduction of Ilan": [31]

I went to lunch with Judge Sweet, whom I had known before. Sweet has tried other of the insider cases and has been a federal judge for eight years. A Yale law graduate, he was formerly an assistant U.S. attorney, deputy mayor of

---

29. The Levine case is discussed supra, p. 153. Levine received a two-year jail term; another investment banker involved with Levine was sentenced to 30 days in jail plus 300 hours of community service. In other cases, Ivan Boesky received a two-year sentence; Winans received 18 months. These sentences are reported in "Boesky Sentence Ends Chapter in Scandal," Wall St. J., Dec. 21, 1987, p. 2. For a "post-Boesky" sentence, see "Wang, Former Morgan Stanley Analyst, Sentenced to 3 years for Insider Trading," Wall St. J., Oct. 27, 1988, p. A3 (3 year sentence against 24-year old analyst who made $200,000; government argued sentence appropriate because conduct took place after Levine and Boesky cases publicized). For a "where are they now" for fifty insider traders, see "After the Fall: Fates Are Disparate For Those Charged with Insider Trading," Wall St. J., Nov. 18, 1987, p. 1.

30. See Guidelines § 5C2.1.

31. Esquire Magazine, May 1987, at p. 76. Reprinted with permission.

New York, and a partner in a major law firm. He has four children and four grandchildren.

Judge Sweet had said he hoped that when Reich had served his term, Sweet's remarks might help get Reich reinstated to the bar.

"If that's in order, I wouldn't have any hesitation," he said. "This fellow is a good lawyer—even a brilliant lawyer. Some day, somebody will hire him."

But why jail? I asked. There were muggers and burglars and drug dealers out there getting off by plea bargaining, and no one seemed to think Ilan Reich was a threat to society.

"You have to set up a deterrent. Forty weekends of community service? That's not enough of a deterrent. If you're going to have laws on the books, then you have to have them obeyed. This fellow had been privileged by society, he went to Columbia Law School, he should have known better—he *did* know better, that's why he felt guilty enough not to take the money. He was a skilled lawyer, an interpreter of the laws."

"Are you holding lawyers to a higher standard than other people?" I asked.

"Maybe I am. Insider trading doesn't seem as bad to some people as burglary, because it doesn't involve a physical threat. And some economists, I know, say the whole notion is fallacious—that we should have *no* rules on insider trading. But we the judiciary don't make the laws, the legislature makes them. Once they're on the books, though, we have to enforce them or the system comes apart.

"Right now the laws on the books say that the public has to believe that markets are fair, and in order to sustain that faith, there has to be no information passed on what is not yet public information."

I asked Judge Sweet how he had decided the sentence.

"Every judge gets a report from a probation officer who investigates the accused," he said. "The probation officer investigated, and he said, 'This guy works—he works all the time—and that's all he does. He's a workaholic. I'm convinced he'll never do anything wrong again.' There are rough guidelines, and if he serves his time well, which I'm sure he will, he will be out in less than a year. But nonetheless, a jail, any jail, is a traumatic experience for an educated, upper-middle-class person."

* * *

Judge Sweet, in the courtroom, made these remarks: "Here is the crux of the problem: that element in our world which has abandoned all that we used to cherish—integrity and honesty—an element that ignores reality and the law of the land, an element which exalts form and discards substance, which is only for the appearance, and the appearance is success."

* * *

I asked him what he meant.

"Ilan Reich confused illusion and reality," he said. "He was seduced. He had an emotional need—he wanted to be part of the world he thought Dennis Levine represented, and he thought Levine really cared about him. But all Levine wanted was money."

Illusion and reality—an interesting phrase for a judge. I thought of all the situations in which many of us blur illusion and reality—the love affairs that end badly, the jobs, or the relationships within the jobs—that are not what they seem. A universal problem—but we do not go to jail for our mistakes.

"No, we don't," said Judge Sweet, "because somewhere there is a line we do not step over."

(3) *How Do We Judge Equality?* Consider *United States v. Rodriguez,* 496 F.Supp. 930 (S.D.N.Y.1980):

BRIEANT, DISTRICT JUDGE.

The Court has considered all papers filed in behalf of defendant in support of his motion for a reduction of sentence pursuant to Rule 35, F.R.Crim.P. Oral argument has been heard. . . .

[I]t should be noted that this sentence was imposed upon an adequate legal and factual foundation and the reasons therefor were fully stated in open court at the time. . . . When sentence was imposed, the Court distinguished this case from that of "the typical mail-sorter * * * who found a preprinted envelope addressed to the March of Dimes and it has quarters in it", finding those persons to be situational offenders but concluding that this defendant committed a calculated crime.

In a supplemental submission, counsel for defendant alludes to a non-custodial sentence subsequently imposed by this Court on September 4, 1979 in the unrelated case of United States v. Shulman, 78 Cr. 890–CLB (aff'd 624 F.2d 384 (2d Cir.1980):

> "I fervently believe that equality under the law invites comparisons. Very shortly after Mr. Rodriguez stood trial before Your Honor, one Max L. Shulman, Chairman of the Board of Mays Department Stores, was tried before you and convicted of offering a Ten Thousand Dollar bribe to a tax agent to reduce a tax assessment by some Four Million Dollars, in order to save about a Half Million Dollars in taxes. I am informed that Mr. Shulman also testified at his own trial, and that worthy gentleman was not suffering from any terminal ailments—except perhaps that of avarice—and that Your Honor saw fit to sentence that captain of commerce to a mere fine, and a suspended jail term of one year. I am informed that Mr. Shulman produced numerous letters from prominent members of the community and politicians, attesting to his various and sundry virtues as a merchant, philanthropist and civic leader. My client Mr. Rodriguez, a modest Puerto Rican mailman living on the lower east side, submitted no such testimonials of course, simply because he does not travel in the same circles as Mr. Shulman. Surely Your Honor must understand that a Nabob of commerce is almost required as a business proposition to cultivate the socially and politically prominent of this world.
>
> Disparity in sentences has always been a troublesome business for the community to understand. It is particularly vexing when this disparity cannot be explained on the basis that different Judges obviously have different views. In these two cases, Your Honor chose to incarcerate for a year and a half, a

very modest hard working first offender who had stolen a watch, but not impose any jail time to a millionaire who sought to enrich himself further still, by corrupting a public official.

There is rampant in the community the feeling that though all men are equal, the rich are more equal than the poor and that these latter ones fare much worse at the hands of sentencing judges. Should Mr. Rodriguez' sentence be permitted to stand as imposed, it might well prove perfectly the accuracy of the community's perception."

This Court shares the concern of counsel that the public shall perceive all this Court's judgments to be just, and does not ignore the current cant in the legal community about sentence disparity. Granted some sentence disparity probably exists in the courts of our nation. The affairs of men have never been conducted with perfection, they never will be, and we should keep striving in our pursuit of Justice. We recognize that sentence disparity when it exists is a serious evil, and all the more so, if as charged here, the claimed disparity favors a "philanthropist and civic leader," to the detriment of a "modest mailman." But at the end of the argument, all that a criminal can demand is a fair sentence, fair to himself and fair to organized society which is the victim of every crime. As noted above, the Court believes movant's sentence meets that test. The Court holds the same view about Shulman's sentence. . . . Only by reference to the entire record of Shulman's trial, including sentencing proceedings and the non-public confidential pre-sentence report, could a successful attempt to compare these two cases be made. Even after such an impracticable comparison, some nuances would be unnoticed.[32]

If the comparison should show that the Court was too lenient with Shulman, and it will not, does this require that a fair sentence in another case be reduced so as to compound one mistake with another? . . .

---

32. [Court's footnote 1.] The analysis of Shulman's case quoted above is factually incorrect even as to matters of public record. To begin with, Shulman, a 76 year old lawyer turned executive, did not "seek to enrich himself by corrupting a public official." The officials, employed in the Valuations Group for federal estate and gift tax audits, were already utterly corrupt. Through a private appraiser whom they used as a bagman, they solicited unlawful payments from executors and others. The amount of the bribe was fixed before the bagman ever solicited Shulman. A strong element of coercion was present in each case, in that excessively high appraisal values were proposed, accompanied by a representation on the part of the bagman that these figures could be reduced somewhat, but "they want to get paid". Of course this coercion did not excuse the payment. Defendant, a person of high standing in the community, could have complained to the authorities and should have done so. Neither Shulman nor his wife nor their children had any financial interest in the funds which would have been saved as a result of the bribe, had the conspiracy been successful. The tax which would have been saved had the bribe been successful was ultimately determined at $41,000.00 (Shulman sentencing minutes, p. 5). Shulman's isolated act was completely inconsistent with all of the positive elements of a long and productive life characterized by patriotic, civic and philanthropic effort, and devotion to duty and family. The probation report in Shulman's case recommended a non-custodial sentence.

It is too simplistic to suggest that because one malefactor has a higher profile than another, the former requires a sentence of greater severity than the latter. Nor should we drive from our Courthouse the concepts that under extenuating circumstances justice may be tempered with mercy, and that it is better to err, if error there be, on the side of lenity.

The motion is denied.

(4) *Examining Disparity in White Collar Crime Cases.* See Nagel and Hagen, The Sentencing of White–Collar Criminals in Federal Courts: A Socio–Legal Exploration of Disparity, 80 Mich.L.Rev. 1427 (1982), a study of 6,518 offenders sentenced in ten federal districts between 1974 and the end of 1977. The authors divided offenses, separating thirty-one "white collar" offenses (including antitrust, mail fraud and tax violations) from "common crimes"; divided offenders by education (college as the dividing line) and income ($13,777 as the dividing line); and assessed severity of the sentence based on various combinations of incarceration, probation, fines, and restitution. One of the districts (denominated "District III") was considerably more active than the others in the prosecution of white collar crimes committed by college educated offenders. The authors concluded:

> [S]etting aside for the moment jurisdictional comparisons, when we consider the sentences meted out in all ten jurisdictions taken together, controlling for all the independent variables, in addition to the white-collar of the offense and offender earlier identified, the purest form of white-collar criminality—college educated persons convicted of white-collar crimes—does not receive preferential treatment in terms of the decision to incarcerate or not (the In/Out decision) nor in terms of our measure of sentence severity. This is a most dramatic finding. Furthermore, only the category of college educated persons convicted of common crimes receives preferential treatment. This is only true when considering the length of sentence for those sentenced to a period of imprisonment. College educated persons sentenced for common crimes receive six months less time than their less educated counterparts similarly convicted of common crimes. At least for those convicted of common crimes, a college education appears to have some positive benefit.
>
> [T]he possibility of jurisdictional variation produces substantial departures from these results in District III. District III had a higher rate of sentencing of college educated persons convicted of white-collar crimes than all other nine districts. In fact, of all the college educated persons convicted of white-collar crimes across the ten districts, 25% were convicted and sentenced in District III, even though District III did not have the largest case base of the ten districts.
>
> In District III, unlike the case for all ten districts considered together, persons convicted of white-collar crimes, whether college

educated or not, fared better in sentencing outcomes than those convicted of common crimes, especially the less educated convicted of common crimes. The advantage of the less educated persons convicted of white-collar crimes becomes pronounced when considering the decision to imprison or not. Finally, persons convicted of white-collar crimes, in District III, whether college educated or not, received sentences more than two years shorter (24 + months) than the average term of imprisonment for the less educated person convicted of common crimes.

Three potential explanations may provide some insight into these findings. First, with respect to our finding of no preferential treatment for both college and less educated persons sentenced for white-collar crimes, across the ten jurisdictions, differences in the time, effort, and care in the prosecution of these cases may result in only the most egregious offenses of the most culpable offenders coming to the sentencing stage. Preferential treatment may occur at the earlier processing stages, but once the most serious offenders and offenses have been weeded out, the courts treat those remaining like all other cases.

Second, with respect to the marked contrast noted for District III, . . . a highly proactive attitude toward the prosecution of white-collar crime may lead to a higher rate of conviction coupled with a pattern of sentence leniency. We explain this by emphasizing that white-collar cases present special evidentiary problems and often involve multiple defendants, some of whom may testify for the state. In the bargaining for testimony, the government may exchange sentence leniency for needed evidence.

Third, our interviews with judges and United States Attorneys in District III lead to the identification of several factors that might contribute to increased convictions and lighter sentences. These factors include expanded manpower enabling more numerous prosecutions; a deliberate emphasis by the U.S. Attorney on public corruption, and sophisticated trial lawyers working closely with other law enforcement agencies. Judges in District III expressed considerable sentiment against imprisoning white-collar offenders, emphasizing many of the arguments for leniency that elsewhere evoke a greater skepticism. Preferential sentencing appears to be the price paid for expanded prosecution of white-collar crime.

The authors also provided these excerpts from interviews with judges in "District III" (at 1455 n. 90):

> [1] "We were suffering from a collective prosecutorial guilt about our inattention to white-collar crimes."
>
> [2] "The Justice Department saw a sophisticated judiciary here and an attitude of trustbusterism."
>
> [3] "Our judges are not going to wink away anti-trust cases. We love them . . . we find them challenging."

As to why the jurisdiction produces a high rate of convictions coupled with a pattern of preferential treatment at sentencing for white-collar criminality, the judges suggested:

> [1] "The white-collar offender can do community service . . . the postal guy stealing watches, what can he teach?"
>
> [2] "A badge of guilt is enough for a white-collar offender. He doesn't need jail. A badge of guilt doesn't, however, punish the nonwhite-collar offender."
>
> [3] "I start with probation. Jail is for violence, harm done to others, danger to hard working people. I identify with the victim. But also know the ramifications of punishment for establishment persons."
>
> [4] "If you give a white-collar guy a long sentence and he goes to the wrong place, he can't cope. They'll totally destroy the guy. The lower class, especially the recidivist, he can cope."

And finally, linking the preference for tough prosecution and modest sentences, one judge said:

> In blue-collar cases, you go after the defendant. In white-collar cases, you're after the system—the industry—the defendant may be less important. The sentence may be less critical than the processing—the prosecution. The publicity of the prosecution may achieve the desired impact. You don't need quite the Greek tragedy of a whole viking funeral.

GUIDELINE FOR ANTITRUST OFFENSES

§ 2R1.1. *Bid–Rigging, Price–Fixing or Market–Allocation Agreements Among Competitors*

(a) Base Offense Level: 9

(b) Specific Offense Characteristics

    (1) If the conduct involved participation in an agreement to submit noncompetitive bids, increase by 1 level.

    (2) If the volume of commerce attributable to the defendant was less than $1,000,000 or more than $4,000,000, adjust the offense level as follows:

	Volume of Commerce	Adjustment to Offense Level
(A)	less than $1,000,000	subtract 1
(B)	$1,000,000—$4,000,000	no adjustment
(C)	$4,000,001—$15,000,000	add 1
(D)	$15,000,001—$50,000,000	add 2
(E)	over $50,000,000	add 3

For purposes of this guideline, the volume of commerce attributable to an individual participant in a conspiracy is the volume of commerce done by him or his principal in goods or services that were affected by the violation. When multiple counts or conspiracies are involved, the volume of commerce should be treated cumulatively to determine a single, combined offense level.

* * *

Commentary

These guidelines apply to violations of the antitrust laws. Although they are not unlawful in all countries, there is near universal agreement that restrictive agreements among competitors such as horizontal price-fixing (including bid rigging) and horizontal market-allocation can cause serious economic harm. There is no consensus, however, about the harmfulness of other types of antitrust offenses, which furthermore are rarely prosecuted and may involve unsettled issues of law. Consequently, only one guideline, which deals with horizontal agreements in restraint of trade, has been promulgated. The controlling consideration is general deterrence.

§ 2R1.1 (15 U.S.C. § 1). The agreements among competitors covered by this section—such as horizontal price-fixing and bid-rigging—are almost invariably covert conspiracies that are intended to and serve no purpose other than to restrict output and raise prices, and that are so plainly anticompetitive that they have been recognized as illegal per se, i.e., without any inquiry in individual cases as to their actual competitive effect. The Commission believes that the most effective method to deter individuals from committing this crime is through imposing short prison sentences coupled with large fines. The guideline is designed with that purpose in mind.

Under the guidelines prison terms should be much more common, and usually longer, than is currently typical. Absent adjustments, the guidelines require confinement of four months or longer in the great majority of cases that are prosecuted, including all bid-rigging cases. The court will have the discretion to impose considerably longer sentences within the guideline ranges. It is the intent of the Commission that alternatives to imprisonment such as community confinement and home confinement not be available for antitrust offenders. Adjustments from Chapter Three, Part E (Acceptance of Responsibility) and, in rare instances, Chapter Three, Part B (Role in the Offense), may decrease these minimum sentences; nonetheless, in very few cases will the guidelines not require that some confinement be imposed. Adjustments will not affect the level of fines.

The guideline imprisonment terms represent a substantial change from present practice. Currently, approximately 39 percent of all individuals convicted of antitrust violations are imprisoned. Considering all defendants sentenced, the average time served is only forty-five days. . . .

Tying the offense level to the scale or scope of the offense is important in order to ensure that the sanction is in fact punitive and that there is an incentive to desist from a violation once it has begun. The offense levels are not based directly on the damage caused or profit made by the defendant because damages are difficult and time consuming to establish. The volume of commerce is an acceptable and more readily measurable substitute. . . .

The Commission believes that the volume of commerce is liable to be an understated measure of seriousness in some bid-rigging cases. For this reason, and consistent with current practice, the Commission has specified a 1 level increase for bid-rigging. Understatement of seriousness is especially likely in cases involving complementary bids. If, for example, the defendant participated in an agreement not to submit a bid, or to submit an unreasonably high bid, on one occasion, in exchange for his being allowed to win a subsequent bid that he did not in fact win, his volume of commerce would be zero, although he would have contributed to harm that possibly was quite substantial. The court should consider sentences near the top of the guideline range in such cases.

* * *

Because the guideline sentences depend on the volume of commerce done by each firm, role in the offense is implicitly taken into account. Thus, an increase for role under § 3B1.1 might be appropriate only where a defendant coerced others into participating in a conspiracy from which his firm did not profit significantly—an unlikely circumstance. Conversely, a decrease for role under § 3B1.2 would not be appropriate merely because a defendant's firm did not profit substantially. An individual should be considered for a downward adjustment for a mitigating role in the offense only if he was responsible merely for a small portion of his firm's participation in the conspiracy. For example, a complementary bidder who did not win a bid would not qualify for a downward adjustment.

Sentences at or even above the guideline maximum may be appropriate for individuals with previous antitrust convictions.

QUERIES

A critical aspect of the Antitrust Guideline is its stated goal of increasing the use of imprisonment in antitrust price-fixing and bid-rigging cases. How did the Commission decide that in this area it should not base sentencing ranges on past practice but should write a Guideline that would increase punishment? Does the Commission assume that past sentences have been inadequate for deterrence purposes? Does the Commission provide any empirical support for such a proposition? (Do you imagine that such support exists?) Might the continued existence of price-fixing be as much the result of a lack of aggressive prosecution by the government as it is an unwillingness by courts to impose jail time (as opposed to other sanctions)? Is the desire to make prison terms "much more common" consistent with views on the proper sanction for first time offenders (which most individual antitrust offenders are)? Review the provisions of the Sentencing Reform Act with regard to first time nonviolent offenders, and the Commission's general approach to this issue, supra.

Consider the question of the defendant's position in the corporation. Does the Guideline distinguish among defendants who are middle managers, high level executives, or those who have a substantial ownership interest in the corporation? Note that the Guideline by its terms is keyed to the volume of commerce "done by him or his principal in goods or services that were affected by the violation." There are separate Guidelines that account for "role in the offense" (§§ 3B1.1, 1.2, referred to in the Commentary, supra), but these appear to be aimed at the general role played by a particular defendant in a large conspiracy, rather than the role played by a defendant within a legitimate business enterprise. Do you think that corporate position should affect culpability?

Do you think culpability should be keyed to the volume of commerce? The absolute dollar amount does not indicate how successful a price-fixing or bid-rigging conspiracy was. Suppose the conspirators had made a very large profit on a small contract. Should the penalty be increased? Suppose, instead, that they made very little profit on a very large contract. Should the penalty be decreased? If the penalty should be keyed to economic harm, shouldn't we pay more attention to the exact amount of harm? On the other hand, is economic harm the key factor? If the conduct involved is bidding to government authorities (which often requires a sworn statement that the bidder did not engage in collusion), should the penalty be increased? Does the Guideline so provide?

Do you think that the antitrust Guideline is severe enough? Remember that the maximum specified by Congress is three years. Doesn't the Commission's Guideline make it virtually impossible to impose this maximum which, after all, was set by our elected legislators?

2. SENTENCING ALTERNATIVES

Jail is not the only sentence that a court can impose on an individual defendant in business crime cases. One obvious alternative (or additional sanction) is a fine. Note, for example, that the Guideline for antitrust offenses requires the court to impose a fine in addition to imprisonment.[33] Surely, however, courts can be more creative than just sticking to jail and fines. When faced with a defendant who poses little future danger to the community and who has skills not possessed by "common criminals," should judges seek alternative sanctions which

---

33. See § 2R1.1(c) (fine to range from 4% to 10% of the volume of commerce done by the defendant or his principal, with a minimum of $20,000). Theories for assessing fines are explored infra pp. 355–364.

are less costly to society than incarceration? The following materials explore some of these alternatives.

RENFREW, THE PAPER LABEL SENTENCES: AN EVALUATION
86 Yale L.J. 590 (1977).[34]

In October 1974, I imposed unorthodox and somewhat controversial sentences upon five corporate executives convicted of conspiring to fix prices in the paper label industry in violation of § 1 of the Sherman Act. Besides giving the defendants suspended jail sentences ranging from three to six months and fining them from $5,000 to $15,000 each, I required, as a special condition of probation, that each defendant "make an oral presentation before twelve (12) business, civic or other groups about the circumstances of this case and his participation therein" and "submit a written report to the Court giving details of each such appearance, the composition of the group, the import of the presentation, and the response thereto."

* * *

This article describes the reasoning underlying my imposition of the paper label sentences. It also discusses my effort to assess the impact of the sentences by eliciting comments from those who heard the defendants speak and from other members of the legal and business community. The purpose of the article is to contribute to the body of knowledge concerning the efficacy of sentencing decisions and to encourage other judges to become more active participants in evaluating the sentences they impose.

I. The Paper Label Sentences

A. The Offense

The paper label case involved a classic violation of the antitrust laws. The paper label industry manufactures the paper labels that are affixed to the containers of a variety of canned and bottled products. Many of the companies in the industry are small in comparison to their customers. The possibility that purchasers will shift to another more competitive supplier forces companies in the industry to keep their costs and prices as low as possible. In general, this is the type of economic situation that the competitive economic model predicts and that the antitrust laws seek to encourage.

Although such a market structure engenders remarkable efficiency, it places the businessmen involved under constant pressure to retain their market positions. As a result, no matter how strongly businessmen support competition in theory, they often tend to be considerably less enthusiastic when the competition is directed against their own

---

34. Reprinted with permission of The Yale Law Journal Company and Fred B. Rothman & Company from The Yale Law Journal Company, Vol. 86, pp. 590–617. Critiques of the Paper Label sentences by Antitrust Division lawyers, a private lawyer, a law professor, and a professor of law and sociology, follow at 86 Yale L.J. 619 (1977).

companies. Manufacturers of paper labels responded to the competitive conditions in their industry by expanding casual social contacts at trade association meetings to include the exchange of increasingly explicit information concerning pricing decisions and policies. These exchanges of information eventually resulted in a division of the market through pricing agreements. The scheme collapsed when a disgruntled former employee revealed the illegal practices, leading to a number of private treble damage actions and a criminal indictment.

. . . Before trial, all eight of the individual defendants moved to change their pleas from not guilty to nolo contendere. Because the private civil actions had preceded the criminal action in this case, and because the Government did not object to the change of plea,[35] I accepted the new pleas and proceeded to consider suitable sentences.

B. The Sentencing Decision

For me, this classic violation posed an extremely difficult sentencing decision. A sentencing judge's recognition that imprisonment may be a necessary response to criminal activity often creates a tension between his sense of duty to society and his concern for the individual defendant. In the instant case, this tension was especially great because, in my view, the only theory of punishment that could justify imprisoning the defendants was one of general deterrence.

All of the defendants were community leaders of previously unsullied reputation who held top executive positions in their corporations. My personal observation of the impact of the prosecution on these defendants convinced me that they did not present a threat of continued violations. Thus, imprisonment could not be justified in terms of such typical sentencing objectives as specific deterrence and isolation. Similarly, in-prison rehabilitation was not at issue because the defendants needed neither psychological counseling nor vocational training.

Retribution did not mandate the incarceration of the defendants because the hardship resulting from the prosecution itself and the fines that I intended to impose constituted sufficient expiation for the violations that had occurred. Being prosecuted placed a considerable emotional burden on the defendants. Furthermore, the cost of counsel had been great and had been borne individually, and the fines that I would impose were large relative to the defendants' ability to pay. According full weight to the societal importance of the antitrust laws—an importance emphasized by the recent enactment of the Antitrust Procedures and Penalties Act, which makes such violations felonies rather than misdemeanors [36]—I believed that the monetary exactions alone constituted firm and proportionate punishment.

35. [Footnote 7 in original.] In my experience the Government regularly opposes the entry of nolo contendere pleas to offenses that it believes are particularly serious. Thus, the Government's agreement to such pleas cannot help but have an important impact on the sentencing decision.

36. [Footnote 8 in original.] Despite the seriousness of antitrust violations, I find a blanket comparison between these crimes and other felonies inappropriate. I

* * *

General deterrence requires both that an unpleasant punishment be imposed upon wrongdoers and that the public have a relatively high degree of knowledge about the activities proscribed by law and the sentences imposed for its violation. After careful consideration, although not without reservation, I decided that the sentences I eventually imposed met these requirements. The emotional and financial burden of the prosecution, the fines imposed, and the defendants' embarrassment in appearing before groups of their peers as convicted criminals would supply the deterrent sting. The requirement that the individual defendants give speeches about their experiences promised greater public awareness of the demands of the law and the consequences of its violation. I expected that media coverage of the sentences would convey the same message to an even wider audience. Indeed, the communicative possibilities of the sentences struck me as their most desirable feature.

I would never advocate that a sentence be fashioned solely to create publicity. I do believe, however, that publicity can serve some of the more fundamental purposes of a criminal sentence. In cases such as this, where general deterrence is the principal purpose of a sentence, it is only logical to attempt to ensure that as many people as possible learn of the prosecution and punishment of the defendants. Violations may be deterred by increasing community awareness that a particular kind of unlawful conduct will be detected and that prosecution and conviction will follow. Moreover, the need for general deterrence appears particularly acute in the field of antitrust, for there seems to be a widespread feeling in the business community that antitrust violations often escape undetected and unpunished.

Of course, I could not be certain what general deterrent effect the paper label sentences would have. Without data to aid me, I relied on my own experience and judgment in designing the sentences I imposed.

II. Evaluating the Sentences

During the months subsequent to the sentencing, my actions were publicized in numerous news reports and feature articles—some highly critical. Although the amount of publicity far exceeded my expectations, it failed to satisfy my curiosity about the impact of my sentences

believe that crimes of violence are, in general, much more destructive of the fabric of society than are nonviolent commercial crimes. The butcher who routinely charges his customers an extra quarter for the weight of his thumb on the scale surely abuses his position. Over time, his activities may result in an economic loss to his customers far exceeding the "take" of an average bank robbery, and, if discovered, his dishonesty would undoubtedly create mistrust and anger among his customers. Yet, however reprehensible the butcher's conduct may be, I feel certain that it entails a smaller social cost than would result if each of his customers were stopped at gunpoint and robbed of a quarter several times a week for the same period of time. Violent crime massively disrupts and distorts the daily social intercourse among human beings upon which any viable society depends. While the two kinds of crime may have a similar economic impact, and may both instill some apprehension in the public, the psychological effect of violent crime is clearly more pernicious.

on the audiences who had listened to the defendants speak and on the legal and business community at large. Therefore, in the fall of 1975 I began systematically to gather evidence pertinent to an evaluation of the sentences.

I designed a questionnaire and sent it to all business, civic, and educational groups that heard one of the presentations. . . . I also solicited by letter the views of many individuals who did not hear the defendants but who are involved with and concerned about antitrust. . . . To facilitate analysis of the data, the questionnaire respondents were divided into two categories. "Category one" included those employed in the business or financial communities; "category two" included attorneys, academics, students, editors, and others less likely to be affected directly by the antitrust laws in the conduct of their own affairs. Fifty-seven respondents constituted the first category and 42 the second. In addition, I received replies to my letter from 18 of the attorneys in the case, 7 other attorneys, 7 federal judges, and 12 law professors. These nonaudience responses were examined separately from the more structured responses elicited by questionnaire.

My inquiry did not employ statistically rigorous techniques of data collection and interpretation. The results, therefore, should not be taken for more than what they are: an impressionistic canvass of the views of people in various walks of life about the sentencing of white-collar criminals.

* * *

The Respondents' Attitudes Toward Antitrust Violations and Penalties

* * *

[T]he responses reveal two inconsistencies. First, although virtually all respondents considered antitrust violations to be serious or moderately serious, only about two-thirds felt antitrust violators deserved to be imprisoned. Second, although two-thirds of the respondents supported imprisonment of antitrust violators in general, virtually none of the respondents thought such a penalty was appropriate in the paper label case.

* * *

. . . The remarks of one respondent, an insurance broker, are particularly illuminating:

> At the dinner meeting where [the defendant] made his talk, I shared a table with about six other people. All said that at one time or another they had engaged in the practices that resulted in [the defendant's] sentence. Two of them (both personally known to me as decent and ethical men) expressed their dismay that on that very day they had engaged in a conversation about a job that one had lost to the other in a bid situation which would have put them in violation of the law, as [the defendant] explained it to us. I have often heard that "ignorance of the law is no excuse," but I feel that maxim must be tempered in times like ours. The body of law is growing at an alarming (and, in my opinion, an unnecessary) rate.

When, despite the best efforts of trade associations, attorneys, accountants and insurance advisors, two honest businessmen can break the law without knowing it, we have a situation that needs correcting. Had my friends been "caught in the act" and received sentences anything [like the defendant's], I would have considered it a gross miscarriage of justice.

[T]he respondents' inclination toward less stigmatizing sentences may have stemmed from their identification with the defendants they heard and their consequently profound appreciation of the costs of criminal liability. Personal exposure to an individual being punished for violating the antitrust laws clearly had a significant impact. Several respondents stressed, for example, that they were impressed by "the anguish that [the speaker] suffered with his family," and the "personal feeling of the speaker's loss of peace of mind and well-being during the entire episode." One respondent wrote:

I consider the opportunity of hearing this man tell his story as a very positive one. It is a long way from headlines in a paper to the thoughts in the mind of the individual involved in the story. The headlines are soon forgotten, but the severe effect on the individual involved, as told by him, will remain for a long time.

Another summarized his views succinctly: "Having seen this man in person impressed me more than *reading* about 10 men having been convicted of violating the anti-trust laws." Several respondents stated that the very thought that they might ever have to make such speeches themselves was truly frightening. It was probably sentiments like these that underlay one of the more striking results of the inquiry: although three-quarters of all respondents stated that they believed the stigma associated with antitrust violations would be increased if the offenders were sentenced to prison, 65% of those in category one and 55% of those in category two stated that prison would be less effective than the paper label sentences in preventing similar offense by others in the future.

The Effect of the Sentences on the Respondents' Business Practices

The highly personal reactions to the speeches often had a practical impact upon respondents' business affairs. Respondents were asked: "What changes, if any, have occurred in your business practice as a result of the speech?" A significant number indicated that the presentation they heard heightened their awareness of the antitrust laws and prompted a review and intensification of their compliance procedures.

[T]he presentations [also] appear to have generated an effort by members of the audiences to convey the defendants' message to others. One respondent, for instance, stated that although he himself had not changed his business practices, he had "related the speech to other businessmen as a warning." A university instructor said that he had tape-recorded the speech and now replays it in each of his classes in basic marketing. . . .

The Letter Responses

* * *

Judges

A . . . wide range of opinion is reflected in the letters received from judges. Two judges declined to express an opinion about the sentences imposed, one believing he lacked sufficient information to assess the sentences, and the other remarking how uncertain we all are in this area: "All things considered, I come out enrolled as student rather than teacher." Two judges viewed the sentences favorably. One stressed that, in his view, "compliance with your sentences was humiliating, perhaps more humiliating than a short prison sentence quietly served out of public view," but also noted that it was his customary practice to impose short prison sentences—two weeks or five weekends, for example—upon income tax violators. Another judge was particularly impressed by the speechmaking requirement, indicating that he might impose similar sentences if an appropriate occasion arose.

Three other judges were in substantial disagreement with the sentences. One voiced a concern mentioned by several others, namely, that businessmen who violate the law must not be treated preferentially. . . .

Professors

The final group whose opinions I solicited consisted of professors in the fields of antitrust, criminal law, and business administration. Eleven professors responded. Their letters display less general agreement with the sentences than the responses of any other group. This is not to say that all of them believed that all antitrust violators should be incarcerated. In fact, three of them were quite adamantly opposed to imprisoning antitrust violators. . . .

* * *

. . . Several professors wrote that "new and imaginative sanctions are needed in antitrust cases," and that it is "commendable for a judge to explore alternatives to incarceration which will achieve a similar deterrent effect upon others." But the consensus was neatly summarized in the following comment: "Although I applaud your effort to find a more suitable penalty and deterrent, I confess considerable doubt that a repeated mea culpa is sufficient."

Finally, the remarks of one law professor, who arranged for one of the defendants to address his antitrust class and was thus uniquely situated to evaluate one of the presentations first-hand, are thought provoking. Having explained his own belief that short periods of incarceration are necessary and appropriate in price-fixing cases and that the sentences in the paper label case were ill-designed, he stated:

> I find it even more difficult to form any judgments as to the effect of the presentation given by the individual defendants pursuant to your sentences. The gentleman who talked to my class was chastened and shaken by his experience. In one sense he did not deny

at any time that he had discussed prices with his competitors and had violated the law; and yet at the same time the tenor of his presentation was that he had not really been fully aware that anything so customary amounted to a legal violation. And he was at pains to explain to the class again and again that such conduct really was illegal. Reactions among the class varied: some were skeptical of his implied naivete, and were slightly hostile in their questioning. Others quite plainly felt sorry for him. But in legal terms, this was an atypically sophisticated audience. It is very difficult for me to guess what the impact of his presentation would have been at a Rotary luncheon or a meeting of the local Chamber of Commerce. My uncertain guess is that the listeners would not have come away with increased insight into the wisdom of the rule prohibiting price fixing or even with deepened resolve that they themselves would never let themselves drift into such circumstances.

Conclusion

* * *

A frequent criticism of the sentences stemmed from a perceived disparity between the treatment of "common criminals," such as those who steal welfare checks or engage in minor embezzlements, who are routinely sent to prison, and white-collar criminals, who are not. I share this concern, but I do not feel it applies to my sentencing. Although I judge each case individually, I rarely impose prison sentences upon first offenders convicted of nonviolent crimes—regardless of the color of their collars.[37] I cannot and will not adapt my sentencing practices to conform to those of other judges, particularly to those that I consider overly harsh.

Were the sentences successful in terms of general deterrence? I cannot be certain. To be sure, the speeches succeeded in stimulating some stronger compliance measures by certain businessmen; but the key question—and the one impossible to answer—is whether those compliance efforts would have been more or less vigorous if the sentences had included incarceration.

This study provides some guidance for judges who may impose such sentences in the future. Closer judicial supervision may be necessary to ensure that the speeches accurately describe the conduct for which the defendant was criminally penalized. Furthermore, judges may wish to require the defendant to address audiences concerned with the laws that were violated.

37. [Footnote 32 in original.] I frequently do impose prison sentences upon first offenders convicted of certain serious crimes, such as widespread trafficking in a controlled substance like heroin. I do not, however, view narcotics distribution as a nonviolent crime. A large-scale drug dealer and his organization routinely engage in violence to safeguard and carry out their operation, and their product inevitably invades the physical and psychological integrity of its consumers.

NOTES AND QUERIES

(1) *Queries.* Consider how the various rationales for imposing criminal punishment influenced Judge Renfrew's decision. Was it necessary for him to choose between deserts and deterrence, or did he believe that his sentence could satisfy both? Did you agree with his view of the seriousness of economic crimes as compared to crimes of violence (see n. 36, supra)? Does the Sentencing Commission? With regard to general deterrence, do you think that this will be the most likely reason for sanctioning business crime violators? If so, does this call for less use of imprisonment in such cases?

(2) *Community Service.* See Fried, "Zaccaro's Punishment Is a Gift for Three Groups," N.Y. Times, March 9, 1986, p. 43: [38]

Over the last year John A. Zaccaro, the husband of Geraldine A. Ferraro, has gone through a decayed building on the Lower East Side and given advice on how it could be turned into an emergency shelter for troubled youths.

He has helped assess the heating and plumbing systems in two other Manhattan buildings used as long-term housing for the homeless. And he has advised tenants of buildings abandoned by their landlords how to manage them themselves.

Mr. Zaccaro, a real estate owner and manager, has provided these services for free as part of the 150 hours of community service he was sentenced to in February 1985 for his admitted involvement in a fraudulent real estate deal. He could not be reached for comment on his community service. Telephone calls to his Manhattan office were answered by associates who said he was not in. The calls were not returned.

"I'm delighted I was able to get him," said Angel Rodriguez, executive director of the Andrew Glover Youth Program, one of the three groups Mr. Zaccaro was directed to assist.

The program is receiving his advice on a building at 100 Avenue B that it plans to rehabilitate into a shelter and counseling facility for delinquent youngsters.

"All the reports I have received have reflected that he has performed well," Acting Justice George F. Roberts of State Supreme Court in Manhattan said of Mr. Zaccaro's community service.

Justice Roberts sentenced Mr. Zaccaro after he pleaded guilty to a misdemeanor charge of scheming to defraud in the second degree. Prosecutors said he had submitted a false sales contract, an altered appraisal and a misleading statement of net worth in connection with a Queens real estate deal intended to yield millions of dollars for him and several associates.

The transaction was among the activities of Mr. Zaccaro that came under scrutiny when his wife ran as the Democratic Vice Presidential candidate in 1984. The offense carried a penalty of up to a year in jail and a $1,000 fine. But under a plea agreement the Manhattan District Attorney's office did not seek a jail term.

---

38. Copyright © 1986 by The New York Times Company. Reprinted by permission.

Mr. Zaccaro has completed about 115 hours of his community service, according to officials.

He has met his original 50-hour requirement with the Glover program, raising money, as well as giving advice on rehabilitating the Avenue B building, according to Mr. Rodriguez. He said Mr. Zaccaro "even got his wife involved with us. She cracked a bottle of champagne on the door of the building to signify the start of construction."

Mr. Zaccaro has completed about 40 of his 50 hours with St. Francis Friends of the Poor, helping it determine heating, plumbing and other improvements needed in the two Manhattan residences it operates, according to the group's vice president, the Rev. John McVean.

He said Mr. Zaccaro had not completed all 50 hours because "we asked him to hold off" so he could advise the group on renovating a third building it is buying.

Mr. Zaccaro has also performed 25 of his 50 hours with the Legal Aid Society, advising its tenant clients and lawyers on operating buildings abandoned by landlords, said Patricia Bath, a society spokesman. . . .

(3) *House Arrest.* Consider *United States v. Murphy*, 108 F.R.D. 437 (E.D.N.Y.1985): [39]

SENTENCING OPINION

WEINSTEIN, CHIEF JUDGE.

The sentencing of Maureen Murphy requires, in the court's opinion, a sentence not heretofore used in this District and almost never used in the country in the federal court. It is used elsewhere in the world and is considered by some to be highly objectionable. The difference, however, is that in other countries it is used to repress political dissent and before trial. Here it will be used after a full trial where the defendant has been found guilty of a serious offense.

The penalty is home detention. Respect for public opinion, the need to explain the reasons for the sentence to the defendant and others and the desirability of providing data for the Federal Sentencing Commission just appointed by the President require a more extensive statement than usual.

After a full trial Ms. Murphy was found guilty of a violation of the Racketeer Influenced and Corrupt Organizations Act (RICO), mail fraud and obstruction of justice charges. For many years as confidential secretary to Norman Teitler, a lawyer, she assisted in committing frauds against insurance companies and helped obtain inflated medical and other expenses following auto accidents. When the Grand Jury began its investigation she attempted to induce key witnesses to change their testimony.

---

39. The sentence is discussed in Note, House Arrest: A Critical Analysis of an Intermediate–Level Penal Sanction, 135 U.Pa.L.Rev. 771 (1987), and Rangel, "Two-Year House Arrest Instead of Jail Term is Ordered for Fraud," N.Y. Times, Sept. 24, 1985, p. 1 (Chief Probation officer applauds sentence as "more humane and economical"; estimates costs of house arrest at $3,000 per year).

Obviously these crimes are serious. They threaten the very foundation of the effective administration of justice in polluting the sources of information available to the Grand Jury. In addition, the corruption of the civil litigation process by lawyers, doctors and others cannot, and will not, be condoned or tolerated.

A sentence such as this must be approached with some general philosophical background.

The prison population in this country is approaching one-half million. Cost estimates of $30,000 a year and upward per prisoner are common. The direct costs are thus in the order of $15 billion a year.

All agree that longer prison terms, and imprisonment for more and more persons cannot be borne indefinitely. Other controls to prevent crime, social policies to avoid criminality and alternative punishments are essential.

* * *

[W]e turn to the defendant's background. . . . In total, she is subject to $56,000 in fines and 50 years in prison. She is now 35 years old, a high school graduate. She attended local parochial schools. She was raised in a close-knit, harmonious and religious family setting by hard-working parents. Her father was a New York City Sanitation Department Engineer. She studied at secretarial schools and is, by all accounts, an excellent and bright worker who has always been steadily employed. Her assets are $150.00 in a savings account and a 1976 Pontiac. She has never been married and lives alone.

Her attorney and she, of course, plead for mercy. The government, in a letter dated September 20, 1975, has taken the unusual step in this District of urging a term of incarceration and the maximum allowable fine. It writes:

> Maureen Murphy was not simply a secretary following instructions of her boss. The evidence showed Maureen Murphy to be a longtime, trusted member of this criminal venture, who attempted to protect that venture when it came under investigation by obstructing the work of the grand jury.
>
> We emphasize the seriousness of these offenses and the flagrantly corrupt nature of the enterprise for which this defendant worked for so many years. This case involved a corruption of the legal process by those charged with its protection. Maureen Murphy was a willing, knowing and active participant in that corruption. Accordingly, the government believes that an appropriate sentence for Maureen Murphy should include a term of incarceration and the maximum allowable fine.

Obviously the maximum fine could never be paid and would accomplish nothing except to make it impossible for the defendant to live and rehabilitate herself. The maximum terms of imprisonment provided by the statutes are much too long to even be considered seriously for this relatively young person who has never, so far as we know, committed another crime.

Putting her in prison for any substantial length of time will undoubtedly help to destroy her. The conditions of imprisonment, even in the best prisons for women, are reprehensible.

Accordingly, the court assesses a fine of $5,000 payable as Probation directs over the next five years. It sentences the defendant on Counts 2, 10 and 27 to 5 years on each count, concurrent, suspending execution of sentence and placing her on probation. Home detention is a condition of the probation on Counts 2, 10 and 27.

* * *

The defendant will be required to remain in her apartment, or other place of abode. She may not change her residence without the consent of Probation. She may leave only as permitted by Probation for medical reasons, employment and religious services and essential shopping for food and the like. She may go directly to and from her job and may seek a new job only as permitted by Probation. She is at all times subject to strict supervision, to surprise visits by Probation and strict control.

* * *

Should the defendant not comply strictly with Probation's orders, she will be ordered to serve out her prison term. She is reminded that the prison term is now suspended, not cancelled.

There will be some who will believe that this sentence is much too lenient. Others will believe it too humiliating. Public humiliation is a part of the punishment. Obviously there is serious danger of depression and worse in the case of home detention. Probation will arrange for suitable psychiatric and other appropriate services for defendant to forestall such problems.

In many respects the colonial use of stocks and equivalent punishment in other societies served a useful goal in providing swift social disapproval as a deterrent. It is obvious that some form of this disapproval is required under modern conditions. How it can be accomplished is not clear. Obviously we will not tolerate branding and the carrying of signs. The matter is a difficult one and will require experimentation and modification of procedures in the light of experience.

[Omitted is an Appendix prepared by the Probation Department describing home detention.]

(4) *Alternative Sanctions Under the Guidelines.* The Guidelines permit a court to order community service or house arrest, either as a

condition of probation or as a condition of supervised release.[40] The major difference between the Guidelines' approach and the approach described in the above Notes is that these punishments may not be used in lieu of a term of imprisonment unless the minimum Guidelines sentence is six months or less (Offense Levels 1 to 10).[41] When the minimum Guidelines sentence is more than six months but less than twelve (Offense Levels 11 and 12), at least half the minimum must be served in jail. Once the minimum Guidelines sentence reaches 12 months (Offense Level 13), a judge must impose a term of imprisonment between the minimum and maximum sentence specified, unless the judge decides to "depart" from the Guidelines. The judge may still impose community service or house arrest as a condition for "supervised release" after the jail term is served; but the jail term is required.

Query. Are the Guidelines overly harsh in refusing to permit alternative sentences as substitutes for imprisonment? Or is this the inevitable result of a system which seeks to eliminate disparities and provide determinate sentences? Given Congress' goals, could you have a system which required, say, a sentence of imprisonment between 24 and 30 months, but then allowed the judge to suspend all of it and place the defendant on probation?

(5) *Occupational Restrictions.* Business crime offenders generally have good jobs; indeed, their jobs often put them in position to commit the offense for which they stand convicted. Would deprivation of their position be more severe punishment than any sentence of imprisonment could be? Consider the following Guideline (§ 5F5.5). Would you use it in insider trading cases? Could Judge Sweet have used it in the *Reich* case, supra?

    (a) The court may impose a condition of probation or supervised release prohibiting the defendant from engaging in a specified occupation, business, or profession, or limiting the terms on which the defendant may do so, only if it determines that:

        (1) a reasonably direct relationship existed between the defendant's occupation, business, or profession and the conduct relevant to the offense of conviction;

        (2) there is a risk that, absent such restriction, the defendant will continue to engage in unlawful conduct similar to that for which the defendant was convicted; and

        (3) imposition of such a restriction is reasonably necessary to protect the public.

    (b) If the court decides to impose a condition of probation or supervised release restricting a defendant's engagement in a

---

40. See Guidelines §§ 5F5.2, 5F5.3. "Supervised release" is virtually identical to probation, except that it follows a term of imprisonment whereas "probation" cannot be ordered if a term of imprisonment is imposed. See 18 U.S.C.A. § 3561(a)(3).

41. Note that if the minimum sentence is between one and six months (Offense Levels 7 to 10), some term of "intermittent confinement" or "community confinement" will also be required.

specified occupation, business, or profession, the court shall impose the condition for the minimum time and to the minimum extent necessary to protect the public.

Commentary

The Comprehensive Crime Control Act authorizes the imposition of occupational restrictions as a condition of probation or supervised release. . . .

. . . The Senate Judiciary Committee Report on the Comprehensive Crime Control Act explains that the provision was "intended to be used to preclude the continuation or repetition of illegal activities while avoiding a bar from employment that exceeds that needed to achieve that result." S.Rep. No. 225, 98th Cong., 1st Sess. 96–97. The condition "should only be used as reasonably necessary to protect the public. It should not be used as a means of punishing the convicted person." Id. at 96. Section 5F5.5 accordingly limits the use of the condition and, if imposed, limits its scope, to the minimum reasonably necessary to protect the public.

(6) *Where Do They Go to Jail?* Under the Guidelines, more business crime offenders will spend more time in jail. Where will they be put? Consider Wilson, "Where the White–Collar Inmate Stays," N.Y. Times, May 29, 1988: [42]

There are no cells or perimeter walls at the Federal Prison Camp at Lompoc, where Ivan F. Boesky, convicted of insider stock trading, is serving a three-year sentence. At the minimum-security prison, a continent away from Wall Street and 150 miles north of Los Angeles, inmates live in former Army barracks lined with bunk beds and cots, sleeping 6 to 40 men per room. Head counts are taken daily, but the harshest visible restriction for the camp's 615 inmates seems to be a "Keep Off the Grass" sign.

The Lompoc camp, one of 20 Federal minimum-security prisons, was home to Watergate alumni H.R. Haldeman, Donald Segretti, Dwight Chapin and John Dean. The sentencing of Mr. Boesky last spring refocused attention on the question of why such camps are appropriate for white-collar criminals—people convicted of fraud, embezzlement, forgery, counterfeiting and regulatory offenses—who, arguably, can do society far more damage than inmates in the maximum-security penitentiaries who were convicted of violent crimes. In any case, Federal officials say, as the prison population in the United States grows, the country may rely more and more on the minimum-security camps.

The camps are often called country-club prisons or "Club Feds," but many criminologists say the boredom and lack of true freedom in a spartan setting is punishment even if it is not harsh. For example, Lompoc's recreational facilities—weight rooms, a single concrete tennis court and an out-of-repair bocce ball alley—are not as good as those at many maximum-security prisons, officials said.

42. Copyright © 1988 by The New York Times Company. Reprinted with permission.

But among Lompoc's inmates, the camp is considered "the outside." What they call "the inside" is the Federal Penitentiary across a grassy field from the camp. The penitentiary's guard towers and double row of barbed fences remind the camp inmates of how fortunate they are.

The mix of relative freedom and dull routine at the prison camps, where inmates work eight-hour days at a slaughterhouse, dairy or garden, and where inmates can earn paid time off from their jobs much as people on the outside receive paid vacations, illustrates what some sociologists say are the contradictions in the American penal system. There is an unclear urge, they maintain, to both punish and rehabilitate.

When not working, Lompoc inmates are free to watch television, exercise or read almost any publication they can afford to subscribe to. Theoretically, they could also spend every free minute either on the telephone or waiting to use one. Calls are limited to 15 minutes each, but the number of calls they are allowed to make is unlimited, provided the inmate goes to the back of line between calls. The prisoners eat in a rather austere cafeteria where the menu recently included selections such as "liver fiesta."

Citing, among other factors, calls for stiffer punishment of white-collar criminals and of people convicted on drug-related crimes—the two most common groups of camp occupants—Government officials say that the population of the Federal prison system is expected to nearly double to 87,000 by 1995. To accommodate the rise, officials say that the Federal system will increasingly rely on minimum-security camps, which on average cost half as much to operate as more secure prisons, where the annual cost per prisoner can climb to $30,000.

Safety for some prisoners also makes the camps a necessity, some experts say. Henry N. Pontell, a criminologist at the University of California at Irvine, said that putting the average white-collar convict—about 29 percent of those at Lompoc—into a maximum-security prison "would be like sentencing the guy to death." "He wouldn't last two days," Mr. Pontell said. People who commit crimes with phone calls and fountain pens would, it is presumed, not mix well with violent criminals. . . .

Dennis E. Curtis, a law professor at the University of Southern California who has worked with camp inmates, suggests that the looser discipline of the minimum-security prisons can actually be more stressful than the tightly structured regime of penitentiaries. "In a pen, you know the rules," Mr. Curtis said. "In a camp, it's not so clear and there's more room for inmates to rat on each other."

C. ENTITY SANCTIONS

SCOPE NOTE

For entity sanctions, the question is: What can be done? The accepted remedy is a fine; but how much should the fine be? If it is too low, it takes on the appearance of a license fee. If it is too high, it might end up unfairly penalizing innocent shareholders or employees (recall the argument made in *New York Central,* supra). If fines are unsatisfactory, however, do we have any alternatives?

The materials in this Section are organized around the issues of fine setting and alternative entity sanctions. In contrast to the situation for individuals, the Sentencing Commission has so far promulgated only one Guideline for organizational sanctions (for antitrust). Thus, our discussion begins by examining a general approach to organizational sanctions proposed by the Commission, but not yet adopted. This approach is based on an economic theory of punishment; it downplays sanctions other than fines. Accordingly, our study of sentencing alternatives for entities moves beyond the proposals of the Sentencing Commission, examining court decisions on corporate probation and the suggestions of various commentators with regard to alternative entity sanctions.

1. FINES

UNITED STATES SENTENCING COMMISSION, DISCUSSION DRAFT OF SENTENCING GUIDELINES AND POLICY STATEMENTS FOR ORGANIZATIONS
(July 1988).

* * *

2. *Principles for Determining an Organization's Sentence*

The draft sentencing guidelines and policy statements embody three basic principles: (a) a total monetary sanction is determined by multiplying the loss caused by the offense times a "multiple" representing the difficulty of detecting and punishing the offender, and adding enforcement costs; (b) non-monetary sanctions are added as necessary to reinforce the monetary sanctions; and (c) criminal and civil sanctions are coordinated.

a. *Monetary Sanctions*

The draft sentencing guidelines and policy statements for organizations rely primarily on the monetary sanctions for both the compensatory purpose of restitution to victims and the punitive purposes of deterrence, just punishment, and crime control. The total monetary sanction—for both compensatory and punitive purposes—is determined from three major factors based on the organization's offense conduct: (1) the "offense loss," based on the total harm (and risk of harm in some instances) caused by the offense; multiplied by (2) the "offense multiple," based on the difficulty of detecting and punishing the offender; plus (3) enforcement costs. The resulting "total monetary sanction" is then distributed among the sentencing options of restitution, forfeitures, and fines.

(1) *Offense Loss*

The "offense loss" includes both the losses to immediate victims and the more general societal losses from organizational offenses, translated to the monetary terms necessary to compute a monetary sanction. For most organizational offenses, the major part of the translation is direct, because the offenses primarily cause economic or monetary losses.

The focus on "offense loss," rather than some other measure such as offender's gain, rests on the rationale that organizational punishment is most appropriately based on the losses created by criminal conduct—to both immediate victims and society as a whole—that the criminal law seeks to prevent. An offender's gain may be a very poor measure of those harmful effects. Some offenses may produce a very small gain and a much larger loss, and nearly all offenses produce less gain than loss. Therefore, a penalty system based primarily on gain often will fail to provide the appropriate incentives for compliance, particularly for organizations that must expend resources to control their agents, and ultimately may produce penalties that are disproportionate to the harmful potential of offenses. The offense loss measures society's interest in controlling the criminal conduct, which is prohibited not because it might confer a gain on the offender, but rather because of its harmful effects on others.

Similarly, the draft guidelines reject the use of an organization's size or financial performance as a principal measure of penalties. The size of an organization may affect the scope of criminal activity and thereby the amount of offense loss, and size or financial resources may affect an organization's ability to pay a loss-based penalty. However, large organizational size alone does not necessarily render an offense more harmful in terms of loss or detectability, and is neither prohibited nor disfavored by the law in general. As with gain, penalties based primarily on size would distort the central focus of the criminal law on harmful effects.

* * *

For offenses involving deceptive or involuntary transfers of property or other economic values, such as fraud and theft, the size of the transfer is the principal component of loss. . . .

* * *

Loss guidelines for environmental and food and drug offenses involve statutes designed to prevent harms or risks of harm to health and safety that often are diffuse and difficult to identify to specific victims. For this type of offense, the guidelines specify higher minimum loss amounts designed to recognize the risks inherent in this type of criminal conduct, and use loss rules based on the reasonable costs of eliminating the risks created by the offense plus property or economic damage. Where the personal safety of identifiable victims is threatened, there is provision for a further increase to reflect the expected loss resulting from such risks.

(2) *Offense Multiple*

The second major factor, the "offense multiple," is determined by the difficulty of detecting and prosecuting the offense, including the offenders' conduct in concealing the offense or impeding enforcement. The multiple is designed to insure that the total monetary sanction is set at a punitive level that will serve the sentencing purposes of deterrence and just punishment. For both purposes, offenders should not be encouraged to gamble on the possibility that they might escape punishment at the expense of their victims, and society at large. Offenders should face an expected sanction that reflects the difficulty of enforcement.

* * *

(3) *Enforcement Costs*

The third major factor in determining monetary sanctions is an estimate of the reasonable expenses of investigating and prosecuting of the offense, and carrying out the monetary sanctions. Enforcement costs represent an additional societal loss caused by the offense, for which the offender should be held accountable.

(4) *The Total Monetary Sanction*

The offense loss multiplied by the offense multiple, plus enforcement costs, equals the total monetary sanction for an organizational offense. That total sanction is then distributed among the sentencing options of restitution, forfeitures, and fines.

First, an order of restitution to victims is required in all cases where restitution is feasible and does not duplicate an available civil or administrative remedy providing compensation to victims. The primacy of compensation to victims in all cases carries out the statutory direction that federal courts consider "the need to provide restitution to any victims of the offense" as a factor in sentencing all federal offenders. 18 U.S.C. § 3553(a)(7).

Second, forfeitures are to be imposed as required by law. . . .

Third, the remainder of the total monetary sanction, after deducting victims' compensation and criminal forfeitures, is the midpoint of the guideline fine range. Within that range, the court may select a fine based on all pertinent sentencing factors. The court's discretion is supplemented by policy statements regarding general rules for departures, the need to consider the passage of time between the crime and its punishment, and several aspects of coordinating the criminal fine with collateral penalties, including sanctions imposed upon the organization through civil or administrative procedures, penalties imposed against the agents of the organization who were responsible for the organization's offense, and penalties imposed against other joint offenders. The intent of the policy statements on collateral penalties is to promote the objective of an appropriate total penalty where multiple sanctions for the same conduct are available.

NOTES AND QUERIES

(1) *Understanding the Theory.* The proposed Guidelines' approach is deterrence based; in the Commission's words, the approach "seeks to provide organizations with measured incentives for assuring their compliance with federal law." To better understand the theory behind the

Commission's proposed solution, consider the following excerpt from R. Posner, Antitrust Law: An Economic Perspective 221–27 (1976):[43]

> The way in which we deter an activity is by making it costly to engage in, and a key question is: how costly? We could fine antitrust violators $1, or hang them. How do we decide what the proper punishment is? The answer depends in the first instance on the gravity of the offense. As a first approximation, the penalty for an antitrust violation should be such as to impose on the violator a cost, whether in pecuniary or nonpecuniary terms, equal to the cost that his violation imposed on society. This criterion is not derived from notions of symmetry or from the biblical notion of "an eye for an eye." It is a criterion of efficiency—and hence an especially appropriate one to use in designing remedies for antitrust violations. If the penalty for violating the antitrust laws were less than the cost of the violation to society, the potential violator, in deciding whether to commit a violation, would reckon the cost to him (the punishment cost, since he presumably cares nothing about the consequences of his conduct for the society at large) at a figure lower than the social cost. This would result in an excessive amount of unlawful activity, just as a divergence between private and social cost will lead to an excessive amount of pollution. If, on the other hand, the penalty for a violation is set at a level higher than the social cost of the violation, we may have too little unlawful activity: some illegal acts will be deterred that confer benefits on society greater than the costs they impose.
>
> * * *
>
> I have said that the penalty should be designed to place the social costs of the violation on the violator. It is easy to jump to the conclusion that the penalty should be equal to those costs, but this conclusion would be incorrect in those cases where the violation was concealable. If, because of concealability, the probability of being punished for a particular antitrust violation is less than unity, the prospective violator will discount (i.e., multiply) the punishment cost by that probability in determining the expected punishment cost for the violation. The result will be to drive a wedge between the social cost of the violation and the private cost to the violator, unless the punishment cost is appropriately higher than the social cost. For example, suppose that the social cost of a particular price-fixing conspiracy is $1 million, but the probability of the conspirators' being apprehended and punished is only .25. If the fine is set at $1 million the conspirators, assuming they are risk neutral,[44] will discount the fine by .25, which yields an expected

---

43. Reprinted with permission.

44. [Footnote 4 in original.] An individual is risk neutral if he is indifferent as between an expected cost (or value) and its certain equivalent. Thus, a risk-neutral individual would be indifferent as between a 1 percent chance of having to pay $100 and the certainty of having to pay $1. A risk-averse individual would consider himself worse off if forced to accept the expected choice rather than its certain equivalent, while a risk preferrer would react the opposite way. Corporations are generally assumed to be risk neutral since any

punishment cost of only $250,000—far below the social cost of the conspiracy. The correct fine is calculated by *dividing* the social cost of the violation by the probability of apprehension and punishment. In the last example this would yield $4 million, the optimal fine.

I have spoken thus far as though the social costs of price fixing . . . could be determined without difficulty. This is of course not the case. In price-fixing cases the courts have used as their measure of cost the difference between the competitive and collusive price, multiplied by the number of units sold at the collusive price during the relevant time period. This is an incorrect measure because it leaves out the cost resulting from the reduced output of the monopolist. It would not be insuperably difficult to measure this additional cost; the only additional information that is necessary is the elasticity of demand at the collusive price.

* * *

Compared to the scheme of antitrust remedies described above, the actual remedial scheme found in the antitrust statutes leaves much to be desired. There is, to begin with, the unnecessary and therefore inappropriate reliance on the criminal sanction, including imprisonment (now for as long as three years). Imprisonment should be regarded as a sanction of last resort, in general and with particular reference to antitrust. First, it is difficult to translate a monetary sum (the costs of a particular price-fixing conspiracy, say) into a nonpecuniary cost—so many days in prison. The effort to do so is almost certain to lead to excessive leniency. Second, imprisonment is a much costlier sanction for society to administer than the collection of a fine. Imprisonment consumes real resources, not the least of which is the legitimate production of the imprisoned individual, which is lost during his term of imprisonment. Fines involve no such waste. Apart from (ordinarily slight) collection costs, the entire loss to the defendant who is fined is offset by an equal benefit to the taxpayers (or whoever else receives the fine). A fine is a transfer payment that only negligibly reduces the aggregate wealth of the society. Not so with imprisonment: the cost to the defendant of being imprisoned is a deadweight loss to society.

Where violators are judgment-proof, society is compelled to resort to imprisonment or some other method of nonpecuniary sanction despite the advantages of the fine. But inability to pay

riskiness involved in the corporation's business can be eliminated or minimized by the individual shareholder; he can combine his shares in the corporation with other shares or other assets so as to create a portfolio that will be as risky or as risk-free as he desires, and therefore the corporation needn't worry about its shareholders' attitude toward risk. Of course, if the corporation's managers are not running the firm in the shareholders' interest—a popular, though unverified, theory—their personal attitudes toward risk may become relevant in determining the impact of antitrust sanctions containing various amounts of risk. However, nothing essential in my analysis would be affected by modifying the assumption of risk neutrality utilized in the text.

judgments is not a problem in the antitrust field. True, individuals are frequently joined as defendants in antitrust suits—the individuals who participated actively in whatever violation the corporate defendant is accused of having committed—and, although they are a good deal more affluent than the common criminal, they might sometimes be unable to pay judgments measured by the social costs of their violations. But I consider this a detail, for it is in general unimportant whether the individual corporate employees are joined as defendants in antitrust cases. A corporation has effective methods of preventing its employees from commiting acts that impose huge liabilities on it. A sales manager whose unauthorized participation in a price-fixing scheme resulted in the imposition of a $1–million fine on his employer would thereafter, I predict, have great difficulty finding responsible employment, and this prospect would appear to be sufficient to exert a substantial deterrent effect, one at least comparable to the generally light individual fines and very short prison sentences of existing law.

(2) *Three Details.* (a) If there is an optimal fine which will produce the correct amount of deterrence (not too much and not too little), how should one account for additional punishment imposed on corporate employees? Note that the Guidelines already require that an individual defendant be fined "in all cases." [45] Given this mandatory fine, plus a fine to be imposed on the corporation, how, theoretically, would the rational potential offender react? Will the individual add the two penalties together before deciding on the improper behavior, and therefore be overdeterred? (And how does imprisonment fit in? Will this further increase overdeterrence?) The Draft Organization Guidelines recognize this problem with the theory, and provide for a downward adjustment in the corporation's fine equal to the monetary penalty "incurred by the individuals responsible for the organization's participation in the offense." The Draft Guidelines also permit a reduction to account for the imprisonment of responsible agents; the amount of the reduction is "the lost value to the organization of the agent's services." [46]

(b) The Draft Organization Guidelines propose adjusting the multiple for characteristics which increase the difficulty of detecting the offense (increase the multiple) or which decrease the difficulty of detection (decrease the multiple). One of the "detectability characteristics" which increases the multiple is active participation by senior management; one which decreases the multiple is "the commission of the offense by open and obvious conduct." [47]

(c) As the Posner excerpt, supra, indicates, the value assigned to the "multiple" is critical for producing the correct amount of deterrence. The Draft Organization Guidelines choose a multiple of 2.0 for

---

45. See Guidelines § 5E4.2. The only exception is where the defendant is unable to pay or the fine would unduly burden the defendant's dependents. See § 5E4.2(f).

46. See § 8C5.6 (Draft Proposal 1988).

47. See § 8B3.2 (Draft Proposal 1988).

"private fraud offenses and property offenses substantially affecting identifiable private victims." The multiple is raised to 2.5 for "all other offenses." [48] The accompanying commentary indicates that the higher multiple would be applicable to government fraud, regulatory reporting offenses, environmental offenses, and food, drug and agricultural offenses.

(3) *Queries.* (a) Do you accept the "deterrence-only" punishment rationale of the Draft Guidelines? Review the materials on corporate criminal liability in Chapter 2. Is a deterrence-only philosophy consistent with the reasons for imposing substantive corporate criminal liability? If you think that fines should reflect other goals (particularly deserts), how would you alter the results chosen by the Commission in the "Three Details" described in Note (2), supra?

(b) In describing its proposed approach to organizational sanctions, the Commission writes: "With few exceptions, organizational defendants in the federal courts are business corporations, which are motivated primarily by monetary profit and loss. Monetary sanctions have the most direct impact on a business firm's fundamental interest." [49] What Model of the corporation is implicit in this approach? How would a different Model affect the penalty structure? Would it necessarily affect the fines structure?

(c) Is a single approach appropriate for all organizations? When you read the proposed Guidelines, what size and kind of corporation were you thinking of? Did you have a major industrial corporation in mind? A brokerage firm? A road paving firm owned only by family members? Should the fines structure take account of the differences among these various potential defendants? Is an equal sized fine appropriate for business firms with different amounts of assets? For people with different amounts of assets? Note that the Sentencing Reform Act provides that in determining the amount of a fine, a court "shall consider" the defendant's "income, earning capacity, and financial resources" and "if the defendant is an organization, the size of the organization." [50]

(d) Is it more appropriate to base fines on losses to society or gains to offenders? Judge Posner, supra, argues that economic theory requires the former measure. The Draft Guidelines agree. Will this measure produce high fines or low fines? For example, what would be the "optimal" fine for a waste disposal firm whose medical waste is illegally dumped and washes up on vacation beaches in the summer? What would be the optimal fine for a payment to a foreign official in violation of the Foreign Corrupt Practices Act? How about for the sale of bootlegged Elvis Presley records? Would basing the fine on gain to the offender work equally well as a deterrent? Would the fines likely be lower? Is "gain" equivalent to "profit"? If the Commission seeks to

---

48. See § 8B3.1(a) (Draft Proposal 1988).

49. Draft Guidelines at p. 8.1.

50. See 18 U.S.C.A. § 3572.

make crime unprofitable, wouldn't it be more theoretically correct to key fines to profits?

(e) The Criminal Fine Improvements Act of 1987, 18 U.S.C. § 3571, amended the Sentencing Reform Act (it is reproduced above). Is there any hope of truly carrying out the theory behind the Draft Guidelines in light of the limits this Act places on fines?

(4) *Collateral Consequences.* A major problem for a theory of fines is taking account of the collateral consequences of a criminal conviction. Collateral consequences may include debarments by federal, state, and/or local governmental agencies (often the result in government fraud or bid-rigging cases); disqualification for certain business licenses; treble civil damages; or (as E.F. Hutton discovered, for example) an effect on business reputation impossible to predict or prevent. These penalties vary more by offender than offense, thereby creating potential disparities in effective sentences. Indeed, it may be that these collateral penalties are more severe than any maxima set as a criminal penalty.

The Draft Organizational Guidelines include a policy statement indicating that a court should consider lowering the fine if collateral penalties are "significantly higher" than is "ordinarily" the case: "For example, if a government fraud was fully and voluntarily reported, and the offender fully cooperated in the investigation and prosecution of the offense, but nonetheless was debarred from government contracting for several years and paid treble damages plus civil penalties equal to another multiple of the loss under the Civil False Claims Act, a large criminal fine on top of the other remedies plainly would be inappropriate."[51] Do you agree?

(5) *Equity Fine.* Is it best to levy fines in dollars? Could we think of a better way to make illegal conduct "unprofitable" (so as to effect deterrence) without punishing innocent shareholders. Consider this proposal from Coffee, "No Soul to Damn: No Body to Kick": An Unscandalized Inquiry Into the Problem of Corporate Punishment, 79 Mich.L.Rev. 386, 413 (1981):[52]

> The time has come for a basic policy assertion: when very severe fines need to be imposed on the corporation, they should be imposed not in cash, but in the equity securities of the corporation. The convicted corporation should be required to authorize and issue such number of shares to the state's crime victim compensation fund as would have an expected market value equal to the cash fine necessary to deter illegal activity. The fund should then be able to liquidate the securities in whatever manner maximizes its return.
>
> This strategy reduces the earlier encountered obstacles to adequate corporate deterrence: (1) the overspill of corporate penalties to workers and consumers is reduced, and the costs of deter-

---

51. See § 8C5.5 (Draft Proposal 1988).   **52.** Reprinted with permission.

rence are concentrated exclusively on the stockholder; (2) in turn, the nullification phenomenon may be reduced, since the latent threat to employees and the community dependent on the corporation that a cash fine carries is no longer present; (3) much higher penalties (in terms of total monetary value) can be imposed, because the market valuation of the typical corporation vastly exceeds the cash resources available to it (with which a cash fine might be paid); (4) the manager's self-interest is better aligned with that of the corporation because the resulting per-share decline in the corporation's common stock following such a penalty will reduce the value of stock options and other incentive compensation available to him; (5) the manager will fear that the creation of a large marketable block of securities makes the corporation an inviting target for a takeover; and (6) the typical stockholder's apparent focus on short-term profit maximization will now have to take into account the risks of illegal behavior; accordingly, the stock value of legally "risky" companies will predictably decline, and stockholders will begin to demand increased internal controls within corporations to reduce such legal exposure. . . .

* * *

. . . For example, the consequence of an equity fine equal to 25% of the outstanding shares after the fine should be to reduce the value of each shareholder's investment in the corporation by 25%. A cash fine in a similar amount would very likely cause bankruptcy or, at the least, a considerably greater decline in the market value of the corporation's shares because of the corporation's reduced capital. In other words, because cash fines reduce the corporation's ability to weather future financial reversals and to undertake new opportunities, the risk of bankruptcy increases, its prospects for growth falter, and investors will discount its shares (to reflect the increased risk) to a degree that is greater than the proportionate dilution incident to the equity fine.

* * *

[Another] consequence of an equity fine is to place a large marketable bloc of the corporation's securities in the hands of the trustee who manages the victim compensation fund. This in turn raises a possibility that the convicted corporation will become the target of a hostile takeover. To the aggressive corporate suitor, such a bloc supplies the necessary toehold acquisition from which to launch a tender offer or other campaign for control. Empirically, it is evident that incumbent managers fear takeovers and take elaborate precautions against them. Thus, to the extent that the equity fine raises the probability of a takeover, we create a sanction—which is virtually costless to society—by which to dissuade corporate managers from criminal behavior. Predictably, where senior management sees its own position in office threatened by the criminal behavior of subordinate middle management officials, it will install greater internal controls than when the only consequence is a modest cash fine to the organization and possibly the criminal prosecution of the subordinate. . . .

2. PROBATION

UNITED STATES v. MISSOURI VALLEY CONSTRUCTION COMPANY

United States Court of Appeals, Eighth Circuit, en banc, 1984.
741 F.2d 1542.

[Digest: Missouri Valley Construction Co., a subsidiary of Peter Kiewit Sons', Inc., pleaded guilty to a two-count indictment charging a violation of the Sherman Act arising out of highway construction bid-rigging. The district court imposed a $1 million fine on each count. The defendant moved the district court to reduce the sentence to a $100,000 fine plus probation. The terms of probation would be to contribute $1.4 million to the University of Nebraska Foundation, either to endow a professorship in ethics or to fund the construction of an addition to the University's College of Engineering and to establish a permanent program of seminars on ethics in business and engineering. The district court reduced the fine to $325,000 and placed the corporation on probation for five years on condition that it contribute $1.475 million to endow a chair in ethics at the University of Nebraska. The chair could not be named nor in any way identify the source of the funds; no officer of the defendant or its parent could participate in administering the chair or endowment; and the contribution would not qualify for any income tax deduction. The defendant and its parent were also ordered to adopt a policy for detecting and reporting bid-rigging and were required to conduct an annual seminar on antitrust compliance.

The United States objected to the payment to the University of Nebraska as a condition of probation.]

BRIGHT, CIRCUIT JUDGE.

This case presents the narrow question whether a federal district court may impose on a willing corporation as a condition of probation, in lieu of a fine, the requirement that it contribute money to a charitable organization that has not suffered actual damages or loss from the corporation's criminal offense. We conclude that the district courts lack authority to impose such conditions of probation. We overrule the decision of a panel of this court in United States v. William Anderson Co., 698 F.2d 911 (8th Cir.1982), insofar as it authorizes the district courts to direct a defendant, as a condition of probation, to pay money to entities that did not suffer actual damages or loss resulting from the defendant's offense.

* * *

The power of the federal courts to suspend sentences and place defendants on probation arises entirely from statute; it is not inherent in the courts. The probation statute, 18 U.S.C. § 3651, gives the trial court wide discretion to fashion probationary conditions appropriate to each case. It provides that the trial court,

> when satisfied that the ends of justice and the best interest of the public as well as the defendant will be served thereby, may suspend the imposition or execution of sentence and place the defendant on probation for such period and upon such terms and conditions as the court deems best.

The statute elaborates upon this general grant of discretion, however, by specifying a number of different conditions of probation that the trial court may impose. With respect to monetary payments, the statute provides that,

> While on probation and among the conditions thereof, the defendant—
>
> May be required to pay a fine in one or several sums; and
>
> May be required to make restitution or reparation to aggrieved parties for actual damages or loss caused by the offense for which conviction was had; and
>
> May be required to provide for the support of any persons, for whose support he is legally responsible.

Though the statute does not expressly forbid the imposition of other kinds of monetary payments than those enumerated, several considerations lead us to conclude that the enumeration should be construed as a limitation on the authority of the courts to exact monetary payments as a condition of probation.

Initially, we are guided by the general principle of statutory construction, which other courts have applied to section 3651, that where a statute contains both general and specific language on a subject, the specific language governs. In section 3651, Congress has with notable specificity defined two permissible categories of money-payment conditions of probation, in addition to the imposition of a fine. First, the sentencing court may require the defendant to make support payments, but only to those "for whose support he is legally responsible." Second, restitution or reparation may be required, but it is to be paid "to aggrieved parties," and it is limited to "actual damages or loss caused by the offense for which conviction was had."

* * *

. . . The consistent strictness with which the courts have applied the provisions in question leads us to conclude that the only monetary payments permissible as conditions of probation are those expressly authorized by the statute: payments to the treasury (fines), to persons for whose support the defendant is legally responsible, or to aggrieved parties who suffered actual damages or loss caused by the offense for which conviction was had, in the amount of such damages or loss.

Both the Fourth Circuit and the Tenth Circuit have reached the same conclusion in cases closely similar to this. In United States v. Wright Contracting Co., 728 F.2d 648, the Fourth Circuit vacated the sentences of two corporations that had pleaded guilty to highway construction contract bid-rigging in Maryland. In one instance, the district court rejected the government's proposed $200,000 fine, imposing instead a $400,000 fine, all but $50,000 of which was suspended on the condition that the defendant corporation contribute $175,000 to a jobs program sponsored by the City of Baltimore. In the other instance, the district court imposed a $40,000 fine, suspending all but $10,000 on the condition that the defendant corporation contribute an additional $10,000 to a charitable organization to be recommended by the probation department and approved by the district court. The Fourth Circuit vacated both sentences, observing that, even though the district court characterized the payments as deterrent and rehabilitative, rather than restitutional or reparative, in nature, they had the effect either of punishing the corporation or of compensating the public at large in some way for the harm the defendants had caused. As the Fourth Circuit construed section 3651, the district court was limited, when exacting monetary payments as punishment, to ordering the payment of a fine to the treasury, and when exacting monetary payments as recompense to those harmed by the defendants' crimes, to ordering payment to parties actually damaged by the offense for which conviction was had, in the legally determined amount of such damage.

In United States v. Clovis Retail Liquor Dealers Trade Association, 540 F.2d 1389, the Tenth Circuit reviewed the sentence imposed on a number of defendants, corporate and individual, who pleaded nolo contendere to indictments charging Sherman Act violations. The district court sentenced each defendant to the maximum statutory fine, $50,000, but suspended the fines on condition that the defendants pay specific amounts (in most cases less than $50,000) as "community restitution" to a nonprofit organization devoted to educating the public about alcoholism. The Tenth Circuit reversed because the record did not show that the recipient organization had been aggrieved by the defendants' Sherman Act violations, or that it had suffered losses, as a result of the violations, equal to the amount it was to receive.

Finally, in United States v. Prescon Corp., 695 F.2d 1236, the Tenth Circuit vacated the sentences imposed on two corporations that pleaded nolo contendere to charges of rigging construction bids. The district court was held to have exceeded its authority under section 3651 in suspending the defendants' fines of $252,000 and $302,000, respectively, on condition that they deposit with the court $50,000 and $75,000, respectively, to be disbursed to community agencies selected by the chief probation officer and approved by the district court. The Tenth Circuit construed section 3651 to limit the district court, in exacting monetary payments as conditions of probation, to ordering those kinds of payments specifically enumerated in the statute.[53] Payments to the

---

53. [Court's footnote 8.] We do not think that United States v. Mitsubishi International Corp., 677 F.2d 785 (9th Cir. 1982) stands for a contrary proposition. In *Mitsubishi*, a number of corporate defendants pleaded guilty to violating railroad freight tariffs imposed under the Elkins Act. The district court imposed the statu-

court for disbursement to community agencies clearly did not, in the eyes of the Tenth Circuit, constitute restitution or reparation to aggrieved parties that had suffered actual damages or loss from the offense for which conviction was had, in the amount of such damages or loss.

The payment to the University of Nebraska Foundation ordered in this case likewise meets none of the statutory criteria. In particular, the Foundation suffered no actual damage or loss from Missouri Valley's bid-rigging, nor does it appear that the amount in question—$1,475,000—is related in any way to the amount of harm caused by the defendants' offense. (Rather, the amount is related only to the amount of the fine in lieu of which it is exacted.) We conclude that the district court lacked authority under the statute to order payments to the University of Nebraska Foundation in this case.

* * *

Finally, some considerations of public policy lead us to conclude that the courts should not direct criminal defendants, as a condition of probation, to pay money to private entities that did not suffer damages or loss resulting from the defendants' offenses. The courts are ill-equipped to pick and choose, among countless worthy causes, which nonaggrieved charitable organizations should receive large sums of money that would otherwise be paid to the treasury as fines. In the absence of clearer authorization from Congress, we reject the concept here that the general grant of discretion in section 3651 empowers the courts to dispense largesse to nonaggrieved parties, however worthy their activities. The involvement of the courts in the selection of the recipients of such benefits raises, additionally, the prospect of conflicts of interest and unnecessary criticism of the courts. . . .

Our decision in this case does not call into question the validity of corporate probation generally, or of the imposition as conditions of probation the requirements that individual defendants perform charitable or community service work, that corporate employees perform such work as part of a corporate defendant's probation, that corporate defendants or their employees (including employees of parent or subsidiary corporations) conduct activities to educate the public, or that corporate employees (including those of parents or subsidiaries) receive

tory maximum fine, $20,000 on each count, but suspended all but $1000 (the statutory minimum) on each count on the probationary condition that each corporate defendant loan an executive for one year to the National Alliance for Business's Community Alliance Program for Ex–Offenders ("CAPE") and contribute $10,000 to CAPE for each count on which the corporation had entered a guilty plea.

On appeal, the corporate defendants contended that the terms of probation, including the loan of the executives, were unlawful because, taken together, they were more punitive than the maximum fine authorized by statute. The Ninth Circuit held that, viewed as a whole, the sentence did not impose a harsher penalty than that authorized by the Elkins Act, because if the defendants regarded compliance with the terms of probation as more burdensome than payment of the statutory maximum fine, they were free to pay the fine. The court expressly declined to consider whether the terms of probation were themselves proper. *Mitsubishi* therefore does not hold that the probation statute authorizes monetary payments to nonaggrieved third parties.

instruction on compliance with the law or subscribe to a statement setting forth corporate compliance policy.

* * *

Reversed and remanded.

HEANEY, CIRCUIT JUDGE, concurring and dissenting.

I concur in the result reached by the majority and join in Judge Gibson's dissenting opinion. I would go one step further and sustain payments to charitable foundations or educational institutions under the guidelines set forth below.

The present practice of punishing corporate crime with fines paid to the United States Treasury has done little to deter corporate crime. Once the payment is made to the Treasury, the public promptly forgets the transgression, and the corporation continues on its way, with its reputation only slightly tarnished by what it usually describes as a "highly technical violation." On the other hand, if a corporation is required to fund a chair in corporate ethics at a distinguished university as a condition of probation, and if the chair is identified as one funded through an involuntary contribution, there is at the very least a strong probability that there will be an improvement in corporate conduct both in the near and long term. Probation conditions similar to those imposed here are used daily for individual defendants. These conditions are generally recognized as being effective in deterring crime and bringing benefits to the communities that have been harmed by the transgression.

We err greatly in shutting the door on probationary conditions of this nature for corporate defendants. To be sure, there are potential problems. The judge must be careful to avoid any conflicts of interest and must make sure that posterity will understand that the chair was established by court order to punish illegal and unethical conduct. But we give district court judges broad discretion in scheduling and trying cases. We are even more loath to interfere with their sentencing discretion, frequently sustaining sentences that we feel are entirely too long. Why then does the Justice Department and a majority of this Court insist on tying the hands of the district courts when it comes to imposing conditions of probation on corporate defendants, when the statutes do not require such restrictions? It seems to me that, in reality, we do so for two reasons: first, in a shortsighted effort to protect government revenues derived from criminal fines, and second, out of an inordinate fear that our district court judges will not have the wisdom to avoid possible conflicts of interest. Neither reason is sufficient for me.

JOHN R. GIBSON, CIRCUIT JUDGE, with whom HEANEY, CIRCUIT JUDGE, joins, concurring in the result and dissenting.

* * *

Contrary to the point of view of the Court today, the broad discretion placed in district courts to tailor probation to the particular circumstances in each case was recognized in Burns v. United States,

287 U.S. 216, 220, 53 S.Ct. 154, 155, 77 L.Ed. 266 (1932). Other courts have held that the conditions enumerated in section 3651 are not exclusive but are simply "among the conditions" which may be imposed; and . . . the legislative history of the act supports the reading that it is not exclusive but provides only general guidelines.

The shortcoming of the probation imposed on Missouri Valley is that. . . . there is no connection between the payment of money and programs in which individual corporate officers will be involved as a part of their probation. What we have in Missouri Valley is simply the payment of money to a designated charity, without any tie to the probation of the individuals. . . .

The sentence in *Missouri Valley* illustrates the particular abuse that is possible when a district court orders payment of funds to an entity other than the governmental institution or the party directly damaged. The record is plain that the Chairman of the Board of Peter Kiewit Sons', Inc., the corporate parent of Missouri Valley, has close ties with the University of Nebraska. The Chairman serves on several boards or committees of the University of Nebraska Foundation. The University of Nebraska was proposed by Missouri Valley as the beneficiary of these payments. I have no difficulty in concluding that there was an abuse of discretion in allowing the corporate defendant to choose a favorite beneficiary for the receipt of these funds. The selection in this manner runs contrary to the purpose of imposing punishment on the defendant.

For these reasons I agree with the holding of the Court today. My dissent is limited to the overruling of *Anderson.*

ROSS, CIRCUIT JUDGE, took no part in the consideration or decision of this case.

NOTES AND QUERIES

(1) *Charitable Contributions Under the Sentencing Reform Act.* The Sentencing Reform Act repealed the Federal Probation Act involved in *Missouri Valley,* replacing that statute with new provisions relating to probation. One section explicitly permits courts to sentence organizations to a fine, or probation, or both.[54] Probation is thus an additional sanction under the Act, not just a substitute for a fine. The Sentencing Reform Act also requires that if probation is imposed, the court must impose at least one or more of the following as a condition of probation: fine, restitution "to a victim," or "work in community service."[55] Finally, the Act has a list of discretionary conditions, ending with "such other conditions as the court may impose." (These provisions are reproduced supra, p. 301.)

Given these statutory provisions, would the result in *Missouri Valley* now be different? Can you make any arguments based on the language of the Sentencing Reform Act in contrast to the Probation

---

54. See 18 U.S.C.A. § 3551(c).   **55.** See 18 U.S.C.A. § 1863.

Act? The legislative history of the Act is not revealing. Although *Missouri Valley* was decided before the Sentencing Reform Act was passed (as were other similar cases striking down charitable contributions as a condition of corporate probation), there is no indication that Congress was either aware of this interpretation of the Probation Act or had formed any view with regard to the propriety of this particular condition of corporate probation.[56]

(2) *The Purposes of Corporate Probation.* Assuming that the Sentencing Reform Act does not explicitly state whether charitable contributions are a proper condition of probation, is the approach to probation in *Missouri Valley* excessively narrow? What are the purposes of corporate probation? Are we only concerned that corporations pay fines to the Treasury and restitution to victims? Can probation achieve other goals with regard to organizational offenders? Review the purposes of sentencing set out in the Sentencing Reform Act, 18 U.S.C.A. § 3553(a)(2), reproduced supra, p. 298. Can you think of any conditions of probation beyond fines and restitution that could meet these purposes?

(3) *Just Desserts.* In *United States v. Danilow Pastry Co.,* 563 F.Supp. 1159 (S.D.N.Y.1983), six major wholesale bakeries in the New York City area were charged with violating the Sherman Act by conspiring to fix the prices of pastry over a period of approximately fifteen years. The district court accepted the corporations' pleas of nolo contendere and imposed fines on each. Portions of each corporation's fine were suspended, however, on condition that the corporation deliver a certain amount of fresh baked goods each week for one year to designated charitable organizations. Danilow Pastry, for example, was sentenced to pay a fine of $162,400; the amount over $100,000 was suspended if Danilow donated weekly $1200 worth of baked goods (using wholesale prices). The designated recipients were Catholic Charities, Citymeals-on-Wheels, Manhattan Youth Residence Center, Pleasantville Cottage School of the Jewish Child Care Association, Community Food Bank, Coalition for the Homeless, Salvation Army, Federation of Protestant Welfare Agencies, Westside Churches Service Alliance, and the New York Philanthropic League. The Government objected to the sentences, arguing (as in *Missouri Valley*) that the donation of pastry was "restitution" under the Probation Act and that the court was accordingly limited to providing it to aggrieved parties in the amount of their actual damages. Judge Edelstein disagreed. He characterized the donations as "community service," and wrote:

> In formulating its sentences, the court sought punishment that would compensate for the reduced deterrent effect of the nolo pleas. After reviewing the extensive financial data submitted by the parties, the court determined that fines substantial enough to achieve the appropriate measure of deterrence would bankrupt the

---

56. See Rush, Corporate Probation: Invasive Techniques for Restructuring Institutional Behavior, 21 Suff.L.Rev. 33, 65–66 (1986) (discussing arguments on interpretation of Sentencing Reform Act; legislative history silent on issue).

corporate defendants. Such a sentence would cause widespread unemployment among the bakeries' employees,[57] damage the economies of the communities in which the plants are located, and ironically, diminish competition. Hence, this is precisely the overly harsh sentence that the Probation Act was designed to avoid.

The sentences have avoided this harsh result, and at the same time have increased the deterrent effect beyond that which would have been provided by fines. These sentences help compensate for the reduced deterrence inherent in the acceptance of the nolo pleas. In addition, criminological literature has shown that symbolic restitution that reaffirms the community's standards is an important element of general criminal deterrence.[58] Finally, deterrence is fostered by the publicity garnered by the sentences.

Rehabilitation and specific deterrence against future price fixing by the six corporations is also enhanced in that the executives and workers of these companies will be made aware, on a continuous basis throughout the next twelve months, of the violations perpetrated by their company, of the need for restitution, and of the need to guard against similar violations in the future. See Fisse, Community Service As A Sanction Against Corporations, 1981 Wis.L.Rev. 970, 977 (1981).

* * *

After determining that community service was the best way to promote these goals, the court then had to determine who would be the beneficiaries of this community service. The court was aware that compensation for many of the defendants' customers had already been arranged through the settlement reached in the private actions. The court [therefore] selected, as beneficiaries, organizations that serve the public in order to further the public awareness and rehabilitative nature of the punishment and to provide symbolic restitution to the community. . . .

* * *

57. [Court's footnote 14.] See e.g., Exhibit B of the Sentencing Memorandum on Behalf of Ernst Ostreicher and the Danilow Pastry Co., Inc. including: letter of Michael Sandroff, Secretary–Treasurer of the Bakers' Union Local 3, dated October 19, 1982 (estimating that 500 Bakers' Union members would lose their jobs if the defendants were forced out of business, and that because of the members' lack of general skills they would be unlikely to find other employment); letter of Murray Gorgo, Business Agent of the Paper Box Makers' Union Local 299, dated October 20, 1982 (stating that Danilow Pastry Co., Inc. alone employs twenty-two of the Union's members, who are mostly unskilled, minority workers and who would be unlikely to find other employment if laid off); and letter of Stanley Berman, Collective Bargaining Representative of the Bakery Drivers' Local 802, dated October 22, 1982 (stating that eighty-one of the Union's members are employed by the defendants and that they would be hard-pressed to find employment elsewhere if laid off, and that they would lose substantial parts of their pensions, which are accrued but still unpaid).

58. [Court's footnote 15.] United States v. William Anderson Co., 698 F.2d 911, 913 (8th Cir.1982); Emil Durkheim, The Division of Labor in Society. Simpson trans. (1933), pp. 108–9; Gahringer, Punishment and Responsibility, 66 J. Philos. 291, 291–93 (1969).

. . . [T]he government asserts that the distribution of baked goods must be confined to organizations that were "injured" by the defendants' price fixing activities.[59] Moreover, the government contends that such restitution may not exceed the actual damages sustained by each organization as a result of the defendants' price fixing activities.

* * *

Were this court to adopt the government's position, then its ability to devise flexible sentences in the interests of justice would be severely curtailed. Any community service condition can be given a monetary value. Under the government's logic any such condition could arguably be limited by the restitution section. Such a construction would severely impede judges from . . . "creative" sentencing . . . .

* * *

. . . Even assuming arguendo that the sentence is controlled by this limitation, the court for two reasons finds the amount of the community service permissible. First, the government lacks standing to complain that the amount of an order of restitution is excessive. Second, the court finds that the amount of damages can not accurately be determined. The value of the community service required, however, even if added to the amount of the negotiated settlement in the private antitrust cases, is well within the actual damages sustained by the consuming public over nearly two decades of price fixing.

CONCLUSION

* * *

These sentences are designed to achieve the following objectives: 1) deterrence, 2) rehabilitation, 3) incorporation in the resolution of this case of as many components of a guilty plea as possible, 4) preservation of jobs at the defendants' plants, and 5) compensation of aggrieved parties. It is also hoped the donations will bring some sweetness to hungry people who probably have missed more than one opportunity to buy the defendants' products because the price, illegally set by the defendants, was too high.

* * *

. . . The government's contention that the beneficiaries of the community service ordered herein must be "aggrieved parties" within the meaning of § 3651 is rejected.

SO ORDERED.

Query. Are you convinced that the pastry donation can be termed "community service"? Note that community service is a recognized condition of probation under the Sentencing Reform Act.

---

59. [Court's footnote 19.] The government does not indicate . . . exactly what beneficiaries would qualify as "injured" parties, but it implied at the sentencing hearing that organizations that serve the needy public in the defendants' market area would not.

(4) *Limits on the Cost of Probationary Conditions.* How much pastry could Judge Edelstein have required the defendants to donate? Should the amount be limited by the statutory cap on fines? In *United States v. United Cigar Co., Inc.,* 801 F.2d 555 (1st Cir.1986), the Court of Appeals, per Judge Breyer, vacated a sentence which, in addition to the maximum fine, placed the corporation on probation (the conditions of probation required the corporation to file monthly financial statements and a sworn certificate that the defendant had not made any kickbacks). The Court indicated that probation could be imposed only as a substitute for some or all of the statutorily authorized fine or imprisonment and thus could not exceed those limits. The Court also pointed out, however, that the sentence involved was not imposed under the Sentencing Reform Act, and that the Sentencing Reform Act reconceives probation "as a form of sentence in itself, not as a sanction that takes the place of fine or imprisonment." If that view is correct (check 18 U.S.C. § 3551, supra), under current law are there any limits on the cost of probationary conditions?

UNITED STATES SENTENCING COMMISSION, DISCUSSION DRAFT OF SENTENCING GUIDELINES AND POLICY STATEMENTS FOR ORGANIZATIONS
(July 1988).

§ 8D2.1 Imposition of Probation

An organization may be sentenced to probation only in the circumstances and upon the conditions specified below:

(a) [where necessary to carry out an order to pay restitution, a fine, or a forfeiture]

(b) [where necessary to carry out an order to give notice to victims]

(c) If (1) the instant offense was a felony, (2) the senior management of the organization participated in or encouraged the offense, (3) the organization or its senior management has a criminal history of one or more felony convictions of the same or similar type as the instant offense, and (4) the court determines that (A) the organization is unlikely to avoid a recurrence of the criminal behavior despite the imposition of a fine, and (B) probation is likely to prevent a recurrence of the criminal behavior in a cost-justified manner, then the organization shall be sentenced to probation upon the conditions set forth in § 8D2.2(c), unless the court finds that available civil or administrative procedures will produce substantially equivalent conditions.

§ 8D2.2 Conditions of Probation

* * *

(c) When a sentence of probation is imposed under § 8D2.1(c), then the following conditions shall be applied:

(1) If deemed necessary by the court to avoid a repetition of the organization's criminal behavior in the instant offense, by facilitating detection of a further offense or correcting a serious deficiency in the organization's internal control procedures, the organization shall be required to develop and submit for approval by the court a plan for avoiding a recurrence of the type of felony offense or offenses of which it was convicted in the instant case or appearing in criminal history of the organization or its senior management. The court shall approve any plan that appears reasonably calculated to avoid such a recurrence. The organization shall not be required to terminate, restrict, or unduly burden any lawful business operation, nor to adopt any compliance measure unless such a measure is reasonably related to the circumstances of the organization's offenses of conviction, and reasonably necessary to avoid a likelihood that there will be a recurrence of the type of felony offense of which the organization was convicted in the instant case. If so ordered by the court, the organization shall distribute copies of an approved plan of operation to employees, equity holders, and creditors of the organization.

(2) The organization shall be required to make periodic reports to the court or probation officer, at intervals specified by the court, regarding the organization's progress in (A) implementing any plan required and approved by the court under subsection (c)(1), and (B) avoiding the commission of further criminal offenses. Such reports should be in a form to be prescribed by the court, but (i) should disclose any criminal prosecution, civil litigation, or administrative proceeding commenced against the organization, or any investigations or formal inquiries by government authorities, of which the organization learned since its last report, (ii) shall not require disclosure of any trade secrets or other confidential business information, including future business plans, and (iii) shall not be unduly or unreasonably burdensome to the organization or its legitimate business activities.

NOTES AND QUERIES

(1) *The Commission's Proposal and the Sentencing Reform Act.* Toward what statutory sentencing purpose is the Sentencing Commission's proposal directed? Do you think the proposal too narrow? Will its conditions likely be satisfied easily? Is that good or bad?

The legislative history of the Sentencing Reform Act does not provide much guidance with regard to more intrusive forms of corporate probation. The Senate Committee Report states: [60]

---

60. See S.Rep. No. 98–225, at 99.

This language [the reference in the probation section to the statutory purposes of sentencing, see 18 U.S.C. § 3563(b)] is designed to allay the fears of such disparate groups as the ACLU and the Business Roundtable that probation conditions might be too restrictive in a particular case or might involve more supervision than is justified by the case. The judge is limited in imposing conditions of probation to imposing only those that carry out the purposes of sentencing in a particular case. He cannot . . . place business conditions on an organization that are unrelated to the purposes of sentencing for the offense of which the organization is convicted. It is not the intent of the Committee that the courts manage organizations as a part of probation supervision, but it is the intent of the Committee that all necessary conditions that are related to the characteristics of the offense and the offender and that are directed to the purposes of sentencing be imposed.

(2) *Alternative Proposal.* Consider the following guideline for corporate probation prepared by Professors Coffee, Gruner, and Stone for consideration by the Sentencing Commission:[61]

§ 8D2.3 Conditions of Probation

* * *

(b) The following "special" conditions of probation are recommended in particular cases, as described below:

(1) *Compliance Plan.* If the court finds . . . that management policies or practices encouraged, facilitated, or otherwise substantially contributed to the criminal behavior or delayed its detection, the court should require (A) the filing by defendant or, if necessary, the probation officer of a compliance plan, satisfactory to the court, detailing the specific procedures that will be implemented to correct such policies, practices, or inadequacies at or prior to the date of sentencing, and (B) the communication of the terms of such plan and the conditions of probation to relevant personnel. Compliance with such plan should, itself, be a condition of probation. Such plan may require:

(A) the conduct of a special audit or other internal investigation or inspections, which may be required periodically during the term of probation;

(B) the appointment of independent counsel or the use, if available, of a special committee of independent directors;

(C) the hiring and use of special consultants;

(D) the adoption of new or revised information gathering procedures and the preservation and centralization of such records or of any other information gathered by the organization;

---

61. Reprinted along with the Commission's Draft Proposals (July 1988).

(E) the designation of a special compliance officer with responsibility for supervising organizational activities related to the criminal offense;

(F) the revision or adoption of formal corporate policies, including those expressed in employee manuals and other written procedures, including notification procedures for the reporting of specific transactions or events to specified personnel with the organization, including the board of directors.

(2) *Internal Investigation.* If . . . the court finds that clarification of the circumstances of the crime, including the possible involvement of any officers or agents of the organization, is appropriate, the court should require the preparation of a special study, to be conducted, as the court shall direct, either by agents of the corporation approved by the court or by special counsel appointed by the court, which report shall set forth a factual account of the criminal behavior, the involvement of corporate personnel therein, and an evaluation of existing and possible internal control systems. When completed, such report shall be filed with the court as a public document, except to the extent that the court permits the substitution of a factual summary therefor in order not to expose the corporation or others to unjustified injury;

* * *

(5) *Community Services.* If the court finds that the organization is able to provide essential community service or interim relief, or to repair or restore specific harms or injuries, for which an order of restitution is either not feasible or not an adequate substitute, the court should specify the specific services that the organization is to provide and require performance of such services for the benefit of its victims as a condition of probation; provided, however, that the costs of such services should not be disproportionate to the maximum fine imposable for the offense.

* * *

(3) *Debarment.* The original proposal for a Federal Criminal Code provided, as one sanction, that an organization could be barred from its "right to affect interstate or foreign commerce" for a period up to the maximum jail sentence that could be imposed on an individual convicted of the relevant offense. In subsequent reform proposals this provision was recast as a condition of probation. Courts were given only the more limited authority either to bar an organization from engaging "in a particular business" or to order an organization to engage in a particular business in a particular way. This modification, however, was not adopted in the Sentencing Reform Act because of business concern that even a limited debarment order might be misapplied "to a business that had committed a regulatory offense but that was otherwise a legitimate business." Accordingly, the debarment section (§ 3563(b)(6)) applies only to individuals. The Committee Report indicates that in the "rare case" in which an organization operates in a "generally illegal manner," the sentencing judge can still use the "such

other conditions" clause [(b)(21)] to set "appropriate conditions" for the organization, as well as using (b)(6) to bar the individuals involved from engaging in the business.[62]

(4) *Imprisonment.* Of course, we all know that a corporation cannot be imprisoned. But is that correct? Consider the following proposal:[63]

> While the suggestion that a lawbreaking corporation should be imprisoned may have a somewhat radical sound, it may, on second thought, appear to be more conservative than the prevailing cry of the day, that negligent directors and dummy officers should pay the penalty of imprisonment for wrongdoing, conceived for the benefit of, and worked out for the profit of, stockholders, who are not legally liable to punishment. . . .
>
> How Can a Corporation be Imprisoned?
>
> The imprisonment of a corporation would be accomplished by a process similar to a receivership. On a sentence of imprisonment being pronounced, the court would place the corporation in the hands of those designated by the statute; perhaps, following the receivership analogy, persons chosen by the court as fitted to manage the business involved, and made officers of the government for that purpose. Under the control of these receivers, whom I may designate marshal receivers, to distinguish them from civil receivers, the corporate entity would be kept alive just as an individual prisoner is fed, given a habitation and permitted to labor for the benefit of his health, and for the benefit of the state. The entire affairs of the corporation would be subject to the scrutiny of the Federal officers; illegal contracts, in violation of the anti-trust law or the interstate commerce law, would be exposed and could be abrogated; and, during the term of imprisonment, suited, not to the offense, but to the proper amount of time necessary to reform a concern, the entire organization could be put on a basis of healthy business, so that it might, at the end, be turned back to its stockholders as a legitimate enterprise. It may be assumed that they would welcome it with all the joy with which a family greets the return of the wage-earning convict. To some it may seem reasonable that a proportion of the legitimate earnings of such a concern should be returned to the stockholders, though, in accordance with the treatment of individual convicts, the entire amount might be appropriated by the state. To maintain stable credit, probably the interest on bonded indebtedness should be paid, if earned, although the debtors of the individual convict are not permitted to require such payments of interest on his loans from the proceeds of his labor in the penitentiary.

62. See S.Rep. No. 98–223, at pp. 65–66.

63. Richberg, The Imprisonment of Criminal Corporations, 18 Case & Comment 527 (1912).

These problems are mere matters of administration, in which broad investigation and practical experience will necessarily modify, and greatly improve upon any program which a theorist could propose in advance. But the main questions in considering such a penalty are:

First: What harm would it do?

Second: What good would it do?

In several years of discussion of this theory with editors, lawyers, publicists, and political economists, I may say that the chief objection urged is one which appeals to me as insecurely founded, that innocent stockholders will suffer. . . .

There are no innocent stockholders in the great enterprises at present being subjected to dissolution, or whose dissolution is being demanded by the government. Every adult person able to read, who has invested in the stock of such corporations, invested on the assumption that he or she was ready and willing to promote, and share in the profits of, an enterprise of doubtful legality. If a man invests money in any apparently legal enterprise, and discovers that he is thereby assisting in violating the law, he has the alternative of accepting his responsibility as a stockholder and demanding lawful management, or he can put his shares up for sale to anyone who wishes to assume the risk and responsibility of the situation. It seems that such a responsibility upon the stockholder might have a healthy effect upon the stock market, in making law-abiding, as well as profit-producing, management a factor in determining the market price of stocks. . . .

Feeling confident that little harm would result from imprisoning criminal corporations, the final question is: What good would it do?

. . . . There is a great clamor for publicity in corporate affairs, yet anyone concerned with business must feel that a reasonable privacy is essential to the profitable conduct of private enterprise. Publicity should be regarded, in a way, as a penalty for failure on the part of a corporation to maintain the standard of conduct which would insure the public against the dangers which might arise from permitting desirable privacy. . . .

Every one of the great incorporated enterprises which have been subjected to governmental prosecution in recent years has been charged with being guilty of numerous kinds and classes of criminality. . . . The imprisonment of such a corporation would place the government in a position where the investigation of its marshal receivers would speedily determine whether or not the charges were true or false. If such charges have been true, it is essential to the common welfare that the proof thereof should be made easy of access to the officers of government. If such charges are false, they should be proved false to the satisfaction of the vast number of people who feel to-day, and perhaps justly, that the large business enterprises of this country are not great organizations of commerce, but merely huge exploitations of the disorganized many, helpless to combat the well-organized few. . . .

As long as we permit at large in the community, artificial persons, through which real persons will work out criminal acts, and permit our hands to be tied by ancient decisions and worn-out reasoning, admitting our inability to confine these Frankensteins, as we would confine human criminals, we will have a constant, unsolved problem on our hands. Provision for the criminal receivership, suggested as a method of confinement, would affect only one phase of that problem. But it may be urged, logically, that a long step would be taken toward its final solution in the passage of such legislation as would provide adequate punishment for the corporate felon,—the imprisonment of the criminal corporation itself.

In *United States v. Allegheny Bottling Co.*, 695 F.Supp. 856 (E.D.Va. 1988), Judge Doumar did sentence a corporation to a term of imprisonment. The corporation, a Pepsi–Cola bottler, had been found guilty of conspiring with a Coca–Cola bottler to fix prices. The government contended that the price-fixing increased the bottlers' revenue by at least $10 to $12 million during the period of the conspiracy. The judge sentenced the corporation to three years in jail and fined it $1 million. He then suspended the sentence of imprisonment and $50,000 of the fine, placing the corporation on probation for three years. Among the conditions of probation were requirements that the corporation provide four employees to perform community service and that the corporation not dispose of any assets without the probation officer's permission.

With regard to imprisonment, Judge Doumar wrote:

> Corporate imprisonment requires only that the Court restrain or immobilize the corporation. Such restraint of individuals is accomplished by, for example, placing them in the custody of the United States Marshal. Likewise, corporate imprisonment can be accomplished by simply placing the corporation in the custody of the United States Marshal. The United States Marshal would restrain the corporation by seizing the corporation's physical assets or part of the assets or restricting its actions or liberty in a particular manner. When this sentence was contemplated, the United States Marshal for the Eastern District of Virginia, Roger Ray, was contacted. When asked if he could imprison Allegheny Pepsi, he stated that he could. He stated that he restrained corporations regularly for bankruptcy court. He stated that he could close the physical plant itself and guard it. He further stated that he could allow employees to come and go and limit certain actions or sales if that is what the Court imposes.
>
> . . . Who am I to say that imprisonment is impossible when the keeper indicates that it can physically be done? Obviously, one can restrain a corporation. If so, why should it be more privileged

than an individual citizen? There is no reason, and accordingly, a corporation should not be more privileged.

Cases in the past have *assumed* that corporations cannot be imprisoned, without any cited authority for that proposition. This Court, however, has been unable to find any case which actually held that corporate imprisonment is illegal, unconstitutional or impossible. . . . Since the Marshal can restrain the corporation's liberty and has done so in bankruptcy cases, there is no reason that he cannot do so in this case as he himself has so stated prior to the imposition of this sentence.

* * *

Incapacitation or restraint of the liberty of Allegheny is certainly accomplished by corporate imprisonment. No more price-fixing by Allegheny Pepsi will occur when the United States Marshal prevents the corporation from acting.

Deterrence of price-fixing will also be achieved by corporate imprisonment of Allegheny Pepsi. Other corporations will be deterred by seeing that violation of the Sherman Act could lead to consequences sufficiently severe as to dictate that the potential cost of price-fixing is seldom worth the potential gain.

The deterrence achieved by corporate imprisonment may in fact be the only effective deterrent to price-fixing, especially regarding corporations as large as the ones in this case. A corporation the size of Allegheny Pepsi will, through price-fixing, make many times the maximum fine by the time the price-fixing is detected. Knowing this, the fine will be ineffective as a deterrent even if the probability of detection is considered great. The fine becomes simply a cost of doing business, which is small in comparison with the potential profits. Corporate imprisonment, in contrast, prevents the cost-benefit analysis to economically justify price-fixing. The corporate decision-makers would know that, if caught, the corporation would lose more than they could gain.

The Department of Justice subsequently objected both to the sentence of imprisonment (it "could adversely affect competition and further injure consumers") and to the community service requirement (no authority to require service from individuals who were not defendants). The district court rejected both arguments (citing *Missouri Valley* as authority for community service).[64] The corporation then paid a $1 million fine and appealed, arguing that other sanctions were beyond the court's power. The government confessed error. The court of appeals agreed with the government and the defendant, holding that the imprisonment and probation terms were "a nullity." The court stated that the $1 million amount was the maximum permitted under the statute and added that a corporation "may not be sent to jail."[65]

---

64. See United States v. Allegheny Bottling Co., 1988–2 Trade Cas. ¶ 68,350 (E.D. Va.1988) (unpublished).

65. See United States v. Harford, 1988–2 Trade Cas. ¶ 68,387, at p. 60,132 (4th Cir. 1989) (unpublished).

(Note, however, that because of the dates of the violation, the Sentencing Reform Act did not apply, see Note (2), supra p. 319. Would the result be different under current law?)

(5) *Endnote.* Review the position the Justice Department has taken in the cases in this Section with regard to non-fine sanctions for corporations. Why do you think the Department has been so consistently opposed to these sanctions? Do you agree with its position?

Part Two

PROBLEMS OF CRIMINAL PROCEDURE

Chapter 4

CORPORATE PRIVILEGES

A. CONSTITUTIONAL

SCOPE NOTE

Dealing with the corporate entity has been a problem not only for substantive criminal law. It has also been a problem for criminal procedure. At the same time that the courts began to struggle with cases involving corporate and managerial criminal liability, very basic litigation problems also emerged. Business crimes, being organizational crimes, were committed in complex ways which often left no complaining witnesses to tell the government what happened (or, indeed, if any crime occurred at all). Further, as it became clear that certain conduct would be held unlawful, particularly with respect to the Sherman Act, corporations took steps to suppress the facts surrounding their activities. Consequently, the Government needed to resort to legal process—primarily the grand jury subpoena—to force information from corporations. This led corporations, or their agents, to attempt to use the Constitution in an effort to block the Government's evidence gathering.

The result is a group of cases decided in the early part of the twentieth century which have had a lasting impact on constitutional criminal procedure for all types of crimes. The lead case in this Section is one of those landmark cases, *Hale v. Henkel*, decided in 1906. *Hale* established the basic framework for the application of the fourth and fifth amendments to corporations. The Notes following *Hale* explore the development of *Hale*'s fifth amendment holding, as well as other constitutional protections available to corporations. Subsequent Chapters will explore more fully the application of the fourth and fifth amendments in specific settings.

HALE v. HENKEL
Supreme Court of the United States, 1906.
201 U.S. 43, 26 S.Ct. 370, 50 L.Ed. 652.

This was an appeal from a final order of the Circuit Court made June 18, 1905, dismissing a writ of habeas corpus and remanding the petitioner Hale to the custody of the marshal.

The proceeding originated in a subpoena duces tecum, issued April 28, 1905, commanding Hale to appear before the grand jury at a time and place named, to "testify and give evidence in a certain action now pending . . . in the Circuit Court of the United States for the Southern District of New York, between the United States of America and the American Tobacco Company and MacAndrews & Forbes Company on the part of the United States, and that you bring with you and produce at the time and place aforesaid":

1. All understandings, agreements, arrangements, or contracts, whether evidenced by correspondence, memoranda, formal agreements, or other writings, between MacAndrews & Forbes Company and six other firms and corporations named, from the date of the organization of the said MacAndrews & Forbes Company.

2. All correspondence by letter or telegram between MacAndrews & Forbes Company and six other firms and corporations.

3. All reports made or accounts rendered by these six companies or corporations to the principal company.

4. Any agreements or contracts or arrangements, however evidenced, between MacAndrews & Forbes Company and the Amsterdam Supply Company or the American Tobacco Company or the Continental Company or the Consolidated Tobacco Company.

5. All letters received by the MacAndrews & Forbes Company since the date of its organization from thirteen other companies named, located in different parts of the United States and also copies of all correspondence with such companies.

Petitioner appeared before the grand jury in obedience to the subpoena, and before being sworn asked to be advised of the nature of the investigation in which he had been summoned; whether under any statute of the United States, and the specific charge, if any had been made, in order that he might learn whether or not the grand jury had any lawful right to make the inquiry, and also that he be furnished with a copy of the complaint, information or proposed indictment upon which they were acting; that he had been informed that there was no action pending in the Circuit Court as stated in the subpoena, and that the grand jury was investigating no specific charge against any one, and he therefore declined to answer: First, because there was no legal warrant for his examination, and, second, because his answers might tend to incriminate him.

After stating his name, residence and the fact that he was secretary and treasurer of the MacAndrews & Forbes Company, he declined to answer all other questions in regard to the business of the company, its officers, the location of its office, or its agreement or arrangements with other companies. He was thereupon advised by the Assistant District Attorney that this was a proceeding under the Sherman Act to protect trade and commerce against unlawful restraint and monopolies; that under the act of 1903, amendatory thereof, no person could be prosecuted or subjected to any penalty or forfeiture on account of any matter or thing concerning which he might testify or produce documentary evidence in any prosecution under said act, and that he thereby offered and assured appellant immunity from punishment. The witness still persisted in his refusal to answer all questions. He also declined to produce the papers and documents called for in the subpoena:

First. Because it would have been a physical impossibility to have gotten them together within the time allowed.

Second. Because he was advised by counsel that he was under no legal obligations to produce anything called for by the subpoena.

Third. Because they might tend to incriminate him.

Whereupon the grand jury reported the matter to the court, and made a presentment that Hale was in contempt, and that the proper proceedings should be taken. Thereupon all the parties appeared before the Circuit judge, who directed the witness to answer the questions and produce the papers. Appellant still persisting in his refusal, the Circuit judge held him to be in contempt, and committed him to the custody of the marshal until he should answer the questions and produce the papers. A writ of habeas corpus was thereupon sued out, and a hearing had before another judge of the same court, who discharged the writ and remanded the petitioner.

MR. JUSTICE BROWN, after making the foregoing statement, delivered the opinion of the court.

Two issues are presented by the record in this case, which are so far distinct as to require separate consideration. They depend upon the applicability of different provisions of the Constitution, and, in determining the question of affirmance or reversal, should not be confounded. The first of these involves the immunity of the witness from oral examination; the second, the legality of his action in refusing to produce the documents called for by the subpoena duces tecum.

* * *

Appellant . . . invokes the protection of the Fifth Amendment to the Constitution, which declares that no person "shall be compelled in any criminal case to be a witness against himself," and in reply to various questions put to him he declined to answer, on the ground that he would thereby incriminate himself.

[The Court pointed out that the witness was protected from prosecution by virtue of the federal immunity statute. For further discussion of the problems associated with immunity grants, see Chapter 6A, infra p. 496.]

But it is further insisted that while the immunity statute may protect individual witnesses it would not protect the corporation of which appellant was the agent and representative. This is true, but the answer is that it was not designed to do so. The right of a person under the Fifth Amendment to refuse to incriminate himself is purely a personal privilege of the witness. It was never intended to permit him to plead the fact that some third person might be incriminated by his testimony, even though he were the agent of such person. A privilege so extensive might be used to put a stop to the examination of every witness who was called upon to testify before the grand jury with regard to the doings or business of his principal, whether such principal were an individual or a corporation. The question whether a corporation is a "person" within the meaning of this Amendment really does not arise, except perhaps where a corporation is called upon to answer a bill of discovery, since it can only be heard by oral evidence in the person of some one of its agents or employés. The Amendment is limited to a person who shall be compelled in any criminal case to be a witness against *himself,* and if he cannot set up the privilege of a third person, he certainly cannot set up the privilege of a corporation. As the combination or conspiracies provided against by the Sherman Anti Trust Act can ordinarily be proved only by the testimony of parties thereto, in the person of their agents or employés, the privilege claimed would practically nullify the whole act of Congress. Of what use would it be for the legislature to declare these combinations unlawful if the judicial power may close the door of access to every available source of information upon the subject? Indeed, so strict is the rule that the privilege is a personal one that it has been held in some cases that counsel will not be allowed to make the objection. We hold that the questions should have been answered.

The second branch of the case relates to the non-production by the witness of the books and papers called for by the subpoena duces tecum. The witness put his refusal on the ground, first, that it was impossible for him to collect them within the time allowed; second, because he was advised by counsel that under the circumstances he was under no obligation to produce them; and, finally, because they might tend to incriminate him.

Had the witness relied solely upon the first ground, doubtless the court would have given him the necessary time. The last ground we have already held untenable. While the second ground does not set forth with technical accuracy the real reason for declining to produce them, the witness could not be expected to speak with legal exactness, and we think is entitled to assert that the subpoena was an infringement upon the Fourth Amendment to the Constitution, which declares that "the right of the people to be secure in their persons, houses, papers and effects, against unreasonable searches and seizures, shall not be violated, and no warrants shall issue but upon probable cause, supported by oath or affirmation, and particularly describing the place to be searched, and the persons or things to be seized."

The construction of this amendment was exhaustively considered in the case of Boyd v. United States, 116 U.S. 616 [1886], which was an information in rem against certain cases of plate glass, alleged to have been imported in fraud of the revenue acts. On the trial it became important to show the quantity and value of the glass contained in a number of cases previously imported; and the district judge, under section 5 of the act of June 22, 1874, directed a notice to be given to the claimants, requiring them to produce the invoice of these cases under penalty that the allegations respecting their contents should be taken as confessed. We held (p. 622) "that a compulsory production of a man's private papers to establish a criminal charge against him, or to forfeit his property, is within the scope of the Fourth Amendment to the Constitution, in all cases in which a search and seizure would be," and that the order in question was an unreasonable search and seizure within that Amendment.

The history of this provision of the Constitution and its connection with the former practice of general warrants, or writs of assistance, was given at great length, and the conclusion reached that the compulsory extortion of a man's own testimony, or of his private papers, to connect him with a crime or a forfeiture of his goods, is illegal (p. 634), "is compelling him to be a witness against himself, within the meaning of the Fifth Amendment to the Constitution, and is the equivalent of a search and seizure—and an unreasonable search and seizure—within the Fourth Amendment.

[The Court then reviewed several cases decided after *Boyd*. The Court believed that these cases treated the fourth and fifth amendments as "quite distinct, having different histories, and performing separate functions." The Court continued:]

If, whenever an officer or employé of a corporation were summoned before a grand jury as a witness he could refuse to produce the books and documents of such corporation, upon the ground that they would incriminate the corporation itself, it would result in the failure of a large number of cases where the illegal combination was determinable only upon the examination of such papers. Conceding that the witness was an officer of the corporation under investigation, and that he was entitled to assert the rights of the corporation with respect to the production of its books and papers, we are of the opinion that there is a clear distinction in this particular between an individual and a corporation, and that the latter has no right to refuse to submit its books and papers for an examination at the suit of the State. The individual may stand upon his constitutional rights as a citizen. He is entitled to carry on his private business in his own way. His power to contract is unlimited. He owes no duty to the State or to his neighbors to divulge his business, or to open his doors to an investigation, so far as it may tend to criminate him. He owes no such duty to the State, since he receives nothing therefrom, beyond the protection of his life and property. His rights are such as existed by the law of the land long antecedent to the organization of the State, and can only be taken from him by due process of law, and in accordance with the Constitution. Among his rights are a refusal to incriminate himself, and the immunity of himself and his property from arrest or seizure except under a warrant of the law. He owes nothing to the public so long as he does not trespass upon their rights.

Upon the other hand, the corporation is a creature of the State. It is presumed to be incorporated for the benefit of the public. It receives certain special privileges and franchises, and holds them subject to the laws of the State and the limitations of its charter. Its powers are limited by law. It can make no contract not authorized by its charter. Its rights to act as a corporation are only preserved to it so long as it obeys the laws of its creation. There is a reserved right in the legislature to investigate its contracts and find out whether it has exceeded its powers. It would be a strange anomaly to hold that a State, having chartered a corporation to make use of certain franchises, could not in the exercise of its sovereignty inquire how these franchises had been employed, and whether they had been abused, and demand the production of the corporate books and papers for that purpose. The defense amounts to this: That an officer of a corporation, which is charged with a criminal violation of the statute, may plead the criminality of such corporation as a refusal to produce its books. To state this proposition is to answer it. While an individual may lawfully refuse to answer incriminating questions unless protected by an immunity statute, it does not follow that a corporation, vested with special privileges and franchises, may refuse to show its hand when charged with an abuse of such privileges.

It is true that the corporation in this case was chartered under the laws of New Jersey, and that it receives its franchise from the legislature of that State; but such franchises, so far as they involve questions of interstate commerce, must also be exercised in subordination to the power of Congress to regulate such commerce, and in respect to this the General Government may also assert a sovereign authority to ascertain whether such franchises have been exercised in a lawful manner, with a due regard to its own laws. Being subject to this dual sovereignty, the General Government possesses the same right to see that its own laws are respected as the State would have with respect to the special franchises vested in it by the laws of the State. The powers of the General Government in this particular in the vindication of its own laws, are the same as if the corporation had been created by an act of Congress. It is not intended to intimate, however, that it has a general visitatorial power over state corporations.

Although, for the reasons above stated, we are of the opinion that an officer of a corporation which is charged with a violation of a statute of the State of its creation, or of an act of Congress passed in the exercise of its constitutional powers, cannot refuse to produce the books and papers of such corporation, we do not wish to be understood as holding that a corporation is not entitled to immunity, under the Fourth Amendment, against *unreasonable* searches and seizures. A corporation is, after all, but an association of individuals under an assumed name and with a distinct legal entity. In organizing itself as a collective body it waives no constitutional immunities appropriate to such body. Its property cannot be taken without compensation. It can only be proceeded against by due process of law, and is protected, under the Fourteenth Amendment, against unlawful discrimination. Corporations are a necessary feature of modern business activity, and their aggregated capital has become the source of nearly all great enterprises.

We are also of opinion that an order for the production of books and papers may constitute an unreasonable search and seizure within the Fourth Amendment. While a search ordinarily implies a quest by an officer of the law, and a seizure contemplates a forcible dispossession of the owner, still, as was held in the *Boyd case*, the substance of the offense is the compulsory production of private papers, whether under a search warrant or a subpoena duces tecum, against which the person, be he individual or corporation, is entitled to protection. Applying the test of reasonableness to the present case, we think the subpoena duces tecum is far too sweeping in its terms to be regarded as reasonable. It does not require the production of a single contract, or of contracts with a particular corporation, or a limited number of documents, but all understandings, contracts or correspondence between the MacAndrews & Forbes Company, and no less than six different companies, as well as all reports made, and accounts rendered by such companies from the date of the organization of the MacAndrews & Forbes Company, as well as all letters received by that company since its organization from more than a dozen different companies, situated in seven different States in the Union.

If the writ had required the production of all the books, papers and documents found in the office of the MacAndrews & Forbes Company, it would scarcely be more universal in its operation, or more completely put a stop to the business of that company. Indeed, it is difficult to say how its business could be carried on after it had been denuded of this mass of material, which is not shown to be necessary in the prosecution of this case, and is clearly in violation of the general principle of law with regard to the particularity required in the description of documents necessary to a search warrant or subpoena. Doubtless many, if not all, of these documents may ultimately be required, but some necessity should be shown, either from an examination of the witnesses orally, or from the known transactions of these companies with the other companies implicated, or some evidence of their materiality produced, to justify an order for the production of such a mass of papers. A general subpoena of this description is equally indefensible as a search warrant would be if couched in similar terms.

Of course, in view of the power of Congress over interstate commerce to which we have adverted, we do not wish to be understood as holding that an examination of the books of a corporation, if duly authorized by act of Congress, would constitute an unreasonable search and seizure within the Fourth Amendment.

But this objection to the subpoena does not go to the validity of the order remanding the petitioner, which is, therefore, *Affirmed.*

MR. JUSTICE HARLAN, concurring.

I concur entirely in what is said in the opinion of the court in reference to the powers and functions of the grand jury and as to the scope of the Fifth Amendment to the Constitution. I concur also in the affirmance of the judgment, but must withhold my assent to some of the views expressed in the opinion. It seems to me that the witness was not entitled to assert, as a reason for not obeying the order of the court, that the subpoena duces tecum was an infringement of the Fourth Amendment, which declares that "the right of the *People* to be secure in their *persons,* houses, papers and effects, against unreasonable searches and seizures, shall not be violated, and no warrants shall issue but upon probable cause, supported by oath or affirmation, and particularly describing the place to be searched, and the *persons* or things to be seized." It may be, I am inclined to think as a matter of procedure and practice, that the subpoena duces tecum was too broad and indefinite. But the action of the court in that regard was, at the utmost, only error, and that error did not affect its jurisdiction to make the order, nor authorize the witness—whose personal rights, let it be observed, were in no wise involved in the pending inquiry—to refuse compliance with the subpoena, upon the ground that it involved an unreasonable search and seizure of the books, papers and records of the corporation whose conduct, so far as it related to the Sherman Anti Trust Act, was the subject of examination. It was not his privilege to stand between the corporation and the Government in the investigation before the grand jury. In my opinion, a corporation—"an artificial being, invisible, intangible and existing only in contemplation of law"—cannot claim the immunity given by the Fourth Amendment; for, it is not a part of the "People," within the meaning of that Amendment. Nor is it embraced by the word "persons" in the Amendment. If a contrary view obtains, the power of the Government by its representatives to look into the books, records and papers of a corporation of its own creation, to ascertain whether that corporation has obeyed or is defying the law, will be greatly curtailed, if not destroyed. If a corporation, when its affairs are under examination by a grand jury proceeding in its work under the orders of the court, can plead the immunity given by the Fourth Amendment against unreasonable searches and seizures, may it not equally rely upon that Amendment to protect it even against a statute authorizing or directing the examination by the agents of the Government creating it, of its papers, documents and records, unless they specify the particular papers, documents and records to be examined? If the order of the court below is to be deemed invalid as an unreasonable search and seizure of the papers, books and records of the corporation, could it be deemed valid if made under the express authority of an act of Congress? Congress could not, any more than a court, authorize an unreasonable seizure or search in violation of the Fourth Amendment. In my judgment when a grand jury seeking, in the discharge of its public duties, to ascertain whether a corporation has violated the law in any particular, requires the production of the books, papers and records of such corporation, no officer of that corporation can rightfully refuse, when ordered to do so by the court, to produce such books, papers and records in his official custody, upon the ground simply that the order was, as to the corporation, an unreasonable search and seizure within the meaning of the Fourth Amendment.

MR. JUSTICE MCKENNA, also concurring.

I concur in the judgment but not in all the propositions declared by the court. . . .

. . . There are certainly strong reasons for the contention that if corporations cannot plead the immunity of the Fifth Amendment, they cannot plead the immunity of the Fourth Amendment. The protection of both Amendments, it can be contended, is against the compulsory production of evidence to be used in criminal trials. Such warrants are used in aid of public prosecutions (Cooley Constitutional Lim. 6th ed. 364), and in Boyd v. United States, 116 U.S. 616, a relation between the Fourth Amendment and the Fifth Amendment was declared. It was said the Amendments throw great light on each other, "for the 'unreasonable searches and seizures' condemned in the Fourth Amendment are almost always made for the purpose of compelling a man to give evidence against himself, which in criminal cases is condemned in the Fifth Amendment; and compelling a man 'in a criminal case to be a witness against himself,' which is condemned in the Fifth Amendment, throws light on the question as to what is an 'unreasonable search and seizure' within the meaning of the Fourth Amendment. And we have been unable to perceive that the seizure of a man's private books and papers to be used in evidence against him is substantially different from compelling him to be a witness against himself." Boyd v. United States is still recognized, and if its reasoning remains unimpaired, and the purpose and effect of the Fourth Amendment receives illumination from the Fifth, or, to express the idea differently, if the Amendments are the complements of each other, directed against the different ways by which a man's immunity from giving evidence against himself may be violated, it would seem a strong, if not an inevitable conclusion, that if corporations have not such immunity they can no more claim the protection of the Fourth Amendment than they can of the Fifth.

[CHIEF JUSTICE FULLER and JUSTICE BREWER, although agreeing with the majority's views, would have set aside the order adjudicating the petitioner in contempt.]

NOTES AND QUERIES

(1) *Understanding the Context of Hale v. Henkel.* The grand jury's investigation of the MacAndrews & Forbes Company, out of which *Hale v. Henkel* arose, was an important part of the federal government's antitrust attack on the American Tobacco Company (the "Tobacco Trust"). Indeed, as early as 1894 the District Attorney in North Carolina had reported a "terrible clamor" to prosecute the American Tobacco Company under the Sherman Act. He had even submitted to

the Attorney General a proposed indictment, but the Attorney General had refused to let him proceed.[1]

Hale was the Secretary and Treasurer, and also a director, of the MacAndrews & Forbes Company, a company that imported licorice root from which it made licorice paste.[2] Licorice paste was the second most important material used in tobacco manufacturing, next to the tobacco leaf itself; it was used extensively in plug (chewing) tobacco, and to some extent in smoking tobacco and snuff (but not in cigarettes or cigars). In 1905 MacAndrews & Forbes supplied approximately 98% of the licorice paste used by tobacco manufacturers.

MacAndrews & Forbes was acquired by the American Tobacco Company in 1904. The grand jury was investigating MacAndrews & Forbes to determine whether the company, following its acquisition by American Tobacco, had raised the price of licorice paste to independent manufacturers and limited the supply, thereby making it more difficult for the independents to compete against American.[3]

A companion case to *Hale v. Henkel*,[4] raising the same legal issues and decided by the Supreme Court on the same day, involved a grand jury request for documents regarding a world-wide division of markets between the American Tobacco Company and the Imperial Tobacco Company (a combination of thirteen British tobacco companies, formed in 1901). An agreement dividing world markets had been signed by the parties in 1902, and was apparently on file in London.[5]

Following the Supreme Court's decision in *Hale,* MacAndrews & Forbes and two of its officers were indicted for conspiring to restrain trade and attempting to monopolize, in violation of the Sherman Act. After a trial by jury the officers were acquitted, but the corporation was convicted and fined.[6] Six months later the government proceeded against the American Tobacco Company by civil suit, rather than criminal prosecution. The civil case alleged monopolization and world division of markets. The government was partially successful in this case, and the American Tobacco Company was subsequently dissolved and split into three firms.[7]

1. See H. Thorelli, The Federal Antitrust Policy: Origination of an American Tradition 388 (1954). An indictment of officers and directors of American Tobacco, brought by New York under state law, was dismissed in 1897. See H. Seager and C. Gulick, Trust and Corporate Problems 170 (1929).

2. The description of the MacAndrews and Forbes Company is found in Report of the Commissioner of Corporations on the Tobacco Industry, Part I, 113, 232–263 (1909).

3. See Taft, The Tobacco Trust Decisions, 6 Colum.L.Rev. 375, 377 (1906).

4. See McAlister v. Henkel, 201 U.S. 90, 26 S.Ct. 385, 50 L.Ed. 671 (1906) (subpoena of the Secretary of the American Tobacco Company).

5. The relevant agreements are reproduced in Report of the Commissioner of Corporations on the Tobacco Industry, Part II, at 431–447 (1909).

6. See United States v. MacAndrews & Forbes Co., 149 Fed. 836, 837 (C.C.S.D.N.Y. 1906). The defendant corporation filed an appeal with the Supreme Court, but had the appeal dismissed shortly before the trial court decision in the civil case against American Tobacco. See 212 U.S. 585, 29 S.Ct. 681, 53 L.Ed. 661 (1908).

7. See United States v. American Tobacco Co., 221 U.S. 106, 31 S.Ct. 632, 55 L.Ed. 663 (1911). The plan of dissolution is

Counsel for the government in *Hale* later wrote that the case "set to rest" fourth and fifth amendment questions involving investigations of corporate conduct "never before presented." [8] He explained that these issues had not arisen before because initial government enforcement of the Sherman Act was through civil injunction. In addition, early cases featured "specific and easily proven" agreements. "In none of these cases was the policy of suppressing the facts resorted to by the defendants, for the reason, probably, that the corporations relied upon the contention that, even conceding that they had made the agreements, they were not in violation of the law." With greater enforcement of the antitrust laws, however, corporations began to resort "to obstructive measures" to keep the government from proving the illegality of their acts.

(2) *Queries.* In large part, counsel for the government was correct in his prediction that *Hale* "set to rest" the basic scope of fourth and fifth amendment protections available to corporations. But do you think that they were set to rest properly?

a) The fifth amendment provides, inter alia: "No person . . . shall be compelled in any criminal case to be a witness against himself, nor be deprived of life, liberty, or property, without due process of law. . . ." Should the Court have simply held that a "corporation" is not a "person"?

b) The fourth amendment provides that the "right of the people to be secure in their persons, houses, papers, and effects, against unreasonable searches and seizures, shall not be violated, and no Warrants shall issue, but upon probable cause, supported by oath or affirmation, and particularly describing the place to be searched, and the persons or things to be seized." Should the Court have simply held that "corporations" are not "people"?

c) The Court in *Hale* held that a corporation is entitled to the protection of the fourth amendment, but also held that this did not give the corporation an immunity from producing incriminating documents. The only protection given by the fourth amendment was from an overly-broad subpoena.

This holding was in some contrast to the Court's decision twenty years before in *Boyd v. United States*,[9] discussed in the opinion in *Hale*. *Boyd* was a civil case for forfeiture of thirty-five cases of plate-glass allegedly imported without payment of the duty. The district court

set out at 191 Fed. 371, 374, 423 (C.C.S.D. N.Y.1911). The relief obtained by the government was criticized by a number of people, including Louis Brandeis. See E. Jones, The Trust Problem in the United States 461–69 (1928). After American Tobacco's dissolution, MacAndrews & Forbes was left with sixty percent of the licorice paste business. See id. at 466. Its business eventually declined with the decline in demand for licorice paste in the industry. See R. Cox, Competition in the American Tobacco Industry 129 n. 19 (1933).

8. See Taft, The Tobacco Trust Decisions, 6 Colum.L.Rev. 375, 375–77 (1906). A third issue in the case, involving the meaning of the fifth amendment grand jury clause, was similarly described. This issue is discussed infra, p. 435.

9. 116 U.S. 616, 6 S.Ct. 524, 29 L.Ed. 746 (1886).

judge, acting pursuant to specific federal statutory authority, ordered E.A. Boyd & Sons (a partnership) to produce invoices for the cases. Boyd refused. The Supreme Court held that the compelled production of the documents would be a per se unreasonable search under the fourth amendment. These invoices were not stolen or forfeited goods, nor were they entries in "books required by law to be kept for their inspection." They were "a man's private books and papers." The Court wrote: "[A]ny forcible and compulsory extortion of a man's testimony or of his private papers to be used as evidence to convict him of crime" is unreasonable, and condemned by the fourth amendment.[10]

The Court in *Hale* thus turned the fourth amendment away from *Boyd*'s view that the fourth amendment can be an absolute bar to seizing certain types of incriminating evidence (e.g., "private" books and records) toward the view that the fourth amendment provides protection only against improperly performed searches and seizures (e.g., overly-broad subpoenas). What are the implications of such a shift? Suppose the fourth amendment had been construed to make certain types of searches per se unlawful?[11] Based on *Boyd*, what types of searches might have qualified? How would such a rule have affected business crime prosecutions?[12]

d) Does *Hale* address the question whether a corporation has any Fifth amendment right to refuse to produce documents (as opposed to refusing to testify orally)?[13]

(3) *Developing Hale's Fifth Amendment Theory.* In *United States v. White*[14] the Supreme Court considered the question whether a labor union official, answering a grand jury subpoena directed at the union, could refuse to produce union records on the ground that the records might incriminate himself and the union. The Court of Appeals, finding that the records of an unincorporated labor union were the property of all its members, had held that if the respondent to the subpoena were a union member and if the records would have incriminated him, he could properly refuse to produce them. The Supreme Court reversed:

> Respondent contends that an officer of an unincorporated labor union possesses a constitutional right to refuse to produce, in

---

10. 116 U.S. at 630, 6 S.Ct. at 532, 29 L.Ed. at 751.

11. There is historical support for the view that the first clause of the fourth amendment (prohibiting "unreasonable" searches) was intended to have some independent force apart from the second ("warrant") clause. See N. Lasson, The History and Development of the Fourth Amendment to the United States Constitution 103 (1937) (after reviewing the legislative history surrounding the drafting of the fourth amendment, concludes "that the prohibition against 'unreasonable' searches was intended, accordingly, to cover something other than the form of the warrant . . .") What this broader scope was intended to be, however, is not clear. See Amsterdam, Perspectives on the Fourth Amendment, 58 Minn.L.Rev. 349, 399 (1974).

12. Reconsider these questions after reading Warden v. Hayden, infra p. 546.

13. For further development of the Fifth Amendment right to resist the compulsory production of documents, see Fisher v. United States, infra p. 598, and cases following.

14. 322 U.S. 694, 64 S.Ct. 1248, 88 L.Ed. 1542 (1944).

compliance with a subpoena duces tecum, records of the union which are in his custody and which might tend to incriminate him. He relies upon the "unreasonable search and seizure" clause of the Fourth Amendment and the explicit guarantee of the Fifth Amendment that no person shall be compelled in any criminal case to be a witness against himself. We hold, however, that neither the Fourth nor the Fifth Amendment, both of which are directed primarily to the protection of individual and personal rights, requires the recognition of a privilege against self-incrimination under the circumstances of this case.

The constitutional privilege against self-incrimination is essentially a personal one, applying only to natural individuals. It grows out of the high sentiment and regard of our jurisprudence for conducting criminal trials and investigatory proceedings upon a plane of dignity, humanity and impartiality. It is designed to prevent the use of legal process to force from the lips of the accused individual the evidence necessary to convict him or to force him to produce and authenticate any personal documents or effects that might incriminate him. Physical torture and other less violent but equally reprehensible modes of compelling the production of incriminating evidence are thereby avoided. The prosecutors are forced to search for independent evidence instead of relying upon proof extracted from individuals by force of law. The immediate and potential evils of compulsory self-disclosure transcend any difficulties that the exercise of the privilege may impose on society in the detection and prosecution of crime. While the privilege is subject to abuse and misuse, it is firmly embedded in our constitutional and legal frameworks as a bulwark against iniquitous methods of prosecution. It protects the individual from any disclosure, in the form of oral testimony, documents or chattels, sought by legal process against him as a witness.

Since the privilege against self-incrimination is a purely personal one, it cannot be utilized by or on behalf of any organization, such as a corporation. Hale v. Henkel, 201 U.S. 43. Moreover, the papers and effects which the privilege protects must be the private property of the person claiming the privilege, or at least in his possession in a purely personal capacity. Boyd v. United States, 116 U.S. 616. But individuals, when acting as representatives of a collective group, cannot be said to be exercising their personal rights and duties nor to be entitled to their purely personal privileges. Rather they assume the rights, duties and privileges of the artificial entity or association of which they are agents or officers and they are bound by its obligations. In their official capacity, therefore, they have no privilege against self-incrimination. And the official records and documents of the organization that are held by them in a representative rather than in a personal capacity cannot be the subject of the personal privilege against self-incrimination, even though production of the papers might tend to incriminate them personally. Such records and papers are not the private records of the individual members or officers of the organization. Usually, if not always, they are open to inspection by the members and this right may be enforced on appropriate occasions by available legal procedures. They therefore embody no element of personal privacy and carry with them no claim of personal privilege.

The reason underlying the restriction of this constitutional privilege to natural individuals acting in their own private capacity is clear. The scope and nature of the economic activities of incorporated and unincorporated organizations and their representatives demand that the constitutional power of the federal and state governments to regulate those activities be correspondingly effective. The greater portion of evidence of wrongdoing by an organization or its representatives is usually to be found in the official records and documents of that organization. Were the cloak of the privilege to be thrown around these impersonal records and documents, effective enforcement of many federal and state laws would be impossible. See Hale v. Henkel, supra, 70, 74. The framers of the constitutional guarantee against compulsory self-disclosure, who were interested primarily in protecting individual civil liberties, cannot be said to have intended the privilege to be available to protect economic or other interests of such organizations so as to nullify appropriate governmental regulations.

The fact that the state charters corporations and has visitorial powers over them provides a convenient vehicle for justification of governmental investigation of corporate books and records. Hale v. Henkel, supra. But the absence of that fact as to a particular type of organization does not lessen the public necessity for making reasonable regulations of its activities effective, nor does it confer upon such an organization the purely personal privilege against self-incrimination. Basically, the power to compel the production of the records of any organization, whether it be incorporated or not, arises out of the inherent and necessary power of the federal and state governments to enforce their laws, with the privilege against self-incrimination being limited to its historic function of protecting only the natural individual from compulsory incrimination through his own testimony or personal records.

It follows that labor unions, as well as their officers and agents acting in their official capacity, cannot invoke this personal privilege. This conclusion is not reached by any mechanical comparison of unions with corporations or with other entities nor by any determination of whether unions technically may be regarded as legal personalities for any or all purposes. The test, rather, is whether one can fairly say under all the circumstances that a particular type of organization has a character so impersonal in the scope of its membership and activities that it cannot be said to embody or represent the purely private or personal interests of its constituents, but rather to embody their common or group interests only. If so, the privilege cannot be invoked on behalf of the organization or its representatives in their official capacity. Labor unions—national or local, incorporated or unincorporated—clearly meet that test.

Structurally and functionally, a labor union is an institution which involves more than the private or personal interests of its members. It represents organized, institutional activity as contrasted with wholly individual activity. This difference is as well defined as that existing between individual members of the union. The union's existence in fact, and for some purposes in law, is as perpetual as that of any corporation, not being dependent upon the life of any member. It normally operates under its own constitution, rules and by-laws which, in controversies between member and union, are often enforced by the courts. The union engages in a multitude of business and other official concerted activities, none of which can be said to be the private undertakings of the members. Duly elected union officers have no authority to do or sanction anything other than that which the union may lawfully do; nor have they authority to act for the members in matters affecting only the individual rights of such members. The union owns separate real and personal property, even though the title may nominally be in the names of its members or trustees. The official union books and records are distinct from the personal books and records of the individuals, in the same manner as the union treasury exists apart from the private and personal funds of the members. And no member or officer has the right to use them for criminal purposes or for his purely private affairs. The actions of one individual member no more bind the union than they bind another individual member unless there is proof that the union authorized or ratified the acts in question. At the same time, the members are not subject to either criminal or civil liability for the acts of the union or its officers as such unless it is shown that they personally authorized or participated in the particular acts.

These various considerations compel the conclusion that respondent could not claim the personal privilege against self-incrimination under these circumstances. The subpoena duces tecum was directed to the union and demanded the production only of its official documents and records. Respondent could not claim the privilege on behalf of the union because the union did not itself possess such a privilege. Moreover, the privilege is personal to the individual called as a witness, making it impossible for him to set up the privilege of a third person as an excuse for a refusal to answer or to produce documents. Hence respondent could not rely upon any possible privilege that the union might have. Hale v. Henkel, supra, 69–70; McAlister v. Henkel, 201 U.S. 90. Nor could respondent claim the privilege on behalf of himself as an officer of the union or as an individual. The documents he sought to place under the protective shield of the privilege were official union documents held by him in his capacity as a representative of the union. No valid claim was made that any part of them constituted his own private papers. He thus could not object that the union's books and records might incriminate him as an officer or as an individual.

* * *

Reversed.

Queries. 1) Is the fifth amendment theory in *White* consistent with the theory in *Hale?* 2) Which Model of the corporation did the Court have in mind for its test to determine whether an organization can be considered "personal"? 3) Can you now answer the question posed above (in Note (2)) as to whether a corporation has any fifth amendment right to refuse to produce documents?

(4) *The Partnership Entity.* In *Bellis v. United States* [15] the Court held that a partner in a three-partner law firm could not invoke his own fifth amendment privilege to resist a subpoena directed at him to produce the partnership's financial records. Justice Marshall wrote:

> In this case . . . we are required to explore the outer limits of the analysis of the Court in *White*. Petitioner argues that in view of the modest size of the partnership involved here, it is unrealistic to consider the firm as an entity independent of its three partners; rather, he claims, the law firm embodies little more than the personal legal practice of the individual partners. Moreover, petitioner argues that he has a substantial and direct ownership interest in the partnership records, and does not hold them in a representative capacity.
>
> Despite the force of these arguments, we conclude that the lower courts properly applied the *White* rule in the circumstances of this case. While small, the partnership here did have an established institutional identity independent of its individual partners. This was not an informal association or a temporary arrangement for the undertaking of a few projects of short-lived duration. Rather, the partnership represented a formal institutional arrangement organized for the continuing conduct of the firm's legal practice. The partnership was in existence for nearly 15 years prior to its voluntary dissolution. Although it may not have had a formal constitution or bylaws to govern its internal affairs, state partnership law imposed on the firm a certain organizational structure in the absence of any contrary agreement by the partners; for example, it guaranteed to each of the partners the equal right to participate in the management and control of the firm and prescribed that majority rule governed the conduct of the firm's business. The firm maintained a bank account in the partnership name, had stationery using the firm name on its

---

15. 417 U.S. 85, 94 S.Ct. 2719, 40 L.Ed. 2d 678 (1974).

letterhead, and, in general, held itself out to third parties as an entity with an independent institutional identity. It employed six persons in addition to its partners, including two other attorneys who practiced law on behalf of the firm, rather than as individuals on their own behalf. It filed separate partnership returns for federal tax purposes, as required by § 6031 of the Internal Revenue Code, 26 U.S.C. § 6031. State law permitted the firm to be sued and to hold title to property in the partnership name, and generally regarded the partnership as a distinct entity for numerous other purposes.

Equally important, we believe it is fair to say that petitioner is holding the subpoenaed partnership records in a representative capacity . . . .

* * *

Petitioner relies heavily on language in the Court's opinion in *White* which suggests that the "test" for determining the applicability of the Fifth Amendment privilege in this area is whether the organization "has a character so impersonal in the scope of its membership and activities that it cannot be said to embody or represent the purely private or personal interests of its constituents, but rather to embody their common or group interests only." We must admit our agreement with the Solicitor General's observation that "it is difficult to know precisely what situations the formulation in *White* was intended to include within the protection of the privilege." Brief for United States 21. The Court in *White*, after stating its test, did not really apply it, nor has any of the subsequent decisions of this Court. On its face, the test is not particularly helpful in the broad range of cases, including this one, where the organization embodies neither "purely . . . personal interests" nor "group interests only," but rather some combination of the two.

In any event, we do not believe that the Court's formulation in *White* can be reduced to a simple proposition based solely upon the size of the organization. It is well settled that no privilege can be claimed by the custodian of corporate records, regardless of how small the corporation may be. Every State has now adopted laws permitting incorporation of professional associations, and increasing numbers of lawyers, doctors, and other professionals are choosing to conduct their business affairs in the corporate form rather than the more traditional partnership. Whether corporation or partnership, many of these firms will be independent entities whose financial records are held by a member of the firm in a representative capacity. In these circumstances, the applicability of the privilege should not turn on an insubstantial difference in the form of the business enterprise.

This might be a different case if it involved a small family partnership, or, as the Solicitor General suggests, Brief for United

States 22–23, if there were some other pre-existing relationship of confidentiality among the partners. But in the circumstances of this case, petitioner's possession of the partnership's financial records in what can be fairly said to be a representative capacity compels our holding that his personal privilege against compulsory self-incrimination is inapplicable.

Affirmed.

JUSTICE DOUGLAS, dissenting.

* * *

. . . Bellis was not holding the records involved here as a representative of some separate, impersonal entity with no rights under the Fifth Amendment. The records he holds are his own, in both a legal and a practical sense. Nor could the grand jury investigation result in any finding of tax liability by the partnership as a separate entity, for the partnership has no tax obligations other than the filing of informational forms that aid in determining the liabilities of the individual partners. It was only Bellis individually, or his two former partners, against whom the investigation could have been directed. If Bellis had been conducting a solo practice, his claim of privilege could not be overridden, as the Government here necessarily conceded. I am unable to perceive why he should be held to have forfeited that constitutional right by joining with two others in a partnership.

* * *

(5) *The Constitutional Rights of Corporations.* The general question of which constitutional protections are available to corporations has been one of continuing controversy. In 1886 Chief Justice Waite announced, prior to oral argument in *Santa Clara County v. Southern Pac. R. Co.,*[16] that:

> The court does not wish to hear argument on the question whether the provision in the Fourteenth Amendment to the Constitution, which forbids a State to deny to any person within its jurisdiction the equal protection of the laws, applies to these corporations. We are all of opinion that it does.[17]

Since that time, however, the Court has not always extended Constitutional protections to corporations. For example, the privileges and immunities clause of the fourteenth amendment does not apply to corporations,[18] nor does the due process protection of "liberty." [19] On

---

16. 118 U.S. 394, 396, 6 S.Ct. 1132, 30 L.Ed. 118 (1886).

17. Waite was positive about this issue because of an earlier oral argument made by Roscoe Conkling, a former member of the Joint Congressional Committee which drafted the fourteenth amendment, to the effect that Congress had deliberately used the word "person" to cover corporations. See San Mateo County v. Southern Pac. R. Co., 116 U.S. 138, 6 S.Ct. 317, 29 L.Ed. 589 (1885). Conkling based his arguments on a hitherto undisclosed manuscript journal of the Joint Committee. Later evidence indicates, however, that Conkling's arguments were not supported by the journal. For further discussion of Conkling's argument, see Graham, The "Conspiracy Theory" of the Fourteenth Amendment, 47 Yale L.J. 371 (1938).

18. See Hague v. CIO, 307 U.S. 496, 514, 59 S.Ct. 954, 963, 83 L.Ed. 1423, 1436 (1939).

19. See note 19 on page 400.

the other hand, the due process protection "of property" is applicable to corporations,[20] as are the protections of the first amendment.[21]

(6) *Double Jeopardy.* The Supreme Court has never directly passed on the question whether a corporation is entitled to the protection of the double jeopardy clause. The closest the Court has come is *United States v. Martin Linen Supply Co.*[22] There the Court held that the United States could not appeal a judgment of acquittal entered in a criminal contempt proceeding brought against two corporations because the federal Criminal Appeals Act barred appeals where the double jeopardy clause "prohibits further prosecution." Justice Powell later cited *Martin Linen* as an example of a decision "affording corporations the protection of constitutional guarantees."[23]

In *United States v. Security Nat'l Bank,*[24] the Second Circuit held that a corporation was protected by the double jeopardy clause, and therefore dismissed a government attempt to appeal from a judgment of acquittal:

> The prohibition against double jeopardy, "one of the oldest ideas found in western civilization", Bartkus v. Illinois, 359 U.S. 121, 151, 79 S.Ct. 676, 696, 3 L.Ed.2d 684 (1959) (Black, J., dissenting), has become "part of our American concept of fundamental fairness." Brock v. North Carolina, 344 U.S. 424, 435, 73 S.Ct. 349, 354, 97 L.Ed. 456 (1953) (Vinson, C.J., dissenting). It represents such a "fundamental ideal in our constitutional heritage" that its basic core must be included within the equally fundamental constitutional right of due process. We see no valid reason why a corporation which is a "person" entitled to both equal protection and due process under the Constitution, should not also be entitled to the constitutional guaranty against double jeopardy.
>
> The Government argues its cause as if all corporations were industrial giants and all corporate crimes were merely regulatory violations punishable by modest fines. Thus, it seeks to avoid the concept of governmental harassment and oppression which is a basic ingredient of the resistance to double jeopardy. Neither corporations nor corporate crimes can be so easily encapsulated. Most New York business corporations, for example, have only a few shareholders, and some have only one. Moreover, many corporations are organized for religious, educational, charitable or social purposes, rather than for the pursuit of profit. It is well-settled,

---

19. See Western Turf Ass'n v. Greenburg, 204 U.S. 359, 363, 27 S.Ct. 384, 386, 51 L.Ed. 520, 522 (1907).

20. See, e.g., Smyth v. Ames, 169 U.S. 466, 18 S.Ct. 418, 42 L.Ed. 819 (1898); Minneapolis & St. L. Ry. Co. v. Beckwith, 129 U.S. 26, 28, 9 S.Ct. 207, 32 L.Ed. 585, 586 (1889).

21. See First Nat. Bank of Boston v. Bellotti, 435 U.S. 765, 98 S.Ct. 1407, 55 L.Ed.2d 707 (1978).

22. 430 U.S. 564, 97 S.Ct. 1349, 51 L.Ed. 2d 642 (1977).

23. See First Nat. Bank of Boston v. Bellotti, 435 U.S. 765, 778 n. 14, 98 S.Ct. 1407, 1417 n. 14, 55 L.Ed.2d 707, 719 n. 14 (1978).

24. 546 F.2d 492 (2d Cir.1976).

also, that a corporate entity may be guilty of a great variety of criminal acts. Indeed, some commentators assert, perhaps a bit enthusiastically, that there is virtually no crime for which a corporation should not be held liable. The financial penalties for some of these offenses can be substantial indeed. Bearing these factors in mind, we are not prepared to accept the Government's contention that "but for the label [a criminal proceeding against a corporation] is little different from a civil case." Government's reply brief at 18.

The small entrepreneur is not spared the embarrassment, expense, anxiety and insecurity resulting from repeated trials on criminal charges, simply because he has incorporated his modest business. That a large corporation may have more substantial financial resources is no more valid ground for depriving it of its constitutional rights than is the possession of greater wealth by an individual. Indeed, the larger the corporation, the more likely it is that its shareholders, who in the end must bear the financial burden consequent upon criminal liability, will be completely innocent and unaware of any corporate wrongdoing.

No corporation, large or small, can escape the "incalculable effect" which a conviction may have on the public attitude toward the company. Like an individual, it must answer to the "verdict of the community." No corporation, no matter how large, can pit its resources against the overwhelming might of the State so as to avoid the harassment and the increasing probability of conviction resulting from reprosecutions. In this unequal contest, "fundamental fairness" requires that the Government, having had a full try at establishing criminal wrongdoing, shall not have another.

B. COMMON LAW: ATTORNEY–CLIENT PRIVILEGE

SCOPE NOTE

The materials in this Section focus on the common law attorney-client privilege (along with its companion, the work-product doctrine). The attorney-client privilege can be used by corporations to achieve the same goal sought originally in *Hale v. Henkel*—protecting corporate documents from compulsory disclosure to the government. As the cases in this Section indicate, however, corporations have had more success with the common law privileges than with the constitutional ones. Students should keep this in mind while reading these materials, and should ask why the courts have been more generous in extending these privileges to the corporation than in extending the constitutional ones.

The main case in this Section is *Upjohn v. United States*, in which the Supreme Court elaborated upon the scope of the attorney-client privilege and work-product doctrine in the context of the corporate client. The Notes following *Upjohn* explore some of the implications of *Upjohn*, particularly as the case relates to corporate internal investigations. Subsequent materials in this Section explore the two major ways for losing the coverage of the privilege, waiver and the crime-fraud exception to the attorney-client privilege.

1. QUALIFYING FOR THE PRIVILEGE

UPJOHN CO. v. UNITED STATES

Supreme Court of the United States, 1981.
449 U.S. 383, 101 S.Ct. 677, 66 L.Ed.2d 584.

JUSTICE REHNQUIST delivered the opinion of the Court.

We granted certiorari in this case to address important questions concerning the scope of the attorney-client privilege in the corporate context and the applicability of the work-product doctrine in proceedings to enforce tax summonses. With respect to the privilege question the parties and various amici have described our task as one of choosing between two "tests" which have gained adherents in the courts of appeals. We are acutely aware, however, that we sit to decide concrete cases and not abstract propositions of law. We decline to lay down a broad rule or series of rules to govern all conceivable future questions in this area, even were we able to do so. We can and do, however, conclude that the attorney-client privilege protects the communications involved in this case from compelled disclosure and that the work-product doctrine does apply in tax summons enforcement proceedings.

I

Petitioner Upjohn manufactures and sells pharmaceuticals here and abroad. In January 1976 independent accountants conducting an audit of one of petitioner's foreign subsidiaries discovered that the subsidiary made payments to or for the benefit of foreign government officials in order to secure government business. The accountants so informed Mr. Gerard Thomas, petitioner's Vice-President, Secretary, and General Counsel. Thomas is a member of the Michigan and New York bars, and has been petitioner's General Counsel for 20 years. He consulted with outside counsel and R.T. Parfet, Jr., petitioner's Chairman of the Board. It was decided that the company would conduct an internal investigation of what were termed "questionable payments." As part of this investigation the attorneys prepared a letter containing a questionnaire which was sent to "all foreign general and area managers" over the Chairman's signature. The letter began by noting recent disclosures that several American companies made "possibly illegal" payments to foreign government officials and emphasized that the management needed full information concerning any such payments made by Upjohn. The letter indicated that the Chairman had asked Thomas, identified as "the company's General Counsel," "to conduct an investigation for the purpose of determining the nature and magnitude of any payments made by the Upjohn Company or any of its subsidiaries to any employee or official of a foreign government." The questionnaire sought detailed information concerning such payments. Managers were instructed to treat the investigation as "highly confidential" and not to discuss it with anyone other than Upjohn employees who might be helpful in providing the requested information. Responses were to be sent directly to Thomas. Thomas and outside counsel also interviewed the recipients of the questionnaire and some 33 other Upjohn officers or employees as part of the investigation.

On March 26, 1976, the company voluntarily submitted a preliminary report to the Securities and Exchange Commission on Form 8–K disclosing certain questionable payments. A copy of the report was simultaneously submitted to the Internal Revenue Service, which immediately began an investigation to determine the tax consequences of the payments. Special agents conducting the investigation were given lists by Upjohn of all those interviewed and all who had responded to the questionnaire. On November 23, 1976, the Service issued a summons pursuant to 26 U.S.C. § 7602 demanding production of:

> "All files relative to the investigation conducted under the supervision of Gerard Thomas to identify payments to employees of foreign governments and any political contributions made by the Upjohn Company or any of its affiliates since January 1, 1971 and to determine whether any funds of the Upjohn Company had been improperly accounted for on the corporate books during the same period.
>
> "The records should include but not be limited to written questionnaires sent to managers of the Upjohn Company's foreign affiliates, and memoranda or notes of the interviews conducted in the United States and abroad with officers and employees of the Upjohn Company and its subsidiaries."

The company declined to produce the documents specified in the second paragraph on the grounds that they were protected from disclosure by the attorney-client privilege and constituted the work product of attorneys prepared in anticipation of litigation. On August 31, 1977, the United States filed a petition seeking enforcement of the summons under 26 U.S.C. §§ 7402(b) and 7604(a) in the United States District Court for the Western District of Michigan. That court adopted the recommendation of a magistrate who concluded that the summons should be enforced. Petitioner appealed to the Court of Appeals for the Sixth Circuit which rejected the magistrate's finding of a waiver of the attorney-client privilege, but agreed that the privilege did not apply "to the extent the communications were made by officers and agents not responsible for directing Upjohn's actions in response to legal advice . . . for the simple reason that the communications were not the 'client's.'" The court reasoned that accepting petitioner's claim for a broader application of the privilege would encourage upper-echelon management to ignore unpleasant facts and create too broad a "zone of silence." Noting that petitioner's counsel had interviewed officials such as the Chairman and President, the Court of Appeals remanded to the District Court so that a determination of who was within the "control group" could be made. In a concluding footnote the court stated that the work-product doctrine "is not applicable to administrative summonses issued under 26 U.S.C. § 7602."

II

Federal Rule of Evidence 501 provides that "the privilege of a witness . . . shall be governed by the principles of the common law as they may be interpreted by the courts of the United States in light of reason and experience." The attorney-client privilege is the oldest of the privileges for confidential communications known to the common law. 8 Wigmore, Evidence § 2290 (McNaughton rev. 1961). Its purpose is to encourage full and frank communication between attorneys and their clients and thereby promote broader public interests in the observance of law and administration of justice. The privilege recognizes that sound legal advice or advocacy serves public ends and that such advice or advocacy depends upon the lawyer being fully informed by the client. As we stated last Term in Trammel v. United States, 445 U.S. 40, 51, 100 S.Ct. 906, 913, 63 L.Ed.2d 186 (1980), "The attorney-client privilege rests on the need for the advocate and counselor to know all that relates to the client's reasons for seeking representation if the professional mission is to be carried out." And in Fisher v. United States, 425 U.S. 391, 403, 96 S.Ct. 1569, 1577, 48 L.Ed.2d 39 (1976), we recognized the purpose of the privilege to be "to encourage clients to make full disclosures to their attorneys." This rationale for the privilege has long been recognized by the Court, see Hunt v. Blackburn, 128 U.S. 464, 470, 9 S.Ct. 125, 127, 32 L.Ed. 488 (1888) (privilege "is founded upon the necessity, in the interest and administration of justice, of the aid of persons having knowledge of the law and skilled in its practice, which assistance can only be safely and readily availed of when free from the consequences or the apprehension of disclosure"). Admittedly complications in the application of the privilege arise when the client is a corporation, which in theory is an artificial creature of the law, and not an individual; but this Court has assumed that the privilege applies when the client is a corporation, United States v. Louisville & Nashville R. Co., 236 U.S. 318, 336, 35 S.Ct. 363, 369, 59 L.Ed. 598 (1915), and the Government does not contest the general proposition.

The Court of Appeals, however, considered the application of the privilege in the corporate context to present a "different problem," since the client was an inanimate entity and "only the senior management, guiding and integrating the several operations, ... can be said to possess an identity analogous to the corporation as a whole." The first case to articulate the so-called "control group test" adopted by the court below, City of Philadelphia v. Westinghouse Electric Corp., 210 F.Supp. 483, 485 (ED Pa.), petition for mandamus and prohibition denied, General Electric Company v. Kirkpatrick, 312 F.2d 742 (CA3 1962), cert. denied, 372 U.S. 943, 83 S.Ct. 937, 9 L.Ed.2d 969 (1963), reflected a similar conceptual approach:

> "Keeping in mind that the question is, Is it the corporation which is seeking the lawyer's advice when the asserted privileged communication is made?, the most satisfactory solution, I think, is that if the employee making the communication, of whatever rank he may be, is in a position to control or even to take a substantial part in a decision about any action which the corporation may take upon the advice of the attorney, . . . then, in effect, *he is (or personifies) the corporation* when he makes his disclosure to the lawyer and the privilege would apply." (Emphasis supplied.)

Such a view, we think, overlooks the fact that the privilege exists to protect not only the giving of professional advice to those who can act on it but also the giving of information to the lawyer to enable him to give sound and informed advice. The first step in the resolution of any legal problem is ascertaining the factual background and sifting through the facts with an eye to the legally relevant. See ABA Code of Professional Responsibility, Ethical Consideration 4–1:

> "A lawyer should be fully informed of all the facts of the matter he is handling in order for his client to obtain the full advantage of our legal system. It is for the lawyer in the exercise of his independent professional judgment to separate the relevant and important from the irrelevant and unimportant. The observance of the ethical obligation of a lawyer to hold inviolate the confidences and secrets of his client not only facilitates the full development of facts essential to proper representation of the client but also encourages laymen to seek early legal assistance."

In the case of the individual client the provider of information and the person who acts on the lawyer's advice are one and the same. In the corporate context, however, it will frequently be employees beyond the control group as defined by the court below—"officers and agents . . . responsible for directing [the company's] actions in response to legal advice"—who will possess the information needed by the corporation's lawyers. Middle-level—and indeed lower-level—employees can, by actions within the scope of their employment, embroil the corporation in serious legal difficulties, and it is only natural that these employees would have the relevant information needed by corporate counsel if he is adequately to advise the client with respect to such actual or potential difficulties. This fact was noted in Diversified Industries, Inc. v. Meredith, 572 F.2d 596 (CA8 1978) (en banc):

> "In a corporation, it may be necessary to glean information relevant to a legal problem from middle management or non-management personnel as well as from top executives. The attorney

dealing with a complex legal problem 'is thus faced with a "Hobson's choice." If he interviews employees not having "the very highest authority" their communications to him will not be privileged. If, on the other hand, he interviews *only* those employees with the "very highest authority," he may find it extremely difficult, if not impossible, to determine what happened.'"

The control group test adopted by the court below thus frustrates the very purpose of the privilege by discouraging the communication of relevant information by employees of the client to attorneys seeking to render legal advice to the client corporation. The attorney's advice will also frequently be more significant to noncontrol group members than to those who officially sanction the advice, and the control group test makes it more difficult to convey full and frank legal advice to the employees who will put into effect the client corporation's policy.

The narrow scope given the attorney-client privilege by the court below not only makes it difficult for corporate attorneys to formulate sound advice when their client is faced with a specific legal problem but also threatens to limit the valuable efforts of corporate counsel to ensure their client's compliance with the law. In light of the vast and complicated array of regulatory legislation confronting the modern corporation, corporations, unlike most individuals, "constantly go to lawyers to find out how to obey the law," Burnham, The Attorney-Client Privilege in the Corporate Arena, 24 Bus.Law. 901, 913 (1969), particularly since compliance with the law in this area is hardly an instinctive matter, see, e.g., United States v. United States Gypsum Co., 438 U.S. 422, 440–441, 98 S.Ct. 2864, 2875–2876, 57 L.Ed.2d 854 (1978) ("the behavior proscribed by the [Sherman] Act is often difficult to distinguish from the gray zone of socially acceptable and economically justifiable business conduct").[25] The test adopted by the court below is difficult to apply in practice, though no abstractly formulated and unvarying "test" will necessarily enable courts to decide questions such as this with mathematical precision. But if the purpose of the attorney-client privilege is to be served, the attorney and client must be able to predict with some degree of certainty whether particular discussions will be protected. An uncertain privilege, or one which purports to be certain but results in widely varying applications by the courts, is little better than no privilege at all. The very terms of the test adopted by the court below suggest the unpredictability of its application. The test restricts the availability of the privilege to those officers who play a "substantial role" in deciding and directing a corporation's legal re-

---

25. [Court's footnote 2.] The Government argues that the risk of civil or criminal liability suffices to ensure that corporations will seek legal advice in the absence of the protection of the privilege. This response ignores the fact that the depth and quality of any investigations to ensure compliance with the law would suffer, even were they undertaken. The response also proves too much, since it applies to all communications covered by the privilege: an individual trying to comply with the law or faced with a legal problem also has strong incentive to disclose information to his lawyer, yet the common law has recognized the value of the privilege in further facilitating communications.

sponse. Disparate decisions in cases applying this test illustrate its unpredictability. Compare, e.g., Hogan v. Zletz, 43 F.R.D. 308, 315–316 (ND Okl.1967), aff'd in part sub nom. Natta v. Hogan, 392 F.2d 686 (CA10 1968) (control group includes managers and assistant managers of patent division and research and development department) with Congoleum Industries, Inc. v. GAF Corp., 49 F.R.D. 82, 83–85 (ED Pa. 1969), aff'd, 478 F.2d 1398 (CA3 1973) (control group includes only division and corporate vice-presidents, and not two directors of research and vice-president for production and research).

The communications at issue were made by Upjohn employees [26] to counsel for Upjohn acting as such, at the direction of corporate superiors in order to secure legal advice from counsel. As the magistrate found, "Mr. Thomas consulted with the Chairman of the Board and outside counsel and thereafter conducted a factual investigation to determine the nature and extent of the questionable payments *and to be in a position to give legal advice to the company with respect to the payments.*" (Emphasis supplied.) Information, not available from upper-echelon management, was needed to supply a basis for legal advice concerning compliance with securities and tax laws, foreign laws, currency regulations, duties to shareholders, and potential litigation in each of these areas. The communications concerned matters within the scope of the employees' corporate duties, and the employees themselves were sufficiently aware that they were being questioned in order that the corporation could obtain legal advice. The questionnaire identified Thomas as "the company's General Counsel" and referred in its opening sentence to the possible illegality of payments such as the ones on which information was sought. A statement of policy accompanying the questionnaire clearly indicated the legal implications of the investigation. The policy statement was issued "in order that there be no uncertainty in the future as to the policy with respect to the practices which are the subject of this investigation." It began "Upjohn will comply with all laws and regulations," and stated that commissions or payments "will not be used as a subterfuge for bribes or illegal payments" and that all payments must be "proper and legal." Any future agreements with foreign distributors or agents were to be approved "by a company attorney" and any questions concerning the policy were to be referred "to the company's General Counsel." This statement was issued to Upjohn employees worldwide, so that even those interviewees not receiving a questionnaire were aware of the legal implications of the interviews. Pursuant to explicit instructions from the Chairman of the Board, the communications were considered "highly confidential" when made and have been kept confidential by the company. Consistent with the underlying purposes of the attorney-

---

26. [Court's footnote 3.] Seven of the 86 employees interviewed by counsel had terminated their employment with Upjohn at the time of the interview. Petitioner argues that the privilege should nonetheless apply to communications by these former employees concerning activities during their period of employment. Neither the District Court nor the Court of Appeals had occasion to address this issue, and we decline to decide it without the benefit of treatment below.

client privilege, these communications must be protected against compelled disclosure.

The Court of Appeals declined to extend the attorney-client privilege beyond the limits of the control group test for fear that doing so would entail severe burdens on discovery and create a broad "zone of silence" over corporate affairs. Application of the attorney-client privilege to communications such as those involved here, however, puts the adversary in no worse position than if the communications had never taken place. The privilege only protects disclosure of communications; it does not protect disclosure of the underlying facts by those who communicated with the attorney:

> "The protection of the privilege extends only to *communications* and not to facts. A fact is one thing and a communication concerning that fact is an entirely different thing. The client cannot be compelled to answer the question, 'What did you say or write to the attorney?' but may not refuse to disclose any relevant fact within his knowledge merely because he incorporated a statement of such fact into his communication to his attorney." City of Philadelphia v. Westinghouse Electric Corp., 205 F.Supp. 830, 831 (ED Pa.1962).

See also State v. Circuit Court, 34 Wis.2d 559, 580, 150 N.W.2d 387, 399 (1967) ("the courts have noted that a party cannot conceal a fact merely by revealing it to his lawyer"). Here the Government was free to question the employees who communicated with Thomas and outside counsel. Upjohn has provided the IRS with a list of such employees, and the IRS has already interviewed some 25 of them. While it would probably be more convenient for the Government to secure the results of petitioner's internal investigation by simply subpoenaing the questionnaires and notes taken by petitioner's attorneys, such considerations of convenience do not overcome the policies served by the attorney-client privilege. . . .

Needless to say, we decide only the case before us, and do not undertake to draft a set of rules which should govern challenges to investigatory subpoenas. Any such approach would violate the spirit of F.R.E. 501. While such a "case-by-case" basis may to some slight extent undermine desirable certainty in the boundaries of the attorney-client privilege, it obeys the spirit of the Rules. At the same time we conclude that the narrow "control group test" sanctioned by the Court of Appeals, in this case cannot, consistent with "the principles of the common law as . . . interpreted . . . in light of reason and experience," F.R.E. 501, govern the development of the law in this area.

III

Our decision that the communications by Upjohn employees to counsel are covered by the attorney-client privilege disposes of the case so far as the responses to the questionnaires and any notes reflecting responses to interview questions are concerned. The summons reaches further, however, and Thomas has testified that his notes and memoranda of interviews go beyond recording responses to his questions. To the extent that the material subject to the summons is not protected by the attorney-client privilege as disclosing communications between an employee and counsel, we must reach the ruling by the Court of Appeals that the work-product doctrine does not apply to summonses issued under 26 U.S.C. § 7602.[27]

The Government concedes, wisely, that the Court of Appeals erred and that the work-product doctrine does apply to IRS summonses. This doctrine was announced by the Court over 30 years ago in *Hickman v. Taylor*, 329 U.S. 495, 67 S.Ct. 385, 91 L.Ed. 451 (1947). In that case the Court rejected "an attempt, without purported necessity or justification, to secure written statements, private memoranda, and personal recollections prepared or formed by an adverse party's counsel in the course of his legal duties." Id., at 510, 67 S.Ct., at 393. The Court noted that "it is essential that a lawyer work with a certain degree of privacy" and reasoned that if discovery of the material sought were permitted

> "much of what is now put down in writing would remain unwritten. An attorney's thoughts, heretofore inviolate, would not be his own. Inefficiency, unfairness and sharp practices would inevitably develop in the giving of legal advice and in the preparation of cases for trial. The effect on the legal profession would be demoralizing. And the interests of the clients and the cause of justice would be poorly served." Id., at 511, 67 S.Ct., at 393–394.

The "strong public policy" underlying the work-product doctrine was reaffirmed recently in United States v. Nobles, 422 U.S. 225, 236–240, 95 S.Ct. 2160, 2169–2171, 45 L.Ed.2d 141 (1975), and has been substantially incorporated in Federal Rule of Civil Procedure 26(b)(3).[28]

. . . While conceding the applicability of the work-product doctrine, the Government asserts that it has made a sufficient showing of necessity to overcome its protections. The magistrate apparently so found. The Government relies on the following language in *Hickman*:

> "We do not mean to say that all written materials obtained or prepared by an adversary's counsel with an eye toward litigation are necessarily free from discovery in all cases. Where relevant

---

27. [Court's footnote 6.] The following discussion will also be relevant to counsels' notes and memoranda of interviews with the seven former employees should it be determined that the attorney-client privilege does not apply to them.

28. [Court's footnote 7.] This provides, in pertinent part:

"A party may obtain discovery of documents and tangible things otherwise discoverable under subdivision (b)(1) of this rule and prepared in anticipation of litigation or for trial by or for another party or by or for that other party's representative (including his attorney, consultant, surety, indemnitor, insurer, or agent) only upon a showing that the party seeking discovery has substantial need of the materials in the preparation of his case and that he is unable without undue hardship to obtain the substantial equivalent of the materials by other means. In ordering discovery of such materials when the required showing has been made, the court shall protect against disclosure of the mental impressions, conclusions, opinions, or legal theories of an attorney or other representative of a party concerning the litigation."

and nonprivileged facts remain hidden in an attorney's file and where production of those facts is essential to the preparation of one's case, discovery may properly be had. . . . And production might be justified where the witnesses are no longer available or may be reached only with difficulty." 329 U.S., at 511, 67 S.Ct., at 394.

The Government stresses that interviewees are scattered across the globe and that Upjohn has forbidden its employees to answer questions it considers irrelevant. The above-quoted language from *Hickman*, however, did not apply to "oral statements made by witnesses . . . whether presently in the form of [the attorney's] mental impressions or memoranda." Id., at 512, 67 S.Ct., at 394. As to such material the Court did "not believe that any showing of necessity can be made under the circumstances of this case so as to justify production. . . . If there should be a rare situation justifying production of these matters petitioner's case is not of that type." Forcing an attorney to disclose notes and memoranda of witnesses' oral statements is particularly disfavored because it tends to reveal the attorney's mental processes, 329 U.S., at 513, 67 S.Ct., at 394–395 ("what he saw fit to write down regarding witnesses' remarks"); id., at 516–517, 67 S.Ct., at 396 ("the statement would be his [the attorney's] language, permeated with his inferences") (Jackson, J., concurring).[29]

* * *

Based on the foregoing, some courts have concluded that *no* showing of necessity can overcome protection of work product which is based on oral statements from witnesses. Those courts declining to adopt an absolute rule have nonetheless recognized that such material is entitled to special protection.

We do not decide the issue at this time. It is clear that the magistrate applied the wrong standard when he concluded that the Government had made a sufficient showing of necessity to overcome the protections of the work-product doctrine. The magistrate applied the "substantial need" and "without undue hardship" standard articulated in the first part of Rule 26(b)(3). The notes and memoranda sought by the Government here, however, are work product based on oral statements. If they reveal communications, they are, in this case, protected by the attorney-client privilege. To the extent they do not reveal communications, they reveal the attorneys' mental processes in evaluating the communications. As Rule 26 and *Hickman* make clear, such work product cannot be disclosed simply on a showing of substantial need and inability to obtain the equivalent without undue hardship.

---

29. [Court's footnote 8.] Thomas described his notes of the interviews as containing "what I consider to be the important questions, the substance of the responses to them, my beliefs as to the importance of these, my beliefs as to how they related to the inquiry, my thoughts as to how they related to other questions. In some instances they might even suggest other questions that I would have to ask or things that I needed to find elsewhere."

While we are not prepared at this juncture to say that such material is always protected by the work product rule, we think a far stronger showing of necessity and unavailability by other means than was made by the Government or applied by the magistrate in this case would be necessary to compel disclosure. Since the Court of Appeals thought that the work-product protection was never applicable in an enforcement proceeding such as this, and since the magistrate whose recommendations the District Court adopted applied too lenient a standard of protection, we think the best procedure with respect to this aspect of the case would be to reverse the judgment of the Court of Appeals for the Sixth Circuit and remand the case to it for such further proceedings in connection with the work-product claim as are consistent with this opinion.

Accordingly, the judgment of the Court of Appeals is reversed, and the case remanded for further proceedings.

NOTES AND QUERIES

(1) *The Court's Choices.* In determining that the communications involved in *Upjohn* were protected by the attorney-client privilege, the Court had several approaches to the question that it could have taken, but did not.[30] Consider:

a) No privilege: Why should a corporation be entitled to assert an "immunity" from document production based on the attorney-client privilege? Note that the Court in *Upjohn* stated that "this Court has assumed that the privilege applies when the client is a corporation" and that government counsel in *Upjohn* did not contest this proposition.[31] In 1962 a district court had held that a corporation was not entitled to assert the attorney-client privilege. Although the district court was reversed on appeal,[32] another court subsequently described the district court's opinion as "supported by a good deal of history and sound logic."[33] What is the "logic" for and against allowing corporations to claim the privilege? How far do you think this logic extends?

b) Control Group Test: Prior to *Upjohn*, the courts were fairly unanimous in extending the attorney-client privilege to corporations, but a majority of the federal courts followed the "control group" test, first enunciated by the district court in *City of Philadelphia v. Westing-*

---

30. These alternate approaches are explored in Sexton, A Post–Upjohn Consideration of the Corporate Attorney–Client Privilege, 57 N.Y.U.L.Rev. 443, 445–56 (1982).

31. The case which the Court cited for its assumption that the privilege applies to corporations was United States v. Louisville & Nashville R. Co., 236 U.S. 318, 35 S.Ct. 363, 59 L.Ed. 598 (1915). As in *Upjohn*, however, the Government in that case conceded that the privilege was applicable to corporations and the Court did not challenge the concession.

32. See Radiant Burners, Inc. v. American Gas Ass'n, 207 F.Supp. 771 (N.D.Ill. 1962), reversed 320 F.2d 314 (7th Cir.1963), certiorari denied 375 U.S. 929, 84 S.Ct. 330, 11 L.Ed.2d 262 (1963).

33. City of Phila. v. Westinghouse Elec. Corp., 210 F.Supp. 483, 484 (E.D.Pa.), mandamus denied sub nom. General Elec. Co. v. Kirkpatrick, 312 F.2d 742 (3d Cir.1962), certiorari denied 372 U.S. 943, 83 S.Ct. 937, 9 L.Ed.2d 969 (1963).

house Electric Corp.³⁴ This test, as noted in *Upjohn,* required the employee who made the communication to have been in a "position to control or even to take a substantial part in a decision about any action which the corporation may take upon the advice of the attorney." Such employees, the district court felt, "personify" the corporation. Do you agree with the reasons given in *Upjohn* for rejecting this test? Does either the control group test or the "test" adopted in *Upjohn* reflect a particular Model of the corporation?

c) *Subject Matter Test:* The competing theory to the control group test was the "subject matter" test. This test covered communications to counsel "at the direction of a superior" where the subject matter of the attorney's advice and of the communication involved "the performance by the employee of the duties of his employment." ³⁵ Does this test differ from the "test" adopted in *Upjohn?* What was the test adopted in *Upjohn?* On what Model of the corporation does the subject matter test rest? Would you be concerned that it might shield too much information from subsequent disclosure?

(2) *Internal Investigations.* Performing internal corporate investigations, like the one described in *Upjohn,* is a growing specialization for law firms.³⁶ These investigations, however, often pose many potential problems, as can be seen in the following article. Ingersoll and Lubove, "Three Top Law Firms Mired in Litigation Involving Ashland Oil," The Wall Street Journal, March 21, 1986, p. 1.³⁷

Three of the nation's leading law firms have become mired in a legal and ethical tar pit involving Ashland Oil Inc.

The prestigious New York firm of Cravath, Swaine & Moore has been disqualified from defending Ashland in federal court here against charges of making illegal foreign payments and then covering them up. Samuel C. Butler, Cravath's presiding partner and an Ashland director, is a defendant in the litigation here, along with other Ashland directors. A former executive's suit also accuses Mr. Butler of improperly trying to influence the legal representation of the executive, who became a whistle blower in the case.

---

34. 210 F.Supp. 483, 485 (E.D.Pa.), mandamus denied sub nom. General Elec. Co. v. Kirkpatrick, 312 F.2d 742 (3d Cir.1962), certiorari denied 372 U.S. 943, 83 S.Ct. 937, 9 L.Ed.2d 969 (1963).

35. See Harper & Row Publishers, Inc. v. Decker, 423 F.2d 487 (7th Cir.1970), affirmed by an equally divided Court, 400 U.S. 348, 91 S.Ct. 479, 27 L.Ed.2d 433 (1971). Two issues were raised in the Supreme Court, the proper test for the attorney client privilege and the question whether the district court's opinion was reviewable by writ of mandamus. It is thus not possible to determine whether the evenly divided vote represented any view with regard to the test for the attorney-client privilege.

36. See "Milbank, Law Firm, Forms Special Team To Do Internal Corporate Investigations," Wall St.J., May 11, 1988, p. 31 (announcing formation of "special team" of three prominent partners, including a former Attorney General of the United States and a former Abscam prosecutor, who will perform independent internal corporate investigations; other lawyers skeptical: "'I don't exactly feel that corporate America is racing to conduct internal investigations of itself,'" says one lawyer). For a discussion of the development of these investigations and some of the problems involved, see Mathews, Internal Corporate Investigations, 45 Ohio St.L.J. 655 (1984).

37. Reprinted by permission of The Wall Street Journal, © Dow Jones & Company, Inc. 1986. All Rights Reserved Worldwide.

A Pittsburgh lawyer who conducted an internal investigation for Ashland is accused in the whistle blower's suit of having played a major role in the alleged cover-up after previously advising the company on the questionable payments. Meanwhile, two House subcommittees are reviewing the Securities and Exchange Commission's recent rejection of its staff recommendation to charge Ashland with violating the antibribery law. The subcommittees have asked for the SEC documents in the case.

All the law firms and Ashland deny any improper actions. But the Kentucky litigation highlights several gray areas of corporate law.

Roles of Counsel and Director

It shows the potential pitfalls for any corporate lawyer who counsels a company while serving on its board of directors. It raises questions about what a lawyer should do to protect a corporate client. And it rekindles the debate about how companies should go about investigating possible wrongdoing in their midst. The suits also provide glimpses of how litigation can strain relations between, and within, law firms.

The legal problems grow out of allegations that Ashland, one of the nation's largest independent oil refiners, made illegal payments in 1980 to obtain oil from Oman. The charges about the lawyers are raised by two former Ashland executives in wrongful-dismissal suits in federal court here. In a third suit in the same court, a shareholder accuses Ashland of squandering corporate funds overseas. . . .

Bill E. McKay Jr., the whistle blower alleges in his suit that a former Ashland chairman, Orin Atkins, undertook several ventures with a mysterious Libyan-born businessman who had ties to the sultan of Oman and who said he could help the company obtain Omani oil. Mr. McKay, formerly the president of an Ashland subsidiary and a vice president of the parent, contends that the ventures were really conduits for illegal foreign payments. In April 1980, Ashland agreed to put up—and eventually lost—$25 million for a 75% stake in a Zimbabwe chromium mine.

In September 1980, Oman agreed to sell the company 20,000 barrels of crude oil a day. Three months later, Ashland wired a $1.35 million payment to Mont d'Or ("mountain of gold"), a Liechtenstein concern owned by the businessman with Omani connections, according to the suit.

Pittsburgh Lawyer's Job

In May 1981, after Mr. McKay objected to the payment and others questioned the chromium venture, Ashland directors retained Charles J. Queenan Jr., a partner in the Pittsburgh law firm of Kirkpatrick & Lockhart, to investigate whether the company had violated the anti-bribery or anti-racketeering laws. Mr. Queenan's report criticized the transactions but exonerated Ashland of any law violations and said the company needn't make any disclosures.

* * *

Butler's Involvement

Mr. Butler, Ashland's outside counsel, who is regarded as one of its most influential directors, . . . is widely regarded as the dean of the corporate-law bar. It was Mr. Butler who recommended Mr. Queenan for the internal investigation. And when Mr. McKay needed a lawyer during the inquiry, Mr.

Butler referred him to the Washington, D.C., law firm of Wilmer, Cutler & Pickering.

The Cravath and Wilmer Cutler firms have long enjoyed a close, lucrative relationship. . . . Lloyd Cutler, a former White House counsel, and John Pickering are Cravath alumni and still feel loyalty toward the Wall Street firm. Messrs. Cutler and Butler play tennis together. . . .

The close ties are a major issue in the legal-ethics dispute. Mr. McKay, in a legal memo, contends that Mr. Butler "took full advantage of this relationship to bring intense pressure on the Washington firm's senior management to rein in the vigorous representation" by two Wilmer Cutler partners assigned to represent him—Michael Klein and Arthur Mathews.

Mr. Klein stirred Mr. Butler's wrath when he wrote every Ashland director in August 1981 to express Mr. McKay's suspicions about the "ostensibly independent" investigation by Mr. Queenan. According to Mr. Mathews' pre-trial testimony in proceedings consolidating the three suits, Mr. Butler told Mr. Cutler that he was "incensed with Mike Klein" and that he "would never send Art Mathews another piece of business again as long as he practiced law."

Mr. Butler says he doesn't recall making those remarks, but he doesn't deny them. He says, "I thought Mike Klein had clearly overstepped the role of a lawyer."

* * *

McKay's Firing

[Subsequently, Wilmer Cutler agreed to defend Mr. McKay against a shareholder's suit filed against Ashland's directors and McKay, but declined to handle any offensive litigation against Ashland because of its relationship with Cravath.]

Consequently, when Mr. McKay was fired in September 1983, he retained the Louisville firm of Brown, Todd & Heyburn to file his wrongful-dismissal suit. Ashland denies that Mr. McKay was fired because of his clashes with higher-ups about overseas payments.

Ultimately, Wilmer Cutler withdrew from the shareholder litigation. . . .

Cravath decided to stay in, . . . [but] Federal Judge William Bertlesman . . . decided that Messrs. Butler and Rolfe [lead counsel] were "essential witnesses" in the proceedings and could no longer represent Ashland. "Mr. Rolfe and, by extension, members of his firm are too close to the case to exercise independent judgment," he added in his Jan. 29 opinion. It was a stunning defeat—Cravath's first disqualification ever.

The plaintiffs also raise ethical questions about Ashland's internal investigation and the role of Mr. Queenan, one of Pittsburgh's leading lawyers and a well-known tax expert. . . .

Omani Connection

After Mr. McKay questioned the Mont d'Or transaction, Mr. Butler asked Wilmer Cutler's Mr. Cutler to look into whether Yehia Omar, the Libyan-born businessman, and Timothy Landon, who was a part owner in the chromium mine acquired by Ashland, were Omani government officials.

In his pretrial testimony, Mr. Cutler says he contacted U.S. intelligence officials and then reported to Mr. Butler: "It appeared more likely than not that they would be regarded as [Omani] officials."

Mr. Omar was apparently persuaded to return the Mont d'Or payment of $1.35 million after the Ashland directors approved a consulting agreement with him, according to a document filed here by Mr. Butler and according to Mr. McKay's complaint. Mr. Butler says in pre-trial testimony that he believed that the return of the money should resolve any legal problem, as "no harm had been done even if there had been an inadvertent violation." Mr. McKay's suit says that a $3 million consulting fee was to have been paid to Mr. Omar as part of an Ashland effort to obtain letters from the Omani government stating that he wasn't an Omani official.

As it turns out, no letters were ever signed. So in May 1981, Ashland's directors decided—at Mr. Butler's suggestion—to hire Mr. Queenan as special independent counsel to investigate the Mont d'Or payment and other transactions. A similar inquiry by Mr. Queenan had led to a 1975 consent decree with the SEC that bars Ashland from using any corporate funds for illegal political contributions and other "unlawful purposes."

Reporting six months later, Mr. Queenan concluded that Ashland hadn't violated the antibribery law or the consent decree. He termed it unlikely that Mr. Omar "would be construed as a government official" under the Foreign Corrupt Practices Act. But Mr. Queenan did acknowledge that he couldn't conclude "with certainty that Mr. Landon would not be construed as a foreign official."

More than Mr. Queenan's conclusions are at issue in the litigation here, John McCall, the Brown Todd partner representing Mr. McKay, asserts in an interview. "Ashland shouldn't hold Mr. Queenan out as an independent investigator because he advised Ashland on the Mont d'Or payment months before he began investigating it."

As evidence, Mr. McCall cites a memo from Ashland's former chairman, Mr. Atkins, saying that Mr. Queenan discussed the "form and substance" of the Mont d'Or payment with an Ashland attorney in December 1980. And the following month, at a New York meeting, Mr. Queenan "cautioned" company officials on the corporate accounting for the transaction, according to the legal memo filed here.

In an affidavit, Mr. Queenan insists that he did nothing more than answer "hypothetical questions" about a possible legal defense against bribery charges and didn't learn until later that Mont d'Or was the payment in question. As for the New York meeting, Mr. Queenan denies rendering any "legal opinion" on Mont d'Or or any other transactions.

* * *

The Kentucky litigation also revives a legal debate from the mid–1970s: Should a company rely on its own lawyers or its regular outside counsel to conduct a so-called business ethics review, or should it hire a law firm that it has never used before?

* * *

Ties to Ex–Chairman

Mr. Queenan's harshest critic is Wilmer Cutler's Mr. Klein, who has done several internal inquiries for major companies. Mr. Klein, in pre-trial testimony in the consolidated suits, depicts Mr. Queenan as a co-opted lawyer who was "somewhat in awe" of former Chairman Atkins and enjoyed jetting about with Mr. Atkins on business, and he asserts that Mr. Queenan's investigative methods "stunk."

* * *

A Kirkpatrick spokesman calls Mr. Klein's criticism "belated sour grapes," coming long after he failed to get a lucrative severance contract for his former client, Mr. McKay. . . . The spokesman denies that Mr. Queenan was co-opted by Mr. Atkins or anybody else. "We were independent in the sense that we were not beholden to anybody, and we were impartial," says the spokesman, who adds: "There was never any attempt by us to manipulate the facts."

(3) *E.F. Hutton Internal Investigation.* As discussed in Chapter 1 (see pp. 9–10, supra), on May 2, 1985, E.F. Hutton & Co. entered guilty pleas to 2,000 counts of mail fraud arising out of its check overdrafting practices. As part of the plea agreement, no individuals from Hutton were charged. Shortly thereafter, Hutton decided to employ Griffin Bell, a former federal court of appeals judge and Attorney General in the Carter Administration, as "special counsel" to investigate the practices that led to the criminal charges and to determine who within Hutton was responsible. Hutton employees were directed to cooperate with Bell. Hutton decided that Bell's final report would be released to the Securities and Exchange Commission, the fifty state Securities Commissioners, and at least two subcommittees of the United States House of Representatives. Hutton wrote of its decision to make the 183–page report public: "[T]he overdrafting matter is vested with a public interest. The thrust of the Department of Justice's investigation was into practices that the Department contended endangered the banking system, and Hutton's business in large part involves activities that require public confidence."

As described in the report, Bell's investigation began with interviews of present and former employees of Hutton's branch offices; the investigators then proceeded to interview regional vice-presidents, regional operations managers, and regional cashiers. After that, interviews were conducted at the New York corporate offices "with all Hutton officials who had any possible responsibility for the Hutton problems" including former officers of the company. After completing these interviews, additional interviews "in the nature of due process hearings" were conducted with those whom it was believed had some responsibility for Hutton's problem. "The purpose of these interviews was to ensure that each individual would have an opportunity to respond to the case that may have been made with regard to that director, officer, or employee."

The investigators also reviewed numerous documents. Included were: 1) 40,000 pages of nonfinancial memoranda, correspondence, reports, and notes; 2) "thousands" of financial documents in connection with the branch and regional interviews; 3) materials supplied by Hutton to the Justice Department in connection with the grand jury investigation; and 4) documents produced in response to Congressional subpoenas. The report did point out, however, that the document review was "necessarily limited" to documents voluntarily disclosed. "We had no subpoena power or other mechanism to ensure access to all documents that may be relevant. . . . We are not aware of any instance in which Hutton refused to provide relevant documents, with the exception of certain documents that Hutton and its counsel considered privileged."

Among the report's recommendations were that the Board of Directors be reorganized to include a majority of outside directors; that an Internal Audit Committee be formed to report to the Board of Directors; and that "sanctions be applied against certain named individuals in a range from removal from office to reprimand, together with fines in some instances."

The report concluded: [38]

> The improper overdrafting problem, while substantial, was not Hutton-wide by any means and could be described more as a failure of management controls, in an organization based on aggressive selling and earnings policies. The real failing seems to us to have been a failing to take note that a sales organization requires much attention to the idea of internal controls where earnings are based on a percentage of profits and the earner can manipulate the system to increase profits.
>
> A new Hutton, with a majority of outside Directors, a reorganized management, with tight internal controls and a renewed commitment to its shareholders, customers and employees should give it a fresh start.
>
> In an effort to ensure that Hutton will never again engage in any questionable or unethical activities Hutton has on its own asked the Ethics Resource Center to propose a plan to establish an ethics program.
>
> Hopefully this report will have served to place the Hutton problem in perspective and that, if followed, it will serve to put the problem to rest and permit Hutton's 17,000 employees to get on with the traditional work of Hutton. Hutton has been punished substantially by pleading guilty to a crime of first impression in the money management area of America's financial life and by having paid substantial fines. It must obey a strong civil decree in its future dealings with banks and must make restitution to those filing claims.
>
> The recommendations of this report, when carried out, should be sufficient punishment both as punishment and as a deterrent to Hutton and to others who may wish to risk violating the law for easy interest profits.

38. See The Hutton Report: A Special Investigation Into the Conduct of E.F. Hutton & Company Inc. That Gave Rise to the Plea of Guilty Entered on May 2, 1985, at 182–183 (Sept. 4, 1985).

Query. Would you have expected the report to "put the problem to rest?" What more could Hutton or Bell have done?[39]

(4) *Lying During an Investigation.* One of the federal obstruction of justice statutes[40] makes it illegal for anyone knowingly to engage in "misleading conduct toward another person, with intent to—1) influence, delay, or prevent the testimony of any person in an official proceeding; . . . or 3) hinder, delay, or prevent the communication to a law enforcement officer or judge of the United States of information relating to the commission or possible commission of a Federal offense." The statute further provides that "an official proceeding need not be pending or about to be instituted at the time of the offense."

United States v. Abrams[41] involved an internal investigation done by Mego International (a manufacturer and distributor of toys) into unauthorized "off the books" cash sales of Mego merchandise. After the corporation completed its investigation, the government indicted three officers of the company (including the former president and chairman of the board) for obstruction of justice, alleging that they had lied to an outside lawyer in the course of his investigation. The indictment alleged that the defendants had willfully prevented "the disinterested members of the Audit Committee of the Mego Board of Directors, its special counsel and the members and employees of his law firm from communicating information relating to a violation of criminal statutes of the United States . . . to the United States Attorney's Office, . . . the Securities and Exchange Commission and to other federal criminal investigators." The district court upheld the indictment against a motion to dismiss, finding that the indictment, "fairly read," implied that the defendants "knew or reasonably believed that the members of the [Audit] committee were about to communicate information to criminal investigators."

At trial, special counsel testified that he advised each person he interviewed that the information conveyed would be disclosed to the Board of Directors and " 'any other body' " the Board deemed appropriate. On cross-examination he testified that at the time he conducted the interviews he was " 'not about to convey any information to any federal agency or any federal investigator' " nor had he formed an intent to do so.[42] The jury acquitted the defendants.[43]

---

39. The report did not put Hutton's problems to rest. Hutton was nearly destroyed by the controversy and was taken over by Shearson–Lehman in 1987. George Ball, who was President of Hutton and exonerated in Bell's report, was censured by the New York Stock Exchange for failing adequately to supervise Hutton employees; the NYSE also fined Hutton $400,000. See N.Y. Times, Jun. 29, 1988, p. D6. Griffin Bell was sued for defamation by one of the former Hutton branch managers whom Bell's report found to be responsible, but successfully defended himself at trial. See "Outside Probers Want Protection," Legal Times, June 27, 1988 p. 8 (despite victory, Bell litigation will likely lead other lawyers to seek indemnification for such suits arising out of future investigations).

40. 18 U.S.C.A. § 1512 (Supp.).

41. 543 F.Supp. 1184 (S.D.N.Y.1982) (brought under 18 U.S.C.A. § 1510, subsequently modified and reenacted).

42. The testimony is quoted in Morvillo, "Obstruction of Criminal, Internal Investigations," N.Y.L.J., Dec. 7, 1982, at p. 2.

43. Note, however, that at the same trial two of the defendants were convicted

Query. Do you favor prosecutions like *Abrams?* What would be the effect of such prosecutions on the way corporate internal investigations are performed? Note that such prosecutions appear to be quite rare.

2. LOSING THE PRIVILEGE

IN RE GRAND JURY PROCEEDINGS (FMC CORP.)

United States Court of Appeals for the Third Circuit, 1979.
604 F.2d 798.

WEIS, CIRCUIT JUDGE.

The crime-fraud exception to the attorney-client privilege permits the disclosure of otherwise protected material. In this case, the district court applied the same rule of disclosure to documents covered by the work product privilege. Finding that the government had presented a prima facie case to support the allegation of the commission of a crime, the district court ordered counsel for the corporate client to produce the documents for a grand jury's inspection. We agree with the court's reasoning but remand for a more specific factual determination as to when the alleged crime occurred.

In 1977, a grand jury sitting in Philadelphia began an investigation into allegations that FMC Corporation had made false statements to the Environmental Protection Agency (EPA) in connection with the discharge of carbon tetrachloride into the Kanawha River in West Virginia. No indictments were returned by that grand jury but a new one was convened in January, 1979. It issued subpoenas duces tecum and ad testificandum to Douglas Kliever, an attorney and partner in the firm of Cleary, Gottlieb, Steen & Hamilton, which had been retained by FMC. The firm represented FMC in its negotiations with the EPA bearing on pollution problems in the Kanawha River near South Charleston, West Virginia, the site of the corporation's carbon tetrachloride manufacturing facilities.

Kliever produced a number of the subpoenaed documents for the grand jury but asserted the attorney-client and work product privileges as to 31 of them. The government filed a motion to compel production of the withheld documents, to which FMC and Kliever responded. Although FMC did not file a formal petition, it was treated as an intervenor by the district court. The documents were submitted to the district judge for his review in camera, and he heard an ex parte in camera presentation by the government. Following these proceedings, the court directed that all of the documents be produced. In his bench opinion, the district judge assumed for purposes of his ruling that the attorney-client privilege had been properly claimed by FMC. He de-

on sixteen counts of mail fraud and one was convicted on a separate obstruction charge in connection with a different incident which occurred during the course of the investigation. The court of appeals subsequently affirmed the convictions on the mail fraud counts, but reversed on the obstruction count. See United States v. Siegel, 717 F.2d 9, 21 (2d Cir.1983).

nied the use of the privilege, however, because the government had "presented prima facie evidence that a crime has been committed by FMC personnel."

The district judge expressed some doubts about the applicability of the work product privilege because the documents were prepared in anticipation of civil matters rather than the grand jury investigations. Assuming that issue in favor of the appellants, the court nonetheless ruled that the work product privilege could not be recognized because of the crime-fraud exception, and because the government had "made a showing of substantial need" for the documents. Both FMC and Kliever promptly filed appeals and petitioned this court for a stay of the order directing Kliever to testify, asserting that the attorney would not disobey the district court nor would FMC ask him to do so. We granted the stay . . . .

* * *

. . . The government contends that the crime-fraud exception operates to permit disclosure of documents that FMC asserts are protected by the work product doctrine as well as those coming within the ambit of the attorney-client relationship. This rule of disclosure is ordinarily viewed as an exception to the attorney-client privilege, and there is no question as to its applicability in that context. Its rationale is straightforward. The attorney-client privilege is designed to encourage clients to make full disclosure of facts to counsel so that he may properly, competently, and ethically carry out his representation. The ultimate aim is to promote the proper administration of justice. That end, however, would be frustrated if the client used the lawyer's services to further a continuing or future crime or tort. Thus, when the lawyer is consulted, not with respect to past wrongdoing but to future illegal activities, the privilege is no longer defensible and the crime-fraud exception comes into play. In determining whether the exception is applicable, the client's intention controls and the privilege may be denied even if the lawyer is altogether innocent.

In the case at bar, the district judge ruled that the crime-fraud exception applied to both the attorney-client and work product privileges. [T]he two privileges are separate and distinct, but there is also an overlap. Information furnished by the client to the lawyer may merge into his work product; moreover, the overriding purpose of the two privileges is the same—to encourage proper functioning of the adversary system. From this viewpoint, there is no actual inconsistency in applying the crime-fraud exception to the work product as well as to the attorney-client privilege. The rationale supporting the exception in both areas is virtually identical. The work product privilege is perverted if it is used to further illegal activities as is the attorney-client privilege, and there are no overpowering considerations in either situation that would justify the shielding of evidence that aids continuing or future criminal activity.

Recognizing a crime-fraud exception to the work product doctrine would be consistent with the precept reiterated by the Supreme Court that "evidentiary privileges are not favored. . . ." As we observed in the context of the attorney-client privilege in In re Grand Jury Proceedings (Sun Co.), in language equally adaptable to the work product setting, "because the privilege obstructs the search for truth and because its benefits are, at best, 'indirect and speculative,' it must be 'strictly confined within the narrowest possible limits consistent with the logic of its principle.'" As a necessary corollary, moreover, we have held that the work product privilege is a qualified one that can be overcome by a showing of good cause. We have no doubt that the crime-fraud exception comes within "good cause" to deny applicability of the work product doctrine. In reaching this conclusion, we find most helpful the principles followed by courts in determining whether the exception applies to defeat the attorney-client privilege. For in a case such as this, where the two privileges substantially overlap, there appear to be no compelling reasons for employing different standards.

Nevertheless, although we agree with the district court that generally the crime-fraud exception applies to the work product as well as to the attorney-client privilege, we have some difficulty in determining whether the principle was properly invoked in this case. We appreciate the district judge's desire to be circumspect in his findings so that in the event of a contrary appellate ruling there would be no premature disclosure of privileged matter. But the district court's finding that "a crime has been committed by FMC" (emphasis ours) does not state whether the crime was committed before or after Mr. Kliever and his firm were retained for the work during which the documents at issue were generated. If the crime had been completed before retention of the Cleary firm, then the privilege should be in effect. If, however, the crime was a continuing one, or one that occurred after the firm was consulted, then the prima facie showing made by the government would suffice to allow inspection by the grand jury.[44]

The district court also indicated some reservations about whether the documents were within the privilege since they had been created for use in the civil proceedings rather than specifically for the grand jury investigations. That issue was raised in In re Grand Jury Proceedings (Sun Co.), supra, and there we discussed the various tests that had been advanced. We found particularly attractive the one set forth in 8 C. Wright and A. Miller, Federal Practice and Procedure § 204, at 198 (1970):

> "Prudent parties anticipate litigation and begin preparation prior to the time suit is formally commenced. Thus, the test should be

---

44. [Court's footnote 6.] . . . The district judge stated, "I further find on the basis of the government showing and my own independent examination of the documents themselves that the documents claimed to be privileged are related to the charges under investigation. Therefore, I conclude that at least for purposes of the grand jury proceedings the crime fraud exception to the attorney-client privilege is established." We consider this an adequate link between the documents and the alleged crime.

whether in light of the nature of the document and the factual situation in the particular case, the document can fairly be said to have been prepared or obtained because of the prospect of litigation."

It appears from the record that at least after mid-1974 Cleary, Gottlieb, Steen & Hamilton, and particularly Mr. Kliever, represented FMC in connection with administrative proceedings before the EPA. These matters included problems caused by the alleged discharge of chemicals into the Kanawha River, the very matter underlying the grand jury investigations. There is thus an identity of subject matter between that pursued in the civil aspects and the grand jury investigations. During some stages, moreover, both the civil and grand jury matters were proceeding at the same time and, therefore, a temporal connection between the civil and criminal litigation was established as well. In these circumstances, we conclude that the documents subpoenaed covering the period from July, 1975 to September, 1978 qualify for consideration of the work product privilege even though they may not have been prepared specifically in connection with the grand jury investigations. We therefore need not decide whether the work product privilege applies to all litigation, related or not.

Since the record does not demonstrate when it was that the alleged crime to which the district court referred may have occurred, we are unable to determine whether there was error in the court's order. We therefore will remand for a more specific finding. If the court determines that the alleged crime occurred before the Cleary firm and Mr. Kliever were consulted in connection with the carbon tetrachloride discharges, then the district court may rule that both privileges should be given effect. If, however, the court determines that the alleged crime occurred after consultation with counsel, then, consistent with this opinion, the court may find that the crime-fraud exception bars use of the privileges.

Accordingly, the matter will be remanded to the district court for further proceedings. . . .

QUERIES

The crime-fraud exception to the attorney-client privilege was given expression by Justice Cardozo in *Clark v. United States:* [45]

> . . . There is a privilege protecting communications between attorney and client. The privilege takes flight if the relation is abused. A client who consults an attorney for advice that will serve him in the commission of a fraud will have no help from the law. He must let the truth be told. There are early cases apparently to the effect that a mere charge of illegality, not supported by any evidence, will set the confidences free. But this conception of the privilege is without support in later rulings. "It

---

45. 289 U.S. 1, 15, 53 S.Ct. 465, 469–70, 77 L.Ed. 993, 1000 (1933).

is obvious that it would be absurd to say that the privilege could be got rid of merely by making a charge of fraud." O'Rourke v. Darbishire, [1920] A.C. 581, 604. To drive the privilege away, there must be "something to give colour to the charge;" there must be "prima facie evidence that it has some foundation in fact." When that evidence is supplied, the seal of secrecy is broken. . . . Nor does the loss of the privilege depend upon the showing of a conspiracy, upon proof that client and attorney are involved in equal guilt. The attorney may be innocent, and still the guilty client must let the truth come out. . . .

The courts have established a two-part test for satisfying the crime-fraud exception: 1) a prima facie showing of a violation (crime or fraud); and 2) a relationship between the material claimed to be protected and the prima facie violation. Re-consider the *FMC* case. What relationship was shown between the violations and the communications which occurred after Cleary, Gottlieb was retained? Is a temporal relationship between the communication (first) and crime (second) adequate? Should the Government have been required to show that FMC had retained Cleary, Gottlieb with the intent of furthering a crime or fraud, as opposed to an attempt to obtain counselling with regard to future behavior? [46]

COMMODITY FUTURES TRADING COMMISSION v. WEINTRAUB

Supreme Court of the United States, 1985.
471 U.S. 343, 105 S.Ct. 1986, 85 L.Ed.2d 372.

JUSTICE MARSHALL delivered the opinion of the Court.

The question here is whether the trustee of a corporation in bankruptcy has the power to waive the debtor corporation's attorney-client privilege with respect to communications that took place before the filing of the petition in bankruptcy.

I

The case arises out of a formal investigation by petitioner Commodity Futures Trading Commission to determine whether Chicago Discount Commodity Brokers (CDCB), or persons associated with that firm,

---

46. See Developments, Privileged Communications, 98 Harv.L.Rev. 1450, 1512–13 (1985) (arguing that the standard two-part test improperly dispenses with proof of intent). See also In re Antitrust Grand Jury, 805 F.2d 155 (6th Cir.1986) (reversing decision that all documents relating to legal assistance involving illegal transaction lose work product protection under crime-fraud exception, and must be turned over to grand jury; district court must review each document to determine whether the communications were made in furtherance of the alleged crime, although law firms need not be "knowing and willing conspirators"); In re Grand Jury Subpoena Duces Tecum, 731 F.2d 1032 (2d Cir.1984) (disclosure ordered for: documents reflecting communications made prior to sale of asset, allegedly sold to avoid payment of fine; documents reflecting communications after sale of asset until the government learned of agreement, on theory that non-disclosure was part of fraudulent plan); Note, The Crime or Fraud Exception to the Attorney–Client Privilege: Marc Rich and the Second Circuit, 51 Brooklyn L.Rev. 913 (1985).

violated the Commodity Exchange Act. CDCB was a discount commodity brokerage house registered with the Commission as a futures commission merchant. On October 27, 1980, the Commission filed a complaint against CDCB in the United States District Court for the Northern District of Illinois alleging violations of the Act. That same day, respondent Frank McGhee, acting as sole director and officer of CDCB, entered into a consent decree with the Commission, which provided for the appointment of a receiver and for the receiver to file a petition for liquidation under Chapter 7 of the Bankruptcy Reform Act of 1978 (Bankruptcy Code). The District Court appointed John K. Notz, Jr., as receiver.

Notz then filed a voluntary petition in bankruptcy on behalf of CDCB. He sought relief under Subchapter IV of Chapter 7 of the Bankruptcy Code, which provides for the liquidation of bankrupt commodity brokers. The bankruptcy court appointed Notz as interim trustee and, later, as permanent trustee.

As part of its investigation of CDCB, the Commission served a subpoena duces tecum upon CDCB's former counsel, respondent Gary Weintraub. The Commission sought Weintraub's testimony about various CDCB matters, including suspected misappropriation of customer funds by CDCB's officers and employees, and other fraudulent activities. Weintraub appeared for his deposition and responded to numerous inquiries but refused to answer 23 questions, asserting CDCB's attorney-client privilege. The Commission then moved to compel answers to those questions. It argued that Weintraub's assertion of the attorney-client privilege was inappropriate because the privilege could not be used to "thwart legitimate access to information sought in an administrative investigation."

Even though the Commission argued in its motion that the matters on which Weintraub refused to testify were not protected by CDCB's attorney-client privilege, it also asked Notz to waive that privilege. In a letter to Notz, the Commission maintained that CDCB's former officers, directors, and employees no longer had the authority to assert the privilege. According to the Commission, that power was vested in Notz as the then-interim trustee. In response to the Commission's request, Notz waived "any interest I have in the attorney/client privilege possessed by that debtor for any communications or information occurring or arising on or before October 27, 1980"—the date of Notz's appointment as receiver.

On April 26, 1982, a United States Magistrate ordered Weintraub to testify. The Magistrate found that Weintraub had the power to assert CDCB's privilege. He added however, that Notz was "successor in interest of all assets, rights and privileges of CDCB, including the attorney/client privilege at issue herein," and that Notz's waiver was therefore valid. The District Court upheld the Magistrate's order on June 9. Thereafter, Frank McGhee and his brother, respondent Andrew McGhee, intervened and argued that Notz could not validly waive the privilege over their objection.[47] The District Court rejected this argument and, on July 27, entered a new order requiring Weintraub to testify without asserting an attorney-client privilege on behalf of CDCB.

The McGhees appealed from the District Court's order of July 27 and the Court of Appeals for the Seventh Circuit reversed. It held that a bankruptcy trustee does not have the power to waive a corporate-debtor's attorney-client privilege with respect to communications that occurred before the filing of the bankruptcy petition. The court recognized that two other Circuits had addressed the question and had come to the opposite conclusion. We granted certiorari to resolve the conflict. We now reverse the Court of Appeals.

II

It is by now well established, and undisputed by the parties to this case, that the attorney-client privilege attaches to corporations as well as to individuals. Upjohn Co. v. United States, 449 U.S. 383, 101 S.Ct. 677, 66 L.Ed.2d 584 (1981). Both for corporations and individuals, the attorney-client privilege serves the function of promoting full and frank communications between attorneys and their clients. It thereby encourages observance of the law and aids in the administration of justice.

The administration of the attorney-client privilege in the case of corporations, however, presents special problems. As an inanimate entity, a corporation must act through agents. A corporation cannot speak directly to its lawyers. Similarly, it cannot directly waive the privilege when disclosure is in its best interest. Each of these actions must necessarily be undertaken by individuals empowered to act on behalf of the corporation. In *Upjohn Co.*, we considered whether the privilege covers only communications between counsel and top management, and decided that, under certain circumstances, communications between counsel and lower-level employees are also covered. Here, we face the related question of which corporate actors are empowered to waive the corporation's privilege.

The parties in this case agree that, for solvent corporations, the power to waive the corporate attorney-client privilege rests with the corporation's management and is normally exercised by its officers and directors. The managers, of course, must exercise the privilege in a manner consistent with their fiduciary duty to act in the best interests of the corporation and not of themselves as individuals.

The parties also agree that when control of a corporation passes to new management, the authority to assert and waive the corporation's attorney-client privilege passes as well. New managers installed as a result of a takeover, merger, loss of confidence by shareholders, or simply normal succession, may waive the attorney-client privilege with respect to communications made by former officers and directors.

47. [Court's footnote 1.] The Court of Appeals found that Andrew McGhee resigned his position as officer and director of CDCB on October 21, 1980. Frank McGhee, however, remained as an officer and director.

Displaced managers may not assert the privilege over the wishes of current managers, even as to statements that the former might have made to counsel concerning matters within the scope of their corporate duties.[48]

The dispute in this case centers on the control of the attorney-client privilege of a corporation in bankruptcy. The Government maintains that the power to exercise that privilege with respect to prebankruptcy communications passes to the bankruptcy trustee. In contrast, respondents maintain that this power remains with the debtor's directors.

III

[The Court here reviewed relevant provisions of the Bankruptcy Code.]

IV

In light of the lack of direct guidance from the Code, we turn to consider the roles played by the various actors of a corporation in bankruptcy to determine which is most analogous to the role played by the management of a solvent corporation. Because the attorney-client privilege is controlled, outside of bankruptcy, by a corporation's management, the actor whose duties most closely resemble those of management should control the privilege in bankruptcy, unless such a result interferes with policies underlying the bankruptcy laws.

A

The powers and duties of a bankruptcy trustee are extensive. Upon the commencement of a case in bankruptcy, all corporate property passes to an estate represented by the trustee. The trustee is . . . directed to investigate the debtor's financial affairs, and is empowered to sue officers, directors, and other insiders to recover, on behalf of the estate, fraudulent or preferential transfers of the debtor's property. Subject to court approval, he may use, sell or lease property of the estate.

Moreover, in reorganization, the trustee has the power to "operate the debtor's business" unless the court orders otherwise. Even in liquidation, the court "may authorize the trustee to operate the business" for a limited period of time. In the course of operating the debtor's business, the trustee "may enter into transactions, including the sale or lease of property of the estate" without court approval.

As even this brief and incomplete list should indicate, the Bankruptcy Code gives the trustee wide-ranging management authority over the debtor. In contrast, the powers of the debtor's directors are

---

48. [Court's footnote 5.] It follows that Andrew McGhee, who is now neither an officer nor a director, retains no control over the corporation's privilege. The remainder of this opinion therefore focuses on whether Frank McGhee has such power.

severely limited. Their role is to turn over the corporation's property to the trustee and to provide certain information to the trustee and to the creditors. Congress contemplated that when a trustee is appointed, he assumes control of the business, and the debtor's directors are "completely ousted."

In light of the Code's allocation of responsibilities, it is clear that the trustee plays the role most closely analogous to that of a solvent corporation's management. Given that the debtor's directors retain virtually no management powers, they should not exercise the traditional management function of controlling the corporation's attorney-client privilege, unless a contrary arrangement would be inconsistent with policies of the bankruptcy laws.

B

We find no federal interests that would be impaired by the trustee's control of the corporation's attorney-client privilege with respect to pre-bankruptcy communications. On the other hand, the rule suggested by respondents—that the debtor's directors have this power—would frustrate an important goal of the bankruptcy laws. In seeking to maximize the value of the estate, the trustee must investigate the conduct of prior management to uncover and assert causes of action against the debtor's officers and directors. It would often be extremely difficult to conduct this inquiry if the former management were allowed to control the corporation's attorney-client privilege and therefore to control access to the corporation's legal files. To the extent that management had wrongfully diverted or appropriated corporate assets, it could use the privilege as a shield against the trustee's efforts to identify those assets. The Code's goal of uncovering insider fraud would be substantially defeated if the debtor's directors were to retain the one management power that might effectively thwart an investigation into their own conduct.

Respondents contend that the trustee can adequately investigate fraud without controlling the corporation's attorney-client privilege. They point out that the privilege does not shield the disclosure of communications relating to the planning or commission of ongoing fraud, crimes, and ordinary torts, see, e.g., Clark v. United States, 289 U.S. 1, 15, 53 S.Ct. 465, 469, 77 L.Ed. 993 (1933). The problem, however, is making the threshold showing of fraud necessary to defeat the privilege. Without control over the privilege, the trustee might not be able to discover hidden assets or looting schemes, and therefore might not be able to make the necessary showing.

In summary, we conclude that vesting in the trustee control of the corporation's attorney-client privilege most closely comports with the allocation of the waiver power to management outside of bankruptcy without in any way obstructing the careful design of the Bankruptcy Code.

V

Respondents do not seriously contest that the bankruptcy trustee exercises functions analogous to those exercised by management outside of bankruptcy, whereas the debtor's directors exercise virtually no management functions at all. Neither do respondents seriously dispute that vesting control over the attorney-client privilege in the trustee will facilitate the recovery of misappropriated corporate assets.

Respondents argue, however, that the trustee should not obtain control over the privilege because, unlike the management of a solvent corporation, the trustee's primary loyalty goes not to shareholders but to creditors, who elect him and who often will be the only beneficiaries of his efforts. Thus, they contend, as a practical matter bankruptcy trustees represent only the creditors.

We are unpersuaded by this argument. First, the fiduciary duty of the trustee runs to shareholders as well as to creditors. Second, respondents do not explain why, out of all management powers, control over the attorney-client privilege should remain with those elected by the corporation's shareholders. Perhaps most importantly, respondents' position ignores the fact that bankruptcy causes fundamental changes in the nature of corporate relationships. One of the painful facts of bankruptcy is that the interests of shareholders become subordinated to the interests of creditors. . . .

VI

Respondents' other arguments are similarly unpersuasive . . . .

[R]espondents argue that giving the trustee control over the attorney-client privilege will have an undesirable chilling effect on attorney-client communications. According to respondents, corporate managers will be wary of speaking freely with corporate counsel if their communications might subsequently be disclosed due to bankruptcy. But the chilling effect is no greater here than in the case of a solvent corporation, where individual officers and directors always run the risk that successor management might waive the corporation's attorney-client privilege with respect to prior management's communications with counsel.

* * *

VII

For the foregoing reasons, we hold that the trustee of a corporation in bankruptcy has the power to waive the corporation's attorney-client privilege with respect to prebankruptcy communications. We therefore conclude that Notz, in his capacity as trustee, properly waived CDCB's privilege in this case. The judgment of the Court of Appeals for the Seventh Circuit is accordingly reversed.

It is so ordered.

Justice Powell took no part in the consideration or decision of this case.

NOTES AND QUERIES

(1) *Who Can Waive the Privilege?* Does the Court in *Weinberg* imply that only "management" can waive the privilege? Would such a rule be consistent with *Upjohn*'s view of who can create privileged communications? Should the rules be consistent? Note that counsel can sometimes waive the privilege inadvertently, and contrary to the express wishes of its corporate client.[49]

Consider, in this connection, *Velsicol Chemical Corp. v. Parsons*, 561 F.2d 671 (7th Cir.1977), certiorari denied 435 U.S. 942, 98 S.Ct. 1521, 55 L.Ed.2d 538 (1978):

> Grant, Senior District Judge.
>
> In September 1975, the U.S. Attorney's office for the Northern District of Illinois initiated an investigation of Velsicol Chemical Corporation and several of its current and former employees and attorneys. The purpose of the investigation was to determine whether Velsicol and/or certain of its officers, employees, and attorneys withheld certain information from the United States Environmental Protection Agency which tended to show pesticides manufactured by Velsicol induced tumors and/or cancers in laboratory animals. . . .
>
> The key people involved in this appeal and mandamus action are Neil Mitchell, General Counsel of Velsicol; Bernant Lorant, an attorney in private practice and former employee of Velsicol; Harvey Gold, an employee of Velsicol; and three attorneys of the law firm of Sellers, Conner & Cuneo, Messrs. Robert L. Ackerly, Charles A. O'Connor and Joe G. Hollingsworth. Mitchell, Lorant and the Sellers law firm were jointly involved in the representation of Velsicol in administrative proceedings before the Environmental Protection Agency. Gold has submitted an affidavit to the Environmental Protection Agency which stated in part that "[a]ll relevant reports and advisory committee proceedings have been submitted to the Environmental Protection Agency and its predecessor agencies". A particular focus of the investigation is Gold's affidavit and a legal memorandum prepared by Mitchell and Lorant with assistance of counsel from the Sellers firm. These two documents were filed by Velsicol in 1973 in opposition to the EPA's motion for a discovery subpoena in an administrative proceeding concerning two pesticides. The Government maintains that the representa-

---

49. See In re Grand Jury Investigation of Ocean Transportation, 604 F.2d 672 (D.C.Cir.) (documents marked "P" produced in response to grand jury subpoena, even though corporation intended them to be protected by the attorney-client privilege; held: privilege waived; counsel acted as corporation's agent within scope of authority), certiorari denied 444 U.S. 915, 100 S.Ct. 229, 62 L.Ed.2d 169 (1979).

tions embodied in those two documents appear to be false because some of the reports on the pesticides reposed in Velsicol's files at the time the legal memorandum and affidavits were filed. After being notified that it, along with several individuals, was under investigation, Velsicol retained Williams, Connolly & Califano (now Williams & Connolly) to represent the corporation in the grand jury investigation. The same firm also represented some of the individual subjects of the investigation, including Mitchell and Lorant. During the early stages of the investigation, government counsel, Assistant United States Attorney Thomas Mulroy, met with Messrs. David Povich and Richard Cooper of the Williams firm. At that meeting, Povich told Mulroy that Velsicol would not assert its attorney-client privilege as to any conversations between Velsicol employees and Mitchell and Lorant. Povich also told the Government that Velsicol would exercise the attorney-client privilege with respect to any communication between Velsicol and its outside counsel, including the Sellers and Williams firms.

From October 1975 to the present, Mitchell and Lorant have appeared before government counsel and the grand jury on a number of occasions and have testified as to numerous communications. Some of these communications have entailed remarks with lawyers from the Sellers firm. Specifically, Mitchell appeared at a sworn deposition in October, 1975, and before the Grand Jury in February 1977, disclosing conversations he had on several subjects with attorneys of the Sellers firm. The Government argues that a waiver evolved out of this program.

On 9 February 1977, grand jury subpoenae were issued directing three attorneys of the Sellers firm to give testimony and produce documents relating to their representation of Velsicol in the on-going EPA proceedings previously mentioned. Velsicol filed a motion to intervene in the grand jury proceeding and motions to quash and for a protective order. Velsicol argued that the subpoena-requested documents and testimony protected against disclosure by the attorney-client privilege and the work product rule.

Mr. Ackerly appeared before the grand jury and refused to answer ten questions propounded by the Government on the grounds that the subject of the inquiries was protected by the attorney-client privilege. A claim was also made that some of the subpoenaed documents were at least in part protected by the work-product rule. The Government then brought Mr. Ackerly before the district court on a motion to compel testimony and production of documents. The court . . . granted . . . the Government's motion to compel Ackerly's testimony. . . .

THE ISSUE OF WAIVER BY VELSICOL

In granting the motion to compel, the district court concluded that there had been an intent on the part of Velsicol "to limit the disclosures" but "that that intent had been exceeded and exceeded under circumstances by which the corporation was bound." Judge Parsons also determined that the waiver was "a general waiver" relating "primarily to subject matter" rather than merely to specific conversations.

Velsicol makes a number of arguments as to why the district court ruling was erroneous. It is suggested that there was no corporate intent to waive and that Mitchell as a corporate officer did not possess the requisite authority to bind the corporation. Therefore, Velsicol concludes he was outside the scope of his authority.

It is generally recognized that a corporation acts through its officers. In the instant suit, Mitchell held the office of "Vice–President–Legal" and as such was senior house counsel. While we believe that a corporate officer must have authority to bind the corporation, the authority of different corporate officers will inevitably vary as to the positions held. Despite the protestations of Velsicol that Mitchell lacked authority to waive the corporation's attorney-client privilege, we are not persuaded his authority was so limited. Although we do not intend to define the precise authority of every Velsicol corporate officer, we have no doubts that Mitchell was within the scope of his authority when he testified. The fact that the corporation has engaged outside counsel does not necessarily circumscribe or revoke the authority of house counsel.

Mitchell's status before the grand jury admittedly has several dimensions. As an individual, he is unquestionably a potential target. He also, however, is an agent of Velsicol and was employed as house counsel when he testified. Because the focus of the investigation is upon possible corporate misconduct within its own legal department, Velsicol is being represented by the Williams firm. While Mitchell's presence before the grand jury may be characterized as a client for purposes of determining attorney-client issues, vis-à-vis communications with outside counsel, he was nonetheless possessed of the office of house counsel of the corporation and as such was an agent of the client corporation with authority to waive the attorney-client privilege. Furthermore, as the Government has pointed out, Velsicol has never produced any corporate resolution or written document purporting to formalize its purported limited waiver of the privilege with regard to its own lawyers or outside counsel.

Velsicol also reasons that the disclosures made by Mitchell were inadvertent because Velsicol did not intend to waive the privilege as to outside counsel. . . . Mitchell, house counsel for Velsicol, was conferring with a Mr. Vincent Fuller (a member of Velsicol's outside counsel team from the Williams firm) during the course of his grand jury testimony in which the waiver occurred. Apparently Mitchell was consulting with Fuller to determine if he could answer particular questions before the grand jury. Fuller suggested at the hearing that Mitchell might have "violated the instructions given him by counsel for Velsicol."

Under these circumstances, we cannot accept Velsicol's thesis that Mitchell's testimony was inadvertent. Mitchell, an attorney himself, answered the questions propounded to him after consultation with outside counsel and Velsicol must accept the legal implications of that testimony. Moreover, the presence of Fuller at the grand jury questioning undermines Velsicol's contention that Mitchell was there in a merely noncorporate capacity. Having afforded Mitchell the benefit of outside counsel for his testimony, it does not seem reasonable that Velsicol should be allowed to disavow the content of that testimony. We have to accept the position that Mitchell was aware of the privilege involved and the surrounding circumstances. Accordingly, the relinquishment of the privilege embodied in his testimony cannot be characterized as inadvertent.

* * *

For reasons discussed above, we are of the opinion that Mitchell's testimony before the grand jury was of such a nature as to effect a waiver of Velsicol's attorney-client privilege as to outside counsel. This being the case, the Government has the right to pursue the investigation with respect to communications between Velsicol and outside counsel as to the allegedly false memorandum and affidavit and to the carcinogenicity data in question. The district court properly granted the Government's motion to compel.

* * *

(2) *Remember—Who Is the Client?* Consider *In re Grand Jury Proceedings, Detroit, Mich.,* 434 F.Supp. 648 (E.D.Mich.1977), affirmed 570 F.2d 562 (6th Cir.1978):

JOINER, DISTRICT JUDGE.

This matter is brought before the court by Edmund W. Faudman to quash a grand jury subpoena directed to Lawrence S. Jackier to appear and give testimony before a grand jury. Mr. Jackier is an attorney at law and was at one time attorney for Arnolds, Inc. At the same time, Mr. Faudman was vice president in charge of the Pharmacy Division of Arnolds, Inc. During this time, Faudman in his capacity as vice president of Arnolds, Inc., consulted Jackier in his capacity as attorney to Arnolds, Inc., concerning a matter about which the grand jury is now investigating. Written and oral communications passed between the two, from Faudman as vice president of Arnolds, Inc., to Jackier, Arnolds' attorney, and from Jackier, Arnolds' attorney, to Faudman as Arnolds' vice president. The subpoena seeks to call Jackier before the grand jury to reveal these communications.

* * *

[I]n this case the client, Arnolds, Inc., has waived the privilege. It has taken formal action to cooperate fully with the grand jury investigation and has directed its general counsel to instruct Jackier not to claim the privilege on its behalf. It is this fact that presents for the first time, as far as this court has been able to determine, the issue of whether an operating official of a corporation . . . can claim the attorney-client privilege and prevent disclosure of communications between himself and the corporation's attorney when the corporation has waived the privilege. This being the first case of its kind that this court can find, it is necessary to step back and put the problem fully in perspective.

In general, privileges are not favored in the law. They are developed and expanded only to accommodate needs that can be narrowly defined and, when so defined, require protection to a greater degree than does the need for testimony.

* * *

As stated the privilege is that of the client. In this case the client is Arnolds, Inc., and it has waived the privilege. Jackier testified that in all conversations with Faudman, he understood that he was acting as Arnolds' attorney and that Faudman was consulting him as Arnolds' attorney. His responses were directed to Arnolds, through Faudman, the vice president.

The concept of a representative of the client comes into the rule and is needed to permit an accurate consideration of how a corporation communicates with a lawyer. Surely Faudman was a representative of the client. Surely his communications with Jackier were privileged, but the privilege was that of Arnolds under the traditional statement of the rule. . . .

If the communicating officer seeks legal advice himself and consults a lawyer about his problems, he may have a privilege. If he makes it clear when he is consulting the company lawyer that he personally is consulting the lawyer and the lawyer sees fit to accept and give communication knowing the possible conflicts that could arise, he may have a privilege. But in the absence of any indication to the company's lawyer that the lawyer is to act in any other capacity than as lawyer for the company in giving and receiving communications . . . ., the privilege is and should remain that of the company and not that of the communicating officer.

Such a rule should not inhibit obtaining legal advice. The vice president is free to get legal advice about his problems at any time from any lawyer. Such a rule should tend to prevent inadvertent conflicts of interest from developing because to create the privilege in someone other than the company it must be made clear to the lawyer that the intended client . . . is someone other than the company, and the lawyer at that time could choose whether to accept the communication on such terms.

Thus, because the privilege in this case is Arnolds' and Arnolds has waived the privilege and, because Faudman was not a client of Jackier and did not have a privilege as to communications with Arnolds' lawyer, the motion to quash the subpoena will be denied.

So ordered.

(3) *Endnote.* Review the cases in this Section relating the ways in which the attorney-client privilege can be lost. In light of these cases do you think the privilege is really very valuable? Review the reasons given in *Upjohn* for allowing corporate employees beyond the control group to create privileged communications. If corporate employees were familiar with all the materials in this Section, would they engage in the "full and frank" communication with corporate counsel that *Upjohn* envisions?

Chapter 5

THE GRAND JURY

A. FUNDAMENTALS OF GRAND JURY POWER

SCOPE NOTE

The grand jury's extensive powers make it the key institution in the investigation of business crime, enabling government attorneys to obtain the documents and testimony necessary to discover and prosecute these complex cases. The grand jury's powers, however, have frequently been criticized as being subject to abuse, criticism which often arises in connection with highly visible political cases. Thus it is that people's views of the grand jury are often shaped by the type of crime they envision the grand jury investigating. Civil libertarians see political prosecutions and tend to forget the critical importance of the grand jury in prosecuting complex crime; and those interested in vigorous prosecution of business crime often forget the important civil liberties interest that all have in properly regulating government power when criminal punishments are involved.

The challenge of the materials in this Section is to evaluate the powers given the grand jury without regard to the crime being investigated. Students who favor business crime prosecutions should keep in mind the grand jury's power to harass those espousing unpopular views; and those who want to restrain the grand jury's investigative powers should remember the effect this might have on business crime prosecutions.

This Section begins with the two cases which are the foundation for the federal grand jury's power, *Hale v. Henkel* and *Blair v. United States*. The Notes which follow provide background historical information on the grand jury to put the cases and the issue of grand jury power in some perspective. The major question posed is whether the courts should tilt toward the grand jury's power to investigate, or toward the grand jury's power to act as a check on prosecutorial abuse.

HALE v. HENKEL
Supreme Court of the United States, 1906.
201 U.S. 43, 26 S.Ct. 370, 50 L.Ed. 652.

[Hale had refused to comply with a subpoena issued by a grand jury in a criminal antitrust investigation. The facts are set out supra, p. 383. The Court's discussion of two of the three issues raised in the case are set out supra, pp. 384–388. The third issue involved the power of the grand jury:]

The appellant justifies his action in refusing to answer the questions propounded to him . . . upon the ground that there was no specific "charge" pending before the grand jury against any particular person. . . .

The . . . objection requires a definition of the word "charge" as used in this connection, which it is not easy to furnish. An accused person is usually charged with crime by a complaint made before a committing magistrate, which has fully performed its office when the party is committed or held to bail, and it is quite unnecessary to the finding of an indictment by a grand jury; or by an information of the district attorney, which is of no legal value in prosecutions for felony; or by a presentment usually made, as in this case, for an offense committed in the presence of the jury; or by an indictment which, as often as not, is drawn after the grand jury has acted upon the testimony. If another kind of charge be contemplated, when and by whom must it be preferred? Must it be in writing, and if so, in what form? Or may it be oral? The suggestion of the witness that he should be furnished with a copy of such charge, if applicable to him is applicable to other witnesses summoned before the grand jury. Indeed, it is a novelty in criminal procedure with which we are wholly unacquainted, and one which might involve a betrayal of the secrets of the grand jury room.

Under the ancient English system, criminal prosecutions were instituted at the suit of private prosecutors, to which the King lent his name in the interest of the public peace and good order of society. In such cases the usual practice was to prepare the proposed indictment and lay it before the grand jury for their consideration. There was much propriety in this, as the most valuable function of the grand jury was not only to examine into the commission of crimes, but to stand between the prosecutor and the accused, and to determine whether the charge was founded upon credible testimony or was dictated by malice or personal ill will.

We are pointed to no case, however, holding that a grand jury cannot proceed without the formality of a written charge. Indeed, the oath administered to the foreman, which has come down to us from the most ancient times, and is found in Rex v. Shaftsbury, 8 Howell's State Trials, 759, indicates that the grand jury was competent to act solely on its own volition. This oath was that "you shall diligently inquire and true presentments make of all such matters, articles, and things as shall be given to you in charge, *as of all other matters, and things as shall come to your own knowledge* touching this present service," etc. This oath has remained substantially unchanged to the present day. There was a difference, too, in the nomenclature of the two cases of accusations by private persons and upon their own knowledge. In the former case their action was embodied in an indictment formally laid before them for their consideration; in the latter case, in the form of a presentment. Says Blackstone in his Commentaries, Book IV, page 301:

"A presentment, properly speaking, is a notice taken by a grand jury of any offense from their own knowledge or observation, without any bill of indictment laid before them at the suit of the King, as the presentment of a nuisance, a libel, and the like; upon which the officer of the court must afterwards frame an indictment, before the party presented can be put to answer it."

* * *

In a case arising in Tennessee the grand jury, without the agency of the district attorney, had called witnesses before them, whom they interrogated as to their knowledge concerning the then late Cuban expedition. Mr. Justice Catron sustained the legality of the proceeding and compelled the witnesses to answer. His opinion is reported in Wharton's Criminal Pleading and Practice, 8th ed. § 337. He says: "The grand jury have the undoubted right to send for witnesses and have them sworn to give evidence generally, and to found presentments on the evidence of such witnesses; and the question here is, whether a witness thus introduced is legally bound to disclose whether a crime has been committed, and also who committed the crime." His charge contains a thorough discussion of the whole subject.

While presentments have largely fallen into disuse in this country, the practice of grand juries acting upon notice, either of their own knowledge or upon information obtained by them, and incorporating their findings in an indictment, still largely obtains. Whatever doubts there may be with regard to the early English procedure, the practice in this country, under the system of public prosecutions carried on by officers of the State appointed for that purpose, has been entirely settled since the adoption of the Constitution. In a lecture delivered by Mr. Justice Wilson of this court, who may be assumed to have known the current practice, before the students of the University of Pennsylvania, he says (Wilson's Works, vol. II, page 213):

"It has been alleged, that grand juries are confined, in their inquiries, to the bills offered to them, to the crimes given them in charge, and to the evidence brought before them by the prosecutor. But these conceptions are much too contracted; they present but a very imperfect and unsatisfactory view of the duty required from grand jurors, and of the trust reposed in them. They are not appointed for the prosecutor or for the court; they are appointed for the government and for the people; and of both the government and people it is surely the concernment that, on one hand, all crimes, whether given or not given in charge, whether described or not described with professional skill, should receive the punishment, which the law denounces; and that, on the other hand, innocence, however strongly assailed by accusations drawn up in regular form, and by accusers, marshalled in legal array, should, on full investigation, be secure in that protection, which the law engages that she shall enjoy inviolate.

"The oath of a grand juryman—and his oath is the commission under which he acts—assigns no limits, except those marked by diligence itself, to the course of his inquiries: Why, then, should it be circumscribed by more contracted boundaries? Shall diligent inquiry be enjoined? And shall the means and opportunities of inquiry be prohibited or restrained?"

Similar language was used by Judge Addison, President of the Court of Common Pleas, in charging the grand jury at the session of the Common Pleas Court in 1791 (Addison's Pa.Rep.Appx. p. 38):

"If the grand jury, *of their own knowledge,* or the knowledge of any of them, or from the examination of witnesses, know of any offense committed in the county, for which no indictment is preferred to them, it is their duty, either to inform the officer, who prosecutes for the State, of the nature of the offense, and desire that an indictment for it be laid before them; or, if they do not, or if no such indictment be given them, it is their duty to give such information of it to the court; stating, without any particular form, the facts and circumstances which constitute the offense. This is called a presentment."

The practice then prevailing, with regard to the duty of grand juries, shows that a presentment may be based not only upon their own personal knowledge, but from the examination of witnesses.

While no case has arisen in this court in which the question has been distinctly presented, the authorities in the state courts largely preponderate in favor of the theory that the grand jury may act upon information received by them from the examination of witnesses without a formal indictment, or other charge previously laid before them. . . .

The rulings of the inferior Federal courts are to the same effect. . . .

* * *

There are doubtless a few cases in the state courts which take a contrary view, but they are generally such as deal with the abuses of the system, as the indiscriminate summoning of witnesses with no definite object in view and in a spirit of meddlesome inquiry. . . .

We deem it entirely clear that under the practice in this country, at least, the examination of witnesses need not be preceded by a presentment or indictment formally drawn up, but that the grand jury may proceed, either upon their own knowledge or upon the examination of witnesses, to inquire for themselves whether a crime cognizable by the court has been committed; that the result of their investigations may be subsequently embodied in an indictment, and that in summoning witnesses it is quite sufficient to apprise them of the names of the parties with respect to whom they will be called to testify, without indicating the nature of the charge against them. So valuable is this inquisitorial power of the grand jury that, in States where felonies may be prosecuted by information as well as indictment, the power is ordinarily reserved to courts of impanelling grand juries for the investigation of riots, frauds and nuisances, and other cases where it is impracticable to ascertain in advance the names of the persons implicated. It is impossible to conceive that in such cases the examination of witnesses must be stopped until a basis is laid by an indictment formally preferred, when the very object of the examination is to ascertain who shall be indicted. As criminal prosecutions are instituted by the State through an officer selected for that purpose, he is vested with a certain discretion with respect to the cases he will call to their attention, the number and character of the witnesses, the form in which the indictment shall be drawn, and other details of the proceedings. Doubtless abuses of this power may be imagined, as if the object of the inquiry were merely to pry into the details of domestic or business life. But were such abuses called to the attention of the court, it would doubtless be alert to repress them. While the grand jury may not indict upon current rumors or unverified reports, they may act upon knowledge acquired either from their own observations or upon the evidence of witnesses given before them.

* * *

BLAIR v. UNITED STATES

Supreme Court of the United States, 1919.
250 U.S. 273, 39 S.Ct. 468, 63 L.Ed. 979.

MR. JUSTICE PITNEY delivered the opinion of the court.

Three of these cases come here on writs of error, the other three on appeals. The writs bring up final orders adjudging plaintiffs in error guilty of contempt of court because of their refusal to obey an order directing them to answer certain questions asked of them before a federal grand jury, and committing them to the custody of the United States marshal until they should comply. The appeals bring under review final orders discharging writs of habeas corpus sued out by appellants to review their detention under the original orders of commitment and remanding them to the custody of the marshal. Blair, Templeton, and Phillips are plaintiffs in error, as well as appellants.

It appears that in October, 1918, the federal grand jury of the Southern District of New York was making inquiry concerning supposed violations of § 125 of the Criminal Code (relating to perjury) and of the so-called Corrupt Practices Act of June 25, 1910, c. 392, 36 Stat. 822, as amended, in connection with the verification and filing in that district of reports to the Secretary of the Senate of the United States made by a candidate for nomination as Senator at a primary election held in the State of Michigan on August 27, 1918. Phillips was served with a subpoena requiring him to appear and testify before this grand jury. Blair and Templeton were subpoenaed to appear and testify and also to produce certain records, correspondence, and other documentary evidence. All were served in the State of Michigan. They appeared before the grand jury in response to the subpoenas, were severally sworn, and were examined by counsel for the United States. Each witness, after answering preliminary questions, asked that he be informed of the object and purpose of the inquiry and against whom it was directed, whereupon he was informed by counsel for the United

States that the inquiry was not directed against him (the witness). After this each witness read to and left with the grand jury a typewritten statement to the effect that upon advice of counsel he refused to answer any questions pertaining to the matter under inquiry, for the reason that the grand jury and the court were without jurisdiction to inquire into the conduct of a campaign in Michigan for the primary election of a United States Senator; that the Federal Corrupt Practices Act as amended was unconstitutional; and that no federal court or grand jury in any State had constitutional authority to conduct an inquiry regarding a primary election for United States Senator. Thereupon each witness was asked by counsel for the United States whether he refused to testify for the reason that to do so would incriminate him, to which he made no other answer than to refer to the reasons for his refusal as set forth in his statement.

The grand jury made a written presentment of these facts to the district court, with a prayer that the parties named might be dealt with as contumacious witnesses.

* * *

The principal contention is that the [statutes] are unconstitutional in so far as they attempt to regulate and control the selection by political parties at primary elections of candidates for United States Senator to be voted for at the general elections; it being insisted that the authority of Congress under § 4 of Art. I of the Constitution extends only to the definitive general election and not to preëlection arrangements or devices such as nominating conventions and primaries.

It is maintained further that, because of the invalidity of these statutes, neither the United States district court nor the federal grand jury has jurisdiction to inquire into primary elections or to indict or try any person for an offense based upon the statutes, and therefore the order committing appellants is null and void.

. . . Considerations of propriety, as well as long-established practice, demand that we refrain from passing upon the constitutionality of an act of Congress unless obliged to do so in the proper performance of our judicial function, when the question is raised by a party whose interests entitle him to raise it.

We do not think the present parties are so entitled, since a brief consideration of the relation of a witness to the proceeding in which he is called will suffice to show that he is not interested to challenge the jurisdiction of court or grand jury over the subject-matter that is under inquiry.

Long before the separation of the American Colonies from the mother country, compulsion of witnesses to appear and testify had become established in England. . . . When it was that grand juries first resorted to compulsory process for witnesses is not clear. But as early as 1612, in the Countess of Shrewsbury's case, Lord Bacon is reported to have declared that "all subjects, without distinction of degrees, owe to the King tribute and service, not only of their deed and hand, but of their knowledge and discovery." . . .

At the foundation of our Federal Government the inquisitorial function of the grand jury and the compulsion of witnesses were recognized as incidents of the judicial power of the United States. . . .

[I]t is clearly recognized that the giving of testimony and the attendance upon court or grand jury in order to testify are public duties which every person within the jurisdiction of the Government is bound to perform upon being properly summoned, and for performance of which he is entitled to no further compensation than that which the statutes provide. The personal sacrifice involved is a part of the necessary contribution of the individual to the welfare of the public. The duty, so onerous at times, yet so necessary to the administration of justice according to the forms and modes established in our system of government, is subject to mitigation in exceptional circumstances; there is a constitutional exemption from being compelled in any criminal case to be a witness against oneself, entitling the witness to be excused from answering anything that will tend to incriminate him; some confidential matters are shielded from considerations of policy, and perhaps in other cases for special reasons a witness may be excused from telling all that he knows.

But, aside from exceptions and qualifications—and none such is asserted in the present case—the witness is bound not only to attend but to tell what he knows in answer to questions framed for the purpose of bringing out the truth of the matter under inquiry.

He is not entitled to urge objections of incompetency or irrelevancy, such as a party might raise, for this is no concern of his.

On familiar principles, he is not entitled to challenge the authority of the court or of the grand jury, provided they have a de facto existence and organization.

He is not entitled to set limits to the investigation that the grand jury may conduct. The Fifth Amendment and the statutes relative to the organization of grand juries recognize such a jury as being possessed of the same powers that pertained to its British prototype, and in our system examination of witnesses by a grand jury need not be preceded by a formal charge against a particular individual. Hale v. Henkel, 201 U.S. 43, 65. It is a grand inquest, a body with powers of investigation and inquisition, the scope of whose inquiries is not to be limited narrowly by questions of propriety or forecasts of the probable result of the investigation, or by doubts whether any particular individual will be found properly subject to an accusation of crime. As has been said before, the identity of the offender, and the precise nature of the offense, if there be one, normally are developed at the conclusion of the grand jury's labors, not at the beginning.

And, for the same reasons, witnesses are not entitled to take exception to the jurisdiction of the grand jury or the court over the particular subject-matter that is under investigation. In truth it is in the ordinary case no concern of one summoned as a witness whether the offense is within the jurisdiction of the court or not. At least, the court and grand jury have authority and jurisdiction to investigate the facts in order to determine the question whether the facts show a case within their jurisdiction.

The present cases are not exceptional, and for the reasons that have been outlined we are of opinion that appellants were not entitled to raise any question about the constitutionality of the statutes under which the grand jury's investigation was conducted.

Final orders affirmed.

NOTES AND QUERIES

(1) *Role and Function of the Grand Jury—Some History.* The grand jury plays a unique role in our system of government. It is empowered to investigate for crimes, at the request of a state prosecutor, the request of the court, or from its own knowledge. At the same time the grand jury is expected to protect citizens from unfounded accusations. It stands, says the Supreme Court, "between the accuser and the accused . . . to determine whether a charge is founded upon reason or was dictated by an intimidating power or by malice and personal ill will." [1]

The grand jury thus performs two roles, inquisitor and protector. In carrying out these roles it uneasily combines executive and judicial functions, determining not only whether a crime has been committed and by whom, but also impartially judging the strength of the charges under consideration. *Blair* stated that the grand jury's inquisitorial function and power to call witnesses were "recognized incidents of the judicial power of the United States." Nevertheless, the historical record indicates that this power has most often been under the effective control of the prosecutor, not the courts. Indeed, *Hale* and *Blair* effectively solidified the prosecutor's control of the grand jury. The question is whether the Supreme Court should have done otherwise.

Some historical perspective can assist consideration of this question. The grand jury traces its roots back to England in 1166, as a body of twelve men whose purpose was to present sworn accusations of crime against suspected offenders.[2] Although it thus began as an instrument of the Crown, it came to exercise sufficient independence in England such that it could be extolled by the Lord Chancellor in 1681 as "our only security" against "malicious" charges: "All our lives are thus by

---

1. Wood v. Georgia, 370 U.S. 375, 390, 82 S.Ct. 1364, 1373, 8 L.Ed.2d 569, 580 (1962). For similar expressions, see, e.g., United States v. Calandra, 414 U.S. 338, 343, 94 S.Ct. 613, 617, 38 L.Ed.2d 561, 568 (1974); Ex parte Bain, 121 U.S. 1, 11, 7 S.Ct. 781, 786–87, 30 L.Ed. 849, 852–53 (1887).

2. See R. Younger, The People's Panel: The Grand Jury in the United States, 1634–1941, at 1 (1963). For an earlier dating, see Schwartz, Demythologizing the Historic Role of the Grand Jury, 10 Am. Crim.L.Rev. 701, 706–707 (1972) (Constitutions of Clarendon in 1163).

law trusted to the care of our grand inquests, that none may be put to answer for their lives, unless they indict them."³

The English colonists brought the grand jury with them to America, and in the pre-Revolutionary period the grand jury played a significant role in blocking criminal prosecutions sought by royal authorities.⁴ After independence, two new state constitutions guaranteed the right to indictment by grand jury and all states enacted laws providing for grand juries.⁵ The Massachusetts, New York, and New Hampshire conventions ratifying the Constitution recommended that the Constitution be amended to include the requirement of grand jury indictment; this amendment, proposed in the first Congress in 1789, was ratified as part of the fifth amendment.⁶ The provision "elicited no recorded debate or opposition."⁷

At the turn of the eighteenth century the grand jury continued to play its independent role of checking prosecutorial abuse, but grand juries also became tangled in political controversies between the federalists and anti-federalists.⁸ Although Justice Wilson's lectures about the grand jury (quoted by the Court in *Hale,* supra p. 437) praised its powerful role as a democratic institution, others were arguing in favor of restricting the broad power of the grand jury.⁹ Bentham criticized the grand jury in England as having become "packed" on behalf of the upper classes, as well as being inefficient in comparison to a professionally trained prosecutor.¹⁰ By the 1850s retention of the grand jury was being debated in a number of states, with reformers seeking the abolition of this " 'crumbling survivor of fallen institutions . . . more akin to the star chamber.' "¹¹

After the Civil War, critics resumed urging that grand juries be confined to investigating matters within their own personal knowledge, or brought to their attention by the court or the prosecutor; independent investigations by the grand jurors were argued to be both dangerous and inefficient. These reformers began convincing legislatures to

3. Somers, The Security of Englishmen's Lives: Or, The Trust, Power and Duty of Grand Juries of England 2, 20 (1766 ed.). The grand jury's reputation rested on its refusal, in the late seventeenth century, to indict two prominent critics of the King (Stephen Colledge and the Earl of Shaftesbury) for treason. For a full treatment of these cases, see Schwartz, supra n. 2, at 710–721 (Colledge indicted by second grand jury and executed; Shaftesbury died in exile while avoiding prosecution).

4. For example, in 1765 Boston jurors refused to indict the leaders of the Stamp Act riots, see Younger, supra, at 28; and in 1743 twice refused to indict John Peter Zenger for seditious libel. See M. Frankel & G. Naftalis, The Grand Jury: An Institution on Trial 11 (1977).

5. Younger, supra, at 37.

6. See I Elliot's Debates 323, 326, 328; II Elliot's Debates 110.

7. Constitution of United States of America, Analysis and Interpretation, Annotations of Cases Decided by the Supreme Court of the United States to July 2, 1982, S.Doc. No. 99–16, 99th Cong., 1st Sess. 1215 (1982).

8. See Younger, supra, at 47–55.

9. Compare 2 The Works of James Wilson 534–37, 688–89 (R. McClosky, Ed., 1967) (praising grand jury) with Alexander Addison, 2 Reports of Cases in the County Courts of the Fifth Circuit 37–46 (1883).

10. See Younger, supra, at 56.

11. Younger, supra, at 68 (quoting report of Judiciary Committee of Michigan House of Representatives from 1859).

change the grand jury system. Wisconsin restricted the grand jury in 1870; Nebraska allowed for its abolition in 1875, as did Colorado in 1876. In 1879 California permitted prosecution by information.[12] In 1884, in *Hurtado v. California,* the Supreme Court upheld this California law, over a vigorous dissent by Justice Harlan, finding that the due process clause of the fourteenth amendment did not include the fifth amendment's requirement of grand jury indictment.[13] The grand jury need not be the only way to initiate prosecutions. The States could "take the best ideas of all systems and of every age" and "mould and shape" the "new and various experiences of our own situation" into new forms.[14]

Given that the Supreme Court at the end of the nineteenth century was not convinced of the critical importance of the grand jury, and that the grand jury was then under strong attack, it is perhaps somewhat surprising that *Hale* emphasized traditional statements supporting the grand jury's power. In contrast to the tone of assurance in the Supreme Court's opinion as to the breadth of the grand jury's power, the lower court in *Hale* had stated: "[A]s to the extent and limitation of this [inquisitorial] power there is pronounced divergence of opinion." The lower court pointed out that the grand jurors had not acted pursuant to their own knowledge or pursuant to any charge given them by either the court or the prosecutor. According to the lower court, this placed the investigation "upon the border line between the legitimate exercise and the abuse of the inquisitorial power of the grand jury." [15]

The Supreme Court in *Hale* seemed less concerned about the grand jury abusing its power. Perhaps this was because the Court understood that the grand jury was *not* acting independently, but was being controlled by the prosecutor. Reconsider the following excerpt from the Court's opinion (supra p. 439):

> As criminal prosecutions are instituted by the State through an officer selected for that purpose, he is vested with a certain discretion with respect to the cases he will call to their attention, the number and character of the witnesses, the form in which the indictment shall be drawn, and other details of the proceedings. Doubtless abuses of this power may be imagined. . . . But were such abuses called to the attention of the court, it would doubtless be alert to repress them.

The Court thus recognizes and accepts the prosecutor's role in directing the grand jury. It willingly shifts the federal grand jury from independent inquisitor to arm of the prosecution, subject only to gener-

---

12. These post-Civil War reform efforts are traced in Younger, supra, pp. 138–154.

13. 110 U.S. 516, 4 S.Ct. 111, 28 L.Ed. 232 (1884).

14. 110 U.S. at 531, 4 S.Ct. at 118–19, 28 L.Ed. at 233.

15. See In re Hale, 139 Fed. 496, 498, 501 (C.C.S.D.N.Y.1905). The court felt, however, that judicial intervention in ordering Hale to appear and answer was "equivalent to an express instruction [by the court] to the grand jury to investigate." See id. at 501.

al court oversight. (Note, in this connection, that the Department of Justice had only been established in 1870.) The Court in *Hale* thus did not approve an undirected grand jury. Rather it gave shape to the modern grand jury, run by government prosecutors, ready to investigate the complexities of crime in the twentieth century.[16]

(2) *Constitutional Protection?* The fifth amendment provides: "No person shall be held to answer for a capital, or otherwise infamous crime, unless on a presentment or indictment of a Grand Jury. . . ." This recognizes the grand jury as a Constitutional protection for citizens in the criminal process, protection which the drafters of the fifth amendment believed necessary to prevent improper charges by the government (as Note (1), supra, indicates).

Neither *Hale* nor *Blair* pay any attention to the constitutional status of the grand jury. Rather, the Court in both cases reaches back into the common law history of the grand jury to judge the propriety of the acts in question. Was this approach correct? Should the Court have paid more attention to the constitutional status of the grand jury, using the two cases to describe a grand jury which could offer citizens greater protection from state power? Should the fifth amendment have been held to emphasize the grand jury's role as impartial judge of the state's case?

If you find no consideration of this issue in either opinion, perhaps this is somewhat understandable in light of the factual settings of both cases. The background of *Hale* is discussed supra, p. 390; recall the language in the Court's opinion (supra, p. 386) demonstrating the Court's interest in seeing effective prosecution of corporate crimes. As for *Blair,* note that the question of the grand jury's power was not the focus of the litigants in the Supreme Court. Rather, the parties were concerned about the constitutionality of the Federal Corrupt Practices Act, passed in 1911. The Act required political campaign committees to maintain records of contributions and expenditures, and limited the amount of money which could be spent by candidates for nomination and election to Congress. Facing a sensitive political issue and a difficult constitutional question (the power of Congress to regulate primary elections), the Court in *Blair* chose the safer decisional route of holding that witnesses could not challenge the grand jury at this point in the investigation.[17] Thus, the Court's sweeping language regarding

---

16. For modern criticisms and reviews of the grand jury, see, e.g., M. Frankel & G. Naftalis, The Grand Jury: An Institution on Trial (1977) (review of grand jury criticisms); L. Clark, The Grand Jury: The Use and Abuse of Political Power (1975) (review of use of grand jury in political cases during 1960s); Dession, From Indictment to Information: Implications of the Shift, 42 Yale L.J. 163 (1932) (supporting grand jury efficacy and reviewing contemporaneous criticism); Dession and Cohen, The Inquisitorial Functions of Grand Juries, 41 Yale L.J. 687 (1932) ("In the normal situation a grand jury is thus designed and in fact operates as a prosecutor's instrument—a highly effective instrument for conducting an investigation ex parte and in secret."); Moley, The Initiation of Criminal Prosecutions by Indictment or Information, 29 Mich.L.Rev. 403 (1931) (critic of grand jury on efficiency grounds, arguing in favor of use of prosecutors' indictments).

17. The district court in *Blair* had similarly based its decision on its view of the

the power of the grand jury may have been less than carefully considered; it certainly seems doubtful that the Court expected this decision to turn out to be the landmark case that it has.

(3) *Coverage of the Grand Jury Clause: States and Corporations.* As indicated in Note (1), supra, the Supreme Court held in 1884, in *Hurtado v. California,* that the grand jury clause does not apply to state prosecutions. This decision has never been overruled.

Should corporations be covered by the clause? Consider *United States v. Armored Transport, Inc.,* 629 F.2d 1313 (9th Cir.1980), certiorari denied 450 U.S. 965, 101 S.Ct. 1481, 67 L.Ed.2d 614 (1981):

NELSON, CIRCUIT JUDGE:

This appeal presents several issues of first impression in this circuit. The primary question is when does a federal grand jury commence service for the purposes of Rule 6(g), Fed.R.Crim.P., which provides that "no grand jury may serve more than 18 months." The District Court held that the life of the grand jury is measured from the date on which it is authorized to begin serving, rather than the date on which it is impaneled and sworn. We disagree. For purposes of Rule 6(g) the life of a grand jury commences on the impanelment date. The indictment against Armored Transport was handed down more than eighteen months after the grand jury in this case was impaneled and is invalid.

We decline to reverse Armored Transport's conviction, however. Because the crimes charged are not infamous within the meaning of the fifth amendment, and because the government could, therefore, have proceeded by information, the conviction is affirmed.

STATEMENT OF FACTS

On March 9, 1979, the grand jury [herein, the Martin grand jury] returned an indictment against appellant Armored Transport, Inc. and two of its officers, Irvin and DeSalvo, alleging felony violations of Section 1 of the Sherman Act. The Martin grand jury was impaneled and given the oath of impanelment on August 26, 1977. Jurors were then excused from the courtroom and told to

issues which could be raised by a witness on a petition for habeas corpus. See In re Blair, 253 Fed. 800 (S.D.N.Y.1918). The Senator under investigation in *Blair* was eventually indicted and convicted. The Supreme Court, forced to deal with the constitutionality of the statute, held it unconstitutional. See Newberry v. United States, 256 U.S. 232, 41 S.Ct. 469, 65 L.Ed. 913 (1921). The Supreme Court has not always been so reluctant to avoid challenges raised by grand jury witnesses who assert that the statute involved in an investigation is unconstitutional. Compare Morrison v. Olson, ___ U.S. ___, 108 S.Ct. 2597, 101 L.Ed.2d 569 (1988) (witness held in contempt for failing to comply with grand jury subpoena; prosecutor failed to raise *Blair* as barring witness from attacking constitutionality of underlying statute; Court holds objection waived) (upholding constitutionality of Special Prosecutor law). See also In re Sealed Case, 827 F.2d 776 (D.C.Cir.1987) (cases subsequent to *Blair* have permitted witnesses to challenge grand jury subpoenas under certain circumstances).

return when notified by the United States Attorney's office by mail. Evidence was first heard on October 17, 1977. The Martin grand jury's term was extended twice by court order to March 10, 1979. The indictments were returned on March 9, 1979.

Pursuant to a plea bargaining agreement, Armored Transport pleaded nolo contendere to the indictment and was fined $200,000. On June 28, 1979, a former Justice Department Antitrust Division lawyer who was once responsible for prosecuting this case, filed and served an amicus curiae motion to vacate judgments, to allow withdrawal of pleas, and to dismiss the indictment. The amicus motion argued that the original indictment was rendered by the grand jury after its term had expired, and was a nullity. . . . The defendants joined the amicus motion in all respects. The district court denied the motions. This appeal follows.

Only the appeal by Armored Transport remains. The appeals by Irvin and DeSalvo were voluntary dismissed.

[After holding that the impanelment date is the start of the eighteen month grand jury term, set out in Rule 6(g) of the Federal Rules of Criminal Procedure, the Court continued:]

Despite the invalid indictment by grand jury, we affirm the district court. Because the crimes charged are not infamous within the meaning of the fifth amendment and because the Government could have proceeded by information, the District Court correctly retained jurisdiction and sustained the plea entered by defendant.

The fifth amendment provides that "capital or otherwise infamous crimes" must be prosecuted by indictment. So, we must decide whether Armored Transport has been charged with an infamous crime. Appellant argues that all felonies are infamous crimes, and that since the Sherman Act expressly defines a violation of 15 U.S.C. § 1 as a felony, any defendant charged with such a violation may only be prosecuted by indictment. The district court rejected this line of reasoning and held that the indictment clause of the fifth amendment does not extend to a corporation.

We need not consider whether corporations can ever be charged with infamous crimes. Our inquiry is concluded when we determine that Armored Transport has not been charged with such a crime. The Supreme Court has provided substantial, if somewhat ambiguous, guidance as to what constitutes an infamous crime. Early cases discuss two possible approaches to the definition of "infamous". A crime may be classified infamous either because of the nature of the crime, or because the potential punishment is infamous. See Mackin v. United States, 117 U.S. 348, 350–51, 6 S.Ct. 777, 778, 29 L.Ed. 909 (1886); Ex parte Wilson, 114 U.S. 417, 422, 5 S.Ct. 935, 937, 29 L.Ed. 89 (1885). The following language from *Mackin* is instructive:

> . . . The test is whether the crime is one for which the statutes authorize the court to award an infamous punishment,

not whether the punishment ultimately awarded is an infamous one; when the accused is in danger of being subjected to an infamous punishment if convicted, he has the right to insist that he shall not be put upon his trial, except on the accusation of a grand jury.

117 U.S. at 350–51, 6 S.Ct. at 778. Subsequent decisions, relying on Mackin and Ex parte Wilson, interpret "infamous" by examination of the punishment imposed. . . .

We now apply the above analysis to the present case. Under the punishment provision of 15 U.S.C. § 1, as amended in 1974, a corporation is potentially subject to a fine not exceeding one million dollars if convicted. Since indictment is constitutionally required only when a defendant is potentially subject to an infamous punishment, Armored Transport has no right to indictment because a fine is not such a punishment.[18] We agree that the public's notion of what constitutes an infamous punishment varies from one age to another, but we disagree that a fine is as infamous a punishment to a corporation as a year of imprisonment or hard labor is to an individual. Deprivation of liberty takes away from an individual his ability to work, to support and live with his family, to engage in social activity, and other highly valued attributes of living in our society. A corporation in violation of 15 U.S.C. § 1 can only suffer a monetary penalty.

While we sympathize with appellant's argument that a one million dollar fine may mean considerable hardship or even economic ruin to a corporation, the gravity of this consequence to a corporation seems no greater than the potential gravity of a large fine upon an individual. Clearly, an individual charged with an offense for which the maximum penalty is a fine is not constitutionally entitled to indictment by grand jury. . . . The potential punishment must be infamous, and a fine, levied against either an individual or a corporation, simply does not fit within the meaning of that word, as interpreted by the Supreme Court.

We recognize the result of our holding is that an individual charged with a violation of 15 U.S.C. § 1 must be indicted but that a corporation charged with the same offense may be proceeded against by information. . . . An individual convicted of a violation of 15 U.S.C. § 1 is potentially subject to three years imprisonment whereas a corporation is potentially subject to no greater penalty than a one million dollar fine. The only punishment that is directly relevant to classification of a crime as infamous is the potential punishment that the statute imposes on the particular defendant being tried. Congress may treat different classes of defendants differently and it has done so here.

18. [Court's footnote 3.] We leave open the question whether infamous punishments might be fashioned in the future that could be inflicted upon corporations.

We conclude, therefore, that the right of indictment guaranteed by the fifth amendment does not extend to a corporation charged under 15 U.S.C. § 1. Because Armored Transport does not have the right to an indictment, the Government could have proceeded against it by information. . . .

* * * [19]

(4) *Executive Control Over the Grand Jury.* From time to time there have been conflicts between the grand jury's independent inquisitorial role and the prosecutorial policies of the executive. A classic example was *United States v. Cox* [20] in which the United States Attorney was instructed by the Attorney General not to sign an indictment that the grand jury sought to bring against two Blacks for alleged perjury in connection with their testimony relating to discrimination in voter registration. The Court of Appeals for the Fifth Circuit, en banc, upheld the prosecutor's independent power to make a final determination as to whether criminal charges should be brought.

More recent concerns relating to the prosecutorial independence of the grand jury have involved questions of foreign policy. Should a grand jury, for example, be free to indict current or former heads of government for criminal acts with direct effects in the United States? [21] Consider Hershey, "Reagan Orders an End to Air Inquiry," New York Times, Nov. 20, 1984, p. D1: [22]

The Justice Department said today that it had closed, at the direction of President Reagan, a criminal antitrust investigation into passenger air travel that has soured relations between the United States and Britain.

The department, in a terse two-sentence statement, said the President's decision was "based on foreign policy reasons." The department's spokesman, Mark T. Sheehan, declined to elaborate on the reasons. "You can't expect the President to explain foreign policy decisions," he said. "It is enough for him to consider the factors and decide, for the good of the country."

Although the Justice Department has never formally said so, it is widely believed that the grand jury investigation, begun in June 1983, was looking into the possibility that various North Atlantic carriers conspired to drive the price-cutting Laker Airways out of business. The British company has been in receivership since February 1982.

19. See also United States v. Yellow Freight System, Inc., 637 F.2d 1248 (9th Cir.1980) (Elkins Act prosecution for giving rate discounts not "infamous"; even if some crimes might be "inherently" infamous regardless of penalty, regulatory crime does not so qualify), certiorari denied 454 U.S. 815, 102 S.Ct. 91, 70 L.Ed.2d 84 (1981).

20. 342 F.2d 167 (5th Cir.), certiorari denied 381 U.S. 935, 85 S.Ct. 1767, 14 L.Ed.2d 700 (1965).

21. See "U.S. Said to Weigh Indicting Marcos," N.Y. Times, July 17, 1988, p. 6 (White House spokesman denies President would have "'veto power'" over indictment, but terms matter one that has "'foreign policy implications'" in which President would make his views "'known to the Justice Department'"; grand jury has been investigating Marcos' activities while President of Philippines). Marcos was subsequently indicted. See "Marcos and Wife, 8 Others Charged By U.S. With Fraud," N.Y. Times, Oct. 22, 1988, p. 1.

22. Copyright © 1984 by The New York Times Company. Reprinted with permission.

British officials have complained about both the antitrust investigation and the penalties that its carriers could suffer as a result of a civil suit brought by Laker's receiver, which is continuing.

One effect of today's decision is likely to be resumed sales by British Airways, Pan American World Airways and other carriers of low-priced tickets between most American gateway cities and London this winter. The fares, as low as $378 round trip, were the subject of a dispute between the two countries, and the British Government announced on Oct. 18 that they would not be approved.

"This would seem to give the fares a new lease on life," Wallace C. Stefany, a spokesman for the Civil Aeronautics Board, said this afternoon.

Laker, which was founded by the entrepreneur Frederick A. Laker in the late 1940's with a few war-surplus planes, was a successful charter company but came to worldwide prominence when, in September 1977, it began offering its no-frills Skytrain service between New York and London. Westbound flights then cost £59, about $102, and eastbound flights, $135.

Although other carriers were forced into drastic price reductions to compete, Laker thrived and expanded the service to the London–Los Angeles route as well. Mr. Laker was later knighted for successfully battling the established carriers on behalf of price-conscious passengers.

Planned to Expand Service

At one time Sir Freddie's line was carrying one of every five trans-Atlantic passengers and he was proposing to expand cut-fare service throughout Europe.

Mr. Sheehan strongly suggested today that Justice Department lawyers sought to continue the investigation and that it was the State Department that inspired President Reagan to overrule them. "If the Justice Department had thought the investigation should be closed on purely legal grounds, the question would not have gone to the President in the first place," Mr. Sheehan said. "There was not complete agreement between the agencies as to which considerations were paramount—legal or foreign relations considerations."

He said he could not recall the last time a President ordered an end to such an inquiry, but noted that this might have occurred without his knowledge. Mr. Sheehan also said that "there was no quid pro quo involved" in today's decision and that it was not tied to fare negotiations between the two countries. "We have never discussed" the two subjects together, he added.

* * *

B. CONDUCTING THE GRAND JURY INQUEST

SCOPE NOTE

The federal grand jury is governed primarily by Rule 6 of the Federal Rules of Criminal Procedure. Rule 6(a) provides for a grand jury consisting of not less than sixteen nor more than twenty-three members; 6(f) requires the concurrence of twelve or more grand jurors to return an indictment. The selection of those eligible to serve on the grand jury is done on the same basis as the selection of those eligible to serve on the petit jury; discrimination on the basis of race or sex is similarly forbidden.²³ Normal rules of evidence do not apply; hearsay may be used, as well as evidence which police agents have seized unconstitutionally.²⁴ All hearings of federal grand juries are held ex parte. Under Rule 6(d), the only people who may be present, in addition to the grand jurors, are the witness under examination, an interpreter, a stenographer to record the proceedings, and government attorneys. A witness has no right to have counsel present in the grand jury room, although a witness may leave the grand jury room to consult with counsel.²⁵ Witnesses may invoke their fifth amendment privilege against self-incrimination; although there is no requirement that witnesses be warned of their privilege, it is the practice of the Justice Department to do so.²⁶ In addition, it is federal practice to inform witnesses as to whether they are considered "targets" or "subjects" of the grand jury's investigation. A "target" is a witness who the prosecutor or grand jury has linked to the crime by "substantial evidence" and who, in the judgment of the prosecutor, is a "putative defendant." A "subject" is a witness whose conduct is "within the scope" of the grand jury's investigation.²⁷

The materials in this Section are not intended to describe exhaustively federal grand jury practice.²⁸ Rather, they concentrate on three major areas of particular relevance to business crime prosecutions: 1) grand jury secrecy; 2) presenting evidence to the grand jury; and 3) the standard for challenging grand jury action.

1. GRAND JURY SECRECY

FEDERAL RULES OF CRIMINAL PROCEDURE RULE 6(e)

(e) Recording and Disclosure of Proceedings

(1) Recording of Proceedings. All proceedings, except when the grand jury is deliberating or voting, shall be recorded stenographically or by an electronic recording device. . . .

(2) General Rule of Secrecy. A grand juror, an interpreter, a stenographer, an operator of a recording device, a typist who tran-

---

23. See Jury Selection and Service Act, 28 U.S.C.A. § 1861 et seq. (Supp.); Vasquez v. Hillery, 474 U.S. 254, 106 S.Ct. 617, 88 L.Ed.2d 598 (1986) (racial discrimination); Ballard v. United States, 329 U.S. 187, 67 S.Ct. 261, 91 L.Ed. 181 (1946) (discrimination against women).

24. The leading case upholding indictments based on hearsay is Costello v. United States, 350 U.S. 359, 76 S.Ct. 406, 100 L.Ed. 397 (1956). On allowing grand juries to use evidence seized unconstitutionally, see United States v. Calandra, 414 U.S. 338, 94 S.Ct. 613, 38 L.Ed.2d 561 (1974), explored further infra, p. 589.

25. In a number of states, counsel for a witness is permitted into the grand jury room, in varying circumstances. For a listing, see D. Emerson, Grand Jury Reform: A Review of Key Issues 16 (1983) (listing 15 states which permit counsel; only one permits counsel to object to questions).

26. See United States v. Washington, 431 U.S. 181, 97 S.Ct. 1814, 52 L.Ed.2d 238 (1977). The practice of the Department of Justice is set out in United States Attorneys' Manual, tit. 9-11.260 (1984).

27. See United States Attorneys' Manual, tit. 9-11.260, .261 (1984).

28. For more comprehensive reviews, see, e.g., W. LaFave & J. Israel, Criminal Procedure chs. 8, 15 (1984); S. Beale & W. Bryson, Grand Jury Law and Practice (1988) (2 vols.).

scribes recorded testimony, an attorney for the government, or any person to whom disclosure is made under paragraph (3)(A)(ii) of this subdivision shall not disclose matters occurring before the grand jury, except as otherwise provided for in these rules. No obligation of secrecy may be imposed on any person except in accordance with this rule. A knowing violation of rule 6 may be punished as a contempt of court.

(3) Exceptions.

(A) Disclosure otherwise prohibited by this rule of matters occurring before the grand jury, other than its deliberations and the vote of any grand juror, may be made to—

>   (i) an attorney for the government for use in the performance of such attorney's duty; and

>   (ii) such government personnel (including personnel of a state or subdivision of a state) as are deemed necessary by an attorney for the government to assist an attorney for the government in the performance of such attorney's duty to enforce federal criminal law.

(B) Any person to whom matters are disclosed under subparagraph (A)(ii) of this paragraph shall not utilize that grand jury material for any purpose other than assisting the attorney for the government in the performance of such attorney's duty to enforce federal criminal law. An attorney for the government shall promptly provide the district court, before which was impaneled the grand jury whose material has been so disclosed, with the names of the persons to whom such disclosure has been made, and shall certify that he has advised such persons of their obligation of secrecy under this rule.

(C) Disclosure otherwise prohibited by this rule of matters occurring before the grand jury may also be made—

>   (i) when so directed by a court preliminarily to or in connection with a judicial proceeding;

>   (ii) when permitted by a court at the request of the defendant, upon a showing that grounds may exist for a motion to dismiss the indictment because of matters occurring before the grand jury; or

>   (iii) when the disclosure is made by an attorney for the government to another federal grand jury; or

>   (iv) when permitted by a court at the request of an attorney for the government, upon a showing that such matters may disclose a violation of state criminal law, to an appropriate official of a state or subdivision of a state for the purpose of enforcing such law.

If the court orders disclosure of matters occurring before the grand jury, the disclosure shall be made in such manner, at such time, and under such conditions as the court may direct.

* * *

(5) Closed Hearing. Subject to any right to an open hearing in contempt proceedings, the court shall order a hearing on matters

affecting a grand jury proceeding to be closed to the extent necessary to prevent disclosure of matters occuring before a grand jury.

(6) *Sealed Records.* Records, orders and subpoenas relating to grand jury proceedings shall be kept under seal to the extent and for such time as is necessary to prevent disclosure of matters occurring before a grand jury.

NOTES AND QUERIES

(1) *Reasons for Secrecy.* Rule 6(e), originally effective in 1946, continued the traditional practice of grand jury secrecy, although it altered the common practice of requiring witnesses before the grand jury to take an oath of secrecy.[29] In *United States v. Procter & Gamble Co.* the Supreme Court set out an often-quoted statement of the reasons for the policy of secrecy:[30]

> (1) To prevent the escape of those whose indictment may be contemplated; (2) to insure the utmost freedom to the grand jury in its deliberations, and to prevent persons subject to indictment or their friends from importuning the grand jurors; (3) to prevent subornation of perjury or tampering with the witnesses who may testify before the grand jury and later appear at the trial of those indicted by it; (4) to encourage free and untrammeled disclosures by persons who have information with respect to the commission of crimes; (5) to protect [the] innocent accused who is exonerated from disclosure of the fact that he has been under investigation, and from the expense of standing trial where there was no probability of guilt.

The Court stressed in *Procter & Gamble* that grand jury secrecy "encourage[s] all witnesses to step forward and testify freely without fear of retaliation." In antitrust suits, the Court wrote, the witnesses "may be employees or even officers of potential defendants, or their customers, their competitors, their suppliers. The grand jury as a public institution serving the community might suffer if those testifying today knew that the secrecy of their testimony would be lifted tomorrow." (Do you agree?)

Courts take the policy of grand jury secrecy extremely seriously. It is of importance not only in the pre-indictment phase, when defense counsel would like very much to learn what the grand jury is doing, but also post-indictment when defense counsel endeavor to obtain grand jury transcripts; and even post-trial, when civil litigants (government and private) seek to discover what the grand jury found out.[31] Reconsider the reasons for grand jury secrecy articulated in *Procter & Gamble*. To what extent do they argue for a broad rule on grand jury secrecy? In light of more modern ideas of litigation, which generally

---

29. For a description of pre-Rules practice, see G. Dession, Criminal Law Administration and Public Order 860–61 (1948).

30. 356 U.S. 677, 681 n. 6, 78 S.Ct. 983, 986 n. 6, 2 L.Ed.2d 1077, 1081 n. 6 (1958) (quoting United States v. Rose, 215 F.2d 617, 628–629 (3d Cir.1954)).

31. The availability of grand jury materials in civil litigation is explored infra, Chapter 7C.

favor broad pretrial discovery by both sides, should grand jury secrecy be less severe? Note that under Rule 16, indicted defendants are entitled to obtain a copy of their grand jury transcripts; where the defendant is a corporation, it is generally entitled to obtain the transcripts of those of its employees who testified before the grand jury.[32]

(2) *Debriefing Witnesses.* It is standard practice for counsel to interview and debrief grand jury witnesses after they have testified. Where possible, counsel might attempt to debrief witnesses whom they do not represent. This is particularly common where corporate counsel seeks to interview those corporate employees who are represented by independent counsel.[33] Is such a practice consistent with maintaining grand jury secrecy? Consider, in this connection, *In re Grand Jury Proceedings,* 558 F.Supp. 532 (W.D.Va.1983):

> TURK, CHIEF JUDGE.
>
> The United States Attorney filed a "Motion to Enjoin Violations of Grand Jury Secrecy" on January 18, 1983 against respondent, a law firm, alleging that the latter was systematically "debriefing" witnesses appearing before the Grand Jury during the course of an ongoing tax fraud investigation. The government, citing the paramount need for secrecy in grand jury proceedings, seeks an injunction . . . .
>
> * * *
>
> The government argues that the paramount need for secrecy in grand jury proceedings commands that the relief sought be granted. Respondent, on the other hand, contends that Fed.R.Crim.P. 6(e)(2) prohibits it. That rule, while imposing an obligation of secrecy on other parties to the proceeding, does not do so with regard to witnesses, and provides that "[n]o obligation of secrecy may be imposed on any person except in accordance with this rule." The Advisory Committee Note following Rule 6(e) explains this provision as follows:
>
>> The rule does not impose any obligation of secrecy on witnesses. The existing practice on this point varies among the districts. The seal of secrecy on witnesses seems an unnecessary hardship and may lead to injustice if a witness is not permitted to make a disclosure to counsel or to an associate.
>
> Respondent relies heavily on In re Grand Jury Summoned October 12, 1970, 321 F.Supp. 238 (N.D.Ohio 1970). In that case, the court restrained government attorneys from in effect imposing a "veil of secrecy" over witnesses by advising them that, "while they were free to discuss their testimony with whomever they pleased, they were to report back to the grand jury in the event they were interrogated regarding the questions presented to them by the

---

32. See F.R.Crim.P. 16(a)(1)(A) (those employees who could legally bind the corporation either when they testified or when they participated in the unlawful conduct).

33. Separate representation might be necessary in conflict of interest situations. For further discussion, see pp. 477–495.

grand jury." The court stated: "The cases show that the secrecy of grand jury proceedings may not be imposed upon witnesses who appear before a grand jury; they may be interviewed after their appearance and repeat what they said before the grand jury or otherwise relate their knowledge on the subject of their inquiry."

* * *

The government counters that the requirement of grand jury secrecy is great. This is beyond dispute. To be weighed against this policy, however, is the First Amendment rights of respondent to communicate with whom it chooses. Respondent's related rights of free speech and association are inconsistent with the relief sought by the government.

To accommodate the values and interests found on each side of the argument, a balancing approach is dictated. An injunction, which would be in effect a disfavored "prior restraint," is not warranted at this point, especially since the government has not demonstrated that the efficacy of the grand jury proceeding has been affirmatively harmed. On the other hand, the government has an interest in guarding against the chilling effect that respondent's practices are likely to have upon potential witnesses. Accordingly, the government attorneys may tell witnesses that, although they have a right to discuss their testimony with third parties, they may also refuse to do so. In addition, the government may indicate to witnesses that it would prefer that they not discuss their testimony with third parties (apart from their own attorneys), although they may do so if they choose. Such a course of action would not violate the rule 6(e) proscription against imposing an obligation of secrecy on witnesses; it would merely convey the government's desires.

* * *

Query. Would you favor amending Rule 6(e) to forbid witness debriefings? Under what circumstances?

(3) *How Secret Are Grand Jury Proceedings?* In 1980 the General Accounting Office issued a report regarding federal grand jury secrecy. Based on data collected in seven judicial districts (out of ninety-five), the GAO reported a total of 492 unauthorized disclosures between 1973 and 1980. None were traced to witnesses; two were traced to grand jurors; four to court reporters; twenty-four to inadequate security; eight-five to government attorneys or agencies; and 292 to public documents or public proceedings. As a result of these disclosures, the report asserted, 343 witnesses were identified before indictments were returned; five were murdered, ten intimidated, and one disappeared. The nature of 168 grand jury investigations were revealed before indictment, and 147 targets were publicly identified. As a result, 23 grand jury investigations had to be dropped or delayed.[34]

34. See General Accounting Office, Comptroller General, Report to the Congress: More Guidance and Supervision Needed Over Federal Grand Jury Proceedings 6, 45 (1980).

The Committee on Criminal Law of the Association of the Bar of the City of New York did a more recent study of grand jury leaks in the press. Although concluding that there was no evidence of an *increase* in press leaks of matters occurring before federal grand juries, the study also detailed press reports of ten controversial cases in the 1970s and 1980s, including Abscam, municipal corruption in New York City, and insider trading. The report concluded that prosecutors were not the "exclusive" source of these disclosures, but that disclosures can also come from witnesses, targets, and federal and state investigative agencies. Among its recommendations were that leaks be investigated by entities independent of the prosecutor involved and that any evidentiary privilege be denied to a reporter subpoenaed to testify as to the identity of a government official who leaked grand jury information.

Review the reasons given for grand jury secrecy in *Procter & Gamble,* supra, and the provisions of Rule 6(e). Do you still think that the grand jury must be a "secret inquest"?

2. PRESENTING EVIDENCE TO THE GRAND JURY

The preindictment phase of criminal litigation may be the most critical in business crime cases. Corporate and individual defendants often believe that much damage is done to their business and reputations by the very fact of indictment; once indicted, corporations often prefer to plead rather than litigate. Defense counsel have thus come to focus more attention on the preindictment phase, in an attempt to affect the grand jury's charging decision. As the following cases make clear, however, the attempt by the defense to "participate" in the grand jury's investigation runs counter to established views on the role of the grand jury and triggers court concern that such attention will turn the grand jury process into a "mini-trial." Students should therefore read the following cases not only to discover how the courts are deciding the particular issues of grand jury practice before them, but also to evaluate the role and function of the grand jury in the criminal justice system.

a. Charge to the Grand Jury

IN RE GRAND JURY 79–01

United States District Court, Northern District of Georgia, 1980.
489 F.Supp. 844.

HORACE T. WARD, DISTRICT JUDGE.

The above matter is pending before this court on the motions of defendants to stay proceedings of Grand Jury 79–01 and to supplement the initial charge to this grand jury. . . .

The movants are individuals and corporations who have been informed by attorneys of the Antitrust Division of the United States Department of Justice that they are targets in a grand jury investigation of alleged Sherman Act violations in connection with the waste disposal business in metropolitan Atlanta. These defendants have joined in this unique and novel motion requesting the court to supplement the initial charge to Grand Jury 79–01.

The movants recognize that the prosecutors would be presenting a statement to the grand jury on the applicable law, but argue that it might be one-sided and that circumstances require an independent charge by the court.

The defendants contend that a clear statement to the grand jury as to what constitutes a criminal antitrust violation is demanded because of the vague and ambiguous nature of the Sherman Act when compared with other criminal statutes and the serious business consequences of a publicized indictment, regardless of the ultimate outcome. This motion is vigorously opposed by the government on the ground that to grant it would seriously imperil the traditional ex parte role of the grand jury procedure and would impose an unnecessary burden on the criminal justice process by adding one more adversary proceeding.

The facts presented at the hearing indicate that the government will recommend to the grand jury that indictments be returned charging the movants with violations of Section 1 of the Sherman Act, 15 U.S.C. § 1. This recommendation appears to be imminent. To date the jurors have only heard a standard charge explaining the nature and function of the grand jury, its weighty responsibilities, its procedures, and its limitations. No specific charge on the elements of an antitrust violation has been read to them. The Assistant United States Attorney informed the court at the hearing on this motion that, contrary to the movants' assertions, it was not his division's standard procedure to merely read the Sherman Act to the panel. Rather, it is the practice (and one which will be followed in this matter) to present the law as it applies to the facts uncovered by the grand jury's investigation.[35]

The court is aware of no federal cases which have required a supplemental charge to a grand jury on the elements of a particular crime prior to the presentation of an indictment. While a number of opinions have found prosecutors' instructions on the applicable law insufficient and misleading, the issue has been invariably presented in the form of a postindictment motion to quash or to dismiss. This does not mean that a court is barred from acting sooner. It is clear that the

35. [Court's footnote 2.] The following statements of the prosecutor from transcript of the hearing should be noted:

* * *

THE COURT: What is the normal procedure? . . .

MR. ORR: The normal procedure is to present the evidence to the grand jury and when the investigation is completed the prosecutor will summarize that evidence in an orderly fashion so that the grand jury can have their recollection refreshed; they are told that they do not accept the description of the prosecutor, it is only for their assistance, but their recollection controls. They are also told what the basic law is, it is not a lengthy procedure, but they are told what the statute is and contrary to what the targets say here, we do strongly disagree with the law as described by the targets in the attachment to their motion . . .

MR. ORR: . . . I did not tell the court we merely read the statute to the grand jury. We read the statute and explain the law as it applied to the facts before the grand jury. We will tell them what customer allocation is and price fixing is.

supervisory power which district courts exercise over the grand juries they impanel is a broad one which can take many forms. . . .

Nevertheless, courts should refrain from exercising their supervisory prerogative at the preindictment, investigatory stage unless serious abuses have been shown. Preindictment attacks will almost always be speculative. If prosecutorial abuse is shown or a substantial likelihood of its occurrence is demonstrated, a court is well within its supervisory authority in determining that a grand jury is properly instructed on the applicable criminal law. This is merely another facet of the court's duty to preserve the traditional independence of this body, and should be done upon a proper showing that a statute is indistinct.

The government's contention that the addition of another adversary proceeding would unduly burden the criminal justice process is certainly worthy of consideration, but is not totally persuasive in the premises here presented. Any increased burden on the criminal justice process must be assessed in relation to other considerations relating to fairness and justice.

The movants' argument rests on a claimed uniqueness in the Sherman Act in that unlike most other criminal statutes it does not clearly set forth the elements of the behavior it penalizes. In making this distinction they rely on a recent United States Supreme Court case, United States v. United States Gypsum, [discussed supra this Casebook, p. 228]. . . .

. . . In the United States Gypsum case, the court observed that the "gray area" of uncertain prohibition created by the lack of preciseness of the Sherman Act standards did not include prohibitions on conduct which is per se illegal. That kind of conduct is clearly subject to criminal sanctions, and includes . . . price fixing arrangements and customer allocation agreements. The movants and the government agree that these are the type of violations involved in the instant investigation.

It is strongly urged by the moving parties that an instruction elucidating the elements of an antitrust offense will not threaten, but strengthen the traditional role of the grand jury. This role has to a great extent been the protection of our citizens from false prosecutions as well as the indictment of lawbreakers. Over a period of centuries, the grand jury grew to be a sturdy bulwark between the Crown and the citizenry, and was highly esteemed for this function at the time of the Continental Congress. When presented by Madison in the first draft of the Bill of Rights the provision was unopposed; it was not even debated. When the English grand jury was transplanted here, it brought its protective function with it, a function which has often been lauded. . . . The courts have authority to intervene during the preindictment stage to ensure that this insulating purpose is not imperiled by prosecutorial misconduct which may mislead grand jurors. Apparently such intervention could even go so far as to include the giving of a supplemental charge when manifestly necessitated by the situation before the judge.

In the present case, any crimes which may be charged will be per se violations of the Sherman Act. These are not vague and indistinct, and there is thus little danger that the broad wording of the Sherman Act will necessarily mislead the grand jurors in this case. Moreover, there has been no intimation of prosecutorial misconduct in this matter or any showing that such is likely to occur. Thus, there is no more danger of an unwarranted prosecution here than where investigations of other criminal violations, based on other statutes, are before the grand jury. The court finds no occasion to use the unprecedented procedure suggested by the movants. Accordingly, the motion of the defendants for supplemental charges on the law to Grand Jury 79–01 is denied. . . . [36]

b. Presentation of Exculpatory Evidence

UNITED STATES V. DEERFIELD SPECIALTY PAPERS, INC.

United States District Court, Eastern District of Pennsylvania, 1980.
501 F.Supp. 796.

HANNUM, DISTRICT JUDGE.

On February 28, 1980, the Grand Jury handed down an indictment charging five (5) corporations and eight (8) individuals with a combination and conspiracy to raise, fix, maintain and stabilize the prices and terms and conditions of sale of glassine and greaseproof paper. The indictment charges that the conspiracy and combination began at least as early as January, 1973 and continued until at least August, 1976. In the prosecution of this case, numerous pre-trial motions have been filed both by the Government and the defendants, jointly and individually. The following discussion and resolution will pertain to these aforementioned motions.

* * *

The defendant Hollis P. Fowler has asserted that the government's failure to present evidence which it knew to be exculpatory . . . constitutes a ground for dismissal of the indictment. The evidence originally referred to would have been in the form of testimony provided by the defendant, himself, and a former employee of the defendant Westfield River Paper Company and associate of the defendant, Dudley Ross. . . . [An] additional issue concerns the government's allegedly

---

36. Courts have been unreceptive to arguments that the grand jury should be given instructions on the relevant law, see, e.g., United States v. Kenny, 645 F.2d 1323, 1347 (9th Cir.) (rejecting "novel argument" that grand jurors must be instructed on the law), certiorari denied sub nom. Parker v. United States, 454 U.S. 828, 102 S.Ct. 121, 70 L.Ed.2d 104 (1981); United States v. Simon, 510 F.Supp. 232, 235–36 (E.D.Pa. 1981) (denying motion alleging inadequate instructions by impaneling judge and prosecutor; instructions need not be as comprehensive as those given a petit jury); or that the prosecutors' failure properly to instruct the grand jury amounts to prosecutorial misconduct, see, e.g., United States v. Roman, 706 F.2d 370 (2d Cir.1983).

selective interrogation before the Grand Jury of the defendant Robert R. Ackley, who has since entered a plea of nolo contendere. . . .

The issue now before the Court is thus postured simply as whether and to what extent the government in its presentation to the Grand Jury was required to present exculpatory information, if such information existed. The inquiries pertaining to the particular testimony which is allegedly exculpatory and which the government failed to either present or elicit may be dealt with collectively and summarily.

As a general proposition by which the Court is guided, case law dictates that a prosecutor is not obligated to submit exculpatory evidence to a Grand Jury. This rule reflects the philosophy that to convert a grand jury proceeding from an investigative one into a minitrial of the merits would be unnecessarily burdensome and wasteful, since, even if an indictment should be filed, the defendant could be found guilty only after a guilty plea or criminal jury trial in which guilt was established beyond a reasonable doubt. It is recognized, however,

> that where a prosecutor is aware of any substantial evidence negating guilt he should, in the interest of justice, make it known to the grand jury, at least where it might reasonably be expected to lead the jury not to indict.

For the reasons that follow, the Court will decline to adopt the arguments of the defendants and will, accordingly, deny their motion.

Initially, the Court notes that the defendant Hollis P. Fowler's representations are essentially that none of his statements were inculpatory but merely provided the government with general information of the glassine paper industry. The defendant also apparently offered statements negating any participation on his part in the alleged conspiracy in restraint of trade. Moreover, it is noted that the defendants represent that had Dudley Ross and Robert R. Ackley been permitted to testify at all or in full, respectively, that exculpatory information would have forthcome for consideration by the Grand Jury. The defendants contend by reference to these witnesses that had their testimony been presented to the Grand Jury a version opposite to that presented by the government may have been considered and may have precluded a return of an indictment.

"An indictment is not defective because the defendant did not have an opportunity to present his version of the facts before the grand jury." United States v. Ciambrone, [601 F.2d] at 623. While the articulation of the general rule as set forth above has been more often presented in a context where a defendant has not been permitted to appear before a grand jury, the philosophy and intent of the rule itself is equally appropriate in cases such as exists here. Essentially, the grand jury tool is used to ascertain whether probable cause exists to believe that a crime has been committed and is not an adversary proceeding in which guilt or innocence is adjudged. . . .

The nature of the proposed testimony viewed in accordance with the defendants' representations, if offered, would amount to a rebuttal of the government's case. This testimony, in most instances, would merely present issues of credibility which could not reasonably be expected to lead the Grand Jury to a conclusion not to indict. To require the submission of this testimony would amount to a preliminary or miniature trial before the Grand Jury. . . .

While the government's argument that the law imposes no duty upon it to present evidence favorable to the accused to the Grand Jury is absolutely accurate, an indictment may nevertheless be dismissed "in a flagrant case, and perhaps only where knowing perjury, relating to a material matter, has been presented to a grand jury. . . ." United States v. Lasky, 600 F.2d 765, 768 (9th Cir.1979), citing Costello v. United States, supra. . . .

In the first instance, the Court notes that the sole matter which could even conceivably be considered as a transgression or impropriety is the alleged selective interrogation of the defendant Robert R. Ackley. [T]he defendants contend that this grand jury witness would have presented evidence negating the existence of a conspiratorial agreement in restraint of trade and that, in any event, the defendant Westfield River Paper Company was not engaged in the conspiracy as it was not even a member of the trade association in which the conspiracy was allegedly formed. . . .

. . . The Court is unwilling to afford such stature to the allegedly selectively controlled and withheld testimony of the defendant Robert R. Ackley. In the absence of additional substantial transgressions, the Court rules that the alleged selective interrogation of the defendant Robert R. Ackley, even if proven or asserted as well-founded, does not arise to the proportions requiring dismissal of the indictment. In essence, selective interrogation of a grand jury witness, as it may have existed in the present case, may not warrant a "flagrant case" characterization requiring the dismissal of an indictment.

* * *

NOTES AND QUERIES

(1) *Should There Be Any Duty?* It is Black Letter Law that the prosecutor is under no duty to offer exculpatory evidence. The farthest that some courts go is to suggest that this rule might not apply in the case of presenting perjured evidence or in the failure to present evidence that "clearly negates guilt."[37] Even under this standard, however, courts are highly unlikely to dismiss an indictment. Despite the state of the law, the Justice Department's United States Attorneys' Manual provides that "it is the Department's internal policy" to present exculpatory evidence under "many" circumstances. The Manual

---

37. See, e.g., United States v. Page, 808 F.2d 723, 727–28 (10th Cir.1987) (evidence not clearly exculpatory); United States v. Ciambrone, 601 F.2d 616, 622–23 (2d Cir. 1979) (prosecutor's statements "fall far short" of misleading conduct or deception). But cf. United States v. Adamo, 742 F.2d 927, 937 (6th Cir.1984) ("no such duty" to present exculpatory evidence), certiorari denied 469 U.S. 1193, 105 S.Ct. 971, 83 L.Ed.2d 975 (1985).

gives one example—where the prosecutor conducting the grand jury inquiry is "personally aware of substantial evidence which directly negates" guilt.[38]

Consider this view of then-Justice Rehnquist, sitting as a Circuit Justice, denying a motion for a stay pending disposition of the defendants' petition for a writ of certiorari in *Bracy v. United States:*[39]

> The chief contention raised by applicants in their petition for certiorari is that a witness committed perjury before the grand jury which indicted them. The witness admitted his perjury at trial, and applicants moved to dismiss the indictment, contending that the prosecutor should have immediately informed the defense and the court when he became aware of the perjury. The District Court denied the motion, and the Court of Appeals affirmed. . . . Because it seems to me that applicants misconceive the function of the grand jury in our system of criminal justice, I cannot conclude that four Justices of this Court are likely to vote to grant their petition. The grand jury does not sit to determine the truth of the charges brought against a defendant, but only to determine whether there is probable cause to believe them true, so as to require him to stand trial. Because of this limited function, we have held that an indictment is not invalidated by the grand jury's consideration of hearsay, Costello v. United States, 350 U.S. 359 (1956). . . . While the presentation of inadmissible evidence at trial may pose a substantial threat to the integrity of that factfinding process, its introduction before the grand jury poses no such threat. . . . The application is denied.

(2) *Tactical Choices.* It is Justice Department policy, "in appropriate cases," to notify a target prior to indictment so as to afford the target an opportunity to present evidence to the grand jury.[40] In addition, the Department recognizes that subjects or targets, "particularly in white collar crime cases," will often request an opportunity to testify before the grand jury. "Reasonable requests . . . ordinarily should be given favorable consideration."[41]

If given the opportunity to present exculpatory evidence, should defense counsel accept? What are the hazards either in having the target testify personally, or in attempting to make a "defense case" before the grand jury? Consider Lempert, "Defense Foray into the Grand Jury Paid Off," Legal Times of Washington, January 12, 1981, p. 1:[42]

> Litigation, just like substantive law, has its blackletter rules—but one of the most important things to know about a rule is when to break it.

---

38. See tit. 9–11.334 (1984).

39. 435 U.S. 1301, 98 S.Ct. 1171, 55 L.Ed.2d 489 (1978).

40. See United States Attorneys' Manual, tit. 9–11.263 (1984).

41. See United States Attorneys' Manual, tit. 9–11.262 (1984).

42. © 1981 by Legal Times. Reprinted by permission.

With that simple lesson in their pockets, Leonard Garment and his colleagues recently emerged victorious from a four-year struggle on behalf of client Warner–Lambert Co. and four company officials, charged with reckless manslaughter and criminally negligent homicide after a tragic factory explosion in 1976.

Was there one strategy decision that, in retrospect, was most responsible . . . ? There was, said Garment in a recent interview: the decision to buck the traditional wisdom and to present testimony before the grand jury. In most cases, defense lawyers steer as far clear of the grand jury as they can, figuring they have little to gain and much to lose by appearing in that prosecutor-dominated forum to tell their tale.

Although the defense witnesses' grand jury testimony did not succeed in goal No. 1 of forestalling an indictment, Garment said, it did lay the groundwork for goal No. 2, dismissal of the indictment—and the judge did in fact, dismiss, saving the defense the risky exposure of a jury trial in a highly emotional case. . . .

What the defense did was to present to the D.A., for appearance before the grand jury, two carefully prepared independent experts who had been retained by the company to determine the cause of the accident. The defense also submitted to the D.A. a detailed memorandum of fact and law. According to the defense argument, the accident had been the result of a "freak cryogenic phenomenon which was unforeseeable."

Most of the lawyers did not really expect that the grand jury could be persuaded not to indict. "I did not have a very profound belief in the fairness of the grand jury system," said [defense counsel] Arkin. As a rule, he said, expressing the notion widely held by defense lawyers, "You don't get a fair shot" because the prosecutor has so much control behind those closed grand jury room doors.

Like most defense lawyers, too, Arkin said he is usually opposed to making a presentation before the grand jury, given the low probability of influencing enough minds.

The risks too far outweigh any possible benefits. "The potential exposure is tremendous," [defense counsel] Hederman said. According to several of the defense lawyers, it's too likely that the unaccompanied defense witnesses will be caught in an unfavorable light; that the prosecutor will learn even more facts to use against the defense than he has already; and that the important element of surprise will be lost, as the prosecutor picks up indicators of likely defenses and trial approaches. Also, Hederman said, in the garden-variety criminal case there is little that a witness for defendants can say, unless there is an alibi defense.

Close Call

But this was not a garden-variety case. There was a lot to say—if the benefits outweighed the risks.

"It was a close, complicated call," said Garment, generally credited with forging the agreement to go forward with the grand jury presentation. The defense, above all, needed a convincing way to get the trial judge to question the legal sufficiency of the evidence. Defense lawyers often ask the judge to inspect the grand jury minutes and dismiss the indictment based on what he finds—or does not find. But the defense has never seen the minutes and knows only as much about the grand jury proceedings as witnesses will tell them. "For the most part, when you make the motion to inspect, it's entirely guesswork," Garment said.

Choosing the course that they did, Garment said, the defense lawyers knew at least that some very precise evidence about the accident, based on comprehensive, on-site examinations, was put before the grand jury. That precise evidence stood in contrast to vague prosecution evidence about the potential hazards—prosecution evidence, however, that would have been damaging if it had been the only information before the grand jury, according to Garment. The defense motion was also able to refer to grand jury testimony by U.S. government experts (surmising what their testimony must have been, based on the official reports that were filed after the accident); the government experts' evidence, which might have been viewed as fairly neutral, tended to help the defense when viewed along with the defense experts' testimony, Garment said.

Technicalities

The defense was especially eager to get its own experts before the grand jury because they wanted, on the record before that body, their interpretation of the scientifically complex evidence. The heart of the legal argument they wanted to make lay in such arcane subjects as the physical properties of liquid nitrogen (sprayed on the machines to cool them) and magnesium stearate. Such technicalities were basic to the question of whether a crime had been committed, because the foreseeability issue was so central to that question.

Garment said he was convinced from the outset that the case should not be a criminal matter—but he was jittery about putting the well-publicized case before a jury. That's why an early ruling from the judge on the legal issue was so important. . . .

D.A. Santucci did not oppose putting the defense experts before the grand jury. "We weren't looking to ramrod anything through," said Santucci, who was credited in the trial judge's opinion with "laborious and exhaustive efforts . . . nothing short of heroic, and in keeping with the finest and highest traditions of the law" in presenting the voluminous and highly technical evidence to the grand jury.

The defense experts testified about matters that would generally be question of fact for a petit jury, Santucci said. Here, though, "they were the very nub of the case, so I was happy to do it. We realized this case was essentially a first."

* * *

Query. The litigation tactics referred to in the above article were ultimately successful because New York law permits a defendant to make a pre-trial motion to dismiss an indictment on the ground that the evidence before the grand jury was not legally sufficient to establish the offense charged.[43] It was in the context of such a motion that the defendants were able to use the expert testimony that they put before the grand jury. Federal law does not allow such challenges to indictments.[44] Why not?

---

43. See New York Crim.Proc.Law § 210.20.1(b).

44. See, e.g., United States v. Olmstead, 7 F.2d 756 (W.D.Wa.1925); United States v. Morse, 292 Fed. 273 (S.D.N.Y.1922); Wright, Federal Practice & Procedure: Criminal 2d § 111 (1982).

3. CHALLENGING THE DECISION TO INDICT

BANK OF NOVA SCOTIA v. UNITED STATES

Supreme Court of the United States, 1988.
___ U.S. ___, 108 S.Ct. 2369, 101 L.Ed.2d 228.

JUSTICE KENNEDY delivered the opinion of the Court.

The issue presented is whether a District Court may invoke its supervisory power to dismiss an indictment for prosecutorial misconduct in a grand jury investigation, where the misconduct does not prejudice the defendants.

I

In 1982, after a 20-month investigation conducted before two successive grand juries, eight defendants, including petitioners William A. Kilpatrick, Declan J. O'Donnell, Sheila C. Lerner, and The Bank of Nova Scotia, were indicted on 27 counts. The first 26 counts charged all defendants with conspiracy and some of them with mail and tax fraud. Count 27 charged Kilpatrick with obstruction of justice. The United States District Court for the District of Colorado initially dismissed the first 26 counts for failure to charge a crime, improper pleading, and, as to charges against the bank, for failure to allege that the bank or its agents had the requisite knowledge and criminal intent. Kilpatrick was tried and convicted on the obstruction of justice count.

The Government appealed the dismissal of the first 26 counts. Before oral argument, however, the Court of Appeals granted a defense motion to remand the case to the District Court for a hearing on whether prosecutorial misconduct and irregularities in the grand jury proceedings were additional grounds for dismissal. United States District Judge Fred M. Winner first presided over the post-trial motions and granted a new trial to Kilpatrick on the obstruction of justice count. The cases were later reassigned to United States District Judge John L. Kane, Jr., to complete the post-trial proceedings. After 10 days of hearings, Judge Kane dismissed all 27 counts of the indictment. The District Court held that dismissal was required for various violations of Federal Rule of Criminal Procedure 6. Further, it ruled dismissal was proper under the "totality of the circumstances," including the "numerous violations of Rule 6(d) and (e), Fed.R.Crim.P., violations of 18 U.S.C. §§ 6002 and 6003, violations of the Fifth and Sixth Amendments to the United States Constitution, knowing presentation of misinformation to the grand jury and mistreatment of witnesses." We shall discuss these findings in more detail below.

The District Court determined that "[a]s a result of the conduct of the prosecutors and their entourage of agents, the indicting grand jury was not able to undertake its essential mission" to act independently of the prosecution. In an apparent alternative holding, the District Court also ruled that: "The supervisory authority of the court must be used in circumstances such as those presented in this case to declare with unmistakable intention that such conduct is neither 'silly' nor 'frivolous' and that it will not be tolerated."

The Government appealed once again, and a divided panel of the Court of Appeals reversed the order of dismissal. The Court of Appeals first rejected the District Court's conclusion that the violations of Federal Rule of Criminal Procedure 6 were an independent ground for dismissal of the indictment. It then held that "the totality of conduct before the grand jury did not warrant dismissal of the indictment," because "the accumulation of misconduct by the Government attorneys did not significantly infringe on the grand jury's ability to exercise independent judgment." Without a showing of such an infringement, the court held, the District Court could not exercise its supervisory authority to dismiss the indictment.

The dissenting judge rejected the "view of the majority that prejudice to the defendant must be shown before a court can exercise its supervisory powers to dismiss an indictment on the basis of egregious prosecutorial misconduct." In her view, the instances of prosecutorial misconduct relied on by the District Court pervaded the grand jury proceedings, rendering the remedy of dismissal necessary to safeguard the integrity of the judicial process notwithstanding the absence of prejudice to the defendants.

We hold that, as a general matter, a District Court may not dismiss an indictment for errors in grand jury proceedings unless such errors prejudiced the defendants.

II

In the exercise of its supervisory authority, a federal court "may, within limits, formulate procedural rules not specifically required by the Constitution or the Congress." United States v. Hasting, 461 U.S. 499, 505 (1983). Nevertheless, it is well established that "[e]ven a sensible and efficient use of the supervisory power . . . is invalid if it conflicts with constitutional or statutory provisions." Thomas v. Arn, 474 U.S. 140, 148 (1985). To allow otherwise "would confer on the judiciary discretionary power to disregard the considered limitations of the law it is charged with enforcing." United States v. Payner, 447 U.S. 727, 737 (1980). Our previous cases have not addressed explicitly whether this rationale bars exercise of a supervisory authority where, as here, dismissal of the indictment would conflict with the harmless error inquiry mandated by the Federal Rules of Criminal Procedure.

We now hold that a federal court may not invoke supervisory power to circumvent the harmless error inquiry prescribed by Federal Rule of Criminal Procedure 52(a). Rule 52(a) provides that "[a]ny error, defect, irregularity or variance which does not affect substantial rights shall be disregarded." . . . Rule 52 is, in every pertinent respect, as binding as any statute duly enacted by Congress, and federal courts have no more discretion to disregard the Rule's mandate than they do to disregard constitutional or statutory provisions. The balance struck by the Rule between societal costs and the rights of the accused may not casually be overlooked "because a court has elected to analyze the question under the supervisory power." United States v. Payner, 447 U.S., at 736.

* * *

Having concluded that our customary harmless error inquiry is applicable where, as in the cases before us, a court is asked to dismiss an indictment prior to the conclusion of the trial, we turn to the standard of prejudice that courts should apply in assessing such claims. We adopt for this purpose, at least where dismissal is sought for nonconstitutional error, the standard articulated by Justice O'Connor in her concurring opinion in United States v. Mechanik [discussed infra this Casebook, p. 472]. Under this standard, dismissal of the indictment is appropriate only "if it is established that the violation substantially influenced the grand jury's decision to indict," or if there is "grave doubt" that the decision to indict was free from the substantial influence of such violations. . . .

To be distinguished from the cases before us are a class of cases in which indictments are dismissed, without a particular assessment of the prejudicial impact of the errors in each case, because the errors are deemed fundamental. These cases may be explained as isolated exceptions to the harmless error rule. We think, however, that an alternative and more clear explanation is that these cases are ones in which the structural protections of the grand jury have been so compromised as to render the proceedings fundamentally unfair, allowing the presumption of prejudice. These cases are exemplified by Vasquez v. Hillery, 474 U.S. 254, 260–264 (1986), where we held that racial discrimination in selection of grand jurors compelled dismissal of the indictment. In addition to involving an error of constitutional magnitude, other remedies were impractical and it could be presumed that a discriminatorily selected grand jury would treat defendants unfairly. We reached a like conclusion in Ballard v. United States, 329 U.S. 187 (1946), where women had been excluded from the grand jury. The nature of the violation allowed a presumption that the defendant was prejudiced, and any inquiry into harmless error would have required unguided speculation. Such considerations are not presented here, and we review the alleged errors to assess their influence, if any, on the grand jury's decision to indict in the factual context of the cases before us.

III

Though the standard we have articulated differs from that used by the Court of Appeals, we reach the same conclusion and affirm its decision reversing the order of dismissal. We review the record to set forth the basis of our agreement with the Court of Appeals that prejudice has not been established.

The District Court found that the Government had violated Federal Rule of Criminal Procedure 6(e) by: (1) disclosing grand jury materials to Internal Revenue Service employees having civil tax enforcement responsibilities; (2) failing to give the court prompt notice of such disclosures; (3) disclosing to potential witnesses the names of targets of the investigation; and (4) instructing two grand jury witnesses, who had represented some of the defendants in a separate investigation of the same tax shelters, that they were not to reveal the substance of their testimony or that they had testified before the grand jury. The court also found that the Government had violated Federal Rule of Criminal Procedure 6(d) in allowing joint appearances by IRS agents before the grand jury for the purpose of reading transcripts to the jurors.

The District Court further concluded that one of the prosecutors improperly argued with an expert witness during a recess of the grand jury after the witness gave testimony adverse to the Government. It also held that the Government had violated the witness immunity statute, 18 U.S.C. §§ 6002, 6003, by the use of "pocket immunity" (immunity granted on representation of the prosecutor rather than by order of a judge), and that the Government caused IRS agents to mischaracterize testimony given in prior proceedings. Furthermore, the District Court found that the Government violated the Fifth Amendment by calling a number of witnesses for the sole purpose of having them assert their privilege against self-incrimination and that it had violated the Sixth Amendment by conducting postindictment interviews of several high-level employees of The Bank of Nova Scotia. Finally, the court concluded that the Government had caused IRS agents to be sworn as agents of the grand jury, thereby elevating their credibility.

As we have noted, no constitutional error occurred during the grand jury proceedings. The Court of Appeals concluded that the District Court's findings of Sixth Amendment postindictment violations were unrelated to the grand jury's independence and decisionmaking process because the alleged violations occurred after the indictment. We agree that it was improper for the District Court to cite such matters in dismissing the indictment. The Court of Appeals also found that no Fifth Amendment violation occurred as a result of the Government's calling seven witnesses to testify despite an avowed intention to invoke their Fifth Amendment privilege. We agree that, in the circumstances of these cases, calling the witnesses was not error. The Government was not required to take at face value the unsworn assertions made by these witnesses outside the grand jury room. Once a witness invoked the privilege on the record, the prosecutors immediately ceased all questioning. Throughout the proceedings, moreover, the prosecution repeated the caution to the grand jury that it was not to draw any adverse inference from a witness' invocation of the Fifth Amendment.

In the cases before us we do not inquire whether the grand jury's independence was infringed. Such an infringement may result in grave doubt as to a violation's effect on the grand jury's decision to indict, but we did not grant certiorari to review this conclusion. We note that the Court of Appeals found that the prosecution's conduct was not "a significant infringement on the grand jury's ability to exercise independent judgment," and we accept that conclusion here. Finally, we note that we are not faced with a history of prosecutorial misconduct, spanning several cases, that is so systematic and pervasive as to raise a substantial and serious question about the fundamental fairness of the process which resulted in the indictment.

We must address, however, whether, despite the grand jury's independence, there was any misconduct by the prosecution that otherwise may have influenced substantially the grand jury's decision to indict, or whether there is grave doubt as to whether the decision to indict was so influenced. Several instances of misconduct found by the District Court—that the prosecutors manipulated the grand jury investigation to gather evidence for use in civil audits; violated the secrecy provisions of Rule 6(e) by publicly identifying the targets and the subject matter of the grand jury investigation; and imposed secrecy obligations in violation of Rule 6(e) upon grand jury witnesses—might be relevant to an allegation of a purpose or intent to abuse the grand jury process. Here, however, it is plain that these alleged breaches could not have affected the charging decision. We have no occasion to consider them further.

We are left to consider only the District Court's findings that the prosecutors: (1) fashioned and administered unauthorized "oaths" to IRS agents in violation of Rule 6(c); (2) caused the same IRS agents to "summarize" evidence falsely and to assert incorrectly that all the evidence summarized by them had been presented previously to the grand jury; (3) deliberately berated and mistreated an expert witness for the defense in the presence of some grand jurors; (4) abused its authority by providing "pocket immunity" to 23 grand jury witnesses; and (5) permitted IRS agents to appear in tandem to present evidence to the grand jury in violation of Rule 6(d). We consider each in turn.

The Government administered oaths to IRS agents, swearing them in as "agents" of the grand jury. Although the administration of such oaths to IRS agents by the Government was unauthorized, there is ample evidence that the jurors understood that the agents were aligned with the prosecutors. . . . . There is nothing in the record to indicate that the oaths administered to the IRS agents caused their reliability or credibility to be elevated, and the effect, if any, on the grand jury's decision to indict was negligible.

The District Court found that, to the prejudice of petitioners, IRS agents gave misleading and inaccurate summaries to the grand jury just prior to the indictment. Because the record does not reveal any prosecutorial misconduct with respect to these summaries, they provide no ground for dismissing the indictment. The District Court's finding that the summaries offered by IRS agents contained evidence that had not been presented to the grand jury in prior testimony boils down to a challenge to the reliability or competence of the evidence presented to the grand jury. We have held that an indictment valid on its face is not subject to such a challenge. To the extent that a challenge is made to the accuracy of the summaries, the mere fact that evidence itself is unreliable is not sufficient to require a dismissal of the indictment. See Costello v. United States, 350 U.S. 359, 363 (1956) (holding that a court may not look behind the indictment to determine if the evidence upon which it was based is sufficient). In light of the record, the finding that the prosecutors knew the evidence to be false or misleading, or that the Government caused the agents to testify falsely, is clearly erroneous. Although the Government may have had doubts about the accuracy of certain aspects of the summaries, this is quite different from having knowledge of falsity.

The District Court found that a prosecutor was abusive to an expert defense witness during a recess and in the hearing of same grand jurors. Although the Government concedes that the treatment of the expert tax witness was improper, the witness himself testified that his testimony was unaffected by this misconduct. The prosecutors instructed the grand jury to disregard anything they may have heard in conversations between a prosecutor and a witness, and explained to the grand jury that such conversations should have no influence on its deliberations. In light of these ameliorative measures, there is nothing to indicate that the prosecutor's conduct toward this witness substantially affected the grand jury's evaluation of the testimony or its decision to indict.

The District Court found that the Government granted "pocket immunity" to 23 witnesses during the course of the grand jury proceedings.[45] Without deciding the propriety of granting such immunity to grand jury witnesses, we conclude the conduct did not have a substantial effect on the grand jury's decision to indict, and it does not create grave doubt as to whether it affected the grand jury's decision. Some prosecutors told the grand jury that immunized witnesses retained their Fifth Amendment privilege and could refuse to testify, while other prosecutors stated that the witnesses had no Fifth Amendment privilege, but we fail to see how this could have had a substantial effect on the jury's assessment of the testimony or its decision to indict. The significant point is that the jurors were made aware that these witnesses had made a deal with the Government.

Assuming the Government had threatened to withdraw immunity from a witness in order to manipulate that witness' testimony, this might have given rise to a finding of prejudice. There is no evidence in the record, however, that would support such a finding. The Government told a witness' attorney that if the witness "testified for Mr. Kilpatrick, all bets were off." The attorney, however, ultimately con-

---

45. [The statutory procedure for granting immunity is discussed infra, p. 506.—Ed.]

cluded that the prosecution did not mean to imply that immunity would be withdrawn if his client testified for Kilpatrick, but rather that his client would be validly subject to prosecution for perjury. Although the District Court found that the Government's statement was interpreted by the witness to mean that if he testified favorably for Kilpatrick his immunity would be withdrawn, neither Judge Winner nor Judge Kane made a definitive finding that the Government improperly threatened the witness. The witness may have felt threatened by the prosecutor's statement, but his subjective fear cannot be ascribed to governmental misconduct and was, at most, a consideration bearing on the reliability of his testimony.

Finally, the Government permitted two IRS agents to appear before the grand jury at the same time for the purpose of reading transcripts. Although allowing the agents to read to the grand jury in tandem was a violation of Rule 6(d), it was not prejudicial. The agents gave no testimony of their own during the reading of the transcripts. The grand jury was instructed not to ask any questions and the agents were instructed not to answer any questions during the readings. There is no evidence that the agents' reading in tandem enhanced the credibility of the testimony or otherwise allowed the agents to exercise undue influence.

In considering the prejudicial effect of the foregoing instances of alleged misconduct, we note that these incidents occurred as isolated episodes in the course of a 20–month investigation, an investigation involving dozens of witnesses and thousands of documents. In view of this context, those violations that did occur do not, even when considered cumulatively, raise a substantial question, much less a grave doubt, as to whether they had a substantial effect on the grand jury's decision to charge.

Errors of the kind alleged in these cases can be remedied adequately by means other than dismissal. For example, a knowing violation of Rule 6 may be punished as a contempt of court. See Fed.R.Crim.Proc. 6(e)(2). In addition, the court may direct a prosecutor to show cause why he should not be disciplined and request the bar or the Department of Justice to initiate disciplinary proceedings against him. The court may also chastise the prosecutor in a published opinion. Such remedies allow the court to focus on the culpable individual rather than granting a windfall to the unprejudiced defendant.

IV

We conclude that the District Court had no authority to dismiss the indictment on the basis of prosecutorial misconduct absent a finding that petitioners were prejudiced by such misconduct. The prejudicial inquiry must focus on whether any violations had an effect on the grand jury's decision to indict. If violations did substantially influence this decision, or if there is grave doubt that the decision to indict was free from such substantial influence, the violations cannot be deemed harmless. The record will not support the conclusion that petitioners can meet this standard. The judgment of the Court of Appeals is affirmed.

It is so ordered.

[The concurring opinion of JUSTICE SCALIA is omitted. JUSTICE MARSHALL, in the course of his dissenting opinion, wrote: "Today's decision reduces Rule 6 to little more than a code of honor that prosecutors can violate with virtual impunity."]

NOTES AND QUERIES

(1) *Queries.* The Court's opinion carefully distinguishes between reversals for constitutional error and reversals in the exercise of "supervisory power." The Court also states that "no constitutional error occurred during the grand jury proceedings." What sorts of constitutional errors might occur during the grand jury proceedings? Does the grand jury clause itself imply any requirements? If it does not, what sort of protection does this constitutional provision provide?

In articulating the correct standard for reviewing non-constitutional errors in the exercise of its supervisory power, the Court puts forward a standard which differs from the one applied by the Court of Appeals. The standard used by the Court of Appeals was "misconduct . . . [which] significantly infringe[s] on the grand jury's ability to exercise independent judgment." What is the difference between this standard and the one adopted by the Court? Note that the Court also writes that it did not inquire whether the grand jury's independence was infringed. "Such an infringement may result in grave doubt as to a violation's effect on the grand jury's decision to indict, but we did not grant certiorari to review this conclusion."

After *Bank of Nova Scotia* would it be reversible error for a prosecutor knowingly to present false evidence to the grand jury? What standard would be used to review this behavior?

(2) *Post–Conviction Attacks on Grand Jury Errors.* *Bank of Nova Scotia* involved review of a district court decision granting a pre-trial motion to dismiss an indictment on the ground of grand jury improprieties. Suppose that the motion had been denied and that review was sought post-trial (remember, only convicted defendants will be seeking such review). If the grand jury improprieties do not meet the "harmless error" standard of *Bank of Nova Scotia,* then, presumably, the improprieties would not warrant appellate court reversal at this point in the proceedings either. But suppose that the improprieties do meet the standard from *Bank of Nova Scotia,* i.e., they "substantially influenced the grand jury's decision to indict"? Would such improprieties be grounds for reversal even after conviction by a petit jury?

Consider in this connection *United States v. Mechanik,* 475 U.S. 66, 106 S.Ct. 938, 89 L.Ed.2d 50 (1986). In *Mechanik* two law enforcement agents were questioned in tandem before the grand jury. The Government had told the defendants pre-trial that no unauthorized persons had appeared before the grand jury, but at trial the defendants learned that the two witnesses had been in the grand jury room at the same time. This violated Rule 6(d), which permits only one witness at a time to appear before the grand jury. Justice Rehnquist, writing for a five-member majority,[46] assumed that the violation of Rule 6(d) would have justified dismissing the indictment pre-trial "had there been actual prejudice." Although finding no fault in defense counsel's failure to make this motion pre-trial, nevertheless the Court held "that the supervening jury verdict made reversal of the conviction and dismissal of the indictment inappropriate." The Court wrote:

> Both the District Court and the Court of Appeals observed that Rule 6(d) was designed, in part, "to ensure that grand jurors, sitting without the direct supervision of a judge, are not subject to undue influence that may come with the presence of an unauthorized person." The Rule protects against the danger that a defendant will be required to defend against a charge for which there is no probable cause to believe him guilty. The error involving Rule 6(d) in these cases had the theoretical potential to affect the grand jury's determination whether to indict these particular defendants for the offenses with which they were charged. But the petit jury's subsequent guilty verdict not only means that there was probable cause to believe that the defendants were guilty as charged, but that they are in fact guilty as charged beyond a reasonable doubt. Measured by the petit jury's verdict, then, any error in the grand jury proceeding connected with the charging decision was harmless beyond a reasonable doubt.[47]
>
> It might be argued in some literal sense that because the Rule was designed to protect against an erroneous charging decision by the *grand jury,* the indictment should not be compared to the evidence produced by the Government at *trial,* but to the evidence produced before the *grand jury.* But even if this argument were accepted, there is no simple way after the verdict to restore the defendant to the position in which he would have been had the

---

46. Chief Justice Burger wrote a concurring opinion; Justice O'Connor, joined by Justices Brennan and Blackmun, wrote a separate concurring opinion; Justice Marshall wrote a dissenting opinion.

47. [Court's footnote 1.] In Vasquez v. Hillery, 474 U.S. 254, 106 S.Ct. 617, 88 L.Ed.2d 598 (1986), the Court set aside a final judgment of conviction because of racial discrimination in the composition of the grand jury that indicted the defendant. It found this result to be compelled by precedent directly applicable to the special problem of racial discrimination. It also reasoned that racial discrimination in the selection of grand jurors is so pernicious, and other remedies so impractical, that the remedy of automatic reversal was necessary as a prophylactic means of deterring grand jury discrimination in the future, and that one could presume that a discriminatorily selected grand jury would treat defendants of excluded races unfairly.

We think that these considerations have little force outside the context of racial discrimination in the composition of the grand jury. No long line of precedent requires the setting aside of a conviction based on a rule violation in the antecedent grand jury proceedings, and the societal interest in deterring this sort of error does not rise to the level of the interest in deterring racial discrimination.

indictment been dismissed before trial. He will already have suffered whatever inconvenience, expense, and opprobrium that a proper indictment may have spared him. In courtroom proceedings as elsewhere, "the moving finger writes, and having writ moves on." Thus reversal of a conviction after a trial free from reversible error cannot restore to the defendant whatever benefit might have accrued to him from a trial on an indictment returned in conformity with Rule 6(d).

We cannot accept the Court of Appeals' view that a violation of Rule 6(d) requires automatic reversal of a subsequent conviction regardless of the lack of prejudice. Federal Rule of Criminal Procedure 52(a) provides that errors not affecting substantial rights shall be disregarded. We see no reason not to apply this provision to "errors, defects, irregularities or variances" occurring before a grand jury just as we have applied it to such error occurring in the criminal trial itself.

The reversal of a conviction entails substantial social costs: it forces jurors, witnesses, courts, the prosecution, and the defendants to expend further time, energy, and other resources to repeat a trial that has already once taken place; victims may be asked to relive their disturbing experiences. The "[p]assage of time, erosion of memory, and dispersion of witnesses may render retrial difficult, even impossible." Engle v. Isaac, 456 U.S. 107, 127–128, 102 S.Ct. 1558, 1571–1572, 71 L.Ed.2d 783 (1982). Thus, while reversal "may, in theory, entitle the defendant only to retrial, in practice it may reward the accused with complete freedom from prosecution," id., at 128, 102 S.Ct., at 1572, and thereby "cost society the right to punish admitted offenders." Id., at 127, 102 S.Ct., at 1572. . . . These societal costs of reversal and retrial are an acceptable and often necessary consequence when an error in the first proceeding has deprived a defendant of a fair determination of the issue of guilt or innocence. But the balance of interest tips decidedly the other way when an error has had no effect on the outcome of the trial.

We express no opinion as to what remedy may be appropriate for a violation of Rule 6(d) that has affected the grand jury's charging decision and is brought to the attention of the trial court before the commencement of trial. We hold only that however diligent the defendants may have been in seeking to discover the basis for the claimed violation of Rule 6(d), the petit jury's verdict rendered harmless any conceivable error in the charging decision that might have flowed from the violation. In such a case, the societal costs of retrial after a jury verdict of guilty are far too substantial to justify setting aside the verdict simply because of an error in the earlier grand jury proceedings. The judgment of the Court of Appeals is therefore reversed to the extent it set aside the conspiracy convictions and dismissed the indictment, but is otherwise affirmed.

It is so ordered.

Query. Is *Mechanik* limited to "technical violations" of rules governing the grand jury? In *United States v. Fountain*,[48] the Seventh Circuit was faced with a post-conviction appeal where the asserted grand jury errors were a failure to present exculpatory evidence and excessive use of hearsay. The Court of Appeals assumed, arguendo, that there might be an exceptional case in which such errors could amount to an improper manipulation of the grand jury, but held the errors harmless under *Mechanik*:

> The function of the grand jury is to screen out cases in which there is not even probable cause to believe a person committed the offense, and it is possible to imagine manipulations of the grand jury that prevent it from fulfilling this mission. But the people harmed by such misdeeds are the innocent, those exposed to the travail and expense of trial even though they were fated to prevail in the end. Once a person is convicted by the petit jury, we may be confident that a full presentation to the grand jury would have ended in indictment. The trial is a full, adversarial presentation, in which the live witnesses and exculpatory evidence missing in the grand jury come to the fore. The grand jury acts by majority vote and uses a lesser burden; it is impossible to imagine evidence sufficient to produce a conviction at trial that would not also produce an indictment. So it would be silly to reverse a conviction on the ground that the evidence before the grand jury was insufficient. We know that this defendant is not a member of the class that is harmed by sloppy or overbearing conduct before the grand jury. We know that he could be reindicted in a trice (using the record of the trial as a basis), and would be tried anew in the same fashion.

[After discussing *Mechanik*, the Court of Appeals continued:]

> Fountain dismisses *Mechanik* as a case concerned with a "technicality". It is fair to apply this label to Rule 6(d); the violation was that two witnesses testified simultaneously, while the Rule regards anyone other than the prosecutor, a court reporter, and a single testifying witness an unauthorized person. The Court's reasoning, however, does not depend on the nature of the rule at hand; the Court assumed that the violation was sufficiently substantial to permit dismissal of the indictment. *Mechanik* proceeds by identifying the purpose of the rule (to protect the innocent from being indicted) and then says that a rule with this purpose should not be enforced by reversing a conviction obtained after trial—because we *know,* as surely as courts "know" anything, that

---

[48]. 840 F.2d 509 (7th Cir.) (Easterbrook, J.), certiorari denied ___ U.S. ___, 109 S.Ct. 533, 102 L.Ed.2d 564 (1988).

the convicted defendant is not a member of the class of beneficiaries of the rule. Most important legal rules, even constitutional ones, may be enforced only by their beneficiaries. . . .

We recognize that at least one court had held that *Mechanik* is limited to "technical violations" before the grand jury. For the reasons we have given, we respectfully disagree . . . .

(3) *Constitutional Error.* In *Vasquez v. Hillery*,[49] cited in *Bank of Nova Scotia* and *Mechanik,* the defendant sought to overturn a state conviction, on habeas corpus, on the ground that the grand jury which had indicted him had been chosen on a racially discriminatory basis. The Supreme Court refused to apply a harmless error rule and set aside the state court's final judgment. Justice Marshall wrote for the majority:

> Nor are we persuaded that discrimination in the grand jury has no effect on the fairness of the criminal trials that result from that grand jury's actions. The grand jury does not determine only that probable cause exists to believe that a defendant committed a crime, or that it does not. In the hands of the grand jury lies the power to charge a greater offense or a lesser offense; numerous counts or a single count; and perhaps most significant of all, a capital offense or a noncapital offense—all on the basis of the same facts. Moreover, "[t]he grand jury is not bound to indict in every case where a conviction can be obtained." United States v. Ciambrone, 601 F.2d 616, 629 (CA2 1979) (Friendly, J., dissenting). Thus, even if a grand jury's determination of probable cause is confirmed in hindsight by a conviction on the indicted offense, that confirmation in no way suggests that the discrimination did not impermissibly infect the framing of the indictment and, consequently, the nature or very existence of the proceedings to come.
>
> When constitutional error calls into question the objectivity of those charged with bringing a defendant to judgment, a reviewing court can neither indulge a presumption of regularity nor evaluate the resulting harm. . . . [W]hen a petit jury has been selected upon improper criteria or has been exposed to prejudicial publicity, we have required reversal of the conviction because the effect of the violation cannot be ascertained. Like these fundamental flaws, which never have been thought harmless, discrimination in the grand jury undermines the structural integrity of the criminal tribunal itself, and is not amenable to harmless-error review.
>
> . . . [A] conviction cannot be understood to cure the taint attributable to a charging body selected on the basis of race. Once having found discrimination in the selection of a grand jury, we simply cannot know that the need to indict would have been assessed in the same way by a grand jury properly constituted. The overriding imperative to eliminate this systemic flaw in the

---

49. 474 U.S. 254, 106 S.Ct. 617, 88 L.Ed. 2d 598 (1986).

charging process, as well as the difficulty of assessing its effect on any given defendant, requires our continued adherence to a rule of mandatory reversal.

Queries. Are you satisfied with the way the Court in *Bank of Nova Scotia* subsequently distinguished *Vasquez?* Are there other types of error which might fall into the *Vasquez* category? Might there be constitutional error related to the protections granted by the fifth amendment grand jury clause?

Compare Justice Marshall's view of the grand jury's function with the view expressed by Chief Justice Rehnquist in *Bracy v. United States,* supra p. 462. With which view do you agree? Which statement represents the Court's view today?

(4) *Endnote—Indict a Ham Sandwich?* Reconsider the materials on the role and function of the grand jury, supra Section A, in light of the Court's decisions in *Bank of Nova Scotia* and *Mechanik.* Have these two decisions completed the process begun in *Hale* and *Blair* of giving the grand jury—and, therefore, the prosecutor—virtually unreviewable discretion to investigate for crime?

Review, as well, the descriptions of grand jury practice in the materials in this Section. It has been said [50] that "given the control that the prosecutor exercises over the grand jury, he or she could indict a ham sandwich." Should we care so long as petit juries don't convict ham sandwiches? Or so long as appellate courts will review such convictions and reverse them?

C. MULTIPLE REPRESENTATION AND CONFLICTS OF INTEREST

PIRILLO v. TAKIFF

Supreme Court of the Commonwealth of Pennsylvania, 1975.
462 Pa. 511, 341 A.2d 896, certiorari denied 423 U.S. 1083, 96 S.Ct. 873, 47 L.Ed.2d 94 (1976).

JONES, CHIEF JUSTICE.

These two petitions present the novel question of whether the supervising judge of a regular grand jury conducting a special investigation may disqualify a single attorney and his associate from representing twelve witnesses subpoenaed to testify before the grand jury. We decline to issue a writ of prohibition to the supervising judge who disqualified the two attorneys/petitioners.

On January 31, 1974, the Honorable Harry A. Takiff, respondent herein, charged the January 1974 Grand Jury as a special investigating grand jury to investigate, inter alia, corruption in the Philadelphia Police Department. On March 26, 1974, the Attorney General of

---

[50]. By Chief Judge Sol Wachtler, of the New York Court of Appeals (correspondence with the author).

Pennsylvania established the Office of the Special Prosecutor by appointing respondent Walter M. Phillips, Jr., as Deputy Attorney General to investigate and prosecute police corruption in Philadelphia. The convening of the grand jury and the appointment of the Special Prosecutor were actions taken in response to a Report by the Pennsylvania Crime Commission on Police Corruption and the Quality of Law Enforcement in Philadelphia.

In June and July of 1974, the twelve policemen/petitioners were subpoenaed to appear before the grand jury. Each officer was represented by petitioner Anthony D. Pirillo, Jr., Esquire and/or by Mr. Pirillo's associate, Salvator J. Cucinotta, Esquire. As was customary, before any witness testified, Judge Takiff held an in camera session with the Special Prosecutor or his representative during which the Judge was informed as to the proposed scope of inquiry for these witnesses. It was revealed by the Special Prosecutor that each witness would be questioned about the conduct of other police officers, and in most cases, about the conduct of each other. Most of the officers had been named in the Crime Commission Report as persons who had taken bribes from the owners of Philadelphia bars.

Because the Special Prosecutor's office brought to Judge Takiff's attention the possibility of a conflict of interest in the multiple representation by Attorney Pirillo and his associate of all the petitioners/witnesses, the supervising judge deferred the testimony of these witnesses pending a determination of the question. After an evidentiary hearing on the conflicts matter, the judge decided that Mr. Pirillo and his associate, Mr. Cucinotta, must be disqualified from representing all twelve of the policemen/witnesses before the grand jury. His decision was based on the following grounds:

(1) The multiple representation interfered with the individual witness's right to effective counsel. For example, if witness A has information about witness B's criminal conduct, one attorney could not represent both. It may be in A's best interest for counsel to advise A to cooperate. However, this would operate to the detriment of B.

(2) The attorneys' fee compensation arrangement with the Fraternal Order of Police, by whom the petitioners/attorneys were referred and paid, constituted a serious question of conflict because of the Fraternal Order of Police's avowed public policy of strenuous opposition to any form of cooperation by individual policemen with the Special Prosecutor's office and with the investigating grand jury. This would not only interfere with the public function of the investigating grand jury but would also jeopardize the rights of the individual witnesses to effective assistance of counsel because the attorneys might be compelled to pursue the dictates of the F.O.P. which pays them rather than the best interests of the witness.

(3) There would be a serious detriment to the investigative function of the grand jury because of the multiple representation. With one attorney representing all witnesses in a particular area of investigation,

the Special Prosecutor could not convince counsel to elicit cooperation of one witness since such cooperation might seriously implicate the attorneys' other clients in illegal activity.

In summary, according to the Special Prosecutor, the practical effect of the multiple representation was the creation of the conspiratorial "stonewall" to the investigation shrouded by the interwoven attorney-client relationships.

I Rights of the Petitioners

In order to assess the legitimacy of the supervising judge's order, it is imperative that we assess the rights asserted and determine whether these rights may be balanced against competing state interests.

The twelve witnesses claim that the order of the supervising judge has impaired their right to counsel of their own choosing. . . .

* * *

[Petitioners, who are attorneys, also claim they have been denied the right to practice law.]

But neither of these rights is absolute; both may be impaired or eliminated by state regulation which is designed to provide for overriding state interests or individual constitutional guarantees which are in conflict with these rights to counsel and to pursue one's profession.

In a third argument, the petitioners assert that the order of the supervising judge has infringed upon their freedom of speech, assembly and petition as guaranteed by the First and Fourteenth Amendments, citing National Association for the Advancement of Colored People v. Button, 371 U.S. 415, 83 S.Ct. 328, 9 L.Ed.2d 405 (1963), Brotherhood of Railway Trainmen v. Virginia, 377 U.S. 1, 84 S.Ct. 1113, 12 L.Ed.2d 89 (1964), United Mine Workers v. Illinois State Bar Association, 389 U.S. 217, 88 S.Ct. 353, 19 L.Ed.2d 426 (1967), and United Transportation Union v. State Bar of Michigan, 401 U.S. 576, 91 S.Ct. 1076, 28 L.Ed.2d 33 (1971).

One of the services the F.O.P. provides for its members is free representation by counsel when they are charged with a crime, questioned during a departmental investigation, or called as witnesses before an investigating grand jury. The attorney who represents the member is paid on a per hour basis by the F.O.P. The common thread running through the decisions in Button, Trainmen, United Mine Workers and United Transportation Union is that collective activity undertaken to obtain meaningful access to the courts is a fundamental right within the protection of the First Amendment. However, all four of these cases acknowledged the fact that a state may constitutionally advance substantial regulatory interests to prevent specific harm from flowing from the particular petitioners' activities, which activities justify the infringement of First Amendment rights.

. . . The United States Supreme Court recognized that a state may act pursuant to its broad power to regulate the practice of law to prevent a serious conflict of interest from arising in the legal representation of its citizens, but held that the record below, in each instance, failed to demonstrate that any actual danger existed or that the state regulation was sufficiently narrow to meet only the particular form of danger present. The primary objectionable feature of state regulation in the First Amendment area is vagueness and overbreadth which result in sweeping and improper application of a regulation. Thus, if regulations affecting First Amendment rights are no greater than necessary to eliminate the substantive evil and protect the substantial governmental interests and individual rights, then the regulation can be constitutionally tolerated.

In summary, none of the three rights asserted by petitioners are absolute ones; they may be weighed against competing state interests.

II State Interests

The history and function of a grand jury charged with a special investigation is amply detailed elsewhere. Suffice it to say that a grand jury charged with a special investigation seeks to discover past and continuing criminal acts which seriously affect or injure the public and with which normal law enforcement is unable to cope. In order to perform its function adequately, the grand jury's scope of inquiry is necessarily broad.

A grand jury proceeding is not an adversary hearing in which the guilt or innocence of an accused is determined. Consequently, certain constitutional and supervisory protections have been held inapplicable to the grand jury proceeding in order to facilitate the jury's quest to determine whether a crime has been committed and whether a prima facie case exists which warrants the institution of criminal proceedings. The supervising judge sought by his order to protect the public function of the grand jury, i.e., to insure that the grand jury's search for the truth in areas of alleged criminality affecting the peace and security of all persons and the Commonwealth would not be unduly impaired.

Secondly, the supervising judge cited the responsibility of the courts to protect the rights of each individual to effective counsel. There are two potential conflicts in this situation which could impair the sanctity of the attorney-client relationship. If an attorney and his associate represent more than one of the officers who have been called to testify, where, as the Special Prosecutor alleges, each officer will be called to testify as to the activity of the other officers, an impermissible conflict purportedly exists. The other potential for conflict arises from the attorney-client relationship between Pirillo and the Fraternal Order of Police, since the organization may have interests adverse to the best interests of the testifying officers.

. . . We do not choose to place substantial reliance, as the supervising judge did, upon the rationale that the order below is justified because of the multiple representation of the witnesses by a single attorney, especially since our result can be sustained on other grounds. The witnesses argue that because they have chosen the particular attorney and his associate knowing full well that the attorneys represent all of the policemen subpoenaed and because the attorneys have, as fully as possible, advised the witnesses of the potentiality of the conflicts involved, therefore the witnesses have waived their constitutional right to effective counsel. Such waiver may very well be defective on the ground that it is not a knowing and intelligent waiver; the client may not be fully and adequately informed as to the nature of the potential conflict, because, in this instance, full disclosure to the client, as required by the Code of Professional Responsibility, D.R. 5–105(C),[51] may be impossible in light of the requirements of secrecy surrounding the grand jury proceeding. But multiple representation, in and of itself, is not condemned. In light of the strenuous assertions by the witnesses that they freely choose the multiple representation, we are not willing to base our result on the existence of multiple representation per se.[52]

The other potential conflict which threatens the individual rights of the witnesses to the effective assistance of counsel stems from Pirillo's representation of the Fraternal Order of Police which is not formally a party to this action or in the grand jury proceeding. The F.O.P. pays the legal fees for its members who require representation before the grand jury. The Special Prosecutor claims that, based on the F.O.P.'s history of demonstrated enmity toward investigations into police corruption, the organization has adopted a tactic of noncooperation, which tactic is inimical to the rights of any witness who might stand to gain from a strategy of cooperation with the Special Prosecutor's office. It is further alleged that such a tactic coupled with the F.O.P.'s payment of fees on behalf of the witnesses could result in a complete frustration of the grand jury's function.

. . . Throughout the investigations into police corruption conducted by the Pennsylvania Crime Commission and the June, 1972, Special Investigating Grand Jury, the F.O.P. has consistently taken the position that these investigations were a threat to its members and made numerous efforts to thwart these investigations. . . . The F.O.P.'s attitude of broad noncooperation is apparently shared by respondent Pirillo, the attorney paid by the F.O.P. to represent its individual members. Thus, petitioner Pirillo testified that whenever a police

---

51. [Court's footnote 4.] D.R. 5–105(C):

"In the situations covered by D.R. 5–105(A) and (B), a lawyer may represent multiple clients if it is obvious that he can adequately represent the interest of each and if each consents to the representation after full disclosure of the possible effect of such representation on the exercise of his independent professional judgment on behalf of each."

52. [Court's footnote 5.] There is another tangential consideration. The existence of multiple representation jeopardizes the time-honored concept of grand jury secrecy. Such secrecy is designed to protect the Commonwealth, the grand jurors, and the witnesses. If one of the witnesses reveals his testimony before the grand jury to his attorney, as he has every right to do, certainly the attorney will feel obliged, perhaps even subconsciously, to reveal to his other clients the testimony of the first witness. With the attorney in such a position, either the attorney-client relationship or the grand jury secrecy must suffer. . . .

officer indicated that he might consider cooperating, he would immediately remove himself as counsel and advise the witness to hire another attorney. This fee arrangement clearly has a chilling effect upon a police witness who is considering cooperation, since his access to F.O.P. paid counsel depends directly on his agreement not to cooperate. Moreover, the limited viability of the options open to a police witness suspected of illegal activity is further demonstrated by petitioner Pirillo's testimony that he would discuss the possibility of a witness cooperating only when the witness had come to him and raised the possibility. The failure of petitioner Pirillo to raise the subject of cooperation, apparently as a result of his fee arrangement with the F.O.P., deprives the witnesses of their right to the full and complete loyalty of their attorney.

* * *

III Balancing of Competing Interests

* * *

None of the petitioners have suggested alternative means by which the interests of the state may be protected without the concomitant infringement upon the petitioners' individual rights. Nor are we able to conjure any plan other than the one ordered by the supervising judge which would adequately protect the various state interests threatened by the multiple representation.

Furthermore, the interests of the state are sufficiently compelling to justify appropriately tailored infringements of constitutional rights. We have earlier pointed out that each right asserted by petitioners is susceptible to curtailment. We have also endeavored to demonstrate that the state interests are sufficiently strong to justify some incursion upon the rights invoked by petitioners. The court in its supervisory capacity over the grand jury must be alert to prevent as far as possible any abridgment of that body's function which is to investigate public wrongs and to bring indictments for the protection of society. The secrecy surrounding grand jury proceedings is a mechanism to insure the safety and reputation of witnesses and grand jurors. The historical and statutory power of courts to regulate the legal profession is one which is inherent in the power to oversee the administration of justice. Surely this power serves the interest of all citizens of the Commonwealth to be secure against the actions of attorneys subservient to clients with competing interests.

The degree of infringement in this instance is especially justified in light of the limited scope of the supervising judge's order, and the problems which are sought to be prevented. . . .

The Opinion makes it clear that in no event may any witness hire an F.O.P.-related attorney. To hold otherwise would allow the witnesses to recreate albeit perhaps to a lesser degree the conflict sought to be eradicated. The order, however, pertains only to the conduct of the grand jury investigation. . . .

It is also manifest in the order of the supervising judge that no two of the subpoenaed witnesses who are parties to this petition may be represented by the same counsel. This portion of the order is essential to secure the secrecy of the grand jury proceeding. We do not mean to imply that multiple representation will never be tolerated at the grand jury level. Here, however, where each witness was a potential defendant, and the Court received information that the testimony of each officer might be expected to incriminate one or more of the other witnesses, and where the extent of the possible multiple cross-involvement in criminal activity is known to the Court but hidden from the individual witnesses by the requirements of secrecy, it is inappropriate for the supervising judge to permit multiple representation.

Attorneys Pirillo and Cucinotta are not suspended from the practice of law, formally disciplined, or precluded from representing the F.O.P. or any of its members in other litigation. They are, however, precluded from representing the twelve witnesses in this proceeding. Because of their relationship with the F.O.P., it would be improper to allow them to represent even one of the witnesses since the attorney-client relationship between the attorneys and the F.O.P. presents a serious danger that the attorney-client relationship with even one witness would be impaired.

In short, the degree of infringement resulting from the supervising judge's order is the minimum necessary to insure the state interests while at the same time the infringement is justified by the scope of the state interests and the extent of harm which is sought to be prevented.

* * *

[JUSTICE NIX did not participate in the decision. The dissenting opinion of JUSTICE MANDERINO is omitted.]

NOTES AND QUERIES

(1) *Tactics—Who Wants Multiple Representation?* In *Pirillo* the prosecutor was in the somewhat anomalous position of urging that the grand jury witnesses were not being effectively represented. What explains the prosecutor's concern for the witnesses? Wouldn't you expect the witnesses to make this argument? Or, is it likely that the witnesses believed that they were best served by multiple representation, that this was a case where they would either hang together or hang separately?

In the business crime context, the issue of multiple representation is often posed at the very beginning of the grand jury's investigation, where the question is whether the corporation's lawyer can or should represent corporate employees who the government would like to talk to or subpoena. The advice which will first need to be given is likely to be whether to cooperate with the government and seek immunity from prosecution. Donald Baker, a former Assistant Attorney General in charge of the Department of Justice's Antitrust Division and now in private practice, describes the problem:[53]

> Can the corporation's lawyer effectively advise the employee at such a juncture? To take the "cooperation and immunity" route may save the employee from risks of jail for himself, if he was involved in the crime; but it will almost certainly do so at the price of making the individual an outcast within his organization. The "hang in with the corporation" route may increase the individual's risk of doing jail time, but may increase the chance that all targets will get off without indictment or conviction. For an executive facing such a choice, this decision may be among the most crucial in his life. "Do I want to rat on my boss or my friends? Or do I want to 'take the Fifth' and take my chances?" No lawyer can make such a decision for the individual employee—but an effective lawyer can help him focus the potential and probable consequences of the alternative options.
>
> A clear *potential* conflict does exist where corporate counsel represents the employee in this situation. But to say this is not to imply . . . that a conflict *almost invariably* exists between the employee and his corporation.
>
> To take the simplest case, if the employee has not participated in the suspected crime, he has no proper grounds for pleading the Fifth Amendment—and hence no basis for seeking immunity to compel testimony. Such an employee can normally be represented by the corporation's attorney if called as witness to the grand jury or trial. Counsel's duty to such an employee-witness is the same as his duty is to the court—to counsel the witness to tell the truth and thereby avoid any dangers of perjury.
>
> The better practice today in the antitrust bar follows from what I have said. Employees will normally be represented by the corporation's lawyer until it appears that the individual is an actual or potential target himself; and at that point the individual is usually given the option of having separate counsel—very often paid for, but not controlled by, the corporation. Often the employee will accept such separate representation, but sometimes he will not.
>
> * * *
>
> One must say a final word about costs. Separate representation of every individual in a major grand jury investigation or criminal trial is costly for *somebody*. The threat of large legal bills may coerce an individual into accepting joint representation in the face of a conflict; and the courts should be vigilant to situations of the *Pirillo* type to assure the checkbook is not being used to thwart the Sixth Amendment. On the other hand, when the corporation

---

53. Baker, Multiple Representation Issue Comes to the Fore with "Pirillo," National L.J., Aug. 7, 1978, p. 32. Copyright 1978. The National Law Journal, reprinted with permission.

(or union) agrees to pay for completely independent counsel, this fact should go some way toward showing that the individual's waiver of such counsel is indeed voluntary. Finally, the expensive truth is that any broad rule or presumption requiring separate representation in almost every case would impose large aggregate costs; this is an independent, non-constitutional reason for treading cautiously in this sensitive area of lawyer-client relations.

(2) *Constitutional Right to Counsel.* Courts have often been called upon to determine whether joint representation at trial is violative of the sixth amendment right to counsel. In *Holloway v. Arkansas*,[54] the Supreme Court held that appointing one lawyer to represent three co-defendants at trial was unconstitutional in a case where counsel had informed the trial court of a conflict among his clients but the court failed to take adequate steps to ascertain whether the risk of conflict was likely or remote. The Court also stated:

> Requiring or permitting a single attorney to represent codefendants, often referred to as joint representation, is not per se violative of constitutional guarantees of effective assistance of counsel. This principle recognizes that in some cases multiple defendants can appropriately be represented by one attorney; indeed, in some cases, certain advantages might accrue from joint representation. In Mr. Justice Frankfurter's view: "Joint representation is a means of insuring against reciprocal recrimination. A common defense often gives strength against a common attack." Glasser v. United States, [315 U.S.] at 92 [1942] (dissenting opinion).

In cases where having conflicted counsel might violate the sixth amendment, could a defendant waive this right? As a normal rule, constitutional rights are waivable, so long as the waiver is knowing and intelligent. In *Pirillo* the witnesses waived their rights to conflict-free counsel. Should not their waivers have been dispositive? Put more strongly, based on the above excerpt from *Holloway*, should an aspect of the constitutional right to counsel be the right to counsel of choice, even if the choice is to have conflicted-counsel?[55]

Consider the Supreme Court's approach to the waiver/right arguments in *Wheat v. United States*, 486 U.S. 153, 108 S.Ct. 1692, 100 L.Ed. 2d 140 (1988):

> CHIEF JUSTICE REHNQUIST delivered the opinion of the Court.
>
> [Digest: Iredale represented two co-defendants (Gomez–Barajas and Bravo) charged with participating in a conspiracy to distribute illegal drugs. Gomez–Barajas was tried first and acquitted; he then negotiated a plea bargain on other charges. Bravo did not go

---

54. 435 U.S. 475, 98 S.Ct. 1173, 55 L.Ed. 2d 426 (1978).

55. Note that this constitutional question is somewhat ambiguous for grand jury witnesses, because technically a grand jury witness has no sixth amendment right to counsel at the stage of a grand jury investigation. Nevertheless, courts have assumed that a witness has a constitutional right to retain counsel of his or her own choice to render advice at this stage.

to trial on the drug charges, but pleaded guilty to a reduced charge. After Bravo's guilty plea hearing, Wheat asked Iredale to represent him as well. The Government objected, arguing that there were serious conflicts of interest among the three defendants. Wheat emphasized his right to counsel of choice, indicating that all three defendants were willing to waive the right to conflict-free counsel. He also argued that the conflicts were highly speculative. The District Court refused to allow Wheat to substitute Iredale as attorney of record. Wheat was subsequently convicted of conspiracy to possess, and possession of, marijuana with intent to distribute. The Court of Appeals for the Ninth Circuit affirmed his convictions and the Supreme Court granted certiorari.]

The Sixth Amendment to the Constitution guarantees that "[i]n all criminal prosecutions, the accused shall enjoy the right . . . to have the Assistance of Counsel for his defence." In United States v. Morrison, 449 U.S. 361, 364, 101 S.Ct. 665, 667, 66 L.Ed.2d 564 (1981), we observed that this right was designed to assure fairness in the adversary criminal process. . . . Thus, while the right to select and be represented by one's preferred attorney is comprehended by the Sixth Amendment, the essential aim of the Amendment is to guarantee an effective advocate for each criminal defendant rather than to ensure that a defendant will inexorably be represented by the lawyer whom he prefers.

The Sixth Amendment right to choose one's own counsel is circumscribed in several important respects. Regardless of his persuasive powers, an advocate who is not a member of the bar may not represent clients (other than himself) in court. Similarly, a defendant may not insist on representation by an attorney he cannot afford or who for other reasons declines to represent the defendant. Nor may a defendant insist on the counsel of an attorney who has a previous or ongoing relationship with an opposing party, even when the opposing party is the Government. The question raised in this case is the extent to which a criminal defendant's right under the Sixth Amendment to his chosen attorney is qualified by the fact that the attorney has represented other defendants charged in the same criminal conspiracy.

In previous cases, we have recognized that multiple representation of criminal defendants engenders special dangers of which a court must be aware. While "permitting a single attorney to represent codefendants . . . is not per se violative of constitutional guarantees of effective assistance of counsel," Holloway v. Arkansas, 435 U.S. 475, 482, 98 S.Ct. 1173, 1178, 55 L.Ed.2d 426 (1978), a court confronted with and alerted to possible conflicts of interest must take adequate steps to ascertain whether the conflict warrants separate counsel. As we said in Holloway,

> "Joint representation of conflicting interests is suspect because of what it tends to prevent the attorney from do-

ing. . . . [A] conflict may . . . prevent an attorney from challenging the admission of evidence prejudicial to one client but perhaps favorable to another, or from arguing at the sentencing hearing the relative involvement and culpability of his clients in order to minimize the culpability of one by emphasizing that of another."

Petitioner insists that the provision of waivers by all affected defendants cures any problems created by the multiple representation. But no such flat rule can be deduced from the Sixth Amendment presumption in favor of counsel of choice. Federal courts have an independent interest in ensuring that criminal trials are conducted within the ethical standards of the profession and that legal proceedings appear fair to all who observe them. Both the American Bar Association's Model Code of Professional Responsibility and its Model Rules of Professional Conduct, as well as the rules of the California Bar Association (which governed the attorneys in this case), impose limitations on multiple representation of clients. Not only the interest of a criminal defendant but the institutional interest in the rendition of just verdicts in criminal cases may be jeopardized by unregulated multiple representation.

For this reason, the Federal Rules of Criminal Procedure direct trial judges to investigate specially cases involving joint representation. In pertinent part, Rule 44(c) provides:

> "[T]he court shall promptly inquire with respect to such joint representation and shall personally advise each defendant of his right to the effective assistance of counsel, including separate representation. Unless it appears that there is good cause to believe no conflict of interest is likely to arise, the court shall take such measures as may be appropriate to protect each defendant's right to counsel."

Although Rule 44(c) does not specify what particular measures may be taken by a district court, one option suggested by the Notes of the Advisory Committee is an order by the court that the defendants be separately represented in subsequent proceedings in the case. . . .

* * *

Thus, where a court justifiably finds an actual conflict of interest, there can be no doubt that it may decline a proffer of waiver, and insist that defendants be separately represented. . . .

Unfortunately for all concerned, a district court must pass on the issue of whether or not to allow a waiver of a conflict of interest by a criminal defendant not with the wisdom of hindsight after the trial has taken place, but in the murkier pre-trial context when relationships between parties are seen through a glass, darkly. The likelihood and dimensions of nascent conflicts of interest are notoriously hard to predict, even for those thoroughly familiar with criminal trials. It is a rare attorney who will be fortunate enough to learn the entire truth from his own client, much less be fully apprised before trial of what each of the Government's witnesses will say on the stand. A few bits of unforeseen testimony or a single previously unknown or unnoticed document may significantly shift the relationship between multiple defendants. These imponderables are difficult enough for a lawyer to assess, and even more difficult to convey by way of explanation to a criminal defendant untutored in the niceties of legal ethics. Nor is it amiss to observe that the willingness of an attorney to obtain such waivers from his clients may bear an inverse relation to the care with which he conveys all the necessary information to them.

For these reasons we think the District Court must be allowed substantial latitude in refusing waivers of conflicts of interest not only in those rare cases where an actual conflict may be demonstrated before trial, but in the more common cases where a potential for conflict exists which may or may not burgeon into an actual conflict as the trial progresses. In the circumstances of this case, with the motion for substitution of counsel made so close to the time of trial, the District Court relied on instinct and judgment based on experience in making its decision. We do not think it can be said that the court exceeded the broad latitude which must be accorded it in making this decision. Petitioner of course rightly points out that the government may seek to "manufacture" a conflict in order to prevent a defendant from having a particularly able defense counsel at his side; but trial courts are undoubtedly aware of this possibility, and must take it into consideration along with all of the other factors which inform this sort of a decision.

Here the District Court was confronted not simply with an attorney who wished to represent two coequal defendants in a straightforward criminal prosecution; rather, Iredale proposed to defend three conspirators of varying stature in a complex drug distribution scheme. The Government intended to call Bravo as a witness for the prosecution at petitioner's trial.[56] The Government might readily have tied certain deliveries of marijuana by Bravo to petitioner, necessitating vigorous cross-examination of Bravo by petitioner's counsel. Iredale, because of his prior representation of Bravo, would have been unable ethically to provide that cross-examination.

Iredale had also represented Gomez–Barajas, one of the alleged kingpins of the distribution ring, and had succeeded in obtaining a verdict of acquittal for him. Gomez–Barajas had agreed with the Government to plead guilty to other charges, but the District Court had not yet accepted the plea arrangement. If the agreement were rejected, petitioner's probable testimony at the resulting trial of

---

56. [Court's footnote 4.] Bravo was in fact called as a witness at petitioner's trial. His testimony was elicited to demonstrate the transportation of drugs that the prosecution hoped to link to petitioner.

Gomez–Barajas would create an ethical dilemma for Iredale from which one or the other of his clients would likely suffer.

Viewing the situation as it did before trial, we hold that the District Court's refusal to permit the substitution of counsel in this case was within its discretion and did not violate petitioner's Sixth Amendment rights. Other district courts might have reached differing or opposite conclusions with equal justification, but that does not mean that one conclusion was "right" and the other "wrong". The District Court must recognize a presumption in favor of petitioner's counsel of choice, but that presumption may be overcome not only by a demonstration of actual conflict but by a showing of a serious potential for conflict. The evaluation of the facts and circumstances of each case under this standard must be left primarily to the informed judgment of the trial court.

The judgment of the Court of Appeals is accordingly affirmed.

JUSTICE MARSHALL, with whom JUSTICE BRENNAN joins, dissenting.

* * *

The right to counsel of choice, as the Court notes, is not absolute. . . . As the Court states, however, the trial court must recognize a presumption in favor of a defendant's counsel of choice. This presumption means that a trial court may not reject a defendant's chosen counsel on the ground of a potential conflict of interest absent a showing that both the likelihood and the dimensions of the feared conflict are substantial. . . .

I do disagree, however, with the Court's suggestion that the trial court's decision as to whether a potential conflict justifies rejection of a defendant's chosen counsel is entitled to some kind of special deference on appeal. . . . The interest at stake in this kind of decision is nothing less than a criminal defendant's Sixth Amendment right to counsel of his choice. The trial court simply does not have "broad latitude" to vitiate this right.

. . . Indeed, I believe that even under the Court's deferential standard, reversal is in order. . . .

At the time of petitioner's trial, Iredale's representation of Gomez–Barajas was effectively completed. . . . The most likely occurrence at the time petitioner moved to retain Iredale as his defense counsel was that the trial court would accept Gomez–Barajas's plea agreement, as the court in fact later did. Moreover, even if Gomez–Barajas had gone to trial, petitioner probably would not have testified. The record contains no indication that petitioner had any involvement in or information about crimes for which Gomez–Barajas might yet have stood trial. . . .

Similarly, Iredale's prior representation of Bravo was not a cause for concern. . . . As all parties were aware at the time, Bravo did not know and could not identify petitioner; indeed, prior to the commencement of legal proceedings, the two men never had heard of each other. Bravo's eventual testimony at petitioner's trial related to a shipment of marijuana in which petitioner was not involved; the testimony contained not a single reference to petitioner. Petitioner's counsel did not cross-examine Bravo, and neither petitioner's counsel nor the prosecutor mentioned Bravo's testimony in closing argument. All of these developments were predictable when the District Court ruled on petitioner's request that Iredale serve as trial counsel; the contours of Bravo's testimony were clear at that time. Given the insignificance of this testimony to any matter that petitioner's counsel would dispute, the proposed joint representation of petitioner and Bravo did not threaten a conflict of interest.[57]

* * *

[In a separate dissenting opinion, JUSTICE STEVENS, joined by JUSTICE BLACKMUN, argued, inter alia, that the Court gave inadequate weight to "the informed and voluntary character of the clients' waiver of their right to conflict-free representation." They concluded that the District Court abused its discretion in denying Wheat's request.]

(3) *Separate Representation and the Joint Defense Privilege.* A major reason for multiple representation is to insure a common presentation of a common defense. If multiple grand jury witnesses or defendants must be represented by separate defense counsel, could they still achieve the same result by meeting and discussing their case and strategy? If they do so, will their communications be protected by the attorney-client privilege?

Consider *In the Matter of Grand Jury Subpoena Duces Tecum Dated November 16, 1974,* 406 F.Supp. 381 (S.D.N.Y.1975):

CONNER, DISTRICT JUDGE:

[Digest: In 1974 the grand jury subpoenaed notes taken by attorneys of interviews held in 1972 and 1973 with a number of people then under investigation by the SEC for broad-ranging securities fraud schemes. These people included Robert Vesco, who was associated with International Controls Corp. (ICC); Norman LeBlanc, an officer of International Overseas Services, Ltd. (IOS); and Stanley Graze, also associated with IOS. The attorneys

---

57. [Footnote 3 from dissenting opinion.] The very insignificance of Bravo's testimony, combined with the timing of the prosecutor's decision to call Bravo as a witness, raises a serious concern that the prosecutor attempted to manufacture a conflict in this case. The prosecutor's decision to use Bravo as a witness was an 11th-hour development. . . . Especially in light of the scarce value of Bravo's testimony, this prosecutorial behavior very plausibly may be viewed as a maneuver to prevent Iredale from representing petitioner at trial. Iredale had proved to be a formidable adversary; he previously had gained an acquittal for the alleged kingpin of the marijuana distribution scheme. As the District Court stated in considering petitioner's motion, "Were I in [petitioner's] position I'm sure I would want Mr. Iredale representing me, too. He did a fantastic job in that [Gomez–Barajas] trial. . . ." The prosecutor's decision to call Bravo as a witness may well have stemmed from a concern that Iredale would do an equally fantastic job at petitioner's trial.

refused to produce their notes for the grand jury, arguing that their notes were protected by the attorney-client privilege. After describing generally the documents sought by the grand jury, the court continued:]

II.

The sine qua non of the attorney-client privilege is, of course, a confidence reposed—and effectively imposed—for the purpose of obtaining or furthering legal assistance. It therefore must follow, and in general principle it is universally acknowledged, that communications between a client and his counsel in the presence of a "third party," i.e., one who stands in a neutral or adverse position vis-a-vis the subject of the communication, bespeaks the absence of such confidentiality and thus belies any subsequent claim to the privilege.

Those cases in which the privilege has been sustained in relation to communications among, or made in the presence of, two or more lay persons and one or more attorneys may be regarded as clarifications of, rather than exceptions to, the rule set forth above. Thus, for example, where there is consultation among several clients and their jointly retained counsel, allied in a common legal cause, it may reasonably be inferred that resultant disclosures are intended to be insulated from exposure beyond the confines of the group; that inference, supported by a demonstration that the disclosures would not have been made but for the sake of securing, advancing, or supplying legal representation, will give sufficient force to a subsequent claim to the privilege.

The Government urges here that the privilege attending joint conferences does not extend to the present case, i.e., where statements have been made, ostensibly for the advancement of a common defense, in the presence of co-defendants or potential co-defendants and their independently retained attorneys. . . .

* * *

The privilege is . . . born of the law's own complexity. The layman's course through litigation must at least be evened by the assurance that he may, without penalty, invest his confidence and confidences in a professional counsellor. That assurance is no less important or appropriate where a cooperative program of joint defense is helpful or, a fortiori, necessary to form and inform the representation of clients whose attorneys are each separately retained. Hence the following observations, in dicta issuing a century ago from a Virginia appellate court:

> "The parties were jointly indicted for a conspiracy * * *. They might have employed the same counsel, or they might have employed different counsel as they did. But whether they did the one thing or the other, the effect is the same, as to their right of communication to each and all of the counsel,

and as to the privilege of such communication. They had the same defence to make, the act of one in furtherance of the conspiracy, being the act of all, and the counsel of each was in effect the counsel of all * * *. They had a right, all the accused and their counsel, to consult together about the case and the defence, and it follows as a necessary consequence, that all the information, derived by any of the counsel from such consultation, is privileged * * *."

Chahoon v. The Commonwealth, 62 Va. (21 Gratt.) 822, 841–42 (1871).

For the reasons stated above, I conclude that the attorney-client privilege covers communications to a prospective or actual co-defendant's attorney when those communications are engendered solely in the interests of a joint defense effort.

III.

The question remains whether these particular respondents in fact reasonably believed at the time of their meetings and interviews that their statements were being made within the context, and in furtherance, of their joint defense. Respondents concede that the burden is theirs on this issue. . . .

In March 1971, the SEC inaugurated a wide-scale formal investigation of the business interrelations and dealings of ICC and Vesco, among others, with IOS and IOS affiliates. During the course of the investigation, respondents ICC and Vesco were represented by Hogan & Hartson, ICC corporate and litigation counsel. On October 6, 1972, SEC staff members advised Hogan & Hartson that a criminal reference might be made with respect to Vesco on the basis of the Commission's findings and suggested that the individual respondent might best be represented by independent counsel. Accordingly, in mid-October 1972, Hogan & Hartson asked Paul, Weiss to serve as co-counsel for Vesco in relation to the SEC proceedings, and Paul, Weiss agreed to do so. Having been advised by the SEC of the charges that the Commission proposed to bring in a forthcoming civil action, attorneys associated with Hogan & Hartson, Paul, Weiss, and Willkie, Farr (the latter acting as counsel for IOS) met on October 23, 1972 in New York, and on October 27, 1972 in Nassau, allegedly to establish the groundwork for a cooperative defense effort in the anticipated litigation.

A portion of the October 27 meeting was addressed to the questions of work product and attorney-client privileges raised by a joint defense. The attorneys concluded that, although the relevant law was not entirely clear, the privileges would probably apply to their own discussions and to their interviews of several potential co-defendants, scheduled to be held on the following day. That conclusion was restated at the outset of the October 28 interview sessions.

* * *

LeBlanc . . . was apparently not represented by individual counsel at the time of his October 28 interview. [He] expressed an active concern that . . . [his] statements might not be preserved from outside exposure . . . [and he] continued with the interview only after receiving repeated assurances from the attorneys present that all disclosures would be privileged on the ground of joint defense.

[T]he SEC civil action, based upon the Commission's twenty-month investigation, was filed in this district on November 27, 1972. Either on that date, or shortly before, Hogan & Hartson discontinued its formal representation of Vesco, leaving Paul, Weiss to act as Vesco's sole counsel with respect to the ensuing litigation; nonetheless, both firms agreed that Hogan & Hartson would continue to "shoulder responsibility" for the Vesco defense, at least to the extent that it would share with Paul, Weiss the benefits of Hogan & Hartson's background knowledge of the case, gained by virtue of the latter's long involvement with the SEC investigation.

On December 3 and 4, 1972, attorneys from Hogan & Hartson, Paul, Weiss, and Steptoe & Johnson (the latter firm then acting as co-counsel for IOS) met, in Vesco's Nassau home, with several of the individuals named as co-defendants in the SEC complaint. Among those present at the December 3 and 4 meetings was Stanley Graze. At those meetings, the attorneys again stressed the need for cooperation among the defendants and their counsel. In addition, discussions were had concerning the assignment of counsel for those defendants who were not then individually represented. Recommendations of counsel were made, partially on the basis that the recommended attorneys could "work cooperatively" on the case.

It was apparently at the December 3 meeting that Graze was first asked to make available certain documents for the inspection of co-defendants' counsel. Graze initially agreed to do so, but that cooperation was immediately thereafter "vetoed" by Graze's individual counsel, who had not attended either the December 3 or 4 session. However, Graze's attorney was contacted by counsel for Vesco, who appears successfully to have "engaged in advocacy" on behalf of the purported joint defense effort then in progress. For, on December 5, 1972, Graze agreed to submit to an interview by attorneys from Hogan & Hartson and Steptoe & Johnson. . . . Within two weeks of that interview, Graze again submitted to questioning by counsel representing other defendants. On that occasion, Graze's individual attorney indicated that he was submitting his client to interview in the presence of additional counsel only because the latter represented other defendants in the SEC action. Requesting a copy of the Hogan & Hartson memorandum that recorded Graze's December 5 statements, Graze's attorney further indicated that additional copies might be distributed to co-defendants and their counsel, but to no others.

. . . Vesco submitted to further interview by Hogan & Hartson on December 6 and December 22, 1972, in the presence of his Paul, Weiss counsel. In addition, on January 10, 1973, a discussion was had between Vesco and a Hogan & Hartson attorney that bore some relation to the SEC action. . . .

During the same period, interviews were conducted by Hogan & Hartson attorneys with additional co-defendants. It had apparently been agreed among the various counsel representing defendants in the SEC litigation that a division of attorney labor and a sharing of information gathered from co-defendants would be necessary to construction of a defense against the SEC's charges. Hence, the task of conducting interviews was assigned primarily to particular firms; the compilation of transcripts and abstracts was assigned to others; the maintenance of a central repository of relevant documents for reference of all defense counsel was assigned to Paul, Weiss. The question of privilege was repeatedly discussed among the various counsel, sometimes alone and sometimes in the presence of their clients. On several occasions, persons not clearly engaged in the defense against the SEC action were excluded from defense strategy sessions and interviews, for the purpose of preserving confidentiality.

All of the above activities, singly and in combination, bear the markings of a conscious and conscientious joint defense undertaking.

The Government nevertheless maintains, on a variety of grounds, that the particular communications recorded in the contested documents were not in fact made under the impetus of a joint defense. For the reasons indicated below, I conclude that the Government's arguments on the facts are without force. . . .

The Government contends that the absence of counsel for LeBlanc and Graze and the presence of individuals other than the interviewing attorneys on October 28, 1972 and December 5, 1972, vitiate the present claims to attorney-client privilege. . . . [But] the rule remains that, where persons confer with counsel for the purpose of advancing their joint defense, the conference is sealed from outside view; . . . that rule applies whether the parties are technically represented by joint or independent counsel. And, on the basis of the record outlined above, this Court concludes that the "third" persons present at the LeBlanc interview—all prospective co-defendants—were without exception among the participants in a common defense effort that had begun to take form by the final week of October 1972.

Moreover, this Court deems it clear that LeBlanc and Graze themselves understood their interviews to be designed as the implements of a joint defense. . . . His eventual cooperation, this Court concludes, would not have been forthcoming unless LeBlanc himself believed that such cooperation would enure to his own benefit, as well as to that of his potential co-defendants.

Similarly, Graze did not submit to interview until his individual attorney was convinced that it was in the interests of Graze's defense to do so. Graze, like LeBlanc, may not reasonably be viewed as a mere disinterested witness following an impulse to satisfy the "need to know" of others.

The Government urges most strongly that the documents recording Vesco's statements to Hogan & Hartson attorneys in December 1972 and January 1973 cannot have been the products of a joint defense embracing Vesco and ICC because, or so the Government contends, Vesco and ICC at that time stood in adverse positions. To support that contention, the Government points to the several occasions on which Hogan & Hartson and Paul, Weiss attorneys were advised by SEC staff members that ICC might well have grounds for its own action against Vesco on the basis of dealings uncovered by the SEC investigation. . . .

[I]f an action by ICC against Vesco might have been foreseeable as early as December 1972 and January 1973, that alone would not have prevented Vesco and ICC from sharing confidential information for the purpose of a joint defense against the immediate SEC action. Those confidences might have placed Vesco at his peril in the event that a private action were eventually instituted by ICC. Nevertheless, assuming arguendo that such peril was anticipated and appreciated by Vesco and his counsel, Vesco was entitled to risk it for the sake of strengthening his immediate defense by cooperation from and with ICC and the other co-defendants. That a joint defense may be made by somewhat unsteady bedfellows does not in itself negate the existence or viability of the joint defense.

* * *

Query. Review the description in the Court's opinion of the joint defense efforts. Does the ability to find counsel who can "work cooperatively," and whose communications will then be protected by the attorney client privilege, mean that efforts (like *Pirillo*) to prevent joint representation produce no gain for the criminal justice system? Are the only beneficiaries of disqualification the multiple lawyers who will need to be retained in these cases?

Chapter 6

GOVERNMENT EVIDENCE GATHERING

A. IMMUNITY

SCOPE NOTE

The grant of immunity from prosecution is one of the most powerful weapons a prosecutor has for obtaining information. As we have already seen in Chapter 4, witnesses have a constitutional privilege to refuse to provide information which will incriminate them. To the extent a prosecutor can overcome this privilege by providing some sort of immunity from prosecution, information about crime can be obtained from those who know the most about the transaction under investigation.

The first part of this Section begins with the development of the constitutional principles which govern the grant of immunity. The two lead cases, *Counselman v. Hitchcock* and *Brown v. Walker,* established the constitutional theory which permits testimony to be compelled in exchange for a grant of immunity. The Notes following these cases explore how these theories have been applied in more recent settings—the constitutionality of the current federal immunity statute, the validity of a perjury prosecution based on immunized testimony, and the question whether one can assert the fifth amendment privilege because of a threatened foreign prosecution.

The second part of this Section deals with immunity which is not the result of a grant under the federal immunity statute. The leading case is *Murphy v. Waterfront Commission,* involving the effect of a state grant of immunity on subsequent federal prosecutions. The Notes following *Murphy* deal with immunity grants to defense witnesses by the court, and the validity of "informal" immunity agreements by prosecutors.

COUNSELMAN v. HITCHCOCK
Supreme Court of the United States, 1892.
142 U.S. 547, 12 S.Ct. 195, 35 L.Ed. 1110.

On the 21st of November, 1890, while the grand jury in attendance upon the District Court of the United States for the Northern District of Illinois was engaged in investigating and inquiring into certain alleged violations, in that district, of an act of Congress entitled "An act to regulate commerce," approved February 4, 1887, by the officers and agents of the Chicago, Rock Island and Pacific Railway Company, and by the officers and agents of the Chicago, St. Paul and Kansas City Railway Company, and by the officers and agents of the Chicago,

Burlington and Quincy Railroad Company, and the officers and agents of various other railroad companies having lines of road in that district, one Charles Counselman appeared before the grand jury, in response to a subpoena served upon him, and after having been duly sworn, testified as follows:

"Q. Your name is Charles Counselman?

"A. Yes, sir.

"Q. You are the sole member of Charles Counselman & Co.?

"A. Yes, sir.

"Q. Engaged in the grain and commission business in the city of Chicago?

"A. Yes, sir.

"Q. Have you been a receiver of grain from the West during the past two years?

"A. Yes, sir.

"Q. Over what roads did you ship grain received by you during the present summer of 1890?

"A. The Rock Island and Burlington, principally.

"Q. Have you during the past year, Mr. Counselman, obtained a rate for the transportation of your grain on any of the railroads coming to Chicago, from points outside of this State, less than the tariff or open rate?

"A. That I decline to answer, Mr. Milchrist, on the ground that it might tend to criminate me.

"Q. During the past year have you received rates upon the Chicago, Rock Island and Pacific from points outside of the State to the city of Chicago, at less than the tariff rates?

"A. That I decline to answer on the same ground.

"Q. I will ask you the same question with reference to the Burlington.

"A. I answer in the same way.

* * *

"Q. Who attends to the freight department of your business?

"A. Myself and Mr. Martin.

"Q. Have you or the firm of Charles Counselman & Co. received any rebate, drawback or commission from the Chicago, Rock Island and Pacific Railroad Company, or the Chicago, Burlington and Quincy Railroad Company, on the transportation of grain from points in the States of Nebraska and Kansas, to the city of Chicago, in the State of Illinois, during the past year, whereby you secured the transportation of said grain at less than the tariff rates established by said railroad?

"A. I decline to answer on the same ground."

* * *

Mr. Justice Blatchford, after stating the case, delivered the opinion of the court.

* * *

It is broadly contended on the part of the appellee that a witness is not entitled to plead the privilege of silence, except in a criminal case against himself; but such is not the language of the Constitution. Its provision is that no person shall be compelled in *any* criminal case to be a witness against himself. This provision must have a broad construction in favor of the right which it was intended to secure. The matter under investigation by the grand jury in this case was a criminal matter, to inquire whether there had been a criminal violation of the Interstate Commerce Act. If Counselman had been guilty of the matters inquired of in the questions which he refused to answer, he himself was liable to criminal prosecution under the act. The case before the grand jury was, therefore, a criminal case. The reason given by Counselman for his refusal to answer the questions was that his answers might tend to criminate him, and showed that his apprehension was that, if he answered the questions truly and fully (as he was bound to do if he should answer them at all), the answers might show that he had committed a crime against the Interstate Commerce Act, for which he might be prosecuted. His answers, therefore, would be testimony against himself, and he would be compelled to give them in a criminal case.

It is impossible that the meaning of the constitutional provision can only be, that a person shall not be compelled to be a witness against himself in a criminal prosecution against himself. It would doubtless cover such cases; but it is not limited to them. The object was to insure that a person should not be compelled, when acting as a witness in any investigation, to give testimony which might tend to show that he himself had committed a crime. The privilege is limited to criminal matters, but it is as broad as the mischief against which it seeks to guard.

* * *

It remains to consider whether § 860 of the Revised Statutes removes the protection of the constitutional privilege of Counselman. That section must be construed as declaring that no evidence obtained from a witness by means of a judicial proceeding shall be given in evidence, or in any manner used against him or his property or estate, in any court of the United States, in any criminal proceeding, or for the enforcement of any penalty or forfeiture. It follows, that any evidence which might have been obtained from Counselman by means of his examination before the grand jury could not be given in evidence or used against him or his property in any court of the United States, in any criminal proceeding, or for the enforcement of any penalty or forfeiture. This, of course, protected him against the use of his testimony against him or his property in any prosecution against him or his property, in any criminal proceeding, in a court of the United States. But it had only that effect. It could not, and would not, prevent the use of his testimony to search out other testimony to be used in evidence against him or his property, in a criminal proceeding in such court. It could not prevent the obtaining and the use of witnesses and evidence which should be attributable directly to the testimony he might give under compulsion, and on which he might be convicted, when otherwise, and if he had refused to answer, he could not possibly have been convicted.

The constitutional provision distinctly declares that a person shall not "be compelled in any criminal case to be a witness against himself;" and the protection of § 860 is not coextensive with the constitutional provision. Legislation cannot detract from the privilege afforded by the Constitution.

* * *

We are clearly of opinion that no statute which leaves the party or witness subject to prosecution after he answers the criminating question put to him, can have the effect of supplanting the privilege conferred by the Constitution of the United States. Section 860 of the Revised Statutes does not supply a complete protection from all the perils against which the constitutional prohibition was designed to guard, and is not a full substitute for that prohibition. In view of the constitutional provision, a statutory enactment, to be valid, must afford absolute immunity against future prosecution for the offence to which the question relates. . . . Section 860, moreover, affords no protection against that use of compelled testimony which consists in gaining therefrom a knowledge of the details of a crime, and of sources of information which may supply other means of convicting the witness or party.

* * *

BROWN v. WALKER
Supreme Court of the United States, 1896.
161 U.S. 591, 16 S.Ct. 644, 40 L.Ed. 819.

MR. JUSTICE BROWN, after stating the case, delivered the opinion of the court.

This case involves an alleged incompatibility between that clause of the Fifth Amendment to the Constitution, which declares that no person "shall be compelled in any criminal case to be a witness against himself," and the act of Congress of February 11, 1893, which enacts that "no person shall be excused from attending and testifying or from producing books, papers, tariffs, contracts, agreements and documents before the Interstate Commerce Commission, or in obedience to the subpoena of the Commission, . . . on the ground or for the reason that the testimony or evidence, documentary or otherwise, required of him, may tend to criminate him or subject him to a penalty or forfeiture. But no person shall be prosecuted or subjected to any penalty or forfeiture for or on account of any transaction, matter or thing, concerning which he may testify, or produce evidence, documentary or otherwise, before said Commission, or in obedience to its subpoena, or the subpoena of either of them, or in any such case or proceeding."

The act is supposed to have been passed in view of the opinion of this court in Counselman v. Hitchcock, 142 U.S. 547, to the effect that section 860 of the Revised Statutes, providing that no evidence given by a witness shall be used against him, his property or estate, in any manner, in any court of the United States, in any criminal proceeding, did not afford that complete protection to the witness which the amendment was intended to guarantee.

* * *

The clause of the Constitution in question is obviously susceptible of two interpretations. If it be construed literally, as authorizing the witness to refuse to disclose any fact which might tend to incriminate, disgrace or expose him to unfavorable comments, then as he must necessarily to a large extent determine upon his own conscience and responsibility whether his answer to the proposed question will have that tendency, . . . the practical result would be, that no one could be compelled to testify to a material fact in a criminal case, unless he chose to do so, or unless it was entirely clear that the privilege was not set up in good faith. If, upon the other hand, the object of the provision be to secure the witness against a criminal prosecution, which might be aided directly or indirectly by his disclosure, then, if no such prosecution be possible—in other words, if his testimony operate as a complete pardon for the offence to which it relates—a statute absolutely securing to him such immunity from prosecution would satisfy the demands of the clause in question.

Our attention has been called to but few cases wherein this provision, which is found with slight variation in the constitution of every State, has been construed in connection with a statute similar to the one before us, as the decisions have usually turned upon the validity of statutes providing, as did section 860, that the testimony given by such witness should never be used against him in any criminal prosecution. It can only be said in general that the clause should be construed, as it was doubtless designed, to effect a practical and beneficent purpose—not necessarily to protect witnesses against every possible detriment which might happen to them from their testimony, nor to unduly impede, hinder or obstruct the administration of criminal justice. That the statute should be upheld, if it can be construed in harmony with the fundamental law, will be admitted. . . .

The maxim *nemo tenetur seipsum accusare* had its origin in a protest against the inquisitorial and manifestly unjust methods of interrogating accused persons, which has long obtained in the continental system, and, until the expulsion of the Stuarts from the British throne in 1688, and the erection of additional barriers for the protection of the people against the exercise of arbitrary power, was not uncommon even in England. While the admissions or confessions of the prisoner, when voluntarily and freely made, have always ranked high in the scale of incriminating evidence, if an accused person be asked to explain his apparent connection with a crime under investigation, the ease with which the questions put to him may assume an inquisitorial character, the temptation to press the witness unduly, to browbeat him if he be timid or reluctant, to push him into a corner, and to entrap him into fatal contradictions, which is so painfully evident in many of the earlier state trials, notably in those of Sir Nicholas Throckmorton, and Udal, the Puritan minister, made the system so odious as to give rise to a demand for its total abolition. The change in the English criminal procedure in that particular seems to be founded upon no statute and no judicial opinion, but upon a general and silent acquiescence of the courts in a popular demand. But, however adopted, it has become firmly embedded in English, as well as in American jurisprudence. So deeply did the iniquities of the ancient system impress themselves upon the minds of the American colonists that the States, with one accord, made a denial of the right to question an accused person a part of their fundamental law, so that a maxim, which in England was a mere rule of evidence, became clothed in this country with the impregnability of a constitutional enactment.

Stringent as the general rule is, however, certain classes of cases have always been treated as not falling within the reason of the rule, and, therefore, constituting apparent exceptions. When examined, these cases will all be found to be based upon the idea that, if the testimony sought cannot possibly be used as a basis for, or in aid of, a criminal prosecution against the witness, the rule ceases to apply, its object being to protect the witness himself and no one else—much less that it shall be made use of as a pretext for securing immunity to others.

1. Thus, if the witness himself elects to waive his privilege, as he may doubtless do, since the privilege is for his protection and not for that of other parties, and discloses his criminal connections, he is not permitted to stop, but must go on and make a full disclosure.

* * *

2. For the same reason if a prosecution for a crime, concerning which the witness is interrogated, is barred by the statute of limitations, he is compellable to answer. . . .

3. If the answer of the witness may have a tendency to disgrace him or bring him into disrepute, and the proposed evidence be material to the issue on trial, the great weight of authority is that he may be compelled to answer, although, if the answer can have no effect upon the case, except so far as to impair the credibility of the witness, he may fall back upon his privilege.

* * *

4. It is almost a necessary corollary of the above propositions that, if the witness has already received a pardon, he cannot longer set up his privilege, since he stands with respect to such offence as if it had never been committed.

* * *

All of the cases above cited proceed upon the idea that the prohibition against his being compelled to testify against himself presupposes a legal detriment to the witness arising from the exposure. . . .

The danger of extending the principle announced in Counselman v. Hitchcock is that the privilege may be put forward for a sentimental reason, or for a purely fanciful protection of the witness against an imaginary danger, and for the real purpose of securing immunity to some third person, who is interested in concealing the facts to which he would testify. Every good citizen is bound to aid in the enforcement of the law, and has no right to permit himself, under the pretext of shielding his own good name, to be made the tool of others, who are desirous of seeking shelter behind his privilege.

* * *

It is entirely true that the statute does not purport, nor is it possible for any statute, to shield the witness from the personal disgrace or opprobrium attaching to the exposure of his crime; but, as we have already observed, the authorities are numerous and very nearly uniform to the effect that, if the proposed testimony is material to the issue on trial, the fact that the testimony may tend to degrade the witness in public estimation does not exempt him from the duty of disclosure. A person who commits a criminal act is bound to contemplate the consequences of exposure to his good name and reputation, and ought not to call upon the courts to protect that which he has himself esteemed to be of such little value. The safety and welfare of an entire community should not be put into the scale against the reputation of a self-confessed criminal, who ought not, either in justice or in good morals, to refuse to disclose that which may be of great public utility, in order that his neighbors may think well of him. The design of the constitutional privilege is not to aid the witness in vindicating his character, but to protect him against being compelled to furnish evidence to convict him of a criminal charge. If he secure legal immunity from prosecution, the possible impairment of his good name is a penalty which it is reasonable he should be compelled to pay for the common good. If it be once conceded that the fact that his testimony may tend to bring the witness into disrepute, though not to incriminate him, does not entitle him to the privilege of silence, it necessarily follows that if it also tends to incriminate, but at the same time operates as a pardon for the offence, the fact that the disgrace remains no more entitles him to immunity in this case than in the other.

* * *

In the case under consideration, the grand jury was engaged in investigating certain alleged violations of the Interstate Commerce Act, among which was a charge against the Allegheny Valley Railway Company of transporting coal of the Union Coal Company from intermediate points to Buffalo, at less than the established rates between the terminal points, and a further charge of discriminating in favor of such coal company by rebates, drawbacks or commissions on its coal, by which it obtained transportation at less than the tariff rates. Brown, the witness, was the auditor of the road, whose duty it was to audit the accounts of the officers, and the money paid out by them. Having audited the accounts of the freight department during the time in question, he was asked whether he knew of any such discrimination in favor of the Union Coal Company, and declined to answer upon the ground that he would thereby incriminate himself.

As he . . . was concerned only in auditing accounts, and passing vouchers for money paid by others, it is difficult to see how, under any construction of section 10 of the Interstate Commerce Act, he could be said to have wilfully done anything. . . . But, however this may be, it is entirely clear that he was not the chief or even a substantial offender against the law, and that his privilege was claimed for the purpose of shielding the railway or its officers from answering a charge of having violated its provisions. To say that, notwithstanding his immunity from punishment, he would incur personal odium and disgrace from answering these questions, seems too much like an abuse of language to be worthy of serious consideration. But, even if this were true, under the authorities above cited, he would still be compelled to answer, if the facts sought to be elucidated were material to the issue.

If, as was justly observed in the opinion of the court below, witnesses standing in Brown's position were at liberty to set up an immunity from testifying, the enforcement of the Interstate Commerce law or other analogous acts, wherein it is for the interest of both parties to conceal their misdoings, would become impossible, since it is only from the mouths of those having knowledge of the inhibited contracts that the facts can be ascertained. While the constitutional provision in question is justly regarded as one of the most valuable prerogatives of the citizen, its object is fully accomplished by the statutory immunity, and we are, therefore, of opinion that the witness was compellable to answer, and that the judgment of the court below must be affirmed.

[The dissenting opinion of MR. JUSTICE SHIRAS, concurred in by MR. JUSTICE GRAY and MR. JUSTICE WHITE, is omitted.]

MR. JUSTICE FIELD, dissenting.

* * *

. . . It is contended . . . that it was not the object of the constitutional safeguard to protect the witness against infamy and disgrace. It is urged that its sole purpose was to protect him against incriminating testimony with reference to the offence under prosecution. But I do not agree that such limited protection was all that was secured. As stated by counsel of the appellant, "it is entirely possible, and certainly not impossible, that the framers of the Constitution reasoned that in bestowing upon witnesses in criminal cases the privilege of silence when in danger of self-incrimination, they would at the same time save him *in all such cases* from the shame and infamy of confessing disgraceful crimes and thus preserve to him some measure of self-respect. . . ." It is true, as counsel observes, that "both the safeguard of the Constitution and the common law rule spring alike from that sentiment of *personal self-respect, liberty, independence and dignity* which has inhabited the breasts of English speaking peoples for centuries, and to save which they have always been ready to sacrifice many governmental facilities and conveniences. In scarcely anything has that sentiment been more manifest than in the abhorrence felt at the legal compulsion upon witnesses to make concessions which must cover the witness with lasting shame and leave him degraded both in his own eyes and those of others. What can be more abhorrent . . . than to compel a man who has fought his way from obscurity to dignity and honor to reveal crimes of which he had repented and of which the world was ignorant?"

* * *

The position that if witnesses are allowed to assert an exemption from answering questions when in their opinion such answers may tend to incriminate them, the proof of offence like those prescribed by the Interstate Commerce act will be difficult and probably impossible— ought not to have a feather's weight against the abuses which would follow necessarily the enforcement of criminating testimony. The abuses and perversions of sound principles which would creep into the law by yielding to arguments like these—to what is supposed to be necessary for the public good—cannot be better stated than it was by the late Justice Bradley in Boyd v. United States, 116 U.S. 616, 635. Said the learned justice:

"Illegitimate and unconstitutional practices get their first footing in that way, namely, by silent approaches and slight deviations from legal modes of procedure. This can only be obviated by adhering to the rule that constitutional provisions for the security of person and property should be liberally construed. *A close and literal construction deprives them of half their efficacy,* and leads to gradual depreciation of the right, as if it consisted more in sound than substance. It is the duty of courts to be watchful for the constitutional rights of the citizens and against any stealthy encroachments thereon. Their motto should be *obsta principiis.*"

* * *

NOTES AND QUERIES

(1) *Resist Beginnings?* The decision in *Brown v. Walker,* although a close one at the time, has never been overruled. Ten years after *Brown* the Court revisited the issue in *Hale v. Henkel,* but unanimously reaffirmed the basic idea that witnesses could be compelled to testify so long as they were given an immunity from prosecution coextensive with the coverage of the privilege.[1] In 1956, in *Ullman v. United States,*[2] the Court was again asked to reconsider *Brown:*

1. See 201 U.S. at 67, 26 S.Ct. at 376, 50 L.Ed. at 662.

2. 350 U.S. 422, 76 S.Ct. 497, 100 L.Ed. 511 (1956).

MR. JUSTICE FRANKFURTER delivered the opinion of the Court.

On November 10, 1954, the United States Attorney for the Southern District of New York filed an application under the Immunity Act of 1954 for an order requiring petitioner to testify before a grand jury. . . . In his application the United States Attorney alleged the following facts. On November 3, 1954, petitioner, pursuant to subpoena, appeared before a duly constituted grand jury of the Southern District of New York which was investigating matters concerned with attempts to endanger the national security by espionage and conspiracy to commit espionage. The grand jury asked him a series of questions relating to his knowledge of such activities, to his and other persons' participation in such activities, and to his and other persons' membership in the Communist Party. Petitioner, invoking the privilege against self-incrimination, refused to answer the questions. The United States Attorney also asserted that he deemed the testimony necessary to the public interest of the United States, and annexed a letter from the Attorney General of the United States approving the application [for immunity].

* * *

Petitioner . . . urges that . . . Brown v. Walker . . . be reconsidered and overruled. He also urges upon us a "return" to a literal reading of the Fifth Amendment. . . . [In Brown v. Walker, as in Counselman v. Hitchcock,] appellant's numerous arguments were presented by James C. Carter, widely acknowledged as the leader of the American bar. The Court was closely divided in upholding the statute, and the opinions reflect the thoroughness with which the issues were considered. Since that time the Court's holding in Brown v. Walker has never been challenged; the case and the doctrine it announced have consistently and without question been treated as definitive by this Court, in opinions written, among others, by Holmes and Brandeis, JJ. The 1893 statute has become part of our constitutional fabric and has been included "in substantially the same terms, in virtually all of the major regulatory enactments of the Federal Government." . . .

We are not dealing here with one of the vague, indefinable, admonitory provisions of the Constitution whose scope is inevitably addressed to changing circumstances. The privilege against self-incrimination is a specific provision of which it is peculiarly true that "a page of history is worth a volume of logic." For the history of the privilege establishes not only that it is not to be interpreted literally, but also that its sole concern is, as its name indicates, with the danger to a witness forced to give testimony leading to the infliction of "penalties affixed to the criminal acts . . . ." Boyd v. United States, 116 U.S. 616, 634. . . . Immunity displaces the danger.

[Justice Douglas, joined by Justice Black, wrote a dissenting opinion arguing that Brown v. Walker be overruled. The opinion first reviewed historical materials to support their view that

> the Framers put it beyond the power of Congress to compel anyone to confess his crimes. The evil to be guarded against was partly self-accusation under legal compulsion. But that was only a part of the evil. The conscience and dignity of man were also involved. So too was his right to freedom of expression guaranteed by the First Amendment. The Framers, therefore, created the federally protected right of silence and decreed that the law could not be used to pry open one's lips and make him a witness against himself.

Justice Douglas also argued that the fifth amendment was designed to protect the accused against "infamy" as well as against prosecution. Tracing the concept of "infamy" based on writings contemporaneous with the Constitution, Justice Douglas continued:]

There is great infamy involved in the present case, apart from the loss of rights of citizenship under federal law which I have already mentioned. The disclosure that a person is a Communist practically excommunicates him from society. School boards will not hire him. A lawyer risks exclusion from the bar; a doctor, the revocation of his license to practice. If an actor, he is on a black list. And he will be able to find no employment in our society except at the lowest level, if at all. . . .

It is no answer to say that a witness who exercises his Fifth Amendment right of silence and stands mute may bring himself into disrepute. If so, that is the price he pays for exercising the right of silence granted by the Fifth Amendment. The critical point is that the Constitution places the right of silence beyond the reach of government. The Fifth Amendment stands between the citizen and his government. When public opinion casts a person into the outer darkness, as happens today when a person is exposed as a Communist, the government brings infamy on the head of the witness when it compels disclosure. That is precisely what the Fifth Amendment prohibits.

(2) *Transactional v. Use Immunity.* The statute upheld in *Brown* provided transactional immunity, that is, immunity from prosecution for the transaction to which the compelled testimony related. This statute then became the model for federal immunity statutes which Congress enacted in connection with subsequent regulatory legislation (such as the Sherman Act). By 1970 Congress had enacted more than fifty such statutes. In that year, however, Congress enacted a new immunity statute to replace all existing federal immunity statutes (other than for bankruptcy). The new statute, set out below, provides only for use and derivative use immunity:

18 U.S.C. § 6002. Immunity generally

Whenever a witness refuses, on the basis of his privilege against self-incrimination, to testify or provide other information in a proceeding before or ancillary to—

> (1) a court or grand jury of the United States,
>
> (2) an agency of the United States, or
>
> (3) either House of Congress, a joint committee of the two Houses, or a committee or a subcommittee of either House,

and the person presiding over the proceeding communicates to the witness an order issued under this part, the witness may not refuse to comply with the order on the basis of his privilege against self-incrimination; but no testimony or other information compelled under the order (or any information directly or indirectly derived from such testimony or other information) may be used against the witness in any criminal case, except a prosecution for perjury, giving a false statement, or otherwise failing to comply with the order.

18 U.S.C. § 6003. Court and grand jury proceedings

(a) In the case of any individual who has been or may be called to testify or provide other information at any proceeding before or ancillary to a court of the United States or a grand jury of the United States, the United States district court for the judicial district in which the proceeding is or may be held shall issue, in accordance with subsection (b) of this section, upon the request of the United States attorney for such district, an order requiring such individual to give testimony or provide other information which he refuses to give or provide on the basis of his privilege against self-incrimination, such order to become effective as provided in section 6002 of this part.

(b) A United States attorney may, with the approval of the Attorney General, the Deputy Attorney General, or any designated Assistant Attorney General, request an order under subsection (a) of this section when in his judgment—

> (1) the testimony or other information from such individual may be necessary to the public interest; and
>
> (2) such individual has refused or is likely to refuse to testify or provide other information on the basis of his privilege against self-incrimination.

The constitutionality of the new statute was challenged in *Kastigar v. United States*.[3] The Court first rejected a request to overrule *Brown* and *Ullman,* writing that immunity statutes "are not incompatible" with the values of the fifth amendment:

---

3. 406 U.S. 441, 92 S.Ct. 1653, 32 L.Ed. 2d 212 (1972).

[T]hey seek a rational accommodation between the imperatives of the privilege and the legitimate demands of government to compel citizens to testify. The existence of these statutes reflects the importance of testimony, and the fact that many offenses are of such a character that the only persons capable of giving useful testimony are those implicated in the crime.

The Court, per Justice Powell, then continued:

Petitioners' second contention is that the scope of immunity provided by the federal witness immunity statute, 18 U.S.C. § 6002, is not coextensive with the scope of the Fifth Amendment privilege against compulsory self-incrimination, and therefore is not sufficient to supplant the privilege and compel testimony over a claim of the privilege. . . .

* * *

Petitioners draw a distinction between statutes that provide transactional immunity and those that provide, as does the statute before us, immunity from use and derivative use. They contend that a statute must at a minimum grant full transactional immunity in order to be coextensive with the scope of the privilege. In support of this contention, they rely on Counselman v. Hitchcock, the first case in which this Court considered a constitutional challenge to an immunity statute. . . .

* * *

The statute's explicit proscription of the use in any criminal case of "testimony or other information compelled under the order (or any information directly or indirectly derived from such testimony or other information)" is consonant with Fifth Amendment standards. We hold that such immunity from use and derivative use is coextensive with the scope of the privilege against self-incrimination, and therefore is sufficient to compel testimony over a claim of the privilege. While a grant of immunity must afford protection commensurate with that afforded by the privilege, it need not be broader. Transactional immunity, which accords full immunity from prosecution for the offense to which the compelled testimony relates, affords the witness considerably broader protection than does the Fifth Amendment privilege. The privilege has never been construed to mean that one who invokes it cannot subsequently be prosecuted. Its sole concern is to afford protection against being "forced to give testimony leading to the infliction of 'penalties affixed to . . . criminal acts.'" Immunity from the use of compelled testimony, as well as evidence derived directly and indirectly therefrom, affords this protection. It prohibits the prosecutorial authorities from using the compelled testimony in any respect, and it therefore insures that the testimony cannot lead to the infliction of criminal penalties on the witness.

Our holding is consistent with the conceptual basis of *Counselman*. The *Counselman* statute, as construed by the Court, was plainly deficient in its failure to prohibit the use against the immunized witness of evidence derived from his compelled testimony. The Court repeatedly emphasized this deficiency. . . .

* * *

Although an analysis of prior decisions and the purpose of the Fifth Amendment privilege indicates that use and derivative-use immunity is coextensive with the privilege, we must consider additional arguments advanced by petitioners against the sufficiency of such immunity. . . .

Petitioners argue that use and derivative-use immunity will not adequately protect a witness from various possible incriminating uses of the compelled testimony: for example, the prosecutor or other law enforcement officials may obtain leads, names of witnesses, or other information not otherwise available that might result in a prosecution. It will be difficult and perhaps impossible, the argument goes, to identify, by testimony or cross-examination, the subtle ways in which the compelled testimony may disadvantage a witness, especially in the jurisdiction granting the immunity.

This argument presupposes that the statute's prohibition will prove impossible to enforce. The statute provides a sweeping proscription of any use, direct or indirect, of the compelled testimony and any information derived therefrom. . . . This total prohibition on use provides a comprehensive safeguard, barring the use of compelled testimony as an "investigatory lead," and also barring the use of any evidence obtained by focusing investigation on a witness as a result of his compelled disclosures.

A person accorded this immunity under 18 U.S.C. § 6002, and subsequently prosecuted, is not dependent for the preservation of his rights upon the integrity and good faith of the prosecuting authorities. . . .

[The goverment's] burden of proof, which we reaffirm as appropriate, is not limited to a negation of taint; rather, it imposes on the prosecution the affirmative duty to prove that the evidence it proposes to use is derived from a legitimate source wholly independent of the compelled testimony.

This is very substantial protection, commensurate with that resulting from invoking the privilege itself. The privilege assures that a citizen is not compelled to incriminate himself by his own testimony. It usually operates to allow a citizen to remain silent when asked a question requiring an incriminatory answer. This statute, which operates after a witness has given incriminatory testimony, affords the same protection by assuring that the compelled testimony can in no way lead to the infliction of criminal penalties. The statute, like the Fifth Amendment, grants neither pardon nor amnesty. Both the statute and the Fifth Amendment allow the government to prosecute using evidence from legitimate independent sources.

* * *

We conclude that the immunity provided by 18 U.S.C. § 6002 leaves the witness and the prosecutorial authorities in substantially the same position as if the witness had claimed the Fifth Amendment privilege. The immunity therefore is coextensive with the privilege and suffices to supplant it.

(3) *Prosecutions for Perjury.* Suppose an immunized witness lies? Can the witness's testimony be used against the witness in a subsequent prosecution for perjury? Note that § 6002 specifically allows such use. Is such use constitutional?

In *United States v. Apfelbaum* [4] the defendant was prosecuted for perjury with regard to testimony given before the grand jury under a grant of immunity. At the perjury trial the Government introduced into evidence parts of the defendant's grand jury testimony which were true, using this testimony to help prove that the defendant knew that his false testimony was false. The Court of Appeals had held that the truthful testimony could not be used consistently with the fifth amendment privilege. The Supreme Court reversed. Justice Rehnquist wrote for the Court:

> The principle that the Fifth Amendment privilege against compulsory self-incrimination provides no protection for the commission of perjury has frequently been cited without any elaboration as to its underlying rationale. . . . Its doctrinal foundation . . . is traceable to Glickstein v. United States, 222 U.S. 139, 142, 32 S.Ct. 71, 73, 56 L.Ed. 128 (1911). *Glickstein* stated that the Fifth Amendment "does not endow the person who testifies with a license to commit perjury," and that statement has been so often repeated in our cases as to be firmly established constitutional law. But just as we have refused to read literally the broad dicta of *Counselman,* supra, we are likewise unwilling to decide this case solely upon an epigram contained in *Glickstein,* supra. Thus, even if, as the Court of Appeals said, a perjury prosecution is but a "narrow exception" to the principle that a witness should be treated as if he had remained silent, it does not follow that the Court of Appeals was correct in its view of the [inadmissibility of the truthful testimony.]

* * *

> [W]e conclude that the Fifth Amendment does not prevent the use of respondent's immunized testimony at his trial for false swearing because, at the time he was granted immunity, the privilege would not have protected him against false testimony that he later might decide to give. Respondent's assertion of his Fifth Amendment privilege arose from his claim that the questions relating to his connection with the Chestnut Hill auto dealership would tend to incriminate him. The government consequently granted him "use" immunity under § 6002, which prevents the use

---

4. 445 U.S. 115, 100 S.Ct. 948, 63 L.Ed. 2d 250 (1980).

and derivative use of his testimony with respect to any subsequent criminal case except prosecutions for perjury and false swearing offenses, in exchange for his compelled testimony.

The government has kept its part of the bargain; this is a perjury prosecution and not any other kind of criminal prosecution. The Court of Appeals agreed that such a prosecution might be maintained, but as noted above severely limited the admissibility of immunized testimony to prove the government's case. We believe that it could not be fairly said that respondent, at the time he asserted his privilege and was consequently granted immunity, was confronted with more than a "trifling or imaginary" hazard of compelled self-incrimination as a result of the possibility that he might commit perjury during the course of his immunized testimony.

[There] is no doctrine of "anticipatory perjury." In the criminal law, both a culpable mens rea and a criminal actus reus are generally required for an offense to occur. Similarly, a future intention to commit perjury or to make false statements if granted immunity because of a claim of compulsory self-incrimination is not by itself sufficient to create a "substantial and 'real'" hazard that permits invocation of the Fifth Amendment. Therefore, neither the immunity statute nor the Fifth Amendment preclude the use of respondent's immunized testimony at a subsequent prosecution for making false statements, so long as that testimony conforms to otherwise applicable rules of evidence. The exception of a perjury prosecution from the use that may be made of immunized testimony may be a narrow one, but it is also a complete one. The Court of Appeals having held otherwise, its judgment is accordingly

Reversed.

Query. Do you agree with Justice Rehnquist's theory for why immunity for use in a perjury prosecution need not be given? Is the theory consistent with the view expressed in *Kastigar* that the federal immunity statute "leaves the witness and the prosecutorial authorities in substantially the same position as if the witness had claimed the Fifth Amendment privilege"? Suppose that an immunized witness could not be prosecuted for perjury? What effect might this have on the utility of immunity statutes?

(4) *Fear of Foreign Prosecution.* Can a witness given immunity under § 6002 still refuse to answer questions on the ground that the answers could subject the witness to prosecution in a foreign country? As federal prosecutors have grown more aggressive in investigating crimes with foreign conduct or effects—from insider trading to international drug cartels—this issue has grown in importance.

In *Zicarelli v. New Jersey State Comm'n of Investigation*,[5] decided the same day as *Kastigar*, the Supreme Court granted certiorari to decide the application of the fifth amendment in the context of a

---

5. 406 U.S. 472, 92 S.Ct. 1670, 32 L.Ed. 2d 234 (1972).

potential foreign prosecution. The Court found, however, that there was no "real and substantial fear" of foreign prosecution and, accordingly, the witness was not entitled to assert the fifth amendment even if it applied in this context.[6] The Court, therefore, did not reach the underlying constitutional issue. Most subsequent lower federal court decisions have similarly concentrated on the issue of fear of foreign prosecution, and have generally been able to avoid the constitutional issue by finding that there was no real and substantial fear.[7]

One case which did reach the constitutional issue is *United States v. (Under Seal).*[8] This case involved a grand jury investigation of corruption in arms contracts with the Philippines. The subpoenaed witnesses, Irene and Gregorio Araneta (the daughter and son-in-law of Ferdinand Marcos), were given immunity under §§ 6002 and 6003. They still refused to answer questions, pointing out that criminal charges had already been filed against them in the Philippines. The Court of Appeals for the Fourth Circuit agreed that they faced a real and substantial fear of foreign prosecution. The Court was thus required to reach the constitutional issue:

> By its terms, the Fifth Amendment does not purport to have effect in foreign countries; and ordinarily, unless specifically stated otherwise, a provision of domestic law, statutory or constitutional, is deemed to apply only to the jurisdiction which enacts it. Thus it seems quite certain that the Fifth Amendment would not prohibit the use of compelled self-incriminatory evidence in a Philippine prosecution if Philippine law countenanced its use.
>
> To determine whether the Fifth Amendment protects from compelled self-incrimination a witness immunized under domestic law but exposed to a substantial risk of foreign prosecution, we reason by analogy to the extension of the Fifth Amendment to prosecutions under state law. When the Fifth Amendment was applied only to the federal government, the Supreme Court held that the protection it afforded did not forbid the United States from compelling testimony from a witness that would incriminate him under state law, nor did it forbid a state government from compelling testimony that would incriminate under federal law. Only when the Fifth Amendment was held applicable to the states, Malloy v. Hogan, 378 U.S. 1, 84 S.Ct. 1489, 12 L.Ed.2d 653 (1964), was the privilege held to protect a witness in state or federal court from incriminating himself under either federal or state law. See Murphy v. Waterfront Commission, [infra this Casebook, p. 514.]

6. For a discussion of the conditions under which a witness may assert the fifth amendment, see p. 653, infra.

7. See, e.g., United States v. Klimavicius, 847 F.2d 28 (1st Cir.1988); United States v. Rubin, 836 F.2d 1096 (8th Cir. 1988); United States v. Joudis, 800 F.2d 159 (7th Cir.1986); United States v. Gilboe, 699 F.2d 71 (2d Cir.1983). Assertion of the privilege has been allowed by several district courts. See Mishima v. United States, 507 F.Supp. 131 (D.Alaska 1981); In re Cardassi, 351 F.Supp. 1080 (D.Conn. 1972) (Newman, J.).

8. 794 F.2d 920 (4th Cir.), certiorari denied sub nom. Araneta v. United States 479 U.S. 924, 107 S.Ct. 331, 93 L.Ed.2d 303 (1986).

From this history, we conclude that the Fifth Amendment privilege applies only where the sovereign compelling the testimony and the sovereign using the testimony are both restrained by the Fifth Amendment from compelling self-incrimination. See, Note, The Reach Of The Fifth Amendment Privilege When Domestically Compelled Testimony May Be Used in A Foreign Country's Court, 69 Va.L.Rev. 875 (1983). Since the Fifth Amendment would not prohibit the use of compelled incriminating testimony in a Philippine court, it affords an immunized witness no privilege not to testify before a federal grand jury on the ground that his testimony will incriminate him under Philippine law.

The privilege against compulsory self-incrimination serves a dual purpose. It protects individual dignity and conscience, and it preserves the accusatorial nature of our system of criminal justice. . . . Our decision that the Aranetas cannot find shelter in the Fifth Amendment does not imperil these values. Insofar as the privilege exists to promote the criminal justice system established by our Constitution, it can have no application to a prosecution by a foreign sovereign not similarly constrained. Comity among nations dictates that the United States not intrude into the law enforcement activities of other countries conducted abroad. With regard to insulating the individual from the moral hazards of self-incrimination, perjury or contempt, the United States has done everything in its power to relieve the pressure by granting the Aranetas use and derivative use immunity. Just as comity among nations requires the United States to respect the law enforcement processes of other nations, our own national sovereignty would be compromised if our system of criminal justice were made to depend on the actions of foreign government beyond our control. It would be intolerable to require the United States to forego evidence legitimately within its reach solely because a foreign power could deploy this evidence in a fashion not permitted within this country. . . .

* * *

Fully mindful of our obligation to decide only the case before us, we nevertheless feel compelled to note what is not at issue in this case. First, there has been no attempt to show that the United States inspired, instigated or controls the Philippine prosecution. In addition, petitioners have not suggested that the United States, in compelling their testimony under a grant of immunity, pursues no legitimate purpose of its own, even if it also has an intention to assist a foreign government whose continued good will is of great strategic importance. In short, petitioners have not presented to us a claim of American participation in a foreign prosecution, either actually, through a joint venture with foreign law enforcement officials, or constructively, by means of employing such individuals as agents. The case before us does not require us to address either of these factual patterns, as we express no views on them at this time.

Queries. The Court of Appeals refers to the principle of "comity" as preventing the United States from intruding into law enforcement in other countries. How would a decision that the fifth amendment protects the witnesses in this case intrude into law enforcement in the Philippines? Suppose that the Court had found that the witnesses were constitutionally entitled to assert the fifth amendment privilege? What would have been the result in this case? Reconsider this question after reading the next case, *Murphy v. Waterfront Comm'n.*

MURPHY v. WATERFRONT COMMISSION
Supreme Court of the United States, 1964.
378 U.S. 52, 84 S.Ct. 1594, 12 L.Ed.2d 678.

MR. JUSTICE GOLDBERG delivered the opinion of the Court.

We have held today that the Fifth Amendment privilege against self-incrimination must be deemed fully applicable to the States through the Fourteenth Amendment. Malloy v. Hogan. This case presents a related issue: whether one jurisdiction within our federal structure may compel a witness, whom it has immunized from prosecution under its laws, to give testimony which might then be used to convict him of a crime against another such jurisdiction.[9]

Petitioners were subpoenaed to testify at a hearing conducted by the Waterfront Commission of New York Harbor concerning a work stoppage at the Hoboken, New Jersey, piers. After refusing to respond to certain questions about the stoppage on the ground that the answers might tend to incriminate them, petitioners were granted immunity from prosecution under the laws of New Jersey and New York. Notwithstanding this grant of immunity, they still refused to respond to the questions on the ground that the answers might tend to incriminate them under *federal* law, to which the grant of immunity did not purport to extend. Petitioners were thereupon held in civil and criminal contempt of court. The New Jersey Supreme Court . . . held that a State may constitutionally compel a witness to give testimony which might be used in a federal prosecution against him.

Since a grant of immunity is valid only if it is coextensive with the scope of the privilege against self-incrimination, Counselman v. Hitchcock, we must now decide the fundamental constitutional question of whether, absent an immunity provision, one jurisdiction in our federal structure may compel a witness to give testimony which might incriminate him under the laws of another jurisdiction. The answer to this question must depend, of course, on whether such an application of the privilege promotes or defeats its policies and purposes.

---

9. [Court's footnote 1.] Since the privilege is now fully applicable to the State and to the Federal Government, the basic issue is the same whether the testimony is compelled by the Federal Government and used by a State, or compelled by a State and used by the Federal Government.

The privilege against self-incrimination "registers an important advance in the development of our liberty—'one of the great landmarks in man's struggle to make himself civilized.'" Ullmann v. United States, 350 U.S. 422, 426. It reflects many of our fundamental values and most noble aspirations: our unwillingness to subject those suspected of crime to the cruel trilemma of self-accusation, perjury or contempt; our preference for an accusatorial rather than an inquisitorial system of criminal justice; our fear that self-incriminating statements will be elicited by inhumane treatment and abuses; our sense of fair play which dictates "a fair state-individual balance by requiring the government to leave the individual alone until good cause is shown for disturbing him and by requiring the government in its contest with the individual to shoulder the entire load," 8 Wigmore, Evidence (McNaughton rev., 1961), 317; our respect for the inviolability of the human personality and of the right of each individual "to a private enclave where he may lead a private life," United States v. Grunewald, 233 F.2d 556, 581–582 (Frank, J., dissenting), rev'd 353 U.S. 391; our distrust of self-deprecatory statements; and our realization that the privilege, while sometimes "a shelter to the guilty," is often "a protection to the innocent." Quinn v. United States, 349 U.S. 155, 162.

Most, if not all, of these policies and purposes are defeated when a witness "can be whipsawed into incriminating himself under both state and federal law even though" the constitutional privilege against self-incrimination is applicable to each. This has become especially true in our age of "cooperative federalism," where the Federal and State Governments are waging a united front against many types of criminal activity.

Respondent contends, however, that we should adhere to the "established rule" that the constitutional privilege against self-incrimination does not protect a witness in one jurisdiction against being compelled to give testimony which could be used to convict him in another jurisdiction . . .

Our decision today in Malloy v. Hogan, supra, necessitates a reconsideration of this rule.[10] [After reviewing pertinent Supreme Court cases and their English antecedents, the Court held that there was "no continuing legal vitality to, or historical justification for, the rule that one jurisdiction within our federal structure may compel a witness to give testimony which could be used to convict him of a crime in another jurisdiction."]

We must now decide what effect this holding has on existing state immunity legislation. In Counselman v. Hitchcock, this Court consid-

10. [Court's footnote 6.] The constitutional privilege against self-incrimination has two primary interrelated facets: The Government may not use compulsion to elicit self-incriminating statements; and the Government may not permit the use in a criminal trial of self-incriminating statements elicited by compulsion. In every "whipsaw" case, either the "compelling" government or the "using" government is a State, and, until today, the States were not deemed fully bound by the privilege against self-incrimination. . . .

ered a federal statute which provided that no "evidence obtained from a party or witness by means of a judicial proceeding . . . shall be given in evidence, or in any manner used against him . . . in any court of the United States. . . ." Notwithstanding this statute, appellant, claiming his privilege against self-incrimination, refused to answer certain questions before a federal grand jury. The Court said "that legislation cannot abridge a constitutional privilege, and that it cannot replace or supply one, at least unless it is so broad as to have the same extent in scope and effect." Applying this principle to the facts of that case, the Court upheld appellant's refusal to answer on the ground that the statute:

> "could not, and would not, prevent the use of his testimony to search out other testimony to be used in evidence against him or his property, in a criminal proceeding in such court . . .,"

that it:

> "could not prevent the obtaining and the use of witnesses and evidence which should be attributable directly to the testimony he might give under compulsion, and on which he might be convicted, when otherwise, and if he had refused to answer, he could not possibly have been convicted . . .,"

and that it:

> "affords no protection against that use of compelled testimony which consists in gaining therefrom a knowledge of the details of a crime, and of sources of information which may supply other means of convicting the witness or party."

Applying the holding of that case to our holdings today that the privilege against self-incrimination protects a state witness against federal prosecution, and that "the same standards must determine whether [a witness'] silence in either a federal or state proceeding is justified," Malloy v. Hogan, we hold the constitutional rule to be that a state witness may not be compelled to give testimony which may be incriminating under federal law unless the compelled testimony and its fruits cannot be used in any manner by federal officials in connection with a criminal prosecution against him. We conclude, moreover, that in order to implement this constitutional rule and accommodate the interests of the State and Federal Governments in investigating and prosecuting crime, the Federal Government must be prohibited from making any such use of compelled testimony and its fruits.[11] This exclusionary rule, while permitting the States to secure information necessary for effective law enforcement, leaves the witness and the Federal Government in substantially the same position as if the witness had claimed his privilege in the absence of a state grant of immunity.

---

11. [Court's footnote 18.] Once a defendant demonstrates that he has testified, under a state grant of immunity, to matters related to the federal prosecution, the federal authorities have the burden of showing that their evidence is not tainted by establishing that they had an independent, legitimate source for the disputed evidence.

It follows that petitioners here may now be compelled to answer the questions propounded to them. . . .

NOTES AND QUERIES

(1) *Queries.* Was the remedy chosen in *Murphy* appropriate? By creating an exclusionary rule, restricting future use by the federal government of this testimony, the Court, in effect, is creating a judicially-fashioned federal immunity outside the structure provided by Congress in §§ 6002 and 6003. Might this confer immunity on witnesses that federal prosecutors would prefer not to give? Note that federal and state governments frequently have statutory authority to investigate similar crimes, particularly in the business crime area. Is the independent source rule (set out in *Murphy* and reaffirmed in *Kastigar*) adequate protection for federal interests?

Consider the Supreme Court's later views in *Pillsbury Co. v. Conboy*.[12] This case involved a civil deposition at which plaintiffs' counsel sought to examine a witness (Conboy) based on his grand jury transcript. Conboy had testified before the grand jury pursuant to a grant of immunity under §§ 6002 and 6003. At the civil deposition Conboy refused to answer questions based on his grand jury transcript, asserting his fifth amendment privilege. Plaintiffs' counsel argued that the answers would have been derived from the immunized testimony and therefore should be excluded under the original grant of immunity. The Court disagreed, holding that the witness had no immunity under § 6002 for his deposition testimony. Accordingly, the witness could assert his fifth amendment privilege.

Justice Powell, in the plurality opinion, wrote:

> Use immunity was intended to immunize and exclude from a subsequent criminal trial only that information to which the Government expressly has surrendered future use. If the Government is engaged in an ongoing investigation of the particular activity at issue, immunizing new information (e.g., the answers to questions in a case like this one) may make it more difficult to show in a subsequent prosecution that similar information was obtained from wholly independent sources. If a District Court were to conclude in a subsequent civil proceeding that the prior immunity order extended to civil deposition testimony closely tracking the immunized testimony, it in effect could invest the deponent with transactional immunity on matters about which he testified at the immunized proceedings. This is precisely the kind of immunity Congress intended to prohibit. The purpose of § 6002 was to limit the scope of immunity to the level that is constitutionally required, as well as to limit the use of immunity to those cases in which the Attorney General, or officials designated by him, determine that gaining the

---

12. 459 U.S. 248, 103 S.Ct. 608, 74 L.Ed. 2d 430 (1983). Pillsbury Co. v. Conboy is explored further infra, p. 645.

witness's testimony outweighs the loss of the opportunity for criminal prosecution of that witness.

Petitioners' interpretation of § 6002 also places substantial risks on the deponent. Unless the grant of immunity assures a witness that his incriminating testimony will not be used against him in a subsequent criminal prosecution, the witness has not received the certain protection of his Fifth Amendment privilege that he has been forced to exchange. No court has authority to immunize a witness. That responsibility, as we have noted, is peculiarly an executive one, and only the Attorney General or a designated officer of the Department of Justice has authority to grant use immunity. See 18 U.S.C. §§ 6002, 6003. Nor should a court, at the time of the civil testimony, pre-determine the decision of the court in a subsequent criminal prosecution on the question whether the Government has met its burden of proving "that the evidence it proposes to use is derived from a legitimate source wholly independent of the compelled testimony." Kastigar, 406 U.S., at 460, 92 S.Ct., at 1664. Yet in holding Conboy in contempt for his Fifth Amendment silence, the District Court below essentially predicted that a court in any future criminal prosecution of Conboy will be obligated to protect against evidentiary use of the deposition testimony petitioners seek. We do not think such a predictive judgment is enough.

Petitioners' interpretation of § 6002 imposes risks on the deponent whether or not the deposition testimony properly can be used against him in a subsequent criminal prosecution. Accordingly, the District Court's compulsion order in this case, in the absence of statutory authority or a new grant of immunity by the United States Attorney, cannot be justified by the subsequent exclusion of the compelled testimony. . . .

The result of compelling testimony—whether it is immunized or excluded—is that the Government's interests, as well as the witness's, suffer. Reliance on judicial exclusion of nonimmunized testimony would be inconsistent with the congressional policy of leaving the granting of immunity to the Executive Branch.

(2) *Defense Witness Immunity.* Under § 6003, an immunity order for testimony in court can be obtained only upon the request of a United States Attorney, which request must be approved by a senior official in the Justice Department. Suppose that the defendant, seeking to prove innocence, wishes to call a witness to testify in his or her defense, but the witness will assert the fifth amendment. Should the defendant be able to provide the witness with immunity so as to compel the testimony?

In *Government of Virgin Islands v. Smith* [13] the Court of Appeals for the Third Circuit stated that the due process clause required an immunity grant to a defense witness in two situations: 1) where the

---

13. 615 F.2d 964 (3d Cir.1980).

government refused to grant such an immunity pursuant to a "deliberate intention of distorting the judicial factfinding process"; or 2) where the preferred testimony is "clearly exculpatory" and "essential," and there are "no strong governmental interests which countervail against a grant of immunity." [14] *Smith* involved the testimony of a witness which inculpated the witness but exculpated three of the four defendants on trial. The witness was a youth under the jurisdiction of juvenile authorities who were willing to grant him immunity so long as the United States Attorney had no objection; the United States Attorney, for reasons never disclosed, refused consent. The Court of Appeals remanded the case for an evidentiary hearing to determine whether immunity was required under either theory.

In *United States v. Turkish*,[15] however, the Court of Appeals for the Second Circuit declined to follow *Smith*. Judge Newman wrote with regard to the due process theory:

> . . . The appeal to constitutionally protected fairness proceeds from two basic arguments. First, . . . unfairness may inhere in some situations because the Government's grant of use immunity to its witnesses affords it an advantage over the defendant's ability to present a defense. Secondly, to the extent that a trial is viewed as a search for the truth, denial of defense witness immunity may in some circumstances unfairly thwart that objective.
>
> The first contention, based on equalizing the powers of the prosecution and the defense, is entirely unpersuasive. A criminal prosecution, unlike a civil trial, is in no sense a symmetrical proceeding. The prosecution assumes substantial affirmative obligations and accepts numerous restrictions, neither of which are imposed on the defendant. The prosecution must prove the defendant's guilt beyond a reasonable doubt to the satisfaction of all the jurors; it may not obtain the defendant's testimony, suppress exculpatory evidence, nor retry the defendant after acquittal, even though errors prejudicial to the Government occurred. The defendant, by contrast, may prevail without offering any proof at all; he need not disclose whatever inculpatory evidence he discovers, may avoid conviction by persuading a single juror that reasonable doubt exists, and may challenge a conviction by direct appeal and subsequent collateral attack.
>
> The system of criminal law administration involves not only this procedural imbalance in favor of the defendant, but also important aspects of the Government's law enforcement power that

---

14. The court of appeals stated that the remedy in the first situation would be to require the United States Attorney to grant immunity under §§ 6002 and 6003 or face dismissal of the charges against the defendants; the remedy in the second situation would be to adopt "judicial" immunity and order that the witness's statements could not be used against him in any future proceeding.

15. 623 F.2d 769 (2d Cir.1980), certiorari denied 449 U.S. 1077, 101 S.Ct. 856, 66 L.Ed.2d 800 (1981).

are not available to the defendant. Subject to constitutional and statutory limits, the Government may arrest suspects, search private premises, wiretap telephones, and deploy the investigative resources of large public agencies. Few would seriously argue that the public interest would be well served either by extending all of these powers to those accused of crime or by equalizing the procedural burdens and restrictions of prosecution and defendant at trial. . . .

The second argument, based on the need to pursue the truth, has somewhat greater force. As a general rule the Government is properly obliged to divulge exculpatory evidence. Brady v. Maryland, 373 U.S. 83, 83 S.Ct. 1194, 10 L.Ed.2d 215 (1963). That principle, however, has heretofore been limited to evidence in the Government's possession and has not been extended to create a Government obligation to assist the defense in extracting from others evidence the Government does not have. Moreover the concept of a trial as a search for the truth has always failed of full realization whenever important facts are shielded from disclosure because of a lawful privilege. . . . Nevertheless, it must be acknowledged that since the advent of immunity statutes, the self-incrimination privilege, unlike any other, can be displaced without any impairment of the legally protected rights of the holder of the privilege. And unlike transactional immunity, use immunity does not improve the legal position of the holder of the privilege; it leaves his legal rights precisely as they were before he testified. However, the grant of use immunity does implicate public interests, and any assessment of a claim for defense witness use immunity must reckon with those public concerns.

In the first place, while the prosecution remains theoretically free under *Kastigar* to prosecute a witness granted use immunity, the obstacles to a successful prosecution can be substantial. The Government has a "heavy burden" to prove that its evidence against the immunized witness has not been obtained as a result of his immunized testimony. While this burden can be met by cataloguing or "freezing" the evidence known to the Government prior to the immunized testimony, that technique is not available when continuing investigations disclose vital evidence after, though not resulting from, the immunized testimony. Moreover, to meet its burden of proving that prosecution of the immunized witness was not benefitted in any way by his immunized testimony the prosecutors most knowledgeable about an investigation may in some circumstances be obliged to forgo any further contact with the witness and arrange for a new team of investigators and prosecutors to pursue the case against him.

Secondly, awareness of the obstacles to successful prosecution of an immunized witness may force the prosecution to curtail its cross-examination of the witness in the case on trial to narrow the scope of the testimony that the witness will later claim tainted his subsequent prosecution. While the witness cannot prevent prosecution and secure an immunity "bath" by broadening the scope of his answers, as he could if testifying under a grant of transactional immunity, his fulsome answers may substantially lessen the likelihood of any successful prosecution.

Finally, there is considerable force to the Government's apprehension that defense witness immunity could create opportunities for undermining the administration of justice by inviting cooperative perjury among law violators. Co-defendants could secure use immunity for each other, and each immunized witness could exonerate his co-defendant at a separate trial by falsely accepting sole responsibility for the crime, secure in the knowledge that his admission could not be used at his own trial for the substantive offense. The threat of a perjury conviction, with penalties frequently far below substantive offenses, could not be relied upon to prevent such tactics. Moreover, this maneuver would substantially undermine the opportunity for joint trials, with consequent expense, delay, and burden upon disinterested witnesses and the judicial system.

How these substantial concerns are to be weighed against the defendant's interest in securing truthful exculpatory testimony through defense witness immunity turns in large part upon whether the balancing of these interests is appropriately a judicial function. The Government suggests it is not, contending that the granting of immunity is pre-eminently a function of the Executive Branch. On the other hand, the judiciary has constitutional responsibilities for the fairness of a trial. . . . Judicially created use immunity, albeit premised on constitutional considerations, was fashioned by the Supreme Court in *Murphy v. Waterfront Commission*. . . .

However, a court cannot determine whether any constitutional provision requires a judicial grant of use immunity without assessing the implications upon the Executive Branch, both those that flow from a grant of use immunity and those that flow from an adjudication of whether such immunity might be appropriate in a particular case. The concerns previously expressed about the risk to other successful prosecutions are matters normally better assessed by prosecutors than by judges. Surely a court is in no position to weigh the public interest in the comparative worth of prosecuting a defendant or his witness, although if a court decides that immunity is required, it can always leave that ultimate assessment with the prosecutor by advising that trial of the defendant will continue only if the witness's testimony is immunized. But confronting the prosecutor with a choice between terminating prosecution of the defendant or jeopardizing prosecution of the witness is not a task congenial to the judicial function.

. . . Either [of the two inquiries required in *Smith*] will propel a trial court into uncharted waters. Focusing upon the prosecutor's intent will often lead to exploration and premature disclosure of the pending status of an investigation against the witness. Moreover, a prosecutor without enough evidence to seek indictment of a witness may legitimately prefer to maintain his option to prosecute on the basis of later information. . . . In the extraordinary fact situation presented by the *Smith* case, where the prosecutor opposing use immunity does not even have jurisdiction to prosecute the witness, the public interest in not granting defense witness immunity appears to be non-existent. But in most situations where defense witness immunity is likely to be sought, some legitimate opposing prosecution interest will exist, and constitutional fairness is not a satisfactory standard against which to assess such interests.

. . . Without precluding the possibility of some circumstances not now anticipated, we simply do not find in the Due Process Clause a general requirement that defense witness immunity must be ordered whenever it seems fair to grant it. The essential fairness required by the Fifth Amendment guards the defendant against overreaching by the prosecutor. . . . It does not create general obligations for prosecutors or courts to obtain evidence protected by lawful privileges.

* * *[16]

(3) *Enforcing "Non–Statutory" Grants of Immunity.* As the preceding cases indicate, there is some tension between viewing immunity as the exclusive prerogative of the Executive acting pursuant to §§ 6002 and 6003, and the need that courts find on occasion to fashion non-statutory immunity. It also appears that even the Executive does not always wish to be confined to the structure of § 6002. An example of the government's practice of granting non-statutory forms of immunity is illustrated in *United States v. Deerfield Specialty Papers.*[17] In that case, Hollis Fowler, one of the defendants, moved to dismiss the indictment on the ground that it was obtained directly or derivatively from information provided the government under a grant of immunity expressed in the following letter written by a Department of Justice Attorney:

---

16. For an early case demonstrating similar reluctance to grant defense witness immunity, see United States v. Standard Sanitary Mfg. Co., 187 Fed. 232 (E.D.Pa. 1911) (despite fact that antitrust immunity statute did not explicitly provide that only government could grant immunity, court refuses to allow defendants in civil suit to compel co-defendants to testify pursuant to immunity; otherwise, might create an immunity bath of all defendants). For later defense witness immunity cases, see, e.g., United States v. Hooks, 848 F.2d 785 (7th Cir.1988) (no showing of distortion of fact finding process by failure to grant immunity); United States v. Lord, 711 F.2d 887 (9th Cir.1983) (accepting prosecutorial abuse theory).

17. 501 F.Supp. 796 (E.D.Pa.1980).

February 22, 1979

Dear Mr. Fowler:

This is to confirm our appointment for February 28 at 12 o'clock. As we discussed, based upon your representation of your medical history and your offer of cooperation with the Government, the Antitrust Division does not intend to prosecute you for any violation of the antitrust laws based on information or testimony you may give in connection with this matter.

If you have any questions, please call me collect at (215) 597–7413.

          Sincerely yours,

          Norma B. Carter

          Attorney

          Middle Atlantic Office

          Antitrust Division

The District Court wrote:

    The government contends that this letter in no way constituted an informal grant of immunity (or an agreement not to prosecute) but rather was merely an invitation for a proffer. According to the government, "Fowler was never told, either on the telephone, by letter, or during the interview, that he would never be subject to prosecution." For the reasons that follow, the Court finds the government's position unpersuasive and concludes that some type of bargain had been struck.

    A review of the language contained in the letter reveals that some type of bargain had been reached by the government and the defendant. In essence, the government promised that it would not prosecute the defendant for violations of the antitrust laws so long as the defendant fulfilled its promise of cooperation. [Thus,] the language of the letter suggests an agreement not to prosecute rather than a blind grant of informal immunity.

          * * *

    In light of the Court's decision that indeed a bargain had been struck between the government and the defendant Hollis P. Fowler, the inquiry turns to the manner and method of considering the defendant's allegations and, if proven, their effects. [A] characterization whether the bargain constitutes a grant of immunity or an agreement not to prosecute dictates the nature of the procedure eventually utilized. If the bargain is determined to constitute a grant of immunity, the procedure adopted to test the defendant's allegations will be of a nature prescribed in Kastigar v. United States, wherein the government bears the burden of establishing that information supportive of the indictment was derived from a source or sources independent of the defendant. If the bargain is determined to constitute merely an agreement not to prosecute, a procedural device similar to a *Kastigar* hearing may be utilized wherein the government bears the burden of establishing that the defendant has breached the agreement.[18] Notwithstanding this cursory dissertation, the Court deems it desirable and, in fact, necessary to defer characterization of the pact, and the conduct of a hearing concomittantly required, until a time post trial. . . . This ruling is made notwithstanding the suggestion made in *Kastigar* that such matters should be considered on a pretrial basis.

* * *

In the present case, the Court finds that the conduct of a *Kastigar* or other type hearing will cause virtually the complete exposure of the government's case. Moreover, and as a result, the trial process will become extremely fragmented. The Court is mindful of the considerable amount of time and money that the defendant will expend in his defense but views the government's prejudice resultant from exposure of its case and fragmentation of the process as at the minimum, countervailing. Accordingly, the hearing to determine the characterization of the agreement and the merits of the defendant's contentions will be delayed pending the completion of trial.

(4) *Talking to the Government.* The immunity statute covers statements made by a witness in a very formal setting, e.g., testifying before a grand jury. Of course, statements may be made to government agents in less formal settings. For example, when counsel discusses a case with a government prosecutor, does counsel run any risk that statements made during the course of such conversations might later be used against the client? Consider *United States v. Valencia*, 826 F.2d 169 (2d Cir.1987):

JON O. NEWMAN, CIRCUIT JUDGE:

This appeal presents the issue, rarely litigated, whether statements made by defense counsel during informal conversations with a prosecutor may be admitted against a criminal defendant as admissions by an agent. The issue arises on an appeal by the United States from a pretrial order of the District Court for the Eastern District of New York (Henry Bramwell, Judge) excluding from evidence out-of-court statements made by a defendant's counsel in his efforts to secure bail for his client. Under the circumstances of this case, we conclude that Judge Bramwell did not exceed his discretion in excluding the attorney's statements, and we therefore affirm the ruling of the District Court.

---

18. [From Court's footnote 3.] Although the difference between a grant of immunity and an agreement not to prosecute may appear to be purely a matter of semantics, it is far more in reality. . . . [I]n the former, the government must establish evidence derived from sources independent of the defendant and supportive of the indictment while, in the latter, the government bears the burden of presenting evidence that the defendant failed to fulfill his part of the bargain.

Background

Freddy Valencia is charged with conspiracy to possess and possession with intent to distribute cocaine. . . . The theory of the prosecution is that Valencia conspired with co-defendant Gladys Bolivar to sell a kilogram of cocaine to a Government informant. On August 19 and 20, 1986, Bolivar negotiated the sale with the informant during a series of phone calls. She later met him by arrangement in a supermarket in Queens and returned there to meet him a second time to deliver the narcotics. Valencia was seen joining Bolivar during the first meeting. He and Bolivar then left the supermarket together in a car driven by Valencia, and he returned with her in the same car for the second meeting. When the informant gave the prearranged signal during the second meeting, Drug Enforcement Administration (DEA) agents arrested both Bolivar and Valencia.

Valencia retained attorney Michael Maloney to represent him. In late August and early September 1986, Maloney initiated several conversations with the case agent and the Assistant United States Attorney (AUSA) in an effort to persuade the Government to release Valencia on bail. One reason for setting bail, he argued, was that his client was innocent. Maloney represented that Valencia had not met Bolivar prior to August 20 and that his encounter with her that day was entirely innocent. In a telephone conversation with the AUSA, Maloney elaborated his contentions. According to Maloney, Valencia first saw Bolivar in the Queens supermarket and decided to try to "pick her up." He approached her and introduced himself. When, two hours later, he happened to see her again standing near a bus stop, he offered her a ride, which she accepted. The Government contends that in recounting this story, Maloney told the AUSA that he was repeating what his client had told him.

The Government later obtained evidence that contradicted Maloney's account of the facts and proved that Bolivar and Valencia had had a longstanding relationship since at least 1985. The Government sought a pretrial ruling that Maloney's remarks were admissible at trial as false exculpatory statements attributable to Valencia. It contended that because Maloney made those statements while acting on Valencia's behalf and within the scope of his employment, they were admissible as admissions of a party-opponent under the agency exceptions to the hearsay rule. Fed.R.Evid. 801(d)(2)(C), (D). The Government sought the right to use Maloney's statements both as substantive evidence to show Valencia's consciousness of guilt and as impeaching evidence if Valencia testified.

Ruling from the bench, Judge Bramwell denied the Government's motion. He ruled that Maloney's statements "may not be directly attributed to the defendant" and that their use would be "contrary to the attorney/client privilege." "To rule as the government asks," he cautioned, "would set a dangerous precedent for the admission of all informal, out-of-court statements by attorneys against their clients." The Government appeals from Judge Bramwell's order. . . .

Discussion

* * *

The Government contends that Maloney's statements to the prosecutor are admissible against Valencia under Rule 801(d)(2) of the Federal Rules of Evidence as admissions of a party-opponent. The Government relies alternatively on subsection 801(d)(2)(C), "a statement by a person authorized by [a party] to make a statement concerning the subject," or subsection 801(d)(2)(D), "a statement by [the party's] agent or servant concerning a matter within the scope of his agency or employment, made during the existence of the relationship." In this case, the Government gains nothing from subsection (C). The only basis relied on for a conclusion that Valencia authorized Maloney to make the offered statements is the fact that Maloney was Valencia's agent, that the subject matter was within the scope of the agency, and that the statements were made during the agency relationship. Thus, the Government's appeal stands or falls on whether Judge Bramwell erred in declining to consider the statements admissible under Rule 801(d)(2)(D).

This Court has recognized that "[s]tatements made by an attorney concerning a matter within his employment *may* be admissible against the party retaining the attorney." United States v. Margiotta, 662 F.2d at 142 (emphasis added) (citations omitted). However, in United States v. McKeon, 738 F.2d 26 (2d Cir.1984), we emphasized that care must be exercised in the criminal context in determining under what circumstances attorney statements may be used against a client, and we declined "to subject such statements to the more expansive practices sometimes permitted under the rule allowing use of admissions by a party-opponent." Our concern arose because the routine use of attorney statements against a criminal defendant risks impairment of the privilege against self-incrimination, the right to counsel of one's choice,[19] and the right to the effective assistance of counsel. In *McKeon* we considered whether an attorney's description of facts during his opening statement in a criminal trial was admissible against his client on retrial to show consciousness of guilt arising from a change in the defense claim between the first trial and the retrial. Noting the analogous example of superseded pleadings in civil

---

19. [Court's footnote 1.] In this case, the Government acknowledges that a ruling allowing Maloney's statements in evidence may require his disqualification as trial counsel. [Attorneys who are expected to testify on behalf of a client at trial are generally precluded from representing that client at trial.—Ed.]

cases, which are viewed as admissions of a party-opponent and are admissible in both the original and subsequent cases, we concluded that opening statements were not per se inadmissible in criminal cases. Nevertheless, "to avoid trenching upon other important policies," we declined to permit expansive use of prior jury argument at a prior trial. Only after canvassing the precise circumstances of the case did we approve the admission at retrial of counsel's opening argument at the prior trial.

The pending case differs from *McKeon* in several respects. First, the statements the Government seeks to use were not made in court but during the course of informal discussions between prosecutor and defense counsel concerning the defendant's release on bail. Unlike an opening statement, which is transcribed, or a written pleading, the statements of Maloney would have to be proved through the testimony of a person who heard them, thereby generating dispute as to precisely what was said. Moreover, a pleading or an opening statement to a jury is more likely to be worded with precision than informal remarks made during discussions with a prosecutor.

Second, unlike *McKeon,* the admission of Maloney's statements would pose some threat to chilling the prospects for plea negotiations. Though the statements were not made during the course of plea negotiations and therefore were not automatically excludable under Fed.R.Evid. 410, see Fed.R.Crim.P. 11(e)(6),[20] a statement by defense counsel protesting a client's innocence may often be the preclude to plea negotiations. A district court is entitled to consider whether trial use of informal attorney statements will lessen the prospects for plea negotiation or inhibit frank discussion between defense counsel and prosecutor on various topics that must be freely discussed in the interest of expediting trial preparation and the conduct of the trial.

* * *

In this case the Government's claim to the statements is not strong. The statements are not offered to show admission of an element of the offense, a use that would directly prove the Govern-

---

20. [F.R.Evid. 410 and F.R.Crim.P. 11(e)(6) are identical. They provide:

(6) *Inadmissibility of Pleas, Plea Discussions, and Related Statements.* Except as otherwise provided in this paragraph, evidence of the following is not, in any civil or criminal proceeding, admissible against the defendant who made the plea or was a participant in the plea discussions:

(A) a plea of guilty which was later withdrawn;

(B) a plea of nolo contendre;

(C) any statement made in the course of any proceedings under this rule regarding either of the foregoing pleas; or

(D) any statement made in the course of plea discussions with an attorney for the government which do not result in a plea of guilty or which result in a plea of guilty later withdrawn.

However, such a statement is admissible (i) in any proceeding wherein another statement made in the course of the same plea or plea discussions has been introduced and the statement ought in fairness be considered contemporaneously with it, or (ii) in a criminal proceeding for perjury or false statement if the statement was made by the defendant under oath, on the record, and in the presence of counsel.

—Ed.]

ment's case and expedite the trial. Weighing against use of the statements are the defendant's interests in retaining the services of his counsel, assuring uninhibited discussions between his counsel and the prosecutor, and avoiding the risk of impairing his privilege against self-incrimination. We cannot say that Judge Bramwell exceeded his discretion in a context involving the substantial concerns we have noted. Moreover, the Government had the option, when presented with Maloney's statements, to invite counsel to furnish an affidavit of his client's version of the facts.

The order of the District Court is affirmed.

[JUDGE MESKILL dissented. Among other things, he disputed the majority's view of the effect that admitting these statements might have on "vigorous advocacy":

> Rather than deter advocacy, however, I suggest that admission of Maloney's statements would cause counsel to be more careful in verifying the accuracy of information offered by the client before communicating the client's statements to the government. An attorney who possesses competent and reliable information favorable to his client will rarely be deterred by Rule 801 from vigorously pursuing his client's interests.

In response to the argument that the statements could be excluded because they "would pose some threat to chilling the prospects for plea negotiations," Judge Meskill wrote:

> [At] the time these statements were made, the parties were conducting bail negotiations, not plea negotiations. Statements made during the course of plea negotiations are fully protected from disclosure by Fed.R.Evid. 410. The federal rules do not provide for the automatic exclusion of statements not made during the course of plea negotiations, even if those statements are a "prelude" to plea negotiations as the majority contends here. The majority's solution, therefore, would give protection to statements that the federal rules were not intended to cover.]

B. SEARCH WARRANTS

SCOPE NOTE

A familiar way for the government to obtain evidence is through searches and seizures. Searches and seizures are governed by the fourth amendment, which provides:

> The right of the people to be secure in their persons, houses, papers, and effects, against unreasonable searches and seizures, shall not be violated, and no Warrants shall issue, but upon probable cause, supported by Oath or affirmation, and particularly

describing the place to be searched, and the persons or things to be seized.

Chapter 4 provided an introduction to the fourth amendment, developing the question of how the fourth amendment applies to corporations. This Section of this Chapter will explore the application of the fourth amendment to certain specific problems which arise in the investigation of business crimes. Our focus will be on searches that government agents perform physically (as opposed to "searches" done through subpoena, which will be explored in the next Section).

Although these materials focus on some specialized areas of fourth amendment law, it is nevertheless necessary to keep in mind the basic structure for analyzing a fourth amendment problem.[21]

1) Has there been a fourth amendment search? Since the Supreme Court's 1967 decision in *Katz v. United States*, this has depended on whether the search violated "reasonable" expectations of privacy.[22]

2) If there has been a fourth amendment intrusion, was it done on adequate cause? The fourth amendment generally requires that the search meet a standard of "probable cause."

3) Was the search performed pursuant to a properly issued and executed warrant? The fourth amendment generally requires that a search be performed pursuant to a warrant issued by a "neutral, detached magistrate" describing "with particularity" what is to be searched for and seized.[23]

4) Does the person objecting to the search have standing? Only those whose rights are violated (i.e., whose privacy is violated) may protest.

5) What remedy is proper? The most common remedy is to suppress the use, at trial, of the illegally seized evidence. Victims of illegal searches can also move for the return of their illegally seized property.

This Section is organized as follows. It begins with cases which deal with the extent to which the fourth amendment protects business premises. The lead case here is *Marshall v. Barlow's, Inc.*, which made clear that business premises are generally covered by the probable cause and warrant requirements of the fourth amendment. The Notes following *Barlow's* explore subsequent developments with regard to the warrant requirement for these intrusions. The second group of cases deals with the scope of a lawful search—what can permissibly be searched for, or who can be searched? The lead case here is *Warden v.*

---

21. For a fuller discussion of these fourth amendment issues, see 3 W. La Fave & J. Israel, Criminal Procedure §§ 3.1–3.4 (1984).

22. See 389 U.S. 347, 361, 88 S.Ct. 507, 516, 19 L.Ed.2d 576, 588 (1967) (Harlan, J., concurring).

23. Note that warrantless searches are often upheld by the courts under numerous "exceptions" to the fourth amendment's preference for a warrant. Indeed, the courts often say that the legality of a search depends, in the end, on whether it was "reasonable."

Hayden, which held that it is permissible to search for "mere evidence." The Note cases explore the effect of *Warden* in the business crime context. The third group of cases involve the question of specificity. Searches in business crime cases often involve large quantities of documents. How specifically must these documents be described to meet fourth amendment standards? *Andresen v. Maryland*, the lead case here, is a major Supreme Court case dealing with this issue. The Section concludes with *Massachusetts v. Sheppard*, an important Supreme Court case which narrowed the scope of the exclusionary rule in a way which is critical for business crime cases.

1. PROTECTION OF BUSINESS PREMISES

MARSHALL v. BARLOW'S, INC.

Supreme Court of the United States, 1978.
436 U.S. 307, 98 S.Ct. 1816, 56 L.Ed.2d 305.

Mr. Justice White delivered the opinion of the Court.

Section 8(a) of the Occupational Safety and Health Act of 1970 (OSHA) [24] empowers agents of the Secretary of Labor (the Secretary) to search the work area of any employment facility within the Act's jurisdiction. The purpose of the search is to inspect for safety hazards and violations of OSHA regulations. No search warrant or other process is expressly required under the Act.

On the morning of September 11, 1975, an OSHA inspector entered the customer service area of Barlow's, Inc., an electrical and plumbing installation business located in Pocatello, Idaho. The president and general manager, Ferrol G. "Bill" Barlow, was on hand; and the OSHA inspector, after showing his credentials, informed Mr. Barlow that he wished to conduct a search of the working areas of the business. Mr. Barlow inquired whether any complaint had been received about his company. The inspector answered no, but that Barlow's Inc. had simply turned up in the agency's selection process. The inspector again asked to enter the nonpublic area of the business; Mr. Barlow's response was to inquire whether the inspector had a search warrant. The inspector had none. Thereupon, Mr. Barlow refused the inspector admission to the employee area of his business. He said he was relying on his rights as guaranteed by the Fourth Amendment of the United States Constitution.

---

24. [Court's footnote 1.] In order to carry out the purposes of this chapter, the Secretary, upon presenting appropriate credentials to the owner, operator, or agent in charge, is authorized—

"(1) to enter without delay and at reasonable times any factory, plant, establishment, construction site, or other area, workplace or environment where work is performed by an employee of an employer; and

"(2) to inspect and investigate during regular working hours and at other reasonable times, and within reasonable limits and in a reasonable manner, any such place of employment and all pertinent conditions, structures, machines, apparatus, devices, equipment, and materials therein, and to question privately any such employer, owner, operator, agent, or employee." 84 Stat. 1590, 29 U.S.C. § 657(a) (1970).

Three months later, the Secretary petitioned the United States District Court for the District of Idaho to issue an order compelling Mr. Barlow to admit the inspector. The requested order was issued on December 30, 1975, and was presented to Mr. Barlow on January 5, 1976. Mr. Barlow again refused admission, and he sought his own injunctive relief against the warrantless searches assertedly permitted by OSHA. A three-judge court was convened. On December 30, 1976, it ruled in Mr. Barlow's favor. . . . An injunction against searches or inspections pursuant to § 8(a) was entered. The Secretary appealed, challenging the judgment, and we noted probable jurisdiction.

I

The Secretary urges that warrantless inspections to enforce OSHA are reasonable within the meaning of the Fourth Amendment. Among other things, he relies on § 8(a) of the Act, 29 U.S.C. § 657(a), which authorizes inspection of business premises without a warrant and which the Secretary urges represents a congressional construction of the Fourth Amendment that the courts should not reject. Regretfully, we are unable to agree.

The Warrant Clause of the Fourth Amendment protects commercial buildings as well as private homes. To hold otherwise would belie the origin of that Amendment, and the American colonial experience. An important forerunner of the first 10 Amendments to the United States Constitution, the Virginia Bill of Rights, specifically opposed "general warrants, whereby an officer or messenger may be commanded to search suspected places without evidence of a fact committed." The general warrant was a recurring point of contention in the colonies immediately preceding the Revolution. The particular offensiveness it engendered was acutely felt by the merchants and businessmen whose premises and products were inspected for compliance with the several Parliamentary revenue measures that most irritated the colonists. "[T]he Fourth Amendment's commands grew in large measure out of the colonists' experience with the writs of assistance .. [that] granted sweeping power to customs officials and other agents of the King to search at large for smuggled goods." United States v. Chadwick, 433 U.S. 1, 7–8, 97 S.Ct. 2476, 2481, 53 L.Ed.2d 538 (1977). Against this background, it is untenable that the ban on warrantless searches was not intended to shield places of business as well as of residence.

This Court has already held that warrantless searches are generally unreasonable, and that this rule applies to commercial premises as well as homes. In Camara v. Municipal Court, 387 U.S. 523, 528–529, 87 S.Ct. 1727, 1731, 18 L.Ed.2d 930 (1967), we held:

> "[E]xcept in certain carefully defined classes of cases, a search of private property without proper consent is 'unreasonable' unless it has been authorized by a valid search warrant."

On the same day, we also ruled:

> "As we explained in *Camara,* a search of private houses is presumptively unreasonable if conducted without a warrant. The businessman, like the occupant of a residence, has a constitutional right to go about his business free from unreasonable official entries upon his private commercial property. The businessman, too, has that right placed in jeopardy if the decision to enter and inspect for violation of regulatory laws can be made and enforced by the inspector in the field without official authority evidenced by a warrant." See v. City of Seattle, 387 U.S. 541, 543, 87 S.Ct. 1737, 1739, 18 L.Ed.2d 943 (1967).

These same cases also held that the Fourth Amendment prohibition against unreasonable searches protects against warrantless intrusions during civil as well as criminal investigations. . . . If the government intrudes on a person's property, the privacy interest suffers whether the government's motivation is to investigate violations of criminal laws or breaches of other statutory or regulatory standards. If therefore appears that unless some recognized exception to the warrant requirement applies, See v. City of Seattle, supra, would require a warrant to conduct the inspection sought in this case.

The Secretary urges that an exception from the search warrant requirement has been recognized for "pervasively regulated business[es]," United States v. Biswell, 406 U.S. 311, 316, 92 S.Ct. 1593, 1596, 32 L.Ed.2d 87 (1972), and for "closely regulated" industries "long subject to close supervision and inspection." Colonnade Catering Corp. v. United States, 397 U.S. 72, 74, 77, 90 S.Ct. 774, 777, 25 L.Ed.2d 60 (1970). These cases are indeed exceptions, but they represent responses to relatively unique circumstances. Certain industries have such a history of government oversight that no reasonable expectation of privacy, see Katz v. United States, 389 U.S. 347, 351–352, 88 S.Ct. 507, 511, 19 L.Ed.2d 576 (1967), could exist for a proprietor over the stock of such an enterprise. Liquor (*Colonnade*) and firearms (*Biswell*) are industries of this type; when an entrepreneur embarks upon such a business, he has voluntarily chosen to subject himself to a full arsenal of governmental regulation.

Industries such as these fall within the "certain carefully defined classes of cases," referenced in *Camara,* supra, 387 U.S., at 528, 87 S.Ct., at 1731. The element that distinguishes these enterprises from ordinary businesses is a long tradition of close government supervision, of which any person who chooses to enter such a business must already be aware. . . .

The clear import of our cases is that the closely regulated industry of the type involved in *Colonnade* and *Biswell* is the exception. . . .

* * *

The Secretary nevertheless stoutly argues that the enforcement scheme of the Act requires warrantless searches, and that the restrictions on search discretion contained in the Act and its regulations already protect as much privacy as a warrant would. The Secretary thereby asserts the actual reasonableness of OSHA searches, whatever the general rule against warrantless searches might be. Because "reasonableness is still the ultimate standard," Camara v. Municipal Court, supra, 387 U.S., at 539, 87 S.Ct., at 1736, the Secretary suggests that the Court decide whether a warrant is needed by arriving at a sensible balance between the administrative necessities of OSHA inspections and the incremental protection of privacy of business owners a warrant would afford. . . .

The Secretary submits that warrantless inspections are essential to the proper enforcement of OSHA because they afford the opportunity to inspect without prior notice and hence to preserve the advantages of surprise. While the dangerous conditions outlawed by the Act include structural defects that cannot be quickly hidden or remedied, the Act also regulates a myriad of safety details that may be amenable to speedy alteration or disguise. The risk is that during the interval between an inspector's initial request to search a plant and his procuring a warrant following the owner's refusal of permission, violations of this latter type could be corrected and thus escape the inspector's notice. To the suggestion that warrants may be issued ex parte and executed without delay and without prior notice, thereby preserving the element of surprise, the Secretary expresses concern for the administrative strain that would be experienced by the inspection system, and by the courts, should ex parte warrants issued in advance become standard practice.

We are unconvinced, however, that requiring warrants to inspect will impose serious burdens on the inspection system or the courts, will prevent inspections necessary to enforce the statute, or will make them less effective. . . . [T]he Secretary has . . . promulgated a regulation providing that upon refusal to permit an inspector to enter the property or to complete his inspection, the inspector shall attempt to ascertain the reasons for the refusal and report to his superior, who shall "promptly take appropriate action, including compulsory process, if necessary." 29 CFR § 1903.4. The regulation represents a choice to proceed by process where entry is refused; and on the basis of evidence available from present practice, the Act's effectiveness has not been crippled by providing those owners who wish to refuse an initial requested entry with a time lapse while the inspector obtains the necessary process. Indeed, the kind of process sought in this case and apparently anticipated by the regulation provides notice to the business operator.[25] If this safeguard endangers the efficient administration of

25. [Court's footnote 14.] The proceeding was instituted by filing an "Application for Affirmative Order to Grant Entry and for an Order to show cause why such affirmative order should not issue." The District Court issued the order to show cause, the matter was argued, and an order then issued authorizing the inspection and enjoining interference by Barlow's. The following is the order issued by the District Court:

"IT IS HEREBY ORDERED, ADJUDGED AND DECREED that [representatives of] the . . . Occupational Safety and Health Administration . . . are enti-

OSHA, the Secretary should never have adopted it, particularly when the Act does not require it. Nor is it immediately apparent why the advantages of surprise would be lost if, after being refused entry, procedures were available for the Secretary to seek an ex parte warrant and to reappear at the premises without further notice to the establishment being inspected.

Whether the Secretary proceeds to secure a warrant or other process, with or without prior notice, his entitlement to inspect will not depend on his demonstrating probable cause to believe that conditions in violation of OSHA exist on the premises. Probable cause in the criminal law sense is not required. For purposes of an administrative search such as this, probable cause justifying the issuance of a warrant may be based not only on specific evidence of an existing violation but also on a showing that "reasonable legislative or administrative standards for conducting an . . . inspection are satisfied with respect to a particular [establishment]." Camara v. Municipal Court, supra, at 538, 87 S.Ct., at 1736. A warrant showing that a specific business has been chosen for an OSHA search on the basis of a general administrative plan for the enforcement of the Act derived from neutral sources such as, for example, dispersion of employees in various types of industries across a given area, and the desired frequency of searches in any of the lesser divisions of the area, would protect an employer's Fourth Amendment rights. We doubt that the consumption of enforcement energies in the obtaining of such warrants will exceed manageable proportions.

* * *

[We do not] agree that the incremental protections afforded the employer's privacy by a warrant are so marginal that they fail to justify the administrative burdens that may be entailed. The authority to make warrantless searches devolves almost unbridled discretion upon executive and administrative officers, particularly those in the field, as to when to search and whom to search. A warrant, by contrast, would provide assurances from a neutral officer that the inspection is reasonable under the Constitution, is authorized by statute, and is pursuant to an administrative plan containing specific neutral criteria.[26] Also, a warrant would then and there advise the

tled to entry upon the premises known as Barlow's Inc., . . . to conduct an inspection and investigation as provided for in Section 8 of the Occupational Safety and Health Act of 1970 . . .; that the inspection and investigation shall be conducted during regular working hours or at other reasonable times, within reasonable limits and in a reasonable manner, all as set forth in the regulations pertaining to such inspections promulgated by the Secretary of Labor, at 29 C.F.R., Part 1903; that . . . the inspection and investigation shall be commenced as soon as practicable after the issuance of this Order and shall be completed within reasonable promptness; that the inspection and investigation shall extend to . . . where work is performed by employees of the employer, Barlow's Inc., and to all pertinent conditions, structures, machines, apparatus, devices, equipment, materials, and all other things therein (including but not limited to records, files, papers, processes, controls, and facilities) bearing upon whether Barlow's Inc. is . . . complying with the . . . Occupational Safety and Health Act. . . ."

26. [Court's footnote 20.] The application for the inspection order filed by the Secretary in this case represented that "the desired inspection and investigation are contemplated as part of an inspection

owner of the scope and objects of the search, beyond which limits the inspector is not expected to proceed. These are important functions for a warrant to perform, functions which underlie the Court's prior decisions that the Warrant Clause applies to inspections for compliance with regulatory statutes.[27] We conclude that the concerns expressed by the Secretary do not suffice to justify warrantless inspections under OSHA or vitiate the general constitutional requirement that for a search to be reasonable a warrant must be obtained.

III

We hold that Barlow was entitled to a declaratory judgment that the Act is unconstitutional insofar as it purports to authorize inspections without warrant or its equivalent and to an injunction enjoining the Act's enforcement to that extent. The judgment of the District Court is therefore affirmed.

So ordered.

MR. JUSTICE BRENNAN took no part in the consideration or decision of this case. [The dissenting opinion of JUSTICE STEVENS, joined by JUSTICES BLACKMUN AND REHNQUIST, is omitted.]

NOTES AND QUERIES

(1) *Constitutional Background—Administrative Searches.* *Marshall v. Barlow's* is an elaboration of two Supreme Court decisions from 1967, *Camara v. Municipal Court*[28] and *See v. Seattle.*[29] Prior to those decisions, administrative searches were not subject to the fourth amendment. In *Camara* the Court held that a warrant was required

---

program designed to assure compliance with the Act and are authorized by Section 8(a) of the Act." The program was not described, however, or any facts presented that would indicate why an inspection of Barlow's establishment was within the program. . . .

27. [Court's footnote 22.] Delineating the scope of a search with some care is particularly important where documents are involved. . . .

In describing the scope of the warrantless inspection authorized by the statute, § 8(a) does not expressly include any records among those items or things that may be examined, and § 8(c) merely provides that the employer is "to make available" his pertinent records and to make periodic reports.

The Secretary's regulation, 29 CFR § 1903.3, however, expressly includes among the inspector's powers the authority "to review records required by the Act and regulations published in this chapter, and other records which are directly related to the purpose of the inspection." Further, 29 CFR § 1903.7 requires inspectors to indicate generally "the records specified in § 1903.3 which they wish to review" but "such designations of records shall not preclude access to additional records specified in § 1903.3." It is the Secretary's position, which we reject, that an inspection of documents of this scope may be effected without a warrant.

The order that issued in this case included among the objects and things to be inspected "all other things therein (including but not limited to records, files, papers, processes, controls and facilities) bearing upon whether Barlow's, Inc., is furnishing to its employees employment and a place of employment that are free from recognizable hazards that are causing or are likely to cause death or serious physical harm to its employees, and whether Barlow's, Inc., is complying with . . ." the OSHA regulations.

28. 387 U.S. 523, 87 S.Ct. 1727, 18 L.Ed. 2d 930 (1967).

29. 387 U.S. 541, 87 S.Ct. 1737, 18 L.Ed. 2d 943 (1967).

for administrative searches of residential premises, overruling *Frank v. Maryland*.[30] In *See* the Court held that a warrant would also be required for administrative searches of business premises (there, a fire department inspection of a locked commercial warehouse).

The Supreme Court recognized in those two cases that administrative searches involve considerations different from the usual police search for weapons or contraband. The Court accordingly discussed what kind of "cause" would amount to "probable cause" so as to justify the issuance of a warrant (an issue also discussed in *Marshall v. Barlow's*). In *Camara* the agency was engaged in a "routine annual inspection" of an apartment house for possible Housing Code violations. There was no reason to suspect any violations in the particular apartment house being searched. The Court wrote:

> [A]ppellant argues . . . that warrants should issue only when the inspector possesses probable cause to believe that a particular dwelling contains violations of the minimum standards prescribed by the code being enforced. We disagree.
>
> In cases in which the Fourth Amendment requires that a warrant to search be obtained, "probable cause" is the standard by which a particular decision to search is tested against the constitutional mandate of reasonableness. To apply this standard, it is obviously necessary first to focus upon the governmental interest which allegedly justifies official intrusion upon the constitutionally protected interests of the private citizen. . . .
>
> Unlike the search pursuant to a criminal investigation, the inspection programs at issue here are aimed at securing city-wide compliance with minimum physical standards for private property. The primary governmental interest at stake is to prevent even the unintentional development of conditions which are hazardous to public health and safety. Because fires and epidemics may ravage large urban areas, because unsightly conditions adversely affect the economic values of neighboring structures, numerous courts have upheld the police power of municipalities to impose and enforce such minimum standards even upon existing structures. In determining whether a particular inspection is reasonable—and thus in determining whether there is probable cause to issue a warrant for that inspection—the need for the inspection must be weighed in terms of these reasonable goals of code enforcement.
>
> There is unanimous agreement among those most familiar with this field that the only effective way to seek universal compliance with the minimum standards required by municipal codes is through routine periodic inspections of all structures. It is here that the probable cause debate is focused, for the agency's decision to conduct an area inspection is unavoidably based on its appraisal of conditions in the area as a whole, not on its knowledge of

---

30. 359 U.S. 360, 79 S.Ct. 804, 3 L.Ed.2d 877 (1959).

conditions in each particular building. Appellee contends that, if the probable cause standard urged by appellant is adopted, the area inspection will be eliminated as a means of seeking compliance with code standards and the reasonable goals of code enforcement will be dealt a crushing blow.

. . . [T]here can be no ready test for determining reasonableness other than by balancing the need to search against the invasion which the search entails. But we think that a number of persuasive factors combine to support the reasonableness of area code-enforcement inspections. First, such programs have a long history of judicial and public acceptance. Second, the public interest demands that all dangerous conditions be prevented or abated, yet it is doubtful that any other canvassing technique would achieve acceptable results. Many such conditions—faulty wiring is an obvious example—are not observable from outside the building and indeed may not be apparent to the inexpert occupant himself. Finally, because the inspections are neither personal in nature nor aimed at the discovery of evidence of crime, they involve a relatively limited invasion of the urban citizen's privacy.

* * *

Having concluded that the area inspection is a "reasonable" search of private property within the meaning of the Fourth Amendment, it is obvious that "probable cause" to issue a warrant to inspect must exist if reasonable legislative or administrative standards for conducting an area inspection are satisfied with respect to a particular dwelling. Such standards, which will vary with the municipal program being enforced, may be based upon the passage of time, the nature of the building (e.g., a multi-family apartment house), or the condition of the entire area, but they will not necessarily depend upon specific knowledge of the condition of the particular dwelling. . . . Such an approach neither endangers time-honored doctrines applicable to criminal investigations nor makes a nullity of the probable cause requirement in this area. It merely gives full recognition to the competing public and private interests here at stake and, in so doing, best fulfills the historic purpose behind the constitutional right to be free from unreasonable government invasions of privacy.

(2) *Pervasively Regulated Industries.* *Marshall v. Barlow's* was followed by *Donovan v. Dewey*[31] in which the Supreme Court upheld a warrantless search of a stone quarry undertaken pursuant to the Federal Mine Safety and Health Act of 1977, which provided for warrantless intrusions. The Court wrote that the

greater latitude to conduct warrantless inspections of commercial property reflects the fact that the expectation of privacy that the owner of commercial property enjoys in such property differs

---

31. 452 U.S. 594, 101 S.Ct. 2534, 69 L.Ed.2d 262 (1981).

significantly from the sanctity accorded an individual's home, and that this privacy interest may, in certain circumstances, be adequately protected by regulatory schemes authorizing warrantless inspections.

The Court held that the Act's regulatory scheme reflected the well-known hazards in the mining industry, that warrantless inspections were necessary for enforcement, and that the Act provided a "constitutionally adequate substitute for a warrant." The Act required semi-annual inspections of surface mines to insure compliance with published standards developed by the Secretary of Labor. If a violation were found, a follow-up inspection was mandatory. If an inspector were denied entry, the Act required the Secretary to file a civil action to enjoin future refusals, thereby providing the target of the search an opportunity to contest legality. Justice Stewart, in dissent, wrote that Congress was now free to avoid the fourth amendment "industry by industry," even though *Barlow's* held that it could not do it wholesale. "Congress after today can define any industry as dangerous, regulate it substantially, and provide for warrantless inspections of its members."

Six years after *Donovan v. Dewey* the Supreme Court decided *New York v. Burger*:[32]

JUSTICE BLACKMUN delivered the opinion of the Court.

This case presents the question whether the warrantless search of an automobile junkyard, conducted pursuant to a statute authorizing such a search, falls within the exception to the warrant requirement for administrative inspections of pervasively regulated industries. . . .

I

Respondent Joseph Burger is the owner of a junkyard in Brooklyn, N.Y. His business consists, in part, of the dismantling of automobiles and the selling of their parts. His junkyard is an open lot with no buildings. A high metal fence surrounds it, wherein are located, among other things, vehicles and parts of vehicles. At approximately noon on November 17, 1982, Officer Joseph Vega and four other plainclothes officers, all members of the Auto Crimes Division of the New York City Police Department, entered respondent's junkyard to conduct an inspection pursuant to N.Y. Veh. & Traf.Law § 415–a5 (McKinney 1986).[33] On any given day,

---

32. 482 U.S. 691, 107 S.Ct. 2636, 96 L.Ed.2d 601 (1987).

33. [Court's footnote 1.] This statute reads in pertinent part:

"Records and identification. (a) . . . Every person required to be registered pursuant to this section shall maintain a record of all motor vehicles, trailers, and major component parts thereof, coming into his possession together with a record of the disposition of any such motor vehicle, trailer or part thereof and shall maintain proof of ownership for any motor vehicle, trailer or major component part thereof while in his possession. . . . Upon request of an agent of the commissioner or of any police officer and during his regular and usual business hours, a vehicle dismantler shall produce such records and permit said agent or

the Division conducts from 5 to 10 inspections of vehicle dismantlers, automobile junkyards, and related businesses.[34]

Upon entering the junkyard, the officers asked to see Burger's license [35] and his "police book"—the record of the automobiles and vehicle parts in his possession. Burger replied that he had neither a license nor a police book. The officers then announced their intention to conduct a § 415–a inspection. Burger did not object. In accordance with their practice, the officers copied down the Vehicle Inspection Numbers (VINs) of several vehicles and parts of vehicles that were in the junkyard. After checking these numbers against a police computer, the officers determined that respondent was in possession of stolen vehicles and parts. Accordingly, Burger was arrested and charged with five counts of possession of stolen property and one count of unregistered operation as a vehicle dismantler, in violation of § 415–a1.

[Burger's motion to suppress was denied by the trial court, which held § 415–a5 constitutional. The Appellate Division affirmed, but the New York Court of Appeals reversed. The grant of certiorari followed.]

II

* * *

Because the owner or operator of commercial premises in a "closely regulated" industry has a reduced expectation of privacy, the warrant and probable-cause requirements, which fulfill the traditional Fourth Amendment standard of reasonableness for a government search, have lessened application in this context. Rather, we conclude that, as in other situations of "special need," where the privacy interests of the owner are weakened and the government interests in regulating particular businesses are concomitantly heightened, a warrantless inspection of commercial premises may well be reasonable within the meaning of the Fourth Amendment.

This warrantless inspection, however, even in the context of a pervasively regulated business, will be deemed to be reasonable only so long as three criteria are met. First, there must be a "substantial" government interest that informs the regulatory scheme pursuant to which the inspection is made.

Second, the warrantless inspections must be "necessary to further [the] regulatory scheme." . . .

---

police officer to examine them and any vehicles or parts of vehicles which are subject to the record keeping requirements of this section and which are on the premises . . . .

34. [Court's footnote 2.] It was unclear from the record why, on that particular day, Burger's junkyard was selected for inspection. The junkyards designated for inspection apparently were selected from a list of such businesses compiled by New York City police detectives.

35. [Court's footnote 3.] An individual operating a vehicle-dismantling business in New York is required to have a license . . . .

Finally, "the statute's inspection program, in terms of the certainty and regularity of its application, [must] provid[e] a constitutionally adequate substitute for a warrant." In other words, the regulatory statute must perform the two basic functions of a warrant: it must advise the owner of the commercial premises that the search is being made pursuant to the law and has a properly defined scope, and it must limit the discretion of the inspecting officers. To perform this first function, the statute must be "sufficiently comprehensive and defined that the owner of commercial property cannot help but be aware that his property will be subject to periodic inspections undertaken for specific purposes." In addition, in defining how a statute limits the discretion of the inspectors, we have observed that it must be "carefully limited in time, place, and scope."

III

A

Searches made pursuant to § 415–a, in our view, clearly fall within this established exception to the warrant requirement for administrative inspections in "closely regulated" businesses. First, the nature of the regulatory statute reveals that the operation of a junkyard, part of which is devoted to vehicle dismantling, is a "closely regulated" business in the State of New York. The provisions regulating the activity of vehicle dismantling are extensive. An operator cannot engage in this industry without first obtaining a license, which means that he must meet the registration requirements and must pay a fee. Under § 415–a5(a), the operator must maintain a police book recording the acquisition and disposition of motor vehicles and vehicle parts, and make such records and inventory available for inspection by the police or any agent of the Department of Motor Vehicles. The operator also must display his registration number prominently at his place of business, on business documentation, and on vehicles and parts that pass through his business. Moreover, the person engaged in this activity is subject to criminal penalties, as well as to loss of license or civil fines, for failure to comply with these provisions. . . .

In determining whether vehicle dismantlers constitute a "closely regulated" industry, the "duration of [this] particular regulatory scheme" has some relevancy. Section 415–a could be said to be of fairly recent vintage, see 1973 N.Y.Laws, ch. 225, § 1 (McKinney), and the inspection provision of § 415–a5 was added only in 1979, see 1979 N.Y.Laws, ch. 691, § 2 (McKinney). But because the automobile is a relatively new phenomenon in our society and because its widespread use is even newer, automobile junkyards and vehicle dismantlers have not been in existence very long and thus do not have an ancient history of government oversight. . . .

The automobile junkyard business, however, is simply a new branch of an industry that has existed, and has been closely regulated, for many years. The automobile junkyard is closely akin to the secondhand shop or the general junkyard. Both share the purpose of recycling salvageable articles and components of items no longer usable in their original form. As such, vehicle dismantlers represent a modern, specialized version of a traditional activity. In New York, general junkyards and secondhand shops long have been subject to regulation. . . .

Accordingly, in light of the regulatory framework governing his business and the history of regulation of related industries, an operator of a junkyard engaging in vehicle dismantling has a reduced expectation of privacy in this "closely regulated" business.

B

The New York regulatory scheme satisfies the three criteria necessary to make reasonable warrantless inspections pursuant to § 415–a5. First, the State has a substantial interest in regulating the vehicle-dismantling and automobile-junkyard industry because motor vehicle theft has increased in the State and because the problem of theft is associated with this industry. In this day, automobile theft has become a significant social problem, placing enormous economic and personal burdens upon the citizens of different States. . . .

Second, regulation of the vehicle-dismantling industry reasonably serves the State's substantial interest in eradicating automobile theft. It is well established that the theft problem can be addressed effectively by controlling the receiver of, or market in, stolen property. . . . [T]he State rationally may believe that it will reduce car theft by regulations that prevent automobile junkyards from becoming markets for stolen vehicles and that help trace the origin and destination of vehicle parts.

Moreover, the warrantless administrative inspections pursuant to § 415–a5 "are necessary to further [the] regulatory scheme." . . . [A] warrant requirement would interfere with the statute's purpose of deterring automobile theft accomplished by identifying vehicles and parts as stolen and shutting down the market in such items. Because stolen cars and parts often pass quickly through an automobile junkyard, "frequent" and "unannounced" inspections are necessary in order to detect them. In sum, surprise is crucial if the regulatory scheme aimed at remedying this major social problem is to function at all.

Third, § 415–a5 provides a "constitutionally adequate substitute for a warrant." The statute informs the operator of a vehicle dismantling business that inspections will be made on a regular basis. Thus, the vehicle dismantler knows that the inspections to which he is subject do not constitute discretionary acts by a government official but are conducted pursuant to statute. Section 415–a5 also sets forth the scope of the inspection and, accordingly, places the operator on notice as to how to comply with the statute. In addition, it notifies the operator as to who is authorized to conduct an inspection.

Finally, the "time, place, and scope" of the inspection is limited, to place appropriate restraints upon the discretion of the inspecting officers. The officers are allowed to conduct an inspection only "during [the] regular and usual business hours." § 415–a5. The inspections can be made only of vehicle-dismantling and related industries. And the permissible scope of these searches is narrowly defined: the inspectors may examine the records, as well as "any vehicles or parts of vehicles which are subject to the record keeping requirements of this section and which are on the premises."

IV

[In this part of its opinion, the Court rejected the argument, accepted by the New York Court of Appeals, that the statute did not qualify for the "closely regulated" exception because the statute was penal rather than administrative and the search was carried out by police officers. "[T]he Court of Appeals failed to recognize that a State can address a major social problem *both* by way of an administrative scheme *and* through penal sanctions."]

V

Accordingly, the judgment of the New York Court of Appeals is reversed and the case is remanded to that court for further proceedings not inconsistent with this opinion.

It is so ordered.

[The dissenting opinion of JUSTICE BRENNAN, with whom JUSTICES MARSHALL and O'CONNOR joined, is omitted.]

(3) *Reasonable Expectations of Privacy*? Was the search in *Donovan v. Dewey* or *New York v. Burger* a "fourth amendment search"? Did the proprietors have any reasonable expectations of privacy given the pervasive regulation of their businesses? Consider *Dow Chemical Co. v. United States,* 476 U.S. 227, 106 S.Ct. 1819, 90 L.Ed.2d 226 (1986):

CHIEF JUSTICE BURGER delivered the opinion of the Court.

[Digest: Dow Chemical Co. operated a 2,000 acre chemical manufacturing facility consisting of numerous covered buildings, but with equipment and piping between the buildings observable from the air. Dow maintained elaborate security on the ground and investigated any low-level flights over the facility. Because of expense, it did not cover all equipment from view. The Environmental Protection Agency made one on-site inspection of the facility with Dow's consent; Dow refused consent for a second visit. The

EPA then hired a commercial aerial photographer, who took approximately 75 photographs of the facility, using a standard floor-mounted, precision aerial mapping camera from altitudes of 12,000, 3,000, and 1,200 feet. Some of the photographs, when enlarged and magnified, could show power lines as small as ½ inch in diameter. Dow sued to enjoin the EPA from violating the fourth amendment.]

We turn now to Dow's contention that taking aerial photographs constituted a search without a warrant, thereby violating Dow's rights under the Fourth Amendment. In making this contention, however, Dow concedes that a simple flyover with naked-eye observation, or the taking of a photograph from a nearby hillside overlooking such a facility, would give rise to no Fourth Amendment problem.

* * *

Two lines of cases are relevant to the inquiry: the curtilage doctrine and the "open fields" doctrine. The curtilage area immediately surrounding a private house has long been given protection as a place where the occupants have a reasonable and legitimate expectation of privacy that society is prepared to accept.

As the curtilage doctrine evolved to protect much the same kind of privacy as that covering the interior of a structure, the contrasting "open fields" doctrine evolved as well. From Hester v. United States, 265 U.S. 57, 44 S.Ct. 445, 68 L.Ed. 898 (1924), to Oliver v. United States, 466 U.S. 170, 104 S.Ct. 1735, 80 L.Ed.2d 214 (1984), the Court has drawn a line as to what expectations are reasonable in the open areas beyond the curtilage of a dwelling; "open fields do not provide the setting for those intimate activities that the [Fourth] Amendment is intended to shelter from governmental interference or surveillance." *Oliver*, 466 U.S., at 179, 104 S.Ct., at 1741. In *Oliver*, we held that "an individual may not legitimately demand privacy for activities out of doors in fields, except in the area immediately surrounding the home." To fall within the open fields doctrine the area "need be neither 'open' nor a 'field' as those terms are used in common speech."

Dow plainly has a reasonable, legitimate, and objective expectation of privacy within the interior of its covered buildings, and it is equally clear that expectation is one society is prepared to observe. E.g., See v. City of Seattle, supra. Moreover, it could hardly be expected that Dow would erect a huge cover over a 2,000-acre tract. In contending that its entire enclosed plant complex is an "industrial curtilage," Dow argues that its exposed manufacturing facilities are analogous to the curtilage surrounding a home because it has taken every possible step to bar access from ground level.

* * *

Admittedly, Dow's enclosed plant complex does not fall precisely within the "open fields" doctrine. The area at issue here can perhaps be seen as falling somewhere between "open fields" and curtilage, but lacking some of the critical characteristics of both.[36] Dow's inner manufacturing areas are elaborately secured to ensure they are not open or exposed to the public from the ground. Any actual physical entry by EPA into any enclosed area would raise significantly different questions, because "[t]he businessman, like the occupant of a residence, has a constitutional right to go about his business free from unreasonable official entries upon his private commercial property." See v. City of Seattle, supra, 387 U.S., at 543, 87 S.Ct., at 1739. The narrow issue raised by Dow's claim of search and seizure, however, concerns aerial observation of a 2,000-acre outdoor manufacturing facility *without* physical entry.[37]

We pointed out in Donovan v. Dewey, 452 U.S. 594, 598–599, 101 S.Ct. 2534, 2537–2538, 69 L.Ed.2d 262 (1981), that the Government has "greater latitude to conduct warrantless inspections of commercial property" because "the expectation of privacy that the owner of commercial property enjoys in such property differs significantly from the sanctity accorded an individual's home." We emphasized that unlike a homeowner's interest in his dwelling, "[t]he interest of the owner of commercial property is not one in being free from any inspections." Id., at 599, 101 S.Ct., at 2538. And with regard to regulatory inspections, we have held that "[w]hat is observable by the public is observable without a warrant, by the Government inspector as well." Marshall v. Barlow's, Inc., 436 U.S., at 315, 98 S.Ct., at 1822 (footnote omitted).

Oliver recognized that in the open field context, "the public and police lawfully may survey lands from the air." 466 U.S., at 179, 104 S.Ct., at 1741 (footnote omitted). Here, EPA was not employing some unique sensory device that, for example, could penetrate the walls of buildings and record conversations in Dow's plants, offices or laboratories, but rather a conventional, albeit precise, commercial camera commonly used in map-making. The Government asserts it has not yet enlarged the photographs to any significant degree, but Dow points out that simple magnification permits identification of objects such as wires as small as one-half inch diameter.

It may well be, as the Government concedes, that surveillance of private property by using highly sophisticated surveillance equipment not generally available to the public, such as satellite

36. [Court's footnote 3.] . . . As *Oliver* recognized, the curtilage surrounding a home is generally a well-defined, limited area. In stark contrast, the areas for which Dow claims enhanced protection covers an area the equivalent of a half dozen family farms.

37. [Court's footnote 4.] We find it important that this is *not* an area immediately adjacent to a private home, where privacy expectations are most heightened. Nor is this an area where Dow has made any effort to protect against aerial surveillance. . . . Simply keeping track of the identification numbers of any planes flying overhead, with a later followup to see if photographs were taken, does not constitute a "procedure[ ] designed to protect the facility from aerial photography."

technology, might be constitutionally proscribed absent a warrant. But the photographs here are not so revealing of intimate details as to raise constitutional concerns. Although they undoubtedly give EPA more detailed information than naked-eye views, they remain limited to an outline of the facility's buildings and equipment. The mere fact that human vision is enhanced somewhat, at least to the degree here, does not give rise to constitutional problems. An electronic device to penetrate walls or windows so as to hear and record confidential discussions of chemical formulae or other trade secrets would raise very different and far more serious questions; other protections such as trade secret laws are available to protect commercial activities from private surveillance by competitors.

We conclude that the open areas of an industrial plant complex with numerous plant structures spread over an area of 2,000 acres are not analogous to the "curtilage" of a dwelling for purposes of aerial surveillance; such an industrial complex is more comparable to an open field and as such it is open to the view and observation of persons in aircraft lawfully in the public airspace immediately above or sufficiently near the area for the reach of cameras.

We hold that the taking of aerial photographs of an industrial plant complex from navigable airspace is not a search prohibited by the Fourth Amendment.

Affirmed.

[The dissenting opinion of JUSTICE POWELL, joined by JUSTICES BRENNAN, MARSHALL, and BLACKMUN, is omitted.] [38]

(4) *Queries.* Do you think that the statutes in *Donovan v. Dewey* and *Burger* were "adequate substitutes" for a warrant issued by a "neutral detached magistrate"? What are the purposes of the warrant requirement? Do you think that the actual procedure (including the court proceeding) followed by OSHA in *Barlow's* was significantly different from the procedures prescribed in *Dewey* or *Burger*?

In reviewing the Court's decisions in this area, do you think that *Camara* and *See* should be reconsidered? Particularly with regard to intrusions onto business premises, is there any reason to provide fourth amendment protection? Is the net effect of the Court's decisions to so water down the application of the fourth amendment in these cases that no effective protection remains anyway? What effect might this have on the application of the fourth amendment outside the business context?

38. See also Florida v. Riley, ___ U.S. ___, 109 S.Ct. 693, 102 L.Ed.2d 835 (1989) (viewing marijuana through openings in greenhouse from helicopter 400 feet above property not a fourth amendment search) (5–4); O'Connor v. Ortega, 480 U.S. 709, 107 S.Ct. 1492, 94 L.Ed.2d 714 (1987) (reasonable expectations of privacy in the workplace of a public employee).

2. SCOPE OF A LAWFUL SEARCH

WARDEN v. HAYDEN
Supreme Court of the United States, 1967.
387 U.S. 294, 87 S.Ct. 1642, 18 L.Ed.2d 782.

Mr. Justice Brennan delivered the opinion of the Court.

We review in this case the validity of the proposition that there is under the Fourth Amendment a "distinction between merely evidentiary materials, on the one hand, which may not be seized either under the authority of a search warrant or during the course of a search incident to arrest, and on the other hand, those objects which may validly be seized including the instrumentalities and means by which a crime is committed, the fruits of crime such as stolen property, weapons by which escape of the person arrested might be effected, and property the possession of which is a crime."

A Maryland court sitting without a jury convicted respondent of armed robbery. Items of his clothing, a cap, jacket, and trousers, among other things, were seized during a search of his home, and were admitted in evidence without objection. . . . The Court of Appeals . . . held that respondent was correct in his contention that the clothing seized was improperly admitted in evidence because the items had "evidential value only" and therefore were not lawfully subject to seizure. We granted certiorari. We reverse.

[After holding that the search itself, although done without a warrant, was lawful, the Court continued:]

We have examined on many occasions the history and purposes of the Amendment. It was a reaction to the evils of the use of the general warrant in England and the writs of assistance in the Colonies, and was intended to protect against invasions of "the sanctity of a man's home and the privacies of life," Boyd v. United States, 116 U.S. 616, 630, from searches under indiscriminate, general authority. Protection of these interests was assured by prohibiting all "unreasonable" searches and seizures, and by requiring the use of warrants, which particularly describe "the place to be searched, and the persons or things to be seized," thereby interposing "a magistrate between the citizen and the police," McDonald v. United States, 335 U.S., at 455.

Nothing in the language of the Fourth Amendment supports the distinction between "mere evidence" and instrumentalities, fruits of crime, or contraband. On its face, the provision assures the "right of the people to be secure in their persons, houses, papers, and effects . . . .," without regard to the use to which any of these things are applied. This "right of the people" is certainly unrelated to the "mere evidence" limitation. Privacy is disturbed no more by a search directed to a purely evidentiary object than it is by a search directed to an instrumentality, fruit, or contraband. A magistrate can intervene in both situations, and the requirements of probable cause and specificity can be preserved intact. Moreover, nothing in the nature of property seized as evidence renders it more private than property seized, for example, as an instrumentality; quite the opposite may be true. Indeed, the distinction is wholly irrational, since, depending on the circumstances, the same "papers and effects" may be "mere evidence" in one case and "instrumentality" in another.

In Gouled v. United States, 255 U.S. 298, 309, the Court said that search warrants "may not be used as a means of gaining access to a man's house or office and papers solely for the purpose of making search to secure evidence to be used against him in a criminal or penal proceeding. . . ." The Court derived from Boyd v. United States, supra, the proposition that warrants "may be resorted to only when a primary right to such search and seizure may be found in the interest which the public or the complainant may have in the property to be seized, or in the right to the possession of it, or when a valid exercise of the police power renders possession of the property by the accused unlawful and provides that it may be taken"; that is, when the property is an instrumentality or fruit of crime, or contraband. Since it was "impossible to say, on the record . . . that the Government had any interest" in the papers involved "other than as evidence against the accused . . .," "to permit them to be used in evidence would be, in effect, as ruled in the Boyd Case, to compel the defendant to become a witness against himself."

The items of clothing involved in this case are not "testimonial" or "communicative" in nature, and their introduction therefore did not compel respondent to become a witness against himself in violation of the Fifth Amendment. This case thus does not require that we consider whether there are items of evidential value whose very nature precludes them from being the object of a reasonable search and seizure.

The Fourth Amendment ruling in *Gouled* was based upon the dual, related premises that historically the right to search for and seize property depended upon the assertion by the Government of a valid claim of superior interest, and that it was not enough that the purpose of the search and seizure was to obtain evidence to use in apprehending and convicting criminals. The common law of search and seizure after Entick v. Carrington, 19 How.St.Tr. 1029, reflected Lord Camden's view, derived no doubt from the political thought of his time, that the "great end, for which men entered into society, was to secure their property." Warrants were "allowed only where the primary right to such a search and seizure is in the interest which the public or complainant may have in the property seized." Lasson, The History and Development of the Fourth Amendment to the United States Constitution 133–134. Thus stolen property—the fruits of crime—was always subject to seizure. And the power to search for stolen property was gradually extended to cover "any property which the private citizen was not permitted to possess," which included instrumentalities of crime (because of the early notion that items used in crime were forfeited to the State) and contraband. Kaplan, Search and Seizure: A No–Man's Land in the Criminal Law, 49 Calif.L.Rev. 474, 475. No separate governmental interest in seizing evidence to apprehend and convict criminals was recognized; it was required that some property interest be asserted. . . .

The premise that property interests control the right of the Government to search and seize has been discredited. Searches and seizures may be "unreasonable" within the Fourth Amendment even though the Government asserts a superior property interest at common law. We have recognized that the principal object of the Fourth Amendment is the protection of privacy rather than property. . . .

* * *

. . . The requirements of the Fourth Amendment can secure the same protection of privacy whether the search is for "mere evidence" or for fruits, instrumentalities or contraband. There must, of course, be a nexus—automatically provided in the case of fruits, instrumentalities or contraband—between the item to be seized and criminal behavior. Thus in the case of "mere evidence," probable cause must be examined in terms of cause to believe that the evidence sought will aid in a particular apprehension or conviction. In so doing, consideration of police purposes will be required.

* * *

The survival of the *Gouled* distinction is attributable more to chance than considered judgment. Legislation has helped perpetuate it. Thus, Congress has never authorized the issuance of search warrants for the seizure of mere evidence of crime. . . . Rule 41(b) of the Federal Rules of Criminal Procedure incorporated the *Gouled* categories as limitations on federal authorities to issue warrants, and Mapp v. Ohio, 367 U.S. 643, only recently made the "mere evidence" rule a problem in the state courts. Pressure against the rule in the federal courts has taken the form rather of broadening the categories of evidence subject to seizure, thereby creating considerable confusion in the law.

The rationale most frequently suggested for the rule preventing the seizure of evidence is that "limitations upon the fruit to be gathered tend to limit the quest itself." United States v. Poller, 43 F.2d 911, 914 (C.A.2d Cir.1930). But privacy "would be just as well served by a restriction on search to the even-numbered days of the month. . . . And it would have the extra advantage of avoiding hair-splitting questions. . . ." Kaplan, op. cit. supra, at 479. The "mere evidence" limitation has spawned exceptions so numerous and confusion so great, in fact, that it is questionable whether it affords meaningful protection. But if its rejection does enlarge the area of permissible searches, the intrusions are nevertheless made after fulfilling the probable cause and particularity requirements of the Fourth Amendment and after the intervention of "a neutral and detached magistrate . . ." The Fourth Amendment allows intrusions upon privacy under these circumstances, and there is no viable reason to distinguish intrusions to secure "mere evidence" from intrusions to secure fruits, instrumentalities, or contraband.

The judgment of the Court of Appeals is reversed.

[JUSTICE BLACK concurred in the result. The concurring opinion of JUSTICE FORTAS, in which CHIEF JUSTICE WARREN joined, is omitted.]

MR. JUSTICE DOUGLAS, dissenting.

We start with the Fourth Amendment which provides:

> "The right of the people to be secure in their persons, houses, papers, and effects, against unreasonable searches and seizures, shall not be violated, and no Warrants shall issue, but upon probable cause, supported by Oath or affirmation, and particularly describing the place to be searched, and the persons or things to be seized."

This constitutional guarantee, now as applicable to the States (Mapp v. Ohio, 367 U.S. 643) as to the Federal Government, has been thought, until today, to have two faces of privacy:

(1) One creates a zone of privacy that may not be invaded by the police through raids, by the legislators through laws, or by magistrates through the issuance of warrants.

(2) A second creates a zone of privacy that may be invaded either by the police in hot pursuit or by a search incident to arrest or by a warrant issued by a magistrate on a showing of probable cause.

The *first* has been recognized from early days in Anglo–American law. . . .

As stated by Lord Camden in Entick v. Carrington, 19 How.St.Tr. 1029, 1067, even warrants authorizing seizure of stolen goods were looked upon with disfavor but "crept into the law by imperceptible practice." . . . Lord Camden's opinion not only outlawed the general warrant but went on to condemn searches "for evidence" with or without a general warrant:

* * *

> "Whether this procedeth from the gentleness of the law towards criminals, or from a consideration that such a power would be more pernicious to the innocent than useful to the public, I will not say.
>
> "It is very certain, that the law obligeth no man to accuse himself; because the necessary means of compelling self-accusation, falling upon the innocent as well as the guilty, would be both cruel and unjust; and it should seem, that search for evidence is disallowed upon the same principle. There too the innocent would be confounded with the guilty."

Thus Lord Camden decided two things: (1) that searches for evidence violated the principle against self-incrimination; (2) that general warrants were void.

This decision, in the very forefront when the Fourth Amendment was adopted, underlines the construction that it covers something other than the form of the warrant and creates a zone of privacy which no government official may enter.

* * *

. . . That there is a zone that no police can enter—whether in "hot pursuit" or armed with a meticulously proper warrant—has been emphasized by *Boyd* and by *Gouled.* They have been consistently and continuously approved. I would adhere to them and leave with the individual the choice of opening his private effects (apart from contraband and the like) to the police or keeping their contents a secret and their integrity inviolate. The existence of that choice is the very essence of the right of privacy. Without it the Fourth Amendment and the Fifth are ready instruments for the police state that the Framers sought to avoid.

NOTES AND QUERIES

(1) *Expanding the Scope of the Search.* Do you agree with the argument made in *Warden v. Hayden* that the mere evidence rule was a poor way to limit the scope of a search? Consider, in this connection, a subsequent Supreme Court decision, *Zurcher v. Stanford Daily.*[39] Involved there was a search of a newspaper's offices for negatives, film, and pictures of a demonstration at a hospital at which nine police officers were injured. No police photographers had been at the demonstration; the newspaper, however, had published articles and photographs about the demonstration. The search was carried out pursuant to a warrant. Four police officers searched photographic laboratories, filing cabinets, desks, and wastepaper baskets. No locked drawers or rooms were opened. The officers had the opportunity to read notes and correspondence during the search. The search only revealed the previously printed photographs and no materials were removed from the newspaper's office.

The Supreme Court, in an opinion by JUSTICE WHITE, held that the search was lawful:

> . . . Nothing on the face of the Amendment suggests that a third-party search warrant should not normally issue. The warrant clause speaks of search warrants issued on "probable cause" and "particularly describing the place to be searched and the persons or things to be seized." In situations where the State does not seek to seize "persons" but only those "things" which there is probable cause to believe are located on the place to be searched, there is no apparent basis in the language of the Amendment for also imposing the requirements for a valid arrest—probable cause to believe that the third party is implicated in the crime.

* * *

---

39. 436 U.S. 547, 98 S.Ct. 1970, 56 L.Ed. 2d 525 (1978).

The critical element in a reasonable search is not that the owner of the property is suspected of crime but that there is reasonable cause to believe that the specific "things" to be searched for and seized are located on the property to which entry is sought. . . .

* * *

. . . As we understand the structure and language of the Fourth Amendment and our cases expounding it, valid warrants to search property may be issued when it is satisfactorily demonstrated to the magistrate that fruits, instrumentalities, or evidence of crime is located on the premises. The Fourth Amendment has itself struck the balance between privacy and public need, and there is no occasion or justification for a court to revise the Amendment and strike a new balance by denying the search warrant in the circumstances present here and by insisting that the investigation proceed by subpoena duces tecum, whether on the theory that the latter is a less intrusive alternative, or otherwise.

* * *

We note finally that if the evidence sought by warrant is sufficiently connected with the crime to satisfy the probable cause requirement, it will very likely be sufficiently relevant to justify a subpoena and to withstand a motion to quash. Further, Fifth Amendment and state shield law objections that might be asserted in opposition to compliance with a subpoena are largely irrelevant to determining the legality of a search warrant under the Fourth Amendment. Of course, the Fourth Amendment does not prevent or advise against legislative or executive efforts to establish non-constitutional protections against possible abuses of the search warrant procedure, but we decline to reinterpret the Amendment to impose a general constitutional barrier against warrants to search newspaper premises, to require resort to subpoenas as a general rule, or to demand prior notice and hearing in connection with the issuance of search warrants.

* * *

[The dissenting opinion of JUSTICES STEWART and MARSHALL, and the concurring opinion of JUSTICE POWELL, are omitted. JUSTICE BRENNAN did not participate in the consideration or decision of the case.]

MR. JUSTICE STEVENS, dissenting.

The novel problem presented by this case is an outgrowth of the profound change in Fourth Amendment law that occurred in 1967, when Warden v. Hayden was decided. The question is what kind of "probable cause" must be established in order to obtain a warrant to conduct an unannounced search for documentary evidence in the private files of a person not suspected of involvement in any criminal activity. The Court holds that a reasonable belief that the files contain relevant evidence is a sufficient justification.

This holding rests on a misconstruction of history and of the Fourth Amendment's purposely broad language.

* * *

In the pre-*Hayden* era warrants were used to search for contraband, weapons and plunder, but not for "mere evidence." The practical effect of the rule prohibiting the issuance of warrants to search for mere evidence was to narrowly limit not only the category of objects, but also the category of persons and the character of the privacy interests that might be affected by an unannounced police search.

Just as the witnesses who participate in an investigation or a trial far outnumber the defendants, the persons who possess evidence that may help to identify an offender, or explain an aspect of a criminal transaction, far outnumber those who have custody of weapons or plunder. Countless law abiding citizens—doctors, lawyers, merchants, customers, bystanders—may have documents in their possession that relate to an ongoing criminal investigation. The consequences of subjecting this large category of persons to unannounced police searches are extremely serious. The ex parte warrant procedure enables the prosecutor to obtain access to privileged documents that could not be examined if advance notice gave the custodian an opportunity to object. The search for the documents described in a warrant may involve the inspection of files containing other private matter. The dramatic character of a sudden search may cause an entirely unjustified injury to the reputation of the persons searched.

Of greatest importance, however, is the question whether the offensive intrusion on the privacy of the ordinary citizen is justified by the law enforcement interest it is intended to vindicate. Possession of contraband or the proceeds or tools of crime gives rise to two inferences: that the custodian is involved in the criminal activity, and that, if given notice of an intended search, he will conceal or destroy what is being sought. The probability of criminal culpability justifies the invasion of his privacy; the need to accomplish the law enforcement purpose of the search justifies acting without advance notice and by force, if necessary. By satisfying the probable cause standard appropriate for weapons or plunder, the police effectively demonstrate that no less intrusive method of investigation will succeed.

Mere possession of documentary evidence, however, is much less likely to demonstrate that the custodian is guilty of any wrongdoing or that he will not honor a subpoena or informal request to produce it. In the pre-*Hayden* era, evidence of that kind was routinely obtained by procedures that presumed that the custodian would respect his obligation to obey subpoenas and to cooperate in the investigation of crime. These procedures had a constitutional dimension. For the innocent citizen's interest in the privacy of his papers and possessions is an aspect of liberty protected by the Due Process Clause of the Fourteenth Amendment. Notice and an opportunity to object to the deprivation of the citizen's liberty are; therefore, the constitutionally mandated general rule. An exception to that rule can only be justified by strict compliance with the Fourth Amendment. That Amendment flatly prohibits the issuance of any warrant unless justified by probable cause.

A showing of probable cause that was adequate to justify the issuance of a warrant to search for stolen goods in the 18th century does not automatically satisfy the new dimensions of the Fourth Amendment in the post-*Hayden* era. . . . The only conceivable justification for an unannounced search of an innocent citizen is the fear that, if notice were given, he would conceal or destroy the object of the search. . . .

(2) *Privacy Protection Act.* Congress enacted the Privacy Protection Act of 1980 [40] in response to the Supreme Court's decision in *Zurcher*. Title I of the Act was directed at "First Amendment Privacy Protection." It made it generally unlawful for any state or federal officer, in connection with the investigation or prosecution of a criminal offense, to search for or seize any "work product materials" in possession of someone reasonably believed to have a purpose "to disseminate to the public a newspaper, book, broadcast, or other similar form of public communication." The statute further provided that documentary material (other than "work product material") possessed by such persons could be seized if there were reasonable cause to believe that the material would be altered or destroyed if a subpoena were issued.

Title II of the Act provided protection for a broader class of persons: [41]

> (a) The Attorney General shall . . . issue guidelines for the procedures to be employed by any Federal officer or employee, in connection with the investigation or prosecution of an offense, to obtain documentary materials in the private possession of a person when the person is not reasonably believed to be a suspect in such offense or related by blood or marriage to such a suspect, and when the materials sought are not contraband or the fruits or instrumentalities of an offense. The Attorney General shall incorporate in such guidelines—
>
> > (1) a recognition of the personal privacy interests of the person in possession of such documentary materials;
> >
> > (2) a requirement that the least intrusive method or means of obtaining such materials be used which do not substantially jeopardize the availability or usefulness of the materials sought to be obtained;

---

40. 42 U.S.C.A. § 2000aa et seq.. For legislative history, see 1980 U.S.Code Cong. & Admin.News p. 3950.

41. 42 U.S.C.A. § 2000aa–11.

(3) a recognition of special concern for privacy interests in cases in which a search or seizure for such documents would intrude upon a known confidential relationship such as that which may exist between clergyman and parishioner; lawyer and client; or doctor and patient; and

(4) a requirement that an application for a warrant to conduct a search governed by this title be approved by an attorney for the government, except that in an emergency situation the application may be approved by another appropriate supervisory official if within 24 hours of such emergency the appropriate United States Attorney is notified.

* * *

Queries. Would you have placed greater restrictions on third party searches than the Privacy Protection Act did? Or do you agree with *Zurcher* that the protections generally applicable to searches should be adequate for these searches? What remedy would you provide for a violation of regulations issued pursuant to the Act? [42]

(3) *Law Office Searches.* Among the most likely "third parties" to have evidence relevant to business crime activity are lawyers. Do law office searches pose any special problems that might make them "unreasonable" if done in cases where there were no particular necessity to proceed by warrant rather than subpoena? Consider the decision of the Minnesota Supreme Court in *O'Connor v. Johnson*, 287 N.W.2d 400 (Minn.1979): [43]

Wahl, Justice.

This is an original proceeding in the Supreme Court pursuant to Rule 120, Rules of Civil Appellate Procedure, for a writ of prohibition directing respondent, a Ramsey County Municipal Court Judge, to quash an order upholding the validity of a search warrant of an attorney's office. Writ granted.

This case arose from an investigation into certain liquor establishments by the St. Paul Police Department. Believing that false written statements had been made in the applications for liquor licenses for Patrick's Lounge, the police applied for a search warrant to obtain the business records of Patrick's Lounge. When the warrant was executed on July 24, 1978, the accountant indicated that the business records of the former owners were in the possession of attorney David O'Connor, petitioner in this case. The police then obtained a warrant to search petitioner's office for these records.

---

42. The Act provides that issues relating to compliance with the regulations "may not be litigated" and may not provide the basis for the suppression or exclusion of evidence. See 42 U.S.C.A. § 2000aa–12. For the regulations issued pursuant to the statute, see 28 C.F.R. §§ 59.1–59.6.

43. Contra, In re Search Warrant B–21778, 513 Pa. 429, 521 A.2d 422 (1987) (upholding warrant to seize client's non-confidential business documents in lawyer's possession; relies on *Zurcher*).

On July 25, 1978, when three police officers appeared at petitioner's office to execute the warrant, petitioner refused to permit the search and indicated that all his records concerning Patrick's Lounge were contained in a box and his work product file. Petitioner accompanied the police officers to respondent's chambers to move to quash the warrant. Respondent permitted petitioner to retain his work product file but ordered him to leave the box of records in the court's custody. On August 4, 1978, respondent held the box of records not privileged and the search warrant valid. He ordered that the box be turned over to the St. Paul Police Department and that a representative of the Ramsey County Attorney's Office obtain all documents pertaining to Patrick's Lounge from petitioner's work product file after determining that the documents were not protected by the attorney-client privilege or the work product doctrine. After petitioner applied to this court for a writ of prohibition to quash the search warrant, respondent amended his order so that the court, rather than a representative of the county attorney's office, would determine which documents were protected by the attorney-client privilege or the work product doctrine. Only those documents which are not so protected would be given to the police department.

In his application for a writ of prohibition petitioner challenges only that portion of the court's order requiring him to turn over his work product file to the court for this determination. He has apparently abandoned his claim to the box of records. Because the attorney was present so that his office was not searched as the officers had a right to do in executing the warrant, and because the officers were willing to allow the attorney to bring the file and box of records before the court to make a determination of privilege before a seizure was made, it would be relatively easy to find on this record no violation of constitutional rights, the attorney-client privilege, or the work product doctrine, and thus to approve a hybrid procedure—part warrant, part subpoena. This we decline to do. We must instead examine the validity of the search warrant upon which the court's order was based to determine the propriety of that order. The case thus presents us with the very difficult and delicate issue of the reasonableness of searching an attorney's office for documents and files of a particular client to find evidence of criminal wrongdoing. We have here no claim of wrongdoing by the attorney. . . .

. . . There is no question in the instant case that the warrant is based on probable cause and supported by an affidavit. We must decide, however, whether the proposed search was reasonable, even though there was compliance with the literal terms of the constitutional and statutory provisions respecting warrants, in light of the attorney-client privilege, client confidentiality, the work product doctrine, and the criminal defendant's constitutional right to counsel.

* * *

. . . The indispensable relationship of trust between client and attorney and the adequate functioning of our adversary system of justice can only be ensured when the client can completely disclose all the facts—favorable and unfavorable—without the fear that the attorney's files will be seized by police officers pursuant to a search warrant.

* * *

To protect confidential communications between an attorney and his clients, the Supreme Court in Hickman v. Taylor, 329 U.S. 495, 67 S.Ct. 385, 91 L.Ed. 451 (1947), developed a qualified privilege which prevented an attorney's work product from being readily discoverable despite the policy of broad discovery under the Federal Rules of Civil Procedure. . . . The work product doctrine is distinct from and broader than the attorney-client privilege and is especially important in criminal cases. . . . If police are permitted to search through an attorney's files for documents listed in an otherwise valid warrant, the protection afforded an attorney's work product by this doctrine will be destroyed.

A criminal defendant's constitutional right to counsel . . . must also be weighed in determining the reasonableness of a search warrant under Article I, section 10 of the Minnesota Constitution and the Fourth Amendment of the United States Constitution. Not only is effective assistance of counsel a constitutional mandate, it is also necessary to an adversary system of justice to protect the fairness and integrity of the system. . . .

In protecting these rights and privileges we must take care to protect not only the rights of the client who is suspected of criminal wrongdoing in the case which prompts the search warrant, but also the rights of all clients of the attorney whose office is being searched. This leads to a consideration of the particularity requirement regarding the place to be searched. . . . Even though the warrant in the instant case describes the things to be seized with particularity and the location of the office in which they may be found, a search of that office for the items specified of necessity involves a general and exploratory search of all of the attorney's files. It was only by chance that the attorney in this case was present when the police officers came to his office to execute the warrant. Had he been absent and this warrant were held valid under these circumstances, the police would have been free to rifle through his files until they found the documents for which they were searching.

The warrant describes the items to be seized as:

> "Business records, including but not limited to contracts or agreements for the lease or purchase of property or liquor licenses, correspondence, accounting records, bookkeeping entries, ledgers, corporate certificates, articles of incorporation,

partnership agreements, payroll records, cancelled checks, money orders, certified checks, cashiers checks, promissory notes, records of cash transactions, copies of liquor license applications and other liquor license transactions, real estate appraisals, inventory appraisals, profit and loss statements, income statements pertaining to: Stephen F. Conroy, John T. Finley, Patrick C. Igo, Patrick M. McGibbon, and Alden D. Landreville, and Knight Kap Inc., Knight & Day, Inc. and Blackie Inc., doing business as Patrick's Lounge at 1318 Larpenteur Ave. St. Paul, Minnesota."

Given this extensive list of items to be seized, there is no way the police officers could be sure that they had found all of the items to be seized unless they searched every file in the attorney's office.

Even the most particular warrant cannot adequately safeguard client confidentiality, the attorney-client privilege, the attorney's work product, and the criminal defendant's constitutional right to counsel of all of the attorney's clients. It is unreasonable, in any case, to permit law enforcement officers to peruse miscellaneous documents in an attorney's office while attempting to locate documents listed in a search warrant. Even if it were possible to meet the particularity requirement regarding the place to be searched, the file would still contain some confidential information that is immune from seizure under the attorney-client privilege or the work product doctrine. Once that information is revealed to the police, the privileges are lost, and the information cannot be erased from the minds of the police.

It will not unreasonably burden prosecutors' offices and effective law enforcement to require officers to proceed by subpoena duces tecum in seeking documents held by an attorney. Attorneys are required by statute, the Code of Professional Responsibility, and the oath of admission to the bar to preserve and protect the judicial process. Thus, attorneys must respond faithfully and promptly, while still being allowed the opportunity to assert applicable privileges by a motion to quash. . . .

We are aware that the United States Supreme Court has held that a rule denying a search warrant for the premises of a third party and requiring a subpoena duces tecum was not constitutionally mandated. Zurcher v. Stanford Daily, 436 U.S. 547, 98 S.Ct. 1970, 56 L.Ed.2d 525 (1978). That case is distinguishable from the present case because the newspaper had announced a policy of destroying any evidence that might aid in the prosecution of protestors, while an attorney has an ethical obligation to the legal system and would be subject to discipline if he destroyed documents which had been subpoenaed. Moreover, there is no indication that the attorney in this case would have attempted to destroy the documents. A more important distinction between this case and *Zurcher* is that our decision rests not only on the Fourth Amendment of the United States Constitution, but also on Article I, section 10 of the Minnesota Constitution. The states may, as the United States Supreme Court has often recognized, afford their citizens greater protection than the safeguards guaranteed in the Federal Constitution. . . .

We hold that a warrant authorizing the search of an attorney's office is unreasonable and, therefore, invalid when the attorney is not suspected of criminal wrongdoing and there is no threat that the documents sought will be destroyed. Since the county attorney and the court had no legal precedent or guidance with regard to such a search, their failure to use the subpoena process does not preclude them from obtaining these documents by use of a timely subpoena.

Writ of Prohibition granted.

Queries. Suppose O'Connor had been suspected of being a coconspirator in the scheme? Would the problems with the search have been any different? Would the Court have required the prosecutor to proceed by subpoena? Is the real problem in *O'Connor* one of particularity? How "particular" can any search for business documents be? Do searches through a lawyer's files present any problems which differ from those encountered in any file search? Consider these questions again after reading the materials on specificity which follow.

3. SPECIFICITY

ANDRESEN v. MARYLAND
Supreme Court of the United States, 1976.
427 U.S. 463, 96 S.Ct. 2737, 49 L.Ed.2d 627.

MR. JUSTICE BLACKMUN delivered the opinion of the Court.

This case presents the issue whether the introduction into evidence of a person's business records, seized during a search of his offices, violates the Fifth Amendment's command that "[n]o person . . . shall be compelled in any criminal case to be a witness against himself." We also must determine whether the particular searches and seizures here were "unreasonable" and thus violated the prohibition of the Fourth Amendment.

I

In early 1972, a Bi–County Fraud Unit, acting under the joint auspices of the State's Attorneys' Offices of Montgomery and Prince George's Counties, Md., began an investigation of real estate settlement activities in the Washington, D.C., area. At the time, petitioner Andresen was an attorney who, as a sole practitioner, specialized in real estate settlements in Montgomery County. During the Fraud Unit's investigation, his activities came under scrutiny, particularly in connection with a transaction involving Lot 13T in the Potomac Woods subdivision of Montgomery County. The investigation, which included interviews with the purchaser, the mortgage holder, and other lienholders of Lot 13T, as well as an examination of county land records, disclosed that petitioner, acting as settlement attorney, had defrauded Standard–Young Associates, the purchaser of Lot 13T. Petitioner had represented that the property was free of liens and that, accordingly, no title insurance was necessary, when in fact, he knew that there were two outstanding liens on the property. In addition, investigators learned that the lienholders, by threatening to foreclose their liens, had forced a halt to the purchaser's construction on the property. When Standard–Young had confronted petitioner with this information, he responded by issuing, as an agent of a title insurance company, a title policy guaranteeing clear title to the property. By this action, petitioner also defrauded that insurance company by requiring it to pay the outstanding liens.

The investigators, concluding that there was probable cause to believe that petitioner had committed the state crime of false pretenses against Standard–Young, applied for warrants to search petitioner's law office and the separate office of Mount Vernon Development Corporation, of which petitioner was incorporator, sole shareholder, resident agent, and director. The application sought permission to search for specified documents pertaining to the sale and conveyance of Lot 13T. A judge of the Sixth Judicial Circuit of Montgomery County concluded that there was probable cause and issued the warrants.

The searches of the two offices were conducted simultaneously during daylight hours on October 31, 1972. Petitioner was present during the search of his law office and was free to move about. Counsel for him was present during the latter half of the search. Between 2% and 3% of the files in the office were seized. A single investigator, in the presence of a police officer, conducted the search of Mount Vernon Development Corporation. This search, taking about four hours, resulted in the seizure of less than 5% of the corporation's files.

Petitioner eventually was charged, partly by information and partly by indictment, with the crime of false pretenses, based on his misrepresentation to Standard–Young concerning Lot 13T, and with fraudulent misappropriation by a fiduciary, based on similar false claims made to three home purchasers. Before trial began, petitioner moved to suppress the seized documents. The trial court held a full suppression hearing. At the hearing, the State returned to petitioner 45 of the 52 items taken from the offices of the corporation. The trial court suppressed six other corporation items on the ground that there was no connection between them and the crimes charged. The net result was that the only item seized from the corporation's offices that was not returned by the State or suppressed was a single file labeled "Potomac Woods General." In addition, the State returned to petitioner seven of the 28 items seized from his law office, and the trial court suppressed four other law office items based on its determination that there was no connection between them and the crime charged.

* * *

After a trial by jury, petitioner was found guilty upon five counts of false pretenses and three counts of fraudulent misappropriation by a fiduciary. He was sentenced to eight concurrent two-year prison terms.

On appeal . . . the Court of Special Appeals rejected petitioner's Fourth and Fifth Amendment claims . . .

We granted certiorari limited to the Fourth and Fifth Amendment issues.

II

[The Court held that the search and seizure did not compel Andresen to testify against himself in violation of the fifth amendment.]

III

We turn next to petitioner's contention that rights guaranteed him by the Fourth Amendment were violated because the descriptive terms of the search warrants were so broad as to make them impermissible "general" warrants, and because certain items were seized in violation of the principles of Warden v. Hayden, 387 U.S. 294, 18 L.Ed.2d 782, 87 S.Ct. 1642 (1967).

The specificity of the search warrants. Although petitioner concedes that the warrants for the most part were models of particularity, he contends that they were rendered fatally "general" by the addition, in each warrant, to the exhaustive list of particularly described documents, of the phrase "together with other fruits, instrumentalities and evidence of crime at this [time] unknown." The quoted language, it is argued, must be read in isolation and without reference to the rest of the long sentence at the end of which it appears. When read "properly," petitioner contends, it permits the search for and seizure of any evidence of any crime.

General warrants, of course, are prohibited by the Fourth Amendment. "[T]he problem [posed by the general warrant] is not that of intrusion per se, but of a general, exploratory rummaging in a person's belongings. . . . [The Fourth Amendment addresses the problem] by requiring a 'particular description' of the things to be seized." Coolidge v. New Hampshire, 403 U.S. 443, 467 (1971). This requirement "'makes general searches . . . impossible and prevents the seizure of one thing under a warrant describing another. As to what is to be taken, nothing is left to the discretion of the officer executing the warrant.'" Stanford v. Texas, 379 U.S. 476, 485 (1965), quoting Marron v. United States, 275 U.S., at 196.

In this case we agree with the determination of the Court of Special Appeals of Maryland that the challenged phrase must be read as authorizing only the search for and seizure of evidence relating to "the crime of false pretenses with respect to Lot 13T." The challenged phrase is not a separate sentence. Instead, it appears in each warrant at the end of a sentence containing a lengthy list of specified and particular items to be seized, all pertaining to Lot 13T.[44] We think it clear from the context that the term "crime" in the warrants refers only to the crime of false pretenses with respect to the sale of Lot 13T. The "other fruits" clause is one of a series that follows the colon after the word "Maryland." All clauses in the series are limited by what precedes that colon, namely, "items pertaining to . . . lot 13, block T." The warrants, accordingly, did not authorize the executing officers to conduct a search for evidence of other crimes but only to search for and seize evidence relevant to the crime of false pretenses and Lot 13T.[45]

The admissibility of certain items of evidence in light of Warden v. Hayden. Petitioner charges that the seizure of documents pertaining to a lot other than Lot 13T violated the principles of Warden v. Hayden and therefore should have been suppressed. His objection appears to be that these papers were not relevant to the Lot 13T charge and were admissible only to prove another crime with which he was charged

---

44. [Court's footnote 10.] "[T]he following items pertaining to sale, purchase, settlement and conveyance of lot 13, block T, Potomac Woods subdivision, Montgomery County, Maryland:

"title notes, title abstracts, title rundowns; contracts of sale and/or assignments from Raffaele Antonelli and Rocco Caniglia to Mount Vernon Development Corporation and/or others; lien payoff correspondence and lien pay-off memoranda to and from lienholders and noteholders; correspondence and memoranda to and from trustees of deeds of trust; lenders instructions for a construction loan or construction and permanent loan; disbursement sheets and disbursement memoranda; checks, check stubs and ledger sheets indicating disbursement upon settlement; correspondence and memoranda concerning disbursements upon settlement; settlement statements and settlement memoranda; fully or partially prepared deed of trust releases, whether or not executed and whether or not recorded; books, records, documents, papers, memoranda and correspondence, showing or tending to show a fraudulent intent, and/or knowledge as elements of the crime of false pretenses, in violation of Article 27, Section 140, of the Annotated Code of Maryland, 1957 Edition, as amended and revised, together with other fruits, instrumentalities and evidence of crime at this [time] unknown."

Petitioner also suggests that the specific list of the documents to be seized constitutes a "general" warrant. We disagree. Under investigation was a complex real estate scheme whose existence could be proved only by piecing together many bits of evidence. Like a jigsaw puzzle, the whole "picture" of petitioner's false-pretense scheme with respect to Lot 13T could be shown only by placing in the proper place the many pieces of evidence that, taken singly, would show comparatively little. The complexity of an illegal scheme may not be used as a shield to avoid detection when the State has demonstrated probable cause to believe that a crime has been committed and probable cause to believe that evidence of this crime is in the suspect's possession. . . .

45. [Court's footnote 11.] The record discloses that the officials executing the warrants seized numerous papers that were not introduced into evidence. Although we are not informed of their content, we observe that to the extent such papers were not within the scope of the warrants or were otherwise improperly seized, the State was correct in returning them voluntarily and the trial judge was correct in suppressing others.

We recognize that there are grave dangers inherent in executing a warrant authorizing a search and seizure of a person's papers that are not necessarily present in executing a warrant to search for physical objects whose relevance is more easily ascertainable. In searches for papers, it is certain that some innocuous documents will be examined, at least cursorily, in order to determine whether they are, in fact, among those papers authorized to be seized. Similar dangers, of course, are present in executing a warrant for the "seizure" of telephone conversations. In both kinds of searches, responsible officials, including judicial officials, must take care to assure that they are conducted in a manner that minimizes unwarranted intrusions upon privacy.

after the search. The fact that these documents were used to help form the evidentiary basis for another charge, it is argued, shows that the documents were seized solely for that purpose.

The State replies that Warden v. Hayden was not violated and that this is so because the challenged evidence is relevant to the question whether petitioner committed the crime of false pretenses with respect to Lot 13T. In Maryland, ... the State is required to prove intent to defraud beyond a reasonable doubt. The State consequently argues that the documents pertaining to another lot in the Potomac Woods subdivision demonstrate that the misrepresentation with respect to Lot 13T was not the result of mistake on the part of petitioner.

In Warden v. Hayden, the Court stated that when the police seize " 'mere evidence,' probable cause must be examined in terms of cause to believe that the evidence sought will aid in a particular apprehension or conviction. In so doing, consideration of police purposes will be required." In this case, we conclude that the trained special investigators reasonably could have believed that the evidence specifically dealing with another lot in the Potomac Woods subdivision could be used to show petitioner's intent with respect to the Lot 13T transaction.

The Court has often recognized that proof of similar acts is admissible to show intent or the absence of mistake. . . . In the present case, when the special investigators secured the search warrants, they had been informed of a number of similar charges against petitioner arising out of Potomac Woods transactions. And, by reading numerous documents and records supplied by the Lot 13T and other complainants, and by interviewing witnesses, they had become familiar with petitioner's method of operation. Accordingly, the relevance of documents pertaining specifically to a lot other than Lot 13T, and their admissibility to show the Lot 13T offense, would have been apparent. Lot 13T and the other lot had numerous features in common. Both were in the same section of the Potomac Woods subdivision; both had been owned by the same person; and transactions concerning both had been handled extensively by petitioner. Most important was the fact that there were two deeds of trust in which both lots were listed as collateral. Unreleased liens respecting both lots were evidenced by these deeds of trusts. Petitioner's transactions relating to the other lot, subject to the same liens as Lot 13T, therefore, were highly relevant to the question whether his failure to deliver title to Lot 13T free of all encumbrances was mere inadvertence. Although these records subsequently were used to secure additional charges against petitioner, suppression of this evidence in this case was not required. The fact that the records could be used to show intent to defraud with respect to Lot 13T permitted the seizure and satisfied the requirements of Warden v. Hayden.

The judgment of the Court of Special Appeals of Maryland is affirmed.

It is so ordered.

Ch. 6   GOVERNMENT EVIDENCE GATHERING   563

[JUSTICES BRENNAN and MARSHALL dissented, arguing that the warrants were impermissibly general.]

NOTES AND QUERIES

(1) *Queries.* What is the purpose of the particularity requirement? Is it just to limit the discretion of the executing officers? Wouldn't a warrant "to seize everything" limit discretion and give direction to the officers in the field? Would such a warrant therefore be lawful?

Is there some connection between the particularity requirement and the probable cause requirement? If so, is this then linked with the rejection of the "mere evidence" rule in *Warden v. Hayden?* Is it easier to particularize and make a probable cause showing for warrants that seek fruits of the crime, contraband, and/or instrumentalities of the crime?

Do you agree that the warrant in *Andresen* was sufficiently particular? Note that the prosecutor voluntarily returned a rather large amount of the materials seized under the warrant. Does this give you confidence in the warrant's particularity? Or are such after-the-fact evaluations of reasonably seized documents inevitable in searches of this sort?

(2) *Is Specificity Possible?* Consider *Application of Lafayette Academy,* 610 F.2d 1 (1st Cir.1979):

> LEVIN H. CAMPBELL, CIRCUIT JUDGE.
>
> The government appeals from the district court's allowance of appellees' motions, filed pursuant to Fed.R.Crim.P. 41(e), for return of property. We affirm the judgment of the district court.
>
> Appellee Lafayette Academy, Inc. owns and operates a vocational home-study school which participated in the Federal Insured Student Loan Program (FISLP). Lafayette Academy and its two subsidiaries came under investigation for possible fraudulent practices in connection with their participation in FISLP. The investigating officer by affidavit set forth the observations, information, and conclusions of various officials of the Department of Health, Education and Welfare, the Office of Education, and former employees of Lafayette Academy as well as his own with respect to Lafayette's irregular practices in recordkeeping and violations of federal regulations respecting the student loan program. Based upon his affidavit, a warrant issued authorizing the seizure of
>
>> "books, papers, rosters of students, letters, correspondence, documents, memoranda, contracts, agreements, ledgers, worksheets, books of account, student files, file jackets and contents, computer tapes/discs, computer operation manuals, computer tape logs, computer tape layouts, computer tape printouts, Office of Education (HEW) documents and forms, cancellation reports and directives, reinstatement reports or forms, Government loan registers, refund ledgers, reports and notes, adminis-

trative reports, financial data cards, lesson and grading cards and registers, registration (corporations) documents, student collection reports, financial documents (corporations), journals of accounts and student survey data, which are and constitute evidence of the commission of violations of the laws of the United States, that is violations of 18 U.S.C., Sections 286, 287, 371, 1001 and 1014; . . ."

from appellees' place of business. The warrant was executed the next day by approximately thirty government agents who seized a substantial percentage of the records on the searched premises, employing four or five trucks to remove the seized material.

We hold with the district court that the warrant does not describe the "things to be seized" with the particularity required by the fourth amendment. The warrant is framed to allow seizure of most every sort of book or paper at the described premises, limited only by the qualification that the seized item be evidence of violations of "the laws of the United States, that is violations of 18 U.S.C. Sections 286, 287, 371, 1001, and 1014." The cited statutes, however, penalize a very wide range of frauds and conspiracies. They are not limited to frauds pertaining to FISLP, and there is no indication from the warrant that the violations of federal law as to which evidence is being sought stem only or indeed at all from Lafayette's participation in FISLP. Thus, the warrant purports to authorize not just a search and seizure of FISLP-related records as the government contends but a general rummaging for evidence of any type of federal conspiracy or fraud. Here, at a minimum, the precise nature of the fraud and conspiracy offenses for evidence of which the search was authorized—fraud and conspiracy in the FISLP—needed to be stated in order to delimit the broad categories of documentary material and thus to meet the particularity requirement of the fourth amendment.[46]

---

46. [Court's footnote 4.] This is not to suggest that a description of those documents which are to be seized from among a large number solely in terms of their relevancy to a particular fraud or other crime—i.e., "all documents evidencing fraud in connection with FISLP"—would necessarily suffice. In many instances of warrants authorizing the seizure of documents from a general file efforts may also be required to narrow the documents by category, time periods, and the like.

It is interesting (although of no help to the government in view of the failure to incorporate—see discussion infra) that the listing of documents in the affidavit reflects an attempt at narrowing along the foregoing lines. Unlike the warrant description, the listing in the affidavit did not commence with the all-inclusive words "books, papers." Rather, more prudently, it listed the following subcategories of records:

"1. Records of student financial accounts

2. Student applications

3. Student account cards

4. Student grade cards

5. Student correspondence files

6. General student files

7. Correspondence files to OE and HEW; to FISL lender banks; to NHSC

8. Student roster 1969 to present

9. Financial statements of Lafayette

10. General books of account, including cash receipts, disbursements, general journals, corporate ledgers

11. Notes receivable and notes payable

The government argues, however, that the requisite specificity is supplied by the affidavit. "The traditional rule is that the generality of a warrant cannot be cured by the specificity of the affidavit which supports it . . . Specificity is required in the warrant itself in order to limit the discretion of the executing officers as well as to give notice to the party searched." United States v. Johnson, 541 F.2d 1311, 1315 (8th Cir.1976). Under some circumstances, however, an affidavit may cure deficiencies which would exist were the warrant to stand alone. In United States v. Klein, 565 F.2d 183 (1st Cir.1977), this court stated,

> "An affidavit may be referred to for purposes of providing particularity if the affidavit accompanies the warrant, *and* the warrant uses suitable words of reference which incorporate the affidavit." (Emphasis in original.)

. . . Here the district court found and the government has not disputed that the affidavit was not served with the warrant. Nor does the warrant language incorporate the affidavit. Hence, the above standard was not satisfied.

The government argues that where, as here, the executing officers have proceeded as if the inadvertently broad warrant language were limited by the affidavit, the omission of the formal requisites—words of incorporation and stapling the affidavit to the warrant—should not invalidate the search and seizure. The government points out that the affiant, who was knowledgeable in the FISLP and its operation, directed and supervised the search and seizure and took steps to insure that only FISLP-related records were seized. Furthermore, HEW Office of Education program compliance officers and auditors, specialists in FISLP, assisted during the search to identify FISLP records. Thus, the executing officers never had any doubt that only FISLP-related records, not records of other types of fraud or conspiracy, were to be searched and seized and consequently there was no danger of the officers

12. Instructors' grade books
13. Savings accounts of Lafayette
14. Printouts on FISL transactions
15. List of refunds to students
16. FISL student financial cards
17. Contracts with FISL lender banks
18. Copies of reports to OE and HEW
19. FISL student extension of graduation date forms, 1970 to present
20. FISL loans paid off by Lafayette
21. Student complaint memos
22. Computer tapes and microfilms
23. Computer tape layouts and computer tape printouts
24. Cancellation reports and directives
25. Refund ledgers"

and then concluded with the tailored catchall

"26. Books, papers, memoranda, which may relate to the above requested documents."

While we need not now determine whether this more particularized approach, had it been followed in the warrant listing, was either essential or, by itself, would have saved the day, we do say without hesitation that it is better practice, and sometimes may be absolutely essential, for prosecutors whenever possible to frame documentary descriptions in particularized terms. . . .

exceeding the scope of their authority as contemplated by the affidavit, the government maintains.

Even if the government were to prove that the executing officers all understood only FISLP-related documents were the subject of the search and seizure, and that they acted as if the warrant had explicitly so stated, we would be compelled to reject the government's attempt to cure the overbreadth of the warrant language by the specificity of the affidavit. This is because the requirement that the warrant itself particularly describe the material to be seized is not only to circumscribe the discretion of the executing officers but also to inform the person subject to the search and seizure what the officers are entitled to take. Even assuming the government is able to prove the first purpose was otherwise served, the second was not. Moreover, self-restraint on the part of the instant executing officers does not erase the fact that under the broadly worded warrant appellees were subject to a greater exercise of power than that which may have actually transpired and for which probable cause had been established. The particularity requirement is a check to just this sort of risk.

We have said that a principle deficiency here is the lack of particularity in the phrase which purports to qualify and delineate the generic categories of items: the description "books, papers . . . letters, correspondence, documents, . . . which are and constitute evidence of the commission of violations of the [federal conspiracy and fraud statutes]" provides insufficient guidance to the executing officer as to what items from among many he should seize. The qualifying phrase in effect does nothing to limit the broad warrant description. If, of course, the generic descriptions were sufficiently specific and particular standing alone, the defect in the qualifying phrase would be of no effect. For the most part, though, the categories listed here are too broad. . . . True, it could be argued that as the above description authorizes in effect the search and seizure of all books, papers, etc., the warrant does not suffer from a lack of particularity. The directions to the executing officer are straightforward—he is to cart away all documents. But while, so interpreted, the description would be particular enough, it would also be too broad to satisfy the probable cause requirements of the fourth amendment. The affidavit does not establish probable cause to search and seize all of those items.

In contrast to the broad categories of items set forth above, certain of the warrant items may be sufficiently particularized standing alone, for example, "rosters of students," "student files, file jackets and contents," "lesson and grading cards and registers," "student collection reports," and "student survey data." However, while these documentary descriptions may be sufficiently specific, they cover documents antedating Lafayette Academy's participation in FISLP. According to the affidavit in support of the warrant, Lafayette Academy was organized as a correspondence school in 1969 but did not participate in FISLP until 1972. While the affidavit establishes the relevance of post–1972 student documents, it does not indicate any nexus between the earlier student documents and alleged criminal behavior. The warrant thus improperly authorizes the seizure of documents that are apparently irrelevant to the fraud.

Two categories remain: "computer operation manuals" and "Office of Education (HEW) documents and forms." The relevance of the first is not apparent from the affidavit. Perhaps the manuals were to assist the agents in procuring and interpreting computer tape printouts, but as the printouts must now be returned, the manuals no longer appear to serve any purpose. The second is too general. The Office of Education operates many programs in addition to FISLP. It is quite conceivable that Lafayette participated in other OE programs and filled out documents and forms in conjunction therewith. The affidavit does not establish probable cause for the seizure of non–FISLP documents and forms, and therefore the description is insufficient.

Since we determine that the description of no item is free from fourth amendment difficulties, we do not reach the issue of severability. Because the warrant does not satisfy fourth amendment requirements we affirm the judgment of the district court granting appellees' Rule 41(e) motions. We express no opinion whether the government may reobtain part or all of the seized material by subpoena, properly limited warrant, or other means.

Affirmed.

Kunzig, Judge (concurring).

I am forced to concur with Judge Campbell's able decision in this case, but only because of the excessively broad and generalized wording of the warrant as drawn.

I would want to caution attorneys and prospective litigants that technical errors will not necessarily always prove the "easy out" that this decision seemingly portends. In this era of expanding white collar fraud, it may be that future court decisions will tend toward narrower interpretations of Fourth Amendment protections in this type of situation. I would hope so.

In the case at bar, however, too many errors (such as failure to incorporate the affidavit in the warrant) make such a decision impossible.

Therefore, with great reluctance, given the factual situation in this close and difficult case, I feel compelled to concur.

Queries. How would you have written the warrant to make it sufficiently specific? Even if the warrant adequately identifies relevant types of documents, won't the executing officers still engage in a great deal of "rummaging" through the specified documents in search for evidentiary information? If we allow document seizures, is it possible adequately to protect a citizen's privacy rights?

4. REMEDY

MASSACHUSETTS v. SHEPPARD

Supreme Court of the United States, 1984.
468 U.S. 981, 104 S.Ct. 3424, 82 L.Ed.2d 737.

JUSTICE WHITE delivered the opinion of the Court.

This case involves the application of the rules articulated today in United States v. Leon, to a situation in which police officers seize items pursuant to a warrant subsequently invalidated because of a technical error on the part of the issuing judge.

I

[Detective Peter O'Malley, in the course of investigating a homicide, applied for a warrant to arrest one of the victim's boyfriends, Osborne Sheppard, and to search Sheppard's house. O'Malley drafted an affidavit stating that the police wished to search for

> "[a] fifth bottle of amaretto liquor, 2 nickel bags of marijuana, a woman's jacket that has been described as black-grey (charcoal), any possessions of Sandra D. Boulware, similar type wire and rope that match those on the body of Sandra D. Boulware, or in the above Thunderbird. A blunt instrument that might have been used on the victim, men's or women's clothing that may have blood, gasoline burns on them. Items that may have fingerprints of the victim."]

Because it was Sunday, the local court was closed, and the police had a difficult time finding a warrant application form. Detective O'Malley finally found a warrant form previously in use in the Dorchester District. The form was entitled "Search Warrant—Controlled Substance G.L. c. 276 §§ 1 through 3A." Realizing that some changes had to be made before the form could be used to authorize the search requested in the affidavit, Detective O'Malley deleted the subtitle "controlled substance" with a typewriter. He also substituted "Roxbury" for the printed "Dorchester" and typed Sheppard's name and address into blank spaces provided for that information. However, the reference to "controlled substance" was not deleted in the portion of the form that constituted the warrant application and that, when signed, would constitute the warrant itself.

Detective O'Malley then took the affidavit and the warrant form to the residence of a judge who had consented to consider the warrant application. The judge examined the affidavit and stated that he would authorize the search as requested. Detective O'Malley offered the warrant form and stated that he knew the form as presented dealt with controlled substances. He showed the judge where he had crossed out the subtitles. After unsuccessfully searching for a more suitable form, the judge informed O'Malley that he would make the necessary changes so as to provide a proper search warrant. The judge then took the form, made some changes on it, and dated and signed the warrant. However, he did not change the substantive portion of the warrant, which continued to authorize a search for controlled substances;[47] nor did he alter the form so as to incorporate the affidavit. The judge returned the affidavit and the warrant to O'Malley, informing him that the warrant was sufficient authority in form and content to carry out the search as requested. O'Malley took the two documents and, accompanied by other officers, proceeded to Sheppard's residence. The scope of the ensuing search was limited to the items listed in the affidavit, and several incriminating pieces of evidence were discovered. Sheppard was then charged with first degree murder.

At a pretrial suppression hearing, the trial judge concluded that the warrant failed to conform to the commands of the Fourth Amendment because it did not particularly describe the items to be seized. The judge ruled, however, that the evidence could be admitted notwithstanding the defect in the warrant because the police had acted in good faith in executing what they reasonably thought was a valid warrant. At the subsequent trial, Sheppard was convicted.

On appeal, Sheppard argued that the evidence obtained pursuant to the defective warrant should have been suppressed. The Supreme Judicial Court of Massachusetts agreed. . . . We granted certiorari and set the case for argument in conjunction with United States v. Leon.

[The Court decided *Leon* on the same day it decided Massachusetts v. Sheppard. The case is excerpted infra this Casebook, Note (1), p. 572. Involved in *Leon* was a search conducted pursuant to a warrant subsequently found to be unsupported by probable cause. The Supreme Court held that the officers' reliance on the magistrate's determination of probable cause was objectively reasonable, and that, accordingly, the evidence seized could be admitted at trial.]

* * *

II

Having already decided that the exclusionary rule should not be applied when the officer conducting the search acted in objectively reasonable reliance on a warrant issued by a detached and neutral magistrate that subsequently is determined to be invalid, the sole issue before us in this case is whether the officers reasonably believed that the search they conducted was authorized by a valid warrant.[48] There

---

47. [Court's footnote 2.] The warrant directed the officers to "search for any controlled substance, article, implement or other paraphernalia used in, for, or in connection with the unlawful possession or use of any controlled substance, and to seize and securely keep the same until final action. . . ."

48. [Court's footnote 5.] Both the trial court, and a majority of the Supreme Judicial Court, concluded that the warrant was constitutionally defective because the description in the warrant was completely inaccurate and the warrant did not incorporate the description contained in the afis no dispute that the officers believed that the warrant authorized the search that they conducted. Thus, the only question is whether there was an objectively reasonable basis for the officers' mistaken belief. Both the trial court and a majority of the Supreme Judicial Court concluded that there was. We agree.

The officers in this case took every step that could reasonably be expected of them. Detective O'Malley prepared an affidavit which was reviewed and approved by the District Attorney. He presented that affidavit to a neutral judge. The judge concluded that the affidavit established probable cause to search Sheppard's residence, and informed O'Malley that he would authorize the search as requested. O'Malley then produced the warrant form and informed the judge that it might need to be changed. He was told by the judge that the necessary changes would be made. He then observed the judge make some changes and received the warrant and the affidavit. At this point, a reasonable police officer would have concluded, as O'Malley did, that the warrant authorized a search for the materials outlined in the affidavit.

Sheppard contends that since O'Malley knew the warrant form was defective, he should have examined it to make sure that the necessary changes had been made. However, that argument is based on the premise that O'Malley had a duty to disregard the judge's assurances that the requested search would be authorized and the necessary changes would be made. Whatever an officer may be required to do when he executes a warrant without knowing beforehand what items are to be seized,[49] we refuse to rule that an officer is required to disbelieve a judge who has just advised him, by word and by action, that the warrant he possesses authorizes him to conduct the search he has requested. . . .

In sum, the police conduct in this case clearly was objectively reasonable and largely error-free. An error of constitutional dimen-

fidavit. Petitioner does not dispute this conclusion.

Petitioner does argue, however, that even though the warrant was invalid, the search was constitutional because it was reasonable within the meaning of the Fourth Amendment. The uniformly applied rule is that a search conducted pursuant to a warrant that fails to conform to the particularity requirement of the Fourth Amendment is unconstitutional. That rule is in keeping with the well-established principle that "except in certain carefully defined classes of cases, a search of private property without proper consent is 'unreasonable' unless it has been authorized by a valid warrant." Camara v. Municipal Court, 387 U.S. 523, 528–529, 87 S.Ct. 1727, 1730–1731, 18 L.Ed.2d 930 (1967). . . .

49. [Court's footnote 6.] Normally, when an officer who has not been involved in the application stage receives a warrant, he will read it in order to determine the object of the search. In this case, Detective O'Malley, the officer who directed the search, knew what items were listed in the affidavit presented to the judge, and he had good reason to believe that the warrant authorized the seizure of those items. Whether an officer who is less familiar with the warrant application or who has unalleviated concerns about the proper scope of the search would be justified in failing to notice a defect like the one in the warrant in this case is an issue we need not decide. We hold only that it was not unreasonable for the police in this case to rely on the judge's assurances that the warrant authorized the search they had requested.

sions may have been committed with respect to the issuance of the warrant, but it was the judge, not the police officers, who made the critical mistake. . . . Suppressing evidence because the judge failed to make all the necessary clerical corrections despite his assurances that such changes would be made will not serve the deterrent function that the exclusionary rule was designed to achieve. Accordingly, federal law does not require the exclusion of the disputed evidence in this case. The judgment of the Supreme Judicial Court is therefore reversed, and the case is remanded for further proceedings not inconsistent with this opinion.

It is so ordered.

[JUSTICE STEVENS concurred in the judgment. Although believing the search was "reasonable" and therefore not violative of the fourth amendment, he disagreed with creating a "good faith" exception to the exclusionary rule:

"[U]nder our cases it has never been "reasonable" for the police to rely on the mere fact that a warrant has issued; the police have always known that if they fail to supply the magistrate with sufficient information, the warrant will be held invalid and its fruits excluded.

The notion that a police officer's reliance on a magistrate's warrant is automatically appropriate is one the Framers of the Fourth Amendment would have vehemently rejected. The precise problem that the Amendment was intended to address was the unreasonable issuance of warrants. As we have often observed, the Amendment was actually motivated by the practice of issuing general warrants—warrants which did not satisfy the particularity and probable cause requirements. . . .

. . . The fact that colonial officers had magisterial authorization for their conduct when they engaged in general searches surely did not make their conduct "reasonable." The Court's view that it is consistent with our Constitution to adopt a rule that it is presumptively reasonable to rely on a defective warrant is the product of constitutional amnesia.]

[JUSTICE BRENNAN wrote a dissenting opinion in which JUSTICE MARSHALL joined. In the course of his opinion, JUSTICE BRENNAN wrote:

Although the Court's opinion tends to overlook this fact, the requirement of particularity is not a mere "technicality," it is an express constitutional command. The purpose of that requirement is to prevent precisely the kind of governmental conduct that the faulty warrant at issue here created a grave risk of permitting—namely, a search that was not narrowly and particularly limited to the things that a neutral and detached magistrate had reason to believe might be found at respondent's home. . . .

What the Framers of the Bill of Rights sought to accomplish through the express requirements of the Fourth Amendment was to define precisely the conditions under which government agents could search private property so that citizens would not have to depend solely upon the discretion and restraint of those agents for the protection of their privacy. Although the self-restraint and care exhibited by the officers in this case is commendable, that alone can never be a sufficient protection for constitutional liberties. I am convinced that it is not too much to ask that an attentive magistrate take those minimum steps necessary to ensure that every warrant he issues describes with particularity the things that his independent review of the warrant application convinces him are likely to be found in the premises. And I am equally convinced that it is not too much to ask that well-trained and experienced police officers take a moment to check that the warrant they have been issued at least describes those things for which they have sought leave to search. These convictions spring not from my own view of sound criminal law enforcement policy, but are instead compelled by the language of the Fourth Amendment and the history that led to its adoption.]

NOTES AND QUERIES

(1) *The Rationale for the "Good Faith Exception"*. In *United States v. Leon*[50] the Court explained the reason for admitting evidence seized in "objective good faith" under a constitutionally defective warrant:

> Whether the exclusionary sanction is appropriately imposed in a particular case . . . must be resolved by weighing the costs and benefits of preventing the use in the prosecution's case-in-chief of inherently trustworthy tangible evidence obtained in reliance on a search warrant issued by a detached and neutral magistrate that ultimately is found to be defective.
>
> The substantial social costs exacted by the exclusionary rule for the vindication of Fourth Amendment rights have long been a source of concern. . . . Particularly when law enforcement officers have acted in objective good faith or their transgressions have been minor, the magnitude of the benefit conferred on such guilty defendants offends basic concepts of the criminal justice system. Indiscriminate application of the exclusionary rule, therefore, may well "generat[e] disrespect for the law and the administration of justice." . . .
>
> * * *
>
> Because a search warrant "provides the detached scrutiny of a neutral magistrate, which is a more reliable safeguard against improper searches than the hurried judgment of a law enforcement officer 'engaged in the often competitive enterprise of ferreting out crime,'" we have expressed a strong preference for warrants and declared that "in a doubtful or marginal case a search under a warrant may be sustainable where without one it would fail."

50. 468 U.S. 897, 104 S.Ct. 3405, 82 L.Ed.2d 677 (1984).

Reasonable minds frequently may differ on the question whether a particular affidavit establishes probable cause, and we have thus concluded that the preference for warrants is most appropriately effectuated by according "great deference" to a magistrate's determination.

Deference to the magistrate, however, is not boundless. It is clear, first, that the deference accorded to a magistrate's finding of probable cause does not preclude inquiry into the knowing or reckless falsity of the affidavit on which that determination was based. Second, the courts must also insist that the magistrate purport to "perform his 'neutral and detached' function and not serve merely as a rubber stamp for the police." A magistrate failing to "manifest that neutrality and detachment demanded of a judicial officer when presented with a warrant application" and who acts instead as "an adjunct law enforcement officer" cannot provide valid authorization for an otherwise unconstitutional search.

Third, reviewing courts will not defer to a warrant based on an affidavit that does not "provide the magistrate with a substantial basis for determining the existence of probable cause." "Sufficient information must be presented to the magistrate to allow that official to determine probable cause; his action cannot be a mere ratification of the bare conclusions of others."

Only in the first of these three situations, however, has the Court set forth a rationale for suppressing evidence obtained pursuant to a search warrant; in the other areas, it has simply excluded such evidence without considering whether Fourth Amendment interests will be advanced. To the extent that proponents of exclusion rely on its behavioral effects on judges and magistrates in these areas, their reliance is misplaced. First, the exclusionary rule is designed to deter police misconduct rather than to punish the errors of judges and magistrates. Second, there exists no evidence suggesting that judges and magistrates are inclined to ignore or subvert the Fourth Amendment or that lawlessness among these actors requires application of the extreme sanction of exclusion.

Third, and most important, we discern no basis, and are offered none, for believing that exclusion of evidence seized pursuant to a warrant will have a significant deterrent effect on the issuing judge or magistrate. Many of the factors that indicate that the exclusionary rule cannot provide an effective "special" or "general" deterrent for individual offending law enforcement officers apply as well to judges or magistrates. And, to the extent that the rule is thought to operate as a "systemic" deterrent on a wider audience, it clearly can have no such effect on individuals empowered to issue search warrants. Judges and magistrates are not adjuncts to the law enforcement team; as neutral judicial officers, they have no stake in the outcome of particular criminal prosecutions. The threat of exclusion thus cannot be expected significantly to deter them. . . .

If exclusion of evidence obtained pursuant to a subsequently invalidated warrant is to have any deterrent effect, therefore, it must alter the behavior of individual law enforcement officers or the policies of their departments. . . . We . . . conclude that suppression of evidence obtained pursuant to a warrant should be ordered only on a case-by-case basis and only in those unusual cases in which exclusion will further the purposes of the exclusionary rule.[51]

We have frequently questioned whether the exclusionary rule can have any deterrent effect when the offending officers acted in the objectively reasonable belief that their conduct did not violate the Fourth Amendment. . . . But even assuming that the rule effectively deters some police misconduct and provides incentives for the law enforcement profession as a whole to conduct itself in accord with the Fourth Amendment, it cannot be expected, and should not be applied, to deter objectively reasonable law enforcement activity.

* * *

This is particularly true, we believe, when an officer acting with objective good faith has obtained a search warrant from a judge or magistrate and acted within its scope.[52] In most such cases, there is no police illegality and thus nothing to deter. It is the magistrate's responsibility to determine whether the officer's allegations establish probable cause and, if so, to issue a warrant comporting in form with the requirements of the Fourth Amendment. In the ordinary case, an officer cannot be expected to question the magistrate's probable-cause determination or his judgment that the form of the warrant is technically sufficient. . . . Penalizing the officer for the magistrate's error, rather than his own, cannot logically contribute to the deterrence of Fourth Amendment violations.

We conclude that the marginal or nonexistent benefits produced by suppressing evidence obtained in objectively reasonable reliance on a subsequently invalidated search warrant cannot justify the substantial costs of exclusion. We do not suggest, however, that exclusion is always inappropriate in cases where an officer has obtained a warrant and abided by its terms. . . . [T]he officer's

---

51. [Court's footnote 19.] Our discussion of the deterrent effect of excluding evidence obtained in reasonable reliance on a subsequently invalidated warrant assumes, of course, that the officers properly executed the warrant and searched only those places and for those objects that it was reasonable to believe were covered by the warrant.

52. [Court's footnote 20.] We emphasize that the standard of reasonableness we adopt is an objective one. Many objections to a good faith exception assume that the exception will turn on the subjective good faith of individual officers. . . . The objective standard we adopt, moreover, requires officers to have a reasonable knowledge of what the law prohibits. . . .

reliance on the magistrate's probable-cause determination and on the technical sufficiency of the warrant he issues must be objectively reasonable, and it is clear that in some circumstances the officer will have no reasonable grounds for believing that the warrant was properly issued.

Suppression therefore remains an appropriate remedy if the magistrate or judge in issuing a warrant was misled by information in an affidavit that the affiant knew was false or would have known was false except for his reckless disregard of the truth. The exception we recognize today will also not apply in cases where the issuing magistrate wholly abandoned his judicial role . . .; in such circumstances, no reasonably well-trained officer should rely on the warrant. Nor would an officer manifest objective good faith in relying on a warrant based on an affidavit "so lacking in indicia of probable cause as to render official belief in its existence entirely unreasonable." Finally, depending on the circumstances of the particular case, a warrant may be so facially deficient—i.e., in failing to particularize the place to be searched or the things to be seized—that the executing officers cannot reasonably presume it to be valid.

(2) *Queries.* Review the First Circuit's decision in *Lafayette Academy,* supra. Would the search in that case have come within the *Sheppard/Leon* test for objective good faith? If you think so, do you also think that this change in the exclusionary rule might lead courts to avoid making substantive decisions on the legality of the search, preferring, instead, to take the easier course of determining good faith?

For an indication of how the search in *Lafayette Academy* might now be handled, consider the First Circuit's subsequent decision in *United States v. Diaz.*[53] There it was alleged that employees of Isla Rica Sales, Inc. (IRSI) were engaged in a fraudulent scheme to have USDA inspectors falsely condemn produce and certify that the produce was destroyed. The produce would then be sold for cash, but IRSI would claim insurance losses. The scheme was brought to light by two IRSI employees, Mr. and Mrs. Novoa, who contacted an FBI agent, Coffey. Coffey subsequently obtained a search warrant to seize a wide variety of business records, including all bank records, dating back to IRSI's inception in 1983. The court of appeals held that the bank records could not properly be seized, there being nothing in Coffey's affidavit implying that these records would have evidentiary value (indeed, since the scheme was carried out in cash, the court held that the agent could not have made the seizure in good faith under *Sheppard/Leon*). Although ordering these records suppressed, the court of appeals did not suppress the documents which had been seized properly. ("This is an especially appropriate measure in this case where the bulk of the warrant and records seized are fully supported by probable

---

53. 841 F.2d 1 (1st Cir.1988).

cause," the Court wrote. What do you think of this remedy?) The Court then addressed another category of documents:

> More troubling is the fact that the warrant included permission to seize records between February 1, 1983, when IRSI first commenced operations, and October 5, 1983, when the first instance of wrongdoing mentioned in the affidavit occurred. The government argues that the affidavit provided the magistrate with "substantial basis" to conclude that there was probable cause to believe the fraud was ongoing, and had not simply begun on October 5. It argues that the affidavit describes a fraudulent scheme of some complexity, with a fairly elaborate infrastructure, and a scheme that had generated substantial profits. The fact that specific documents suggesting improprieties dated October 5 and 10, 1983, and February 1 and April 26, 1984, were included as corroborative examples, should not defeat such a finding, appellants argue.
>
> Appellees respond that the affidavit does not state the belief that the scheme enjoyed such a permanent status. They argue that the magistrate did not even know how long the Novoas had worked for IRSI, or that the Novoas had told Coffey that the fraud started as soon as IRSI opened for business. All the magistrate had before him was a description of the fraudulent scheme and evidence that fraud may have taken place as far back as October 5, 1983. Nothing in the affidavit is at all inconsistent with an October starting date for the fraud.
>
> We find that the government should have advised the magistrate of its belief regarding the duration of the suspected scheme, and the basis for that belief. This would have allowed the magistrate to reach a reasoned decision as to the first date on which there is probable cause to believe that evidence of criminal acts was recorded in IRSI's business records. In essence, then, the warrant describes and allows, within each category, the seizure of documents as to which there is no probable cause, as well as documents that were properly seizable.
>
> * * *
>
> Before applying the exclusionary rule, however, we must determine whether the agents were acting in objective good faith. "In the absence of an allegation that the magistrate abandoned his detached and neutral role, suppression is appropriate only if the officers were dishonest or reckless in preparing their affidavit or could not have harbored an objectively reasonable belief in the existence of probable cause." United States v. Leon, 468 U.S. 897, 926, 104 S.Ct. 3405, 3422, 82 L.Ed.2d 677 (1984). A court must inquire into the "objectively ascertainable question whether a reasonably well trained officer would have known that the search was illegal despite the magistrate's authorization." *Leon,* 468 U.S. at 922, n. 23, 104 S.Ct. at 3420, n. 23. The Court explained that "a

warrant may be so facially deficient—i.e., in failing to particularize . . . the things to be seized—that the executing officers cannot reasonably presume it to be valid." Id. at 923, 104 S.Ct. at 3421.

In this case, the district court found that since there was no proof in the affidavit of illicit activity occurring before October 5, 1983, no experienced FBI agent could reasonably believe that the warrant was limited to properly seizable documents. We note, however, that Coffey attempted to ensure that the search was conducted properly. He prepared an affidavit which was duly approved by a magistrate. He conducted four interviews with two witnesses in order to glean all the necessary information. The Novoas, in fact, had told the agent that the fraud had been in motion since IRSI was founded. He was entitled to believe, as the magistrate implicitly found, that he had set forth enough information in the affidavit to support the search he wished to conduct. The complexity of the fraudulent scheme, its description as an ongoing enterprise bolstered by evidence that illegal activity had continued for at least seven months, and the agent's reasonable belief that the fraud had begun already at IRSI's inception, all demonstrate that a reasonably well trained officer would not necessarily have known that the search was illegal. Suppression of all the evidence seized is not, therefore, mandated.

We realize that this is a close case, but . . . seizing business records in a fraud investigation presents special problems for investigators attempting to draft warrants. Especially difficult is the case where the files contain a mixture of "bad" material (supported by probable cause) and "innocent" material. In a case such as this one, where it is virtually impossible to limit the scope of the warrant any further, a closer judgment call arises as to the acceptability of broader warrants than in cases where the documents can more easily be sub-classified. We must also recognize that the inherent difficulty in segregating "good" from "bad" records, and consequently in drawing up an adequately limited warrant, makes it difficult for even a "reasonably well-trained officer," who is not expected to be a legal technician and is entitled to rely on the greater sophistication of the magistrate—to know precisely where to draw the line.

* * *

(3) *Motions for Return of Unlawfully Seized Evidence.* The exclusionary rule is not the only remedy for an unlawful search. Under Rule 41(e), a person aggrieved by an unlawful search may move for return of unlawfully seized property of which "he is entitled to lawful possession." Any property so returned is not admissible in evidence "at any hearing or trial."

Should *Leon* apply to evidence returnable under Rule 41(e)? Consider *Roberts v. United States*,[54] which involved an extensive search of a

---

54. 656 F.Supp. 929 (S.D.N.Y.1987).

business premises; the search produced a 73 page index of items seized, and government counsel represented at the Rule 41 hearing that "he could not think of a single office record not covered by the warrant." The district court first held the warrant overbroad. Noting that the officers in the field ended up seizing less than they were permitted to seize under the warrant, the court concluded that this proved the warrant violated "the cardinal rule of Fourth Amendment law"—that nothing be left to the discretion of the officer executing the warrant. The court then continued:

> . . . Rule 41(e) plainly provides for pre-indictment adjudication of the legality of a seizure, and . . . it is not the court's place to "ignor[e] what the Rule provides in plain language." Accepting the Rule as "meaning what it says," this is indeed the proper time to pass on the legality of the search.

The government argues that even if the warrant is illegal, the agents' reliance on it falls well within the good faith standard announced in United States v. Leon, 468 U.S. 897, 104 S.Ct. 3405, 82 L.Ed.2d 677 (1984), and Massachusetts v. Sheppard, 468 U.S. 981, 104 S.Ct. 3424, 82 L.Ed.2d 737 (1984), and that, therefore, the evidence at issue should not be suppressed. In making this argument, the government has confused the "judicially implied" constitutional remedy available under the Fourth Amendment with the explicit textual remedy available under Rule 41(e). The two are distinct, and this case concerns the latter.

By now it is well established that a violation of the Fourth Amendment is analytically and legally distinct from the award of any remedy for the violation. Gone are the days when it was thought that the exclusionary rule was "a necessary corollary of the Fourth Amendment." Today it is understood that, "Whether the exclusionary sanction is appropriately imposed in a particular case . . . is 'an issue separate from the question whether the Fourth Amendment rights of the party seeking to invoke the rule were violated by police conduct.'" [*Leon*, 468 U.S.] at 906.

The "good faith" exception set out in *Leon*, and urged on the court here by the Assistant United States Attorney, is a judicially crafted qualification of a judicially fashioned remedy. In contrast, this case concerns a remedy for illegal searches that was explicitly codified in Rule 41(e) and was left intact by Congress when it later modified another portion of Rule 41. That is, in applying Rule 41(e), a court is *not* making a Fourth Amendment exclusion decision; it is applying a procedural remedy dictated by the Federal Rules.

To apply Rule 41(e), courts must determine whether: "(1) the person is entitled to lawful possession *and* (2) the seizure was illegal." Fed.R.Crim.P. 41 (Commentary to 1972 Amendment) (emphasis in original). The first of the two criteria was provided so that "the judge in the district of seizure does not have to decide the legality of the seizure in cases involving contraband which, even if seized illegally, is not to be returned." Id. It is a criterion beyond that required in a Fourth Amendment suppression motion brought under Fed.R.Crim.P. 12(b)(3). If the goods in question are not contraband—and here the government has made no such claim—then the court proceeds to determine whether the seizure was legal. A seizure in violation of the Fourth Amendment certainly counts as an "illegal" search under the Rule. If both of these criteria are met, then the Rule's remedial procedures are triggered: "the property shall be restored and it shall not be admissible in evidence at any hearing or trial." (emphasis added)

Unquestionably, the remedy that Rule 41(e) provides is more stringent than required by the Constitution as construed in *Leon*, just as other of the Federal Criminal Rules are likewise more exacting than the Constitution demands. . . .

The government has offered no authority to require this court to create a good faith exception out of the explicit language chosen by the drafters of Rule 41(e). . . .

The Court of Appeals reversed, holding that the good faith exception applied. See 852 F.2d 671 (2d Cir.1987), certiorari denied ___ U.S. ___, 109 S.Ct. 556, 102 L.Ed.2d 583 (1988). Noting that a Rule 41(e) motion for return of property applies only before indictment (after indictment, the motion is treated as a motion to suppress), the Court of Appeals pointed out that the District Court's interpretation would therefore give persons who had not yet been indicted greater fourth amendment rights than those who had been indicted. "Although Congress might see fit to provide greater protection to people who are not yet indicted, this would be inconsistent with the presumption of innocence that indicted persons enjoy, and there is nothing in the legislative history to indicate that . . . Congress intended such an anomalous result." Id. at 675.

5. ENDNOTE

In reviewing the developments in fourth amendment law in the past quarter century, it could be argued that the Supreme Court has gradually, but consistently, increased the power of government to intrude on businesses and to obtain the evidence necessary for business crime convictions. Despite the apparent extension of fourth amendment protection in *Camara* and *See*, the Court has subsequently adopted doctrines which inevitably provide less protection to businesses than to individuals. Indeed, it could be argued that the Supreme Court's direction is simply a latter-day reflection of the attitude toward fourth amendment protection that was originally expressed in *Hale v. Henkel* in 1906. Business crime is complex crime; if the government is to be able to prosecute it (and it must), then fourth amendment protections must bend.

If this description of the direction of fourth amendment doctrine is accurate, does this development of fourth amendment doctrine constitute either good law or good policy? To what extent has the Court deserted the historical underpinnings of the fourth amendment? If the powerful in society get watered-down protection, what protection can the weak expect?

C. SUBPOENAS AND SUMMONSES

SCOPE NOTE

If the government wishes to obtain documents from a suspect, it need not proceed by a warrant to search for and seize the documents. As we saw in *Hale v. Henkel,* for example, the government may seek process to order a party to bring documents in for the government's inspection and review. In *Hale,* the process was a grand jury subpoena. As we will see in this Section, Congress often grants administrative agencies the power in their basic enabling statutes to issue an administrative subpoena or summons, the statutory analogue to the grand jury's subpoena.

Although the subpoena is used for the same purpose as the search and seizure warrant, there are significant differences between the two. The subpoena relies on the recipient of the process to bring the documents into the government's offices. There is no physical intrusion by government agents into the "privacy" of the recipient. The subpoena does compel production of evidence, but the compulsion is supplied by the judicial power of contempt for failure to comply rather than by the physical compulsion of a direct physical seizure. Thus the use of a subpoena or summons relies more on the voluntary compliance of the recipient who is given the opportunity to decide what documents should be produced in response to the process. Finally, the recipient of a subpoena or summons can obtain judicial review of the validity of the request (at a contempt hearing or on a motion to quash) prior to the time the Government sees the documents. Unlike the warrant, issued ex parte and then executed, the legality of the subpoena or summons can thus be tested prior to execution.

The materials in this Section explore the fourth and fifth amendment issues which arise in the course of enforcing subpoenas and summonses. The first lead case, *Oklahoma Press Publishing Co. v. Walling,* provides the doctrinal foundation for evaluating fourth amendment coverage. The Notes following explore the difference in fourth amendment protection between warrants and subpoenas, as well as alternative remedies for unreasonably broad subpoenas. The second lead case is one of the most important cases dealing with subpoenas, *Fisher v. United States.* This case dramatically altered the development of fifth amendment law in this area, significantly narrowing the extent to which recipients of subpoenas can assert the privilege against self-incrimination as a way of avoiding production of documents. The Notes following *Fisher* explore how the case has developed.

OKLAHOMA PRESS PUBLISHING CO. v. WALLING

Supreme Court of the United States, 1946.
327 U.S. 186, 66 S.Ct. 494, 90 L.Ed. 614.

MR. JUSTICE RUTLEDGE delivered the opinion of the Court.

These cases bring for decision important questions concerning the Administrator's right to judicial enforcement of subpoenas duces tecum issued by him in the course of investigations conducted pursuant to § 11(a) of the Fair Labor Standards Act. His claim is founded directly upon § 9, which incorporates the enforcement provisions of §§ 9 and 10 of the Federal Trade Commission Act. The subpoenas sought the production of specified records to determine whether petitioners were violating the Fair Labor Standards Act, including records relating to coverage. Petitioners, newspaper publishing corporations, maintain that the Act is not applicable to them, for constitutional and other reasons, and insist that the question of coverage must be adjudicated before the subpoenas may be enforced.

In No. 61, involving the Oklahoma Press Publishing Company, the Circuit Court of Appeals for the Tenth Circuit has rejected this view, holding that the Administrator was entitled to enforcement upon showing of "probable cause," which it found had been made. Accordingly it affirmed the district court's order directing that the Administrator be given access to the records and documents specified.

In No. 63, the Circuit Court of Appeals for the Third Circuit likewise rejected the company's position, one judge dissenting on the ground that probable cause had not been shown. It accordingly reversed the district court's order of dismissal in the proceeding to show cause, which in effect denied enforcement for want of a showing of coverage.

* * *

The issues have taken wide range. . . . In addition to an argument from Congress' intent, reliance falls upon various constitutional provisions, including the First, Fourth and Fifth Amendments, as well as the limited reach of the commerce clause, to show that the Administrator's conduct and the relief he seeks are forbidden.

I.

[The Court held that the first amendment did not "knock out" the application of the Fair Labor Standard Act to the newspaper business.]

II.

Other questions pertain to whether enforcement of the subpoenas as directed by the circuit courts of appeals will violate any of petitioners' rights secured by the Fourth Amendment and related issues concerning Congress' intent. It is claimed that enforcement would permit the Administrator to conduct general fishing expeditions into petitioners' books, records and papers, in order to secure evidence that they have violated the Act, without a prior charge or complaint and simply to secure information upon which to base one, all allegedly in violation of the Amendment's search and seizure provisions.

* * *

The short answer to the Fourth Amendment objections is that the records in these cases present no question of actual search and seizure, but raise only the question whether orders of court for the production of specified records have been validly made; and no sufficient showing appears to justify setting them aside. No officer or other person has sought to enter petitioners' premises against their will, to search them, or to seize or examine their books, records or papers without their assent, otherwise than pursuant to orders of court authorized by law and made after adequate opportunity to present objections, which in fact were made. Nor has any objection been taken to the breadth of the subpoenas or to any other specific defect which would invalidate them.

What petitioners seek is not to prevent an unlawful search and seizure. It is rather a total immunity to the Act's provisions, applicable to all others similarly situated, requiring them to submit their pertinent records for the Administrator's inspection under every judicial safeguard, after and only after an order of court made pursuant to and in exact compliance with authority granted by Congress. This broad claim of immunity no doubt is induced by petitioners' First Amendment contentions. But beyond them it is rested also upon conceptions of the Fourth Amendment equally lacking in merit.

* * *

III.

The primary source of misconception concerning the Fourth Amendment's function lies perhaps in the identification of cases involving so-called "figurative" or "constructive" search with cases of actual search and seizure.[55] Only in this analogical sense can any question related to search and seizure be thought to arise in situations which, like the present ones, involve only the validity of authorized judicial orders.

The confusion is due in part to the fact that this is the very kind of situation in which the decisions have moved with variant direction, although without actual conflict when all of the facts in each case are taken into account. Notwithstanding this, emphasis and tone at times are highly contrasting, with consequent overtones of doubt and confusion for validity of the statute or its application. The subject matter

---

55. [Court's footnote 28.] "In other words, the subpoena is equivalent to a search and seizure and to be constitutional it must be a *reasonable* exercise of the power." Lasson, Development of the Fourth Amendment to the United States Constitution, 137, citing . . . Hale v. Henkel, 201 U.S. 43, 76. . . .

perhaps too often has been generative of heat rather than light, for the border along which the cases lie is one where government intrudes upon different areas of privacy and the history of such intrusions has brought forth some of the stoutest and most effective instances of resistance to excess of governmental authority.

The matter of requiring the production of books and records to secure evidence is not as one-sided, in this kind of situation, as the most extreme expressions of either emphasis would indicate. With some obvious exceptions, there has always been a real problem of balancing the public interest against private security. The cases for protection of the opposing interests are stated as clearly as anywhere perhaps in the summations, quoted in the margin,[56] of two former members of this Court, each of whom was fully alive to the dual necessity of safeguarding adequately the public and the private interest. But emphasis has not always been so aptly placed.

The confusion obscuring the basic distinction between actual and so-called "constructive" search has been accentuated where the records and papers sought are of corporate character, as in these cases. Historically private corporations have been subject to broad visitorial power, both in England and in this country. And it long has been established that Congress may exercise wide investigative power over them, analogous to the visitorial power of the incorporating state, when their activities take place within or affect interstate commerce. Correspondingly it has been settled that corporations are not entitled to all of the

---

56. [Court's footnote 30.] The case for protection of the public interest was stated as follows: "The opinion of the court reminds us of the dangers that wait upon the abuse of power by officialdom unchained. The warning is so fraught with truth that it can never be untimely. But timely too is the reminder, as a host of impoverished investors will be ready to attest, that there are dangers in untruths and half truths when certificates masquerading as securities pass current in the market. There are dangers in spreading a belief that untruths and half truths, designed to be passed on for the guidance of confiding buyers, are to be ranked as peccadillos, or even perhaps as part of the amenities of business. . . . A Commission which is without coercive powers, which cannot arrest or amerce or imprison though a crime has been uncovered, or even punish for contempt, but can only inquire and report, the propriety of every question in the course of the inquiry being subject to the supervision of the ordinary courts of justice, is likened with denunciatory fervor to the Star Chamber of the Stuarts. Historians may find hyperbole in the sanguinary simile." Mr. Justice Cardozo, with whom joined the present Chief Justice and Mr. Justice Brandeis, dissenting in Jones v. Securities & Exchange Commission, 298 U.S. 1, 32–33. See also Handler, Constitutionality of Investigations of the Federal Trade Commission (1928) 28 Col.L.Rev. 708, 905, particularly at 933 ff.

On the other hand, the case for protected privacy was put by Mr. Justice Brandeis, dissenting, in Olmstead v. United States, 277 U.S. 438, 478–479: "The makers of our Constitution undertook to secure conditions favorable to the pursuit of happiness. They recognized the significance of man's spiritual nature, of his feelings and of his intellect. They knew that only a part of the pain, pleasure and satisfactions of life are to be found in material things. They sought to protect Americans in their beliefs, their thoughts, their emotions and their sensations. They conferred, as against the Government, the right to be let alone—the most comprehensive of rights and the right most valued by civilized men. To protect that right, every unjustifiable intrusion by the Government upon the privacy of the individual, whatever the means employed, must be deemed a violation of the Fourth Amendment. And the use, as evidence in a criminal proceeding, of facts ascertained by such intrusion must be deemed a violation of the Fifth."

constitutional protections which private individuals have in these and related matters. As has been noted, they are not at all within the privilege against self-incrimination, although this Court more than once has said that the privilege runs very closely with the Fourth Amendment's search and seizure provisions.[57] It is also settled that an officer of the company cannot refuse to produce its records in his possession, upon the plea that they either will incriminate him or may incriminate it.[58] . . .

* * *

Without attempt to summarize or accurately distinguish all of the cases, the fair distillation, in so far as they apply merely to the production of corporate records and papers in response to a subpoena or order authorized by law and safeguarded by judicial sanction, seems to be that the Fifth Amendment affords no protection by virtue of the self-incrimination provision, whether for the corporation or for its officers; and the Fourth, if applicable, at the most guards against abuse only by way of too much indefiniteness or breadth in the things required to be "particularly described," if also the inquiry is one the demanding agency is authorized by law to make and the materials specified are relevant. The gist of the protection is in the requirement, expressed in terms, that the disclosure sought shall not be unreasonable.

As this has taken form in the decisions, the following specific results have been worked out. It is not necessary, as in the case of a warrant, that a specific charge or complaint of violation of law be pending or that the order be made pursuant to one. It is enough that the investigation be for a lawfully authorized purpose, within the power of Congress to command. This has been ruled most often perhaps in relation to grand jury investigations,[59] but also frequently in respect to general or statistical investigations authorized by Congress. The requirement of "probable cause, supported by oath or affirmation," literally applicable in the case of a warrant, is satisfied in that of an order for production by the court's determination that the investigation is authorized by Congress, is for a purpose Congress can order, and the documents sought are relevant to the inquiry. Beyond this the requirement of reasonableness, including particularity in "describing the place to be searched, and the persons or things to be seized," also literally applicable to warrants, comes down to specification of the documents to

---

57. [Court's footnote 33.] In the leading case of Boyd v. United States, 116 U.S. 616, 630, Mr. Justice Bradley, speaking for the Court in relation to the compelled production of "a man's own testimony or of his private papers [specifically a business invoice] to be used as evidence to convict him of crime or to forfeit his goods," said in a much quoted statement: "In this regard the Fourth and Fifth Amendments run almost into each other." The opinion, quoting at length from Lord Camden's discussion in the historic case of Entick v. Carrington, 19 Howell's State Trials 1029, relies strongly in this phase upon his conjunction of the right to freedom from search and seizure "where the law forceth evidence out of the owner's custody by process" and the privilege against self-incrimination. 116 U.S. at 629. Cf. also the statement of Mr. Justice Brandeis, quoted supra note 56.

58. [Court's footnote 34.] Wilson v. United States, 221 U.S. 361; Hale v. Henkel, 201 U.S. 43. . . .

59. [Court's foonote 42.] E.g., Hale v. Henkel, 201 U.S. 43. . . .

be produced adequate, but not excessive, for the purposes of the relevant inquiry. Necessarily, as has been said, this cannot be reduced to formula; for relevancy and adequacy or excess in the breadth of the subpoena are matters variable in relation to the nature, purposes and scope of the inquiry.

When these principles are applied to the facts of the present cases, it is impossible to conceive how a violation of petitioners' rights could have been involved. Both were corporations. The only records or documents sought were corporate ones. No possible element of self-incrimination was therefore presented or in fact claimed. All the records sought were relevant to the authorized inquiry,[60] the purpose of which was to determine two issues, whether petitioners were subject to the Act and, if so, whether they were violating it. These were subjects of investigation authorized by § 11(a). . . . It is not to be doubted that Congress could authorize investigation of these matters. In all these respects, the specifications more than meet the requirements long established by many precedents.

* * *

[T]he basic compromise has been worked out in a manner to secure the public interest and at the same time to guard the private ones affected against the only abuses from which protection rightfully may be claimed. The latter are not identical with those protected against invasion by actual search and seizure, nor are the threatened abuses the same. They are rather the interests of men to be free from officious intermeddling, whether because irrelevant to any lawful purpose or because unauthorized by law, concerning matters which on proper occasion and within lawfully conferred authority of broad limits are subject to public examination in the public interest. Officious examination can be expensive, so much so that it eats up men's substance. It can be time consuming, clogging the processes of business. It can become persecution when carried beyond reason.

On the other hand, petitioners' view, if accepted, would stop much if not all of investigation in the public interest at the threshold of inquiry and, in the case of the Administrator, is designed avowedly to do so. This would render substantially impossible his effective discharge of the duties of investigation and enforcement which Congress has placed upon him. And if his functions could be thus blocked, so might many others of equal importance.

---

60. [Court's footnote 46.] The subpoena in No. 61 called for production of:

"All of your books, papers and documents showing the hours worked by and wages paid to each of your employees between October 28, 1938, and the date hereof, including all payroll ledgers, time sheets, time cards and time clock records, and all your books, papers and documents showing the distribution of papers outside the State of Oklahoma, the dissemination of news outside the State of Oklahoma, the source and receipt of news from outside the State of Oklahoma, and the source and receipt of advertisements of nationally advertised goods."

The specification in No. 63 was substantially identical except for the period of time covered by the demand.

We think, therefore, that the courts of appeals were correct in the view that Congress has authorized the Administrator, rather than the district courts in the first instance, to determine the question of coverage in the preliminary investigation of possibly existing violations; in doing so to exercise his subpoena power for securing evidence upon that question, by seeking the production of petitioners' relevant books, records and papers; and, in case of refusal to obey his subpoena, issued according to the statute's authorization, to have the aid of the district court in enforcing it. No constitutional provision forbids Congress to do this. On the contrary, its authority would seem clearly to be comprehended in the "necessary and proper" clause, as incidental to both its general legislative and its investigative powers.

IV.

What has been said disposes of petitioners' principal contention upon the sufficiency of the showing. Other assignments, however, present the further questions whether any showing is required beyond the Administrator's allegations of coverage and relevance of the required materials to that question; and, if so, of what character. Stated otherwise, they are whether the court may order enforcement only upon a finding of "probable cause," that is, probability in fact, of coverage. . . .

* * *

Congress has made no requirement in terms of any showing of "probable cause"; and, in view of what has already been said, any possible constitutional requirement of that sort was satisfied by the Administrator's showing in this case, including not only the allegations concerning coverage, but also that he was proceeding with his investigation in accordance with the mandate of Congress and that the records sought were relevant to that purpose. . . .

The result therefore sustains the Administrator's position that his investigative function, in searching out violations with a view to securing enforcement of the Act, is essentially the same as the grand jury's, or the court's in issuing other pretrial orders for the discovery of evidence, and is governed by the same limitations. These are that he shall not act arbitrarily or in excess of his statutory authority, but this does not mean that his inquiry must be "limited . . . by forecasts of the probable result of the investigation . . ." Blair v. United States, 250 U.S. 273, 282; cf. Hale v. Henkel, 201 U.S. 43. Nor is the judicial function either abused or abased, as has been suggested, by leaving to it the determination of the important questions which the Administrator's position concedes the courts may decide.

Petitioners stress that enforcement will subject them to inconvenience, expense and harassment. . . . There is no harassment when the subpoena is issued and enforced according to law. The Administrator is authorized to enter and inspect, but the Act makes his right to do so subject in all cases to judicial supervision. Persons from whom he seeks relevant information are not required to submit to his demand, if in any respect it is unreasonable or overreaches the authority Congress has given. To it they may make "appropriate defence" surrounded by every safeguard of judicial restraint. In view of these safeguards, the expressed fears of unwarranted intrusions upon personal liberty are effective only to recall Mr. Justice Cardozo's reply to the same exaggerated forebodings in Jones v. Securities & Exchange Commission: "Historians may find hyperbole in the sanguinary simile."

Nor is there room for intimation that the Administrator has proceeded in these cases in any manner contrary to petitioners' fundamental rights or otherwise than strictly according to law. It is to be remembered that petitioners' are not the only rights which may be involved or threatened with possible infringement. Their employees' rights and the public interest under the declared policy of Congress also would be affected if petitioners should enjoy the practically complete immunity they seek.

No sufficient reason was set forth in the returns or the accompanying affidavits for not enforcing the subpoenas, a burden petitioners were required to assume in order to make "appropriate defence."

Accordingly the judgments in both causes, No. 61 and No. 63, are *Affirmed.*

MR. JUSTICE JACKSON took no part in the consideration or decision of these cases.

[The dissenting opinion of MR. JUSTICE MURPHY is omitted.]

NOTES AND QUERIES

(1) *The Correct Analogy?* The process in *Oklahoma Press Publishing* was issued by an administrative agency for the purpose of carrying out its enforcement duties. In permitting the agency to obtain judicial enforcement without proof of "probable cause," the Court relies on cases like *Hale v. Henkel* involving the power of the grand jury to issue subpoenas. Is this the correct analogy? Is there a difference (historically? in fact?) between the position of the grand jury as a prosecuting agency and the position of an administrative agency?

Although the Court concedes that the fourth amendment's requirement of "reasonableness" is broadly applicable to administrative process, the Court rejects imposing the same requirements as are imposed on search warrants. Do you think the distinction justified on the ground asserted by the Court, that the search is "figurative"? Compare the description of the subpoena (footnote 46 of the Court's opinion, supra p. 585) with the inspection order issued in *Marshall v. Barlow's* (footnote 14, supra p. 533) which the Court held unconstitutional because not issued by a magistrate. Would the order have been constitutional if issued by OSHA as an administrative summons? In placing so much reliance on the fact of intrusion, as opposed to the fact of seizure, has the Court divorced fourth amendment protection of documents from its historical roots? Recall Justice Stevens' dissenting opinion in *Zurcher* regarding the importance of protecting the privacy of documents, supra p. 551.

If an administrative summons is not perfectly analogous either to a grand jury subpoena or to a search warrant, should the Court, in defining "reasonableness," have imposed a set of protections tailored to the potential for abuse posed by administrative agencies? If so, what would these protections include?

Consider *United States v. Powell*,[61] where the Internal Revenue Service had summoned Powell to appear before a Special Agent to give testimony and produce records. When Powell refused to produce the documents, the IRS sought court enforcement of its summons, providing an agent's affidavit that the agent suspected tax fraud. In court, however, the IRS refused to provide any basis for its suspicion. Justice Harlan determined that the relevant provisions of the Internal Revenue Code did not require a showing of "probable cause" (a reading reinforced, he argued, by the general principles enunciated in *Oklahoma Press Publishing*). He continued:

> [The Commissioner] must show that the investigation will be conducted pursuant to a legitimate purpose, that the inquiry may be relevant to the purpose, that the information sought is not already within the Commissioner's possession, and that the administrative steps required by the Code have been followed—in particular, that the "Secretary or his delegate," after investigation, has determined the further examination to be necessary and has notified the taxpayer in writing to that effect. This does not make meaningless the adversary hearing to which the taxpayer is entitled before enforcement is ordered. At the hearing he "may challenge the summons on any appropriate ground." Nor does our reading of the statutes mean that under no circumstances may the court inquire into the underlying reasons for the examination. It is the court's process which is invoked to enforce the administrative summons and a court may not permit its process to be abused. Such an abuse would take place if the summons had been issued for an improper purpose, such as to harass the taxpayer or to put pressure on him to settle a collateral dispute, or for any other purpose reflecting on the good faith of the particular investigation. The burden of showing an abuse of the court's process is on the taxpayer, and it is not met by a mere showing, as was made in this case, that the statute of limitations for ordinary deficiencies has run or that the records in question have already been once examined.[62]

Query. Is the protection provided in *Powell* any broader than the fourth amendment protection for grand jury subpoenas enunciated in *Hale v. Henkel?*

---

61. 379 U.S. 48, 85 S.Ct. 248, 13 L.Ed.2d 112 (1964).

62. Justice Douglas dissented, joined by Justices Stewart and Goldberg.

(2) *Grand Jury Subpoenas.* The overall fourth amendment protection provided in the context of grand jury subpoenas has been explored earlier in *Hale v. Henkel,* supra p. 382. As *Hale* indicated, and as *Oklahoma Press Publishing* reaffirmed, in the grand jury context the fourth amendment protects only against overbreadth; probable cause and specificity need not be shown. This view that the fourth amendment protects only against extreme abuses in gathering evidence also fits into the general theory underlying the broad scope of the grand jury's investigative powers, particularly its freedom to consider evidence that would otherwise be inadmissible before a petit jury at trial (see p. 451, supra). However broad the grand jury's power, however, the Supreme Court has indicated that the grand jury "may not itself violate a valid privilege, whether established by the Constitution, statutes, or the common law." [63] This applies not only to subpoenas for documentary evidence, but also to subpoenas to appear and testify. Thus, even though a witness cannot generally refuse to appear before a grand jury when summoned,[64] the witness can refuse to answer questions on the basis of the fifth amendment self-incrimination clause or on the basis of the attorney-client or spousal privilege.[65]

(3) *Searches Followed by Subpoenas—The Fruits Problem.* Suppose the government obtains documents through an unlawful fourth amendment search (for example, an overbroad warrant). Could the Government return the documents and then issue a grand jury subpoena for them? Could the government copy the documents before returning them, present the copies to the grand jury, and thereby obtain an indictment?

Consider Justice Holmes' opinion for the Court in *Silverthorne Lumber Co. v. United States,* 251 U.S. 385, 40 S.Ct. 182, 64 L.Ed. 319 (1920):

> This is a writ of error brought to reverse a judgment of the District Court fining the Silverthorne Lumber Company two hundred and fifty dollars for contempt of court and ordering Frederick W. Silverthorne to be imprisoned until he should purge himself of a similar contempt. The contempt in question was a refusal to obey subpoenas and an order of Court to produce books and documents of the company before the grand jury to be used in regard to alleged violation of the statutes of the United States by the said

---

63. United States v. Calandra, 414 U.S. 338, 346, 94 S.Ct. 613, 619, 38 L.Ed.2d 561 (1974) (refusing to apply exclusionary rule to prevent the use before the grand jury of evidence seized by the police in violation of the fourth amendment).

64. See, e.g., Branzburg v. Hayes, 408 U.S. 665, 92 S.Ct. 2646, 33 L.Ed.2d 626 (1972) (reporter); In re Walsh, 623 F.2d 489 (7th Cir.) (attorney), certiorari denied 449 U.S. 994, 101 S.Ct. 531, 66 L.Ed.2d 291 (1980); United States v. Wolfson, 282 F.Supp. 772 (S.D.N.Y.1967) (target), reversed on other grounds 437 F.2d 862 (2d Cir.1970).

65. For attorney-client and work product protections, see Chapter 4B, supra. For spousal privilege, see, e.g., In re Grand Jury Empanelled October 18, 1979 (Malfitano), 633 F.2d 276 (3d Cir.1980); cf. Trammel v. United States, 445 U.S. 40, 100 S.Ct. 906, 63 L.Ed.2d 186 (1980) (limiting spousal privilege to allow it to be claimed only by testifying spouse; confidences privately disclosed between husband and wife remain fully protected).

Silverthorne and his father. One ground of the refusal was that the order of the Court infringed the rights of the parties under the Fourth Amendment of the Constitution of the United States.

The facts are simple. An indictment upon a single specific charge having been brought against the two Silverthornes mentioned, they both were arrested at their homes early in the morning of February 25, 1919, and were detained in custody a number of hours. While they were thus detained representatives of the Department of Justice and the United States marshal without a shadow of authority went to the office of their company and made a clean sweep of all the books, papers and documents found there. All the employees were taken or directed to go to the office of the District Attorney of the United States to which also the books, &c., were taken at once. An application was made as soon as might be to the District Court for a return of what thus had been taken unlawfully. It was opposed by the District Attorney so far as he had found evidence against the plaintiffs in error, and it was stated that the evidence so obtained was before the grand jury. Color had been given by the District Attorney to the approach of those concerned in the act by an invalid subpoena for certain documents relating to the charge in the indictment then on file. Thus the case is not that of knowledge acquired through the wrongful act of a stranger, but it must be assumed that the Government planned or at all events ratified the whole performance. Photographs and copies of material papers were made and a new indictment was framed based upon the knowledge thus obtained. The District Court ordered a return of the originals but impounded the photographs and copies. Subpoenas to produce the originals then were served and on the refusal of the plaintiffs in error to produce them the Court made an order that the subpoenas should be complied with, although it had found that all the papers had been seized in violation of the parties' constitutional rights. The refusal to obey this order is the contempt alleged. The Government now, while in form repudiating and condemning the illegal seizure, seeks to maintain its right to avail itself of the knowledge obtained by that means which otherwise it would not have had.

The proposition could not be presented more nakedly. It is that although of course its seizure was an outrage which the Government now regrets, it may study the papers before it returns them, copy them, and then may use the knowledge that it has gained to call upon the owners in a more regular form to produce them; that the protection of the Constitution covers the physical possession but not any advantages that the Government can gain over the object of its pursuit by doing the forbidden act. . . . In our opinion such is not the law. It reduces the Fourth Amendment to a form of words. The essence of a provision forbidding the acquisition of evidence in a certain way is that not merely evidence so acquired shall not be used before the Court but that it shall not be used at all. Of course this does not mean that the facts thus obtained become sacred and inaccessible. If knowledge of them is gained from an independent source they may be proved like any others, but the knowledge gained by the Government's own wrong cannot be used by it in the way proposed. . . . In Linn v. United States, 251 Fed.Rep. 476, 480, it was thought that a different rule applied to a corporation, on the ground that it was not privileged from producing its books and papers. But the rights of a corporation against unlawful search and seizure are to be protected even if the same result might have been achieved in a lawful way.[66]

In 1974, however, the Supreme Court decided *United States v. Calandra*.[67] In *Calandra* the Court held that a witness summoned before a grand jury could be asked questions even if the questions were derived from evidence seized in violation of the fourth amendment ("fruits"). The Court, per Justice Powell, distinguished *Silverthorne:* [68]

> *Silverthorne* is distinguishable from the present case in several significant respects. There, plaintiffs in error had previously been indicted by the grand jury and thus could invoke the exclusionary rule on the basis of their status as criminal defendants. Moreover, the Government's interest in recapturing the original documents was founded on a belief that they might be useful in the criminal prosecution already authorized by the grand jury. It did not appear that the grand jury needed the documents to perform its investigative or accusatorial functions. Thus, the primary consequence of the Court's decision was to exclude the evidence from the subsequent criminal trial. Finally, prior to the issuance of the grand jury subpoenas, there had been a judicial determination that the search and seizure were illegal. The claim of plaintiffs in error was not raised for the first time in a pre-indictment motion to suppress requiring interruption of grand jury proceedings.
>
> By contrast, in the instant case respondent had not been indicted by the grand jury and was not a criminal defendant. Under traditional principles, he had no standing to invoke the exclusionary rule. The effect of the District Court's order was to deprive the grand jury of testimony it needed to conduct its investigation. Furthermore, respondent's motion to suppress had not been previously made and required interruption of the grand jury proceedings. In these circumstances, *Silverthorne* is certainly not controlling. To the extent that the Court's broad dictum might be construed to suggest a different result in the present case, we note that it has been substantially undermined by later cases. See Parts III and IV of this opinion [which discuss the purpose of the exclusionary role (to deter unlawful police behavior) and the rule in the context of grand jury proceedings].

66. The Chief Justice and Justice Pitney dissented.

67. 414 U.S. 338, 94 S.Ct. 613, 38 L.Ed. 2d 561 (1974).

68. 414 U.S. at 352 n. 8, 94 S.Ct. at 622 n. 8, 38 L.Ed.2d at 573 n. 8.

Query. How do these two cases affect the hypothetical situations raised at the beginning of the Note? Might the Court's subsequent construction of the exclusionary rule in *Leon* and *Sheppard* affect the resolution of such cases?

(4) *Subpoenas to Third Parties—Notice to Targets.* As has already been observed with search warrants, the government will frequently attempt to discover documentary evidence in the hands of third parties. With a search warrant, the party being searched has no right to present objections to the search prior to execution; all objections are made after the search has been carried out. A subpoena, on the other hand, does provide the recipient with an opportunity to object to its legality prior to its execution. If the subpoena is served on a third party, however, the third party may have no interest in objecting. In such circumstances, should the government be required to give notice to the target of the investigation, so that the target will not be deprived of an opportunity to object to the legality of the subpoena prior to compliance?

The Supreme Court considered this question in *SEC v. Jerry T. O'Brien, Inc.,* 467 U.S. 735, 104 S.Ct. 2720, 81 L.Ed.2d 615 (1984):

> [Digest: In the course of investigating Harry Magnuson for stock fraud, the SEC subpoenaed financial records in the possession of O'Brien, a broker-dealer firm. In response to inquiry by O'Brien's counsel, SEC staff informed O'Brien that it was a "subject" of the investigation. (See p. 541 supra this Casebook for the distinction between "target" and "subject" status.) The SEC subsequently issued several subpoenas to third parties. Magnuson and O'Brien then sought to enjoin the SEC from issuing such subpoenas without providing them notice. The Court of Appeals for the Ninth Circuit held that "targets" of an SEC investigation have a right to notice of subpoenas to third parties so that they can enforce their right "to be investigated consistently with the *Powell* standards." The Supreme Court granted certiorari and reversed. After reviewing the facts, Justice Marshall wrote for a unanimous Court:]
>
> No provision in the complex of statutes governing the SEC's investigative power expressly obliges the Commission to notify the "target" of an investigation when it issues a subpoena to a third party. If such an obligation is to be imposed on the Commission, therefore, it must be derived from one of three sources: a constitutional provision; an understanding on the part of Congress, inferable from the structure of the securities laws, regarding how the SEC should conduct its inquiries; or the general standards governing judicial enforcement of administrative subpoenas enunciated in United States v. Powell, 379 U.S. 48, 85 S.Ct. 248, 13 L.Ed.2d 112 (1964), and its progeny. Examination of these three potential bases for the Court of Appeals' ruling leaves us unpersuaded that the notice requirement fashioned by that court is warranted.

A

[R]espondents cannot invoke the Fourth Amendment in support of the Court of Appeals' decision. It is established that, when a person communicates information to a third party even on the understanding that the communication is confidential, he cannot object if the third party conveys that information or records thereof to law enforcement authorities. United States v. Miller, 425 U.S. 435, 443, 96 S.Ct. 1619, 1624, 48 L.Ed.2d 71 (1976). Relying on that principle, the Court has held that a customer of a bank cannot challenge on Fourth Amendment grounds the admission into evidence in a criminal prosecution of financial records obtained by the Government from his bank pursuant to allegedly defective subpoenas, despite the fact that he was given no notice of the subpoenas. These rulings disable respondents from arguing that notice of subpoenas issued to third parties is necessary to allow a target to prevent an unconstitutional search or seizure of his papers.

B

The language and structure of the statutes administered by the Commission afford respondents no greater aid. The provisions vesting the SEC with the power to issue and seek enforcement of subpoenas are expansive. . . .

* * *

. . . Congress intended to vest the SEC with considerable discretion in determining when and how to investigate possible violations of the statutes administered by the Commission. We discern no evidence that Congress wished or expected that the Commission would adopt any particular procedures for notifying "targets" of investigations when it sought information from third parties.

The inference that the relief sought by respondents is not necessary to give effect to congressional intent is reinforced by the fact that, in one special context, Congress has imposed on the Commission an obligation to notify persons directly affected by its subpoenas. In 1978, in response to this Court's decision in United States v. Miller, supra, Congress enacted the Right to Financial Privacy Act, 92 Stat. 3697, 12 U.S.C. § 3401 et seq. That statute accords customers of banks and similar financial institutions certain rights to be notified of and to challenge in court administrative subpoenas of financial records in the possession of the banks. The most salient feature of the Act is the narrow scope of the entitlements it creates. Thus, it carefully limits the kinds of customers to whom it applies, and the types of records they may seek to protect. A customer's ability to challenge a subpoena is cabined by strict procedural requirements. For example, he must assert his claim within a short period of time, and cannot appeal an adverse determination until the Government has completed its investigation. Perhaps most importantly, the statute is drafted in a fashion that minimizes the risk that customers' objections to subpoenas will delay or frustrate agency investigations. Thus, a court presented with such a challenge is required to rule upon it within seven days of the Government's response, and the pertinent statutes of limitations are tolled while the claim is pending. Since 1980, the SEC has been subject to the constraints of the Right to Financial Privacy Act. When it made the statute applicable to the SEC, however, Congress empowered the Commission in prescribed circumstances to seek ex parte orders authorizing it to delay notifying bank customers when it subpoenas information about them, thereby further curtailing the ability of persons under investigation to impede the agency's inquiries.

* * *

C

The last of the three potential footings for the remedy sought by respondents is some other entitlement that would be effectuated thereby. Respondents seek to derive such an entitlement from a combination of our prior decisions. Distilled, their argument is as follows: A subpoena issued by the SEC must comport with the standards set forth in our decision in United States v. Powell, 379 U.S., at 57–58, 85 S.Ct., at 254–255. Not only the recipient of an SEC subpoena, but also any person who would be affected by compliance therewith, has a substantive right, under *Powell*, to insist that those standards are met. A target of an SEC investigation may assert the foregoing right in two ways. First, . . . the target may seek permissive intervention in an enforcement action brought by the Commission against the subpoena recipient. Second, if the recipient of the subpoena threatens voluntarily to turn over the requested information, the target "might restrain compliance" by the recipient, thereby forcing the Commission to institute an enforcement suit. A target can avail himself of these options only if he is aware of the existence of subpoenas directed at others. To ensure that ignorance does not prevent a target from asserting his rights, respondents conclude, the Commission must notify him when it issues a subpoena to a third party.

There are several tenuous links in respondent's argument. Especially debatable are the proposition that a target has a substantive right to be investigated in a manner consistent with the *Powell* standards and the assertion that a target may obtain a restraining order preventing voluntary compliance by a third party with an administrative subpoena. Certainly we have never before expressly so held. For the present, however, we may assume, arguendo, that a target enjoys each of the substantive and procedural rights identified by respondents. Nevertheless, we conclude that it would be inappropriate to elaborate upon those entitlements by mandating notification of targets whenever the Commission issues subpoenas.

Two considerations underlie our decision on this issue. First, administration of the notice requirement advocated by respondents would be highly burdensome for both the Commission and the courts. The most obvious difficulty would involve identification of the persons and organizations that should be considered "targets" of investigations. The SEC often undertakes investigations into suspicious securities transactions without any knowledge of which of the parties involved may have violated the law. To notify all potential wrongdoers in such a situation of the issuance of each subpoena would be virtually impossible. The Commission would thus be obliged to determine the point at which enough evidence had been assembled to focus suspicion on a manageable subset of the participants in the transaction, thereby lending them the status of "targets" and entitling them to notice of the outstanding subpoenas directed at others. The complexity of that task is apparent. Even in cases in which the Commission could identify with reasonable ease the principal targets of its inquiry, another problem would arise. In such circumstances, a person not considered a target by the Commission could contend that he deserved that status and therefore should be given notice of subpoenas issued to others. To assess a claim of this sort, a district court would be obliged to conduct some kind of hearing to determine the scope and thrust of the ongoing investigation. Implementation of this new remedy would drain the resources of the judiciary as well as the Commission.

Second, the imposition of a notice requirement on the SEC would substantially increase the ability of persons who have something to hide to impede legitimate investigations by the Commission. A target given notice of every subpoena issued to third parties would be able to discourage the recipients from complying, and then further delay disclosure of damaging information by seeking intervention in all enforcement actions brought by the Commission. More seriously, the understanding of the progress of an SEC inquiry that would flow from knowledge of which persons had received subpoenas would enable an unscrupulous target to destroy or alter documents, intimidate witnesses, or transfer securities or funds so that they could not be reached by the Government. Especially in the context of securities regulation, where speed in locating and halting violations of the law is so important, we would be loathe to place such potent weapons in the hands of persons with a desire to keep the Commission at bay.

We acknowledge that our ruling may have the effect in practice of preventing some persons under investigation by the SEC from asserting objections to subpoenas issued by the Commission to third parties for improper reasons. However, to accept respondents' proposal "would unwarrantedly cast doubt upon and stultify the [Commission's] every investigatory move." Particularly in view of Congress' manifest disinclination to require the Commission to notify targets whenever it seeks information from others, we refuse so to curb the Commission's exercise of its statutory power.

* * *

(5) *Subpoenas to Third Parties—Paying the Costs.* If a subpoena is not so burdensome or abusive that it violates the fourth amendment or the statute under which it is issued, is there anything further that the recipient of the subpoena can do? Consider *United States v. Farmers & Merchants Bank*, 397 F.Supp. 418 (C.D.Cal.1975):

FERGUSON, DISTRICT JUDGE.

Respondent bank asks that the United States be ordered to reimburse it for the expenses incurred in complying with an IRS summons which required production of the bank's records of transactions by several of its customers. The facts are as follows.

1. On November 27, 1973, an agent of the Internal Revenue Service served a summons on the assistant manager of the bank, demanding production of various books, records, and papers of customers of the bank.

2. Respondents appeared on the date set forth in the summons, December 10, 1973, but did not supply the requested materials.

3. On May 30, 1974, the United States filed in this court a petition to enforce the summons.

4. The bank's objection to the summons was that the privacy of all its customers would be breached were the IRS to be allowed to go through all of the bank's records for five years in the search for any transaction by the parties being investigated. The bank said that it was willing to conduct the search itself, thereby protecting the customers' privacy, but that it would want to be reimbursed for the costs of such a search. It made no contention that the summons was not pursuant to a legitimate investigation, or that it was overbroad or ambiguous.

5. On July 10, 1974, this court ordered the bank to comply immediately with the summons. Jurisdiction was explicitly retained for the purpose of entertaining a motion by respondents for the costs incurred, should respondents wish to file such a motion after compliance was completed.

6. On May 1, 1975, respondents filed a motion for reimbursement, asserting that they had expended $2,545.28 in complying with the summons.

7. At oral argument the government made clear that it does not dispute the accuracy of the amount claimed by respondents— only their legal entitlement to it.

* * *

The court is here involved in a very delicate balancing act. There is no doubt but that citizens—both individuals and corporations—owe to their government certain duties, many of which cost time and money. For example, a bank incurs costs of time and money in complying with governmental regulations, but receives no compensation from the government. When, however, the government takes land from a private party for public use, it reimburses that party. That reimbursement is required by the Due Process Clause of the Fifth Amendment. Because these cases are so familiar to us, it seems relatively easy to see why one activity is reimbursed and the other isn't. Yet it's not easy to come up with a rationale which fairly divides all the costs of complying with various government mandates into two groups: those to be reimbursed, and those not.

There are, however, some principles on which we can seize. The regulation of banks is an exercise of fundamental governmental powers by a legislature which has presumably considered an issue of public concern and has determined that banks, in order to operate within the pale of government protection and approval, must do certain things. Banks are aware of this kind of regulation when they first open their doors, and are entitled to rally their legitimate political resources against them, or any other such measures, if they feel that the laws ought to be changed. But they are always bound to the current law because the legislature has determined that the public interest requires certain costs to be borne by banks in doing business. In addition, these regulations fall equally on all of the regulated class—all banks must comply, and bear the related costs. It is, for all, a cost of doing business.

That situation is quite different from our case, even though the government would label the costs of complying with a summons as a "cost of doing business." This "cost" is not predictably part of the banking business, does not fall upon all equally, and was not specifically evaluated by the legislature and imposed by it upon all those who do a banking business. Although the statute demands compliance with legitimate summonses, it is silent on the issue of reimbursement. Given that silence, and the dictates of the Due Process Clause, this court feels that it would be unreasonable to expect a party such as respondent to bear anything other than nominal costs in complying with a government summons. The duties of a citizen to his government, see United States v. Nixon, 418 U.S. 683, 94 S.Ct. 3090, 41 L.Ed.2d 1039 (1974), do not run so far as absorbing a $2500 expense in aid of a government investigation of a third party.

* * *

It will therefore be ordered that the United States reimburse respondent for the $2545.28 which it expended in complying with the summons in this case.

Query. If, as the Court argued in *SEC v. Jerry T. O'Brien, Inc.,* it is difficult to tell at the subpoena stage who the target is, could the approach in *Farmers & Merchants* be employed by any recipient who has not yet been formally identified as a target? Could it be used for grand jury subpoenas? Would you advocate legislation providing some payment by the government for compliance with subpoenas?

FISHER v. UNITED STATES
Supreme Court of the United States, 1976.
425 U.S. 391, 96 S.Ct. 1569, 48 L.Ed.2d 39.

MR. JUSTICE WHITE delivered the opinion of the Court.

In these two cases we are called upon to decide whether a summons directing an attorney to produce documents delivered to him by his client in connection with the attorney-client relationship is enforceable over claims that the documents were constitutionally immune from summons in the hands of the clients and retained that immunity in the hands of the attorneys.

I

In each case, an Internal Revenue agent visited the taxpayer or taxpayers and interviewed them in connection with an investigation of possible civil or criminal liability under the federal income tax laws. Shortly after the interviews—one day later in No. 74–611 and a week or two later in No. 74–18—the taxpayers obtained from their respective accountants certain documents relating to the preparation by the accountant of their tax returns. Shortly after obtaining the documents—later the same day in No. 74–611 and a few weeks later in No. 74–18—the taxpayers transferred the documents to their lawyers—respondent Kasmir and petitioner Fisher, respectively—each of whom was retained to assist the taxpayer in connection with the investigation. Upon learning of the whereabouts of the documents, the Internal Revenue Service served summonses on the attorneys directing them to produce documents listed therein. In No. 74–611, the documents were described as "the following records of Tannebaum Bindler & Lewis [the accounting firm]:

"1. Accountant's workpapers pertaining to Dr. E.J. Mason's books and records of 1969, 1970 and 1971.[69]

"2. Retained copies of E.J. Mason's income tax returns for 1969, 1970 and 1971.

"3. Retained copies of reports and other correspondence between Tannebaum Bindler & Lewis and Dr. E.J. Mason during 1969, 1970 and 1971."

---

69. [Court's footnote 2.] The "books and records" concerned taxpayer's large medical practice.

In No. 74–18, the documents demanded were analyses by the accountant of the taxpayers' income and expenses which had been copied by the accountant from the taxpayers' cancelled checks and deposit receipts.[70] . . . In each case, the lawyer declined to comply with the summons directing production of the documents, and enforcement actions were commenced by the Government under 26 U.S.C. §§ 7402(b) and 7604(a). . . .

[The Third Circuit enforced the summons; the Fifth Circuit did not.] We granted certiorari to resolve the conflict created. Because in our view the documents were not privileged either in the hands of the lawyers or of their clients, we affirm the judgment of the Third Circuit in No. 74–18 and reverse the judgment of the Fifth Circuit in No. 74–611.

II

All of the parties in this case and the Court of Appeals for the Fifth Circuit have concurred in the proposition that if the Fifth Amendment would have excused a *taxpayer* from turning over the accountant's papers had he possessed them, the *attorney* to whom they are delivered for the purpose of obtaining legal advice should also be immune from subpoena. Although we agree with this proposition for the reasons set forth in Part III, infra, . . . it is not the taxpayer's Fifth Amendment privilege that would excuse the *attorney* from production.

The relevant part of that Amendment provides:

> "No person . . . shall be *compelled* in any criminal case to be a *witness against himself*." (Emphasis added.)

The taxpayer's privilege under this Amendment is not violated by enforcement of the summonses involved in these cases because enforcement against a taxpayer's lawyer would not "compel" the taxpayer to do anything—and certainly would not compel him to be a "witness" against himself. The Court has held repeatedly that the Fifth Amendment is limited to prohibiting the use of "physical or moral compulsion" exerted on the person asserting the privilege.

* * *

Respondents argue, and the Fifth Circuit Court of Appeals apparently agreed, that if the summons was enforced, the taxpayers' Fifth Amendment privilege would be, but should not be, lost solely because they gave their documents to their lawyers in order to obtain legal advice. But this misconceives the nature of the constitutional privilege. The amendment protects a person from being compelled to be a witness against himself. Here, the taxpayers retained any privilege they ever had not to be compelled to testify against themselves and not to be compelled themselves to produce private papers in their possession. *This* personal privilege was in no way decreased by the transfer. It is simply that by reason of the transfer of the documents to the

---

70. [Court's footnote 3.] The husband taxpayer's checks and deposit receipts related to his textile waste business. The wife's related to her women's wear shop.

attorneys, those papers may be subpoenaed without compulsion on the taxpayer. The protection of the Fifth Amendment is therefore not available. "A party is privileged from producing evidence but not from its production."

The Court of Appeals for the Fifth Circuit suggested that because legally and ethically the attorney was required to respect the confidences of his client, the latter had a reasonable expectation of privacy for the records in the hands of the attorney and therefore did not forfeit his Fifth Amendment privilege with respect to the records by transferring them in order to obtain legal advice. It is true that the Court has often stated that one of the several purposes served by the constitutional privilege against compelled testimonial self-incrimination is that of protecting personal privacy. But the Court has never suggested that every invasion of privacy violates the privilege. Within the limits imposed by the language of the Fifth Amendment, which we necessarily observe, the privilege truly serves privacy interests; but the Court has never on any ground, personal privacy included, applied the Fifth Amendment to prevent the otherwise proper acquisition or use of evidence which, in the Court's view, did not involve compelled testimonial self-incrimination of some sort.

. . . The Framers addressed the subject of personal privacy directly in the Fourth Amendment. They struck a balance so that when the State's reason to believe incriminating evidence will be found becomes sufficiently great, the invasion of privacy becomes justified and a warrant to search and seize will issue. They did not seek in still another Amendment—the Fifth—to achieve a general protection of privacy but to deal with the more specific issue of compelled self-incrimination.

We cannot cut the Amendment completely loose from the moorings of its language, and make it serve as a general protector of privacy—a word not mentioned in its text and a concept directly addressed in the Fourth Amendment. . . .

Insofar as private information not obtained through compelled self-incriminating testimony is legally protected, its protection stems from other sources—the Fourth Amendment's protection against seizures without warrant or probable cause and against subpoenas which suffer from "too much indefiniteness or breadth in the things required to be 'particularly described,'" Oklahoma Press Publishing Co. v. Walling, 327 U.S. 186, 208, 66 S.Ct. 494, 505, 90 L.Ed. 614, 629 (1946); the First Amendment; or evidentiary privileges such as the attorney-client privilege.[71]

71. [Court's footnote 7.] The taxpayers and their attorneys have not raised arguments of a Fourth Amendment nature before this Court and could not be successful if they had. The summonses are narrowly drawn and seek only documents of unquestionable relevance to the tax investigation. Special problems of privacy which might be presented by subpoena of a personal diary, are not involved here.

First Amendment values are also plainly not implicated in this case.

III

Our above holding is that compelled production of documents from an attorney does not implicate whatever Fifth Amendment privilege the taxpayer might have enjoyed from being himself compelled to produce them. The taxpayers in these cases, however, have from the outset consistently urged that they should not be forced to expose otherwise protected documents to summons simply because they have sought legal advice and turned the papers over to their attorneys. The government appears to agree unqualifiedly. The difficulty is that taxpayers have erroneously relied on the Fifth Amendment without urging the attorney-client privilege in so many words. They have nevertheless invoked the relevant body of law and policies that govern the attorney-client privilege. In this posture of the case, we feel obliged to inquire whether the attorney-client privilege applies to documents in the hands of an attorney which would have been privileged in the hands of the client by reason of the Fifth Amendment.

Confidential disclosures by a client to an attorney made in order to obtain legal assistance are privileged. The purpose of the privilege is to encourage clients to make full disclosure to their attorneys. . . . As a practical matter, if the client knows that damaging information could more readily be obtained from the attorney following disclosure than from himself in the absence of disclosure, the client would be reluctant to confide in his lawyer and it would be difficult to obtain fully informed legal advice. However, since the privilege has the effect of withholding relevant information from the fact-finder, it applies only where necessary to achieve its purpose. Accordingly it protects only those disclosures—necessary to obtain informed legal advice—which might not have been made absent the privilege. . . . This Court and the lower courts have thus uniformly held that pre-existing documents which could have been obtained by court process from the client when he was in possession may also be obtained from the attorney by similar process following transfer by the client in order to obtain more informed legal advice. The purpose of the privilege requires no broader rule. Pre-existing documents obtainable from the client are not appreciably easier to obtain from the attorney after transfer to him. Thus, even absent the attorney-client privilege, clients will not be discouraged from disclosing the documents to the attorney and their ability to obtain informed legal advice will remain unfettered. It is otherwise if the documents are not obtainable by subpoena duces tecum or summons while in the exclusive possession of the client, for the client will then be reluctant to transfer possession to the lawyer unless the documents are also privileged in the latter's hands. Where the transfer is made for the purpose of obtaining legal advice, the purposes of the attorney-client privilege would be defeated unless the privilege is applicable. "It follows, then, that *when the client himself would be privileged* from production of the document either as a party at common law

... or as exempt from self-incrimination, the attorney having possession of the document is not bound to produce." ...

Since each taxpayer transferred possession of the documents in question from himself to his attorney, in order to obtain legal assistance in the tax investigations in question, the papers, if unobtainable by summons from the client, are unobtainable by summons directed to the attorney by reason of the attorney-client privilege. We accordingly proceed to the question whether the documents could have been obtained by summons addressed to the taxpayer while the documents were in his possession. The only bar to enforcement of such summons asserted by the parties or the courts below is the Fifth Amendment's privilege against self-incrimination. ...

IV

The proposition that the Fifth Amendment prevents compelled production of documents over objection that such production might incriminate stems from Boyd v. United States, 116 U.S. 616, 68 S.Ct. 524, 29 L.Ed. 746 (1886). *Boyd* involved a civil forfeiture proceeding brought by the Government against two partners for fraudulently attempting to import 35 cases of glass without paying the prescribed duty. The partnership had contracted with the Government to furnish the glass needed in the construction of a government building. The glass specified was foreign glass, it being understood that if part or all of the glass was furnished from the partnership's existing duty-paid inventory, it could be replaced by duty-free imports. Pursuant to this arrangement, 29 cases of glass were imported by the partnership duty free. The partners then represented that they were entitled to duty-free entry of an additional 35 cases which were soon to arrive. The forfeiture action concerned these 35 cases. The government's position was that the partnership had replaced all of the glass used in construction of the government building when it imported the 29 cases. At trial, the government obtained a court order directing the partners to produce an invoice the partnership had received from the shipper covering the previous 29-case shipment. The invoice was disclosed, offered in evidence and used, over the Fifth Amendment objection of the partners, to establish that the partners were fraudulently claiming a greater exemption from duty than they were entitled to under the contract. This Court held that the invoice was inadmissible and reversed the judgment in favor of the Government. The Court ruled that the Fourth Amendment applied to court orders in the nature of subpoenas duces tecum in the same manner in which it applies to search warrants; and that the Government may not, consistent with the Fourth Amendment, seize a person's documents or other property as evidence unless it can claim a proprietary interest in the property superior to that of the person from whom the property is obtained. ...

Among its several pronouncements, *Boyd* was understood to declare that the seizure, under warrant or otherwise, of any purely evidentiary materials violated the Fourth Amendment and that the Fifth Amendment rendered these seized materials inadmissible. That rule applied to documents as well as to other evidentiary items . . . .

Several of *Boyd*'s express or implicit declarations have not stood the test of time. The Application of the Fourth Amendment to subpoenas was limited by Hale v. Henkel, 201 U.S. 43, 26 S.Ct. 370, 50 L.Ed. 652 (1906), and more recent cases. See, for example, Oklahoma Press Publishing Co. v. Walling, 327 U.S. 186, 66 S.Ct. 494, 90 L.Ed. 614 (1946). Purely evidentiary (but "non-testimonial") [72] materials, as well as contraband and fruits and instrumentalities of crime, may now be searched for and seized under proper circumstances, Warden v. Hayden, 387 U.S. 294, 87 S.Ct. 1642, 18 L.Ed.2d 782 (1967). . . .

It is also clear that the Fifth Amendment does not independently proscribe the compelled production of every sort of incriminating evidence but applies only when the accused is compelled to make a *testimonial* communication that is incriminating. We have, accordingly, declined to extend the protection of the privilege to the giving of blood samples, to the giving of handwriting exemplars, voice exemplars, or the donning of a blouse worn by the perpetrator. Furthermore, despite *Boyd*, neither a partnership nor the individual partners are shielded from compelled production of partnership records on self-incrimination grounds. Bellis v. United States, 417 U.S. 85, 94 S.Ct. 2179, 40 L.Ed.2d 678 (1974). It would appear that under that case the precise claim sustained in *Boyd* would now be rejected for reasons not there considered.

The pronouncement in *Boyd* that a person may not be forced to produce his private papers has nonetheless often appeared as dictum in later opinions of this Court. . . . To the extent, however, that the rule against compelling production of private papers rested on the proposition that seizures of or subpoenas for "mere evidence," including documents, violated the Fourth Amendment and therefore also transgressed the Fifth, the foundations for the rule have been washed away. In consequence, the prohibition against forcing the production of private papers has long been a rule searching for a rationale consistent with the proscriptions of the Fifth Amendment against compelling a person to give "testimony" that incriminates him. Accordingly, we turn to the question of what, if any, incriminating testimony within the Fifth Amendment's protection, is compelled by a documentary summons.

A subpoena served on a taxpayer requiring him to produce an accountant's work papers in his possession without doubt involves substantial compulsion. But it does not compel oral testimony; nor

---

72. [Court's footnote 9.] . . . Warden v. Hayden reserved the question "whether there are items of evidential value whose very nature precludes them from being the object of a reasonable search and seizure."

would it ordinarily compel the taxpayer to restate, repeat or affirm the truth of the contents of the documents sought. Therefore, the Fifth Amendment would not be violated by the fact alone that the papers on their face might incriminate the taxpayer, for the privilege protects a person only against being incriminated by his own compelled testimonial communications. The accountants' work papers are not the taxpayer's. They were not prepared by him, and they contain no testimonial declarations by him. Furthermore, as far as this record demonstrates, the preparation of all of the papers sought in these cases was wholly voluntary, and they cannot be said to contain compelled testimonial evidence, either of the taxpayer or of anyone else. The taxpayer cannot avoid compliance with the subpoena merely by asserting that the item of evidence which he is required to produce contains incriminating writing, whether his own or that of someone else.

The act of producing evidence in response to a subpoena nevertheless has communicative aspects of its own, wholly aside from the contents of the papers produced. Compliance with the subpoena tacitly concedes the existence of the papers demanded and their possession or control by the taxpayer. It also would indicate the taxpayer's belief that the papers are those described in the subpoena. The elements of compulsion are clearly present, but the more difficult issues are whether the tacit averments of the taxpayer are both "testimonial" and "incriminating" for purposes of applying the Fifth Amendment. These questions perhaps do not lend themselves to categorical answer; their resolution may instead depend on the facts and circumstances of particular cases or classes thereof. In light of the records now before us, we are confident that however incriminating the contents of the accountant's work papers might be, the act of producing them—the only thing which the taxpayer is compelled to do—would not itself involve testimonial self-incrimination.

It is doubtful that implicitly admitting the existence and possession of the papers rises to the level of testimony within the protection of the Fifth Amendment. The papers belong to the accountant, were prepared by him and are the kind usually prepared by an accountant working on the tax returns of his client. Surely the Government is in no way relying on the "truth telling" of the taxpayer to prove the existence of or his access to the documents. The existence and location of the papers are a foregone conclusion and the taxpayer adds little or nothing to the sum total of the government's information by conceding that he in fact has the papers. . . .

When an accused is required to submit a handwriting exemplar he admits his ability to write and impliedly asserts that the exemplar is his writing. But in common experience, the first would be a near truism and the latter self-evident. In any event, although the exemplar may be incriminating to the accused and although he is compelled to furnish it, his Fifth Amendment privilege is not violated because nothing he has said or done is deemed to be sufficiently testimonial for purposes of the privilege. This Court has also time and again allowed subpoenas against the custodian of corporate documents or those belonging to other collective entities such as unions and partnerships and those of bankrupt businesses over claims that the documents will incriminate the custodian despite the fact that producing the documents tacitly admits their existence and their location in the hands of their possessor. The existence and possession or control of the subpoenaed documents being no more in issue here than in the above cases, the summons is equally enforceable.

* * *

As for the possibility that responding to the subpoena would authenticate the work papers, production would express nothing more than the taxpayer's belief that the papers are those described in the subpoena. The taxpayers would be no more competent to authenticate their accountant's work papers or reports by producing them than they would be to authenticate them if testifying orally. They did not prepare the papers and could not vouch for their accuracy. The documents would not be admissible in evidence against the taxpayers without authenticating testimony. Without more, responding to the subpoena in the circumstances before us would not appear to represent a substantial threat of self-incrimination. . . .

Whether the Fifth Amendment would shield the taxpayer from producing his own tax records in his possession is a question not involved here; for the papers demanded here are not his "private papers," see Boyd v. United States, supra, 116 U.S., at 634, 6 S.Ct., at 534, 29 L.Ed., at 752. We do hold that compliance with a summons directing the taxpayer to produce the accountant's documents involved in this case would involve no incriminating testimony within the protection of the Fifth Amendment.

The judgment of the Court of Appeals for the Fifth Circuit in No. 74–611 is reversed. The judgment of the Court of Appeals for the Third Circuit in No. 74–18 is affirmed.

So ordered.

Affirmed in part; reversed in part.

Mr. Justice Stevens took no part in the consideration or disposition of these cases.

Mr. Justice Brennan, concurring in the judgment.

I concur in the judgment. Given the prior access by accountants retained by the taxpayers to the papers involved in these cases and the wholly business rather than personal nature of the papers, I agree that the privilege against compelled self-incrimination did not in either of these cases protect the papers from production in response to the summons. I do not join the Court's opinion, however, because of the portent in much of what is said of a serious crippling of the protection secured by the privilege against compelled production of one's private books and papers. . . .

[After developing the view that "the protection of personal privacy is a central purpose of the privilege" and that this protection extends not only to oral declarations but also to books and papers, Justice Brennan continued:] [I]t is not enough that the production of a writing, or books and papers, is compelled. Unless those materials are such as to come within the zone of privacy recognized by the amendments, the privilege against compulsory self-incrimination does not protect against their production.

* * *

A precise cataloguing of private papers within the ambit of the privacy protected by the privilege is probably impossible. Some kinds, however, do lend themselves to classification. Production of documentary materials created or authenticated by the State or Federal Governments, such as automobile registrations or property deeds, would seem ordinarily to fall outside the protection of the privilege. They hardly reflect an extension of the person.

Economic and business records may present difficulty in particular cases. The records of business entities generally fall without the scope of the privilege. But, as noted, the Court has recognized that the privilege extends to the business records of the sole proprietor or practitioner. Such records are at least an extension of an aspect of a person's activities, though concededly not the more intimate aspects of one's life. Where the privilege would have protected one's mental notes of his business affairs in a less complicated day and age, it would seem that that protection should not fall away because the complexities of another time compel one to keep business records. Non-business economic records in the possession of an individual, such as cancelled checks or tax records, would also seem to be protected. They may provide clear insights into a person's total life style. They are, however, like business records and the papers involved in these cases, frequently, though not always, disclosed to other parties, and disclosure, in proper cases, may foreclose reliance upon the privilege. Personal letters constitute an integral aspect of a person's private enclave. And while letters, being necessarily interpersonal, are not wholly private, their peculiarly private nature and the generally narrow extent of their disclosure would seem to render them within the scope of the privilege. Papers in the nature of a personal diary are a fortiori protected under the privilege.

The Court's treatment in the instant cases of the question whether the evidence involved here is within the protection of the privilege is, with all respect, most inadequate. The gaping hole is in the omission of any reference to the taxpayer's privacy interests and to whether the subpoenas impermissibly invade those interests. . . . For the reasons I have stated at the outset, however, I do not believe that the evidence involved in these cases falls within the scope of privacy protected by the Fifth Amendment.

* * *

[The concurring opinion of JUSTICE MARSHALL is omitted.]

NOTES AND QUERIES

(1) *Developing Fifth Amendment Doctrine.* *Fisher* presents the student with an excellent opportunity to review the historical development of fifth amendment doctrine in the twentieth century. For example, looking at the cases which have attempted to limit the fifth amendment's self-incrimination clause as it applies to corporations, can you discern what the Court at various times believed the fifth amendment would have covered had it been applicable? Review *United States v. White,* supra p. 393. Does the Court there indicate the extent of protection available to those "natural persons" eligible for fifth amendment protection? Is that view consistent with the view taken by the Court in *Fisher?* Put another way, if *Fisher* is the correct view of the extent to which the fifth amendment protects documents, why did the Court spend three-quarters of a century worrying about whether particular entities qualified for this protection?

Looking at this constitutional history from the position taken by Justice Brennan, can it be said that the "central purpose" of the fifth amendment's self-incrimination clause is personal privacy? If so, how do the immunity cases fit in? Isn't the central purpose of the self-incrimination clause to keep you from being forced to put yourself in jail? Indeed, doesn't the majority's rejection of the centrality of privacy merely complete the process, begun in *Hale,* of splitting the fifth and fourth amendments?

After *Fisher,* is there anything which the fifth amendment prevents the government from obtaining by subpoena? Could the government subpoena a diary which contains the diarist's confession of murder? Could the government subpoena someone to bring in their marijuana?

(2) *What Does Fisher Mean—Round 1.* The Supreme Court's first opportunity to apply *Fisher* did not come until 1984. *United States v. Doe*[73] involved five grand jury subpoenas seeking numerous documents relating to several of "Doe's" companies, all of which he was the sole owner. JUSTICE POWELL delivered the Court's opinion:

> This case presents the issue whether, and to what extent, the Fifth Amendment privilege against compelled self-incrimination applies to the business records of a sole proprietorship.
>
> * * *
>
> II
>
> Respondent filed a motion in federal district court seeking to quash the subpoenas. The District Court for the District of New Jersey granted his motion. . . . In reaching its decision, the District Court noted that the Government had conceded that the materials sought in the subpoena were or might be incriminating.

[73]. 465 U.S. 605, 104 S.Ct. 1237, 79 L.Ed.2d 552 (1984).

The court stated that, therefore, "the relevant inquiry is . . . whether the *act* of producing the documents has communicative aspects which warrant Fifth Amendment protection." The court found that the act of production would compel respondent to "admit that the records exist, that they are in his possession, and that they are authentic." . . .

The Court of Appeals for the Third Circuit affirmed. It first addressed the question whether the Fifth Amendment ever applies to the records of a sole proprietorship. After noting that an individual may not assert the Fifth Amendment privilege on behalf of a corporation, partnership, or other collective entity under the holding of Bellis v. United States, 417 U.S. 85, 94 S.Ct. 2179, 40 L.Ed.2d 678 (1974), the Court of Appeals reasoned that the owner of a sole proprietorship acts in a personal rather than a representative capacity. As a result, the court held that respondent's claim of the privilege was not foreclosed by the reasoning of *Bellis*.

The Court of Appeals next considered whether the documents at issue in this case are privileged. The court noted that this Court held in Fisher v. United States that the contents of business records ordinarily are not privileged because they are created voluntarily and without compulsion. The Court of Appeals nevertheless found that respondent's business records were privileged under either of two analyses. First, the court reasoned that, notwithstanding the holdings in *Bellis* and *Fisher*, the business records of a sole proprietorship are no different from the individual owner's personal records. Noting that Third Circuit cases had held that private papers, although created voluntarily, are protected by the Fifth Amendment, the court accorded the same protection to respondent's business papers. Second, it held that respondent's act of producing the subpoenaed records would have "communicative aspects of its own." The turning over of the subpoenaed documents to the grand jury would admit their existence and authenticity. Accordingly, respondent was entitled to assert his Fifth Amendment privilege rather than produce the subpoenaed documents.

The Government contended that the court should enforce the subpoenas because of the Government's offer not to use respondent's act of production against respondent in any way. The Court of Appeals noted that no formal request for use immunity under 18 U.S.C. §§ 6002 and 6003 had been made. In light of this failure, the court held that the District Court did not err in rejecting the Government's attempt to compel delivery of the subpoenaed records.

We granted certiorari to resolve the apparent conflict between the Court of Appeals holding and the reasoning underlying this Court's holding in *Fisher*. We now affirm in part, reverse in part, and remand for further proceedings.

III

A

The Court in *Fisher* expressly declined to reach the question whether the Fifth Amendment privilege protects the contents of an individual's tax records in his possession. The rationale underlying our holding in that case is, however, persuasive here. As we noted in *Fisher,* the Fifth Amendment protects the person asserting the privilege only from *compelled* self-incrimination. Where the preparation of business records is voluntary, no compulsion is present. A subpoena that demands production of documents "does not compel oral testimony; nor would it ordinarily compel the taxpayer to restate, repeat, or affirm the truth of the contents of the documents sought." . . .

. . . Respondent does not contend that he prepared the documents involuntarily or that the subpoena would force him to restate, repeat, or affirm the truth of their contents. The fact that the records are in respondent's possession is irrelevant to the determination of whether the creation of the records was compelled. We therefore hold that the contents of those records are not privileged.

B

Although the contents of a document may not be privileged, the act of producing the document may be. A government subpoena compels the holder of the document to perform an act that may have testimonial aspects and an incriminating effect. . . .

. . . Unlike the Court in *Fisher,* we have the explicit finding of the District Court that the act of producing the documents would involve testimonial self-incrimination. The Court of Appeals agreed.[74] The District Court's finding essentially rests on its determination of factual issues. Therefore, we will not overturn that finding unless it has no support in the record. Traditionally, we also have been reluctant to disturb findings of fact in which two courts below have concurred. We therefore decline to overturn the finding of the District Court in this regard, where, as here, it has been affirmed by the Court of Appeals.[75]

---

74. [Court's footnote 12.] The Court of Appeals stated:

"In the matter sub judice, however, we find nothing in the record that would indicate that the United States knows, as a certainty, that each of the myriad documents demanded by the five subpoenas in fact is in the appellee's possession or subject to his control. The most plausible inference to be drawn from the broad-sweeping subpoenas is that the Government, unable to prove that the subpoenaed documents exist—or that the appellee even is somehow connected to the business entities under investigation—is attempting to compensate for its lack of knowledge by requiring the appellee to become, in effect, the primary informant against himself."

75. [Court's footnote 13.] The Government concedes that the act of producing the subpoenaed documents might have had some testimonial aspects, but it argues that any incrimination would be so trivial

IV

The Government, as it concedes, could have compelled respondent to produce the documents listed in the subpoena. Sections 6002 and 6003 of Title 18 provide for the granting of use immunity with respect to the potentially incriminating evidence. . . .

The Government did state several times before the District Court that it would not use respondent's act of production against him in any way. But counsel for the Government never made a statutory request to the District Court to grant respondent use immunity. We are urged to adopt a doctrine of constructive use immunity. Under this doctrine, the courts would impose a requirement on the Government not to use the incriminatory aspects of the act of production against the person claiming the privilege even though the statutory procedures have not been followed.

We decline to extend the jurisdiction of courts to include prospective grants of use immunity in the absence of the formal request that the statute requires. As we stated in Pillsbury Co. v. Conboy, [excerpted supra this Casebook, p. 517], in passing the use immunity statute, "Congress gave certain officials in the Department of Justice exclusive authority to grant immunities." "Congress foresaw the courts as playing only a minor role in the immunizing process: . . ." The decision to seek use immunity necessarily involves a balancing of the Government's interest in obtaining information against the risk that immunity will frustrate the Government's attempts to prosecute the subject of the investigation. Congress expressly left this decision exclusively to the Justice Department. If, on remand, the appropriate official concludes that it is desirable to compel respondent to produce his business records, the statutory procedure for requesting use immunity will be available.[76]

---

that the Fifth Amendment is not implicated. On the basis of the findings made in this case we think it clear that the risk of incrimination was "substantial and real" and not "trifling or imaginary." Respondent did not concede in the District Court that the records listed in the subpoena actually existed or were in his possession. Respondent argued that by producing the records, he would tacitly admit their existence and his possession. Respondent also pointed out that if the Government obtained the documents from another source, it would have to authenticate them before they would be admissible at trial. See Fed. R.Evid. 901. By producing the documents, respondent would relieve the Government of the need for authentication. These allegations were sufficient to establish a valid claim of the privilege against self-incrimination. This is not to say that the Government was foreclosed from rebutting respondent's claim by producing evidence that possession, existence, and authentication were a "foregone conclusion." In this case, however, the Government failed to make such a showing.

76. [Court's footnote 17.] Respondent argues that any grant of use immunity must cover the contents of the documents as well as the act of production. We find this contention unfounded. To satisfy the requirements of the Fifth Amendment, a grant of immunity need be only as broad as the privilege against self-incrimination. As discussed above, the privilege in this case extends only to the act of production. Therefore, any grant of use immunity need only protect respondent from the self-incrimination that might accompany the act of producing his business records.

V

We conclude that the Court of Appeals erred in holding that the contents of the subpoenaed documents were privileged under the Fifth Amendment. The act of producing the documents at issue in this case is privileged and cannot be compelled without a statutory grant of use immunity pursuant to 18 U.S.C. §§ 6002 and 6003. The judgment of the Court of Appeals is, therefore, affirmed in part, reversed in part, and the case is remanded to the District Court for further proceedings in accordance with this decision.

It is so ordered.

Affirmed in part, reversed in part, and remanded.

JUSTICE O'CONNOR, concurring.

I concur in both the result and reasoning of Justice Powell's opinion for the Court. I write separately, however, just to make explicit what is implicit in the analysis of that opinion: that the Fifth Amendment provides absolutely no protection for the contents of private papers of any kind. The notion that the Fifth Amendment protects the privacy of papers originated in Boyd v. United States, but our decision in Fisher v. United States sounded the death-knell for *Boyd*. "Several of *Boyd's* express or implicit declarations [had] not stood the test of time[,]" id., at 407, 96 S.Ct., at 1579, and its privacy of papers concept "had long been a rule searching for a rationale. . . ." Id., at 409, 96 S.Ct., at 1580. Today's decision puts a long-overdue end to that fruitless search.

JUSTICE MARSHALL, with whom JUSTICE BRENNAN joins, concurring in part and dissenting in part.

* * *

Contrary to what Justice O'Connor contends, I do not view the Court's opinion in this case as having reconsidered whether the Fifth Amendment provides protection for the contents of "private papers of any kind." This case presented nothing remotely close to the question that Justice O'Connor eagerly poses and answers. . . . [T]he documents at stake here are business records which implicate a lesser degree of concern for privacy interests than, for example, personal diaries.

Were it true that the Court's opinion stands for the proposition that "the Fifth Amendment provides absolutely no protection for the contents of private papers of any kind," I would assuredly dissent. I continue to believe that under the Fifth Amendment "there are certain documents no person ought to be compelled to produce at the Government's request." Fisher v. United States, 425 U.S. 391, 431–432, 96 S.Ct. 1569, 1590–91, 48 L.Ed.2d 39 (Justice Marshall, concurring).

[The opinion of JUSTICE STEVENS, concurring in part and dissenting in part, is omitted.]

(3) *What Does Fisher Mean—Round 2.* Corporate subpoenas are often directed at a particular employee of the corporation, as "custodian" of the corporation's records. Prior to *Fisher*, custodians had not been successful in asserting the fifth amendment to block production of corporate documents whose contents might incriminate the custodian. After all, the corporation, owner of the documents, had no fifth amendment privilege to assert.[77] After *Fisher*, however, subpoenaed corporate employees began to assert that their act of production (rather than the contents of the documents) might be personally incriminating and that they could therefore refuse to produce.

It was in this context that the Supreme Court had its second opportunity to apply *Fisher*. In *Braswell v. United States*,[78] the grand jury issued a subpoena to the sole shareholder of a corporation to produce certain corporate books and records:

> CHIEF JUSTICE REHNQUIST delivered the opinion of the Court.
>
> * * *
>
> Had petitioner conducted his business as a sole proprietorship, *Doe* [supra this Casebook, Note (2)] would require that he be provided the opportunity to show that his act of production would entail testimonial self-incrimination. But petitioner has operated his business through the corporate form, and we have long recognized that for purposes of the Fifth Amendment, corporations and other collective entities are treated differently from individuals. This doctrine—known as the collective entity rule—has a lengthy and distinguished pedigree.
>
> The rule was first articulated by the Court in the case of Hale v. Henkel, 201 U.S. 43, 26 S.Ct. 370, 50 L.Ed. 652 (1906). Hale, a corporate officer, had been served with a subpoena ordering him to produce corporate records and to testify concerning certain corporate transactions. Although Hale was protected by personal immunity, he sought to resist the demand for the records by interposing a Fifth Amendment privilege on behalf of the corporation. The Court rejected that argument: "[W]e are of the opinion that there is a clear distinction . . . between an individual and a corporation, and . . . the latter has no right to refuse to submit its books and papers for an examination at the suit of the State." The Court explained that the corporation "is a creature of the State," with powers limited by the State. As such, the State may, in the exercise of its right to oversee the corporation, demand the production of corporate records.
>
> The ruling in *Hale* represented a limitation on the prior holding in Boyd v. United States, 116 U.S. 616, 6 S.Ct. 524, 29 L.Ed.

---

77. The lead case is Wilson v. United States, 221 U.S. 361, 31 S.Ct. 538, 55 L.Ed. 771 (1911). Cf. Curcio v. United States, 354 U.S. 118, 77 S.Ct. 1145, 1 L.Ed.2d 1225 (1957) (cannot force custodian to testify orally as to whereabouts of nonproduced records; would require him "to disclose the contents of his own mind"; protected by fifth amendment).

78. ___ U.S. ___, 108 S.Ct. 2284, 101 L.Ed.2d 98 (1988).

746 (1886), which involved a court order directing partners to produce an invoice received by the partnership. The partners had produced the invoice, but steadfastly maintained that the court order ran afoul of the Fifth Amendment. This Court agreed. After concluding that the order transgressed the Fourth Amendment, the Court declared: "[A] compulsory production of the *private* books and papers of the owner of goods sought to be forfeited . . . is compelling him to be a witness against himself, within the meaning of the Fifth Amendment to the Constitution. . . ." Id., at 634–635, 6 S.Ct., at 534 (emphasis added). *Hale* carved an exception out of *Boyd* by establishing that corporate books and records are not "private papers" protected by the Fifth Amendment.

[The Court then reviewed other cases dealing with an entity's right to assert the fifth amendment, including United States v. White and Bellis v. United States, supra this Casebook pp. 393, 397. The Court continued:]

The plain mandate of these decisions is that without regard to whether the subpoena is addressed to the corporation, or as here, to the individual in his capacity as a custodian, a corporate custodian such as petitioner may not resist a subpoena for corporate records on Fifth Amendment grounds. Petitioner argues, however, that this rule falls in the wake of Fisher v. United States and United States v. Doe.

To be sure, the holding in *Fisher*—later reaffirmed in *Doe*—embarked upon a new course of Fifth Amendment analysis. We cannot agree, however, that it rendered the collective entity rule obsolete. The agency rationale undergirding the collective entity decisions, in which custodians asserted that production of entity records would incriminate them personally, survives. [T]he Court has consistently recognized that the custodian of corporate or entity records holds those documents in a representative rather than a personal capacity. Artificial entities such as corporations may act only through their agents, and a custodian's assumption of his representative capacity leads to certain obligations, including the duty to produce corporate records on proper demand by the Government. Under those circumstances, the custodian's act of production is not deemed a personal act, but rather an act of the corporation. Any claim of Fifth Amendment privilege asserted by the agent would be tantamount to a claim of privilege by the corporation—which of course possesses no such privilege.

* * *

We note further that recognizing a Fifth Amendment privilege on behalf of the records custodians of collective entities would have a detrimental impact on the Government's efforts to prosecute "white-collar crime," one of the most serious problems confronting law enforcement authorities.[79] . . . If custodians could assert a privilege, authorities would be stymied not only in their enforcement efforts against those individuals but also in their prosecutions of organizations. . . .

Petitioner suggests, however, that these concerns can be minimized by the simple expedient of either granting the custodian statutory immunity as to the act of production, 18 U.S.C. §§ 6002, 6003, or addressing the subpoena to the corporation and allowing it to choose an agent to produce the records who can do so without incriminating himself. We think neither proposal satisfactorily addresses these concerns. Taking the last first, it is no doubt true that if a subpoena is addressed to a corporation, the corporation "must find some means by which to comply because no Fifth Amendment defense is available to it." The means most commonly used to comply is the appointment of an alternate custodian. But petitioner insists he cannot be required to aid the appointed custodian in his search for the demanded records, for any statement to the surrogate would itself be testimonial and incriminating. If this is correct, then petitioner's "solution" is a chimera. In situations such as this—where the corporate custodian is likely the only person with knowledge about the demanded documents—the appointment of a surrogate will simply not ensure that the documents sought will ever reach the grand jury room; the appointed custodian will essentially be sent on an unguided search.

This problem is eliminated if the Government grants the subpoenaed custodian statutory immunity for the testimonial aspects of his act of production. But that "solution" also entails a significant drawback. All of the evidence obtained under a grant of immunity to the custodian may of course be used freely against the corporation, but if the Government has any thought of prosecuting the custodian, a grant of act of production immunity can have serious consequences. Testimony obtained pursuant to a grant of statutory use immunity may be used neither directly nor derivatively. 18 U.S.C. § 6002; Kastigar v. United States, 406 U.S. 441, 92 S.Ct. 1653, 32 L.Ed.2d 212 (1972). And "[o]ne raising a claim under [the federal immunity] statute need only show that he testified under a grant of immunity in order to shift to the government the heavy burden of proving that all of the evidence it proposes to use was derived from legitimate independent sources." Id., at 461–462, 92 S.Ct., at 1665. Even in cases where the Government does not employ the immunized testimony for any purpose—direct or derivative—against the witness, the Government's inability to meet the "heavy burden" it

---

79. [Court's footnote 9.] White-collar crime is "the most serious and all-pervasive crime problem in America today." Conyers, Corporate and White–Collar Crime: A View by the Chairman of the House Subcommittee on Crime, 17 Am. Crim.L.Rev. 287, 288 (1980). Although this statement was made in 1980, there is no reason to think the problem has diminished in the meantime.

bears may result in the preclusion of crucial evidence that was obtained legitimately.

Although a corporate custodian is not entitled to resist a subpoena on the ground that his act of production will be personally incriminating, we do think certain consequences flow from the fact that the custodian's act of production is one in his representative rather than personal capacity. Because the custodian acts as a representative, the act is deemed one of the corporation and not the individual. Therefore, the Government concedes, as it must, that it may make no evidentiary use of the "individual act" against the individual.[80] For example, in a criminal prosecution against the custodian, the Government may not introduce into evidence before the jury the fact that the subpoena was served upon and the corporation's documents were delivered by one particular individual, the custodian. The Government has the right, however, to use the corporation's act of production against the custodian. The Government may offer testimony—for example, from the process server who delivered the subpoena and from the individual who received the records—establishing that the corporation produced the records subpoenaed. The jury may draw from the corporation's act of production the conclusion that the records in question are authentic corporate records, which the corporation possessed, and which it produced in response to the subpoena. And if the defendant held a prominent position within the corporation that produced the records, the jury may, just as it would had someone else produced the documents, reasonably infer that he had possession of the documents or knowledge of their contents. Because the jury is not told that the defendant produced the records, any nexus between the defendant and the documents results solely from the corporation's act of production and other evidence in the case.[81]

Consistent with our precedent, the United States Court of Appeals for the Fifth Circuit ruled that petitioner could not resist the subpoena for corporate documents on the ground that the act of production might tend to incriminate him. The judgment is therefore affirmed.

---

80. [Query: Is this the normal rule when corporations and their agents are prosecuted criminally?—Ed.]

81. [Court's footnote 11.] We reject the suggestion that the limitation on the evidentiary use of the custodian's act of production is the equivalent of constructive use immunity barred under our decision in *Doe* [supra this Casebook, p. 607]. Rather, the limitation is a necessary concomitant of the notion that a corporate custodian acts as an agent and not an individual when he produces corporate records in response to a subpoena addressed to him in his representative capacity.

We leave open the question whether the agency rationale supports compelling a custodian to produce corporate records when the custodian is able to establish, by showing for example that he is the sole employee and officer of the corporation, that the jury would inevitably conclude that he produced the records.

JUSTICE KENNEDY, with whom JUSTICE BRENNAN, JUSTICE MARSHALL, and JUSTICE SCALIA join, dissenting.

Our long course of decisions concerning artificial entities and the Fifth Amendment served us well. It illuminated two of the critical foundations for the constitutional guarantee against self-incrimination: first, that it is an explicit right of a natural person, protecting the realm of human thought and expression; second, that it is confined to governmental compulsion.

It is regrettable that the very line of cases which at last matured to teach these principles is now invoked to curtail them, for the Court rules that a natural person forfeits the privilege in a criminal investigation directed against him and that the Government may use compulsion to elicit testimonial assertions from a person who faces the threat of criminal proceedings. A case that might have served as the paradigmatic expression of the purposes served by the Fifth Amendment instead is used to obscure them.

The Court today denies an individual his Fifth Amendment privilege against self-incrimination in order to vindicate the rule that a collective entity which employs him has no such privilege itself. To reach this ironic conclusion, the majority must blur an analytic clarity in Fifth Amendment doctrine that has taken almost a century to emerge. After holding that corporate employment strips the individual of his privilege, the Court then attempts to restore some measure of protection by its judicial creation of a new zone of immunity in some vaguely defined circumstances. This exercise admits what the Court denied in the first place, namely that compelled compliance with the subpoena implicates the Fifth Amendment self-incrimination privilege.

The majority's apparent reasoning is that collective entities have no privilege and so their employees must have none either. The Court holds that a corporate agent must incriminate himself even when he is named in the subpoena and is a target of the investigation, and even when it is conceded that compliance requires compelled, personal, testimonial, incriminating assertions. I disagree with that conclusion; find no precedent for it; maintain that if there is a likelihood of personal self-incrimination the narrow use immunity permitted by statute can be granted without frustrating the investigation of collective entities; and submit that basic Fifth Amendment principles should not be avoided and manipulated, which is the necessary effect of this decision.

* * *

The collective entity rule provides no support for the majority's holding. . . . In none of the collective entity cases cited by the majority, and in none that I have found, were we presented with a claim that the custodian would be incriminated by the act of production, in contrast to the contents of the documents.

* * *

The question before us is not the existence of the collective entity rule, but whether it contains any principle which overrides the personal Fifth Amendment privilege of someone compelled to give incriminating testimony. Our precedents establish a firm basis for assertion of the privilege. Randy Braswell, like the respondent in *Doe I*, is being asked to draw upon his personal knowledge to identify and to deliver documents which are responsive to the Government's subpoena. Once the Government concedes there are testimonial consequences implicit in the act of production, it cannot escape the conclusion that compliance with the subpoena is indisputably Braswell's own act. . . .

* * *

(4) *What Is Testimonial?* As indicated in *Fisher*, the Court had previously held that compelling a person to undergo a blood test, or to create a handwriting or voice exemplar (an example for identification), or to stand in a line-up did not violate the fifth amendment because it did not compel "testimony." The compelled action, of course, helped convict the compelled party, but the Court, nevertheless, felt that the conduct was not "testimonial or communicative."

Consider *Doe v. United States*,[82] a post-*Fisher* case, which involved the efforts of a grand jury to obtain records from banks in the Cayman Islands and Bermuda. Banking laws in those countries forbade the disclosure of such records without the customer's consent. The Government sought a court order requiring the witness to sign twelve forms which stated that he consented to disclosure of records of twelve accounts which the Government believed the witness controlled. After the motion was denied, the Government presented a revised form which the Fifth Circuit ruled he could be forced to sign. The revised consent form provided (reproduced in note 2 of the Court's opinion):

"I, _____, of the State of Texas in the United States of America, do hereby direct any bank or trust company at which I may have a bank account of any kind or at which a corporation has a bank account of any kind upon which I am authorized to draw, and its officers, employees and agents, to disclose all information and deliver copies of all documents of every nature in your possession or control which relate to said bank account to Grand Jury 84–2, empaneled May 7, 1984 and sitting in the Southern District of Texas, or to any attorney of the District of Texas, or to any attorney of the United States Department of Justice assisting said Grand Jury, and to give evidence relevant thereto, in the investigation conducted by Grand Jury 84–2 in the Southern District of Texas, and this shall be irrevocable authority for so doing. This direction has been executed pursuant to that certain order of the United States District Court for the Southern District of Texas issued in connection with the aforesaid investigation, dated _____. This direction is intended to apply to the Confidential

---

[82] __ U.S. __, 108 S.Ct. 2341, 101 L.Ed.2d 184 (1988).

Relationships (Preservation) Law of the Cayman Islands, and to any implied contract of confidentiality between Bermuda banks and their customers which may be imposed by Bermuda common law, and shall be construed as consent with respect thereto as the same shall apply to any of the bank accounts for which I may be a relevant principal."

After being held in contempt for failing to sign the form, the witness obtained review in the Supreme Court. JUSTICE BLACKMUN wrote for the Court:

The execution of the consent directive at issue in this case obviously would be compelled, and we may assume that its execution would have an incriminating effect.[83] The question on which this case turns is whether the act of executing the form is a "testimonial communication." The parties disagree about both the meaning of "testimonial" and whether the consent directive fits the proposed definitions.

A

Petitioner contends that a compelled statement is testimonial if the Government could use the content of the speech or writing, as opposed to its physical characteristics, to further a criminal investigation of the witness. The second half of petitioner's "testimonial" test is that the statement must be incriminating, which is, of course, already a separate requirement for invoking the privilege. Thus, Doe contends, in essence, that every written and oral statement significant for its content is necessarily testimonial for purposes of the Fifth Amendment. Under this view, the consent directive is testimonial because it is a declarative statement of consent made by Doe to the foreign banks, a statement that the Government will use to persuade the banks to produce potentially incriminating account records that would otherwise be unavailable to the grand jury.

The Government, on the other hand, suggests that a compelled statement is not testimonial for purposes of the privilege, unless it implicitly or explicitly relates a factual assertion or otherwise conveys information to the Government. It argues that, under this view, the consent directive is not testimonial because neither the directive itself nor Doe's execution of the form discloses or communicates facts or information. Petitioner disagrees.

The Government's view of the privilege . . . is derived largely from this Court's decisions in *Fisher* and *Doe*. The issue presented in those cases was whether the act of producing subpoenaed docu-

---

83. [Court's footnote 5.] [T]he District Court concluded that the consent directive was incriminating in that it would furnish the Government with a link in the chain of evidence leading to Doe's indictment. Because we ultimately find no testimonial significance in either the contents of the directive or Doe's execution of it, we need not, and do not, address the incrimination element of the privilege.

ments, not itself the making of a statement, might nonetheless have some protected testimonial aspects. The Court concluded that the act of production could constitute protected testimonial communication because it might entail implicit statements of fact: by producing documents in compliance with a subpoena, the witness would admit that the papers existed, were in his possession or control, and were authentic. Thus, the Court made clear that the Fifth Amendment privilege against self-incrimination applies to acts that imply assertions of fact.

We reject petitioner's argument that this test does not control the determination as to when the privilege applies to oral or written statements. While the Court in *Fisher* and *Doe* did not purport to announce a universal test for determining the scope of the privilege, it also did not purport to establish a more narrow boundary applicable to acts alone. To the contrary, the Court applied basic Fifth Amendment principles. [I]n order to be testimonial, an accused's communication must itself, explicitly or implicitly, relate a factual assertion or disclose information. Only then is a person compelled to be a "witness" against himself.

* * *

It is consistent with the history of and the policies underlying the Self–Incrimination Clause to hold that the privilege may be asserted only to resist compelled explicit or implicit disclosures of incriminating information. Historically, the privilege was intended to prevent the use of legal compulsion to extract from the accused a sworn communication of facts which would incriminate him. Such was the process of the ecclesiastical courts and the Star Chamber—the inquisitorial method of putting the accused upon his oath and compelling him to answer questions designed to uncover uncharged offenses, without evidence from another source. The major thrust of the policies undergirding the privilege is to prevent such compulsion. . . . These policies are served when the privilege is asserted to spare the accused from having to reveal, directly or indirectly, his knowledge of facts relating him to the offense or from having to share his thoughts and beliefs with the Government.

We are not persuaded by petitioner's arguments that our articulation of the privilege fundamentally alters the power of the Government to compel an accused to assist in his prosecution. There are very few instances in which a verbal statement, either oral or written, will not convey information or assert facts. The vast majority of verbal statements thus will be testimonial and, to that extent at least, will fall within the privilege. . . .

B

. . . We turn, then, to consider whether Doe's execution of the consent directive at issue here would have testimonial significance. We agree with the Court of Appeals that it would not, because neither the form, nor its execution, communicates any factual assertions, implicit or explicit, or conveys any information to the Government.

The consent directive itself is not "testimonial." It is carefully drafted not to make reference to a specific account, but only to speak in the hypothetical. Thus, the form does not acknowledge that an account in a foreign financial institution is in existence or that it is controlled by petitioner. Nor does the form indicate whether documents or any other information relating to petitioner are present at the foreign bank, assuming that such an account does exist. The form does not even identify the relevant bank. Although the executed form allows the Government access to a potential source of evidence, the directive itself does not point the Government toward hidden accounts or otherwise provide information that will assist the prosecution in uncovering evidence. . . . As in *Fisher*, the Government is not relying upon the " 'truthtelling' " of Doe's directive to show the existence of, or his control over, foreign bank account records.

Given the consent directive's phraseology, petitioner's compelled act of executing the form has no testimonial significance either. By signing the form, Doe makes no statement, explicit or implicit, regarding the existence of a foreign bank account or his control over any such account. Nor would his execution of the form admit the authenticity of any records produced by the bank. . . . Authentication evidence would have to be provided by bank officials.

Finally, we cannot agree with petitioner's contention that his execution of the directive admits or asserts Doe's consent. The form does not state that Doe "consents" to the release of bank records. Instead, it states that the directive "shall be construed as consent" with respect to Cayman Islands and Bermuda bank-secrecy laws. Because the directive explicitly indicates that it was signed pursuant to a court order, Doe's compelled execution of the form sheds no light on his actual intent or state of mind.[84] The form does "direct" the bank to disclose account information and

---

84. [Court's footnote 14.] The consent directive at issue here differs from the form at issue in [In Re Grand Jury Proceedings (Ranauro), 814 F.2d 791 (1st Cir. 1987)] which suggested that the witness, in fact, had consented: "I, [witness], consent to the production to the [District Court and Grand Jury] of any and all records related to any accounts held by, or banking transactions engaged in with, [bank X], which are in the name of, or on behalf of: [witness], if any such records exist." Further, the *Ranauro* form, unlike the directive here, did not indicate that it was executed under court order. It is true that the First Circuit made clear that its conclusion that the *Ranauro* form was testimonial did not turn on these distinctions, but we are not sanguine that the differences are irrelevant. Even if the Self–Incrimination Clause was not implicated, it might be argued that the compelled signing of such a "consent" form raises due process concerns. Neither issue, of course, is presented by this case, and we take no position on whether such compulsion in fact would violate Fifth Amendment or due process principles.

release any records that "may" exist and for which Doe "may" be a relevant principal. But directing the recipient of a communication to do something is not an assertion of fact or, at least in this context, a disclosure of information. In its testimonial significance, the execution of such a directive is analogous to the production of a handwriting sample or voice exemplar: it is a nontestimonial act. . . .

We read the directive as equivalent to a statement by Doe that, although he expresses no opinion about the existence of, or his control over, any such account, he is authorizing the bank to disclose information relating to accounts over which, in the bank's opinion, Doe can exercise the right of withdrawal. When forwarded to the bank along with a subpoena, the executed directive, if effective under local law,[85] will simply make it possible for the recipient bank to comply with the Government's request to produce such records. As a result, if the Government obtains bank records after Doe signs the directive, the only factual statement made by anyone will be the *bank's* implicit declaration, by its act of production in response to the subpoena, that *it* believes the accounts to be petitioner's. . . .

III

Because the consent directive is not testimonial in nature, we conclude that the District Court's order compelling petitioner to sign the directive does not violate his Fifth Amendment privilege against self-incrimination. Accordingly, the judgment of the Court of Appeals is affirmed.

It is so ordered.

JUSTICE STEVENS, dissenting.

A defendant can be compelled to produce material evidence that is incriminating. Fingerprints, blood samples, voice exemplars, handwriting specimens or other items of physical evidence may be extracted from a defendant against his will. But can he be compelled to use his mind to assist the prosecution in convicting him of a crime? I think not. He may in some cases be forced to surrender a key to a strong box containing incriminating documents, but I do not believe he can be compelled to reveal the combination to his wall safe—by word or deed.

---

85. [Court's footnote 16.] The Government of the Cayman Islands maintains that a compelled consent, such as the one at issue in this case, is not sufficient to authorize the release of confidential financial records protected by Cayman law. The Grand Court of the Cayman Islands has held expressly that a consent directive signed pursuant to an order of a United States court and at the risk of contempt sanctions, could not constitute "consent" under the Cayman confidentiality law. . . .

The effectiveness of the directive under foreign law has no bearing on the constitutional issue in this case. Nevertheless, we are not unaware of the international comity questions implicated by the Government's attempts to overcome protections afforded by the laws of another nation. We are not called upon to address those questions here.

* * *

If John Doe can be compelled to use his mind to assist the Government in developing its case, I think he will be forced "to be a witness against himself." The fundamental purpose of the Fifth Amendment was to mark the line between the kind of inquisition conducted by the Star Chamber and what we proudly describe as our accusatorial system of justice. It reflects "our respect for the inviability of the human personality." . . . In my opinion that protection gives John Doe the right to refuse to sign the directive authorizing access to the records of any bank account that he may control. Accordingly, I respectfully dissent.

* * *

Chapter 7

INTERPLAY BETWEEN CIVIL AND CRIMINAL PROCEEDINGS

SCOPE NOTE

Prosecuting and defending business crime is not solely a matter of criminal litigation. Conduct which gives rise to criminal liability can also trigger civil litigation. Government administrative agencies may want to impose sanctions under a regulatory act. Private plaintiffs may want to sue for damages caused by the conduct about which the government is complaining. Although any criminal case has the possibility of spawning companion civil litigation brought by victims, business crimes are more likely to do so, in part because some of the statutes provide treble damages for violations (e.g., the Sherman Act) and in part because defendants in business crime cases often have sufficient assets to pay the damages sustained by crime victims.

This Chapter explores some of the problems which arise from this interplay of civil and criminal enforcement. The Chapter is organized on the following plan. Section A deals with order of litigation problems. The basic question here is whether there are any restraints on the Government's ability to choose to proceed through civil or criminal process, or even whether it can proceed simultaneously with both. The lead case is *United States v. LaSalle National Bank,* dealing with the use of civil process prior to a formal decision to refer the case to the Department of Justice for criminal prosecution. Section B explores a number of fifth amendment issues which arise when there are parallel civil and criminal proceedings. The lead case is *Pillsbury Co. v. Conboy,* involving the use of immunized grand jury testimony in subsequent civil depositions. Issues raised in the Notes include the standards for asserting the fifth amendment in civil litigation and the potential effects of its assertion. Section C focuses on the ability of civil litigants to obtain grand jury transcripts to assist their litigation. The lead case here is *Douglas Oil Co. v. Petrol Stops Northwest,* where private plaintiffs sought grand jury transcripts. The Notes explore the standards for disclosure of grand jury transcripts to other parties.

A. ORDER OF LITIGATION

UNITED STATES V. LaSALLE NATIONAL BANK
Supreme Court of the United States, 1978.
437 U.S. 298, 98 S.Ct. 2357, 57 L.Ed.2d 221.

MR. JUSTICE BLACKMUN delivered the opinion of the Court.

This case . . . . presents the issue whether the District Court correctly refused to enforce Internal Revenue Service summonses when it specifically found that the special agent who issued them "was conducting his investigation solely for the purpose of unearthing evidence of criminal conduct."

I

In May 1975, John F. Olivero, a special agent with the Intelligence Division of the Chicago District of the Internal Revenue Service (hereinafter IRS or the Service), received an assignment to investigate the tax liability of John Gattuso for his taxable years 1970–1972. Olivero testified that he had requested the assignment because of information he had received from a confidential informant and from an unrelated investigation. The case was not referred to the IRS from another law enforcement agency, but the nature of the assignment, Olivero testified, was "[t]o investigate the possibility of any criminal violations of the Internal Revenue Code." . . .

. . . In order to determine the accuracy of Gattuso's income reports, Olivero proceeded to issue two summonses, under the authority of § 7602 of the Internal Revenue Code of 1954, 26 U.S.C. § 7602, to respondent bank. [A] . . . vice president of the bank appeared in response to the summonses but, on advice of counsel, refused to produce any of the material requested.

* * *

[The District Court denied the Government's petition for enforcement of the summonses. The Seventh Circuit Court of Appeals affirmed and the Supreme Court granted certiorari.]

II

In Donaldson v. United States, 400 U.S. 517, 91 S.Ct. 534, 27 L.Ed. 2d 580 (1971), . . . [t]his Court addressed the taxpayer's contention that the summonses were unenforceable because they were issued in aid of an investigation that could have resulted in a criminal charge against the taxpayer. . . .

. . . The validity of the summonses depended ultimately on whether they were among those authorized by Congress. Having reviewed the statutory scheme, the Court concluded that Congress had authorized the use of summonses in investigating potentially criminal conduct. The statutory history, particularly the use of summonses under the Internal Revenue Code of 1939, supported this conclusion, as did consistent IRS practice and decisions concerning effective enforcement of other comparable federal statutes. The Court saw no reason to force the Service to choose either to forgo the use of congressionally authorized summonses or to abandon the option of recommending criminal prosecutions to the Department of Justice. As long as the summonses were issued in good-faith pursuit of the congressionally authorized purposes, and prior to any recommendation to the Department for prosecution, they were enforceable.

III

The present case requires us to examine the limits of the good-faith use of an Internal Revenue summons issued under § 7602. As the preceding discussion demonstrates, *Donaldson* does not control the facts now before us. There, the taxpayer had argued that the mere potentiality of criminal prosecution should have precluded enforcement of the summons. Here, on the other hand, the District Court found that Special Agent Olivero was investigating Gattuso "solely for the purpose of unearthing evidence of criminal conduct." The question then becomes whether this finding necessarily leads to the conclusion that the summonses were not issued in good-faith pursuit of the congressionally authorized purposes of § 7602.

A

The Secretary of the Treasury and the Commissioner of Internal Revenue are charged with the responsibility of administering and enforcing the Internal Revenue Code. . . . With regard to suspected fraud, these duties encompass enforcement of both civil and criminal statutes. The willful submission of a false or fraudulent tax return may subject a taxpayer not only to criminal penalties under §§ 7206 and 7207 of the Code, but, as well, to a civil penalty, under § 6653(b), of 50% of the underpayment. And § 6659(a) provides that the civil penalty shall be considered as part of the tax liability of the taxpayer. Hence, when § 7602 permits the use of a summons "[f]or the purpose of ascertaining the correctness of any return, . . . determining the liability of any person for any internal revenue tax . . ., or collecting any such liability," it necessarily permits the use of the summons for examination of suspected tax fraud and for the calculation of the 50% civil penalty. . . . This result is inevitable because Congress has created a law enforcement system in which criminal and civil elements are inherently intertwined. When an investigation examines the possibility of criminal misconduct, it also necessarily inquires about the appropriateness of assessing the 50% civil tax penalty.

The legislative history of the Code supports the conclusion that Congress intended to design a system with interrelated criminal and civil elements. . . .

In short, Congress has not categorized tax fraud investigations into civil and criminal components. Any limitation on the good faith use of an Internal Revenue summons must reflect this statutory premise.

B

The preceding discussion suggests why the primary limitation on the use of a summons occurs upon the recommendation of criminal prosecution to the Department of Justice. Only at that point do the criminal and civil aspects of a tax fraud case begin to diverge. We recognize, of course, that even upon recommendation to the Justice Department, the civil and criminal elements do not separate completely. The Government does not sacrifice its interest in unpaid taxes just because a criminal prosecution begins. Logically, then, the IRS could use its summons authority under § 7602 to uncover information about the tax liability created by a fraud regardless of the status of the criminal case. But the rule forbidding such is a prophylactic intended to safeguard the following policy interests.

A referral to the Justice Department permits criminal litigation to proceed. The IRS cannot try its own prosecutions. Such authority is reserved to the Department of Justice and, more particularly, to the United States attorneys. Nothing in § 7602 or its legislative history suggests that Congress intended the summons authority to broaden the Justice Department's right of criminal litigation discovery or to infringe on the role of the grand jury as a principal tool of criminal accusation. The likelihood that discovery would be broadened or the role of the grand jury infringed is substantial if post-referral use of the summons authority were permitted. For example, the IRS, upon referral, loses its ability to compromise both the criminal and the civil aspects of a fraud case. After the referral, the authority to settle rests with the Department of Justice. Interagency cooperation on the calculation of the civil liability is then to be expected and probably encourages efficient settlement of the dispute. But such cooperation, when combined with the inherently intertwined nature of the criminal and civil elements of the case, suggests that it is unrealistic to attempt to build a partial information barrier between the two branches of the executive. Effective use of information to determine civil liability would inevitably result in criminal discovery. The prophylactic restraint on the use of the summons effectively safeguards the two policy interests while encouraging maximum interagency cooperation.

C

Prior to a recommendation for prosecution to the Department of Justice, the IRS must use its summons authority in good faith. . . .

. . . For a fraud investigation to be solely criminal in nature [(and therefore in bad faith)] would require an extraordinary departure from the normally inseparable goals of examining whether the basis exists for criminal charges and for the assessment of civil penalties.

In this case, respondents submit that such a departure did indeed occur because Special Agent Olivero was interested only in gathering evidence for a criminal prosecution. We disagree. The institutional responsibility of the Service to calculate and to collect civil fraud penalties and fraudulently reported or unreported taxes is not necessarily overturned by a single agent who attempts to build a criminal case. The review process over and above his conclusions is multilayered and thorough. Apart from the control of his immediate supervisor, the agent's final recommendation is reviewed by the district chief of the Intelligence Division. . . . The Office of Regional Counsel also reviews the case before it is forwarded to the National Office of the Service or to the Justice Department. If the Regional Counsel and the Assistant Regional Commissioner for Intelligence disagree about the disposition of a case, another complete review occurs at the national level centered in the Criminal Tax Division of the Office of General Counsel. Only after the officials of at least two layers of review have concurred in the conclusion of the special agent does the referral to the Department of Justice take place. At any of the various stages, the Service can abandon the criminal prosecution, can decide instead to assert a civil penalty, or can pursue both goals. While the special agent is an important actor in the process, his motivation is hardly dispositive.

* * *

[We cannot] draw the line between permissible civil and impermissible criminal purposes . . . on the basis of the agent's personal intent. To do so would unnecessarily frustrate the enforcement of the tax laws by restricting the use of the summons according to the motivation of a single agent without regard to the enforcement policy of the Service as an institution. Furthermore, the inquiry into the criminal enforcement objectives of the agent would delay summons enforcement proceedings while parties clash over, and judges grapple with, the thought processes of each investigator. This obviously is undesirable and unrewarding. As a result, the question whether an investigation has solely criminal purposes must be answered only by an examination of the institutional posture of the IRS. Contrary to the assertion of respondents, this means that those opposing enforcement of a summons do bear the burden to disprove the actual existence of a valid civil tax determination or collection purpose by the Service. After all, the purpose of the good-faith inquiry is to determine whether the agency is honestly pursuing the goals of § 7602 by issuing the summons.

Without doubt, this burden is a heavy one. Because criminal and civil fraud liabilities are coterminous, the Service rarely will be found to have acted in bad faith by pursuing the former. On the other hand, we cannot abandon this aspect of the good-faith inquiry altogether.¹ We shall not countenance delay in submitting a recommendation to the Justice Department when there is an institutional commitment to make the referral and the Service merely would like to gather additional evidence for the prosecution. Such a delay would be tantamount to the use of the summons authority after the recommendation and would permit the Government to expand its criminal discovery rights. Similarly, the good-faith standard will not permit the IRS to become an information gathering agency for other departments, including the Department of Justice, regardless of the status of criminal cases.

* * *

IV

[T]he District Court refused enforcement because it found that Olivero's personal motivation was to gather evidence solely for a criminal prosecution. The court, however, failed to consider whether the Service in an institutional sense had abandoned its pursuit of Gattuso's civil tax liability. The Court of Appeals did not require that inquiry. On the record presently developed, we cannot conclude that such an abandonment has occurred.

The judgment of the Court of Appeals is therefore reversed with instructions to that court to remand the case to the District Court for further proceedings consistent with this opinion.

It is so ordered.

MR. JUSTICE STEWART, with whom THE CHIEF JUSTICE, MR. JUSTICE REHNQUIST, and MR. JUSTICE STEVENS join, dissenting.

[The dissenting opinion urged the use of a "bright line test"— enforcement should be granted if the summons is issued prior to a recommendation for criminal prosecution, so long as the summons was otherwise in good faith. The dissent also argued:]

The Court concedes that the task of establishing the "purpose" of an individual agent is "undesirable and unrewarding." Yet the burden it imposes today—to discover the "institutional good faith" of the entire Internal Revenue Service—is, in my view, even less desirable and less rewarding. The elusiveness of "institutional good faith" as described by the Court can produce little but endless discovery proceedings and ultimate frustration of the fair administration of the Internal Revenue

---

1. [Court's footnote 18.] The dissent would abandon this aspect of the good-faith inquiry. It would permit the IRS to use the summons authority solely for criminal investigation. It reaches this conclusion because it says the Code contains no limitation to prevent such use. Its argument reveals a fundamental misunderstanding about the authority of the IRS. The Service does not enjoy inherent authority to summon production of the private papers of citizens. It may exercise only that authority granted by Congress. We . . . could uncover nothing in the Code or its legislative history to suggest that Congress intended to permit exclusively criminal use of summonses. As a result, the IRS employs its authority in good faith when it pursues the four purposes of § 7602, which do not include aiding criminal investigations solely.

Code. In short, I fear that the Court's new criteria will prove wholly unworkable.

NOTES AND QUERIES

(1) *Aftermath of LaSalle.* As the Court's opinion in *LaSalle* indicates, its interpretation of the IRS's power to issue a subpoena in aid of criminal enforcement depended on the Court's view of Congress' intent in enacting Section 7602. Thus, Congress was left free to overrule *LaSalle* and give the IRS broader power. Congress accepted this invitation by amending Section 7602 when it enacted the Tax Equity and Fiscal Responsibility Act of 1982 (TEFRA). The TEFRA amendment first made it clear that a summons could be issued for inquiring into criminal violations of the internal revenue laws. The amendment also adopted the "bright line" test of the dissenters in *LaSalle* by providing that a summons may not be issued if a Justice Department referral is "in effect" (defined as occurring if the Secretary of the Treasury has recommended a criminal prosecution to the Attorney General). If there has been no official referral, summons enforcement cannot be denied on the basis that there was, nevertheless, some other evidence of an institutional commitment to recommend criminal prosecution.[2]

(2) *Institutional Good Faith.* Review the three Models of institutional behavior described supra, p. 167. Which Model does Justice Blackmun have in mind for determining whether the IRS has "acted" in good faith? Which Model would have looked solely at Agent Olivero's intent? Which approach would be more likely to lead to "undesirable and unrewarding" proceedings for determining the IRS's intent?

Although the TEFRA amendments mooted the issue of the IRS's intent with regard to criminal referrals, the issue of the IRS's good faith can still arise in subpoena enforcement proceedings. For example, it might be asserted that the IRS is using a summons to harass a taxpayer or to act solely as an information gatherer for another agency (such as the Department of Justice).[3] To determine the IRS's intent, should the courts look exclusively at the IRS's internal procedures and whether the agent followed them, or would an agent's intent be relevant? Suppose the agent didn't follow procedures, but was just inexperienced?[4]

---

2. See Pub.L. 97–248, 96 Stat. 324 (1982). For legislative history regarding the intent to avoid the "institutional commitment" inquiry of *LaSalle*, see 1982 U.S. Code Cong. & Admin.News pp. 1031–1032.

3. See, e.g., United States v. Pickel, 746 F.2d 176, 184 (3d Cir.1984). For a statement of the general test for issuing a valid IRS summons, see United States v. Powell, supra p. 588.

4. See Groder v. United States, 816 F.2d 139 (4th Cir.1987) (although agent probably violated IRS' regulations by failing to stop inquiry upon discovering "firm indication of fraud," agent was inexperienced; no evidence of intent to deceive on part of agent or her supervisors).

(3) *Agency Investigation and the Criminal Referral.* Consider Justice Blackmun's policy reasons for terminating agency investigatory authority once a decision has been made to refer the case for criminal prosecution. Review the materials on the grand jury, supra Chapter 5. Are you concerned that "discovery would be broadened" by permitting an administrative agency to continue its investigation at the same time that the grand jury was investigating? Do you think that the grand jury's role might be infringed by such investigations? Do you think that such parallel enforcement proceedings might be unduly burdensome on targets? The limits adopted in *LaSalle* appear to be non-Constitutional. Should Congress amend Section 7602 to permit an IRS summons to issue after criminal referral?

Consider the above questions in connection with *Securities & Exchange Comm'n v. Dresser Industries,* 628 F.2d 1368 (D.C.Cir.) (en banc), certiorari denied 449 U.S. 993, 101 S.Ct. 529, 66 L.Ed.2d 289 (1980):

J. SKELLY WRIGHT, CHIEF JUDGE.

[Digest: This case grew out of the SEC's investigation of "questionable payments" made by United States corporations to agents of foreign governments (these investigations are described in *Upjohn v. United States,* supra p. 402). Although Dresser disclosed to the SEC the fact that it had made several such payments, it refused to disclose the documents upon which its admissions were based. The SEC staff accordingly recommended that the Commission issue a formal order of investigation authorizing the issuance of an administrative subpoena for the underlying documents. During this same period the Department of Justice had begun its own investigation of illegal foreign payments. As a result of this investigation, on April 21, 1978, a grand jury issued a subpoena for Dresser's documents. On May 4, 1978, the SEC issued its own subpoena, seeking, inter alia, the same documents sought by the grand jury. Dresser's motion to quash the grand jury subpoena was denied, although in response to Dresser's claim that subpoena enforcement might jeopardize the lives of its employees abroad, the District Court imposed a protective order requiring "strict confidentiality." The SEC then sought enforcement of its subpoena, and on June 30, 1978, the District Court ordered Dresser to comply. Dresser appealed.]

The case at bar concerns enforcement of the securities laws of the United States, especially the Securities Act of 1933 and the Securities Exchange Act of 1934. These statutes explicitly empower the SEC to investigate possible infractions of the securities laws with a view to both civil and criminal enforcement, and to transmit the fruits of its investigations to Justice in the event of potential criminal proceedings. . . . Under the . . . '34 Act the SEC may "transmit such evidence as may be available concerning such acts or practices * * * to the Attorney General, who may, in his discretion, institute the necessary criminal proceedings under this chapter." The '33 Act is to similar effect.

Effective enforcement of the securities laws requires that the SEC and Justice be able to investigate possible violations simultaneously. Dissemination of false or misleading information by companies to members of the investing public may distort the efficient workings of the securities markets and injure investors who rely on the accuracy and completeness of the company's public disclosures. If the SEC suspects that a company has violated the securities laws, it must be able to respond quickly: it must be able to obtain relevant information concerning the alleged violation and to seek prompt judicial redress if necessary. Similarly, Justice must act quickly if it suspects that the laws have been broken. Grand jury investigations take time, as do criminal prosecutions. If Justice moves too slowly the statute of limitations may run, witnesses may die or move away, memories may fade, or enforcement resources may be diverted. The SEC cannot always wait for Justice to complete the criminal proceedings if it is to obtain the necessary prompt civil remedy; neither can Justice always await the conclusion of the civil proceeding without endangering its criminal case. Thus we should not block parallel investigations by these agencies in the absence of "special circumstances" in which the nature of the proceedings demonstrably prejudices substantial rights of the investigated party or of the government.

III. Applicability of United States v. LaSalle Nat'l Bank

Dresser principally relies on an analogy to United States v. LaSalle Nat'l Bank, 437 U.S. 298, 98 S.Ct. 2357, 57 L.Ed.2d 221 (1978), in which the Supreme Court said in dictum that the Internal Revenue Service (IRS) may not use its summons authority to investigate possible violations of the tax laws after it has referred those violations to Justice for criminal prosecution. Dresser argues that the SEC's transmittal of Dresser's file to Justice was equivalent to a "referral" under *LaSalle,* and thus that the SEC's power to enforce investigative subpoenas against Dresser in connection with that file lapsed at that time. Alternatively, Dresser suggests that, even if transmittal of the file was not analogous to a "referral" under *LaSalle,* initiation of the grand jury investigation precluded subsequent enforcement of SEC investigative subpoenas into the same matters.

These two alternatives are vulnerable to the same objection: the *LaSalle* rule applies solely to the statutory scheme of the Internal Revenue Code, in which the IRS's civil authority ceases for all practical purposes upon referral of a taxpayer's case to Justice; it does not apply to the securities laws, in which the SEC's civil enforcement authority continues undiminished after Justice initiates a criminal investigation by the grand jury.

* * *

The investigative provisions of the securities laws are far broader than Section 7602 of the Internal Revenue Code, as interpreted in *LaSalle*. SEC investigations are not confined to "four purposes only." Rather, the SEC may, "*in its discretion,* make such investigations as *it deems necessary* to determine whether any person has violated, is violating, or is about to violate any provision" of the '34 Act, Section 21(a) of the '34 Act, 15 U.S.C. § 78u(a) (1976) (emphasis added). Moreover, the SEC is "authorized *in its discretion* * * * to investigate *any* facts, conditions, practices, or matters which *it may deem necessary or proper* to aid in the enforcement of such provisions, in the prescribing of rules and regulations under this chapter, or in securing information to serve as a basis for recommending further legislation concerning matters to which this chapter relates." Id. (emphasis added). Given this broad statutory mandate, there is virtually no possibility that in issuing this subpoena the SEC was acting ultra vires. The investigation of Dresser—based as it was on the staff's conclusion that Dresser may have engaged in conduct seriously contravening the securities laws—falls squarely within the Commission's explicit investigatory authority. Unlike the Internal Revenue Code as interpreted in *LaSalle,* the securities laws offer no suggestion that the scope of the SEC's investigative authority shrinks when a grand jury begins to investigate the same matters. Since the validity of summonses or subpoenas "depend[s] ultimately on whether they were among those authorized by Congress," United States v. LaSalle Nat'l Bank, 437 U.S. at 307, 98 S.Ct. at 2362, we conclude that this subpoena is enforceable under the rule of that case.

Fulfillment of the SEC's civil enforcement responsibilities requires this conclusion. Unlike the IRS, which can postpone collection of taxes for the duration of parallel criminal proceedings without seriously injuring the public, the SEC must often act quickly, lest the false or incomplete statements of corporations mislead investors and infect the markets. Thus the Commission must be able to investigate possible securities infractions and undertake civil enforcement actions even after Justice has begun a criminal investigation. For the SEC to stay its hand might well defeat its purpose.

Dresser attempts to prevent enforcement of this subpoena by invoking the "policy interests" identified by the *LaSalle* Court: to avoid broadening Justice's right of criminal litigation discovery and to avoid infringing the role of the grand jury as a principal tool of criminal accusation. We reject this argument for two reasons.

First, Dresser disregards the context in which these "policy interests" arose in *LaSalle.* Only after the Court had determined that the IRS had no practical authorized purpose for issuing a summons after referral of a case to Justice did it direct its attention to these "policy interests." Then it did so solely to explain its imposition of a "prophylactic" rule forbidding *any use* of the IRS summons authority after referral to Justice, as opposed to forbidding only such uses as are unrelated to the purposes of Section 7602. The Court did not impose such a "prophylactic" rule in any situation where it would significantly restrict the legitimate investigative authority of the IRS. In the case of an SEC investigation there is no call for a "prophylactic rule," and thus no need to ponder the import of these "policy interests," because the SEC's authority to issue the subpoena remains undiminished after the start of a grand jury investigation.

Second, the "policy interests" of *LaSalle* have little practical significance in this context. The first—to avoid broadening Justice's right to criminal discovery—is flatly inapplicable. . . . The strict limitations on discovery in criminal cases, embodied in Federal Rules of Criminal Procedure 15–17, do not take effect until after a grand jury has returned an indictment. Until then there is no danger that Justice might broaden its discovery rights, because the subpoena power of the grand jury is as broad as—perhaps broader than—that of the SEC. Justice can procure from Dresser directly whatever materials it might procure indirectly through the SEC. In fact, a party investigated under SEC rules instead of grand jury procedures is accorded far greater procedural protection, and has no cause to complain.

In its brief Dresser has concentrated upon the second "policy interest" identified in *LaSalle:* avoiding infringement upon the role of the grand jury. Dresser suggests two ways in which the SEC civil investigation might infringe the role of the grand jury. First, it argues that enforcement of the SEC subpoena would undermine the secrecy protections of the grand jury because the SEC subpoena covers many or all of the Dresser documents that have already been subpoenaed by the grand jury. In this argument Dresser misconceives the nature of the secrecy protections of the grand jury.

* * *

. . . The fact that a grand jury has subpoenaed documents concerning a particular matter does not insulate that matter from investigation in another forum. In fact, if the grand jury proceedings are genuinely secret, other agencies and courts will not know the subject matter of the grand jury investigation and thus will not be able to determine whether their own inquiry would overlap that of the grand jury.

In this case Dresser is obligated under the securities laws to provide documents to the SEC in obedience to a lawful subpoena. The existence of a grand jury proceeding neither adds to nor detracts from Dresser's rights before the SEC. Whatever rights to secrecy or confidentiality Dresser may have are the product solely of the laws governing the SEC; they are unaffected by the parallel grand jury proceeding.

* * *

We conclude that the danger that enforcement of this subpoena might infringe the role of the grand jury is too speculative and remote at this point to justify so extreme an action as denying enforcement of this subpoena.

In essence, Dresser has launched this attack on the parallel SEC and Justice proceedings in order to obtain protection against the bare SEC proceeding, which it fears will result in public disclosure of sensitive corporate documents. The prejudice Dresser claims it will suffer from the parallel nature of the proceedings is speculative and undefined—if indeed Dresser would suffer any prejudice from it at all. Any entitlement to confidential treatment of its documents must arise under the laws pertaining to the SEC; the fortuity of a parallel grand jury investigation cannot expand Dresser's rights in this SEC enforcement action. Thus Dresser's invocation of *LaSalle* can avail the company nothing.

IV. Cooperation Between SEC and Justice

In its initial decision in this case a panel of this court ruled that "the broad prophylactic rule enunciated in *LaSalle* is inappropriate where the SEC and the Justice Department are simultaneously pursuing civil and criminal investigations." The panel therefore affirmed the District Court and ordered enforcement of the SEC subpoena. Out of a concern that the SEC subpoena might somehow "subvert the limitations of criminal discovery," however, the panel, with one judge dissenting, modified the terms of the subpoena enforcement order. It required that "once the Justice Department initiates criminal proceedings by means of a grand jury, the SEC may not provide the Justice Department with the fruits of the Commission's civil discovery gathered after the decision to prosecute." We affirm the judgment of the District Court and reject the panel's modification.

* * *

The Foreign Corrupt Practices Act outlaws corporate bribery of foreign officials and associated inaccurate or misleading financial recordkeeping. Both the Senate and the House reports on the bill acknowledged the SEC's dual investigative role in preparing cases for civil and criminal enforcement actions. They also recognize the necessity of close cooperation between the SEC and Justice in preparing such cases. The Senate Committee said:

The committee expects that close cooperation will develop between the SEC and the Justice Department at the earliest stage of any investigation in order to insure that the evidence needed for a criminal prosecution does not become stale.

* * *

It stated that it expected the SEC and Justice to "work out" between themselves certain "arrangements * * * on criminal matters" that would preserve the authority of each within its jurisdiction. The House Committee said:

Traditionally, there has been a close working relationship between the Justice Department and the SEC. The Committee fully expects that this cooperation between the two agencies will continue with respect to the enforcement of the provisions of this bill.

H.R.Rep. No. 640, 95th Cong., 1st Sess. 10 (1977).

Although the legislative history of the Foreign Corrupt Practices Act is not directly probative of congressional intent governing the '33 and '34 Acts, these statements by the 95th Congress are nevertheless entitled to some weight. The remarks in the committee reports concerning the investigative practices of the SEC and Justice were not intended to change, but to reaffirm, past practice. This indicates that Congress understands and approves of the "close working relationship" between the agencies in their investigative capacities. Since such a "close working relationship" will govern the activities of the agencies in enforcing the laws against questionable foreign payments under the new statute, it would be impractical for us to attempt to screen the agencies from each other when they are investigating the same sort of offense under the former statutes.

Congress manifestly did not intend that the SEC be forbidden to share information with Justice at this stage of the investigation. Under the panel majority's theory of the case the SEC would be foreclosed from sharing the fruits of its investigation with Justice as soon as Justice begins its own investigation through a grand jury. Only by waiting until the close of the SEC proceeding before initiating its own grand jury investigation could Justice obtain access to the evidence procured by the SEC. In view of Congress' concern that the agencies share information "at the earliest stage of any investigation in order to insure that the evidence needed for a criminal prosecution does not become stale," and that the agencies avoid "a costly duplication of effort," it would be unreasonable to prevent a sharing of information at this point in the investigation.

* * *

[The concurring opinion of JUDGE EDWARDS is omitted.]

(4) *Why Permit Simultaneous Government Civil and Criminal Proceedings?* The importance of permitting the Government to proceed

simultaneously through civil and criminal proceedings was emphasized by the Supreme Court in *United States v. Kordel,* 397 U.S. 1, 90 S.Ct. 763, 25 L.Ed.2d 1 (1970). The proceeding began in 1960 with an investigation by the federal Food and Drug Administration of Detroit Vital Foods, Inc. Within a month the FDA instituted (through the office of the United States Attorney) a civil seizure of certain of the company's products; interrogatories were subsequently prepared and filed in that action. At the same time the FDA notified the corporation that it contemplated a criminal action with regard to the products involved in the civil case. The corporation moved to stay the civil action, but the motion was denied, and on September 5, 1961, the corporation accordingly answered the interrogatories. On June 13, 1962, the Department of Health, Education, and Welfare requested the Justice Department to institute criminal proceedings. In November 1962 the civil case was settled with a consent decree. Eight months later the Government obtained the indictment upon which the defendants were convicted. The defendants, president and vice-president of the company, appealed. JUSTICE STEWART delivered the opinion for a unanimous Court:

> The respondents urge that . . . the Government's conduct . . . reflected such unfairness and want of consideration for justice as . . . to require the reversal of their convictions. On the record before us, we cannot agree that the respondents have made out either a violation of due process or a departure from proper standards in the administration of justice requiring the exercise of our supervisory power. The public interest in protecting consumers throughout the Nation from misbranded drugs requires prompt action by the agency charged with responsibility for administration of the federal food and drug laws. But a rational decision whether to proceed criminally against those responsible for the misbranding may have to await consideration of a fuller record than that before the agency at the time of the civil seizure of the offending products. It would stultify enforcement of federal law to require a governmental agency such as the FDA invariably to choose either to forgo recommendation of a criminal prosecution once it seeks civil relief, or to defer civil proceedings pending the ultimate outcome of a criminal trial.
>
> We do not deal here with a case where the Government has brought a civil action solely to obtain evidence for its criminal prosecution or has failed to advise the defendant in its civil proceeding that it contemplates his criminal prosecution; nor with a case where the defendant is without counsel or reasonably fears prejudice from adverse pretrial publicity or other unfair injury; nor with any other special circumstances that might suggest the unconstitutionality or even the impropriety of this criminal prosecution.
>
> Overturning these convictions would be tantamount to the adoption of a rule that the Government's use of interrogatories

directed against a corporate defendant in the ordinary course of a civil proceeding would always immunize the corporation's officers from subsequent criminal prosecution. The Court of Appeals was correct in stating that "the Government may not use evidence against a defendant in a criminal case which has been coerced from him under penalty of either giving the evidence or suffering a forfeiture of his property." But on this record there was no such violation of the Constitution, and no such departure from the proper administration of criminal justice.

Accordingly, the judgment of the Court of Appeals is reversed, and the case is remanded to that court for further proceedings consistent with this opinion.

It is so ordered.

MR. JUSTICE BLACK did not take part in the decision of this case.

(5) *Bargaining Over the Criminal Referral.* As you might imagine, a major goal of a target of an agency investigation is to convince the agency not to refer the matter to the Justice Department for criminal investigation. Of course, this gives the administrative agency some bargaining power. Are there any limits on what the agency can do? Consider *United States v. Fields,* 592 F.2d 638 (2d Cir.1978):

TIMBERS, CIRCUIT JUDGE.

[This is an appeal by the United States from the dismissal of an indictment on the ground of misconduct by SEC attorneys in obtaining settlement of civil charges. The indictment alleged securities fraud involving kickbacks and stock manipulation in two corporations (TDA and Westcalind). The defendants Fields, Friedman, Davis, Sandberg, and Berge were officers and directors of the two corporations; defendant Davis was general counsel.

In early 1975, counsel for the defendants were informed by New York state prosecutors investigating the kickbacks that the kickbacks did not violate state law. Anticipating that the state prosecutor would then inform the SEC about the investigation, defense counsel (Gould and Kantor) arranged a meeting for January 14, 1975, at the SEC's New York regional office. Attending were William Moran, the SEC regional administrator, Jeffrey Tucker, a branch chief, and Stuart Perlmutter, a staff attorney.]

At this meeting Gould and Kantor disclosed to the SEC employees the three kickback transactions which had been under investigation by the District Attorney's office. They did not disclose to the SEC then, or at any other time, the scheme to manipulate the price of TDA stock. . . . The upshot of the January 14 meeting was that Gould proposed negotiations looking toward a possible civil settlement of the transactions disclosed, on the assumption that the SEC's investigation would not turn up something new. Moran said that he first would have to obtain authorization from the SEC's Division of Enforcement for a formal investigation of the alleged *civil* violations. Such authorization was granted on February 19.

The chief purpose of the disclosures which defendants' counsel made at the January 14 meeting was to avoid a criminal reference to the Department of Justice. Defendants' counsel, being thoroughly experienced in SEC procedure and in criminal matters, recognized from the outset that defendants' activities constituted criminal offenses under the federal securities laws. Their best hope, so they urged, was to work out some sort of a package by which defendants would accept the imposition of civil sanctions in return for the avoidance of a criminal reference. Defendants' experienced counsel of course also were aware of the SEC's long standing and well known policy *against* settling civil actions in a manner that would impair subsequent criminal prosecutions.

As the result of the SEC's investigation which had been authorized on February 19 and after a number of conversations between defendants' counsel and the SEC employees regarding a possible civil settlement, the SEC commenced a civil action on September 16, 1975 in the Southern District of New York, entitled SEC v. TDA Industries, Inc., et al., 75 Civ. 4519–LWP. The complaint named as defendants TDA, Westcalind and the five individual defendants later charged in the instant indictment. The complaint was based on the three kickback transactions which Gould and Kantor disclosed to the SEC at the January 14 meeting. The complaint sought injunctive and other relief, including an order that defendants disgorge the fraudulently obtained "finder's fees" and the appointment of receivers for the two corporate defendants.

During settlement negotiations between defendants' counsel and the SEC employees, both before and after the commencement of the SEC civil action on September 16, defendants' counsel repeatedly stated their desire to avoid a criminal reference if a consent judgment could be worked out in the civil proceedings.

Throughout these negotiations Tucker and Perlmutter of the SEC were aware of the stated objective of defense counsel to avoid a criminal reference if a consent judgment could be agreed upon. Tucker and Perlmutter remained silent during this period in response to the statements of defense counsel as to their objective. Such silence was interpreted by defense counsel as assent by Tucker and Perlmutter to defense counsel's proposal to avoid a criminal reference. Nevertheless, as we state below, Tucker and Perlmutter were in touch with the United States Attorney's office as early as September 16 on the subject of a prospective criminal reference of the TDA matter.

As for the negotiations to settle the civil action, on December 1 a settlement offer was made . . . to Tucker and Perlmutter, both of whom viewed the offer favorably. They recommended to their superiors that it be accepted. It was. Consents to the entry of judgment in the civil action were signed by Fields, Friedman and Davis on December 10 and 11, and judgments in the action as to them were entered on February 5, 1976. Similar consents were signed by Sandberg and Berge on January 6 and February 10, and judgments as to them were entered on January 16 and February 23. None of the defendants or their counsel knew, when the consents to the entry of judgment in the civil action were signed, that Tucker had communicated with the United States Attorney's office concerning the TDA matter on December 1, as stated below.

As indicated above, Tucker and Perlmutter, beginning in September 1975, had been in touch with the United States Attorney's office about a criminal reference of the TDA matter. These contacts with Assistant United States Attorney Sorkin continued during October and November. During this period Tucker and Perlmutter urged the United States Attorney's office to investigate the TDA matter but they made it clear that they wanted to conclude a settlement in the civil action before making a criminal reference.

On December 1, shortly after Gould . . . had made the offer to settle the civil action, Tucker, in the presence of the Assistant Regional Administrator of the SEC's New York Regional Office, communicated regarding the TDA matter with Assistant United States Attorney Wing, Chief of the Fraud Unit of the United States Attorney's office. This was done by telephone, followed by a letter dated December 1 from Tucker to Wing enclosing the SEC's pleadings file in the TDA case.

There followed an investigation of the TDA matter by the United States Attorney's office, presentation of the case to a grand jury, and the return of the instant indictment on November 8, 1976.

III.

Before getting to the chief issue on this appeal as stated above, we shall take up as a preliminary matter the claim asserted by some of the appellees, namely, that the communications regarding this case by the Commission's staff to the United States Attorney's office on December 1, 1975 were contrary to the applicable statutes, rules and regulations. This ground for dismissal of the indictment was urged upon the district court, as it is upon us. The district court rejected it. We also reject it.

The claim in essence is that the statutes authorize only the "Commission" to transmit evidence to the Attorney General for criminal proceedings, and that therefore the informal criminal reference on December 1, 1975 by the SEC's New York regional office to the United States Attorney's office "constituted an invalid criminal reference requiring dismissal of the resulting indictment." We hold that this claim is totally without merit.

It is important to bear in mind the distinctions, under SEC procedure, between preliminary communications between the Commission's staff and the United States Attorney's office, which may occur in the context of either a formal or informal investigation, and Commission criminal references, which may in turn be either formal or informal.

With respect to the investigation procedure, the *informal,* or *preliminary, investigation* does not require members of the staff to obtain Commission authorization before turning over public or nonpublic investigative materials to the United States Attorney's office. On the other hand, a *formal investigation* of alleged criminal violations, where issuance of process or compulsion of testimony is necessary, does require Commission authorization. A formal investigation may or may not be preceded by an informal or preliminary one. 17 C.F.R. § 202.5(a) (1977).

As for the criminal reference procedure, whether formal or informal, it is authorized by statute and by Commission rules and regulations. In view of the fraudulent transactions charged in the instant indictment, we look to the Securities Act of 1933 [5] and the Securities Exchange Act of 1934,[6] each of which provides the statutory authorization for the Commission to transmit to the Attorney General available evidence of violations of the statutes involved for possible criminal proceedings. Moreover, the Commission is authorized by statute to delegate "any of its functions" to an employee, among others. In its Manual of Administrative Regulations, the Commission has delegated its authority to act to Directors of Divisions and Regional Administrators, and further has empowered these officials to redelegate such authority to designated members of their respective staffs. The Commission's Manual specifically authorizes and *encourages* the disclosure of non public information to other federal law enforcement officials even when it has been developed in other than a formal investigation.

The district court below found that during recent years it has been the SEC policy in the Southern District of New York for the Regional Administrator to redelegate his authority to lower echelon attorneys for the purpose of conferring with the United States Attorney's office at an early stage of either a formal or informal

---

5. [Court's footnote 13.] Section 20(b) of the 1933 Act, 15 U.S.C. § 77t(b) (1976), in relevant part provides:

"The Commission may transmit such evidence as may be available concerning such acts or practices to the Attorney General who may, in his discretion, institute the necessary criminal proceedings under this subchapter. . . ."

6. [Court's footnote 14.] Section 21(d) of the 1934 Act, 15 U.S.C. § 78u(d) (1976), in relevant part provides:

"The Commission may transmit such evidence as may be available concerning such acts or practices as may constitute a violation of any provision of this chapter or the rules or regulations thereunder to the Attorney General, who may, in his discretion, institute the necessary criminal proceedings under this chapter."

investigation. We hold that the district court correctly declined to dismiss the indictment on this ground.

As the SEC points out in its amicus brief, the procedure permitting preliminary communications with the United States Attorney has significant advantages. Allowing early participation in the case by the United States Attorney minimizes statute of limitations problems. The more time a United States Attorney has, the easier it is for him to become familiar with the complex facts of a securities fraud case, to prepare the case, and to present it to a grand jury before expiration of the applicable statute of limitations. Earlier initiation of criminal proceedings moreover is consistent with a defendant's right to a speedy trial. We decline, as the district court likewise declined, to interfere with this commendable example of inter-agency cooperation.

IV.

This brings us to what we regard as the chief issue in the case—whether the district court in this *criminal* action abused its discretion in dismissing and striking substantial portions of the indictment because of alleged misconduct by employees of the SEC in attempting to settle the *civil* action. On this issue we hold that the district court did abuse its discretion. We reverse and remand with directions to reinstate the unexpurgated indictment.

The district court recognized that, aside from *the most drastic remedy* of dismissing the indictment (as urged by all defendants), there were available at least two alternative remedies, i.e. "admonishment to the SEC" and "[p]ermitting the defendants to reopen the consent judgments entered in the civil suit".

We believe on the facts of this case that the district court, in opting for the most drastic remedy available to it, abused its discretion. The relief granted was wholly out of proportion to the wrong sought to be corrected. And it was contrary to the law of this circuit or any other circuit, so far as we are aware.

The extreme sanction of dismissal of an indictment is justified in order to achieve one or both of two objectives: first, to eliminate prejudice to a defendant in a criminal prosecution; second, to "help to translate the assurances of the United States Attorneys into consistent performances by their assistants." Here, dismissal of the indictment served neither objective.

We agree with the district court that the conduct of the SEC employees in concealing their reference of this case to the United States Attorney and in leading defense counsel to believe the opposite was improper. But we fail to see any resulting harm to defendants. By that time defendants, with their backs to the wall because of the New York County District Attorney's anticipated reference of the matter to the SEC, had long since disclosed enough facts to the SEC to enable the government to marshal the evidence and to proceed both civilly and criminally against them. Thus, even assuming arguendo that the SEC was engaged in enforcement of federal *criminal* laws when it negotiated the *civil* consent decree—a proposition about which we have considerable doubt—it clearly was an abuse of discretion for the district court to employ such a severe sanction against the government on the facts of this case.

Even when a *prosecutorial* arm of the government unlawfully obtains evidence, we normally limit the permissible sanction to suppression of the illegally obtained evidence. It is only in the rare case, where it is impossible to restore a criminal defendant to the position that he would have occupied vis-a-vis the prosecutor, that the indictment may be dismissed.

The improper conduct here certainly was not as egregious as that in United States v. Rodman, 519 F.2d 1058 (1 Cir.1975), where the SEC not only broke its promise but obtained incriminating evidence from the defendant in reliance on that promise. Moreover, the promise there was to "strongly recommend" against prosecution.

As for the deterrence objective of the district court's order here, proper regard for the public interest in the prosecution of crimes counsels restraint in dismissing an indictment for deterrence purposes unless the course of official misconduct is a demonstrated, long-standing one. We have approved this extreme sanction only when the pattern of misconduct is widespread or continuous.

What we have here is an isolated instance of misconduct by two employees of a large government agency. There is no contention that SEC employees generally fail to disclose to defense counsel the release of relevant information or a criminal reference to the Department of Justice. We know of no other instance where this has occurred.

Since the district court's extreme sanction of dismissal of the indictment is not justified on grounds of eliminating prejudice to the defendants in this criminal prosecution or of deterring widespread or continuous official misconduct, we reverse the order and remand with directions to reinstate the unexpurgated indictment.

* * *

MANSFIELD, CIRCUIT JUDGE (concurring):

I concur in Judge Timbers' carefully considered opinion.

I would only add that in my view the conduct of the SEC representatives (Tucker and Perlmutter) in continuing to negotiate a civil settlement after appellants' counsel had repeatedly stated that they were negotiating on the basis that there would not be any criminal reference was deceitful and duplicitous.

Judge Haight found that at the very first meeting between defense counsel and Messrs. Tucker and Perlmutter, which took place on January 14, 1975, Tucker was advised that defense counsel's objective was "the avoidance of a criminal reference" and this was made clear to the same SEC counsel at a meeting on February 28, 1975. Moreover, after rejecting Tucker's testimony to the effect that he had in September 1975 told defense counsel that there was "no deal on criminal" Judge Haight further found that on September 30, 1975, former Judge Streit, who was substituting for Mr. Gould as chief defense counsel, advised that "in light of the fact that there [was] to be no criminal prosecution," he would endeavor to obtain the amount of the repayment demanded by the SEC, to which Tucker and Perlmutter made no response even though Perlmutter had in the interim been in communication with the U.S. Attorney about the case. In October 1975 Perlmutter confirmed to a lawyer representing a prospective outside director of TDA that there would be no criminal reference, and an attorney for appellant Sandberg told Tucker and Perlmutter that he would advise his client to settle, since settlement was "better than going over to the golden dome [U.S. Courthouse]," to which the SEC counsel made no response.

Once they were advised by appellants' counsel of the basis on which the latter were proceeding, SEC counsel surely owed an ethical obligation immediately to correct the record by advising counsel that they had already initiated an informal criminal reference or at least that they felt free to do so. However, since appellants' counsel, with no viable alternative, faced the prospect that the incriminating evidence would in any event be forwarded by the New York County District Attorney to the SEC without restrictions on its use no prejudice warranting dismissal of the indictment is shown.

Queries. This case provides students with a description of the statutory and administrative procedures for an SEC criminal referral. It also provides some idea of the strategies involved in making the decision. If you had been defense counsel, could you have done anything more to insure that there would be no criminal referral? Would you have done anything more? Do you think that there should be more formal requirements before attorneys investigating a matter at an administrative agency begin talking with attorneys at the Justice Department? What are the potential abuses?

NOTE: STAYING PARALLEL PROCEEDINGS

The Supreme Court has long held that the government has broad discretion to decide the order of litigation. The issue was presented in the early days of Sherman Act enforcement. *Standard Sanitary Manufacturing Co. v. United States,* 226 U.S. 20, 33 S.Ct. 9, 57 L.Ed. 107 (1912), was a civil antitrust suit brought by the government. At the time of trial there was a pending government criminal proceeding. One of the defendants called witnesses who refused to testify for fear of self-incrimination in the criminal case. The defendants argued that this prevented them from properly presenting their defense. They accordingly moved that the civil proceedings be stayed pending the outcome of the criminal case. The Supreme Court wrote:

> The Sherman Act provides for a criminal proceeding to punish violations and suits in equity to restrain such violations, and the suits may be brought simultaneously or successively. The order of their bringing must depend upon the Government; the dependence of their trials cannot be fixed by a hard and fast rule or made imperatively to turn upon the character of the suit. Circumstances may determine and are for the consideration of the court. An imperative rule that the civil suit must await the trial of the criminal action might result in injustice or take from the statute a great deal of its power. Besides a suit by the Government there may be an action for damages by a "person injured by reason of anything forbidden by the Act." Must it also wait? Indeed, the reasons urged for the rule, if logically extended, would compel the postponement of the enforcement of the civil remedies until the exhaustion of criminal prosecutions or their expiration by lapse of time. Until either event occurs the danger of incrimination cannot be said to have passed. It is manifest, therefore, that the most favorable view which can be taken of the rights of defendants in such situation is that they depend upon the discretion of the court in the particular case. We find no abuse of such discretion in the case at bar.

The fact that the Supreme Court has given discretion to the trial court with regard to a stay in civil proceedings does not mean that this discretion is always exercised against granting the stay. There are a number of cases in which a defendant's request for a stay of civil proceedings has been granted; these cases have involved stay requests in government and in private civil actions. Although the cases tend to be rather fact-specific, the courts have articulated five factors relevant to the exercise of their discretion: [7]

> (1) the interest of the plaintiffs in proceeding expeditiously with this litigation or any particular aspect of it, and the potential prejudice to plaintiffs of a delay;
>
> (2) the burden which any particular aspect of the proceedings may impose on defendants;
>
> (3) the convenience of the court in the management of its cases, and the efficient use of judicial resources;
>
> (4) the interests of persons not parties to the civil litigation; and,

---

7. Golden Quality Ice Cream Co. v. Deerfield Specialty Papers, Inc., 87 F.R.D. 53, 56 (E.D.Pa.1980).

(5) the interest of the public in the pending civil and criminal litigation.

Using this standard, the District Court in *White v. Mapco Gas Products, Inc.*,[8] granted a stay in a private civil antitrust case pending the completion of the grand jury's investigation and, if an indictment should issue, "until the conclusion of the presentation of evidence in a criminal trial." Relevant to the court was the likelihood that the criminal case could result in a narrowing of the issues; the burden of protecting fifth amendment privileges; and the fact that the civil case was brought only on behalf of one individual (rather than as a class action) while the Government was devoting substantial resources to its investigation.

As a general matter, however, courts appear to be reluctant to grant extensively long stays, even though litigating parallel civil and criminal proceedings may present the defense with some difficult tactical choices.[9] Students should review the question of the proper standard for a stay after considering subsequent materials relating, in particular, to assertion of the fifth amendment in civil litigation. It may be that granting a stay pending the outcome of a criminal case will only postpone some of these difficult issues, rather than resolving them (unless, of course, the outcome of the criminal case convinces the parties to settle).

B. FIFTH AMENDMENT ISSUES

PILLSBURY CO. v. CONBOY
Supreme Court of the United States, 1983.
459 U.S. 248, 103 S.Ct. 608, 74 L.Ed.2d 430.

JUSTICE POWELL delivered the opinion of the Court.

Pursuant to the federal use immunity provisions, 18 U.S.C. §§ 6001–6005 (1976), a United States Attorney may request an order from a federal court compelling a witness to testify even though he has asserted his privilege against self-incrimination. Section 6002 provides, however, that "no testimony or other information compelled under the order (or any information directly or indirectly derived from such testimony or other information) may be used against the witness in any criminal case. . . ." The issue presented in this case is whether a deponent's civil deposition testimony, repeating verbatim or closely tracking his prior immunized testimony, is immunized "testimony" that can be compelled over the valid assertion of his Fifth Amendment privilege.

---

8. 116 F.R.D. 498 (E.D.Ark.1987).

9. See, e.g., United States v. Amrep Corp., 405 F.Supp. 1053 (S.D.N.Y.1976) (permitting FTC proceedings to continue through completion of government's case-in-chief because there would be no conflict with preparation for the criminal trial; all subsequent proceedings in FTC case stayed until one month after entry of jury's verdict in criminal case).

I

Respondent John Conboy is a former executive of a defendant in the In re Corrugated Container Antitrust Litigation, M.D.L. 310 (S.D. Tex.). In January 1978, United States Department of Justice attorneys interviewed Conboy following a promise of use immunity. Conboy subsequently appeared before a grand jury investigating price-fixing activities and, pursuant to 18 U.S.C. § 6002, was granted formal use immunity for his testimony.

Following the criminal indictment of several companies, numerous civil antitrust actions were filed in various United States district courts. Those actions were consolidated for discovery in the District Court for the Southern District of Texas. Petitioners here are purchasers of corrugated containers who elected to opt out of the class-action proceedings and pursue their own causes of action against manufacturers. The District Court ordered that portions of the immunized government interview and grand-jury testimony of certain witnesses, including that of Conboy, be made available to lawyers for the class and opt-outs.

Pursuant to a subpoena issued by the District Court for the Northern District of Illinois, Conboy appeared in Chicago for a deposition at which he, his counsel, and petitioners' counsel had copies of his immunized testimony. The transcripts were marked as deposition exhibits so that all could follow the intended examination. The questioning fell into the following pattern: a question was read from the transcript; it then was rephrased to include the transcript answer (i.e., "Is it not the fact that. . . ."); finally, Conboy was asked if he had "so testified" in his immunized interview and grand-jury examination.[10] Conboy refused to answer each question, asserting his Fifth Amendment privilege against self-incrimination.

The District Court granted petitioners' motion to compel Conboy to answer the questions.[11] When Conboy continued to claim his privilege, the District Court held him in contempt, but stayed its order pending appeal. A panel of the Court of Appeals for the Seventh Circuit affirmed the contempt order. . . .

On rehearing en banc, the Court of Appeals reversed the District Court. . . .

We granted certiorari to resolve the conflict in the Courts of Appeals, and now affirm.

---

10. [Court's footnote 2.] An example of this three-question pattern is as follows:

Q. Who did you have price communications with at Alton Box Board?

Q. Is it not the fact that you had price communications with Fred Renshaw and Dick Herman . . .?

Q. Did you not so testify in your government interview of January 10, 1978?

11. [Court's footnote 3.] Chief Judge John V. Singleton, Jr. of the District Court for the Southern District of Texas expressly exercised the powers of the District Court for the Northern District of Illinois pursuant to 28 U.S.C. § 1407(b). The contempt hearing was conducted by telephone with his chambers in Houston.

II

[The Court reviewed the legislative purpose of § 6002 and its decision in *Kastigar v. United States,* discussed supra this Casebook, Chapter 6A.]

III

With the foregoing statutory history and relevant principles in mind, we turn now to this case. It is not disputed that the *questions* asked of Conboy were directly or indirectly derived from his immunized testimony. The issue as presented to us is whether the causal connection between the questions and the answers is so direct that the *answers* also are derived from that testimony and therefore should be excluded under the grant of immunity.

Petitioners' argument is based on the language of § 6002 and on a common understanding of the words "derived from." The questions formulated on the basis of immunized testimony are clearly "derived from" the prior testimony. Thus, the answers that repeat verbatim or closely track a deponent's testimony are necessarily also "derived from" and "tainted by" such testimony. . . .

Conboy's position is also straightforward: Questions do not incriminate; answers do. Unlike the questions, answers are not directly or indirectly derived from the immunized grand jury or interview transcripts, but from the deponent's current, independent memory of events. Even when a deponent's deposition answers are identical to those he gave to the grand jury, he is under oath to tell the truth, not necessarily as he told it before the grand jury, but as he knows it now. Each new statement of the deponent creates a new "source." In sum, the initial grant of immunity does not prevent the prosecutor from prosecuting; it merely limits his sources of evidence.

Although the parties make their arguments in terms tracking those of the statute—whether the deposition testimony is "derived from" the prior testimony—it is clear that the crux of their dispute is whether the earlier grant of immunity itself compelled Conboy to talk. Petitioners contend that the prior grant of immunity *already* had supplanted Conboy's Fifth Amendment privilege at the time of the civil deposition. Petitioners would limit this immunity, of course, to testimony that "closely tracks" his prior immunized testimony. It is argued that this would not threaten the Government's need for admissible evidence or the individual's interest in avoiding self-incrimination. In the absence of such a threat, admissible evidence should be available to civil antitrust plaintiffs. But we cannot accept the assumptions upon which petitioners' conclusion rests. In our view, a District Court cannot compel Conboy to answer deposition questions, over a valid assertion of his Fifth Amendment right, absent a duly authorized assurance of immunity at the time.

We note at the outset that although there may be practical reasons for not testifying,[12] as far as the deponent's Fifth Amendment right is concerned he should be indifferent between the protection afforded by silence and that afforded by immunity. A deponent's primary interest is that the protection be certain. The Government's interest, however, may be affected seriously by whether the deponent relies at the civil deposition on his Fifth Amendment privilege or on his prior grant of immunity. With due recognition of petitioners' need for admissible evidence, our inquiry then is whether this need can be met without jeopardizing the Government's interest in limiting the scope of an immunity grant or encroaching upon the deponent's certainty of protection.

A

Questions taken verbatim from a transcript of immunized testimony could evoke one of several responses from a deponent: (i) he could repeat or adopt his immunized answer; (ii) he could affirm that the transcript of his immunized answers accurately reflects his prior testimony; (iii) he could recall additional information responsive to the question but not disclosed in his immune testimony; or (iv) he could disclose information that is not responsive to the question. Petitioners do not contend, nor could they, that the prior grant of use immunity affords protection for *all* self-incriminating information disclosed by the immunized witness on *any* occasion after the giving of the immunized testimony. Rather, petitioners argue that only the first three responses would be "derived from" his immune testimony and therefore would be unavailable for use against the deponent in any subsequent criminal prosecution.

Petitioners' premise is that the deposition of Conboy is designed not to discover new information,[13] but to obtain evidence that simply repeats the statements in the immunized transcript.[14] Because there will be little opportunity for the grant of immunity to sweep in statements on direct examination that the Government did not intend to immunize, or for the deponent to give responses that may fall outside

---

12. [Court's footnote 14.] Besides the costs of testifying against close associates, any witness increases the risk of committing perjury the more he talks.

13. [Court's footnote 16.] Direct examination may not be as limited as petitioners assume. The District Court's civil contempt order stated that the questions asked in the deposition "were taken directly" from the immunized transcripts, but did not define exactly what deposition questions petitioners could ask. Other Courts of Appeals have permitted direct questioning to go beyond mere restatements of the prior testimony. See In re Corrugated Container Antitrust Litigation, Appeal of Fleischacker, 644 F.2d 70, 79 (CA2 1981) (compelling answers to questions "concerning specific subjects that actually were touched upon by questions appearing in the transcript of the immunized testimony"); Little Rock School District v. Borden, Inc., 632 F.2d 700, 705 (CA8 1980) (compelling answers as long as deposition questions confined to " 'the same time, geographical and substantive frame work as the [witness' immunized] grand jury testimony' ") (quoting Appeal of Starkey, 600 F.2d 1043, 1048 (CA8 1979)). . . .

14. [Court's footnote 17.] For purposes of this case, we assume that the grand jury transcripts are inadmissible as evidence in a civil trial because the testimony is not subject to cross examination. . . .

of the grant of immunity and later be used against him in a subsequent criminal prosecution, petitioners argue that Conboy's deposition will yield only a carbon copy of the grand-jury transcript. In such a situation, it would be desirable for civil plaintiffs, particularly those bringing private suits that supplement the criminal enforcement of the federal antitrust laws, to have access to the available, probative information.

But even if the direct examination is limited to the questions and answers in the immunized transcript, there remains the right of cross examination, a right traditionally relied upon expansively to test credibility as well as to seek the truth. Petitioners recognize this problem, but maintain that the antitrust defendants "would be entitled to test the accuracy and truthfulness of Conboy's repeated immunized testimony without going beyond the confines of that testimony." Regardless of any limitations that may be imposed on its scope, however, cross examination is intended to and often will produce information not elicited on direct. We must assume that, to produce admissible evidence, the scope of cross examination at the deposition cannot easily be limited to the immunized testimony. This assumption implicates both the Government's and the individual's interests embodied in § 6002.

B

Use immunity was intended to immunize and exclude from a subsequent criminal trial only that information to which the Government expressly has surrendered future use. If the Government is engaged in an ongoing investigation of the particular activity at issue, immunizing new information (e.g., the answers to questions in a case like this one) may make it more difficult to show in a subsequent prosecution that similar information was obtained from wholly independent sources. If a District Court were to conclude in a subsequent civil proceeding that the prior immunity order extended to civil deposition testimony closely tracking the immunized testimony, it in effect could invest the deponent with transactional immunity on matters about which he testified at the immunized proceedings. This is precisely the kind of immunity Congress intended to prohibit. The purpose of § 6002 was to limit the scope of immunity to the level that is constitutionally required, as well as to limit the use of immunity to those cases in which the Attorney General, or officials designated by him, determine that gaining the witness's testimony outweighs the loss of the opportunity for criminal prosecution of that witness.

C

Petitioners' interpretation of § 6002 also places substantial risks on the deponent. Unless the grant of immunity assures a witness that his incriminating testimony will not be used against him in a subsequent criminal prosecution, the witness has not received the certain protection of his Fifth Amendment privilege that he has been forced to exchange. No court has authority to immunize a witness. That responsibility, as we have noted, is peculiarly an executive one, and only the Attorney General or a designated officer of the Department of Justice has authority to grant use immunity. See 18 U.S.C. §§ 6002, 6003. Nor should a court, at the time of the civil testimony, predetermine the decision of the court in a subsequent criminal prosecution on the question whether the Government has met its burden of proving "that the evidence it proposes to use is derived from a legitimate source wholly independent of the compelled testimony." *Kastigar,* 406 U.S., at 460, 92 S.Ct., at 1664. Yet in holding Conboy in contempt for his Fifth Amendment silence, the District Court below essentially predicted that a court in any future criminal prosecution of Conboy will be obligated to protect against evidentiary use of the deposition testimony petitioners seek. We do not think such a predictive judgment is enough.

Petitioners' interpretation of § 6002 imposes risks on the deponent whether or not the deposition testimony properly can be used against him in a subsequent criminal prosecution. Accordingly, the District Court's compulsion order in this case, in the absence of statutory authority or a new grant of immunity by the United States Attorney, cannot be justified by the subsequent exclusion of the compelled testimony. . . .

* * *

IV

This Court has emphasized the importance of the private action as a means of furthering the policy goals of certain federal regulatory statutes, including the federal antitrust laws. But private civil actions can only supplement, not supplant, the primary responsibility of Government. Petitioners' proposed construction of § 6002 sweeps further than Congress intended and could hinder governmental enforcement of its criminal laws by turning use immunity into a form of transactional immunity for subjects examined in the immunized proceeding. It also puts the deponent in some danger of criminal prosecution unless he receives an assurance of immunity or exclusion that the courts cannot properly give. Silence, on the other hand, preserves the deponent's rights and the Government's interests, as well as the judicial resources that otherwise would be required to make the many difficult judgments that petitioners' interpretation of § 6002 would require.

V

We hold that a deponent's civil deposition testimony, closely tracking his prior immunized testimony, is not, without duly authorized assurance of immunity at the time, immunized testimony within the meaning of § 6002, and therefore may not be compelled over a valid assertion of his Fifth Amendment privilege. The judgment of the Court of Appeals accordingly is affirmed.

[The concurring opinions of JUSTICES MARSHALL, BLACKMUN, and BRENNAN are omitted. Justice Marshall's view was that Conboy's answers could not properly have been admitted at a subsequent trial because they were "derived from" immunized testimony. Nevertheless, he did not believe that meant Conboy could be compelled to answer. The witness retained his fifth amendment right and, unlike the situation of a government grant under § 6002, there is "no similar justification for compelling a witness to give incriminating testimony for the benefit of a private litigant." Justice Blackmun's view was that had Conboy testified without asserting his fifth amendment right, his answers would have been admissible at a subsequent trial. They would not have been "derived from" the immunized testimony, within the meaning of the statute, because they would not have been the "fruits" of his immunized testimony, but, rather, would have been given as an "independent act of free will." Accordingly, Conboy was free to assert his fifth amendment right at the deposition. Nevertheless, Justice Blackmun also stated that once the privilege was asserted, testimony incorrectly compelled by a trial court's contempt order would not be admissible in any subsequent prosecution. Justice Brennan stated that he was not "in entire agreement" with everything in either the majority's opinion or in Justice Blackmun's, but that his "small matters" of difference did not warrant a separate lengthy opinion.

The dissenting opinion of JUSTICE STEVENS, in which JUSTICE O'CONNOR joined, is omitted. The dissenters' view was that Conboy's answers at the deposition were "quite plainly 'information directly or indirectly derived from such [immunized] testimony'" and were accordingly inadmissible at a subsequent trial. Conboy therefore had no greater right to assert the fifth amendment at the deposition than he originally had at the grand jury after immunity was given under § 6002.]

NOTES AND QUERIES

(1) *Blocking Civil Litigation.* Conboy was deposed in this case after the Department of Justice had finished its criminal investigation. In fact, the criminal trial had already been held and the jury had acquitted all the defendants who stood trial. Is it clear to you that the Court's interpretation of § 6002 is the best way to advance the "primary responsibility of Government" to enforce federal law? Isn't private enforcement an important component of many federal regulatory statutes, including the antitrust laws? Consider Justice Stevens' argument in dissent in *Conboy:*

> A federal prosecutor does not offer immunity to a suspected criminal unless he expects to obtain important testimony that would not otherwise be available. The prosecutor realizes that, in almost all cases, an offer of immunity—even of use immunity—means sacrificing the chance to prosecute the witness for his own

role in the criminal enterprise. The question is what kind of return society will get on the prosecutor's investment in immunity. Once the prosecutor pays the immunity price, he will normally wish to probe deeply for evidence that will implicate the witness's criminal associates as thoroughly as possible. The primary law enforcement interest is to maximize the amount of information that the witness provides. A broad construction of the immunity grant serves that purpose; a narrow construction can only motivate witnesses to be as unresponsive as possible.

Yet the Court suggests that the Government prosecutors take a different attitude towards immunized witnesses. Even though the Government itself has not promoted such a view in the deposition proceedings in this case or by argument in this Court, the opinion of the Court suggests that when a prosecutor immunizes a witness in order to obtain particular information, he harbors an intent to indict the witness afterwards and would therefore prefer that the witness remain in the same peril of prosecution as before being immunized. Yet it defies human nature to presume that the witness would be just as cooperative during a 24-hour truce, knowing that hostilities will resume immediately thereafter, as he would be after signing a peace treaty.

* * *

The Court's reference to "transactional immunity" suggests a fear that ordering the respondent to answer a deposition question may somehow jeopardize legitimate efforts to prosecute him. Consideration of the facts of this particular case demonstrates that the Court's apparent fear is baseless. Unless some prosecutor already has an independent basis for prosecuting the respondent—and nothing in the record suggests that any such independent basis exists—the Government has already agreed that he will not be prosecuted for engaging in illegal price discussions with Fred Renshaw and Dick Herman of the Alton Box Board. If, at the deposition, he is required to confirm that such discussions took place, how can that confirmation affect his criminal liability? If some prosecutor has a demonstrably independent basis for proving the respondent's participation in the discussions, his confirmation will not make that basis any less demonstrably independent. And if that prosecutor has an independent basis for showing that the respondent participated in the discussions, that basis will be no less demonstrably independent if the respondent is required to identify the time, place, and other persons who participated in the discussions.

Furthermore, one should not overlook the societal costs—law enforcement costs—of the Court's expansion of the Fifth Amendment. The public interest in obtaining the full and candid testimony of a witness with knowledge of the inner workings of a price-fixing conspiracy is both real and significant. . . .

(2) *When Are You Entitled to Assert the Fifth?* Is the real problem in *Conboy* whether the witness had a legitimate fear of criminal prosecution? The leading Supreme Court case for testing when a witness is entitled to assert the fifth amendment privilege is *Hoffman v. United States*.[15] *Hoffman* involved a federal grand jury convened to investigate various federal offenses, including violations of the customs, narcotics, and internal revenue laws. When called before the grand jury he refused to answer questions about what he did and whether he had seen or talked to one William Weisberg in the past week. He was held in contempt by the district court and his conviction was affirmed by the court of appeals. The Supreme Court reversed.

> The privilege afforded not only extends to answers that would in themselves support a conviction under a federal criminal statute but likewise embraces those which would furnish a link in the chain of evidence needed to prosecute the claimant for a federal crime. But this protection must be confined to instances where the witness has reasonable cause to apprehend danger from a direct answer. The witness is not exonerated from answering merely because he declares that in so doing he would incriminate himself—his say-so does not of itself establish the hazard of incrimination. It is for the court to say whether his silence is justified, and to require him to answer if "it clearly appears to the court that he is mistaken." Temple v. Commonwealth, 75 Va. 892, 899 (1881). However, if the witness, upon interposing his claim, were required to prove the hazard in the sense in which a claim is usually required to be established in court, he would be compelled to surrender the very protection which the privilege is designed to guarantee. To sustain the privilege, it need only be evident from the implications of the question, in the setting in which it is asked, that a responsive answer to the question or an explanation of why it cannot be answered might be dangerous because injurious disclosure could result. The trial judge in appraising the claim "must be governed as much by his personal perception of the peculiarities of the case as by the facts actually in evidence." See Taft, J., in Ex parte Irvine, 74 F. 954, 960 (C.C.S.D. Ohio, 1896).

After reviewing the background circumstances, including the fact that Weisberg had been summoned by the grand jury but had not appeared and that Hoffman had a police record and had been publicly labeled as a racketeer, the Court stated:

> The [district] court should have considered, in connection with the business questions, that the chief occupation of some persons involves evasion of federal criminal laws, and that truthful answers by petitioner to these questions might have disclosed that he was engaged in such proscribed activity.

15. 341 U.S. 479, 71 S.Ct. 814, 95 L.Ed. 1118 (1951).

Also, the court should have recognized, in considering the Weisberg questions, that one person with a police record summoned to testify before a grand jury investigating the rackets might be hiding or helping to hide another person of questionable repute sought as a witness. . . . Petitioner could reasonably have sensed the peril of prosecution for federal offenses ranging from obstruction to conspiracy.

In this setting it was not *"perfectly clear,* from a careful consideration of all the circumstances in the case, that the witness is mistaken, and that the answer[s] *cannot possibly* have such tendency" to incriminate. Temple v. Commonwealth, 75 Va. 892, 898 (1881), cited with approval in Counselman v. Hitchcock, 142 U.S. 547, 579–580 (1892).

* * *

(3) *Taking the Fifth After Conviction.* In 1976, R. Harper Brown pleaded nolo contendere to fixing prices in the folding carton industry from 1960 to 1974. In 1978 he was deposed in private treble-damage litigation. He refused to answer any questions other than his name and residence, asserting the fifth amendment. He had never been granted immunity under § 6002. In *In Re Folding Carton Antitrust Litigation,*[16] the court of appeals vacated the district court's contempt order entered after Brown's refusal to testify:

. . . When a witness can demonstrate any possibility of prosecution which is more than fanciful he has demonstrated a reasonable fear of prosecution sufficient to meet constitutional muster.

Appellees argue that their stated oral assurance to restrict their deposition questions to the pre-December 1974 activities of Brown in reference to folding cartons affords Brown a complete protection against subsequent prosecution pursuant to the law of double jeopardy. Further, appellee asserts that since the possibility of Brown's indictment for state offenses committed before 1974 is "trifling," it was proper for the district court to discount that possibility of prosecution and compel the testimony. While appellees correctly claim that the conviction of Brown on the one count Sherman Act violation nullifies any claim of privilege for liability for that offense, we cannot agree that Brown does not remain open to further state or federal prosecutions. A valid state indictment filed within the statute of limitations could cover any alleged illegal activities engaged in by Brown regardless of the time of occurrence or product-line. Appellant argues that it is not fanciful to say that a federal prosecution could use pre–1974 evidence to substantiate claims of a felony conspiracy (after December 1974) in the folding carton product-line, or a conspiracy involving other product-lines. . . . It is argued that the pre–1974 evidence could be used in a subsequent prosecution not to substantiate guilt on the

---

16. 609 F.2d 867 (7th Cir.1979).

subsequent charges but to show a common plan or scheme, or motive. . . .

. . . To the extent that an assessment of the probability of prosecution is significant in the trial court's evaluation of an asserted privilege, it is more properly accomplished through examination of the more traditional tests, viz, statute of limitations, immunity, double jeopardy. Short of the existence of one of these indicia of an absolute bar to subsequent prosecution, a judge's prediction as to the likelihood of a prosecutor filing an indictment [17] is not dispositive in ascertaining the permissible scope of a claim of fifth amendment privilege.

* * *

On remand, the district court upheld Brown's refusal to testify, despite the receipt of a letter from a Justice Department Attorney stating that the Department "has no intention of bringing an enforcement action against R. Harper Brown based upon activities in the folding carton industry for which he was prosecuted." [18] The court emphasized, in particular, Ohio's "limitless" statute of limitations for criminal enforcement (Brown "may have had substantial contact" with Ohio), pointing out that it was a "difficult question" whether the Justice Department letter could give immunity in Ohio. The district court concluded:

> We continue to be concerned about the use by key witnesses in civil cases of their fifth amendment privilege to preclude normal discovery where the possibility of any criminal prosecution is highly remote though not completely fanciful and believe some procedure or formula must be developed to prevent this device from being widely used substantially to limit discovery in civil cases. It is a rare civil case, indeed, where some criminal prosecution might not theoretically be possible against, e.g., the driver of a vehicle involved in an accident, a party to a contract allegedly fraudulently induced, etc. Yet the possibility of such a prosecution is very remote even though not "fanciful."

(4) *The Costs of Taking the Fifth.* In civil litigation there are many occasions for testimonial assertions, from filing an answer, to responding to interrogatories or depositions, to testifying at a trial. If you assert the fifth amendment on any of these occasions, can the invocation of the privilege then be used against you in the litigation? In *Baxter v. Palmigiano* [19] the Supreme Court was faced with the question whether an inmate's invocation of the fifth amendment in a

---

17. [Court's footnote 10.] Appellees buttress their assertion that the federal authorities are not likely to reopen their massive completed investigation by noting that all known federal grand juries investigating the folding carton industry have now been disbanded. However, we do not view the pendency of grand jury proceedings as being dispositive of the issue of possibility of prosecution.

18. See 1980–2 Trade Cas. ¶ 63,469 (N.D.Ill.1980).

19. 425 U.S. 308, 96 S.Ct. 1551, 47 L.Ed. 2d 810 (1976).

prison disciplinary proceeding could be used against him. The Supreme Court held that it could.

> [A] prison inmate in Rhode Island electing to remain silent during his disciplinary hearing, as respondent Palmigiano did here, is not in consequence of his silence automatically found guilty of the infraction with which he has been charged. . . . Here, Palmigiano remained silent at the hearing in the face of evidence that incriminated him; and, as far as this record reveals, his silence was given no more evidentiary value than was warranted by the facts surrounding his case. . . .
>
> Our conclusion [that drawing an adverse inference from silence does not violate the Fifth Amendment] is consistent with the prevailing rule that the Fifth Amendment does not forbid adverse inferences against parties to civil actions when they refuse to testify in response to probative evidence offered against them: the Amendment "does not preclude the inference where the privilege is claimed by a party to a civil cause." 8 J. Wigmore, Evidence 439 (McNaughton rev. 1961).

(5) *Answering the Complaint.* In *National Acceptance Co. of America v. Bathalter*[20] the plaintiff finance corporation sued its former employee for breach of fiduciary duty, fraud, and unjust enrichment arising out of a loan scheme which allegedly cost the finance corporation $8.6 million. The defendant, in his answer, declined to respond to the allegations in the complaint "on the ground that his answers might incriminate him," pointing out that the subject matter of the complaint had been the basis for at least one grand jury investigation. The plaintiff moved for judgment on the pleadings, arguing that because defendant did not admit, deny, or plead lack of knowledge, its allegations must be deemed admitted under F.R.Civ.P. 8(d). The district court agreed, and granted judgment for the plaintiff. Judge Fairchild, for the Seventh Circuit Court of Appeals, wrote:

> There is no question that the language of Rule 8 requires exactly the result reached by the district court. . . . The question facing us here is whether the literal language of Rule 8 must give way in order to protect the defendant's constitutional right to avoid self-incrimination.
>
> * * *
>
> After Baxter [v. Palmigiano] there is no longer any doubt that at trial a civil defendant's silence may be used against him, even if that silence is an exercise of his constitutional privilege against self-incrimination. Thus, if this case were to go to trial, NAC would be entitled to the benefit of an adverse inference against Bathalter if he declined to answer a question and invoked his Fifth Amendment privilege, although *Baxter* does not hold that an adverse finding could properly rest on the silence, without other evidence. The question we must address, is whether this inference

---

20. 705 F.2d 924 (7th Cir.1983).

is available at the pleading stage. NAC contends that it is so available. We disagree.

* * *

In a later case, the Supreme Court described its holding [in *Baxter*] as follows:

> *Baxter* did no more than permit an inference to be drawn in a civil case from a party's refusal to testify. Respondent's silence in *Baxter* was only one of a number of factors to be considered by the finder of fact in assessing a penalty, and was given no more probative value than the facts of the case warranted; here, refusal to waive the Fifth Amendment leads automatically and without more to imposition of sanctions.

Lefkowitz v. Cunningham, 431 U.S. 801, 808 n. 5, 97 S.Ct. 2132, 2137 n. 5, 53 L.Ed.2d 1 (1977).

* * *

Thus *Baxter* established that the drawing of an adverse inference from privileged silence in a civil case does not make the exercise of the privilege sufficiently "costly" to amount to compulsion when there is other evidence of the fact. NAC seeks to persuade that it does not make such silence "costly" to treat it as an admission of an allegation.

The Fifth Circuit also considered *Baxter* as it bears upon the exercise of the privilege against self-incrimination in a civil case. U.S. v. White, 589 F.2d 1283, 1286–87 (5th Cir.1979). Keno, a defendant in a criminal case, had testified as a defendant in a civil case, and contended that he had been forced to choose between preserving his Fifth Amendment privilege and losing the civil suit. In rejecting Keno's contention, the court quoted from *Baxter* and said:

> Similarly, there is no indication that invocation of the fifth amendment in this case would have resulted in an adverse judgment. Alside, as plaintiff, was put to the proof of its case . . . and there is no indication that under Georgia law silence on the part of defendant would compel a verdict for plaintiff.

* * *

The "cost" to a defendant of treating his claim of privilege in his answer as an admission is at least that plaintiff is excused from presenting proof of his averment and defendant is subjected without more, to an adverse judgment on that issue. We think *Baxter* indicates that this is too great a cost.

It is our best judgment, in the light of *Baxter,* that even in a civil case a judgment imposing liability cannot rest solely upon a privileged refusal to admit or deny at the pleading stage. We conclude that defendant's claim of privilege should not have been deemed an admission, and that plaintiff should have been put to its proof, either by way of evidentiary support for a motion for summary judgment or at trial.

* * *

(6) *Taking the Fifth Amendment at Trial.* See *Marine Midland Bank v. John E. Russo Produce,*[21] where the plaintiff bank was suing two corporations and its officers for fraud and conversion arising out of alleged check kiting (drawing checks against other checks which have not yet cleared through the bank collection process). Judge Fuchsberg wrote for the New York Court of Appeals:

> In the ensuing 21–day jury trial, as part of its own case Marine Midland called John and Rita Russo, in turn, to the stand. Upon the advice of their own counsel, and in light of an ongoing FBI investigation of the transactions, however, each invoked the privilege against self incrimination when queried about whether he or she had signed any of the checks, had directed others to do so or had known there were then insufficient funds in the accounts to cover them. Over objection, the court later charged the jury that no inference adverse to these defendants could be drawn from their refusal to answer.
>
> * * *
>
> Whether a jury in the context of a conventional civil case may be instructed to consider a party's invocation of the privilege against self incrimination when called to the stand has not previously been addressed by this court. Nonetheless, rulings on closely related issues trace a well-marked path to the answer. So, we have long held that an attorney's failure to testify in his own behalf in a disciplinary proceeding may count against him, and we have even concluded that a grant of immunity coextensive with the privilege will not preclude the use of Grand Jury testimony in a disbarment proceeding.
>
> If it be true, then, that the underlying policy of the privilege is to protect the individual from oppression at the hands of a State exercising its awesome powers of investigation to ferret out wrongdoing, the constitutionality of allowing its assertion to count against the target of a disciplinary proceeding—a quasi-criminal matter . . .—suggests that a like result would obtain in a purely civil case. For, here the parties are on an equal footing and the only disadvantage threatened is liability to compensate an adversary for damages. We therefore decline to extend to civil cases a rule originally designed as a safeguard in criminal prosecutions.
>
> Essentially, then, the issue becomes one akin to that arising when a party fails or refuses to produce a material witness who is within his control. It is now well established that such an event may be considered by a jury in assessing the strength of evidence

---

21. 50 N.Y.2d 31, 427 N.Y.S.2d 961, 405 N.E.2d 205 (1980).

offered by the opposite party on the issue which the witness was in a position to controvert. . . .

Accordingly, we conclude that the court's charge was in error.

IN RE GRAND JURY SUBPOENA
United States Court of Appeals, Fourth Circuit, 1988.
836 F.2d 1468, certiorari denied ___ U.S. ___, 108 S.Ct. 2914,
101 L.Ed.2d 945 (1988).

HARRISON L. WINTER, CHIEF JUDGE:

Four third-party deponents in a civil action in the Eastern District of Virginia appeal from a judgment of the district court of Maryland denying their motion to quash two grand jury subpoenas issued by a special grand jury in Maryland to an attorney in Virginia requiring production of their sealed depositions taken during the civil litigation in Virginia. The appellants-deponents moved to quash the subpoenas in the district court of Maryland on the ground that the depositions were sealed by a protective order issued by the district court in Virginia. The district court of Maryland denied the motion to quash, concluding that a civil protective order cannot be used to shield discovery materials from a subpoena issued by a grand jury. We affirm.

I.

A special grand jury in the district of Maryland is investigating the events surrounding the collapse in September, 1985, of Community Savings & Loan (Community), which was part of a group of affiliated organizations whose parent corporation is Equity Programs Investment Corporation (EPIC). The appellants-deponents in this case are former officers and directors of EPIC and its subsidiaries. In 1985, the state of Maryland placed Community into conservatorship and EPIC filed for bankruptcy. Subsequently, several private mortgage insurance companies which had insured mortgages held by EPIC brought suit in the Eastern District of Virginia against EPIC Mortgage, Inc. (a subsidiary of EPIC), numerous banks, and the Maryland Deposit Insurance Corporation, the conservator for Community. The appellants-deponents are not parties to the litigation in the Eastern District of Virginia.

In 1986, plaintiffs in the civil action in Virginia noticed the depositions of the appellants. Some of these deponents became concerned about complying with this order because of the ongoing grand jury investigation in Maryland. The deponents moved for a stay of discovery pending completion of the grand jury investigation in order to avoid being forced to choose between the possibility of self-incrimination and asserting their fifth amendment rights. After a hearing, the Virginia district court denied the motion for a stay. With the consent of all parties and the deponents, the court instead orally issued a protective order sealing the deposition transcripts and limiting access to the transcripts to the parties in the civil action. The district court requested that the parties prepare a written protective order for the district court to consider. The parties submitted the written order to the district judge on October 8, and it was signed the next day.

The written protective order sealed deposition transcripts that were filed with the court and limited access to these transcripts to necessary court personnel, the deponents, and the parties to the civil action and their counsel. The protective order specifically stated:

> IT IS FURTHER ORDERED that the transcript or record of the sealed depositions and the information contained therein shall not be made available to any state or federal investigating agency or authority, and shall not be used in connection with any proceedings other than these actions, except by further order of this Court.

The protective order also provided for possible modification:

> IT IS FURTHER ORDERED that this Order may be modified only by further order of this Court or any other court having jurisdiction over the trial of any of these cases upon notice to the deponents and the parties to this case with reasonable opportunity to respond.

In late 1986, following the taking of these depositions, the Assistant United States Attorney guiding the special grand jury investigation in Maryland requested copies of the deposition transcripts in the Virginia litigation from an attorney for a defendant in that action. The attorney provided the grand jury with the requested materials, except for those depositions sealed by the protective order. On December 16, 1986, the grand jury issued a subpoena duces tecum requiring an attorney for the plaintiffs in the Virginia action to produce the deposition transcripts of two of the appellants in this action. On January 21, 1987, the grand jury issued a second subpoena requiring an attorney to produce the deposition transcripts of the remaining appellants. Appellants subsequently filed their motion to quash.

Following a hearing on the motion to quash, the deponents, at the request of the Maryland district judge, scheduled an appearance before the Virginia district court in order to clarify the protective order. During that hearing, the district judge in Virginia explained that the protective order was intended to bar access to the transcripts by the Maryland grand jury and that the deponents were entitled to rely on the order to protect their fifth amendment rights. The government subsequently stipulated that the protective order was intended to apply to the Maryland grand jury. On April 21, 1987, the district court of Maryland denied the motion to quash.

II.

The appellants seek to employ a civil protective order as a defense against compliance with a grand jury subpoena demanding production of deposition transcripts obtained during discovery in a civil action to which they were not parties. The issue of the need to comply with the grand jury subpoena is properly before this court. The government had two options in seeking to obtain the deposition transcripts: it could seek permissive intervention in the civil action in Virginia pursuant to Fed.R.Civ.P. 24(b) to request that the protective order be modified or vacated, or it could subpoena the transcripts as part of the ongoing grand jury investigation. The government validly chose the latter course in this action.

The issue presented in this case is an important one of first impression in the circuit courts concerning the legal authority of the grand jury. The Maryland district court denied the motion to quash the subpoena on the ground that it lacked the authority to quash the grand jury's subpoena duces tecum notwithstanding that the deposition transcripts sought to be obtained were sealed under the terms of a valid civil protective order issued by another federal district court. In reaching this decision, the Maryland district court assumed that the deponents relied on the protective order during the taking of depositions and that the protective order was validly issued. The district court appropriately framed the legal issue for consideration, and we agree with its conclusion.

The question of the grand jury's authority presented in this case involves the intersection of three interests: the authority of a grand jury to gather evidence in a criminal investigation; the deponents' right against self-incrimination; and the goals of liberal discovery and efficient dispute resolution in civil proceedings. We begin by discussing these respective interests.

A.

[The Court here discussed the broad power of the grand jury, citing, inter alia, *Blair v. United States,* supra this Casebook, p. 439.]

B.

The grand jury subpoena in this case seeks discovery materials which, we assume for purposes of this appeal, were produced in reliance on the Virginia district court's protective order. At first blush, resolution of this case might appear to depend on balancing the deponents' right against self-incrimination as secured by the protective order and the grand jury's interest in effective investigation of crime. But this is not so, because the deponents' fifth amendment right against self-incrimination did not require, nor may it depend on, the shield of civil protective orders. Deponents were entitled to rely only on their own silence or a grant of immunity to protect their rights, otherwise they risked waiving those rights.

In contrast with a grant of immunity, the government may not use a protective order to compel a witness to testify during a criminal or civil proceeding. Absent a grant of immunity, the deponents were entitled, with or without a protective order, to assert their fifth amendment privilege in answer to potentially incriminating questions in a civil proceeding. In Pillsbury Co. v. Conboy, the Supreme Court established this principle by reversing a contempt order entered against a civil litigant who had not received a grant of immunity and who asserted his fifth amendment privilege against self-incrimination in deposition testimony. The Court ruled that a party to a civil action has a right to assert the privilege until immunity is granted by officials of the Department of Justice.

Deponents argue that the burden of silence in civil litigation may unduly punish an individual for asserting the right against self-incrimination. A party's silence, for example, may bar that party from asserting facts which would allow him to prevail in litigation which will have severe financial consequences for the loser. Silence may also create inferences which are relevant and adverse to the party maintaining such silence. On the facts of this case, these concerns are remote because the deponents had no stake in the outcome of the civil litigation.

Even if such a risk were present, however, the burden placed on an individual's right to avoid self-incrimination by the institution of a civil lawsuit by a private party does not implicate values protected by the fifth amendment. In Baxter v. Palmigiano, for example, the Supreme Court held that the fifth amendment privilege does not protect state prison inmates against the drawing of adverse inferences from the failure to testify during disciplinary proceedings which could result in punitive action. The Court, in part, relied on the prevailing rule that "the fifth amendment does not forbid adverse inferences against parties to civil actions when they refuse to testify in response to probative evidence offered against them." Justice Brennan, joined by Justice Marshall, dissented from the conclusion that the fifth amendment privilege did not extend to prison disciplinary hearings, but agreed that he would "have difficulty holding such an inference impermissible in civil cases involving only private parties." Thus, the security given to the deponent's interest in avoiding self-incrimination by a civil protective order does not outweigh the substantial government interest present in this case.

C.

While protective orders do not significantly advance fifth amendment interests, they do aid the civil courts in facilitating resolution of private disputes. Federal Rule of Civil Procedure 26(c) authorizes the district courts to issue protective orders to encourage full disclosure of all relevant evidence in order to "secure the just, speedy, and inexpensive determination" of civil disputes. Fed.R.Civ.P. 1. Absent such orders, witnesses would be deterred from providing essential testimony in civil litigation, thus undermining the adversary process.

Assertion of the privilege against self-incrimination may disrupt or thwart civil litigation and discovery in a wide variety of cases. The privilege may slow or thwart the efficient resolution of many civil cases because the privilege applies not only to information which is itself incriminating but also to information relevant to civil liability which provides a clue leading to evidence of criminal conduct. Hoffman v. United States. Thus, the privilege may apply in antitrust litigation, commercial litigation and securities actions involving fraud, personal injury actions involving criminal negligence, or civil rights actions involving assault, because these civil actions may elicit information tending to demonstrate the element or elements of a crime. See, generally, Heidt, The Conjurer's Circle: The Fifth Amendment Privilege in Civil Cases, 91 Yale L.J. 1062, 1065–1071 (1982).

The assertion of the privilege against self-incrimination in civil cases can impose severe burdens on civil litigants. Invocation may occur in the answer to a complaint or in response to interrogatories, deposition questions, or requests for admissions. The assertion of the privilege prior to trial may thus significantly reduce a party's chances of prevailing on the merits of his claim. The lack of direct access to such information may also prolong civil litigation and increase its costs. As a result, assertion of the privilege forces civil litigants to share the cost of the right to silence of the individual asserting the privilege.

We must therefore weigh the extent to which protective orders insure the efficient resolution of civil disputes against the interest of obtaining all relevant evidence during a grand jury's criminal investigation.

III.

[The Court here reviewed four decisions from the Second Circuit involving the enforceability of protective orders.]

IV.

[W]e conclude that the balance in this case must be struck in favor of the grand jury's need to gather evidence. . . .

A civil protective order may seriously impede a criminal investigation by a grand jury. Uncoerced testimony given in a civil action may provide important and relevant information to a grand jury investigation. In addition, the government has an interest in obtaining this information for purposes of impeachment should the deponents testify in a manner materially inconsistent with their deposition testimony in any future criminal trial. . . .

In addition, a protective order issued by a civil court for the purpose of protecting a deponent's fifth amendment privilege if given paramount effect would usurp the proper authority of the executive branch to balance the public interest in confidentiality against the interest in effective criminal investigation. For this reason, the power to apply to a court for a grant of immunity is limited to the United States Attorney under federal law. 18 U.S.C. § 6003; Pillsbury v. Conboy, supra. . . .

These limitations on judicial power thus counsel against authorizing district courts to give civil deponents de facto grants of immunity in the guise of Rule 26 protective orders.[22] The deponents here, in seeking a civil order on which they could rely to protect their privilege against self-incrimination, desired such a de facto grant of immunity. This circuit has properly refrained from allowing such judicial intervention into executive prerogatives. . . .

Another consideration is that while a protective order, if given full effect, would impede the investigating function of a grand jury, it is not totally effective in furthering the civil court's interest in facilitating discovery. Of course, a protective order may encourage deponents to provide relevant evidence because the order reduces the risk that incriminating information will be brought to the attention of law enforcement officials. . . . Even with a protective order in place, incriminating statements still create the risk that parties to a civil action will leak sealed information or materials to relevant law enforcement authorities. In the event of a leak of information to law enforcement authorities, a protective order, unlike a grant of immunity, provides no assurance that incriminating statements will not be used against a deponent in a criminal proceeding or that the statements will not be used to obtain other relevant evidence. Moreover, a protective order, such as the order in this case, is normally subject to modification under Rule 26 for sufficient cause.

In addition, a protective order cannot serve as more than a stopgap measure to seal discovery materials. Incriminating information will normally be disclosed at trial even if the information is effectively suppressed prior to that time. The temporary benefit of pretrial secrecy will not appeal to many individuals as a substitute for formal immunity or cause them to cooperate with civil discovery motions by waiving their fifth amendment privilege. . . .

Apart from a protective order, a civil court has available other tools to ensure successful resolution of a civil action which is threatened by a deponent's privileged silence. One commonly used alternative to allay the fears of a deponent is to delay discovery until a pending grand jury investigation has been completed. Such a stay, which was denied by the Virginia district court in this case, has the salutary effect of minimizing the conflict between criminal investigations and fair discovery in civil litigation. . . .

In some cases, invocation of the privilege by a party may justify shifting the burden of proof in a civil action in accordance with the doctrine that the burden of proof should be placed on the party who is in the best position to provide relevant proof. . . . [U]se of the traditional rules of burden-shifting may allow civil litigation to proceed in the face of silence during discovery.

22. [Court's footnote 12.] Separation of powers principles also counsel courts against intervening in a criminal investigation being conducted by a grand jury.

Finally, to avoid invocation of the privilege aimed at thwarting discovery, testimony waiving the privilege against incrimination during trial might be excluded where the privilege was asserted in response to questions during discovery. Exclusion, like a protective order, would be justified under Rule 26 which authorizes a court to issue such orders as may be needed to protect a party from oppression.

In summary, a district court has alternatives available to encourage parties to comply with the goal of liberal discovery short of entry of a protective order. Where discovery is nonetheless impeded by a genuine fear of future prosecution, these alternatives also provide tools for resolution of private disputes in the face of pretrial silence. In cases such as this one, where deponents to a civil action are not parties to the suit, these devices will not burden the exercise of the constitutional right to silence. In other cases involving deponents who are parties to an action, these alternatives may burden a party's decision to maintain silence due to the risk of self-incrimination, but such burden in the civil context, where equitable under the circumstances, does not implicate values with which the fifth amendment is concerned.

V.

In our view, a reasonable balancing of the respective interests of the civil courts and grand jury investigations favors enforcement of a grand jury subpoena despite the existence of an otherwise valid protective order. Deponents suggest, however, that the per se rule favoring enforcement of a grand jury subpoena which we adopt is unwarranted. They suggest that a case-by-case approach of balancing these competing interests would be appropriate, with the right on the part of the government to seek modification of a protective order upon a showing of compelling need under Rule 26. . . .

* * *

. . . The adoption of a compelling need test for disclosure of sealed discovery materials would deprive federal grand juries of relevant evidence in some cases. Despite the availability of protective orders, however, parties with self-incrimination concerns would still have the option of resisting discovery requests by asserting their fifth amendment privilege. Uncertainty about the ultimate outcome of a protective order will mean that no deponent may always effectively rely on a protective order to secure his right against self-incrimination. Only an absolute, unmodifiable protective order could thus hope to provide the civil courts with a tool to entice deponents to forsake their right to assert a fifth amendment privilege.

* * *

AFFIRMED.

SPROUSE, CIRCUIT JUDGE, dissenting:

I respectfully dissent. . . .

* * *

The majority's argument that a protective order "may seriously impede a criminal investigation by a grand jury" both overstates the reach of the Rule 26(c) shield and understates the retained power of the grand jury. Rule 26(c) provides only limited protection for evidence that, here, would not exist but for the protective order itself. Unlike a grant of immunity, a protective order has no effect on the continued conduct of the grand jury's investigation. The government remains free to call the deponents before the grand jury to explore their fifth amendment claims and to prosecute or grant immunity. If the deponents are immunized, the grand jury can then demand the sought-after evidence and the balance would tilt conclusively towards enforcing a subpoena for previous deposition testimony.

* * *

The majority argues that Rule 26(c) is ineffective and should be supplanted by other methods of eliciting evidence from recalcitrant witnesses. I disagree. The vitality of the protective order has made it a valuable method of facilitating discovery.

Placing higher burdens of proof upon those who invoke the fifth amendment in civil litigation could well retard the truth-seeking function of civil discovery, and it unnecessarily penalizes the exercise of a constitutional right. . . .

In sum, I feel that Rule 26(c) has worked long and quietly to effect the efficient and just management of civil discovery. The emasculation of protective orders by today's decision replaces the rule with a new presence in civil litigation—the roving eye of government and the attendant rush by affected civil litigants to invoke the fifth amendment in discovery.

NOTES AND QUERIES

(1) *Queries.* Doesn't the protective order offer a good way to advance everyone's interests? The civil litigants are able to obtain discovery which might lead to a resolution of the civil claims. The witness does not have to incur the cost of asserting his or her constitutional privilege. And the Government is in no worse position than it would otherwise have been if the witness had asserted the fifth amendment protection. Why not honor the protective order? Note that *In Re Grand Jury* arises in a "strong" procedural setting. The Government sought the depositions through use of a grand jury subpoena; the witnesses created a clear record that they were willing to be deposed only because of the protective order. In other cases either the party's fifth amendment rights were not asserted, or the Government was seeking the testimony through a modification of the protective order.[23]

23. See Palmieri v. New York, 779 F.2d 861 (2d Cir.1985) (state government motion to intervene in private antitrust litigation to "unseal" private settlement; settlement entered into in reliance on protective order; held: error to modify protective order absent error in initial grant or showing of compelling need); United States v. GAF Corp., 596 F.2d 10 (2d Cir.1979) (government civil investigative demand for documents produced in private discovery under protective order; held: enforceable); Mar-

(2) *Granting a Stay.* Another possible remedy for the witness' dilemma is to grant a stay of the civil proceedings pending the resolution of the criminal case (although, as we have seen, completion of parallel criminal proceedings might not remove the witness' right to assert the fifth amendment). Note that the district court in *In re Grand Jury Subpoena* refused such a request. Consider *Wehling v. CBS, Inc.*,[24] in which plaintiff claimed that CBS defamed him in a television news story dealing with his trade schools. Prior to filing his lawsuit he had been subpoenaed five times by a grand jury investigating student loan programs. When deposed by CBS, Wehling asserted the fifth amendment nineteen times, stating that the grand jury investigation was continuing. Wehling then sought a stay in the proceedings. The district court denied his motion. When he indicated that he would continue to assert his fifth amendment privilege, the district court dismissed his complaint with prejudice. Wehling appealed. The Court of Appeals reversed:

> We hold that the district court erred in concluding that plaintiff's assertion of his self-incrimination privilege during pretrial discovery automatically required the dismissal of his libel action. First, we find no provision in the federal discovery rules which authorizes a court to impose sanctions on a party who resists discovery by asserting a valid claim of privilege. . . .
>
> Second, we believe that dismissing a plaintiff's action with prejudice solely because he exercises his privilege against self-incrimination is constitutionally impermissible. Wehling had, in addition to his Fifth Amendment right to silence, a due process right to a judicial determination of his civil action. When the district court ordered Wehling to answer CBS' questions or suffer dismissal, it forced plaintiff to choose between his silence and his lawsuit. The Supreme Court has disapproved of procedures which require a party to surrender one constitutional right in order to assert another. . . .
>
> We recognize, of course, that Wehling is not the only party to this action who has important rights that must be respected. . . . CBS should not be required to defend against a party who refuses to reveal the very information which might absolve defendant of all liability. . . . Therefore we emphasize that a civil plaintiff has no absolute right to both his silence and his lawsuit. Neither, however, does the civil defendant have an absolute right to have the action dismissed anytime a plaintiff invokes his constitutional privilege. When plaintiff's silence is constitutionally guaranteed, dismissal is appropriate only where other, less burdensome, reme-

---

tindell v. International Tel. & Tel. Corp., 594 F.2d 291 (2d Cir.1979) (government, requesting modification of protective order, seeks deposition transcripts; deposed witnesses had not invoked fifth amendment, relying on protective order; held: in view of importance of enforcing protective orders so as to foster civil discovery, district court properly refused access).

24. 608 F.2d 1084 (5th Cir.1979).

dies would be an ineffective means of preventing unfairness to defendant.

* * *

. . . Wehling filed his suit against CBS on August 17, 1976, the last day before limitations ran on any libel action arising out of the August 18, 1975 broadcast. Wehling had disposed of his last interest in the trade schools in August of 1975 and, under the applicable statute of limitations, was threatened with potential criminal prosecution until approximately September 1, 1980. Thus, . . . he in effect was asking the court to stay further discovery for approximately three years. Although a three-year hiatus in the lawsuit is undesirable from the standpoint of both the court and the defendant, permitting such inconvenience seems preferable at this point to requiring plaintiff to choose between his silence and his lawsuit. Because staying discovery would not impose undue hardship on defendant and, therefore, would protect the party exercising a constitutional privilege from *unnecessary* adverse consequences, we believe the court abused its discretion in denying Wehling's [m]otion . . . and dismissing the lawsuit.

* * *

C. GRAND JURY MATERIALS

DOUGLAS OIL CO. v. PETROL STOPS NORTHWEST

Supreme Court of the United States, 1979.
441 U.S. 211, 99 S.Ct. 1667, 60 L.Ed.2d 156.

Mr. Justice Powell delivered the opinion of the Court.

This case presents two intertwined questions concerning a civil litigant's right to obtain transcripts [25] of federal criminal grand jury proceedings. First, what justification for disclosure must a private party show in order to overcome the presumption of grand jury secrecy applicable to such transcripts? Second, what court should assess the strength of this showing—the court where the civil action is pending, or the court that acts as custodian of the grand jury documents?

I

Respondent Petrol Stops Northwest is a gasoline retailer unaffiliated with any major oil company. In 1973, it operated 104 service stations located in Arizona, California, Oregon, Washington, and several other States. On December 13, 1973, respondent filed an antitrust action in the District of Arizona against 12 large oil companies, including petitioners Douglas Oil Company of California and Phillips Petroleum Company. In its complaint, respondent alleged that on January 1, 1973, there had been a sharp reduction in the amount of gasoline offered for sale to it, and that this reduction had resulted from a

---

25. [Court's footnote 1.] "Transcripts" is used herein to refer to the verbatim recordings of testimony given before a grand jury.

conspiracy among the oil companies to restrain trade in gasoline, in violation of §§ 1 and 2 of the Sherman Act. As a part of this conspiracy, respondent charged, petitioners and their codefendants had fixed the prices of gasoline at the retail and wholesale distribution levels in California, Oregon and Washington.

Respondents Gas–A–Tron of Arizona and Coinoco also independently sell gasoline through service stations they own or lease. . . . On November 2, 1973, Gas–A–Tron and Coinoco filed an antitrust complaint in the District of Arizona naming as defendants nine large oil companies, including petitioner Phillips Petroleum Company. Like respondent Petrol Stops Northwest, Gas–A–Tron and Coinco alleged that as of January 1, 1973, their supply of gasoline had been sharply reduced, and attributed this reduction to a conspiracy to restrain trade in violation of the Sherman Act. . . .

. . . In February 1974, respondents served upon petitioners a set of interrogatories which included a request that petitioners state whether either of their companies at any time between January 1, 1968, and December 14, 1974, had had any communication with any of their competitors concerning the wholesale price of gasoline to be sold to unaffiliated retailers. Petitioners also were asked to produce any documents they had concerning such communications. Petitioners responded that they were aware of no such communications, and therefore could produce no documents pertinent to the request.

In the meantime, the Antitrust Division of the Department of Justice had been investigating since 1972 the pricing behavior on the West Coast of several major oil companies, including petitioners. As part of this investigation, employees of petitioners were called to testify before a grand jury empanelled in the Central District of California. The Government's investigation culminated on March 19, 1975, when the grand jury returned an indictment charging petitioners and four other oil companies with having conspired to fix the price of "rebrand gasoline" in California, Oregon, Washington, Nevada, and Arizona.[26] The indictment alleged that the price-fixing conspiracy had begun in July 1970 and had continued at least until the end of 1971.

Although initially all six defendants charged in the criminal indictment pled not guilty, by December of 1975, each had pled nolo contendere and was fined $50,000. Before changing their pleas, petitioners, acting pursuant to Fed.Rule Crim.Proc. 16(a)(1)(A), asked the District Court for the Central District of California to give them copies of the transcripts of testimony given by their employees before the grand jury. Their request was granted, and it appears that petitioners continue to possess copies of these transcripts.

In October of 1976 respondents served upon petitioners requests under Fed.Rule Civ.Proc. 34 for production of the grand jury transcripts

---

26. [Court's footnote 7.] . . . It appears to be undisputed that the gasoline purchased by respondents from the major oil companies was "rebrand gasoline" within the meaning of the indictment.

in petitioners' possession. Petitioners objected to the requests for production, arguing that the transcripts were not relevant to the private antitrust actions and that they were not likely to lead to any admissible evidence. Respondents did not pursue their discovery requests by making a motion in the Arizona trial court under Fed.Rule Civ.Proc. 37 to compel discovery. Rather, they filed a petition in the District Court for the Central District of California asking that court, as guardian of the grand jury transcripts under Fed.Rule Crim.Proc. 6(e), to order them released to respondents. An attorney from the Antitrust Division of the Department of Justice appeared and indicated that the Government had no objection to respondents' receiving the transcripts already made available to petitioners under Fed.Rule Crim.Proc. 16(a)(1)(A). He suggested to the court, however, that the real parties in interest were petitioners, and therefore that they should be given an opportunity to be heard. The California District Court accepted this suggestion, and petitioners participated in the proceedings as parties adverse to respondents.

After briefing and oral argument, the court ordered the Chief of the Antitrust Division's Los Angeles Office "to produce for [respondents'] inspection and copying all grand jury transcripts previously disclosed to Phillips Petroleum Company or Douglas Oil Company of California or their attorneys relating to the indictment in United States v. Phillips, et al., Criminal Docket No. 75–377." The production order was subject, however, to several protective conditions. The transcripts were to "be disclosed only to counsel for [respondents] in connection with the two civil actions" pending in Arizona. Furthermore, under the court's order the transcripts of grand jury testimony "may be used . . . solely for the purpose of impeaching or refreshing the recollection of a witness, either in deposition or at trial" in the Arizona actions. Finally, the court forbade any further reproduction of the matter turned over to respondents, and ordered that the material be returned to the Antitrust Division "upon completion of the purposes authorized by this Order."

On appeal the Ninth Circuit affirmed the disclosure order. The Court of Appeals noted that under United States v. Procter & Gamble Co. [supra this Casebook, p. 453], a party seeking access to grand jury transcripts must show a "particularized need." In evaluating the strength of the need shown in the present case, the Ninth Circuit considered two factors: the need for continued grand jury secrecy and respondents' need for the requested material. The court found the former need to be insubstantial, as the grand jury proceeding had concluded three years before and the transcripts already had been released to petitioners. As to respondents' claim, the court conceded that it knew little about the Arizona proceedings, but speculated that the transcripts would facilitate the prosecution of respondents' civil suits: Petitioners' answers to the 1974 interrogatories concerning price communications with competitors appeared to be at odds with their pleas of nolo contendere in the California criminal action.

II

Petitioners contend that the courts below erred in holding that, because the grand jury had dissolved and the requested material had been disclosed already to the defendants, respondents had to show only a "slight need" for disclosure. According to petitioners, this approach to disclosure under Fed.Rule Crim.Proc. 6(e) is contrary to prior decisions of this Court indicating that, "a civil litigant must demonstrate a compelling necessity for specified grand jury materials before disclosure is proper."

We consistently have recognized that the proper functioning of our grand jury system depends upon the secrecy of grand jury proceedings. In particular, we have noted several distinct interests served by safeguarding the confidentiality of grand jury proceedings. First, if pre-indictment proceedings were made public, many prospective witnesses would be hesitant to come forward voluntarily, knowing that those against whom they testify would be aware of that testimony. Moreover, witnesses who appeared before the grand jury would be less likely to testify fully and frankly, as they would be open to retribution as well as to inducements. There also would be the risk that those about to be indicted would flee, or would try to influence individual grand jurors to vote against indictment. Finally, by preserving the secrecy of the proceedings, we assure that persons who are accused but found innocent by the grand jury will not be held up to public ridicule.

For all of these reasons, courts have been reluctant to lift unnecessarily the veil of secrecy from the grand jury. At the same time, it has been recognized that in some situations justice may demand that discrete portions of transcripts be made available for use in subsequent proceedings. Indeed, recognition of the occasional need for litigants to have access to grand jury transcripts led to the provision in Fed.Rule Crim.Proc. 6(e)(2)(C)(i) that disclosure of grand jury transcripts may be made "when so directed by a court preliminarily to or in connection with a judicial proceeding."

In United States v. Procter & Gamble, supra, the Court sought to accommodate the competing needs for secrecy and disclosure by ruling that a private party seeking to obtain grand jury transcripts must demonstrate that "without the transcript a defense would be greatly prejudiced or that without reference to it an injustice would be done." Moreover, the Court required that the showing of need for the transcripts be made "with particularity" so that "the secrecy of the proceedings [may] be lifted discretely and limitedly."

In Dennis v. United States, 384 U.S. 855, 86 S.Ct. 1840, 16 L.Ed.2d 973 (1966), the Court considered a request for disclosure of grand jury records in quite different circumstances. It was there held to be an abuse of discretion for a district court in a criminal trial to refuse to disclose to the defendants the grand jury testimony of four witnesses who some years earlier had appeared before a grand jury investigating activities of the defendants. The grand jury had completed its investigation, and the witnesses whose testimony was sought already had testified in public concerning the same matters. The Court noted that "[n]one of the reasons traditionally advanced to justify nondisclosure of grand jury minutes" was significant in those circumstances, whereas the defendants had shown it to be likely that the witnesses' testimony at trial was inconsistent with their prior grand jury testimony.

From *Procter & Gamble* and *Dennis* emerges the standard for determining when the traditional secrecy of the grand jury may be broken: Parties seeking grand jury transcripts under Rule 6(e) must show that the material they seek is needed to avoid a possible injustice in another judicial proceeding, that the need for disclosure is greater than the need for continued secrecy, and that their request is structured to cover only material so needed.[27] Such a showing must be made even when the grand jury whose transcripts are sought has concluded its operations, as it had in *Dennis*. For in considering the effects of disclosure on grand jury proceedings, the courts must consider not only the immediate effects upon a particular grand jury, but also the possible effect upon the functioning of future grand juries. Persons called upon to testify will consider the likelihood that their testimony may one day be disclosed to outside parties. Fear of future retribution or social stigma may act as powerful deterrents to those who would come forward and aid the grand jury in the performance of its duties. Concern as to the future consequences of frank and full testimony is heightened where the witness is an employee of a company under investigation. Thus, the interests in grand jury secrecy, although reduced, are not eliminated merely because the grand jury has ended its activities.[28]

It is clear from *Procter & Gamble* and *Dennis* that disclosure is appropriate only in those cases where the need for it outweighs the public interest in secrecy, and that the burden of demonstrating this balance rests upon the private party seeking disclosure. It is equally clear that as the considerations justifying secrecy become less relevant, a party asserting a need for grand jury transcripts will have a lesser burden in showing justification. . . .

In sum, as so often is the situation in our jurisprudence, the court's duty in a case of this kind is to weigh carefully the competing interests in light of the relevant circumstances and the standards announced by

---

27. [Court's footnote 12.] As noted in United States v. Procter & Gamble, 356 U.S. 677, 683, 78 S.Ct. 983, 987, 2 L.Ed.2d 1077 (1958), the typical showing of particularized need arises when a litigant seeks to use "the grand jury transcript at the trial to impeach a witness, to refresh his recollection, to test his credibility and the like." Such use is necessary to avoid misleading the trier of fact. Moreover, disclosure can be limited strictly to those portions of a particular witness' testimony that bear upon some aspect of his direct testimony at trial.

28. [Court's footnote 13.] The transcripts sought by respondents already had been given to the target companies in the grand jury investigation. Thus, release to respondents will not enhance the possibility of retaliatory action by employers in this case. But the other factors supporting the presumption of secrecy remain and must be considered.

this Court. And if disclosure is ordered, the court may include protective limitations on the use of the disclosed material, as did the District Court in this case. Moreover, we emphasize that a court called upon to determine whether grand jury transcripts should be released necessarily is infused with substantial discretion.

Applying these principles to the present case, we conclude that neither the District Court nor the Court of Appeals erred in the standard by which it assessed the request for disclosure under Rule 6(e). The District Court made clear that the question before it was whether a particularized need for disclosure outweighed the interest in continued grand jury secrecy. Similarly, the Court of Appeals correctly understood that the standard enunciated in *Procter & Gamble* requires a court to examine the extent of the need for continuing grand jury secrecy, the need for disclosure, and the extent to which the request was limited to that material directly pertinent to the need for disclosure.[29]

III

Petitioners contend, irrespective of the legal standard applied, that the District Court for the Central District of California was not the proper court to rule on respondents' motion for disclosure. . . .

. . . The federal courts that have addressed the question generally have said that the request for disclosure of grand jury minutes under Rule 6(e) must be directed toward the court under whose auspices the grand jury was empanelled. . . . Indeed, those who seek grand jury transcripts have little choice other than to file a request with the court that supervised the grand jury, as it is the only court with control over the transcripts.[30]

Quite apart from practical necessity, the policies underlying Rule 6(e) dictate that the grand jury's supervisory court participate in reviewing such requests, as it is in the best position to determine the continuing need for grand jury secrecy. . . . We conclude, therefore, that, in general, requests for disclosure of grand jury transcripts should be directed to the court that supervised the grand jury's activities.

29. [Court's footnote 14.] As petitioners point out, the Court of Appeals did say that, because of the circumstances, "the party seeking disclosure should not be required to demonstrate a large compelling need," and that a "minimal showing of particularized need" would suffice. In a different context, these statements could be read as an unjustified lowering of the standard of proof required by *Procter & Gamble* and *Dennis*. We cannot say, however, that the Court of Appeals applied an incorrect standard in view of the circumstances of this case and the discussion thereof in the opinion below.

30. [Court's footnote 17.] As we have noted, by virtue of a prior order petitioners have possession of the transcripts sought by respondents. We were informed at argument by counsel for the Government that under the terms of that order, the transcripts were to be returned upon completion of the criminal proceeding in the Central District of California and were to be used only for purposes of defending against the criminal charges in that case. . . .

It does not follow, however, that in every case the court in which the grand jury sat should make the final decision whether a request for disclosure under Rule 6(e) should be granted. Where, as in this case, the request is made for use in a case pending in another district, the judges of the court having custody of the grand jury transcripts will have no first-hand knowledge of the litigation in which the transcripts allegedly are needed, and no practical means by which such knowledge can be obtained. In such a case, a judge in the district of the grand jury cannot weigh in an informed manner the need for disclosure against the need for maintaining grand jury secrecy. Thus, it may well be impossible for that court to apply the standard required by the decisions of this Court, reiterated above, for determining whether the veil of secrecy should be lifted.

* * *

In the present case, the District Court for the Central District of California was called upon to make an evaluation entirely beyond its expertise. The District Judge readily conceded that he had no knowledge of the civil proceedings pending several hundred miles away in Arizona. Nonetheless, he was asked to rule whether there was a "particularized need" for disclosure of portions of the grand jury transcript and whether this need outweighed the need for continued grand jury secrecy. . . .

* * *

Under these circumstances, the better practice would have been for the District Court, after making a written evaluation of the need for continued grand jury secrecy and a determination that the limited evidence before it showed that disclosure might be appropriate, to have sent the requested materials to the courts where the civil cases were pending. The Arizona court, armed with their special knowledge of the status of the civil actions, then could have considered the requests for disclosure in light of the California court's evaluation of the need for continued grand jury secrecy. In this way, both the need for continued secrecy and the need for disclosure could have been evaluated by the courts in the best position to make the respective evaluations.

We do not suggest, of course, that such a procedure would be required in every case arising under Rule 6(e). Circumstances that dictate the need for cooperative action between the courts of different districts will vary, and procedures to deal with the many variations are best left to the rulemaking procedures established by Congress. Undoubtedly there will be cases in which the court to whom the Rule 6(e) request is directed will be able intelligently on the basis of limited knowledge to decide that disclosure plainly is inappropriate or that justice requires immediate disclosure to the requesting party, without reference of the matter to any other court. Our decision today therefore is restricted to situations, such as that presented by this case, in which the District Court having custody of the grand jury records is unlikely to have dependable knowledge of the status of, and the needs of the parties in, the civil suit in which the desired transcripts are to be used.

The judgment of the Court of Appeals is reversed, and the case remanded for further proceedings consistent with this opinion.

[JUSTICE STEVENS, joined by CHIEF JUSTICE BURGER and JUSTICE STEWART, dissented from the Court's "readiness to review the District Judge's exercise of his broad discretion" and would not have found his order an abuse of discretion. The concurring opinion of JUSTICE REHNQUIST is omitted.][31]

NOTES AND QUERIES

(1) *Queries.* As in cases previously reviewed in this Chapter, the Court appears to be anxious to safeguard the integrity of the criminal justice process even if it is to the disadvantage of private plaintiffs whose enforcement efforts could actually further the goals of the statute under which prosecution was sought. Do you think that the Court is being overly restrictive? Review the materials on grand jury secrecy, supra Chapter 5B, p. 451. Is there that much secrecy to be guarded? Consider, also, that in *Douglas Oil* the transcripts in question had already been disclosed to the employers of the witnesses pursuant to Rule 16. Indeed, although the terms of disclosure apparently required return of the transcripts to the district court in California at the conclusion of the criminal case (a requirement which does not appear in Rule 16), apparently no one had bothered. If the defendants had the transcripts, why shouldn't the plaintiffs?[32]

(2) *Particularized Need—Taking the Fifth.* In *In Re Corrugated Container Antitrust Litigation*[33] the plaintiffs sought the grand jury testimony of four witnesses who had taken the fifth amendment during depositions. The witnesses had previously testified before the grand jury under a grant of immunity. (This was the same litigation that gave rise to *Pillsbury v. Conboy,* supra p. 645.) The district court refused to compel the witnesses to testify over their claim of fifth amendment privilege, but did order their grand jury testimony disclosed. Invocation of the fifth amendment helped to make out "particularized need." The district court wrote: "Despite extensive discovery procedures, Messrs. McCain, Fryburg, Lindeman, Stalder, and Barnum are key witnesses due to their pricing responsibility. They can best

---

31. For remand, see 647 F.2d 1005 (9th Cir.) (interest in secrecy slight; outweighed by need to use transcripts to test credibility of witnesses) (affirming district court grant of motion to disclose), certiorari denied 454 U.S. 1098, 102 S.Ct. 672, 70 L.Ed. 2d 639 (1981). In 1983 Rule 6 was amended to adopt the two-court process spelled out in *Douglas Oil.* See F.R.Crim. P. 6(e)(3)(C), (D).

32. See In re Screws Antitrust Litigation, M.D.L. No. 443, 91 F.R.D. 47 (D.Mass. 1981) (defendants in civil litigation had partial or complete transcripts of testimony of 60 persons; court grants disclosure of transcripts of three of four witnesses requested "to assure the accuracy of testimony at trial and equalize the access to relevant facts which each side possesses").

33. M.D.L. No. 310, 556 F.Supp. 1117 (S.D.Tex.), affirmed 687 F.2d 52 (5th Cir. 1982).

support allegations of a price fixing conspiracy. Failure of memory and selective use of the Fifth Amendment prevent meaningful discovery of information crucial to the trial in this litigation." The court of appeals affirmed, finding no abuse of discretion.

(3) *Government as Civil Plaintiff.* Are the concerns expressed in *Douglas Oil* lessened when the government is the civil plaintiff? In *United States v. Sells Engineering, Inc.*,[34] the defendants had pleaded guilty to conspiring to defraud the government. The Government then moved for an order permitting disclosure of all grand jury materials to attorneys in the Civil Division of the Justice Department for use in a possible civil suit under the False Claims Act. The district court granted the motion, but the court of appeals reversed on the ground that the Government was required to show particularized need under Rule 6(e)(3)(C)(i). The Supreme Court granted certiorari and affirmed the court of appeals. Justice Brennan wrote for the majority:

> [There is no] support for breaching grand jury secrecy in favor of Government attorneys *other than prosecutors* —either by allowing them into the grand jury room, or by granting them uncontrolled access to grand jury materials. An attorney with only civil duties lacks both the prosecutor's special role in supporting the grand jury, and the prosecutor's own crucial need to know what occurs before the grand jury.[35]
>
> Of course, it would be of substantial help to a Justice Department civil attorney if he had free access to a storehouse of evidence compiled by a grand jury; but that is of a different order from the prosecutor's need for access. The civil lawyer's need is ordinarily nothing more than a matter of saving time and expense. The same argument could be made for access on behalf of any lawyer in another government agency, or indeed, in private practice. We have consistently rejected the argument that such savings can justify a breach of grand jury secrecy. In most cases, the same evidence that could be obtained from the grand jury will be available through ordinary discovery or other routine avenues of investigation. If, in a particular case, ordinary discovery is insufficient for some reason, the Government may request disclosure under a (C)(i) court order.
>
> Not only is disclosure for civil use unjustified by the considerations supporting prosecutorial access, but it threatens to do affirmative mischief. The problem is threefold.
>
> First, disclosure to government bodies raises much the same concerns that underlie the rule of secrecy in other contexts. Not only does disclosure increase the number of persons to whom the

34. 463 U.S. 418, 103 S.Ct. 3133, 77 L.Ed.2d 743 (1983).

35. [Court's footnote 15.] This case involves only access by Civil Division attorneys who played no part in the criminal prosecution of respondents. It does not present any issue concerning continued use of grand jury materials, in the civil phase of a dispute, by an attorney who himself conducted the criminal prosecution. We decline to address that problem in this case.

information is available (thereby increasing the risk of inadvertent or illegal release to others), but it renders considerably more concrete the threat to the willingness of witnesses to come forward and to testify fully and candidly. If a witness knows or fears that his testimony before the grand jury will be routinely available for use in governmental civil litigation or administrative action, he may well be less willing to speak for fear that he will get himself into trouble in some other forum.

Second, because the Government takes an active part in the activities of the grand jury, disclosure to government attorneys for civil use poses a significant threat to the integrity of the grand jury itself. If prosecutors in a given case knew that their colleagues would be free to use the materials generated by the grand jury for a civil case, they might be tempted to manipulate the grand jury's powerful investigative tools to root out additional evidence useful in the civil suit, or even to start or continue a grand jury inquiry where no criminal prosecution seemed likely. Any such use of grand jury proceedings to elicit evidence for use in a civil case is improper per se. . . . Our concern is based less on any belief that grand jury misuse is in fact widespread than on our concern that, if and when it does occur, it would often be very difficult to detect and prove. . . .

Third, use of grand jury materials by government agencies in civil or administrative settings threatens to subvert the limitations applied outside the grand jury context on the Government's powers of discovery and investigation. While there are some limits on the investigative powers of the grand jury, there are few if any other forums in which a governmental body has such relatively unregulated power to compel other persons to divulge information or produce evidence. Other agencies, both within and without the Justice Department, operate under specific and detailed statutes, rules, or regulations conferring only limited authority to require citizens to testify or produce evidence. Some agencies have been granted special statutory powers to obtain information and require testimony in pursuance of their duties. Others (including the Civil Division) are relegated to the usual course of discovery under the Federal Rules of Civil Procedure. In either case, the limitations imposed on investigation and discovery exist for sound reasons—ranging from fundamental fairness to concern about burdensomeness and intrusiveness. If government litigators or investigators in civil matters enjoyed unlimited access to grand jury material, though, there would be little reason for them to resort to their usual, more limited avenues of investigation. To allow these agencies to circumvent their usual methods of discovery would not only subvert the limitations and procedural requirements built into those methods, but would grant to the Government a virtual ex parte form of discovery, from which its civil litigation opponents are excluded unless they make a strong showing of particularized need. . . .

In short, if grand juries are to be granted extraordinary powers of investigation because of the difficulty and importance of their task, the use of those powers ought to be limited as far as reasonably possible to the accomplishment of the task. The policies of Rule 6 require that any disclosure to attorneys other than prosecutors be judicially supervised rather than automatic.

* * *

Since we conclude that the Government must obtain a (C)(i) court order to secure the disclosure it seeks in this case, we must consider what standard should govern the issuance of such an order.

* * *

The Government points out that *Douglas Oil* and its forerunners all involved private parties seeking access to grand jury materials. It contends that the *Douglas Oil* standard ought not be applied when government officials seek access "in furtherance of their responsibility to protect the public weal." Earlier this Term, however, we rejected a similar argument in [Illinois v.] Abbott, 460 U.S. 557, 103 S.Ct. 1356, 75 L.Ed.2d 281. . . . We held . . . that the particularized need standard applies to disclosure to state attorneys general. . . .

* * *

The Government further argues that "disclosure of grand jury materials to government attorneys typically implicates few, if any, of the concerns that underlie the policy of grand jury secrecy." The contention is overstated, but it has some validity. Nothing in *Douglas Oil,* however, requires a district court to pretend that there are no differences between governmental bodies and private parties. The *Douglas Oil* standard is a highly flexible one, adaptable to different circumstances and sensitive to the fact that the requirements of secrecy are greater in some situations than in others. Hence, although . . . [there is no] special dispensation from the *Douglas Oil* standard for government agencies, the standard itself accommodates any relevant considerations, peculiar to government movants, that weigh for or against disclosure in a given case. For example, a district court might reasonably consider that disclosure to Justice Department attorneys poses less risk of further leakage or improper use than would disclosure to private parties or the general public. . . . And "under the particularized need standard, the district court may weigh the public interest, if any, served by disclosure to a governmental body. . . ." *Abbott,* 460 U.S., at 567, n. 15, 103 S.Ct., at 1362, n. 15. On the other hand, for example, in weighing the need for disclosure, the court could take into account any alternative discovery tools available by statute or regulation to the agency seeking disclosure.

* * *

The Court of Appeals correctly held that disclosure to government attorneys and their assistants for use in a civil suit is permissible only with a court order under Rule 6(e)(3)(C)(i), and that the District Court did not apply correctly the particularized need standard for issuance of such an order. Accordingly, the judgment of the Court of Appeals is *Affirmed*.[36]

The Supreme Court had a subsequent opportunity to apply the particularized need standard to intra-Justice Department disclosures. In *United States v. John Doe, Inc., I,*[37] Antitrust Division attorneys completed a grand jury investigation of three corporations without returning indictments. The same attorneys then began a civil investigation of the three corporations, tentatively concluding that the corporations had violated the False Claims Act and the Foreign Assistance Act, in addition to the Sherman Act. Believing that they should consult with lawyers in the Civil Division and in the United States Attorneys Office regarding the non-Sherman Act claims, they obtained a 6(e) order to permit disclosure of grand jury materials to six named government attorneys. The Supreme Court, in an opinion by Justice Stevens, first held that the civil use of grand jury materials by the Antitrust Division attorneys themselves after they ended the criminal investigation was not covered by Rule 6 because it was not a "disclosure." The Court then held that disclosure to other Justice Department attorneys was permissible under the *Douglas Oil* "flexible" standard. Disclosure was limited to named Justice Department attorneys for consultation purposes and thus the threat to grand jury secrecy was minimal. There were also strong "public interests served" by the consultation. The fact that the Government might have been able to obtain the materials through other means of discovery, does not, of itself, make disclosure improper. Justices Brennan, Marshall, and Blackmun dissented.

36. Chief Justice Burger, joined by Justices Powell, Rehnquist, and O'Connor, dissented. They reviewed what they believed to be "more than 30 years of consistent Justice Department practice of using grand jury materials without court order in investigating and prosecuting civil actions." They also argued that many federal civil enforcement actions seek "precisely the same object" as criminal enforcement and that civil and criminal provisions often form "an integrated law enforcement scheme."

37. 481 U.S. 102, 107 S.Ct. 1656, 95 L.Ed.2d 94 (1987).

APPENDIX

A. SELECTED FEDERAL STATUTES

The Sherman Act, 15 U.S.C. §§ 1 & 2:

§ 1. Trusts, etc., in restraint of trade illegal; penalty

Every contract, combination in the form of trust or otherwise, or conspiracy, in restraint of trade or commerce among the several States, or with foreign nations, is declared to be illegal. Every person who shall make any contract or engage in any combination or conspiracy hereby declared to be illegal shall be deemed guilty of a felony, and, on conviction thereof, shall be punished by fine not exceeding one million dollars if a corporation, or, if any other person, one hundred thousand dollars, or by imprisonment not exceeding three years, or by both said punishments, in the discretion of the court.

§ 2. Monopolizing trade a felony; penalty

Every person who shall monopolize, or attempt to monopolize, or combine or conspire with any other person or persons, to monopolize any part of the trade or commerce among the several States, or with foreign nations, shall be deemed guilty of a felony, and, on conviction thereof, shall be punished by fine not exceeding one million dollars if a corporation, or, if any other person, one hundred thousand dollars, or by imprisonment not exceeding three years, or by both said punishments, in the discretion of the court.

Clayton Act of 1914, 15 U.S.C. § 24:

§ 14. That whenever a corporation shall violate any of the penal provisions of the antitrust laws, such violation shall be deemed to be also that of the individual directors, officers, or agents of such corporation who shall have authorized, ordered, or done any of the acts constituting in whole or in part such violation, and such violation shall be deemed a misdemeanor, and upon conviction therefor of any such director, officer, or agent he shall be punished by a fine of not exceeding $5,000 or by imprisonment for not exceeding one year, or by both, in the discretion of the court.

The Securities Act of 1933, 15 U.S.C. § 77x:

§ 77x. Penalties

Any person who willfully violates any of the provisions of this subchapter, or the rules and regulations promulgated by the Commission under authority thereof, or any person who willfully, in a registration statement filed under this subchapter, makes any untrue statement of a material fact or omits to state any material fact required to be stated therein or necessary to make the statements therein not misleading, shall upon conviction be fined not more than $10,000 or imprisoned not more than five years, or both.

Securities Exchange Act of 1934, 15 U.S.C. § 78ff:

§ 77ff. Penalties

(a) Any person who willfully violates any provision of this chapter, or any rule or regulation thereunder the violation of which is made unlawful or the observance of which is required under the terms of this chapter, or any person who willfully and knowingly makes, or causes to be made, any statement in any application, report, or document required to be filed under this chapter or any rule or regulation thereunder or any undertaking contained in a registration statement as provided in subsection (d) of section 78o of this title, or by any self-regulatory organization in connection with an application for membership or participation thereof or to become associated with a member thereof which statement was false or misleading with respect to any material fact, shall upon conviction be fined not more than $1,000,000, or imprisoned not more than ten years, or both, except that when such person is a person other than a natural person, a fine not exceeding $2,500,000 may be imposed; but no person shall be subject to imprisonment under this section for the violation of any rule or regulation if he proves that he had no knowledge of such rule or regulation.

Note: The 1934 Act originally provided for the following penalties: for individuals, $10,000 fine and/or five years in prison; for securities exchanges, $500,000 fine. The fine for individuals was increased to $100,000 in 1984. The current penalty provisions were enacted in 1988.

Conspiracy, 18 U.S.C. § 371:

§ 371. Conspiracy to commit offense or to defraud United States

If two or more persons conspire either to commit any offense against the United States or to defraud the United States, or any agency thereof in any manner or for any purpose, and one or more of such persons do any act to effect the object of the conspiracy, each shall be fined not more than $10,000 or imprisoned not more than five years, or both.

If, however, the offense, the commission of which is the object of the conspiracy, is a misdemeanor only, the punishment for such conspiracy shall not exceed the maximum punishment provided for such misdemeanor.

Mail Fraud Statute, 18 U.S.C. § 1341:

§ 1341. Frauds and swindles

Whoever, having devised or intending to devise any scheme or artifice to defraud, or for obtaining money or property by means of false or fraudulent pretenses, representations, or promises, or to sell, dispose of, loan, exchange, alter, give away, distribute, supply, or furnish or procure for unlawful use any counterfeit or spurious coin, obligation, security, or other article, or anything represented to be or intimated or held out to be such counterfeit or spurious article, for the purpose of executing such scheme or artifice or attempting so to do, places in any post office or authorized depository for mail matter, any matter or thing whatever to be sent or delivered by the Postal Service, or takes or receives therefrom, any such matter or thing, or knowingly causes to be delivered by mail according to the direction thereon, or at the place at which it is directed to be delivered by the person to whom it is addressed, any such matter or thing, shall be fined not more than $1,000 or imprisoned not more than five years, or both.

Wire Fraud Statute, 18 U.S.C. § 1343:

§ 1343. Fraud by wire, radio, or television

Whoever, having devised or intending to devise any scheme or artifice to defraud, or for obtaining money or property by means of false or fraudulent pretenses, representations, or promises, transmits or causes to be transmitted by means of wire, radio, or television communications in interstate or foreign commerce, any writings, signs, signals, pictures, or sounds for the purpose of executing such scheme or artifice, shall be fined not more than $1,000 or imprisoned not more than five years, or both.

Note: The Mail Fraud and Wire Fraud Statutes were amended by the Anti–Drug Abuse Act of 1988, which provides:

For the purposes of this chapter [which includes mail fraud, wire fraud, and bank fraud], the term "scheme or artifice to defraud" includes a scheme or artifice to deprive another of the intangible right of honest services.

Racketeer–Influenced and Corrupt Organizations (RICO), 18 U.S.C. § 1961 et seq.:

§ 1961. Definitions

As used in this chapter—

(1) "racketeering activity" means (A) any act or threat involving murder, kidnapping, gambling, arson, robbery, bribery, extortion, dealing in obscene matter, or dealing in narcotic or other dangerous drugs, which is chargeable under State law and punishable by imprisonment for more than one year; (B) any act which is indictable under any of the following provisions of title 18, United

States Code: Section 201 (relating to bribery), section 224 (relating to sports bribery), sections 471, 472, and 473 (relating to counterfeiting), section 659 (relating to theft from interstate shipment) if the act indictable under section 659 is felonious, section 664 (relating to embezzlement from pension and welfare funds), section 891–894 (relating to extortionate credit transactions), section 1084 (relating to the transmission of gambling information), section 1341 (relating to mail fraud), section 1343 (relating to wire fraud), sections 1461–1465 (relating to obscene matter), section 1503 (relating to obstruction of justice), section 1510 (relating to obstruction of criminal investigations), section 1511 (relating to the obstruction of State or local law enforcement), section 1512 (relating to tampering with a witness, victim, or an informant), section 1513 (relating to retaliating against a witness, victim, or an informant), section 1951 (relating to interference with commerce, robbery, or extortion), section 1952 (relating to racketeering), section 1953 (relating to interstate transportation of wagering paraphernalia), section 1954 (relating to unlawful welfare fund payments), section 1955 (relating to the prohibition of illegal gambling businesses), section 1956 (relating to the laundering of monetary instruments), section 1957 (relating to engaging in monetary transactions in property derived from specified unlawful activity), sections 2312 and 2313 (relating to interstate transportation of stolen motor vehicles), sections 2314 and 2315 (relating to interstate transportation of stolen property), section 2320 (relating to trafficking in certain motor vehicles or motor vehicle parts), sections 2341–2346 (relating to trafficking in contraband cigarettes), sections 2421–24 (relating to white slave traffic), (C) any act which is indictable under title 29, United States Code, section 186 (dealing with restrictions on payments and loans to labor organizations) or section 501(c) (relating to embezzlement from union funds), (D) any offense involving fraud connected with a case under title 11, fraud in the sale of securities, or the felonious manufacture, importation, receiving, concealment, buying, selling, or otherwise dealing in narcotic or other dangerous drugs, punishable under any law of the United States, or (E) any act which is indictable under the Currency and Foreign Transactions Reporting Act;

(2) "State" means any State of the United States, the District of Columbia, the Commonwealth of Puerto Rico, any territory or possession of the United States, any political subdivision, or any department, agency, or instrumentality thereof;

(3) "person" includes any individual or entity capable of holding a legal or beneficial interest in property;

(4) "enterprise" includes any individual, partnership, corporation, association, or other legal entity, and any union or group of individuals associated in fact although not a legal entity;

(5) "pattern of racketeering activity" requires at least two acts of racketeering activity, one of which occurred after the effective date of this chapter and the last of which occurred within ten years (excluding any period of imprisonment) after the commission of a prior act of racketeering activity;

(6) "unlawful debt" means a debt (A) incurred or contracted in gambling activity which was in violation of the law of the United States, a State or political subdivision thereof, or which is unenforceable under State or Federal law in whole or in part as to principal or interest because of the laws relating to usury, and (B) which was incurred in connection with the business of gambling in violation of the law of the United States, a State or political subdivision thereof, or the business of lending money or a thing of value at a rate usurious under State or Federal law, where the usurious rate is at least twice the enforceable rate;

(7) "racketeering investigator" means any attorney or investigator so designated by the Attorney General and charged with the duty of enforcing or carrying into effect this chapter;

(8) "racketeering investigation" means any inquiry conducted by any racketeering investigator for the purpose of ascertaining whether any person has been involved in any violation of this chapter or of any final order, judgment, or decree of any court of the United States, duly entered in any case or proceeding arising under this chapter;

(9) "documentary material" includes any book, paper, document, record, recording, or other material; and

(10) "Attorney General" includes the Attorney General of the United States, the Deputy Attorney General of the United States, any Assistant Attorney General of the United States, or any employee of the Department of Justice or any employee of any department or agency of the United States so designated by the Attorney General to carry out the powers conferred on the Attorney General by this chapter. Any department or agency so designated may use in investigations authorized by this chapter either the investigative provisions of this chapter or the investigative power of such department or agency otherwise conferred by law.

CONGRESSIONAL STATEMENT OF FINDINGS AND PURPOSE

Section 1 of Pub.L. 91–452 provided in part that:

"The Congress finds that (1) organized crime in the United States is a highly sophisticated, diversified, and widespread activity that annually drains billions of dollars from America's economy by unlawful conduct and the illegal use of force, fraud, and corruption; (2) organized crime derives a major portion of its power through money obtained from such illegal endeavors as syndicated gambling, loan sharking, the theft and fencing of property, the importa-

"POSITIVELY MAGICAL"

Hubert "Geese" Ausbie
Coach   College: Philander Smith College

©2000 HARLEM GLOBETROTTERS INTERNATIONAL, Inc., A Division of MJA, Inc.
To join the Harlem Globetrotters Fan Club Call: (602) 258-0000
www.harlemglobetrotters.com

tion and distribution of narcotics and other dangerous drugs, and other forms of social exploitation; (3) this money and power are increasingly used to infiltrate and corrupt legitimate business and labor unions and to subvert and corrupt our democratic processes; (4) organized crime activities in the United States weaken the stability of the Nation's economic system, harm innocent investors and competing organizations, interfere with free competition, seriously burden interstate and foreign commerce, threaten the domestic security, and undermine the general welfare of the Nation and its citizens; and (5) organized crime continues to grow because of defects in the evidence-gathering process of the law inhibiting the development of the legally admissible evidence necessary to bring criminal and other sanctions or remedies to bear on the unlawful activities of those engaged in organized crime and because the sanctions and remedies available to the Government are unnecessarily limited in scope and impact.

"It is the purpose of this Act [see Short Title note above] to seek the eradication of organized crime in the United States by strengthening the legal tools in the evidence-gathering process, by establishing new penal prohibitions, and by providing enhanced sanctions and new remedies to deal with the unlawful activities of those engaged in organized crime."

LIBERAL CONSTRUCTION OF PROVISIONS; SUPERSEDURE OF FEDERAL OR STATE LAWS; AUTHORITY OF ATTORNEYS REPRESENTING UNITED STATES

Section 904 of Pub.L. 91–452 provided that:

"(a) The provisions of this title [enacting this chapter and amending sections 1505, 2516, and 2517 of this title] shall be liberally construed to effectuate its remedial purposes.

"(b) Nothing in this title shall supersede any provision of Federal, State, or other law imposing criminal penalties or affording civil remedies in addition to those provided for in this title.

"(c) Nothing contained in this title shall impair the authority of any attorney representing the United States to—

"(1) lay before any grand jury impaneled by any district court of the United States any evidence concerning any alleged racketeering violation of law;

"(2) invoke the power of any such court to compel the production of any evidence before any such grand jury; or

"(3) institute any proceeding to enforce any order or process issued in execution of such power or to punish disobedience of any such order or process by any person."

§ 1962. Prohibited activities

(a) It shall be unlawful for any person who has received any income derived, directly or indirectly, from a pattern of racketeering activity or through collection of an unlawful debt in which such person has participated as a principal within the meaning of section 2, title 18, United States Code, to use or invest, directly or indirectly, any part of such income, or the proceeds of such income, in acquisition of any interest in, or the establishment or operation of, any enterprise which is engaged in, or the activities of which affect, interstate or foreign commerce. A purchase of securities on the open market for purposes of investment, and without the intention of controlling or participating in the control of the issuer, or of assisting another to do so, shall not be unlawful under this subsection if the securities of the issuer held by the purchaser, the members of his immediate family, and his or their accomplices in any pattern of racketeering activity or the collection of an unlawful debt after such purchase do not amount in the aggregate to one percent of the outstanding securities of any one class, and do not confer, either in law or in fact, the power to elect one or more directors of the issuer.

(b) It shall be unlawful for any person through a pattern of racketeering activity or through collection of an unlawful debt to acquire or maintain, directly or indirectly, any interest in or control of any enterprise which is engaged in, or the activities of which affect, interstate or foreign commerce.

(c) It shall be unlawful for any person employed by or associated with any enterprise engaged in, or the activities of which affect, interstate or foreign commerce, to conduct or participate, directly or indirectly, in the conduct of such enterprise's affairs through a pattern of racketeering activity or collection of unlawful debt.

(d) It shall be unlawful for any person to conspire to violate any of the provisions of subsections (a), (b), or (c) of this section.

§ 1963. Criminal penalties

(a) Whoever violates any provision of section 1962 of this chapter shall be fined not more than $25,000 or imprisoned not more than twenty years, or both, and shall forfeit to the United States, irrespective of any provision of State law—

    (1) any interest the person has acquired or maintained in violation of section 1962;

    (2) any—

        (A) interest in;

        (B) security of;

        (C) claim against; or

        (D) property or contractual right of any kind affording a source of influence over;

any enterprise which the person has established, operated, controlled, conducted, or participated in the conduct of in violation of section 1962; and

(3) any property constituting, or derived from, any proceeds which the person obtained, directly or indirectly, from racketeering activity or unlawful debt collection in violation of section 1962.

The court, in imposing sentence on such person shall order, in addition to any other sentence imposed pursuant to this section, that the person forfeit to the United States all property described in this subsection. In lieu of a fine otherwise authorized by this section, a defendant who derives profits or other proceeds from an offense may be fined not more than twice the gross profits or other proceeds.

(b) Property subject to criminal forfeiture under this section includes—

(1) real property, including things growing on, affixed to, and found in land; and

(2) tangible and intangible personal property, including rights, privileges, interests, claims and securities.

(c) All right, title, and interest in property described in subsection (a) vests in the United States upon the commission of the act giving rise to forfeiture under this section. Any such property that is subsequently transferred to a person other than the defendant may be the subject of a special verdict of forfeiture and thereafter shall be ordered forfeited to the United States, unless the transferee establishes in a hearing pursuant to subsection (*l*) that he is a bona fide purchaser for value of such property who at the time of purchase was reasonably without cause to believe that the property was subject to forfeiture under this section.

(d)(1) Upon application of the United States, the court may enter a restraining order or injunction, require the execution of a satisfactory performance bond, or take any other action to preserve the availability of property described in subsection (a) for forfeiture under this section—

(A) upon the filing of an indictment or information charging a violation of section 1962 of this chapter and alleging that the property with respect to which the order is sought would, in the event of conviction, be subject to forfeiture under this section; or

(B) prior to the filing of such an indictment or information, if, after notice to persons appearing to have an interest in the property and opportunity for a hearing, the court determines that—

(i) there is a substantial probability that the United States will prevail on the issue of forfeiture and that failure to enter the order will result in the property being destroyed, removed from the jurisdiction of the court, or otherwise made unavailable for forfeiture; and

(ii) the need to preserve the availability of the property through the entry of the requested order outweighs the hardship on any party against whom the order is to be entered:

Provided, however, That an order entered pursuant to subparagraph (B) shall be effective for not more than ninety days, unless extended by the court for good cause shown or unless an indictment or information described in subparagraph (A) has been filed.

(2) A temporary restraining order under this subsection may be entered upon application of the United States without notice or opportunity for a hearing when an information or indictment has not yet been filed with respect to the property, if the United States demonstrates that there is probable cause to believe that the property with respect to which the order is sought would, in the event of conviction, be subject to forfeiture under this section and that provision of notice will jeopardize the availability of the property for forfeiture. Such a temporary order shall expire not more than ten days after the date on which it is entered, unless extended for good cause shown or unless the party against whom it is entered consents to an extension for a longer period. A hearing requested concerning an order entered under this paragraph shall be held at the earliest possible time, and prior to the expiration of the temporary order.

(3) The court may receive and consider, at a hearing held pursuant to this subsection, evidence and information that would be inadmissible under the Federal Rules of Evidence.

(e) Upon conviction of a person under this section, the court shall enter a judgment of forfeiture of the property to the United States and shall also authorize the Attorney General to seize all property ordered forfeited upon such terms and conditions as the court shall deem proper. Following the entry of an order declaring the property forfeited, the court may, upon application of the United States, enter such appropriate restraining orders or injunctions, require the execution of satisfactory performance bonds, appoint receivers, conservators, appraisers, accountants, or trustees, or take any other action to protect the interest of the United States in the property ordered forfeited. Any income accruing to, or derived from, an enterprise or an interest in an enterprise which has been ordered forfeited under this section may be used to offset ordinary and necessary expenses to the enterprise which are required by law, or which are necessary to protect the interests of the United States or third parties.

(f) Following the seizure of property ordered forfeited under this section, the Attorney General shall direct the disposition of the property by sale or any other commercially feasible means, making due provision for the rights of any innocent persons. Any property right or interest not exercisable by, or transferable for value to, the United States shall expire and shall not revert to the defendant, nor shall the defendant or any person acting in concert with or on behalf of the defendant be eligible to purchase forfeited property at any sale held by the United States. Upon application of a person, other than the defendant or a person acting in concert with or on behalf of the defendant, the court may restrain or stay the sale or disposition of the property pending the conclusion of any appeal of the criminal case giving rise to the forfeiture, if the applicant demonstrates that proceeding with the sale or disposition of the property will result in irreparable injury, harm or loss to him. Notwithstanding 31 U.S.C. 3302(b), the proceeds of any sale or other disposition of property forfeited under this section and any moneys forfeited shall be used to pay all proper expenses for the forfeiture and the sale, including expenses of seizure, maintenance and custody of the property pending its disposition, advertising and court costs. The Attorney General shall deposit in the Treasury any amounts of such proceeds or moneys remaining after the payment of such expenses.

(g) With respect to property ordered forfeited under this section, the Attorney General is authorized to—

(1) grant petitions for mitigation or remission of forfeiture, restore forfeited property to victims of a violation of this chapter, or take any other action to protect the rights of innocent persons which is in the interest of justice and which is not inconsistent with the provisions of this chapter;

(2) compromise claims arising under this section;

(3) award compensation to persons providing information resulting in a forfeiture under this section;

(4) direct the disposition by the United States of all property ordered forfeited under this section by public sale or any other commercially feasible means, making due provision for the rights of innocent persons; and

(5) take appropriate measures necessary to safeguard and maintain property ordered forfeited under this section pending its disposition.

(h) The Attorney General may promulgate regulations with respect to—

(1) making reasonable efforts to provide notice to persons who may have an interest in property ordered forfeited under this section;

(2) granting petitions for remission or mitigation of forfeiture;

(3) the restitution of property to victims of an offense petitioning for remission or mitigation of forfeiture under this chapter;

(4) the disposition by the United States of forfeited property by public sale or other commercially feasible means;

(5) the maintenance and safekeeping of any property forfeited under this section pending its disposition; and

(6) the compromise of claims arising under this chapter.

Pending the promulgation of such regulations, all provisions of law relating to the disposition of property, or the proceeds from the sale thereof, or the remission or mitigation of forfeitures for violation of the customs laws, and the compromise of claims and the award of compensation to informers in respect of such forfeitures shall apply to forfeitures incurred, or alleged to have been incurred, under the provisions of this section, insofar as applicable and not inconsistent with the provisions hereof. Such duties as are imposed upon the Customs Service or any person with respect to the disposition of property under the customs law shall be performed under this chapter by the Attorney General.

(i) Except as provided in subsection (l), no party claiming an interest in property subject to forfeiture under this section may—

(1) intervene in a trial or appeal of a criminal case involving the forfeiture of such property under this section; or

(2) commence an action at law or equity against the United States concerning the validity of his alleged interest in the property subsequent to the filing of an indictment or information alleging that the property is subject to forfeiture under this section.

(j) The district courts of the United States shall have jurisdiction to enter orders as provided in this section without regard to the location of any property which may be subject to forfeiture under this section or which has been ordered forfeited under this section.

(k) In order to facilitate the identification or location of property declared forfeited and to facilitate the disposition of petitions for remission or mitigation of forfeiture, after the entry of an order declaring property forfeited to the United States the court may, upon application of the United States, order that the testimony of any witness relating to the property forfeited be taken by deposition and that any designated book, paper, document, record, recording, or other material not privileged be produced at the same time and place, in the same manner as provided for the taking of depositions under Rule 15 of the Federal Rules of Criminal Procedure.

(*l*)(1) Following the entry of an order of forfeiture under this section, the United States shall publish notice of the order and of its intent to dispose of the property in such manner as the Attorney General may direct. The Government may also, to the extent practicable, provide direct written notice to any person known to have alleged an interest in the property that is the subject of the order of forfeiture as a substitute for published notice as to those persons so notified.

(2) Any person, other than the defendant, asserting a legal interest in property which has been ordered forfeited to the United States pursuant to this section may, within thirty days of the final publication of notice or his receipt of notice under paragraph (1), whichever is earlier, petition the court for a hearing to adjudicate the validity of his alleged interest in the property. The hearing shall be held before the court alone, without a jury.

(3) The petition shall be signed by the petitioner under penalty of perjury and shall set forth the nature and extent of the petitioner's right, title, or interest in the property, the time and circumstances of the petitioner's acquisition of the right, title, or interest in the property, any additional facts supporting the petitioner's claim, and the relief sought.

(4) The hearing on the petition shall, to the extent practicable and consistent with the interests of justice, be held within thirty days of the filing of the petition. The court may consolidate the hearing on the petition with a hearing on any other petition filed by a person other than the defendant under this subsection.

(5) At the hearing, the petitioner may testify and present evidence and witnesses on his own behalf, and cross-examine witnesses who appear at the hearing. The United States may present evidence and witnesses in rebuttal and in defense of its claim to the property and cross-examine witnesses who appear at the hearing. In addition to testimony and evidence presented at the hearing, the court shall consider the relevant portions of the record of the criminal case which resulted in the order of forfeiture.

(6) If, after the hearing, the court determines that the petitioner has established by a preponderance of the evidence that—

> (A) the petitioner has a legal right, title, or interest in the property, and such right, title, or interest renders the order of forfeiture invalid in whole or in part because the right, title, or interest was vested in the petitioner rather than the defendant or was superior to any right, title, or interest of the defendant at the time of the commission of

the acts which gave rise to the forfeiture of the property under this section; or

(B) the petitioner is a bona fide purchaser for value of the right, title, or interest in the property and was at the time of purchase reasonably without cause to believe that the property was subject to forfeiture under this section;

the court shall amend the order of forfeiture in accordance with its determination.

(7) Following the court's disposition of all petitions filed under this subsection, or if no such petitions are filed following the expiration of the period provided in paragraph (2) for the filing of such petitions, the United States shall have clear title to property that is the subject of the order of forfeiture and may warrant good title to any subsequent purchaser or transferee.

(n)[1] If any of the property described in subsection (a), as a result of any act or omission of the defendant—

(1) cannot be located upon the exercise of due diligence;

(2) has been transferred or sold to, or deposited with, a third party;

(3) has been placed beyond the jurisdiction of the court;

(4) has been substantially diminished in value; or

(5) has been commingled with other property which cannot be divided without difficulty;

the court shall order the forfeiture of any other property of the defendant up to the value of any property described in paragraphs (1) through (5).

§ 1964. Civil remedies

(a) The district courts of the United States shall have jurisdiction to prevent and restrain violations of section 1962 of this chapter by issuing appropriate orders, including, but not limited to: ordering any person to divest himself of any interest, direct or indirect, in any enterprise; imposing reasonable restrictions on the future activities or investments of any person, including, but not limited to, prohibiting any person from engaging in the same type of endeavor as the enterprise engaged in, the activities of which affect interstate or foreign commerce; or ordering dissolution or reorganization of any enterprise, making due provision for the rights of innocent persons.

(b) The Attorney General may institute proceedings under this section. Pending final determination thereof, the court may at any

---

1. So in original.

time enter such restraining orders or prohibitions, or take such other actions, including the acceptance of satisfactory performance bonds, as it shall deem proper.

(c) Any person injured in his business or property by reason of a violation of section 1962 of this chapter may sue therefor in any appropriate United States district court and shall recover threefold the damages he sustains and the cost of the suit, including a reasonable attorney's fee.

(d) A final judgment or decree rendered in favor of the United States in any criminal proceeding brought by the United States under this chapter shall estop the defendant from denying the essential allegations of the criminal offense in any subsequent civil proceedings brought by the United States.

§ 1965. Venue and process

(a) Any civil action or proceeding under this chapter against any person may be instituted in the district court of the United States for any district in which such person resides, is found, has an agent, or transacts his affairs.

(b) In any action under section 1964 of this chapter in any district court of the United States in which it is shown that the ends of justice require that other parties residing in any other district be brought before the court, the court may cause such parties to be summoned, and process for that purpose may be served in any judicial district of the United States by the marshal thereof.

(c) In any civil or criminal action or proceeding instituted by the United States under this chapter in the district court of the United States for any judicial district, subpenas issued by such court to compel the attendance of witnesses may be served in any other judicial district, except that in any civil action or proceeding no such subpena shall be issued for service upon any individual who resides in another district at a place more than one hundred miles from the place at which such court is held without approval given by a judge of such court upon a showing of good cause.

(d) All other process in any action or proceeding under this chapter may be served on any person in any judicial district in which such person resides, is found, has an agent, or transacts his affairs.

B. UNITED STATES SENTENCING COMMISSION

Sentencing Table

Criminal History Category

Offense Level	I 0 or 1	II 2 or 3	III 4, 5, 6	IV 7, 8, 9	V 10, 11, 12	VI 13 or more
1	0–1	0–2	0–3	0–4	0–5	0–6
2	0–2	0–3	0–4	0–5	0–6	1–7
3	0–3	0–4	0–5	0–6	2–8	3–9
4	0–4	0–5	0–6	2–8	4–10	6–12
5	0–5	0–6	1–7	4–10	6–12	9–15
6	0–6	1–7	2–8	6–12	9–15	12–18
7	1–7	2–8	4–10	8–14	12–18	15–21
8	2–8	4–10	6–12	10–16	15–21	18–24
9	4–10	6–12	8–14	12–18	18–24	21–27
10	6–12	8–14	10–16	15–21	21–27	24–30
11	8–14	10–16	12–18	18–24	24–30	27–33
12	10–16	12–18	15–21	21–27	27–33	30–37
13	12–18	15–21	18–24	24–30	30–37	33–41
14	15–21	18–24	21–27	27–33	33–41	37–46
15	18–24	21–27	24–30	30–37	37–46	41–51
16	21–27	24–30	27–33	33–41	41–51	46–57
17	24–30	27–33	30–37	37–46	46–57	51–63
18	27–33	30–37	33–41	41–51	51–63	57–71
19	30–37	33–41	37–46	46–57	57–71	63–78
20	33–41	37–46	41–51	51–63	63–78	70–87
21	37–46	41–51	46–57	57–71	70–87	77–96
22	41–51	46–57	51–63	63–78	77–96	84–105
23	46–57	51–63	57–71	70–87	84–105	92–115
24	51–63	57–71	63–78	77–96	92–115	100–125
25	57–71	63–78	70–87	84–105	100–125	110–137
26	63–78	70–87	78–97	92–115	110–137	120–150
27	70–87	78–97	87–108	100–125	120–150	130–162
28	78–97	87–108	97–121	110–137	130–162	140–175
29	87–108	97–121	108–135	121–151	140–175	151–188
30	97–121	108–135	121–151	135–168	151–188	168–210
31	108–135	121–151	135–168	151–188	168–210	188–235
32	121–151	135–168	151–188	168–210	188–235	210–262
33	135–168	151–188	168–210	188–235	210–262	235–293
34	151–188	168–210	188–235	210–262	235–293	262–327
35	168–210	188–235	210–262	235–293	262–327	292–365

Offense Level	I 0 or 1	II 2 or 3	III 4, 5, 6	IV 7, 8, 9	V 10, 11, 12	VI 13 or more
36	188–235	210–262	235–293	262–327	292–365	324–405
37	210–262	235–293	262–327	292–365	324–405	360–life
38	235–293	262–327	292–365	324–405	360–life	360–life
39	262–327	292–365	324–405	360–life	360–life	360–life
40	292–365	324–405	360–life	360–life	360–life	360–life
41	324–405	360–life	360–life	360–life	360–life	360–life
42	360–life	360–life	360–life	360–life	360–life	360–life
43	life	life	life	life	life	life

Notes:

(1) Sentencing ranges are in months.

(2) Criminal History Category I includes first offenders.

INDEX
References are to Pages

AIR QUALITY ACT
Generally, 5

AMERICAN TOBACCO COMPANY
Antitrust prosecutions against, 390–391

ANTI-DRUG ABUSE ACT OF 1988, pp. 137–138

ANTIPOLLUTION LAWS
See also Water Pollution Control Act, Federal, of 1972
Criminal prosecutions, 259

ANTITRUST
See Sentencing Guidelines; Sherman Act

ASHLAND OIL INC.
Internal investigation, 412

ATTORNEY–CLIENT PRIVILEGE
See also Work Product Doctrine
Bankruptcy trustee, assertion by, 423
Conflict of interest, among clients, 130, 412, 480
Control group test, 404–405, 411
Corporations, application to, 402, 411 n. 31, 425, 428
Counsel, constitutional right to,
   Grand jury, 451
   Own choice, 479, 485
Crime-fraud exception,
   Application of, 419, 421
   Purpose, 420, 422
   Test for, 423
Fees, see Multiple Representation, infra this heading
Fifth amendment, privilege against self-incrimination,
   Assertion on behalf of client, 601
Grand jury subpoena, for notes, 490
Joint defense,
   Purpose, 492
   Test for, 491
Multiple representation,
   Code of Professional Responsibility, 481 n. 51
   Corporation and employee, 484
   Federal Rule of Criminal Procedure 44(c), 487
   Fees, payment of, 481
   Grand jury, 478
   Trial, 485
Purpose, generally, 404, 406
Search and seizure, attorney files, 555

ATTORNEY–CLIENT PRIVILEGE—Cont'd
Subject matter test, 412
Waiver,
   Generally, 424, 431, 433
   Conflicts of interest, 481, 487
   Corporation, of employee communications, 432
   Inadvertent, 429 n. 49
   Management, 428

BANK OF BOSTON
See Bank Secrecy Act

BANK SECRECY ACT
Generally, 10
Bank of Boston, 11, 224–225
Cash Transaction Report ("CTR"), 10
Currency and Foreign Transactions Reporting Act, 11 n. 40
Money laundering,
   Generally, 10
   Civil liability, 11 n. 49
   Money Laundering Control Act of 1986, p. 11
Structured transactions, prosecution for, 219–224

BANKS
See also Financial Institutions; Fraud
History of protection, 67–68

BENEFIT, ACTING FOR
See Corporate Criminal Liability

BIBLIOGRAPHY
General, 12

BOESKY, IVAN, 153, 155–159, 353

BOYCOTTS
See Export Administration Act; Sherman Act

BRANDEIS, LOUIS, 27

CIVIL PROCEEDINGS
See also Self-Incrimination Privilege, Civil Proceedings
Before criminal enforcement,
   Internal Revenue Service, 624
   Securities and Exchange Commission, 637
Complaint, assertion of self-incrimination privilege when answering, 656

CIVIL PROCEEDINGS—Cont'd
Depositions,
  Immunized testimony, use of, 517, 645, 648 n. 13
  Protective order, as shield to grand jury subpoena, 659
  Self-incrimination, assertion of privilege during, 654, 675
Grand jury transcripts, discovery of, 668, 676
Settlement, misconduct during, 641
Simultaneous proceedings,
  Food and Drug Administration, 636
  Securities and Exchange Commission, 630
Stay, 643–645, 667

CLAYTON ACT OF 1914
Generally, 3
Managerial liability under Section 14, pp. 261, 281

CODE OF PROFESSSIONAL RESPONSIBILITY
See Professional Responsibility, Code of

COLLECTIVE KNOWLEDGE
See Corporate Criminal Liability

COMPLIANCE PROGRAMS
See Corporate Criminal Liability

COMPREHENSIVE CRIME CONTROL ACT OF 1984
See also Sentencing Reform Act of 1984
Banks,
  Bribery, 9
  Fraud, 9

COMPREHENSIVE FORFEITURE ACT OF 1984, pp. 102–103

CONFIDENTIAL INFORMATION
See National Stolen Property Act; Trade Secrets

CONFLICT OF INTEREST
See Attorney-Client Privilege; Grand Jury, Counsel

CONSTITUTIONAL RIGHTS
See Corporations; specific constitutional protection

CONSUMER PRODUCT SAFETY ACT OF 1972
Generally, 5

COPYRIGHT ACT
Criminal penalties, 39
Piracy and Counterfeiting Amendments Act of 1982, p. 40

CORPORATE CRIMINAL LIABILITY
See also Employee Criminal Liability; Managerial Criminal Liability; Organizational Crime; Partnerships
Authority, agent acting within, 177
Benefit, acting for, 195–196, 197 nn. 29, 30, 201–202, 205 n. 35
Blackstone, view of, 176, 180
Collective knowledge, 198–202, 219–224
Compliance programs,
  As a defense to, 202, 206
  Example of, 212
  Sentence, relevance to, 207 n. 43
Constitutional objections to, 176
Governmental entities, 182
History of, 179–181
Homicide, 184, 186, 187
Imputation Rule, 177, 179, 203, 207, 210
Insider trading, 159
Instructions, agent acting against, as defense, 177, 203
Knowing and willful violations, liability therefor, 184, 198
Management involvement, as necessary for, 207, 208
Manslaughter, involuntary, 187
National Commission on Reform of Federal Criminal Laws, proposal, 209
Orders, see Instructions supra this heading
Organizational crime, theory of, 225
RICO, 93
Strict liability, 217
Workplace injuries, liability for, 185, 187

CORPORATE EMPLOYEE
Criminal liability of, see Employee Criminal Liability
Grand jury transcripts, right of corporation to obtain, 454

CORPORATE OFFICER
Criminal liability of, see Managerial Criminal Liability
Fifth amendment, assertion of, see Self-Incrimination Privilege

CORPORATIONS
See also Attorney-Client Privilege; Fourth Amendment; Grand Jury; Internal Investigations; Sanctions; Self-Incrimination Privilege; Work Product Doctrine; Specific statutes
Constitutional rights,
  Generally, 399
  Double Jeopardy, 400
  Indictment, 446

CORRUPT PRACTICES
See also Foreign Corrupt Practices Act of 1977
Corrupt Practices Act, Federal, 439, 445

COUNSEL
See Attorney-Client Privilege, Counsel

INDEX

References are to Pages

CRIME–FRAUD EXCEPTION
See Attorney-Client Privilege

CRIMINAL CODE, PROPOSED FEDERAL
Generally, 12
Corporate criminal liability, 209–211
Managerial liability, 287–288

CRIMINAL FINE IMPROVEMENTS ACT OF 1987, pp. 302 n. 2, 362

CURRENCY AND FOREIGN TRANSACTIONS REPORTING ACT, 11 n. 40

CUSTODIAN OF RECORDS
See Immunity; Self-Incrimination Privilege, Corporations

DARROW, CLARENCE, 62

DATA
Business crime prosecutions, 14 n. 55
Insider trading, 152
RICO, 103 n. 25, 104 n. 28
Violators, list of, 53–62

DEPARTMENT OF JUSTICE
See Justice, United States Department of, Guidelines for Prosecution

DIRECTORS
See Managerial Criminal Liability

DOUBLE JEOPARDY
Corporation, application to, 400

DRUGS
See also Bank Secrecy Act
Anti-Drug Abuse Act of 1988, pp. 137–138

ELKINS ACT
See Interstate Commerce Act

EMPLOYEE CRIMINAL LIABILITY
Generally, 227
Employer,
  Consistent verdicts with, 227–228
  Same crime, liability for, 227
Following orders, defense, 294, 295–296, 296 n. 12
Representative capacity defense, 227

ENTITY CRIMINAL LIABILITY
See Corporate Criminal Liability; Partnerships

EXPORT ADMINISTRATION ACT
Generally, 7
Criminal prosecutions under, 9

FAIR LABOR STANDARDS ACT
Subpoena issued under, 581

FEDERAL (Listed under remainder of title)

FIFTH AMENDMENT
See Grand Jury; Immunity; Self-Incrimination Privilege

FINANCIAL INSTITUTIONS
Consent forms, compulsory signing, 617, 620 n. 84
Criminal liability, generally, 9
Hutton, E.F.,
  Internal investigation of, 416–417
  Overdrafting by, 9–10
Right to Financial Privacy Act, 593

FOOD AND DRUG ACT OF 1906
See Food, Drug and Cosmetic Act

FOOD, DRUG AND COSMETIC ACT
Generally, 3
Criminal prosecution, 262, 267
Public welfare offense, 263–264

FOREIGN CORRUPT PRACTICES ACT OF 1977
Generally, 7
Amendments, 1988, p. 8
Criticism, 8
Criminal prosecutions under, 8 n. 28
Grease payments, 212
International Telephone and Telegraph Co. ("ITT"), investigation by, 211
Pre-transaction review, 7 n. 22

FORFEITURE
See also Racketeer Influenced and Corrupt Organizations Act
Comprehensive Forfeiture Act of 1984, pp. 102–103

FOURTH AMENDMENT
Aerial searches, application to, 542, 545 n. 38
Administrative searches,
  Generally, 535
  Fair Labor Standards Act, 581
  Occupational Safety and Health Administration, by, 530
  Probable cause, nature of, 534, 536
Attorney, search and seizure of files, 554, 558
Commercial premises, application to, 531, 536
Constructive search, 583
Corporation,
  Books and records, 385, 584, 586
  Documents, 385
  Officer, assertion on behalf of corporation, 385
  Right to assert, 387
Curtilage doctrine, 543
Documents, see, this heading, Corporation; Papers
Exclusionary rule,
  Fruits of unlawful search, 590
  Good faith exception, 568, 572, 576

FOURTH AMENDMENT—Cont'd
  Grand jury, application to, 589, 591
  Purpose, 573–574
  Independent source, 591
  Return of illegally seized evidence, 578
General warrants, 531, 546, 560
Grand jury subpoena, application to, 388, 584, 589, 591
History, 393 n. 11, 547, 549
Mere evidence rule, 546, 552, 603
Objects of search,
  Contraband, 547
  Evidence, 551, 603
  Fruits of the crime, 547, 551
  Instrumentalities, 551
Open fields doctrine, 543
Papers, private, 386, 393, 584, 603, 605
Particularity, 558, 563, 569, 584
Privacy, reasonable expectations of, 529, 542
Privacy Protection Act of 1980, text, 553–554
Reasonableness, 388, 393, 533, 537, 557
Right to Financial Privacy Act, 593
Specificity, see Particularity, supra this heading
Subpoena,
  Application to, 581, 582
  Particularity, 584
  Probable cause, 586, 588
  Scope, reasonableness, 388
Summons,
  See also Subpoena, supra this heading
  Internal Revenue Service, 588, 598
Target, notice to, 592
Text, 528–529
Third party search,
  Notice of, to target, 592
  Payment for, by government, 596
  Search of, 550, 553
Warrant, necessity for,
  Generally, 529 n. 23, 539, 572
  Commercial premises, 531, 537–538
  Fire department inspection, 536
  Housing code violations, 536
  Junkyards, 538
  OSHA, 530
  Purpose, 534
  Regulated business, 532, 538, 539–540

FRAUD
  See also Mail Fraud; Securities Exchange Act of 1934
Bank, 9

FRIEDMAN, LAWRENCE, 71

GOVERNMENTAL ENTITIES
See Corporate Criminal Liability

GRAND JURY
  See also Attorney-Client Privilege; Justice, United States Department of, guidelines for prosecution

GRAND JURY—Cont'd
Accusation, need for prior to investigation, 436
Attorneys' notes, subpoena for, 490
Charge, see Instructions to, infra this heading
Composition,
  Discrimination,
    Race, 467, 473 n. 47, 476
    Sex, 467
  Number, 450
Constitutional right to, in state prosecution, 444
Constitutional violations by, 589
Corporation, right to indictment by, 446
Counsel,
  See also Attorney-Client Privilege, Multiple Representation
  Conflict of interest, multiple representation, 478
  Employee, representation by corporate counsel, 484
  Fees, payment of, 481
  Right to, 451
  Waiver, 481
Deposition testimony, subpoena for, 659
Dismissal of indictment,
  Constitutional error, 476
  Harmless error, 466
  Insufficient evidence,
    Federal law, 464 n. 44, 470
    New York law, 464
  Post-trial, standard for, 472
  Pretrial, standard for, 467
  Prosecutorial misconduct, 465
Evidence before,
  Exculpatory, 460, 461 n. 37, 463–464, 475
  Hearsay, 451 n. 24
  Perjured, 461, 462
Executive power over, see Prosecutor, control over, infra this heading
Function, 442
Hearsay, use of, 451 n. 24
History,
  England, 442
  United States,
    Bill of rights, legislative history, 443, 458
    Pre-twentieth century, 443–444
Infamous crime, 447, 449 n. 19
Impanelment, date of, 447
Inquisitorial power, scope of, 437–438, 440
Instructions to,
  By court, 458, 459 n. 36
  By government counsel, 457 n. 36
Jurisdiction, objection to by witness, 441
Multiple representation of clients, see Counsel, supra this heading
Oath of grand juror, 436
Presentment, defined, 437
Procedures, generally, 450
Prosecutor, control over, 439, 442, 449, 477
Protective order, sealing deposition transcripts, 659

INDEX

References are to Pages

GRAND JURY—Cont'd
Rules of Criminal Procedure, Federal,
  Rule 6(d), pp. 451, 471, 473
  Rule 6(e), pp. 451, 469, 471, 670, 671
  Rule 6(e), history, 453
  Rule 16, pp. 454, 670
Secrecy,
  Data, 455
  Exceptions, generally, 452
  Multiple representation, 481 n. 52
  Reasons for, 453
  Rule 6(e), text, 451
  Witness, 453
Subject status,
  Defined, 451
Supervisory power over, 458, 466
Subpoena, application of fourth amendment to, 388, 584, 589, 591
Target status,
  Defined, 451
  Notification before indictment, 462
Transcripts,
  Disclosure, in civil case, 668, 675
  Employee testimony, corporation's right to, 454
  Government request, 676, 679
  Particularized need, 672 n. 27, 674, 675 n. 31, 679
Witness,
  Attorney client privilege, assertion of, 589
  Challenge to grand jury authority, 441
  Challenge to subpoena, 445 n. 17
  Debriefing, 454
  Duty to testify, 441
  Spousal privilege, assertion of, 589 n. 65
  Warning, fifth amendment privilege, 451

GUIDELINES
See Justice, United States Department of, guidelines for prosecution; Sentencing Guidelines

HALL, JEROME, 66

HOMICIDE
See Corporate Criminal Liability

HUTTON, E.F., AND CO.
See Financial Institutions

IMMUNITY
See also Self-Incrimination Privilege
Agreement not to prosecute, 524 n. 18
Constructive immunity, 610
Custodian of records, for act of production, 610, 614
Defense witness, 518, 522 n. 16
Derivative use,
  Civil deposition, 517, 645, 648 n. 13
  Defined, 508
Foreign prosecution, 511, 512 n. 7
Independent evidence, prosecutor's burden of proof, 509, 520, 614

IMMUNITY—Cont'd
Letter grant, 523
Non-statutory grant, 516, 610
Other jurisdiction, prosecution by, 512, 514
Perjury, by immunized witness, 510
Plea negotiations, 524
Pocket, 468
Statutory grant,
  Constitutionality of, 498, 499, 505, 508
  Federal, text, 507
  Interstate Commerce Act, text, 499
  Preference for, 517, 610, 650
Transactional, 506
Use, 508, 649

INDICTMENT
See Grand Jury

INFAMOUS CRIME
See Grand Jury

INSIDER TRADING
See also Sentencing Guidelines
Boesky, Ivan, prosecution of, 153 n. 83
Civil penalty, 163
Controlling person, liability for, 163
Corporate liability for, 159
Doonesbury, views on, 166
Drexel Burnham Lambert, prosecution of, 153 n. 84
Duty to disclose,
    Generally, 140
  Corporate insider, 140
  Employee, 142, 148
  Financial printer, 138
  Market information, 141
  Securities analyst, 147
  Tippee, 146
Enforcement policy, 152
Insider Trading Sanctions Act of 1984, p. 163
Insider Trading and Securities Fraud Enforcement Act of 1988, p. 163
Levine, Dennis, prosecution of, 153 n. 82
Misappropriation theory, 143, 149
Penalties for violation, 163–164
Purpose of prohibition, 143–144, 150, 164
RICO, charge for, 154
Rule 10b–5, text, 139
Sentences for, 324
Siegel, Martin, prosecution of, 154
Tippee liability, 146

INSIDER TRADING AND SECURITIES FRAUD ENFORCEMENT ACT OF 1988, p. 163

INSIDER TRADING SANCTIONS ACT OF 1984, p. 163

INTELLECTUAL PROPERTY
See Copyright Act; National Stolen Property Act; Trade Secrets; Trademarks

INTERNAL INVESTIGATIONS
Ashland Oil Inc., 412
Conflicts of interest, 412–416
E.F. Hutton & Co., investigation of, 416
International Telephone and Telegraph Co. ("ITT"), 211
Obstruction of justice during, 418
Perjury during, 418

INTERNAL REVENUE CODE
Criminal prosecutions, 247–256
Section 7602, pp. 624, 629
Summons under,
    Criminal referral, prior to, 624
    Fifth amendment application to, 598
    Standard for abuse, 588
    Work product doctrine, application to, 409
Tax Equity and Fiscal Responsibility Act of 1982 ("TEFRA"), 629
Work product privilege, application to summons, 409

INTERNATIONAL TELEPHONE AND TELEGRAPH CO. ("ITT")
Internal investigation of, 211

INTERSTATE COMMERCE ACT
Criminal liability, 2
Elkins Act, 2, 174 n. 2, 179
Hepburn Act, 2
Immunity under, 498, 499
Motor Carrier Act, 2 n. 5, 183, 198
Price discrimination, criminal liability for, 2, 3 n. 12, 497, 502

JAPAN
Japanese corporations, criminal investigations, 32

JOINT REPRESENTATION
See Attorney-Client Privilege; Grand Jury, Multiple representation of clients

JURIES
Verdict, consistency, 227–228

JUSTICE, UNITED STATES DEPARTMENT OF, GUIDELINES FOR PROSECUTION
Grand jury,
    Exculpatory evidence, presentation of, 461
    Notice to targets prior to indictment, 462
    Status of witnesses, 451 n. 26
Requests to prosecute, 50
RICO, 99–100

KADISH, SANFORD, 76

KNOWING AND WILLFUL
    See also Corporate Criminal Liability; Mistake of Law; Partnership
Bank Secrecy Act, 259
Definition, 200, 220, 236

KNOWING AND WILLFUL—Cont'd
Internal Revenue Code, prosecution under, 247
Knowledge of law, when required, 242, 247 n.77
Organizational crime, 227

LABOR UNIONS
See Unions

LEVER ACT
Constitutionality, 25–26

LEVINE, DENNIS, 153

MAIL FRAUD
Anti-Drug Abuse Act of 1988, pp. 137–138
Attorney, application to, 125
Confidential information, disclosure of, 135
Constructive trustee doctrine, 133 n. 63
Corporations, committed by, 132
Duty to disclose,
    Attorney, 125
    Employee, 122, 133
    Public official, 121
Elements, 116
Employees, application to, 122, 132, 133
Fraud, definition of, 119
Government corruption, application to, 118
Intangible rights doctrine,
    Generally, 107
    Anti-Drug Abuse Act of 1988, pp. 137–138
    Case examples, 112 nn. 35–38
Legislative history, 109–110, 116
Mails, use of, 116 n. 44, 131, 137

MANAGERIAL CRIMINAL LIABILITY
    See also Employee Criminal Liability
Aiding and abetting, 261
Authorization, 261
Clayton Act of 1914, pp. 261, 281
National Commission on Reform of Federal Criminal Laws, proposal, 287
Responsible share test, 265, 272, 274, 277, 279 n. 5
Sherman Act, 279
War, supervision of troops, 282–287

MENS REA
See Strict Liability

MINE SAFETY AND HEALTH ACT, FEDERAL, OF 1977
Searches pursuant to, 537

MISTAKE OF LAW
Counsel, reliance on advice of, 258–259
Good faith defense, 247, 256, 257 n. 84
Knowledge of law, requirement, 242, 243, 247 n. 77
Official interpretation, reliance on, 259
Sherman Act, 242

INDEX

References are to Pages

MONEY LAUNDERING CONTROL ACT OF 1986
See Bank Secrecy Act

MOTOR CARRIER ACT
See Interstate Commerce Act

MULTIPLE REPRESENTATION
See Attorney Client Privilege; Grand Jury

NATIONAL COMMISSION ON REFORM OF FEDERAL CRIMINAL LAWS
See also Criminal Code, Proposed Federal
History, 12

NATIONAL STOLEN PROPERTY ACT
Confidential information, theft of, 43, 45
Phonorecords, transportation of, 33

OBSTRUCTION OF JUSTICE
Statute, 418

OCCUPATIONAL SAFETY AND HEALTH
Occupational Safety and Health Act of 1970,
  Generally, 5
  Preemption, of state criminal prosecution, 187 n. 23
  Search, pursuant to section 8(a), p. 530
Occupational Safety and Health Administration ("OSHA"),
  Criticism of, 191–192
  Prosecution by, 207–208
  Regulations, for searches, 533
State prosecutions, 185, 187–189
Statistics concerning, 190–191

OFFICERS, CORPORATE
Criminal liability of, see Managerial Liability
Fifth amendment, assertion of, see Self-Incrimination

OMNIBUS TRADE AND COMPETITIVENESS ACT OF 1988
Corrupt practices, 8 n. 30

ORGANIZATION THEORY
Generally, 167
Bureaucratic politics, 172
Model I, 168–169
Model II, 169–172, 226, 277–279
Model III, 172–174
Organizational process, 169
Rational actor, 168
Standard operating procedures, 170, 226, 277
Use of, generally, 207, 361, 397, 629

ORGANIZATIONAL CRIME
Theory of, 225–227

ORGANIZED CRIME CONTROL ACT OF 1970
See Racketeer Influenced and Corrupt Organizations Act ("RICO")

OSHA
See Occupational Safety and Health

PARALLEL PROCEEDINGS
See Civil Proceedings; Referrals to Justice Department for Criminal Prosecution

PARTNERSHIPS
Criminal liability, 182–184
Fifth amendment, assertion on behalf of, 397
Knowing and willful violations, liability therefor, 184

PERJURY
Internal investigation, during, 418

PIRACY AND COUNTERFEITING AMENDMENTS ACT OF 1982, p. 40

POLLUTION
See Antipollution Laws

PRESUMPTIONS
Constitutional limitations, 239–241
Sherman Act prosecution, 231

PRICE DISCRIMINATION
See Interstate Commerce Act; Robinson Patman Act of 1935

PRICE FIXING
See Sherman Act

PRICE VERIFICATION
See Robinson Patman Act of 1935

PRIVACY PROTECTION ACT OF 1980, p. 553

PRIVILEGE
See Attorney-Client Privilege; Self-Incrimination Privilege; Work Product Doctrine

PROBATION ACT, FEDERAL, 365

PROFESSIONAL RESPONSIBILITY, CODE OF
D.R. 5–105, p. 130
D.R. 5–105(C), p. 481 n. 51
Ethical Consideration 4–1, p. 405

PROTECTIVE ORDER
See Civil Proceedings; Grand Jury

PUBLIC WELFARE OFFENSES
See Strict Liability

PURE FOOD AND DRUG ACT OF 1906
See Food, Drug and Cosmetic Act

QUESTIONABLE PAYMENTS
See also Foreign Corrupt Practices Act
International Telephone and Telegraph Co., 211–213
Upjohn Co., 402

RACKETEER INFLUENCED AND CORRUPT ORGANIZATIONS ACT ("RICO")
Amendments, proposed, 105 n. 30
Civil remedy, 103–106
Corporations, as criminal defendants, 93, 97 n.13
Enterprise,
  Legitimate, application to, 81
  Case examples, 87 n. 5
Forfeiture,
  Generally, 100–103
  Comprehensive Forfeiture Act of 1984, pp. 102–103
  Profits, 103
Government corruption, application to, 87 n. 4
Justice, United States Department of, guidelines for prosecution, 99
Legislative history, 85–87, 87 n. 3, 89–91
Multiplicious charges, 92
Pattern, 89, 105–106
Securities cases, use in, 154 nn. 85, 86

RAILROADS
See Interstate Commerce Act

REBATES
See Interstate Commerce Act, Price Discrimination

REFERRALS TO JUSTICE DEPARTMENT FOR CRIMINAL PROSECUTION
Food and Drug Administration, by, 636
Internal Revenue Service, by, 626
Securities and Exchange Commission, by, 635, 638–639, 640 nn. 5, 6

RESOURCE CONSERVATION AND RECOVERY ACT (RCRA)
Generally, 6
Criminal prosecutions under, 6 n. 21

RICO
See Racketeer Influenced and Corrupt Organizations Act ("RICO")

RIGHT TO FINANCIAL PRIVACY ACT, 593

ROBINSON PATMAN ACT OF 1935
Criminal provisions, 3 n. 12
Meeting competition, defense, 230 n. 58
Price verification, 242

RULES OF CRIMINAL PROCEDURE, FEDERAL
Rule 6(e),
  History, 453
  Transcripts, 674
  (2)(C)(i), p. 671
  (3)(C)(i), pp. 676, 679
Rule 11(e)(6), p. 527
Rule 16, p. 454
Rule 41(e), p. 578
Rule 44(c), p. 487

SANCTIONS
See also Sentencing Guidelines; Listing under specific offense
Alternative sanctions,
  Charitable contributions, 364, 366, 370
  Community service, 348, 352 n. 40, 370
  Guidelines provisions for, 352
  House arrest, 349, 352 n. 40
  Justice Department, opposition to, 372, 380
  Occupational restrictions, 352
  Speeches, 341
Collateral effects, 362
Corporations, see Organizations, infra this heading
Criminal Fine Improvements Act of 1987, pp. 302 n. 2, 362
Debarment, 376
Disparity, 333, 335
Entities, see Organizations, infra this heading
Fines,
  Equity, 362
  Theory for determination, 355, 358
History, 306–308
Imprisonment,
  Club Feds, 353
  Corporations, 377, 379
  White collar, generally, 335, 353
Indeterminate sentences, 307
Insider trading, 324, 331 n. 29
Jail, see Imprisonment, supra this heading
Organizations,
  Equity fines, 362
  Charitable contributions, 366, 370
  Community service, 370, 376
  Debarment, 376
  Monetary, 355
  Overspill, 362
  Imprisonment, 377, 379
  Internal investigation, 376
  Probation, conditions of, 364, 373
Probation, 300–301, 318, 364
Probation Act, Federal, 365
Purposes, 298
Restitution, 299

SEARCH AND SEIZURE
See Fourth Amendment

SEC
See Securities and Exchange Commission

INDEX
References are to Pages

SECURITIES ACT OF 1933
Generally, 4

SECURITIES AND EXCHANGE COMMISSION
See also Referrals to Justice Department for Criminal Prosecution
Subpoena, issuance, 592, 630

SECURITIES EXCHANGE ACT OF 1934
See also Insider Trading
Generally, 4
Criminal prosecutions, 288
Fraud, 4
Rule 10b–5, text, 139

SELF–INCRIMINATION PRIVILEGE
See also Immunity
Act of production doctrine, 605, 609, 612
Assertion, grounds for,
    Generally, 512, 653
    Civil proceedings, after conviction, 654
Civil litigation,
    Assertion of privilege, effect on, 655, 656, 658, 662, 675
    Protective order, 659
Collective entity rule, 612
Communications, see Testimonial communications, infra this heading
Consent forms, compulsory signing, 617
Corporations,
    Books and records, 384, 585, 602
    Custodian, assertion by, 612, 615
    Officer, assertion by, 384, 584
    Right to assert, generally, 584
Custodian, see Corporations, supra this heading
Documents,
    Authentication of, by production, 605, 609
    Compulsory production, 598
    Corporate, 384, 394, 613
    Sole proprietorship, 607
Handwriting exemplars, 604
Partnership, assertion on behalf of, 397
Personal nature of, 394
Privacy, protection of, 600
Private papers,
    See also Fourth Amendment, Papers, private
    Application to, 611
Purpose of, 502, 515
Sole proprietorship, assertion by, 607
Testimonial communications, 603, 617
Third party, assertion on behalf, 385, 599
Unions, application to, 393

SENTENCES
See Sanctions; Sentencing Reform Act of 1984

SENTENCING COMMISSION
Composition, 303

SENTENCING COMMISSION—Cont'd
Constitutionality,
    Delegation of power, 309
    Separation of powers, 311
Duties, 304

SENTENCING GUIDELINES
See also Sentencing Commission; Sentencing Reform Act of 1984
Alternative sentences, 351, 352 n. 40
Antitrust offenses, 337–339, 340 n. 33
Application, how to, 319
Basic approach, 316
Bid-rigging, 337, 340 n. 33
Corporations, see Organizations, infra this heading
Departures from, 317
Effective date, 320
Fines,
    Individuals, 340 n. 33, 360
    Offense multiple, 356
    Organizations, 355
General requirements, 304–305
History of, 319
Insider trading, 324, 327
Model Acts, 308 n. 10
Occupational restrictions, 352
Organizations,
    Fines, proposed, 355
    Offense multiple, 356
    Probation,
        Proposed, 373
        Sentencing Reform Act, legislative history, 375
Plea bargaining, 317–318
Price-fixing, 337, 340 n. 33
Probation,
    Generally, 318
    Organizations, proposed, 373
Split sentences, 318
State statutes, 308 n. 11
Supervised release, 352 n. 40

SENTENCING REFORM ACT OF 1984
See also Sentencing Commission
Classification, offenses, 300
Criminal Fine Improvements Act of 1987, p. 302
Debarment, 376
Fines, 302
Guidelines, general requirements, 304
Imprisonment, factors to be considered, 303
Individuals, penalties, 298, 302
Organizations, penalties, 298, 302
Probation,
    Generally, 300
    Corporate, 370 n. 56
    Legislative history, 375
Restitution, 299
Text, 297–306
Victims, notice to, 299

SHERMAN ACT
Generally, 2
Airline industry, grand jury investigation, 449
Bid-rigging,
    Charitable contributions, as penalty, 364, 366
    Guideline for penalty, 337
Boycott,
    Arab, 2–3
    Criminal liability for, 202
Constitutionality, 24
Fines, guideline for, 340 n. 33
Intent requirement,
    Generally, 231, 235–236
    Legislative history, 239
Managerial liability, 279–282
Market allocation, guideline for penalty, 337
Monopolization, prosecution for, 15, 27
Penalties, 2, 235 n. 63, 337
Price-fixing,
    Charitable contributions, as penalty, 370
    Guideline for penalty, 337
    Prosecution for, 228
    Speeches, as penalty, 341
Vagueness, 21, 24

SIEGEL, MARTIN, 154–159, 160

SIMULTANEOUS PROCEEDINGS
See Civil Proceedings; Referrals to Justice Department for Criminal Prosecution

SOFT PROPERTY
See Copyright Act; National Stolen Property Act; Trade Secrets; Trademarks

STANDARD OPERATING PROCEDURES
See Organization Theory

STAY
Civil proceedings, 643–645, 667

STRICT LIABILITY
See also Food, Drug and Cosmetic Act
Disfavored status, 232
Food stamp fraud, 246
Migratory Bird Act, 217
Purpose of, 234 n. 62, 264
Sherman Act, 231

SUBJECT STATUS
See Grand Jury

SUBORDINATE CRIMINAL LIABILITY
See Employee Criminal Liability

SUBPOENA
See also Fourth Amendment; Grand Jury
SEC, issued by, 630

SUMMONS
Abuse, test for, 588

SUMMONS—Cont'd
Civil case, before criminal referral, 624
Internal Revenue Service, 409, 588, 624

SUPERVISOR CRIMINAL LIABILITY
See Managerial Criminal Liability

SUPERVISORY POWER, 458, 466

SUTHERLAND, EDWIN, 73

TARGET STATUS
See Fourth Amendment; Grand Jury

TAX EQUITY AND FISCAL RESPONSIBILITY ACT OF 1982 ("TEFRA")
Summons under, 629

TAX PROSECUTIONS
See Internal Revenue Code; Mistake of Law

THEFT
History, 71

TOBACCO TRUST
Antitrust prosecutions against, 390–391

TOXIC SUBSTANCES CONTROL ACT
Generally, 6

TRADE
See Omnibus Trade and Competitiveness Act of 1988

TRADE SECRETS
Confidential information, misappropriation of, 149
Mail fraud prosecution, 132
State criminal law, 133 n. 62
Theft of, 44, 45

TRADEMARKS
Act of 1870, constitutionality, 46
Criminal penalties for infringement, 41 n. 77
Private criminal prosecutions, 48
Trademark Counterfeiting Act of 1984, p. 46

TRUCKING
See Interstate Commerce Act, Motor Carriers

UNIONS
Self-incrimination clause, application to, 393

UNITED STATES ATTORNEYS MANUAL
See Justice, United States Department of, guidelines for prosecution

UNITED STATES SENTENCING COMMISSION
See Sentencing Commission

INDEX

References are to Pages

VAGUENESS
Lever Act, 26
RICO, 106
Robinson Patman Act, 3 n. 12
Sherman Act, 24–25, 233

WARRANTS
See Fourth Amendment

WATER POLLUTION CONTROL ACT, FEDERAL, OF 1972
Generally, 5
Criminal prosecutions under, 6 n. 21

WILLFUL
See Knowing and Willful

WORK PRODUCT DOCTRINE
Civil litigation, application in criminal litigation to documents prepared for, 422
Corporations, application to, 409
Crime-fraud exception, application to, 420
Necessity, overcoming privilege, 410
Search and seizure, attorney files, 556
Witness interviews, application to, 410

WORKPLACE SAFETY
See Occupational Safety and Health

†